A New Star-Rating System & Other Exciting News from Frommer's!

In our continuing effort to publish the savviest, most up-to-date, and most appealing travel guides available, we've added some great new features.

Frommer's guides now include a new **star-rating system.** Every hotel, restaurant, and attraction is rated from 0 to 3 stars to help you set priorities and organize your time.

We've also added **seven brand-new features** that point you to the great deals, in-the-know advice, and unique experiences that separate travelers from tourists. Throughout the guide, look for:

Finds	Special finds—those places only insiders know about
Fun Fact	Fun facts—details that make travelers more informed and their trips more fun
Kids	Best bets for kids—advice for the whole family
Moments	Special moments—those experiences that memories are made of
Overrated	Places or experiences not worth your time or money
Tips	Insider tips—some great ways to save time and money
Value	Great values—where to get the best deals

We've also added a **"What's New"** section in every guide—a timely crash course in what's hot and what's not in every destination we cover.

D0067499

Here's what the critics say about Frommer's:

"Amazingly easy to use. Very portable, very complete."

—*Booklist*

"Detailed, accurate, and easy-to-read information for all price ranges."
—*Glamour Magazine*

"Hotel information is close to encyclopedic."
—*Des Moines Sunday Register*

"Frommer's Guides have a way of giving you a real feel for a place."
—*Knight Ridder Newspapers*

Frommer's®

New England

11th Edition

by Wayne Curtis, Herbert Bailey Livesey, Marie Morris & Laura M. Reckford

Wiley Publishing, Inc.

917.4
FRO

Published by:

Wiley Publishing, Inc.

909 Third Ave.
New York, NY 10022

ISBN 0-7645-6630-X
ISSN 1044-2286

Editor: Leslie Shen
With special thanks to Amy Lyons
Production Editor: M. Faunette Johnston
Cartographer: Nicholas Trotter
Photo Editor: Richard Fox
Production by Wiley Indianapolis Composition Services

For information on our other products and services or to obtain technical support, please contact our Customer Care Department within the U.S. at 800-762-2974, outside the U.S. at 317-572-3993 or fax 317-572-4002.

Wiley also publishes its books in a variety of electronic formats. Some content that appears in print may not be available in electronic formats.

Manufactured in the United States of America

5 4 3 2

Contents

13 Maine 540

by Wayne Curtis

Appendix: New England in Depth 623

by Wayne Curtis

Index 633

List of Maps

About the Authors

Wayne Curtis (chapters 2, 3, 11 through 13, and the appendix) is a freelance writer who's also the author of *Frommer's Nova Scotia, New Brunswick & Prince Edward Island.* He writes for the *Atlantic Monthly,* the *New York Times, Preservation,* and *Yankee,* among others. He lives on the Maine coast a few hundred yards from the Canadian border, and can be reached at curtis@maine.com.

Herbert Bailey Livesey (chapters 8 through 10) is a native New Yorker and a former NYU administrator. After leaving his career in higher education, he worked briefly as an artist before devoting himself to writing full time. He is the author of several travel guides, nine books on education and sociology, and a novel.

Marie Morris (chapters 4 and 5) is a native New Yorker and a graduate of Harvard, where she studied history. She has worked for the *New York Times, Boston* magazine, and the *Boston Herald,* and is also the author of *Frommer's Boston.* She lives in Boston.

Laura M. Reckford (chapters 6 and 7) is a writer and editor who lives on Cape Cod. Formerly the managing editor of *Cape Cod Life Magazine,* she has also been on the editorial staffs of *Good Housekeeping Magazine* and *Entertainment Weekly.*

An Invitation to the Reader

In researching this book, we discovered many wonderful places—hotels, restaurants, shops, and more. We're sure you'll find others. Please tell us about them so that we can share the information with your fellow travelers in upcoming editions. If you were disappointed with a recommendation, we'd love to know that, too. Please write to:

Frommer's New England, 11th Edition
Wiley Publishing, Inc. • 909 Third Ave. • New York, NY 10022

An Additional Note

Please be advised that travel information is subject to change at any time—and this is especially true of prices. We therefore suggest that you write or call ahead for confirmation when making your travel plans. The authors, editors, and publisher cannot be held responsible for the experiences of readers while traveling. Your safety is important to us, however, so we encourage you to stay alert and be aware of your surroundings. Keep a close eye on cameras, purses, and wallets, all favorite targets of thieves and pickpockets.

New! Frommer's Star Ratings & Icons

Every hotel, restaurant, and attraction listing in this guide has been ranked for quality, value, service, amenities, and special features using a star-rating scale. In country, state, and regional guides, we also rate towns and regions to help you narrow down your choices and budget your time accordingly. Hotels and restaurants in the Very Expensive and Expensive categories are rated on a scale of one (highly recommended) to three stars (exceptional). Those in the Moderate and Inexpensive categories rate from zero (recommended) to two stars (very highly recommended). Attractions, towns, and regions are rated according to the following scale: zero stars (recommended), one star (highly recommended), two stars (very highly recommended), and three stars (must-see).

In addition to the rating system, we also use seven icons to highlight insider information, useful tips, special bargains, hidden gems, memorable experiences, kid-friendly venues, places to avoid, and other useful information:

(**Finds** (**Fun Fact** (**Kids** (**Moments** (**Overrated** (**Tips** (**Value**

The following abbreviations are used for credit cards:

AE	American Express	DISC	Discover	V	Visa
DC	Diners Club	MC	MasterCard		

FROMMERS.COM

Now that you have the guidebook to a great trip, visit our website at **www.frommers.com** for travel information on nearly 2,500 destinations. With features updated regularly, we give you instant access to the most current trip-planning information available. At Frommers.com, you'll also find the best prices on airfares, accommodations, and car rentals—and you can even book travel online through our travel booking partners. At Frommers.com, you'll also find the following:

- Online updates to our most popular guidebooks
- Vacation sweepstakes and contest giveaways
- Newsletter highlighting the hottest travel trends
- Online travel message boards with featured travel discussions

What's New in New England

BOSTON & CAMBRIDGE **Amtrak** (© 800/USA-RAIL; www. amtrak.com) has restored rail service between Boston and Portland. The *Downeaster* (www.thedowneaster.com) now operates four times daily.

The **Ritz-Carlton, Boston Common,** 10 Avery St. (© 800/241-3333; www.ritzcarlton.com), a posh, modern hotel whose guests have access to the enormous Sports Club/LA, opened last year. After extensive renovations, the **Ritz-Carlton, Boston,** 15 Arlington St., is scheduled to reopen in October 2002, in time to celebrate its 75th anniversary.

For security reasons, the **John Hancock Observatory** has closed permanently.

SIDE TRIPS FROM BOSTON Salem's **Peabody Essex Museum,** East India Square (© 800/745-4054; www.pem.org), is wrapping up an ambitious expansion project. Celebrations and special exhibits will accompany the opening of the new galleries in the spring of 2003; meanwhile, visitors can track the progress of the construction.

CAPE COD Falmouth finally has a fun restaurant on Main Street. **Roo-Bar,** 285 Main St. (© 508/548-8600), opened to rave reviews, and the place, especially the bar, is packed nightly in season.

Even other innkeepers are calling the **Scallop Shell Inn,** 16 Mass. Ave. (© 800/249-4587; www.scallop-shellinn.com), Falmouth's best new lodging. It's just steps from popular Falmouth Heights Beach. (Cars need a sticker to park here, so it's convenient to be able to walk to it.)

At press time, renovations to the **Salt Pond Visitor Center,** in Eastham (© 508/255-3421), are scheduled to begin in late 2002. The center will be closed during this time, but visitors will still be able to walk the trails. They can also travel up to the **Province Lands Visitor Center** (© 508/487-1256), which has similar displays and programs.

MARTHA'S VINEYARD & NANTUCKET Everyone is talking about the intimate **Park Corner Bistro,** 20H Kennebec Ave., Oak Bluffs (© 508/696-9922), in the heart of the Vineyard's most hopping town.

On Nantucket, the luxurious **White Elephant,** 50 Easton St. (© 800/475-2673; www.white elephanthotel.com), has undergone a multimillion-dollar renovation. Guests can watch the ferries and yachts come and go in Nantucket Harbor as they relax in the largest bedrooms on the island.

CENTRAL & WESTERN MASSACHUSETTS **The Mount,** 2 Plunkett St. (© 413/637-1899; www.edithwharton.org), Edith Wharton's mansion in Lenox, remains in the throes of a $15-million restoration. Tours continue. **Shakespeare & Company** (© 413/637-1199; www.shakespeare.org), which long staged its productions at the Mount, has nearly completed its staged withdrawals to its new home close to Lenox center.

In North Adams, that long-depressed former factory town, the ambitious new **Massachusetts Museum of Contemporary Art,** 87 Marshall St. (© **413/662-2111;** www.massmoca.org), is exceeding all hopes. Known as MASS MoCA, it has inspired other efforts to recycle the local building stock into restaurants, shops, and galleries. Check out **Eleven,** 1111 MASS MoCA Way (© **413/622-2004**), next to the museum entrance.

CONNECTICUT Up in Ridgefield, new proprietors have breathed life into the near-somnolent Inn at Ridgefield, with its reconstituted dining room, **Bernard's,** 20 West Lane (© **203/438-8282**). Romance is revived by candlelit evenings with piano music.

New Haven's reputation as a dining destination continues to grow, and not only for pizza. Hottest of the hot is **Roomba,** 1044 Chapel St. (© **203/ 562-7666**), a Nuevo Latino dazzler with surprises on every plate.

New lodgings in the Mystic/casinos region include the jazzy **Mystic Marriott Hotel & Spa,** on Route 117 in Groton (© **860/446-2600;** www. marriotthotels.com), with a super health club and Elizabeth Arden Spa, and the tranquil **Inn at Stonington,** 60 Water St., in Stonington (© **860/ 535-2000;** www.innatstonington. com).

RHODE ISLAND In Providence, watch for news of the opening of the new **Heritage Harbor Museum,** an affiliate of the Smithsonian Institution, scheduled to open this year in a former power plant.

In Newport, the owners of the exemplary **Cliffside Inn,** 2 Seaview Ave. (© **800/845-1811;** www.cliffsideinn.com), have purchased an existing inn not far away and renamed it the **Adele Turner Inn,** 93 Pelham St.

(© **800/845-1811;** www.adeleturner inn.com). It has been successfully brought up to the lofty standards of its sister property.

VERMONT At the Latchis Hotel in Brattleboro, **Lucca Bistro & Brasserie,** 6 Flat St. (© **802/254-4747**), has replaced the Latchis Grille. While local microbrews are still available from the Windham Brewery, the food has migrated toward French country and bistro fare. A sign of Brattleboro's growing upscale-ism: There's now an oyster and martini bar at street level above the restaurant.

Links are falling into place along the excellent **Burlington Bike Path.** At press time, it looked promising that funding would be found to pay for two bike ferries spanning critical gaps in the emerging bike loop around Lake Champlain. Call Burlington Parks and Recreation at © **802/864-0123** for up-to-date information.

And as if you needed another reason to visit the terrific **Shelburne Museum,** Route 7, Shelburne (© **802/985-3346;** www.shelburne museum.org), this innovative institution has recently opened the "Collector's House," made of prefab metal structures and featuring folk-art displays. It's a spectacular collision of old and new.

NEW HAMPSHIRE Since **Jumpin' Jay's Fish Café,** 150 Congress St. (© **603/766-3474**), opened two summers ago, it's become our favorite spot in Portsmouth. And though it's not technically *new,* it's still new enough to be little known to travelers.

Who says lift tickets never get any cheaper? In a very welcome reversal of a very unwelcome trend in the escalating cost of downhill skiing, **Waterville Valley** (© **800/468-2553;** www. waterville.com) slashed its ticket prices for 2001–2002 on most weekends by $10. Whether this is a one-time deal or a more enduring change remains to be seen.

Other good news in the North Country: The **Mountain View Grand,** in Whitefield ((C) **603/837-2100;** www.mountainviewgrand. com), is slated to open in 2002. The sprawling 19th-century resort has been thoroughly restored, with 146 rooms and many modern amenities.

MAINE Longtime favorite **Cape Neddick Inn Restaurant,** 1233 Rte. 1, Cape Neddick ((C) **207/363-2899**), was purchased in 2001 by Johnathan Pratt, who has worked at such noted establishments as Restaurant Daniel and Jean George in New York. No surprise: His menu features French-inspired American fare, and it's well worth a splurge.

Portland's **Percy Inn,** 15 Pine St. ((C) **207/871-7638;** www.percyinn. com), has expanded into the adjacent town house and carriage house. One of the new rooms is in an old art gallery, complete with track lighting.

Cedarholm Garden Bay, Route 1, north of Camden in Lincolnville Beach (tel] **207/236-3886**), has added two new cottages along Penobscot Bay. The older cottages were among our favorites for their privacy and craftsmanship; the new ones are a tad smaller, but no less appealing.

Finally, in Bar Harbor, the 1932 **Criterion Theater,** Cottage Street ((C) **207/288-3441;** www.criterion theatre.com), is under new ownership—the new owner happens to be the guy who operates our favorite restaurant in town, Havana. The theater continues to offer a summer lineup of first-run movies, but now there's food available in the loge and live musical acts appearing regularly in summer and fall.

1

The Best of New England

One of the greatest challenges of traveling in New England is choosing from an abundance of superb restaurants, accommodations, and attractions. Where to start? Here's an entirely biased list of our favorite destinations and experiences. Over years of traveling through the region, we've discovered that these are places worth more than just a quick stop—they're all worth a major detour.

1 The Best of Small-Town New England

- **Marblehead** (Mass.): The "Yachting Capital of America" has major picture-postcard potential, especially in summer, when the harbor fills with boats of all sizes. From downtown, a short distance inland, make your way toward the water down the narrow, flower-dotted streets. The first glimpse of blue sea and sky is breathtaking. See "Marblehead" in chapter 5.

- **Chatham** (Cape Cod, Mass.): Located on the "elbow" of the Cape, Chatham is proof that Main Street, U.S.A, is alive and well. Families throng here to enjoy the beach and to browse through shops brimming with upscale gifts. In summer, visitors and locals gather every Friday night for festive outdoor concerts, while the looming Chatham Lighthouse, built in 1828, keeps a close eye on the Atlantic. See "The Lower Cape" in chapter 6.

- **Edgartown** (Martha's Vineyard, Mass.): For many visitors, Edgartown *is* Martha's Vineyard, its regal captains' houses and manicured lawns a symbol of a more refined way of life. The old-fashioned Fourth of July parade harks back to small-town America, as hundreds line Main Street cheering the loudest for the floats with the most heart. See "Martha's Vineyard" in chapter 7.

- **Stockbridge** (Mass.): Norman Rockwell made a famous painting of the main street of this, his adopted hometown. Facing south, it uses the southern Berkshires as backdrop for the sprawl of the Red Lion Inn and the other late-19th-century buildings that make up the commercial district. Then as now, they service a beguiling mix of unassuming saltboxes and Gilded Age mansions that have sheltered farmers, artists, and aristocrats since the days of the French and Indian Wars. See "The Berkshires" in chapter 8.

- **Washington** (Conn.): A classic, with a Congregational church facing a village green surrounded by clapboard colonial houses—all of them with black shutters. See "The Litchfield Hills" in chapter 9.

- **Essex** (Conn.): A widely circulated survey voted Essex tops on its list of the 100 best towns in the United States. That judgment is largely statistical, but a walk past white-clapboard houses to the active waterfront on this unspoiled stretch of the Connecticut River rings all the bells. There is not an artificial note, a cookie-cutter franchise, nor a costumed docent to muddy its near-perfect image. See "The Connecticut River Valley" in chapter 9.

- **Grafton** (Vt.): Grafton was once a down-at-the-heels mountain town slowly being reclaimed by termites and the elements. A wealthy family took it on as a pet project, and has lovingly restored the village to its former self—even burying the electric lines to reclaim the landscape. It doesn't feel like a living-history museum; it just feels right. See "Brattleboro & the Southern Green Mountains" in chapter 11.

- **Woodstock** (Vt.): Woodstock has a stunning village green, a whole range of 19th-century homes, woodland walks leading just out of town, and a settled, old-money air. This is a good place to explore on foot or by bike, or to just sit and watch summer unfold. See "Woodstock" in chapter 11.

- **Montpelier** (Vt.): This is the way all state capitals should be: slow-paced, small enough so you can walk everywhere, and full of shops that still sell nails and strapping tape. Montpelier also shows a more sophisticated edge, with its Culinary Institute, an art-house movie theater, and several fine bookshops. But at heart it's a small town, where you just might run into the governor buying a wrench at the corner store. See "Montpelier & Barre" in chapter 11.

- **Hanover** (N.H.): It's the perfect college town: the handsome brick buildings of Dartmouth College, a tidy green, a small but select shopping district, and a scattering of good restaurants. Come in the fall and you'll be tempted to join in the touch football game on the green. See "Hanover & Environs" in chapter 12.

- **Castine** (Maine): Soaring elm trees, a peaceful harborside setting, plenty of grand historic homes, and a few good inns make this a great spot to soak up some of Maine's coastal ambience off the beaten path. See "The Blue Hill Peninsula" in chapter 13.

2 The Best Places to See Fall Foliage

- **Walden Pond State Reservation** (Concord, Mass.): Walden Pond is hidden from the road by the woods where Henry David Thoreau built a small cabin and lived from 1845 to 1847. When the leaves are turning and the trees are reflected in the water, it's hard to imagine why he left. See p. 141.

- **Bash-Bish Falls State Park** (Mass.): Head from the comely village of South Egremont up into the forested hills of the extreme southwest corner of Massachusetts. The roads, which change from macadam to gravel to dirt and back, wind between crimson clouds of sugar maples and white birches feather-stroked against banks of black evergreens. The payoff is a three-state view from a promontory above a 50-foot (15m) cascade notched into a bluff, with carpets of russet and gold stretching all the way to the Hudson River. See p. 298.

- **The Litchfield Hills** (Conn.): Route 7, running south to north through the rugged northwest corner of Connecticut, roughly along the course of the Housatonic River, explodes with color in the weeks before and after Columbus Day. Leaves drift down to the water and whirl down the foaming river. See "The Litchfield Hills" in chapter 9.

New England

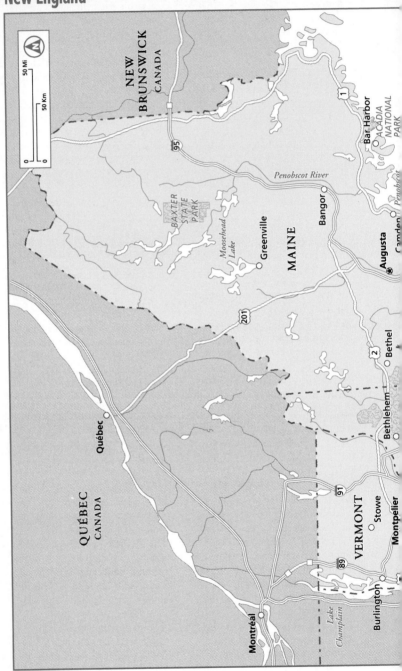

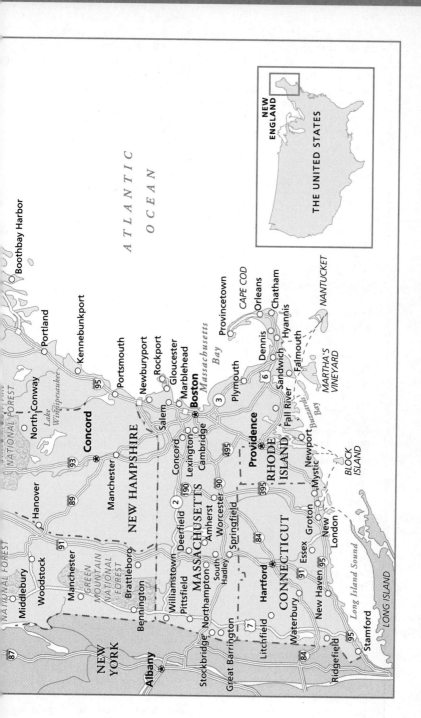

- **I-91** (Vt.): An interstate? Don't scoff (the traffic can be terrible on narrow state roads). If you like your foliage viewing wholesale, cruise I-91 from Brattleboro to Newport. You'll be overwhelmed with gorgeous terrain, from the gentle Connecticut River Valley to the sloping hills of the Northeast Kingdom. See chapter 11.
- **Route 100** (Vt.): Route 100 winds the length of Vermont from Readsboro to Newport. It's the major north-south route through the center of the Green Mountains, and it's surprisingly undeveloped along most of its length. You won't have it to yourself along the southern stretches on autumn weekends, but as you head further north, you'll leave the crowds behind. See chapter 11.
- **The MV *Mount Washington*** (N.H.): One of the more majestic views of the White Mountains is from Lake Winnipesaukee to the south. The vista is especially appealing as seen from the deck of the *Mount Washington,* an uncommonly handsome vessel that offers a variety of tours through mid-October, when the lake is trimmed with a fringe of fall color along the shoreline. See p. 512.
- **Crawford Notch** (N.H.): Route 302 passes through this scenic valley, where you can see the brilliant red maples and yellow birches high on the hillsides. In fall, Mount Washington, in the background, is likely to be dusted with an early snow. See "The White Mountains" in chapter 12.
- **Camden** (Maine): The dazzling fall colors that cover the rolling hills are reflected in Penobscot Bay on the east side, and in the lakes on the west. Ascend the coastal peaks for views out to the color-splashed islands in the bay. Autumn usually comes a week or two later on the coast, so you can stretch out your viewing pleasure. See "Penobscot Bay" in chapter 13.

3 The Best Ways to View Coastal Scenery

- **Strolling Around Rockport** (Mass.): The town surrounds the small harbor and spreads out along the rugged, rocky coastline of Cape Ann. From the end of Bearskin Neck, the view is spectacular—fishing and pleasure boats in one direction, roaring surf in the other. See "Cape Ann" in chapter 5.
- **Getting Back to Nature on Plum Island** (Mass.): The Parker River National Wildlife Refuge, in Newburyport, offers two varieties of coastal scenery: picturesque salt marshes packed with birds and other animals, and gorgeous ocean beaches where the power of the Atlantic is evident. See "Newburyport, Ipswich & Plum Island" in chapter 5.
- **Biking or Driving the Outer Cape** (Mass.): From Eastham through Wellfleet and Truro, all the way to Provincetown, Cape Cod's outermost towns offer dazzling ocean vistas and a number of exceptional bike paths, including the Province Lands, just outside Provincetown, that are bordered by spectacular swooping dunes. See "The Outer Cape" in chapter 6.
- **Heading "Up-Island" on Martha's Vineyard** (Mass.): Many visitors never venture beyond the port towns of Vineyard Haven, Oak Bluffs, and Edgartown. Though each has its charms, the scenery actually gets more spectacular "up-island," in towns like Chilmark, where you'll pass moorlike meadows and family farms

surrounded by stone walls. Follow State Road and the scenic Moshup Trail to the westernmost tip of the island, where you'll experience the dazzling colored cliffs of Aquinnah and the quaint fishing port of Menemsha. See "Martha's Vineyard" in chapter 7.

- **Cruising Newport's Ocean Drive** (R.I.): After a tour of the fabulously overwrought "cottages" of the hyper-rich that are strung along Bellevue Avenue, emerging onto the shoreline road that dodges the spray of the boiling Atlantic is a cleansing reminder of the power of nature over fragile monuments to the conceits of men. To extend the experience, take a 3½-mile (6km) hike along the Cliff Walk that skirts the edge of the bluff commanded by the largest mansions. See "Newport" in chapter 10.

- **Sitting in a Rocking Chair** (Maine): The views are never better than when you're caught unawares—such as suddenly looking up from an engrossing book on the front porch of an oceanside inn. Throughout the Maine chapter, look for mention of inns right on the water, such as Black-Point Inn (p. 559), Grey Havens (p. 568), Samoset Resort (p. 580), Inn on the Harbor (p. 589), and the Claremont (p. 608).

- **Hiking Monhegan Island** (Maine): The village of Monhegan is clustered around the harbor, but the rest of this 700-acre (284-hectare) island is all picturesque wildlands, with miles of trails crossing open meadows and winding along rocky bluffs. See "The Mid Coast" in chapter 13.

- **Driving the Park Loop Road at Acadia National Park** (Maine): This is the region's premier ocean drive. You'll start high along a ridge with views of Frenchman Bay and the Porcupine Islands, then dip down along the rocky shores to watch the surf crash against the dark rocks. Plan to do this 20-mile (32km) loop at least twice to get the most out of it. See p. 595.

- **Cruising on a Windjammer** (Maine): See Maine as it was first seen for centuries—from the ocean looking inland. A handsome fleet of sailing ships departs from various harbors along the coast, particularly Rockland and Camden. Spend from a night to a week exploring the dramatic shoreline. See p. 579.

4 The Best Places to Rediscover America's Past

- **Paul Revere House** (Boston, Mass.): The history of the American Revolution is often told through stories of governments and institutions. At this little home in the North End, you'll learn about a real person. The self-guided tour is particularly thought-provoking, allowing you to linger on the artifacts that hold your interest. Revere had 16 children with two wives, supported them with his thriving silversmith's trade—and put the whole operation in jeopardy with his role in the events that led to the Revolutionary War. See p. 107.

- **Old State House** (Boston, Mass.): Built in 1713, the once-towering Old State House is dwarfed by modern-day skyscrapers. It stands as a reminder of British rule (the exterior features a lion and a unicorn) and its overthrow—the Declaration of Independence was read from the balcony, which overlooks a traffic island where a circle of bricks represents the site of the Boston Massacre. See p. 106.

- **Faneuil Hall** (Boston, Mass.): Although Faneuil Hall is best known nowadays as a shopping destination, if you head upstairs, you'll be transported back in time. The second-floor auditorium is in tip-top shape, and park rangers are on hand to talk about the building's role in the Revolution. Tune out the sound of sneakers squeaking across the floor, and you can almost hear Samuel Adams (his statue is out front) exhorting the Sons of Liberty. See p. 107.

- **"Old Ironsides"** (Boston, Mass.): Formally named USS *Constitution,* the frigate was launched in 1797 and made a name for itself battling Barbary pirates and seeing action in the War of 1812. Last used in battle in 1815, it was periodically threatened with destruction until a complete renovation in the late 1920s started its career as a floating monument. The staff includes sailors on active duty who wear 1812 dress uniforms. See p. 107.

- **North Bridge** (Concord, Mass.): British troops headed to Concord after putting down the uprising in Lexington, and the bridge (a replica) stands as a testament to the Minutemen who fought here. The Concord River and its peaceful green banks give no hint of the bloodshed that took place. On the path in from Monument Street, placards and audio stations provide a fascinating narrative. See "Concord" in chapter 5.

- **Plymouth Rock** (Plymouth, Mass.): Okay, it's a fraction of its original size and looks like something you might find in your garden. Nevertheless, Plymouth Rock makes a perfect starting point for exploration. Close by is the *Mayflower II,* a replica of the alarmingly small original vessel. The juxtaposition reminds you of what a dangerous undertaking the Pilgrims' voyage was. See "Plymouth" in chapter 5.

- **Sandwich** (Mass.): The oldest town on Cape Cod, Sandwich was founded in 1637. Glassmaking brought notoriety and prosperity to this picturesque town in the 19th century. Visit the Sandwich Glass Museum for the whole story, or tour one of the town's glassblowing studios. Don't leave without visiting the 76-acre (31-hectare) Heritage Plantation, which has a working carousel, a sparkling antique-car collection, and a wonderful collection of Americana. See "The Upper Cape" in chapter 6.

- **Nantucket** (Mass): It looks like the whalers just left, leaving behind their grand houses, cobbled streets, and a gamut of enticing shops offering luxury goods from around the world. The Nantucket Historical Association owns more than a dozen properties open for tours, and the Whaling Museum is one of the most fascinating sites in the region. Tourism may be rampant, but not its tackier side effects, thanks to stringent preservation measures. See "Nantucket" in chapter 7.

- **Deerfield** (Mass.): Arguably the best-preserved colonial village in New England, Deerfield has scores of houses dating back to the 17th and 18th centuries. None of the clutter of modernity has intruded here. Fourteen houses on the main avenue can be visited through tours conducted by the organization known as Historic Deerfield. See "The Pioneer Valley" in chapter 8.

- **Newport** (R.I.): A key port of the clipper trade long before the British surrendered their colony, Newport retains abundant recollections of its maritime past. In addition to its great harbor, clogged with cigarette boats, tugs, ferries, and majestic sloops, the City by the Sea has kept three distinctive enclaves preserved: the waterside homes of colonial seamen, the hillside Federal houses of port-bound merchants, and the ostentatious mansions of America's post–Civil War industrial and financial grandees. See "Newport" in chapter 10.

- **Plymouth** (Vt.): President Calvin Coolidge was born in this high upland valley, and the state has done a superb job preserving his hometown village. You'll get a good sense of the president's roots, but also gain a greater understanding of how a New England village works. See p. 457.

- **Shelburne Museum** (Shelburne, Vt.): Think of this sprawling museum as New England's attic. Located on the shores of Lake Champlain, the Shelburne features not only the usual exhibits of quilts and early glass, but also whole buildings preserved like specimens in formaldehyde. Look

for the lighthouse, the railroad station, and the stagecoach inn. This is one of northern New England's "don't miss" destinations. See p. 483.

- **Portsmouth** (N.H.): Portsmouth is a salty coastal city that just happens to boast some of the most impressive historic homes in New England. Start at Strawbery Banke, a historic compound of 42 buildings dating from 1695 to 1820. Then visit the many other grand homes in nearby neighborhoods, like the house John Paul Jones occupied while building his warship during the Revolution. See "Portsmouth" in chapter 12.

- **Victoria Mansion** (Portland, Maine): Donald Trump had nothing on the Victorians when it came to material excess. You'll see Victorian decorative arts at their zenith in this elaborate Italianate mansion built during the Civil War years by a prosperous hotelier. It's open to the public for tours throughout the summer. See p. 558.

5 The Best Literary Landmarks

- **Concord** (Mass.): Concord is home to a legion of literary ghosts. The homes of Ralph Waldo Emerson, Nathaniel Hawthorne, Henry David Thoreau, and Louisa May Alcott are popular destinations, and look much as they did during the "flowering of New England" in the mid–19th century. See "Concord" in chapter 5.

- **Salem** (Mass.): Native son Nathaniel Hawthorne might still feel at home here. A hotel and a boulevard bear his name, the Custom House where he found an embroidered scarlet "A" still stands, and his birthplace is open for tours. It has been moved into

the same complex as the House of the Seven Gables, a cousin's home that inspired the classic novel. See "Salem" in chapter 5.

- **The Outer Cape** (Mass.): In the late 19th and early 20th centuries, the communities at the far end of the Cape—Wellfleet, Truro, and particularly Provincetown—were a veritable headquarters of Bohemia. Henry David Thoreau walked the 28 miles (45km) from Eastham to Provincetown and wrote about it in his classic *Cape Cod.* Distinguished literati such as Edna St. Vincent Millay, Mary McCarthy, Edmund Wilson, Tennessee Williams, Norman Mailer, and many others have also taken refuge among the dunes here. See "The Outer Cape" in chapter 6.

- **The Frost Place** (Franconia Notch, N.H.): Two of the most famous New England poems—"The Road Not Taken" and "Stopping by Woods on a Snowy Evening"—were composed by Robert Frost at this farm just outside of Franconia. Explore the woods and read the verses posted along the pathways, then tour the farmhouse where Frost lived with his family. See p. 534.

6 The Best Activities for Families

- **Exploring the Museum of Fine Arts** (Boston, Mass.): Parents hear "magnificent Egyptian collections," but kids think: "Mummies!" Even the most hyper youngster manages to take it down a notch in these quiet, refined surroundings, and the collections at the MFA simultaneously tickle visitors' brains. See p. 103.

- **Visiting the Museum of Science** (Boston, Mass.): Built around demonstrations, experiments, and interactive displays that never feel like homework, this museum is wildly popular with kids—and adults. Explore the exhibits, and then take in a show at the planetarium or the Mugar Omni Theater. Before you know it, everyone will have learned something, painlessly. See p. 104.

- **Catching a Free Friday Flick at the Hatch Shell** (Boston, Mass.): Better known for the Boston Pops' Fourth of July concert, the Esplanade is also famous for family films (*The Wizard of Oz* or *Pocahontas,* for example) shown on Friday nights in summer. The lawn in front of the Hatch Shell turns into a giant, carless drive-in as hundreds of people picnic and wait for the sky to grow dark. See p. 123.

- **Visiting the Heritage Plantation of Sandwich** (Cape Cod, Mass.): This site with museum buildings spread over 76 acres (31 hectares) will delight both children and adults. Kids will especially love the gleaming antique cars, the collections of soldiers and Native American clothing, and the 1912 carousel that offers unlimited rides. Outdoor concerts free with admission take place most Sunday afternoons in season. See p. 184.

- **Whale-Watching off Provincetown** (Cape Cod, Mass.): Boats leave MacMillan Wharf for the 8-mile (13km) journey to Stellwagen Bank National Marine Sanctuary, a rich feeding ground for several types of whales. Nothing can prepare you for the thrill of spotting these magnificent creatures feeding, breaching, and even flipper slapping. Hands down, the best outfit in town is the *Dolphin Fleet* (© 800/826-9300), which is affiliated with the Center for Coastal Studies. See p. 230.

- **Deep-Sea Fishing:** Charter fishing boats these days usually have high-tech fish-finding gear—imagine how your kids will react to reeling in one big bluefish after another. The top spots to mount such an expedition are Barnstable Harbor or Rock Harbor in Orleans, on Cape Cod; Point Judith, at the southern tip of Rhode Island; and the Maine coast. See chapters 6, 10, and 13, respectively.

- **Riding the Flying Horses Carousel in Oak Bluffs** (Martha's Vineyard, Mass.): Some say this is the oldest carousel in the country, but your kids might not notice the genuine horsehair, sculptural details, or glass eyes. They'll be too busy trying to grab the brass ring to win a free ride. After your ride, stroll around the town of Oak Bluffs. Children will be enchanted with the clustered "gingerbread" houses, a carryover from the 19th-century revivalist movement. See p. 253.

- **Biking Nantucket** (Mass.): Short, flat trails crisscross the island, and every one leads to a beach. The shortest rides lead to Children's Beach, with its own playground, and Jetties Beach, with a skate park and watersports equipment for rent; older kids will be able to make the few miles to Surfside and Madaket. See "Nantucket" in chapter 7.

- **Learning to Ski at Jiminy Peak** (Mass.): More than 70 percent of Jiminy Peak's trails are geared toward beginners and intermediates, making it one of the premier places to learn to ski in the East. The mountain is located in the heart of the Berkshires, near Mount Greylock. See p. 315.

- **Visiting Mystic Seaport and Mystic Aquarium** (Conn.): The double-down winner in the family-fun sweepstakes has to be this combination: performing dolphins and whales, full-rigged tall ships, penguins and sharks, and river rides on a perky little 1906 motor launch. These are the kinds of G-rated attractions that have no age barriers. See p. 363.

- **Exploring the Lake Champlain Bikeway** (Burlington, Vt.): A lovely bike path follows the shores of the lake on an abandoned railbed. Efforts to link up this trail with others to the north include two new bike ferries that span rivers and causeway gaps. Lakeshore beaches and leafy parks dot the route. See p. 484.

- **Visiting the Montshire Museum of Science** (Norwich, Vt.): This handsome children's museum, in a soaring, barnlike space on the Vermont–New Hampshire border, has interactive exhibits that put the wonder back into science. Afterward, stroll the nature trails along the Connecticut River. See p. 503.

- **Riding the Mount Washington Cog Railway** (Crawford Notch, N.H.): It's fun! It's terrifying! It's a great glimpse into history. Kids love this ratchety climb to the top of New England's highest peak aboard trains that were specially designed to scale the mountain in 1869. As a technological marvel, the railroad attracted tourists by the thousands a century ago. They still come to marvel at the sheer audacity of it all. See p. 526.

- **Exploring Monhegan Island** (Maine): Kids from 8 to 12 especially enjoy overnight excursions to Monhegan Island. The mailboat from Port Clyde is rustic and intriguing, and the hotels are an adventure. Leave at least an afternoon to sit atop the high, rocky bluffs scouting the glimmering ocean for whales. See "The Mid Coast" in chapter 13.

7 The Best Country Inns

- **Hawthorne Inn** (Concord, Mass.; ✆ **978/369-5610**): Everything here—the 1870 building, the garden setting a stone's throw from the historic attractions, the antique furnishings, the eclectic decorations, the accommodating innkeepers—is top of the line. See p. 142.

- **Longfellow's Wayside Inn** (Sudbury, Mass.; ✆ **800/339-1776**): A gorgeous inn, an unusual setting, excellent food, the imprimatur of a distinguished New

England author, nearly 300 years of history, and the schoolhouse the little lamb followed Mary to. What's not to like? See p. 142.

- **Captain's House Inn** (Chatham, Cape Cod, Mass.; © 800/315-0728): An elegant country inn positively dripping with good taste, this is among the best small inns in the region. Most rooms have fireplaces, elegant paneling, and antiques; they're sumptuous yet cozy. This could be the ultimate spot to enjoy Chatham's Christmas Stroll festivities. See p. 217.

- **Charlotte Inn** (Edgartown, Martha's Vineyard, Mass.; © 508/627-4751): Edgartown tends to be the most formal enclave on Martha's Vineyard, and this compound of exquisite buildings is by far the fanciest address in town. The rooms are distinctively decorated: One boasts a baby grand, another its own thematic dressing room. The conservatory restaurant, L'étoile, is among the finest you'll find this side of France. See p. 255.

- **Mayflower Inn** (Washington, Conn.; © 860/868-9466): Not a tough call at all for this part of the region: Immaculate in taste and execution, the Mayflower is as close to perfection as any such enterprise is likely to be (points off for whiffs of excess pretension). A genuine Joshua Reynolds hangs in the hall. See p. 335.

- **Griswold Inn** (Essex, Conn.; © 860/767-1776): "The Griz" has been accommodating sailors and travelers as long as any inn in the country, give or take a decade. For all that time, it has been the focus of life and commerce in the lower Connecticut River Valley, always ready with a mug of suds, a haunch of beef, and a roaring fire. The walls are layered with nautical paintings and memorabilia, and there's music every night in the schoolhouse-turned-tavern. See p. 357.

- **The Equinox** (Manchester Village, Vt.; © 800/362-4747): This is southern Vermont's grand resort, with nearly 200 rooms in a white-clapboard compound that seems to go on forever. The rooms are pleasant enough, but the real draws are the grounds and the resort's varied activities—it's set on 2,300 acres (932 hectares) with pools, tennis courts, an 18-hole golf course, and even its own mountainside. Tried everything on vacation? How about falconry classes or backcountry driving at the Range Rover school? See p. 433.

- **Windham Hill Inn** (West Townshend, Vt.; © 800/944-4080): New innkeepers have added welcome amenities like air-conditioning in the rooms and a conference room in the barn while still preserving the antique charm of this 1823 farmstead. It's at the end of a remote dirt road in a high upland valley, and guests are welcome to explore 160 private acres (65 hectares) on a network of walking trails. See p. 445.

- **Jackson House Inn** (Woodstock, Vt.; © 800/448-1890): The constant improvements and the meticulous attention to service have made this a longtime favorite for visitors to Woodstock. The meals are stunning, the guest rooms the very picture of antique elegance. The only downside? It fronts a sometimes noisy road. See p. 454.

- **Twin Farms** (Barnard, Vt.; © 800/894-6327): Just north of Woodstock may be the most elegant inn in New England. Its rates are a tad breathtaking, but guests are certainly pampered here.

Novelist Sinclair Lewis once lived on this 300-acre (122-hectare) farm, and today it's an aesthetic retreat that offers serenity and exceptional food. See p. 454.

- **The Pitcher Inn** (Warren, Vt.; ☎ **888/867-8424**): Even though this place was built in 1997, it's possessed of the graciousness of a longtime, well-worn inn. It combines traditional New England form and scale with modern and luxe touches, plus a good dollop of whimsy. See p. 467.

- **Basin Harbor Club** (Vergennes, Vt.; ☎ **800/622-4000**): Established in 1886, this lakeside resort has the sort of patina that only comes with age. It's a classic old-fashioned family resort, with golf, boating on Lake Champlain, jackets-required dining, evening lectures on the arts, and even a private airstrip. Bring books and board games, and re-learn what summer's all about. See p. 484.

- **Balsams Grand Resort Hotel** (Dixville Notch, N.H.; ☎ **800/ 255-0600**): The designation "country inn" is only half correct.

You've got plenty of country—it's set on 15,000 acres (6,075 hectares) in far northern New Hampshire. But this historic resort is more castle than inn. The Balsams has been offering superb hospitality and gracious comfort since 1866. It has two golf courses, miles of hiking trails, and, in winter, its own downhill and cross-country ski areas. See p. 538.

- **White Barn Inn** (Kennebunkport, Maine; ☎ **207/967-2321**): Many of the White Barn staff hail from Europe, and guests are treated with a Continental graciousness. The rooms are a delight, and the meals (served in the barn) are among the best in Maine. See p. 553.

- **The Claremont** (Southwest Harbor, Maine; ☎ **800/244-5036**): The 1884 Claremont is a Maine classic. This waterside lodge has everything a Victorian resort should, including sparely decorated rooms, creaky floorboards in the halls, great views of water and mountains, and a perfect croquet pitch. See p. 608.

8 The Best Moderately Priced Accommodations

- **Newbury Guest House** (Boston, Mass.; ☎ **800/437-7668**) and **Harborside Inn** (Boston, Mass.; ☎ **617/723-7500**): These sister properties would be good deals even if they weren't ideally located—the former in the Back Bay, the latter downtown. Rates at the Guest House even include breakfast. See p. 76 and p. 82.

- **Harvard Square Hotel** (Cambridge, Mass.; ☎ **800/458-5886**): Smack in the middle of Cambridge's most popular destination, this hotel is a comfortable place to stay in a great location. See p. 88.

- **John Carver Inn** (Plymouth, Mass.; ☎ **800/274-1620**): This

hotel is centrally located, whether you're immersing yourself in Pilgrim lore or passing through on the way from Boston to Cape Cod. Ask about the "Destination Plymouth" packages for a good deal. See p. 178.

- **Isaiah Hall B&B Inn** (Dennis, Cape Cod, Mass.; ☎ **800/736-0160**): Nestled amid oak trees in Dennis, this B&B has been welcoming visitors for more than 50 years. The inn and its gregarious owner are popular with actors starring in summer stock at the nearby Cape Playhouse. Guests enjoy country-cozy rooms and a communal breakfast. See p. 206.

- **Nauset House Inn** (East Orleans, Cape Cod, Mass.; ℂ **508/255-2195**): This romantic 1810 farmhouse is like a sepia-toned vision of old Cape Cod. Recline in a wicker divan surrounded by fragrant flowers while the wind whistles outside. Better yet, stroll to Nauset Beach and take a quiet walk as the sun sets. Your genial hosts also prepare one of the finest breakfasts in town. See p. 221.
- **Hopkins Inn** (New Preston, Conn.; ℂ **860/868-7295**): This yellow farmhouse bestows the top view of gorgeous Lake Waramaug, at its best on soft summer days when robust Alpine dishes can be taken out on the terrace. The somewhat spartan rooms don't tempt winding-down guests with either phones or TVs. See p. 337.
- **Bee and Thistle Inn** (Old Lyme, Conn.; ℂ **800/622-4946**): Known for decades for its highly regarded cuisine, this 1756 house also has a detached cottage and 11 pretty guest rooms, two of which have fireplaces. Easily one of the area's most romantic weekend getaways, there are musicians underscoring the mood in the dining rooms on weekends. See p. 356.
- **Inn at the Mad River Barn** (Waitsfield, Vt.; ℂ **800/631-0466**): It takes a few minutes to adapt to the spartan rooms and no-frills accommodations here. But you'll soon discover that the real action takes place in the living room and dining room, where skiers relax and chat after a day on the slopes, and share heaping helpings at mealtime. See p. 467.
- **Thayers Inn** (Littleton, N.H.; ℂ **800/634-8179**): This old-fashioned downtown inn has 48 eclectic rooms and a whole lot of relaxed charm. Ulysses S. Grant and Richard Nixon slept here, among others. Rooms start at just $40 if you're willing to share a bathroom; from $60 for a private bathroom. See p. 536.
- **Philbrook Farm Inn** (Shelburne, N.H.; ℂ **603/466-3831**): Come here if you're looking for a complete getaway. The inn has been taking in travelers since the 1850s, and the owners know how to do it right. The farmhouse sits on 1,000 acres (405 hectares) between the Mahoosuc Mountains and the Androscoggin River, and guests can hike with vigor or relax in leisure with equal aplomb. See p. 538.
- **Franciscan Guest House** (Kennebunk, Maine; ℂ **207/967-2011**): No daily maid service, cheap paneling on the walls, and industrial carpeting. What's to like? Plenty, including the location (on the lush riverside grounds of a monastery), price (doubles from $65), and a great Lithuanian-style breakfast spread in the morning. You can bike to the beach or walk to Dock Square in Kennebunkport. See p. 552.
- **Driftwood Inn & Cottages** (Bailey Island, Maine; ℂ **207/833-5461**): Where else can you find rooms at the edge of the rocky Maine coast for $70? This classic shingled compound dates from 1910 and mostly offers rooms with shared bathrooms—but it's worth that small inconvenience for the views alone. See p. 567.

9 The Best Restaurants

- **Aujourd'hui** (Boston, Mass.; ℂ **617/351-2071**): The exquisite setting, spectacular view, telepathic service, and, of course, marvelous food combine to transport you to a plane where you might not even notice (or care) how much it's costing. See p. 95.

- **Rialto** (Cambridge, Mass.; ✆ **617/661-5050**): This is a don't-miss destination if your plans include fine dining. The contemporary setting is a great match for chef Jody Adams's inventive cuisine, and the service is efficient without being too familiar—surely a draw for the visiting celebrities who flock here. See p. 97.

- **Chester** (Provincetown, Cape Cod, Mass.; ✆ **508/487-8200**): A singular dining experience awaits beyond the colonnaded portico of this Commercial Street restaurant. Chester specializes in local seafood, meats, and vegetables prepared simply yet with a flourish, and the service is exceptional. See p. 235.

- **L'étoile** (Edgartown, Martha's Vineyard, Mass.; ✆ **508/627-5187**): The most exemplary dining experience on Martha's Vineyard can be found in this exquisite conservatory at the renowned Charlotte Inn. The nouvelle-cuisine offerings vary seasonally, but the chef consistently dazzles with a menu of delicacies flown in from the four corners of the earth. See p. 260.

- **Òran Mór** (Nantucket, Mass.; ✆ **508/228-8655**): Climb up the stairs of this historic building and prepare yourself for an extravagant dining experience. Chef/owner Peter Wallace has created an intimate setting for his creative international cuisine, served with utmost professionalism. The best sommelier on the island will assist you in choosing a wine to go with your elegant meal. See p. 277.

- **Truc Orient Express** (West Stockbridge, Mass.; ✆ **413/232-4204**): The artists who live in this funky Berkshires hamlet deserve something outside the prevailing red-sauce and red-meat modes. They get it in this converted warehouse, with eye-opening Thai, Vietnamese, and Southeast Asian dishes that rarely emerge from kitchens this far west of Ho Chi Minh City. Tastes range from delicate to sinus-clearing. See p. 305.

- **Union League Café** (New Haven, Conn.; ✆ **203/562-4299**): This august setting of arched windows and high ceilings is more than a century old and was long the sanctuary of an exclusive club. It still looks good, but the tone has been lightened into an approximation of a Lyonnaise brasserie. The menu observes the southern French tastes for curry, olive oil, pastas, lamb, and shellfish. See p. 346.

- **Scales & Shells** (Newport, R.I.; ✆ **401/846-3474**): Ye who turn aside all ostentation, get yourselves hence. There's nary a frill nor affectation anywhere near this place, and because the wide-open kitchen is right at the entrance, there are no secrets, either. What we have here are marine critters mere hours from the depths, prepared and presented free of any but the slightest artifice. This might well be the purest seafood joint on the southern New England coast. See p. 405.

- **Chantecleer** (Manchester Center, Vt.; ✆ **802/362-1616**): Swiss chef Michel Baumann has been turning out dazzling dinners here since 1981, and the kitchen hasn't gotten stale in the least. The dining room in an old barn is magical, the staff helpful and friendly. It's a great spot for those who demand top-notch Continental fare but don't like the fuss of a fancy restaurant. See p. 434.

- **T. J. Buckley's** (Brattleboro, Vt.; © 802/257-4922): This tiny diner on a dark side street serves up outsized tastes prepared by talented chef Michael Fuller. Forget about stewed-too-long diner fare; get in your mind big tastes blossoming from the freshest of ingredients prepared just right. See p. 443.

- **Jackson House Inn** (Woodstock, Vt.; © 800/448-1890): Situated in a modern addition to an upscale country inn, the Jackson House Inn serves meals that are ingeniously conceived, deftly prepared, and artfully arranged. The three-course meals cost around $55, and offer excellent value at that. See p. 453.

- **Hemingway's** (Killington, Vt.; © 802/422-3886): Killington seems an unlikely place for a serious culinary adventure, yet Hemingway's will meet the loftiest expectations. The menu changes frequently to ensure only the freshest of ingredients. If it's available, be sure to order the wild mushroom and truffle soup. See p. 460.

- **Arrows** (Ogunquit, Maine; © 207/361-1100): The emphasis at this elegant spot is local products—often very local, including many ingredients from the large organic vegetable gardens. Prices are not for the fainthearted (it's expensive even by New York City standards), but the experience is top-rate, from the cordial service to the silver and linens. Expect New American fare informed by an Asian sensibility. See p. 549.

- **White Barn Inn** (Kennebunkport, Maine; © 207/967-2321): The setting, in an ancient, rustic barn, is magical. The tables are set with floor-length tablecloths, and the chairs feature imported Italian upholstery. The food? To die for. Enjoy entrees such as grilled duckling breast with ginger and sun-dried cherry sauce, or a roast rack of lamb with pecans and homemade barbecue sauce. See p. 553.

- **Fore Street** (Portland, Maine; © 207/775-2717): Fore Street is one of New England's most celebrated restaurants—the place was listed as one of *Gourmet* magazine's 100 best restaurants in 2001, and the chef has been getting lots of press elsewhere as well. His secret? Simplicity, and lots of it. Some of the most memorable meals are prepared over an applewood grill. See p. 561.

10 The Best Local Dining Experiences

- **Durgin-Park** (Boston, Mass.; © 617/227-2038): A meal at this landmark restaurant might start with a waitress dropping a handful of cutlery in front of you and saying, "Here, give these out." The surly service usually seems to be an act, but it's so much a part of the experience that some people are disappointed when the waitresses are nice (as they often are). In any case, it's worked since 1827. See p. 93.

- **Woodman's of Essex** (Essex, Mass.; © 800/649-1773): This busy North Shore institution is not for the faint of heart—or the hard of artery, unless you like eating corn and steamers while everyone around you is gobbling fried clams and onion rings. The food at this glorified clam shack is fresh and delicious, and a look at the organized pandemonium behind the counter is worth the (reasonable) price. See p. 159.

- **The Bite** (Menemsha, Martha's Vineyard, Mass.; © 508/645-9239): This is your quintessential "chowdah" and clam shack, serving up exceptional chowder, potato salad, and fried fish. Those in the know bring their picnic dinner over to nearby Menemsha Beach, where the sunsets are awesome. See p. 263.

- **Louis' Lunch—The Very First (Well, Probably) Burgers** (New Haven, Conn.; ✆ 203/562-5507): Not a lot of serious history has happened in New Haven, but boosters claim it was here that hamburgers were invented in 1900. This boxy little luncheonette lives on, moved from its original site in order to save it. The patties are freshly ground daily, thrust into vertical grills, and served on white toast. Garnishes are tomato, onion, and cheese. No ketchup and no fries, so don't even ask. See p. 346.

- **Wooster Street Pizza** (New Haven, Conn.): New Haven's claim to America's first pizza is a whole lot shakier, but it has few equals as purveyor of the ultra-thin, charred variety of what they still call "apizza" in these parts, pronounced "ah-peetz." Old-timer **Frank Pepe's,** 157 Wooster St. (✆ 203/865-5762), is usually ceded top rank among the local parlors, but it is joined at the summit by such contenders as **Sally's,** 237 Wooster St. (✆ 203/624-5271) and the upstart brewpub **Brü Rm,** 254 Crown St. (✆ 203/495-1111). See p. 345.

- **Abbott's Lobster in the Rough** (Noank, Conn.; ✆ 860/536-7719): Places like this frill-free shack abound along more northerly reaches of the New England coast, but here's a little bit o' Maine a Sunday drive from Manhattan. Shore dinners rule, so roll up sleeves, tie on napkins and feedbags, dive into bowls of chowder and platters of boiled shrimp and steamed mussels, and dunk

hot lobster chunks in pots of drawn butter. See p. 366.

- **Johnnycakes and Stuffies** (R.I.): Sooner or later, most worthy regional food faves become known to the wider world (witness Buffalo wings). The Ocean State still clutches a couple of taste treats within its borders. "Johnnycakes" are flapjacks made with cornmeal, which come small and plump or wide and lacy, depending upon family tradition. "Stuffies" are the baby-fist-sized quahog (*KWAH*-og or *KOE*-hog) clams barely known elsewhere in New England. The flesh is chopped up, combined with minced bell peppers and bread crumbs, and packed back into both halves of the shell. See chapter 10.

- **Blue Benn Diner** (Bennington, Vt.; ✆ 802/442-5140): This classic 1945 Silk City diner has a barrel ceiling, acres of stainless steel, and a vast menu. Don't overlook specials scrawled on paper and taped all over the walls. And leave room for a slice of delicious pie, such as blackberry, pumpkin, or chocolate cream. See p. 428.

- **Al's** (South Burlington, Vt.; ✆ 802/862-9203): This is where Ben and Jerry go to eat french fries—as does every other potato addict in the state. See p. 486.

- **Lou's** (Hanover, N.H.; ✆ 603/643-3321): Huge crowds flock to Lou's, just down the block from the Dartmouth campus, for breakfast on weekends. Fortunately, breakfast is served all day here, and the sandwiches on fresh-baked bread are huge and delicious. See p. 505.

- **Becky's** (Portland, Maine; ✆ 207/773-7070): Five different kinds of home fries on the menu? It's breakfast nirvana at this local institution on the working waterfront. It's a favored hangout of fishermen, high-school kids, businessmen, and just about everyone else. See p. 562.

- **Silly's** (Portland, Maine; © **207/ 772-0360**): Hectic and fun, this tiny, informal, kitschy restaurant serves up delicious finger food, like pita wraps, hamburgers, and pizza. The milkshakes alone are worth the detour. See p. 562.

- **Fisherman's Friend** (Stonington, Maine; © **207/367-2442**): This is a lively and boisterous kind of place, where you'll get your fill of both local color and what may be Maine's most succulent lobster stew. See p. 590.

11 The Best of the Performing Arts

- **Symphony Hall** (Boston, Mass.; © **617/266-1492**): Home to the Boston Symphony Orchestra, the Boston Pops, and other local and visiting groups and performers, this is a perfect (acoustically and otherwise) destination for classical music. See p. 123.

- **Hatch Shell** (Boston, Mass.; © **617/727-5215**): This amphitheater on the Charles River Esplanade plays host to free music and dance performances and films almost every night in summer. Around the Fourth of July, the Boston Pops provide the entertainment. Bring a blanket to sit on. See p. 123.

- **Boston's Theater District:** The area's performance spaces are in the midst of a nearly unprecedented boom, and this is the epicenter. Previews and touring companies of Broadway hits, local music and dance troupes, and other productions of every description make this part of town hop every night. See p. 124.

- *The Nutcracker* (Boston, Mass.; © **617/695-6955** for tickets): New England's premier family-oriented holiday event is Boston Ballet's extravaganza. When the Christmas tree grows through the floor, even fidgety preadolescents forget that they think they're too cool to be here. See p. 124.

- **The Comedy Connection at Faneuil Hall** (Boston, Mass.; © **888/398-5100**): Even in the Athens of America, it's not all high culture. The biggest national names and the funniest local comedians take the stage at this Quincy Market hot spot. See p. 125.

- **The Berkshire Theatre Festival** (Stockbridge, Mass.; © **413/298-5576**): An 1887 "casino" and converted barn mount both new and classic plays from June to late August in one of the prettiest towns in the Berkshires. Name artists on the order of Joanne Woodward and Dianne Wiest are often listed as actors and directors in the annual playbill. See p. 302.

- **The Jacob's Pillow Dance Festival** (Becket, Mass.; © **413/243-0745**): Celebrated dancer/choreographer Martha Graham made this her summertime performance space for decades. Guest troupes are among the world's best, often including Dance Theatre of Harlem, the Merce Cunningham Dance Company, and the Paul Taylor Company, supplemented by repertory companies working with jazz, flamenco, or world music. See p. 305.

- **Tanglewood Music Festival** (Lenox, Mass.; © **617/266-1492** in Boston, 413/637-5165 in Lenox): By far the most dominating presence on New England's summer cultural front, the music festival that takes place on this magnificent Berkshires estate is itself in thrall to the Boston Symphony Orchestra (BSO). While the BSO reigns, room is made for such guest soloists as Jessye Norman and Itzhak Perlman as well as practitioners of other forms, from jazz (Dave Brubeck) to folk (James Taylor) and the Boston Pops. See p. 308.

- **The Williamstown Theatre Festival** (Williamstown, Mass.; ✆ 413/597-3400): Classic, new, and avant-garde plays are all presented during the June-through-August season at this venerable festival. There are two stages, one for works by established playwrights, the smaller second venue for less mainstream or experimental plays. There is usually a Broadway headliner on hand; Frank Langella has been a frequent presence. See p. 318.

- **The Norfolk Chamber Music Festival** (Norfolk, Conn.; ✆ 860/542-3000): A century-old "Music Shed" on the Ellen Battell Stoeckel Estate in this Litchfield Hills town shelters such important chamber performance groups as the Tokyo String Quartet and the Vermeer Quartet. Young professional musicians perform morning recitals. See p. 341.

- **Summer in Newport** (R.I.): From Memorial Day to Labor Day, only a scheduling misfortune will deny visitors the experience of an outdoor musical event. In calendar order, the highlights (well short of all-inclusive) are the July Newport Music Festival, the August Ben & Jerry's Folk Festival and JVC Jazz Festival, and the Waterfront Irish Festival in September. See p. 390.

- **The Marlboro Music Festival** (Marlboro, Vt.; ✆ 215/569-4690 off-season, 802/254-2394 in summer): Pablo Casals participated in this highly regarded festival between 1960 and 1973. He's gone, but today you can hear accomplished masters and talented younger musicians in a 700-seat auditorium amid the rolling hills of southern Vermont. Performances are held weekends from mid-July to mid-August. See p. 436.

12 The Best Destinations for Antiques Hounds

- **Charles Street** (Boston, Mass.): Beacon Hill is one of the city's oldest neighborhoods, and at the foot of the hill is a thoroughfare that's equally steeped in history. Hundreds of years' worth of furniture, collectibles, and accessories jam the shops along its 5 blocks. See p. 121.

- **Main Street, Essex** (Mass.): The treasures on display in this North Shore town run the gamut, from one step above yard sales to one step below nationally televised auctions. Follow Route 133 west of Route 128 through downtown and north almost all the way to the Ipswich border. See "Cape Ann" in chapter 5.

- **Route 6A: The Old King's Highway** (Cape Cod, Mass.): Antiques buffs, as well as architecture and country-road connoisseurs, will have a field day along scenic Route 6A. Designated a Regional Historic District, this former stagecoach route winds through a half dozen charming Cape Cod villages and is lined with scores of antiques shops. The largest concentration is in Brewster, but you'll find good pickings all along this meandering road, from Sandwich to Orleans. See chapter 6.

- **Brimfield Antique and Collectible Shows** (Brimfield, Mass.): This otherwise undistinguished town west of Sturbridge erupts with three monster shows every summer, in mid-May, mid-July, and early September. Upward of 6,000 dealers set up tented and tabletop shops in fields around town. Call ⓒ **800/628-8379** for details, and book room reservations far in advance. See p. 282.
- **Sheffield** (Mass.): This southernmost town in the Berkshires is home to at least three dozen dealers in collectibles, Americana, military memorabilia, English furniture of the Georgian period, silverware, and weather vanes . . . even antique birdhouses. Most of them are strung along Route 7, with a worthwhile detour west along Route 23 in South Egremont. See p. 296.
- **Woodbury** (Conn.): More than 30 dealers strung along Main Street offer a diversity of precious treasures, near-antiques, and simply funky old stuff. American and European furniture and other pieces are most evident, but there are forays into crafts and assorted whimsies as well. Pick up the directory of the Woodbury Antiques Dealers Association, available in most of the shops. See p. 332.
- **Newfane and Townshend** (Vt.): A handful of delightful antiques shops are hidden in and around these picture-perfect towns. But the real draw is the Sunday flea market, held just off Route 30 north of Newfane, where you never know what might turn up. See p. 443.
- **Portsmouth** (N.H.): Picturesque downtown Portsmouth is home to a half dozen or so antiques stores and some fine used-book shops. For more meaty browsing, head about 25 miles (40km) northwest on Route 4 to Northwood, where a dozen good-size shops flank the highway. See "Portsmouth" in chapter 12.
- **Route 1, Kittery to Scarborough** (Maine): Antiques scavengers delight in this 37-mile (60km) stretch of less-than-scenic Route 1. Antiques minimalls and high-class junk shops alike are scattered all along the route, though there's no central antiques zone. See "The South Coast" in chapter 13.

2

Planning Your Trip to New England

by Wayne Curtis

This chapter provides most of the nuts-and-bolts information you'll need before setting off for New England. Browse through this section before you hit the road to ensure you've touched all the bases.

1 The Regions in Brief

BOSTON Oliver Wendell Holmes dubbed Boston the "Hub of the Universe," and the label stuck. Today, "The Hub" is the region's largest and most vibrant city. This alluring metropolis of historic and modern buildings, world-class museums, and top-notch restaurants is an important stop for travelers on any trip to New England.

CAPE COD & THE ISLANDS The ocean is writ large on Cape Cod, a low peninsula with miles of sandy beaches and grassy dunes that whisper in the wind. The carnival-like atmosphere of Provincetown is a draw, as are the genteel charms of Martha's Vineyard and Nantucket, two islands just offshore.

THE PIONEER VALLEY Extending through Massachusetts along the Connecticut River, the area takes its name from the early settlers who arrived here in the 17th century. Among the many picturesque towns is unspoiled Historic Deerfield.

THE BERKSHIRES Massachusetts's rolling hills at the state's western edge are home to historic old estates, graceful villages, and an abundance of festivals and cultural events, including the Tanglewood Music Festival and Jacob's Pillow Dance Festival.

THE LITCHFIELD HILLS The historic northwest corner of Connecticut has sleepy villages, hidden hiking trails, and a surfeit of New England charm—all just a couple of hours from New York City.

THE CONNECTICUT COAST The eastern coast is home to the historic towns of Mystic and New London, where you can get a glimpse of the shipbuilding trade at the Mystic Seaport museum and the Navy submarine base in nearby Groton.

NEWPORT, RHODE ISLAND AREA The lifestyles of the truly rich and famous are on parade in Newport, once home to the likes of the Astors and Vanderbilts. A tour of the oceanfront mansions never fails to astonish.

GREEN MOUNTAINS Extending the length of Vermont from Massachusetts to Canada, this mostly gentle chain of forested hills and low mountains offers great hiking, scenic back-road drives, fantastic inns, and superb bicycling.

WHITE MOUNTAINS Since the mid–19th century, New Hampshire's White Mountains have drawn travelers to its rugged, windswept peaks and forests dotted with glacial boulders and clear, rushing streams. New

England's best backcountry hiking and camping are found here.

COASTAL MAINE Maine's rocky coast is the stuff of legend, art, and poetry. The southern coast features most of the state's beaches; farther "down east," you'll find rocky headlands and Acadia National Park, New England's only national park.

MAINE'S NORTH WOODS Consisting of millions of acres of uninhabited terrain, the North Woods is almost entirely owned by timber companies that harvest trees to feed their mills. Within this vast tree plantation are pockets of undisturbed wildlands that recall the era when Thoreau paddled and portaged his way north.

2 Visitor Information

Chamber addresses and phone numbers are provided for each region in the chapters that follow. If you're a highly organized traveler, you'll call in advance and ask for information to be mailed to you long before you depart. If you're like the rest of us, you'll swing by when you reach town and hope the office is still open.

All six New England states are pleased to send out general visitor information packets and maps to those who call or write ahead. Here's the contact information:

- **Connecticut Office of Tourism,** Department of Economic and Community Development, 505 Hudson St., Hartford, CT 06106 (© **800/282-6863** or 860/270-8080; www.ctbound.com).
- **Maine Tourism Association,** P.O. Box 2300, Hallowell, ME 04347 (© **800/533-9595** outside Maine, or 207/623-0363; www. visitmaine.com).

- **Massachusetts Office of Travel and Tourism,** State Transportation Building, 10 Park Plaza, Suite 4510, Boston, MA 02116 (© **800/227-6277** or 617/973-8500; www.mass-vacation.com).
- **New Hampshire Office of Travel and Tourism,** P.O. Box 1856, Concord, NH 03302 (© **800/ 386-4664** or 603/271-2343; www.visitnh.gov).
- **Rhode Island Department of Economic Development,** 1 West Exchange St., Providence, RI 02903 (© **800/556-2484** or 401/277-2601; www.visitrhode island.com).
- **Vermont Travel and Tourism,** 134 State St., Montpelier, VT 05602 (© **800/837-6668** or 802/828-3237 for general information, or 800/833-9756 to receive information by fax; www.travel-vermont.com).

3 Money

ATMs ATMs are commonly found in New England's more populated areas and in regions that cater to tourists, but don't count on finding machines in the most remote locales. ATMs are linked to a network that most likely includes your bank at home. **Cirrus** (© **800/424-7787;** www.mastercard.com) and **PLUS** (© **800/843-7587;** www.visa.com) are the two most popular networks in

the U.S.; call or check online for ATM locations at your destination. You'll get the best exchange rate if you withdraw money from an ATM, but keep in mind that many banks impose a fee every time a card is used at an ATM in a different city or bank. On top of this, the bank from which you withdraw cash may charge its own fee.

TRAVELER'S CHECKS Note that many hotels, restaurants, and shops

New England's Regions

Tips Saving Money on Accommodations

Budget travelers might be in for a bit of sticker shock in New England. Boston is one of the nation's more expensive cities when it comes to hotels, and in midsummer, there's simply no such thing as a cheap room in popular areas like Cape Cod, Newport, or Bar Harbor. To save money, consider these alternatives:

- **Travel in the off-season.** At summer destinations, inexpensive rooms are often available in April, May, November, and early December. Granted, it's a bit bleak then, but you can find good deals if you're just looking for a quiet retreat. The best "off-season" period to my mind is September. The weather is great, and many lodgings cut prices between the summer and foliage seasons.

- **Commute from lower-priced areas.** If you're willing to drive a half hour or an hour to reach prime destinations, you can often find cheaper lodging in less glamorous settings. Chain hotels ring the Boston area, and Bangor, Maine, is within striking distance of Acadia National Park. Study a map and be creative.

- **Camp out.** You can often find camping at both public and private campgrounds near popular attractions, with prices ranging from $9 to $25 per night. That's especially true in the northern three states, where you can often find camping within a short drive of even major cities.

will accept traveler's checks with no transaction fee, but some banks may charge as much as $10 just to cash a traveler's check. Be sure to keep a record of the serial numbers separate from the checks; in case of loss or theft, you'll need this information.

American Express offers traveler's checks with a service charge ranging from 1% to 4%. You can get them over the phone by calling © 800/221-7282; Amex gold and platinum cardholders who use this number are exempt from the 1% fee. AAA members can obtain checks without a fee at most AAA offices.

Visa offers traveler's checks at Citibank locations as well as several other banks. The service charge ranges from 1.5% to 2%. Call © 800/732-1322 for information. **Master-Card** also offers traveler's checks. Call © 800/223-9920 for a location near you.

CREDIT CARDS Credit cards are invaluable when traveling. They're a safe way to carry money and provide a convenient record of all your expenses. You can also withdraw cash advances from your credit cards at any bank (though you'll start paying hefty interest on the advance the moment you receive the cash). Cards widely accepted in New England include American Express, Discover, Master-Card, and Visa.

4 When to Go

The well-worn joke about New England's weather is that the region has just two seasons: winter and August. There's a kernel of truth to that, especially in the north, but it's mostly a canard to keep outsiders from moving here. In fact, the individual seasons are among those elements that make New England so distinctive.

SUMMER Peak summer season runs from July 4th to Labor Day, when crowds surge into New England's tourist areas in the mountains and along the coast. Summers are verdant and lush, and in the mountains, warm (rarely hot) days are the rule, followed by cool nights. Along the coast, ocean breezes keep temperatures down; Cape Cod and the Islands, for example, are generally 10 degrees cooler than the mainland in summer.

The weather typically follows the winds. Southerly breezes bring haze, heat, and humidity. Northwest winds bring cool weather and knife-sharp vistas. These systems tend to alternate, often with rain between them, and the change from hot to cool will sometimes occur in a matter of minutes. Rain is never far away—some days it's a quick afternoon thunderstorm; other times it's a steady drizzle that brings a 4-day soaking. Travelers should come prepared.

For most of the region, especially the coastal areas, midsummer is the prime season for travel. Expect to pay premium prices at hotels and restaurants except near the empty ski resorts of northern New England, where you can often find bargains. Also be aware that early summer (generally mid-May through June) brings out voracious black flies and mosquitoes, especially in the North Country. Outdoorsy types are better off waiting until July before heading into the deep woods.

AUTUMN In northern New England, don't be surprised to smell the tang of fall approaching as early as mid-August. Fall comes early here, puts its feet up on the couch, and stays for a time. The foliage season begins in earnest in the northern part of the region by the third week in September; in the south, it reaches its peak by mid- to late October. The change in

seasons in southern Connecticut runs 3 to 4 weeks behind northern Maine. And the higher elevations of the Green and White mountains likewise start to feel wintry a month or so before coastal locations.

Fall in New England is one of America's great natural spectacles, with miles of rolling hills blanketed with brilliant reds and stunning oranges. Along winding country roads you'll find heaps of pumpkins for sale beneath blazing red sugar maples, and crisp apples available by the bushel.

Keep in mind that this is the most popular time of year to travel—bus tours fill the roads and hotels throughout October. Advance reservations are essential; you can also expect to pay a foliage premium of $20 or more at many inns.

WINTER New England winters are like wine—some years are good, some lousy. During a good season, plenty of light, fluffy snow covers the deep woods and ski slopes, and exploring the forest on snowshoes or cross-country skis is a magical experience.

During the *other* winters, the weather brings a nasty mélange of rain and sleet. It's bone-numbing cold, and bleak, bleak, bleak. Look into the eyes of the residents on the streets during this time. They are all thinking about the Caribbean.

The higher you go and the farther north you head, the better your odds of finding snow and avoiding rain. Winter coastal vacations can be spectacular (nothing beats cross-country skiing at the edge of the pounding surf), but it's a high-risk venture that could yield rain rather than snow.

Ski areas naturally are crowded during the winter months. They're especially so during school vacations, when most resorts tend to jack up their rates.

SPRING New England is famous for its elusive spring, which some residents claim lasts only a weekend or so, typically around mid-May, but sometimes as late as June. One day the ground is muddy, the trees are barren, and gritty snow is piled in shady hollows. The next day, temperatures are in the 80s, trees are blooming, and kids are swimming in the lakes. It's a little weird, frankly. Travelers must be very alert if they want to experience spring in New England. Spring is also known as the mud season, and a time when many innkeepers and restaurateurs close up for a few weeks for either vacation or renovation.

Be aware that New England is home to hundreds of colleges, universities, and prep schools. As graduation nears (mid- to late May and early June), the region is afflicted with unusually high hotel occupancy rates in towns near schools. As always, it's best to book rooms well in advance.

Burlington, Vt.'s Average Temperatures (°F/°C)

	Jan	Feb	Mar	Apr	May	June	July	Aug	Sept	Oct	Nov	Dec
Avg. High	25/-4	27/-3	38/3	53/12	66/19	76/24	80/27	78/26	69/21	57/14	44/7	30/-1
Avg. Low	8/-13	9/-13	21/-6	33/1	44/7	54/12	59/15	57/14	49/9	39/4	30/-1	15/-9

Boston's Average Temperatures (°F/°C)

	Jan	Feb	Mar	Apr	May	June	July	Aug	Sept	Oct	Nov	Dec
Avg. High	36/2	38/3	43/6	54/12	67/19	76/24	81/27	79/26	72/22	63/17	49/9	40/4
Avg. Low	20/-7	22/-6	29/-2	38/3	49/9	58/14	63/17	63/17	56/13	47/8	36/2	25/-4

NEW ENGLAND CALENDAR OF EVENTS

January

New Year's and First Night Celebrations, regionwide. Boston, Mass.; Portland, Maine; Providence, R.I.; Hartford, Conn.; Portsmouth, N.H.; Burlington, Vt.; and many other cities and towns, including on Cape Cod and Martha's Vineyard, celebrate the coming of the New Year with an abundance of festivities. Check with local chambers of commerce for details. New Year's Eve.

Wildflower Inn Sleigh Rally, East Burke, Vt. About a dozen sleighs, horse teams, and drivers trot their stuff at this 4-hour wintertime rally, which harkens back to the days before cars. Call the Wildflower Inn (© **800/627-8310**) for date and time. Late January.

February

U.S. National Toboggan Championships, Camden, Maine. This is a raucous and lively athletic event where being overweight is actually an advantage. Held at the toboggan chute of the Camden Snow Bowl. Call © **207/236-3438.** Early February.

Dartmouth Winter Carnival, Hanover, N.H. Huge and elaborate ice sculptures grace the village green during this festive celebration of winter, which includes numerous sporting events and other winter-related activities. Call © **603/646-1110.** Mid-February.

Stowe Derby, Stowe, Vt. The oldest downhill/cross-country ski race in the nation pits racers who scramble from the wintry summit of Mount Mansfield into the village on the Stowe Recreation path. Call © **802/253-3423.** Late February.

March

New England Spring Flower Show, Dorchester, Mass. This annual harbinger of spring presented by the Massachusetts

Horticultural Society (© **617/536-9280**) draws huge crowds starved for a glimpse of green. Second or third week in March.

St. Patrick's Day/Evacuation Day, Boston, Mass. (Parade, South Boston; celebration, Faneuil Hall Marketplace). The 5-mile (8km) parade salutes the city's Irish heritage and the day British troops left Boston in 1776. Head to Faneuil Hall Marketplace for music, dancing, food, and plenty of Irish spirit. Call © **800/888-5515.** March 17.

Maine Boatbuilders Show, Portland, Maine. More than 200 exhibitors and 9,000 boat aficionados gather as winter fades to make plans for the coming summer. A great place to meet boatbuilders and get ideas for your dream craft. Call © **207/774-1067.** Mid- to late March.

April

Patriot's Day, Boston area (Paul Revere House, Old North Church, Lexington Green, Concord's North Bridge), Mass. The events of April 18 and 19, 1775, which signified the start of the Revolutionary War, are commemorated and reenacted. Participants dressed as Paul Revere and William Dawes ride to Lexington and Concord to warn the Minutemen that "the regulars are out" (not that "the British are coming"—most colonists considered themselves British). Mock battles are fought at Lexington and Concord. Call the Lexington Visitor Center (© **781/862-1450**) or the Concord Chamber of Commerce (© **978/369-3120**). Third Monday in April; a state holiday in Massachusetts and Maine.

Boston Marathon, from Hopkinton to Boston, Mass. International stars and local amateurs run in the world's oldest and most famous marathon. The noon start means elite runners hit Boston around 2pm; weekend runners stagger across the Boylston Street finish line as late as 4 hours after that. Call the Boston Athletic Association (© **617/236-1652;** www.boston marathon.org). Patriot's Day, the third Monday in April.

Sugarbush Celebration, Waitsfield, Vt. Ski-related events herald the coming of spring and the most inviting season for skiing. Special events for kids are held. Call © **802/583-2381.** Mid-April.

Daffodil Festival, Nantucket, Mass. Spring's arrival is trumpeted with masses of yellow blooms adorning everything in sight, including a cavalcade of antique cars. Call © **508/228-1700.** Late April.

May

Brimfield Antique and Collectible Show, Brimfield, Mass. Up to 6,000 dealers fill several fields near this central Massachusetts town, with similar fairs in July and September. Call © **800/628-8379** or 508/347-2761, or go to www. brimfieldshow.com. Mid-May.

Cape Maritime Week, Cape Cod, Mass. A multitude of cultural organizations mount special events—such as lighthouse tours—highlighting the region's nautical history. Call © **508/362-3828.** Mid-May.

Lilac Festival, Shelburne, Vt. See the famed lilacs (more than 400 bushes) at the renowned Shelburne Museum when they're at their most beautiful. Call © **802/985-3346.** Mid- to late May.

MooseMainea, Greenville, Maine. A variety of low-key events, from an antique-car show to a black-fly festival, are staged deep in the heart of moose territory. But the real attraction is the possibility of spotting one of the gangly beasts on a forest safari. Call ⓒ **207/695-2702.** Mid-May to mid-June.

Figawi Sailboat Race, Hyannis (on Cape Cod) to Nantucket, Mass. The largest and wildest sailboat race on the East Coast. Intensive partying in Hyannis and on Nantucket surrounds this popular event. Call ⓒ **508/771-3333.** Late May.

June

Old Port Festival, Portland, Maine. A block party in the heart of Portland's historic district with live music, food vendors, and activities for kids. Call ⓒ **207/772-2249.** Early June.

Yale-Harvard Regatta, on the Thames River in New London, Conn. One of the oldest collegiate rivalries in the country. Call ⓒ **617/495-4848.** Early June.

Taste of Hartford, Hartford, Conn. One of New England's largest outdoor festivals, where many area restaurants serve up their specialties. You'll also get a "taste" of local music, dance, magic, and comedy. Call ⓒ **860/728-3089.** Early June.

Market Square Weekend, Portsmouth, N.H. This lively street fair attracts 300 vendors and revelers from throughout southern New Hampshire and Maine into downtown Portsmouth to dance, listen to music, sample food, and enjoy summer's arrival. Call ⓒ **603/431-5388.** Second Saturday in June.

Motorcycle Week, Loudon and Weirs Beach, N.H. Tens of thousands of bikers descend on the Lake Winnipesaukee region early each summer to compare their machines and cruise the strip at Weirs Beach. The Gunstock Hill Climb and the Loudon Classic race are the centerpieces of the week's activities. Call ⓒ **603/783-4931.** Mid-June.

Boston Globe Jazz & Blues Festival, Boston, Mass. Big names and rising stars of the jazz world appear at lunchtime, after-work, evening, and weekend events, some of which are free. For the current schedule, call ⓒ **617/267-4301,** or go to www.boston.com/jazzfest. Third week in June.

Stowe Flower Festival, Stowe, Vt. Nearly three dozen events celebrate the joys of making the earth bloom, with offerings as diverse as garden tours and seminars by the experts. Call ⓒ **800/247-8693.** Last week in June.

Whatever Family Festival, Augusta, Maine. A community celebration to mark the cleaning up of the Kennebec River, culminating in a wacky race involving all manner of watercraft, some more seaworthy than others. Call ⓒ **207/623-4559.** Late June to early July.

Jacob's Pillow Dance Festival, Becket, Mass. The oldest dance festival in America features everything from ballet to modern dance and jazz. For a season brochure, call ⓒ **413/243-0745.** Late June through August.

Williamstown Theater Festival, Williamstown, Mass. This nationally distinguished theater festival presents everything from the classics to uproarious comedies and contemporary works. Scattered among the drama are literary readings and cabarets. Call ⓒ **413/597-3399.** Late June through August.

July

Tanglewood Music Festival, near Lenox, Mass. The Boston Symphony Orchestra makes its summer home at this fine estate, bringing symphonies, chamber groups, and soloists to the Berkshire Hills. Call the Tanglewood Concert Line at ⓒ **413/637-1666** (July and Aug only) or Symphony Hall at

© **617/266-1492;** or go to www. bso.org. July through August.

Boston Harborfest, downtown Boston (along Boston Harbor and the Harbor Islands), Mass. The city puts on its Sunday best for the Fourth of July, which has become a gigantic weeklong celebration of Boston's maritime history and an excuse to just get out and have fun. Events include concerts, guided tours, cruises, fireworks, the Boston Chowderfest, and the annual turn-around of the USS *Constitution.* Call © **617/227-1528.** First week in July.

Boston Pops Concert and Fireworks Display, Hatch Memorial Shell on the Esplanade, Boston, Mass. Independence Week culminates in the famous Boston Pops' Fourth of July concert. People wait from dawn 'til dark for the music to start. The program includes Tchaikovsky's *1812 Overture* with actual cannon fire that segues into the fireworks. Call © **617/727-5215.** July 4th.

Independence Day, regionwide. Communities throughout New England celebrate the Fourth of July with parades, cookouts, road races, and fireworks. Contact local chambers of commerce for details. July 4th.

Wickford Art Festival, Wickford, R.I. More than 200 artists gather in this quaint village for one of the East Coast's oldest art festivals. Wickford is the ancestral home of author John Updike and is said to be the setting for his book *The Witches of Eastwick.* Call © **401/294-6840,** or go to www.wickford art.org. Weekend after July 4th.

Newport Music Festival, Newport, R.I. Chamber-music concerts are held inside Newport's opulent mansions. Call © **401/846-1133.** Second and third weeks in July.

Brimfield Antique and Collectible Show, Brimfield, Mass. Up to 6,000 dealers fill several fields near this central Massachusetts town, with similar fairs in May and September. Call © **800/628-8379** or 508/347-2761, or go to www. brimfieldshow.com. Mid-July.

Friendship Sloop Days, Rockland, Maine. This 3-day event is a series of boat races that culminates in a parade of sloops. Call © **207/596-0376.** Mid-July.

Vermont Quilt Festival, Northfield, Vt. Displays are only part of the allure of New England's largest (and oldest) quilt festival. You can also attend classes and have your heirlooms appraised. See class and event descriptions at www.vqf.org, or call © **802/485-7092** for more information. Mid-July.

Revolutionary War Days, Exeter, N.H. Learn all you need to know about the War of Independence during this historic community festival, which features a Revolutionary War encampment and dozens of re-enactors. Call © **603/772-2622.** Third weekend in July.

Barnstable County Fair, East Falmouth (on Cape Cod), Mass. An old-time county fair complete with rides, food, and livestock contests. Call © **508/563-3200.** Late July.

Marlboro Music Festival, Marlboro, Vt. This is a popular 6-week series of classical concerts featuring talented student musicians and seasoned artists performing in the peaceful hills outside of Brattleboro. Call © **802/254-2394** (or © 215/569-4690 in winter) for information. Weekends from July to mid-August.

Maine Lobster Festival, Rockland, Maine. Fill up on the local harvest at this event marking the importance and delectability of Maine's favorite crustacean. Enjoy a boiled lobster or two, and take in the ample entertainment during this informal waterfront gala. Call ℂ **800/562-2529** or 207/596-0376. Late July/early August.

August

Maine Festival, Brunswick, Maine. A 3-day festival showcasing Maine-made crafts, music, foods, and performers. It's boisterous, fun, and filling. Call ℂ **207/772-9012.** Early August.

Southern Vermont Crafts Fair, Manchester, Vt. More than 200 artisans show off their fine work at this popular festival, which also features creative food and good music. Held on the grounds of Hildene, a grand historic home. Call ℂ **802/362-1788.** Early August.

Newport Folk Festival. Newport, R.I. Thousands of music lovers congregate at Fort Adams State Park for a heavy dose of performances on an August weekend. It's one of the nation's premier folk festivals. Call ℂ **401/847-3700,** or go to www.newportfolk.com. Early August.

Annual Star Party, St. Johnsbury, Vt. The historic Fairbanks Museum and Planetarium hosts special events and shows, including night-viewing sessions during the Perseid Meteor Shower. Call ℂ **802/748-2372.** Mid-August.

Blueberry Festival, Machias, Maine. A festival marking the harvest of the region's wild blueberries. Eat to your heart's content. Call ℂ **207/794-3543.** Mid-August.

JVC Jazz Festival. Newport, R.I. This 3-day jazz festival brings together some of the best in the music industry to play for a sizzling weekend at Fort Adams State Park. Call ℂ **401/847-3700.** Mid-August.

Martha's Vineyard Agricultural Fair, West Tisbury, Mass. An old-fashioned country fair featuring horse pulls, livestock shows, musicians, and woodsman contests, along with plenty of carnival action. Call ℂ **508/693-4343.** Third weekend in August.

Blue Hill Fair, Blue Hill, Maine. A classic country fair just outside one of Maine's most elegant villages. Call ℂ **207/374-9976.** Late August to Labor Day.

September

Windjammer Weekend, Camden, Maine. Come visit Maine's impressive fleet of old-time sailing ships, which host open houses throughout the weekend at this scenic harbor. Call ℂ **207/236-4404.** Labor Day weekend.

Brimfield Antique and Collectible Show, Brimfield, Mass. Up to 6,000 dealers fill several fields near this central Massachusetts town, with similar fairs in May and July. Call ℂ **800/628-8379** or 508/347-2761, or go to www.brimfieldshow.com. Early September.

Vermont State Fair, Rutland, Vt. All of Vermont seems to show up for this grand event, with a midway, live music, and plenty of agricultural exhibits. Call ℂ **802/775-5200.** Early September.

Providence Waterfront Festival, Providence, R.I. Musical performances are the highlight of this weekend event, especially the jazz festival on Sunday. A food court and children's tent round out the activities. Call ℂ **401/621-1992.** Weekend after Labor Day.

Norwalk Oyster Festival, Norwalk, Conn. This waterfront festival celebrates Long Island Sound's seafaring past. Highlights include oyster-shucking and -slurping contests, harbor cruises, concerts, and fireworks. Call ℂ **203/838-9444.** Weekend after Labor Day.

Convergence International Festival of the Arts, Providence, R.I. Various Providence arts organizations pull together for this week-long citywide event, which includes sculptural installations, musical performances, and other arts events. Call ✆ **401/621-1992.** Mid-September.

Eastern States Exhibition, West Springfield, Mass. "The Big E" is New England's largest agricultural fair with a midway, games, rides, rodeo and lumberjack shows, country-music stars, and lots of eats. Call ✆ **413/737-2443.** Mid- to late September.

Provincetown Arts Festival, Provincetown (on Cape Cod), Mass. One of the country's oldest art colonies celebrates its past and present with local artists opening their studios. It's a great opportunity for collecting 20th-century works. Call ✆ **508/487-3424.** Late September.

Common Ground Fair, Windsor, Maine. A sprawling, old-time state fair with a twist: The emphasis is on organic foods, recycling, and wholesome living. Call ✆ **207/623-5115.** Late September.

October

Northeast Kingdom Fall Foliage Festival, Vt. A cornucopia of events staged in towns and villages throughout Vermont's northeast corner heralds the arrival of the fall foliage season. Be the first to see colors at their peak. Call ✆ **802/748-3678.** Early October.

Fryeburg Fair, Fryeburg, Maine. Cotton candy, tractor pulls, live music, and huge vegetables and barnyard animals at Maine's largest agricultural fair. There's also harness racing in the evening. Call ✆ **207/985-3278.** One week in early October.

Mystic Chowderfest, Mystic, Conn. A festival of soup served from bubbling cauldrons set on wood fires. Call ✆ **860/572-5315.** Mid-October.

Harvest Day, Canterbury, N.H. A celebration of the harvest season, Shaker style. Lots of autumnal exhibits and children's games. Call ✆ **603/783-9511.** Mid-October.

Cranberry Harvest Festival, Nantucket, Mass. Tour scenic cranberry bogs and local inns just when foliage is at its burnished prime. Call ✆ **508/228-1700.** Mid-October.

Head of the Charles Regatta, Boston and Cambridge, Mass. High school, college, and post-collegiate rowing teams and individuals—some 4,000 in all—race in front of hordes of fans along the banks of the Charles River. This event always seems to fall on the crispest, most picturesque Sunday of the season. Call the Metropolitan District Commission Harbor Master (✆ **617/727-0537**) for information. Late October.

November

Brookfield Holiday Craft Exhibition & Sale, Brookfield, Conn. Thousands of unique, elegant, and artful gifts are displayed in gallery settings on three floors of a restored grist mill. Call ✆ **203/775-4526.** Mid-November through late December.

Thanksgiving Celebration, Plymouth, Mass. The holiday that put Plymouth on the map is observed with a "stroll through the ages," showcasing 17th- and 19th-century Thanksgiving preparations in historic homes. Nearby Plimoth Plantation, where the colony's first years are re-created, wisely offers a Victorian Thanksgiving feast (reservations required). Call Plymouth

Visitor Information (© **800/872-1620**) or the Plimoth Plantation (© **508/746-1622**). Thanksgiving Day.

Victorian Holiday, Portland, Maine. Portland decorates its Old Port in a Victorian Christmas theme: Enjoy the window displays, take a free hayride, and listen to costumed carolers sing. Call © **207/772-6828** for details. Late November through Christmas.

December

Christmas Tree Lighting, Prudential Center, Boston, Mass. Carol singing precedes the lighting of a magnificent tree from Nova Scotia—an annual expression of thanks from the people of Halifax for Bostonians' help in fighting a devastating fire more than 70 years ago. Call the Greater Boston Convention & Visitors Bureau (© **888/SEE-BOSTON** or 617/536-4100). Early December.

Christmas Prelude, Kennebunkport, Maine. This scenic coastal village greets Santa's arrival in a lobster boat, and marks the coming of Christmas with street shows, pancake breakfasts, and tours of the town's splendid inns. Call © **207/967-3286.** Early December.

Candlelight Stroll, Portsmouth, N.H. Historic Strawbery Banke gets in a Christmas way with old-time decorations and more than 1,000 candles lighting the 10-acre (4-hectare) grounds. Call © **603/433-1100.** First two weekends in December.

Boston Tea Party Reenactment, Congress Street Bridge, Boston, Mass. Chafing under British rule, the colonists rose up on December 16, 1773, to strike a blow where it would cause real pain—in the pocketbook. Call © **617/338-1773.** Mid-December.

Woodstock Wassail Celebration, Woodstock, Vt. Enjoy classic English grog, along with parades and dances at this annual event. Call © **802/457-3555.** Mid-December.

Christmas Eve and Christmas Day, special festivities throughout New England. In Newport, R.I., several of the great mansions offer special tours; Mystic, Conn., has a program of Christmas festivities; Nantucket, Mass., features carolers in Victorian garb, art exhibits, and tours of historic homes. December 24 and 25.

5 Health & Insurance

THE HEALTHY TRAVELER

You shouldn't face any serious health risks when traveling in New England, though you may find yourself at higher risk when exploring the outdoors, particularly the backcountry. Those planning longer outdoor excursions may find a first-aid kit with basic salves and medicines handy to have along. Those traveling mostly in towns and villages should have little trouble finding a local pharmacy to stock up on common medicines (like calamine lotion or aspirin) to aid with minor ailments.

If you suffer from a chronic illness, consult your doctor before your departure. For conditions such as epilepsy, diabetes, or heart problems, wear a **Medic Alert Identification Tag** (© 800/825-3785; www.medicalert.org), which will immediately alert doctors to your condition and give them access to your records through Medic Alert's 24-hour hot line.

A few things to watch for when venturing off the beaten track:

POISON IVY The shiny, three-leafed plant is common throughout the region. If touched, you may develop a nasty, itchy rash. If you're unfamiliar with what poison ivy looks like, ask at a ranger station or visitor center for more information. Many have posters or books to help with identification.

GIARDIA That crystal-clear stream coursing down a backcountry peak may seem as pure as pure gets, but consider the possibility that it may be contaminated with animal feces. Gross, yes, and also dangerous. Giardia cysts may be present in some streams and rivers; when ingested by humans, the cysts can result in copious diarrhea and weight loss. Symptoms may not surface until well after you've left the backcountry. Carry your own water for day trips, or bring a small filter (available at most sporting-goods shops) to treat backcountry water. Failing that, at least boil water or treat it with iodine before using it for cooking, drinking, or washing. If you detect symptoms, see a doctor immediately.

LYME DISEASE Lyme disease has been a growing problem in New England since 1975, when the disease was identified in the town of Lyme, Conn. It's transmitted by tiny deer ticks—smaller than the more common, relatively harmless wood ticks. Look for a bull's-eye shaped rash, 3 to 8 inches (8–20cm) in diameter; it may feel warm but usually doesn't itch. Symptoms include muscle and joint pain, fever, and fatigue. If left untreated, heart damage may occur. It's more easily treated in early phases than later, so it's best to seek medical attention as soon as any symptoms are noted.

RABIES Since 1989, rabies has been spreading northward from New Jersey through New England. The disease is spread by animal saliva and is especially prevalent in skunks, raccoons, bats, and foxes. It is always fatal if left untreated in humans. Infected animals tend to display erratic and aggressive behavior. The best advice is to keep a safe distance between yourself and any wild animal you may encounter. If bitten, wash the wound as soon as you can and immediately seek medical attention. Treatment is no longer as painful as it once was, but still involves a series of shots.

TRAVEL INSURANCE

Check your existing insurance policies before you buy travel insurance to cover trip cancellation, lost luggage, medical expenses, or car rentals. You're likely to have partial or complete coverage. If you do need to purchase insurance, ask your travel agent about a comprehensive package. The cost of travel insurance varies widely, depending on the cost and length of your trip, your age and overall health, and the type of trip you're taking.

Some credit cards (American Express and certain gold and platinum Visa and MasterCards, for example) offer automatic flight insurance against death or dismemberment in case of an airplane crash if you charged the cost of your ticket.

For information, contact one of the following major insurers:

- **Access America** (℡ **800/284-8300;** www.accessamerica.com)
- **Travelex Insurance Services** (℡ **800/228-9792;** www.travelex-insurance.com)
- **Travel Guard International** (℡ **800/826-1300;** www.travelguard.com)
- **Travel Insured International** (℡ **800/243-3174;** www.travelinsured.com)

6 Tips for Travelers with Special Needs

FOR TRAVELERS WITH DISABILITIES Prodded by the Americans with Disabilities Act, a growing number of inns and hotels are retrofitting some of their rooms for guests with special needs. Outdoor-recreation areas, especially on state and federal lands, are also providing more trails and facilities for those who've been effectively barred in the past. Accessibility is improving region-wide, but improvements are far from universal. When in doubt, call ahead to ensure that you'll be accommodated.

The **Society for Accessible Travel & Hospitality** (© 212/447-7284; www.sath.org) offers informed recommendations on destinations, guides, travel agents, tour operators, and vehicle rentals. Annual membership costs $45 for adults, $30 for seniors and students. Its *Open World for Disability and Mature Travel* magazine is full of information; a year's subscription is $13.

The **Moss Rehab Hospital** (© 215/456-9603; www.moss resourcenet.org) provides helpful phone assistance through its Travel Information Service.

Mobility International USA (© 541/343-1284; www.miusa.org) publishes *A World of Options,* a 658-page book of resources, covering everything from biking trips to scuba outfitters, and a biannual newsletter, *Over the Rainbow.* Annual membership is $35.

Access Adventures (© 716/889-9096) offers customized itineraries for travelers with disabilities. **Accessible Journeys** (© 800/TINGLES or 610/521-0339; www.disabilitytravel.com) caters specifically to slow walkers and wheelchair travelers. **Flying Wheels Travel** (© 800/535-6790; www.flyingwheelstravel.com) offers escorted tours and cruises that emphasize sports.

FOR SENIORS Mention the fact that you're a senior citizen when you first make your travel reservations. All major airlines and many hotels offer discounts for seniors. Major airlines also offer coupons for domestic travel for those over 60. Typically, a book of four coupons costs less than $700, which means you can fly anywhere in the continental U.S. for under $350 round-trip. In most cities, seniors qualify for reduced admission to theaters, museums, and other attractions, as well as discounted fares on public transportation.

New England offers older travelers a wide array of activities and discounts. It's wise to request a discount at hotels or motels when booking the room, not when you arrive. An identification card from **AARP,** formerly known as the American Association of Retired Persons (© 800/424-3410 or 202/434-2277; www.aarp.org), can aid in getting discounts on hotels, airfares, and car rentals. AARP offers members a wide range of benefits, including *Modern Maturity* magazine and a monthly newsletter. Anyone over 50 can join.

The **Alliance for Retired Americans** (© 301/578-8422; www.retired americans.org) offers a newsletter and discounts on hotel and car rentals; annual dues are $13. *Note:* Members of the former National Council of Senior Citizens receive automatic membership in the Alliance.

Grand Circle Travel (© 800/221-2610 or 617/350-7500; www.gct.com) features packages for the 50-plus market, mostly of the tour-bus variety. It also offers the publication *101 Tips for the Mature Traveler.*

Elderhostel (© 877/426-8056; www.elderhostel.org) arranges study programs for those 55 and over in more than 80 countries. Most courses in the U.S. last 5 to 7 days, and many include airfare, accommodations in university dormitories or modest inns, meals, and tuition.

Interhostel (© 800/733-9753; www.learn.unh.edu/interhostel), organized by the University of New Hampshire, also offers educational travel for those 50 and over. On these escorted tours, the days are packed with seminars, lectures, and field trips, with sightseeing led by academic experts.

The Book of Deals is a collection of more than 1,000 senior discounts on airfare, lodging, tours, and attractions around the country; it's available for $9.95 by calling ℂ **800/460-6676.**

FOR GAY & LESBIAN TRAVELERS

Provincetown, on the tip of Cape Cod, is one of the first and still one of the most famous gay resort communities. Gay entrepreneurs and politicians are well represented in the town's businesses and politics, and much of the nightlife revolves around gay culture.

Outside of Provincetown, New England isn't exactly a hotbed of gay culture, although there are noted pockets, like Ogunquit, Maine (see www.gayogunquit.com). Providence, Boston, and Burlington tend to be very welcoming to alternative lifestyles. For a small city, Portland has an active gay population and hosts a sizable gay pride festival early each summer.

Vermont became the first state in the nation (in 2000) to permit same-sex couples to be joined in civil union—at this point, the closest thing to gay marriage available. One needn't be a state resident to establish a civil union; many same-sex couples have traveled here, paid their $20 fee, and exchanged legally recognized vows before a judge or clergy member, even though such unions generally aren't recognized outside of Vermont. A good guide to the law is found at www.sec.state.vt.us/pubs/civilunions. htm.

Vermont has a fine monthly newsletter covering gay, lesbian, and bisexual issues and happenings called *Out in the Mountain* (www.mountain pridemedia.org). It's free at many Vermont bookstores and other shops.

For a more detailed directory of gay-oriented enterprises in New England, track down a copy of *The Pink Pages* (ℂ **800/338-6550;** www.pink web.com).

More adventurous souls should consider linking up with the **Chiltern Mountain Club** (ℂ **617/859-2843;** www.chiltern.org), which organizes trips to northern New England for gays and lesbians.

For more general information about gay travel, the following resources are helpful:

The **International Gay & Lesbian Travel Association** (IGLTA; ℂ **800/ 448-8550** or 954/776-2626; www. iglta.org) links travelers up with gay-friendly hoteliers, tour operators, and airline and cruise-line representatives. Membership is $150 yearly, plus a $100 administration fee for new members.

Above and Beyond Tours (ℂ **800/ 397-2681;** www.abovebeyondtours. com) offers gay and lesbian tours worldwide and is the exclusive gay and lesbian tour operator for United Airlines.

Now, Voyager (ℂ **800/255-6951;** www.nowvoyager.com) is a San Francisco–based, gay-owned-and-operated travel service.

Olivia Cruises & Resorts (ℂ **800/ 631-6277** or 510/655-0364; http:// oliviatravel.com) charters entire resorts and ships for lesbian vacations all over the world.

Out and About (ℂ **800/929-2268** or 415-644-8044; www.outand about.com) offers guidebooks and a newsletter packed with information on the global gay and lesbian scene.

Spartacus International Gay Guide and *Odysseus* are good annual guidebooks focused on gay men, with some information for lesbians.

Gay Travel A to Z: The World of Gay & Lesbian Travel Options at Your Fingertips (Ferrari Publications) is a very good gay and lesbian guide-book series.

FOR FAMILIES Be sure to ask about family discounts when visiting attractions. Many places offer a flat family rate that is cheaper than paying for each ticket individually. Some parks and beaches charge by the car rather than the head.

Be aware that a number of inns cater to couples and prefer that children be over a certain age. We note in this guide the recommended age where restrictions apply, but it's still best to ask first just to be safe.

Recommended destinations for families include Boston, with its plethora of museums; Cape Cod, with its miles of famous beaches and dunes; and Martha's Vineyard, with bike paths, beaches, and kid-scaled architecture in the cottage section of Oak Bluffs. Other destinations good for kids are Weirs Beach on New Hampshire's Lake Winnipesaukee, Hampton Beach on New Hampshire's tiny coast, and York Beach and Acadia National Park in Maine.

North Conway, N.H., also makes a good base for exploring with younger kids. The town has lots of motels with pools, and there are nearby train rides, aquaboggans, streams for splashing around, easy hikes, and the always-entertaining StoryLand. Excellent children's museums are located in Mystic, Boston, Portsmouth, Portland, and Norwich.

Several specialized guides offer more detailed information for families on the go. Try *The Unofficial Guide to New England & New York with Kids* (Frommer's, 2001), *Fun Places to Go With Children in New England* (Chronicle Books, 1998), and *Great Family Vacations Northeast* (Globe Pequot, 2001). *How to Take Great Trips with Your Kids* (The Harvard Common Press, 1995) is full of good general advice that can apply to travel anywhere.

Travel with Your Children (www.travelwithyourkids.com) is a comprehensive site offering sound advice for traveling with children. **Family Travel Network** (www.family travelnetwork.com) offers travel tips and reviews of family-friendly destinations, vacation deals, and thoughtful features such as "Kid-Style Camping."

FOR TRAVELERS WITH PETS No surprise: Some places allow pets, some don't. We've noted hotels and inns that allow pets (it doesn't hurt to inquire, even if the pet policy isn't explicitly mentioned in these pages), but we still don't recommend showing up with a pet in tow unless you've cleared it over the phone first. Note that many establishments have only one or two rooms (often a cottage or room with exterior entrance) set aside for guests traveling with pets, and they won't be happy to meet Fido if the pet rooms are already occupied. Also expect a surcharge of $10 or $20 to pay for the extra cleaning.

An excellent resource is **www.petswelcome.com**, which dispenses medical tips, names of animal-friendly lodgings and campgrounds, and lists of kennels and veterinarians. Also check out *The Portable Petswelcome.com: The Complete Guide to Traveling with Your Pet* (Howell, 2001). Another resource is *Pets-R-Permitted Hotel, Motel & Kennel Directory: The Travel Resource for Pet Owners Who Travel* (Annenberg Communications, 1997).

If you plan to fly with your pet, the FAA has compiled a list of all requirements for transporting live animals at www.dot.gov/airconsumer/animals.htm. Note that summer may not be the best time to fly with your pet: Many airlines will not check pets as baggage in the hotter months. The ASPCA discourages travelers from checking pets as luggage at any time, as storage conditions on planes are loosely monitored, and fatal accidents are not unprecedented. Your other option is to ship your pet with a professional carrier, which can be expensive.

Keep in mind that dogs are prohibited on hiking trails and must be leashed at all times on federal lands administered by the National Park Service. Pets are allowed to hike off-leash in the White Mountains National Forest in New Hampshire and the Green Mountains National Forest in Vermont.

7 Getting There

BY PLANE

Airlines serving New England include **American** (© 800/433-7300), **Comair** (© 800/354-9822), **Continental** (© 800/525-0280), **Delta** (© 800/221-1212), **Jet Blue** (© 800/538-2583), **Northwest** (© 800/225-2525), **Pan Am** (© 800/359-7262), **Southwest** (© 800/435-9792), **United** (© 800/241-6522), and **US Airways** (© 800/247-8786).

Carriers to Cape Cod and the Islands include several of the above, plus **Cape Air/Nantucket Air** (© 800/352-0714 or 508/771-6944) and **Island Airlines** (© 800/248-7779 or 508/775-6606). Charter flights throughout the region are offered by Cape Air/Nantucket Air, as well as by **Cape Flight Limited** (© 508/775-8171) and **King Air Charters** (© 800/247-2427).

The traditional gateways to New England have been Boston, New York City, and Montréal. Major commercial carriers also serve Hartford, Conn. (Bradley International); Burlington, Vt.; and Bangor and Portland, Maine. Note that if you're heading to southwest Vermont or northwest Massachusetts, the closest major airport is Albany, N.Y.

In the last few years, Providence, R.I., and Manchester, N.H., have grown in prominence thanks to the arrival of **Southwest Airlines,** which has brought competitive, low-cost airfares and improved service. Manchester in particular has gone from a sleepy backwater airport to a bustling destination serving an increasing number of flights.

Another discount carrier is **Pan Am,** once a dominant (then bankrupt) air carrier, and now back to life (under the auspices of entrepreneurs who purchased the name) and operating out of Portsmouth, N.H., also serving Bangor, Maine; and Worcester, Mass. Pan Am is the only airline that serves Portsmouth; it connects to a limited but growing roster of second-tier airports, including Gary, Ind.; Sanford, Fla.; and Allentown, Penn.

Upstart discounter **Jet Blue** offers direct service between Burlington, Vt., and New York City.

Travelers should note that Boston's Logan Airport can be very congested. Following the September 11, 2001, terrorist attacks, increased security has led to periodic but massive delays during check-in and screening. With far fewer flights, the smaller airports (such as Bangor and Burlington) have not been subject to such wholesale disruptions. No matter what airport you use, remember that new security measures allow travelers in the U.S. only one carry-on bag, plus one personal bag (such as a purse or briefcase). At press time, Pan Am disallows all carry-ons except for a purse or wallet. The Transportation Security Administration (TSA) has also issued a list of newly restricted carry-on items. Knives, box cutters, corkscrews, straight razors, metal scissors, ice picks, golf clubs, baseball bats, pool cues, hockey sticks, and ski poles are not permitted as carry-on items. Permitted items include nail clippers, nail files, tweezers, eyelash curlers, safety razors (including disposable razors),

> ### Tips   Flight Plans
>
> If your flight is canceled, don't book a new fare at the ticket counter. Instead, find the nearest phone and call the airline directly to reschedule. You'll be relaxing while other passengers are still standing in line.

syringes (with documented proof of medical need), and walking canes and umbrellas (which must be inspected first). For more information, go to www.tsa.gov. Note that your airline may have additional restrictions; call ahead to avoid problems.

BY CAR

From the south, I-95 is the major interstate highway serving Connecticut, Rhode Island, Massachusetts, and Maine. The least stressful route (with fewer tractor-trailers) from New York to Boston is via Hartford, Conn., using I-84 and the Massachusetts Turnpike. The easiest approach to northern New England from southern New England is along one of the three main interstate highway corridors. I-91 heads more or less due north from Hartford along the Vermont–New Hampshire border, then angles through northern Vermont. I-93 departs from I-95 near Boston, and then cuts through New Hampshire to connect with I-91 near St. Johnsbury, Vt. For Maine, take I-95 north; it parallels the southern Maine coast before veering inland.

If scenery is your priority, the most picturesque way to enter New England is from the west. The most scenic way to arrive in northern Vermont is to drive I-87 to Exit 34 near Port Kent on Lake Champlain, then catch the car ferry across the lake to Burlington. For a more southern route, take one of the smaller state highways that cross from New York State into Connecticut or Massachusetts. These routes, while often slow, take you through rolling hills and farmland and are exceptionally scenic.

Be aware that the interstates out of New York and Boston can be sluggish on Friday afternoons and evenings in summer, especially along the routes from Boston leading to Cape Cod and Maine. A handful of choke points (particularly the Bourne and Sagamore bridges to Cape Cod and the Maine tollbooths on I-95) can back up for miles. North Conway, N.H., is also famed for its nightmarish weekend traffic, especially during foliage season.

BY TRAIN

Amtrak (© **800/872-7245;** www. amtrak.com) operates Northeast Direct service from Newport News, Va., to Boston via Washington, Baltimore, Philadelphia, and New York City. North of New Haven, Conn., the line divides into two branches, both of which reunite in Boston. Stops along the Hartford branch include Springfield and Worcester; stops on the Providence, R.I., branch include New London, Mystic, and Kingston. The route through Providence is about 15 minutes faster.

Train service is limited in northern New England. Amtrak's **Vermonter** departs Washington, D.C., with stops in Baltimore, Philadelphia, and New York before following the Connecticut River northward. Stops in Vermont include Brattleboro, Bellows Falls, Claremont (N.H.), White River Junction, Randolph, Montpelier, Waterbury, Burlington/Essex Junction, and St. Albans. A bus connection takes passengers on to Montréal.

The **Ethan Allen Express** departs New York and travels north up the Hudson River Valley and into the

Driving Distances

Numbers on roads indicate distances between cities in miles.
For long distances between widely separated points,
add all intervening mileages.

Adirondacks before veering over to Vermont and terminating at Rutland. Buses continue on to Killington and north to Middlebury and Burlington.

The nation's first high-speed rail service went into operation in 2000 with Amtrak's *Acela* making stops between Washington, D.C., and Boston.

After more than a decade of delays, Amtrak relaunched rail service to Maine in December 2001, restoring a line that had been discontinued in the 1960s. The *Downeaster* now operates between Boston's North Station and Portland, with intermediate stops at Haverhill, Mass.; Exeter, Durham, and Dover, N.H.; and Wells, Saco, and Old Orchard Beach, Maine. Travel time is about 2 hours and 45 minutes between Boston and Portland, with that expected to decrease as track upgrades are completed. Bikes may be loaded and off-loaded at Boston, Wells, and Portland. Four trips are offered daily.

For rail service between New York and Connecticut, try cheaper **Metro North** (© **800/METRO-INFO** or 212/532-4900; www.mta.nyc.ny.us/ mnr), which runs commuter trains connecting many towns from New Haven to New York City.

BY BUS

Bonanza (© **800/556-3815** or 617/ 720-4110) operates largely in Connecticut. **Concord Trailways** (© **800/639-3317** or 617/426-8080) serves New Hampshire and Maine, including some smaller towns in the Lake Winnipesaukee and White Mountains areas. **Greyhound** (© **800/231-2222** or 617/526-1810) is nationwide, and serves many destinations in New England. **Peter Pan** (© **800/343-9999** or 617/426-7838) serves western Massachusetts and Connecticut. **Plymouth & Brockton** (© **508/746-0378**) serves Massachusetts's south shore and onward to Cape Cod. And **Vermont Transit** (© **800/ 451-3292**) is affiliated with Greyhound and serves Vermont, New Hampshire, and Maine with frequent departures from Boston.

8 The Active Vacation Planner

Don't let New England's outsized reputation for quaint villages and pastoral landscapes obscure another fact: It's also a superb destination for outdoor adventures.

Of course, New England isn't the Rockies—you won't find endless acres of wilderness populated by grizzlies and bighorn sheep. But you may be surprised at the amount of undeveloped terrain. While the three northern states are the least densely populated and offer the best chances for slipping away from the crowds, you'll still find plenty of outdoor opportunities throughout the region.

The state and regional chapters that follow offer a number of tips on specific adventures (such as biking trips and kayaking tours). This section offers a general overview, as well as contact information for guided tours and recreation specialists.

For more detailed information on where to go and what to do in New England's backcountry, see *Frommer's Great Outdoor Guide to New England.* The **Appalachian Mountain Club** (© 617/523-0636; www.outdoors. org) publishes a number of definitive guides to hiking and boating in the region. And, an exhaustive collection of regional outdoor guidebooks for sale can be found at **www.mountain wanderer.com**.

OUTFITTERS & ORGANIZED TOURS Reputable resources for New England excursions include the following:

Appalachian Mountain Club (© 603/466-2727; www.outdoors. org), New England's largest outdoor club, hosts workshops and tours throughout the year, many based out of its Pinkham Notch compound in New Hampshire's White Mountains. (Other workshops are held at Mount Greylock in the Massachusetts Berkshires.) One- to 5-day classes range from introductory rock climbing to identifying wild mushrooms to tracking wild animals; tours include backcountry canoeing and hiking trips.

Away.com (© **800/843-5630;** www.away.com), one of the best managed of the outdoor-adventure websites, has extensive trip-planning information for those seeking thrills; packaged tours are also available online. Adventure specialists promptly answer any queries you might have. You can search by state and activity.

Backroads (© **800/462-2848** or 510/527-1555; www.backroads.com), the venerable Berkeley-based retailer of packaged soft-adventure trips, offers multi-sport trips to Maine (biking, walking, and sea kayaking), as well as biking and walking excursions through Vermont. This is one of the higher-end outfitters; accommodations typically consist of luxe inns.

Elderhostel (© **877/426-8056;** www.elderhostel.org) has a number of excellent programs in New England (and throughout the world) for those over 55 (or traveling with someone who is); many offerings focus on learning about the outdoors through hiking, kayaking, canoeing, and more. Accommodations vary, but the price is right—averaging $500 for 6 days, including meals and instruction. Courses are so popular that catalogs are distributed via a lottery system to ensure that everyone gets an even shot at signing up for the classes most in demand.

Gorp Travel (© **877/532-4677;** www.gorptravel.gorp.com), one of the first online resources for outdoor adventure, also offers dozens of adventure packages around the globe. More than 100 New England trips are listed, ranging from 1-day canoe excursions in Connecticut to 6-day kayaking and hiking trips along the Maine coast. Overnights typically find travelers at upscale inns.

L.L.Bean (© **888/552-3261;** www.llbean.com), the region's premier outdoor retailer, offers workshops on activities ranging from ice climbing to sporting clays. The outdoor discovery program features a 3-day fly-fishing school, 3-day canoe and kayak symposiums, and a weekend cross-country ski workshop.

Sierra Club (© **415/977-5500;** www.sierraclub.org/chapters), the venerable environmental organization, has chapters in all six New England states. All host outings ranging from area hikes and bike rides to ice-skating parties open to nonmembers. To view a schedule of upcoming events, visit the website and follow links by state.

Zoar Outdoor (© **800/532-7483;** www.zoaroutdoor.com), an all-purpose adventure center on Route 2 (the Mohawk Trail) in western Massachusetts, is a great destination for river sports, including white-water rafting and kayaking, as well as rock climbing. Ask about the family adventure packages.

ALPINE SKIING   New England's most challenging alpine ski resorts are located in the three northernmost states, although western Massachusetts also offers skiing that's popular with families. All of the major ski areas offer packages (including accommodations and lift tickets); see the state or regional chapters that follow for resort contact information.

Moguls Ski and Snowboard Tours (© **800/666-4857;** www.skimoguls.com) sells packaged ski vacations in Maine, New Hampshire, and Vermont.

For information on resorts and current ski conditions, contact **Ski Maine Association** (© **207/761-3774;**

www.skimaine.com), **Ski New Hampshire** (𝒞 **800/887-5464,** or 603/745-9396 in N.H.; www.skinh. com), or **Ski Vermont** (𝒞 **800/837-6668;** www.skivermont.com).

BACKPACKING Contact the **Appalachian Mountain Club** (see above) for information on trail guidebooks and organized backpacking trips in the White Mountains and beyond. Contact information for ranger stations in the Green and White mountains national forests is in chapters 11 and 12.

Appalachian Trail Conference (𝒞 **304/535-6331;** www.atconf.org) is the best single source for information on hiking New England's premier long-distance pathway, which passes through five of the region's six states. (Rhode Island is the exception.) This nonprofit organization publishes detailed trail guides for every step along the route.

Green Mountain Club, on Route 100 between Waterbury and Stowe (𝒞 **802/244-7037;** www.greenmountainclub.org), is the best source of information on Vermont's Long Trail, the oldest long-distance hiking trail in the nation. The club publishes the definitive *Long Trail Guide.* The information center and bookstore are open Monday through Friday, usually until about 4:30pm.

Baxter State Park (𝒞 **207/723-5140**) consists of more than 200,000 wild acres (81,000 hectares) in the north-central part of Maine. The park maintains about 180 miles (290km) of backcountry hiking trails and more than 25 backcountry sites, some accessible only by canoe. Most hikers coming to the park are intent on ascending 5,267-foot (1,580m) Mount Katahdin, but dozens of other peaks are well worth scaling, and just traveling through the deep woods hereabouts is a sublime experience. Reservations, which can be made by mail or in person (but not by phone), are required for backcountry camping; many of the best spots fill up shortly after the first of the year.

Note: Backcountry camping is not permitted at Acadia National Park in Maine.

BIKING With its human scale and quiet back roads, New England offers great opportunities for road bikers and mountain bikers alike. Bikes are easy to rent throughout the region, and bike shops are great sources of information on the best routes. Look for tips in the regional chapters that follow.

Bike Riders (𝒞 **800/473-7040;** www.bikeriderstours.com), out of Boston, runs excellent 6-day tours of Martha's Vineyard and Nantucket, as well as other excursions around New England, Canada, and Europe.

The **Massachusetts Bicycle Coalition** (𝒞 **617/542-2453;** www.massbike.org) strives to improve the biking experience around the state through the development of bikeways. The group's website offers information on state bikeways and numerous links to local bike groups.

Organized inn-to-inn bike tours through the rolling hills of Vermont are a great way to see the countryside by day while relaxing in luxury at night. Tours are typically self-guided, with luggage transferred for you each day by vehicle. Try **Bike Vermont** (𝒞 **800/257-2226;** www.bikevt. com), **Country Inns Along the Trail** (𝒞 **800/838-3301;** www.inntoinn. com), or **Vermont Bicycle Touring** (**VBT;** 𝒞 **800/245-3868;** www.vbt. com). VBT also offers three trips in Maine, including a 6-day Acadia trip with some overnights at the grand Claremont Hotel.

Bike the Whites (𝒞 **800/448-3534;** www.bikethewhites.com) offers self-guided biking tours between three inns in the White Mountains, with each day involving a relaxed 20 miles

(32km) of biking. Luggage is shuttled from inn to inn.

BIRDING Each state has one or more birding hot lines, which offer recorded announcements of recent unusual sightings: Cape Cod (© **508/ 349-9464**); Western Massachusetts (© **413/253-2218**); Eastern Massachusetts (© **781/259-8805**); Connecticut (© **203/254-3665**); Rhode Island (© **401/949-3870**); Vermont (© **802/457-2779**); New Hampshire (© **603/224-9900**); and Maine (© **207/781-2332**).

Many experienced birders sign up for whale-watching trips to view pelagic birds; some birder-only trips are scheduled, usually in conjunction with a statewide birding group. For tips on upcoming offshore birding expeditions in Massachusetts, see **www.neseabirds.com**.

The **Maine Audubon Society** (© **207/781-2330**) offers a series of superb in-depth bird-watching workshops each summer on a beautiful 333-acre (135-hectare) island in Mucongus Bay, just northeast of Pemaquid Point. The highlight is a boat trip to an offshore island to see nesting puffins.

CANOEING Upper Valley Land Trust (© **603/643-6626**; www.uvlt. org) has established a network of primitive campsites along the Connecticut River; canoeists can paddle and portage its length and camp along the riverbanks. Two of the campsites are accessible by car.

Battenkill Canoe Ltd. (© **800/ 421-5268** or 802/362-2800; www. battenkill.com) runs 2- to 6-night canoeing and walking excursions in Vermont. Nights are spent at inns.

The **Allagash Wilderness Waterway,** in Maine, is considered by many to be the region's premier canoe trip. Some 80 campsites are spaced along the nearly 100-mile (161km) route, which includes a 9-mile (14km) stretch of Class I to II white water. For a map and brochure, contact the Bureau of Parks and Recreation, Maine Department of Conservation, State House Station #22, Augusta, ME 04333 (© **207/287-3821**). The Allagash is also served by several outfitters, including **Allagash Canoe Trips** (© **207/695-3668;** www.allagash canoetrips.com), which leads 5- to 7-day excursions. Bring a sleeping bag; everything else is taken care of.

See also Appalachian Mountain Club and Zoar Outdoor, under "Outfitters and Organized Tours," above.

CROSS-COUNTRY SKIING Western Massachusetts Cross Country Ski Areas Association (no phone; www.xcskimass.com) produces a website with current ski conditions, upcoming events, and information on the association's eight members.

Vermont Department of Travel and Tourism (© **802/828-3239;** www.1-800-vermont.com) updates a recorded cross-country ski report for the state each Thursday.

Catamount Trail Association (© **802/864-5794;** www.catamount trail.org) oversees the 200-mile (322km) Catamount Trail, which runs the length of Vermont.

Ski New Hampshire (© **800/887- 5464,** or 603/745-9396 in N.H.; www.skinh.com) offers current information on conditions at cross-country ski resorts, as well as assistance in finding a resort that's suited to your skills and interests.

Maine Nordic Council (© **800/ 754-9263**) prepares a recorded guide to conditions at cross-country ski areas throughout the state; it's updated Fridays in winter.

DEEP-SEA FISHING Ports up and down the New England coast are home to charter fishing boats; inquire with the chamber of commerce at your destination for more information. Other resources include the following:

Cape Cod Charter Association (© 508/945-6052; www.capecod outdoors.com) books fishing trips on various charter boats sailing from the Cape and the Islands.

Rhode Island Party & Charterboat Association (© 401/737-5812; www.rifishing.com) is a good contact for setting up trips from this state. Many of the boats sail from bustling Port Judith.

Fish-Maine.com (© 207/273-3474; www.fish-maine.com) manages a handy website featuring information and links to about three dozen charter boats based along the Maine coast and rivers.

FRESHWATER FISHING Housatonic Anglers (© 860/672-4457; www.housatonicanglers.com) offers 3-day fly-fishing classes in summer and fall on the scenic Housatonic River in Connecticut. Ask also about guide services and the guest cottages located on 14 private acres (6 hectares) along the river.

Orvis Catalog Store, in Manchester, Vt. (© 802/362-3750; www. orvis.com), sells the company's well-regarded equipment and features small ponds to try out gear before you buy. Orvis also offers top-rated fly-fishing classes, in which an expert will critique your technique and offer pointers.

Maine Professional Guides Association (© 207/549-5631; www. maineguides.org) represents dozens of registered guides, who pass stringent proficiency tests before being licensed. The website features links to numerous Maine guide services.

Maine Sporting Camp Association (no phone; www.mainesporting-camps.com) represents some 50 traditional backcountry lodges scattered in the more remote sections of the state. Fishing guides are often available for hire by the day.

See also L.L.Bean, under "Outfitters and Organized Tours," above, for fly-fishing equipment and workshops.

HIKING Hikers have dozens of specialized guidebooks to choose from, each offering detailed information on thousands of trails that wind through New England hills and mountains. Local bookstores are amply stocked with guides, which can also be ordered in advance through Amazon.com or other online booksellers. See "Backpacking," above, for additional information on regional trails.

Country Walkers (© 800/464-9255 or 802/244-1387; www.country walkers.com) has a glorious color catalog (more like a wishbook) outlining supported walking trips around the world, among them 4- or 5-night tours in coastal Maine and north-central Vermont. Trips include all meals and lodging at appealing inns.

New England Hiking Holidays (© 800/869-0949; www.nehiking holidays.com) offers an extensive inventory of options, including weekend trips in the White Mountains as well as more extended excursions to the Maine coast and Vermont. Trips typically involve moderate day hiking coupled with nights at comfortable lodges.

HORSEBACK RIDING Horse rentals.com (© 877/446-7730; www.horserentals.com) features a directory of stables that offer horse rentals and guided trail rides in all six New England states.

Kedron Valley Stables (© 802/457-1480) runs 4- to 6-day trips in the Green Mountains of Vermont. You'll be guided through secluded woods and historic towns like South Woodstock, Tyson, and Window, staying at inns and eating at wonderful country restaurants.

Vermont Icelandic Horse Farm (© 802/496-7141) leads ½- to 3-day trips on tiny Icelandic ponies, which move at a steady gait without much rocking—much like driving with good shocks.

SAILING JWorld Sailing School
(© **800/343-2255** or 401/849-5492;
www.jworldschool.com) is a performance sailing school founded in Newport, R.I., in 1981. (It also has
locations in Key West, Annapolis, and
San Diego.) Offerings include a 5-day
learn-to-sail course; each class has just
four students and includes 6-hour
days on the water.

Winds of Ireland (© **800/
458-9301** or 802/863-5090; www.
windsofireland.com), in South
Burlington, Vt., on "New England's
West Coast," charters seven Hunters,
ranging from 28 to 41 feet (8–12m).

School of Ocean Sailing (© **800/
732-6281;** www.sailingschool.com)
offers classes in open-water sailing and
navigation (technical as well as celestial) aboard a 52-foot (16m) steel
ketch. The 5-day classes begin and end
in Portland, and cruise along the scenic mid-coast area of Maine.

Maine Windjammer Association
(© **800/807-9463;** www.sailmaine
coast.com) is a consortium of more
than a dozen handsome vintage and
replica sailing ships that take passengers on crewed trips of between 1 and
7 days. Most are based in the Camden
and Rockland area. An array of excursions are available, from simple day
sails to 1-week expeditions.

Hinckley Yacht Charters (© **800/
492-7245;** www.acadia.net/hyc) is on
the southwestern shores of Mount
Desert Island in Maine, and features
more than 20 of the internationally
famous boats available for weekly
rental (from $2,750) to qualified
sailors. Those without experience
should contact **Hinckley Crewed
Charters** (© **800/504-2305** or 207
/244-0122; www.hinckleyyacht.com)
for information on fully outfitted
charters.

**SEA   KAYAKING Adventure
Learning** (© **800/649-9728** or
978/346-9728;   www.adventure

-
learning.com) offers 1-day sea-kayaking workshops and tours, including a
whale-watching paddle that departs
from Newburyport, Mass.

Collinsville Canoe & Kayak
(© **860/693-6977;** www.cckstore.
com), in Collinsville, Conn., leads 4-
to 6-hour trips around some of the
appealing lakes and estuaries of coastal
Connecticut. Lessons and rentals are
also available.

Maine Island Trail Association
(© **207/596-6456** or 207/761-8225;
www.mita.org) oversees the nation's
first long-distance water trail. Established in 1987, this 325-mile (523km)
waterway winds along the coast from
Portland to Machias, and incorporates
some 70 state- and privately-owned
islands along the route. Members of
the association, a private nonprofit
group, help maintain and monitor the
islands and in turn are granted permission to visit and camp on them
provided they follow certain restrictions. Membership is $40 per year.

Maine Island Kayak Co. (© **207/
766-2373;** www.sea-kayak.com) has a
fleet of seaworthy kayaks it employs
on camping trips up and down the
Maine coast. The firm has a number
of 2- and 3-night expeditions each
summer, and the staff has plenty of
experience training novices.

Maine Sport Outfitters (© **800/
244-8799** or 207/236-8797; www.
mainesport.com) offers rentals and
guided tours from a convenient
Penobscot Bay location.

See also L.L.Bean, under "Outfitters and Organized Tours," earlier in
this chapter, for information on the
store's kayak classes and symposia.

**SNOWMOBILING Snowmobile
Vermont** (© **860/916-0937;** www.
snowmobilevt.com) runs a website
with everything you need to know—
where to rent, where to stay, how to
contact area snowmobile clubs, what
regulations are in force, and more.

Spas for Sybarites

New England's Puritan work ethic and its inhabitants' preference for austere forms of recreation (fly-fishing in Apr, ice-skiing in Jan) don't necessarily mean that sybarites will be left out in the cold. Spas have made some inroads in New England, and now offer guests the sort of pampering that the Pilgrims would have found altogether bewildering. Below is a sampling of some reputable spas in the region.

Canyon Ranch, 165 Kemble St., Lenox, MA 01240 (© 800/742-9000; www.canyonranch.com), is the region's premier spa. It's located in the Berkshires at the Bellefontaine mansion, an extraordinary 1897 replica of a palace at Versailles. The spa mixes athletic and outdoor endeavors with nutritional dining, and tops it all off with massages and other body work, including mud treatments, relexology, shiatsu, and herbal wraps. The rates are not for the budget-minded (a 3-night stay for two typically runs more than $2,100), but they do include treatments, gratuities, and other activities that are priced separately at many other spas.

Kripalu Center for Yoga and Health, P.O. Box 793, Lenox, MA 01240 (© 800/967-3577; www.kripalu.org/programguide.html), is a superb destination for those who use "quest" as a verb. The emphasis is on spirit and soul, with weekend retreats offering programs such as "Raw Juice Fasting" and "The Practice of Thai Yoga Massage." It's located in the Berkshires on the grounds of a former Jesuit seminary, and the accommodations range from dormitories to rather spartan private rooms.

The **New Hampshire Snowmobile Association** (© 603/224-8906; www.nhsa.com) provides information on the nearly 6,000 miles (9,660km) of groomed trails that lace the state, including information on how to register your machine (mandatory) through any of the 248 off-highway recreational-vehicle agents. For current trail conditions, call © 603/743-5050 or go to the website.

The **Maine Snowmobile Association** (© 207/622-6983; www.mesnow.com) has information on more than 12,000 miles (19,320km) of maintained snowmobile trails. The website lists current conditions, sled-friendly accommodations, and outfitters.

WHITE-WATER RAFTING The region's big-water rivers are in northern and western Maine, but white-water rafting trips are available in Massachusetts, Vermont, and Connecticut as well.

North American Whitewater Expeditions (© 800/727-4379; www.nawhitewater.com) runs early-spring trips on Connecticut's Housatonic River and Vermont's West River, as well as summer trips in Maine.

Raft Maine (© 800/723-8633 or 207/824-3694; www.raftmaine.com) is a trade association of white-water outfitters running descents on Maine's popular rivers, including the Penobscot, Kennebec, and Dead. See chapter 13 for more information on the rivers.

See also Zoar Outdoor under "Outfitters and Organized Tours," earlier in this section for information on rafting rivers in western Massachusetts.

(Make your own bed.) The center publishes an extensive bulletin of classes and events; you can browse upcoming programs on the website.

Norwich Inn & Spa, 607 W. Thames St., Route 32, Norwich, CT 06369 (© 800/ASK-4-SPA; www.norwichinnandspa.com), is an intimate retreat in a brick Georgian mansion on 40 acres (16 hectares) not far from Mystic. It offers a long list of services, such as invigorating loofah scrubs, clay wraps, and thalassotherapy, a seawater-based treatment. It also has tennis courts and an 18-hole golf course next door.

Topnotch at Stowe, Mountain Road, Stowe, VT 05672 (© 800/451-8686; www.topnotch.com), is considered a resort spa rather than a destination spa, but it has an attractive indoor pool and fitness facility situated on 120 acres (49 hectares) a short drive from Stowe's ski area and is near great summer hiking trails. A variety of treatments are available, and there's easy access to year-round outdoor activities, like hiking in the Green Mountains and horseback riding on superb local trails. Spa and non-spa meals are served in the elegant on-site restaurant.

Northern Pines Health Resort, 559 State Rte. 85, Raymond, ME 04071 (© 207/655-7624; www.maine.com/norpines), is 40 minutes west of Portland and is less extravagant than other spas. Located on 70 acres (28 hectares) that border a lovely lake (it's a former girls' summer camp), this intimate bed-and-breakfast/resort emphasizes a holistic approach to stress control and weight loss. Meals are vegetarian, and teatime is yoga time.

9 Planning Your Trip Online

Internet users today can tap into the same travel-planning databases that were once accessible only to travel agents. Sites such as **Frommers.com**, **Travelocity.com**, **Expedia.com**, and **Orbitz.com** allow consumers to comparison shop for airfares, access special bargains, and reserve hotel rooms and rental cars.

But don't fire your travel agent just yet. Although online booking sites offer tips and hard data to help you bargain shop, they cannot endow you with the experience that makes a seasoned travel agent an invaluable resource, even in the Internet age. And for consumers with a complex itinerary, a trusty travel agent is still the best way to arrange the most direct flights to and from the best airports.

Still, there's no denying the Internet's emergence as a powerful tool in plotting travel time. The benefits of researching your trip online can be well worth the effort.

Last-minute specials, offered by airlines to fill empty seats, are usually announced on Tuesdays or Wednesdays and must be purchased online. Sign up for weekly e-mail alerts at sites that compile comprehensive lists of such specials, like **Smarter Living** (smarterliving.com) or **WebFlyer** (www.webflyer.com).

TRAVEL PLANNING & BOOKING SITES Keep in mind that because several airlines are no longer willing to pay commissions on tickets sold by online travel agencies, these agencies may assess a $10 surcharge if

Tips   Easy Internet Access Away from Home

There are a number of ways to get your e-mail on the web, using any computer.

- Your **Internet Service Provider (ISP)** may have a web-based interface that lets you access your e-mail on computers other than your own. Just find out how it works before you leave home. The major ISPs maintain local access numbers around the world so that you can go online by placing a local call. Check your ISP's website or call its toll-free number and ask how you can use your current account away from home, and how much it will cost.
- You can open an account on a free, web-based **e-mail provider** before you leave home, such as Microsoft's **Hotmail** (hotmail.com) or **Yahoo! Mail** (mail.yahoo.com). Your home ISP may be able to forward your home e-mail to the web-based account automatically.
- Check out **www.mail2web.com**. This amazing free service allows you to type in your regular e-mail address and password and retrieve your e-mail from any web browser, anywhere, so long as your home ISP hasn't blocked it with a firewall.
- Call your hotel in advance to see whether Internet access is possible from your room.

you book on that carrier—or neglect to offer that carrier's schedule altogether.

The list below is selective, not comprehensive. Some sites will have evolved or disappeared by the time you read this.

- **Travelocity** (www.travelocity.com or www.frommers.travelocity.com) and **Expedia** (www.expedia.com) are among the most popular sites, each offering an excellent range of options. Travelers search by destination, dates, and cost.
- **Orbitz** (www.orbitz.com) is a popular site launched by United, Delta, Northwest, American, and Continental airlines. (Stay tuned:

At press time, travel-agency associations were waging an antitrust battle against this site.)
- **Qixo** (www.qixo.com) is another powerful search engine that allows you to search for flights and accommodations from some 20 airline and travel-planning sites (such as Travelocity) at once.
- **Priceline** (www.priceline.com) lets you "name your price" for airline tickets, hotel rooms, and rental cars. For airline tickets, you must accept any flight between 6am and 10pm on the dates you've selected, and you may have to make one or more stopovers.

10 Getting Around

BY CAR New England airports all host national car rental chains. Useful phone numbers include: **Avis** (✆ 800/831-2847), **Budget** (✆ 800/527-0700), **Enterprise** (✆ 800/325-8007), **Hertz** (✆ 800/654-3131), **National**

(✆ 800/227-7368), **Rent-A-Wreck** (✆ 800/535-1391), and **Thrifty** (✆ 800/367-2277).

Before you drive off in a rental car, be sure you're insured. The basic insurance coverage offered by most car rental companies, known as the **Loss/Damage Waiver** (LDW) or **Collision Damage Waiver** (CDW), can cost $20 per day or more. It usually covers the full value of the vehicle with no deductible if an outside party causes damage to the car. In all states but California, you will probably be covered in case of theft as well. Liability coverage varies according to company policy and state law, but the minimum is usually at least $15,000. If you are at fault in an accident, however, you will be covered for the full replacement value of the car but not for liability.

Most major credit cards provide some degree of coverage as well—provided they were used to pay for the rental. Terms vary widely, however, so be sure to call your credit card company directly before you rent. The credit card will cover damage or theft of a rental car for the full cost of the vehicle. If you already have insurance, your credit card will provide secondary coverage—which basically covers your deductible. Credit cards will not cover liability.

The speed limit on interstate highways in the region is generally 65 miles (105km) per hour, although this is reduced to 55 miles (89km) per hour near cities. State highways are a less formal network, and the speed limits vary widely. Watch for speed limits to drop as you approach a town; that's where the local police often lurk in search of speeders.

If you're a connoisseur of back roads and off-the-beaten-track exploring, **DeLorme Atlases** are invaluable. They offer an extraordinary level of detail, right down to logging roads and public boat launches on small ponds. DeLorme's headquarters and map store (© **888/227-1656**) is in Yarmouth, Maine, but its products are widely available at bookshops and convenience stores throughout the region.

BY BUS See "Getting There," earlier in this chapter, for a list of bus companies serving New England. While express bus service to major cities and tourist areas is quite good, quirky schedules and routes between regional destinations may send you miles out of the way and increase trip time significantly.

11 Tips on Accommodations

What's the difference between an inn and a B&B? The difference narrows by the day. Until relatively recently, inns were always full-service affairs, whereas B&Bs consisted of private homes with an extra bedroom or two and a homeowner looking for some extra income. A few of these old-style B&Bs still exist, but they seem to be fading to the margins, in large part driven by the fact that Americans generally don't want to share bathrooms with other guests.

Today, the only difference between an inn and a B&B is that inns serve dinner (and sometimes lunch), whereas B&Bs provide breakfast only. At least that's the distinction we employ for this guide. Readers shouldn't infer that B&Bs in this guide are necessarily more informal or in any way inferior to a full-service inn. Indeed, many of the B&Bs listed have the air of gracious inns that have accidentally overlooked dinner.

B&Bs today are by and large professionally run affairs, where guests enjoy sumptuous breakfasts, attentive service, private bathrooms (we note exceptions to this in our reviews), and a common area that's separate from the owner's living quarters.

As innkeeping evolves into the more complex and demanding "hospitality industry," you're bound to bump up against more restrictions, rules, and regulations. It's always best to ask in advance to avoid unpleasant surprises.

A few notes on recent trends:

SMOKING Smokers looking to light up are being edged out the door to smoke on front lawns and porches. It's no different in the region's inns and B&Bs than in other public spaces. A decade or two ago, only a handful of places prohibited smoking. Today, the great majority of inns and B&Bs have banned smoking within their buildings entirely, and some have even exiled smokers from their property—front lawn included.

Frommer's has stopped mentioning whether smoking is allowed or not in inns because it has rapidly become a non-issue—almost everyone has banned it. Assume that no smoking is allowed at any of the accommodations listed in this guide. (As in other regions, the larger, more modern hotels—say a Radisson or Holiday Inn—will have guest rooms set aside for smokers.) If being able to smoke in your room or the lobby is paramount to your vacation happiness, be sure to inquire first. Likewise, if you're a non-smoker who finds the smell of cigarette smoke obnoxious in the extreme, it also wouldn't hurt to ask and make sure you're at a fully smoke-free establishment.

ADDITIONAL GUESTS The room rates published in this guide are for two people sharing a room. Many places charge $10 and up for each extra guest sharing the room. Don't assume that children traveling with you are free; ask first about extra charges. Also don't assume that all places are able to accommodate children or extra guests; the rooms at some inns are quite cozy and lack space for a cot. Ask first if you don't want to end up four to a bed.

MINIMUM STAY It's become increasingly common for inns to require guests to book a minimum of 2 nights or more during busy times. These times typically include weekends in summer (or in winter near ski areas), holiday periods, and the fall foliage season. These policies are mentioned in the following pages when known, but they're in constant flux, so don't be surprised if you're told you need to reserve an extra day when you make reservations.

Note that minimum-stay policies typically apply only to those making advance reservations. If you stop by an inn on a Saturday night and find a room available, innkeepers won't make you stay a second night. Also, thanks to erratic travel planning, the occasional stray night sometimes becomes available during minimum-stay periods. Don't hesitate to call and ask if a single night is available when planning your itinerary.

DEPOSITS Many establishments now require guests to provide a credit card number to hold a room. What happens if you cancel? The policies are Byzantine at best. Some places have a graduated refund—cancel a week in advance, and you'll be charged for one night's stay; cancel a day in advance, and you're charged for your whole reserved stay—unless they can fill the room. Then you'll be charged for half. Other places are quite generous about refunding your deposit. It's more than a bit tedious to figure it all out if you're booking a half dozen places over the course of your trip, and the policies can often seem irrational.

Most hotels and inns are fair and will scrupulously spell out their cancellation policy when you make reservations, but always ask about it before you divulge your credit card number, and, if possible, ask to have it e-mailed, faxed, or sent to you before you agree to anything.

PETS Sometimes yes, sometimes no. Always ask. See "Tips for Travelers with Special Needs," earlier in this chapter.

SERVICE CHARGES   Rather than increase room rates in the face of rising competition, many lodgings are increasingly tacking on unpublicized fees to guests' bills. Most innkeepers will tell you about these when you reserve or check in; the less scrupulous will surprise you at checkout. In our opinion, this is not a welcome trend.

The most common surcharge is an involuntary "service charge" of 10% to 15%. Coupled with state lodging taxes (even "sales-tax-free" New Hampshire hits tourists with an 8% levy), that bumps the cost of a bed up by nearly 25%. (The rates listed in this guide don't include service charges or sales tax.)

Other charges might include a pet fee (as much as $10 per day extra), a foliage-season surcharge ($10 or more per room), or a "resort fee."

 ***FAST FACTS:* New England**

American Express American Express offers travel services, including check cashing and trip planning, through a number of affiliated agencies in the region. Call ✆ **800/221-7282** for the nearest location.

Car Rentals See "Getting Around," earlier in this chapter.

Climate See "When to Go," earlier in this chapter.

Embassies/Consulates See chapter 3, "For International Visitors."

Emergencies In the event of an emergency, find any phone and dial ✆ **911.** You do not need a coin to make this call from a pay phone. If this fails, dial "0" (zero) and tell the operator you need to report an emergency.

Internet Access Many public libraries have free terminals with web access, allowing travelers to check their e-mail through a web-based e-mail service such as Yahoo! or Hotmail. Internet cafes have come and gone in the last few years; it's best to ask around locally, or check **www.netcafeguide.com** or **www.cybercafe.com**.

Liquor Laws The legal age to consume alcohol is 21. In Maine, New Hampshire, and Vermont, liquor is sold at government-operated stores only; in Connecticut, Massachusetts, and Rhode Island, liquor is sold in privately owned shops. Restaurants that don't have liquor licenses sometimes allow patrons to bring in their own. Ask first.

Newspapers/Magazines The *Boston Globe, Wall Street Journal,* and *New York Times* are distributed throughout New England, although they can sometimes be hard to find in more remote villages. Almost every small town has a daily or weekly newspaper covering local happenings. These are good sources of information for events and restaurant specials.

Taxes Current state sales taxes (as of 2002): Connecticut, 6% (12% on lodging); Maine, 5% (7% on meals and lodging); Massachusetts, 5% (local sales taxes may also apply on lodging); New Hampshire, no general sales tax but 8% tax on lodging and meals; Rhode Island, 7% (plus 5% surtax on lodging); and Vermont, 5% (9% on meals and lodging).

Time All of New England is in the eastern time zone, the same as New York. All states shift to daylight saving time (1 hr. ahead) on the first Sunday in April, and back to standard time on the last Sunday in October.

3

For International Visitors

by Wayne Curtis

Most of the general information you'll need to ensure a pleasant trip can be found in chapter 2, "Planning Your Trip to New England." Some aspects of U.S. laws, customs, and culture that might be perplexing to visitors from overseas are covered in this chapter.

1 Preparing for Your Trip

ENTRY REQUIREMENTS

Immigration laws may be subject to broad changes following the September 11, 2001, terrorist attacks, and the following requirements may have changed by the time you plan your trip. For up-to-date information on requirements for visiting the U.S., go to the State Department's website at **http://state.gov.**

VISAS Canadian citizens need only present some form of identification at the border; a passport isn't necessary unless you plan to stay more than 90 days, although it may be helpful as identification.

As of 2002, 29 countries participate in the **visa waiver program,** which allows travelers from selected countries to enter the U.S. with just a valid passport and a visa waiver form. Check with your travel agency for the program's current status, or go to http://travel.state.gov. The countries in the program at present are Andorra, Argentina, Australia, Austria, Belgium, Brunei, Denmark, Finland, France, Germany, Iceland, Ireland, Italy, Japan, Liechtenstein, Luxembourg, Monaco, the Netherlands, New Zealand, Norway, Portugal, San Marino, Singapore, Slovenia, Spain, Sweden, Switzerland, the United Kingdom, and Uruguay.

Other foreign visitors should apply for a U.S. visa at the embassy or consulate with jurisdiction over their permanent residence. You can apply for a visa in any country, but it's generally easier to get a visa at home. Applicants must have a passport that's valid for at least 6 months beyond the dates they propose to visit, a passport-sized photo (1½ in. sq.), and some indication that they have a residence outside the U.S. to which they plan to return. Applicants must also fill out Form OF-156 (available free at all U.S. embassies and consulates). If you have a letter of invitation from a U.S. resident, that's sometimes helpful.

Once in the country, foreign visitors come under the jurisdiction of the Immigration and Naturalization Service (INS). If you'd like to change the length or the status of your visa (for instance, from non-immigrant to immigrant), call the INS Customer Information Center at *C* **800/375-5283.**

Be sure to carefully check the valid dates on your visa. If you overstay 1 or 2 days, it's probably no big deal. If it's more than that, you may be on the receiving end of an interrogation by Customs officials on your way out of the country, and it may hinder efforts to get another visa the next time you apply.

MEDICAL REQUIREMENTS

Unless you've recently been in an area suffering from an epidemic (such as yellow fever or cholera), no inoculations are needed to enter the United States. Not all prescription drugs that are sold overseas are necessarily available in the U.S. If you bring your own supplies of prescription drugs (and especially syringes), carry a physician's prescription in case you need to convince Customs officials that you're not a smuggler or drug addict.

HIV-positive visitors should contact the **National Center for HIV** (✆ **404/332-4559;** www.hivatis.org) or the **Gay Men's Health Crisis** (✆ **212/367-1000;** www.gmhc.org) for up-to-date information on traveling to the U.S.

CUSTOMS Jet and ship passengers will be asked to fill out a Customs form declaring what goods they are bringing into the United States. Foreign visitors planning to spend at least 72 hours in the U.S. may bring up to $100 worth of merchandise without paying import duties; this amount may include 1 liter of alcohol, plus 200 cigarettes *or* 4.4 pounds of smoking tobacco *or* 100 cigars (but no Cuban cigars). Anything over these amounts will be taxed. No food may be brought into the country (this includes canned goods); live plants are also prohibited. Up to US$10,000 in cash may be brought in or out of the country without any formal notification. If you are carrying more than that amount, you must notify Customs officials when either entering or departing the country. For more information, visit the official website of the U.S. Customs Service at www. customs.gov/travel/travel.htm.

MONEY

The basic unit of U.S. currency is the dollar, which consists of 100 cents. Common coins include the penny (1¢), nickel (5¢), dime (10¢), and quarter (25¢); gold-tinted $1 coins were introduced in 2000 but are not in wide circulation. Bills and coins are accepted everywhere, but some smaller shops won't accept larger bills ($50 or $100) because they lack sufficient change or are fearful of counterfeit bills. It's best to travel with a plentiful supply of $10 and $20 bills.

CURRENCY EXCHANGE Some banks will exchange foreign currency for dollars, but it's often a time-consuming and expensive process, especially for less common currencies. It's best to plan ahead and obtain dollars or dollar-based traveler's checks in your own country before departure.

Canadian dollars are frequently accepted in border communities in Maine, New Hampshire, and Vermont, but often at an unfavorable exchange rate.

TRAVELER'S CHECKS Traveler's checks are considered as good as cash in most U.S. shops and banks. Widely recognized brands include American Express, Barclay's, and Thomas Cook. With other types of traveler's checks, you might meet with some resistance, particularly in smaller towns. Some small shops may not be willing to cash checks of $100 or more if they have insufficient change; it's best to cash these at hotels or banks. Many banks will cash traveler's checks denominated in U.S. dollars without charge, although some levy high fees; always ask first. *Tip:* Supermarkets are usually happy to cash a traveler's check without a fee if you make a small purchase and have ID such as a passport.

CREDIT CARDS Credit cards are the most common form of payment throughout the United States for everything from expensive hotel rooms to inexpensive gifts. Among the most commonly accepted cards are American Express, Discover, MasterCard, and Visa. Because American Express charges a higher rate for processing its transactions, some hotels and restaurants refuse to accept it.

It's highly recommended that you have at least one credit card when you travel in the United States. Credit cards are commonly accepted in lieu of deposits when renting a car or a hotel room. Many ATMs will debit your credit card and provide cash on the spot. Don't ever give your card to anyone as a deposit; they should always record the information on it and return it to you. Also be careful with your credit card receipts, as the information on them may be used by the unscrupulous to make purchases.

INSURANCE

Foreign visitors who are not insured are strongly urged to take out a traveler's insurance policy to cover any emergencies that may arise during their stay here. The United States does not offer national medical coverage for its own residents; medical services are paid for either in cash or, more commonly, by an individual's insurance company. Be aware that hospitals' and doctors' fees are extremely high in the United States, and even a minor medical emergency could result in a huge expense for those traveling without insurance.

Comprehensive policies available in your country may also cover other problems, including bail (in the event you are arrested), car accidents, theft or loss of baggage, and emergency evacuation to your country in the event of a dire medical situation. Check with your local automobile association or insurance company for detailed information on travelers' insurance.

Packages such as "Worldwide Assistance" in Europe are sold by automobile clubs and travel agencies at attractive rates. **Travel Assistance International** (TAI; ✆ **800/821-2828** or 202/347-2025) is the agent for Worldwide Assistance, so holders of this company's policies can contact TAI for assistance while in the United States.

Canadians should check with their provincial health offices or call **HealthCanada** (✆ **613/957-2991**) to find out the extent of their coverage and what documentation and receipts they must take home in case they are treated in the United States.

SAFETY

New England—with the notable exception of parts of Boston—boasts some of the lowest crime rates in the country. The odds of anything untoward happening during your visit here are very slight. But all travelers are advised to take the usual precautions against theft, robbery, and assault. *Tip:* Be sure to keep a copy of your travel papers separate from your wallet or purse, and leave a copy with someone at home should you need it faxed to you in an emergency.

2 Getting to the United States

Most international travelers come to New England from Canada, via Boston's Logan Airport, or via one of the three New York City–area airports. Dozens of airlines serve New York and Boston airports from overseas. But because New York gets far more air traffic from abroad, the fares there and back are often more competitive. Some helpful numbers (all in London) include: **Air Canada** (✆ 0181/759-2636), **American Airlines** (✆ 0181/572-5555), **British Airways** (✆ 0345/222-111), **Continental** (✆ 01293/776-464), **Delta** (✆ 0800/414-767), **United** (✆ 0845/844-4747), and **Virgin Atlantic** (✆ 0293/747-747).

Those coming from Latin America, Asia, Australia, or New Zealand will probably arrive in New England through gateway cities like Miami, Los Angeles, or San Francisco, clearing Customs before connecting onward. Airports with regularly scheduled flights into the region include—in addition to Boston—Hartford, Conn.; Providence, R.I.; Portland, Maine; Manchester, N.H.; and Burlington, Vt. Albany, N.Y., is another option, especially if your destination is southern Vermont. See "Getting There," in chapter 2.

Bus service is fairly extensive throughout the region, and you can connect to all major cities and many smaller ones through hubs in Boston or New York. Most buses leave Boston from **South Station,** 700 Atlantic Ave., and New York from the **Port Authority Bus Terminal,** Eighth Avenue and 42nd Street.

Travelers seeking to explore more remote regions such as the Litchfield Hills, the Berkshires, or the White Mountains are advised to rent a car. Cars may be easily rented at most airports and at many in-town locations in larger cities. See chapter 2 for a listing of phone numbers for car rental firms.

 FAST FACTS: **For the International Traveler**

Automobile Organizations Becoming a member of an automobile club is handy for obtaining maps and route suggestions, and can be helpful should an emergency arise with your car. AAA (© **800/222-4357**) has nearly 1,000 offices nationwide. AAA offers reciprocal arrangements with many overseas automobile clubs; if you're a member of a club at home, find out whether your privileges extend to the United States.

Business Hours Most offices are open from 8 or 9am to 5 or 6pm. Shops usually open around 10am. Banks typically close at 3pm, but many have ATMs available 24 hours. A few supermarkets are open 24 hours a day, but they're not terribly common in this part of the country. If you need quick provisions, look for one of the brightly lit convenience stores, which are usually open until at least 10pm.

Climate See "When to Go," in chapter 2.

Currency See "Money," under "Preparing for Your Trip," above.

Drinking Laws You must be 21 to legally drink alcohol in the U.S. No matter what your age, state laws in New England are notoriously harsh on those who drive drunk.

Driving A current overseas license is valid on U.S. roads. If your license is in a language other than English, it's recommended that you obtain an International Driver's Permit from the AAA affiliate or other automobile organization in your own country prior to departure (see "Automobile Organizations," above).

Drivers may make a right turn at a red light, provided that they first stop fully and confirm that no other driver is approaching from the left. At some intersections, signs prohibit such a turn.

Electricity Electrical incompatibility makes it tricky to use appliances manufactured for Europe in the United States. The current here is 110 to 120 volts, 60 cycles, compared to the 220 to 240 volts, 50 cycles, used in much of Europe. If you're bringing an electric camera flash, laptop computer, or other gadget that requires electricity, be sure to bring the appropriate converter and plug adapter.

Embassies/Consulates Embassies for countries with which the United States maintains diplomatic relations are located in Washington, D.C. Call directory assistance (© **202/555-1212**) and request the phone number.

A handful of countries maintain consulates in Boston, including Canada, 3 Copley Place, Suite 400 (© 617/262-3760); Great Britain, Federal Reserve Plaza, 600 Atlantic Ave., 25th floor (© 617/248-9555); Ireland, 535 Boylston St. (© 617/267-9330); and Israel, 1020 Statler Office Building, 20 Park Plaza (© 617/535-0200). For other countries, contact directory assistance (© 617/555-1212).

Emergencies In the event of any type of emergency, simply dial © **911** from any phone. You do not need a coin to make this call from a pay phone. A dispatcher will send medics, the police, or the fire department to assist you. If 911 doesn't work (some of the more remote areas haven't yet been connected to the network), dial "0" (zero) and report your situation to the operator.

Gasoline Gasoline is widely available throughout the region, with the exception of the North Woods region of Maine, where you can travel many miles without seeing a filling station. Gas tends to be cheaper farther to the south and in larger town and cities; you're better off filling up before setting off into remote or rural areas. (The exception is in Connecticut, where state taxes drive the price of gasoline to above the regional average.)

Many of the filling stations in New England have both "self-serve" and "full-service" pumps; look for signs as you pull up. The full-service pumps are slightly more expensive per gallon, but an attendant will pump your gas and check your oil. (You might have to ask for this.) The self-serve pumps often have simple directions posted on them. If you're at all confused, ask anyone who happens to be around for instructions.

Holidays With some important exceptions, national holidays usually fall on Mondays to allow workers to enjoy a 3-day weekend. The exceptions are New Year's Day (Jan 1), Independence Day (July 4th), Veterans Day (Nov 11), Thanksgiving (last Thurs in Nov), and Christmas (Dec 25). Other holidays include Martin Luther King, Jr., Day (third Mon in Jan), Presidents' Day (third Mon in Feb), Easter (first Sun following a full moon occurring Mar 21 or later), Memorial Day (last Mon in May), Labor Day (first Mon in Sept), and Columbus Day (second Mon in Oct). In Maine and Massachusetts, Patriot's Day is celebrated on the third Monday in April. Banks, government offices, and post offices are closed on these holidays. Shops are sometimes open, but assume almost all will be closed on Thanksgiving and Christmas.

Languages Some of the larger hotels may have multilingual employees, but don't count on it. Outside of the cities, English is the only language spoken. The exception is along the Canadian border and in some Maine locales (including Old Orchard Beach), where French is commonly spoken, or at least understood.

Legal Aid If a foreign tourist accidentally breaks a law, it's most likely to be for exceeding the posted speed limit on a road. (It's the law U.S. residents frequently run afoul of.) If you are pulled over by a police officer, don't attempt to pay the fine directly—that may be interpreted as a bribe, and you may find yourself in graver trouble. If pulled over, your best bet is to put on a display of confusion or ignorance of local laws (this may be feigned or legitimate), combined with a respect for authority. You may be let off with a warning. Failing that, you'll be issued a summons with a court date and a fine listed on it; if you pay the fine by mail, you don't have to appear in court. If you are arrested for a more serious infraction, you'll be allowed one phone call from jail. It's advisable to contact your embassy or consulate for further instruction.

Mail Virtually every small town and village has a post office. Mail may also be deposited at blue mailboxes with the inscription U.S. MAIL or UNITED STATES POSTAL SERVICE, located on many streets.

Mail within the United States costs 37¢ for a 1-ounce letter, and 23¢ for each additional ounce; postcards are 23¢. At press time, overseas mail to Europe, Australia, New Zealand, Asia, and South America is 80¢ up to an ounce, or 70¢ for a postcard. A 1-ounce letter to Mexico or Canada is 60¢; a postcard is 50¢. Ask a postal clerk for current rates.

If you need to receive mail during your travels, have your correspondents address it to your name, "c/o General Delivery" at the city you are visiting. Go in person to the main post office to collect it; you'll be asked for identification (a passport is ideal) before it's given to you.

Newspapers/Magazines Overseas newspapers and magazines are commonly found in Boston and Cambridge, but are harder to track down elsewhere in New England. Your best bet is to check in the phone book for Borders or Barnes & Noble, two of the largest chain bookstores in New England.

Taxes Visitors to the United States are assessed a $10 Customs tax upon entering the country and a $6 tax on departure. The United States does not have a value-added tax (VAT). The tax you most commonly come across is a sales tax (typically 5%–7%) added to the price of goods and some services. New Hampshire does not have a sales tax on goods but does levy an 8% tax on hotel rooms and meals at restaurants.

Telephone & Fax Pay phones are not hard to find except in the more remote regions. Shops that have public phones inside usually display a blue sign featuring a bell within a circle.

Telephone numbers beginning with "800," "877," "888," or "866" are toll-free. Press "1" before dialing a toll-free number.

Phone directories include the Yellow Pages (stores and services, listed by category) and the White Pages (names, listed alphabetically). Some White Pages are divided into commercial and residential listings. Phone books are sometimes found at pay phones; failing that, ask to see one at a friendly shop or restaurant. To find a specific local phone number, dial "411" and an operator will take your request. Sometimes this is a free call from a pay phone, sometimes it's not.

Local calls usually cost 50¢ for an unlimited amount of time; the price of a local call will appear on the phone. If you're uncertain whether a call is long distance or not, try it as a local call. If a recorded voice comes on telling you to deposit more money for the first 3 minutes, that means it's a long-distance call.

Long-distance calls at pay phones tend to be very expensive, and you'll need a lot of coins. There are other options. At some phones, you can use your credit card. Prepaid phone cards are available at many convenience stores and other outlets, typically for $5 or $10. Long-distance charges using the cards are typically between 5¢ and 25¢ per minute; ask about per-call charges or minimum fees per call before you buy. The cards are less expensive and more convenient than feeding coins into a pay phone.

Be aware that many hotels tack on a surcharge for calls made from your room. Even toll-free calls can cost you $1.50 or more. Ask about phone charges when you check in. If your hotel does add a high surcharge and you plan to make a number of local calls, you're better off using a pay phone.

To charge the phone call to the person receiving your call, dial "0" (zero), then the area code and the number you're calling. An operator will come on the line and ask your name, and will then call the number to ask permission to reverse the charges. If the person you're calling accepts, the call will be put through.

If you need to send or receive a fax (facsimile), ask at your hotel or look in the Yellow Pages under "Fax Transmission Service."

Time All of New England is in the eastern time zone, the same as New York. All states shift to daylight saving time (1 hr. ahead) on the first Sunday in April, and back to standard time on the last Sunday in October.

Tipping Tipping is commonly practiced in the United States to recognize good service. In virtually every restaurant, servers are paid a bare minimum and depend on tips for their wage. Tipping isn't considered optional, unless the service is unspeakably bad. For decent to good service, tip 15%; for outstanding service, 20%. Other suggestions for tipping include: bartenders, 10% to 15%; bellhops, $1 per bag; cab drivers, 10% of the fare; chambermaids, $1 to $2 per day; checkroom attendants, $1 per garment; and parking attendants, $1 to $2. No tipping is expected at gas stations or fast-food restaurants.

Toilets Public toilets (often called "restrooms") are increasingly scarce in the United States, and where they do exist, they're often not fit for use. Restaurants have restrooms for their customers; some will let people off the street use them, but many have signs indicating FOR PATRONS ONLY. This is remedied by buying a pack of gum or a cup of coffee. Fast-food restaurants are a good bet for reasonably clean toilets when traveling on the highways.

4

Boston & Cambridge

by Marie Morris

Boston embodies contrasts and contradictions—it's blue blood and blue collar, Yankee and Irish, home to budget-conscious graduate students and free-spending computer wizards (still!). Rich in colonial history and 21st-century technology, it's a living landmark whose unofficial mascot is the construction worker. A new highway, a dramatic new bridge, and new buildings of all sizes are altering the landscape of eastern Massachusetts. One notable structure (in suburban Foxboro) is a state-of-the-art stadium for the Super Bowl champion New England Patriots. In this traditionally sports-mad region, their victory in 2002 sparked weeks of celebration.

The most prominent sign of Boston's transformation, the $14.5-billion "Big Dig," is nearing completion—in early 2005, if it stays on schedule. The largest construction project in the world, which is moving an elevated expressway underground, has dominated the downtown waterfront for much of a decade. One section, a breathtaking white bridge over the Charles River between Boston and Cambridge, is slated to open to traffic in 2003.

Cambridge and Boston are so close that many people believe they're the same—a notion both cities' residents and politicians are happy to dispel. Cantabrigians are often considered more liberal and better educated than Bostonians, which is another idea that's sure to get you involved in a heated discussion. Harvard dominates Cambridge's history and geography, but there's more to the city than just the university.

Take a few days (or weeks) to get to know the Boston area, or use it as a gateway to the rest of New England. Here's hoping your experience is memorable and delightful.

1 Orientation

ARRIVING

BY PLANE   The major domestic carriers that serve Boston's Logan International Airport are **AirTran** (© 800/247-8726), **American** (© 800/433-7300), **America West** (© 800/235-9292), **Continental** (© 800/523-3273), **Delta** (© 800/221-1212), **Frontier** (© 800/432-1359), **Midway** (© 800/446-4392), **Midwest Express** (© 800/452-2022), **Northwest** (© 800/225-2525), **United** (© 800/241-6522), and **US Airways** (© 800/428-4322). Many major international carriers also fly into Boston.

Southwest (© 800/435-9792) serves **T. F. Green Airport,** in the Providence suburb of Warwick, R.I. (© 888/268-7222; www.pvd-ri.com), and New Hampshire's **Manchester International Airport** (© 603/624-6556; www.fly manchester.com). Several other major carriers serve both, and prices often undercut fares to Boston. **Bonanza** (© 800/556-3815; www.bonanzabus.com)

offers bus service from T. F. Green to Boston's South Station; the fare is $18 one-way, $32 round-trip. Allow at least 90 minutes. From Manchester, **Vermont Transit** (© 800/552-8737; www.vermonttransit.com) runs buses to South Station; some continue to Logan. The fare is $11 one-way, $22 round-trip. Allow 60 to 90 minutes.

The regional commuter airline **Shuttle America** (© 888/999-3273; www.shuttleamerica.com) serves **Hanscom Field,** off Route 2A in Bedford (© 781/869-8000; www.massport.com). Hanscom is handy if you're visiting the western suburbs, but handles only propeller aircraft, no jets.

Logan Airport is in East Boston at the end of the Sumner, Callahan, and Ted Williams tunnels, 3 miles (5km) across the harbor from downtown. All five terminals have ATMs, Internet kiosks, pay phones with dataports, fax machines, and information booths (near baggage claim). Terminals C and E have bank branches that handle currency exchange; A and C have children's play spaces.

The Massachusetts Port Authority, or **MassPort** (© 800/23-LOGAN; www.massport.com), coordinates airport transportation. Access to the city is by subway (the "T"), cab, and boat. The **subway** is fast and cheap—10 minutes to Government Center and $1 for a token (good for one ride). Free **shuttle buses** run from each terminal to the Airport station on the Blue Line of the T daily from 5:30am to 1am. The Blue Line stops at State Street and Government Center, downtown points where you can exit or transfer (free) to the other lines.

A **cab** from the airport to downtown or the Back Bay costs about $18 to $24. The ride into town takes 10 to 45 minutes, depending on traffic and the time of day. If you must travel during rush hour or on Sunday afternoon, allow extra time, or plan to take the subway or water shuttle (and pack accordingly).

The trip to the downtown waterfront (near cab stands and several hotels) in a weather-protected **boat** takes 7 minutes, dock to dock. The free no. 66 shuttle bus connects all terminals to the Logan ferry dock. The **Airport Water Shuttle** (© 617/330-8680) runs to Rowes Wharf on Atlantic Avenue Monday through Friday from 6am to 8pm, Saturday and Sunday from 10am to 8pm. The one-way fare is $10 for adults, $5 for seniors, and free for children under 12. **Harbor Express** (© 617/376-8417; www.harborexpress.com) runs from the airport to Long Wharf Monday through Friday from 6:30am to 9pm (to 11pm on Fri), less frequently on weekends. (The return trip goes through Quincy, so the Airport Water Shuttle is much faster.) The one-way fare is $8 for adults, $4 for children 6 to 12, and $1 for children under 6.

Some hotels have **limousines** or **shuttle vans;** ask when you make your reservations. To arrange private service, call ahead for a reservation, especially at busy times. Your hotel can recommend a company, or try **Carey Limousine Boston** (© 800/336-4646 or 617/623-8700) or **Commonwealth Limousine Service** (© 800/558-LIMO outside Mass., or 617/787-5575).

BY CAR   Boston is 218 miles (351km) from New York; driving time is about 4½ hours. From Washington, it takes about 8 hours to cover the 468 miles (753km); the 992-mile (1,597km) drive from Chicago takes around 21 hours.

Driving to Boston is not difficult, but between the cost of parking and the hassle of traffic, the savings on airfare may not be worth the aggravation. The **Big Dig** dominates the area near the Central Artery, which is being moved underground without being closed. If you're thinking of using the car to get around town, think again—you won't need one to explore Boston and Cambridge.

The major highways are **I-90,** the Massachusetts Turnpike ("Mass. Pike"), an east-west toll road that leads to the New York State Thruway; **I-93/U.S. 1,** which extends north to Canada; and **I-93/Route 3,** the Southeast Expressway, which connects with the south, including Cape Cod. **I-95** (Mass. Rte. 128) is a beltway about 11 miles (18km) from downtown that connects to I-93 and to highways in Rhode Island, Connecticut, and New York to the south and New Hampshire and Maine to the north. The **Mass. Pike** extends into the city and connects with the **Central Artery** (the John F. Fitzgerald Expressway). To avoid Big Dig construction, exit at Cambridge/Allston or Prudential Center in the Back Bay.

To reach Cambridge, take **Storrow Drive** or **Memorial Drive** (on either side of the Charles River). The Mass. Pike's Allston/Brighton exit connects with Storrow Drive. It has a Harvard Square exit; cross the Anderson Bridge to John F. Kennedy Street to reach the square. Memorial Drive intersects with Kennedy Street; turn away from the bridge to reach the square.

AAA (© **800/AAA-HELP;** www.aaa.com) provides members with maps, itineraries, and other information, and arranges free towing if you break down. The privately operated Mass. Pike arranges its own towing; if you break down, wait in your car until a patrol arrives.

BY TRAIN   Boston has three rail centers: **South Station,** on Atlantic Avenue; **Back Bay Station,** on Dartmouth Street across from the Copley Place mall; and **North Station,** on Causeway Street near the FleetCenter. **Amtrak** (© **800/USA-RAIL** or 617/482-3660; www.amtrak.com) serves all three. Each train station is also a rapid-transit station. See the "Boston Transit & Parking" map on p. 69.

Amtrak serves Boston from the south and, as of 2001, the north. The new *Downeaster* service (www.thedowneaster.com) runs from North Station to Portland, Maine, in just under 3 hours. Acela Express high-speed service has cut trip time from New York to just under 4 hours and from Washington to about 6 hours. Standard Northeast Corridor service takes 4 to 5 hours and 8 hours, respectively.

South Station is a stop on the Red Line, which runs to Cambridge by way of Park Street, the hub of the **subway** (© **800/392-6100** outside Mass., or 617/222-3200; www.mbta.com). At Park Street you can connect to the Green, Blue, and Orange lines. The Orange Line links Back Bay Station with Downtown Crossing (where there's a walkway to Park Street station) and other points. The **commuter rail** serves Ipswich, Rockport, and Fitchburg from North Station, and points south and west of Boston, including Plymouth, from South Station.

BY BUS   The **South Station Transportation Center,** on Atlantic Avenue next to the train station, is the city's bus-service hub. It's served by regional and national lines, including **Greyhound** (© **800/231-2222** or 617/526-1801; www.greyhound.com), **Bonanza** (© **800/556-3815** or 617/720-4110; www.bonanzabus.com), and **Peter Pan** (© **800/237-8747** or 617/426-8554; www.peterpanbus.com).

VISITOR INFORMATION
BEFORE YOU LEAVE HOME   Contact the **Greater Boston Convention & Visitors Bureau,** 2 Copley Place, Suite 105, Boston (© **888/SEE-BOSTON** or 617/536-4100; 0171/431-3434 in the U.K.; fax 617/424-7664; www.bostonusa.com). It offers a comprehensive information kit ($6.25) with a planner, guidebook, map, and coupon book; and a *Kids Love Boston* guide ($5). Free smaller planners for specific seasons or events are often available.

The **Cambridge Office for Tourism,** 18 Brattle St., Cambridge (© **800/862-5678** or 617/441-2884; fax 617/441-7736; www.cambridge-usa.org), distributes information about Cambridge.

Tips   **Area Code Alert**

You must dial all 10 digits—area code plus number—to complete a local call in eastern Massachusetts. If you accidentally dial "1" first, the call still goes through as a local call.

The **Massachusetts Office of Travel and Tourism,** 10 Park Plaza, Suite 4510, Boston (© **800/227-6277** or 617/973-8500; fax 617/973-8525; www.massvacation.com), distributes the *Getaway Guide,* a free magazine with information on attractions and lodgings, a map, and a seasonal calendar.

An excellent resource for travelers with disabilities is **Very Special Arts Massachusetts,** 2 Boylston St., Boston (© **617/350-7713;** TTY 617/350-6836; www.vsamass.org). Its comprehensive website includes general access information and specifics on more than 200 arts and entertainment facilities.

IN PERSON   The **Boston National Historic Park Visitor Center,** 15 State St. (© **617/242-5642;** www.nps.gov/bost), across the street from the Old State House and the State Street T, is a good place to start exploring. National Park Service rangers staff the center and lead free tours of the Freedom Trail. The audiovisual show provides basic information on 16 historic sites on the trail. The center is wheelchair accessible and has restrooms. Open daily from 9am to 5pm.

The Freedom Trail begins at the **Boston Common Information Center,** 146 Tremont St., on the Common. The center is open Monday through Saturday from 8:30am to 5pm, Sunday from 9am to 5pm. The **Prudential Information Center,** on the main level of the Prudential Center, is open Monday through Friday from 8:30am to 6pm, Saturday and Sunday from 10am to 6pm. The **Greater Boston Convention & Visitors Bureau** (© **888/SEE-BOSTON** or 617/536-4100) operates both centers.

There's an outdoor information booth at **Faneuil Hall Marketplace** between Quincy Market and the South Market Building. It's staffed in the spring, summer, and fall from 10am to 6pm Monday through Saturday, noon to 6pm Sunday.

In Cambridge, there's an **information kiosk** (© **800/862-5678** or 617/497-1630) in the heart of Harvard Square, near the T entrance at the intersection of Mass. Ave., John F. Kennedy Street, and Brattle Street. It's open Monday through Saturday from 9am to 5pm, Sunday from 1 to 5pm.

CITY LAYOUT

Parts of Boston reflect the city's original layout, a seemingly haphazard plan that can disorient even longtime residents. Old Boston abounds with alleys, dead ends, one-way streets, streets that change names, and streets named after extinct geographical features. On the plus side, every "wrong" turn **downtown,** in the **North End,** or on **Beacon Hill** is a chance to see something you might otherwise have missed.

FINDING AN ADDRESS   There's no rhyme or reason to the street pattern, compass directions are virtually useless, and there aren't enough street signs. The best way to find an address is to call ahead and ask for directions, including landmarks, or leave time for wandering around. If the directions involve a T stop, be sure to ask which exit to use—most stations have more than one.

It's a Big, Big, Big, Big Dig

In a city with glorious water views, historic architecture, and gorgeous parks, the most prominent physical feature is a giant highway-construction project. The Central Artery/Third Harbor Tunnel Project, better known as the "Big Dig," is a $14.5 billion undertaking that will move Interstate 93 underground—without closing the road—and connect the Mass. Pike to the airport. It encompasses a new bridge over the Charles River (north of North Station), reconfigured Mass. Pike access (south of South Station), and a giant construction site (in between).

If it's on schedule, the Big Dig will be completed in early 2005; meanwhile, it's causing countless traffic nightmares and making engineering history. Many of the construction techniques are so unusual that professionals come from all over the world just to see them. To learn more, visit www.bigdig.com, or just go for a walk downtown.

STREET MAPS Free maps of downtown Boston and the transit system are available at visitor centers around the city. *Where* and other tourism-oriented magazines, available free at most hotels, include maps of central Boston and the T. *Streetwise Boston* ($5.95) and *Artwise Boston* ($5.95) are sturdy, laminated maps available at most bookstores.

BOSTON NEIGHBORHOODS IN BRIEF

See the map on p. 74 to locate these areas. When Bostonians say **"downtown,"** they usually mean the first six neighborhoods defined here.

The Waterfront This narrow area along **Atlantic Avenue** and **Commercial Street,** once filled with wharves and warehouses, now boasts luxury condos, marinas, restaurants, offices, and hotels. Also here are the New England Aquarium and departure points for harbor cruises and whale-watches.

The North End One of the city's oldest neighborhoods has been an immigrant stronghold for much of its history. It's now less than half Italian American, but you'll still hear Italian spoken and find many Italian restaurants, *caffès,* and shops. **Hanover Street** is the main street of the North End, which lies across **I-93** from the rest of downtown. Clubs and restaurants cluster on and near **Causeway Street** in the North Station area (between N. Washington St. and Beacon Hill), but it's not a good place to wander alone at night.

Faneuil Hall Marketplace & Haymarket Employees aside, Boston residents tend to be scarce at Faneuil Hall Marketplace (also called Quincy Market). An irresistible draw for out-of-towners and suburbanites, the cluster of restored market buildings across **I-93** from the North End is the city's most popular attraction. **Haymarket,** along Blackstone Street, is home to an open-air produce market on Friday and Saturday. **Congress Street** separates the marketplace from Government Center.

Government Center Here, modern design strays into the red-brick facade of traditional Boston architecture. Across **Cambridge Street** from Beacon Hill, Government Center is home to state and federal office towers, Boston City Hall, and a central T stop.

Financial District In the city's banking, insurance, and legal center, skyscrapers surround the landmark Custom House Tower. This area is frantic during the day and practically empty at night. **State Street** separates it from Faneuil Hall Marketplace.

Downtown Crossing The Freedom Trail runs through this shopping and business district east of Boston Common, which hops during the day and slows at night. The intersection that gives Downtown Crossing its name is where Winter Street becomes Summer Street at **Washington Street,** the most "main" street downtown. The one-time "Combat Zone" (red-light district) has been the object of a PR campaign pushing the **Ladder District** designation for the area between Tremont and Washington streets, opposite the Common.

Beacon Hill Narrow, tree-lined streets and architectural showpieces make up this residential area near the State House. **Charles Street** is the main drag of "the Hill." Louisburg (say "Lewis-burg") Square and Mount Vernon Street, two of the city's loveliest and most exclusive spots, are on Beacon Hill. It's also home to Massachusetts General Hospital, off **Cambridge Street.** On the south side, **Beacon Street** borders Boston Common, as does **Park Street,** which is just 1 block long (but looms large in the geography of the **T**).

Charlestown One of the oldest areas of Boston is where you'll see the Bunker Hill Monument, USS *Constitution* ("Old Ironsides"), and one of the city's best restaurants, Olives (p. 89). Yuppification has brought some diversity to the mostly white residential neighborhood, but pockets remain that have earned their reputation for insularity. To get here, follow **North Washington Street** from the North End.

South Boston Waterfront (Seaport District) The city's newest neighborhood has several names; these are the most popular. Across **Fort Point Channel** from downtown, it's where you'll find the World Trade Center, Seaport Hotel, Fish Pier, federal courthouse, Museum Wharf, and a lot of construction.

Chinatown The fourth-largest Chinese community in the country is a small but growing area jammed with Asian restaurants, groceries, and other businesses. As the "Combat Zone," or red-light district, has nearly disappeared, Chinatown has expanded to fill the area between Downtown Crossing and the Mass. Pike extension. Its main street is **Beach Street.** Also in this neighborhood, the tiny **Theater District** extends about 1½ blocks in each direction from the intersection of Tremont and Stuart streets; be careful here at night after the crowds thin out.

South End Cross **Huntington Avenue** or Stuart Street to reach this landmark district packed with Victorian row houses and little parks. Known for its ethnic, economic, and cultural diversity, as well as its galleries and boutiques, the South End has a large gay community and some of the city's best restaurants. Main thoroughfares include **Tremont** and **Washington streets,** which originate downtown, and **Columbus Avenue.** *Note:* Don't confuse the South End with

South Boston, a residential neighborhood across I-93.

Back Bay Fashionable since its creation out of landfill over a century ago, the Back Bay overflows with gorgeous architecture and chic shops. It extends from **Arlington Street,** in the plush area near the **Public Garden,** to the student-dominated sections near Massachusetts Avenue, or **Mass. Ave.** Unlike downtown, it's laid out in a grid. The main streets include the prime shopping areas of **Boylston** and **Newbury streets** and largely residential Commonwealth Avenue, or **Comm. Ave.,** and **Beacon Street.** The cross streets go in alphabetical order.

Huntington Avenue Landmarks dot the "Avenue of the Arts." Not a formal neighborhood, Huntington Avenue is where you'll find Symphony Hall (at the corner of **Mass. Ave.**), Northeastern University, and the Museum of Fine Arts. Parts of Huntington can be a little risky; if you're leaving the museum at night, grab a cab or the Green Line, and travel in a group.

Kenmore Square The landmark white-and-red Citgo sign above the intersection of **Comm. Ave., Beacon Street,** and **Brookline Avenue** tells you you're approaching Kenmore Square. Boston University students throng its shops, bars, restaurants, and clubs. The college-town atmosphere goes out the window when the Red Sox are in town and baseball fans flock to Fenway Park, 3 blocks away.

Cambridge The backbone of Boston's neighbor across the Charles River is **Mass. Ave.,** which originates in Roxbury and extends into Cambridge, Arlington, and Lexington, 9 miles (14km) away. The Red Line subway parallels Mass. Ave. in the areas you're likeliest to visit, around the following T stops: **Kendall/MIT, Central, Harvard,** and **Porter.**

2 Getting Around

It's impossible to say this often enough: When you reach your hotel, *leave your car in the garage and walk or use public transportation.* If you must drive in town, ask at the front desk for a route around or away from Big Dig construction.

BY PUBLIC TRANSPORTATION

The **Massachusetts Bay Transportation Authority,** or **MBTA** (✆ **800/392-6100** outside Mass., or 617/222-3200; www.mbta.com), is known as the "T," and its logo is the letter in a circle. It runs subways, trolleys, buses, and ferries in Boston and many suburbs, as well as the commuter rail. Its website includes maps, schedules, and other information.

Newer stations on the Red, Blue, and Orange lines are wheelchair accessible; the Green Line is being converted. All T buses have lifts or kneelers; call ✆ **800/LIFT-BUS** for information. To learn more, call the **Office for Transportation Access** (✆ **617/222-5438** or TTY 617/222-5854).

The **Boston Visitor Pass** (✆ **877/927-7277** or 617/222-5218; www.mbta.com) includes unlimited travel on the subway and local buses, in commuter rail zones 1A and 1B, and on two ferries. The cost is $6 for 1 day (thus tokens are cheaper for fewer than six trips), $11 for 3 days, and $22 for 7 days. The $12.50 **weekly combo pass** covers subways and buses but not ferries, and is good only from Sunday through Saturday. You can buy a pass in advance by phone or online, or when you arrive at the Airport T station, South Station, Back Bay

---

Tips **Late-Night Transit**

The MBTA's **Night Owl** bus service extends curfews on Friday and Saturday nights. It operates until 2:30am on popular bus routes and on supplemental routes that parallel subway lines. Originally a 1-year program, it proved so successful that it should (budget permitting) still be operating when you visit. The fare is $1 in coins or a token. For information and schedules, contact the MBTA (© **800/392-6100** outside Mass., or 617/222-3200; www.mbta.com).

Station, or North Station. They're also for sale at the Government Center and Harvard T stations; the Boston Common, Prudential Center, and Faneuil Hall Marketplace information centers; and some hotels.

BY SUBWAY & TROLLEY   Red, Blue, and Orange line trains and Green Line trolleys make up the **subway** system, which runs partly aboveground. The local fare is $1—you'll need a token—and can be as much as $2.50 for some surface line extensions. Transfers are free. Route and fare information and timetables are available through the website and at centrally located stations. Service begins around 5:15am and ends around 12:30am. On New Year's Eve, closing time is 2am and service is free after 8pm. A sign on the token booth in every station gives the time of the last train in either direction.

The oldest system in the country, the T dates to 1897. The Green Line is the most unpredictable—leave early if you're taking it to a vital appointment. Note that downtown stops are so close together that walking is often faster. The system is generally safe, but always watch out for pickpockets, especially during the holiday season.

BY BUS   T buses and "trackless trolleys" (buses with electric antennae) provide service around town and to and around the suburbs. The local bus fare is 75¢; express buses are $1.50 and up. Exact change is required. You can use a token, but you won't get change. Important local routes include **no. 1** (Mass. Ave. from Dudley Sq. in Roxbury through the Back Bay and Cambridge to Harvard Sq.); **nos. 92** and **93** (between Haymarket and Charlestown); and **no. 77** (Mass. Ave. from Harvard Sq. north to Porter Sq. and Arlington).

BY FERRY   Two useful routes (both included in the T visitor pass) run on the Inner Harbor. The first connects **Long Wharf** (near the New England Aquarium), the **Charlestown Navy Yard**—it's a good final leg of the Freedom Trail—and **Lovejoy Wharf,** off Causeway Street behind North Station. The other runs between **Lovejoy Wharf** and the **World Trade Center.** The fare is $1.25. Call © **617/227-4321** for information.

BY TAXI

Taxis are expensive and not always easy to flag—find a cab stand or call a dispatcher. Stands are usually near hotels. There are also busy ones at Faneuil Hall Marketplace (on North St.), South Station, Back Bay Station, and on either side of Mass. Ave. in Harvard Square, near the Coop and Au Bon Pain.

To call ahead, try the **Independent Taxi Operators Association** (© **617/426-8700**), **Boston Cab** (© **617/536-5010** or 617/262-2227), **Metro Cab** (© **617/242-8000**), or **Town Taxi** (© **617/536-5000**). In Cambridge, call **Ambassador Brattle** (© **617/492-1100**) or **Yellow Cab** (© **617/547-3000**).

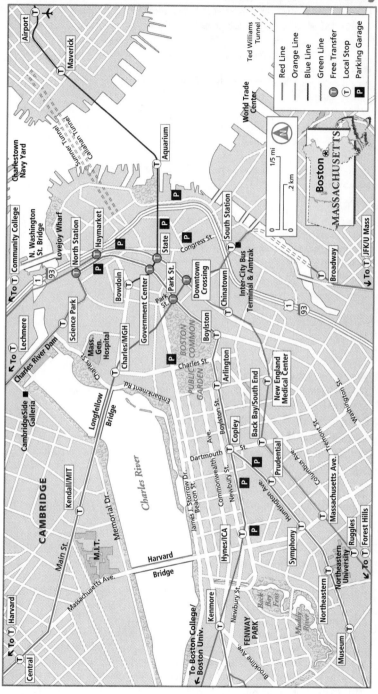

Boston Cab can dispatch a wheelchair-accessible vehicle; advance notice is recommended. If you want to report a problem or have lost something in a cab, call the police department's **Hackney Hot Line** (© **617/536-8294**).

The fare structure at press time (subject to a pending increase): the first quarter mile (when the flag drops), $1.50; each additional eighth of a mile, 25¢. Wait time is extra, and the passenger pays tolls as well as the $1.50 airport fee on trips entering and leaving Logan. Charging a flat rate is not allowed in the city; the police department publishes a list (available at www.massport.com/logan) of distances to the suburbs that establishes the flat rate for those trips.

BY WATER TAXI   From April to mid-October, on-call service in small boats connects 11 stops on the Inner Harbor, including the airport. It operates daily from 7am to 7pm. The fare at press time is $10. Call © **617/422-0392** for information.

BY CAR

If you plan to visit only Boston and Cambridge, you do not need a car. Construction, expensive parking, and confusing geography make Boston in particular a motorist's nightmare. If you arrive by car, park at the hotel and walk or use public transit. For day trips, you'll probably want a car.

RENTALS   The major car-rental firms have offices at Logan Airport and in Boston; some have other area branches. Boston levies a $10 surcharge on car rentals that goes toward the construction of a new convention center. If you're traveling at a busy time, especially during foliage season, reserve well in advance. Most agencies offer shuttle service from the airport to their offices.

Companies with offices at the airport include **Alamo** (© 800/327-9633), **Avis** (© 800/831-2847), **Budget** (© 800/527-0700), **Dollar** (© 800/800-4000), **Hertz** (© 800/654-3131), and **National** (© 800/227-7368). **Enterprise** (© 800/325-8007) and **Thrifty** (© 800/367-2277) are nearby but not on the grounds; leave time for the shuttle ride.

PARKING   It's difficult to find your way around Boston and practically impossible to park in some areas. Most spaces on the street are metered (and patrolled until 6pm on the dot Mon–Sat), have strict time limits, or both. Rates vary (usually $1 an hour downtown); bring plenty of quarters. Time limits range from 15 minutes to 2 hours. The penalty is a $25 ticket, but should you blunder into a tow-away zone, retrieving the car will take at least $100 and a lot of running around. The city tow lot is at 200 Frontage Rd., South Boston (© **617/635-3900**).

It's best to leave the car in a garage or lot and walk. A full day at most lots costs no more than $25 (in other words, cheaper than a parking ticket), but some downtown facilities charge as much as $35. Some restaurants offer discounts at nearby garages; ask when you make reservations.

The reasonably priced city-run **Boston Common Garage,** off Charles Street (© **617/954-2096**), accepts vehicles under 6 feet, 3 inches tall (2m). The **Prudential Center Garage** (© 617/267-1002) has entrances on Boylston Street, Huntington Avenue, and Exeter Street, and at the Sheraton Boston Hotel. Parking is discounted if you buy something at the Shops at Prudential Center and have your ticket validated. The **Copley Place Garage,** off Huntington Avenue (© **617/375-4488**), offers a similar deal. Many businesses in Faneuil Hall Marketplace validate parking at the **75 State St. Garage** (© 617/742-7275).

Good-size garages downtown are at **Government Center,** off Congress Street (© **617/227-0385**); **Sudbury Street** off Congress Street (© **617/973-6954**); the **New England Aquarium** (© **617/723-1731**); and **Zero Post Office Square,** in the Financial District (© **617/423-1430**). In the Back Bay, there's a large garage near the Hynes Convention Center on **Dalton Street** (© **617/247-8006**).

DRIVING RULES   When traffic permits, you may turn right at a red light after stopping, unless a sign says otherwise. Seat belts are mandatory for adults and children, children under 12 may not ride in the front seat, and infants and children under 5 must be in car seats. Pedestrians in the crosswalk and vehicles already in a rotary (traffic circle or roundabout) have the right of way.

 FAST FACTS: Boston & Cambridge

American Express The main local office is at 1 State St. (© **617/723-8400**), opposite the Old State House. Other offices are in the Back Bay, 222 Berkeley St., at Boylston Street (© **617/236-1334**), and in Cambridge, 39 John F. Kennedy St., Harvard Square (© **617/868-2600**).

Area Codes Eastern Massachusetts has eight area codes: Boston proper, **617** and **857**; immediate suburbs, **781** and **339**; northern and western suburbs, **978** and **351**; southern suburbs, **508** and **774**. *Note:* To complete a local call, you must dial all 10 digits.

Car Rentals See "Getting Around," above.

Dentists Ask at your hotel's front desk or try the **Massachusetts Dental Society** (© **800/342-8747** or 508/651-7511; www.massdental.org).

Doctors Your hotel concierge should be able to help you. Hospital referral services include **Brigham and Women's** (© **800/294-9999**), **Massachusetts General** (© **800/711-4MGH**), and **Tufts New England Medical Center** (© **617/636-9700**). An affiliate of Mass. General, **MGH Back Bay,** 388 Comm. Ave. (© **617/267-7171**), offers walk-in service and honors most insurance plans.

Drinking Laws The legal drinking age is 21. In many bars, particularly near college campuses, and at sporting events, you will probably be asked for ID. Retail liquor outlets are closed on Sunday. Some suburban towns, notably Rockport, are "dry."

Embassies/Consulates See "Fast Facts: For the International Traveler," in chapter 3.

Emergencies Call © **911** for fire, ambulance, or police. For the state police, call © **617/523-1212**.

Hospitals **Massachusetts General Hospital,** 55 Fruit St. (© **617/726-2000**), and **Tufts New England Medical Center,** 750 Washington St. (© **617/636-5000**), are closest to downtown. In Cambridge are **Mount Auburn Hospital,** 330 Mt. Auburn St. (© **617/492-3500**), and **Cambridge Hospital,** 1493 Cambridge St. (© **617/498-1000**).

Hot Lines AIDS Hotline (© **800/590-2437** or 617/451-5155); Poison Control (© **800/682-9211**); Rape Crisis (© **617/492-7273**); and Travelers Aid Society (© **617/542-7286**).

Information See "Visitor Information," earlier in this chapter. For directory assistance, dial ⓒ **411**.

Internet Access The ubiquitous **Kinko's** charges 10¢ to 20¢ a minute. Locations include 2 Center Plaza, Government Center (ⓒ **617/973-9000**); 187 Dartmouth St., Back Bay (ⓒ **617/262-6188**); and 1 Mifflin Place, off Mount Auburn Street near Eliot Street, Harvard Square (ⓒ **617/497-0125**).

Newspapers/Magazines The daily papers are the *Boston Globe* and *Boston Herald*. The "Calendar" section of the Thursday *Globe* contains extensive cultural listings. The Friday *Herald* has a similar insert called "Scene." The arts-oriented *Boston Phoenix*, published on Thursday, has entertainment and restaurant listings.

Where, a free monthly magazine, contains information on shopping, nightlife, attractions, museums, and galleries. Newspaper boxes around both cities dispense the free weekly *Phoenix* and *Tab*, and biweekly *Improper Bostonian* and *Stuff@Night*. *Boston* magazine is a lifestyle-oriented monthly.

Pharmacies Downtown Boston has no 24-hour drugstore. The **CVS** at 155–157 Charles St. (ⓒ **617/523-1028**), next to the Charles/MGH Red Line T stop, is open until midnight. The **CVS** at the Porter Square Shopping Center, off Mass. Ave. in Cambridge (ⓒ **617/876-5519**), is open 24 hours. Some emergency rooms can fill your prescription at the hospital's pharmacy.

Police Call ⓒ **911** for emergencies. For the state police, call ⓒ **617/523-1212**.

Restrooms The visitor center at 15 State St. has public restrooms, as do most tourist attractions, hotels, department stores, shopping centers, coffee bars, and public buildings. Free-standing, self-cleaning pay toilets (25¢) occupy eight locations downtown, including City Hall Plaza and Commercial Street at Snowhill Street, off the Freedom Trail.

Safety On the whole, Boston and Cambridge are safe cities for walking. As in any urban area, stay out of parks (including Boston Common, the Public Garden, and the Esplanade) at night unless you're in a crowd. Areas to avoid at night include Boylston Street between Tremont and Washington, and Tremont Street from Stuart to Boylston. Try not to walk alone late at night in the Theater District and around North Station. Public transportation is busy and safe, but service stops between 12:30 and 1am.

Smoking Massachusetts is an anti-tobacco stronghold. Most public places and all office buildings ban smoking, and many cities and towns prohibit smoking in restaurants. Brookline also forbids smoking in bars.

Taxes The 5% sales tax does not apply to food, prescription drugs, newspapers, or clothing that costs less than $175; the tax on meals and takeout food is 5%. The lodging tax in Boston and Cambridge is 12.45%.

Taxis See "Getting Around," earlier in this chapter.

Transit Info ⓒ **617/222-3200** for the T (subways, local buses, commuter rail), and ⓒ **800/23-LOGAN** for MassPort (airport transportation).

3 Where to Stay

Boston has one of the busiest hotel markets in the country, with some of the highest prices. Demand was softening before the travel turmoil of late 2001, and after business picked up, uncertainty continued to plague the market. Even with decreased demand, however, supply is limited, so you'll need to do some planning. Rates at most downtown hotels are lower on weekends than on weeknights, when business and convention travelers fill rooms; leisure hotels offer discounts during the week. If you don't mind cold and the possibility of snow, aim for January through March, when you'll find great deals, especially on weekends.

It's always a good idea to make a reservation, especially during foliage season. The area is also busy during spring and fall conventions, July and August vacations, and college graduation season (May and early June).

Before you rule out a hotel because of its location, consult a map. Especially downtown, neighborhoods are so small that the borders are somewhat arbitrary. The division to consider is **downtown vs. the Back Bay vs. Cambridge** and not, say, Downtown Crossing vs. the Financial District. For example, if your interests lie primarily in Cambridge, the Back Bay is not the most convenient place to stay. But if your companion has business downtown and you have the Newbury Street shopping bug, the Theater District may be a good compromise.

The state **hotel tax** is 5.7%. Boston and Cambridge (like Worcester and Springfield) add a 2.75% convention-center tax to the 4% city tax, bringing the total tax to 12.45%.

The Convention & Visitors Bureau **Hotel Hot Line** (© 800/777-6001) can help make reservations even at the busiest times. It's staffed Monday through Friday until 8pm, Saturday and Sunday until 4pm. If you're driving from the west, stop at the Mass. Pike's Natick rest area and try the **reservations service** at the visitor center.

BED-AND-BREAKFASTS   Most lodgings require a minimum stay of at least 2 nights. The following organizations can help you find a B&B:

- **Bed & Breakfast Agency of Boston** (© **800/248-9262** or 617/720-3540, 0800/89-5128 from the U.K.; fax 617/523-5761; www.boston-bnbagency.com).
- **Host Homes of Boston** (© **800/600-1308** or 617/244-1308; fax 617/244-5156; www.hosthomesofboston.com).
- **Bed & Breakfast Reservations North Shore/Greater Boston/Cape Cod** (© **800/832-2632** outside Mass., 617/964-1606 or 978/281-9505; fax 978/281-9426; www.bbreserve.com).
- **Bed & Breakfast Associates Bay Colony** (© **800/347-5088** or 781/647-4949; fax 781/647-7437; www.bnbboston.com).
- **New England Bed & Breakfast** (© **617/244-2112**).

THE WATERFRONT & FANEUIL HALL MARKETPLACE

These areas are convenient to the Financial District and other downtown destinations, but not as handy if you plan to spend a lot of time in the Back Bay or Cambridge. *Tip:* Ask for a room on a high floor—you'll want to be as far as possible from the noise and disarray of the Big Dig.

VERY EXPENSIVE

Boston Harbor Hotel ★★★   The Boston Harbor Hotel is one of the finest in town, an excellent choice for both business and leisure travelers. The 16-story

Boston Accommodations

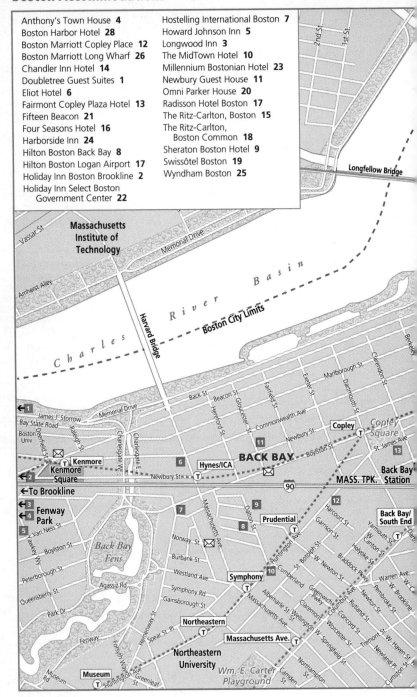

Anthony's Town House **4**
Boston Harbor Hotel **28**
Boston Marriott Copley Place **12**
Boston Marriott Long Wharf **26**
Chandler Inn Hotel **14**
Doubletree Guest Suites **1**
Eliot Hotel **6**
Fairmont Copley Plaza Hotel **13**
Fifteen Beacon **21**
Four Seasons Hotel **16**
Harborside Inn **24**
Hilton Boston Back Bay **8**
Hilton Boston Logan Airport **17**
Holiday Inn Boston Brookline **2**
Holiday Inn Select Boston
   Government Center **22**

Hostelling International Boston **7**
Howard Johnson Inn **5**
Longwood Inn **3**
The MidTown Hotel **10**
Millennium Bostonian Hotel **23**
Newbury Guest House **11**
Omni Parker House **20**
Radisson Hotel Boston **17**
The Ritz-Carlton, Boston **15**
The Ritz-Carlton,
   Boston Common **18**
Sheraton Boston Hotel **9**
Swissôtel Boston **19**
Wyndham Boston **25**

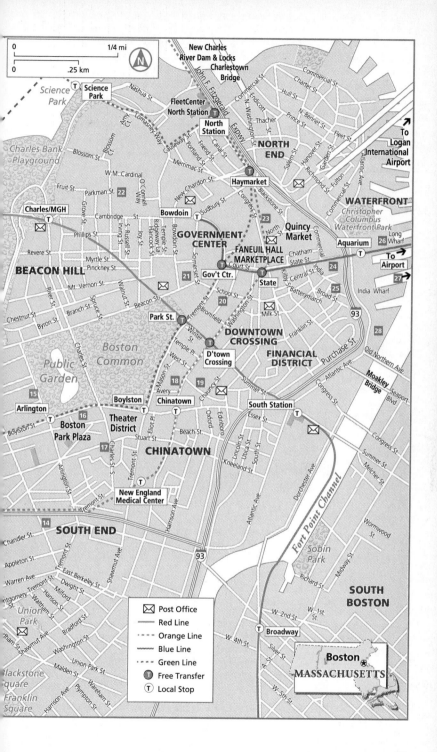

brick building is within walking distance of downtown and the waterfront attractions; the Airport Water Shuttle stops behind the hotel. Each plush guest room is a luxurious combination of bedroom and living room, with mahogany furnishings and comfortable chairs. Rooms with city views are less expensive than those that face the harbor. We'd opt for the savings and an up-close look at the Big Dig—the water will always be there; the construction won't. If you don't share our fascination with the project, the best units are suites with private terraces and dazzling water vistas.

Rowes Wharf (entrance on Atlantic Ave.), Boston, MA 02110. (℄ **800/752-7077** or 617/439-7000. Fax 617/330-9450. www.bhh.com. 230 units. $365–$555 double; from $455 suite. Extra person $50. Children under 18 stay free in parents' room. Weekend packages available. AE, DC, DISC, MC, V. Valet parking $20–$28; self-parking $15–$26. T: Red Line to South Station or Blue Line to Aquarium. Pets accepted. **Amenities:** Restaurant (New England), cafe, bar; 60-ft. (18m) indoor lap pool; well-appointed health club and spa; concierge; courtesy car; business center; 24-hr. room service; in-room massage; babysitting; laundry service; dry cleaning; video rentals. In room: A/C, TV, dataport, minibar, hair dryer.

Boston Marriott Long Wharf ⭐ The chief appeal of this standard-issue Marriott is its location, a stone's throw from the New England Aquarium. It attracts business travelers with its proximity to the Financial District, and families with its easy access to downtown and waterfront attractions. Rooms and bathrooms underwent renovation in 2000 and 2001. Big Dig construction is directly under the windows of the rooms near the street. Ask to be as close to the water as possible, and you'll have good views of the wharves and waterfront without the attendant noise.

296 State St. (at Atlantic Ave.), Boston, MA 02109. (℄ **800/228-9290** or 617/227-0800. Fax 617/227-2867. www.marriotthotels.com/BOSLW. 400 units. Apr–Nov $379–$450 double, Dec–Mar $269–$379 double; $450–$490 suite year-round. Weekend packages from $179 per night. AE, DC, DISC, MC, V. Parking $30. T: Blue Line to Aquarium. **Amenities:** Restaurant (seafood), cafe and lounge, bar and grill; indoor pool; exercise room; Jacuzzi; sauna; game room; concierge; business center; limited room service; laundry service; dry cleaning. In room: A/C, TV, dataport, coffeemaker, hair dryer.

Millennium Bostonian Hotel ⭐⭐ The relatively small Bostonian offers excellent service and features that make it competitive with larger hotels. It's popular with business travelers who want a break from convention-oriented giants, and with vacationers who enjoy the boutique atmosphere. The traditionally appointed guest rooms contain top-of-the-line furnishings and amenities. They're soundproofed, an important feature in this busy location. Half of the units have French doors that open onto small balconies; the plushest rooms are suites with working fireplaces or Jacuzzis. Three brick 19th-century buildings make up the hotel; the 38 units in the new wing, added in 1999, include a suite and four rooms on the glass-enclosed top floor.

At Faneuil Hall Marketplace, 40 North St., Boston, MA 02109. (℄ **800/343-0922** or 617/523-3600. Fax 617/523-2454. www.millennium-hotels.com/boston. 201 units. $245–$420 double; $265–$450 deluxe double; $500–$775 suite. Extra person $20. Children under 18 stay free in parents' room. Weekend and other packages available. AE, DC, DISC, MC, V. Valet parking $30. T: Orange Line to Haymarket, or Green or Blue Line to Government Center. **Amenities:** Restaurant (contemporary American), lounge; access to nearby health club with pool; small fitness room; exercise equipment delivery on request; concierge; morning limo service; secretarial services; 24-hr. room service; in-room massage; babysitting; laundry service; dry cleaning. In room: A/C, TV w/ pay movies, dataport, minibar, hair dryer, iron, safe.

MODERATE

Harborside Inn ⭐⭐ Under the same management as the Newbury Guest House in the Back Bay, the Harborside Inn offers a similar combination of location and (for this neighborhood) value. The renovated 1858 warehouse is near Faneuil Hall Marketplace, the harbor, the Financial District, and the Big Dig.

The nicely appointed guest rooms have hardwood floors, Oriental rugs, and Victorian-style furniture. They surround a skylit atrium; city-view units are more expensive but can be noisier. Still, they're preferable to the interior rooms, whose windows open only to the atrium. Units on the top floors of the eight-story building have lower ceilings but better views.

185 State St. (between I-93 and the Custom House Tower), Boston, MA 02109. © **617/723-7500.** Fax 617/670-2010. www.hagopianhotels.com. 54 units. $120–$210 double; $235–$310 suite. Extra person $15. Rates may be higher during special events. AE, DC, DISC, MC, V. No parking. T: Blue Line to Aquarium or Orange Line to State. **Amenities:** Restaurant (international bistro); access to nearby health club ($15 fee); limited room service; laundry service; dry cleaning. *In room:* A/C, TV, dataport, hair dryer.

AT THE AIRPORT
EXPENSIVE

Hilton Boston Logan Airport ★★   This hotel smack in the middle of the airport draws most of its guests from meetings, conventions, and canceled flights. Walkways lead directly to Terminals A (close) and E (distant). The hotel is convenient for business travelers, and an excellent fallback for vacationers who don't mind a short commute to downtown. Guest rooms are tastefully furnished; the best units, on higher floors of the 10-story building, afford sensational views. Soundproofing throughout the hotel, which opened in 1999, is excellent. The closest competition, the Hyatt Harborside, is farther from the T but right at the ferry dock.

85 Terminal Rd., Logan International Airport, Boston, MA 02128. © **800/HILTONS** or 617/568-6700. Fax 617/568-6800. www.hilton.com. 599 units. $149–$399 double; from $500 suite. Children under 19 stay free in parents' room. Weekend and other packages from $159 per night. AE, DC, DISC, MC, V. Valet parking $20; self-parking $18. T: Blue Line to Airport, then take shuttle bus. **Amenities:** Restaurant (American), Irish pub, coffee counter; indoor lap pool; health club and spa; 24-hr. shuttle bus to airport destinations (including car rental offices and ferry dock); business center; 24-hr. room service; laundry service; dry cleaning. *In room:* A/C, TV, dataport, minibar, coffeemaker, hair dryer, iron.

MODERATE

Comfort Inn & Suites Logan Airport   Although it loses points for the misleading name—the airport is about 3½ miles (5.5km) south—the well-equipped Comfort Inn ranks high in other areas. The eight-story hotel, which opened in 2001, offers a good range of amenities. The somewhat inconvenient location translates to reasonable rates, and the North Shore is easily accessible if you plan to take a day trip.

85 American Legion Hwy. (Rte. 60), Revere, MA 02151. © **888/283-9300,** 800/228-5150, or 781/485-3600. Fax 781/485-3601. www.comfortinnboston.com. 208 units. $129–$199 double; $139–$229 suite. Rates include continental breakfast. Senior and AAA discounts available. AE, DC, DISC, MC, V. Free parking. T: Blue Line to Wonderland, then take shuttle bus. Pets accepted ($10). **Amenities:** Restaurant (Italian/American), lounge; indoor pool; exercise room; shuttle to subway and airport; business center; coin-op laundry. *In room:* A/C, TV w/ pay movies, dataport, coffeemaker, hair dryer, iron.

FINANCIAL DISTRICT
VERY EXPENSIVE

Wyndham Boston ★★   This meticulously designed luxury hotel draws business travelers during the week and leisure travelers on weekends. The 14-story building is near Faneuil Hall Marketplace and the waterfront, but not all that close (by downtown standards) to the T. The spacious guest rooms have 9½-foot (3m) ceilings that make them feel even larger. The best units, on the upper floors, have great views of the harbor and downtown. Soundproofing throughout makes the whole building exceptionally quiet. The closest competitor, literally and figuratively, is Le Meridien, which is less convenient to public transit but has a pool.

89 Broad St., Boston, MA 02110. © **800/WYNDHAM** or 617/556-0006. Fax 617/556-0053. www.wyndham. com. 362 units. Double $215–$415 weekdays, $159–$279 weekends; suite $290–$490 weekdays, $234– $354 weekends. Children under 13 stay free in parents' room. Weekend, holiday, and other packages available. AE, DC, DISC, MC, V. Valet parking $16–$30. T: Blue or Orange Line to State, or Red Line to South Station. **Amenities:** Restaurant (California/Italian); bar; fitness center; concierge; business center; laundry service. *In room:* A/C, TV, dataport, minibar, coffeemaker, hair dryer, iron.

DOWNTOWN CROSSING & BEACON HILL

The **Holiday Inn Select Boston Government Center,** 5 Blossom St., at Cambridge Street (© **800/HOLIDAY** or 617/742-7630), offers all the features you'd expect of the international chain, including a heated outdoor pool.

VERY EXPENSIVE

Fifteen Beacon ★★ Nonstop pampering, high-tech appointments, and outrageously luxurious rooms make this boutique hotel *the* name to drop with the expense-be-hanged set. The hotel has attracted demanding travelers, especially businesspeople, since it opened in 2000. Management bends over backward to keep them returning, with attentive service and lavish perks that include personalized business cards listing the direct phone and fax numbers guests will have during their stay. The individually decorated rooms, opulent yet understated, contain queen-size canopy beds with Italian linens (300 thread count, of course), surround-sound stereo systems, gas fireplaces, and 4-inch (10cm) TVs in the bathrooms. The lobby restaurant, though overpriced and a bit cramped, is one of the best places in the city to see (or be) movers and shakers, especially at breakfast.

15 Beacon St., Boston, MA 02108. © **877/XV-BEACON** or 617/670-1500. Fax 617/670-2525. www.xv beacon.com. 61 units. From $395 double; from $1,200 suite. Valet parking $28. AE, DC, DISC, MC, V. T: Red or Green Line to Park, or Blue Line to Government Center. **Amenities:** Restaurant (French); bar; fitness room; access to nearby health club; concierge; in-town courtesy car; 24-hr. room service; laundry service; dry cleaning. *In room:* A/C, TV w/ pay movies, fax/copier/printer, dataport, minibar, hair dryer, safe.

Swissôtel Boston ★★ (Value) This centrally located 22-story hotel lives two lives. It's a busy convention and business destination during the week, and the excellent weekend packages make it a magnet for sightseers. The plain exterior contrasts with the elegant European style and luxurious appointments that take over in the second-floor lobby. Guest rooms, clustered around four atriums, are large enough to hold sitting areas, desks, and settees. Ask for a room on a high floor; this neighborhood was ugly even before construction began all along Washington Street.

1 Avenue de Lafayette (off Washington St.), Boston, MA 02111. © **888/73-SWISS** or 617/451-2600. Fax 617/451-0054. www.swissotel.com. 501 units. $250–$395 double; $280–$465 deluxe double; from $500 suite or Swiss Butler Executive Level. Extra person $25. Children under 12 stay free in parents' room. Weekend packages from $139 per night. AE, DC, DISC, MC, V. Valet parking $30; self-parking $26. T: Red Line to Downtown Crossing, or Green Line to Boylston. Small pets accepted. **Amenities:** Restaurant (international); lounge; 52-ft. (16m) indoor pool; health club; sauna; concierge; business center; 24-hr. room service; laundry service; dry cleaning. *In room:* A/C, TV, fax, dataport, minibar, coffeemaker, hair dryer.

EXPENSIVE

Omni Parker House ★ The Parker House offers a great combination of nearly 150 years of history and extensive renovations. It has been in continuous operation longer than any other hotel in America, since 1855. Since the detail-oriented Omni chain took over in the late 1990s, the hotel has been upgraded throughout. Guest rooms, a patchwork of more than 50 configurations, aren't huge, but they are thoughtfully laid out and nicely appointed. Business travelers can book a room with an expanded work area, while sightseers can economize by requesting a smaller, less expensive unit.

60 School St., Boston, MA 02108. ℂ **800/THE-OMNI** or 617/227-8600. Fax 617/742-5729. www.omni hotels.com. 552 units (some with shower only). $189–$309 double; $249–$385 superior double; $279–$445 suite. Children under 18 stay free in parents' room. Weekend packages and AARP discount available. AE, DC, DISC, MC, V. Valet parking $27; self-parking $20. T: Green or Blue Line to Government Center, or Red Line to Park St. Pets under 25 lbs. accepted ($50). **Amenities:** Restaurant (New England), 2 bars; fitness center; concierge; business center; 24-hr. room service; in-room massage; laundry service; same-day dry cleaning. *In room:* A/C, TV w/ pay movies, dataport, minibar, hair dryer, iron.

CHINATOWN/THEATER DISTRICT
VERY EXPENSIVE

The Ritz-Carlton, Boston Common ★★   This plush, ultramodern hotel is at the heart of an enormous new complex of offices, condos, a 19-screen movie theater, and the state-of-the-art Sports Club/LA. Challenging the Four Seasons' claim to A-list celebrities, the "new Ritz" opened in September 2001. It boasts the cachet and service of the original (see "Back Bay/South End," below), without a ruffle in sight. Guest rooms occupy the top four floors of the 12-story building; you'll pay more for a room with a view of the Common. The accommodations contain the latest in indulgent amenities, including luxury linens, feather duvets, and phones in the large bathrooms. The neighborhood is the urban-planning equivalent of a self-fulfilling prophecy: It's not the greatest, but the presence of the hotel automatically improves it.

10 Avery St. (between Tremont and Washington sts.), Boston, MA 02111. ℂ **800/241-3333** or 617/574-7100. Fax 617/574-7200. www.ritzcarlton.com. 193 units. From $495 double; from $595 Club Level; from $695 suite. Weekend and other packages available. AE, DC, DISC, MC, V. Valet parking $32; self-parking $28. T: Green Line to Boylston. Pets accepted. **Amenities:** Restaurant (contemporary American), bar, lounge; access to adjoining Sports Club/LA (with lap pool, spa, basketball court, weight room, steam rooms, saunas, and squash courts); concierge; courtesy car to Financial District (weekdays); business center; 24-hr. room service; babysitting; laundry service; same-day dry cleaning. *In room:* A/C, TV w/ pay movies, dataport, minibar, hair dryer, iron, safe.

EXPENSIVE

Radisson Hotel Boston ★★   The chain only recently started expanding in the Northeast and the location isn't the most attractive, so this hotel can be a pleasant surprise. It's convenient to both the Back Bay and downtown, and the guest rooms are among the largest in the city, each with a private balcony and sitting area. The well-maintained hotel has become as popular with business travelers as it already was with tour groups and families. The best units are the executive-level rooms on the top five floors of the 24-story building.

200 Stuart St. (at Charles St. S.), Boston, MA 02116. ℂ **800/333-3333** or 617/482-1800. Fax 617/451-2750. www.radisson.com/bostonma. 356 units (some with shower only). $159–$359 double. Extra person $20; cot $20; cribs free. Children under 18 stay free in parents' room. Weekend, theater, and other packages available. AE, DC, DISC, MC, V. Valet parking $21; self-parking $19. T: Green Line to Boylston, or Orange Line to New England Medical Center. **Amenities:** Restaurant (steakhouse), cafe; Stuart Street Playhouse (ℂ **617/ 426-4499**), a small theater that often books one-person shows; heated indoor pool; exercise room; concierge; business center; limited room service; laundry service; dry cleaning. *In room:* A/C, TV, dataport, coffeemaker, hair dryer, iron.

BACK BAY/SOUTH END
VERY EXPENSIVE

The **Ritz-Carlton, Boston,** 15 Arlington St. (ℂ **800/241-3333** or 617/536-5700; www.ritzcarlton.com), was shrouded in tarpaulins at press time, undergoing top-to-bottom renovations. The 278-room hotel is expected to reopen in October 2002, allowing for a year-end 75th-anniversary celebration.

Eliot Hotel ★★★ This exquisite hotel combines the flavor of Yankee Boston with European-style service and amenities. On tree-lined Comm. Ave., it feels more like a classy apartment building than a hotel, with a romantic atmosphere that belies the top-notch business features. Every unit is a spacious suite with antique furnishings and traditional chintz fabrics. French doors separate the living rooms and bedrooms, and bathrooms are outfitted in Italian marble. Many suites have pantries with microwaves. The hotel is near Boston University and MIT (across the river), and the location contrasts pleasantly with the bustle of Newbury Street, a block away.

370 Comm. Ave. (at Mass. Ave.), Boston, MA 02215. ℂ **800/44-ELIOT** or 617/267-1607. Fax 617/536-9114. www.eliothotel.com. 95 units. $315–$435 1-bedroom suite for 2; $600–$750 2-bedroom suite. Extra person $20. Children under 18 stay free in parents' room. AE, DC, MC, V. Valet parking $28. T: Green Line B, C, or D to Hynes/ICA. Pets accepted. **Amenities:** Restaurant (see review of Clio, later in this chapter); concierge; business center; 24-hr. room service; in-room massage; babysitting; laundry service; dry cleaning. *In room:* A/C, TV/VCR, fax/copier/printer, dataport, minibar, hair dryer, iron.

The Fairmont Copley Plaza Hotel ★★ The "grande dame of Boston" is a true grand hotel, an old-fashioned lodging that recalls the days when an out-of-town trip (by train, of course) was an event, not an ordeal. Built in 1912, the six-story Renaissance Revival building faces Copley Square. Already known for superb service, the Copley Plaza has enjoyed a renaissance of its own since becoming a Fairmont property in 1996. Extensive renovations included restoration of the spacious guest rooms, which contain reproduction Edwardian antiques. The traditional furnishings reflect the elegance of the opulent public spaces. Rooms that face the lovely square afford better views than those that overlook busy Dartmouth Street.

138 St. James Ave., Boston, MA 02116. ℂ **800/441-1414** or 617/267-5300. Fax 617/247-6681. www.fairmont.com/copleyplaza. 379 units. From $249 double; from $429 suite. Extra person $30. Weekend and other packages available. AE, DC, MC, V. Valet parking $32. T: Green Line to Copley, or Orange Line to Back Bay. Pets up to 20 lbs. accepted ($25 per day). **Amenities:** 2 restaurants (steakhouse, American), bar, lounge; exercise room; access to nearby health club; concierge; tour desk; car-rental desk; business center; 24-hr. room service; babysitting; laundry service; same-day dry cleaning. *In room:* A/C, TV/VCR, fax, dataport, minibar, hair dryer, iron.

Four Seasons Hotel ★★★ Many hotels offer exquisite service, a beautiful location, elegant guest rooms and public areas, a terrific health club, and wonderful restaurants. However, no other hotel in Boston—indeed, in New England—combines every element of a luxury hotel as seamlessly as the Four Seasons. If we were traveling with someone else's credit cards, we'd head straight here. Overlooking the Public Garden, the 16-story brick-and-glass building (the hotel occupies eight floors) blends traditional and contemporary style. The best units overlook the Public Garden; city views from the back of the hotel aren't as desirable. Children receive bedtime snacks and toys, and can ask at the concierge desk for duck food to take to the Public Garden. Small pets even enjoy a special menu and amenities.

200 Boylston St., Boston, MA 02116. ℂ **800/332-3442** or 617/338-4400. Fax 617/423-0154. www.fourseasons.com. 274 units. $535–$775 double; $1,450–$1,950 1-bedroom suite; $2,050–$2,300 2-bedroom suite. Weekend packages available. AE, DC, DISC, MC, V. Valet parking $27. T: Green Line to Arlington. Pets under 15 lbs. accepted. **Amenities:** Restaurant (see review of Aujourd'hui under "Where to Dine," later in this chapter), lounge; 51-ft. (15m) pool; well-equipped health club and spa; Jacuzzi; concierge; limo to downtown; business center; 24-hr. room service; in-room massage; laundry service; dry cleaning. *In room:* A/C, TV/VCR w/ free videos, dataport, minibar, hair dryer, safe.

EXPENSIVE

Boston Marriott Copley Place ⭐   This 38-story tower feels generic, but it does offer something for everyone—complete business facilities, a good-sized pool, and easy access to Boston's shopping wonderland. Guest rooms have Queen Anne–style mahogany furniture and are large enough to hold a desk, table, and sitting area. As at the Back Bay's other high-rise lodgings, ask for the highest possible floor and you'll enjoy excellent views. This is New England's biggest convention hotel (the Sheraton Boston is larger but attracts more vacationers), so solo travelers may feel out of place—but a hotel this large offers pretty good odds of finding a room at busy times.

110 Huntington Ave., Boston, MA 02116. ✆ **800/228-9290** or 617/236-5800. Fax 617/236-5885. www. marriotthotels.com/BOSCO. 1,147 units. $139–$399 double; $500–$1,200 suite. Children stay free in parents' room. Weekend and other packages available. AE, DC, DISC, MC, V. Valet parking $29; self-parking $27. T: Orange Line to Back Bay, or Green Line E to Prudential. **Amenities:** 3 restaurants (Italian, American, sushi), sports bar, lounge; heated indoor pool; well-equipped health club; concierge; car-rental desk; business center; 24-hr. room service; massage; dry cleaning. *In room:* A/C, TV w/ pay movies, dataport, coffeemaker, hair dryer, iron.

Hilton Boston Back Bay ⭐⭐   Across the street from the Prudential Center complex, the Hilton is primarily a business hotel, but families also find it convenient. Rooms in the 26-story tower are large, soundproofed, and furnished in modern style. The weekend packages, especially in winter, can be a great deal. The closest competitor is the Sheraton, across the street. It's three times the Hilton's size (which generally means less personalized service), has a better pool, and books more vacation and function business.

40 Dalton St., Boston, MA 02115. ✆ **800/874-0663**, 800/HILTONS, or 617/236-1100. Fax 617/867-6104. www.hilton.com. 385 units (some with shower only). $179–$295 double; $450 minisuite; $650 1-bedroom suite; $850 2-bedroom suite. Extra person $20; rollaway $20. Children stay free in parents' room. Packages and AAA discount available. AE, DC, DISC, MC, V. Valet parking $24; self-parking $17. T: Green Line B, C, or D to Hynes/ICA. Small pets accepted. **Amenities:** Restaurant (steakhouse), bar, nightclub; indoor pool; well-equipped fitness center; concierge; business center; limited room service; laundry service; dry cleaning. *In room:* A/C, TV, dataport, coffeemaker, hair dryer, iron.

Sheraton Boston Hotel ⭐⭐   Its central location, range of accommodations, lavish convention and function facilities, and huge pool make this recently refurbished 29-story hotel one of the most popular in the city. It attracts both business and leisure travelers with direct access to the Hynes Convention Center and the Prudential Center complex; because it's so big, it often has rooms available when smaller properties are full. A $100-million overhaul in 2001 upgraded the entire property. The fairly large guest rooms are decorated in sleek contemporary style and contain Starwood's signature pillowtop beds. Units on higher floors afford gorgeous views, especially to the west and north.

39 Dalton St., Boston, MA 02199. ✆ **800/325-3535** or 617/236-2000. Fax 617/236-1702. www.sheraton.com. 1,215 units. $149–$369 double; from $400 suite. Children under 17 stay free in parents' room. Weekend packages available. 25% discount for students, faculty, and retired persons with ID, depending on availability. AE, DC, DISC, MC, V. Valet parking $28; self-parking $25. T: Green Line E to Prudential, or B, C, or D to Hynes/ICA. Small pets accepted. **Amenities:** Restaurant (New England), lounge; heated indoor/outdoor pool; well-equipped health club; Jacuzzi; sauna; concierge; car-rental desk; courtesy car; 24-hr. room service; in-room massage; laundry service; dry cleaning. *In room:* A/C, TV, dataport, coffeemaker, hair dryer, iron.

MODERATE

Chandler Inn Hotel ⭐ *Value*   The Chandler Inn is a bargain for its location, just 2 blocks from the Back Bay. It underwent $1 million in renovations in

2000, and even with the accompanying price hike, the comfortable, unpretentious hotel is a deal. Guest rooms have individual climate control and tasteful contemporary-style furniture. Each unit holds a queen or double bed or two twin beds, without enough room to squeeze in a cot. Bathrooms are tiny, and the one elevator in the eight-story inn can be slow, but the staff is welcoming and helpful. This is a gay-friendly hotel—Fritz, the bar next to the lobby, is a neighborhood hangout—that often books up early.

26 Chandler St. (at Berkeley St.), Boston, MA 02116. © **800/842-3450** or 617/482-3450. Fax 617/542-3428. www.chandlerinn.com. 56 units. Apr–Dec $139–$169 double; Jan–Mar $129–$139 double. Rates include continental breakfast. Children under 12 stay free in parent's room. AE, DC, DISC, MC, V. No parking. T: Orange Line to Back Bay. Pets accepted with prior approval. *In room:* A/C, TV, hair dryer.

The MidTown Hotel ⭐ *(Value)*   Even without free parking and an outdoor pool, this centrally located two-story hotel would be a good deal for families and budget-conscious businesspeople; it also books a lot of tour groups. It's on a busy street within walking distance of Symphony Hall and the Museum of Fine Arts. The well-maintained rooms are large, bright, and attractively outfitted, although bathrooms are on the small side. Some units have connecting doors that allow families to spread out. The best rooms are on the side of the building that faces away from Huntington Avenue.

220 Huntington Ave., Boston, MA 02115. © **800/343-1177** or 617/262-1000. Fax 617/262-8739. www. midtownhotel.com. 159 units. Apr–Aug $139–$209 double; Sept to mid-Nov $159–$259; mid-Nov to Dec $109–$169; Jan–Mar $99–$159. Extra person $15. Children under 18 stay free in parents' room. AAA, AARP, and government employee discount available, subject to availability. AE, DC, DISC, MC, V. Free parking. T: Green Line E to Prudential, or Orange Line to Mass. Ave. **Amenities:** Restaurant (breakfast only); heated outdoor pool (in season); tour desk; babysitting; dry cleaning; video rentals. *In room:* A/C, TV, dataport, coffeemaker, hair dryer, iron.

Newbury Guest House ⭐⭐ *(Value)*   After just a little shopping in the Back Bay, you'll appreciate what a find this cozy inn is: a bargain on Newbury Street. It's a pair of brick town houses built in the 1880s and combined into a refined guesthouse. It offers comfortable furnishings, a pleasant staff, nifty architectural details, and a buffet breakfast served in the dining room, which adjoins a brick patio. Rooms are modest in size, but nicely appointed. Since opening in 1991, it has operated near capacity all year, drawing business travelers during the week and sightseers on weekends. At these prices in this location, there's only one caveat: Reserve early.

261 Newbury St. (between Fairfield and Gloucester sts.), Boston, MA 02116. © **800/437-7668** or 617/437-7666. Fax 617/670-6100. www.newburyguesthouse.com. 32 units (some with shower only). $130–$195 double; winter $115–$160 double. Rates include continental breakfast. Extra person $15. Rates may be higher during special events. 2-night minimum stay on weekends. AE, DC, DISC, MC, V. Parking $15 (reservation required). T: Green Line B, C, or D to Hynes/ICA. *In room:* A/C, TV, hair dryer.

INEXPENSIVE

Hostelling International–Boston   This hostel near the Berklee College of Music and Symphony Hall caters to students, youth groups, and other travelers in search of comfortable, no-frills lodging. Accommodations are dorm-style, with six beds per room; there are also a couple of private units. The hostel has two kitchens, 19 bathrooms, and a large common room. It provides linens, or you can bring your own; sleeping bags are not permitted. The enthusiastic staff organizes free and inexpensive cultural, educational, and recreational programs.

Note: To get a bed in summer, you must be a member of Hostelling International–American Youth Hostels. For information, contact HI–AYH

(© 202/783-6161; www.hiayh.org). If you are not a U.S. citizen, apply to your home country's hostelling association.

12 Hemenway St., Boston, MA 02115. © 888/HOST222, HI–AYH 800/909-4776, or 617/536-9455. Fax 617/424-6558. www.bostonhostel.org. 205 beds. Members $29 per bed; nonmembers $32 per bed. Members $81 per private room; nonmembers $84 per private room. MC, V. T: Green Line B, C, or D to Hynes/ICA. **Amenities:** Coin-op laundry. *In room:* No phone.

OUTSKIRTS & BROOKLINE

Staying in this area means commuting to downtown Boston. Because of the unwieldy public transit connections, it's not a great choice if your destination is Cambridge.

EXPENSIVE

Doubletree Guest Suites *ﬁﬁ* *Value*   This hotel is one of the best deals in town—every unit is a two-room suite. Overlooking the Charles River, the hotel is near Cambridge and the riverfront bike path, but not in a real neighborhood. Van service to and from attractions and business areas in Boston and Cambridge makes the location easier to handle. The large, attractively furnished suites surround a 15-story atrium. Most bedrooms have a king-size bed and writing desk. Each living room contains a sofa bed and dining table. The Hyatt Regency Cambridge, the hotel's nearest rival, is more convenient but generally more expensive.

400 Soldiers Field Rd., Boston, MA 02134. © 800/222-TREE or 617/783-0090. Fax 617/783-0897. www.doubletree.com. 308 units. $129–$309 double. Extra person $20. Children under 18 stay free in parents' room. Weekend packages $154–$264. AARP and AAA discounts available. AE, DC, DISC, MC, V. Parking $20. **Amenities:** Restaurant (American), lounge, Scullers Jazz Club (see below); indoor pool; exercise room; Jacuzzi; sauna; concierge; car-rental desk; business center; 24-hr. room service; coin-op laundry; dry cleaning. *In room:* A/C, TV w/ pay movies, dataport, minibar, fridge, coffeemaker, hair dryer, iron.

MODERATE

Many options in this price range and area are chain hotels, including the **Holiday Inn Boston Brookline,** 1200 Beacon St., Brookline (© **800/HOLIDAY** or 617/277-1200), and the **Howard Johnson Inn,** 1271 Boylston St., Boston (© **800/654-2000** or 617/267-8300).

Longwood Inn   In a residential area 3 blocks from the Boston–Brookline border, this three-story Victorian guesthouse offers comfortable accommodations at modest rates. Guests have the use of a full kitchen, dining room, and TV lounge. There's one apartment with a private bathroom, kitchen, and balcony. Tennis courts, a running track, and a playground at the school next door are open to the public. Public transportation is easily accessible, and the Longwood Medical Area and busy Coolidge Corner neighborhood are within walking distance.

123 Longwood Ave., Brookline, MA 02446. © 617/566-8615. Fax 617/738-1070. http://go.boston.com/long woodinn. 22 units, 17 with private bathroom (some with shower only). Apr–Nov $109–$129 double; Dec–Mar $89–$109 double. Apartment (sleeps 4-plus) $89–$119. Weekly rates available. No credit cards. Free parking. T: Green Line D to Longwood, or C to Coolidge Corner. **Amenities:** Coin-op laundry. *In room:* A/C.

INEXPENSIVE

Anthony's Town House   The Anthony family has operated this four-story brownstone guesthouse since 1944, and a stay here feels like a visit to Grandma's. Many patrons are Europeans accustomed to accommodations with shared bathrooms, but budget-minded Americans won't be disappointed. Each floor has three high-ceilinged rooms furnished in Queen Anne or Victorian style, plus a bathroom with enclosed shower. The large front rooms have bay windows. The guesthouse is 1 mile (1.6km) from Kenmore Square, about 15 minutes from downtown by subway, and 2 blocks from a busy commercial strip.

1085 Beacon St., Brookline, MA 02446. ℭ 617/566-3972. Fax 617/232-1085. www.anthonystownhouse. com. 12 units (none with private bathroom). $68–$98 double. Extra person $10. Weekly rates and winter discounts available. No credit cards. Limited free parking. T: Green Line C to Hawes St. *In room:* A/C, TV, no phone.

CAMBRIDGE
VERY EXPENSIVE

The Charles Hotel 👍👍👍   This nine-story brick hotel a block from Harvard Square has been *the* place for business and leisure travelers in Cambridge since it opened in 1985. Much of its fame derives from its excellent restaurants, jazz bar, and day spa; the service is equally impeccable. In the posh guest rooms, the style is contemporary country, with custom adaptations of early American Shaker furniture. The austere design contrasts with the indulgent amenities, which include down quilts and Bose Wave radios; bathrooms contain telephones and TVs.

1 Bennett St., Cambridge, MA 02138. ℭ 800/882-1818 outside Mass., or 617/864-1200. Fax 617/864-5715. www.charleshotel.com. 293 units. $380–$460 double; $500–$3,000 suite. Extra person $20. Weekend packages available. AE, DC, MC, V. Valet and self-parking $20. T: Red Line to Harvard. Pets accepted. **Amenities:** 2 restaurants (including Rialto, p. 97), bar, Regattabar jazz club (p. 126); access to adjacent health club with pool, Jacuzzi, and exercise room; access to adjacent spa and salon; concierge; car-rental desk; business center; 24-hr. room service; in-room massage; babysitting; laundry service; same-day dry cleaning; video rentals. *In room:* A/C, TV, dataport, minibar, hair dryer, iron.

Royal Sonesta Hotel 👍👍 *Kids*   This luxurious hotel is in a curious location—it's close to only a few things but convenient to everything, making it a good choice for both businesspeople and families. Features for both, from the business center to the indoor/outdoor pool with retractable roof, are excellent. The CambridgeSide Galleria mall is across the street, and the Museum of Science is around the corner on the bridge to Boston, which is closer than Harvard Square. MIT and Kendall Square are 10 minutes away on foot. Most of the spacious rooms have lovely views of the river or the city. (Higher prices are for better views.) Everything is custom designed in modern yet comfortable style.

5 Cambridge Pkwy., Cambridge, MA 02142. ℭ 800/SONESTA or 617/806-4200. Fax 617/806-4232. www.sonesta.com/boston. 400 units. $239–$279 standard double; $259–$299 superior double; $279–$319 deluxe double; $329–$950 suite. Extra person $25. Children under 18 stay free in parents' room. Weekend and other packages available. AE, DC, DISC, MC, V. Valet and self-parking $19. T: Green Line to Lechmere; 10-min. walk. Pets accepted with prior approval. **Amenities:** Restaurant (northern Italian), cafe; heated indoor/outdoor pool; well-equipped health club and spa; bike rental (seasonal); concierge; courtesy van; business center; limited room service; massage; laundry service; dry cleaning. *In room:* A/C, TV, Sony PlayStation, dataport, minibar, coffeemaker, hair dryer, iron, safe.

EXPENSIVE

The Inn at Harvard 👍👍   The red-brick Inn at Harvard looks almost like a college dorm—it's adjacent to Harvard Yard, and its Georgian-style architecture would fit nicely on campus. Inside, there's no mistaking it for anything other than an elegant hotel, popular with business travelers and university visitors. The guest rooms, which were redecorated in 2002, have cherry furniture; each holds a lounge chair or two armchairs, a work area, and an original painting from the Fogg Art Museum. Some units have dormer windows and window seats. The four-story skylit atrium holds the "living room," a huge, well-appointed guest lounge that's suitable for meeting with a visitor if you don't want to conduct business in your room.

1201 Mass. Ave. (at Quincy St.), Cambridge, MA 02138. © **800/458-5886** or 617/491-2222. Fax 617/491-6520. www.theinnatharvard.com. 109 units (some with shower only). $199–$359 double; $650 presidential suite. AAA and AARP discounts available. AE, DC, DISC, MC, V. Valet parking $30. T: Red Line to Harvard. **Amenities:** Restaurant (New England), dining privileges at the nearby Harvard Faculty Club; access to nearby health club; concierge; car-rental desk; limited room service; laundry service; dry cleaning. *In room:* A/C, TV, dataport, hair dryer, iron.

Sheraton Commander Hotel ★

This six-story hotel in the heart of Cambridge's historic district opened in 1927, and it's exactly what you'd expect of a traditional hostelry within sight of the Harvard campus. The colonial-style decor begins in the elegant lobby and extends to the guest rooms, which are attractively furnished and well maintained. Ask the pleasant front-desk staff for a room facing Cambridge Common; even if you aren't on a (relatively) high floor, you'll have a decent view. The Sheraton Commander doesn't have the cachet and amenities of the Charles Hotel—but with the money you save, you can buy your own cachet.

16 Garden St., Cambridge, MA 02138. © **800/325-3535** or 617/547-4800. Fax 617/868-8322. www.sheratoncommander.com. 175 units. $139–$385 double; $295–$750 suite. Extra person $20. Children under 18 stay free in parents' room. Weekend packages and AAA and AARP discounts available. AE, DC, DISC, MC, V. Valet parking $18. T: Red Line to Harvard. **Amenities:** Restaurant (American), lounge; small fitness center; concierge; limited room service; laundry service; same-day dry cleaning. *In room:* A/C, TV w/ pay movies, dataport, coffeemaker, hair dryer, iron.

MODERATE

The **Holiday Inn Express Hotel and Suites,** 250 Msgr. O'Brien Hwy., Cambridge (© **888/887-7690** or 617/577-7600; fax 617/354-1313; www.bristol hotels.com), is a limited-service lodging on a busy street a 5-minute walk from Lechmere station on the Green Line. The neighborhood is busy and noisy, but the hotel is convenient.

Best Western Homestead Inn ★

The busy commercial neighborhood is no prize, but this four-story motel is comfortable and convenient for motorists. Guest rooms are spacious, with contemporary or reproduction colonial furnishings, and at least one floor up from the busy street. The pool, free parking, and breakfast help make up for the less-than-scenic location, and a 2½-mile (4km) jogging trail around Fresh Pond is across the street. There's a restaurant next door, and a shopping center with a 10-screen movie theater nearby. Boston is about a 15-minute drive or a 30-minute T ride away; Lexington and Concord are less than 30 minutes away by car.

220 Alewife Brook Pkwy., Cambridge, MA 02138. © **800/491-4914** or 617/491-8000. Fax 617/491-4932. www.bestwestern.com/homestead. 69 units. Mid-Mar to Oct $129–$299 double; Nov to mid-Mar $109–$159 double. Rates include continental breakfast. Extra person $10. Children under 16 stay free in parents' room. Rates may be higher during special events. AE, DC, MC, V. Free parking. T: Red Line to Alewife; 10-min. walk. **Amenities:** Indoor pool; access to nearby health club; Jacuzzi; same-day dry cleaning. *In room:* A/C, TV, dataport, coffeemaker, hair dryer, iron.

A Cambridge House Bed & Breakfast Inn ★★

A Cambridge House feels almost like a country inn but is on a busy stretch of Cambridge's main street, set back from the sidewalk by a lawn. The beautifully restored 1892 Victorian contains well-maintained guest rooms, warmly decorated with Waverly-Schumacher fabrics and period antiques. Most contain fireplaces and four-poster canopy beds. The best units face away from the street. The inn serves a generous breakfast and afternoon refreshments.

Cambridge Accommodations & Dining

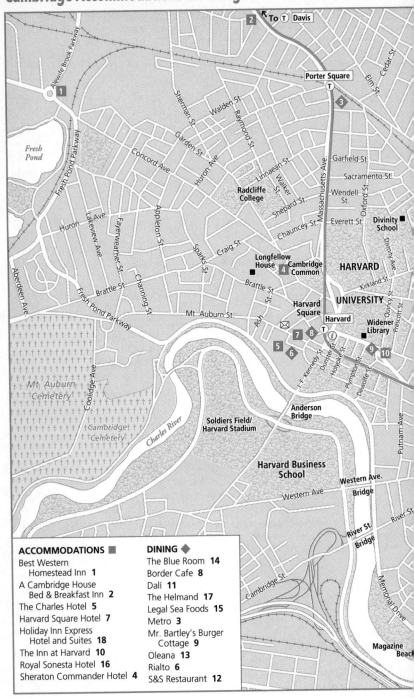

ACCOMMODATIONS ■

Best Western
   Homestead Inn **1**
A Cambridge House
   Bed & Breakfast Inn **2**
The Charles Hotel **5**
Harvard Square Hotel **7**
Holiday Inn Express
   Hotel and Suites **18**
The Inn at Harvard **10**
Royal Sonesta Hotel **16**
Sheraton Commander Hotel **4**

DINING ◆

The Blue Room **14**
Border Cafe **8**
Dalí **11**
The Helmand **17**
Legal Sea Foods **15**
Metro **3**
Mr. Bartley's Burger
   Cottage **9**
Oleana **13**
Rialto **6**
S&S Restaurant **12**

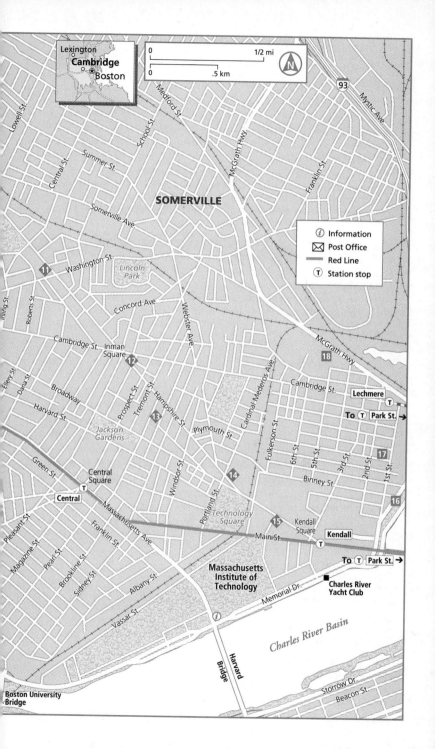

2218 Mass. Ave., Cambridge, MA 02140. (© 800/232-9989 or 617/491-6300, or 800/96-2079 in the U.K. Fax 617/868-2848. www.acambridgehouse.com. 15 units (some with shower only). $139–$350 double. Rates include buffet breakfast. Extra person $35. AE, DISC, MC, V. Free parking. T: Red Line to Porter. **Amenities:** Concierge. *In room:* A/C, TV, fax, dataport, hair dryer.

Harvard Square Hotel ✦   Smack in the middle of Harvard Square, this six-story brick hotel is a favorite with visiting parents and budget-conscious business travelers. The unpretentious guest rooms were renovated in early 2000. They're relatively small but comfortable; some overlook Harvard Square. The front desk handles fax and copy services.

110 Mount Auburn St., Cambridge, MA 02138. (© 800/458-5886 or 617/864-5200. Fax 617/864-2409. www.doubletree.com. 73 units. $129–$209 double. Extra person $10. Children under 17 stay free in parents' room. Corporate rates and AAA and AARP discounts available. AE, DC, DISC, MC, V. Parking $20. T: Red Line to Harvard. **Amenities:** Dining privileges at the Harvard Faculty Club; car-rental desk; laundry service; dry cleaning. *In room:* A/C, TV, dataport, fridge, hair dryer, iron.

4 Where to Dine

Travelers from around the world relish the variety of skillfully prepared seafood available in the Boston area. Lunch is an excellent, economical way to check out a fancy restaurant without breaking the bank. At restaurants that accept reservations, it's always a good idea to make them, particularly for dinner.

WATERFRONT
EXPENSIVE

A branch of **Legal Sea Foods,** at 255 State St. ((© **617/227-3115**), sits across from the New England Aquarium. See "Back Bay," later in this section.

Sel de la Terre ✦✦ PROVENÇAL   Side by side with the Big Dig, Sel de la Terre is a peaceful taste of southern France. The subtly flavorful food—scallops handled so gently that they're still sweet, juicy roasted chicken, and haddock infused with rosemary—relies on fresh local ingredients. The relaxing atmosphere belies the mayhem outside as well as the go-go business-lunch crowd. (Dinner is calmer.) The unusual pricing structure feels like a deal when you're tucking into a generous portion of roasted lamb, less of a bargain if you're eating pasta. Whatever you're eating, try the sublime pommes frites. The boulangerie at the entrance sells the out-of-this-world breads to go.

255 State St. (© **617/720-1300.** www.seldelaterre.com. Reservations recommended. Main courses $15 lunch, $23 dinner. Children's menu $7. AE, DISC, MC, V. Daily 11:30am–2:30pm and 5:30–10pm. T: Blue Line to Aquarium.

THE NORTH END & CHARLESTOWN

Many North End restaurants don't serve dessert, but you can satisfy your sweet tooth at a *caffè*. Favorites include **Caffè dello Sport,** 308 Hanover St. (no phone), and **Caffè Vittoria,** 296 Hanover St. ((© **617/227-7606**). There's also table service at **Mike's Pastry,** 300 Hanover St. ((© **617/742-3050**), which is better known for its bustling takeout business.

VERY EXPENSIVE

Mamma Maria ✦✦✦ NORTHERN ITALIAN   In a town house overlooking North Square and the Paul Revere House, this traditional-looking restaurant offers innovative seasonal cuisine and a level of sophistication that's unusual for the casual North End. The excellent entrees are unlike anything else in this neighborhood, except in size—portions are more than generous. Fork-tender osso buco is almost enough for two, but you'll want it all for yourself. You can't go wrong with main-course pastas, either, and the fresh seafood specials are uniformly marvelous. The pasta, bread, and desserts are homemade, and the shadowy, whitewashed rooms make this a popular spot for getting engaged.

3 North Sq. ✆ 617/523-0077. www.mammamaria.com. Reservations recommended. Main courses $19–$35. AE, DC, DISC, MC, V. Sun–Thurs 5–9:30pm; Fri–Sat 5–10:30pm. Closed 1 week in Jan. Valet parking available. T: Green or Orange Line to Haymarket.

Olives ✹✹ ECLECTIC   This informal bistro, the flagship of celebrity chef Todd English's growing empire, is a perennial hotspot with an infuriating reservations policy. A line often forms shortly after 5pm; if you don't arrive by 5:45pm, expect the charm-free front-desk staff to banish you for at least 2 hours. Once you're seated, you'll find the noise level high, the service uneven, and the ravenous customers festive. Happily, the food is worth the ordeal. Classics on the regularly changing menu include the delicious Olives tart (olives, caramelized onions, and anchovies) and spit-roasted chicken flavored with herbs and garlic. Grilling is a popular technique—yellowfin tuna, atop parsley mashed potatoes and accented with perfect mussels, demonstrates why, and any lamb dish is sure to please. When you order your entree, the server will ask if you want falling chocolate cake for dessert. Say yes.

10 City Sq. ✆ 617/242-1999. Reservations accepted for parties of 6 or more. Main courses $18–$32. AE, DC, MC, V. Mon–Fri 5:30–10pm; Sat 5–10:30pm. Valet parking available. T: Orange or Green Line to North Station; 15-min. walk.

MODERATE

Billy Tse Restaurant CHINESE/PAN-ASIAN/SUSHI   This casual spot on the edge of the Italian North End serves excellent renditions of the usual Chinese dishes and especially good fresh seafood. The Thai- and Vietnamese-influenced selections are just as enjoyable. Main dishes range from seven kinds of fried rice to the house special noodles, topped with shrimp, calamari, and scallops in a scrumptious sauce.

240 Commercial St. ✆ 617/227-9990. Reservations recommended for dinner on weekends. Main courses $5–$20; lunch specials $5.50–$7.50. AE, DC, DISC, MC, V. Mon–Thurs 11:30am–11:30pm; Fri–Sat 11:30am–midnight; Sun 11:30am–11pm. T: Blue Line to Aquarium, or Green or Orange Line to Haymarket.

Daily Catch ✹ SOUTHERN ITALIAN/SEAFOOD   This storefront restaurant is about the size of a large kitchen (it seats just 20), but it packs a wallop—of garlic. It's a North End classic, with excellent food, chummy service, and very little elbowroom. The surprisingly varied menu includes Sicilian-style calamari (squid stuffed with bread crumbs, raisins, pine nuts, parsley, and garlic), fresh clams, squid-ink pasta puttanesca, and a variety of broiled, fried, and sautéed fish and shellfish. All food is prepared to order, and some dishes arrive still in the frying pan.

323 Hanover St. ✆ 617/523-8567. Reservations not accepted. Main courses $12–$19. No credit cards. Sun–Thurs 11:30am–10pm; Fri–Sat 11:30am–11pm. T: Green or Orange Line to Haymarket.

Giacomo's Ristorante ✹✹ ITALIAN/SEAFOOD   The line snakes out the door and down the street, especially on weekends. No reservations, cash only, a tiny dining room with an open kitchen—what's the secret? Terrific food, plenty of it, and the we're-all-in-this-together atmosphere. To start, try fried calamari or mozzarella with excellent marinara sauce. Take the chef's advice or put together your own main dish from the list of daily ingredients on a board on the wall. The best suggestion is salmon and sun-dried tomatoes in tomato cream sauce over fettuccine. Nonseafood offerings such as butternut-squash ravioli are equally

Boston Dining

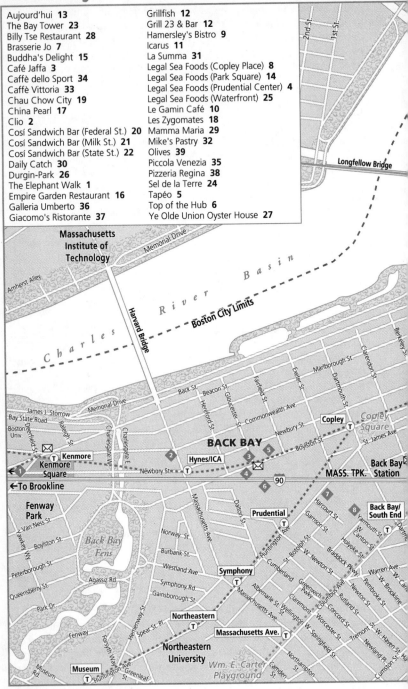

Aujourd'hui **13**
The Bay Tower **23**
Billy Tse Restaurant **28**
Brasserie Jo **7**
Buddha's Delight **15**
Café Jaffa **3**
Caffè dello Sport **34**
Caffè Vittoria **33**
Chau Chow City **19**
China Pearl **17**
Clio **2**
Cosí Sandwich Bar (Federal St.) **20**
Cosí Sandwich Bar (Milk St.) **21**
Cosí Sandwich Bar (State St.) **22**
Daily Catch **30**
Durgin-Park **26**
The Elephant Walk **1**
Empire Garden Restaurant **16**
Galleria Umberto **36**
Giacomo's Ristorante **37**

Grillfish **12**
Grill 23 & Bar **12**
Hamersley's Bistro **9**
Icarus **11**
La Summa **31**
Legal Sea Foods (Copley Place) **8**
Legal Sea Foods (Park Square) **14**
Legal Sea Foods (Prudential Center) **4**
Legal Sea Foods (Waterfront) **25**
Le Gamin Café **10**
Les Zygomates **18**
Mamma Maria **29**
Mike's Pastry **32**
Olives **39**
Piccola Venezia **35**
Pizzeria Regina **38**
Sel de la Terre **24**
Tapéo **5**
Top of the Hub **6**
Ye Olde Union Oyster House **27**

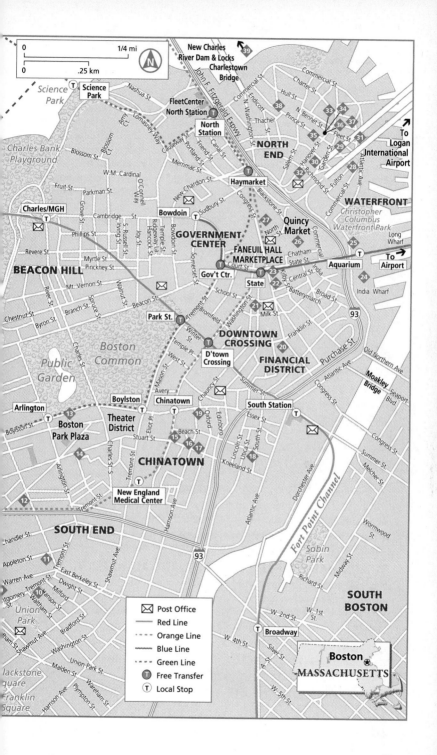

memorable. Service is friendly but incredibly swift. (Those hungry people want your seat.) After a 40-minute dinner, dessert at a caffè is practically a necessity.

355 Hanover St. © 617/523-9026. Reservations not accepted. Main courses $11–$18. No credit cards. Mon–Thurs 5–10pm; Fri–Sat 5–10:30pm; Sun 4–10pm. T: Green or Orange Line to Haymarket.

La Summa ⊕ SOUTHERN ITALIAN Away from the restaurant rows of Hanover and Salem streets, La Summa maintains a cozy neighborhood atmosphere. It's worth seeking out for wonderful homemade pasta and desserts; the more elaborate entrees are scrumptious, too. Try any seafood special, lobster ravioli, *pappardelle e melanzane* (eggplant strips tossed with ethereal fresh pasta), or the house special—veal, chicken, sausage, shrimp, artichokes, pepperoncini, olives, and mushrooms in white-wine sauce. Desserts, especially tiramisu, are terrific.

30 Fleet St. © 617/523-9503. Reservations recommended. Main courses $11–$24. AE, DC, DISC, MC, V. Mon–Sat 4:30–10:30pm; Sun 2–10:30pm. T: Green or Orange Line to Haymarket.

Piccola Venezia ITALIAN Piccola Venezia's glass front wall faces the Freedom Trail—a touristy location with a neighborhood feel. Portions are large, and the homey food tends to be heavy on red sauce. Spaghetti and meatballs, eggplant rolatini, and pasta puttanesca are always on the menu. This is a good place to try traditional Italian-American favorites such as home-style polenta, *baccala* (reconstituted salt cod), or the house specialty, tripe.

263 Hanover St. © 617/523-3888. Reservations recommended for dinner. Main courses $10–$20; lunch specials $5–$8. AE, DISC, MC, V. Daily 11am–10pm (lunch Mon–Fri until 4pm). T: Green or Orange Line to Haymarket.

INEXPENSIVE

An excellent eat-and-run spot just off the Freedom Trail is the cafeteria-style **Galleria Umberto,** 289 Hanover St. (© **617/227-5709**). Join the line for tasty pizza, *arancini* (a rice ball filled with ground beef, peas, and cheese), or calzones. Lunch is served Monday through Saturday; cash only.

Pizzeria Regina ⊕⊕ PIZZA Regina's looks like a movie set, but it's the real thing. Busy waitresses weave through the boisterous dining room, delivering peerless pizza hot from the brick oven. The list of toppings includes nouveau ingredients such as sun-dried tomatoes, but that's not authentic. House-made sausage, maybe some pepperoni, and a couple of beers—now, *that's* authentic.

11½ Thacher St. © 617/227-0765. Reservations not accepted. Pizza $9–$16. No credit cards. Mon–Thurs 11am–11:30pm; Fri–Sat 11am–midnight; Sun noon–11pm. T: Green or Orange Line to Haymarket.

FANEUIL HALL MARKETPLACE & FINANCIAL DISTRICT

The **food court** at Faneuil Hall Marketplace is a great place to pick up picnic fare. Eat here, or cross under the Expressway and pass the Marriott to reach the plaza at the end of Long Wharf. Or, head to the left of the hotel and dine in Christopher Columbus Waterfront Park.

EXPENSIVE

Les Zygomates ⊕⊕ FRENCH/ECLECTIC The construction maze near South Station surrounds this delightful bistro and wine bar. It offers a great selection of wines by the bottle, glass, and 2-ounce "taste." The efficient staff will guide you toward a good accompaniment for chef and co-owner Ian Just's delicious food. Roasted salmon is toothsome; rack of lamb with garlic crust and Italian couscous is succulent. For dessert, try not to fight over the lemon mousse. There's live music nightly.

⌜*Overrated* **Sky-High Dining: The Lowdown**

First, a disclaimer: This is not to disparage the food at either of these elegant places, which is quite good. But the fact is, you—and the rest of the special-occasion and business-meal clientele—are paying for the view. Make a reservation, and if you can't get a table *by the window* (the odds are better at the Bay Tower), have a drink in the lounge, then eat somewhere else.

The **Bay Tower** (✆ 617/723-1666; www.baytower.com) is on the 33rd floor of 60 State St., overlooking Faneuil Hall Marketplace, the waterfront, and the airport. It serves international fusion cuisine at dinner Monday through Saturday. The service and desserts are exquisite.

Top of the Hub (✆ 617/536-1775) is on the 52nd floor of the Prudential Tower, 800 Boylston St. It serves lunch Monday through Saturday, Sunday brunch, and dinner daily. The contemporary American menu includes excellent clam chowder.

---

129 South St. ✆ **617/542-5108.** www.winebar.com. Reservations recommended. Main courses $15–$25; prix fixe $15 lunch, $21 dinner (Mon–Thurs). AE, DC, DISC, MC, V. Mon–Fri 11:30am–1am (lunch until 2pm, dinner until 10:30pm); Sat 6pm–1am (dinner until 11:30pm). Valet parking available at dinner. T: Red Line to South Station.

Ye Olde Union Oyster House ⭐ NEW ENGLAND/SEAFOOD   America's oldest restaurant in continuous service, the Union Oyster House opened in 1826. Its tasty New England fare is popular with tourists on the adjacent Freedom Trail as well as savvy locals. They're not here for anything fancy; the best bets are simple, classic preparations. Try oyster stew or a cold seafood sampler of oysters, clams, and shrimp. Follow with a broiled or grilled dish such as scrod or salmon, or perhaps fried seafood or grilled pork loin. A "shore dinner" (chowder, steamers, lobster, corn, and dessert) is an excellent introduction to local favorites. *Tip:* A plaque marks John F. Kennedy's favorite booth (no. 18), where he often read the Sunday papers.

41 Union St. (between North and Hanover sts.). ✆ **617/227-2750.** www.unionoysterhouse.com. Reservations recommended. Main courses $10–$21 lunch, $15–$31 dinner. Children's menu $5–$11. AE, DC, DISC, MC, V. Sun–Thurs 11am–9:30pm (lunch until 5pm); Fri–Sat 11am–10pm (lunch until 6pm). Union Bar daily 11am–midnight (lunch until 3pm, late supper until 11pm). Valet parking available. T: Green or Orange Line to Haymarket.

MODERATE

Durgin-Park ⭐⭐ *Kids* NEW ENGLAND   For huge portions of delicious food, a rowdy atmosphere where CEOs share tables with students, and famously cranky waitresses, Bostonians have flocked to Durgin-Park since 1827. Politicians rub shoulders with grandmothers, and everyone's disappointed when the waitresses are nice (as they often are). Approximately 2,000 people a day join the line that stretches down a flight of stairs to the first floor of Faneuil Hall Marketplace's North Market building. They come for prime rib the size of a hubcap, piles of fried seafood, fish dinners broiled to order, and bounteous portions of roast turkey. Steaks and chops are broiled on an open fire over wood charcoal. Vegetables come a la carte—now is the time to try Boston baked beans. For dessert, the strawberry shortcake is justly celebrated.

340 Faneuil Hall Marketplace. ✆ 617/227-2038. www.durgin-park.com. Reservations accepted for parties of 15 or more. Main courses $7–$25; specials $19–$40. AE, DC, DISC, MC, V. Daily 11:30am–10pm (Sun to 9pm). Validated parking available. T: Green or Blue Line to Government Center, or Orange Line to Haymarket.

INEXPENSIVE

Cosí Sandwich Bar ✦ ITALIAN/ECLECTIC   Flavorful fillings on delectable bread make Cosí a downtown lunch favorite. This location, right on the Freedom Trail, makes a fantastic refueling stop. Tasty Italian flatbread is filled with your choice of meat, fish, vegetables, cheese, and spreads. Other branches are at 14 Milk St., near Downtown Crossing (✆ **617/426-7565**), and 133 Federal St. (✆ **617/292-2674**), which has patio seating.

53 State St. (at Congress St.). ✆ 617/723-4447. Sandwiches $6–$9; soups and salads $3–$7. AE, DC, MC, V. Mon–Thurs 7am–6pm; Fri 7am–5pm. T: Orange or Blue Line to State.

CHINATOWN/THEATER DISTRICT

The best way to sample Chinese food is by trying **dim sum,** the traditional midday meal featuring a variety of appetizer-style dishes. It's especially popular on weekends, when the variety of offerings is greatest. Our favorite dim sum is at **Empire Garden Restaurant,** also known as Emperor's Garden, 690–698 Washington St., 2nd floor (✆ **617/482-8898**); other good destinations are **China Pearl,** 9 Tyler St., 2nd floor (✆ **617/426-4338**), and **Chau Chow City,** 83 Essex St. (✆ **617/338-8158**).

INEXPENSIVE

Buddha's Delight ✦ VEGETARIAN/VIETNAMESE   Fresh and healthful meet cheap and filling on the menu here. It lists "chicken," "pork," and even "lobster"—in quotes because the chefs substitute fried and barbecued tofu and gluten for meat, poultry, fish, or dairy (some beverages have condensed milk) to create more-than-reasonable facsimiles of traditional dishes. Between pondering how they do it and savoring the strong, clear flavors, you might not miss your usual protein. Try spring rolls—fresh (in paper-thin mung-bean wrappers) are better than fried—then "shrimp" or "pork" with rice noodles, or excellent chow fun. The grim stairwell at the entrance is off-putting, but the food is worth the climb.

5 Beach St., 2nd floor. ✆ 617/451-2395. Main courses $6–$12. MC, V. Sun–Thurs 11am–9:30pm; Fri–Sat 11am–10:30pm. T: Orange Line to Chinatown.

SOUTH END
VERY EXPENSIVE

Hamersley's Bistro ✦✦ ECLECTIC   This is the place that put the South End on Boston's culinary map, a pioneering restaurant that's both classic and contemporary. One of its many claims to fame is its status as a Julia Child favorite. The seasonal menu offers entrees noted for their emphasis on local ingredients and classic techniques. The signature roast chicken with garlic is a bit tame, but cassoulet with pork, duck confit, and garlic sausage is a gorgeously executed combination of flavors and textures. The kitchen also has a way with fish—perhaps salmon au poivre with sorrel, leeks, and fingerling potatoes. The wine list is excellent.

553 Tremont St. ✆ 617/423-2700. www.hamersleysbistro.com. Reservations recommended. Main courses $23–$38; tasting menu varies. AE, DISC, MC, V. Mon–Fri 6–10pm; Sat 5:30–10pm; Sun 5:30–9:30pm. Closed 1 week in Jan. Valet parking available. T: Orange Line to Back Bay.

Icarus ✦✦✦ AMERICAN   This shamelessly romantic subterranean restaurant offers every element of a great dining experience. Chef/owner Christopher Douglass uses choice local ingredients to create imaginative dishes that often seem more like alchemy than cooking. The menu changes regularly—you might start with braised exotic mushrooms on polenta, or perhaps succulent lobster salad. Move on to pine-nut-and-lemon-crusted lamb chops served with lamb osso buco, or lemony grilled chicken with garlic mashed potatoes so good you'll want to ask for a plate of them. Don't—save room for an unbelievable dessert. The seasonal fruit sorbets are especially delicious.

3 Appleton St. ☎ 617/426-1790. www.icarusrestaurant.com. Reservations recommended. Main courses $21–$32.50. AE, DC, DISC, MC, V. Mon–Thurs 6–10pm; Fri 6–10:30pm; Sat 5:30–10:30pm; Sun 5:30–10pm. Valet parking available. T: Green Line to Arlington or Orange Line to Back Bay.

MODERATE

Grillfish SEAFOOD   A splash of Florida style in conservative Boston, this sassy interloper specializes in reasonably priced seafood. An open-fire grill and a PG-13-rated mural over the bar dominate the high-ceilinged room. Shrimp scampi (an unusual version, with tomatoes) is available as an appetizer or entree. Grilled fish—from a regular roster augmented with specials—comes with sweet onion or garlic-tomato sauce. Sautéed dishes have Marsala or piccata sauce, and several types of shellfish are available over pasta. Diners shout to be heard over the loud music; sit near the windows or on the patio if you prefer a quieter atmosphere. Grillfish is a small chain with branches in the Miami and Washington areas.

162 Columbus Ave. ☎ 617/357-1620. www.grillfish.com. Reservations accepted for parties of 6 or more. Main courses $10–$22. AE, DISC, MC, V. Sun–Mon 5:30–10pm; Tues–Thurs 5:30–11pm; Fri–Sat 5:30pm–midnight. T: Green Line to Arlington, or Orange Line to Back Bay.

INEXPENSIVE

Le Gamin Café ✪ FRENCH   The waiter has a heavy French accent. The posters on the walls do, too. The signature sandwiches—with three fillings mixed and matched from a list of more than a dozen—are splendid. The perfect crêpes include an orange-filled version with swooningly good homemade caramel sauce. The tuna in the salade Niçoise is a tad dry and the room a bit noisy, but everything else is just so. Part of a small chain that originated in Manhattan, this is a perfect spot for lingering over morning coffee or an afternoon glass of wine.

550 Tremont St. ☎ 617/654-8969. www.legamin.com. Main courses $5–$12; crêpes $3–$10. MC, V. Daily 8am–midnight. T: Orange Line to Back Bay.

BACK BAY
VERY EXPENSIVE

Aujourd'hui ✪✪✪ CONTEMPORARY AMERICAN   On the second floor of the city's premier luxury hotel, the most beautiful restaurant in town offers incredible service and food to its special-occasion and expense-account clientele. Yes, the cost is astronomical, but how often is it true that you get what you pay for? Here, it is. The menu encompasses basic hotel dining room offerings and creations that characterize an inventive kitchen, and the wine list is excellent. Entrees might include pepper-crusted tuna with balsamic vinegar sauce, grilled beef tenderloin with oxtail ravioli, and a lobster option. The dessert menu includes picture-perfect soufflés and homemade sorbets.

In the Four Seasons Hotel, 200 Boylston St. ☎ 617/351-2071. Reservations recommended (required on holidays). Main courses $19–$24 lunch, $35–$45 dinner; Sun buffet brunch $58 adults, $28 children. AE, DC, DISC, MC, V. Mon–Fri 6:30–11am, Sat 7–11am; Mon–Fri 11:30am–2:30pm, Sun brunch 11:30am–2:30pm; Mon–Sat 5:30–10:30pm, Sun 6–10:30pm. Valet parking available. T: Green Line to Arlington.

Clio ⭐⭐ ECLECTIC   Popular with businesspeople and couples, Clio is a plush room with funky accents—check out the leopard-print rug—that match the mood of food. Chef Ken Oringer's lofty reputation rests on exotic ingredients and elaborate preparations. The menu changes daily—more than at any other restaurant in town. Rely on the good-natured servers' advice. A common complaint is that portions are too small for the price, but this chowhound disagrees. They're not so skimpy, and you wouldn't want too much of food this rich and complicated, anyway. You'll be more than satisfied—and you'll have room for dessert, which Oringer, a former pastry chef, takes as seriously as anything else.

In the Eliot Hotel, 370A Comm. Ave. © 617/536-7200. www.cliorestaurant.com. Reservations recommended. Main courses $29–$45. AE, DC, DISC, MC, V. Sun and Tues–Thurs 5:30–10pm; Fri–Sat 5:30–10:30pm. Valet parking available. T: Green Line B, C, or D to Hynes/ICA.

EXPENSIVE

The Spanish tapas restaurant **Dalí** (p. 98), has a Back Bay outpost called **Tapéo,** at 266 Newbury St. (© **617/267-4799**).

Legal Sea Foods ⭐⭐⭐ SEAFOOD   The food at Legal Sea Foods ("Legal's," to Bostonians) isn't the fanciest, cheapest, or trendiest. It's the freshest, and management's commitment to that policy has produced a thriving chain. The menu includes regular selections plus whatever looked good at the market that morning, prepared in every imaginable way. It's all splendid. The clam chowder is famous, the fish chowder lighter but equally good. We suggest the Prudential Center branch because it takes reservations (at lunch only), a deviation from a long tradition. Equally annoying but equally traditional is the policy of serving each dish when it's ready, instead of one table at a time.

In the Prudential Center, 800 Boylston St. © 617/266-6800. www.legalseafoods.com. Reservations recommended at lunch, not accepted at dinner. Main courses $7–$15 lunch, $14–$35 dinner; lobster priced daily. AE, DC, DISC, MC, V. Mon–Thurs 11am–10:30pm; Fri–Sat 11am–11:30pm; Sun noon–10pm. T: Green Line B, C, or D to Hynes/ICA or E to Prudential. Also at 255 State St. © 617/227-3115. T: Blue Line to Aquarium. 36 Park Sq. (between Columbus Ave. and Stuart St.). © 617/426-4444. T: Green Line to Arlington. Copley Place, 2nd level. © 617/266-7775. T: Orange Line to Back Bay or Green Line to Copley. 5 Cambridge Center, Cambridge. © 617/864-3400. T: Red Line to Kendall/MIT.

MODERATE

Brasserie Jo ⭐ REGIONAL FRENCH   One of the most discriminating diners we know lit up like a marquee on hearing that Boston has a branch of this Chicago favorite. The food is classic—fresh baguettes, Alsatian onion tart, *choucroute,* coq au vin—but never boring. The house beer, an Alsace-style draft, is a good accompaniment. This casual, all-day brasserie and bar is a good bet before or after the symphony or during a shopping break. The only drawbacks are the noise level and the uneven service.

In the Colonnade Hotel, 120 Huntington Ave. © 617/425-3240. Reservations recommended for dinner. Main courses $6–$15 lunch, $15–$27 dinner; *plats du jour* $18–$32. AE, DC, DISC, MC, V. Mon–Fri 6:30am–11pm; Sat 7am–11pm; Sun 7am–10pm; late-night menu daily until 1am. T: Green Line E to Prudential.

INEXPENSIVE

Café Jaffa MIDDLE EASTERN   A long, narrow brick room with a glass front, Café Jaffa looks more like a snazzy pizza place than the excellent Middle Eastern restaurant it is. Reasonable prices, high quality, and large portions draw hordes of young people for traditional dishes such as falafel, baba ghanoush, and hummus, as well as burgers and steak tips. For dessert, try the baklava if it's fresh. (Give it a pass if not.)

48 Gloucester St. © **617/536-0230**. Main courses $5–$13. AE, DC, DISC, MC, V. Mon–Thurs 11am–10:30pm; Fri–Sat 11am–11pm; Sun 1–10pm. T: Green Line B, C, or D to Hynes/ICA.

KENMORE SQUARE

MODERATE

The Elephant Walk ★★ FRENCH/CAMBODIAN   France meets Cambodia on the menu at this madly popular spot 4 blocks from Kenmore Square. Many Cambodian dishes have part-French names, such as *poulet dhomrei* (chicken with Asian basil, bamboo shoots, fresh pineapple, and kaffir lime leaves) and *curry de crevettes* (shrimp curry with picture-perfect vegetables). Or try *loc lac,* fork-tender beef cubes in addictively spicy sauce. On the French side, you'll find classics like filet mignon with pommes frites. The pleasant staff will help out if you need guidance.

900 Beacon St. © **617/247-1500**. www.elephantwalk.com. Reservations recommended for dinner Sun–Thurs; not accepted Fri–Sat. Main courses $7–$19 lunch, $11–$27 dinner. AE, DC, DISC, MC, V. Mon–Sat 11:30am–2:30pm; Mon–Thurs 5–10pm, Fri 5–11pm, Sat 4:30–11pm, Sun 4:30–10pm. Valet parking available at dinner. T: Green Line C to St. Mary's St.

CAMBRIDGE

The Red Line runs from downtown Boston to Harvard Square. Many of the restaurants listed here can be reached on foot from there. To go in search of inexpensive ethnic food, head for Central and Inman squares.

   Note: See the "Cambridge Accommodations & Dining" map on p. 86 for the locations of the restaurants reviewed below.

VERY EXPENSIVE

Rialto ★★★ MEDITERRANEAN   This is our favorite Boston-area restaurant. It attracts a chic crowd, but it's not such a scene that out-of-towners will feel left behind. The dramatic but comfortable room has floor-to-ceiling windows overlooking Harvard Square. Chef Jody Adams's menu changes regularly, and main courses are so good that you might as well close your eyes and point. Tuscan-style steak with portobello-and-arugula salad is wonderful, and any seafood is a guaranteed winner—say, native bluefish in curried mussel broth. For dessert, seasonal sorbets are a great choice.

In the Charles Hotel, 1 Bennett St. © **617/661-5050**. www.rialto-restaurant.com. Reservations recommended. Main courses $20–$36. AE, DC, MC, V. Sun–Thurs 5:30–10pm; Fri–Sat 5:30–11pm. Bar Sun–Thurs 4:30pm–midnight; Fri–Sat 5pm–1am. Valet and validated parking available. T: Red Line to Harvard.

EXPENSIVE

There's a **Legal Sea Foods** branch in Kendall Square; see "Back Bay," above.

The Blue Room ★★★ ECLECTIC   The Blue Room sits below plaza level in an office-retail complex, a slice of foodie paradise in high-tech heaven. The cuisine is a rousing combination of top-notch ingredients and aggressive flavors, the service excellent, and the crowded dining room not as noisy as it looks. Main courses tend to be roasted, grilled, or braised, with at least one well-conceived vegetarian choice. Roast chicken, served with garlic mashed potatoes, is world-class. Seafood is always a good choice, and pork loin with cider glaze will make you think twice the next time you skip over pork on a menu to get to steak. In warm weather, there's seating on the patio.

1 Kendall Sq. © **617/494-9034**. Reservations recommended. Main courses $18–$24. AE, DC, DISC, MC, V. Sun–Thurs 5:30–10pm; Fri–Sat 5:30–11pm; Sun brunch 11am–2:30pm. T: Red Line to Kendall/MIT; 10-min. walk.

Dalí ★★★ SPANISH   The bar at this festive restaurant fills with people cheerfully waiting an hour or more for a table. The payoff is authentic Spanish food, notably tapas. Entrees include excellent paella, but most people come in a group and explore the three dozen or more tapas offerings, all perfect for sharing. They include delectable garlic potatoes, salmon balls with not-too-salty caper sauce, pork tenderloin with blue goat cheese, and delicious sausages. The staff sometimes seems rushed, but never fails to supply bread for sopping up juices, and sangria for washing it all down. Finish with excellent flan, or try the rich *tarta de chocolates.*

The owners of Dalí also run **Tapéo,** 266 Newbury St. (© **617/267-4799**), between Fairfield and Dartmouth streets in Boston's Back Bay.

415 Washington St., Somerville. © **617/661-3254.** www.DaliRestaurant.com. Reservations not accepted. Tapas $4–$8; main courses $19–$24. AE, DC, MC, V. Daily summer 6–11pm; winter 5:30–11pm. T: Red Line to Harvard; follow Kirkland St. to intersection of Washington and Beacon sts. (20-min. walk).

Metro REGIONAL FRENCH   Metro is a slavish copy of a traditional French brasserie, with a zinc bar and tile floor that help crank up the noise level at busy times. The classic menu includes mussels in savory cider-based broth, meltingly good coq au vin, and superb steak frites (with some of the best french fries in town). Another high point is the dessert menu, loaded with modern interpretations of established favorites.

In the Porter Exchange Building, 1815 Mass. Ave. © **617/354-3727.** Reservations recommended for dinner. Main courses $7–$15 lunch, $17–$32 dinner. AE, DC, DISC, MC, V. Mon–Thurs 7:30am–10pm; Fri–Sat 7:30am–11pm; Sun 11am–10pm. T: Red Line to Porter.

Oleana ★★ MEDITERRANEAN   Both casual neighborhood eatery and culinary travelogue, Oleana opened in 2001 and quickly cemented the rising-star status of chef and co-owner Ana Sortun. The seasonal menu might include traditional Portuguese clams *cataplana,* with sausage in an aromatic tomatoey broth; almond-fried chicken, a great contrast of crunchy crust and juicy flesh; and spicy tuna, in a perfectly matched peppery sauce that trades intense heat for intense flavor. Service is polished, portions generous, and the dessert menu heavy on house-made ice cream. In warm weather, there's seating on the patio.

134 Hampshire St., Inman Sq. © **617/661-0505.** Reservations recommended. Main courses $17–$24. AE, MC, V. Sun–Thurs 5:30–10pm; Fri–Sat 5:30–11pm. Free parking. T: Red Line to Central; 10-min. walk.

MODERATE

Border Cafe TEX-MEX/CAJUN   This unbelievably crowded restaurant has been a Harvard Square favorite for over 15 years. Patrons loiter at the bar while waiting for a table, enhancing the festival atmosphere. Portions are generous, and the beleaguered staff keeps the chips and salsa coming. Try the excellent chorizo appetizer, seafood enchiladas, or popcorn shrimp. Fajitas for one or two, sizzling noisily in a large iron frying pan, are also popular. Ask to be seated downstairs if you want to be able to hear your companions.

32 Church St. © **617/864-6100.** Reservations not accepted. Main courses $7–$15. AE, MC, V. Mon–Thurs 11am–1am; Fri–Sat 11am–2am; Sun noon–11pm. T: Red Line to Harvard.

The Helmand ★ AFGHAN   Never exactly a secret, the Helmand enjoyed a burst of publicity when the manager's brother took over the provisional government of Afghanistan, and it's hardly had a slow night since. Unusual cuisine, an elegant setting, and reasonable prices had already made this spacious spot near the CambridgeSide Galleria mall a local favorite. Afghan food is vegetarian friendly; many non-veggie dishes use meat as one element rather than the centerpiece. *Aushak,* pasta pockets filled with leeks or potatoes and topped with split-pea-and-carrot sauce, also comes with meat sauce. Other entrees include stews like *deygee kabob,* an excellent mélange of lamb, yellow split peas, onion, and red peppers. For dessert, don't miss the Afghan version of baklava.

143 First St. ☎ 617/492-4646. Reservations recommended. Main courses $10–$18. AE, MC, V. Sun–Thurs 5–10pm; Fri–Sat 5–11pm. T: Green Line to Lechmere.

INEXPENSIVE

Mr. Bartley's Burger Cottage ★★ AMERICAN   Great burgers and the best onion rings in the world make Bartley's a perennial favorite with a cross section of Cambridge. The 40-year-old family business is a high-ceilinged, crowded room plastered with signs and posters. Anything you can think of to put on ground beef is available, from American cheese to béarnaise sauce. There are also some good dishes that don't involve meat, notably veggie burgers and creamy, garlicky hummus.

1246 Mass. Ave. ☎ 617/354-6559. Most items under $9. No credit cards. Mon–Wed and Sat 11am–9pm; Thurs–Fri 11am–10pm. T: Red Line to Harvard.

S&S Restaurant ★★ DELI   *Es* is Yiddish for "eat," and this Cambridge classic is as straightforward as its name ("eat and eat"). Founded in 1919 by the current owners' great-grandmother, the wildly popular brunch spot draws huge crowds at busy times on weekends. It looks contemporary, but the brunch offerings are traditional: pancakes, waffles, fruit salad, fantastic omelets. You'll also find traditional deli items (corned beef, pastrami, potato pancakes, blintzes), and breakfast anytime. Arrive early for brunch, or plan to spend a good chunk of your Saturday or Sunday people-watching and getting hungry. Or dine on a weekday and soak up the neighborhood atmosphere.

1334 Cambridge St., Inman Sq. ☎ 617/354-0777. www.sandsrestaurant.com. Main courses $4–$12. AE, MC, V. Mon–Wed 7am–11pm; Thurs–Fri 7am–midnight; Sat 8am–midnight; Sun 8am–10pm (brunch Sat–Sun until 4pm). T: Red Line to Harvard, then no. 69 (Harvard–Lechmere) bus to Inman Sq. Or Red Line to Central; 10-min. walk on Prospect St.

5 Seeing the Sights in Boston

If you'll be in town for more than a couple of days, make your first stop a **BosTix** (☎ 617/262-8632; www.bostix.org) booth for a coupon book that offers discounts on admission to many area attractions. It's not worth the money ($9) for single travelers, as many of the coupons offer two-for-one deals, but couples and families can take good advantage. For locations, see "Boston & Cambridge After Dark," later in this chapter. Books are also available by phone, online, and by mail, subject to a handling charge.

A **CityPass** offers great savings in money and time. It's a booklet of tickets to the Harvard Museum of Natural History, Kennedy Library, Museum of Fine Arts, Museum of Science, New England Aquarium, and Prudential Center Skywalk. The price (at press time, $30.25 for adults, $18.50 for children 3–17) represents a 50% savings for adults who visit all six attractions, and having a ticket means you can go straight to the entrance without waiting in line. The passes, good for 9 days from the date of purchase, are on sale at participating attractions, the Boston Common and Prudential Center visitor centers, through the **Greater Boston Convention & Visitors Bureau** (☎ 800/SEE-BOSTON; www.bostonusa.com), and at www.citypass.com.

Boston Attractions

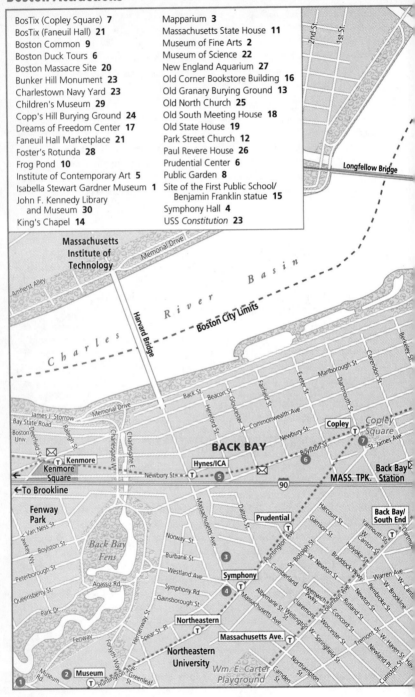

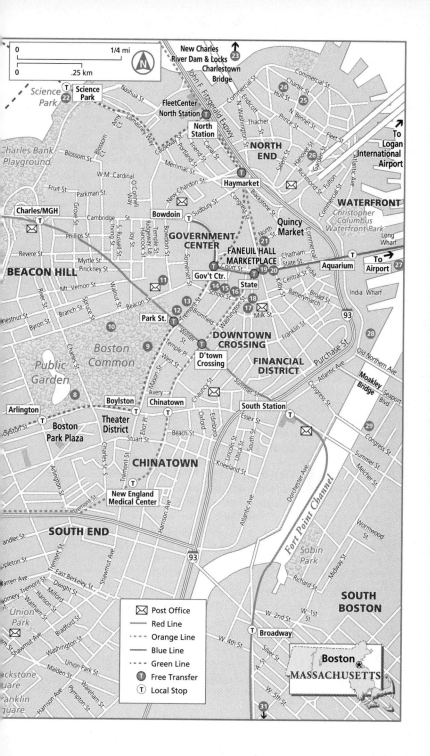

THE TOP ATTRACTIONS

Dreams of Freedom Center ✲ *Kids*   The Freedom Trail isn't just about colonial Boston. If you need proof, detour from the trail to the city's museum of immigration. Boston native Ben Franklin is the "host" of a multimedia show about the changing face of the population. It's an interactive experience unlike the city's typically low-tech attractions—a plus if you're traveling with wired (in both senses) kids. You'll have your passport stamped as you make your way through the thought-provoking exhibits. They include a gallery of bags and suitcases that offers a look at what people brought to the New World, and the interiors of two important modes of transportation: an early-20th-century ship and a jet liner.

1 Milk St., off Washington St. ✆ 617/338-6022. www.dreamsoffreedom.org. Admission $7.50 adults, $3.50 children 6–17. Apr–Dec daily 10am–6pm; Jan–Mar Tues–Sun 10am–5pm. T: Orange or Blue Line to State, or Red Line to Downtown Crossing.

Faneuil Hall Marketplace ✲✲ *Kids*   Since Boston's most popular attraction opened in 1976, cities all over the country have imitated the "festival market" concept. The complex of shops, food counters, restaurants, bars, and public spaces is such a magnet for tourists and suburbanites that you could be forgiven for thinking that the only Bostonians in the crowd are employees.

The five-structure complex sits on brick-and-stone plazas that teem with crowds shopping, eating, performing, watching performers, and people-watching. In warm weather, it's busy from just after dawn until well past dark. **Quincy Market** (you'll hear the whole complex called by that name) is the central Greek Revival–style building; its central corridor is an enormous food court. On either side, glass canopies cover full-service restaurants as well as pushcarts that hold everything from crafts created by New England artisans to hokey souvenirs. In the plaza between the **South Canopy** and the South Market building is an **information kiosk,** and throughout the complex you'll find an enticing mix of chain stores and unique shops. On summer evenings, people fill the tables that spill outdoors from the restaurants and bars. One constant since the year after the original market opened (in 1826) is **Durgin-Park,** a traditional New England restaurant with traditionally crabby waitresses (p. 93). **Faneuil Hall** ✲ itself—nicknamed the "Cradle of Liberty"—sometimes gets overlooked, but it's well worth a visit. National Park Service rangers give free 20-minute talks every half hour from 9am to 5pm in the second-floor auditorium.

Between North, Congress, and State sts. and I-93. ✆ 617/523-1300. www.faneuilhallmarketplace.com. Marketplace Mon–Sat 10am–9pm; Sun noon–6pm. Food court opens earlier; some restaurants close later. T: Green or Blue Line to Government Center, Orange Line to Haymarket, or Blue Line to Aquarium.

The Institute of Contemporary Art   Across from the Hynes Convention Center, the ICA mounts rotating exhibits of 20th- and 21st-century art, including painting, sculpture, photography, and video and performance art. The institute also offers films, lectures, music, video, poetry, and educational programs for children and adults. Check at this location for updates on the ICA's new home, at Fan Pier on the South Boston waterfront, scheduled to open in 2004.

955 Boylston St. ✆ 617/266-5152. www.icaboston.org. Admission $6 adults, $4 seniors and students, free for children under 12; free to all Thurs 5–9pm. Wed and Fri noon–5pm; Thurs noon–9pm; Sat–Sun 11am–5pm. T: Green Line B, C, or D to Hynes/ICA.

Isabella Stewart Gardner Museum ✲✲   Isabella Stewart Gardner (1840–1924) was an incorrigible individualist long before such behavior was acceptable for a woman in polite Boston society, and her iconoclasm paid off for

Kids **Up, Up & Away: A Great View**

The **Prudential Center Skywalk** 🛰, on the 50th floor of 800 Boylston St. (📞 **617/859-0648**), offers a 360-degree view of Boston and beyond. When it's clear, you can see as far as the mountains of New Hampshire and the beaches of Cape Cod. Open 10am to 10pm daily; call before visiting, as the space sometimes closes for private events. Admission is $7 for adults, $4 for seniors and children 2 to 10. T: Green Line E to Prudential or B, C, or D to Hynes/ICA.

art lovers. "Mrs. Jack" designed her exquisite home in the style of a 15th-century Venetian palace and filled it with European, American, and Asian painting and sculpture. You'll see works by Titian, Botticelli, Raphael, Rembrandt, Matisse, and Mrs. Gardner's friends James McNeill Whistler and John Singer Sargent. Titian's magnificent *Europa* is one of the most important Renaissance paintings in the United States. If you enjoy representational art and ornate architecture, run right over; if not, you'll probably be happier at the nearby Museum of Fine Arts.

The building holds a hodgepodge of furniture and architectural details imported from European churches and palaces. The pièce de résistance is the magnificent skylit courtyard, filled year-round with fresh flowers from the museum greenhouse. A special exhibition gallery features two or three changing shows a year, often by contemporary artists in residence.

280 The Fenway. 📞 617/566-1401. www.gardnermuseum.org. Admission $11 adults Sat–Sun, $10 adults Mon–Fri; $7 seniors; $5 college students; free for children under 18. Tues–Sun and some Mon holidays 11am–5pm. T: Green Line E to Museum.

John F. Kennedy Library and Museum 🛰🛰 *Kids*   The Kennedy era springs to life at this dramatic library, museum, and research complex overlooking Dorchester Bay. It captures the 35th president's accomplishments in sound and video recordings as well as fascinating displays of memorabilia and photos. Far from being a static experience, it changes regularly, with temporary shows and reinterpreted displays that highlight and complement the permanent exhibits. A visit begins with a 17-minute film about Kennedy's early life. The exhibits start with the 1960 campaign and end with a tribute to Kennedy's legacy. There's a film about the Cuban Missile Crisis, along with displays on Attorney General Robert F. Kennedy, the civil-rights movement, the Peace Corps, the space program, First Lady Jacqueline Bouvier Kennedy, and the Kennedy family.

Columbia Point. 📞 877/616-4599 or 617/929-4500. www.jfklibrary.org. Admission $8 adults, $6 seniors and college students, $4 youths 13–17, free for children under 13. Surcharges may apply for special exhibitions. Daily 9am–5pm (last film at 3:55pm). T: Red Line to JFK/UMass, then free shuttle bus, which runs every 20 min. By car, take Southeast Expressway (I-93/Rte. 3) south to Exit 15 (Morrissey Blvd./JFK Library), turn left onto Columbia Rd., and follow signs to free parking lot.

Museum of Fine Arts 🛰🛰🛰 *Kids*   One of the world's great museums, the MFA works constantly to become even more accessible and interesting. The museum's not-so-secret weapon in its quest is a powerful one: its magnificent collections. Every installation reflects a curatorial attitude that makes even those who go in with a feeling of obligation leave with a sense of discovery and wonder. That includes children, who can launch a scavenger hunt, admire the mummies, or participate in family-friendly programs scheduled year-round.

The MFA is especially noted for its **Impressionist paintings** ✫✫✫ (including 43 Monets—the largest collection outside Paris), Asian and Old Kingdom Egyptian collections, classical art, Buddhist temple, and medieval sculpture and tapestries. The American and European paintings and sculpture are a remarkable assemblage of timeless works that may seem as familiar as the face in the mirror or as unexpected as a comet. There are also magnificent holdings of prints, photography, furnishings, and decorative arts, including the finest collection of Paul Revere silver in the world. The museum has two restaurants, a cafe, and a cafeteria. Pick up a floor plan at the information desk, or take a free **guided tour** (weekdays except Mon holidays at 10:30am and 1:30pm; Wed at 6:15pm; and Sat at 10:30am and 1pm).

None of this comes cheap: The MFA's admission fees are among the highest in the country. A Boston CityPass (see the introduction to this section) is a great deal if you plan to visit enough of the other included attractions.

Tip: The Huntington Avenue entrance is usually much less busy than the West Wing lobby—though farther from the gift shop, restaurants, and garage. To use it, walk back along Huntington Avenue when you leave the T, enter from the driveway, and stop to take in the recently restored John Singer Sargent murals.

465 Huntington Ave. ✆ 617/267-9300. www.mfa.org. Admission $14 adults, $12 seniors and students (when entire museum is open; $12 and $10, respectively, when only West Wing is open), $5 children 7–17 on school days before 3pm, otherwise free. Admission good for 2 visits within 30 days. Voluntary contribution ($14 suggested) Wed 4–9:45pm. Surcharges may apply for special exhibitions. Free admission for museum shop, library, restaurants, and auditoriums. Entire museum Mon–Tues 10am–4:45pm; Wed 10am–9:45pm; Thurs–Fri 10am–5pm; Sat–Sun 10am–5:45pm. West Wing only Thurs–Fri 5–9:45pm. T: Green Line E to Museum or Orange Line to Ruggles.

Museum of Science ✫✫✫ *(Kids)* For the ultimate pain-free educational experience, head to the Museum of Science. The demonstrations, experiments, and interactive displays introduce facts and concepts so effortlessly that everyone winds up learning something. Take a couple of hours or a whole day to explore the permanent and temporary exhibits, most of them hands-on and all of them great fun. Among the 600-plus exhibits, you might meet an iguana or a dinosaur, find out how much you'd weigh on the moon, or climb into a space module. Activity centers focus on fields of interest—natural history (with live animals), light and optics, computers, and the human body—as well as interdisciplinary approaches. **Investigate!** teaches visitors to think like scientists, analyzing questions through activities such as sifting through an archaeological dig. **Science in the Park** uses familiar tools such as playground equipment and skateboards to look at Newtonian physics.

The separate-admission theaters are worth planning for, even if you're skipping the exhibits. Buy all your tickets at once, not only because it's cheaper but also because shows sometimes sell out. Tickets are for sale in person and, subject to a service charge, over the phone and online (www.tickets.mos.org). The **Mugar Omni Theater** ✫✫✫, which shows IMAX movies on a five-story screen, is an intense experience (but not a 3D experience—for that, head to the Simons IMAX Theatre at the New England Aquarium). The **Charles Hayden Planetarium** ✫✫ takes you into space with daily star shows as well as shows on special topics that change several times a year. On weekends, rock-music laser shows take over.

Many fascinating interactive exhibits from the defunct Computer Museum now delight patrons of the Museum of Science. The most popular is **Virtual Fish-Tank** ✫✫✫, which uses 3D computer graphics and character-animation software to allow visitors to program their own virtual fish. You can even "build" fish at home (through www.virtualfishtank.com) and launch them at the museum.

Science Park. ℂ 617/723-2500. www.mos.org. Admission to exhibit halls $12 adults, $8 seniors and children 3–11. Mugar Omni Theater, Hayden Planetarium, or laser shows $7.50 adults, $5.50 seniors and children 3–11. Discounted tickets to 2 or 3 parts of complex available. July 5–Labor Day Sat–Thurs 9am–7pm, Fri 9am–9pm; day after Labor Day to July 4th Sat–Thurs 9am–5pm, Fri 9am–9pm. T: Green Line to Science Park.

New England Aquarium ⚜ *(Kids*   This entertaining complex is home to more than 7,000 fish and aquatic mammals. At busy times in summer, it seems to contain at least that many people—try to make this your first stop of the day, especially on weekends. You'll want to spend at least half a day, and afternoon crowds can make getting around painfully slow. Also consider buying a Boston CityPass (p. 99); it allows you to skip the ticket line, which can be uncomfortably long. The new **Simons IMAX Theatre** ⚜⚜⚜, which has its own hours and admission fees, is worth planning ahead for, too. It shows 3D films that concentrate on the natural world.

The focal point of the main building is the four-story, 200,000-gallon **Giant Ocean Tank.** It holds a replica of a Caribbean coral reef, a vast assortment of sea creatures, and, five times a day, scuba divers who plunge in to feed the sharks. Other exhibits focus on freshwater and tropical specimens, sea otters, the Aquarium Medical Center, denizens of the Amazon, and the ecology of Boston Harbor. The hands-on **Edge of the Sea** exhibit contains a tide pool with resident sea stars, sea urchins, and horseshoe crabs. The aquarium runs naturalist-led **harbor tours** daily in spring, summer, and fall. Discounts are available when you combine a visit to the aquarium with an IMAX film, harbor tour, or whale-watch (see "Organized Tours," below).

Central Wharf. ℂ 617/973-5200. www.neaq.org. Admission summer weekends and holidays $14.50 adults, $12.50 seniors, $8 children 3–11; weekdays year-round and off-season weekends $13 adults, $11 seniors, $7 children. Harbor tours $13 adults, $10 seniors and college students, $9 youths 12–18, $8.50 children 3–11. Free admission for outdoor exhibits, cafe, and gift shop. July–Labor Day Mon–Tues and Fri 9am–6pm, Wed–Thurs 9am–8pm, Sat–Sun and holidays 9am–7pm; day after Labor Day to June Mon–Fri 9am–5pm, Sat–Sun and holidays 9am–6pm. Simons IMAX Theatre: ℂ 866/815-4629. Tickets $7.50 adults, $5.50 seniors and children 3–11. Daily 10am–9pm. T: Blue Line to Aquarium.

THE FREEDOM TRAIL ⚜⚜⚜

A line of red paint or red brick on the sidewalk, the 3-mile (5km) Freedom Trail links 16 historic sights. Markers identify the stops, and plaques point the way from one to the next. The trail begins at **Boston Common,** where the Information Center, 146 Tremont St., distributes pamphlets that describe a self-guided tour. For a preview, visit the Freedom Trail Foundation's website at **www.thefreedomtrail.org**.

You can also explore the **Black Heritage Trail** ⚜⚜ from here. Stops include stations on the Underground Railroad and homes of famous citizens as well as the African Meeting House, the oldest standing black church in the country. A 2-hour guided tour starts at the visitor center at 46 Joy St. (ℂ 617/742-5415; www.nps.gov/boaf), daily in summer and by request at other times.

As you follow the Freedom Trail, you'll come to another information center, the **Boston National Historic Park Visitor Center,** 15 State St. (ℂ 617/ 242-5642; www.nps.gov/bost). From here, rangers lead free tours of the heart of the trail. An audiovisual show provides basic information on the stops. The wheelchair-accessible center has restrooms and a bookstore. It's open daily from 9am to 5pm.

The hard-core history fiend who peers at every artifact and reads every plaque along the trail will wind up at Bunker Hill some 4 hours later, weary but rewarded. The family with restless children will probably appreciate the enforced efficiency of the 90-minute ranger-led tour.

Space doesn't permit detailing every stop on the trail, but here's a concise listing:

- **Boston Common.** In 1634, when their settlement was just 4 years old, the town fathers paid the Rev. William Blackstone £30 for this property. In 1640, it was set aside as common land. Be sure to stop at Beacon and Park streets, where a **memorial** ★★★ designed by Augustus Saint-Gaudens celebrates Col. Robert Gould Shaw and the Union Army's 54th Massachusetts Colored Regiment, who fought in the Civil War. You may remember the story of the first American army unit made up of free black soldiers from the movie *Glory.*

- **Massachusetts State House** (© **617/727-3676**). Charles Bulfinch designed the "new" State House, and Gov. Samuel Adams laid the cornerstone of the state capitol in 1795. Free tours (guided and self-guided) leave from the second floor Monday through Friday from 10am to 3:30pm; call ahead to see whether weekend hours have been reinstated.

- **Park Street Church,** 1 Park St. (© **617/523-3383;** www.parkstreet.org). The plaque at the corner of Tremont Street describes this Congregational church's storied past. In July and August, it's open for tours Tuesday through Saturday from 9am to 3pm. Year-round Sunday services are at 8:30am, 11am, 4:30pm, and 5:30pm.

- **Old Granary Burying Ground.** This cemetery, established in 1660, contains the graves of Samuel Adams, Paul Revere, John Hancock, and the wife of Isaac Vergoose, believed to be the "Mother Goose" of nursery-rhyme fame. It's open daily from 9am to 5pm (until 3pm in winter).

- **King's Chapel,** 58 Tremont St. (© **617/523-1749**). Completed in 1754, this church was built by erecting the granite edifice around the existing wooden chapel. The **burying ground** (1630), facing Tremont Street, is the oldest in Boston. It's open daily from 8am to 5:30pm (until 3pm in winter).

- **Site of the First Public School.** Founded in 1634, the school is commemorated with a colorful mosaic in the sidewalk on (of course) School Street. Inside the fence is the 1856 statue of **Benjamin Franklin,** the first portrait statue erected in Boston.

- **Old Corner Bookstore Building,** 3 School St. Built in 1718, it's on a plot of land that was once home to the religious reformer Anne Hutchinson.

- **Old South Meeting House,** 310 Washington St. (© **617/482-6439**). Originally built in 1670 and replaced by the current structure in 1729, it was the starting point of the Boston Tea Party. It's open daily, April to October from 9:30am to 5pm, November to March from 10am to 4pm. Admission is $3 for adults, $2.50 for seniors, and $1 for children 6 to 18. Across the street is the **Dreams of Freedom** museum (p. 102).

- **Old State House** ★, 206 Washington St. (© **617/720-1713;** www.boston history.org). Built in 1713, it served as the seat of colonial government in Massachusetts before the Revolution, and as the state capitol until 1797. It houses the Bostonian Society's fascinating museum of the city's history, open daily from 9am to 5pm. Admission is $3 for adults, $2 for seniors and students, and $1 for children 6 to 18.

- **Boston Massacre Site.** On a traffic island in State Street, across from the T station under the Old State House, a ring of cobblestones marks the place where the skirmish took place on March 5, 1770.
- **Faneuil Hall** ✦. Built in 1742 (and enlarged using a Charles Bulfinch design in 1805), it was a gift to the city from the merchant Peter Faneuil. National Park Service rangers give free 20-minute talks every half hour from 9am to 5pm in the second-floor auditorium.
- **Paul Revere House** ✦✦, 19 North Sq. (✆ **617/523-2338**; www.paul reverehouse.org). The oldest house in downtown Boston (built around 1680) presents history on a human scale. It's open April 15 through October daily from 9:30am to 5:15pm; November through April 14 from 9:30am to 4:15pm (closed Mon Jan–Mar). Admission is $2.50 for adults, $2 for seniors and students, and $1 for children 5 to 17.
- **Old North Church** ✦, 193 Salem St. (✆ **617/523-6676**; www.old north.com). Paul Revere saw a signal in this church's steeple and set out on his "midnight ride." Officially named Christ Church, this is the oldest church building in Boston (1723). It's open daily from 9am to 5pm; donations are appreciated. The quirky gift shop and museum, in a former chapel, are also open daily from 9am to 5pm. Sunday services (Episcopal) are at 9am, 11am, and 5pm.
- **Copp's Hill Burying Ground,** off Hull Street. The second-oldest cemetery (1659) in the city, it contains the graves of Cotton Mather and Prince Hall, who established the first black Masonic lodge. It's open daily from 9am to 5pm (until 3pm in winter).
- **USS** *Constitution* ✦✦, Charlestown Navy Yard (✆ **617/242-5670**). Active-duty sailors in 1812 dress uniforms give free tours of "Old Ironsides" daily between 9:30am and 3:50pm. The **USS** *Constitution* **Museum** ✦ (✆ **617/426-1812;** www.ussconstitutionmuseum.org) is open daily, May through October from 9am to 6pm, November through April from 10am to 5pm. Admission is free.
- **Bunker Hill Monument** (✆ **617/242-5644**), Charlestown. The 221-foot (66m) granite obelisk honors the memory of the men who died in the Battle of Bunker Hill on June 17, 1775. A punishing flight of 294 stairs leads to the top. National Park Service rangers staff the monument, which is open daily from 9am to 4:30pm. Admission is free.

PARKS & GARDENS

The best-known park in Boston is the spectacular **Public Garden** ✦✦✦, bordered by Arlington, Boylston, Charles, and Beacon streets. Something lovely is in bloom at the country's first botanical garden at least half of the year. For 5 months, the lagoon is home to the celebrated **swan boats** (✆ **617/522-1966;** www.swanboats.com). The pedal-powered vessels—the attendants pedal, not the passengers—come out of hibernation on the Saturday before Patriot's Day

---

(*Tips* **Out to Sea**

A fun way to return to downtown from Charlestown is on the **ferry** that connects the Navy Yard to Long Wharf (near the Aquarium) or Lovejoy Wharf (near North Station). It costs $1.25 and is included in the MBTA Boston Visitor Pass.

Finds **Eye in the Sky**

For a smashing view of the airport, the harbor, and the South Boston waterfront, stroll along the water or Atlantic Avenue to the Boston Harbor Hotel complex. Above the landmark arch is Foster's Rotunda. Enter through the lobby of 30 Rowes Wharf, sign in (a security measure), and take the elevator that runs to the ninth-floor rotunda. Step out onto the balcony and soak up the scenery. There's no admission charge, but open hours are limited: Monday through Friday from 11am to 4pm.

(the third Mon of Apr). They operate in summer daily from 10am to 5pm; in spring daily from 10am to 4pm; and from Labor Day to mid-September Monday through Friday from noon to 4pm and Saturday and Sunday from 10am to 4pm. The 15-minute ride costs $2 for adults, $1.50 for seniors, and $1 for children under 16.

The most spectacular garden is the **Arnold Arboretum** ⭐⭐, 125 Arborway, Jamaica Plain (© **617/524-1718;** www.arboretum.harvard.edu). One of the oldest parks in the United States, founded in 1872, it is open daily from sunrise to sunset. Admission is free. Its 265 acres (107 hectares) contain more than 15,000 ornamental trees, shrubs, and vines from all over the world. Lilac Sunday, in May, is the only time picnicking is allowed. To get here, take the Orange Line to Forest Hills and follow signs to the entrance. The visitor center is open Monday through Friday from 9am to 4pm, Saturday and Sunday from noon to 4pm.

The world-famous **Emerald Necklace,** Frederick Law Olmsted's vision for a loop of green spaces, threads through the city. See "Organized Tours," below, for information on seeing part or all of the Emerald Necklace with a Boston Park Ranger.

ORGANIZED TOURS

WALKING TOURS ⭐⭐ From May to October, the nonprofit **Boston by Foot** ⭐⭐, 77 N. Washington St. (© 617/367-2345, or 617/367-3766 for recorded info; www.bostonbyfoot.com), conducts excellent historical and architectural tours that focus on neighborhoods or themes. The rigorously trained volunteer guides encourage questions. Buy tickets ($9) from the guide; reservations are not required. The 90-minute tours take place rain or shine.

The **Society for the Preservation of New England Antiquities** (© 617/227-3956; www.spnea.org) offers a fascinating 2-hour tour that describes life in the mansions and garrets of Beacon Hill in 1800. "Magnificent and Modest" ($10) starts at the Harrison Gray Otis House, 141 Cambridge St., at 11am on Saturdays from mid-May to October. The price includes a tour of the Otis House; reservations are recommended.

The **Boston Park Rangers** (© 617/635-7383; www.ci.boston.ma.us/parks) offer free guided walking tours. The best-known focus is the Emerald Necklace, a loop of green spaces designed by pioneering landscape architect Frederick Law Olmsted. They include Boston Common, the Public Garden, the Commonwealth Avenue Mall, the Muddy River in the Fenway, Olmsted Park, Jamaica Pond, the Arnold Arboretum, and Franklin Park. Call for schedules.

The nonprofit **Boston History Collaborative** (© 617/350-0358; www.bostonhistorycollaborative.org) coordinates several heritage trails. Presented as guided and self-guided walking tours, longer excursions by bus and boat, and copiously documented websites, they focus on maritime history (www.bostonbysea.org), immigration (www.BostonFamilyHistory.org), literary history (www.Lit-Trail.org), and inventions (www.innovationtrail.org).

TROLLEY TOURS   Because Boston is so pedestrian friendly, this isn't the best choice for the able-bodied and unencumbered making a long visit. But if you're short on time, unable to walk long distances, or traveling with children, a trolley tour can be worth the money. The narrated tour can give you an overview before you focus on specific attractions, or you can use your all-day pass to hit as many places as possible in 8 hours or so.

The various companies cover the major attractions and offer informative narratives in their 90- to 120-minute tours. Most offer free reboarding if you want to visit the sites. Tickets cost $18 to $24 for adults, $12 or less for children. Boarding spots are at hotels, historic sites, and tourist information centers. Each company paints its cars a different color. Orange-and-green **Old Town Trolleys** (© **617/269-7150;** www.historictours.com) are the most numerous. Minuteman Tours' **Boston Trolley Tours** (© **617/269-3626;** www.historic tours.com) are blue; **Beantown Trolleys** (© **800/343-1328** or 781/968-6100; www.bostontrolley.com) say "Gray Line" but are red; and **CityView Luxury Trolleys** (© **800/525-2489** outside the 617 area code, or 617/363-7899) are silver. The **Discover Boston Multilingual Trolley Tours** (© **617/742-0767**) vehicle is white, and conducts tours in Japanese, Spanish, French, German, and Italian.

SIGHTSEEING CRUISES ★★   The season runs from April to October, with spring and fall offerings often restricted to weekends. If you're prone to seasickness, check the size of the vessel (larger equals more comfortable) before buying tickets.

Boston Harbor Cruises, 1 Long Wharf (© **617/227-4321;** www.boston harborcruises.com), is the largest company. Ninety-minute historic sightseeing cruises, which tour the Inner and Outer harbors, depart daily at 11am, 1pm, 3pm, and 6 or 7pm (the sunset cruise), with extra excursions at busy times. Tickets are $17 for adults, $14 for seniors, and $12 for children under 12. The

---

Kids Boston by Duck

The most unusual and enjoyable way to see Boston is with **Boston Duck Tours** ★★★ (© **800/226-7442** or 617/723-DUCK; www.bostonducktours. com). The tours, offered from April to November, are pricey but great fun. Sightseers board a "duck," a reconditioned Second World War amphibious landing craft, on the Boylston Street side of the Prudential Center (the Pru). The 80-minute narrated tour begins with a quick but comprehensive jaunt around the city. Then the duck lumbers down a ramp, splashes into the Charles River, and takes a spin around the basin. Tickets cost $23 for adults, $20 for seniors and students, $13 for children 4 to 12, and 25¢ for children under 4. Tours run every half hour from 9am to a half hour before sunset. You can buy tickets online or in person (inside the Pru or outside the New England Aquarium). Try to buy sameday tickets early in the day, or ask about the limited number of tickets available 2 days in advance. Reservations are not accepted (except for groups of more than 15). No tours are offered December through March.

45-minute USS *Constitution* cruise takes you around the Inner Harbor and docks at the Charlestown Navy Yard so you can visit "Old Ironsides." Tours leave Long Wharf hourly from 10:30am to 4:30pm, and on the hour from the Navy Yard from 11am to 5pm. Tickets are $10 for adults, $9 for seniors, and $8 for children. The same company offers service to Georges Island, where free water-taxi service to the rest of the Boston Harbor Islands is available (see "A Vacation in the Islands," later in this chapter).

Massachusetts Bay Lines operates the **Boston Steamship Company** (© 617/542-8000; www.bostonsteamship.com), which offers 55-minute harbor tours. Cruises leave from Long Wharf on the hour from 11am to 6pm; the price is $10 for adults, $7 for children and seniors. The 90-minute sunset cruise ($17 for adults, $13 for children and seniors) leaves at 7pm.

The **Charles Riverboat Company** (© 617/621-3001; www.charlesriver boat.com) offers 55-minute narrated cruises around the lower Charles River basin. Boats leave the CambridgeSide Galleria mall seven times a day daily from June to August, and weekends in April, May, and September. Tickets cost $9 for adults, $8 for seniors, and $6 for children 2 to 12.

WHALE-WATCHING 👫👫   For information on Cape Ann excursions, see "A Whale of an Adventure," in chapter 5.

The **New England Aquarium** (p. 105) runs whale-watching trips (© 617/973-5277) daily from May to mid-October and on weekends in April and late October. They travel several miles out to Stellwagen Bank, the feeding ground for whales as they migrate from Newfoundland to Provincetown. Allow 3½ to 5 hours. Tickets are $28.35 for adults, $22.58 for seniors and college students, $20.48 for youths 12 to 18, and $17.85 for children 3 to 11. Children must be at least 3 years old and 30 inches tall. Reservations are strongly recommended; you can also buy tickets online.

With its on-board exhibits and vast experience, the Aquarium offers the best whale-watches in Boston. If they're booked, try **Boston Harbor Cruises** (© 617/227-4321; www.bostonharborcruises.com), which has a high-speed catamaran; Massachusetts Bay Lines' **Beantown Whale Watch** (© 617/542-8000; www.beantownwhalewatch.com); and, on Sunday only, **A. C. Cruise Line** (© 617/261-6633; www.accruiseline.com).

ESPECIALLY FOR KIDS

Destinations with something for every family member include **Faneuil Hall Marketplace** (© 617/523-1300) and the **Museum of Fine Arts** (© 617/267-9300), which offers special weekend and after-school programs. Hands-on exhibits and large-format films are the headliners at the **New England Aquarium** (© 617/973-5200) and the **Museum of Science** (© 617/723-2500). A **Red Sox game** (see "Spectator Sports," later in this chapter) is another sure-fire kid pleaser.

The allure of seeing people the size of ants draws young visitors to the **Prudential Center Skywalk** (© 617/236-3318). They can see actual ants—though they might prefer dinosaurs—at the Museum of Comparative Zoology, part of the **Harvard Museum of Natural History** (© 617/495-3045; see "Exploring Cambridge," below).

Older children who have studied American history will enjoy a visit to the **John F. Kennedy Library and Museum** (© 617/929-4523). Middle-schoolers who enjoyed Esther Forbes's *Johnny Tremain* might get a kick out of the **Paul Revere House** (© 617/523-2338). Young visitors who have read Robert

McCloskey's children's classic *Make Way for Ducklings* will relish a visit to the **Public Garden,** as will fans of E. B. White's *The Trumpet of the Swan,* who certainly will want to ride on the **swan boats.** Considerably less tame and much longer are **whale-watches** (see "Organized Tours," above, and "A Whale of an Adventure," in chapter 5); **sightseeing cruises** fall somewhere in the middle.

The **Boston Tea Party Ship & Museum** (℗ 617/338-1773; www.boston teapartyship.com) closed indefinitely after a fire in late 2001. Call ahead to see whether the complex has reopened; it makes an entertaining stop on the way to or from the Children's Museum. The season runs from March to November.

The walking-tour company **Boston by Foot** ⋆⋆ (℗ 617/367-2345, or 617/367-3766 for recorded info; www.bostonbyfoot.com) has a special program, **Boston by Little Feet,** geared to children 6 to 12. The 1-hour walk gives a child's-eye view of the architecture along the Freedom Trail and of Boston's role in the American Revolution. Children must be accompanied by an adult. Tours ($6 per person) run May through October and meet at the statue of Samuel Adams on the Congress Street side of Faneuil Hall, Saturday at 10am, Sunday at 2pm, and Monday at 10am, rain or shine.

The **Historic Neighborhoods Foundation,** 99 Bedford St. (℗ 617/426-1885; www.historic-neighborhoods.org), offers a 90-minute "Make Way for Ducklings" tour ($8 for adults, $6 for children). It follows the path of the Mallard family described in Robert McCloskey's famous book, and ends at the Public Garden. Reservations are required.

Children's Museum ⋆⋆ *Kids*   A delightful destination for kids under 11, the Children's Museum is great fun for adults, too. Children can stick with the family or wander on their own. The centerpiece of the renovated warehouse building is a two-story-high maze, the **New Balance Climb,** which incorporates motor skills and problem-solving. The hands-on exhibits include, among many others, **Grandparents' Attic,** a souped-up version of playing dress-up at Grandma's; **Under the Dock,** an environmental exhibit that teaches about the Boston waterfront; physical experiments (such as creating giant soap bubbles); and **Boats Afloat,** which has an 800-gallon play tank and a replica of the bridge of a working boat. A special room, **Playspace,** is packed with toys and activities for children under 4 and their caregivers. Check ahead for information on traveling exhibitions, participatory plays, and other special programs.

300 Congress St. (Museum Wharf). ℗ 617/426-8855. www.bostonkids.org. Admission $7 adults, $6 seniors and children 2–15, $2 children age 1, free for children under 1; Fri 5–9pm $1 for all. Sat–Thurs 10am–5pm; Fri 10am–9pm. T: Red Line to South Station. Walk north on Atlantic Ave. 1 block (past Federal Reserve Bank), turn right onto Congress St., walk 2 blocks (across bridge). Call for information on discounted parking.

6 Exploring Cambridge

Harvard Square ⋆ is a people-watching paradise of students, instructors, commuters, and sightseers. Restaurants and stores pack the three streets that radiate from the center of the square and the streets that intersect them. On weekend afternoons and evenings year-round, you'll hear music and see street performers. To get away from the urban bustle, stroll down to the paved paths along the Charles River.

From Boston, take the Red Line toward Alewife. In Cambridge, the subway stops at Kendall/MIT, and Central, Harvard, and Porter squares. If you're staying in or visiting the Back Bay, a longer and more colorful route is the no. 1 bus (Harvard–Dudley), which runs along Mass. Ave.

By car from Boston, follow Mass. Ave., or take Storrow Drive along the south bank of the river to the Harvard Square exit. Memorial Drive runs along the north side of the river near MIT, Central Square, and Harvard. Traffic in and around Harvard Square is almost as bad as in downtown Boston. Once you get to Cambridge, park the car and walk.

HARVARD UNIVERSITY

Harvard is the oldest college in the country, and if you suggest aloud that it's not the best, you may encounter the attitude that inspired the saying, "You can always tell a Harvard man, but you can't tell him much." The university encompasses the college and 10 graduate and professional schools in more than 400 buildings around Boston and Cambridge. Free student-led tours of the main campus leave from the **Events & Information Center,** in Holyoke Center, 1350 Mass. Ave. (© **617/495-1573**), during the school year twice a day Monday through Friday and once on Saturday (except during vacations), and during the summer four times a day Monday through Saturday and twice on Sunday. Call for exact times; reservations aren't necessary. You're also free to wander on your own. The Events & Information Center has maps, illustrated booklets, and self-guided walking-tour directions. You might want to check out the university's website, www.harvard.edu.

Harvard Museum of Natural History and Peabody Museum of Archaeology & Ethnology ✪ *Kids*   These fascinating museums house the university's collections of items and artifacts related to the natural world. The world-famous academic resource offers interdisciplinary programs and exhibitions that tie in elements of all the associated fields. You'll certainly find something interesting here, be it a dinosaur skeleton, a hunk of meteorite, a Native American artifact, or the world-famous Glass Flowers.

The Museum of Natural History comprises three institutions. The best known is the **Botanical Museum,** and the best-known display is the **Glass Flowers** ✪✪✪, 3,000 models of more than 840 plant species devised between 1887 and 1936 by the German father-and-son team of Leopold and Rudolph Blaschka. You may have heard about them, and you may be skeptical, but it's true: They look real. Children love the **Museum of Comparative Zoology** ✪✪, where dinosaurs share space with preserved and stuffed insects and animals that range in size from butterflies to giraffes. The **Mineralogical & Geological Museum** is the most specialized—hold off unless there's an interesting interdisciplinary display or you're really into rocks.

Young visitors enjoy the dollhouse-like "Worlds in Miniature" display at the **Peabody Museum** ✪, which represents people from all over the world in scaled-down homes. The Peabody also boasts the **Hall of the North American Indian,** where 500 artifacts representing 10 cultures are on display.

Museum of Natural History: 26 Oxford St. © 617/495-3045. www.hmnh.harvard.edu. Peabody Museum: 11 Divinity Ave. © **617/496-1027.** www.peabody.harvard.edu. Admission to both $6.50 adults, $5 seniors and students, $4 children 3–13; free to all Sun until noon year-round and Wed 3–5pm Sept–May. Daily 9am–5pm. T: Red Line to Harvard. Cross Harvard Yard, keeping John Harvard statue on right, and turn right at Science Center. First left is Oxford St.

Harvard University Art Museums ✪   The Harvard art museums house a total of about 150,000 works in three collections. The exhibit spaces also serve as teaching and research facilities. You can take a 1-hour guided tour on weekdays September through June, and Wednesdays only in July and August.

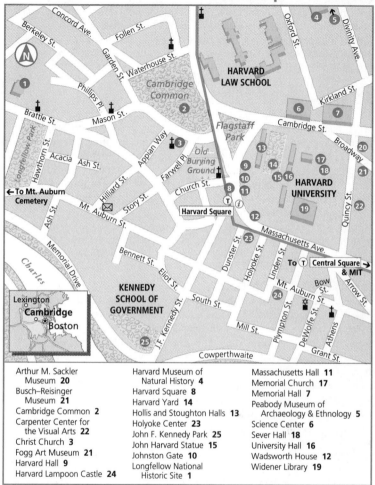

Arthur M. Sackler
  Museum **20**
Busch–Reisinger
  Museum **21**
Cambridge Common **2**
Carpenter Center for
  the Visual Arts **22**
Christ Church **3**
Fogg Art Museum **21**
Harvard Hall **9**
Harvard Lampoon Castle **24**

Harvard Museum of
  Natural History **4**
Harvard Square **8**
Harvard Yard **14**
Hollis and Stoughton Halls **13**
Holyoke Center **23**
John F. Kennedy Park **25**
John Harvard Statue **15**
Johnston Gate **10**
Longfellow National
  Historic Site **1**

Massachusetts Hall **11**
Memorial Church **17**
Memorial Hall **7**
Peabody Museum of
  Archaeology & Ethnology **5**
Science Center **6**
Sever Hall **18**
University Hall **16**
Wadsworth House **12**
Widener Library **19**

The **Fogg Art Museum,** 32 Quincy St., near Broadway, centers on an impressive 16th-century Italian stone courtyard. Each of the 19 galleries holds something different—17th-century Dutch and Flemish landscapes, 19th-century British and American paintings and drawings, French paintings and drawings from the 18th century through the Impressionist period, contemporary sculpture, and changing exhibits.

The **Busch-Reisinger Museum,** in Werner Otto Hall (enter through the Fogg), is the only museum in North America devoted to the art of northern and central Europe, specifically Germany. The early-20th-century collections include works by Klee, Feininger, Kandinsky, and artists and designers associated with the Bauhaus.

The **Arthur M. Sackler Museum,** 485 Broadway, at Quincy Street, houses the university's collections of Asian, ancient, and Islamic art. They include internationally renowned Chinese jades and cave reliefs, superb Roman sculpture,

Korean ceramics, Greek vases, and Persian miniature paintings and calligraphy.

32 Quincy St. and 485 Broadway. ℂ **617/495-9400.** www.artmuseums.harvard.edu. Admission to all three museums $5 adults, $4 seniors, $3 students, free for children under 18; free to all Wed and until noon Sat. Mon–Sat 10am–5pm; Sun 1–5pm. T: Red Line to Harvard. Cross Harvard Yard diagonally from the T station and cross Quincy St.

A HISTORIC HOUSE

Longfellow National Historic Site ✪ By the time you visit, this ravishing yellow mansion, a unit of the National Park Service, should have reopened after more than 3 years of refurbishment. The books and furniture have remained intact since the poet Henry Wadsworth Longfellow died here in 1882. During the siege of Boston in 1775 and 1776, the house served as the headquarters of Gen. George Washington, with whom Longfellow was fascinated. On the absorbing tour—the only way to see the house—you'll learn about the history of the building and its famous occupants.

105 Brattle St. ℂ **617/876-4491.** www.nps.gov/long. Guided tours $2 adults, free for seniors and children under 17. Call ahead to confirm hours and tour times. Mid-Mar to mid-Dec Wed–Sun 10am–4:30pm. Tours 10:45am, 11:45am, 1pm, 2pm, 3pm, and 4pm. Closed mid-Dec to mid-Mar. T: Red Line to Harvard, then follow Brattle St. about 7 blocks; house is on the right.

A CELEBRATED CEMETERY

Dedicated in 1831, **Mount Auburn Cemetery** ✪, 580 Mt. Auburn St. (ℂ **617 547-7105**), was the first of America's rural, or garden, cemeteries. Since the day it opened, Mount Auburn has been a popular place to retreat and reflect. The graves of Henry Wadsworth Longfellow, Oliver Wendell Holmes, James Russell Lowell, and Winslow Homer are here. In season, you'll see gorgeous flowering trees and shrubs. The cemetery is open daily from 8am to dusk; there is no admission fee. Pets, picnicking, and jogging are not allowed. Bus routes no. 71 and 73 start at Harvard station and stop near the gates; they run frequently on weekdays, less often on weekends. From Harvard Square by car (5 min.) or on foot (30 min.), take Mount Auburn Street or Brattle Street west; just after they intersect, the gate is on the left. Stop at the office to pick up brochures and a map or to rent the 60-minute audio tour ($5; a $12 deposit is required), which you can play in your car or on a portable tape player. The **Friends of Mount Auburn Cemetery** (ℂ **617/864-9646**) conducts workshops and coordinates walking tours. Call for topics, schedules, and fees.

A STROLL AROUND CAMBRIDGE

To explore Harvard and the surrounding area, begin your walk in **Harvard Square.** Town and gown meet at this lively intersection, where you'll get a taste of the improbable mix of people drawn to the crossroads of Cambridge.

Start at the Harvard T station, with the **Harvard Coop** at your back. Walk half a block, crossing Dunster Street. To your right is **Holyoke Center,** an administration building designed by the Spanish architect Josep Luis Sert, the dean of the university's Graduate School of Design from 1953 to 1969, and a disciple of Le Corbusier.

Across the street is **Wadsworth House,** 1341 Mass. Ave., a yellow wood structure built in 1726 as a residence for Harvard's fourth president. Its claim to fame is a classic: George Washington slept here. Turn left and follow the outside of the brick wall along Mass. Ave. to another T entrance. Pass through **Johnston Gate,** which guards the oldest part of **Harvard Yard.** "The Yard" was just a patch of grass with grazing animals when Harvard College was established in

1636 to train young men for the ministry. The Continental Army, under Washington's command, spent the winter of 1775–76 here.

With Johnston Gate at your back, to your right is **Massachusetts Hall** (1720), the university's oldest surviving building. It houses the president's office and rooms for first-year students. To your left is **Harvard Hall** (1765), a class-room building. The matching side-by-side buildings behind Harvard Hall are **Hollis** and **Stoughton halls.** Hollis dates to 1763 and has been home to many students who went on to great fame, among them Ralph Waldo Emerson, Henry David Thoreau, and Charles Bulfinch.

Across the Yard is **University Hall,** the college's main administration build-ing, designed by Bulfinch and constructed in 1812 and 1813. It's the backdrop of the **John Harvard statue** ✿✿, one of the most photographed objects in the Boston area. Designed by Daniel Chester French in 1884, it's known as the "Statue of Three Lies" because the inscription reads "John Harvard—Founder—1638." In fact, the college was established in 1636; Harvard (one of many people involved) wasn't the founder, but donated money and his library; and this isn't John Harvard, anyway. No portraits of him survive, so the model was, according to various accounts, either his nephew or a student. Walk over to the statue and join the throng of tourists posing for pictures with the benevolent-looking gentleman.

Walk around University Hall into the adjoining quadrangle; you're leaving the "Old Yard" for the "New Yard," where commencement and other university-wide ceremonies take place. On your right is **Widener Library,** the centerpiece of the world's largest university library system. It was built in 1913 as a memo-rial to Harry Elkins Widener, a 1907 Harvard graduate who died when the *Titanic* sank in 1912. Legend has it that he was unable to swim 50 yards to a lifeboat, and his mother donated $2 million for the library on the condition that every undergraduate pass a 50-yard (46m) swimming test.

Facing the library is **Memorial Church,** built in 1931 and topped with a tower and weather vane 197 feet (59m) tall. You're welcome to look around this Georgian Revival–style edifice unless services are going on. The entrance is on the left. The south wall, toward the Yard, lists the names of Harvard graduates who died in World Wars I and II, Korea, and Vietnam. One is Joseph P. Kennedy, Jr., '38, the president's brother.

Continue across the Yard onto Quincy Street. To your right is the curvilinear **Carpenter Center for the Visual Arts,** 24 Quincy St. Designed by the Swiss-French architect **Le Corbusier,** along with the team of Sert, Jackson, and Gourley, it was constructed from 1961 to 1963. It's the only Le Corbusier build-ing in North America.

Re-enter the Yard, pass Memorial Church, and turn right. Follow the path out of the Yard to the **Science Center,** Zero Oxford St. The 10-story monolith supposedly resembles a Polaroid camera. (Edwin H. Land, founder of Cambridge-based Polaroid Corporation, was one of its main benefactors.) Sert also designed this structure, which was built from 1970 to 1972.

To your right as you face the Science Center is **Memorial Hall,** a Victorian structure built from 1870 to 1874. The hall of memorials (enter from Kirkland or Cambridge sts.) is a transept where you can read the names of the Harvard men who died fighting for the Union during the Civil War—but not those who died for the Confederacy.

With the Science Center behind you and "Mem Hall" to your left, turn right, and follow the walkway for the equivalent of a block and a half as it curves around to the right. The **Harvard Law School** campus is on your right. Carefully cross Mass. Ave. to **Cambridge Common.** Memorials and plaques dot this well-used plot of greenery and bare earth. Turn left and head back toward Harvard Square; after a block or so you'll walk near or over **horseshoes** embedded in the concrete. This is the path William Dawes, Paul Revere's fellow alarm-sounder, took from Boston to Lexington on April 18, 1775.

Turn right onto Garden Street and find **Christ Church,** Zero Garden St. The oldest church in Cambridge, it was designed by Peter Harrison of Newport, R.I. (also the architect of King's Chapel in Boston), and opened in 1761. Note the square wooden tower. Inside the vestibule you can still see bullet holes made by British muskets.

With the church at your back, turn right and return to Mass. Ave. Turn right again, then walk 2 blocks into the middle of the square and 1 more block on John F. Kennedy Street. Turn left onto Mount Auburn Street. Stay on the left side of the street as you cross Dunster, Holyoke, and Linden streets.

The corner of Mount Auburn and Linden streets is a good vantage point for viewing the **Harvard Lampoon Castle,** designed by Wheelwright & Haven in 1909. Listed on the National Register of Historic Places, this is the home of Harvard's undergraduate humor magazine, the *Lampoon.* The main tower looks like a face, with windows as the eyes, nose, and mouth, topped by what looks like a miner's hat.

Follow Mount Auburn Street back to John F. Kennedy Street and turn left. Cross the street at some point, and follow it toward the Charles River, almost to Memorial Drive. On your right is **John F. Kennedy Park** and the adjacent Graduate School of Government. Walk away from the street to the fountain, engraved with excerpts from the president's speeches. This is an excellent place to take a break and plan the rest of your day.

7 Spectator Sports & Outdoor Pursuits

SPECTATOR SPORTS

Boston's reputation as a great sports town derives in part from the days when at least one pro team was one of the world's best. In 2002, the New England Patriots (who play in suburban Foxboro) continued that tradition by winning the Super Bowl. Although the other pro teams haven't enjoyed that level of success recently, passions still run deep. That enthusiasm also applies to college sports, particularly hockey, in which the Division I schools are fierce rivals.

BASEBALL   No other experience in sports matches watching the **Boston Red Sox** play at **Fenway Park** ★★★, which they do from April to early October, and later if they make the playoffs. The team changed hands in 2002, throwing into limbo tentative plans to demolish most of the current park. Adding to the Fenway mystique is the quirkiness of the oldest park in the major leagues (1912) and the fact that (at press time) the team last won the World Series in 1918.

The Fenway Park **ticket office** (© **617/267-1700** for tickets, 617/482-4SOX for touch-tone ticketing; www.redsox.com) is at 4 Yawkey Way, off Brookline Avenue. Tickets go on sale in January; order early. Prices start at $18. Forced to choose between tickets for a low-numbered grandstand section (say, 10 or below) and less expensive bleacher seats, go for the bleachers and the better view. Throughout the season, a limited number of standing-room tickets and (if you're lucky) returned tickets go on sale the day of the game. Take the Green Line B, C, or D to Kenmore or D to Fenway.

Booked seat 6A, open return.

Rented red 4-wheel drive.

Reserved cabin, no running water.

Discovered space.

over 700 airlines, 50,000 hotels, 50 rental car companies and
0 cruise and vacation packages, you can create the perfect get-
y for you. Choose the car, the room, even the ground you walk on.

Travelocity.com
A Sabre Company
Go Virtually Anywhere.

Book your air, hotel, and transportation all in one place.

Hotel or hostel? Cruise or canoe? Car? Plane? Camel? Wherever you're going, visit Yahoo! Travel and get total control over your arrangements. Even choose your seat assignment. So. One hump or two? travel.yahoo.com

YAHOO!
Travel

Tours (© **617/236-6666**) are offered May through September, Monday through Friday at 9am, 11am, noon, and 1pm, plus 2pm when the team is away. There are no tours on holidays or before day games. The cost is $5 for adults, $4 for seniors, and $3 for children under 16.

BASKETBALL   Sixteen NBA championship banners hang in the FleetCenter, testimony to the history of the **Boston Celtics.** Unfortunately, the most recent is from 1986. The Celtics play from early October to April or May; when a top contender is visiting, you may have trouble getting tickets. Prices are as low as $10 for some games and top out at $85. For information, call the **FleetCenter** (© **617/624-1000;** www.nba.com/celtics); for tickets, call **Ticketmaster** (© **617/931-2000;** www.ticketmaster.com). To reach the FleetCenter, take the Green or Orange Line to North Station. *Note:* Spectators may not bring any bags, including backpacks and briefcases, into the arena.

FOOTBALL   The **New England Patriots** (© **800/543-1776;** www.patriots. com) were playing to sellout crowds even before they won the Super Bowl in 2002 and moved to a snazzy new stadium. The Pats play from August to December or January at CMGI Field on Route 1 in Foxboro, about a 45-minute drive south of the city. Tickets sell out well in advance. Call or check the website for information on individual ticket sales and public-transit options.

HOCKEY   The **Boston Bruins** are exciting but expensive to watch. Tickets often sell out early despite being among the priciest ($23–$70) in the league. For information, call the **FleetCenter** (© **617/624-1000;** www.bostonbruins.com); for tickets, call **Ticketmaster** (© **617/931-2000;** www.ticketmaster.com). To reach the FleetCenter, take the Green or Orange Line to North Station. *Note:* Spectators may not bring any bags, including backpacks and briefcases, into the arena.

Economical fans will be pleasantly surprised by the quality of local **college hockey** ✦. Even for sold-out games, standing-room tickets are usually available shortly before game time. Local teams include **Boston College,** Conte Forum, Chestnut Hill (© **617/552-3000); Boston University,** Walter Brown Arena, 285 Babcock St. (© **617/353-3838); Harvard University,** Bright Hockey Center, North Harvard Street, Allston (© **617/495-2211);** and **Northeastern University,** Matthews Arena, St. Botolph Street (© **617/373-4700).**

THE MARATHON   Every year on Patriot's Day (the third Mon in Apr), the **Boston Marathon** ✦✦✦ rules the roads from Hopkinton to Copley Square in Boston. An especially nice place to watch is tree-shaded Comm. Ave. between Kenmore Square and Mass. Ave., but you'll be in a crowd wherever you stand, particularly near the finish line in front of the Boston Public Library. For information about qualifying, contact the **Boston Athletic Association** (© **617/ 236-1652;** www.bostonmarathon.org).

ROWING   In late October, the **Head of the Charles Regatta** ✦ (© **617/ 868-6200;** www.hocr.org) attracts some 4,000 oarsmen and oarswomen. The largest crew event in the country draws hundreds of thousands of spectators who socialize and occasionally even watch the action.

OUTDOOR PURSUITS

The incredibly helpful site maintained by the **Metropolitan District Commission** (© **617/727-9547;** www.state.ma.us/mdc) includes descriptions of properties and activities, and has a planning area to help you make the most of your time.

Finds **A Vacation in the Islands**

Majestic ocean views, hiking trails, historic sights, rocky beaches, nature walks, campsites, and picnic areas abound in New England. The **Boston Harbor Islands** ★★ (© 617/223-8666; www.bostonislands.com) have them all. Their unspoiled beauty makes a welcome break from the urban landscape 45 minutes to the west, but they're not well known, even to many longtime Bostonians. Bring a sweater or jacket, and note that fresh water is available only on Georges Island. (Management strongly suggests that you bring your own.)

There are 30 islands in the Outer Harbor, and at least a half dozen are open to the public. Ferries run to the most popular, **Georges Island,** home of Fort Warren (1834), which held Confederate prisoners during the Civil War. You can investigate on your own or take a ranger-led tour. The island has a visitor center, refreshment area, fishing pier, picnic area, and wonderful view of Boston's skyline. Allow at least half a day, longer if you plan to take the free water taxi to **Lovell, Gallops, Peddocks, Bumpkin,** or **Grape Island,** all of which have picnic areas and campsites.

Boston Harbor Cruises (© 617/227-4321; www.bostonharbor cruises.com) serves Georges Island from Long Wharf; the trip takes 45 minutes, and tickets cost $8 for adults, $7 for seniors, and $6 for children under 12. Cruises depart daily at 10am, noon, 2pm, and 4pm in spring and fall, and daily on the hour from 10am to 5pm in summer. Water taxis and admission to the islands are free.

The Boston Harbor Islands National Recreation Area (www.nps. gov/boha) is the focus of a public-private project designed to make the islands more interesting and accessible. For more information, visit the website, consult the staff at the **kiosk on Long Wharf,** stop at the **Discovery Center** in the courthouse on Fan Pier (on Northern Ave. across the Fort Point Channel from the Boston Harbor Hotel), or contact the **Friends of the Boston Harbor Islands** (© 617/740-4290; www.fbhi.org).

BEACHES   The beaches in Boston proper are not worth the trouble. Boston Harbor water is not only bone-chilling, but also subject to being declared unsafe for swimming. If you want to swim, book a hotel with a pool. If you want the sand-between-your-toes experience, add some time to your excursion to the North Shore or to Walden Pond in Concord. See chapter 5 for information on suburban beaches.

BIKING   Even expert cyclists who feel comfortable with Boston's layout will be better off in Cambridge, which has bike lanes, or on the area's many bike paths. The 18-mile (29km) **Dr. Paul Dudley White Charles River Bike Path** follows the river from the Museum of Science to Watertown and back. You can enter and exit at many points along the way. Bikers share the path with lots of pedestrians, joggers, and in-line skaters. On summer Sundays from 11am to 7pm, **Memorial Drive** from Central Square to west Cambridge is closed to cars.

State law requires that children under 12 wear helmets. Bicycles are forbidden on buses and the Green Line, and on other lines during rush hours.

Most rental shops charge around $5 per hour or $25 per day. They include **Back Bay Bikes & Boards,** 336 Newbury St., near Mass. Ave. (© 617/ 247-2336; www.backbaybicycles.com), and **Community Bicycle Supply,** 496 Tremont St., near East Berkeley Street (© 617/542-8623; www.community bicycle.com). Across the river, try **Cambridge Bicycle,** 259 Mass. Ave., near MIT (© 617/876-6555), or **Ata Cycle,** 1773 Mass. Ave., near Porter Square (© 617/354-0907; www.atabike.com). For more information, contact **Mass Bike** (© 617/542-2453; www.massbike.org).

GOLF   The **Massachusetts Golf Association** (© 781/449-3000; www. mgalinks.org) represents more than 310 courses around the golf-mad state. Given a choice, play on a weekday, when you'll find lower prices and smaller crowds than on weekends.

One of the best public courses in the area, **Newton Commonwealth Golf Course,** 212 Kenrick St., Newton (© 617/630-1971; www.sterlinggolf.com), is a challenging 18-hole Donald Ross design. It's 5,305 yards (4,828m) from the blue tees, par is 70, and greens fees are $23 on weekdays, $30 on weekends. Within the city limits is the legendary 6,009-yard (5,469m) **William J. Devine Golf Course,** in Franklin Park, Dorchester (© 617/265-4084; www.sterling golf.com). As a Harvard student, Bobby Jones sharpened his game on the 18-hole, par-70 course. Greens fees are $23 on weekdays, $26 on weekends. Less challenging but with more of a neighborhood feel is 9-hole, par-35 **Fresh Pond Golf Course,** 691 Huron Ave., Cambridge (© 617/349-6282; www.fresh pondgolf.com). The 3,161-yard (2,877m) layout adjoins the Fresh Pond Reservoir (there's water on four holes) and charges $17, or $27 to go around twice, on weekdays; $22 and $35 on weekends.

GYMS   The concierge at your hotel can recommend a health club. Guests at the new Ritz-Carlton, Boston Common, have the use of the over-the-top facilities at the Sports Club/LA, which is otherwise closed to nonmembers. Other hotels with good health clubs (see "Where to Stay," earlier in this chapter) include the Boston Harbor Hotel, the Four Seasons Hotel, the Hilton Boston Logan Airport, and the Royal Sonesta Hotel. The best combination of facilities and value is at the **Wang YMCA of Chinatown,** 8 Oak St. W., off Washington Street (© 617/426-2237), close to downtown; or the **Central Branch YMCA,** 316 Huntington Ave. (© 617/536-7800), near Symphony Hall. A day pass costs $10.

ICE-SKATING   The rink at the Boston Common **Frog Pond** (© 617/ 635-2120) is an extremely popular cold-weather destination. It's an open surface with an ice-making system and a clubhouse. Admission is $3 for adults and free for children under 14; skate rental costs $7 for adults, $5 for kids. Try to go on a weekday; huge crowds descend on weekends.

IN-LINE SKATING   Unless you're confident of your ability and your knowledge of Boston traffic, stay off the streets. A favorite car-free spot is the **Esplanade,** between the Back Bay and the Charles River. It continues onto the bike path that runs to Watertown and back, but once you leave the Esplanade, the pavement isn't totally smooth. Your best bet is to wait for a summer Sunday, when **Memorial Drive** in Cambridge closes to cars. It's a perfect surface. The **InLine Club of Boston** offers event and safety information on its website (www.sk8net.com).

Expect to pay about $15 for rentals. Try the **Beacon Hill Skate Shop,** 135 Charles St. S. (© 617/482-7400), not far from the Esplanade, or **Blades Board & Skate,** at 349A Newbury St. (© 617/437-6300; www.blades.com), near Mass. Ave., and 38 John F. Kennedy St., Cambridge (© 617/491-4244), near Memorial Drive.

JOGGING The **Dr. Paul Dudley White Charles River Bike Path** (see "Biking," above) is the area's busiest jogging trail. It's so popular because it's car-free (except at intersections), scenic, and generally safe. The bridges along the river allow for circuits of various lengths, but be careful around abutments, where you can't see far ahead. Don't jog at night, and try not to go alone. Visit the MDC website (www.state.ma.us/mdc) to view a map that gives distances. If the river's not convenient, check with the concierge or desk staff at your hotel for a map with suggested routes.

SAILING The best deal in town is **Community Boating, Inc.,** 21 David Mugar Way, on the Esplanade (© 617/523-1038; www.community-boating.org). It's open April through November, and the fleet includes 13- to 23-foot (4–7m) sailboats as well as windsurfers and kayaks. Visitors pay $100 for 2 days of unlimited use in the Charles River basin.

TENNIS Public courts maintained by the **Metropolitan District Commission** (© 617/727-5114; www.state.ma.us/mdc) are available throughout the city at no charge. To find the one nearest you, call the MDC or ask the concierge at your hotel. Well-maintained courts near downtown that seldom get busy until after work are on the Southwest Corridor Park in the South End. (There's a nice one near **W. Newton St.**) The courts on **Boston Common** and in **Charlesbank Park,** overlooking the river next to the bridge to the Museum of Science, are more crowded during the day.

8 Shopping

Boston-area shopping represents a tempting blend of classic and contemporary. Boston and Cambridge boast tiny boutiques and sprawling malls, esoteric bookshops and national chain stores, classy galleries and snazzy secondhand-clothing outlets.

Note: Massachusetts has no sales tax on clothing priced below $175 or on food. All other items are taxed at 5% (as are restaurant meals and takeout food). The state no longer prohibits stores from opening before noon on Sunday, but many still wait until noon or don't open at all—call ahead before setting out.

BACK BAY This is the area's premier shopping district. Dozens of classy galleries, shops, and boutiques make **Newbury Street** 𝄞𝄞𝄞 a world-famous destination. Nearby, a weatherproof walkway across Huntington Avenue links upscale **Copley Place** (© 617/375-4400) and the **Shops at Prudential Center** (© 800/SHOP-PRU). This is where you'll find the tony department stores **Neiman Marcus** (© 617/536-3660), **Lord & Taylor** (© 617/262-6000), and **Saks Fifth Avenue** (© 617/262-8500).

If you're passionate about art, set aside a couple of hours for strolling along Newbury Street. Besides being a prime location for upscale boutiques, it boasts an infinite variety of styles and media in the dozens of art galleries at street level and on the higher floors. (Remember to look up.) Most galleries are open Tuesday through Sunday from 10 or 11am to 5:30 or 6pm. For specifics, pick up a copy

(Finds) **By the Book**

Bookworms flock to Cambridge; Harvard Square in particular caters to general and specific audiences. Check out the basement of the **Harvard Book Store,** 1256 Mass. Ave. (© **800/542-READ** outside 617, or 617/661-1515; www.harvard.com), for great deals on remainders and used books; and **WordsWorth Books,** 30 Brattle St. (© **800/899-2202** or 617/354-5201; www.wordsworth.com), for a huge discounted selection. Up the street, children's books have their own store at **Curious George Goes to WordsWorth,** 1 John F. Kennedy St. (© **617/498-0062;** www. curiousg.com). Barnes & Noble runs the book operation at the **Harvard Coop,** 1400 Mass. Ave. (© **617/499-2000;** www.thecoop.com), which stocks textbooks, academic works, and a large general selection.

Two excellent Boston stores with huge selections of used merchandise are the **Avenue Victor Hugo Bookshop,** 339 Newbury St. (© **617/266-7746;** www.avenuevictorhugobooks.com), in the Back Bay, and the **Brattle Book Shop,** 9 West St. (© **800/447-9595** or 617/542-0210; www. brattlebookshop.com), near Downtown Crossing. Also near Downtown Crossing are **Barnes & Noble,** 395 Washington St. (© **617/426-5184;** www.barnesandnoble.com), and **Borders,** 24 School St. (© **617/557-7188;** www.borders.com). There's also a **Borders** (© **617/679-0887)** at the CambridgeSide Galleria mall.

---

of the free monthly *Gallery Guide* at businesses along Newbury Street, or check with the **Newbury Street League** (© **617/267-7961;** www.newbury-st.com).

DOWNTOWN **Faneuil Hall Marketplace** (© **617/523-1300)** is the busiest attraction in Boston not only for its smorgasbord of food outlets, but also for its shops, boutiques, and pushcarts. Although it has more upscale chain outlets than only-in-Boston shops, the latter category is a fun one. The best example is the **Boston City Store** (© **617/635-2911;** www.cityofboston.gov/citystore), on the lower level. It sells the equivalent of the municipal attic and basement—clothing, office equipment, even old street signs and mounted-police horseshoes.

If the hubbub here is too much for you, stroll over to **Charles Street,** at the foot of Beacon Hill. A short but commercially dense (and picturesque) street, it's home to perhaps the best assortment of gift and antiques shops in the city. Be sure to check out the contemporary home accessories at **Koo De Kir,** 34 Charles St. (© **617/723-8111;** www.koodekir.com), the well-edited selection at **Upstairs Downstairs Antiques,** 93 Charles St. (© **617/367-1950**), and the engagingly funky gifts at **Black Ink,** 101 Charles St. (© **617/723-3883**).

One of Boston's oldest shopping areas is **Downtown Crossing.** Now a traffic-free pedestrian mall along Washington, Winter, and Summer streets near Boston Common, it's home to two major department stores (**Filene's** and **Macy's**); tons of smaller clothing, shoe, and music stores; food and merchandise pushcarts; and outlets of two major bookstore chains, **Barnes & Noble** and **Borders.** The first Boston location of the Swedish discount-fashion phenomenon **H&M** is at 350 Washington St. (© **617/482-0071**). **Filene's Basement** 𝘈𝘈𝘈, 426 Washington St. (© **617/542-2011**), is a New England legend. The famed automatic markdown policy (25% off the already-discounted price after 2 weeks on the selling floor, up to 75% after 7 weeks) applies only here, at the flagship store. We happen to love this sort of thing, but you may find that battling the crowds isn't worth the payoff—the selling floors are pretty wild at busy times.

CAMBRIDGE The bookstores, boutiques, and T-shirt shops of **Harvard Square** lie about 15 minutes from downtown Boston by subway. Despite the neighborhood association's efforts, chain stores have swept over the Square. You'll find a mix of national and regional outlets, and more than a few persistent independent retailers. They include the delightful children's store **Calliope,** 33 Brattle St. (© **617/876-4149**); **Colonial Drug,** 49 Brattle St. (© **617/ 864-2222**), which stocks hard-to-find perfume and other high-end cosmetics; and **Oona's,** 1210 Mass. Ave. (© **617/491-2654**), a trove of lovely "experienced" clothing and accessories.

For a less generic experience, walk along **Mass. Ave.** in either direction to the next T stop. The stroll takes about an hour. Heading north toward Porter Square, be sure to stop at **Joie de Vivre,** 1792 Mass. Ave. (© **617/864-8188**), a top-notch gift shop, and the retro home-accessories emporium **Abodeon,** 1713 Mass. Ave. (© **617/497-0137**). Going southeast to Central, pop into **Pearl Art & Craft Supplies,** 579 Mass. Ave. (© **617/547-6600**), an excellent link in the national discount chain.

And if you just can't manage without a trip to a mall, head to East Cambridge. Take the Green Line to Lechmere, or the Red Line to Kendall/MIT and the free shuttle bus to the **CambridgeSide Galleria,** 100 CambridgeSide Place (© **617/ 621-8666**).

9 Boston & Cambridge After Dark

For up-to-date entertainment listings, consult the "Calendar" section of the Thursday *Boston Globe,* the "Scene" section of the Friday *Boston Herald,* or the Sunday arts sections of both papers. Three free publications, available at newspaper boxes around town, publish nightlife listings: the *Boston Phoenix,* the *Stuff@Night* (a *Phoenix* offshoot), and the *Improper Bostonian.* The *Phoenix* website (www.bostonphoenix.com) archives the paper's season preview issues; especially before a summer or fall visit, it's a worthwhile planning tool.

GETTING TICKETS Some companies and venues sell tickets over the phone or online; many will refer you to a ticket agency. The major agencies that serve Boston, **Ticketmaster** (© 617/931-2000; www.ticketmaster.com), **Next Ticketing** (© 617/423-NEXT; www.nextticketing.com), and **Tele-charge** (© 800/447-7400 or TTY 888/889-8587; www.telecharge.com), calculate service charges per ticket, not per order. To avoid the fee, visit the box office in person. If you wait until the day before or day of a performance, you'll sometimes have access to tickets that were held back and have just gone on sale.

DISCOUNT TICKETS Visit a **BosTix** (© 617/482-2849; www.bostix.org) booth at Faneuil Hall Marketplace (on the south side of Faneuil Hall) or in Copley Square (at the corner of Boylston and Dartmouth sts.). Same-day tickets to musical and theatrical performances are half price, subject to availability. Credit cards are not accepted, and there are no refunds or exchanges. Check the board for the day's offerings. BosTix also sells coupon books ($9) with discounted and two-for-one admission to many area museums; full-price advance tickets; and tickets to museums, historic sites, and attractions in and around town. The booths, which are also Ticketmaster outlets, are open Tuesday through Saturday from 10am to 6pm (half-price tickets go on sale at

11am), Sunday from 11am to 4pm. The Copley Square location is also open Monday from 10am to 6pm.

THE PERFORMING ARTS

The city's premier classical performance venue is **Symphony Hall,** 301 Mass. Ave. (© 617/266-1492; www.bso.org), which turned 100 in 2000. It plays host to other notable groups and artists when the BSO and the Pops are away. The **Hatch Shell** on the Esplanade (© 617/727-5215) is an amphitheater best known as the home of the Boston Pops' Fourth of July concerts. On summer nights, free music and dance performances and films take over the stage to the delight of crowds on the lawn.

Other venues that attract big-name visitors include the **Berklee Performance Center,** 136 Mass. Ave. (© 617/266-1400, ext. 8820; www.berkleebpc.com); the **Boston Center for the Arts,** 539 Tremont St. (© 617/426-7700; www.bcaonline.org); **Jordan Hall,** 30 Gainsborough St. (© 617/536-2412; www.newenglandconservatory.edu/jordanhall); and **Sanders Theatre,** 45 Quincy St., Cambridge (© 617/496-2222; www.fas.harvard.edu/~memhall).

THE MAJOR COMPANIES

In addition to the companies listed below, the **Boston Lyric Opera** (© 617/542-6772 or 617/542-4912; www.blo.org) performs classical and contemporary works. The season runs from October to March. Performances are at the **Shubert Theatre,** 265 Tremont St., and tickets cost $27.50 to $108.

Boston Symphony Orchestra (BSO)   The Boston Symphony, one of the world's greatest, was founded in 1881. You might want to schedule your trip to coincide with a particular performance, or with a visit by a celebrated guest artist or conductor. The season runs from October to April, with performances most Tuesday, Thursday, and Saturday evenings; Friday afternoons; and some Friday evenings. Explanatory talks (included in the ticket price) begin 30 minutes before the curtain. If you can't get tickets in advance, check at the box office for returns from subscribers 2 hours before showtime. A limited number of rush tickets are available on the day of the performance for Tuesday and Thursday evening and Friday afternoon programs. Some Wednesday evening and Thursday morning rehearsals are open to the public. Symphony Hall, 301 Mass. Ave. (at Huntington Ave.). © 617/266-1492 or 617/CONCERT (program information). SymphonyCharge © 888/266-1200 (outside 617) or 617/266-1200. www.bso.org. Tickets $25–$87. Rush tickets $8 (on sale 9am Fri, 5pm Tues and Thurs). Rehearsal tickets $14.50. T: Green Line E to Symphony, or Orange Line to Mass. Ave.

Boston Pops   From May to July, members of the BSO lighten up. Tables and chairs replace the floor seats at Symphony Hall, and drinks and light refreshments are served. The Pops play a range of music from light classical to show tunes to popular music, sometimes with celebrity guest stars. Performances are Tuesday through Sunday evenings. Special holiday performances in December ($20–$95) usually sell out well in advance, but it can't hurt to check. The regular season ends with a week of free outdoor concerts at the Hatch Shell on the Esplanade along the Charles River. It includes the traditional Fourth of July concert. Symphony Hall, 301 Mass. Ave. (at Huntington Ave.). © 617/266-1492 or 617/CONCERT (program information). SymphonyCharge © 888/266-1200 (outside 617) or 617/266-1200. www.bso.org. Tickets $35–$55 for tables; $14–35 for balcony seats. T: Green Line E to Symphony, or Orange Line to Mass. Ave.

Finds **Boston Common Culture**

An excellent summer diversion is a free, top-quality performance on historic Boston Common. Bring a picnic, spread out a blanket, and enjoy the sunset. The **Commonwealth Shakespeare Company** (© 617/423-7600; www.commonwealthshakespeare.org) performs Tuesday through Sunday nights in July and early August. The **Boston Landmarks Orchestra** (© 617/520-2200; www.landmarksorchestra.org) schedules classical concerts in parks around town, including the Common, on weekend afternoons and evenings in July and August.

Boston Ballet   Boston Ballet's reputation seems to jump a notch every time someone says, "So it's not just *The Nutcracker.*" The country's fourth-largest dance company performs the holiday staple from Thanksgiving to New Year's. During the rest of the season (Oct–May), it presents an eclectic mix of classic ballets and contemporary works. Because the Wang was originally a movie theater, the pitch of the seats makes the top two balconies less than ideal for ballet—paying more for a better seat is a good investment. 19 Clarendon St. © 617/695-6955 or 800/447-7400 (Tele-charge). www.bostonballet.com. Performances at the Wang Theatre, 270 Tremont St. (box office Mon–Sat 10am–6pm). Tickets $23–$73. Student rush tickets (1 hr. before curtain) $12.50, except for The Nutcracker. T: Green Line to Boylston.

THEATER & PERFORMANCE ART

Boston is one of the last cities for pre-Broadway tryouts, allowing an early look at a classic (or classic flop) in the making. It's also a popular destination for touring companies of established hits. You'll find most of the shows headed to or coming from Broadway in the **Theater District,** at the **Colonial Theatre,** 106 Boylston St. (© 617/426-9366); the **Shubert Theatre,** 265 Tremont St. (© 617/482-9393); the **Wang Theatre,** 270 Tremont St. (© 617/482-9393; www.wangcenter.org); and the **Wilbur Theater,** 246 Tremont St. (© 617/423-4008). The promoter often is **Broadway in Boston** (© 617/880-2400; www.broadwayinboston.com).

The excellent local theater scene boasts the **Huntington Theatre Company,** which performs at the Boston University Theatre, 264 Huntington Ave. (© 617/266-0800; www.huntington.org), and the **American Repertory Theatre,** which makes its home at Harvard University's Loeb Drama Center, 64 Brattle St., Cambridge (© 617/547-8300; www.amrep.org).

The off-Broadway performance-art sensation **Blue Man Group** branched out from New York to Boston in 1995. The trio of cobalt-colored entertainers uses music, percussion, food, and audience participants—props include social commentary, Twinkies, marshmallows, breakfast cereal, toilet paper, and lots of blue paint. Older children and teenagers enjoy the mayhem as much as adults. Shows are at the **Charles Playhouse,** 74 Warrenton St. (© 617/426-6912), in the Theater District, at 8pm Tuesday and Wednesday; 7 and 10pm Thursday and Friday; 4, 7, and 10pm Saturday; and 3 and 6pm Sunday. Tickets are $53 and $43 at the box office and through Ticketmaster (© 617/931-ARTS).

CHURCH CONCERTS

Fridays at Trinity   This landmark church features 30-minute organ recitals by local and visiting artists on Fridays at 12:15pm. Take advantage of the chance to look around the architectural showpiece. Trinity Church, Copley Sq. © 617/536-0944. Donations accepted. T: Green Line to Copley or Orange Line to Back Bay.

King's Chapel Noon Hour Recitals   Organ, instrumental, and vocal solos fill this historic building with music and make for a pleasant break along the Freedom Trail. Concerts are at 12:15pm on Tuesdays. 58 Tremont St. © 617/227-2155. $2 donation requested. T: Red or Green Line to Park St.

THE CLUB & MUSIC SCENE

The Boston-area club scene changes constantly, and somewhere out there is a good time for everyone. Check the "Calendar" section of the Thursday *Globe,* the *Phoenix,* the "Scene" section of the Friday *Herald, Stuff@Night,* or the *Improper Bostonian* while you're planning.

Bars close at 1am, clubs at 2am. The subway shuts down between 12:30 and 1am; Night Owl bus service operates until 2:30am on Friday and Saturday (see "Late-Night Transit," on p. 68). The drinking age is 21; a valid driver's license or passport is required as proof of age. The law is strictly enforced, especially near college campuses (in other words, practically everywhere). Be prepared to show ID if you appear to be younger than 35 or so, and try to be patient while the amazed 30-year-old ahead of you fishes out a license.

Big-name rock and pop artists play the **FleetCenter,** 150 Causeway St. (© 617/624-1000; www.fleetcenter.com), when it's not in use by the Bruins (hockey), the Celtics (basketball), the circus (in Oct), and touring ice shows. Concerts are in the round or on the arena stage.

COMEDY

The Comedy Connection at Faneuil Hall   The oldest original comedy club in town (established in 1978) draws top-notch talent from near and far. Shows are nightly at 8pm, plus Friday and Saturday at 10:15pm. The cover seldom tops $15 during the week, but jumps for a big name appearing on a weekend. The Backstage restaurant-club next door offers dinner-show packages. Quincy Market. © 888/398-5100 or 617/248-9700. www.comedyconnectionboston.com. Cover $10–$37. T: Green or Blue Line to Government Center or Orange Line to Haymarket.

The Comedy Studio *(Finds*   Nobody here is a sitcom star—yet. With a growing reputation for ferreting out undiscovered talent, the no-frills Comedy Studio draws connoisseurs, students, and network scouts. Sketches and improv spice up the standup. Shows Thursday through Sunday nights. At the Hong Kong restaurant, 1236 Mass. Ave., Cambridge. © 617/661-6507. www.thecomedystudio.com. Cover $5–$7. T: Red Line to Harvard.

DANCE CLUBS

Avalon   A cavernous space divided into several levels, Avalon is either great fun or sensory overload. They Might Be Giants and Elliott Smith have played here recently; when the stage isn't in use, DJs spin for the crowd of 20- and 30-somethings. On Saturday (suburbanites' night out), expect more mainstream dance hits. The dress code calls for jackets and shirts with collars, and no jeans or athletic wear. Open Thursday (international night) through Sunday (gay night) from 10pm to 2am. 15 Lansdowne St. © 617/262-2424. Cover $5–$20. T: Green Line B, C, or D to Kenmore.

The Roxy   This former hotel ballroom boasts excellent DJs and live music, a huge dance floor, a stage, and a balcony. Occasional concerts and boxing cards take good advantage of the sight lines. No jeans or athletic shoes. Open from

8pm to 2am Thursday through Saturday, plus some Wednesdays and Sundays. In the Tremont Boston hotel, 279 Tremont St. ℂ **617/338-7699**. Cover $10–$15. T: Green Line to Boylston.

FOLK & ECLECTIC

Club Passim   Joan Baez, Suzanne Vega, and Tom Rush all started out in this legendary basement coffeehouse, on the street between buildings of the Harvard Coop. There's live music nightly, and coffee and food (no alcohol is served) until 10pm. Open Sunday through Thursday from 11am to 11pm, Friday and Saturday until 4am. 47 Palmer St., Cambridge. ℂ **617/492-7679**. www.clubpassim.org. Cover $5–$25; most shows $12 or less. T: Red Line to Harvard.

Johnny D's Uptown Restaurant & Music Club *Finds*   This family-owned establishment draws a congenial post-collegiate-and-up crowd for performers on international tours as well as local acts. The music ranges from zydeco to rock, blues to ska. It's only two stops past Harvard Square on the Red Line (about a 15-min. ride at night). Open daily from 11:30am to 1am. Brunch starts at 9am on weekends; dinner runs from 4:30 to 9:30pm Tuesday through Saturday, with lighter fare until 11pm. 17 Holland St., Davis Sq., Somerville. ℂ **617/776-2004** or 617/776-9667 (concert line). www.johnnyds.com. Cover $2–$16, usually $5–$10. T: Red Line to Davis.

JAZZ & BLUES

On summer Fridays at 6:30pm, the **Waterfront Jazz Series** (ℂ **617/635-3911**) brings amateurs and professionals to Christopher Columbus Park, on the waterfront, for a refreshing interlude of free music and cool breezes. On summer Thursdays at 6pm, the **Boston Harbor Hotel** (ℂ **617/439-7000**) stages performances on the "Blues Barge," which floats in the water behind the hotel. The *Boston Globe* **Jazz & Blues Festival** (ℂ **617/267-4301;** www. boston.com/jazzfest) is usually scheduled for the third week of June. Constellations of jazz and blues stars appear, often outdoors. The festival wraps up with a free Sunday program at the Hatch Shell.

House of Blues *Kids*   The original House of Blues, near Harvard Square, packs 'em in every evening and on weekend afternoons. It attracts tourists, music buffs, and big names—Mighty Sam McClain, Junior Brown, Entrain, and the Fabulous Thunderbirds have played recently. The restaurant is open Monday through Saturday from 11:30am to 11pm, Sunday from 4:30 to 11pm; the music hall Sunday through Wednesday until 1am, Thursday through Saturday until 2am. **Sunday gospel buffet brunch** seatings are at 10am, noon, and 2pm; advance tickets ($26 for adults, $13 for children) are highly recommended. 96 Winthrop St., Cambridge. ℂ **617/491-2583**, or 617/497-2229 for tickets. Dining reservations (ℂ 617/491-2100) accepted for parties of 25 or more. www.hob.com. Cover $6–$30; no cover Fri–Sat matinee. T: Red Line to Harvard.

Limbo   A see-and-be-seen scene, Limbo books jazz, blues, hip-hop, and soul. Live artists play on the lowest of the three levels nightly; DJs spin on weekends on the other two floors (otherwise a bar and restaurant). 49 Temple Place. ℂ **617/ 338-0280**. www.limboboston.com. No cover. T: Red or Green Line to Park Street, or Orange Line to Downtown Crossing.

Regattabar   The Regattabar's lineup of local and international artists is often considered the best in the area—a title that Scullers (see below) is happy to dispute. Branford Marsalis, Joe Lovano, and Rebecca Parris have appeared recently. The third-floor room holds about 200 and, unfortunately, can get a little noisy. Buy tickets in advance from Concertix or try your luck at the door an hour before showtime. In the Charles Hotel, 1 Bennett St., Cambridge. © 617/661-5000. Concertix: 12 Arrow St., Cambridge. © 617/876-7777. Tickets $8–$35. T: Red Line to Harvard.

Scullers Jazz Club Overlooking the Charles River, Scullers is a lovely room that books top singers and instrumentalists—recent notables include Abbey Lincoln, Jane Monheit, and Bobby Short. Patrons tend to be more hard-core and quieter than the crowds at the Regattabar, but it really depends on who's performing. The box office is open Monday through Saturday from 11am to 6:30pm. Ask about dinner packages. In the Doubletree Guest Suites hotel, 400 Soldiers Field Rd. © 617/562-4111 or 617/931-2000 (Ticketmaster). www.scullersjazz.com. Tickets $10–$45. Validated parking available.

Wally's Cafe This Boston institution, near a busy corner in the South End, opened in 1947. It draws a notably diverse crowd—black, white, straight, gay, affluent, indigent—and features nightly live music by local ensembles, students and instructors from the Berklee College of Music, and (on occasion) internationally renowned musicians. 427 Mass. Ave. © 617/424-1408. www.wallyscafe.com. No cover; 1-drink minimum. T: Orange Line to Mass. Ave.

ROCK & ALTERNATIVE

The Middle East The best rock club in the area books an impressive variety of progressive and alternative acts in two rooms (upstairs and downstairs) every night. Showcasing top local talent as well as bands with international reputations, it's a popular hangout that gets crowded, hot, and *loud*. 472–480 Mass. Ave., Central Sq., Cambridge. © 617/864-EAST or 617/931-2000 (Ticketmaster). www.mideastclub. com. Cover $7–$15. T: Red Line to Central.

Paradise Rock Club Hard by the Boston University campus, the medium-sized Paradise draws enthusiastic, student-intensive crowds for top local rock and alternative performers. You might see national names or locals who aren't ready to headline a big show. 967 Comm. Ave. © 617/562-8800, or 617/423-NEXT for tickets. www.dlclive.com. T: Green Line B to Pleasant St.

Toad *Value* Essentially a bar with a stage, this smoky, claustrophobic space attracts a savvy three-generation clientele with big local names and no cover. Toad enjoys good acoustics but not much elbowroom—a plus when restless musicians wander into the crowd. 1912 Mass. Ave., Cambridge. © 617/497-4950 (info line). No cover. T: Red Line to Porter.

T. T. the Bear's Place This no-frills spot generally attracts a young crowd, but 30-somethings will feel comfortable, too. Bookings range from cutting-edge alternative rock to ska to up-and-coming pop acts. New bands predominate early in the week, with more established artists on weekends. Open Sunday and Monday from 7pm to midnight, Tuesday through Saturday from 6pm to 1am. 10 Brookline St., Cambridge. © 617/492-0082 or 617/492-BEAR (concert line). www.ttthe bears.com. Cover $3–$15, usually less than $10. T: Red Line to Central.

BARS & LOUNGES

The Bay Tower This posh 33rd-floor lounge affords a mesmerizing view of the harbor, airport, and Faneuil Hall Marketplace. There's dancing to live music Monday through Saturday (piano on weeknights, jazz quartet Fri and Sat). No denim or athletic shoes. 60 State St. © 617/723-1666. www.baytower.com. T: Orange or Blue Line to State.

The Black Rose Purists might sneer at the Black Rose's touristy location, but performers don't. Sing along with the authentic entertainment at this jam-packed pub and restaurant at the edge of Faneuil Hall Marketplace. 160 State St. ⓒ 617/742-2286. www.irishconnection.com. Cover $3–$5. T: Orange or Blue Line to State.

Bristol Lounge An elegant room with cushy seating and a fireplace, the Bristol is an oasis anytime, and features a fabulous dessert buffet on weekend nights. There's live jazz every evening, and food until 11:30pm (12:30am on Fri and Sat). In the Four Seasons Hotel, 200 Boylston St. ⓒ 617/351-2053. T: Green Line to Arlington.

Bull & Finch Pub If you're out to impersonate a native, try not to be shocked when you enter "the *Cheers* bar" and it looks nothing like the bar on the TV show. (A new bar in Faneuil Hall Marketplace fills that niche—see the "Cheers" listing, below.) The Bull & Finch really is a neighborhood bar, but it's far better known for attracting legions of out-of-towners, who find good pub grub and plenty of souvenirs. 84 Beacon St. ⓒ 617/227-9605. www.cheersboston.com. T: Green Line to Arlington.

Casablanca Students and professors jam this legendary Harvard Square watering hole, especially on weekends. It offers an excellent jukebox, excellent food, and excellent eavesdropping. 40 Brattle St., Cambridge. ⓒ 617/876-0999. T: Red Line to Harvard.

Cheers Blatantly but good-naturedly courting fans of the sitcom, this bar centers on an area that exactly replicates the set of the TV show. Go ahead, you know you want to. Quincy Market Building, South Canopy, Faneuil Hall Marketplace. ⓒ 617/227-0150. www.cheersboston.com. T: Green or Blue Line to Government Center, or Orange Line to Haymarket.

Grendel's Den A vestige of pre-franchise Harvard Square, this cozy subterranean space is *the* place to celebrate turning 21. Recent grads and grad students dominate, but Grendel's has been so popular for so long that it also gets its share of Gen Y's parents. 89 Winthrop St., Cambridge. ⓒ 617/491-1050. T: Red Line to Harvard.

Hard Rock Cafe *(Kids)* This link in the chain is a fun one—just ask the other tourists in line with you. The bar is shaped like a guitar, and the stained-glass windows glorify rock stars. Memorabilia of Jimi Hendrix, Elvis Presley, Madonna, local favorites Aerosmith and the Cars, and others decorates the walls. 131 Clarendon St. ⓒ 617/424-ROCK. www.hardrock.com. T: Orange Line to Back Bay or Green Line to Copley.

John Harvard's Brew House This subterranean Harvard Square hangout pumps out terrific English-style brews in a clublike setting and prides itself on its food. 33 Dunster St., Cambridge. ⓒ 617/868-3585. www.johnharvards.com. T: Red Line to Harvard.

Mr. Dooley's Boston Tavern Sometimes an expertly poured Guinness is all you need. If one of the nicest bartenders in the city pours it, so much the better. This Financial District after-work spot offers many imported beers on tap, live music, and a menu of pub favorites. 77 Broad St. ⓒ 617/338-5656. www.somerspubs.com. Cover $3–$5 Fri–Sat. T: Orange Line to State or Blue Line to Aquarium.

The Purple Shamrock This rowdy, fun place near Faneuil Hall Marketplace attracts wall-to-wall 20-somethings with DJs, cover bands, and, we're obliged to report, karaoke (on Tues). 1 Union St. ⓒ 617/227-2060. www.irishconnection.com. Cover $3–$6 Thurs–Sat. T: Green or Blue Line to Government Center, or Orange Line to Haymarket.

The Rack Across the street from Faneuil Hall Marketplace, this enormous space is more nightspot than pool hall. It courts the after-work crowd with 22 tournament-size tables, two bars, and a lounge. You can order food until 1am and maybe do a little star-gazing—pro athletes turn up periodically. In good weather, the action spills onto the patio. 24 Clinton St. (at North St.). © 617/725-1051. www.therackboston.com. No cover. T: Green or Blue Line to Government Center, or Orange Line to Haymarket.

Samuel Adams Brew House Despite being in a plush hotel, this dark, sometimes noisy bar has a friendly vibe. It's an excellent place to try the signature local brew, guaranteed to be served fresh. Choose from the dozen beers on tap or order a sampler of four. In the Lenox Hotel, 710 Boylston St. © 617/536-2739. T: Green Line to Copley.

Top of the Hub The 52nd-story view of greater Boston from this appealing lounge is especially lovely at sunset. There's music and dancing nightly. Dress is casual but neat. Prudential Center, 800 Boylston St. © 617/536-1775. T: Green Line E to Prudential.

Whiskey Park New York wannabes congregate outside the Boston incarnation of the nightclub chain cropping up around the country under the direction of Rande (don't call me Mr. Cindy Crawford) Gerber. A dark, plush space with wood and copper accents, Whiskey Park packs in the black-clad 20-somethings who line up outside to seek admission. Be sure to check out the space-age restrooms (on the lower level). In the Boston Park Plaza Hotel, 64 Arlington St. © 617/542-1482. T: Green Line to Arlington.

5

Side Trips from Boston: Lexington & Concord, the North Shore & Plymouth

by Marie Morris

Besides being, in the words of Oliver Wendell Holmes, "the hub of the solar system," Boston is the hub of a network of wonderful day trips and longer excursions. The destinations in this chapter are lively communities where you'll find sights and attractions of great beauty and historical significance. Exploring can take as little as half a day or as long as a week or more.

WEST OF BOSTON If time is short, combine a visit to Cambridge (see chapter 4) with a trip to Lexington and Concord for a hefty dose of American history. The route that Paul Revere took out of Boston on April 18, 1775, is tough to follow—he started by crossing the harbor in a rowboat, for one thing—but his fellow rider William Dawes cut through Harvard Square. Both proceeded to warn the colonists that British troops were on the march.

NORTH OF BOSTON Great prosperity came to eastern Massachusetts after the Revolution, as the new nation took advantage of the lifting of British trade barriers. Today, the spoils of the China trade adorn mansions and public edifices in seaside locales such as Marblehead, Salem, and Cape Ann. Fishing is still an important industry, but these days the area caters more to commuters and tourists than to those who make their living from the sea. A worthwhile detour from the north or west is Lowell, a once-decrepit mill town where tourism is now the largest industry.

SOUTH OF BOSTON The communities between Boston and Cape Cod are mostly commuter suburbs. The prime sightseeing destination is Plymouth, one of the oldest permanent European settlements in North America. It's a pleasant place where you can walk in the footsteps of the Pilgrims—and of the countless out-of-towners who flock here in summer and at Thanksgiving. Farther south, the old whaling port of New Bedford makes an interesting detour.

1 Lexington ⓕ★

9 miles (14km) NW of downtown Boston; 6 miles (10km) NW of Cambridge; 6 miles (10km) E of Concord

A country village turned prosperous suburb, Lexington takes great pride in its history. It's a pleasant town with some engaging destinations, but it lacks the atmosphere and abundant attractions of nearby Concord. Being sure to leave time for a tour of the Buckman Tavern, you can schedule as little as a couple of hours to explore downtown Lexington, possibly en route to Concord. A visit can

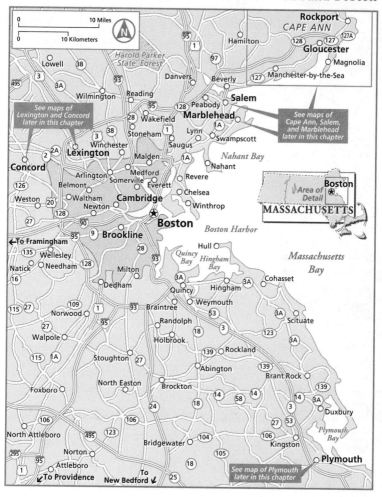

See maps of Lexington and Concord later in this chapter

See maps of Cape Ann, Salem, and Marblehead later in this chapter

See map of Plymouth later in this chapter

also fill a half or full day. The town contains part of Minute Man National Historical Park, which is definitely worth a visit.

The shooting phase of the Revolutionary War started here, with a skirmish on the town green. It began when British troops clashed with local militia members, who were known as "Minutemen" for their ability to assemble on short notice. British soldiers marched from Boston to Lexington late on April 18, 1775. Tipped off, Paul Revere and William Dawes rode ahead to sound the warning. They did their job so well that the alarm came long before the advancing forces. The Lexington Minutemen, under the command of Capt. John Parker, got the word shortly after midnight, but the redcoats were still several hours away. The colonists repaired to their homes and the Buckman Tavern. Five hours later, some 700 British troops under Major Pitcairn arrived.

A tense standoff ensued. Three times Pitcairn ordered them to disperse, but the patriots—fewer than 100, and some accounts say 77—refused. Parker called: "Stand your ground. Don't fire unless fired upon, but if they mean to have a war,

---

Tips Planning Pointers

If you have a few days to explore and history is your main motivation, consider approaching the area in roughly chronological order. Start in Plymouth with the Pilgrims, and then move on to Lexington and Concord to learn about the rebellious colonists. Finally, visit the North Shore and Cape Ann, which flourished after the Revolution. If you lack the time or inclination to make your own arrangements, consider an escorted tour. One reliable company is Gray Line's **Brush Hill Tours,** 435 High St., Randolph (© **800/343-1328** or 781/986-6100; www.grayline.com).

---

let it begin here!" Finally the captain, perhaps realizing as the sky grew light how badly outnumbered his men were, gave the order to fall back.

As the Minutemen began to scatter, a shot rang out. One British company charged into the fray, and the colonists attempted to regroup as Pitcairn tried unsuccessfully to call off his troops. Nobody knows who started the shooting, but when it was over, eight militia members, including a drummer boy, lay dead, and 10 were wounded.

ESSENTIALS

GETTING THERE From downtown Boston, take Storrow or Memorial Drive to Route 2. Follow Route 2 from Cambridge through Belmont, exit at Route 4/225, and follow signs to downtown Lexington. Or take Route 128 (I-95) to Exit 31A and follow signs. If it's not rush hour, allow about 35 minutes. **Mass. Ave.** (the same street as in Boston and Cambridge) runs through the center of town. There's metered parking on the street and in several municipal lots.

The **Massachusetts Bay Transportation Authority,** or **MBTA,** (© **800/ 392-6100** outside Mass., or 617/222-3200; www.mbta.com) runs bus routes no. 62 (Bedford) and 76 (Hanscom) to Lexington from Alewife station, the last stop on the Red Line. The one-way fare is 75¢; the trip takes about 25 minutes. Buses operate Monday through Saturday every hour during the day and every half hour during rush periods. There's no Sunday service.

At press time, there was no public transportation between Lexington and Concord, but it may have begun by the time you visit; contact the Chamber of Commerce in either town for details.

VISITOR INFORMATION The Chamber of Commerce **visitor center,** 1875 Mass. Ave. (© **781/862-2480;** www.lexingtonchamber.org), distributes maps and information. The town website (http://ci.lexington.ma.us) has a section for visitors. You can also contact the **Greater Merrimack Valley Convention & Visitors Bureau** (© **800/443-3332** or 978/459-6150; www.merrimackvalley.org).

GETTING AROUND Downtown Lexington is easily negotiable on foot, and most of the attractions are within walking distance. If you prefer not to walk to the Munroe Tavern and the Museum of Our National Heritage (see below), buses no. 62 and 76 pass by on Mass. Ave.

SPECIAL EVENTS Patriot's Day, a state holiday observed on the third Monday in April, commemorates the start of the Revolution. Celebrations include a re-enactment of the battle and other festivities. Make your Patriot's Day reservations well in advance: It's the day of the Boston Marathon and the start of a school vacation week.

Lexington

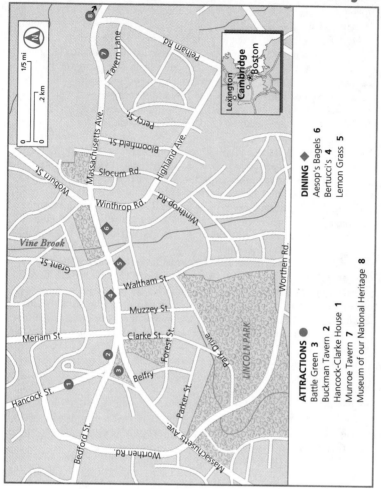

ATTRACTIONS
Battle Green **3**
Buckman Tavern **2**
Hancock-Clarke House **1**
Munroe Tavern **7**
Museum of our National Heritage **8**

DINING
Aesop's Bagels **6**
Bertucci's **4**
Lemon Grass **5**

EXPLORING THE HISTORIC SITES

Minute Man National Historical Park is in Lexington, Concord, and Lincoln (see "Concord," below).

Start your visit to Lexington at the **visitor center,** on the town common or "Battle Green," next to a bustling business district. It's open daily from 9am to 5pm (Nov through mid-Apr from 10am–4pm). A diorama and accompanying narrative illustrate the Battle of Lexington. The **Minuteman statue** (1900) on the green is of Capt. John Parker, who commanded the militia. The **Old Revolutionary Monument** (1799) marks the grave of seven of the eight colonists who died in the conflict, which the **Line of Battle Boulder** commemorates. The **Memorial to the Lexington Minutemen** bears the names of the men who fell in the battle. Across Mass. Ave., near Clarke Street, is the **Old Belfry,** a reproduction of the freestanding bell that sounded the alarm the day of the battle. **Ye Olde Burying Ground,** at the west end of the green, dates to

1690 and contains Parker's grave. A stop at the visitor center and a walk around the monuments takes about half an hour, and gives a good sense of what went on here and why the participants are still held in such high esteem.

Three important destinations in Lexington were among the country's first historic houses when their restoration began in the 1920s. The **Lexington Historical Society** (✆ 781/862-1703; www.lexingtonhistory.org) operates all three. Currently headquartered in the Munroe Tavern, the society is in the process of restoring a building on Depot Square (downtown, off Mass. Ave. near the Battle Green) that will hold exhibits, offices, and a gift shop.

The **Buckman Tavern** ★★, 1 Bedford St. (✆ 781/862-5598), built around 1710, is the only building still on the green that was here on April 19, 1775. If time is short and you have to pick just one house to visit, this is it. The interior has been restored to its appearance on the day of the battle. You'll see the original bar and front door, which has a hole in it from a British musket ball. The Minutemen gathered here to wait for word of British troop movements, and brought their wounded here after the conflict. On the excellent tour, costumed guides describe the history of the building and its inhabitants, explain the battle, and discuss colonial life.

Within walking distance is the **Hancock-Clarke House,** 36 Hancock St. (✆ 781/861-0928). Samuel Adams and John Hancock, who had left Boston several days earlier upon learning that the British were after them, were sleeping here (or trying to) when Revere arrived. They fled to nearby Woburn. Built around 1698 by Hancock's grandfather and lavishly improved by his uncle, the house, restored and furnished in colonial style, contains the Historical Society's museum.

The British took over the **Munroe Tavern** ★, 1332 Mass. Ave. (about 1 mile/ 1.6km east of the green), to use as their headquarters and field hospital. The taproom ceiling still has a bullet hole made by a careless soldier. The 1690 building holds many fascinating artifacts. The furniture, carefully preserved by the Munroe family, includes the table and chair where President Washington dined in 1789. The historically accurate gardens at the rear (free admission) are beautifully planted and maintained.

All three houses are open for guided tours April through October, Monday through Saturday from 10am to 5pm and Sunday from 1 to 5pm. The Buckman Tavern is also open in late March and November. Admission for adults is $5 per house, $8 for two houses, $12 for all three; for seniors, $7 for two houses, $11 for all three; for children 6 to 16, $3 per house, $5 for two or three. The last tour starts 30 minutes before closing time; tours take 30 to 45 minutes. Call for information about group tours, which are offered by appointment.

Museum of Our National Heritage ★ _Kids_   This fascinating museum explores history through popular culture. It makes an entertaining complement to the colonial focus of the rest of the town. The installations in the six exhibition spaces change regularly; you can start with another dose of the Revolution,

---

Tips Poetry in Motion

Before you set out for Lexington and Concord, you might want to read **"Paul Revere's Ride,"** Henry Wadsworth Longfellow's classic but historically questionable poem that dramatically chronicles the events of April 18 and 19, 1775.

the permanent exhibit *Let It Begin Here.* Other topics have ranged from Route 66 to George Washington, banjos to American circus posters. Lectures, concerts, and family programs are also offered, and the cafe serves lunch daily. The Scottish Rite of Freemasonry sponsors the museum.

33 Marrett Rd., Rte. 2A (at Mass. Ave.). ℂ 781/861-6559 or 781/861-9638. www.monh.org. Free admission. Mon–Sat 10am–5pm; Sun noon–5pm. Closed Jan 1, Thanksgiving, Dec 25. Bus: 62 or 76 from downtown Lexington to Rte. 2A.

SHOPPING

A stroll along **Mass. Ave.** near the center of town won't disappoint. Start at **The Muse's Window,** 1656 Mass. Ave. (ℂ **781/274-6873**), an excellent crafts gallery. As you head back toward the green, check out **Waldenbooks,** 1713 Mass. Ave. (ℂ **781/862-7870**); **Upper Story Books,** 1730 Mass. Ave. (ℂ **781/862-0999**); and the **Crafty Yankee,** 1838 Mass. Ave. (ℂ **781/861-1219**). One of the best-known yarn shops in eastern Massachusetts is **Wild & Woolly Studio,** 7A Meriam St., off Mass. Ave. (ℂ **781/861-7717**).

WHERE TO STAY

Bedford is 15 minutes from downtown Lexington on Route 4/225, across I-95. The **Ramada Sovereign Inn,** 340 Great Rd., Bedford (ℂ **888/298-2054** or 781/275-6700), is a pleasant motor inn with an indoor pool. Rates are about $109 to $129 in high season.

Renaissance Bedford Hotel ⭐ The sights in Lexington and Concord are convenient to this three-story, lodge-style hotel, which neatly makes the transition from a weekday business destination to a weekend family resort. There's also plenty to do without leaving the property. The well-maintained guest rooms contain oversize work desks; larger units have king-size beds. The hotel shuttle transports guests to destinations within 5 miles (8km), including the Burlington Mall.

44 Middlesex Tpk., Bedford, MA 01730. ℂ 800/HOTELS-1 or 781/275-5500. Fax 781/275-3042. www.renaissancehotels.com/BOSSB. 284 units. Sun–Thurs $159–$249 double; Fri–Sat $119–$229 double. Extra person $15. Children under 19 stay free in parents' room. Weekend packages and senior discounts available. AE, DC, DISC, MC, V. **Amenities:** Restaurant (eclectic), lounge; indoor pool; indoor/outdoor tennis courts; fitness center; Jacuzzi; sauna; shuttle; business center; 24-hr. room service; laundry service; dry cleaning. *In room:* A/C, TV, dataport, minibar, coffeemaker, hair dryer, iron.

Sheraton Lexington Inn Overlooking the interstate but sheltered from the noise by a stand of trees, this two-story hotel is 5 minutes from downtown by car. It offers the usual chain amenities—reliable, if generic. Rooms are large enough to hold a wing chair or couch, and some have balconies. It's a decent choice for families, and popular with travelers who have business on the Route 128 high-tech corridor.

727 Marrett Rd. (Exit 30B off I-95), Lexington, MA 02173. ℂ 800/325-3535 or 781/862-8700. Fax 781/863-0404. www.sheraton.com. 119 units. $89–$219 double; $199–$369 suite. Extra person $10. AAA and AARP discounts available. AE, DC, DISC, MC, V. **Amenities:** Restaurant (American), lounge; outdoor pool; exercise room. *In room:* A/C, TV, dataport, coffeemaker, iron.

WHERE TO DINE

The cafe at the **Museum of Our National Heritage** (see above) is a popular spot for lunch. **Bertucci's,** 1777 Mass. Ave. (ℂ **781/860-9000**), is a branch of the family-friendly pizzeria chain. **Aesop's Bagels,** 1666 Mass. Ave. (ℂ **781/674-2990**), is a good place to pick up a light meal.

Lemon Grass THAI   This popular restaurant is a former coffee shop disguised with bamboo decorations and the aroma of Asian spices. You might start with *satay* (skewers of meat served with delectable peanut sauce) or chicken coconut soup, with a kick of pepper. Entrees include a tasty rendition of traditional pad Thai and excellent curry dishes. The accommodating staff will adjust the heat and spice to suit your tastes.

1710 Mass. Ave. ✆ **781/862-3530.** Main courses $7–$9 lunch, $8–$16 dinner. AE, DISC, MC, V. Mon–Fri 11:30am–3pm; Mon–Thurs 5–9:30pm, Fri–Sat 5–10pm, Sun 4–9pm.

2 Concord ✫✫✫

18 miles (29km) NW of Boston; 15 miles (24km) NW of Cambridge; 6 miles (10km) W of Lexington.

Concord (say "conquered") revels in its legacy as a center of groundbreaking thought and its role in the country's political and intellectual history. A visit can easily fill a day; if your interests are specialized or time is short, a half-day excursion is reasonable. For an excellent overview of town history, start your explorations at the Concord Museum.

After just a little time in this lovely town, you may find yourself adopting the local attitude toward two of its most famous residents: Ralph Waldo Emerson, who comes across as a well-respected uncle figure, and Henry David Thoreau, everyone's favorite eccentric cousin. Long before they wandered the countryside, the first official battle of the Revolutionary War took place at the North Bridge, now part of Minute Man National Historical Park. By the middle of the 19th century, Concord was the center of the Transcendentalist movement. Homes of Emerson, Thoreau, Nathaniel Hawthorne, and Louisa May Alcott are open to visitors, as is the authors' final resting place, Sleepy Hollow Cemetery.

ESSENTIALS

GETTING THERE   From Lexington (10 min. by car), take Route 2A west from Mass. Ave. (Rte. 4/225) at the Museum of Our National Heritage; follow the BATTLE ROAD signs. From Boston and Cambridge (30–40 min.), take Route 2 into Lincoln and stay in the right lane. Where the main road makes a sharp left, go straight onto Cambridge Turnpike, and follow signs to HISTORIC CONCORD. To go directly to Walden Pond, use the left lane, take what's now Route 2/2A another mile or so, and turn left onto Route 126. There's parking throughout town and at the attractions.

The **commuter rail** (✆ **800/392-6100** outside Mass., or 617/222-3200; www.mbta.com) takes about 45 minutes from North Station in Boston, with a stop at Porter Square in Cambridge. The round-trip fare is $8. The station is about ¾ of a mile (1km) over flat terrain from the town center. There is no bus service from Boston to Concord.

At press time, there was no public transportation between Lexington and Concord, but it may have begun by the time you visit; contact the Chamber of Commerce in either town for details.

VISITOR INFORMATION   The **Chamber of Commerce,** 155 Everett St. (✆ **978/369-3120;** www.concordmachamber.org), maintains an information booth on Heywood Street, 1 block southeast of Monument Square. It's open from 9:30am to 4:30pm on weekends in April and daily May through October. Ninety-minute tours are available Friday through Sunday and on Monday holidays. Weekday and group tours are available by appointment. The community (**www.concordma.com**) and town (**www.concordnet.org**) websites include visitor information. You can also contact the **Greater Merrimack Valley**

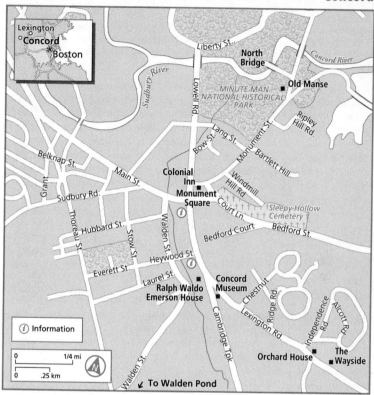

Convention & Visitors Bureau (© 800/443-3332 or 978/459-6150; www. merrimackvalley.org).

GETTING AROUND Major attractions are within walking distance of downtown. If you're trying to stop everywhere in a day or are visiting Walden Pond or Great Meadows, you'll need a car.

SEEING THE SIGHTS
LITERARY LANDMARKS & HISTORIC ATTRACTIONS

Concord Museum ★★ *Kids*   Just when you're (understandably) suspecting that everything interesting in this area started on April 18, 1775, and ended the next day, this superb museum sets you straight. It's a great place to start your visit to the town. The **History Galleries** ★★ explore the question "Why Concord?" Artifacts, murals, films, maps, documents, and other presentations illustrate the town's role as a Native American settlement, Revolutionary War battleground, 19th-century intellectual center, and focal point of the 20th-century historic preservation movement. One of the lanterns that signaled Paul Revere from the Old North Church is on display. You'll also see the contents of Ralph Waldo Emerson's study and a large collection of Henry David Thoreau's belongings. Pick up a **family activity pack** ★ as you enter and use the games and reproduction artifacts (including a quill pen and powder horn) to give the kids a hands-on feel for life in the past.

200 Lexington Rd. (at Cambridge Tpk.). © **978/369-9609** (recorded info) or 978/369-9763. www.concord museum.org. Admission $7 adults, $6 seniors and students, $3 children under 16; $16 per family. Apr–Dec Mon–Sat 9am–5pm, Sun noon–5pm; Jan–Mar Mon–Sat 11am–4pm, Sun 1–4pm. Parking allowed on road. Follow Lexington Rd. out of Concord Center and bear right at museum onto Cambridge Tpk.; entrance is on left.

The Old Manse ✦　The engaging history of this home touches on the military and the literary, but it's mostly the story of a family. The Rev. William Emerson built the Old Manse in 1770 and watched the Battle of Concord from his yard. For almost 170 years, the house was home to his widow, her second husband, their descendants, and two famous friends. Nathaniel Hawthorne and his bride, Sophia Peabody, moved in after their marriage in 1842 and stayed for 3 years. As a wedding present, Henry David Thoreau sowed the vegetable garden for them. This is also where William's grandson Ralph Waldo Emerson wrote the essay "Nature." Today, you'll see mementos and memorabilia of the Emerson and Ripley families and of the Hawthornes, who scratched notes on two windows with Sophia's diamond ring.

269 Monument St. (at North Bridge). © **978/369-3909**. www.thetrustees.org. Guided tours $6.50 adults, $5.50 seniors and students, $4.50 children 6–12; $20 per family. Mid-Apr to Oct Mon–Sat 10am–5pm, Sun and holidays noon–5pm (last tour at 4:30pm). Closed Nov to mid-Apr. From Concord Center, follow Monument St. to North Bridge parking lot (on right); Old Manse is on left.

Orchard House ✦✦✦ (Kids)　*Little Women* (1868), Louisa May Alcott's best-known and most popular work, was written and set at Orchard House. Seeing the family home brings the Alcotts to life for legions of female visitors and their pleasantly surprised male companions. Fans won't want to miss the excellent tour, copiously illustrated with heirlooms. Serious buffs can check in advance for information on holiday programs and other special events, some of which require reservations.

　　Louisa's father, the writer and educator Amos Bronson Alcott, created Orchard House by joining and restoring two homes. The family lived here from 1858 to 1877, socializing in the same circles as Emerson, Thoreau, and Hawthorne. Other relatives served as the models for the characters in *Little Women*. Anna ("Meg"), the eldest, was an amateur actress, and May ("Amy") a talented artist. Elizabeth ("Beth"), a gifted musician, died before the family moved to this house. Their mother, the social activist Abigail May Alcott, frequently assumed the role of breadwinner—Bronson, Louisa wrote in her journal, had "no gift for money making."

　　Note: Call before visiting; an extensive preservation project is under way and may be continuing when you're here.

399 Lexington Rd. © **978/369-4118**. www.louisamayalcott.org. Guided tours $7 adults, $6 seniors and students, $4 children 6–17; $16 per family. Apr–Oct Mon–Sat 10am–4:30pm, Sun 1–4:30pm; Nov–Mar Mon–Fri 11am–3pm, Sat 10am–4:30pm, Sun 1–4:30pm. Closed Jan 1–15, Easter, Thanksgiving, Dec 25. Follow Lexington Rd. out of Concord Center and bear left at Concord Museum; house is on left. Overflow parking across the street.

Ralph Waldo Emerson House　This house offers an instructive look at the days when a philosopher could attain the status we now associate with rock stars. Emerson, also an essayist and poet, lived here from 1835 until his death, in 1882. He moved here after marrying his second wife, Lydia Jackson, whom he called "Lydian"; she called him "Mr. Emerson," as the staff still does. The tour gives a good look at his personal side and at the fashionably ornate interior decoration of the time. You'll see original furnishings and some of Emerson's personal effects.

28 Cambridge Tpk. © **978/369-2236.** Guided tours $6 adults, $4 seniors and students. Call to arrange group tours (10 people or more). Mid-Apr to Oct Thurs–Sat 10am–4:30pm, Sun 2–4:30pm. Closed Nov to mid-Apr. Follow Cambridge Tpk. out of Concord Center; just before Concord Museum, house is on right.

Sleepy Hollow Cemetery ✦ Follow the signs for AUTHOR'S RIDGE and climb the hill to the graves of some of the town's literary lights, including the Alcotts, Emerson, Hawthorne, and Thoreau. Emerson's grave bears no religious symbols, just an uncarved quartz boulder. Thoreau's grave is nearby; at his funeral, in 1862, his old friend Emerson concluded his eulogy with these words: ". . . wherever there is knowledge, wherever there is virtue, wherever there is beauty, he will find a home."

Entrance on Rte. 62 W. © **978/318-3233.** Daily 7am to dusk. Call ahead for wheelchair access. No buses allowed.

The Wayside ✦ The Wayside was Nathaniel Hawthorne's home from 1852 until his death, in 1864. The Alcotts also lived here (the girls called it "the yellow house"), as did Harriett Lothrop, who wrote the *Five Little Peppers* books under the pen name Margaret Sidney and owned most of the current furnishings. The Wayside is part of Minute Man National Historical Park, and the fascinating 45-minute ranger-led tour illuminates the occupants' lives and the house's crazy-quilt architecture. The exhibit in the barn (free admission) consists of audio presentations and figures of the authors.

455 Lexington Rd. © **978/369-6975.** www.nps.gov/mima/wayside. Guided tours $4 adults, free for children under 17. May–Oct Thurs–Tues 10am–4:30pm. Closed Nov–Apr. Follow Lexington Rd. out of Concord Center past Concord Museum and Orchard House. Parking across the street.

MINUTE MAN NATIONAL HISTORICAL PARK ✦✦

This 900-acre (365-hectare) park preserves the scene of the first Revolutionary War battle, on April 19, 1775. Encouraged by their victory at Lexington, the British continued to Concord in search of stockpiled arms (which the colonists had already moved). Warned of the advance, the Minutemen crossed the North Bridge, evading the "regulars" standing guard, and awaited reinforcements on a hilltop. The British searched nearby homes and burned any guns they found, and the Minutemen, seeing the smoke, mistakenly thought the soldiers were burning the town. The gunfire that ensued, the opening salvo of the Revolution, is remembered as "the shot heard round the world."

The park is open daily year-round. A visit can take as little as half an hour—for a jaunt to the North Bridge—or as long as half a day (or more), if you stop at both visitor centers and perhaps participate in a ranger-led program. To reach the bridge (a reproduction) from Concord Center, follow Monument Street until you see the parking lot on the right. Walk a short distance to the bridge, stopping along the unpaved path to read and hear the narratives. On one side of the bridge is a plaque commemorating the British soldiers who died in the Revolutionary War. On the other side is Daniel Chester French's ***Minute Man*** statue, engraved with a stanza of the poem Emerson wrote for the dedication ceremony in 1876.

You can also start at the **North Bridge Visitor Center** ✦, 174 Liberty St., off Monument Street (© **978/369-6993;** www.nps.gov/mima), which overlooks the Concord River and the bridge. A diorama and video illustrate the Battle of Concord; exhibits include uniforms, weapons, and tools of colonial and British soldiers. Park rangers lead programs and answer questions. Outside, picnicking is allowed, and the scenery (especially the fall foliage) is lovely. The bridge isn't far; you'll want to see the exhibits here, too. The center is open daily from 9am to 5:30pm (until 4pm in winter).

At the Lexington end of the park, the **Minute Man Visitor Center** (② 781/862-7753; www.nps.gov/mima) ⊛, off Route 2A, about ½ a mile (1km) mile west of I-95, Exit 30B, is open daily from 9am to 5pm (until 4pm in winter). The park includes the first 4 miles (6.5km) of the Battle Road, the route the defeated British troops took as they left Concord. At the visitor center, you'll see a fascinating multimedia program on the Revolution, informational displays, and a 40-foot (12m) mural illustrating the battle. On summer weekends, rangers lead tours of the park—call ahead for times. The **Battle Road Trail,** a 5½-mile (9km) interpretive path, carries pedestrian, wheelchair, and bicycle traffic. Panels and granite markers display information about the area's military, social, and natural history.

Also on the park grounds, on Old Bedford Road, is the **Hartwell Tavern.** Costumed interpreters demonstrate daily life on a farm and in a tavern in colonial days. It's not Disney, but it is interesting. It's open from 9:30am to 5pm, daily June through August and weekends only in April, May, September, and October. Admission is free.

NEARBY SIGHTS

DeCordova Museum and Sculpture Park ⊛⊛   Indoors and out, the DeCordova shows the work of American contemporary and modern artists, with an emphasis on living New England residents. The main building, on a leafy hilltop, overlooks a pond and the area's only outdoor public sculpture park. The museum also has a roof garden and a sculpture terrace that displays the work of one sculptor per year. Picnicking is allowed in the sculpture park; bring your lunch or buy it at the cafe (open Wed–Sun 11am–3pm). Free tours of the main galleries start at 2pm Wednesday and Sunday year-round; sculpture-park tours run May through October on Saturday and Sunday at 1pm.

51 Sandy Pond Rd., Lincoln. ② 781/259-8355. www.decordova.org. Museum: $6 adults; $4 seniors, students, and children 6–12. Tues–Sun and Mon holidays 11am–5pm. Sculpture park: Free admission. Daily daylight hours. Closed Jan 1, July 4, Thanksgiving, Dec 25. From Rte. 2 East, take Rte. 126 to Baker Bridge Rd. (first left after Walden Pond). When it ends, go right onto Sandy Pond Rd.; museum is on left. From Rte. 2 West, take I-95 to Exit 28B, follow Trapelo Rd. 2½ miles (4km) to Sandy Pond Rd., then follow signs.

Gropius House ⊛   Architect Walter Gropius (1883–1969), founder of the Bauhaus school of design, built this home for his family in the prosperous suburb of Lincoln in 1937. Having taken a job at the Harvard Graduate School of Design, he worked with Marcel Breuer to design the hilltop house, now maintained by the Society for the Preservation of New England Antiquities. They used traditional materials such as clapboard, brick, and fieldstone, with components then seldom seen in domestic architecture, including glass blocks and welded steel. Breuer designed many of the furnishings, which were made for the family at the Bauhaus. Decorated as it was in the last decade of Gropius's life, the house affords a revealing look at his life, career, and philosophy. Call for information on special tours and workshops.

68 Baker Bridge Rd., Lincoln. ② 781/259-8098 or 617/227-3957, ext. 300. www.spnea.org. Guided tours $8 adults, $4 students. Tours on the hour June–Oct 15 Wed–Sun 11am–4pm; Oct 16–May Sat–Sun 11am–4pm. Take Rte. 2 to Rte. 126 south to left on Baker Bridge Rd.; house is on right. From I-95, Exit 28B, follow Trapelo Rd. to Sandy Pond Rd., go left onto Baker Bridge Rd.; house is on left.

WILDERNESS RETREATS

The titles of Henry David Thoreau's first two published works can serve as starting points: *A Week on the Concord and Merrimack Rivers* (1849) and *Walden* (1854).

To see the area from water level, there's no need to take a week; 2 hours or so should suffice. Rent a **canoe** ★ at the **South Bridge Boathouse,** 496 Main St. (© **978/369-9438;** www.sbridge.qpg.com), about seven-tenths of a mile (1km) west of the center of town, and paddle to the North Bridge and back. Rates are about $11 per hour on weekends, less on weekdays.

At the **Walden Pond State Reservation** ★★, 915 Walden St., Route 126 (© **978/369-3254;** www.state.ma.us/dem/parks/wldn.htm), a pile of stones marks the site of the cabin where Thoreau lived from 1845 to 1847. Today the picturesque reservation is an extremely popular destination for walking (a path circles the pond), swimming, and fishing. Although crowded, it's well preserved and insulated from development, making it less difficult than you might expect to imagine Thoreau's experience. Call for the schedule of interpretive programs. No dogs or bikes are allowed. From Memorial Day to Labor Day, a daily parking fee is charged and the lot fills early every day—call before setting out, as the rangers turn away visitors if the park has reached capacity (1,000). To get here from Concord Center, take Walden Street (Rte. 126) south, cross Route 2, and follow signs to the parking lot.

Another Thoreau haunt, an especially popular destination for birders, is **Great Meadows National Wildlife Refuge** ★, Weir Hill Road, Sudbury (© **978/443-4661;** http://northeast.fws.gov/ma/grm.htm). The Concord portion of the 3,400-acre (1,377-hectare) refuge includes 2½ miles (4km) of walking trails around man-made ponds that attract abundant wildlife. More than 200 species of native and migratory birds have been recorded. The refuge is open daily from sunrise to sunset; admission is free. Follow Route 62 (Bedford St.) east out of Concord Center for 1⅓ miles (2km), then turn left onto Monsen Road.

SHOPPING

Downtown Concord, off **Monument Square,** is a terrific shopping destination. Here you'll find the **Concord Toy Shop,** 4 Walden St. (© **978/369-2553**); the **Grasshopper Shop,** 36 Main St. (© **978/369-8295**), which carries women's clothing and accessories; jewelry and art at **Catseye,** 48 Monument Sq. (© **978/369-8377**); and the **Concord Bookshop,** 65 Main St. (© **978/371-2672**). The compact shopping district in **West Concord,** along Route 62, boasts the old-fashioned **West Concord 5 & 10,** 106 Commonwealth Ave. (© **978/369-9011**), which carries everything from light bulbs to lace.

WHERE TO STAY

The **Best Western at Historic Concord,** 740 Elm St. (© **800/528-1234** or 978/369-6100), is just off Route 2, about 2 miles (3km) from the center of town. The motel has a fitness room and a seasonal outdoor pool; doubles go for $119 to $129.

Colonial Inn ★   The main building of the Colonial Inn has overlooked Monument Square since 1716. Like many historic inns, it's not luxurious, but it is comfortable and centrally located. Additions since it became a hotel in 1889 have left the inn large enough to offer modern conveniences and small enough to feel friendly. It's popular with local businesspeople as well as vacationers, especially during foliage season. The 12 original guest rooms—one of which (room 24) supposedly is haunted—are in great demand. Reserve early if you want to stay in the main inn, which is decorated (surprise, surprise) in colonial style. Rooms in the Prescott wing are larger, with country-style decor; a cottage annex holds two good-sized apartments.

Tips **Road Trips North of Boston**

For convenience and flexibility, drive if you can. The trip from Boston to Cape Ann on I-93 and Route 128 takes about an hour. A more leisurely excursion on Routes 1A, 129, and 114 allows you to explore Marblehead and Salem. You can also follow Route 1 to I-95 and Route 128, but don't attempt it during rush hour. To take Route 1A, leave downtown through the Callahan Tunnel, which is in the middle of the Big Dig. If you miss the tunnel and wind up on I-93, follow signs to Route 1 and pick up Route 1A in Revere. The **North of Boston Convention & Visitors Bureau** (© **800/ 742-5306** or 978/977-7760; www.northofboston.org) publishes a visitor guide that covers many destinations in this chapter.

The dining options are pleasant, though hardly exciting—you're here for the atmosphere, not the cuisine. Two lounges serve light meals; sit on the porch and you'll have a front-row seat for the action on Monument Square. The lovely restaurant serves salads, sandwiches, and pasta at lunch, and traditional American fare at dinner. Afternoon tea is served Wednesday through Sunday; reservations required (© **978/369-2373**).

48 Monument Sq., Concord, MA 01742. © **800/370-9200** or 978/369-9200. Fax 978/369-2170. www. concordscolonialinn.com. 45 units (some with shower only). Apr–Oct $195–$205 main inn, $159–$189 Prescott wing, $325 cottage; Nov–Mar $165 main inn, $145 Prescott wing, $250 cottage. AE, DC, DISC, MC, V. **Amenities:** Restaurant (American), 2 lounges, bar with live jazz and blues on weekends; laundry service; dry cleaning. *In room:* A/C, TV.

Hawthorne Inn ★★   This is the quintessential country inn. Built around 1870, it sits on a tree-shaded property across the street from Nathaniel Hawthorne's home, the Wayside. Antiques and handmade quilts enhance the rooms, which aren't huge but are meticulously maintained and gorgeously decorated. Original art is on display throughout, and there's a small pond in the peaceful garden. Personable innkeepers Gregory Burch and Marilyn Mudry, who have been in business for more than 20 years, acquaint interested guests with the philosophical, spiritual, military, and literary aspects of Concord's history.

462 Lexington Rd., Concord, MA 01742. © **978/369-5610.** Fax 978/287-4949. www.concordmass.com. 7 units (some with shower only). $175–$295 double. Rates include continental breakfast. Extra person $20. Off-season discounts available. AE, DISC, MC, V. From Concord Center, take Lexington Rd. ¼ mile (0.5km) east; inn is on right. *In room:* A/C, TV.

A HISTORIC INN NEARBY

Longfellow's Wayside Inn ★★   Worth a visit even if you're not spending the night, this delightful institution dates to 1716 and got its name when Henry Wadsworth Longfellow published *Tales of a Wayside Inn* in 1863. Part of a non-profit educational and charitable trust, it claims to be the country's oldest operating inn. All 10 guest rooms are attractively decorated and furnished with antiques, but only two (the most popular, of course) are in the original building. Reserve as early as possible.

In addition to being a popular wedding and honeymoon destination, the inn is the centerpiece of what amounts to a tiny theme park. Buildings on the 106-acre (43-hectare) property include the Redstone School of "Mary Had a Little Lamb" fame, a wedding chapel, and a working gristmill. The mill stone grinds the wheat flour and cornmeal used in the inn's baked goods. Old grindstones dot the lawn, a pleasant spot for sunbathing.

In the rambling **dining rooms** ⟨⟩, costumed staff members dish up generous portions of traditional New England fare, which often incorporates produce grown at the inn. The menu changes daily; favorite choices include prime rib, lobster casserole, and strawberry shortcake. You'll see lots of families—this seems to be *the* place for grandparents' birthdays. Food is served Monday through Saturday from 11:30am to 3pm and 5 to 9pm, Sunday from noon to 8pm (dinner menu only). Main courses are $9 to $15 at lunch, $17 to $30 at dinner. Reservations are recommended, especially on weekends.

Wayside Inn Rd., Sudbury, MA 01776. ⟨⟩ **800/339-1776** or 978/443-1776. Fax 978/443-8041. www.wayside.org. 10 units (some with shower only). Summer $122–$155 double. Rates include breakfast. Extra person $15. Off-season discounts available. AE, DC, DISC, MC, V. Closed July 4th and Dec 25. From Main St. in Concord, follow Sudbury Rd. to Rte. 20 west; 11 miles (18km) after passing I-95, bear right onto Wayside Inn Rd.; inn is on the right. *In room:* A/C.

WHERE TO DINE

See also the **Colonial Inn** and **Longfellow's Wayside Inn,** above. For basic to lavish picnic provisions, stop in downtown Concord at the **Cheese Shop,** 25–31 Walden St. (⟨⟩ **978/369-5778**).

Nashoba Brook Bakery & Café ⟨⟩ AMERICAN   The enticing variety of artisan breads, baked goods, pastries, and from-scratch soups, salads, and sandwiches makes this airy cafe a popular destination throughout the day. The industrial-looking building off West Concord's main street backs up to little Nashoba Brook, which is visible through the glass back wall. Order and pick up at the counter, then grab a seat along the window or near the children's play area. Or order takeout—this is great picnic food.

152 Commonwealth Ave., West Concord. ⟨⟩ 978/318-1999. www.slowrise.com. Sandwiches $5–$6; salads $6–$8 per pound. Mon–Sat 8am–8pm. From Concord Center, follow Main St. (Rte. 62) west, across Rte. 2; bear right at traffic light in front of train station and go 3 blocks.

3 Marblehead ⟨⟩⟨⟩⟨⟩

15 miles (24km) NE of Boston; 4 miles (6km) SE of Salem

Like an attractive person with a great personality, Marblehead has it all. Scenery, history, architecture, and shopping combine to make it one of the area's most popular day trips for both locals and visitors. The narrow streets of historic "Old Town" lead down to the magnificent harbor that helps make this the self-proclaimed "Yachting Capital of America." The homes along the way have plaques bearing the dates of construction as well as the names of the builders and original occupants—a history lesson without any studying.

Many of the houses have stood since before the Revolutionary War, when Marblehead was a center of merchant shipping. Two historic homes are open for tours. Allow at least a full morning to visit Marblehead, but be flexible, because you may want to hang around.

ESSENTIALS

GETTING THERE   From Boston, take Route 1A north until you see signs in Lynn for Swampscott and Marblehead. Take Lynn Shore Drive to Route 129, and follow it into Marblehead. Or take I-93 or Route 1 to Route 128, then Route 114 through Salem into Marblehead. Except at rush hour, allow 35 to 40 minutes. Parking is tough, especially in Old Town—grab the first spot you see.

MBTA (© 800/392-6100 outside Mass., or 617/222-3200; www.mbta.com) bus no. 441/442 runs from Haymarket (Orange or Green Line) in Boston to downtown Marblehead. During weekday rush periods, bus no. 448/449 connects Marblehead to Downtown Crossing. The trip takes about an hour; the one-way fare is $2.75.

VISITOR INFORMATION The **Marblehead Chamber of Commerce,** 62 Pleasant St. (© 781/631-2868; www.marbleheadchamber.org), is open Monday through Friday from 9am to 5pm. The **information booth** (© 781/ 639-8469) on Pleasant Street near Spring Street is open May through October, daily from 10am to 6pm. The chamber publishes a visitor guide and a map that includes an event calendar; ask for a business directory if you want a description of a walking tour.

GETTING AROUND Wear good walking shoes—the car or bus can get you to Marblehead, but it can't negotiate many of the narrow streets of Old Town. The downtown area is fairly compact and moderately hilly.

SPECIAL EVENTS Sailing regattas take place all summer. **Race Week,** in mid- to late July, draws competitors from across the country. During the **Christmas Walk,** on the first weekend in December, Santa Claus arrives by lobster boat.

EXPLORING THE TOWN

A stroll through the winding streets of **Old Town** 𝒜𝒜𝒜 invariably leads to shopping, snacking, or gazing at something picturesque, be it the harbor or a beautiful home. If you prefer more structure, consult the Chamber of Commerce's business directory, which includes a walking tour. Be sure to spend some time in **Crocker Park** 𝒜𝒜, on the water off Front Street. Especially in warm weather, when boats jam the harbor, the view is breathtaking. The park has benches and allows picnicking. The view from **Fort Sewall,** at the other end of Front Street, is just as mesmerizing. The ruins of the fort, built in the 17th century and rebuilt late in the 18th, are another excellent picnic spot.

Just inland, the **Lafayette House** is a private home at the corner of Hooper and Union streets. Legend has it that one corner of the first floor was chopped off in 1824 to allow Lafayette's carriage to negotiate the turn. In Market Square, on Washington Street near State Street, is the **Old Town House,** a public meeting and gathering place since 1727.

By car or bicycle, the swanky residential community of **Marblehead Neck** 𝒜 is worth a look. Follow Ocean Avenue across the causeway and visit the **Audubon Bird Sanctuary** (look for the tiny sign at the corner of Risley Ave.), or continue to **Castle Rock** for another eyeful of scenery. At the end of "the Neck," at Harbor and Ocean avenues, is **Chandler Hovey Park,** which has a (closed) lighthouse and a panoramic view. Many inns and B&Bs provide bikes for guests' use; to rent, visit **Marblehead Cycle,** 25 Bessom St., 1 block off Pleasant Street (© 781/631-1570). Bikes go for $14 for a half day, $20 for a full day.

Abbot Hall A 5-minute stop here (look for the clock tower) is just the ticket if you want to be able to say you did some sightseeing. The town offices and Historical Commission share Abbot Hall with Archibald M. Willard's famous painting *The Spirit of '76* 𝒜, on display in the Selectmen's Meeting Room. The thrill of recognizing the ubiquitous drummer, drummer boy, and fife player is the main reason to stop here. Cases in the halls contain objects and artifacts from the Historical Society's collections.

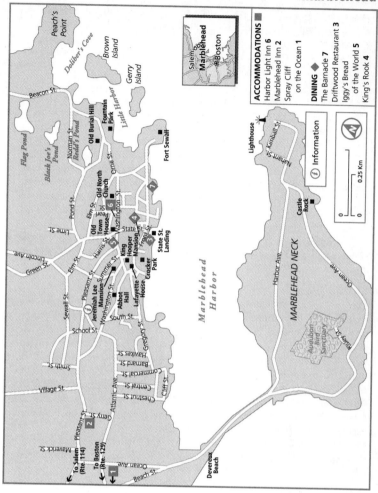

Washington Sq. Ⓒ **781/631-0528.** Free admission. Year-round Mon–Tues and Thurs 8am–5pm, Wed 7:30am–7:30pm, Fri 8am–1pm; May–Oct also open Fri 8am–5pm, Sat 9am–6pm, Sun 11am–6pm. From the historic district, follow Washington St. up the hill.

Jeremiah Lee Mansion 🐟🐟 The prospect of seeing original hand-painted wallpaper in an 18th-century home is reason enough to visit this house, built in 1768 for a wealthy merchant and considered an outstanding example of pre-Revolutionary Georgian architecture. Original rococo carving and other details complement historically accurate room arrangements, and ongoing restoration and interpretation by the Marblehead Historical Society place the 18th- and 19th-century furnishings and artifacts in context. The friendly guides welcome questions and are well versed in the history of the home. The lawn and gardens are open to the public.

The Historical Society's headquarters, across the street, house the **J. O. J. Frost Folk Art Gallery** and a changing exhibition gallery. Frost, a noted primitivist painter, was a Marblehead native. The society occasionally offers candlelight tours of the house and walking tours of the town. Call ahead for schedules.

© 781/631-1768. www.marbleheadhistory.org. Mansion: 161 Washington St. Guided tours $5 adults, $4.50 seniors and students. June to mid-Oct Mon–Sat 10am–4pm, Sun 1–4pm. Closed mid-Oct to May. Historical Society: 170 Washington St. Free admission. Year-round Tues–Sat 10am–4pm. Follow Washington St. until it curves right and heads uphill toward Abbot Hall; mansion is on right.

King Hooper Mansion Shipping tycoon Robert Hooper got his nickname because he treated his sailors so well, but it's easy to think he was called "King" because he lived like royalty. Around the corner from the home of Jeremiah Lee (whose sister was the second of Hooper's four wives), the 1728 King Hooper Mansion gained a Georgian addition in 1745. The period furnishings, although not original, give a sense of the life of an 18th-century merchant prince, from the wine cellar to the third-floor ballroom. The building houses the headquarters of the Marblehead Arts Association, which stages exhibits and runs a gift shop that sells members' work. The mansion has a lovely garden; enter through the gate at the right of the house.

8 Hooper St. © 781/631-2608. Donation requested for tour. Mon–Sat 10am–4pm; Sun 1–5pm. Call ahead; no tours during private parties. Where Washington St. curves at the foot of hill near Lee Mansion, look for the colorful sign.

SHOPPING 🏵🏵
One of Marblehead's claims to fame is its excellent retail scene. Shops, boutiques, and galleries abound in **Old Town** and on **Atlantic Avenue** and the east end of **Pleasant Street.**

The most unusual shop in town is **Antiquewear,** 82 Front St. (© 781/ 639-0070; http://users.primushost.com/~antiquew), near the town pier. It sells 19th-century buttons ingeniously fashioned into women's and men's jewelry of all descriptions. Other good stops include **Local Color,** 1 Pleasant St. (© 781/ 631-7166), a quirky gift shop; **Cargo Unlimited,** 82 Washington St. (© 781/ 631-1112; www.cargounlimited.com), for home furnishings and accessories; an excellent antiquarian bookstore, **Much Ado,** 108 Washington St. (© 781/ 639-0400; www.muchadobooks.com); **Arnould Gallery and Framery,** 111 Washington St. (© 781/631-6366); and the **Toy Shop,** 44–48 Atlantic Ave. (© 781/631-9900).

WHERE TO STAY
The accommodations listings of the **Chamber of Commerce** (© 781/631-2868; www.marbleheadchamber.org) include many of the town's innumerable inns and B&Bs. Contact the chamber or consult one of the agencies listed in chapter 4 under "Accommodations."

Harbor Light Inn 🏵🏵 Two Federal-era mansions make up this gracious inn, a stone's throw from the Old Town House. From the wood floors to the 1729 beams (in a third-floor room) to the swimming pool, it's both historic and relaxing. Rooms are comfortably furnished in period style, with some lovely antiques; most have canopy or four-poster beds. Eleven have working fireplaces, and five of those have double Jacuzzis. VCRs and free video rentals are available. The best rooms, on the top floor at the back of the building (away from the street), have gorgeous harbor views. If you don't book one, you can still take in the scenery from the roof deck. Undeniably romantic, the inn also attracts business travelers during the week.

58 Washington St., Marblehead, MA 01945. © 781/631-2186. Fax 781/631-2216. www.harborlightinn. com. 21 units (some with shower only). $125–$245 double; $195–$295 suite. Rates include breakfast.

Corporate rate available midweek. 2- to 3-night minimum stay weekends and holidays. AE, MC, V. Free parking. **Amenities:** Heated outdoor pool. *In room:* A/C, TV, dataport, hair dryer.

Marblehead Inn ★ *Kids*

This 1872 Victorian mansion just outside the historic district is an all-suite inn. It's not as convenient and romantic as the Harbor Light Inn, but offers better amenities and a more family-friendly atmosphere. Each attractive unit contains a living room, bedroom, and workstation. This is a good choice for businesspeople making an extended stay as well as families, who can make good use of the self-catering kitchenette. (Breakfast provisions are supplied.) Most suites have Jacuzzis, and some have fireplaces and small patios.

264 Pleasant St. (Rte. 114), Marblehead, MA 01945. ☏ 800/399-5843 or 781/639-9999. Fax 781/639-9996. www.marbleheadinn.com. 10 units (some with shower only). $129–$219 double. Rates include continental breakfast. Extra person $25. Children under 10 stay free in parents' room. Winter discounts and long-term rates available. 2- to 3-night minimum stay weekends and holidays. AE, MC, V. Free parking. *In room:* A/C, TV, fax, dataport, kitchenette, coffeemaker, hair dryer.

Spray Cliff on the Ocean ★

Spray Cliff, a three-story Victorian Tudor built in 1910 on a cliff overlooking the ocean, is 5 minutes from town and a world away. The romantic inn is on a quiet residential street just a minute from the beach. It books honeymooners, vacationers in search of isolation, and midweek business travelers. The most desirable of the large, sunny rooms are the five that face the water. Three units have fireplaces, and all are luxuriously decorated in contemporary style with bright accents.

25 Spray Ave., Marblehead, MA 01945. ☏ 800/626-1530 or 781/631-6789. Fax 781/639-4563. www.spray cliff.com. 7 units (some with shower only). May–Oct $200–$250 double. Rates include continental breakfast and evening refreshments. Extra person $25. Off-season discounts available. 2- to 3-night minimum stay weekends and holidays. AE, MC, V. Free parking. Take Atlantic Ave. (Rte. 129) to traffic light at Clifton Ave. and turn east (right driving north, left driving south); parking is at end of street. No children. **Amenities:** Free bikes. *In room:* No phone.

A SEASIDE INN NEARBY

Diamond District Bed & Breakfast ★★

This comfortable Georgian-style mansion, built in 1911 as a private home, now attracts both business and leisure travelers. The Atlantic is a block away; the 3-mile (5km) public beach (a good place to burn off the inn's generous breakfast) is popular for jogging, skating, and biking as well as swimming. It's visible from many of the good-sized rooms, tastefully decorated with elaborate Victorian touches. The best are third-floor units with ocean views and Jacuzzis. Two rooms have cozy electric fireplaces. The large living room and porch overlook houses on Lynn Shore Drive and, just past them, the ocean. The whirlpool spa, on the back lawn, also has a water view.

The **1882 Stewart House,** across the street (away from the water), contains a common living room, a double room, two doubles that share a bathroom (a good choice for families), and a tiny single room.

142 Ocean St., Lynn, MA 01902. ☏ 800/666-3076 or 781/599-4470. Fax 781/599-5122. www.diamond districtinn.com. 15 units, 13 with private bathroom (some with shower only). $135–$265 double. Rates include breakfast. Extra person $20. Winter discounts available. 2-night minimum stay on holiday, summer, and fall weekends. AE, DC, DISC, MC, V. Take Rte. 1A north to signs for Swampscott/Marblehead; after rotary, take Lynn Shore Dr. north, past two lights and Christian Science Church. Turn left onto Wolcott Rd., then right onto Ocean St.; inn is on the right. **Amenities:** Outdoor whirlpool. *In room:* A/C, TV, dataport.

WHERE TO DINE

You can stock up for a picnic at a number of places along the water in Old Town. **Shubie's,** 32 Atlantic Ave. (☏ 781/631-0149), carries a good selection of specialty foods. **Iggy's Bread of the World** ★, 5 Pleasant St.

(② **781/639-4717**), serves fabulous gourmet baked goods and coffee. It has a small seating area—but really, go outside.

The Barnacle SEAFOOD This unassuming spot affords a shorebird's-eye view of the harbor from the deck, the counter, and the crowded dining room. The food is tasty and plentiful. It's not innovative, but it is fresh—the restaurant's lobster boat delivers daily—and popular with local residents, which is always a good sign. The chowder and fried seafood are terrific. This is an agreeable place to quaff a beer and watch the boats.

141 Front St. ② **781/631-4236.** Reservations not accepted. Main courses $5–$15 lunch, $13–$18 dinner. No credit cards. Daily 11:30am–4pm; Sun–Thurs 5–9pm, Fri–Sat 5–10pm. Closed Tues in winter.

Driftwood Restaurant ✦ DINER/SEAFOOD At the foot of State Street next to Clark Landing (the town pier) is an honest-to-goodness local hangout. Join the crowd at a table or the counter for generous portions of breakfast (served all day) or lunch. Try pancakes or hash, chowder or a seafood "roll" (a hot-dog bun filled with, say, fried clams or lobster salad). The house specialty, served on weekends and holidays, is fried dough, which is exactly as delicious and indigestible as it sounds.

63 Front St. ② **781/631-1145.** Main courses $3–$10; breakfast items under $6. No credit cards. Summer daily 6:30am–5pm; winter daily 6:30am–2pm.

King's Rook ✦ CAFE/WINE BAR This cozy spot serves coffees, teas, hot chocolate, soft drinks, and more than 20 wines by the glass, and the food has a sophisticated flair. The intimate side-street atmosphere and racks of newspapers and magazines make this a great place to linger over a pesto pizza, excellent spinach soup, a tasty salad, or a rich dessert.

12 State St. ② **781/631-9838.** Reservations not accepted. Main courses $5–$10. DISC, MC, V. Mon–Fri noon–2:30pm; Tues–Fri 5:30–11:30pm; Sat–Sun noon–11:30pm. Closed Mon in winter.

4 Salem ✦✦

16 miles (26km) NE of Boston; 4 miles (6km) NW of Marblehead

Settled in 1626 (4 years before Boston) and later known around the world as a center of merchant shipping, Salem is internationally famous today for a 7-month episode in 1692. The witchcraft trials led to 20 deaths, centuries of notoriety, countless lessons on the evils of prejudice, and innumerable bad puns ("Stop by for a spell" is a favorite slogan). Today, the city abounds with witch-associated attractions. Most are historically accurate, but you'll also see a fair number of goofy souvenirs and opportunistic tourist traps. An excellent antidote is the Peabody Essex Museum. Salem is a family-friendly destination that's worth at least a half-day visit, perhaps after a stop in Marblehead; it can easily fill a day.

Visitors concentrating on wall-to-wall witches will miss another important part of the city's history. Salem's merchant vessels circled the globe in the 17th and 18th centuries, returning laden with treasures. The city peaked between the Revolutionary War and the War of 1812, with the opening of the China trade—many overseas merchants even believed that Salem was an independent country. One reminder of that era, a replica of the 1797 East Indiaman tall ship *Friendship,* is anchored near the Salem Maritime National Historic Site.

ESSENTIALS

GETTING THERE From Marblehead, take Route 114 west into downtown Salem. From Boston, take I-93 or Route 1 to Route 128, then Route 114 east.

Salem

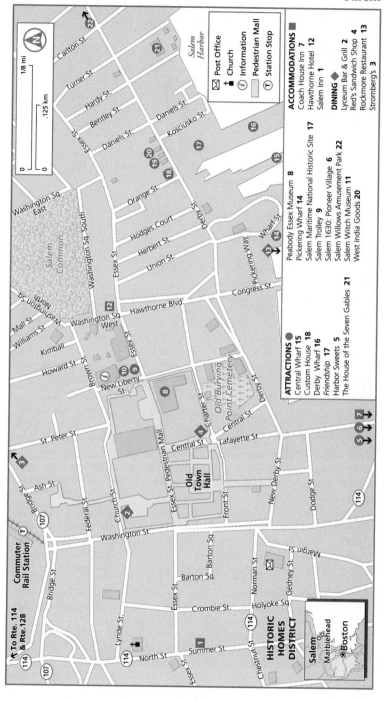

Post Office
Church
Information
Pedestrian Mall
Station Stop

ACCOMMODATIONS ■
Coach House Inn **7**
Hawthorne Hotel **12**
Salem Inn **1**

DINING ◆
Lyceum Bar & Grill **2**
Red's Sandwich Shop **4**
Rockmore Restaurant **13**
Stromberg's **3**

ATTRACTIONS ●
Central Wharf **15**
Custom House **18**
Derby Wharf **16**
Friendship **17**
Harbor Sweets **5**
The House of the Seven Gables **21**

Peabody Essex Museum **8**
Pickering Wharf **14**
Salem Maritime National Historic Site **17**
Salem Trolley **9**
Salem 1630: Pioneer Village **6**
Salem Willows Amusement Park **22**
Salem Witch Museum **11**
West India Goods **20**

Salem Harbor

Salem Common

Old Town Hall

HISTORIC HOMES DISTRICT

Salem
Marblehead
★ Boston

Commuter Rail Station

To Rte. 114 & Rte. 128

1/8 mi
.125 km

Or take Route 1A north from Boston, being careful in Lynn, where the road turns left and immediately right. There's metered street parking and a reasonably priced garage opposite the visitor center.

From Boston, the **MBTA** (© 800/392-6100 outside Mass., or 617/222-3200; www.mbta.com) runs commuter trains from North Station and bus route no. 450 from Haymarket (Orange or Green Line). The train is more comfortable but runs less frequently. It takes 30 to 35 minutes; the round-trip fare is $5.50. The station is about 5 blocks from the downtown area. The one-way fare for the 35- to 55-minute bus trip is $2.75. June through October, **ferries** (© 617/227-4321; www.bostonharborcruises.com) run from Long Wharf in Boston to the Blaney Street Ferry Terminal, off Derby Street. Call for schedules and other details, such as access to downtown from the terminal. The 75-minute trip costs about $10 for adults, less for seniors and children under 12.

VISITOR INFORMATION   A good place to start is the **National Park Service Regional Visitor Center,** 2 New Liberty St. (© 978/740-1650; www.nps.gov/sama), open daily from 9am to 5pm. Exhibits highlight early settlement, maritime history, and the leather and textiles industries. The center distributes brochures and pamphlets, including one that describes a walking tour of the historic district, and has an auditorium where a free film on Essex County provides an overview.

The Office of Tourism & Cultural Affairs, **Destination Salem** (© 877/SALEM-MA or 978/744-3663; www.salem.org), and the Chamber of Commerce collaborate on a free visitor guide that includes a good map. The **Salem Chamber of Commerce,** 32 Derby Sq. (© 978/744-0004; www.salem-chamber.org), maintains a rack of brochures and pamphlets at its office on the first floor of Old Town Hall. It's open Monday through Friday from 9am to 5pm. Salem has an excellent community website, **www.salemweb.com**.

GETTING AROUND   In the congested downtown area, walking is the way to go. If it's hot or you plan lots of sightseeing, you might prefer to ride. **Salem Trolley** (© 508/744-5469; www.salemtrolley.com) offers a 1-hour narrated tour and unlimited reboarding at any of its 15 stops. The tour starts at the Essex Street side of the visitor center. It operates from 10am to 5pm (last tour at 4pm), daily April through October, and weekends only in March and November. Tickets ($10 for adults, $9 for seniors, $5 children for 5–12, or $25 per family) are good all day.

SPECIAL EVENTS   The city's 3-week Halloween celebration, **Haunted Happenings** 🎃🎃 (© 978/744-0013; www.hauntedhappenings.org), includes parades, parties, tours, and a ceremony on the big day. During **Heritage Days,** a weeklong event in mid-August, the city celebrates its multicultural history with musical and theatrical performances, a parade, and fireworks.

EXPLORING SALEM

The **historic district** extends well inland from the waterfront; ask at the visitor center for the walking-tour pamphlet. Many 18th-century houses, some with original furnishings, still stand. Ship captains lived near the water at the east end of downtown, in relatively small houses crowded close together. The captains' employers, the shipping-company owners, built their homes away from the water (and the accompanying aromas). Many lived on the grand thoroughfare of **Chestnut Street** 🎃🎃, now a National Historic Landmark.

By car or trolley, the **Salem Willows** (© 978/745-0251) amusements are 5 minutes away; many signs point the way. The strip of rides and snack bars has a honky-tonk air, and the waterfront park is a good place to bring a picnic and wander along the shore. Admission is free; metered parking is available. To enjoy the great view without the arcades and rides, have lunch one peninsula over at **Winter Island Park.**

The House of the Seven Gables ✿ Nathaniel Hawthorne's cousin lived here, and stories and legends of the house and its inhabitants inspired his 1851 book. If you haven't read the eerie novel, don't let that keep you away—begin with the audiovisual program, which tells the story. The house, built by Capt. John Turner in 1668, holds six rooms of period furniture, including pieces referred to in the book, and a secret staircase. Tours include a visit to Hawthorne's birthplace and descriptions of what life was like for the house's 18th-century inhabitants. The costumed guides can get a little silly as they mug for young visitors, but they're well versed and eager to answer questions. Also on the grounds, overlooking Salem Harbor, are period gardens, the Retire Beckett House (1655), the Hooper-Hathaway House (1682), and a counting house (1830).

54 Turner St. ✆ **978/744-0991.** www.7gables.org. Guided tours $8.50 adults, $7.50 seniors, $5.50 children 5–12. Tour and Salem 1630 admission $14.50 adults, $12.50 seniors, $10.50 children 5–12. Surcharges may apply for special exhibitions. Mid-Apr to June and Nov–Dec daily 10am–5pm; July–Oct daily 10am–7pm; late Jan to mid-Apr Mon–Sat 10am–5pm, Sun noon–5pm. Closed first 3 weeks of Jan, Thanksgiving, Dec 25. From downtown, follow Derby St. east 3 blocks past Derby Wharf.

Peabody Essex Museum ✿✿ *Kids* The Peabody Essex is a treasure trove of art and cultural history peeking out from behind a figure wearing a pointy black hat. Though sometimes overshadowed by Salem's every-witch-way reputation, the museum's encyclopedic collections offer an engaging look at nearly 4 centuries in a fascinating seaport (including the witchcraft trials). A huge expansion project is expected to be complete in May 2003; surf or call ahead for information about special exhibitions and events surrounding the opening of the new galleries.

The permanent collections blend "the natural and artificial curiosities" Salem's sea captains and merchants brought back from around the world with the local artifacts of the county historical society. The well-planned displays help you understand the significance of each item, and interpretive materials (including interactive and hands-on activities) get children involved. You might see objects related to the history of the port of Salem (including gorgeous furniture), the whaling trade, the witchcraft trials, and East Asian art. Portraits of area residents include Charles Osgood's omnipresent rendering of Nathaniel Hawthorne.

Sign up for a fascinating tour of one of the museum's nine historic houses. They include the 1804 **Gardner-Pingree House** ✿✿, a magnificent Federal mansion where a notorious murder was committed in 1830. You can also take a gallery tour or select from about a dozen pamphlets that describe self-guided tours.

East India Sq. ✆ **800/745-4054** or 978/745-9500. www.pem.org. Admission $10 adults, $8 seniors and students, free for children under 17. House tour only $6. Surcharges may apply for special exhibitions. Apr–Oct Mon–Sat 10am–5pm, Sun noon–5pm; Nov–March Tues–Sat 10am–5pm, Sun noon–5pm. Closed Jan 1, Thanksgiving, Dec 25. Take Hawthorne Blvd. to Essex St., following signs for visitor center. Enter on Essex St. or New Liberty St.

Salem Maritime National Historic Site ✿ *Kids* An entertaining introduction to Salem's seagoing history, this complex includes an exciting attraction: a real live ship. The *Friendship* ✿✿ is a full-size replica of a 1797 East Indiaman

Trying Times: The Salem Witch Hysteria

The Salem witch trials took place in 1692, a product of Old World superstition, religious control of government, and plain old boredom.

The crisis began quietly in Salem Village (now the town of Danvers). The Rev. Samuel Parris's household included his 9-year-old daughter, Elizabeth, her cousin Abigail, and a West Indian slave named Tituba who told stories to amuse the girls during the long, harsh winter. Entertained by tales of witchcraft, sorcery, and fortune-telling, the girls and their friends began to act out the stories, claiming to be under a spell, rolling on the ground and wailing. The settlers—aware that thousands of people in Europe had been executed as witches in the previous centuries—took the behavior seriously.

At first, only Tituba and two other women were accused of casting spells. The infighting typical of the Puritan theocracy surfaced soon enough, and an accusation of witchcraft became a handy way to settle a score. Anyone "different" was a potential target, from the elderly to the deaf to the poor. A special court convened in Salem proper, and although the girls recanted, the trials began. Defendants had no counsel, and pleading not guilty or objecting to the proceedings was considered equivalent to a confession. From March 1 to September 22, of the more than 150 people who were accused, 27 were convicted.

In the end, 19 people went to the gallows, and one man who refused to plead, Giles Corey, was pressed to death by stones piled on a board on his chest. Finally, cooler heads prevailed. Leading cleric Cotton Mather and his father, Harvard president Increase Mather, led the call for tolerance. With the jails overflowing, the court called off the trials and freed the remaining prisoners, including Tituba.

The episode's lessons about open-mindedness and tolerance have echoed through the years. Salem was the backdrop for Arthur Miller's 1953 play *The Crucible*. It is both a story about the witch trials and an allegory about the McCarthy Senate hearings—another kind of witch hunt in a time when those lessons needed to be taught again.

merchant vessel, a three-masted 171-footer (51m) that disappeared during the War of 1812. The tall ship is a faithful replica with some concessions to the modern era, such as diesel engines and accessibility for people with disabilities. The guided ranger tour includes a tour of the ship.

Central Wharf holds a warehouse (ca. 1800) that houses the orientation center. Tours, which vary seasonally, expand on Salem's maritime history. Yours might include the Derby House (1762), a wedding gift to shipping magnate Elias Hasket Derby from his father, and the Custom House (1819). Legend (myth, really) has it that this is where Nathaniel Hawthorne was working when he found an embroidered scarlet "A." If you prefer to explore on your own, you can see the free film at the orientation center and wander around Derby Wharf, the West India Goods Store, the Bonded Warehouse, the Scale House, and Central Wharf.

174 Derby St. ℂ **978/740-1660.** www.nps.gov/sama. Free admission. Guided tours $5 adults, $3 seniors and children 6–16. Daily 9am–5pm. Closed Jan 1, Thanksgiving, Dec 25. Take Derby St. east; just past Pickering Wharf, Derby Wharf is on the right.

Salem 1630: Pioneer Village *Kids*   This is a popular destination for school and day-camp field trips; adults traveling alone may feel out of place. The Puritan village re-creates life in Salem just 4 years after European settlement. Costumed interpreters lead tours, demonstrate crafts, and tend farm animals. They escort visitors around the various dwellings—wear sneakers, as the village isn't paved—and explain their activities.

Forest River Park, off West Ave. ℂ **978/744-0991.** www.7gables.org. Admission $7.50 adults, $6.50 seniors, $5.50 children 5–12. Admission and House of the Seven Gables tour $14.50 adults, $12.50 seniors, $10.50 children 5–12. Late Apr to early Nov Mon–Sat 10am–5pm, Sun noon–5pm. Closed early Nov to late Apr. Take Lafayette St. (Rtes. 114 and 1A) south from downtown to West Ave., turn left, and follow signs.

Salem Witch Museum ★★ *Kids*   This is one of the most memorable attractions in eastern Massachusetts—it's both interesting and scary. The main draw of the museum (a former church) is a three-dimensional audiovisual presentation with life-size figures. The show takes place in a huge room lined with displays that are lighted in sequence. The 30-minute narration tells the story of the witchcraft trials and the accompanying hysteria. The well-researched presentation tells the story accurately, if somewhat overdramatically. One of the victims was crushed to death by rocks piled on a board on his chest—smaller kids may need a reminder that he's not real.

19½ Washington Sq., on Route 1A. ℂ **978/744-1692.** www.salemwitchmuseum.com. Admission $6.50 adults, $6 seniors, $4.50 children 6–14. Daily July–Aug 10am–7pm; Sept–June 10am–5pm. Closed Jan 1, Thanksgiving, Dec 25. Follow Hawthorne Blvd. to the northwest corner of Salem Common.

ORGANIZED TOURS & CRUISES

Salem Trolley (see "Getting Around," above) offers the best value, but it's land-locked. Check to see whether **Moby Duck Tours** ★ (ℂ **508/741-4386;** www.mobyduck.com) has resolved its conflict with the city; tours were suspended at press time. When it's operating, Moby Duck's amphibious vehicle cruises the streets of the city, then plunges into the harbor, delighting the kids on board.

SHOPPING

Pickering Wharf, at the corner of Derby and Congress streets (ℂ **978/ 740-6990;** www.pickeringwharf.com), is a waterfront complex of boutiques, restaurants, and condos. It's popular for strolling, snacking, and shopping, and the central location makes it a local landmark.

Several shops specialize in witchcraft accessories. Bear in mind that Salem is home to many practicing witches who take their beliefs very seriously. The **Broom Closet,** 3–5 Central St. (ℂ **978/741-3669**), and **Crow Haven Corner,** 125 Essex St. (ℂ **978/745-8763**), stock everything from crystals to clothing.

Shops throughout New England sell the chocolate confections of **Harbor Sweets** ★★, Palmer Cove, 85 Leavitt St., off Lafayette Street (ℂ **978/ 745-7648**). The retail store overlooks the floor of the factory. The deliriously good sweets are expensive, but candy bars and small assortments are available. Closed Sunday.

WHERE TO STAY

The busiest and most expensive time of year is **Halloween week;** reserve well in advance if you plan to travel anytime in October.

Most major chains are represented on or near Route 1 north of I-95, within 30 minutes of downtown Salem. The **Clipper Ship Inn,** 40 Bridge St., Route 1A (✆ **978/745-8022**), is a comfortable, modern motel northeast of downtown. Doubles in high season run $110 to $150.

Coach House Inn   Built in 1879 for a ship's captain, this inn is 2 blocks from the harbor and a 20-minute walk or 5-minute drive from downtown. The three-story mansion was redecorated in 1998. The good-size guest rooms are elegantly furnished in traditional style. All have high ceilings, and most have (nonworking) fireplaces. Breakfast arrives at your door in a basket.

284 Lafayette St. (Rtes. 1A and 114), Salem, MA 01970. ✆ **800/688-8689** or 978/744-4092. Fax 978/745-8031. www.coachhousesalem.com. 11 units, 9 with private bathroom (2 with shower only). $80–$98 double with shared bathroom; $95–$145 double with private bathroom; $150–$185 suite. Rates include continental breakfast. 2- to 3-night minimum stay weekends and holidays. AE, DISC, MC, V. Free parking. *In room:* A/C, TV, coffeemaker.

Hawthorne Hotel ✪   This historic hotel, built in 1925, is both convenient and comfortable. It attracts vacationers and business travelers, and is popular for functions. The six-story building is centrally located and well maintained, with a traditional atmosphere. The guest rooms, renovated between 1997 and 1999, are attractively furnished and adequate in size. The best units, on the Salem Common (north) side of the building, have better views than rooms that face the street. Ask to be as high up as possible, as the neighborhood is busy.

18 Washington Sq. (at Salem Common), Salem, MA 01970. ✆ **800/729-7829** or 978/744-4080. Fax 978/745-9842. www.hawthornehotel.com. 89 units (some with shower only). $104–$204 double; $204–$309 suite. Extra person $12. Children under 16 stay free in parents' room. Off-season discounts, senior discounts, and weekend and other packages available. 2-night minimum stay May–Oct weekends. AE, DC, DISC, MC, V. Limited self-parking. Small pets accepted ($15). **Amenities:** Restaurant (American), cafe; exercise room; limited room service; laundry service; dry cleaning. *In room:* A/C, TV, dataport.

Salem Inn ✪✪   The Salem Inn, which consists of three properties, occupies the comfortable niche between too-big hotel and too-small B&B. Its clientele includes honeymooners as well as sightseers and families, and the variety of rooms means the innkeepers can make a good match of guest and accommodations. Rooms are large and tastefully decorated; some have fireplaces, canopy beds, and whirlpool baths. The best units are the honeymoon and family suites in the 1874 Peabody House. Guests of all three houses can relax in the peaceful rose garden at the rear of the main building.

7 Summer St. (Rte. 114), Salem, MA 01970. ✆ **800/446-2995** or 978/741-0680. Fax 978/744-8924. www.SalemInnMA.com. 39 units (some with shower only). Nov–Sept $129–$229 double; Oct $180–$290 double. Rates include continental breakfast. 2- to 3-night minimum stay during holidays and special events. AE, DC, DISC, MC, V. Free parking. Pets accepted by prior arrangement ($15). *In room:* A/C, TV, coffeemaker, hair dryer.

WHERE TO DINE

Pickering Wharf has a food court as well as a link in the **Victoria Station** (✆ **978/744-7644**) chain, with a great view of the marina from the deck.

Lyceum Bar & Grill ✪✪ CONTEMPORARY AMERICAN   The elegance of the Lyceum's dining rooms matches the quality of the food, which attracts local businesspeople and out-of-towners. Grilling is a favorite cooking technique— try the signature marinated grilled portobellos. They're available as an appetizer and scattered throughout the menu—say, in delectable pasta with chicken, red peppers, and Swiss chard in wine sauce, or with beef tenderloin, red pepper sauce, and garlic mashed potatoes. Spicy vegetable lasagna is also tasty. Save room for one of the traditional yet sophisticated desserts—the brownie sundae is out of this world.

43 Church St. (at Washington St.). ✆ **978/745-7665**. www.lyceumsalem.com. Reservations recommended. Main courses $7–$11 lunch, $17–$26 dinner. AE, DISC, MC, V. Mon–Fri 11:30am–3pm; Sun brunch 11am–3pm; daily 5:30–10pm.

Red's Sandwich Shop NEW ENGLAND   Locals and visitors feel equally comfortable at this no-frills hangout. Hunker down at the counter or a table and be ready for your waitress to call you "dear" as she brings you pancakes and eggs at breakfast, or soup (opt for chicken over chowder) and a burger at lunch. **Red's Winter Island Grille** (✆ **978/744-0203**), under the same management, is open seasonally at Winter Island Park.

15 Central St. ✆ **978/745-3527**. www.redssandwichshop.com. Most items under $7. No credit cards. Mon–Sat 5am–3pm; Sun 6am–1pm.

Rockmore Restaurant ✆ SEAFOOD/AMERICAN   If you're going to eat at a restaurant with a gimmick, it might as well be a good gimmick. This is: It's on a float in the middle of Salem Harbor. The Rockmore serves burgers, sandwiches, and fresh seafood in an extremely casual atmosphere, usually to local boaters. The food is fine, but nobody's here for the food. (Did we mention it's on a *float?*) If you're not traveling by boat, ferry service is available from 94 Wharf St., Pickering Wharf.

Salem Harbor. ✆ **978/740-1001**. www.rockmoreco.com. Main courses $7–$15. AE, DISC, MC, V. Memorial Day–Labor Day daily 11am–10pm, weather permitting.

Stromberg's ✆ *Kids* SEAFOOD   For generous portions of well-prepared seafood and a view of the water, seek out this local favorite at the foot of the bridge to Beverly. You won't care that Beverly Harbor isn't the most exciting spot, especially if it's summer and you're out on the deck. The fish and clam chowders are excellent, daily specials are numerous, and there are more chicken, beef, and pasta options than you might expect. Crustacean lovers in the mood to splurge will fall for the world-class lobster roll.

2 Bridge St. (Rte. 1A). ✆ **978/744-1863**. www.strombergs.com. Reservations recommended for dinner. Main courses $6–$11 lunch, $11–$18 dinner; children's menu $5. AE, DISC, MC, V. Sun and Tues–Thurs 11am–9pm; Fri–Sat 11am–10pm.

5 Cape Ann

Gloucester, Rockport, Essex, and Manchester-by-the-Sea make up Cape Ann, a rocky peninsula so enchantingly beautiful that when you hear the slogan "Massachusetts's *Other* Cape," you may forget what the first one was. Cape Ann and Cape Cod do share some attributes—scenery, shopping, seafood, and traffic. The smaller cape's proximity to Boston and manageable scale make it a wonderful day trip and a good choice for a longer stay.

With the decline of the fishing industry that brought great prosperity to the area in the 19th century, Cape Ann has played up its long-standing reputation as a haven for artists. Along with galleries and crafts shops, you'll find historical attractions, beaches—and oh, that scenery!

Although all four towns have large year-round populations, this is hardly a four-season destination. Many establishments close in fall or early winter through April or May; some open on weekends in December.

Milling Around: A Trip to Lowell

A 19th-century textile center that later fell into disrepair, Lowell is a 21st-century success story. A city built around restored mills and industrial canals will never be a glamorous vacation spot, but thousands of visitors a year find Lowell a fascinating and rewarding destination. The sights concentrate on the history of the Industrial Revolution and the textile industry. They include boardinghouses where the "mill girls" lived; the workers, some as young as 10 years old, averaged 14-hour days weaving cloth on power looms.

Start at the **Lowell National Historical Park Visitor Center,** 246 Market St. (© 978/970-5000; www.nps.gov/lowe), open daily from 9am to 5pm. Rangers lead free programs and tours, and canal cruises and free trolley tours operate in summer. Ask for a map of the area, and use it to find your way around downtown. Two interesting museums are within walking distance: the **American Textile History Museum,** 491 Dutton St. (© 978/441-0400; www.athm.org), and the **New England Quilt Museum** 🞳, 18 Shattuck St. (© 978/452-4207; www.nequilt museum.org). For more information, consult the **Greater Merrimack Valley Convention & Visitors Bureau,** 9 Central St., Suite 201, Lowell (© 800/443-3332 or 978/459-6150; www.merrimackvalley.org).

To drive to Lowell, take Route 3 or I-495 to the Lowell Connector and follow signs north to Exit 5B and the historic district. The **commuter rail** (© 800/392-6100 outside Mass., or 617/222-3200; www.mbta.com) from Boston's North Station takes about 45 minutes and costs $8.50 round-trip.

The **Cape Ann Transportation Authority** (© 978/283-7916; www.canntran.com) runs buses from town to town on Cape Ann and operates special summer routes.

The **Cape Ann Chamber of Commerce,** 33 Commercial St., Gloucester (© 800/321-0133 or 978/283-1601; www.capeannvacations.com), and the **North of Boston Convention & Visitors Bureau** (© 800/742-5306 or 978/977-7760; www.northofboston.org) provide abundant visitor information.

MANCHESTER-BY-THE-SEA

The scenic route to Gloucester from points south is Route 127, which runs through Manchester-by-the-Sea, a lovely village incorporated in 1645. Now a prosperous suburb of Boston, Manchester is probably best known for **Singing Beach** (see "Life's a Beach," below). The **commuter rail** (© 800/392-6100 outside Mass., or 617/222-3200; www.mbta.com) from Boston costs $8.50 round-trip and stops in the center of the compact downtown area, where there are many shops and restaurants. Nearby **Masconomo Park** overlooks the harbor.

The home of the Manchester Historical Society is the **Trask House,** 10 Union St. (© 978/526-7230), a 19th-century sea captain's home. Tours show off the period furnishings, including pieces produced in Manchester, and the society's costume collections. It's specialized, but intriguing to devotees of house tours. Open late June through August, Saturday from 10am to 4pm, Sunday from noon to 4pm, and by appointment. A donation is requested.

MAGNOLIA

Pay close attention as you head north from Manchester or south from Gloucester on Route 127—Magnolia is easy to miss, but the village (technically part of Gloucester) is worth a detour. Notable for its lack of waterfront commercial property, the village center is unremarkable. The homes surrounding it, many of them former summer residences now occupied year-round, are magnificent.

Just up the coast are two noteworthy geological formations. **Rafe's Chasm** is a huge cleft in the shoreline rock, opposite the reef of **Norman's Woe,** which figures in Henry Wadsworth Longfellow's scary poem "The Wreck of the Hesperus." About ¾ of a mile (1km) out of the center, look for a small parking area on the right. After a ¼-mile (0.5km) walk through the woods, you'll find a gorgeous panorama of stone and surf.

Life's a Beach

Paradoxically, Cape Ann is almost as well known for its sandy beaches as for its rocky coastline. Things to know: First, the water is *cold*. Second, parking can be scarce, especially on weekends, and pricey—as much as $15. If you can't set out before breakfast, wait until midafternoon and hope that the early birds have had enough. During the summer, lifeguards are on duty from 9am to 5pm at larger public beaches. Surfing is generally permitted outside of those hours. The beaches listed here all have bathhouses and snack bars. Swimming or not, watch out for greenhead flies in July and August. They don't sting—they take little bites of flesh. Bring or buy insect repellent.

The best-known North Shore beach is **Singing Beach** 𝒦𝒦, off Masconomo Street in Manchester-by-the-Sea. Because it's accessible by public transportation, it attracts the most diverse crowd—carless singles, local families, and other beach bunnies of all ages. From the train station, they walk about ½ a mile (1km) on Beach Street to find sparkling sand and lively surf. Take the commuter rail (© **800/392-6100** outside Mass., or 617/222-3200; www.mbta.com) from Boston's North Station.

Nearly as famous and popular is **Crane Beach** 𝒦, off Argilla Road in Ipswich, part of a 1,400-acre (567-hectare) barrier beach reservation. Fragile dunes and a white-sand beach lead down to Ipswich Bay. The surf is calmer than that at less sheltered Singing Beach, but still quite chilly. Pick up Argilla Road south of Ipswich Center near the intersection of Routes 1A and 133. Also on Ipswich Bay is Gloucester's **Wingaersheek Beach** 𝒦, on Atlantic Street off Route 133. From Exit 13 off Route 128, the beach is about 15 minutes away (mind the speed limits). Wingaersheek has beautiful white sand, a glorious view, and more dunes. Because these beaches are harder to get to, they attract more locals—but also lots of day-tripping families.

Most other good beaches in Gloucester have almost no nonresident parking. Two exceptions are **Half Moon Beach** and **Cressy's Beach,** at Stage Fort Park, off Route 127 near Route 133 and downtown. The sandy beaches and the park snack bar are popular local hangouts.

The **Hammond Castle Museum,** 80 Hesperus Ave. (© **978/283-2080** or 978/283-7673; www.hammondcastle.org), is a medieval-style edifice designed by eccentric inventor John Hays Hammond, Jr. Constructed of Rockport granite from 1926 to 1929, the castle cost more than $6 million. Guided tours aren't offered, so you're on your own with a pamphlet to direct you—not the best way to explore such a peculiar place, but if you like the medieval era, you'll definitely enjoy this. It has 85-foot (26m) towers, battlements, stained-glass windows, and a great hall 60 feet (18m) high. Many 12th-, 13th-, and 14th-century furnishings, tapestries, paintings, and architectural fragments fill the rooms. Admission is $6.50 for adults, $5.50 for seniors and students, and $4.50 for children 4 to 12. It's open weekends year-round from 10am to 3pm, plus June through December weekdays from 10am to 6pm.

ESSEX 🦀

West of Gloucester (past Rte. 128) on Route 133 lies a beautiful little town known for Essex clams, salt marshes, a long tradition of shipbuilding, a plethora of antiques shops, and one celebrated restaurant.

Legend has it that **Woodman's of Essex** 🦀🦀🦀, on Main Street (© **800/ 649-1773** or 978/768-6451; www.woodmans.com), was the birthplace of the fried clam in 1916. Today the thriving family business is a great spot to join legions of locals and visitors from around the world for lobster "in the rough," chowder, steamers, corn on the cob, onion rings, and (you guessed it) superb fried clams. Expect the line to be long, even in winter, but it moves quickly and offers a view of the regimented commotion in the food-preparation area. Eat in a booth, upstairs on the deck, or out back at a picnic table. You'll want to be well fed before you set off to explore the numerous antiques shops along Main Street.

The water views in town are of the Essex River, a saltwater estuary. Narrated 90-minute tours that put you in prime birding territory are available through **Essex River Cruises** 🦀, Essex Marina, 35 Dodge St. (© **800/748-3706** or 978/768-6981; www.essexcruises.com), open daily April through October. The pontoon boat, which allows for excellent sightseeing, is screened and has restrooms. Call for reservations.

GLOUCESTER ★★

The ocean has been Gloucester's lifeblood since long before the first European settlement in 1623. The most urban of Cape Ann's communities, Gloucester (which rhymes with "roster") is a working city, not a cutesy tourist town. Miles of gorgeous coastline surround the densely populated downtown area. If you read or saw *The Perfect Storm,* you'll have some sense of what to expect. Gloucester is home to one of the last commercial fishing fleets in New England, an internationally celebrated artists' colony, a large Portuguese-American community, and just enough historic attractions. Allow at least half a day, perhaps combined with a visit to the tourist magnet of Rockport; a full day would be better, especially if you plan a cruise or whale-watch.

ESSENTIALS
GETTING THERE   From Boston, the quickest route is I-93 (or Rte. 1, if it's not rush hour) to Route 128, which ends at Gloucester. From Salem, a slower but prettier approach is Route 1A across the bridge at Beverly to Route 127. It runs through Manchester to Gloucester. The Manchester exits from Route 128

Finds *The Perfect Storm*

Sebastian Junger's best-selling book *The Perfect Storm,* a thrilling but tragic nonfiction account of the "no-name" hurricane of 1991, became a blockbuster movie in 2000. Even before that, fans of the book were arriving in Gloucester and asking to be pointed toward the neighborhood tavern that co-stars in both accounts. The **Crow's Nest,** 334 Main St. (© **978/281-2965**), a bit east of downtown, is a no-frills place with a horseshoe-shaped bar and a crowd of regulars who seem amused that their favorite hangout is a tourist attraction. The Crow's Nest plays a major role in Junger's story, but its ceilings weren't high enough for it to be a movie set—so the crew built an exact replica nearby.

allow access to Route 127. There's street parking and a free lot on the causeway to Rocky Neck. Gloucester is 33 miles (53km) northeast of Boston, 16 miles (26km) northeast of Salem, and 7 miles (11km) south of Rockport.

The **commuter rail** (✆ 800/392-6100 outside Mass., or 617/222-3200; www.mbta.com) runs from Boston's North Station. The trip takes about 1 hour; the round-trip fare is $9. The station is across town from downtown, about 10 blocks, so allow time for getting to the waterfront. The **Cape Ann Transportation Authority** (✆ 978/283-7916; www.canntran.com) runs buses from town to town as well as special summer routes.

VISITOR INFORMATION The **Gloucester Tourism Commission** (✆ 800/ 649-6839 or 978/281-8865; www.gloucesterma.com) operates an excellent **Visitors Welcoming Center** at Stage Fort Park, off Route 127 near the intersection with Route 133. It's open in summer daily from 9am to 5pm. The **Cape Ann Chamber of Commerce,** 33 Commercial St. (✆ 800/321-0133 or 978/283-1601; www.capeannvacations.com), is open year-round—in summer, Monday through Friday from 8am to 6pm, Saturday from 10am to 6pm, and Sunday from 10am to 4pm; in winter, Monday through Friday from 8am to 5pm. It also operates a seasonal information booth on Rogers Street at Harbor Loop.

GETTING AROUND Downtown is fairly compact and walkable, but there's more to Gloucester than that. If you can manage it, travel by car. You'll be able to make the best use of your time, especially if you plan several stops. The **Cape Ann Transportation Authority** (see above) serves Gloucester.

SPECIAL EVENTS Gloucester holds summer festivals and street fairs at the drop of a hat. They honor everything from clams to schooners. The best known is **St. Peter's Fiesta,** a colorful 4-day event at the end of June. The Italian-American fishing colony's festival has more in common with a carnival midway than a religious observation, but it's great fun. There are parades, rides, music, food, sporting events, and, on Sunday, the blessing of the fleet. On summer Sunday nights, the **Concerts in the Park** series (✆ 978/281-0543) brings live jazz, country, and traditional music to Stage Fort Park.

EXPLORING THE TOWN

Start at the water, as visitors have done for centuries. The French explorer Samuel de Champlain called the harbor "Le Beauport" in 1604—some 600 years after the Vikings first visited—and its configuration and proximity to good fishing gave it the reputation it enjoys to this day. Fishing is still Gloucester's leading industry (as your nose will tell you), with tourism a close second. The city is exceptionally welcoming—residents seem genuinely happy to see out-of-towners and to offer directions and insider info. The **Gloucester Maritime Trail** brochure, available at visitor centers, describes four excellent self-guided tours.

On Stacy Boulevard (west of downtown) is a reminder of the sea's danger. Leonard Craske's bronze statue of the **Gloucester Fisherman,** known as "The Man at the Wheel," bears the inscription "They That Go Down to the Sea in Ships 1623–1923." To the west is a memorial to the women and children who waited at home. As you take in the glorious view, consider this: More than 10,000 fishermen lost their lives during the city's first 300 years.

Stage Fort Park, off Route 127 near the intersection with Route 133, offers an excellent view of the harbor and has a busy seasonal snack bar. It's a good spot for picnicking, swimming, or playing on the cannons in the Revolutionary War fort.

To reach **East Gloucester,** follow signs as you leave downtown or go directly from Route 128, Exit 9. On East Main Street, you'll see signs for the world-famous **Rocky Neck Art Colony** 𝄐𝄐, the oldest continuously operating art colony in the country. Park in the lot on the tiny causeway and head west along Rocky Neck Avenue, which abounds with studios, galleries, restaurants, and people. The attraction is the presence of working artists, not just shops that happen to sell art. In summer, most galleries are open daily from 10am to 10pm. The prestigious **North Shore Arts Association,** 197 E. Main St. (© 978/ 283-1857), founded in 1922, is open from late May to October, Monday through Saturday from 10am to 5pm, Sunday from 1 to 5pm. Admission is free.

Also in East Gloucester, the **Gloucester Stage Company,** 267 E. Main St. (© 978/281-4099; www.cape-ann.com/stageco.html), is one of the best repertory troupes in New England. Founder and artistic director Israel Horovitz, a prizewinning playwright and screenwriter, schedules six plays a season (June to mid-Sept).

Beauport (Sleeper-McCann House) 𝄐𝄐

The Society for the Preservation of New England Antiquities, which operates Beauport, describes it as a "fantasy house," and that's putting it mildly. Interior designer Henry Davis Sleeper accumulated vast stores of American and European decorative arts and antiques in his summer home. From 1907 to 1934, he decorated the 40 rooms, 26 of which are open to the public, to illustrate literary and historical themes. The entertaining tour concentrates more on the house in general than on the countless objects. You'll see architectural details from other buildings, magnificent arrangements of colored glassware, the "Red Indian Room" (with a majestic view of the harbor), and "Strawberry Hill," the master bedroom. Note that the house is closed on summer weekends.

75 Eastern Point Blvd. © **978/283-0800.** www.spnea.org. Guided tours $10 adults, $9 seniors, $5 students and children 6–12. Tours on the hr. May 15–Sept 14 Mon–Fri 10am–4pm; Sept 15–Oct 15 daily 10am–4pm. Closed Oct 16–May 14 and summer weekends. Take E. Main St. south to Eastern Point Blvd. (a private road), continue ½ mile (1km) to house, park on left.

Cape Ann Historical Museum 𝄐

This meticulously curated museum makes an excellent introduction to Cape Ann's history and artists. It devotes an entire gallery to the extraordinary work of **Fitz Hugh Lane** 𝄐𝄐𝄐, the Luminist painter whose light-flooded canvases show off the best of his native Gloucester. The nation's single largest collection of his paintings and drawings is here. Other galleries feature works on paper by 20th-century artists such as Maurice Prendergast and Milton Avery, work by other contemporary artists, and granite-quarrying tools and equipment. There's also an outdoor sculpture court. The maritime and fisheries galleries display entire vessels, exhibits on the fishing industry, ship models, and historic photographs and models of the Gloucester waterfront. The Capt. Elias Davis House (1804), decorated and furnished in Federal style, is part of the museum.

27 Pleasant St. © **978/283-0455.** www.cape-ann.com/historical-museum. Admission $5 adults, $4.50 seniors, $3.50 students, free for children under 6. Mar–Jan Tues–Sat 10am–5pm. Closed Feb. Follow Main St. west through downtown and turn right onto Pleasant St.; the museum is 1 block up on right. Metered parking on street or in lot across street.

ORGANIZED TOURS & CRUISES

For information on whale-watches, see "A Whale of an Adventure," below.

Moby Duck Tours 𝄐 (© 978/281-3825; www.mobyduck.com) are 55-minute sightseeing expeditions that travel on land before plunging into the water. They're just the right length for kids, who delight in the transition from street to sea. The amphibious vehicles leave from Harbor Loop downtown.

(Kids) A Whale of an Adventure

The waters off the Massachusetts coast are prime **whale-watching** ✮✮ territory, and Gloucester is a center of cruises. Stellwagen Bank, which runs from Gloucester to Provincetown about 27 miles (43km) east of Boston, is a rich feeding ground for the magnificent mammals, which dine on sand eels and other fish that gather on the ridge. The whales often perform for their audience by jumping out of the water, and dolphins occasionally join the show. Naturalists on board narrate the trip for the companies listed here, pointing out the whales and describing birds and fish that cross your path.

Whale-watching is not particularly time- or cost-effective, especially if restless children are along, but it's so popular for a reason: The payoff is, literally and figuratively, huge. This is an "only in New England" experience that kids (and adults) will remember for a long time.

The season runs from May to October. Dress warmly—it's much cooler at sea than on land—and wear a hat and rubber-soled shoes. Pack sunglasses, sunscreen, a camera, and plenty of film. If you're prone to motion sickness, take precautions, because you'll be at sea for 4 to 6 hours.

This is an extremely competitive business—they'd deny it, but the companies are virtually indistinguishable. Most guarantee sightings, offer morning and afternoon cruises and deep-sea fishing excursions, honor other firms' coupons, and offer AARP and AAA discounts. Check ahead for sailing times, prices ($28–$30 for adults, less for seniors and children), and reservations, which are strongly recommended. In downtown Gloucester, **Cape Ann Whale Watch** (© **800/877-5110** or 978/283-5110; www.caww.com), is the oldest and best-known operation. Also downtown are **Captain Bill's Whale Watch** (© **800/33-WHALE** or 978/283-6995; www.captainbillswhalewatch.com) and **Seven Seas Whale Watch** (© **800/238-1776** or 978/283-1776; www.7seas-whalewatch.com). At the Cape Ann Marina, off Route 133, is **Yankee Whale Watch** (© **800/WHALING** or 978/283-0313; www.yankeewhalewatch.com).

Tickets cost $14 for adults, $12 for seniors, and $8 for children under 12. Tours operate daily from Memorial Day to Labor Day, plus weekends in September.

Also at Harbor Loop, you can tour the two-masted schooner *Adventure* ✮✮ (© **978/281-8079;** www.schooner-adventure.org), a 121-foot (36m) fishing vessel built in Essex in 1926, undergoing extensive restoration. It doesn't move, so it's not as thrilling as the *Thomas E. Lannon* (see below), but it's quicker and cheaper and can be more interesting, depending on what's being worked on. The "living museum," a National Historic Landmark, is open to visitors from Memorial Day to Labor Day, Thursday through Sunday from 10am to 4pm. The suggested donation is $5 for adults, $4 for children. The *Adventure* serves **breakfast** on Sundays from 9:30am to 1pm. The hearty meal includes typical American breakfast items, plus whatever the volunteer cooks decide to add. This is a great way to check out the ship, fuel up for sightseeing, and—most important—mingle with the locals. Adults pay $8, children $5; reservations are recommended.

The schooner ***Thomas E. Lannon*** ☆ (© **978/281-6634**; www.schooner.org) is a lovely reproduction of a Gloucester fishing vessel. The 65-foot (20m) tall ship sails from Seven Seas Wharf downtown; 2-hour excursions ($30 for adults, $25 for seniors, $20 for children under 17) leave about four times a day from mid-June to mid-October, less often on weekends from mid-May to mid-June. Reservations are recommended. The company offers music and dining cruises (including Fri lobster bakes) and "storytelling sails."

SHOPPING

Rocky Neck (see "Exploring the Town," above) offers great browsing. If you admired the wardrobe design in *The Perfect Storm,* check out the shirts and caps at **Cape Pond Ice,** 104 Commercial St., near the Chamber of Commerce (© **978/283-0174**; www.capepondice.com). Downtown, Main Street between Pleasant and Washington streets is a good destination. Agreeable stops include **Fun Among Us,** 186 Main St. (© **978/282-0339**), a toy and gift shop for kids and adults; **Mystery Train,** 178 Main St. (© **978/281-8911**; www.mystrain.com), which carries used LPs, CDs, tapes, and videos; **Ménage Gallery,** 134 Main St. (© **978/283-6030**), which shows work by artists and artisans; and the **Dogtown Book Shop,** 2 Duncan St. (© **978/281-5599**), noted for its used and antiquarian selection.

WHERE TO STAY

The 40-unit **Vista Motel,** 22 Thatcher Rd. (Rte. 127A), Gloucester (© **866/ VISTA-MA** or 978/281-3410; www.vistamotel.com), is a comfortable establishment on a hilltop near the Rockport border. Summer rates run $120 to $130.

Atlantis Oceanfront Motor Inn   This motor inn sits across the street from the water, affording stunning views from every window. It's more basic than the neighboring Bass Rocks Ocean Inn, but the views are the same. The good-sized guest rooms are decorated in comfortable, contemporary style. Every unit has a terrace or balcony. The view from second-floor accommodations is a little better.

125 Atlantic Rd., Gloucester, MA 01930. © 800/732-6313 or 978/283-0014. Fax 978/281-8994. www.atlantismotorinn.com. 40 units (some with shower only). Late June–Labor Day $140–$160 double; spring and fall $90–$140 double. Extra person $8. Off-season packages available. Closed Nov to mid-Apr. 2- to 3-night minimum stay on weekends. AE, MC, V. Follow Rte. 128 to the end (Exit 9, East Gloucester), turn left onto Bass Ave. (Rte. 127A), and follow it ½ mile (1km). Turn right and follow Atlantic Rd. **Amenities:** Coffee shop (breakfast only); heated outdoor pool. *In room:* A/C, TV.

Best Western Bass Rocks Ocean Inn   A family operation since 1946, the Bass Rocks Ocean Inn offers gorgeous views and modern accommodations in a traditional setting. The spacious guest rooms take up a sprawling, comfortable two-story motel across the road from the rocky shore. A Colonial Revival mansion built in 1899 and known as the "wedding-cake house" holds the office and public areas, including a billiard room and library. The inn has larger rooms and more of a resort feel than the neighboring Atlantis. Each unit has a balcony or patio; second-floor rooms have slightly better views. In the afternoon, the staff serves coffee, tea, lemonade, and cookies.

107 Atlantic Rd., Gloucester, MA 01930. © 800/528-1234 or 978/283-7600. Fax 978/281-6489. www. bestwestern.com/bassrocksoceaninn. 48 units. Late June to Labor Day $150–$250 double. Spring and fall discounts available. Extra person $8; rollaway or crib $12. Children under 12 stay free in parents' room. Rates include continental breakfast. 3-night minimum stay summer weekends, some spring and fall weekends.

Closed Nov to late Apr. AE, DC, DISC, MC, V. Follow Rte. 128 to the end (Exit 9, East Gloucester), turn left onto Bass Ave. (Rte. 127A), and follow it ½ mile (1km); turn right and follow Atlantic Rd. **Amenities:** Heated outdoor pool; free bikes. *In room:* A/C, TV, dataport, fridge, coffeemaker, hair dryer, iron.

WHERE TO DINE

See "Essex," above, for information on the celebrated **Woodman's of Essex,** which is about 20 minutes from downtown Gloucester.

Boulevard Oceanview Restaurant ✦ PORTUGUESE/SEAFOOD This is a friendly neighborhood place in a high-tourist-traffic location. Across the street from the waterfront promenade just west of downtown, it's a dinerlike spot with water views from the front windows and the small deck. It serves ultra-fresh seafood (crane your neck and you can almost see the processing plants) and lunch-counter sandwiches. Try shrimp *a la plancha* (in irresistible lemon-butter sauce) or one of the several unusual casseroles.

25 Western Ave. (Stacy Blvd.). ✆ **978/281-2949.** Reservations recommended for dinner in summer. Sandwiches $4–$8; main courses $7–$16; lobster priced daily. DISC, MC, V. Summer daily 11am–10pm; winter daily 11am–9:30pm.

The Franklin Cape Ann ✦✦ BISTRO A sophisticated offshoot of a neighborhood favorite in Boston's South End, the Franklin is a welcome addition to the fried-seafood-focused local dining scene. It does serve seafood, but in inventive preparations such as panko-crusted scallops accompanied by delectable lemon sauce, and pan-seared Atlantic cod with oyster mushrooms, scallions, and ginger. Meat dishes are equally creative. A narrow room with a welcoming bar at the back, it also offers fabulous martinis and live jazz at least one night a week, making it a popular late-evening destination.

118 Main St. ✆ **978/283-7888.** Reservations not accepted. Main courses $10–$16. AE, MC, V. Daily 5pm–midnight.

The Gull Restaurant ✦✦ *Kids* SEAFOOD/AMERICAN Floor-to-ceiling windows show off the Annisquam River from almost every seat at the Gull. The big, welcoming restaurant is known for prime rib as well as excellent seafood. It draws locals, visitors, boaters, and families for large portions at reasonable prices. The seafood chowder is famous, appetizers tend toward bar food, and the french fries are terrific. Daily specials run from simple lobster (market price) to sophisticated fish and meat dishes. At lunch, there's an extensive sandwich menu.

75 Essex Ave. (Rte. 133), at Cape Ann Marina. ✆ **978/281-6060.** Reservations recommended for parties of 8 or more. Main courses $5–$13 lunch, $8–$22 dinner; breakfast $3.45–$7.95. DISC, MC, V. Late Apr to Oct daily 6am–9pm. Closed Nov to late Apr. Take Rte. 133 west from intersection with Rte. 127, or take Rte. 133 east from Rte. 128.

Halibut Point Restaurant SEAFOOD/AMERICAN A local legend for its chowders and burgers, Halibut Point is a friendly tavern that serves generous portions of good food. The "Halibut Point Special"—$12 for a cup of chowder, a burger, and a beer—hits the high points. Although the clam chowder is terrific, the spicy Italian fish chowder is so good that some people come to Gloucester just for that. There's also a raw bar. Main courses are simple (mostly sandwiches) at lunch, more elaborate at dinner. Be sure to check the specials board—you didn't come all this way to a fishing port not to have fresh fish, did you?

289 Main St. ✆ **978/281-1900.** Main courses $5–$11 lunch, $9–$16 dinner. AE, DISC, MC, V. Daily 11:30am–11pm.

ROCKPORT ★

This lovely little town at the tip of Cape Ann was settled in 1690. Over the years it has been a fishing port, a center of granite excavation, and a thriving summer community whose specialty seems to be selling fudge and refrigerator magnets to out-of-towners. But there's more to Rockport than just gift shops. It's home to a lovely state park, and popular with photographers, sculptors, jewelry designers, and painters. Winslow Homer, Fitz Hugh Lane, and Childe Hassam are among the famous artists who have captured the local color. At times, especially on summer weekends, you'll be hard-pressed to find much local color in this tourist-weary destination. But for every year-round resident who seems genuinely startled when people with cameras around their necks descend each June, there are dozens who are proud to show off their town. Rockport makes an entertaining half-day trip, perhaps combined with a visit to Gloucester.

ESSENTIALS

GETTING THERE Rockport is north of Gloucester along Route 127 or 127A. At the end of Route 128, turn left at the signs for Rockport to take 127, which is shorter but more commercial. To take 127A, continue on 128 to the sign for East Gloucester and turn left. Parking is next to impossible, especially on summer Saturday afternoons. Make one loop around downtown, and then head to the free parking lot on Upper Main Street (Rte. 127). The shuttle bus to downtown costs $1. Rockport is 40 miles (64km) northeast of Boston, 7 miles (11km) north of Gloucester.

The **commuter rail** (✆ **800/392-6100** outside Mass., or 617/222-3200; www.mbta.com) runs from Boston's North Station. The trip takes 60 to 70 minutes; the round-trip fare is $10. The station is about 6 blocks from the downtown waterfront. **Cape Ann Transportation Authority** (✆ **978/283-7916;** www.canntran.com) buses serve Rockport.

VISITOR INFORMATION The **Rockport Chamber of Commerce and Board of Trade,** 3 Main St. (✆ **978/546-6575;** www.rockportusa.com), is open in summer daily from 9am to 5pm, and in winter Monday through Friday from 10am to 4pm. From mid-May to mid-October, it operates an information booth on Upper Main Street (Rte. 127), about a mile (1.6km) from the town line and a mile (1.6km) from downtown—look for the WELCOME TO ROCKPORT sign. At either location, ask for the walking-tour pamphlet, which has a good map. Out of season, from January to mid-April, Rockport is pretty but somewhat desolate, though some businesses stay open and keep reduced hours.

GETTING AROUND For traffic and congestion, downtown Boston has nothing on Rockport on a summer weekend afternoon. If you can schedule only one weekday trip, make it this one. When you arrive, park and walk, especially downtown. The Cape Ann Transportation Authority (see above) runs within the town.

SPECIAL EVENTS The **Rockport Chamber Music Festival** (✆ **978/546-7391;** www.rcmf.org) takes place in June and early July at the Rockport Art Association, 12 Main St. Events include performances, family concerts, lectures, and discussions. The annual **Christmas pageant,** on Main Street in early December, is a crowded, kid-friendly event with carol singing and live animals.

EXPLORING THE TOWN

The most famous sight in Rockport has something of an "Emperor's New Clothes" aura—it's a wooden fish warehouse on the town wharf, or T-Wharf, in the harbor. The barn-red shack known as **Motif No. 1** is the most frequently painted and photographed object in a town filled with lovely buildings and surrounded by rocky coastline. The color certainly catches the eye in the neutrals of the surrounding seascape, but you may find yourself wondering what the big deal is. Originally constructed in 1884 and destroyed during the blizzard of 1978, Motif No. 1 was rebuilt using donations from residents and visitors. It stands again on the same pier, duplicated in every detail, reinforced to withstand storms.

Nearby is **Bearskin Neck,** named after an unfortunate ursine visitor who washed ashore in 1800. It holds perhaps the highest concentration of gift shops anywhere. The narrow peninsula has one main street (South Rd.) and several alleys crammed with galleries, snack bars, antiques shops, and ancient houses. The peninsula ends in a plaza with a magnificent water view.

Throughout town, more than two dozen **art galleries** display the work of local and nationally known artists. The **Rockport Art Association,** 12 Main St. (© 978/546-6604), open daily year-round, sponsors major exhibitions and special shows.

The 1922 **Paper House,** 52 Pigeon Hill St., Pigeon Cove (© 978/546-2629), is an unusual experience. Everything in it (including the walls and furniture) was built entirely out of 100,000 newspapers. Every item is made from papers of a different period. It's open April through October, daily from 10am to 5pm. Admission is $1.50 for adults, $1 for children. Follow Route 127 north from downtown until you see signs at Curtis Street pointing to the left.

SHOPPING
Bearskin Neck is the obvious place to start. Dozens of little shops stock clothes, gifts, toys, jewelry, souvenirs, inexpensive novelties, and expensive handmade crafts and paintings. Another enjoyable stroll is along Main and Mount Pleasant streets. Good stops include the nonprofit **Toad Hall Bookstore,** 47 Main St. (© 978/546-7323); **New England Goods,** 57 Main St. (© 978/546-9677), where the stock is exclusively local; and **Willoughby's,** 20 Main St. (© 978/546-9820), a women's clothing and accessories shop.

Two favorite stops are retro delights. Downtown, you can watch taffy being made at **Tuck's Candy Factory,** 7 Dock Sq. (© 800/569-2767 or 978/546-6352), a local landmark since the 1920s. Near the train station, **Crackerjacks,** 27 Whistlestop Mall, off Railroad Avenue (© 978/546-1616), is an old-fashioned variety store with a great crafts department.

A TRIP TO THE EDGE OF THE SEA
The very tip of Cape Ann is accessible to the public, and well worth the 2½-mile (4km) trip north on Route 127 to **Halibut Point State Park** (© 978/546-2997; www.state.ma.us/dem/parks/halb.htm). The surf-battered point got its name not from the fish, but because sailing ships heading for Rockport and Gloucester must "haul about" when they reach the jutting promontory.

About 10 minutes from the parking area, you'll come to a huge water-filled quarry next to a visitor center, where staffers dispense information, brochures, and bird lists. Swimming in the water-filled quarry is absolutely forbidden. There are walking trails, tidal pools, a World War II observation tower, and a rocky beach where you can climb around on giant boulders. Guided tours ($2.50) are available on Saturday mornings in summer, and there are also bird, wildflower, and tidal-pool tours; call the park for information and schedules. From Memorial Day to Labor Day, there's a daily parking fee. This is a great place to just wander around and admire the scenery. On a clear day, you can see Maine.

WHERE TO STAY

When Rockport is busy, it's very busy, and when it's not, it's practically empty. If you haven't made summer reservations well in advance, cross your fingers and call the Chamber of Commerce to ask about cancellations. For those not driving, most innkeepers will arrange for guests to be picked up at the train station; be sure to ask about this service when you reserve.

On Route 127 about ½ mile (1km) from downtown is the **Sandy Bay Motor Inn,** 173 Main St. (© **800/437-7155** or 978/546-7155; www.sandybay motorinn.com). A modern building overlooking the road, it has an indoor pool, accepts pets, and offers doubles from $115 in summer.

In Town

Captain's Bounty Motor Inn   This modern, well-maintained motor inn is on the water. In fact, it's almost *in* the water, and nearly as close to the center of town as to the harbor. Each rather plain unit in the three-story building overlooks the water and has its own balcony. Rooms are spacious and soundproofed, with good cross-ventilation but no air-conditioning. The best units are on the adults-only top floor. Kitchenette units are available. Although it's hardly plush, and the pricing structure is a bit peculiar (note the charge for children), you can't beat the location.

1 Beach St., Rockport, MA 01966. © **978/546-9557.** www.cape-ann.com/capt-bounty. 24 units. May to mid-June $88 double, $92 efficiency, $100 efficiency suite; mid-June to early Sept $115 double, $135 efficiency, $150 efficiency suite; early Sept–Oct $95 double, $100 efficiency, $105 efficiency suite. Extra person $10; $5 for each child over 5. 2- to 3-night minimum weekends and holidays. DISC, MC, V. Closed Nov–Apr. *In room:* TV.

Inn on Cove Hill   This attractive Federal-style inn was built in 1791 using the proceeds of pirates' gold found nearby. Although it's just 2 blocks from the town wharf, the inn is set back from the road and has a hideaway feel. Guest rooms are decorated in period style; most units have colonial furnishings and handmade quilts, and some have canopy beds. Water views from rooms at the back of the house are worth the climb on the narrow stairs. In warm weather, the morning meal is served at the garden tables; in inclement weather, breakfast in bed arrives on individual trays.

37 Mt. Pleasant St., Rockport, MA 01966. © **888/546-2701** or 978/546-2701. Fax 978/546-1095. www.cape-ann.com/covehill. 9 units, 7 with private bathroom (some with shower only). $90–$135 double with private bathroom; $55 double with shared bathroom. Extra person $25. Rates include continental breakfast. 2-night minimum stay June–Oct weekends. AE, MC, V. *In room:* A/C, no phone.

Peg Leg Inn   The Peg Leg Inn consists of five houses with front porches, attractive living rooms, and well-kept flower-bordered lawns that run down to the ocean's edge. It's not luxurious, but is convenient and comfortable. Vacationing couples make up much of the clientele; families will probably prefer a more relaxed establishment (such as the Sandy Bay Motor Inn, above). Rooms are good-sized and neatly furnished in colonial style. The best units open onto excellent oceanviews. There's a sandy beach across the road.

2 King St., Rockport, MA 01966. © **800/346-2352** or 978/546-2352. www.pegleginn.com. 29 units (some with shower only). Mid-June to Labor Day, holiday and fall weekends $95–$155 double; $165 two-bedroom. Extra person $15. Rates include continental breakfast. Off-season discounts available. 2- to 3-night minimum stay on summer and holiday weekends. AE, MC, V. Closed Nov–Mar. *In room:* TV, no phone.

On the Outskirts

Emerson Inn by the Sea   Somewhere in an old guest register, you might find Ralph Waldo Emerson's name—the philosopher stayed at the original

(1840) inn. He wouldn't recognize it today: The oceanfront building expanded in 1912, and innkeepers Bruce and Michele Coates have transformed it into a mini-resort. Still, the inn retains a relaxing old-fashioned feel, with modern conveniences like a heated outdoor saltwater pool. Traditional furnishings such as four-poster beds grace the rooms, which are nicely appointed but not terribly large. If you can manage the stairs, the view from the top-floor units is worth the exertion. The best units have private balconies, fireplaces, or hot tubs; the regular oceanview rooms offer the same scenery. Public areas include a lounge with a wide-screen TV and a selection of videos. The dining room (© 978/546-9500) is open to the public; reservations are required.

1 Cathedral Ave., Rockport, MA 01966. © 800/964-5550 or 978/546-6321. Fax 978/546-7043. www. emersoninnbythesea.com. 35 units (some with shower only). May–Oct $249–$325 "best" double, $199–$209 oceanview double, $145–$169 double without view; Nov–Apr $179–$259 "best," $159–$169 with view, $95–$125 without view. Extra person $25; crib or cot $25. Rates include full breakfast in summer, continental breakfast in spring and fall. Weekly rates available. 2-night minimum stay weekends mid-May to Oct. AE, DC, DISC, MC, V. Follow Rte. 127 north from the center of town for 2 miles (3km); turn right at Phillips Ave. **Amenities:** Dining room; outdoor pool; Jacuzzi; sauna. *In room:* A/C.

WHERE TO DINE

Rockport is a "dry" community—no alcoholic beverages can be sold or served—but you can bring your own bottle, sometimes subject to a corking fee.

The birthplace of the fried clam, **Woodman's of Essex** (see "Essex," earlier in this chapter), is about half an hour from Rockport.

Brackett's Oceanview Restaurant *Kids* SEAFOOD/AMERICAN The dining room at Brackett's has a gorgeous view of the water. The nautical decor suits the seafood-intensive menu, which offers enough variety to make this a good choice for families—burgers are always available. The service is friendly and the fresh seafood quite good, if not particularly adventurous. Try the moist, plump codfish cakes if you're looking for a traditional New England dish, or something with Cajun spices for variety. The most exciting offerings are on the extensive dessert menu, where anything homemade is a great choice.

29 Main St. © 978/546-2797. www.bracketts.com. Reservations recommended for dinner. Main courses $7–$20 lunch, $10–$26 dinner. AE, DC, DISC, MC, V. Mid-Apr to Memorial Day Thurs–Sun 11:30am–8pm; Memorial Day–Oct Sun–Fri 11:30am–8pm, Sat 11:30am–9pm. Closed Nov to mid-Apr.

The Greenery *Kids* SEAFOOD/AMERICAN The Greenery could get away with serving so-so food because of its great location near Bearskin Neck—but it doesn't. The cafe at the front serves light fare to stay or go; the dining rooms, at the back, boast great harbor views. The food ranges from tasty crab salad quiche at lunch to lobster at dinner to steamers and fresh-caught fish anytime. As in any town with working fishermen, check out the daily specials. All baking is done in-house, which explains the lines at the front counter for muffins and pastries. When the restaurant is busy, the cheerful service tends to drag. This is a good place to launch a picnic on the beach, and an equally good spot for lingering over coffee and dessert while watching the action around the harbor.

15 Dock Sq. © 978/546-9593. Reservations recommended for dinner. Main courses $7–$12 lunch, $10–$22 dinner; breakfast items $2–$7. AE, DC, DISC, MC, V. Apr–Oct Mon–Fri 8am–11pm, Sat–Sun 7am–11pm; off-season Sun–Thurs 8am–5pm, Fri–Sat 8am–7pm. Off-season hours vary; call ahead.

My Place By-the-Sea SEAFOOD The lure of My Place By-the-Sea is its location at the very end of Bearskin Neck, where its touristy clientele finds Rockport's only outdoor oceanfront deck. The two decks and shaded patio afford excellent views of Sandy Bay. The menu is reliable, with many options dictated by the daily catch. The baked fish and seafood pasta entrees are good choices.

68 South Rd., Bearskin Neck. ✆ **978/546-9667.** Reservations recommended for dinner; accepted same day after noon. Main courses $7–$13 lunch, $15–$22 dinner. AE, DC, DISC, MC, V. Apr–Nov daily 11:30am–9:30pm. Closed Dec–Mar.

Portside Chowder House CHOWDER/SEAFOOD   The crowds at this busy restaurant are here for chowder—clam and whatever else looked good that day. It comes by the cup, pint, and quart, to go or to eat in. You can also get seafood platters and surprisingly good burgers and lobster rolls, but the best reason to come here is for tasty chowder to carry to the edge of the sea for a picnic.

Tuna Wharf, off Bearskin Neck. ✆ **978/546-7045.** Reservations not accepted. Most items less than $8. No credit cards. Late June to Labor Day daily 11am–8pm; Labor Day to late June daily 11am–3pm. Closed Thanksgiving, Dec 25.

6 Newburyport, Ipswich & Plum Island

The area between Cape Ann and the New Hampshire border is magnificent, with outdoor sights and sounds that can only be described as natural wonders, and enough impressive architecture to keep any city slicker happy.

In a part of the world where the word "charming" is used almost as often as "hello," Newburyport is a singular example of a picturesque waterfront city. Downtown Newburyport is on the Merrimack River. On the town's Atlantic coast, Plum Island contains one of the country's top nature preserves. On the other side of Ipswich Bay, Ipswich is a lovely town that's home to Crane Beach, on another wildlife reservation.

NEWBURYPORT 🐿🐿

To get here directly from Boston, take I-93 (or Rte. 1 if it's not rush hour) to I-95—*not* Route 128, as for most other destinations in this chapter—and follow it to Exit 57, a solid 45-minute ride. Signs point to downtown, where you can park and explore. The **commuter rail** (✆ **800/392-6100** outside Mass., or 617/222-3200; www.mbta.com) from North Station takes about 75 minutes and costs $10 round-trip.

Newburyport has a substantial year-round population that lends it a less touristy atmosphere than its appearance might suggest. Start your visit at the **Greater Newburyport Chamber of Commerce and Industry,** 29 State St. (✆ **978/462-6680;** www.newburyportchamber.org), in the heart of the red-brick downtown shopping district. It also runs a seasonal information booth on Merrimac Street near Green Street.

Market Square, at the foot of State Street near the waterfront, is the center of a neighborhood packed with boutiques, gift shops, plain and fancy restaurants, and antiques stores. You can also wander to the water, take a stroll on the boardwalk, and enjoy the action on the river. Architecture buffs will want to climb the hill to High Street, where the **Charles Bulfinch**–designed building (1805) that houses the Superior Court is only one of several Federal-era treasures. Ask at the Chamber of Commerce for the walking-tour map.

If you haven't gone out to sea yet, now is a good time, and here's a good place: **Newburyport Whale Watch** 🐿🐿, Hilton's Dock, 54 Merrimac St. (✆ **800/ 848-1111** or 978/499-0832; www.newburyportwhalewatch.com), offers 4½-hour cruises on a 100-foot (30m) boat with on-board marine biologists as guides. Tickets are $28 for adults, $24 for seniors, and $18 for children 4 to 16;

More Whale Tales: A Trip to New Bedford

The masses that flock to eastern Massachusetts aren't yet swarming the cobblestone streets of New Bedford, which makes it a good destination for families on the verge of crowd-phobia. The **New Bedford Whaling National Historical Park,** which encompasses the downtown historic district, commemorates the city's past as the world's leading whaling port.

The downtown area near the waterfront has been restored, and the attractions are reasonably close together. Start your visit at the **National Park Service Visitor Center,** 33 William St. (© **508/996-4095;** www.nps.gov/nebe), open daily from 9am to 5pm. The exhibits include a film about whaling and the city's history. Take a guided walking tour (daily in summer, some off-season weekends) or pick up a brochure that describes self-guided excursions around the historic district.

The centerpiece of the Historical Park is the **New Bedford Whaling Museum** ⟨, 18 Johnny Cake Hill (© **508/997-0046;** www.whaling museum.org). It's the world's premier whaling museum, which sounds terribly specialized but is actually quite absorbing. On display in the lobby is the skeleton of a 65-foot (20m) juvenile blue whale, Kobo (short for "king of the blue ocean"). Admission to the lobby is free, but the rest of the museum is worth a visit. Children love the half-scale model of the whaling bark *Lagoda,* the world's largest ship model. The museum is open daily from 9am to 5pm, until 9pm on the second Thursday of each month. Admission is $6 for adults, $5 for seniors and students, and $4 for children 6 to 14.

The **Seamen's Bethel,** 15 Johnny Cake Hill (© **508/992-3295**), a nondenominational chapel described in Herman Melville's classic novel *Moby-Dick,* is across the street. Up the hill from the water, the **Rotch-Duff-Jones House & Garden Museum,** 396 County St. (© **508/997-1401**), is an 1834 Greek Revival mansion with magnificent formal gardens.

To get here, take the Southeast Expressway south to I-93 (Rte. 128), then Route 24 south. Follow signs to Route 140 south to I-195. From Plymouth, take Route 44 west to Route 24 south. **American Eagle** (© **800/453-5040** or 508/993-2040) buses take 75 minutes from Boston's South Station ($18 round-trip). For more information, contact the **New Bedford Office of Tourism** (© **508/979-1745;** www.ci.new-bedford.ma.us, click "visitors") or the **Bristol County Convention & Visitors Bureau** (© **800/288-6263** or 508/997-1250; www.bristol-county.org).

reservations are suggested. (See "A Whale of an Adventure," on p. 162, for more information.)

Or, head to the ocean using an inland route: From downtown, take Water Street south until it becomes Plum Island Turnpike and follow it to the Parker River National Wildlife Refuge.

PARKER RIVER NATIONAL WILDLIFE REFUGE ⫷⫸

The 4,662-acre (1,888-hectare) refuge (℗ **978/465-5753;** northeast.fws. gov/ma/pkr.htm) on **Plum Island** is a complex of barrier beaches, dunes, and salt marshes, one of the few remaining in the Northeast. The refuge is flat-out breathtaking, whether you're exploring the marshes or the seashore. More than 800 species of plants and animals (including more than 300 bird species) visit or make their home on the narrow finger of land between Broad Sound and the Atlantic Ocean.

The refuge offers some of the best **birding** ⫷⫸⫸ anywhere, as well as observation of mammals and plants. Wooden boardwalks with observation towers and platforms wind through marshes and along the shore—most lack handrails, so this isn't an activity for rambunctious children. You might see native and migratory species such as owls, hawks, martins, geese, warblers, ducks, snowy egrets, swallows, monarch butterflies, Canada geese, foxes, beavers, and harbor seals.

The ocean beach closes April 1 to allow piping plovers, listed by the federal government as a threatened species, to nest. The areas not being used for nesting reopen July 1; the rest open in August, when the birds are through. The currents are strong and can be dangerous, and there are no lifeguards—swimming is allowed but not encouraged. Surf fishing is popular, though; striped bass and bluefish are found in the area. A permit is required for night fishing and vehicle access to the beach.

The refuge is open from dawn to dusk year-round. There's a daily entrance fee of $5 for motorists, $2 for bikers and pedestrians. The seven parking lots fill quickly on weekends when the weather is good, so plan to arrive early. South of lot 4 (Hellcat Swamp), the access road is flat and well maintained but not paved.

IPSWICH ⫷

Across Ipswich Bay from Plum Island is the town of Ipswich. It's accessible from Route 1A (which you can pick up in Newburyport or at Route 128 in Hamilton) and from Route 133 (which intersects with Rte. 128 in Gloucester and I-95 in Georgetown). The **visitor center,** in the Hall Haskell House, 36 S. Main St., Rte. 133 (℗ **978/356-8540**), is open daily from Memorial Day to Columbus Day. Visitor information is also available from the **Ipswich Community Chamber of Commerce,** 46 Newmarch St. (℗ **978/356-3231**), and the business association's website (**www.ipswichma.com**).

Settled in 1630, Ipswich is dotted with **17th-century houses** ⫷—reputedly the largest concentration in the United States. Many are private homes; ask at the visitor center for a map of a tour that passes three dozen of them. House-tour aficionados can go inside the **John Whipple House,** 1 South Village Green (℗ **978/356-2811**). Built between 1655 and 1700, it's decorated with period furnishings. May through October, tours ($7 for adults, $3 for children) start on the hour from 10am to 3pm Wednesday through Saturday, 1 to 3pm Sunday.

Ipswich is also known for two more contemporary structures. The **Clam Box,** 206 High St., Route 1A/133 (℗ **978/356-9707**), is a restaurant shaped like— what else?—a red-and-white-striped takeout clam box. It's a great place to try Ipswich clams, and not easy to sneak past if you have children in the car. Heading south from Newburyport, it's on the right. Closed December through February.

South of Ipswich Center, near the intersection of Routes 1A and 133, look carefully for the Argilla Road sign (on the east side of the street). If you're traveling west on Route 133 from Gloucester and Essex, watch for a sign on the right pointing to Northgate Road, which intersects with Argilla Road. Follow it east to the end, where you'll find the 1,400-acre (567-hectare) Crane Estate.

The property is home to **Crane Beach** (see "Life's a Beach," on p. 158), the **Crane Wildlife Refuge** ⍟⍟, a network of hiking trails, and **Castle Hill,** 290 Argilla Rd. (② **978/356-4351;** www.thetrustees.org). One of the Boston area's most popular wedding locations, the exquisite Stuart-style seaside mansion known as the Great House was built by Richard Teller Crane, Jr., who made his fortune in plumbing and bathroom fixtures early in the 20th century. If you can't wangle an invitation to a wedding, tours of the house ($7 for adults, $5 for seniors and children) are given on Wednesday and Thursday in summer and two Sundays a year, spring and fall. You can also explore the estate ($8 per car on summer weekends, otherwise $5 per car) without entering the house.

Children who can't get excited about a tour might be pacified by a stop just before Castle Hill. **Russell Orchards Store and Winery** ⍟, 143 Argilla Rd. (② **978/356-5366;** www.russellorchardsMA.com), is open daily May through November. It has a picnic area, farm animals, and an excellent country store. Depending on the season, you might go on a hayride or taste fruit wines. Be sure to try some cider and doughnuts.

7 Plymouth ⍟⍟

Everyone educated in the United States knows at least a little about Plymouth—about how the Pilgrims, fleeing religious persecution, left England on the *Mayflower* and landed at Plymouth Rock in 1620. Many also know that the Pilgrims endured disease and privation, and that just 51 people from the original group of 102 celebrated the first Thanksgiving in 1621 with Squanto, a Pawtuxet Indian associated with the Wampanoags, and his cohorts.

What you won't know until you visit is how small everything was. The *Mayflower* (a replica) seems perilously tiny, and when you contemplate how dangerous life was at the time, it's hard not to be impressed by the settlers' accomplishments. The *Mayflower* passengers weren't even aiming for Plymouth. They originally set out for what they called "Northern Virginia," near the mouth of the Hudson River. On November 11, 1620, rough weather and high seas forced them to make for Cape Cod Bay and anchor at Provincetown. The captain then announced that they had found a safe harbor, and refused to continue to their original destination. On December 16, Provincetown having proven an unsatisfactory location, the weary travelers landed at Plymouth.

Today, Plymouth is in many ways a model destination, where the 17th century coexists with the 21st, and most historic attractions are both educational and fun. Tourists jam the downtown area in summer, but the year-round population is so large that Plymouth feels more like the working community it is than like a warm-weather day-trip destination. It's a manageable excursion from Boston, particularly enjoyable if you're traveling with children. It also makes a good stop between Boston and Cape Cod.

ESSENTIALS
GETTING THERE   By car, follow the Southeast Expressway (I-93) from Boston to Route 3. From Cape Cod, take Route 3 north. Take Exit 6A to Route 44 east, and follow signs to the historic attractions. The 40-mile (64km) trip from Boston takes 45 to 60 minutes if it's not rush hour. Take Exit 5 to the **Regional Information Complex** for maps, brochures, and information. Take Exit 4 to go directly to **Plimoth Plantation.**

Plymouth

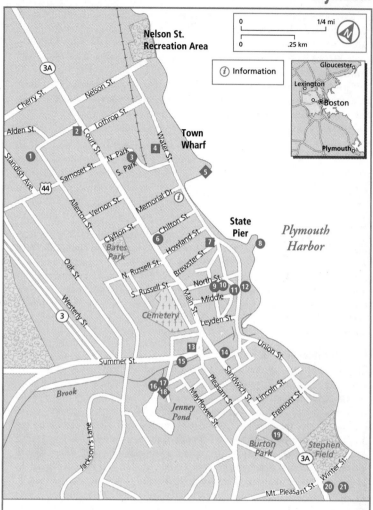

Nelson St.
Recreation Area

0   1/4 mi

0   .25 km

(i) Information

Gloucester

Lexington

Boston

Plymouth

Town
Wharf

State
Pier

*Plymouth
Harbor*

Cherry St.

Nelson St.

Alden St.

Lothrop St.

Court St.

Standish Ave.

Samoset St.

N. Park

S. Park

Water St.

Vernon St.

Allerton St.

Memorial Dr.

Clyfton St.

Chilton St.

*Bates
Park*

Howland St.

Brewster St.

Oak St.

N. Russell St.

S. Russell St.

North St.

Main St.

Middle

Westerly St.

Cemetery

Leyden St.

Union St.

Summer St.

Sandwich St.

Lincoln St.

Brook

Pleasant St.

Mayflower St.

Fremont St.

*Jenney
Pond*

Jackson's Lane

*Burton
Park*

*Stephen
Field*

Winter St.

Mt. Pleasant St.

ACCOMODATIONS ■

Cold Spring Motel **2**

Governor Bradford
on the Harbour **7**

John Carver Inn **13**

Pilgrim Sands Motel **21**

Sheraton Inn Plymouth **4**

DINING ◆

Lobster Hut **5**

Run of the Mill Tavern **18**

ATTRACTIONS ●

Harlow Old Fort House **19**

Hedge House **3**

Jabez Howland House **14**

Jenney Grist Mill **17**

Mayflower II **8**

Mayflower Society
Museum **10**

National Monument
to the Forefathers **1**

Pilgrim Hall Museum **6**

Plimoth Plantation **20**

Plymouth National
Wax Museum **12**

Plymouth Rock **11**

Sparrow House **15**

Spooner House **9**

Town Brook Park **16**

The **commuter rail** (© 800/392-6100 outside Mass., or 617/222-3200; www.mbta.com) serves Cordage Park, on Route 3A north of downtown, from South Station. The round-trip fare is $10. The **Plymouth Area Link bus** (© 508/222-6106; www.gatra.org/pal.htm) runs between the train station and downtown. The fare is 75¢.

Plymouth & Brockton buses (© 617/773-9401 or 508/746-0378; www. p-b.com) run more often and cost more than the train: $9 one-way, $17 round-trip. The ride takes about an hour from South Station.

VISITOR INFORMATION If you haven't visited the Regional Information Complex (see "Getting There," above), pick up a map at the **visitor center** (© 508/747-7525), open seasonally at 130 Water St., across from the town pier. To plan ahead, contact Plymouth Visitor Information, known as **Destination Plymouth** (© 800/USA-1620 or 508/747-7525; www.visit-plymouth.com). The **Plymouth County Convention & Visitors Bureau** (© 508/747-0100; www.plymouth-1620.com), publishes a vacation guide.

GETTING AROUND The downtown attractions are accessible on foot. A shallow hill slopes from the center of town to the waterfront. **Plymouth Rock Trolley Company** (© 800/698-56636 or 508/747-4161; www.plymouthrock trolley.com) offers a 40-minute narrated tour and unlimited reboarding daily from Memorial Day to October and weekends until Thanksgiving. It serves marked stops downtown (every 20 min.) and Plimoth Plantation (once an hour in summer). Tickets are $10 for adults, $9 for seniors and AAA members, and $8 for children 3 to 12.

EXPLORING THE HISTORIC SITES

No matter how many times you suffered through elementary-school pageants wearing a big black hat and paper buckles on your shoes, you can still learn something about Plymouth and the Pilgrims. The logical place to begin is where the Pilgrims first set foot—at **Plymouth Rock** *❀❀*. The rock, accepted as the landing place of the *Mayflower* passengers, was originally 15 feet (5m) long and 3 feet (1m) wide. It was moved on the eve of the Revolution and several times thereafter. In 1867, it assumed its present position at tide level. The Colonial Dames of America commissioned the portico around the rock, designed by McKim, Mead & White and erected in 1920. The rock isn't much to look at, but the accompanying descriptions are interesting, and the atmosphere curiously inspiring.

To get away from the waterfront crowds, make your way to **Town Brook Park,** at Jenney Pond, across Summer Street from the John Carver Inn. Near the tree-bordered pond is the **Jenney Grist Mill,** 6 Spring Lane (© 508/747-3715). It's a working museum where you can see a reconstructed water-powered mill that operates in summer, daily from 10am to 5pm. Admission is $2.50 for adults, $2 for children 5 to 12. The specialty shops in the complex, including the ice-cream shop, are open year-round, daily from 10am to 6pm. Ducks and geese live in the pond, and there's room to run around.

Also removed from the waterfront is the **National Monument to the Fore-fathers** (© 508/746-1790), a granite behemoth inscribed with the names of the *Mayflower* passengers. Heading away from the harbor on Route 44, look carefully on the right for the turn onto Allerton Street, and climb the hill. The 81-foot-high (24m) monument is elaborately decorated with figures represent-ing moral and political virtues and scenes of Pilgrim history—a style of public statuary so unfashionable that it seems quite rebellious. The monument is incongruous in its little park in a residential neighborhood, but it's also quite impressive. The view from the hilltop is excellent.

Mayflower II ✿ *(Kids)*   Berthed a few steps from Plymouth Rock, *Mayflower II* is a full-scale reproduction of the type of ship that brought the Pilgrims from England to America in 1620. Even at full scale, the 106½-foot (32m) vessel seems remarkably small. Although little technical information about the original *Mayflower* survives, William A. Baker, designer of *Mayflower II,* incorporated the few references in Governor Bradford's account of the voyage with other research to re-create the ship as authentically as possible. Costumed guides provide interesting first-person narratives about the vessel and voyage. Displays describe and illustrate the journey and the Pilgrims' experience, including 17th-century navigation techniques.

State Pier. ⓒ 508/746-1622. www.plimoth.org. Admission $8 adults, $6 children 6–12. *Mayflower II* and Plimoth Plantation admission $22 adults, $20 seniors, $14 children 6–12. Apr–Nov daily 9am–5pm.

Pilgrim Hall Museum ✿   This is a great place to get a sense of the day-to-day lives of Plymouth's first European residents. Many original possessions of the early Pilgrims and their descendants are on display, including Myles Standish's sword, Governor Bradford's Bible, and an uncomfortable chair (you can sit in a replica) that belonged to William Brewster. Regularly changing exhibits explore aspects of the settlers' lives, such as home construction or the history of prominent families. Through April 2003, *Patriots and Pilgrims* will focus on Plymouth's role in the Revolution. Among the permanent exhibits is the skeleton of the *Sparrow-Hawk,* a ship wrecked on Cape Cod in 1626 that lay buried in the sand until 1863.

75 Court St. ⓒ 508/746-1620. www.pilgrimhall.org. Admission $5 adults, $4.50 seniors and AAA members, $3 children 5–17; $15 per family. Feb–Dec daily 9:30am–4:30pm. Closed Jan, Dec 25. From Plymouth Rock, walk north on Water St. and up the hill on Chilton St.

Plimoth Plantation ✿✿ *(Kids)*   Allow at least half a day to explore this re-creation of the 1627 Pilgrim village, which children and adults find equally interesting. Enter by the hilltop fort that protects the "villagers" and walk down the hill to the farm area, visiting homes and gardens constructed with careful attention to historic detail. The "Pilgrims" are actors who, in speech, dress, and manner, assume the personalities of members of the original community. You can watch them framing a house, splitting wood, shearing sheep, preserving foodstuffs, or cooking a pot of fish stew over an open hearth, all as it was done in the 1600s. Wear comfortable shoes—you'll be walking a lot, and the plantation isn't paved.

The plantation is as accurate as research can make it. The planners combined accounts of the original colony with archaeological research, old records, and the history written by the Pilgrims' leader, William Bradford (who often used the spelling "Plimoth"). There are daily militia drills with matchlock muskets that are fired to demonstrate the community's defense system. In fact, little defense was needed, because the Native Americans were friendly. Local tribes included the Wampanoags, who are represented near the village at Hobbamock's Homesite (included in plantation admission). Museum staffers show off native foodstuffs, agricultural practices, and crafts.

At the main entrance are two buildings with an interesting orientation show, exhibits, a gift shop, a bookstore, and a cafeteria. There's also a picnic area. Call or surf ahead for information on special events, lectures, tours, workshops, theme dinners, and family programs.

Rte. 3. ℂ 508/746-1622. www.plimoth.org. Admission $20 adults, $12 children 6–12. Plimoth Plantation and *Mayflower II* admission $22 adults, $20 seniors, $14 children 6–12. Apr–Nov daily 9am–5pm. From Rte. 3, take Exit 4, Plimoth Plantation Hwy.

Plymouth National Wax Museum ★★ *Kids*   Adults who visited this entertaining museum as children can still tell you all about the Pilgrims. The galleries hold more than 180 life-size figures arranged in scenes. Dramatic soundtracks tell the story of the move to Holland to escape persecution in England, the harrowing trip across the ocean, the first Thanksgiving, and even the tale of Myles Standish, Priscilla Mullins, and John Alden. This museum is a must if children are in your party, and adults will enjoy it, too. On the hill outside is a monument at the gravesite of the Pilgrims who died during the settlement's first winter.

16 Carver St. ℂ 508/746-6468. Admission $6 adults, $5.50 seniors, $2.75 children 5–12. Daily Mar–May 9am–5pm; June 9am–7pm; July–Aug 9am–9pm; Sept–Oct 9am–7pm; Nov 9am–5pm. Closed Dec–Feb. From Plymouth Rock, turn around and walk up the hill or the steps.

THE HISTORIC HOUSES

You can't stay in Plymouth's historic houses, but they're worth a visit to see the changing styles of architecture and furnishings since the 1600s. Costumed guides explain the homemaking and crafts of earlier generations. Most of the houses are open Memorial Day through Columbus Day, during Thanksgiving celebrations, and around Christmas; call for schedules.

Tip: Unless you have a sky-high tolerance for house tours, pick just one or two from eras that you find particularly interesting. This advice applies especially if you're sightseeing with children.

Six homes are open to visitors. The 1640 **Sparrow House,** 42 Summer St. (ℂ **508/747-1240;** admission $1), and the 1666 **Jabez Howland House,** 33 Sandwich St. (ℂ **508/746-9590;** $4 adults, $2 children), are most engaging for those curious about the original settlers. The other houses are the 1677 **Harlow Old Fort House,** 119 Sandwich St. (ℂ **508/746-0012;** $4 adults, $2 children); the 1749 **Spooner House,** 27 North St. (ℂ **508/746-0012;** $4 adults, $2 children); the 1754 **Mayflower Society Museum,** 4 Winslow St. (ℂ **508/746-2590;** $2.50 adults, 75¢ children); and the 1809 **Hedge House,** 126 Water St. (ℂ **508/746-9697;** $4 adults, $2 children).

ORGANIZED TOURS & CRUISES

To follow in the Pilgrims' footsteps, take a **Colonial Lantern Tour** ★★ (ℂ **800/698-5636** or 508/747-4161; www.lanterntours.com). Participants carry pierced-tin lanterns on a 90-minute walking tour of the original settlement under the direction of a knowledgeable guide. It might seem a bit hokey at first, but it's fascinating. Tours run nightly April through Thanksgiving. Tickets are $10 for adults, $8 for children; check the meeting place when you call for reservations.

Narrated cruises run from April or May to November. **Splashdown Amphibious Tours** ★ (ℂ **800/225-4000** or 508/747-7658; www.ducktours plymouth.com) takes you around town on land and water. The kid-friendly 1-hour excursions (half on land, half on water) leave from Harbor Place, near the Governor Bradford motel, on Water Street—and wind up in the harbor. They cost $17 for adults, $10 for children 3 to 12, and $3 for children under 3. **Capt. John Boats,** Town Wharf (ℂ **800/242-2469** or 508/747-2400; www.captjohn.com), offers several tours. The most eye-catching option is the *Pilgrim Belle* paddle-wheeler. Its 75-minute narrated tours of the harbor ($10 for adults, $8 for seniors, $7 for children) leave from State Pier; dining and entertainment cruises and whale-watches are also available.

A LEGENDARY ATTRACTION NEARBY

The narrow-gauge **Edaville Railroad** ☆☆ (© **877/EDAVILLE** or 508/866-8190; www.edaville.org) is a longtime favorite with young New Englanders. The main attraction is an entertaining 45-minute train ride on a 5½-mile (9km) loop of tracks that takes you past cranberry bogs. Also on the premises are a carousel, kiddie rides, railroad museum, and cafe. It's a retro experience—no high-tech multimedia stuff, just good clean fun.

The railroad, which dates to 1947, reopened in 1999 after being shuttered for 7 years, and has tinkered with its schedule ever since. Definitely call ahead to confirm hours. It's currently open in July and August Friday through Sunday from 11am to 6pm; September and October weekends from 11am to 5pm; and November through early January (the Christmas Light Festival) weekdays from 4 to 9pm and weekends from 2 to 10pm. The railroad is extremely crowded when the weather is good; try to arrive when it opens. Admission is $12.50 for adults, $10.50 for seniors, and $7.50 for children 3 to 12. The railroad is in South Carver. From Plymouth, follow Route 44 west to Route 58 south, continue about 3 miles (5km) to Rochester Road, and turn right.

SHOPPING

Water Street, on the harbor, boasts an inexhaustible supply of souvenir shops. A less kitschy destination, just up the hill, is Route 3A, known as Court, Main, and Warren street as it runs through town. **Lily's Apothecary,** 6 Main St. Extension, in the old post office (© **508/747-7546;** www.lilysapothecary.com), carries a big-city-style selection of skin- and hair-care products. **Main Street Antiques,** 46 Main St. (© **508/747-8887**), is home to dozens of dealers. **Pilgrim's Progress,** 13 Court St. (© **508/746-6033**), carries women's and men's clothing. **Great Giraffe Graphic Co.,** 11 Court St. (© **508/830-1990**), is an entertaining card and gift shop. Plymouth has a pawnshop, **Peggy's,** 37 Court St. (© **508/746-1952**), that sells jewelry, electronic equipment, and power tools.

WHERE TO STAY

Just about every establishment in town participates in a **Destination Plymouth** (© **800/USA-1620;** www.visit-plymouth.com) program that piles on the deals and discounts. Especially in the off-season, this can represent great savings. On busy summer weekends, it's not unusual for every room in town to be taken; make reservations well in advance.

Cold Spring Motel & Guest Suites ☆ *Value*   Convenient to downtown and the historic sights, this fastidiously maintained motel and the adjacent cottages surround nicely landscaped lawns. A $2-million project completed in 2001 updated the existing accommodations and added 30 units. Rooms are pleasantly decorated and big enough for a family to spread out; if the adults want some privacy, book a two-bedroom cottage. The location, a bit removed from the water, makes the Cold Spring a good deal. The complex is 2 blocks inland, set back from the street in a quiet part of town.

188 Court St. (Rte. 3A), Plymouth, MA 02360. © 800/678-8667 or 508/746-2222. Fax 508/746-2744. www.coldspringmotel.com. 62 units (some with shower only). $89–$139 double; $139–$169 suite; $109–$139 cottage. Extra person $10; rollaway $10; crib $5. Children under 12 stay free in parents' room. Off-season discounts available. Mid-May to Oct rates include continental breakfast. AE, DISC, MC, V. Closed Dec–Mar. *In room:* A/C, TV, dataport, coffeemaker, hair dryer.

Governor Bradford on the Harbour   This well-maintained motor inn occupies a great location across the street from the waterfront and only a block from Plymouth Rock and the *Mayflower II.* Each attractively decorated room contains modern furnishings; all were redone in 2000. The more expensive units on the top floor offer excellent water views—if that's what you care about, they're worth the money.

98 Water St., Plymouth, MA 02360. ℂ 800/332-1620 or 508/746-6200. Fax 508/747-3032. www.governor bradford.com. 94 units (some with shower only). From $138 double. Extra person $10. Children under 16 stay free in parents' room. Off-season, AAA, and AARP discounts available. 2-night minimum stay weekends and holidays. AE, DC, DISC, MC, V. **Amenities:** Small heated outdoor pool; coin-op laundry. *In room:* A/C, TV, dataport, fridge.

John Carver Inn ⭐ *(Kids)*   A three-story colonial-style building with a landmark portico, this hotel offers comfortable, modern accommodations and plenty of amenities, including two pools. The indoor "theme pool," a big hit with families, has a large water slide and a Pilgrim ship model. Business features, including meeting space, make this the Sheraton's main competition for corporate travelers. The good-sized guest rooms are decorated in colonial style. The best units are the lavish suites with private Jacuzzis; "four-poster" rooms contain king beds and sleeper sofas. The inn is within walking distance of the main attractions on the edge of the downtown business district.

25 Summer St., Plymouth, MA 02360. ℂ 800/274-1620 or 508/746-7100. Fax 508/746-8299. www.john carverinn.com. 85 units. Mid-Apr to mid-June and mid-Oct to Nov $99–$149 double, $209 suite; mid-June to mid-Oct $129–$179 double, $239 suite; Dec to mid-Apr $89–$129 double, $189 suite. Extra person $20; rollaway $20; cribs free. Children under 19 stay free in parents' room. Packages and senior and AAA discounts available. AE, DC, DISC, MC, V. **Amenities:** Restaurant (American/seafood); outdoor and indoor pools; room service; laundry service; dry cleaning. *In room:* A/C, TV, dataport.

Pilgrim Sands Motel ⭐⭐ *(Kids)*   This attractive motel sits on its own private beach 3 miles (5km) south of town, within walking distance of Plimoth Plantation. If you want to avoid the bustle of downtown and still be near the water, it's an excellent choice. The good-sized rooms are tastefully furnished and well maintained. If you can swing it, book a beachfront room—the view is worth the money, especially when the surf is rough.

150 Warren Ave. (Rte. 3A), Plymouth, MA 02360. ℂ 800/729-7263 or 508/747-0900. Fax 508/746-8066. www.pilgrimsands.com. 64 units. Summer $118–$160 double, spring and early fall $98–$130 double, Apr and late fall $80–$99 double, Dec–Mar $70–$85 double; $130–$250 suite year-round. Extra person $6–$8 (suite $10–$15). 2-night minimum stay on holiday weekends. Rates may be higher on holiday weekends. AE, DC, DISC, MC, V. **Amenities:** Coffee shop; indoor and outdoor pools; Jacuzzi. *In room:* A/C, TV, dataport, fridge, hair dryer.

Sheraton Inn Plymouth   If you need the amenities of a chain and want to be near the historic sights, this is your only choice. Happily, it's a good one. Vacationers enjoy the central location, and the facilities for business travelers are the most extensive in town. The four-story hotel sits on a hill across the street from the waterfront. Rooms are tastefully furnished in contemporary style; some have small balconies that overlook the indoor pool. The best units, facing the harbor on the top two floors, afford excellent views.

180 Water St., Plymouth, MA 02360. ℂ 877/500-0050, 800/325-3535 (Sheraton), or 508/747-4900. Fax 508/746-2609. www.sheratonplymouth.com. 175 units. Apr–Oct $145–$190 double; Nov–Mar $90–$135 double. Extra person $15. Children under 18 stay free in parents' room. AE, DC, DISC, MC, V. **Amenities:** Restaurant (American); pub; indoor pool; exercise room; Jacuzzi; sauna; laundry service; dry cleaning. *In room:* A/C, TV, dataport, coffeemaker, hair dryer.

WHERE TO DINE

Plimoth Plantation (p. 175) has a cafeteria and a picnic area, and occasionally schedules theme dinners. The family-friendly **Hearth 'n' Kettle** chain has a branch at the John Carver Inn (see above), and there's a lively Southwestern restaurant, **Sam Diego's** (© 508/747-0048), at 51 Main St.

Lobster Hut ✿ SEAFOOD   The Lobster Hut is a busy self-service restaurant with a great view. It's popular with both locals and sightseers. Order and pick up at the counter, then head to an indoor table or out onto the large deck that overlooks the bay. To start, try clam chowder or lobster bisque. The seafood "rolls" (hot-dog buns with your choice of filling) are excellent. The many fried seafood options include clams, scallops, shrimp, and haddock. There are also boiled and steamed items, burgers, chicken tenders—and lobster, of course. Beer and wine are served, but only with meals.

25 Town Wharf. © 508/746-2270. Reservations not accepted. Lunch specials $5–$8; main courses $6–$14; sandwiches $3–$7; lobster priced daily. MC, V. Summer daily 11am–9pm; winter daily 11am–7pm. Closed Jan.

Run of the Mill Tavern ✿ AMERICAN   This friendly restaurant sits 3 blocks inland, across from Town Brook Park. You won't mind not having a water view—the food is tasty and reasonably priced, and the comfortable wood-paneled tavern is a popular hangout. The unconventional clam chowder, made with red potatoes, is fantastic. Other appetizers include nachos, potato skins, and mushrooms. Entrees are well-prepared versions of familiar meat, chicken, and fish dishes, plus sandwiches, burgers, and fresh seafood specials (fried, broiled, or baked).

Jenney Grist Mill Village, off Summer St. © 508/830-1262. Reservations not accepted. Main courses $6–$12; children's menu $3–$4. AE, DC, DISC, MC, V. Sun–Thurs 11:30am–10pm; Fri–Sat 11:30am–11pm. Bar closes at 1am.

6

Cape Cod

by Laura M. Reckford

Only 75 miles (121km) long, Cape Cod is a curling peninsula encompassing miles of beaches, hundreds of freshwater ponds, more than a dozen richly historic New England villages, scores of classic clam shacks and ice cream shops—and it's just about everyone's idea of the perfect summer vacation spot.

More than 13 million visitors flock to the Cape to enjoy summertime's nonstop carnival. In full swing, the Cape is, if anything, perhaps a bit too popular for some tastes. Connoisseurs are discovering the subtler appeal of the off-season, when prices plummet along with the population. For some select travelers, the prospect of sunbathing en masse on sizzling sand can't hold a candle to a long, solitary stroll on a windswept beach with only the gulls as company. Come Labor Day, the crowds clear out—even the stragglers are gone by Columbus Day—and the whole place hibernates until Memorial Day weekend, the official start of "the season."

We've listed mostly summer rates for the accommodations in this chapter, because that's when the vast majority of travelers plan their trips, but if you decide to explore the Cape off-season, you'll get the added benefit of lower prices everywhere you go.

The **Cape Cod Chamber of Commerce,** Routes 6 and 132, Hyannis (© **888/332-2732** or 508/862-0700; fax 508/362-2156; www.capecod-chamber.org), is a clearinghouse of information. You can also stop in at the **Route 25 Visitor Center** (© **508/759-3814;** fax 508/759-2146), open daily year-round.

1 The Upper Cape

Because the Upper Cape towns are so close to Boston by car (just over an hour), they've become bedroom as well as summer communities. They are perhaps a bit more staid than those towns further east, but they are also spared some of the fly-by-night qualities that come with a transient populace. Shops and restaurants—many catering to an older, affluent crowd—tend to stay open year-round.

SANDWICH ★★
Sandwich is both the oldest town in this part of the Cape and the most quaint. Towering oak trees, 19th-century churches, and historic houses line its Main Street. A 1640 gristmill still grinds corn beside bucolic Shawme Pond. Further east, Sandy Neck, one of the Cape's most beautiful beaches, reaches out into the Cape Cod Bay.

Sandwich's claim to fame is its prominence as the home of the nation's first glass factories in the early to mid–19th centuries. The town still supports a number of highly skilled glassmakers.

The town is popular with families and nature buffs, who will find excellent spots for hiking, biking, and canoeing. Sandwich also makes a convenient base for exploring other parts of the Cape that may offer more lively activities, like the nightlife of Hyannis or the ocean beaches of Wellfleet.

ESSENTIALS

GETTING THERE   Cross the Cape Cod Canal on either the Bourne or the Sagmore Bridge. At the Bourne Bridge rotary, take Sandwich Road along the canal; it turns into Route 6A as it nears Sandwich Center. If you cross the Sagamore Bridge, take Exit 1 or 2, and follow Sandwich Road/Route 6A or Route 130, respectively, to Sandwich Center. It's 3 miles (5km) east of Sagamore, 16 miles (26km) northwest of Hyannis.

VISITOR INFORMATION   The **Cape Cod Canal Region Chamber of Commerce,** 70 Main St., Buzzards Bay (© **508/759-6000;** fax 508/759-6965; www.capecodcanalchamber.org), is open daily from 10am to 5pm. An excellent walking guide is available at most inns in town.

BEACHES & OUTDOOR PURSUITS

BEACHES   For the beaches listed below, nonresident parking stickers—$20 for the length of your stay—are available at **Town Hall Annex,** 145 Main St. (© **508/833-8012**). Note that there's no swimming allowed within the Cape Cod Canal, as the currents are much too swift and dangerous.

- **Sandy Neck Beach** ★★★, off Sandy Neck Road in East Sandwich: This 6-mile (10km) stretch of silken barrier beach with low, rounded dunes is one of the Cape's most beautiful beaches; in summer, its parking lot tends to fill up early. It's also popular with endangered piping plovers—and their nemesis, off-road vehicles (ORV). That means that ORV trails are closed for most, if not all, of the summer while the chicks hatch. ORV permits ($80 per season for nonresidents) can be purchased at the gatehouse (© **508/362-8300**). ORV drivers must be equipped with supplies like a spare tire, jack, shovel, and tire-pressure gauge. Parking costs $10 per day in season; up to 3 days of camping in self-contained vehicles is permitted at $10 per night.
- **Town Neck Beach,** off Town Neck Road in Sandwich: A bit rocky but ruggedly pretty, this narrow beach offers a busy view of passing ships, plus restrooms and a snack bar, but no lifeguards. Parking costs $4, or you can hike from town (about 1½ miles/2.5km) via the community-built boardwalk, which offers picturesque salt-marsh views.
- **Wakeby Pond,** Ryder Conservation Area, John Ewer Road (off S. Sandwich Rd. on the Mashpee border): This beach, on the Cape's largest freshwater pond, has lifeguards, restrooms, and parking ($4).

BICYCLING   The **Cape Cod Canal bike path** ★★★ is a flat, 14-mile (23km) loop maintained by the U.S. Army Corps of Engineers (© **508/759-5991** for recreation hot line). Park free at the Bourne Recreation Area, north of the Bourne Bridge, on the Cape side. The closest rentals can be found at **Cape Cod Bike Rental,** 40 Rte. 6A (© **508/833-2453**), which charges around $22 per day.

BOATING   To explore by canoe, rent one in Falmouth (see below) and paddle around Old Sandwich Harbor, Sandy Neck, or the salt-marsh maze of Scorton Creek, which leads out to Talbot Point.

FISHING   Sandwich has eight fishable ponds; for licenses, inquire at **Town Hall,** in the center of town (© **508/888-0340**). No permit is required for

Cape Cod

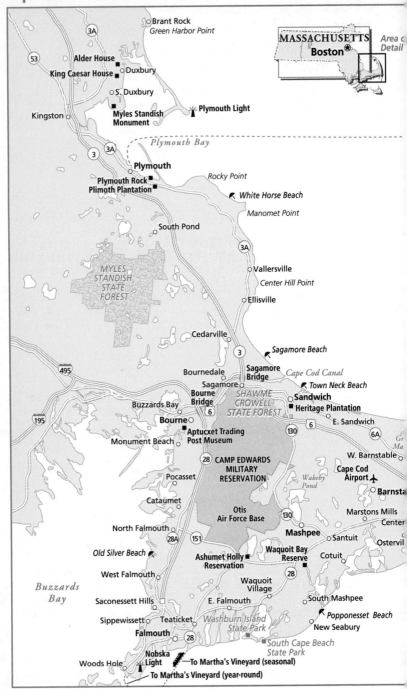

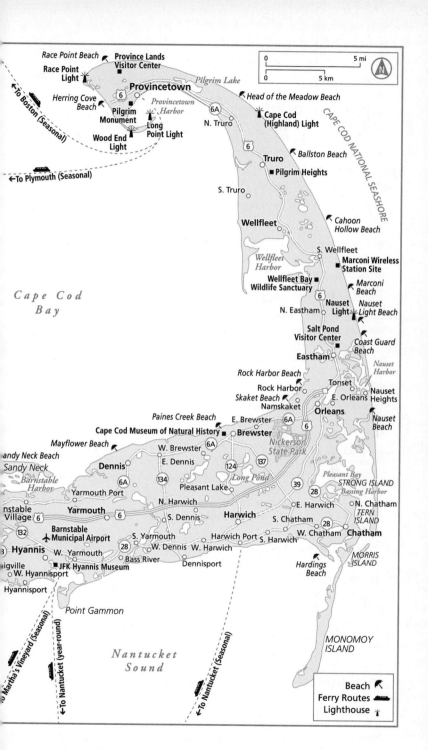

Race Point Beach 🏖 Province Lands
Visitor Center

Race Point
Light ⚲

🚢 To Boston (Seasonal)

Herring Cove
Beach

Pilgrim
Monument

Wood End
Light

Long
Point Light

Provincetown

Pilgrim Lake

Provincetown
Harbor

🚢 To Plymouth (Seasonal)

6A

N. Truro

6

🏖 Head of the Meadow Beach

⚲ Cape Cod
(Highland) Light

🏖 Ballston Beach

Truro

Pilgrim Heights

S. Truro

Wellfleet

CAPE COD NATIONAL SEASHORE

🏖 Cahoon
Hollow Beach

Wellfleet
Harbor

S. Wellfleet 🏖 Marconi Wireless
Station Site

Wellfleet Bay ■
Wildlife Sanctuary

6

🏖 Marconi
Beach

Nauset   Nauset
N. Eastham ○ Light ⚲ Light Beach

Cape Cod
Bay

Salt Pond
Visitor Center

Coast Guard
Beach

Eastham

Nauset
Harbor

Rock Harbor Beach 🏖

Rock Harbor ○
Skaket Beach 🏖
Namskaket

Tonset
○ Nauset
E. Orleans Heights

Orleans

Paines Creek Beach 🏖

E. Brewster 6A

Nauset
Beach

Cape Cod Museum of Natural History ■ Brewster

Mayflower Beach 🏖

W. Brewster 6A

E. Dennis

Nickerson
State Park

andy Neck Beach

Sandy Neck

Dennis ○

6A

Barnstable
Harbor

Yarmouth Port

124

134

Long Pond

Pleasant Lake

137

Pleasant Bay

STRONG ISLAND
Bassing Harbor

nstable
Village 6

Yarmouth

N. Harwich

6

S. Dennis

39   28

E. Harwich ○

○ N. Chatham

TERN
ISLAND

Harwich

132

Barnstable
✈ Municipal Airport

S. Yarmouth 28

Hyannis

W. Yarmouth

W. Dennis

W. Harwich

igville ○
○ W. Hyannisport

Hyannisport

JFK Hyannis Museum

Bass River

S. Chatham 28

Harwich Port S. Harwich

Dennisport

W. Chatham Chatham

Hardings
Beach

MORRIS
ISLAND

Point Gammon

Nantucket
Sound

MONOMOY
ISLAND

Beach 🏖
Ferry Routes 🚢
Lighthouse ⚲

fishing from the banks of the Cape Cod Canal. Call the **Army Corps of Engineers** (© 508/759-5991) for canal tide and fishing information. Local deep-water charters include the *Tigger Two,* at the Sandwich Marina (© 508/888-8372).

NATURE & WILDLIFE AREAS   The **Shawme-Crowell State Forest,** off Route 130 (© 508/888-0351), offers 285 campsites and 742 acres (301 hectares) to roam. Entrance is free; parking costs $2. The **Sandwich Boardwalk** links the town and Town Neck Beach by way of salt marshes that attract a great many birds, including great blue herons. The 57-acre (23-hectare) **Green Briar Nature Center & Jam Kitchen** ⊛, 6 Discovery Hill, off Route 6A (© 508/888-6870), has a mile-long (1.6km) path crossing marsh and stands of white pine.

MUSEUMS

Heritage Plantation of Sandwich ★★★ *Finds Kids*   This is one of those rare museums that appeals equally to adults and children. The 76 beautifully landscaped acres (31 hectares) are crisscrossed with walking paths and riotous with color in late spring. Scattered buildings house a wide variety of collections, from Native American artifacts to outstanding primitive portraits. The high point for most kids will be a ride on the 1912 carousel. There's also a replica Shaker round barn packed with gleaming antique automobiles. Outdoor summer concerts are usually held Sundays at 2pm.

Grove and Pine sts. (about a ½ mile/1km southwest of the town center). © 508/888-3300. Admission $9 adults, $8 seniors, $4.50 children 6–18. Mid-May to mid-Oct daily 10am–5pm; no tickets sold after 4:15pm. Closed late Oct to mid-May.

Sandwich Glass Museum ★★ *Finds*   Even if you don't consider yourself a glass fan, make an exception for this fascinating museum, which captures the history of the town above and beyond its legendary industry. A brief video introduces Deming Jarves's brilliant 19th-century endeavor: bringing glassware—a hitherto rare commodity available only to the rich—within reach of the middle classes. All went well until Midwestern factories undercut Jarves by using coal to fire their furnaces. Unable to keep up with their level of mass production, Jarves switched back to handblown techniques just as his workforce was ready to revolt. An excellent gift shop stocks Sandwich-glass replicas and original works. In summer, volunteers demonstrate glassmaking techniques.

129 Main St. (in the center of town). © 508/888-0251. Admission $3.50 adults, $1 children 6–16. Apr–Dec daily 9:30am–5pm; Feb–Mar Wed–Sun 9:30am–4pm. Closed Jan, Thanksgiving, and Dec 25.

WHERE TO STAY

Route 6A has a number of motels, but the one with the best location is **Sandy Neck Motel,** 669 Rte. 6A, East Sandwich (© 800/564-3992 or 508/362-3992; www.sandyneck.com), which sits at the entrance of the road leading to Sandy Neck Beach. Rates are $89 to $99 double. Closed November through March.

The Belfry Inne ★★ *Finds*   This Victorian rectory and the former church next door have been converted into Sandwich's most stylish lodging. Rooms in the rectory have retrofitted queen-size antique beds, claw-foot tubs (or Jacuzzis), and a scattering of fireplaces and balconies. The third floor, with its single attic rooms and delightful *Alice in Wonderland* mural leading up to the belfry, is perfect for families. Next door in the Abbey are six deluxe guest rooms and a very fine restaurant (see "Where to Dine," below). The Abbey rooms are painted vivid colors and tucked cleverly into sections of the old church. One has a stained-glass window, while another has angel windows.

8 Jarves St. (in the center of town), Sandwich, MA 02563. ✆ 800/844-4542 or 508/888-8550. Fax 508/888-3922. www.belfryinn.com. 14 units. Summer $95–$195 double. Rates include continental breakfast. AE, MC, V. **Amenities:** Restaurant (New American).

The Dan'l Webster Inn ★★ *Kids*   This popular inn is a dependable bet for a comfortable stay or a hearty meal. The modern main building sits on the site of a colonial tavern favored by Daniel Webster, the famous orator and Boston lawyer. Guest rooms are nicely furnished with reproductions; deluxe suites offer perks like balconies, gas fireplaces, whirlpool tubs, and heated tile bathroom floors. Especially appealing are the suites located in nearby historic houses. The inn's common spaces are convivial, if bustling; the restaurant is a tour-bus lunch stop that turns out surprisingly sophisticated fare.

149 Main St. (in the center of town), Sandwich, MA 02563. ✆ 800/444-3566 or 508/888-3622. Fax 508/888-5156. www.danlwebsterinn.com. 54 units. Summer $149–$189 double; $219–$349 suite. Off-season rates include continental breakfast. AE, DC, DISC, MC, V. **Amenities:** Restaurant (New American), tavern/bar; small outdoor heated pool; access to local health club; limited room service. *In room:* AC, TV, dataport, hair dryer, iron.

Spring Hill Motor Lodge ★   Of the many motels on Route 6A, this one boasts the most amenities. Especially impressive are the night-lit tennis court and the large pool. The interiors are cheerfully contemporary, the grounds elegantly landscaped. In addition to the motel rooms, there are four cottages that are light, airy, and comfortable.

351 Rte. 6A (about 2½ miles/4km east of the town center), East Sandwich, MA 02537. ✆ 800/647-2514 or 508/888-1456. Fax 508/833-1556. www.sunsol.com/springhill. 28 units (4 with shower only). Summer $95–$125 double; $160 efficiency; $1,100–$1,400 per week for cottage. AE, DC, DISC, MC, V. **Amenities:** Heated outdoor pool; tennis court. *In room:* A/C, TV, fridge, coffeemaker.

The Village Inn at Sandwich ★★ *Finds*   Why envy the guests relaxing in rockers on the wraparound porch of this 1837 Federal house when you could be among them? You'll enjoy airy sleeping quarters with gleaming bleached floors and splashes of colorful fabric. From the French country–style dining room to the cozy dormer attic, the mood is one of carefree comfort. Innkeeper Susan Fehlinger, an artist, runs a program called Sandwich Artworks with workshops by well-known Cape Cod artists.

4 Jarves St. (in the center of town), Sandwich, MA 02563. ✆ 800/922-9989 or 508/833-0363. Fax 508/833-2063. www.capecodinn.com. 8 units, 2 with shared bathroom. Summer $85–$105 double. Rates include full breakfast. AE, DISC, MC, V. *In room:* No phone.

Wingscorton Farm Inn ★★ *Finds* *Kids*   This colonial farmhouse inn on 7 acres (3 hectares) will delight youngsters and animal lovers of all ages. It's been a working farm since 1758 and still houses a cheerful brood of sheep, goats, chickens, a pet turkey, and a potbellied pig. The paneled guest rooms have canopy beds, fireplaces, and braided rugs. Modernists might prefer the carriage house, with its skylit loft bedroom, kitchen (with woodstove), and deck. A private bay beach is a short walk down a country lane.

11 Wing Blvd. (off Rte. 6A, about 5 miles/8km east of the town center), East Sandwich, MA 02537. ✆ 508/888-0534. Fax 508/888-0545. 4 units. Summer $155 suite; $175 carriage house; $1,000 per week for cottage. Rates for suites and carriage house include full breakfast. AE, MC, V. Pets welcome.

WHERE TO DINE

Aquagrille ★ SEAFOOD   Overlooking the town's picturesque marina and not-so-picturesque power plant, this dining spot wants to be the premier place for fish in Sandwich. The towering lobster salad with haricot vert, tomato, avocado, chives, and crème fraîche is the perfect antidote to a steamy summer night. Those with larger appetites may want to choose their grilled fish (tuna, salmon, swordfish, or scrod) and sauce (Cajun rémoulade, chipotle aioli, béarnaise, or dill mayonnaise). Ask for a table that doesn't face the power plant.

14 Gallo Rd. (next to Sandwich Marina). ✆ **508/888-8889.** Reservations recommended. Main courses $7–$20. AE, MC, V. May–Oct Mon–Fri noon–2:30pm and 5–9pm, Sat–Sun noon–9pm; call for off-season hours.

The Bee-Hive Tavern ★ *Kids* AMERICAN   A cut above the rather characterless restaurants clustered along this stretch of road, this modern-day tavern employs some atmospheric old-time touches: Green-shaded banker's lamps illuminate the dark wood booths, and vintage prints convey a clubby feel. The food is straightforward but tasty. Steaks, chops, and fresh fish are among the pricier choices, while burgers and salads cater to lighter appetites (and wallets). At lunch, try the lobster roll, one of the Cape's best.

406 Rte. 6A (about a ½ mile/1km east of the town center), East Sandwich. ✆ **508/833-1184.** Main courses $7–$16. MC, V. Mon–Sat 11:30am–9pm; Sun 8am–9pm.

The Belfry Bistro ★★ *Finds* NEW AMERICAN   Sandwich's most romantic dining option is located in a restored 19th-century church (see the Belfry Inne under "Where to Stay," above). Entrees range from delicate shrimp scampi with artichoke hearts to hearty grilled filet mignon served with garlic and leek mashed potatoes. There is also a lighter menu, with main courses starting at $10. Desserts are clearly a specialty; especially good is the Victorian gingerbread with fresh berries. There's a piano bar Friday and Saturday nights. Because this restaurant hosts many weddings and other events, it is sometimes closed to the public; be sure to call ahead.

8 Jarves St. (in the center of town). ✆ **508/888-8550.** Reservations recommended. Main courses $14–$25. AE, MC, V. Apr to mid-Oct Tues–Sat 5–10pm; call for off-season hours.

The Dan'l Webster Inn ★★ *Kids* AMERICAN   You have a choice of four main dining rooms at this popular establishment—from a casual, colonial-motif tavern to a skylit conservatory fronting a splendid garden. The atmospheric Tavern at the Inn, with its own pub-style menu, is fast becoming the most popular. A restaurant on this scale could probably get away with ho-hum food, but the output is on a par with that of the Cape's best boutique restaurants. Try a classic dish like *fruits de mer* in white wine. A children's menu is available.

149 Main St. (in the center of town). ✆ **508/888-3622.** Reservations recommended. Main courses $18–$29; tavern menu $7–$14. AE, DC, DISC, MC, V. Daily 8am–9pm; call for off-season hours.

Marshland Restaurant *Value* DINER   Locals have been digging this diner for 2 decades. This is home-cooked grub, slung fast and cheap. You'll gobble up the hearty breakfast and be back in time for dinner.

109 Rte. 6A. ✆ **508/888-9824.** Most items under $10. No credit cards. Tues–Sat 6am–9pm; Sun 7am–1pm; Mon 6am–2pm. Open year-round.

FALMOUTH & WOODS HOLE ★★★

Falmouth is a classic New England town, complete with church steeples encircling the town green and a walkable and bustling Main Street. With over 30,000 year-round residents, it's the second-largest town on the Cape, after Barnstable.

Woods Hole ★★★, one of nine villages in Falmouth, has been a world-renowned oceanic research center since 1871, when the U.S. Commission of Fish and Fisheries set up a primitive seasonal collection station. Today the various scientific institutes—the National Marine Fisheries Service, the Marine

Biological Laboratory, and the Woods Hole Oceanographic Institute—employ thousands of scientists. They offer a unique opportunity to get in-depth—and often hands-on—exposure to marine biology. Woods Hole is also one of the hipper communities on the Cape, with a number of restaurants, bars, and shops making crowded Water Street (don't even think of parking here in summer) a very pleasant place to stroll.

Falmouth Heights ★★★, a cluster of shingled Victorian summer houses on a bluff east of Falmouth's harbor, is as popular as it is picturesque; its narrow ribbon of beach is a magnet for all, especially families.

ESSENTIALS

GETTING THERE   After crossing the Bourne Bridge, take Route 28 south. It's 18 miles (29km) south of Sagamore, 20 miles (32km) southwest of Hyannis.

Falmouth's bus station, near the center of town, is serviced by **Bonanza Bus Lines** (✆ **508/548-7588;** www.bonanzabus.com). There are daily buses from Boston, Providence, and New York.

GETTING AROUND   To get around Falmouth and Woods Hole (where parking in summer is a mathematical impossibility due to ferry traffic to Martha's Vineyard), use the **Whoosh Trolley,** which makes a circuit every 20 minutes down Falmouth's Main Street to Woods Hole. You can flag it down anywhere along the route. A second **trolley** travels from North Falmouth down Route 28A through Falmouth Center to Falmouth Mall, hourly from 7am to 5pm. Trolley fares are $1 for adults, 50¢ for seniors.

The **Sea Line Shuttle** (✆ **800/352-7155**) connects Woods Hole, Falmouth, and Mashpee with Hyannis year-round (except Sun and holidays); the fare ranges from $1 to $3.50, depending on distance.

VISITOR INFORMATION   Contact the **Falmouth Chamber of Commerce,** Academy Lane (✆ **800/526-8532** or 508/548-8500; fax 508/548-8521; www.falmouth-capecod.com).

SPECIAL EVENTS   The **Falmouth Road Race** (www.falmouthroadrace. com), on the second Sunday in August, is a 7.3-mile (12km) run from the Captain Kidd Bar in Woods Hole to the British Beer Company in Falmouth Heights. It all started nearly 30 years ago when two buddies decided to race from one bar to the other. Now the race attracts 10,000 participants from all over the world. Those who want to run need to apply in April to the lottery.

BEACHES & OUTDOOR PURSUITS

BEACHES   While Old Silver Beach, Surf Drive Beach, and Menauhaut Beach will sell a day pass for $10, most other Falmouth public beaches require a parking sticker. Renters can obtain temporary beach parking stickers ($50 per week or $75 per month) at **Falmouth Town Hall,** 59 Town Hall Sq. (✆ **508/548-7611**), or in season at the **Surf Drive Beach Bathhouse** (✆ **508/548-8623**). The town beaches for which a parking fee is charged all have lifeguards, restrooms, and concession stands. Falmouth's public shores include:

- **Falmouth Heights Beach** ★★★, off Grand Avenue in Falmouth Heights: Once a rowdy spot, this is now primarily a family beach. Parking is sticker-only. This neighborhood supported the Cape's first summer colony; the grand Victorian mansions still overlook the beach.
- **Grew's Pond** ★, in Goodwill Park off Palmer Avenue in Falmouth: This freshwater pond in a large town forest tends to stay fairly uncrowded. While everyone else is trying to find parking at Falmouth's popular saltwater

beaches, here you can park for free and wander shady paths around the pond. There's a playground, picnic tables, barbecue grills, lifeguards, and restrooms.

- **Menauhant Beach** ★★, off Central Avenue in East Falmouth: A bit off the beaten track, Menauhant is a little less mobbed than Falmouth Heights Beach and better protected from the winds. Parking costs $10.
- **Old Silver Beach** ★★★, off Route 28A in North Falmouth: Western-facing (great for sunsets) and relatively calm, this warm Buzzards Bay beach is the chosen spot for the college crowd. Families cluster on the opposite side of the street, where a shallow pool formed by a sandbar is perfect for toddlers. Parking costs $10.
- **Surf Drive Beach** ★★★, off Shore Street in Falmouth: About a ½ mile (1km) from downtown, this is an easy-to-get-to choice. The tidal beach between the jetties is a shallow, calm area called the "kiddie pool." Parking is limited and costs $10.

BICYCLING   The **Shining Sea Bikeway** ★★★ (© **508/548-8500**) is a 3⅓-mile (5.5km) beauty following the coast from Falmouth to Woods Hole with plenty of swimmable beach along the way. (Unfortunately, most of the beach here is rocky.) You can park at the trailhead on Locust Street in Falmouth. (Parking in Woods Hole is scarce.) The closest bike shop is **Corner Cycle,** at Palmer Avenue and North Main Street (© **508/540-4195**), near the village green.

BOATING   **Patriot Party Boats,** 227 Clinton Ave., Falmouth (© **800/734-0088** or 508/548-2626; www.patriotpartyboats.com or www.TheLiberte.com), offers scenic cruises around Vineyard Sound aboard the three-masted schooner *Liberte* ★★. Two-hour sails cost $25 for adults and $18 for children 12 and under. Also offered in July and August are 2-hour sunset cruises on the *Patriot II.*

 Cape Cod Kayak (© **508/540-9377;** www.capecodkayak.com) rents kayaks and offers lessons and ecotours. **Waquoit Kayak Company** at **Edward's Boat Yard,** 1209 E. Falmouth Hwy., East Falmouth (© **508/548-9722**), rents canoes and kayaks for exploring Waquoit Bay (see "Nature & Wildlife Areas," below). **Washburn Island** ★★★, a protected reserve with wooded trails and pristine beaches, is about a 1-hour paddle via canoe.

FISHING   Falmouth has six fishable ponds. A free guide is available from the Chamber of Commerce. Freshwater fishing and shellfishing licenses can be obtained at **Town Hall,** 59 Town Hall Sq. (© **508/548-7611,** ext. 219). Freshwater fishing licenses can also be obtained at **Eastman's Sport & Tackle,** 150 Main St. (© **508/548-6900**).

 Surf Drive Beach is a great spot for surf casting, once the crowds have dispersed. Other good locations are Nobska Point in Woods Hole and Bristol Beach on Menauhant Road in East Falmouth.

 To go after bigger prey, head out with a group on one of the **Patriot Party Boats** (© **800/734-0088** or 508/548-2626; www.patriotpartyboats.com). For sportfishing, call Captain Bob MacGregor of the **Hop-Tuit** (© **508/540-7642**) or Captain Dan Junker of **Cool Running Charters** (© **508/457-9445**).

NATURE & WILDLIFE AREAS   **Ashumet Holly and Wildlife Sanctuary** ★★, operated by the Massachusetts Audubon Society at 186 Ashumet Rd., off Route 151 (© **508/362-1426**), is an intriguing 49-acre (20-hectare) collection of more than 1,000 holly trees, along with over 130 species of birds and a kettle pond that's covered with a carpet of Oriental lotus blossoms in summer. The trail fee is $3 for adults, $2 for seniors and children under 16.

Near the center of Falmouth (follow Depot Rd. to the end) is the 650-acre (263-hectare) **Beebe Woods** ⚐⚐, a treasure for hikers and dog walkers. From here, you can wind your way to the 90-acre (36-hectare) **Peterson Farm** ⚐⚐ (entrance off Woods Hole Rd.; take a right at the Quisset farmstand), with paths through woods and fields near historic farm buildings.

The 2,250-acre (911-hectare) **Waquoit Bay National Estuarine Research Reserve,** 149 Waquoit Hwy., East Falmouth (✆ **508/457-0495;** www.waquoit bayreserve.org), maintains a 1-mile (1.6km) nature trail. Also inquire about the boat ride to **Washburn Island** ⚐⚐⚐, on Saturdays in season by reservation. After the 20-minute boat trip to the island, naturalist-led walks are offered.

WATERSPORTS   Falmouth is something of a sailboarding mecca, prized for its unflagging southwesterly winds. While Old Silver Beach in North Falmouth is the most popular spot for windsurfing, it is allowed there only before 9am and after 5pm. Windsurfers are allowed during the day at the Trunk River area on the west end of Falmouth's Surf Drive Beach and in a portion of Chappaquoit Beach.

SEA SCIENCE
Woods Hole Oceanographic Institution Exhibit Center and Gift Shop
This world-class research organization—locally referred to by its acronym, WHOI (pronounced "Hooey")—is dedicated to the study of marine science. Kids might enjoy looking through microscopes at organisms or listening to sounds of marine animals on a computer. *Titanic* fans will enjoy the brief video, displays, and life-size model of the submersible that discovered the wreck. Walking tours of WHOI are offered twice a day Monday through Friday in July and August, reservations required (✆ **508/289-2252**).

15 School St. (off Water St.), Woods Hole. ✆ 508/289-2663. $2 donation requested. Late May to early Sept Mon–Sat 10am–4:30pm, Sun noon–4:30pm; call for off-season hours. Closed Jan–Mar.

Woods Hole Science Aquarium ⚐ *Kids*   A little beat up after more than a century of service, this aquarium—the first such institution in the country—may not be state-of-the-art, but it's a treasure nonetheless. The displays, focusing on local waters, might make you think twice before taking a dip. Children show no hesitation, though, in getting up to their elbows in the touch tanks. A key exhibit concerns the effect of plastic trash on the marine environment. The seals who live here are fed at 11am and 4pm.

Albatross St. (off the western end of Water St.), Woods Hole. ✆ 508/495-2001. Donations accepted. Mid-June to early Sept daily 10am–4pm; mid-Sept to mid-June Mon–Fri 10am–4pm.

WHERE TO STAY
Expensive
Coonamessett Inn ⚐⚐   A gracious inn built around the core of a 1796 homestead, the Coonamessett is Falmouth's most traditional lodging. Set on 7 lush acres (3 hectares) overlooking a pond, it has the feel of a country club. Some of the bedrooms, decorated with reproductions, can be a bit somber, so try to get one with good light. The dining room is unabashedly formal and fairly good, though inconsistent. A better choice is the adjoining tavern, Eli's, where a jazz combo holds forth on weekends in season.

Jones Rd. and Gifford St. (about 1½ mile/1km north of Main St.), Falmouth, MA 02540. ✆ 508/548-2300. Fax 508/540-9831. www.capecodrestaurants.org. 28 units. Summer $180–$260 double. Rates include continental breakfast. AE, MC, V. **Amenities:** Restaurant, tavern. *In room:* A/C, TV, coffeemaker, hair dryer.

Inn at West Falmouth 🐾🐾 One of the loveliest small inns on the Cape and the most stylish in Falmouth, this shingle-style house is set high on a wooded hill with distant views to Buzzards Bay. The living room with fireplace has heaps of bestsellers begging to be borrowed, while the spacious guest rooms are lavished with custom linens and unusual antiques. Some units have small balconies and whirlpool tubs. After a leisurely breakfast, you might carry off a tome to the small deck pool or wander the landscaped grounds. Chappaquoit Beach is about a 10-minute walk away.

66 Frazar Rd. (off Rte. 28A), West Falmouth, MA 02574. ✆ **508/540-7696.** www.innatwestfalmouth.com. 8 units. Summer $175–$300 double. Rates include continental breakfast. AE, MC, V. **Amenities:** Small heated outdoor pool; tennis court.

Scallop Shell Inn 🐾🐾🐾 *Finds* Some call this deluxe B&B, located just steps from Falmouth Heights Beach, Falmouth's best. There are wonderful views of Vineyard Sound and Martha's Vineyard, and guests are apt to be found lounging on the wide front porch. Several bedrooms have gas fireplaces and two-person whirlpool tubs. Two units have balconies; several have private entrances. In the billiard and sitting room, guests can enjoy a drink from the wet bar; they also have free reign in the guest kitchenette, stocked with beverages and home-made treats. The four-course gourmet breakfast could include an omelet of lobster, asparagus, and Gruyère.

16 Massachusetts Ave., Falmouth Heights, MA 02540. ✆ **800/249-4587** or 508/495-4900. Fax 508/495-4600. www.scallopshellinn.com. 7 units. Summer $225–$330 double. Rates include full breakfast. AE, DISC, MC, V. **Amenities:** Free laundry facilities. *In room:* A/C, TV/VCR, safe.

Moderate

The **Tides Motel,** at the west end of Grand Avenue in Falmouth Heights (✆ **508/548-3126**), is a basic lodging with a great location: on the beach at the head of Falmouth Harbor, facing out toward Vineyard Sound. Rates are $130 to $180. Closed late October through April.

Inn on the Sound 🐾🐾 *Finds* The ambience here is as breezy as the setting, high on a bluff beside Falmouth's premier sunning beach, with a sweeping view of Nantucket Sound from the front deck. Innkeeper Renee Ross is an interior decorator, and it shows: There's none of the usual frilly/cutesy stuff in these well-appointed guest rooms, several of which have private decks. The focal point of the living room is a handsome boulder hearth (nice for those nippy nights). Breakfast—a bountiful basket of home-baked goodies—is delivered to your room.

313 Grand Ave., Falmouth Heights, MA 02540. ✆ **800/564-9668** or 508/457-9666. Fax 508/457-9631. www.innonthesound.com. 10 units. Summer $150–$275 double. Rates include continental breakfast. AE, DISC, MC, V. No children under 16. *In room:* TV, no phone.

Sands of Time Motor Inn & Harbor House 🐾🐾 This property, across the street from the ferry terminal for Martha's Vineyard, consists of a two-story motel and a shingled 1879 Victorian mansion. The motel rooms feature crisp, above-average decor, plus private porches overlooking the harbor. The rooms in the Harbor House are more lavish—some with four-poster beds and fireplaces.

549 Woods Hole Rd., Woods Hole, MA 02543. ✆ **800/841-0114** or 508/548-6300. Fax 508/457-0160. www.sandsoftime.com. 36 units (2 with shared bathroom). Summer $120–$170 double. Rates include continental breakfast. AE, DC, DISC, MC, V. Closed Nov–Mar. **Amenities:** Small heated pool; tennis courts. *In room:* A/C, TV.

Wildflower Inn 🐾🐾 Though located on a busy stretch of road, this B&B is immaculately appointed and full of welcoming touches, like the row of rocking chairs lining the front porch. Guest rooms are creatively decorated with wicker furnishings and country quilts. An attached apartment features a loft bedroom served by a spiral staircase. The five-course breakfast might include apple-pie French toast garnished with edible flowers. The inn is across the street from the satellite parking lot for the Martha's Vineyard ferries, so you can easily hop a bus down to the terminal in Woods Hole.

167 Palmer Ave. (2 blocks north of Main St.), Falmouth, MA 02540. ☎ **800/294-5459** or 508/548-9524. Fax 508/548-9524. www.wildflower-inn.com. 6 units. Summer $140–$195 double; $225 cottage. Rates include full breakfast. AE, MC, V. **Amenities:** Bikes for guests' use. *In room:* A/C, hair dryer, no phone.

Inexpensive

Inn at One Main   Though built back in 1892, this shingled house with Queen Anne flourishes still has a youthful air. The bedrooms embody barefoot romance, rather than the Victorian brand. Lace, chintz, and wicker have been laid on lightly, leaving plenty of room to kick about. The Turret Room, with its big brass bed, is perhaps the most irresistible. Breakfasts feature gingerbread pancakes, orange-pecan French toast, homemade scones—it's a good thing the Shining Sea Bikeway is right at hand.

1 Main St. (1 block northwest of the village green), Falmouth, MA 02540. ☎ **888/281-6246** or 508/540-7469. Fax 603/462-5680. www.innatonemain.com. 6 units. Summer $110–$150 double. Rates include full breakfast. AE, DISC, MC, V. *In room:* A/C, hair dryer, no phone.

WHERE TO DINE

Betsy's Diner ★ *Value* DINER   This is hearty food like your mother used to make, if your mother was a variation of June Cleaver. The menu features turkey dinner, breakfast all day, and scrumptious homemade pies. Some say the fried clams are the best in town. Each booth is equipped with its own jukebox with retro hits.

457 Main St. (in the center of town). ☎ **508/540-0060**. Main courses $4–$10. AE, MC, V. Daily 6am–8pm.

The Clam Shack ★ SEAFOOD   This classic clam shack, at the head of Falmouth Harbor, offers steaming plates of fried seafood that you carry to a picnic table inside, outside, or up on the roof deck. It's basic fare, but the fish is fresh and you can't beat the view.

227 Clinton Ave., off Scranton Ave., about 1 mile (1.6km) south of Main St. ☎ **508/540-7758**. Main courses $5–$15. No credit cards. Daily 11:30am–7:45pm. Closed mid-Sept to late May.

Fishmonger's Cafe ★★ NATURAL FOODS   This sunny cafe jutting out into the harbor attracts young people, scientists, and tourists for an array of imaginatively prepared dishes, with vegetarian choices a specialty. Lunch could be a tempeh burger or a regular beef version. The eclectic changing dinner menu includes some Thai entrees. Regulars sit at the counter to enjoy a bowl of the Fisherman's Stew, while newcomers usually go for the tables by the window, where you can watch boats come and go from Eel Pond.

56 Water St. (at the Eel Pond drawbridge), Woods Hole. ☎ **508/540-5376**. Main courses $15–$25. AE, MC, V. Mid-June to Oct Mon–Fri 7–11am, 11:30am–4pm, and 5–10pm; Sat–Sun 7–11:30am, noon–4:30pm, and 5:30–10:30pm. Call for off-season hours. Closed mid-Dec to mid-Feb.

The Flying Bridge ★ *Kids* AMERICAN   Seafood predominates at this harborside mega-restaurant (capacity: some 600). With three bars tossed into the mix and live music upstairs on weekends, things can get a bit crazy; you'll find comparative peace and quiet—as well as tip-top views—out on the deck. In addition to basic bar food, you'll find fish in many guises, from fish-and-chips to appealing blackboard specials. Kids will enjoy wandering onto the attached dock to watch the ducks in the harbor.

220 Scranton Ave. (about a ½ mile/1km south of Main St.). ✆ 508/548-2700. Main courses $8–$20. AE, MC, V. Apr–Dec daily 11:30am–10pm; call for off-season hours.

Landfall ★★ *Kids* AMERICAN   A terrific setting and good service make this Woods Hole restaurant stand out. Besides the usual fish and pasta dishes, there's "lite fare" like burgers and fish-and-chips. This is a great place to bring the kids, who get their own menu that comes with games and crayons. Or come for a drink just to enjoy this massive wooden building constructed of salvage, both marine and terrestrial. A large bank of windows looks out onto the harbor— when the Martha's Vineyard ferry docks, it appears to be making a beeline straight for your table.

Luscombe Ave. (just south of Water St.), Woods Hole. ✆ 508/548-1758. Reservations recommended. Main courses $7–$26. AE, MC, V. Mid-May to Sept daily 11am–10pm; call for off-season hours. Closed Dec to mid-Apr.

RooBar ★★ NEW AMERICAN   RooBar is the best thing that has happened to Falmouth, restaurant-wise, in decades. The decor of this stylish bistro features handblown glass lamps and metal wall sconces. The food is exceptionally yummy, if pricey. Creative appetizers include red curry coconut shrimp and crisp fried polenta. Pizzas from the wood-burning oven come with unusual toppings like scallops and prosciutto. The professional and charming service here is unusual on Cape Cod.

285 Main St. (at Cahoon Court). ✆ 508/548-8600. Reservations not accepted. Main courses $15–$25. AE, MC, V. Daily noon–2pm and 4–10pm; call for off-season hours.

Trabica ★ ITALIAN/NEW AMERICAN   The unfortunate name of this establishment is supposed to be a cute way of saying, "We're a trattoria, a bistro, and a cafe!" It's actually a good Italian restaurant serving creative main courses. In addition to pastas, the menu features such traditional choices as rosemary roasted chicken and eclectic options such as roasted pork loin with pecan stuffing and maple-Marsala demi-glace.

327 Gifford St. (5 blocks north of town). ✆ 508/548-9861. Reservations recommended. Main courses $13–$16. MC, V. Daily 5–9pm.

The Waterfront ★★ NEW AMERICAN   This upscale restaurant, with a deck overlooking Eel Pond, is in the same building as the down-and-dirty Captain Kidd (see "Falmouth After Dark," below). The food is fairly standard for these parts: fresh fish, steaks, and chicken prepared with an attempt at a flourish. A good choice is sole stuffed with crab and topped with a rich lobster sauce. It's perhaps a tad pricey for what it is, but the atmosphere is top-notch.

77 Water St. (next to the Captain Kidd), Woods Hole. ✆ 508/548-8563. Reservations accepted (after 4pm). Main courses $19–$30. AE, MC, V. Mid-June to early Sept daily 5:30–10pm. Closed early Sept to mid June.

FALMOUTH AFTER DARK

Choose from over 18 drafts at the **British Beer Company** ★, 263 Grand Ave., Falmouth Heights (✆ 508/540-9600), as you ponder views of the beach across the street. God knows whom you'll meet in the rough-and-tumble **Captain Kidd** ★, 77 Water St., Woods Hole (✆ 508/548-9206): maybe a lobsterwoman, maybe a Nobel Prize winner. Good grub, too. Everyone heads to **Liam McGuire's Irish Pub** ★, 273 Main St., Falmouth (✆ 508/548-0285), for a taste of the Emerald Isle. The town's newest bar is **RooBar,** 285 Main St.,

Falmouth (© **508/548-8600**), which has a hip crowd and a great menu (see "Where to Dine," above).

2 The Mid Cape

Visitors who want to be centrally located on the Cape choose the Mid Cape, which is just over an hour from Boston (without traffic), an easy (less than an hour) drive to the Outer Cape, and a 1-hour ferry ride from Nantucket. This is the Cape's most populous area and also the prime location for its cheapest motels, which line Route 28 from Hyannis to Dennis.

Hyannis is the Cape's unofficial capital. It's a sprawling concrete jungle of strip malls and chain stores where the Kennedy mystique of the 1960s had the unfortunate side effect of spurring heedless development over the ensuing decades—a period during which the Cape's year-round population doubled to more than 200,000. The summer population is about three times that, and you'd swear every single person had daily errands to run in Hyannis. And yet this overrun town still has pockets of charm, especially the waterfront area and Main Street.

But the real beauty of the Mid Cape lies in its smaller places: old-money hideaways like **Osterville** ✫ to the west, and charming villages like **West Barnstable** ✫✫ and **Yarmouth Port** ✫✫✫, which can be found along the **Old King's Highway** ✫✫✫ (Rte. 6A) on the northern bay side of the Cape. A drive along this winding two-lane road reveals the early architectural history of the region, from humble colonial saltboxes to ostentatious captains' mansions. Scores of intriguing antiques shops subtly compete to draw a closer look, and each village seems a throwback to a kinder, gentler era.

HYANNIS & ENVIRONS ✫

Hectic Hyannis is the commercial center and transportation hub of the Cape, with the enormous Cape Cod Mall and busy Barnstable Municipal Airport. It also has a diverse selection of restaurants, bars, and nightclubs. But if you were to confine your visit to this one town, you'd get a warped view of the Cape. Along Routes 132 and 28, you could be visiting Anywhere, USA: The roads are lined with the standard chain stores and mired with maddening traffic.

While Hyannis's impersonal hotels and motels have more beds at better prices than anywhere else on the Cape, there's little reason to choose them unless you happen to have missed the last ferry out to Nantucket. We recommend staying in Hyannisport or heading due north to Barnstable Village, where you'll find a myriad of charming B&Bs along the scenic Old King's Highway. Once you're settled, you can visit Hyannis to sample some of the Cape's best restaurants and nightlife. See "Barnstable Village & Environs," later in this section.

ESSENTIALS

GETTING THERE   After crossing the Sagamore Bridge, head east on Route 6 or 6A. Route 6A passes through Barnstable Village; Route 132 (Exit 6 off Rte. 6) leads to Hyannis. You can also fly into Hyannis, and there is good bus service from Boston and New York.

VISITOR INFORMATION   Contact the **Hyannis Area Chamber of Commerce,** 1481 Rte. 132, Hyannis (© **800/449-6647,** 877/492-6647, or 508/362-5230; fax 508/362-9499; www.hyannis.com).

BEACHES & OUTDOOR PURSUITS

BEACHES Most of the Nantucket Sound beaches are fairly protected and offer little in the way of surf. Parking costs $10 a day, usually payable at the lot; for a 1-week parking sticker ($40), visit the **Recreation Department,** 141 Basset Lane, at the Kennedy Memorial Skating Rink (© 508/790-6345).

- **Craigville Beach** ⚡⚡⚡, off Craigville Beach Road in Centerville: This broad expanse of sand has lifeguards and restrooms. A destination for the bronzed and buffed, it's known as "Muscle Beach." It's a short walk to Craigville Village, a former Methodist camp meeting site with Carpenter Gothic cottages.
- **Kalmus Beach** ⚡⚡, off Gosnold Street in Hyannisport: This 800-foot (240m) spit of sand stretching toward the mouth of the harbor makes an ideal launching site for windsurfers. The surf is tame, the slope shallow, and the conditions ideal for kids. Lifeguards, a snack bar, and restrooms facilitate family outings.
- **Orrin Keyes Beach** ⚡⚡ (Sea Street Beach), at the end of Sea Street in Hyannis: This little beach at the end of a residential road is popular with families.
- **Veterans Beach,** off Ocean Street in Hyannis: A small stretch of harborside sand adjoining the John F. Kennedy Memorial, this spot is not tops for swimming, unless you're very young and easily wowed. Parking is usually easy, though, and it's walkable from town. The snack bar, restrooms, and playground will see to a family's needs.

FISHING Among the charter boats berthed in Barnstable Harbor is the 36-foot (11m) *Drifter* (© 508/398-2061), offering half- and full-day trips. The **Tightlines Sport Fishing Service,** 65 Camp St., Hyannis (© 508/790-8600), conducts saltwater fly-fishing expeditions. **Hy-Line Cruises** (© 508/790-0696) offers seasonal sonar-aided "bottom" or blues fishing from its Ocean Street dock in Hyannis. **Helen H Deep-Sea Fishing,** 137 Pleasant St., Hyannis (© 508/790-0660), offers year-round expeditions aboard a 100-foot (30m) boat with a heated cabin and full galley.

GOLF The **Hyannis Golf Club,** Route 132 (© 508/362-2606), offers a 46-station driving range and an 18-hole championship course. Smaller but scenic is the nine-hole **Cotuit High Ground Country Club,** 31 Crockers Neck Rd., Cotuit (© 508/428-9863).

WATERSPORTS **Eastern Mountain Sports,** 1513 Iyannough Rd./Rte. 132 (© 508/362-8690), rents kayaks, tents, and sleeping bags. It also sponsors free clinics and walks, such as a full-moon hike.

SIGHTSEEING TOURS BY STEAMER

Hy-Line Harbor Cruises For a fun and informative introduction to the harbor and its residents, take a leisurely 1- to 2-hour tour aboard one of Hy-Line's 1911 steamer replicas. The Sunday "Ice-Cream Float" includes a design-your-own Ben & Jerry's sundae, while the Thursday "Jazz Boat" features a Dixieland band. There's also a lobster luncheon cruise on Monday and Wednesday.

Ocean St. Dock, Hyannis. © 508/790-0696. www.hy-linecruises.com. Tickets $10–$16 adults, free–$8 children 12 and under. Late June to Sept departures daily; call for schedule. Closed Nov to mid-April.

THE KENNEDY LEGACY

Don't even bother trying to track down the Kennedy Compound in Hyannis-port; it's effectively screened from view. You'll see more at the following

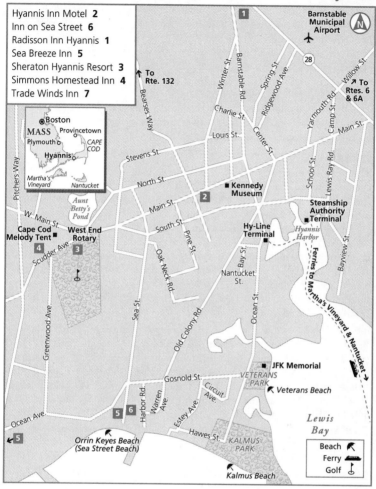

Hyannis Inn Motel **2**
Inn on Sea Street **6**
Radisson Inn Hyannis **1**
Sea Breeze Inn **5**
Sheraton Hyannis Resort **3**
Simmons Homestead Inn **4**
Trade Winds Inn **7**

museum. Or if you absolutely must satisfy your curiosity, take a harbor cruise (see "Sightseeing Tours by Steamer," above).

John F. Kennedy Hyannis Museum *Overrated* This multimedia display captures the Kennedys during the glory days from 1934 to 1963. The death of John F. Kennedy, Jr., in a plane crash in 1999 made visitation jump five times higher than average. A special exhibit of photos of John, Jr., will be on display for an indefinite period of time.

397 Main St., Hyannis. ✆ **508/790-3077.** Admission $3 adults, free for children under 17. Apr–Oct Mon–Sat 10am–4pm, Sun and holidays 1–4pm; last admission at 3:30pm. Call for off-season hours.

SHOPPING

Although Hyannis is undoubtedly the commercial center of the Cape, the stores here are fairly standard. Head to the wealthy enclaves west of Hyannis, such as Osterville, and along the Old King's Highway (Rte. 6A) to the north, to locate the real gems.

The Farmhouse, 1340 Main St., about 1 mile (1.6km) south of Route 28, Osterville (© **508/420-2400**), built in 1742, is set up like a well-decorated home filled with antiques and reproductions.

Ex-Nantucketer Bob Marks fashions the only authentic Nantucket lightship baskets crafted off-island; as aficionados know, they don't come cheap. You'll find them at **Oak and Ivory,** 112 Main St., about 1 mile (1.6km) south of Route 28, Osterville (© **508/428-9425**).

Cape Cod Potato Chips, Breed's Hill Road (at Independence Way, off Rte. 132), Hyannis (© **508/775-7253**), offers free factory tours Monday through Saturday in July and August. Call for off-season hours.

WHERE TO STAY

There are a variety of generic but convenient lodgings in Hyannis. Within strolling distance of restaurants, shops, and the ferries is the 77-unit **Hyannis Inn Motel,** 473 Main St. (© **800/922-8993** or 508/775-0255; www.hyannis inn.com), with an indoor pool and summer rates of $88 to $120. If you need a full health club, try the **Radisson Inn Hyannis,** 287 Iyannough Rd./Rte. 28 (© **800/333-3333** or 508/771-1700; www.radisson.com/capecod); it has an uninspiring location, but is within spitting distance of the airport. Rooms start at $145. Another option is the **Sheraton Hyannis Resort,** at the West End rotary just off Main Street (© **800/598-4559** or 508/775-7775; www. sheraton.com), which boasts a golf course, tennis courts, pools, and restaurants. Doubles start at $189.

Inn on Sea Street ✪   Just a short walk from Orrin Keyes Beach (Sea St. Beach), this establishment comprises two historic houses and a tiny cottage. The main house is decorated in Victorian style; some of its rooms have four-poster beds and claw-foot tubs. The mansard-roofed house across the street has larger rooms outfitted with English country antiques, as well as TVs and air-conditioning. Breakfast might feature such treats as rhubarb coffeecake and quiche with cheese and bacon.

358–363 Sea St., Hyannis, MA 02601. © **508/775-8030.** Fax 508/771-0878. www.innonseastreet.com. 10 units, 2 with shared bathroom. Summer $85–$135 double; $130 cottage. Rates include full breakfast. AE, DISC, MC, V. *In room:* No phone.

Sea Breeze Inn ✪ *Kids*   Within whistling distance of the beach, this classic shingled beach house has been decked out with the totems of small-town America: a picket fence, exuberant plantings, even a wooden rocker built for two couples. The coast used to be lined with superior guesthouses of this sort, and to find one still in its prime is a real treat. Also on the grounds are four cottages, including one with a double Jacuzzi.

270 Ocean Ave. (about 1 mile/1.6km south of the West End rotary), Hyannis, MA 02601. © **508/771-7213.** Fax 508/862-0663. www.seabreezeinn.com. 18 units. Summer $80–$140 double; $1,200–$2,500 per week for cottage. Rates include continental breakfast (except in large cottages). AE, DISC, MC, V. *In room:* A/C, TV.

Simmons Homestead Inn ✪✪ *Finds*   The first thing passersby notice is all the classic red sports cars: 40 at last count. A former ad exec and race-car driver, innkeeper Bill Putman likes to collect. Each room in this rambling 1820s captain's manse has an animal theme represented by stuffed toys, sculptures, even needlepoint and wallpaper. Guests who prefer privacy may book the spiffily updated "servants' quarters," a spacious wing with its own deck. This is the kind of place where you'll find everyone mulling around the hearth sipping complimentary wine while they compare notes and nail down dinner plans. To help guests plan their days, Putman has typed up extensive notes on day trips, bike routes, and his own quirky restaurant reviews. In accordance with the permissive (read: fun) atmosphere here, dogs are allowed, as is smoking in the common room.

288 Scudder Ave. (about ¼ mile/0.5km west of the West End rotary), Hyannisport, MA 02647. ℂ 800/637-1649 or 508/778-4999. Fax 508/790-1342. www.simmonshomesteadinn.com. 14 units. Summer $180–$250 double; $330 suite. Rates include full breakfast. AE, DISC, MC, V. Dogs welcome. **Amenities:** Outdoor Jacuzzi; free bikes. *In room:* Hair dryer, iron, no phone.

Trade Winds Inn ★ *Finds* *Kids*   Many rooms in this attractive motel have wonderful views of Craigville Beach. And because it's hard to see the sand once the summer crowds hit, this property also has its own 500-foot (150m) stretch of private beach. On cloudy days, guests may enjoy strolling up to the Craigville Campground next door, a compound of 19th-century cottages that still serves as a Methodist camp meeting site.

780 Craigville Beach Rd. (across the street from Craigville Beach), Centerville, MA 02632. ℂ 877/444-7966 or 508/775-0365. www.twicapecod.com. 46 units. Summer $129–$189 double; $199–$239 suite. Rates in high season include continental breakfast. AE, MC, V. Closed Nov–Apr. **Amenities:** Small bar; putting green. *In room:* A/C, TV.

WHERE TO DINE
Expensive
The Black Cat ★★ NEW AMERICAN   Located less than a block from the Hy-Line ferries, this is a fine place to catch a quick bite while you wait for your boat to come in. The menu is pretty basic—steak, pasta, and, of course, fish—but attention is paid to the details; the onion rings, for instance, are made fresh. The dining room, with its bar of gleaming mahogany and brass, will appeal to chilled travelers on a blustery day; in fine weather, you might prefer the porch. There's live jazz on weekends in season.

165 Ocean St. (opposite the Ocean St. Dock), Hyannis. ℂ 508/778-1233. Reservations not accepted. Main courses $15–$29. AE, DC, DISC, MC, V. Apr–Oct daily 11:30am–10pm; call for off-season hours.

Keepers Restaurant ★★ *Finds* NEW AMERICAN   You'll really feel like an insider as you wind your way through the fancy neighborhoods of Osterville to this small restaurant (10 tables) set in the old Crosby boatyard. Despite the high prices, there's a homey feeling to this place. As you would expect, fish is a specialty. To start, there's often an unusual preparation of pan-seared scallops, plump and juicy. For a main course, you might splurge on the grilled lobster tail or the striped bass, fresh off the boat.

72 Crosby Circle (on the harbor at the Crosby Boatyard), Osterville. ℂ 508/428-6719. Reservations recommended. Main courses $22–$30. MC, V. June–Aug Wed–Sun 11am–3:30pm and 4:30–9:30pm; call for off-season hours.

The Regatta of Cotuit at the Crocker House ★★★ NEW AMERICAN   One of the best restaurants on Cape Cod, the Regatta serves fine-dining cuisine in the Federal-era rooms of a 1790 Cape. Some may find the atmosphere a wee bit stuffy, but the food and service are always top-notch. Specials might include roasted buffalo tenderloin with blackberry Madeira sauce, served with braised fresh greens and a Stilton sage bread pudding. For budget-minded gourmands, the Regatta also serves a fixed-price ($22–$26) three-course "early dinner," Sunday through Friday from 5 to 6pm.

4631 Rte. 28 (near the intersection of Rte. 130), Cotuit. ℂ 508/428-5715. Reservations recommended. Main courses $26–$35. AE, MC, V. Apr–Dec daily 5–10pm; Jan–Mar Tues–Sun 5–10pm.

Ristorante Barolo ★★ *Finds* NORTHERN ITALIAN   Part of a smart-looking brick office complex, this place does everything right, from offering extra-virgin olive oil for dunking the crusty bread to getting those pastas perfectly al dente. Entrees include a number of tempting veal choices, as well as such favorites as *linguine al frutti di mare,* with littlenecks, mussels, shrimp, and calamari. The desserts are brought in daily from Boston's North End.

1 Financial Place (297 North St., just off the West End rotary), Hyannis. ℂ 508/778-2878. Reservations recommended. Main courses $10–$27. AE, DC, MC, V. June–Sept Sun–Thurs 4:30–10pm, Fri–Sat 4:30–11pm; call for off-season hours.

Roadhouse Cafe ★★ AMERICAN/NORTHERN ITALIAN   This is neither a roadhouse nor a cafe, but it is a solid entry in the Hyannis dining scene. The menu is split between American standards and real Italian cooking. Among the appetizers are beef carpaccio with fresh-shaved Parmesan, and vine-ripened tomatoes and buffalo mozzarella drizzled with balsamic vinaigrette. The latter also makes a tasty marinade for native swordfish headed for the grill. A lighter-fare menu (including what some have called the best burger in the world) is served in the snazzy bistro in back, which also features live jazz Monday nights (see "Hyannis & Environs After Dark," below).

488 South St. (off Main St., near the West End rotary), Hyannis. ℂ 508/775-2386. Reservations recommended. Main courses $12–$25. AE, DC, DISC, MC, V. Daily 4–11pm.

Moderate

Tugboats ★★ *Kids* AMERICAN   Yet another harborside perch for munching and ogling, this one's especially appealing. Forget fancy dining and chow down on blackened-swordfish bites or lobster fritters. Among the desserts is a Key lime pie purportedly lifted straight from Papa's of Key West.

21 Arlington St. (at the Hyannis Marina, off Willow St.), Hyannis. ℂ 508/775-6433. Reservations not accepted. Main courses $11–$15. AE, DC, DISC, MC, V. Late May to late Oct daily 11:30am–10:30pm; mid-Apr to late May Tues–Sun 11:30am–10:30pm. Closed Nov to mid-Apr.

Inexpensive

Baxter's Boat House *Kids* SEAFOOD   A shingled shack on a jetty jutting out into the harbor, Baxter's caters to the boating crowd with fried clams and fish virtually any way you like it, served on paper plates at picnic tables.

177 Pleasant St. (near the Steamship Authority ferry), Hyannis. ℂ 508/775-7040. Main courses $8–$14. AE, MC, V. Late May to early Sept Mon–Sat 11:30am–10pm, Sun 11:30am–9pm; hours may vary at the beginning and end of the season. Closed mid-Oct to Mar.

Common Ground Cafe ★ *Value* AMERICAN   Talk about an out-of-body experience: Step off tacky Main Street Hyannis into this New Age-y sandwich shop run by a commune. The barn-board walls and wide-board floors surround alcoves with private booths containing amorphous tree-stump tables. But enough about atmosphere; this place makes the best iced tea on Cape Cod. The sandwiches and salads are wholesome and delicious, and the burrito with turkey is a winner.

420 Main St., Hyannis. ℂ 508/778-8390. Most items under $6. AE, DC, DISC, MC, V. Mon–Thurs 10am–10pm; Fri 10am–3pm.

Ying's ★★ *Value* THAI/JAPANESE/KOREAN   Not only is this the best Asian food in town, but the atmosphere also provides a much-needed dose of tranquility in hectic Hyannis. While specializing in three distinct Asian cuisines may seem risky, Ying's handles the challenge with aplomb. The sushi menu is extensive, but there are also Thai and Korean specialties, including many vegetarian dishes.

59 Center St. (Center Plaza, 1 block north of Main St.), Hyannis. © **508/790-2432**. All items under $15. AE, MC, V. Daily 11:30am–10:30pm.

HYANNIS & ENVIRONS AFTER DARK

From July to early September, try to catch a show at the **Cape Cod Melody Tent** ★★, West End rotary, Hyannis (© **508/775-9100**). Built as a summer theater in 1950, this billowy big-top proved even better suited to variety shows. A nonprofit venture since 1990, the Melody Tent has hosted the major performers of the past 50 years, from jazz greats to comedians, crooners to rockers. There's children's theater Wednesdays at 11am.

The congenial lounge at **Baxter's Boat House,** 177 Pleasant St. (see "Where to Dine," above), Hyannis (© **508/775-7040**), with low-key blues piano, draws an attractive crowd. A good place for after-dinner entertainment is **Roadhouse Cafe** ★, 488 South St. (see "Where to Dine," above), Hyannis (© **508/ 775-2386**), a dark-paneled bar that stocks 48 boutique beers. Insiders show up Monday nights to hear local jazz great Dave McKenna. **RooBar,** 586 Main St., Hyannis (© **508/778-6515**), feels very Manhattan, with ultra-cool servers, a sleek bar area, and lots of attitude. The bistro food is good, too.

The cramped dance floor makes for instant camaraderie at **Harry's** ★★, 700 Main St., Hyannis (© **508/778-4188**), which features live blues and rockabilly nightly in season and about five nights a week the rest of the year. The cover is $3 to $4 Thursday through Saturday. **Sophie's,** 334 Main St., Hyannis (© **508/ 775-1111**), is a happening scene; check out Velvet Thursdays, with DJs playing the latest house and dance tunes. The cover is $3 to $4 Thursday through Saturday.

BARNSTABLE VILLAGE & ENVIRONS ★★

Just a couple miles from Hyannis, the bucolic village of Barnstable houses the county courthouse and government offices for the region. In this peaceful setting are some of the most charming B&Bs around. The bay area along historic Route 6A, the Old King's Highway, unfolds in a blur of greenery and well-kept colonial houses.

BEACHES & OUTDOOR PURSUITS

BEACHES   Barnstable's primary bay beach is **Sandy Neck,** accessed through East Sandwich (see "The Upper Cape," earlier in this chapter).

BOATING   You can rent a canoe from **Eastern Mountain Sports** (see "Watersports," under "Hyannis & Environs," earlier in this chapter) and paddle around Scorton Creek, Sandy Neck, and Barnstable Harbor.

FISHING   Barnstable has 11 ponds for freshwater fishing; for permits, visit **Town Hall,** 367 Main St., Hyannis (© **508/790-6240**), or **Sports Port,** 149 W. Main St., Hyannis (© **508/775-3096**). Shellfishing permits are available from the **Department of Natural Resources,** 1189 Phinneys Lane, Centerville (© **508/790-6272**). Surf casting without a license is permitted on Sandy Neck. Among the charter boats berthed in Barnstable Harbor is the *Drifter* (© **508/ 398-2061**), a 36-foot (11m) boat offering half- and full-day trips.

SHOPPING

The **Blacks' Handweaving Shop,** 597 Rte. 6A, about ¾ miles (1km) west of Route 149, West Barnstable (© **508/362-3955**), is the only place in the United States where you'll find a weaver making Jacquard designs by hand. Bob Black specializes in custom coverlets on commission. His wife, Gabrielle, contributes colorful fashion accessories—hats, scarves, shawls, and even ties.

Tao Water Art Gallery, 1989 Rte. 6A, West Barnstable (© **508/375-0428**), is a former garage that has been converted into a very Zen-like space. It features paintings by Chinese artists as well as museum reproductions of Chinese antiques and jade.

At **West Barnstable Tables,** 2454 Meetinghouse Way (off Rte. 149 near Rte. 6A), West Barnstable (© **508/362-2676**), Richard Kiusalas and Steven Whittlesey salvage antique lumber and turn it into cupboards, tables, and chairs, among other things.

WHERE TO STAY

Ashley Manor Inn ★★ *Finds*   A lovely country inn along the Old King's Highway, this 1699 mansion still retains many of its original features, including a hearth with beehive oven and wide-board floors, many of them brightened with Nantucket-style splatter paint. The rooms, all but one with working fireplaces, are spacious and inviting. A deluxe unit has a separate entrance, whirlpool tub, and canopy bed. The 2-acre (1-hectare) property itself is shielded from the road by an enormous privet hedge. Breakfast on the patio is worth waking up for.

3660 Rte. 6A (just east of Hyannis Rd.), Barnstable, MA 02630. © **888/535-2246** or 508/362-8044. Fax 508/362-9927. www.ashleymanor.net. 6 units. Summer $145–155 double; $190–$210 suite. Rates include full breakfast. AE, DISC, MC, V. **Amenities:** Tennis court; free bikes. *In room:* A/C, dataport, coffeemaker, hair dryer.

Beechwood Inn ★★ *Finds*   Look for a butterscotch-colored 1853 Queen Anne Victorian all but enshrouded in weeping beech trees. Admirers of late-19th-century decor are in for a treat: The interior is dark and rich, with a red-velvet parlor and tin-ceilinged dining room. Two of the upstairs bedrooms embody distinctive period styles from the 1860s and 1880s. Each affords a distant view of the bay. Rooms range from spacious (the Lilac) to snug (the Garret).

2839 Rte. 6A (about 1½ miles/2.5km east of Rte. 132), Barnstable, MA 02630. © **800/609-6618** or 508/362-6618. Fax 508/362-0298. www.beechwoodinn.com. 6 units. Summer $145–$185 double. Rates include full breakfast. AE, DISC, MC, V. *In room:* A/C, no phone.

WHERE TO DINE

Dolphin Restaurant ★★ NEW AMERICAN   Never mind the corny 1950s decor in what looks like just another run-of-the-mill roadside eatery. The finesse is to be found in the menu, where amid the more typical fried fish you'll find such delicacies as Chilean sea bass with roasted corn salsa and lime vinaigrette, or roast duck with mango glaze and toasted coconut.

3250 Rte. 6A (in the center of town), Barnstable. © **508/362-6610**. Main courses $17–$23. AE, MC, V. May–Oct Mon–Sat 11:30am–3pm, daily 5–9pm (Sun until 9:30pm); call for off-season hours.

Mattakeese Wharf ★ SEAFOOD   This place, with great views and average food, is always packed; don't even bother on summer weekends. The broad decks jut out into the harbor and afford sunset views to Sandy Neck. The fish is fresh, but preparations are bland. The bouillabaisse, however, is always good. And you can't go wrong if you stick to the varied combinations of pasta, seafood, and sauce, from Alfredo to *fra diavolo*. There's live piano music most nights in season.

271 Mill Way (about a ½ mile/1km north of Rte. 6A), Barnstable. © **508/362-4511**. Reservations recommended. Main courses $14–$28. AE, DC, DISC, MC, V. June–Oct daily 11:30am–10pm; call for off-season hours. Closed Nov–Apr.

YARMOUTH

Yarmouth represents the Cape at its best—and worst. **Yarmouth Port**   , on Cape Cod Bay, is an enchanting village, whereas the soundside villages of West to South Yarmouth are a lesson in unbridled development run amok. This section of Route 28 is a nightmarish gauntlet of mostly tacky accommodations and "attractions."

ESSENTIALS

GETTING THERE   After crossing the Sagamore Bridge, head east on Route 6 or 6A. The section of Route 6A north of Exit 7, Route 6, passes through the village of Yarmouth Port. West Yarmouth, Bass River, and South Yarmouth are located along Route 28, east of Hyannis; to reach them from Route 6, take Exit 7 (Yarmouth Rd.) or Exit 8 (Station St.) south.

VISITOR INFORMATION   Contact the **Yarmouth Area Chamber of Commerce,** 657 Rte. 28, West Yarmouth (© **800/732-1008** or 508/778-1008; fax 508/778-5114; www.yarmouthcapecod.com).

BEACHES & OUTDOOR PURSUITS

BEACHES   Yarmouth boasts 11 saltwater and two pond beaches open to the public. The body-per-square-yard ratio can be pretty intense along Nantucket Sound on the south side, but so's the social scene, so no one seems to mind. The beachside parking lots charge $10 a day and sell 1-week stickers for $40.

- **Bass River Beach**   , off South Shore Drive in Bass River (South Yarmouth): Located at the mouth of the largest tidal river on the eastern seaboard, this sound beach offers restrooms and a snack bar, plus a wheelchair-accessible fishing pier. The beaches along the south shore (Nantucket Sound) tend to be clean and sandy with comfortable water temps, but they can also be quite crowded. You'll need a beach sticker to park here.
- **Grays Beach,** off Center Street in Yarmouth Port: This isn't much of a beach, but tame waters make the tiny spit of dark sand good for young children. It adjoins the Callery-Darling Conservation Area, with a 2½-mile (4km) trail. The Bass Hole boardwalk offers one of the most scenic walks in the Mid Cape. Parking is free, and there's a picnic area.
- **Parker's River Beach**   , off South Shore Drive in Bass River: This choice has the usual amenities like restrooms and a snack bar, plus a gazebo for the sun-shy.
- **Seagull Beach**   , off South Sea Avenue in West Yarmouth: Rolling dunes, a boardwalk, and all the necessary facilities, like restrooms and a snack bar, attract a young crowd. Bring bug spray, though: Greenhead flies get the munchies in July.

FISHING   Of the five fishing ponds in the Yarmouth area, Long Pond, near South Yarmouth, is known for its largemouth bass and pickerel. For details and a license (shellfishing is another option), visit **Town Hall,** 1146 Rte. 28, South Yarmouth (© **508/398-2231**), or **Riverview Bait and Tackle,** 1273 Rte. 28, South Yarmouth (© **508/394-1036**). Full-season licenses for out-of-state residents cost $38.50. You can cast for striped bass and bluefish off the pier at Bass River Beach (see "Beaches," above).

NATURE & WILDLIFE AREAS   For a pleasant stroll, follow the 2 miles (3km) of trails maintained by the Historical Society of Old Yarmouth. Park

271 Mill Way (about a ½ mile/1km north of Rte. 6A), Barnstable. ✆ **508/362-4511.** Reservations recommended. Main courses $14–$28. AE, DC, DISC, MC, V. June–Oct daily 11:30am–10pm; call for off-season hours. Closed Nov–Apr.

YARMOUTH 🍂🍂

Yarmouth represents the Cape at its best—and worst. **Yarmouth Port** 🍂🍂, on Cape Cod Bay, is an enchanting village, whereas the soundside villages of West to South Yarmouth are a lesson in unbridled development run amok. This section of Route 28 is a nightmarish gauntlet of mostly tacky accommodations and "attractions."

ESSENTIALS

GETTING THERE   After crossing the Sagamore Bridge, head east on Route 6 or 6A. The section of Route 6A north of Exit 7, Route 6, passes through the village of Yarmouth Port. West Yarmouth, Bass River, and South Yarmouth are located along Route 28, east of Hyannis; to reach them from Route 6, take Exit 7 (Yarmouth Rd.) or Exit 8 (Station St.) south.

VISITOR INFORMATION   Contact the **Yarmouth Area Chamber of Commerce,** 657 Rte. 28, West Yarmouth (✆ **800/732-1008** or 508/778-1008; fax 508/778-5114; www.yarmouthcapecod.com).

BEACHES & OUTDOOR PURSUITS

BEACHES   Yarmouth boasts 11 saltwater and two pond beaches open to the public. The body-per-square-yard ratio can be pretty intense along Nantucket Sound on the south side, but so's the social scene, so no one seems to mind. The beachside parking lots charge $10 a day and sell 1-week stickers for $40.

- **Bass River Beach** 🍂, off South Shore Drive in Bass River (South Yarmouth): Located at the mouth of the largest tidal river on the eastern seaboard, this sound beach offers restrooms and a snack bar, plus a wheelchair-accessible fishing pier. The beaches along the south shore (Nantucket Sound) tend to be clean and sandy with comfortable water temps, but they can also be quite crowded. You'll need a beach sticker to park here.

- **Grays Beach,** off Center Street in Yarmouth Port: This isn't much of a beach, but tame waters make the tiny spit of dark sand good for young children. It adjoins the Callery-Darling Conservation Area, with a 2½-mile (4km) trail. The Bass Hole boardwalk offers one of the most scenic walks in the Mid Cape. Parking is free, and there's a picnic area.

- **Parker's River Beach** 🍂, off South Shore Drive in Bass River: This choice has the usual amenities like restrooms and a snack bar, plus a gazebo for the sun-shy.

- **Seagull Beach** 🍂, off South Sea Avenue in West Yarmouth: Rolling dunes, a boardwalk, and all the necessary facilities, like restrooms and a snack bar, attract a young crowd. Bring bug spray, though: Greenhead flies get the munchies in July.

FISHING   Of the five fishing ponds in the Yarmouth area, Long Pond, near South Yarmouth, is known for its largemouth bass and pickerel. For details and a license (shellfishing is another option), visit **Town Hall,** 1146 Rte. 28, South Yarmouth (✆ **508/398-2231**), or **Riverview Bait and Tackle,** 1273 Rte. 28, South Yarmouth (✆ **508/394-1036**). Full-season licenses for out-of-state residents cost $38.50. You can cast for striped bass and bluefish off the pier at Bass River Beach (see "Beaches," above).

Kids Family-Friendly Accommodations

There are tons of hotels and motels lining Route 28 and along the shore in West and South Yarmouth. For those staying on Route 28, the town runs frequent beach shuttles in season. Families looking for a reasonably priced beach vacation may want to consider one of the following options, all near or on the beach.

The attractive 101-unit white-clapboard **Tidewater Motor Lodge,** 135 Main St. (Rte. 28), West Yarmouth (© **800/338-6322** or 508/775-6322; www.tidewaterml.com), has indoor and outdoor pools. Doubles go for $165 to $199 in summer. The 114-unit **All Seasons Motor Inn,** 1199 Main St. (Rte. 28), South Yarmouth (© **800/527-0359** or 508/394-7600; www.allseasons.com), has a game room and indoor and outdoor pools. Summer rates are $105 to $135. The 63-unit **Ocean Mist,** ⊛, 97 S. Shore Dr., South Yarmouth (© **800/248-6478** or 508/398-2633; www.capecodtravel.com/oceanmist), is right on the beach. There's also an indoor pool, just in case it rains. Doubles range from $199 to $249.

NATURE & WILDLIFE AREAS   For a pleasant stroll, follow the 2 miles (3km) of trails maintained by the Historical Society of Old Yarmouth. Park behind the post office. The in-season trail fee (50¢ for adults, 25¢ for children) includes a keyed trail guide. Your path will cross the transplanted 1873 **Kelley Chapel** ⊛, said to have been built by a Quaker grandfather to comfort his daughter after the death of her child.

MUSEUMS

Winslow Crocker House ⊛⊛   The only property on the Cape currently preserved by the prestigious Society for the Preservation of New England Antiquities, this 1780 house deserves every honor. Not only is it a lovely example of the shingled Georgian style, but it's also packed with outstanding antiques collected in the 1930s by Mary Thacher, a descendent of the town's first land grantee. Anthony Thacher and his family had a rougher crossing than most: Their ship foundered off Cape Ann in 1635, and though their four children drowned, Thacher and his wife were able to make it to shore, clinging to the family cradle. You'll come across a 1690 replica in the parlor.

250 Rte. 6A (about a ½ mile/1km east of the town center), Yarmouth Port. © 508/362-4385. www.spnea.org. Admission $5 adults, $4 seniors, $2.50 children 6–12, free to Cape Cod residents and SPNEA members. June to mid-Oct Sat–Sun tours hourly 11am–5pm (last tour at 4pm). Closed mid-Oct to May.

SHOPPING

Driving Route 6A, the Old King's Highway, in Yarmouth Port, you'll pass a number of antiques stores and shops for the home. Ron Kusins's pewter designs range from the traditional to the contemporary. You can watch this nearly extinct art in action at **Pewter Crafters of Cape Cod** ⊛, 933 Rte. 6A (near the Dennis border), Yarmouth Port (© **508/362-3407**).

The most colorful bookshop on the Cape is **Parnassus Books,** 220 Rte. 6A, Yarmouth Port (© **508/362-6420**), housed in an 1858 Swedenborgian church. Relevant new stock, including the Cape-related reissues published by Parnassus

Imprints, is offered alongside older treasures. The outdoor racks, maintained on an honor system, are open 24 hours a day.

WHERE TO STAY

Captain Farris House ✮✮ Sumptuous is the only way to describe this 1845 inn, improbably set a block off bustling Route 28. Fine antiques and striking contemporary touches lift this inn's interiors way above the average B&B decor. Some suites are apartment-size, with fireplaces and whirlpool tubs. Welcoming touches include chocolates, fresh flowers, and plush robes. Next door, the 1825 Elisha Jenkins House contains an additional suite with its own deck.

308 Old Main St. (just west of the Bass River Bridge), Bass River, MA 02664. ✆ **800/350-9477** or 508/760-2818. Fax 508/398-1262. www.captainfarris.com. 10 units. Summer $110–$160 double; $175–$225 suite. Rates include full breakfast. AE, DISC, MC, V. *In room:* A/C, TV/VCR, dataport, hair dryer, iron.

Red Jacket ✮✮ *Kids* Of the huge resort motels lining Nantucket Sound in South Yarmouth, Red Jacket has the best location. It's at the end of the road and borders Parker's River on the west, so sunsets are particularly fine. Families who want all the fixings will find them, though the atmosphere can be a bit impersonal. All rooms have a balcony or a porch. Off-season rates can be as low as $85.

S. Shore Dr. (P.O. Box 88), South Yarmouth, MA 02664. ✆ **800/672-0500** or 508/398-6941. Fax 508/398-1214. www.redjacketinns.com/redjacket. 163 units. Summer $210–$290 double; $325–$570 cottage ($3,100 per week). MC, V. Closed Nov to mid-Apr. **Amenities:** Restaurant, bar/lounge; indoor and outdoor heated pools; putting green; tennis court; exercise room; Jacuzzi; sauna; watersports rentals (parasailing, kayaks, paddle boats, and sailboats); summer children's programs (which may include miniature golf, shuffleboard, horseshoes, and badminton); concierge; basketball and volleyball courts; catamaran cruises. *In room:* A/C, TV, fridge.

Wedgewood Inn ✮✮ This elegant 1812 Federal house sits atop its sloping lawn with unabashed pride. In the main house, the formal front bedrooms have pencil-post beds, Oriental rugs, and wood-burning fireplaces, while the downstairs rooms have screened porches. The two romantic hideaways under the eaves are decorated in a cheerful country style. The picturesque barn contains three very private suites, with canopy beds, fireplaces, and decks. These suites also include phones and TVs.

83 Main St./Rte. 6A (in the center of town), Yarmouth Port, MA 02675. ✆ **508/362-5157** or 508/362-9178. Fax 508/362-5851. www.wedgewood-inn.com. 9 units. Summer $140–$205 double. Rates include full breakfast. AE, DC, MC, V. *In room:* A/C, hair dryer, no phone (except in barn units).

WHERE TO DINE

At **Hallet's,** 139 Rte. 6A, Yarmouth Port (✆ **508/362-3362**), an 1889 drugstore, you can get a float from the original marble soda fountain.

abbicci ✮✮ NORTHERN ITALIAN This sophisticated spot serves cuisine that's a cut above most of the New England-y fare you'll find around these parts. While the exterior is a modest 18th-century Cape, the stylish interior features

---

Kids Especially for Kids

If the kids get sick of all the miscellaneous go-cart and mini-golf concessions on Route 28, they can take in a show. On Friday mornings in season, at 9:30 and 11:30am, the **Cape Playhouse** (✆ **508/385-3911**) ✮✮, 820 Rte. 6A, Dennis hosts visiting companies that mount theater geared toward children 4 and up. At only $6, tickets go fast.

mosaic floors and mural-covered walls. The menu offers seafood dishes as well as veal, lamb, and, of course, pasta. A taste of the veal *nocciole* (with toasted hazelnuts and a splash of balsamic vinegar), and you'll be transported straight to Tuscany. This small restaurant can get overburdened on summer weekends; expect a wait even with a reservation.

43 Main St./Rte. 6A (near the Cummaquid border), Yarmouth Port. ✆ 508/362-3501. Reservations recommended. Main courses $17–$28. AE, DC, DISC, MC, V. Daily 11:30am–2:30pm and 5–10pm.

Inaho ✪✪ *Finds* JAPANESE   What better application of the Cape's oceanic bounty than fresh-off-the-boat sushi? From the front, Inaho is a typical Cape Cod cottage, but park in the back so you can enter through the Japanese garden. Inside, it's a veritable sanctuary, with minimalist decor softened by tranquil music and service. On chilly days, opt for the tempura or a steaming bowl of shabu-shabu.

157 Main St./Rte. 6A (in the village center), Yarmouth Port. ✆ 508/362-5522. Reservations recommended. Main courses $13–$23; nigiri sushi and rolls $4–$7. MC, V. Tues–Sun 5–10pm; call for off-season hours.

Jack's Out Back ✪ *Finds* *Kids* AMERICAN   This neighborhood cafe is hyperactive and full of fun. Chef/owner Jack Braginton-Smith makes a point of dishing out good-natured insults along with the home-style grub, which you bus yourself from the open kitchen. This is a perfect place for impatient children, who'll find lots of familiar, approachable dishes.

161 Main St./Rte. 6A (behind Main St. buildings, in the center of town), Yarmouth Port. ✆ 508/362-6690. Most items under $7. No credit cards. Daily 6:30am–2pm.

DENNIS ✪✪

In Dennis, as in Yarmouth, virtually all the good stuff—pretty drives, inviting shops, and restaurants with personality—are in the north, along Route 6A. Route 28, on the other hand, is chockablock with generic motels and strip malls.

ESSENTIALS
GETTING THERE   After crossing the Sagamore Bridge, head east on Route 6 or 6A. Route 6A passes through Dennis and East Dennis (which can also be reached via northbound Rte. 134 from Rte. 6, Exit 9). Route 134 south leads to South Dennis; if you follow Route 134 all the way to Route 28, the village of West Dennis will be a couple of miles to your west, and Dennisport a couple of miles east.

VISITOR INFORMATION   Contact the **Dennis Chamber of Commerce,** 242 Swan River Rd., West Dennis (✆ **800/243-9920** or 508/398-3568; www.dennischamber.com).

BEACHES & OUTDOOR PURSUITS
BEACHES   Dennis harbors more than a dozen saltwater and two freshwater beaches open to nonresidents. The bay beaches are charming and a big hit with families. The beaches on the sound tend to attract wall-to-wall families, but the parking lots are usually not too crowded, because so many beachgoers stay within walking distance. The lots charge $10 per day; for a 1-week permit ($34), visit **Town Hall,** on Main Street in South Dennis (✆ **508/760-6159**).

- **Chapin Beach** ✪✪, off Route 6A in Dennis: A nice, long bay beach pocked with occasional boulders and surrounded by dunes. No lifeguard, but there are restrooms.
- **Corporation Beach** ✪✪, off Route 6A in Dennis: This bay beach boasts a wheelchair-accessible boardwalk, lifeguards, snack bar, restrooms, and children's play area.

- **Mayflower Beach** ★★, off Route 6A in Dennis: This 1,200-foot (360m) bay beach has the necessary amenities, plus an accessible boardwalk. The tidal pools attract lots of children.
- **Scargo Lake** ★, in Dennis: This large kettle-hole pond (formed by a melting fragment of a glacier) has two pleasant beaches: Scargo Beach, accessible right off Route 6A, and Princess Beach, off Scargo Hill Road, where there are restrooms and a picnic area.
- **West Dennis Beach** ★★, off Route 28 in West Dennis: This long (1½ miles, or 2.5km) but narrow beach along the sound has lifeguards, a playground, a snack bar, restrooms, and a special kite-flying area. The eastern end is reserved for residents; the western end tends to be less packed.

BICYCLING The 25-mile (40km) **Cape Cod Rail Trail** ★★★ (© 508/896-3491) starts here, on Route 134, a ½ mile (1km) south of Route 6, Exit 9. Once a Penn Central track, this paved bikeway extends all the way to Wellfleet (with a few on-road lapses), passing through woods, marshes, and dunes. At the trailhead is **Bob's Bike Shop,** 430 Rte. 134, South Dennis (© 508/760-4723), which rents bikes and in-line skates. Rates are $10 for a couple hours, up to $22 for the full day. Another bike path runs along Old Bass Road, 3½ miles (6km) north to Route 6A.

FISHING Fishing is allowed in Fresh Pond and Scargo Lake; for a license (shellfishing is also permitted), visit **Town Hall,** on Main Street in South Dennis (© 508/394-8300), or **Riverview Bait and Tackle,** 1273 Rte. 28, South Yarmouth (© 508/394-1036). Plenty of people drop a line off the Bass River Bridge, along Route 28 in West Dennis. Several charter boats operate out of the Northside Marina in East Dennis's Sesuit Harbor, including the *Albatross* (© 508/385-3244).

NATURE & WILDLIFE AREAS Behind the Town Hall parking lot on Main Street in South Dennis, a ½-mile (1km) walk along the **Indian Lands Conservation Trail** leads to the Bass River, where blue herons and kingfishers often take shelter. Dirt roads off South Street in East Dennis, beyond the Quivet Cemetery, lead to **Crow's Pasture,** a patchwork of marshes and dunes bordering the bay; this trail is about 2½ miles (4km) round-trip.

WATERSPORTS Located on the small and placid Swan River, **Cape Cod Waterways,** 16 Rte. 28, Dennisport (© 508/398-0080), rents canoes, kayaks, and paddle boats for exploring 200-acre (81-hectare) Swan Pond or Nantucket Sound. A full-day rental costs $30 to $40.

MUSEUMS

Cape Museum of Fine Arts ★★ Part of the prettily landscaped Cape Playhouse complex, this small museum has done a great job of acquiring hundreds of works by area artists dating back to the turn of the 20th century.

60 Hope Lane (off Rte. 6A in the center of town). © 508/385-4477. www.cmfa.org. Admission $7 adults, free for children under 18. May–Oct Mon–Sat 10am–5pm, Sun 1–5pm; Oct–May Tues–Sat 10am–5pm, Sun 1–5pm. Open year-round.

SHOPPING

There's a growing cluster of flea market–style antiques shops in Dennisport, but you may want to save your time and money for the better shops along Route 6A, where you'll also find fine contemporary crafts.

More than 136 dealers stock the co-op **Antiques Center of Cape Cod,** 243 Rte. 6A, about 1 mile (1.6km) south of Dennis Village center (© **508/ 385-6400**); it's the largest such enterprise on the Cape.

Dennis along Route 6A has become a magnet for interesting small galleries. Among the finest is **Scargo Stoneware Pottery and Art Gallery** ✪, 30 Dr. Lord's Rd. S., off Route 6A, about 1 mile (1.6km) east of the town center (© **508/385-3894**).

WHERE TO STAY

Corsair & Cross Rip Resort Motels ✪ *Kids*   Of the many family-oriented motels lining this part of Nantucket Sound, these two neighbors are among the nicest, with fresh contemporary decor, two beachview pools, and their own chunk of sand. As a rainy-day backup, there's an indoor pool, a game room, and a toddler playroom equipped with toys.

41 Chase Ave. (off Depot St., 1 mile/1.6km southeast of Rte. 28), Dennisport, MA 02639. © **800/201-1072** or 508/398-2279. Fax 508/760-6681. www.corsaircrossrip.com. 47 units. Summer $135–$255 double, $175–$255 efficiency. Special packages and family weekly rates available. AE, MC, V. **Amenities:** 2 outdoor pools; indoor pool; Jacuzzi; playground; game room; coin-op washers and dryers; barbecue grills. *In room:* A/C, TV w/ pay movies, fax, dataport, fridge, coffeemaker, hair dryer, iron.

The Four Chimneys Inn ✪   Scargo Lake is directly across the street, and the village is a brief walk away from this imposing 1880 Victorian. Opulent tastes are evident in the high ceilings and marble fireplace of the front parlor. Guest rooms are appealing, with hand-painted stenciling and wicker furnishings. Two units have decks overlooking the lovely grounds. Five rooms are equipped with TVs; two also have air-conditioning.

946 Rte. 6A (about ½ a mile/1km east of the town center), Dennis, MA 02638. © **800/874-5502** or 508/385-6317. Fax 508/385-6285. www.fourchimneysinn.com. 7 units. Summer $90–$155 double. Rates include full breakfast. AE, MC, V. Open year-round. *In room:* No phone.

Isaiah Hall B&B Inn ✪✪   This inn's location, on a quiet side street in a residential neighborhood, bodes well for a good night's sleep, but it's also just a short walk to restaurants and Corporation Beach. Animated hostess Marie Brophy has been entertaining the entertainers from the nearby Cape Playhouse for over 15 years. Breakfasts are served at the long plank table that dominates the 1857 country kitchen. Bedroom styles range from 1940s knotty pine to spacious and spiffy.

152 Whig St. (1 block northwest of the Cape Playhouse), Dennis, MA 02638. © **800/736-0160** or 508/385-9928. Fax 508/385-5879. www.isaiahhallinn.com. 10 units. Summer $107–$148 double; $179 suite. Rates include continental breakfast. AE, DISC, MC, V. Closed mid-Oct to late Apr. No children under 7. *In room:* A/C, TV/VCR, dataport, hair dryer.

Lighthouse Inn ✪✪ *Kids*   Set smack dab on placid West Dennis Beach, this resort has been welcoming families for over 60 years. In 1938, Everett Stone acquired a decommissioned 1885 lighthouse and built a charming inn and a cottage colony around it. With amusements such as miniature golf right on the premises, there's plenty to do. The rooms aren't what you'd call fancy, but some have great views. Lunch is served on the deck overlooking the sound, a delightful setting to enjoy a club sandwich.

1 Lighthouse Inn Rd. (off Lower County Rd., ½ a mile/1km south of Rte. 28), West Dennis, MA 02670. © **508/398-2244**. Fax 508/398-5658. www.lighthouseinn.com. 68 units. Summer $208–$338 double; $432–$650 2-bedroom cottage; $645–760 3-bedroom cottage. MC, V. Rates include full breakfast and all gratuities. Closed mid-Oct to mid-May. **Amenities:** Restaurant, pool snackbar; bar with entertainment; outdoor heated pool with pool house/changing rooms; tennis court; children's programs (July–Aug); game room; shuffleboard; volleyball; miniature golf. *In room:* TV/VCR, fridge, hair dryer, safe.

WHERE TO DINE

For a time-travel treat, visit **Sundae School** ⊛, 387 Lower County Rd., at Sea Street, about ⅓ mile (0.5km) south of Route 28, Dennisport (© **508/ 394-9122**). The spacious barn has been retrofitted with a marble soda fountain and other artifacts from the golden age of ice cream.

Bob Briggs' Wee Packet Restaurant and Bakery ⊛⊛ *Finds* *Kids*

SEAFOOD   Since 1949, this tiny joint has served all the requisite seafood staples, plus steak and chicken dishes. Grab a Formica table for a traditional summer feast topped off by a timeless dessert such as blueberry shortcake.

79 Depot St. (at Lower County Rd., about a third of a mile/0.5km south of the town center), Dennisport. © **508/398-2181**. Main courses $6–$15. MC, V. Late June to late Sept daily 8am–8:30pm; early May to late June daily 11:30am–8:30pm. Closed late Sept to early May.

The Dog House ⊛ *Finds* HOT DOGS

Hot dogs, cheese dogs, and chili dogs are the specialty at this tiny hut, but there are also hamburgers and salmon burgers. Onion rings are hand-battered, and the chili's homemade. Grab a picnic table, and wash it all down with fresh lemonade.

189 Lower County Rd., Dennisport. © **508/398-7774**. All items under $10. No credit cards. Mid-May to mid-Sept daily 11am–8pm; call for off-season hours. Closed Nov–Apr.

Gina's by the Sea ⊛⊛ ITALIAN

A landmark amid Dennis's "Little Italy" beach community since 1938, this intimate restaurant specializes in traditional Italian comfort food. Save room for Mrs. Riley's Chocolate Rum Cake, made daily by the owner's mother. This place fills up fast, so if you want to eat before 8:30pm, arrive before 5:30pm.

134 Taunton Ave., about 1½ miles (2.5km) northwest of Rte. 6A (turn north across from the Public Market and follow the signs). © **508/385-3213**. Reservations not accepted. Main courses $10–$23. AE, MC, V. June–Sept daily 5–10pm; Apr–May and Oct–Nov Thurs–Sun 5–10pm. Closed Dec–Mar.

The Marshside ⊛ DINER

Overlooking a picturesque marsh is one of the Cape's best diners. There's a relaxed atmosphere here that comes from having a year-round staff that knows what it's doing (a rarity on the Cape). The food is fresh and tasty, be it a fried-fish platter, cheeseburger, or veggie melt. Homemade desserts are good, too.

28 Bridge St. (at the junction of Rtes. 134 and 6A), East Dennis. © **508/385-4010**. Main courses $7–$17. AE, DC, DISC, MC, V. Daily 7:30am–9:30pm. Open year-round.

Olde Inn at West Dennis ⊛⊛ *Finds* NEW ENGLAND

A walk through the doors of this Irish pub/roadhouse, with wide wooden floorboards and a low beamed ceiling, is a step back in time. Large families of several generations sit at big round tables, and everyone seems to know one another. Later in the evening, someone takes out a guitar or a fiddle and starts to play; everyone sings along. The food is about as traditional as it gets. Stick with the basics, like baked scrod, prime rib, or roasted chicken.

348 Main St. (Rte. 28), West Dennis. © **508/760-2627**. Reservations not accepted. Main courses $10–$19. MC, V. June–Sept daily 4–9:30pm; call for off-season hours.

The Red Pheasant Inn ⊛⊛ NEW AMERICAN

An enduring Cape favorite since 1977, this handsome space—an 18th-century barn turned chandlery—has managed not only to keep pace with trends, but also to remain a front-runner. Favorites include roast rack of lamb, sole meunière, and, in the fall, game specials like venison. Two massive brick fireplaces tend to be the focal point in the off-season. In fine weather, sit out in the garden room.

905 Main St. (about a ½ mile/1km east of the town center). ℂ **508/385-2133.** Reservations recommended. Main courses $18–$30. DISC, MC, V. Apr–Dec daily 5–10pm; Jan–Mar Wed–Sun 5–10pm.

Swan River Seafood ⭐ SEAFOOD   Every town has its own version of the "fish place with a fantastic view." Here, the scenic vista is a marsh punctuated by an old windmill, and the fish is available deep-fried, broiled, or sautéed. The difference is that the seafood is snapping fresh—unloaded at the adjoining market every day from the fishing boats. Go for the scrod San Sebastian, poached in a garlic-infused broth.

5 Lower County Rd. (at Swan Pond River, southeast of the town center), Dennisport. ℂ **508/394-4466.** Reservations recommended. Main courses $13–$22. AE, DISC, MC, V. Late May to Sept daily noon–11pm. Closed Oct to late May.

DENNIS AFTER DARK

The oldest continuously active straw-hat theater in the country and still one of the best, the **Cape Playhouse** ⭐⭐, 820 Rte. 6A (ℂ **877/385-3911** or 508/385-3911; www.capeplayhouse.com), was the 1927 brainstorm of Raymond Moore, who'd spent a few summers as a playwright in Provincetown and quickly tired of the strictures of "little theater." Salvaging an 1838 meetinghouse, he plunked it amid a meadow and got his New York buddy, designer Cleon Throckmorton, to turn it into a proper theater. It was an immediate success, and a parade of stars have trod the boards in the decades since, from Humphrey Bogart to Jane Fonda. Not all of today's headliners are quite as impressive, but the theater can be counted on for a varied season of polished work. Performances are staged from mid-June to early September. Tickets range from $15 to $35.

The **Cape Cinema** ⭐⭐, 36 Hope Lane, off Route 6A in the center of town (ℂ **508/385-2503** or 508/385-5644; www.capecinema.com), is an Art Deco surprise, with a Prometheus-themed ceiling mural. George Mansour, curator of the Harvard Film Archive, sees to the art-house programming. The setting and seating—black leather armchairs—may spoil you forever.

3 The Lower Cape

The Lower Cape towns tend to attract a more elite crowd of vacationers. Not surprisingly, the area supports the Cape's priciest shops, restaurants, inns, and rental cottages.

Located on the easternmost portion of historic Route 6A, **Brewster** still enjoys much the same cachet that it boasted as a high roller in the maritime trade. But for a relatively recent incursion of condos—and with it, increased car traffic—it looks much as it might have in the late 19th century, with its general store still serving as a social centerpiece. Perhaps because excellence breeds competition, Brewster has spawned several fine restaurants and has become something of a magnet for gourmands.

Chatham, the Cape's most chichi town, is touted by realtors as "the Nantucket of the Cape." Its Main Street offers appealing shops and eateries, complemented by a scenic lighthouse and plentiful beaches nearby.

As the gateway to the Outer Cape, where all roads merge, **Orleans** offers more variety in the way of shops and entertainment than some of its neighbors. The village of East Orleans is on the upswing as a destination, offering a couple of fun restaurants and—best of all—a goodly chunk of magnificent, unspoiled Cape Cod National Seashore.

BREWSTER ★★

With miles of placid Cape Cod Bay beach and acres of state park, Brewster is an attractive place for families. Route 6A, the Old King's Highway, becomes Brewster's Main Street and houses a bevy of B&Bs, pricey restaurants, and the Cape's finest antiques shops. The town has managed to absorb an intrusively huge development within its borders, the 380-acre (154-hectare) condo complex known as Ocean Edge. Brewster also welcomes tens of thousands of campers and day-trippers headed for Nickerson State Park.

ESSENTIALS

GETTING THERE   After crossing the Sagamore Bridge, head east on Route 6 or 6A. Route 6A passes through the villages of West Brewster, Brewster, and East Brewster. You can also reach Brewster by taking Route 6, Exit 10 north, along Route 124.

VISITOR INFORMATION   The **visitor center** is behind Brewster Town Hall, 2198 Main St./Rte. 6A (© **508/896-3500;** fax 508/896-1086; www.capecodtravel.com/brewster).

BEACHES & OUTDOOR PURSUITS

BEACHES   Brewster's eight bay beaches have minimal facilities. When the tide is out, the beach extends as much as 2 miles (3km), leaving behind tidal pools to splash in and explore. On a clear day, you can see the whole curve of the Cape, from Sandwich to Provincetown. Purchase a beach parking sticker ($8 per day, $25 per week) at the **visitor center** behind Town Hall, 2198 Main St./Rte. 6A (© **508/896-4511**).

- **Breakwater Beach** ★★, off Breakwater Road, Brewster: Only a brief walk from the center of town, this calm, shallow beach (the only one with restrooms) is ideal for young children.
- **Flax Pond** ★★, in Nickerson State Park (see "Nature & Wildlife Areas," below): This freshwater pond offers a bathhouse and watersports rentals. The park contains two more ponds with beaches—Cliff and Little Cliff. Access and parking are free.
- **Linnells Landing Beach** ★, on Linnell Road in East Brewster: This is a ½-mile (1km), wheelchair-accessible bay beach.
- **Paines Creek Beach** ★, off Paines Creek Road, West Brewster: With 1½ miles (2.5km) to stretch out on, this bay beach has something to offer sun lovers and nature lovers alike. Your kids will love it if you arrive when the tide's coming in—the current will give an air mattress a nice little ride.

BICYCLING   The **Cape Cod Rail Trail** ★★★ intersects with the 8-mile (13km) **Nickerson State Park** trail system at the park entrance, where there's plenty of free parking; you could follow the Rail Trail back to Dennis (about 12 miles/19km) or onward toward Wellfleet (13 miles/21km). In season, **Idle Times** (© 508/255-8281) provides rentals within the park. Another good place to jump in is on Underpass Road about a ½ mile (1km) south of Route 6A. Here you'll find **Brewster Bicycle Rental,** 442 Underpass Rd. (© **508/896-8149**), and **Brewster Express,** which makes sandwiches to go. Just up the hill is the well-equipped **Rail Trail Bike & Blade,** 302 Underpass Rd. (© **508/896-8200**). Both shops offer free parking. Bike rentals range from $12 for 4 hours to $18 for 24 hours.

Biking the Cape Cod Rail Trail ★★★

The 25-mile (40km) Cape Cod Rail Trail is one of New England's longest and most popular bike paths. Once a bed of the Penn Central Railroad, the trail is relatively flat and straight. On weekends in summer, you'll have to contend with dogs, in-line skaters, families, and bikers who whip by you on their way to becoming the next Lance Armstrong. Still, if you want to venture away from the coast and see some of the Cape's countryside without having to deal with motorized traffic, this is one of the best ways to do it.

The trail starts in South Wellfleet on Lecount Hollow Road or in South Dennis on Route 134, depending on which way you want to ride. Beginning in South Wellfleet, the path cruises by purple wild-flowers, flowering dogwood, and small maples, where red-winged blackbirds and goldfinches nest. In Orleans, you'll have to ride on Rock Harbor and West roads until the City Council decides to complete the trail. Fortunately, the roads provide a good view of the boats lining Rock Harbor. Clearly marked signs lead back to the Rail Trail. You'll soon enter Nickerson State Park bike trails, or continue straight through Brewster to a series of swimming holes—Seymour, Long, and Hinckleys ponds. A favorite picnic spot is the Pleasant Lake General Store in Harwich. Shortly afterwards, you'll cross over Route 6 on Route 124 before veering right through farmland, soon ending in South Dennis.

—by Stephen Jermanok

BOATING   You can rent a canoe from **Goose Hummock** ⚑, in Orleans (© **508/255-2620**), and paddle around Paines Creek and Quivett Creek, as well as Upper and Lower Mill ponds.

FISHING   Brewster offers more ponds for fishing than any other town: 14 in all. Among the most popular are Cliff and Higgins ponds (within Nickerson State Park). For a license, visit **Town Hall,** 2198 Rte. 6A (© **508/896-4506**).

GOLF   The 18-hole championship **Ocean Edge Golf Course,** 832 Villages Dr. (© **508/896-5911**), is the most challenging in town, followed closely by **Captain's Golf Course,** 1000 Freemans Way (© **508/896-5100**).

NATURE & WILDLIFE AREAS   Admission is free to the two trails maintained by the **Cape Cod Museum of Natural History** (below). The **South Trail,** covering a ¾-mile (1km) round-trip south of Route 6A, crosses a natural cranberry bog beside Paines Creek to reach a hardwood forest of beeches and tupelos; toward the end of the loop, you'll come upon a "glacial erratic," a huge boulder dropped by a receding glacier. Before heading out on the ¼-mile (0.5km) **North Trail,** stop in at the museum for a free guide describing the local flora. Also accessible from the museum parking lot is the **John Wing Trail** ⚑, a 1½-mile (2.5km) network traversing 140 acres (57 hectares) of preservation land, including upland, salt marsh, and beach. (*Note:* This can be a soggy trip. Be sure to heed the posted warnings about high tides, especially in spring, or you might find yourself stranded.)

As it crosses Route 6A, Paines Creek Road becomes Run Hill Road. Follow it to the end to reach **Punkhorn Park Lands,** an 800-acre (324-hectare) tract popular with mountain bikers; it features several kettle ponds, a "quaking bog," and 45 miles (72km) of dirt paths.

The 25-acre (10-hectare) **Spruce Hill Conservation Area,** behind the Brewster Historical Society Museum, includes a 600-foot (180m) stretch of beach reached by a former carriage road.

Just east of the museum is the 1,955-acre (792-hectare) **Nickerson State Park,** at Route 6 and Crosby Lane (☎ **508/896-3491**). This preserve encompasses 418 campsites (reservations pour in a year in advance, but some are held open for new arrivals willing to wait a day or two) and 8 miles (13km) of bike paths.

WATERSPORTS   Kayaks, canoes, and more are available seasonally at **Jack's Boat Rentals,** on Flax Pond in Nickerson State Park (☎ **508/896-8556**).

MUSEUMS

Cape Cod Museum of Natural History ★★ (Kids)   Long before "ecology"

became a buzzword, noted naturalist writer John Hay helped to found a museum dedicated to preserving Cape Cod's unique landscape. Children's exhibits include a "live hive"—like an ant farm, only with busy bees—and marine-room tanks. The bulk of the museum is outdoors, where 85 acres (34 hectares) invite exploration (see "Nature & Wildlife Areas," above). There's an on-site archaeology lab on Wing Island, thought to have sheltered one of Brewster's first settlers—the Quaker John Wing, driven from Sandwich in the mid–17th century by religious persecution—and before him, native tribes dating back 10 millennia. The museum sponsors lectures, concerts, astronomy cruises, bike tours, and "eco-treks"—including a sleepover on uninhabited Monomoy Island off Chatham.

869 Rte. 6A, about 2 miles (3km) west of the town center. ☎ 800/479-3867 in eastern Mass., or 508/896-3867. www.ccmnh.org. Admission $5 adults, $4.50 seniors, $2 children 5–12. Mon–Sat 9:30am–4:30pm; Sun 11am–4:30pm. Closed major holidays. Open year-round.

SHOPPING

Brewster's stretch of Route 6A offers the best antiquing on the entire Cape. The artifacts at **Kingsland Manor Antiques,** 440 Rte. 6A, about 1 mile (1.6km) east of the Dennis border (☎ **800/486-2305** or 508/385-9741), tend to be on the flamboyant side, which makes browsing all the more fun. **Monomoy Antiques,** 3425 Rte. 6A (☎ **508/896-6570**), often has fascinating finds from local estate sales. Specialties include rare books, English china, Native American artifacts, sterling silver, and decoys.

Imagine a town dump full of treasures, and you'll get an idea of what's in store at **Diane Vetromile's Antiques,** 3884 Rte. 6A (no phone). If the sign that reads ANTIQUES is out, it's open. This place is a tad kooky, but any junk aficionado will be thrilled by the pickings: hubcaps, wooden nails, iron rakes, wood shutters—the more peeled paint, the better. Owner Diane Vetromile is herself a sculptor, who works with (surprise) found objects; her work is on view at Jacob Fanning Gallery and Farmhouse Antiques, both in Wellfleet.

No one should miss the venerable **Brewster Store** ★★, 1935 Main St./Rte. 6A, in the center of town (☎ **508/896-3744**), built as a church in 1852. You'll find everything from penny candy to comics to the bestselling Brewster Store coffee. Neighbors meet on the wide front porch to catch up on village gossip.

WHERE TO STAY

Beechcroft Inn ★ Though it looks every inch the gracious summer home, this 1828 building started out as a meetinghouse. Subtract one steeple, relocate atop a little hillock crowned with magnificent beeches, and presto—a made-to-order country retreat. The innkeepers, Jan and Paul Campbell-White from England, have spruced up the place with English antiques. The Brewster Tea Pot serves lunch and an authentic afternoon tea.

1360 Rte. 6A (about 1 mile/1.6km west of the town center), Brewster, MA 02631. ℂ **877/233-2446** or 508/896-9534. Fax 508/896-8812. www.beechcroftinn.com. 10 units. Summer $110–$165. Rates include full breakfast. AE, DISC, MC, V. Open year-round. **Amenities:** Restaurant (lunch and tea); bikes. *In room:* A/C, coffeemaker, hair dryer.

The Bramble Inn ★★ (Value) Cliff and Ruth Manchester oversee two rambling mid-19th-century homes, decorated in a breezy, country-casual manner. The main inn, built in 1861, houses one of the Cape's best restaurants (see "Where to Dine," below). The 1849 Greek Revival house next door has cozy and quaint bedrooms, with antique touches like crocheted bedspreads. Cliff's creative breakfasts, such as mixed-fruit Swedish pancakes, are served in the courtyard garden. The inn is about ½ a mile (1km) from calm beaches on Cape Cod Bay.

2019 Rte. 6A (about ⅓ of a mile/0.5km east of the town center), Brewster, MA 02631. ℂ **508/896-7644.** Fax 508/896-9332. www.brambleinn.com. 8 units. Summer $138–$188 double. Rates include full breakfast. AE, DISC, MC, V. Closed Jan–March. **Amenities:** Restaurant (international). *In room:* A/C, TV, hair dryer, iron.

Captain Freeman Inn ★★ This 1866 Victorian inn has a terrific location, right next to the Brewster Store and within walking distance of a pretty bay beach. The "luxury rooms" incorporate every extra you could hope to encounter: a canopied, four-poster bed; a fireplace; a TV/VCR; and a private porch with a two-person hot tub. The plainer rooms are just as pretty. Innkeeper Carol Edmondson teaches cooking classes here, so you can be sure the breakfasts are top-notch.

15 Breakwater Rd. (off Rte. 6A, in the town center), Brewster, MA 02631. ℂ **800/843-4664** or 508/896-7481. Fax 508/896-5618. www.captainfreemaninn.com. 12 units. Summer $145–$250 double. Rates include full breakfast and afternoon tea. AE, MC, V. No children under 10. **Amenities:** Outdoor pool; bikes. *In room:* A/C, hair dryer.

Old Sea Pines Inn ★★ (Value) (Kids) This inn's former days as the Sea Pines School of Charm and Personality for Young Women can be seen today in the double parlor, the expansive porch lined with rockers, and the handful of rather minuscule bedrooms in the main house. These bargain rooms with shared bathrooms are the only ones in the inn without air-conditioning, but at $75 per night, who cares? The annex rooms are playful, with colorful accoutrements such as pink TVs. Sunday evenings from mid-June to mid-September, Old Sea Pines is the site of a dinner-theater performance by the Cape Cod Repertory Theatre.

2553 Main St. (about 1 mile/1.6km east of the town center), Brewster, MA 02631. ℂ **508/896-6114.** Fax 508/896-7387. www.oldseapinesinn.com. 24 units, 5 with shared bathroom. Summer $75–$150 double; $135–$165 suite. Rates include full breakfast and afternoon tea. AE, DC, DISC, MC, V. Closed Jan–Mar. *In room:* TV, hair dryer, iron.

WHERE TO DINE
Very Expensive

The Bramble Inn Restaurant ★★★ INTERNATIONAL Often named among the best restaurants on Cape Cod, the Bramble Inn is also one of the most expensive—but worth it for a special night out. Five dining rooms are each imbued with a distinct personality, from sporting (the Tack Room) to best-Sunday-behavior (the Parlor). But the highlight is Ruth Manchester's extraordinary cuisine. Her assorted seafood curry (with lobster, cod, scallops, and shrimp in a light curry sauce with grilled banana, toasted almonds, coconut, and chutney) and her rack of lamb (with deep-fried beet-and-fontina polenta, pan-seared zucchini, and mustard port cream) have been written up in the *New York Times*.

2019 Main St. ✆ **508/896-7644**. Reservations suggested. Fixed-price dinners $48–$58. AE, DISC, MC, V. June to mid-Oct Tues–Sun 6–9pm; call for off-season hours. Closed Jan–Mar.

Chillingsworth ✿✿ FRENCH This longtime contender for the title of fanciest restaurant on the Cape now has two dining options: formal with jackets suggested for men, and more casual with no reservations. The fancy dining room boasts antique appointments and a six-course table d'hôte menu that will challenge the most shameless gourmands. Specialties include seared and roasted boneless rib-eye of veal with fresh morels, mushroom torte, and asparagus. Finish with warm chocolate cake with pistachio ice cream and chocolate drizzle. Or try the moderately priced Bistro, which serves meals in the adjoining greenhouse or on the shady lawn. There are also three deluxe guest rooms on the premises.

2449 Main St., about 1 mile (1.6km) east of the town center. ✆ **800/430-3640** or 508/896-3640. www. chillingsworth.com. Reservations suggested. Jackets advised for men in fine-dining section. Fixed-price meals $50–$68. Bistro main courses $13–$24. AE, DC, MC, V. Mid-June to mid-Oct Tues–Sun 11:30am–2:30pm and 6–9:30pm; call for off-season hours. Closed Dec–Apr.

Moderate

The Brewster Fish House ✿✿ NEW AMERICAN Spare and handsome as a Shaker refectory, this small restaurant bills itself as "nonconforming," and delivers on the promise. Its approach to seafood borders on genius: Consider, for instance, squid delectably tenderized in a marinade of soy and ginger, or walnut-crusted ocean catfish accompanied by kale sautéed in Marsala. There are always beef and vegetarian options as well.

2208 Main St., about ½ a mile (1km) east of the town center. ✆ **508/896-7867**. Reservations not accepted. Main courses $15–$26. MC, V. May–Aug Mon–Sat 11:30am–3pm and 5–10pm, Sun noon–3pm and 5–9:30pm; call for off-season hours. Closed Jan–Mar.

Inexpensive

Brewster Inn & Chowder House ✿ ECLECTIC To get the gist of the expression "chow down," just observe the early-evening crowd happily doing so at this century-old restaurant. The draw is hearty staples at prices geared to ordinary people rather than splurging tourists. This place also makes the best martinis in town, and there's a good old bar, the Woodshed, out back.

1993 Rte. 6A (in the center of town). ✆ **508/896-7771**. Main courses $12–$18. AE, DISC, MC, V. Late May to mid-Oct daily 11am–3pm, Sun–Thurs 5–9:30pm, Fri–Sat 5–10pm; call for off-season hours. Open year-round.

Cobie's ✿ *Kids* AMERICAN Accessible to cars whizzing along Route 6A and within collapsing distance for cyclists exploring the Rail Trail, this picture-perfect clam shack has been dishing out exemplary fried clams, lobster rolls, foot-long hot dogs, and all the other beloved staples of summer since 1948.

3260 Rte. 6A, about 2 miles (3km) east of Brewster center. ✆ **508/896-7021**. Most items under $15. No credit cards. Late May to mid-Sept daily 11am–9pm. Closed mid-Sept to late May.

CHATHAM ✿✿✿

Chatham (say *Chatt*-um) is small-town America the way Norman Rockwell imagined it. Roses climb white picket fences in front of simple Cape cottages, all within a stone's throw of the ocean. The Cape's fanciest town is also its prettiest. As a result, inn rooms are pricier here and rentals are snapped up more quickly. But those looking for a picture-perfect New England town will love Chatham's winding Main Street, filled with pleasing shops and leading to a beautiful beach with lighthouse.

Sticking out from the peninsula like a sore elbow, Chatham was one of the first spots to attract early explorers. Samuel de Champlain stopped by in 1606, but got into a tussle with the prior occupants and left in a hurry. The first colonist to stick around was William Nickerson, who befriended a local *sachem* (tribal leader) and built a house beside his wigwam in 1656. To this day, listings for Nickersons occupy a half page in the Cape Cod phone book.

Chatham is one of the few areas on the Cape to support a commercial fishing fleet—against increasing odds. Overfishing has resulted in closely monitored limits to give the stock time to bounce back. Boats must now go out as far as 100 miles (161km) to catch their fill. Despite the difficulties, it's a way of life few locals would willingly relinquish.

ESSENTIALS

GETTING THERE   After crossing the Sagamore Bridge, head east on Route 6 and take Exit 11 south (Rte. 137) to Route 28. From this intersection, South Chatham is about a ½ mile (1km) west, and West Chatham is about 1½ miles (2.5km) east. Chatham itself is 2 miles (3km) farther east on Route 28. The town lies 32 miles (52km) east of Sandwich, 24 miles (39km) south of Provincetown.

VISITOR INFORMATION   Visit the **Chatham Chamber of Commerce,** 533 Main St. (© **800/715-5567** or 508/945-5199; www.chathamcapecod.org), or the new **Chatham Chamber booth,** at the intersection of Routes 137 and 28 (no phone).

BEACHES & OUTDOOR PURSUITS

BEACHES   Chatham has an unusual array of beach styles, from the peaceful shores of Nantucket Sound to the treacherous, shifting shoals along the Atlantic. For beach stickers ($8 per day, $35 per week), call the **Permit Department,** on George Ryder Road in West Chatham (© **508/945-5180**).

- **Chatham Light Beach** 🐾🐾: Located directly below the lighthouse parking lot (where stopovers are limited to 30 min.), this narrow stretch of sand is easy to get to: Just walk down the stairs. Currents here can be tricky and swift, so swimming is discouraged.
- **Cockle Cove Beach, Ridgevale Beach,** and **Hardings Beach** 🐾🐾: Lined up along the sound, each at the end of its namesake road south of Route 28, these family-pleasing beaches offer gentle surf and full facilities. Ridgevale Beach also has kayak and sailboat rentals.
- **Forest Beach** 🐾: No longer an officially recognized town beach (there's no lifeguard), this sound landing near the Harwich border is still popular, especially among surfboarders.
- **Oyster Pond Beach,** off Route 28: Only a block from Chatham's Main Street, this sheltered saltwater pond (with restrooms) swarms with children.
- **South Beach** 🐾🐾: A former island jutting out slightly to the south of the Chatham Light, this glorified sandbar can be dangerous, so heed posted warnings and content yourself with strolling.
- **North Beach** 🐾🐾: Extending all the way south from Orleans, this 5-mile (8km) barrier beach is accessible from Chatham only by boat; you can take

the **Beachcomber** (℃ 508/945-5265), a water taxi, which leaves from the fish pier. The round-trip costs $12 for adults, $8 for children.

BICYCLING Though Chatham has no separate recreational paths per se, a demarcated biking/skating lane makes a scenic 8-mile (13km) circuit of town, heading south onto "The Neck," east to the Chatham Light, up Shore Road all the way to North Chatham, and back to the center of town. A brochure prepared by the **Chamber of Commerce** (℃ 800/715-5567 or 508/945-5199) shows the route. Rentals are available at **Bikes & Blades,** 195 Crowell Rd. (℃ 508/945-7600).

FISHING Chatham has five ponds and lakes that permit fishing; Goose Pond off Fisherman's Landing is among the top spots. For saltwater fishing sans boat, try the fishing bridge on Bridge Street at the southern end of Mill Pond. First, though, get a license at **Town Hall,** 549 Main St. (℃ 508/945-5101). If you hear the deep sea calling, sign on with the *Booby Hatch* (℃ 508/430-2312) or the *Banshee* (℃ 508/945-0403). Sportfishing rates average $550 to $600 for 8 hours. Shellfishing licenses are available at the **Permit Department,** on George Ryder Road in West Chatham (℃ 508/945-5180).

NATURE & WILDLIFE AREAS Heading southeast from the Hardings Beach parking lot, the 2-mile (3km) round-trip **Seaside Trail** offers beautiful parallel panoramas of Nantucket Sound and Oyster Pond River. Access to 40-acre (16-hectare) Morris Island, southwest of the Chatham Light, is easy: Walk or drive across and start right in on a marked ¾-mile (1km) trail. Heed the high tides as advised—they can come in surprisingly quickly, leaving you stranded.

The **Beachcomber** (℃ 508/945-5265) runs seal-watching cruises out of Stage Harbor. Parking is behind the former Main Street School just on the left before the rotary. The cruises cost $18 for adults, $12 for children 3 to 15.

The uninhabited **Monomoy Island**   , 2,750 acres (1,114 hectares) of brush-covered sand favored by some 285 species of migrating birds, is the perfect pit stop along the Atlantic flyway. Harbor and gray seals are catching on, too: Hundreds now carpet the coastline from late November to May. Both the **Wellfleet Bay Wildlife Sanctuary,** operated by the Audubon Society (℃ 508/349-2615), and Brewster's **Cape Cod Museum of Natural History** (℃ 508/896-3867) offer guided trips. The Audubon's trips take place April through November; the cost is $30 to $60. About a dozen times each summer, the museum organizes sleepovers in the island's only surviving structure—a clapboard "keeper's house" flanked by an 1849 lighthouse.

WATERSPORTS Seaworthy vessels, from surfboards to Sunfish, can be rented from **Monomoy Sail and Cycle,** 275 Rte. 28, North Chatham (℃ 508/945-0811). Pleasant Bay, the Cape's largest bay, is the best place to play for those with sufficient experience; if the winds don't seem to be going your way, try Forest Beach on the South Chatham shore. Kayaks and sailboards rent for $45 per day.

SHOPPING

Chatham's tree-shaded Main Street offers a terrific opportunity to shop and stroll. **The Spyglass**   , 618 Main St. (℃ 508/945-9686), stocks antique telescopes, sextants, captains' desks, maps, and charts. Headed for such prestigious outlets as Neiman Marcus, the handblown glassworks at **Chatham Glass**   , 758 Main St., just west of the Chatham rotary (℃ 508/945-5547), are objects that demand to be coveted. Also of note is **Chatham Pottery,** the **Beachcomber** (© 508/945-5265), a water taxi, which leaves from the fish pier. The round-trip costs $12 for adults, $8 for children.

BICYCLING   Though Chatham has no separate recreational paths per se, a demarcated biking/skating lane makes a scenic 8-mile (13km) circuit of town, heading south onto "The Neck," east to the Chatham Light, up Shore Road all the way to North Chatham, and back to the center of town. A brochure prepared by the **Chamber of Commerce** (© 800/715-5567 or 508/945-5199) shows the route. Rentals are available at **Bikes & Blades,** 195 Crowell Rd. (© 508/945-7600).

FISHING   Chatham has five ponds and lakes that permit fishing; Goose Pond off Fisherman's Landing is among the top spots. For saltwater fishing sans boat, try the fishing bridge on Bridge Street at the southern end of Mill Pond. First, though, get a license at **Town Hall,** 549 Main St. (© 508/945-5101). If you hear the deep sea calling, sign on with the *Booby Hatch* (© 508/430-2312) or the *Banshee* (© 508/945-0403). Sportfishing rates average $550 to $600 for 8 hours. Shellfishing licenses are available at the **Permit Department,** on George Ryder Road in West Chatham (© 508/945-5180).

NATURE & WILDLIFE AREAS   Heading southeast from the Hardings Beach parking lot, the 2-mile (3km) round-trip **Seaside Trail** offers beautiful parallel panoramas of Nantucket Sound and Oyster Pond River. Access to 40-acre (16-hectare) Morris Island, southwest of the Chatham Light, is easy: Walk or drive across and start right in on a marked ¾-mile (1km) trail. Heed the high tides as advised—they can come in surprisingly quickly, leaving you stranded.

The **Beachcomber** ✦✦ (© 508/945-5265) runs seal-watching cruises out of Stage Harbor. Parking is behind the former Main Street School just on the left before the rotary. The cruises cost $18 for adults, $12 for children 3 to 15.

The uninhabited **Monomoy Island** ✦✦, 2,750 acres (1,114 hectares) of brush-covered sand favored by some 285 species of migrating birds, is the perfect pit stop along the Atlantic flyway. Harbor and gray seals are catching on, too: Hundreds now carpet the coastline from late November to May. Both the **Wellfleet Bay Wildlife Sanctuary,** operated by the Audubon Society (© 508/349-2615), and Brewster's **Cape Cod Museum of Natural History** (© 508/896-3867) offer guided trips. The Audubon's trips take place April through November; the cost is $30 to $60. About a dozen times each summer, the museum organizes sleepovers in the island's only surviving structure—a clapboard "keeper's house" flanked by an 1849 lighthouse.

WATERSPORTS   Seaworthy vessels, from surfboards to Sunfish, can be rented from **Monomoy Sail and Cycle,** 275 Rte. 28, North Chatham (© 508/945-0811). Pleasant Bay, the Cape's largest bay, is the best place to play for those with sufficient experience; if the winds don't seem to be going your way, try Forest Beach on the South Chatham shore. Kayaks and sailboards rent for $45 per day.

SHOPPING

Chatham's tree-shaded Main Street offers a terrific opportunity to shop and stroll. **The Spyglass** ✦, 618 Main St. (© 508/945-9686), stocks antique telescopes, sextants, captains' desks, maps, and charts. Headed for such prestigious outlets as Neiman Marcus, the handblown glassworks at **Chatham Glass** ✦, 758 Main St., just west of the Chatham rotary (© 508/945-5547), are objects that demand to be coveted. Also of note is **Chatham Pottery,** 2058 Rte. 28, east of Route 137 (© **508/430-2191**).

WHERE TO STAY

Chatham's accommodations tend to be more expensive than those of neighboring towns, as it's considered a fancy place to vacation. But for those allergic to fussy inns, Chatham has several decent motels.

Practically across the street from the Chatham Bars Inn, the very basic **Hawthorne** ⊛, 196 Shore Rd. (© **508/945-0372;** www.thehawthorne.com), boasts one of the best locations in town: right on the water, with striking views of Chatham Harbor, Pleasant Bay, and the Atlantic. Rates are $150 to $180 double.

The personable **Seafarer of Chatham,** 2079 Rte. 28, about a ½ mile (1km) east of Route 137 in West Chatham (© **800/786-2772** or 508/432-1739; www.chathamseafarer.com), lacks a pool, but is only about a ½ mile (1km) from Ridgevale Beach. Rates are $125 to $145 double.

The cheapest option is the **Chatham Motel,** 1487 Main St./Rte. 28, Chatham (© **800/770-5545** or 508/945-2630; www.chathammotel.com), 1½ miles (2.5km) from Hardings Beach. It has an outdoor pool; summer rates are $115.

Very Expensive

Chatham Bars Inn ⊛⊛⊛ (Kids) Set majestically above the beach in Chatham with commanding views out to a barrier beach and the Atlantic beyond, the grand old Chatham Bars Inn is the premier hotel on Cape Cod. The colonnaded 1914 brick building is surrounded by 26 shingled cottages on 20 acres (8 hectares). Take in the sweeping views on the breezy veranda, where you can order a drink and recline in an Adirondack chair. Many guest rooms have balconies with views of the beach or the landscaped grounds. Cottage rooms are cheery with painted furniture and Waverly fabrics. (*Note:* A dozen or so units have not yet been renovated; inquire when you reserve.) Guests can take meals in the formal Main Dining Room (see "Where to Dine," below), the Tavern, or the seasonal Beach House Grill right on the private beach.

Shore Rd. (off Seaview St., about ½ a mile/1km northwest of the town center), Chatham, MA 02633. © 800/527-4884 or 508/945-0096. Fax 508/945-5491. www.chathambarsinn.com. 205 units. Summer $210–$420 double; $425–$540 1-bedroom suite; $580–$1,300 2-bedroom suite. AE, DC, MC, V. **Amenities:** 3 restaurants; outdoor heated pool; putting green; public 9-hole golf course next door; tennis courts; basic fitness room; summer children's programs; concierge; limited room service; babysitting; shuffleboard; croquet; volleyball; complimentary launch to Nauset Beach. *In room:* A/C, TV/VCR, fridge, hair dryer, iron.

Wequassett Inn Resort and Golf Club ⊛⊛⊛ (Kids) Fans of golf, sailing, and tennis will enjoy this 22-acre (9-hectare) resort occupying its own little peninsula sticking out into Pleasant Bay. Adjacent is the private Cape Cod National Golf Club, where inn guests enjoy exclusive privileges. Tucked amid the woods along the shore, 15 modest dwellings, built in the 1940s, harbor roomy quarters done up in an opulent country style. These cost a bit more than the more modern "villa" rooms, but are worth it for their bay views. All units have either a balcony or a patio. The 18th-century Eben Ryder House is home to an elegant restaurant, open to the public (jackets and ties preferred for men at dinner). The pool is set at the neck of Clam Point, a calm beach. North Beach is a 15-minute ride via the inn's Power Skiff ($10). Bay tours and fishing charters can also be arranged.

2173 Rte. 28 (about 5 miles/8km northwest of the town center, on Pleasant Bay), Chatham, MA 02633. © 800/225-7125 or 508/432-5400. Fax 508/432-5032. www.wequassett.com. 104 units. Summer

$315–$895 double. AE, DC, DISC, MC, V. Closed late Nov to Mar. **Amenities:** 2 restaurants (Main Dining Room, Outer Bar and Grille); heated outdoor pool; van service to 2 public golf courses (in Harwich and in Brewster) and the private Cape Cod National Golf Course; tennis courts (extra fee) and pro shop; fitness room; watersports-equipment rental (sailboards, Sunfish, Daysailers, Hobie Cats); bike rental; children's programs; concierge; secretarial services; limited room service; yoga and massage; babysitting; croquet; volleyball; van service to Chatham and Orleans villages for shopping. *In room:* A/C, TV, minibar, coffeemaker, hair dryer, iron.

Expensive

Captain's House Inn ★★★ *(Finds* Set on 2 meticulously maintained acres (1 hectare), this 1839 Greek Revival house, along with a cottage and carriage house, is a shining example of 19th-century style. Bedrooms are richly furnished, with canopied four-posters, beamed ceilings, and, in some cases, brick hearths and Jacuzzis. Breakfast is served at noncommunal tables—a thoughtful touch for those of us slow to rev up, sociability-wise.

369–377 Old Harbor Rd. (about ½ a mile/1km north of the rotary), Chatham, MA 02633. © **800/315-0728** or 508/945-0127. Fax 508/945-0866. www.captainshouseinn.com. 19 units. Summer $175–$425 double. Rates include full breakfast and afternoon tea. AE, DISC, MC, V. **Amenities:** Bikes. *In room:* A/C, TV/VCR, fax, dataport, fridge, coffeemaker, hair dryer, iron.

Chatham Wayside Inn ★★ *(Kids* Centrally located on Chatham's Main Street, this 1860 stagecoach stop has undergone a thoroughly modern renovation. Don't expect any musty antique trappings: It's all lush carpeting, Waverly fabrics, and polished reproductions. The prize rooms boast patios or balconies overlooking the town bandstand. The restaurant serves sophisticated New American fare (see "Where to Dine," below).

512 Main St. (in the center of town), Chatham, MA 02633. © **800/391-5734** or 508/945-5550. Fax 508/945-3407. www.waysideinn.com. 56 units. Summer $185–$265 double, $285–$385 suite; off-season packages available. DISC, MC, V. **Amenities:** Restaurant/bar; outdoor heated pool. *In room:* A/C, TV/VCR, hair dryer, iron.

Pleasant Bay Village ★★ *(Kids* Set across the street from Pleasant Bay, a few minutes' walk from Pleasant Bay Beach, this is one fancy motel. Over the past 25 years, owner Howard Gamsey has transformed this property into a playful Zen paradise, where waterfalls cascade through rock gardens into a stone-edged pool dotted with lily pads and flashing koi. Guest rooms, done up in restful pastels, are unusually pleasant. Many bathrooms feature marble counters and stone floors. In summer, you can order lunch from the grill without having to leave your place at the pool.

1191 Orleans Rd./Rte. 28 (about 3 miles/5km north of Chatham center), Chathamport, MA 02633. © **800/547-1011** or 508/945-1133. Fax 508/945-9701. www.pleasantbayvillage.com. 58 units. Summer $165–$255 double; $355–$455 suite. AE, MC, V. Closed Nov–Apr. **Amenities:** Restaurant (breakfast, plus lunch by the pool and dinner in season); heated pool; limited room service. *In room:* A/C, TV, dataport, fridge, hair dryer, iron.

Moderate

The Dolphin of Chatham ★ *(Value* With an 1805 main building, motel units, and cottages, the Dolphin offers a wide range of lodging options in the heart of town. Even on exquisitely groomed Main Street, this property's colorful gardens stand out. The main inn has seven rooms with romantic touches like beamed ceilings and canopy beds. The rest of the units are standard motel issue, except for the honeymoon suite, which is housed in a whimsical windmill. The inn has a terrific bar area, where guests can enjoy light dinner fare from a screened porch. Lighthouse Beach is a pleasant stroll away.

352 Main St. (at the east end), Chatham, MA 02633-2428. ☎ **800/688-5900** or 508/945-0070. Fax 508/945-5945. www.dolphininn.com. 37 units. Summer $150–$210 double; $209–$275 2-bedroom suite; $1,900 per week for cottage. Rates include continental breakfast. AE, DC, DISC, MC, V. **Amenities:** Bar (light dinners), pool bar (lunch and drinks); outdoor heated pool; Jacuzzi. *In room:* A/C, TV, fax, fridge, coffeemaker, hair dryer, iron.

The Moorings Bed & Breakfast ☆
Whether you end up in the main house, a Victorian beauty, or the carriage houses out back, you'll enjoy breakfast in the gazebo surrounded by flower gardens. Several rooms in the carriage houses are spacious, with kitchenettes and private decks. Some units have VCRs and fridges. All are immaculate and quaintly decorated, joined by a central courtyard and porches lined with rocking chairs.

326 Main St. (at the east end), Chatham, MA 02633. ☎ **800/320-0848** or 508/945-0848. Fax 508/945-1577. www.mooringscapecod.com. 16 units. Summer $142–$208 double; $230–$235 suite; $2,100 per week for cottage. Rates include full breakfast. AE, DISC, MC, V. **Amenities:** Bikes. *In room:* A/C, TV, hair dryer.

WHERE TO DINE

Chatham Wayside Inn ☆ NEW AMERICAN
The Wayside's central location makes it a good spot for a reasonably priced meal in town. Diners have several seating choices: the clubby tavern with gleaming wood tables and comfy Windsor chairs, the front room's cozy booths, or the screened terrace (the perfect people-watching spot at lunchtime). More important, perhaps, is what's on the plate. Specialties include crab cakes, rack of lamb, and pesto cod. For something a little different, try the Portuguese-style chowder, with double-smoked bacon, fresh quahogs, and red bliss potatoes.

512 Main St. (in the center of town). ☎ **508/945-5550.** Main courses $16–$25. DISC, MC, V. May–Oct daily 8–11am, 11:30am–4pm, and 5–9pm; Nov–Apr Tues–Sun 8–11am, 11:30am–4pm, and 5–9pm. Closed Jan.

Christian's ☆ NEW AMERICAN
This popular boîte, owned by the Chatham Wayside Inn, is a good choice for a medium-priced dinner. The downstairs dining rooms enjoy a French country decor, whereas **Upstairs at Christian's** is British clubby, with leather couches, mahogany paneling, a piano bar, and a smattering of classic movie posters. The same cinematic-motif menu applies to both venues: Famous movie titles are accorded to such specialties as salmon sautéed with mushrooms, capers, white wine, and lemon—a.k.a. A Fish Called Wanda. In the bar and on the deck, you can also order small pizzas, burgers, and fries.

443 Main St. (in the center of town). ☎ **508/945-3362.** Reservations not accepted. Main courses $9–$24. DISC, MC, V. May–Dec daily 5–10pm; call for off-season hours. Open year-round.

The Main Dining Room at the Chatham Bars Inn ☆☆ NEW AMERICAN
If it's grandeur you're after, the setting here supplies a surplus. The dining room is vast, and the view of the Atlantic is of the million-dollar variety. Your fellow diners are decked out in their summer finery, and in the background, a pianist tickles the ivories. Dinners consist of hearty traditional fare like roast duckling with mandarin ginger sauce. This is not delicate food, but it is delicious—and the chowder may be the best on Cape Cod.

Shore Rd. ☎ **508/945-0096.** Reservations recommended. Jackets and collared shirts required for men. Main courses $21–$35. A 17% service charge (gratuity) is added onto your check. AE, DC, MC, V. Mid-May to early Sept daily 7:30–11am and 6:30–9pm; call for off-season hours.

Vining's Bistro ☆☆ (Finds) FUSION
If you're looking for cutting-edge cuisine in a sophisticated setting, venture upstairs at Chatham's minimall and into this cool cafe. The film-noirish murals suggest a certain Bohemian abandon, but the

food is up-to-the-minute. The menu offers compelling juxtapositions such as warm lobster tacos with salsa fresca and crème fraîche.

595 Main St. (in the center of town). ⓒ **508/945-5033**. Reservations not accepted. Main courses $16–$24. AE, DC, MC, V. June to mid-Oct daily 5:30–10pm; call for off-season hours. Closed Jan–Mar.

CHATHAM AFTER DARK

Chatham's free **band concerts** ★★ are arguably the best on the Cape and attract crowds in the thousands. This is small-town America at its most nostalgic, as the band plays old standards that never go out of style. Held in Kate Gould Park (off Chatham Bars Ave.) from July to early September, they kick off at 8pm every Friday. Come early to claim your square of lawn—it'll be checkered with blankets by late afternoon. Call ⓒ **508/945-5199** for information.

A great leveler, the **Chatham Squire** ★★, 487 Main St. (ⓒ **508/945-0942**), attracts CEOs, seafarers, and collegiates alike. The piano bar **Upstairs at Christian's** ★, 443 Main St. (ⓒ **508/945-3362**), has the air of a vintage frat house with leather couches and purloined movie posters. Live music is offered nightly in season and on weekends year-round.

ORLEANS ★★

Orleans is where the "Narrow Land" (the early Algonquin name for the Cape) starts to get very narrow indeed: From here on up—or "down," in paradoxical local parlance—it's never more than a few miles wide from coast to coast. This is also where the oceanside beaches open up into a glorious expanse some 40 miles (64km) long, framed by dramatic dunes and serious surf.

The Cape's three main roads (Rtes. 6, 6A, and 28) converge here, too, so on summer weekends, it acts as a rather frustrating funnel. Nevertheless, Main Street boasts some appealing restaurants and shops. The village of East Orleans, near the entrance to Nauset Beach, may be the best place to base yourself. The 10-mile (16km) beach, which is the southernmost stretch of the Cape Cod National Seashore preserve, is a magnet for families and young folks.

ESSENTIALS

GETTING THERE   After crossing the Sagamore Bridge, head east on Route 6 or 6A (the long but scenic route); both converge with Route 28 in Orleans. The town is 31 miles (50km) east of Sandwich, 25 miles (40km) south of Provincetown.

VISITOR INFORMATION   Contact the **Orleans Chamber of Commerce,** 44 Main St. (ⓒ **800/865-1386** or 508/255-1386; www.capecod-orleans.com). There's an **information booth** at the corner of Route 6A and Eldredge Parkway (ⓒ **508/240-2484**).

BEACHES & OUTDOOR PURSUITS

BEACHES   From here all the way to Provincetown on the Cape's eastern side, you're dealing with the wild Atlantic. Current conditions are clearly posted at the entrance to Nauset Beach. One-week parking permits ($25 for renters, $40 for transients) may be obtained from **Town Hall,** on School Road (ⓒ **508/240-3775**). Day-trippers who arrive early enough—better make that before 10am on weekends in July and August—can pay at the gate (ⓒ **508/240-3780**).

- **Crystal Lake** ★, off Monument Road about ¾ of a mile (1km) south of Main Street: Parking—if you can find a space—is free, but there are no facilities here.

- **Nauset Beach** ✿✿✿, in East Orleans (© **508/240-3780**): Stretching southward all the way past Chatham, this barrier beach, which is part of the Cape Cod National Seashore but is managed by the town, has long been one of the Cape's gonzo beach scenes—good surf, big crowds, lots of young people. Once you get past the swarms near the parking lot, you'll have about 9 miles (14km) of beach mostly to yourself. Full facilities, including a terrific snack bar, can be found within the 1,000-car parking lot; the in-season fee is $10 per car, which is also good for same-day parking at Skaket Beach (see below). Substantial waves make for good surfing and boogie-boarding in the special section to the far left reserved for that purpose. In July and August, there are concerts from 7 to 9pm in the gazebo.
- **Pilgrim Lake** ✿, off Monument Road about 1 mile (1.6km) south of Main Street: This small freshwater beach is covered by a lifeguard in season. You must have a beach parking sticker.
- **Skaket Beach** ✿, off Skaket Beach Road to the west of town (© **508/255-0572**): This peaceful bay beach is a better choice for families. When the tide recedes, little kids will enjoy splashing about in the tidal pools left behind. Parking costs $8, and you'd better turn up early.

BICYCLING   Orleans presents the one slight gap in the 25-mile (40km) off-road **Cape Cod Rail Trail** ✿✿✿ (© **508/896-3491**): Just east of the Brewster border, the trail merges with town roads for about 1½ miles (2.5km). The best way to avoid cars is to zigzag west to scenic Rock Harbor. Rentals are available at **Orleans Cycle,** 26 Main St. (© **508/255-9115**).

BOATING   In season, **Arey's Pond Boat Yard,** off Route 28 in South Orleans (© **508/255-7900**), offers sailing lessons on Little Pleasant Bay. Individual lessons are $60 per hour; weekly group lessons are $160 to $250. The **Goose Hummock Outdoor Center,** 15 Rte. 6A, south of the rotary (© **508/255-2620;** www.goose.com), rents canoes, kayaks, and more; the northern half of Pleasant Bay is the perfect place to use them.

FISHING   Fishing is allowed in Baker Pond, Pilgrim Lake, and Crystal Lake. For licenses, visit **Town Hall,** at Post Office Square in the center of town (© **508/240-3700,** ext. 305), or **Goose Hummock** (see above). Surf casting—no license needed—is permitted on Nauset Beach South, off Beach Road. **Rock Harbor** ✿✿, a former packet landing on the bay (about 1¼ miles/2km, northwest of the town center), shelters New England's largest sportfishing fleet: some 18 boats at last count. One call (© **800/287-1771** in Mass., or 508/255-9757) will get you information on them all—or go look them over in person.

WATERSPORTS   The **Pump House Surf Co.,** 9 Cranberry Hwy./Rte. 6A (© **508/240-2226**), rents wet suits, body boards, and surfboards. Stop by for up-to-date reports on where to find the best waves. **Nauset Sports,** Jeremiah Square, Route 6A at the rotary (© **508/255-4742**), also rents surfboards, body boards, skim boards, and wet suits.

SHOPPING
Though shops are somewhat scattered, Orleans is full of great finds for browsers. **Continuum Antiques** ✿, 7 S. Orleans Rd./Rte. 28, south of the junction with Route 6A (© **508/255-8513**), carries some 400 vintage light fixtures. The proprietor of **Countryside Antiques,** 6 Lewis Rd., south of Main Street in the center of East Orleans (© **508/240-0525**), roams the world in search of stylish

furnishings. Stop by **Kemp Pottery,** 9 Cranberry Hwy./Rte. 6A, just south of the rotary (© **508/255-5853**), and check out the turned and slab-built creations—from soup tureens to fanciful sculptures.

WHERE TO STAY

The Cove ⭑ *Kids*   This motel on busy Route 28 also fronts placid Town Cove, where guests are offered a free minicruise in season. The interiors are adequate, if not dazzling, and a small pool and restful gazebo overlook the waterfront. Some rooms have balconies.

13 S. Orleans Rd./Rte. 28 (north of Main St.), Orleans, MA 02653. © **800/343-2233** or 508/255-1203. Fax 508/255-7736. www.thecoveorleans.com. 47 units. Summer $109–$189 double; $169–$189 suite or efficiency. Open year-round. AE, DC, DISC, MC, V. **Amenities:** Small heated outdoor pool. *In room:* A/C, TV/VCR, fridge, coffeemaker, hair dryer, microwave.

Kadee's Gray Elephant ⭑⭑ *Value* *Kids*   These exuberantly decorated studios are extremely cheery. All but one have kitchenettes, with a breakfast basket (milk, juice, pastry, yogurt, and cereal) supplied for your first morning. There's a friendly restaurant next door (see "Where to Dine," below), and the little minigolf course out back is geared just right for kids. Nauset Beach is a few miles down the road.

216 Main St., East Orleans, MA 02643. © **508/255-7608.** Fax 508/240-2976. 6 units. Summer $110–$140 double. Weekly rates available. Closed mid-Oct to Mar. MC, V. **Amenities:** Restaurant (clam shack); gift shop. *In room:* A/C, TV, fridge, coffeemaker, iron.

Nauset House Inn ⭑⭑ *Value*   Just ½ a mile (1km) from Nauset Beach, this inn is for those seeking a quiet retreat. Several of the rooms in greenery-draped outbuildings feature such extras as sunken bathtubs or private decks. Most romantic is a 1907 conservatory appended to the 1810 farmhouse. Breakfast would seem relatively workaday, were it not for the setting—a rustic refectory—and the innkeeper's memorable pastries.

143 Beach Rd./P.O. Box 774 (about 1 mile/1.6km east of the town center), East Orleans, MA 02643. © **508/255-2195.** Fax 508/240-6276. www.nausethouseinn.com. 14 units, 6 with shared bathroom. Summer $75–$150 double. Rates include full breakfast. DISC, MC, V. Closed Nov–Mar. No children under 12. *In room:* No phone.

Nauset Knoll Motor Lodge ⭑⭑ *Value* *Kids*   You can't get any closer to Nauset Beach than this. Each room in the nothing-fancy motel has picture windows looking out over the dunes to the ocean. The simple accommodations are well maintained, and by staying here, you'll save on daily parking charges at Nauset Beach. The whole complex is owned by Uncle Sam and is under the supervision of the National Park Service.

237 Beach Rd. (at Nauset Beach, about 2 miles/3km east of the town center), East Orleans, MA 02643. © **508/255-2364.** www.capecodtravel.com. 12 units. Summer $140 double. MC, V. Closed late Oct to early Apr. *In room:* TV, no phone.

The Orleans Inn ⭑   You can't miss this mansard-roofed 1875 beauty, perched right on the edge of Town Cove. Absolutely ask for one of the rooms facing the water. The simple units are cheerful with modern amenities and extra touches like a box of chocolates on the bureau. The bar and restaurant have wonderful views.

Rte. 6A/P.O. Box 188 (just south of the Orleans rotary), Orleans, MA 02653. © **508/255-2222.** Fax 508/255-6722. www.orleansinn.com. 11 units. Summer $125–$250 double. Rates include continental breakfast. AE, DC, DISC, MC, V. **Amenities:** Restaurant/bar. *In room:* TV.

WHERE TO DINE

Stop by the charming **Fancy's Farm** ⭑, 199 Main St., East Orleans (© **508/255-1949**), for fresh pastries, sandwiches, salads, and soups to go.

Tips **Recommended Reading**

In *Midnights: A Year with the Wellfleet Police,* frequent *New Yorker* contributor Alec Wilkinson chronicles his stint with the police department in this small Cape Cod town, earning the nickname "Crash." A sense of the Cape, and of New England life, is nicely captured here.

The Barley Neck Inn ★★ FRENCH   This 1857 captain's house is one of the top places to dine in Orleans. The owners have recruited a superb chef in Franck Champely, who arrived from Taillevent and Maxim's by way of New York's Four Seasons. His background shines in straightforward yet subtle dishes such as grilled Atlantic salmon with a red-pepper coulis and basil vinaigrette. For a less expensive menu from the same kitchen, go next door to Joe's Beach Road Bar and Grille.

5 Beach Rd., about ½ a mile (1km) east of the town center. ✆ **800/281-7505** or 508/255-0212. Reservations recommended. Main courses $14–$24. AE, DC, MC, V. June to early Sept daily 5–10pm; call for off-season hours. Open year-round.

Kadee's Lobster & Clam Bar ★ *Kids* SEAFOOD   This is the best clam shack in town, and also one of those cheerful businesses that you leave with a smile on your face. Fine weather calls for a lobster roll, or perhaps the Fisherman's Feed combo platter splurge. On the other hand, there's nothing like the classic chowders and stews to take the chill off.

212 Main St., East Orleans. ✆ **508/255-6184.** Reservations not accepted. Main courses $7–$24. MC, V. Late June to early Sept Fri–Sun noon–4pm, daily 4:30–9pm; late May to late June Fri–Sun noon–4pm and 4:30–9pm. Closed early Sept to late May.

The Lobster Claw Restaurant ★ *Kids* SEAFOOD   This sprawling, family-owned business has been serving up quality seafood for almost 30 years. Get the baked stuffed lobster with all the fixings.

Rte. 6A (just south of the rotary), Orleans. ✆ **508/255-1800.** Main courses $10–$19. AE, DC, DISC, MC, V. Daily 11:30am–9pm. Closed Nov–Mar.

Mahoney's Atlantic Bar & Grill ★ NEW AMERICAN   Seafood is the specialty at this casual restaurant. Dishes like tuna sashimi, grilled sea bass, and pan-seared lobster are why you came to Cape Cod. There are also poultry, meat, pasta, and vegetarian options. Some nights in season, there's live jazz and blues.

28 Main St. (in the center of town). ✆ **508/255-5505.** Reservations recommended. Main courses $12–$21. AE, MC, V. Daily 11:30am–10pm; call for off-season hours.

Nauset Beach Club ★ NORTHERN ITALIAN   The first thing you may notice about this trattoria is the tantalizing aromas. Unfortunately, the next impression is apt to be a surfeit of attitude, when, for example, the maitre d' informs you, unbidden, that each person in your party must order an entree—no exceptions made for young diners. If you're willing to play by the rules, the reward is worth it: luscious pastas and other Italian-accented regional fare.

222 Main St., about ½ a mile (1km) east of the town center. ✆ **508/255-8547.** Reservations suggested. Main courses $14–$19. AE, DISC, MC, V. Late May to mid-Oct daily 5:30–9:30pm; mid-Oct to late May Tues–Sat 5:30–9:30pm.

ORLEANS AFTER DARK

Joe's Beach Road Bar & Grille ⭐⭐, at the Barley Neck Inn (© **508/ 255-0212**), is a big old barn of a bar that might as well be town hall: It's where you'll find all the locals. On Sundays in season, there's live "Jazz at Joe's." Other nights feature Jim Turner, a blind piano player who entertains with show tunes and boogie-woogie. There's never a cover.

There's live music on weekends at the **Land Ho!** ⭐⭐, 38 Main St. (© **508/ 255-5165**), the best pub in town on Monday and Tuesday nights in season, and Thursday and Saturday nights off-season. There's usually no cover.

4 The Outer Cape

It's only on the Outer Cape that the landscape and even the air feel really beachy. You can smell the seashore just over the horizon—in fact, everywhere you go, because you're never more than a mile or two away from sand and surf. You won't find any high-rise hotels along the shoreline or tacky amusement arcades—just miles of pristine beaches and dune grass rippling in the wind. That's because in the early 1960s, 27,000 acres (10,935 hectares) here became the federally protected Cape Cod National Seashore.

WELLFLEET ⭐⭐⭐

With the well-tended look of a classic New England village and surrounded by pristine beaches, Wellfleet is the chosen destination for artists, writers, off-duty psychiatrists, and other contemplative types. Distinguished literati such as Edna St. Vincent Millay and Edmund Wilson put this rural village on the map in the 1920s, in the wake of Provincetown's Bohemian heyday.

To this day, Wellfleet remains remarkably unspoiled. Once you leave Route 6, commercialism is kept to a minimum, though the town boasts plenty of appealing shops, distinguished galleries, and a couple of excellent restaurants. It's hard to imagine any other community on the Cape supporting so sophisticated an undertaking as the Wellfleet Harbor Actors' Theatre, or hosting such a wholesome event as public square dancing on the adjacent Town Pier. And where else could you find a thriving drive-in movie theater right next door to an outstanding nature preserve?

ESSENTIALS

GETTING THERE   After crossing the Sagamore Bridge, head east on Route 6 to Orleans, and then north on Route 6 to Wellfleet. Wellfleet is 42 miles (68km) northeast of Sandwich, 14 miles (23km) south of Provincetown.

VISITOR INFORMATION   Contact the **Wellfleet Chamber of Commerce,** off Route 6 (© **508/349-2510;** fax 508/349-3740; www.wellfleetchamber.com).

BEACHES & OUTDOOR PURSUITS

BEACHES   Wellfleet's fabulous ocean beaches tend to sort themselves demographically: LeCount Hollow is popular with families, Newcomb Hollow with high-schoolers, White Crest with the college crowd, and Cahoon with 30-somethings. Only the latter two beaches permit parking by nonresidents ($10 per day). To enjoy the other two, as well as Burton Baker Beach on the harbor and Duck Harbor on the bay, plus three freshwater ponds, you'll have to walk or bike in, or see if you qualify for a sticker ($25 per week). Bring proof of residency to the seasonal **Beach Sticker Booth** on the Town Pier, or call the **Wellfleet Recreation Department** (© **508/349-9818**). Parking is free at all beaches and ponds after 4pm.

- **Marconi Beach** ⟨★★⟩, off Marconi Beach Road in South Wellfleet: A National Seashore property, this cliff-lined beach (with restrooms) charges an entry fee of $7 per day, or $20 for the season. *Note:* The bluffs are so high that the beach lies in shadow by late afternoon.
- **Mayo Beach** ⟨★⟩, Kendrick Avenue (near the Town Pier): Right by the harbor, facing south, this warm, shallow bay beach (with restrooms) is hardly secluded, but will please young waders. Parking is free. You can grab a bite (and a paperback) at the Bookstore Restaurant across the street.
- **White Crest Beach** ⟨★★⟩ and **Cahoon Hollow Beach** ⟨★★★⟩, off Ocean View Drive in Wellfleet: These two town-run ocean beaches—big with surfers—are open to all. Both have snack bars and restrooms. Parking costs $10 per day.

BICYCLING   The end (to date) of the 25-mile (40km) **Cape Cod Rail Trail** ⟨★★★⟩ (© 508/896-3491), Wellfleet is among its more desirable destinations: A country road off the bike path leads right to LeCount Hollow Beach. At the end of the trail, the **Black Duck Sports Shop,** 1446 Rte. 6, at LeCount Hollow Road (© **508/349-9801**), stocks everything from bikes to belly boards. The deli at the adjoining **South Wellfleet General Store** (© **508/349-2335**) can see to your snacking needs.

BOATING   **Jack's Boat Rentals,** on Gull Pond off Gull Pond Road, about a ½ mile (1km) south of the Truro border (© **508/349-9808**), rents canoes, kayaks, sailboards, and sea cycles. Gull Pond connects to Higgins Pond by way of a placid channel lined with red maples and choked with water lilies. Needless to say, it's a great place to paddle. If you'd like a canoe for a few days, you'll need to go to the Jack's Boat Rentals location on Route 6 in Wellfleet (next to the Cumberland Farms). In addition to watercraft to go, Jack's is also the place for information about **Eric Gustavson's guided kayak tours** (© **508/349-1429**) of kettle ponds and tidal rivers from Chatham to Truro.

The **Chequessett Yacht & Country Club,** on Chequessett Neck Road in Wellfleet (© **508/349-3704**), offers group sailing lessons. For experienced sailors, **Wellfleet Marine Corp.,** on the Town Pier (© **508/349-2233**), rents sailboats in season.

FISHING   For a license to fish at Long Pond, Great Pond, or Gull Pond, visit **Town Hall,** 300 Main St. (© **508/349-0301**), or the **Town Pier** (© **508/ 349-9818**). Surf casting, which doesn't require a license, is permitted at the town beaches. Shellfishing licenses—Wellfleet's oysters are world-famous—can be obtained from the **Shellfish Department,** on the Town Pier off Kendrick Avenue (© **508/349-0300**).

Heading out from Wellfleet Harbor in season is the party fishing boat *Navigator* (© **508/349-6003**) and three charter boats: the *Erin-H* (© **508/ 349-9663;** www.virtualcapecod.com/erinh), *Jac's Mate* (© **508/255-2978**), and *Snooper* (© **508/349-6113**).

NATURE & WILDLIFE AREAS   Right in town, the short, picturesque boardwalk known as **Uncle Tim's Bridge,** off East Commercial Street, crosses Duck Creek to access a tiny island crisscrossed by paths.

The Cape Cod National Seashore maintains two spectacular self-guided trails. The 1¼-mile (2km) **Atlantic White Cedar Swamp Trail** ⟨★★⟩, off the parking area for the Marconi Wireless Station (see "Cape Cod National Seashore," later in this chapter), shelters a rare stand of the lightweight species prized by Native Americans as wood for canoes; the moss-choked swamp is a magical place, refreshingly cool even at the height of summer. A boardwalk will see you over the muck, but the return trip does entail a calf-testing ½-mile (1km) trek through deep sand. Consider it a warm-up for magnificent **Great Island,** jutting 4 miles (6km) into the bay (off the western end of Chequessett Neck Rd.) to cup Wellfleet Harbor. Before attaching itself to the mainland in 1831, Great Island harbored a busy whaling post. Be sure to cover up, wear sturdy shoes, bring water, and venture to Jeremy Point—the very tip—only if you're sure the tide is going out.

You'll find 6 miles (10km) of scenic trails lined with lupines and bayberries—Goose Pond, Silver Spring, and Bay View—within the **Wellfleet Bay Wildlife Sanctuary** ★★★, off Route 6 north of the Eastham border, in South Wellfleet (© **508/349-2615;** fax 508/349-2632; www.wellfleetbay.org). A spiffy ecofriendly visitor center serves as both introduction and gateway to this 1,000-acre (405-hectare) refuge, maintained by the Massachusetts Audubon Society. Passive solar heat and composting toilets are just a few of the waste-cutting elements incorporated into the seemingly simple building. You'll see plenty of red-winged blackbirds and osprey as you follow the looping trails through pine forests, salt marsh, and moors. The sanctuary offers naturalist-guided tours and workshops for children; inquire about canoeing, birding, and seal-watching excursions. Trail use is free for Massachusetts Audubon Society members; otherwise, the fee is $3 for adults and $2 for seniors and children. Trails are open July through August from 8am to 8pm, September through June from 8am to dusk. The visitor center is open from Memorial Day to Columbus Day daily from 8:30am to 5pm; off-season, it's closed Mondays.

WATERSPORTS   Surfing is restricted to White Crest Beach, and sailboarding to Burton Baker Beach at Indian Neck during certain tide conditions. Ask for a copy of the regulations at the Beach Sticker Booth on the Town Pier.

SHOPPING

A stroll from Main Street down Bank Street and then along Commercial Street will take you past a dozen galleries worth a look. Crafts make a strong showing in Wellfleet, as do women's clothing and eclectic home furnishings. But unlike Provincetown, Wellfleet pretty much closes up come Columbus Day, so buy while the getting's good.

The **Cove Gallery,** 15 Commercial St., by Duck Creek (© **508/349-2530**)—with a waterside sculpture garden—carries the paintings and prints of many well-known artists, including Barry Moser and Leonard Baskin. John Grillo's work astounds during his annual show in July. **Jules Besch Stationers** ★, 15 Bank St. (© **508/349-1231**), specializes in stationery products, including papers, ribbons, handmade journals, and unusual gift items.

WHERE TO STAY

Aunt Sukie's Bayside Bed & Breakfast ★   Sue and Dan Hamar's 1830 house is perched on a bluff in an exclusive residential neighborhood overlooking Cape Cod Bay. All bedrooms have sweeping bay views; the Nickerson Suite has wide-board floors and a fireplace. In front of the house are beautiful gardens; out back is a large deck where guests can eat breakfast and sunbathe. A boardwalk leads to a private beach. The Hamars also own a two-bedroom cottage located about a mile (1.6km) away in the pines.

525 Chequessett Neck Rd., Wellfleet, MA 02667. © **800/420-9999** or 508/349-2804. www.auntsukies.com. 4 units. Summer $150–$210 double; $1,200–$1,600 per week for cottage. Room rates include continental breakfast. MC, V. Closed Nov to mid-Apr.

Provincetown

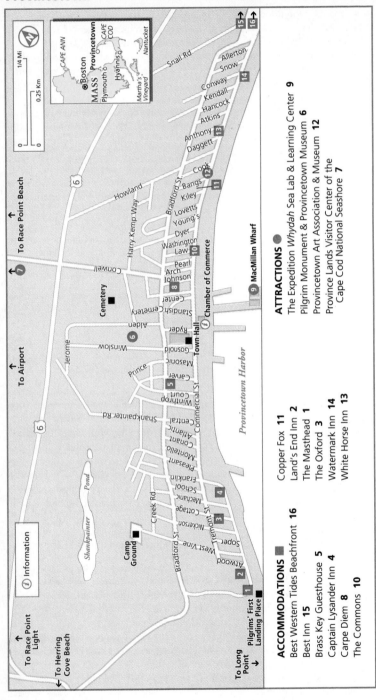

ATTRACTIONS

The Expedition *Whydah* Sea Lab & Learning Center **9**
Pilgrim Monument & Provincetown Museum **6**
Provincetown Art Association & Museum **12**
Province Lands Visitor Center of the
  Cape Cod National Seashore **7**

ACCOMMODATIONS

Best Western Tides Beachfront **16**
Best Inn **15**
Brass Key Guesthouse **5**
Captain Lysander Inn **4**
Carpe Diem **8**
The Commons **10**

Copper Fox **11**
Land's End Inn **2**
The Masthead **1**
The Oxford **3**
Watermark Inn **14**
White Horse Inn **13**

Even'tide ✪ *Kids*   Set back from busy Route 6, this well-run motel is a good base for families. In case of rain, there's a 60-foot (18m) indoor pool, unusual in this part of the Cape. On the property are seven cottages and four apartments. The Rail Trail goes right by, and a 1-mile (1.6km) path through the woods leads to Marconi Beach.

650 Rte. 6 (about 1 mile/1.6km north of the Eastham border), South Wellfleet, MA 02663. ✆ **800/368-0007** in Mass., or 508/349-3410. Fax 508/349-7804. www.eventidemotel.com. 31 units. Summer $98–$175 double; $129–$150 efficiency. AE, DISC, MC, V. **Amenities:** Heated indoor pool; playground; coin-op washers and dryers. *In room:* A/C, TV, fridge, coffeemaker.

The Inn at Duck Creeke *Value*   This historic complex is set on 5 woodsy acres (2 hectares) overlooking a tidal creek and salt marsh. The 1880s captain's house features wide-board floors and charming but basic bedrooms, many with shared bathrooms; the carriage house contains a few light and airy cabin-style rooms; and the 1715 saltworks building has smaller rooms with antique decor. In the main building, each shared bathroom adjoins two rooms, which might not suit those in search of privacy; the third-floor rooms have air-conditioning. The carriage house and saltworks building are quieter and can be downright romantic. But there's definitely a no-frills quality to this place—towels are thin, and so are walls. A big plus: two good on-site restaurants, Sweet Seasons (see "Where to Dine," below) and the Duck Creeke Tavern, with live entertainment in season.

70 Main St. (P.O. Box 364), Wellfleet, MA 02667. ✆ **508/349-9333.** Fax 508/349-0234. www.innatduck creeke.com. 27 units, 8 with shared bathroom. Summer $70–$100 double. Rates include continental breakfast. AE, MC, V. Closed Nov–Apr. **Amenities:** 2 restaurants (seafood, tavern). *In room:* No phone.

Surfside Cottages ✪✪ *Kids*   This is where you want to be: smack dab on a spectacular beach with 50-foot (15m) dunes, within biking distance of Wellfleet Center and a short drive to Provincetown for dinner. All of the one- to three-bedroom cottages have kitchens, fireplaces, barbecues, and screened porches. Some even have roof decks. Bring your own sheets and towels—renting a set costs $10 per person.

Ocean View Dr., at LeCount Hollow Rd. (P.O. Box 937), South Wellfleet, MA 02663. ✆ and fax **508/ 349-3959.** www.surfsidevacation.com. 18 units. Summer $825–$1,500 per week; off-season $75–$130 per day. MC, V. Pets allowed off-season. *In room:* Kitchen, fridge, microwave.

WHERE TO DINE

Hatch's Fish & Produce Market ✪, 310 Main St., behind Town Hall (✆ **508/ 349-6734** for produce, **508/349-2810** for fish market), is the unofficial heart of Wellfleet. You'll find the best of local bounty, from fresh-picked corn to fruit-juice Popsicles to steaming lobsters. Closed from late September to late May.

Aesop's Tables ✪✪ NEW AMERICAN   This delightful restaurant has it all: a historic setting, a relaxed atmosphere, and delectable food turned out by chef Patricia Worthington. Owner Brian Dunne oversees the sourcing of the superb local provender, even growing some of the edible flowers and delicate greens that go into the Monet's Garden salad. The scallops and oysters come straight from the bay. For dessert, try Clementine's Citrus Tart.

316 Main St. (in the center of town). ✆ **508/349-6450.** Reservations recommended. Main courses $15–$27. AE, DISC, MC, V. July–Aug Wed–Sun noon–3pm; daily 5:30–9:30pm; call for off-season hours. Closed mid-Oct to Apr.

Finely JP's ✪ *Value* NEW AMERICAN   The passing motorist who happens upon this roadside eatery will feel like a clever explorer indeed, even if locals have long been in on the secret. Were it not for the venue—a rather nondescript wood-paneled box right by the busy roadway—chef/owner John Pontius could charge a lot more for his polished cuisine. Feast on baked oysters Bienville and an improvised "Wellfleet paella."

554 Rte. 6, about 1 mile (1.6km) north of the Eastham border. ℂ 508/349-7500. Reservations not accepted. Main courses $13–$21. DISC, MC, V. June–Aug daily 5–10pm; call for off-season hours. Closed mid-Dec to mid-Jan.

Mac's Seafood Market and Harbor Grill Restaurant 𝒢 *Finds* *Kids* Located on the town pier, this takeout shack with picnic tables features fresh seafood unloaded from the boats just steps away. Besides grilled fish, there's homemade chowders, sushi, and a raw bar.

Wellfleet Town Pier. ℂ **508/349-9611.** Reservations not accepted. Main courses $6–$15. MC, V. Daily 11am–10pm. Closed mid-Oct to late May.

Sweet Seasons Restaurant 𝒢 NEW AMERICAN   Chef/owner Judith Pihl's Mediterranean-influenced fare is still appealing after 20-plus years, as is this dining room's peaceful pond view. Some of the dishes can be a bit heavy by contemporary standards, but there's usually a healthy alternative: Wellfleet littlenecks and mussels in an aromatic tomato-and-cumin broth, for instance, as opposed to Russian oysters with smoked salmon, vodka, and sour cream. Specialties include sage-and-asparagus ravioli and Seasons shrimp with feta and ouzo.

At the Inn at Duck Creek, 70 Main St. (just west of Rte. 6). ℂ **508/349-6535.** Reservations recommended. Main courses $18–$23. AE, MC, V. Late June to mid-Sept daily 5:30–10pm. Closed mid-Sept to late June.

WELLFLEET AFTER DARK

The Beachcomber 𝒢𝒢, 1220 Old Cahoon Hollow Rd., off Ocean View Drive (ℂ **508/349-6055;** www.beachcomber.com), arguably the best dance club on Cape Cod, is definitely the most scenic. It's right on Cahoon Hollow Beach— so close, in fact, that late beachgoers on summer weekends can count on a free concert of reggae, blues, ska, or rock. The cover varies. Closed from early September to late May.

Local talent—jazz, pop, folk, and blues—accompanies the light fare at **Duck Creeke Tavern,** at the Inn at Duck Creeke, 70 Main St. (ℂ **508/349-7369**). Closed from mid-October to late May; no cover. The cozy attic at the **Upstairs Bar at Aesop's Tables** 𝒢, 316 Main St. (ℂ **508/349-6450**), is usually inhabited by local blues and jazz performers.

The **Wellfleet Drive-In Theater,** 51 Rte. 6, just north of the Eastham border (ℂ **800/696-3532** or 508/349-2520), built in 1957, is the only drive-in left on Cape Cod and one of a scant half dozen surviving in the state. The rituals are unbending and endearing as ever: the playtime preceding the cartoons, the countdown plugging the allures of the snack bar, and, finally, two full first-run features. It's open daily from late May to mid-September; showtime is at dusk. Call for off-season hours.

The principals behind the **Wellfleet Harbor Actors' Theatre** 𝒢𝒢, 1 Kendrick Ave., near the Town Pier (ℂ **508/349-6835**), aim to provoke—and usually succeed, even amid this very sophisticated, seen-it-all summer colony. Performances are given from late May to October, daily at 8pm.

PROVINCETOWN 𝒢𝒢𝒢

You've made it all the way to the end of the Cape, to one of the most interesting spots on the eastern seaboard. Explorer Bartholomew Gosnold must have felt much the same thrill in 1602, when he and his crew happened upon a "great stoare of codfysshes" here. The Pilgrims, of course, were overjoyed when they slogged into the harbor 18 years later: Never mind that they'd landed several hundred miles off course.

And Charles Hawthorne, the painter who "discovered" this near-derelict fishing town in the late 1890s and introduced it to the Greenwich Village intelligentsia, was besotted by this "jumble of color in the intense sunlight accentuated by the brilliant blue of the harbor."

He'd probably be aghast at the commercial circus his enthusiasm has wrought—though pleased, no doubt, to find the Provincetown Art Association & Museum, which he helped found in 1914, still going strong. The whole town, in fact, is dedicated to creative expression, both visual and verbal. The general atmosphere of open-mindedness plays a pivotal role, allowing a very varied assortment of individuals to explore their creative urges.

That same open-mindedness may account for Provincetown's ascendancy as a gay and lesbian resort. In peak season, the streets are a celebration of the individual's freedom to be as "out" as imagination allows. But the street life also includes families, art lovers, and gourmands. In short, Provincetown has something for just about everyone.

ESSENTIALS

GETTING THERE   After crossing the Sagamore Bridge, head east on Route 6 to Orleans, then north on Route 6 to Provincetown. Provincetown is 56 miles (90km) northeast of Sandwich, 42 miles (68km) northeast of Hyannis.

If you plan to spend your entire vacation in Provincetown, you won't need a car—everything is within walking or biking distance. And because parking is a hassle, consider leaving your car at home and taking a boat from Boston or Plymouth. You'll get to skip the horrendous Sagamore Bridge traffic jams and arrive by sea like the Pilgrims did.

In season, **Bay State Cruises** (© 617/748-1428; www.baystatecruise company.com) makes daily round-trips from Boston. Its regular ferry, *Provincetown II,* makes one 3-hour trip daily. From mid-May to early October, its new high-speed *Provincetown Express* makes three round-trips daily, taking 1½ hours. **Captain John Boats** (© 508/747-2400) connects Plymouth and Provincetown daily from mid-June to early September.

GETTING AROUND   Parking is at a premium. Illegally parked cars are ticketed (even on Sun), and repeat offenders will be towed. If your inn provides parking, you may want to keep your car there and get around on foot, by bike, or by shuttle. Provincetown's **Summer Shuttle** (© 508/432-3400) loops through town and to the beach daily in season.

VISITOR INFORMATION   Contact the **Provincetown Chamber of Commerce,** 307 Commercial St. (© 508/487-3424; fax 508/487-8966; www.ptownchamber.com), or the gay-oriented **Provincetown Business Guild,** 115 Bradford St. (© 800/637-8696 or 508/487-2313; fax 508/487-1252; www.ptown.org).

BEACHES & OUTDOOR PURSUITS

BEACHES   With nine-tenths of its territory (basically, all but the downtown area) protected by the Cape Cod National Seashore, Provincetown has miles of beaches. The 3-mile (5km) bay beach that lines the harbor, though certainly swimmable, is not all that inviting compared to the magnificent ocean beaches overseen by the National Seashore. The two official access areas (see below) tend to be crowded; however, you can always find a less densely populated stretch if you're willing to hike down the beach a bit.

- **Herring Cove Beach** ✿✿✿: This popular west-facing National Seashore beach is known for its spectacular sunsets. The long stretches of pristine sand front a calmer beach than Race Point (see below) because Herring Cove faces Cape Cod Bay. This is a haven for same-sex couples, who tend to gather to the far left side of the beach. Parking costs $7 per day, $20 per season.
- **Long Point** ✿: Trek out over the breakwater at the far west end of Commercial Street and walk about 1½ miles (2.5km) over sand—or catch a water shuttle ($10 round-trip) from Flyer's Boat Rental (see "Boating," below)— to visit this very last spit of land, capped by an 1827 lighthouse. Shuttles run hourly in July and August.
- **Race Point Beach** ✿✿✿: Facing the Atlantic, Race Point offers rougher surf than Herring Cove, and you might actually spot whales en route to Stellwagen Bank. Parking costs $7 per day, $20 per season.

BICYCLING   North of town, nestled amid the Cape Cod National Seashore preserve, is one of the more spectacular bike paths in New England, the 7-mile (11km) **Province Lands Trail** ✿✿, a heady swirl of steep dunes anchored by wind-stunted scrub pines. With its free parking, the **Province Lands Visitor Center** ✿✿ (✆ 508/487-1256) is a good place to start: You can survey the landscape from the observation tower before setting off amid the dizzying maze. With any luck, you'll find a spur path leading to one of the beaches—Race Point or Herring Cove—lining the shore. Rentals are offered in season by **Nelson's Bike Shop,** 43 Race Point Rd. (✆ 508/487-8849). It's also an easy jaunt from town, where you'll find plenty of good bike shops, such as **Ptown Bikes,** 42 Bradford St. (✆ 508/487-8735); reserve several days in advance.

BOATING   In addition to operating a Long Point shuttle from its own dock (see "Beaches," above), **Flyer's Boat Rental,** 131 Commercial St., in the West End (✆ 508/487-0898), offers all sorts of craft, from kayaks to sailboats; sailing lessons and fishing-gear rentals are also available. **Off the Coast Kayak Company,** 3 Freeman St., in the center of town (✆ 508/487-2692), offers tours and rentals in season.

FISHING   Surf casting is permitted at Herring Cove Beach (off Rte. 6) and Race Point Beach (near the Race Point Coast Guard Station); many people drop a hand-line or light tackle right off the West End breakwater. For low-cost deep-sea fishing via party boat, board the *Cee Jay* (✆ 800/675-6723 or 508/487-4330). For serious sportfishing, sign on for the *Shady Lady II* (✆ 508/487-0182). Both depart from MacMillan Wharf.

NATURE TRAILS   Within the Province Lands (off Race Point Rd., a ½ mile/ 1km north of Rte. 6), the National Seashore maintains the 1-mile (1.6km) **Beech Forest Trail** ✿, a shaded path that circles a shallow freshwater pond blanketed with water lilies before heading into the woods. You can see the shifting dunes gradually encroaching on the forest.

A wonderful walk for hearty hikers is along the **West End breakwater** ✿✿ out to the end of **Long Point,** about 5 miles (8km) round-trip. Walking just to the end of the wide breakwater, located at the end of Commercial Street next to the Provincetown Inn, is quite popular. You'll see all ages maneuvering the layered boulders, about a 30-minute walk each way. If you want to continue to Long Point, the very tip of Cape Cod, it's about an hour's walk across soft sand. At low tide, the distance can be shortened by cutting across the salt flats. **Wood**

End Light is directly across the spit of sand near the breakwater. **Long Point Light** is at the end of the point. Hikers determined to reach the end of Long Point will want to bring a hat, water, and sunscreen. The inside of the arm has views of Provincetown and Provincetown Harbor, and a couple of shipwrecks.

WHALE-WATCHING ★★★   Stellwagen Bank, 8 miles (13km) off Province-town, is a rich feeding ground for whales. The ***Dolphin* Fleet** ★★★, MacMillan Wharf (℃ **800/826-9300** or 508/349-1900), was the first, and by most accounts is still the best, outfitter running whale-watching trips to Stellwagen. Most cruises carry a naturalist to provide running commentary; on the *Dolphin,* these are scientists from the Center for Coastal Studies out doing research crucial to the whales' survival, and part of the proceeds goes to further their worthwhile efforts. Tickets for the 3½-hour trips are $20 for adults, $18 for seniors, and $17 for children 7 to 12. Call to reserve. Closed November through March.

Tips for first-timers: Dress very warmly, in layers, and take along a waterproof windbreaker. If you're prone to seasickness, consider taking a motion-sickness pill at the start of the trip. (They're provided free as you board the vessel.)

ORGANIZED TOURS & CRUISES

Art's Dune Tours ★★ is at the corner of Commercial and Standish streets (℃ **800/894-1951** or 508/487-1950; www.artsdunetours.com). In 1946, Art Costa started driving sightseers out to ogle the decrepit "dune shacks" where such transient luminaries as Eugene O'Neill, Jack Kerouac, and Jackson Pollock found their respective muses. The Park Service wanted to raze these eyesores, but luckily saner heads prevailed: They're now National Historic Landmarks. The tours typically take 1 to 1½ hours. Tickets are $13 to $16 for adults, $8 to $10 for children 4 to 11. There's also a sunset clambake dune tour ($40) and Race Point Lighthouse tour ($18).

Bay Lady II (℃ **508/487-9308;** www.sailcapecod.com) leaves from Macmillan Wharf. The sunset trip aboard this 73-foot (22m) reproduction gaff-rigged Grand Banks schooner is especially spectacular. Tickets cost $12 to $16 for adults, $7 for children under 12. There are four 2-hour sails daily from mid-May to mid-October.

MUSEUMS

The Expedition Whydah Sea Lab & Learning Center *(Overrated*   Though the subject matter here is fascinating, this site is a bit of a tourist trap. Cape Cod native Barry Clifford made headlines in 1984 when he tracked down the wreck of the 17th-century pirate ship *Whydah* (pronounced "*Wid*-dah") 1,500 feet (450m) off the coast of Wellfleet, where it had lain undisturbed since 1717. Only 10 percent excavated to date, it has already yielded over 100,000 artifacts. Visitors can supposedly observe the reclamation work being done, though it's unusual to actually see scientists or scholars at work.

MacMillan Wharf (just past the whale-watching fleet). ℃ 508/487-8899. www.whydah.com. Admission $6 adults, $3 children 6–12. June–Aug daily 10am–8pm; Sept–Dec and Apr–May daily 10am–5pm. Closed Jan–Mar.

Pilgrim Monument & Provincetown Museum ★★ *(Finds*   Anywhere you go in town, this granite tower looms, ever ready to restore your bearings. Climb up the 60 gradual ramps interspersed with 116 steps—a surprisingly easy lope—and you'll get a gargoyle's-eye view of the spiraling coast and, in the distance, Boston against a backdrop of New Hampshire's mountains. Definitely devote some time to the curious exhibits in the museum, chronicling P-town's checkered past as both fishing port and arts nexus. Among the memorabilia, you'll see polar bears brought back from MacMillan's expeditions, early programs for the Provincetown Players, and a replica dune shack.

High Pole Hill Rd. (off Winslow St., north of Bradford St.). ℂ 508/487-1310. www.pilgrim-monument.org. Admission $6 adults, $3 children 4–12. July–Aug daily 9am–7pm; off-season daily 9am–5pm. Last admission 45 min. before closing. Closed Dec–Mar.

Province Lands Visitor Center of the Cape Cod National Seashore ★★
Though much smaller than the Salt Pond Visitor Center, this satellite does a good job of explaining this special environment, where plant life must fight a fierce battle to maintain its toehold amid shifting sands buffeted by salty winds. Be sure to circle the observation deck for great views. Inquire about special events, such as guided walks, family campfires, and canoe programs (reservations required).

Race Point Rd., about 1½ miles (2.5km) northwest of the town center. ℂ 508/487-1256. Free admission. Mid-Apr to late Nov daily 9am–5pm. Closed late Nov to mid-Apr.

Provincetown Art Association & Museum ★★
This extraordinary cache of 20th-century American art began with five paintings donated by local artists, including Charles Hawthorne, the charismatic teacher who first "discovered" this picturesque outpost. Founded in 1914, only a year after New York's revolutionary Armory Show, the museum was the site of innumerable "space wars," as classicists and modernists vied for square footage. In today's less competitive atmosphere, it's not unusual to see a tame still life next to an unrestrained abstract. The museum sponsors a full schedule of concerts, lectures, readings, and classes.

460 Commercial St. (in the East End). ℂ 508/487-1750. www.paam.org. Suggested donation $5 adults, $1 seniors and children under 12. July–Aug daily noon–5pm and 8–10pm; call for off-season hours. Open year-round.

SHOPPING
ART GALLERIES Of the several dozen galleries in town, only a handful are reliably worthwhile. In season, most of the galleries and even some of the shops open around 11am, then take a siesta from around 5 to 7pm, reopening and greeting visitors up to as late as 10 or 11pm. Shows usually open on Friday evenings, prompting a "stroll" tradition spanning the many receptions.

Berta Walker is a force to be reckoned with, having nurtured many top artists through her association with the Fine Arts Work Center before opening her own gallery in 1990, the **Berta Walker Gallery** ★, 208 Bradford St., in the East End (ℂ **508/487-6411**). Closed from late October to late May.

DNA (Definitive New Art) Gallery ★, 288 Bradford St., in the East End (ℂ **508/487-7700**), has attracted such talents as photographer Joel Meyerowitz, Provincetown's favorite portraitist, known for such tomes as *Cape Light;* sculptor Conrad Malicoat, whose free-form brick chimneys and hearths can be seen around town; and local conceptualist/provocateur Jay Critchley. Readings by cutting-edge authors add to the buzz. Closed from mid-October to late May.

Julie Heller started collecting early Provincetown paintings as a child—and a tourist at that. She chose so incredibly well, her roster at **Julie Heller Gallery** ★, 2 Gosnold St., on the beach in the center of town (ℂ **508/487-2169**), reads like a who's who of local art. Hawthorne, Avery, Hofmann, Lazzell, Hensche—all the big names from Provincetown's past are here, as well as some contemporary artists. Closed weekdays January through April.

Schoolhouse Center for Art and Design ✪, 494 Commercial St., in the East End (© **508/487-4800**), is an impressive setup with two galleries, studios, arts programs, and an events series.

DISCOUNT SHOPPING   Marine Specialties ✪, 235 Commercial St. (© **508/487-1730**), is packed to the rafters with useful stuff, from discounted Doc Martens to cut-rate Swiss Army knives. Hung from the ceiling are some real antiques, including several carillons' worth of ship's bells. **Provincetown Second Hand Store,** 389 Commercial St., in the center of town (© **508/487-9163**), is a local institution selling drag for Guys and Dolls.

FASHION   Mad as a Hatter, 360 Commercial St. (© **508/487-4063**), has hats to suit every style, from folksy to downright diva-esque. Closed from January to mid-February. **Moda Fina** ✪, 349 Commercial St. (© **508/ 487-6632**), specializes in women's clothing and accessories, including shoes, lingerie, and unique summer dresses. **Silk & Feathers,** 377 Commercial St., in the East End (© **508/487-2057**), features seasonal styles, lingerie almost too pretty to cover up, seaweed soaps, and statement jewelry.

WHERE TO STAY
Very Expensive

Brass Key Guesthouse ✪✪✪ *Finds*   Brass Key is the fanciest place to stay in Provincetown. With Ritz-Carlton–style amenities and service in mind, the innkeepers have created a paean to luxury. They've thought of everything: down pillows, jetted showers, and gratis iced tea and lemonade delivered poolside. Rooms in the 1828 Federal-style Captain's House and the Gatehouse are outfitted in a playful country style, while the Victorian-era building is classically elegant, with materials like mahogany, walnut, and marble. Most deluxe rooms have gas fireplaces and whirlpool tubs. In high season, the clientele here is primarily gay men, though all are made to feel welcome.

67 Bradford St. (in the center of town), Provincetown, MA 02657. © **800/842-9858** or 508/487-9005. Fax 508/487-9020. www.brasskey.com. 33 units. Summer $230–$425 double; $280–$425 cottage. Rates include continental breakfast and afternoon wine and cheese. AE, DISC, MC, V. Closed mid-Nov to early Apr. No children under 18. **Amenities:** Heated outdoor pool; 17-ft. (5m) Jacuzzi. *In room:* A/C, TV/VCR, fridge, hair dryer, safe.

Expensive

Best Western Tides Beachfront ✪✪ *Kids*   Families will be delighted with this beachfront motel, set on 6 acres (2 hectares) well removed from Provincetown's bustle and North Truro's ticky-tacky congestion. Every inch of this complex has been groomed to the max, including the ultra-green grounds, the Wedgwood-blue breakfast room, and the spotless guest rooms decorated in a soothing pastel palette.

837 Commercial St. (near the Truro border), Provincetown, MA 02657. © **800/528-1234** or 508/487-1045. Fax 508/487-1621. www.bwprovincetown.com. 64 units. Summer $199–$229 double; $299–$319 suite. AE, DC, DISC, MC, V. Closed Nov to mid-May. **Amenities:** Heated outdoor pool; coin-op washers and dryers. *In room:* A/C, TV, dataport, fridge, coffeemaker.

The Masthead ✪✪ *Value* *Kids*   This is one of the few places in town, other than the impersonal motels, that actively welcomes families, and the placid 450-foot (135m) private beach will delight young splashers. The cottages are fun, some with wicker furniture and antiques. In the water-view rooms perched above the surf, with their 7-foot (2m) picture windows overlooking the bay and Long Point, you may feel as if you're on board a ship.

31–41 Commercial St. (in the West End), Provincetown, MA 02657. © 800/395-5095 or 508/487-0523. Fax 508/487-9251. www.themasthead.com. 25 units, 2 with shared bathroom. Summer $86–$210 double; $169–$203 efficiency; $245 2-bedroom apartment; $1,500–$2,038 per week for cottage. Off-season $63–$115 double; $81–$113 efficiency; $105–$134 apartment; $105–$179 cottage. AE, DC, DISC, MC, V. Open year-round. *In room:* A/C, TV, fridge, coffeemaker, iron, safe.

Watermark Inn ★★ (Kids)   If you'd like to experience P-town without being stuck in the thick of it (the carnival atmosphere can get tiring at times), this contemporary inn at the peaceful edge of town is the perfect choice. The beachfront manor contains dazzling suites; the prize ones, on the top floor, have picture windows and sweeping deck views. Handmade quilts brighten up the clean, monochromatic rooms.

603 Commercial St. (in the East End), Provincetown, MA 02657. © 508/487-0165. Fax 508/487-2383. www.watermark-inn.com. 10 units. Summer $170–$340 suite. From mid-May to mid-Sept, suites rent by the week only ($1,050–$2,175 per week). AE, MC, V. Open year-round. *In room:* TV, fridge, coffeemaker.

Moderate

Best Inn ★   This no-surprises motel, on the waterfront at the east edge of town, is a good choice for first-timers not quite sure what they're getting into. Guests in waterfront rooms get a nice view of town. In season, free movies are shown on a 100-foot (30m) screen in the restaurant/lounge. An in-season town shuttle will whisk you down Commercial Street or to the beaches.

698 Commercial St. (at Rte. 6A, in the East End), Provincetown, MA 02657. © 800/422-4224 or 508/487-1711. Fax 508/487-3929. www.capeinn.com. 78 units. Summer $139–$179 double. Rates include continental breakfast. AE, DC, DISC, MC, V. Closed Nov–Apr. Dogs allowed. **Amenities:** Restaurant; outdoor pool. *In room:* A/C, TV, dataport, fridge, coffeemaker, hair dryer, iron.

Carpe Diem ★★   Rainer and Jurgen, two young, urbane Germans, run this stylish 1884 house whose theme is "seize the day." The location, a quiet side street right in the center of town, suits most P-town habitués to a T. Guest rooms are exquisitely outfitted with antiques, brightly painted walls, down comforters, and robes. Two deluxe garden suites boast private entrances, Jacuzzis, and fireplaces. The cottage has a two-person Jacuzzi and a wet bar. Breakfasts feature homemade German bread and muffins served at the family-size dining-room table. On clear days, sun worshippers prefer the patio.

12 Johnson St. (in the center of town), Provincetown, MA 02657. © 800/487-0132 or 508/487-4242. Fax 508/487-4242. www.carpediemguesthouse.com. 13 units. Summer $135–$195 double; $265 suite; $235 cottage. Rates include continental breakfast. AE, MC, V. Open year-round. **Amenities:** Jacuzzi. *In room:* A/C, TV/VCR, dataport.

The Commons ★★   Right in the thick of town, but removed from the hurly-burly by a streetside bistro (see "Where to Dine," below) and peaceful brick patio, is this venerable guesthouse. The bedrooms, with their marble-look tubs and (in most cases) bay views, are stylish and spacious. At the pinnacle is a beamed attic studio with its own deck overlooking MacMillan Wharf. All the delights of town are within easy reach, including—right on the property—one of Provincetown's best restaurants.

386 Commercial St. (in the center of town), Provincetown, MA 02657. © 800/487-0784 or 508/487-7800. Fax 508/487-6114. www.commonsghb.com. 14 units. Summer $119–$175 double; $175 suite. Rates include continental breakfast. AE, MC, V. Closed Nov–Mar. Pets allowed. **Amenities:** Restaurant (bistro). *In room:* A/C, TV.

Copper Fox ★★   This majestic 1856 captain's house is just a short walk from the galleries and restaurants of the East End. The expansive lawn, unusual in Provincetown where space is at a premium, is dotted with urns and a birdbath.

The inn has a large wraparound porch and a second-floor deck, which offers a perfect view of the harbor across the street. Several bedrooms also have bay views. Two apartments have private entrances and kitchens; one has a private garden, and the other is large enough to accommodate six people.

448 Commercial St. (in the East End), Provincetown, MA 02657. © and fax **508/487-8583**. www. provincetown.com/copperfox. 7 units. Summer $140–$179 double; $195 apartment. Rates include continental breakfast and afternoon tea. MC, V. Open year-round. *In room:* A/C, TV, no phone.

The Oxford 𝕲 *(Value)* This 1853 house offers truly affordable elegance. All bedrooms have amenities like down comforters, robes, and voice mail. A one-bedroom cottage offers more privacy. The drawing room is especially cozy, with sofas and armchairs arranged in front of a fireplace and TV. In the morning, the inn fills with the scrumptious aroma of home-baked breads and coffeecake. You may want to enjoy your coffee out on the veranda overlooking the courtyard's fountain and pond.

8 Cottage St. (in the West End), Provincetown, MA 02657. © **888/456-9103** or 508/487-9103. www.oxfordguesthouse.com 7 units, 2 with shared bathroom. Summer $100–$275 double. Rates include continental breakfast. AE, DC, DISC, MC, V. *In room:* A/C, TV/VCR, CD player, dataport, fridge, hair dryer, iron.

Inexpensive

Captain Lysander Inn 𝕲 *(Value)* Set back from the street in the quiet West End, this 1840 Greek Revival is fronted by a flower-lined path leading to a sunny patio. The conservatively furnished rooms are quite nice for the price, and some have partial water views. Tall windows make these rooms feel light and airy. The whole gang can fit in either the apartment or the cottage, both with TV/VCRs and kitchenettes.

96 Commercial St. (in the West End), Provincetown, MA 02657. © **508/487-2253**. Fax 508/487-7579. 14 units, 6 with shared bathroom. Summer $105 double with shared bathroom, $115 double with private bathroom; efficiency $135 per day, $1,400 per week; apartment $200 per day, $1,200 per week; cottage $250 per day, $1,400 per week. Room and efficiency rates include continental breakfast. MC, V. Open year-round. *In room:* No phone.

White Horse Inn 𝕲𝕲 *(Value)* Look for the house with the bright yellow door in the East End. The rates are terrific, especially given the fact that this inn is the very embodiment of Provincetown's Bohemian mystique. Frank Schaefer has been tinkering with this late-18th-century house since 1963; the rooms may be a bit austere, but each is enlivened by some of the 300 paintings he has collected over the decades. A number of his fellow artists helped him out in cobbling together the studio apartments out of salvage: There's an aura of beatnik improv about them still. Guests over the years have embodied a range of low and high art—cult filmmaker John Waters has stayed here often, as has poet laureate Robert Pinsky.

500 Commercial St. (in the East End), Provincetown, MA 02657. © **508/487-1790**. 24 units, 10 with shared bathroom. Summer $60 single with shared bathroom; $70–$80 double; $125–$140 efficiency. No credit cards. *In room:* No phone.

WHERE TO DINE

Spiritus, 190 Commercial St. (© **508/487-2808**), is an extravagant pizza parlor open until 2am. The pizza's good, as are the fruit drinks and premium ice cream. For a peaceful morning repast, check out the little garden in back. Peruse the scrumptious meat pies and pastries at the beloved **Provincetown Portuguese Bakery,** 299 Commercial St. (© **508/487-1803**). Both establishments are closed November through March.

Very Expensive

Chester ★★★ NEW AMERICAN   Step through the colonnaded portico for a singular dining experience. Chester specializes in local seafood, meats, and vegetables prepared simply yet with a flourish. Service is exceptional, the food beautifully presented. Starters like spinach and scallop risotto take advantage of local provender, as does the entree Chatham cod with prosciutto and sage. The extensive wine list has won *Wine Spectator* awards. For dessert, look no further than the warm chocolate cake with homemade ice cream.

404 Commercial St. ✆ **508/487-8200**. Reservations recommended. Main courses $19–$32. AE, MC, V. July to mid-Sept daily 6–10pm; mid-April to June and mid-Sept to late October Thurs–Mon 6–10pm; call to verify off-season hours. Closed Nov to mid-Apr, except New Year's Eve.

The Dancing Lobster Cafe Trattoria ★ MEDITERRANEAN   This waterfront restaurant has a well-known chef and great location, but it's a tad pricey for the offerings. Chef/owner Nils "Pepe" Berg's establishment is a popular place, so expect to wait, even with a reservation. The mainstay here is seafood, but the menu also features Venetian specialties. Main courses may include steak al "Pepe" with green and black peppercorns, brandy, demi-glace, and cream.

373 Commercial St. (in the center of town). ✆ **508/487-0900**. Reservations recommended. Main courses $17–$30. MC, V. July–Sept Tues–Sun 11:30am–5pm and 5:30–11pm; May–June and Oct 6–9pm. Closed Nov–Apr.

Martin House ★★★ FUSION   Easily one of the most charming restaurants on the Cape, this snuggery of rustic, softly lit rooms happens to contain one of the region's most forward-thinking kitchens. The chef favors local delicacies, such as the littlenecks that appear in a kafir-lime-tamarind broth with Asian noodles. Main courses might include grilled rack of pork with mango salsa and cactus-pear demi-glace on spicy masa. In season, there's seating on the rose-covered garden terrace.

157 Commercial St. ✆ **508/487-1327**. Reservations recommended. Main courses $16–$33. AE, DC, DISC, MC, V. May–Oct daily 6–11pm; Jan–May and Nov–Dec Thurs–Mon 6–10pm. Closed mid-Dec.

Expensive

The Commons Bistro & Bar ★★ *Finds* ECLECTIC/BISTRO   It's a toss-up: The sidewalk cafe provides a prime opportunity for studying P-town's inimitable street life, whereas the plum-colored dining room affords a refuge adorned with the owners' extraordinary collection of Toulouse-Lautrec prints. Either way, you'll get to partake of tasty and creative fare. At lunch, the lobster club sandwich on country bread is unbeatable. The Commons boasts the only wood-fired oven in town to date, which comes in handy in preparing gourmet pizzas with unique toppings. At dinner, try the gingered smoked salmon with scallion basmati rice and orange-soy vinaigrette.

386 Commercial St. (see "Where to Stay," earlier in this section). ✆ **508/487-7800**. Reservations recommended. Main courses $10–$26. AE, MC, V. Mid-June to early Sept daily 11:30am–10:30pm; call for off-season hours. Closed Nov–Mar.

The Mews & Cafe Mews ★★★ INTERNATIONAL/FUSION   Bank on fine food and suave service at this beachfront restaurant, an enduring favorite since 1961. Upstairs is the cafe, with its century-old mahogany bar and lighter menu. The dining room downstairs sits right on the beach. The best soup in the region is the chilled cucumber miso bisque with curry shrimp timbale. Among the showier entrees is "captured scallops": prime Wellfleet specimens enclosed with a shrimp-and-crab mousse in a crisp wonton pouch, served atop a petite filet mignon with chipotle aioli. Desserts and coffees—take them upstairs in the cafe, to the accompaniment of soft-jazz piano—are delectable.

429 Commercial St. ℂ **508/487-1500.** Reservations recommended. Main courses $18–$27. AE, DC, DISC, MC, V. Late May to mid-Oct Mon–Fri 6–10pm, Sat–Sun 11am–2:30pm and 6–10pm; mid-Feb to late May and mid-Oct to late Dec Thurs–Mon 6–10pm, Sun 11am–2:30pm. Open year-round.

Moderate

Bubala's by the Bay ✸ ECLECTIC   This trendy bistro promises "serious food at sensible prices." And that's what it delivers: from buttermilk waffles to creative focaccia sandwiches to ostrich, served with a grilled pepper crust and a caramelized onion and balsamic glaze. The huge patio facing Commercial Street is particularly popular in the morning. In season, there's entertainment nightly from 10pm to 1am.

183 Commercial St. (in the West End). ℂ **508/487-0773.** Main courses $10–$21. AE, DISC, MC, V. Apr–Oct daily 8am–11pm. Closed Nov–Mar.

Cafe Heaven ✸ AMERICAN   Prized for its leisurely country breakfasts (served until midafternoon, for reluctant risers), this modern storefront—adorned with big, bold paintings by acclaimed Wellfleet artist John Grillo—also turns out substantive sandwiches, such as avocado and goat cheese on a baguette. The dinner choices have expanded to include local seafood, steaks, chops, and poultry; create-your-own pastas; and "heavenly" burgers with a choice of toppings. Expect long lines in July and August.

199 Commercial St. (in the center of town). ℂ **508/487-9639.** Reservations not accepted. Most items $11–$18. No credit cards. July–Aug daily 8am–3pm and 6:30–10pm; call for off-season hours. Closed Feb–May.

Little Fluke Cafe ✸✸ *Value* NEW AMERICAN   This tiny cafe with outdoor tables is a perfect people-watching spot at breakfast (try the famous blueberry cornmeal pancakes) as well as an intimate place for dinner. Considering the quality of the food, the four-course prix-fixe dinner is good value for Provincetown. The small menu changes weekly, with tasty choices for carnivores, fish lovers, and vegetarians. A good starter is the Parmesan and asparagus risotto cakes with fig vinaigrette. As a main course, try apple-smoked chicken breast with roasted garlic custard and Beluga lentil ragout.

401½ Commercial St. (in the East End). ℂ **508/487-4773.** Reservations recommended. Fixed-price dinners $28–$38. AE, MC, V. June–Sept daily 8am–1pm, Wed–Sun 6–10pm; Apr–May and Oct Fri–Mon 8am–1pm and 6–10pm. Call for off-season hours. Closed Nov–Mar.

Lorraine's ✸✸ MEXICAN/NEW AMERICAN   Lorraine's occupies a prestigious waterfront location—the site of Provincetown's oldest restaurant, the Flagship, where literati like Gertrude Stein and Anaïs Nin once flocked. Even those who shy away from Mexican restaurants should try Lorraine's—the cuisine here is truly unique. Abandon all caution and begin with *chile relleno de queso,* fresh chile peppers stuffed with the chef's choice nightly, rolled in corn meal and corn flour, and lightly deep-fried. For a main course, consider *viere verde*—sea scallops sautéed with tomatillos, flambéed in tequila, and cloaked in a green-chile sauce. On Fridays and Saturdays, tapas are served until midnight. This place is hopping, with entertainment nightly in season.

463 Commercial St. (in the East End). ℂ **508/487-6074.** Reservations suggested. Main courses $17–$26. DISC, MC, V. June–Sept daily 6–10pm; call for off-season hours. Closed mid-Dec to Mar.

Napi's ✸✸ INTERNATIONAL   Napi Van Dereck can be credited with bringing P-town's restaurant scene up to speed—back in the early 1970s. His namesake restaurant still reflects that Zeitgeist, with its rococo-hippie carpentry, select outtakes from his sideline in antiques, and some rather outstanding art. The cuisine is a lot less granola than it once was, or maybe we've just caught up—hearty peasant fare never really goes out of style. And these peasants really get around, culling dumplings from China, falafel from Syria, and, from Greece, shrimp feta flambéed with ouzo and Metaxa.

7 Freeman St. (at Bradford St.). ⓒ **800/571-6274** or 508/487-1145. Reservations recommended. Main courses $14–$26. DISC, MC, V. May–Oct daily 5–10pm; Nov–Apr daily 11:30am–4pm and 5–9pm.

Inexpensive

Clem and Ursie's ★★ *Finds* *Kids* SEAFOOD/BARBECUE   Grab a picnic table for a big family dinner of fried seafood and barbecued ribs. More elaborate choices include bouillabaisse and udon. The children's menu offers a choice of $5 entrees, which come with fries, dessert, and a surprise. Takeout is popular here, as is the separate ice-cream section.

85 Shankpainter Rd. (off Bradford St., a few blocks south of town). ⓒ **508/487-2333.** Main courses $6–$17. MC, V. Apr–Oct daily 11am–10pm. Closed Nov–Apr.

Takeout & Picnic Fare

Mojo's, 5 Ryder St. Ext. (ⓒ **508/487-3140**), a fried-seafood shack, is known for its lightly breaded fish and hand-cut fries. There are also veggie burgers, burritos, and chicken tenders. Eat at one of the picnic tables on the patio or take it to the beach. Closed November through April.

The best gourmet takeout shop is **Angel Foods,** 467 Commercial St., in the East End (ⓒ **508/487-6666**), which offers Italian specialties and other prepared foods.

The rollwiches—pita bread packed with a wide range of fillings—at **Box Lunch** ★, 353 Commercial St., in the center of town (ⓒ **508/487-6026**), are ideal for a strolling lunch.

At **Flying Cups & Saucers,** the Aquarium Shops, 205 Commercial St., in the center of town (ⓒ **508/487-3780**), the offerings are limited but to the point: juices, java, and pastries. Closed November through May.

PROVINCETOWN AFTER DARK

There's so much going on in season on any given night that you might want to simplify your search by calling or stopping by the **Provincetown Reservations System office,** 293 Commercial St., in the center of town (ⓒ **508/487-6400**).

The hottest club in town for the last few years, **Antro,** 258 Commercial St., 2nd floor, beside Town Hall (ⓒ **508/487-8800**), is the current home of "Two Fags and a Drag" and the ever-popular all-star musical comedy drag revue "Big Boned Barbies," starring Kandi Kane. Closed October through May.

Perhaps the nation's premier gay bar, the **Atlantic House** ★, 6 Masonic Place, off Commercial Street (ⓒ **508/487-3821**), is open year-round. The "A-house" welcomes straight folks, except in the leather-oriented Macho Bar upstairs. In the little bar downstairs, check out the Tennessee Williams memorabilia, including a portrait *au naturel.*

Come late afternoon, if you're wondering where all the beachgoers have gone, it's a safe bet that a number are attending the gay-lesbian tea dance held daily in season from 3:30 to 6:30pm on the pool deck at the **Boatslip Beach Club** ★, 161 Commercial St. (ⓒ **508/487-1669**). The action then shifts to the **Pied,** 193A Commercial St. (ⓒ **508/487-1527;** www.thepied.com), for its After Tea T-Dance from 5 to 10pm, but returns here later in the evening for disco. Closed November through April.

> **Tips Recommended Reading**
>
> Henry David Thoreau's *Cape Cod* is an entertaining account of the author's journeys on the Cape in the late 19th century. The writer/naturalist walked along the beach from Eastham to Provincetown, and you can follow in his footsteps. Henry Beston's *The Outermost House* describes a year of living on the beach in Eastham in a simple one-room dune shack. The shack washed out to sea about 20 years ago, but "The Great Beach" remains.

Crown & Anchor ★★, 247 Commercial St. (© **508/487-1430;** www.thecrownandanchor.net), houses a number of bars spanning leather, disco, comedy, drag shows, and cabaret. Facilities include a pool bar and game room. Closed November through April.

Last year, **Tropical Joe's** ★, 135 Bradford St., at Standish Street (© **508/487-9941**), had the number-one cabaret act in town. Who knows what's in store for the future? But it's bound to be intriguing. Good tropical-inspired food, too. Closed November through April.

The women's bar **Vixen** ★, at the Pilgrim House, 336 Commercial St. (© **508/487-6424**), occupies the lower floors of a former hotel. On the roster are jazz, blues, and comedy acts. There are also pool tables. Closed November through April.

CAPE COD NATIONAL SEASHORE ★★★

No trip to Cape Cod would be complete without a visit to the Cape Cod National Seashore on the Outer Cape. Take an afternoon barefoot stroll along the "The Great Beach," and see why the Cape attracts so many artists and poets. On August 7, 1961, President John F. Kennedy signed a bill designating 27,000 acres (10,935 hectares) in the 40 miles (64km) from Chatham to Provincetown as the Cape Cod National Seashore, a new national park. However, as early as the 1930s, the National Park Service had been interested in Cape Cod's ocean beach; back then the land would have cost taxpayers about $10 an acre! Unusual in a national park, the Seashore includes 500 private residences, the owners of which lease land from the park service. Convincing residents that a National Seashore would be a good thing for Cape Cod was an arduous task back then, and Provincetown still grapples with Seashore officials over town land issues.

ESSENTIALS

GETTING THERE Take Route 6, the Mid-Cape Highway, to Eastham; it's about 50 miles (81km) from the Sagamore Bridge.

VISITOR INFORMATION Pick up a map of the National Seashore at the **Salt Pond Visitor Center,** in Eastham (© **508/225-3421**). It's open daily: late May to early September from 9am to 5pm, early September to late May from 9am to 4:30pm. There is also the **Province Lands Visitor Center** (p. 230), a smaller site, in Provincetown. Both centers have ranger activities, gift shops, and restrooms. Seashore beaches are all clearly marked off Route 6. Additional beaches along this stretch are run by individual towns; you must have a sticker or pay a fee to park.

BEACHES & OUTDOOR PURSUITS

7

Martha's Vineyard & Nantucket

by Laura M. Reckford

Megastars and CEOs, vacationing families, and penniless students all seek refuge on Martha's Vineyard and Nantucket, two picturesque islands off the coast of Cape Cod. Both islands have much to offer families with children and couples seeking a romantic getaway. Their fame as summer resorts doesn't begin to take into account their rich history, diverse communities, and artistic traditions. But the popularity of these islands means that if you must go in the middle of summer, expect crowds and even—yikes!—traffic jams.

While only about 25 nautical miles apart, each island has its own distinct personality. Martha's Vineyard, large enough to support a year-round population spanning a broad socioeconomic spectrum, is not quite as rarefied as Nantucket. Vineyarders pride themselves on their liberal stances. True, a prime oceanside estate might fetch millions here, but the residents still dicker over the price of zucchini at the local farmers' market.

Nantucket, flash-frozen in the mid–19th century through zealous zoning, has long been considered a Republican haven. It's rich and traditional. Social scene aside, Nantucket has more pristine public shores than the Vineyard, as well as the best upscale shopping in the region. But there's something for everyone on both islands, and an island vacation is bound to be one that's cherished for many years.

1 Martha's Vineyard ★★★

With 100 square miles, Martha's Vineyard is New England's largest island, yet each of its six communities is blessed with endearing small-town charm. When the former First Family vacationed here, locals joked that the Clintons tested their reputed nonchalance toward famous faces. But don't visit the Vineyard for the celebrities. Instead, savor the decidedly laid-back pace of this unique place.

Most visitors never take the time to explore the entire island, staying in the "down-island" towns of **Vineyard Haven** ★ (officially called Tisbury), **Edgartown** ★★★, and **Oak Bluffs** ★★★. The "up-island" towns—**West Tisbury** ★★, **Chilmark** ★ (including the fishing village of **Menemsha** ★★★), and **Aquinnah** ★ (formerly known as Gay Head)—tend to be far less touristy.

By all means, admire the regal sea captains' homes in Edgartown. Stroll down Circuit Avenue in Oak Bluffs with a Mad Martha's ice-cream cone, then ride the Flying Horses Carousel, said to be the oldest working carousel in the nation. Check out the cheerful "gingerbread" cottages behind Circuit Avenue, where the echoes of 19th-century revival meetings still ring out from the imposing tabernacle.

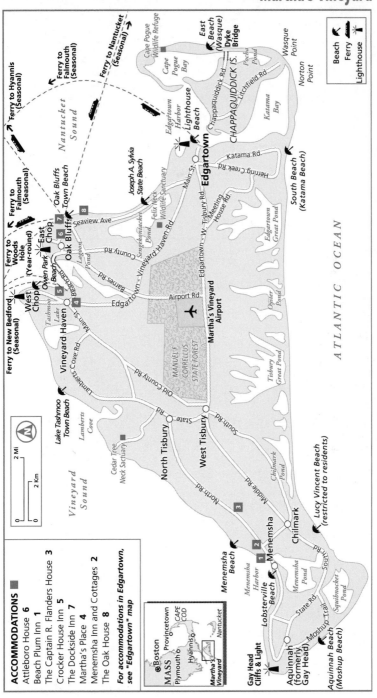

Martha's Vineyard

ACCOMMODATIONS ■
Attleboro House **6**
Beach Plum Inn **1**
The Captain R. Flanders House **3**
Crocker House Inn **5**
The Dockside Inn **7**
Martha's Place **4**
Menemsha Inn and Cottages **2**
The Oak House **8**

For accommodations in Edgartown,
see "Edgartown" map

Beach · Ferry · Lighthouse

East Beach (Wasque) · Dyke Bridge
Cape Pogue Wildlife Refuge
Cape Pogue Bay
Pocha Pond
Wasque Point
Norton Point
CHAPPAQUIDDICK IS.
Chappaquiddick Rd.
Litchfield Rd.
Katama Bay

Edgartown Harbor Lighthouse
Edgartown Lighthouse Beach
Main St.
Edgartown
Katama Rd.
Herring Creek Rd.
South Beach (Katama Beach)
Edgartown Great Pond
Meeting House Rd.
Edgartown–W. Tisbury Rd.
Edgartown–Vineyard Haven Rd.

Joseph A. Sylvia State Beach
Oak Bluffs Town Beach
Seaview Ave.
Oak Bluffs
East Chop
Owen Park Beach
Ferry to Woods Hole (Year-round)

Ferry to Nantucket (Seasonal)
Ferry to Falmouth (Seasonal)
Ferry to Hyannis (Seasonal)
Ferry to Falmouth (Seasonal)
Ferry to New Bedford (Seasonal)

Nantucket Sound

Felix Neck Wildlife Sanctuary
Sengekontacket Pond
County Rd.
Lagoon Pond
Barnes Rd.
Beach Rd.

West Chop
Vineyard Haven
Main St.
Lambert's Cove Rd.
Tashmoo Lake
Airport Rd.
Martha's Vineyard Airport

MANUEL F. CORRELLUS STATE FOREST
Old County Rd.
State Rd.
South Rd.
Oyster Pond

ATLANTIC OCEAN

Lake Tashmoo Town Beach
Lamberts Cove
Cedar Tree Neck Sanctuary
North Tisbury
West Tisbury
North Rd.
Middle Rd.
Chilmark Pond

Tisbury Great Pond

Vineyard Sound

Menemsha Beach
Menemsha Harbor
Menemsha
Lobsterville Beach
Chilmark
Lucy Vincent Beach (restricted to residents)
Menemsha Pond
State Rd.
Squibnocket Pond
Moshup Trail

Gay Head Cliffs & Light
Aquinnah (formerly Gay Head)
Aquinnah Beach (Moshup Beach)

N
0   2 Mi
0   2 Km

Boston
MASS   Provincetown
CAPE COD
Plymouth   Hyannis
Martha's Vineyard   Nantucket

⌢ Tips **Car Passage to Martha's Vineyard**

Reservations are required to bring your car to Martha's Vineyard on Friday, Saturday, Sunday, and Monday from mid-June to mid-September, plus Memorial Day weekend. During these months, standby is in effect only on Tuesday, Wednesday, and Thursday. Technically, reservations can be made up to 1 hour in advance of departure, but in summer ferries are almost always full. Be aware that your space may be forfeited if you have not checked into the ferry terminal 30 minutes prior to sailing time. Reservations may be changed to another date and time with at least 24 hours' notice; otherwise, you will have to pay for an additional ticket for your car.

If you arrive without a reservation on a day that allows standby, come early and be prepared to wait in line for hours. Your passage is guaranteed if you're in line by 2pm on designated standby days. For up-to-date Steamship Authority information, go to **www.islandferry.com**.

But don't forget to journey "up-island" to marvel at the red-clay cliffs of Aquinnah, a national historic landmark. Or, bike the country roads of West Tisbury and Chilmark. Buy a lobster roll in the fishing village of Menemsha. There's a surprising degree of diversity here, for those who take the time to discover it.

ESSENTIALS
GETTING THERE

BY FERRY   Most visitors take ferries from the mainland to the Vineyard. You'll most likely catch a boat from Woods Hole in the town of Falmouth on Cape Cod; however, boats also run from Falmouth Inner Harbor, Hyannis, New Bedford, and Nantucket. It's easy to get a passenger ticket on almost any of the ferries, but space for cars is extremely limited, especially on summer weekends, when reservations must be made months in advance. Unless you absolutely must have your car with you, leave it on the mainland. Traffic and parking on the island can be brutal in summer, and it's easy to take the shuttle buses (see below) from town to town or simply bike around.

From Woods Hole in Falmouth   The state-run **Steamship Authority** (© **508/477-8600** from Apr 4–Sept 7, daily from 7am–9pm, with reduced hours the rest of the year; or 508/693-9130 daily from 8am–5pm; www.island ferry.com) operates daily year-round, weather permitting. It maintains the only ferries to Martha's Vineyard that accommodate cars. These large ferries make the 45-minute trip to Vineyard Haven throughout the year; some boats go to Oak Bluffs from late May to late October (call for seasonal schedules). The cost of a round-trip car passage from mid-May to mid-October is $104; off-season, it drops to $62. Car rates do not include drivers or passengers.

Many people prefer to leave their cars on the mainland, take the ferry (often with their bikes), and then travel around the island by shuttle bus or taxi, or rent a bicycle, car, or Jeep on the island. You can park your car at the Woods Hole lots (always full in summer) or at one of the many lots in Falmouth that absorb the overflow of cars. Parking costs $10 per day. Free shuttle buses (some equipped for bikes) run regularly from the outlying lots to the Woods Hole ferry terminal. If you're leaving your car on the mainland, plan to arrive at the parking lots in Falmouth at least 45 minutes before sailing time.

The cost of a round-trip passenger ticket to Martha's Vineyard is $11 for adults and $5.50 for children 5 to 12. Bringing a bike costs an extra $6 round-trip. You do not need a ferry reservation if you're traveling without a car, and there are no reservations needed for parking.

From Falmouth Inner Harbor   You can board the *Island Queen* (© 508/548-4800; www.islandqueen.com) for a 35-minute cruise to Oak Bluffs (passengers only). The boat runs from late May to mid-October; round-trip fare costs $10 for adults, $5 for children under 13, and $6 for bikes. There are seven crossings a day in season (8 on Fri and Sun), and no reservations are needed. Parking runs $10 or $12 a day.

The **Falmouth-Edgartown Ferry Service,** 278 Scranton Ave. (© 508/548-9400; www.falmouthferry.com), operates a 1-hour passenger ferry, called the *Pied Piper,* from Falmouth Inner Harbor to Edgartown on Martha's Vineyard. The boat runs from late May to mid-October; reservations are required. In season, there are five crossings a day (6 on Fri). Round-trip fares are $24 for adults and $18 for children under 12. Bicycles are $6 round-trip. Parking is $12 per day.

From Hyannis   May through October, **Hy-Line** (© 508/778-2600; www.hy-linecruises.com) operates from the Ocean Street Dock to Oak Bluffs on Martha's Vineyard. It runs three trips a day; travel time is about 1 hour and 45 minutes. A round-trip costs $27 for adults and $13.50 for children 5 to 12 ($10 extra for bikes). In July and August, it's a good idea to reserve a parking spot in Hyannis; the all-day fee is $10.

From Nantucket   From early June to mid-September, **Hy-Line** (© 508/778-2600; www.hy-linecruises.com) runs three passenger ferries to Oak Bluffs on Martha's Vineyard. There is no car-ferry service between the islands. The trip time is 2 hours and 15 minutes. The one-way fare is $13.50 for adults, $6.75 for children 5 to 12, and $5 extra for bikes.

From New Bedford   The *Schamonchi,* at Billy Woods Wharf (© 508/997-1688; www.mvferry.com), which is also run by the Steamship Authority, makes runs to Vineyard Haven from mid-May to mid-September. Trip time is about 1½ hours. A round-trip ticket is $20 for adults, $10 for children under 12, and $5 extra for bikes. Parking is $8 per calendar day. No reservations are needed. This is a great way to avoid Cape traffic.

BY PLANE   You can fly into **Martha's Vineyard Airport,** also known as Dukes County Airport (© 508/693-7022), in West Tisbury, about 5 miles (8km) outside Edgartown.

Airlines serving the Vineyard include **Cape Air/Nantucket Airlines** (© 800/352-0714 or 508/771-6944), which connects the island year-round with Boston (trip time is 33 min.; hourly shuttle service in summer costs about $240 round-trip), Hyannis (20 min.; $80), Nantucket (15 min.; $76), and New Bedford (20 min.; $83); **Continental Express/Colgan Air** (© 800/525-0280), which has seasonal nonstop flights from Newark (75 min.; $240); and **US Airways Express** (© 800/428-4322), which has seasonal weekend service from La Guardia (80 min.; $300).

Direct Flight (© 508/693-6688) is the only company offering year-round charter service. **Westchester Air** (© 800/759-2929) also runs some charters from White Plains, N.Y.

BY BUS   **Bonanza Bus Lines** (© 800/556-3815; www.bonanzabus.com) connects the Woods Hole ferry port with Boston (from South Station), New

> **Tips** **A Note on Mopeds**
>
> Several major accidents and deaths of moped-riding tourists last year has plunged the island into a debate about whether to allow these vehicles on the road. If you do rent a moped, be aware that they are considered quite dangerous on the island's busy, narrow, winding, and sandy roads. Also, note that there is a lot of negative feeling toward mopeds among islanders. (The renting of mopeds is banned in Edgartown.)

York City, and Providence, R.I. The trip from South Station takes about 1 hour and 35 minutes and costs about $15 one-way; from Boston's Logan Airport, it's $20 one-way; from New York, it's about a 6-hour bus trip to Hyannis or Woods Hole, costing approximately $47 one-way or $84 round-trip.

Relax and Ride is a new bus service, run by the Steamship Authority that leaves from the Route 128 MBTA/Amtrak station in Westwood, south of Boston, and takes passengers directly to the Woods Hole ferry terminal. The service operates from late June to early September. Your ticket allows you to board the ferry from the Woods Hole terminal to the Vineyard. A one-way bus/ferry ticket costs $15.50 for adults and $12.75 for children. An additional $10 will buy you a 3-day pass on the Vineyard's public bus system. Parking in Westwood is $10 per day.

BY LIMO Cape Cod Livery (© **800/235-5669** or 508/563-5669) will pick you up at Boston's Logan Airport and take you to meet your ferry in Woods Hole (or anywhere else in the Upper Cape area). The trip takes about 1 hour and 45 minutes depending on traffic, and costs about $115 one-way for a carload or vanload of people. Book the service a couple of days in advance.

GETTING AROUND

BY BICYCLE & MOPED The best way to explore the Vineyard is on two wheels, even if only for a couple of hours. There's a little of everything for cyclists, from paved paths to hilly country roads. (See "Exploring the Vineyard on Two Wheels," later in this chapter, for details on where to ride.)

Mopeds are also a way to navigate the Vineyard, but remember that some roads tend to be narrow and rough—the number of accidents involving mopeds seems to rise every year. You'll need a driver's license to rent one.

Bike-, scooter-, and moped-rental shops are clustered throughout all three down-island towns. Bike rentals cost about $15 to $30 a day; scooters and mopeds, $30 to $80. In Vineyard Haven, try **Strictly Bikes,** Union Street (© **508/693-0782**). In Oak Bluffs, there's **Anderson's** (© **508/693-9346**), which rents bikes only; and **DeBettencourt's Bike Shop** (© **508/693-0011**), both on Circuit Avenue Extension. In Edgartown, you'll find **Wheel Happy,** 204 Upper Main St. and 8 S. Water St. (© **508/627-5928**), which rents only bikes.

BY CAR If you're here for a long visit or you want to do some exploring up-island, you may want to bring a car or rent one on the island. Keep in mind that car-rental rates can soar during peak season, and gas is also much more expensive on the island. Representatives of the national car rental chains are located at the airport and in Vineyard Haven and Oak Bluffs. Local agencies also operate out of all three port towns, and many of them rent Jeeps, mopeds, and bikes as well.

The national chains include **Budget** (℗ **800/527-0700** or 508/693-1911), **Hertz** (℗ **800/654-3131**), and **Thrifty** (℗ **800/874-4389**). Local agencies include **Adventure Rentals,** Beach Road, Vineyard Haven (℗ **508/693-1959**); **AAA Island Rentals,** with locations at 141 Main St., Edgartown (℗ **508/627-6800**), and Five Corners, Vineyard Haven (℗ **508/696-5300**); and **All Island Rent-a-Car,** at the airport (℗ **508/693-6868**).

BY SHUTTLE BUS In season, shuttle buses run often enough to make them a practical means of getting around. Connecting Vineyard Haven (across from the ferry terminal), Oak Bluffs (near the Civil War statue in Ocean Park), and Edgartown (Church St., near the Old Whaling Church), the **Island Transport** **(508/693-0058)** yellow school buses cost about $1.50 to $4, depending on distance. From late June to early September, they run from 6am to midnight every 15 or 30 minutes. Hours are reduced in spring and fall. Late June through August, buses go out to Gay Head (via the airport, West Tisbury, and Chilmark), leaving every couple of hours from down-island towns.

In season, the **Martha's Vineyard Transit Authority** (℗ **508/627-7448** or 508/627-9663) operates several shuttles (white buses with a purple logo). The Edgartown downtown shuttle and the South Beach buses circle throughout town or out to South Beach every 20 minutes. They also stop at the free parking lots just north of the town center. Parking here and shuttling to town is a great way to avoid searching for a spot on busy weekends. A one-way trip in town is 50¢; a trip to South Beach (leaving from Edgartown's Church St. visitor center) is $1.50.

BY TAXI Upon arrival, you'll find taxis at all ferry terminals and at the airport, as well as permanent taxi stands in Oak Bluffs (at the Flying Horses Carousel) and Edgartown (next to the Town Wharf). Most taxi companies operate cars as well as vans for larger groups and travelers with bikes. Options on the island include **Accurate Cab** (℗ **888/557-9798** or 508/627-9798), which is the only all-night service; **Adam Cab** (℗ **800/281-4462** or 508/693-3332); **All Island Taxi** (℗ **800/693-TAXI** or 508/693-2929); and **Martha's Vineyard Taxi** (℗ **508/693-9611** or 508/693-8660). In summer, rates from town to town are generally flat fees based on distance and the number of passengers. A trip from Vineyard Haven to Edgartown costs around $15 for two people. Late-night revelers should keep in mind that rates double from midnight until 7am.

BY CHAPPAQUIDDICK FERRY From June to mid-October, the **On-Time Ferry** (℗ **508/627-9427**) runs the 5-minute trip from Memorial Wharf, on Dock Street in Edgartown, to Chappaquiddick Island. It leaves every 5 minutes from 7am to midnight. Passengers, bikes, mopeds, dogs, and cars (3 at a time) are all welcome. The one-way fare is $1 per person, $4 for one car and one driver, $2.50 for one bike and one person, and $3.50 for one moped or motorcycle and one person.

VISITOR INFORMATION

Contact the **Martha's Vineyard Chamber of Commerce,** Beach Road, 2 blocks from the ferry terminal in Vineyard Haven (℗ **508/693-0085;** fax 508/693-7589; www.mvy.com). There are also information booths at the ferry terminal in Vineyard Haven, across from the Flying Horses Carousel in Oak Bluffs, and on Church Street in Edgartown. For information on current events, check the two local newspapers *Vineyard Gazette* (www.mvgazette.com) and the *Martha's Vineyard Times* (www.mvtimes.com).

In case of medical emergency, the **Martha's Vineyard Hospital,** Linton Lane, Oak Bluffs (© **508/693-0410**), has a 24-hour emergency room.

A STROLL AROUND EDGARTOWN ★★★

A good way to get acclimated to the pace and flavor of the Vineyard is to walk the streets of Edgartown. This walk starts at the Dr. Daniel Fisher House and meanders along for about a mile (1.6km); it takes about 2 to 3 hours.

If you're driving, park at one of the free lots at the edge of town (you'll see signs on the roads from Vineyard Haven and West Tisbury) and bike or take the shuttle bus to the Edgartown visitor center on Church Street.

The **Dr. Daniel Fisher House** ★, 99 Main St. (© **508/627-8017**), is a prime example of Edgartown's trademark Greek Revival opulence. A key player in the 19th-century whaling trade, Dr. Fisher amassed a fortune sufficient to found the Martha's Vineyard National Bank. Built in 1840, his proud mansion boasts colonnaded porticos and a delicate roof walk.

Note: The only way to view the interior (now headquarters for the Martha's Vineyard Preservation Trust) is on a guided **Vineyard Historic Walking Tour** (© **508/627-8619**). This tour, which also takes in the neighboring Old Whaling Church, originates next door at the Vincent House Museum. Tours are offered June through September, Monday through Saturday from 10:30am to 3pm. The cost is $7 to $10 for adults, free for children 12 and under.

The **Vincent House Museum** ★, off Main Street between Planting Field Way and Church Street, is a transplanted 1672 full Cape and is considered to be the oldest surviving dwelling on the island. The **Old Whaling Church** ★★, 89 Main St., a magnificent 1843 Greek Revival edifice designed by local architect Frederick Baylies, Jr., was built as a whaleboat would have been, out of massive pine beams; it boasts 27-foot (8m) windows and a 92-foot (28m) tower. Maintained by the Preservation Trust and still supporting a Methodist parish, the building is now used primarily as a performance venue.

Continuing down Main Street and turning right onto School Street, you'll pass another Baylies monument, the 1839 **Baptist Church,** which, having lost its spire, was converted into a private home with a rather grand, column-fronted facade. Two blocks farther is the **Vineyard Museum** ★★, 59 School St. (© **508/627-4441**), a fascinating complex assembled by the Dukes County Historical Society. This cluster of buildings contains exhibits of Native American crafts, an entire 1765 house, an extraordinary array of maritime art, and the Gay Head Light Tower's decommissioned Fresnel lens.

Give yourself enough time to explore the museum's curiosities before heading south 1 block on Cooke Street. Cater-corner across South Summer Street, you'll spot the first of Baylies's impressive endeavors, the 1828 **Federated Church.** One block left are the offices of the *Vineyard Gazette,* 34 S. Summer St. (© **508/627-4311**). Operating out of a 1760 house, this exemplary small-town newspaper has been going strong since 1846.

Walk down South Summer Street to Main Street and take a right toward the water, stopping at any inviting shops along the way. Veer left on Dock Street to reach the **Old Sculpin Gallery,** 58 Dock St. (© **508/627-4881**), open from late June to early September. The output of the Martha's Vineyard Art Association is displayed here. The real draw is the stark old building itself, which started out as a granary and spent the better part of the 20th century as a boatbuilding shop.

Cross the street to survey the harbor from the dock at Town Wharf. It's from here that the tiny On-Time Ferry makes its 5-minute crossing to **Chappaquiddick Island** ★★. (Don't bother looking for the original **Dyke Bridge,** infamous

Edgartown

Inset map: Boston, MASS, Plymouth, Provincetown, CAPE COD, Edgartown, Martha's Vineyard, Nantucket

SHERIFFS MEADOW
Eel Pond
Planting Field Lane
To Oak Bluffs
To Vineyard Haven
Pine St.
Upper Main St.
Cooke St.
Robinson Rd.
Pease's Point Way
Pierce Lane
Pease's Point Way
Church St.
Winter St.
Morse St.
Cottage St.
Fuller St.
Starbuck Neck
N. Water St.
Edgartown Light
Pent Lane
Davis Lane
Main St.
Daggett
Kelley St.
Lighthouse Beach
Edgartown Harbor
Ferry to Falmouth (Seasonal)
Norton St.
High St.
School St.
S. Summer St.
S. Water St.
Town Wharf
Katama Bay
CHAPPAQUIDDICK ISLAND
Mullins Way
Katama Rd.
Atwood Circle
Dunham Rd.
To South Beach & Katama Beach

Beach
Ferry
Lighthouse

ACCOMMODATIONS ■
Charlotte Inn **9**
Colonial Inn of
    Martha's Vineyard **11**
Edgartown Inn **12**
Harbor View Hotel **13**
Hob Knob Inn **2**
Inn at 148 Main **1**
The Jonathan Munroe
    House **4**
The Point Way Inn **3**
Victorian Inn **10**
The Winnetu Inn
    & Restaurant **14**

ATTRACTIONS ●
Dr. Daniel Fisher House **5**
Old Whaling Church **6**
Vincent House Museum **7**
Vineyard Museum **8**

scene of the Kennedy/Kopechne debacle; it has been dismantled and, at long last, replaced.)

Stroll down North Water Street to admire the many formidable captains' homes, several of which have been converted into inns. Each has a tale to tell. The 1750 **Daggett House** (no. 59), for instance, expanded upon a 1660 tavern, and the original beehive oven is flanked by a "secret" passageway. Nathaniel Hawthorne holed up at the **Edgartown Inn** (no. 56) in 1789 while writing *Twice Told Tales*—and, it is rumored, romancing a local maiden who inspired *The Scarlet Letter*. On your way back to Main Street, you'll pass the **Gardner-Colby Gallery** (no. 27), filled with beautiful island-inspired paintings.

After all that walking, stop for a drink at **The Newes from America,** 23 Kelley St., off North Water Street (© **508/627-4397**). This colonial basement pub serves up hearty food (p. 261).

BEACHES & OUTDOOR PURSUITS

BEACHES Most down-island beaches in Vineyard Haven, Oak Bluffs, and Edgartown are open to the public and just a walk or a short bike ride from town. In season, shuttle buses make stops at **State Beach,** between Oak Buffs and Edgartown. Most of the Vineyard's magnificent up-island shoreline is privately owned or restricted to residents, and thus off-limits to visitors. Renters in up-island communities, however, can obtain a beach sticker (around $35–$50 for a season sticker) for those private beaches by applying with a lease at the relevant town hall: West Tisbury (① **508/696-0147**), Chilmark (① **508/645-2113** or 508/645-2100), or Aquinnah (① **508/645-2300**). Also, many up-island inns offer the perk of temporary passes to the beautiful up-island beaches. In addition to the public beaches listed below, you might want to track down a few hidden coves by requesting a map of conservation properties from the **Martha's Vineyard Land Bank** (① **508/627-7141**). Below is a list of visitor-friendly beaches:

- **Aquinnah Beach** ★★ (Moshup Beach), off Moshup Trail: Parking costs $15 a day in season at this peaceful ½-mile (0.8km) beach just east (Atlantic side) of the colorful cliffs. Although it is against the law, nudists tend to gravitate toward this beach. Because of rapid erosion, climbing the cliffs or taking clay for a souvenir is forbidden. Restrooms are near the parking lot, which is a 10-minute walk from the beach. Lifeguards are on duty here.

- **East Beach** ★★, Wasque (pronounced *Way*-squee) Reservation, Chappaquiddick: Relatively few people go to the bother of biking or hiking (or four-wheel driving) this far, so you should be able to find all the privacy you crave. Take the On-Time Ferry to Chappaquiddick, then go straight 2½ miles (4km), and continue straight for another ½ mile (0.8km) on a dirt road. Biking on Chappaquiddick is one of the great Vineyard experiences, but the roads can be quite sandy, and you may have to dismount for the final leg to Wasque. Because of its exposure on the east shore of the island, the surf is rough here. Still, it's one of the Vineyard's best-kept secrets and an ideal spot for bird-watching. Pack a picnic; there are no stores on Chappy. There is a portable toilet in the parking lot. Pay at the gatehouse ($3 per car and $3 per person) for access in season.

- **Joseph A. Sylvia State Beach** ★★★, midway between Oak Bluffs and Edgartown: Stretching a mile (1.6km) and flanked by a paved bike path, this placid beach on Nantucket Sound has views of Cape Cod and is prized for its gentle and (relatively) warm waves, which make it perfect for swimming. The drawbridge is a local landmark, and visitors and islanders alike have been jumping off it for years. Be aware that State Beach is one of the Vineyard's most popular; in midsummer, it's packed. The shuttle bus stops here, and roadside parking is also available—but it fills up fast, so stake your claim early. There are no restrooms, and only the Edgartown end of the beach, known as Bend-in-the-Road Beach, has lifeguards.

- **Lake Tashmoo Town Beach** ★, off Herring Creek Road, Vineyard Haven: The only spot on the island where lake meets ocean, this tiny strip is good for swimming and surf casting but is somewhat marred by limited parking and often brackish waters. Nonetheless, it's a popular spot, as beachgoers enjoy a choice between the Vineyard Sound beach with mild surf or the placid lake beach. Bikers will have no problem getting here from Vineyard Haven; otherwise, you need a car to get to this beach.

- **Menemsha Beach** 🏖🏖, next to Dutchers Dock in Menemsha Harbor: The gentle surface of this small and well-trafficked strand, with lifeguards and restrooms, is quite popular with families. In season, it's virtually wall-to-wall umbrellas. Nearby vendors in Menemsha—selling everything from ice cream and hot dogs to shrimp cocktail—are a plus here.

- **Oak Bluffs Town Beach,** Seaview Avenue: This sandy strip extends from both sides of the ferry wharf, which makes it a convenient place to linger while waiting for the next boat. This is an in-town beach, within walking distance for visitors staying in Oak Bluffs. The surf is consistently calm and the sand smooth, so it's ideal for families with small children. Restrooms are available at the ferry dock, but there are no lifeguards.

- **Owen Park Beach,** off Main Street in Vineyard Haven: A tiny strip of harborside beach adjoining a town green with swings and a bandstand will suffice for young children, who, by the way, get lifeguard supervision. There are no restrooms, but this is an in-town beach, so it's probably a quick walk from your Vineyard Haven inn.

- **South Beach** 🏖🏖🏖 (Katama Beach), about 4 miles (6km) south of Edgartown on Katama Road: If you have time for only one trip to the beach and you can't get up-island, go with this popular 3-mile (5km) barrier strand that boasts heavy wave action (check with lifeguards for swimming conditions), sweeping dunes, and, most important, relatively ample parking space. It's also accessible by bike path or shuttle bus. Lifeguards patrol some sections, and there are sparsely scattered toilet facilities. The rough surf here is popular with surfers. *Tip:* Families tend to head to the left, college kids to the right.

FISHING   For shellfishing, get information and a permit from the appropriate town hall (for phone numbers, see "Beaches," above). Popular spots for surf casting include Wasque Point on Chappaquiddick, South Beach, and the jetty at Menemsha Pond.

The party boat *Skipper* (© 508/693-1238) offers half-day trips out of Oak Bluffs Harbor in season. The cost is $25 for adults and $15 for children 12 and under. Bring your own poles and bait. Deep-sea excursions can be arranged aboard **Big Eye Charters** (© 508/627-3649) out of Edgartown, or **Summer's Lease** (© 508/693-2880) out of Oak Bluffs. Up-island, there's **North Shore Charters** (© 508/645-2993) and **Flashy Lady Charters** (© 508/645-2462; www.flashyladycharters.com) out of Menemsha, locus of the island's commercial fishing fleet.

IGFA world-record holder Capt. Leslie S. Smith operates **Backlash Charters** (© 508/627-5894; backlash@tiac.net), specializing in light tackle and fly-fishing, out of Edgartown. Cooper Gilkes III, proprietor of **Coop's Bait & Tackle,** 147 W. Tisbury Rd., Edgartown (© 508/627-3909), which offers rentals as well as supplies, is another acknowledged authority. He's available as an instructor or charter guide.

GOLF   The nine-hole **Mink Meadows Golf Course,** off Franklin Street in Vineyard Haven (© 508/693-0600), is open to the public, while the championship-level 18-hole **Farm Neck Golf Club,** off Farm Neck Road in Oak Bluffs (© 508/693-3057), is semiprivate.

NATURE TRAILS   About a fifth of the Vineyard's land mass has been set aside for conservation, and it's all accessible to bikers and hikers. The **West Chop Woods,** off Franklin Street in Vineyard Haven, comprise 85 acres (34 hectares) with marked trails. Midway between Vineyard Haven and Edgartown,

Exploring the Vineyard on Two Wheels

Biking on the Vineyard is a memorable experience, not only for the smooth, well-maintained paths, but also for the long stretches of virtually untrafficked up-island roads that reveal breathtaking country landscapes and sweeping ocean views.

A triangle of paved bike paths, roughly 8 miles (13km) to a side, links the down-island towns of Oak Bluffs, Edgartown, and Vineyard Haven. The Vineyard Sound portion along Beach Road, flanked by water on both sides, is especially enjoyable. From Edgartown, you can also follow the bike path to South Beach. For a more woodsy ride, there are paved paths and mountain-biking trails in the **Manuel F. Corellus State Forest** (© 508/693-2540), a vast spread of scrub oak and pine in the middle of the island. The bike paths are accessible off Edgartown–West Tisbury Road.

The up-island roads leading to West Tisbury, Chilmark, Menemsha, and Aquinnah are a cyclist's paradise, with unspoiled pastureland, old farmhouses, and brilliant sea views reminiscent of Ireland's countryside. But keep in mind that the terrain is often hilly, and the roads are narrow and a little rough around the edges. From West Tisbury to Chilmark Center, try **South Road**—about 5 miles (8km)—which passes stone walls rolling over moors, clumps of pine and wildflowers, verdant marshes and tidal pools, and, every once in awhile, an Old Vineyard farmhouse. **Middle Road** is another lovely ride with a country feel and will also get you from West Tisbury to Chilmark. (It's usually less trafficked, too.)

Our favorite up-island route is the 6-mile (10km) stretch from Chilmark Center out to Aquinnah via **State Road** and **Moshup Trail** . The ocean views along this route are spectacular. Don't miss the **Quitsa Pond Lookout,** about 2 miles (3km) down State Road, which provides a panoramic vista of Nashaquitsa and Menemsha ponds, beyond which you can see Menemsha, Vineyard Sound, and the Elizabeth Islands. A bit farther, just over the Aquinnah town line, is the Aquinnah spring, a roadside iron pipe where you can refill your water bottle with the freshest and coldest water on the island. At the fork after the spring, turn left on Moshup Trail—in fact, a regular road—and follow the coast, which offers gorgeous views of the ocean and the sweeping sand dunes. You'll soon wind up in Aquinnah, where you can explore the red-clay cliffs and pristine beaches. On the return trip, you can take the handy bike ferry ($7 round-trip) from Aquinnah to Menemsha. It runs daily in summer and on weekends in May.

There are lots of bike-rental operations near the ferry landings in Vineyard Haven and Oak Bluffs, as well as a few rental shops in Edgartown. For information rentals, see "Getting Around," earlier in this chapter.

A very good outfitter out of Boston called **Bike Riders** (© 800/473-7040; www.bikeridertours.com) runs 6-day island-hopping tours of Martha's Vineyard and Nantucket. The cost is $1,395 per person, plus $60 if you need to borrow a bike. It's a perfect way to experience both islands.

the **Felix Neck Wildlife Sanctuary** ⚘⚘ includes a 6-mile (10km) network of trails over varying terrain, from woodland to beach.

The 633-acre (256-hectare) **Long Point Wildlife Refuge** ⚘⚘, off Waldron's Bottom Road in West Tisbury (© **508/693-7392** for gatehouse), offers heath and dunes, freshwater ponds, a family-oriented beach, and interpretive nature walks for children.

Up-island, along the sound, the **Menemsha Hills Reservation** ⚘, off North Road in Chilmark (© **508/693-7662**), encompasses 210 acres (85 hectares) of rocks and bluffs, with steep paths, lovely views, and even a public beach. The **Cedar Tree Neck Sanctuary** ⚘, off Indian Hill Road southwest of Vineyard Haven (© **508/693-5207**), offers some 300 forested acres (122 hectares) that end in a stony beach. Swimming and sunbathing are prohibited.

Some remarkable botanical surprises can be found at the 20-acre (8-hectare) **Polly Hill Arboretum** ⚘⚘, 809 State Rd., West Tisbury (© **508/693-9426**). Legendary horticulturist Polly Hill has developed this property over the past 40 years and allows the public to wander the grounds Thursday through Tuesday from 7am until 7pm. This is a magical place, particularly from mid-June to July, when the Dogwood Allee is in bloom. Wanderers will pass old stone walls on the way to the Tunnel of Love, an arbor of plaited hornbeam. To get here from Vineyard Haven, go south on State Road, bearing left at the junction of North Road. There's a requested donation of $5 for adults and $3 for children under 12.

WATERSPORTS   Wind's Up, 199 Beach Rd., Vineyard Haven (© **508/693-4252**), rents canoes, kayaks, and various sailing craft, including windsurfers, and offers instruction on a placid pond. Canoes and kayaks rent for $18 to $20 per hour.

MUSEUMS & HISTORIC LANDMARKS

Cottage Museum ⚘   This little museum, a cottage in the center of Oak Bluffs' famous "campground," displays 19th-century artifacts: bulky black bathing costumes, and a melodeon used for hymnal singalongs. The campground is a 34-acre (14-hectare) circle with more than 300 multicolored, elaborately trimmed Carpenter Gothic cottages, which look very much the way they might have more than 100 years ago. These adorable little houses were loosely modeled on the revivalists' canvas tents that inspired them. In 1867, when these cottages were built, campers typically attended three lengthy prayer services daily. Opportunities for worship remain: within the park at the 1878 Trinity Methodist Church, or just outside, on Samoset Avenue, at the nonsectarian 1870 Union Chapel, a magnificent octagonal structure with superb acoustics.

At the very center of the grounds is the striking **Trinity Park Tabernacle** ⚘⚘. Built in 1879, the open-sided chapel is the largest wrought-iron structure in the country. Thousands can be accommodated on its long wooden benches, which are usually filled to capacity for the Sunday-morning services in summer, as well as for community sings (Wed in July and Aug) and occasional concerts.

1 Trinity Park (within the Camp Meeting Grounds), Oak Bluffs. © 508/693-7784. Admission $1 (donation). Mid-June to Sept Mon–Sat 10am–4pm. Closed Oct to mid-June.

Flying Horses Carousel ⚘⚘ *Kids*   You don't have to be a kid to enjoy what is considered to be the oldest working carousel in the country. Built in 1876 at Coney Island, this National Historic Landmark predates the era of horses that "gallop." Lacking the necessary gears, these mounts merely glide smoothly in place to the joyful strains of a calliope. Take a moment to admire the intricate hand-carving and real horsehair manes, and gaze into the horses' glass eyes for a surprise: tiny animal charms glinting within.

33 Circuit Ave. (at Lake Ave.), Oak Bluffs. © **508/693-9481**. Tickets $1 per ride, or $8 for 10. Late May to early Sept daily 9:30am–10pm; call for off-season hours. Closed mid-Oct to mid-Apr.

Martha's Vineyard Historical Society/Vineyard Museum ★★   All of Martha's Vineyard's colorful history is captured here, in a compound of historic buildings. To acclimate yourself chronologically, start with the pre-colonial arti-facts—from arrowheads to colorful Gay Head clay pottery—displayed in the 1845 Captain Francis Pease House. The Gale Huntington Reference Library houses rare documentation of the island's history, from genealogical records to whale-ship logs. Some extraordinary memorabilia, including scrimshaw and portraiture, are on view in the adjoining Francis Foster Maritime Gallery.

To get a sense of daily life during the era when the waters of the East Coast were the equivalent of a modern highway, visit the Thomas Cooke House, a shipwright-built colonial, built in 1765, where the Customs collector lived and worked. The Fresnel lens on display outside the museum was lifted from the Gay Head Lighthouse in 1952, after nearly a century of service. Though it no longer serves to warn ships of dangerous shoals (that light is automated now), it still lights up the night every evening in summer, just for show.

59 School St. (at Cooke St., 2 blocks southwest of Main St.), Edgartown. © **508/627-4441**. Fax 508/627-4436. www.marthasvineyardhistory.org. Admission in season $7 adults, $4 children 6–15. Early June to mid-Oct Tues–Sat 10am–5pm; off-season Wed–Fri 1–4pm, Sat 10am–4pm.

ORGANIZED TOURS & CRUISES

Hugh Taylor (James's brother) alternates with a couple of other captains in taking the helm of *Arabella* ★, docked in Menemsha Harbor at the end of North Road (© **508/645-3511**). This swift 50-foot (15m) catamaran makes daily trips to Cuttyhunk and offers sunset cruises around the Aquinnah cliffs. It's a great way to see lovely coves and vistas otherwise denied the ordinary tourist. Day sails are $60 for adults, $30 for children under 12. From mid-June to mid-September, departures are daily at 10:30am and 6pm (or 2 hours before sunset). Reservations are required.

The Trustees of Reservations, a statewide land conservation group, offers fascinating 2½-hour **Natural History Tours** ★★★ (© **508/627-3599;** www.vineyard.net/org/trustees) by safari vehicle or canoe around Cape Pogue on Chappaquiddick Island. The canoe tour on Poucha Pond and Cape Pogue Bay is designed for all levels. The cost for the safari tour is $15 for adults and $10 for children; the canoe tour is $30 for adults, $15 for children. Call for reservations.

SHOPPING

ANTIQUES & COLLECTIBLES   For the most exquisite Asian furniture, porcelains, and jewelry, visit **All Things Oriental,** 123 Beach Rd., Vineyard Haven (© **508/693-8375**). The treasures here are handpicked in China by the owner.

You don't have to be a bona-fide collector to marvel over the museum-quality findings at **C. W. Morgan Marine Antiques,** Beach Road, just east of the town center, Vineyard Haven (© **508/693-3622**). The collection encompasses paint-ings and prints, intricate models, nautical instruments, and scrimshaw.

ARTS & CRAFTS   No visit to Edgartown would be complete without a peek at the wares of scrimshander Thomas J. DeMont, Jr., at **Edgartown Scrimshaw**

Gallery, 43 Main St. (© **508/627-9439**). All the scrimshaw in the gallery is hand-carved using ancient mammoth ivory or antique fossil ivory.

The **Field Gallery,** State Road (in the center of town), West Tisbury (© **508/ 693-5595**), is where Marc Chagall meets Henry Moore and where Tom Maley's playful figures have enchanted locals and passersbys for decades. You'll also find cartoons by Jules Feiffer. The Sunday-evening openings are high points of the summer social season. Closed from mid-October to mid-May.

Don't miss the **Granary Gallery at the Red Barn,** Old County Road (off Edgartown–West Tisbury Road), West Tisbury (© **800/472-6279** or 508/693-0455), which displays astounding prints by the late longtime summer resident Alfred Eisenstaedt and dazzling photos by local luminary Alison Shaw.

Another rather unique local artisans' venue is **Martha's Vineyard Glass Works,** State Road, North Tisbury (© **508/693-6026**). The three resident artists—Andrew Magdanz, Susan Shapiro, and Mark Weiner—have shown nationwide to considerable acclaim.

GIFTS/HOME DECOR   Craftworks, 149 Circuit Ave., Oak Bluffs (© **508/ 693-7463**), is filled to the rafters with whimsical contemporary American crafts. **Paper Tiger,** 29 Main St., Vineyard Haven (© **508/693-8970**), is an old-fashioned stationery store with wonderful papers and cards.

Carly Simon's **Midnight Farm,** 18 Water-Cromwell Lane, Vineyard Haven (© **508/693-1997**), offers a world of high-end, imaginative gift items from candles to children's clothes to furniture and glassware.

WHERE TO STAY

Before deciding where to stay on Martha's Vineyard, consider the type of vacation you prefer. The down-island towns of Vineyard Haven, Oak Bluffs, and Edgartown provide shops, restaurants, beaches, and harbors all within walking distance, and frequent shuttles to get you all over the island. But all three can be overly crowded on busy summer weekends. Vineyard Haven is the gateway for most of the ferry traffic; Oak Bluffs is a raucous town with most of the Vineyard's bars and nightclubs. And many visitors make a beeline to Edgartown's manicured Main Street. Up-island inns provide more peace and quiet, but you'll probably need a car to get around. Also, you may not be within walking distance of the beach.

We've provided only summer rates below, because the Vineyard is so seasonal. If you do visit in the off-season, you may find substantial discounts at establishments that remain open year-round.

EDGARTOWN
Very Expensive

Charlotte Inn ✦✦✦   Ask anyone to recommend the best inn on the island, and this is the name you're most likely to hear. It's one of only two Relais & Châteaux properties on the Cape and Islands. Linked by formal gardens, each of the 18th- and 19th-century houses has a distinctive look and feel, though the predominant mode is English Country. All but one of the rooms have TVs; some have VCRs. The bathrooms are luxurious, and some are bigger than most standard hotel rooms. However sterling the accommodations here, the restaurant may actually gather more laurels: L'étoile is one of the island's finest (p. 260).

27 S. Summer St. (in the center of town), Edgartown, MA 02539. © **508/627-4751**. Fax 508/627-4652. 25 units. Summer $295–$525 double; $695–$850 suite. Rates include continental breakfast; full breakfast

offered for $15 extra. AE, MC, V. Open year-round. No children under 14. **Amenities:** Restaurant (French). *In room:* A/C, TV (in most units), hair dryer, no phone.

Harbor View Hotel ☆

The grand exterior of this Gilded Age hotel unfortunately masks a rather bland interior with generic motel-style rooms. Nevertheless, it does have a rather fine location; its 300-foot (90m) veranda overlooks Edgartown Harbor and the lighthouse. Front bedrooms with that pretty view cost quite a bit more; in back, there's a large pool surrounded by newer annexes, where some rooms and suites have kitchenettes. The hotel is just far enough from "downtown" to avoid the traffic, but close enough for a pleasant walk past regal captains' houses. The Coach House (p. 260) serves three meals in an elegant setting.

131 N. Water St. (about a ½ mile/0.8 km northwest of Main St.), Edgartown, MA 02539. © 800/255-6005 or 508/627-7000. Fax 508/627-8417. www.harbor-view.com. 124 units. Summer $285–$475 double; $485–$675 suite. AE, DC, MC, V. Open year-round. **Amenities:** 2 restaurants (fine dining; casual cigar bar); heated outdoor pool; tennis courts; concierge; room service; babysitting; same-day laundry service. In room: A/C, TV, hair dryer, iron, safe.

Hob Knob Inn ★★★

Owner Maggie White has reinvented this 19th-century Gothic Revival inn as an exquisite destination now vying for top honors as one of the Vineyard's best places to stay. Her style is peppy/preppy, with crisp floral fabrics and striped patterns creating a clean and comfortable look. The farm breakfast is a delight, served at beautifully appointed individual tables in the sunny dining rooms. Bovine lovers will enjoy the agrarian theme, a decorative touch throughout the inn. The attentive staff will pack a splendid picnic basket or plan a charter fishing trip on Maggie's 27-foot (8m) Boston Whaler.

128 Main St. (on upper Main St., in the center of town), Edgartown, MA 02539. © 800/696-2723 or 508/627-9510. Fax 508/627-4560. www.hobknob.com. 21 units. Summer $200–$525 double; $7,500 per week for cottage. Rates include full breakfast and afternoon tea. AE, MC, V. Open year-round. **Amenities:** Exercise room with top-notch equipment; bike rental; business center; massage (extra charge). *In room:* A/C, TV, dataport, hair dryer.

The Winnetu Inn & Resort ☆☆

This is the island's newest lodging, a large luxury hotel on 11 acres (4 hectares) overlooking South Beach in Katama. Guests can walk down a 250-yard (228m) path to get to the private beach, which is next to South Beach on the Atlantic Ocean. A 3-mile (5km) bike path links the inn to Edgartown, but the inn also runs a shuttle service in season that can pick up guests at the Edgartown ferry. Most units are comfortable two- and three-bedroom suites with kitchenettes, and there is one deluxe cottage with Jacuzzi and roof deck. Some have ocean views and washer/dryers; most have decks or patios.

South Beach, Edgartown, MA 02539. © 978/443-1733 for reservations, or 508/627-4747. www.winnetu. com. 48 units. Summer $275 studio; $475–$1,140 suite. 3- to 4-night minimum stay in high season. MC, V. Closed Dec–Mar. **Amenities:** Restaurant (fine dining); outdoor heated pool; putting green; tennis courts with pro; fitness room; children's programs; laundry facilities. *In room:* A/C, TV/VCR, fridge, coffeemaker, iron, microwave.

Expensive

Colonial Inn of Martha's Vineyard ☆☆ *Kids*

This 1911 inn in the center of Edgartown has been transformed into a fine modern hotel, and recent renovations have elevated it to what can accurately be described as "affordable luxury." Its lobby serves as a conduit to the Nevins Square shops beyond. Guest rooms are decorated in soothing, contemporary tones, with pine furniture, hardwood floors, and beadboard wainscoting. Many units have fridges and VCRs; some have balconies and awesome views. All guests are free to enjoy a cocktail on one of the four harborview decks. Be sure to visit the roof deck around sunset or, if you're up for it, sunrise.

38 N. Water St., Edgartown, MA 02539. ℂ 800/627-4701 or 508/627-4711. Fax 508/627-5904. www. colonialinnmvy.com. 43 units. Summer $195–$350 double; $375 suite or efficiency. Rates include continental breakfast. AE, MC, V. Closed Dec–Mar. **Amenities:** 2 restaurants (Italian, New American); shopping arcade. *In room:* A/C, TV, dataport, hair dryer.

The Jonathan Munroe House ⭐ *Finds*   With its graceful wraparound, colon-naded front porch, the Jonathan Munroe House stands out from the other inns and captain's homes on this stretch of upper Main Street. Guest rooms are immaculate, antique-filled, and dotted with clever details. Many units have fire-places. At breakfast, don't miss the homemade waffles and pancakes, served on the sunny porch. Request the garden cottage if you're in a honeymooning mood.

100 Main St., Edgartown, MA 02539. ℂ 877/468-6763 or 508/627-5536. Fax 508/627-5536. www.jonathanmunroe.com. 8 units. Summer $190–$255 double; $355 cottage. Rates include full breakfast. AE, DC, MC, V. Open year-round. No children under 12. *In room:* A/C, hair dryer.

The Point Way Inn ⭐⭐   This inn has recently undergone a multimillion-dollar sprucing up, and is just as pretty as can be. While some of the bedrooms are on the small side, they are cheerfully decorated in contemporary style. The garden room is an especially cozy unit with a separate entrance. Hearty break-fasts might include crepes or stuffed French toast. In the afternoons, there are homemade cookies, and in the evenings, wine and cheese. An unusual feature here is a complimentary guest car available for exploring the island.

104 Main St. (on upper Main St.), Edgartown, MA 02539. ℂ 888/711-6633 or 508/627-8633. Fax 508/627-3338. www.pointway.com. 13 units. Summer $225–$325 double; $375–$525 suite. Rates include full breakfast. AE, DISC, MC, V. Closed Jan to mid-Feb. Well-behaved dogs allowed in 2 rooms ($50). **Amenities:** Courtesy car. *In room:* A/C, TV, hair dryer, no phone.

Victorian Inn ⭐⭐   Do you long to stay at a quaint, reasonably priced inn that's bigger than a B&B but smaller than a Marriott? The Victorian Inn is a freshened-up version of those old-style hotels that used to exist in every New England town. There are enough rooms here so you don't feel like you are tres-passing in someone's home, yet there's a personal touch. With three floors of long, graceful corridors, the Victorian could serve as a stage set for a 1930s romance. Several units have canopy beds and balconies. Innkeepers Stephen and Karen Caliri are quick to dispense helpful advice.

24 S. Water St. (in the center of town), Edgartown, MA 02539. ℂ 508/627-4784. www.thevic.com. 14 units. Summer $165–$350 double. Rates include full breakfast and afternoon tea. MC, V. Open year-round. Dogs welcome Nov–Mar. *In room:* A/C, hair dryer, no phone.

Moderate

Edgartown Inn ⭐ *Value*   This centrally located inn offers perhaps the best value on the island. Nathaniel Hawthorne holed up here for nearly a year, and Daniel Webster also spent time here. It's a lovely 1798 Federal manse, a show-place even here on captains' row. Rooms are no-frills but pleasantly traditional; some have TVs and harbor views. Modernists may prefer the cathedral-ceilinged quarters in the annex, which offers lovely light and a sense of seclusion. Service is excellent; be sure to say hello to Henry King, who has been on staff for over 50 years.

56 N. Water St., Edgartown, MA 02539. ℂ 508/627-4794. Fax 508/627-9420. www.edgartowninn.com. 20 units, 4 with shared bathroom. Summer $100–$225 double. Breakfast available for extra charge. No credit cards. Closed Nov–Mar. *In room:* A/C, no phone.

OAK BLUFFS

Those looking for a basic motel with a central location can try **Surfside Motel,** across from the ferry dock on Oak Bluffs Avenue (© **800/537-3007** or 508/693-2500). Doubles are $150 to $160; well-behaved pets are allowed.

Expensive

The Oak House ★★ *Finds* This 1872 Queen Anne bay-front beauty has preserved all the luxury of the Victorian age. Innkeeper Betsi Convery-Luce trained at Johnson & Wales; her pastries are sublime. The common areas are furnished in an opulent Victorian mode, as are the 10 guest rooms. Those toward the back are quieter, but those in front have Nantucket Sound views. This inn is very service-oriented, and requests for feather beds, down pillows, or non-allergenic pillows are accommodated. Anyone intent on decompressing is sure to benefit from this immersion into another era—the one that invented the leisure class.

75 Seaview Ave. (on the sound), Oak Bluffs, MA 02557. © 800/245-5979 or 508/693-4187. Fax 508/696-7385. www.vineyard.net/inns. 10 units. Summer $180–$220 double; $275–$280 suite. Rates include continental breakfast and afternoon tea. AE, DISC, MC, V. Closed late Oct to early May. *In room:* A/C, TV.

Moderate

The Dockside Inn ★ *Kids* Set close to the harbor, the Dockside is geared toward families and is perfectly located for exploring Oak Bluffs. The welcoming exterior, with its colonnaded porch and balconies, duplicates the inns of yesteryear. Once inside, the whimsical Victorian touches will transport you into the spirit of this rollicking town. Most of the cheerfully decorated rooms have either garden or harbor views; some have private decks. Location, charm, and flair make this a popular place, so book early.

9 Circuit Ave. Extension (Box 1206), Oak Bluffs, MA 02557. © 800/245-5979 or 508/693-2966. Fax 508/696-7293. www.vineyard.net/inns. 22 units. Summer $150–$200 double; $250–$350 suite. Rates include continental breakfast. AE, DISC, MC, V. Closed late Oct to early Apr. *In room:* A/C, TV, hair dryer, iron.

Inexpensive

Attleboro House *Value* As old-fashioned as the afghans that proprietor Estelle Reagan crochets for every bed, this harborside guesthouse—serving Camp Meeting visitors since 1874—epitomizes the simple, timeless joys of summer. None of the rooms have private bathrooms, but the rates are so retro that you may not mind. What was good enough for 19th-century tourists more than suffices today.

42 Lake Ave. (on the harbor), Oak Bluffs, MA 02557. © 508/693-4346. 11 units, all with shared bathroom. Summer $75–$115 double; $105–$175 suite. MC, V. Closed Oct–May. *In room:* No phone.

VINEYARD HAVEN (TISBURY)

Expensive

Crocker House Inn ★ Jynell and Jeff Kristal have renovated this 1920s home near the harbor into a comfortable, casually elegant place to stay. Rooms are light and airy; they've all been completely redone with a country flavor. Jynell has Marriott experience, and it shows in the service-oriented hospitality. Jeff bakes blueberry muffins in the morning, and guests rave about his chocolate-chip cookies set out with iced tea and lemonade in the afternoon.

12 Crocker Ave./P.O. Box 1658 (off Main St.), Vineyard Haven, MA 02568. © 800/772-0206 or 508/693-1151. Fax 508/693-1123. www.crockerhouseinn.com. 8 units. Summer $195–$285 double; $385 suite. Rates include continental breakfast. AE, MC, V. Open year-round. Children over 12 welcome. *In room:* A/C, TV.

Martha's Place ★★ Martha's Place is exceptional for its elegance in the heart of this bustling port town. It's across the street from Owen Park, a harbor beach, and a block from the center of Vineyard Haven. The owners have lovingly restored the stately Greek Revival home and surrounded it with rosebushes. Swags and jabots line the windows; every knob has a tassel, every fabric a trim. If you admire neoclassical armoires or antique beds draped in blue velvet, Martha's is the place. Most units have harbor views. The bathrooms are quite luxurious—ever seen one with a fireplace? Breakfast is served at the large dining-room table set with china and silver, or you can have your meal in bed, if you prefer.

114 Main St. (in the center of town), Vineyard Haven, MA 02568. © **508/693-0253.** Fax 508/693-1890. www.marthasplace.com. 6 units. Summer $175–$425 double. Rates include continental breakfast. DISC, MC, V. **Amenities:** Mountain bikes; luxury boat charters (extra charge). *In room:* A/C, TV, dataport, hair dryer.

CHILMARK (INCLUDING MENEMSHA), WEST TISBURY & AQUINNAH
Very Expensive

Beach Plum Inn ★★ This family-owned country inn is on 8 lush acres (3 hectares), with a lawn sloping graciously down to Vineyard Sound. The interior decor is predominantly cottage-y, though some rooms lean towards elegance. All but one have decks, some with views of Menemsha Harbor. Some units have canopy beds and are quite romantic. Linens are 300 count and above; towels are Egyptian cotton; and five rooms have whirlpool tubs.

Beach Plum Lane (off North Rd., a ½ mile/0.8km northeast of the harbor), Menemsha, MA 02552. © **877/645-7398** or 508/645-9454. Fax 508/645-2801. www.beachpluminn.com. 9 units. Summer $200–$400 double or cottage. Rates include full breakfast in season, continental breakfast off-season. AE, DC, DISC, MC, V. Closed Jan–Apr. **Amenities:** Restaurant (Continental); private beach passes; tennis court; exercise room; bike rental; in-room massage (by arrangement); babysitting (by arrangement); laundry service; croquet. *In room:* A/C, TV, fridge, hair dryer, iron.

Expensive

Menemsha Inn and Cottages ★★ There's an almost Quaker-like plainness to this weathered waterside compound, with guest rooms and cottages set in the pines near Menemsha Harbor. Mostly it's a place to revel in the outdoors (on 11 seaside acres, or 4 hectares) without distractions. A ½-mile (0.8km) walk on a wooded path leads to the beach. There's no restaurant here—just a restful breakfast room. Cottages have hair dryers, TV/VCRs, dataports, outdoor showers, barbecue grills, and kitchenettes. The most luxurious suites are located in the Carriage House, which has a spacious common room with a fieldstone fireplace. All units have private decks, most with water views. Guests have access to complimentary passes and shuttle service to the Lucy Vincent and Squibnocket private beaches.

Off North Rd. (about a ½ mile/0.8km northeast of the harbor), Menemsha, MA 02552. © **508/645-2521.** Fax 508/645-9500. www.menemshainn.com. 27 units. Summer $200–$250 double; $315 suite; cottage $1,800–$2,750 per week. Rates for rooms and suites include continental breakfast. No credit cards. Closed Nov to mid-Apr. **Amenities:** Private beach passes; tennis court; fitness room. *In room:* TV.

Moderate

The Captain R. Flanders House ★ *(Finds)* Set amid 60 acres (24 hectares) of rolling meadows crisscrossed by stone walls, this late-18th-century farmhouse has remained much the same for 2 centuries. The living room, with its broadplank floors, is full of astonishing antiques, but there's none of that "for show" feel that's prevalent in more self-conscious B&Bs. Two countrified cottages overlook the pond. The owners will provide guests with a coveted pass to nearby Lucy Vincent Beach.

North Rd. (about 1 mile/1.6km northeast of Menemsha), Chilmark, MA 02535. © **508/645-3123.** 7 units, 2 with shared bathroom. Summer $175–$195 double; $275 cottage. Rates include continental breakfast. AE, DISC, MC, V. Closed Nov–Apr. **Amenities:** Private beach passes. *In room:* No phone.

WHERE TO DINE

Outside Oak Bluffs and Edgartown, all of Martha's Vineyard (including Vineyard Haven) is "dry," so bring your own bottle; some restaurants charge a small fee for uncorking.

EDGARTOWN
Very Expensive

L'étoile ☆☆☆ FRENCH   Every signal (starting with the price) tells you this is going to be one very special meal. To get to the restaurant, you first pass through a pair of sitting rooms before coming to a summery conservatory, sparkling with the light of antique brass sconces and fresh with the scent of potted citrus trees. Everything is perfection, from the table settings (gold-rimmed Villeroy & Boch) to the seasonal nouvelle-cuisine menu. Chef Michael Brisson is determined to dazzle, with an ever-evolving selection of delicacies flown in from the four corners of the earth. Sevruga usually makes an appearance—perhaps as a garnish for chilled leek soup. A roasted pheasant breast in a cider, apple-brandy, and thyme sauce may be accompanied by apple, sun-dried cherry, and mascarpone-filled wild-rice crepes.

Charlotte Inn, 27 S. Summer St. (off Main St.). © **508/627-5187.** Reservations required. Jackets recommended for men. Fixed-price menu $72; chef's tasting menu $120. AE, MC, V. July–Aug daily 6:30–9:45pm; call for off-season hours. Closed Jan to mid-Feb.

Expensive

Alchemy ☆ FRENCH BISTRO   This spiffy restaurant is a little slice of Paris on Main Street. Such esoteric choices as oyster brie soup and Burgundy Vintners salad share the bill with escargot and chantarelle fricassee. As befits a true bistro, there's also a large selection of cocktails, liqueurs, and wines. In addition to lunch and dinner, a bar menu is served from 2:30 to 11pm. This place isn't for everyone, but sophisticated diners will enjoy the Continental flair here.

71 Main St. (in the center of town). © **508/627-9999.** Reservations recommended. Main courses $22–$33. AE, MC, V. Apr–Nov daily noon–11pm; call for off-season hours. Open year-round.

The Coach House ☆☆ NEW AMERICAN   With wraparound windows and views of the harbor and lighthouse, this restaurant in Edgartown's grand hotel is an elegant place to dine. The mirrored bar is the swankiest place in town for a drink. The menu is simple but stylish. To start, there's soft-shell crab with arugula and teardrop tomatoes. As a main course, try the caramelized sea scallops with a salad of Asian pears and apples. Service here is excellent; these are trained waiters, not your usual college surfer dudes. At the end of your meal, you may want to sit in the rockers on the hotel's porch and just watch the lights twinkling in the harbor. © **508/627-7000.**

Harbor View Hotel, 131 N. Water St. © **508/627-7000.** Reservations recommended. Main courses $22–$36. AE, MC, V. Mon–Sat 7–11am and noon–2pm; Sun 8am–1:30pm; daily 6–10pm. Call for off-season hours. Open year-round.

Lattanzi's ☆☆ NORTHERN ITALIAN   Some say Al Lattanzi cooks the best veal chops on Martha's Vineyard. Lattanzi's would be the ideal place to eat in the dead of winter, by the glow of the paneled living room's handsome fireplace. Service is exceptional, and the wine list has a range of well-priced bottles. Back to

Finds **The Quintessential Lobster Dinner**

When the basics—a lobster and a sunset—are what you crave, head to **The Home Port** ⭑⭑, on North Road in Menemsha (☎ **508/645-2679**). At first glance, prices for the lobster dinners may seem a bit high, but note that they include an appetizer (go with the stuffed quahog), salad, amazing fresh-baked breads, non-alcoholic beverage (remember, it's BYOB in these parts), and dessert. The decor is on the simple side, but who cares? It's the riveting harbor views that have drawn fans to this family-friendly place for over 60 years. Locals not keen on summer crowds order takeout (less than half price), then head down to Menemsha Beach for a private sunset supper. Fixed-price platters range from $25 to $45. Reservations are required. Open mid-June to Labor Day, daily from 5 to 10pm. Closed early October to mid-May. Call for off-season hours.

the veal chop. You have two choices: *Piccolo Fiorentina,* which is hickory-grilled veal porterhouse chop with black peppercorns and lemon, or *Lombatina di Vitello al Porcini,* which is served with porcini-mushroom cream. If it's July, get the luscious striped-bass special.

Lattanzi also owns the very good **brick-oven pizza joint** next door (☎ **508/ 627-9084**).

19 Church St. (Old Post Office Sq., off Main St. in the center of town). ☎ **508/627-8854**. Reservations recommended. Main courses $22–$38. AE, DC, DISC, MC, V. June–Sept daily 6–10pm; call for off-season hours. Open year-round.

Moderate

Among the Flowers Cafe ⭑⭑ *(Value* AMERICAN   Everything's appealing at this small outdoor cafe near the dock. The breakfasts are the best around, and the comfort-food dinners are among the most affordable options in this pricey town. There's almost always a wait, not just because it's so picturesque, but also because the food is homey, hearty, and kind on the wallet.

Mayhew Lane. ☎ **508/627-3233**. Main courses $10–$18. AE, DC, DISC, MC, V. July–Aug daily 8am–10pm; May–June and Sept–Oct daily 8am–4pm. Closed Nov–Apr.

Chesca's ⭑⭑ *(Finds* ITALIAN   Chesca's is a solid entry, with yummy food at reasonable prices. You're sure to find favorites like paella (with roasted lobster and other choice seafood), risotto, and ravioli (with portobello and asparagus). Smaller appetites can fill up on homemade soup and salad.

Colonial Inn, 38 N. Water St. ☎ **508/627-1234**. Reservations not accepted. Main courses $13–$32. AE, MC, V. Late June to early Sept daily 5:30–10pm; call for off-season hours. Closed Nov–Mar.

Inexpensive

The Newes from America ⭑ *(Finds* PUB FARE   The food is better than average at this subterranean tavern, built in 1742. Beers are a specialty: Try a rack of five esoteric brews, or let your choice of food—from a wood-smoked oyster "Island Poor Boy" sandwich to a porterhouse steak—dictate your draft; the menu comes handily annotated with recommendations. Don't miss the seasoned fries.

The Kelley House, 23 Kelley St. ☎ **508/627-4397**. Main courses $7–$10. AE, MC, V. Daily 11am–11pm. Open year-round.

OAK BLUFFS
Expensive

Park Corner Bistro ★★ NEW AMERICAN   Locals and visitors have been keeping this quaint bistro packed all summer. Favorite appetizers are the beet salad and the Parmesan gnocchi with chanterelle and black trumpet mushrooms. Move on to a main course of Australian lamb loin with sweet-corn flan. For dessert, don't miss the warm fruit cobbler with vanilla ice cream.

20H Kennebec Ave. (across from the post office). ⓒ **508/696-9922.** Reservations suggested. Main courses $26–$33. AE, MC, V. Wed–Mon 6:30–11am, noon–3pm, and 6–11pm. Open year-round.

Sweet Life Cafe ★★★ FRENCH/NEW AMERICAN   Locals are crazy about this pearl of a restaurant, set in a restored Victorian house on upper Circuit Avenue. In season, sit outside in the gaily lit garden. Fresh local produce is featured, with seafood specials an enticing draw. If it's offered, go for the roasted lobster with potato-Parmesan risotto and smoked-salmon chive fondue.

63 Circuit Ave. ⓒ **508/696-0200.** Reservations recommended. Main courses $23–$36. AE, DISC, MC, V. Mid-May to mid-Sept daily 5:30–10pm; Apr to mid-May and mid-Sept to Dec Thurs–Mon 5:30–9:30pm. Closed Jan–Apr.

Tsunami ★★ *(Finds* ASIAN/INTERNATIONAL   For something a little different, look for the bright-red cottage on Oak Bluffs Harbor. Once you enter the second-floor dining room, you'll feel like you've discovered something very special indeed. There's a picture-perfect view from a spare room with Asian accents. The chef's specialty is seared tuna with mango-mint mashed potatoes, served with mixed vegetables and onion soy relish. While the restaurant specializes in seafood, there's also pheasant, duck, pork, and filet mignon. The downstairs bar has become quite a summer hangout.

6 Circuit Ave. Ext., Oak Bluffs Harbor. ⓒ **508/696-8900.** Reservations recommended. Main courses $22–$35. AE, MC, V. June–Aug daily 11am–4pm and 5:30–10:30pm; call for off-season hours. Closed mid-Oct to mid-May.

Moderate

Lola's Southern Seafood ★ SOUTHERN   This sultry New Orleans–style restaurant drips with atmosphere: chandeliers, wrought iron, and starched linens in an ochre palette. Specialties include chicken-and-seafood jambalaya and rib-eye steak spiced "from heaven or hell." There's live entertainment nightly (plus Sun brunch) in high season, Thursday through Saturday nights off-season. A pub menu is served in the bar.

Island Inn, Beach Rd. ⓒ **508/693-5007.** Reservations accepted for parties of 5 or more. Main courses $20–$36. DC, MC, V. Sun 10am–2pm; daily 5[nd11pm. Open year-round.

Inexpensive

Coup de Ville ★ SEAFOOD   This harborfront seafood shack serves up tasty beer-battered shrimp, grilled swordfish, and "world-famous" chicken wings. It's a fun place to people-watch as boaters cruise around the harbor.

Dockside Market Place, Oak Bluffs Harbor. ⓒ **508/693-3420.** Most items $9–$20. MC, V. June–Aug daily 11am–10pm; call for off-season hours. Closed mid-Oct–April.

VINEYARD HAVEN (TISBURY)

Just around the corner from the Black Dog Tavern, on Water Street near the ferry terminal, is the **Black Dog Bakery** (ⓒ **508/693-4786**). The doors open at 5am, and from midmorning on, it's elbowroom only as customers line up for freshly baked breads, muffins, and desserts that can't be beat. Don't forget some homemade doggie biscuits for your pooch.

Expensive

Black Dog Tavern ✶ NEW AMERICAN   How does a humble harbor shack come to be a national icon? Location helps. So do cool T-shirts. Soon after *Shenandoah* captain Robert Douglas decided, in 1971, that this hard-working port could use a good restaurant, influential vacationers stuck waiting for the ferry began to wander into this saltbox to tide themselves over with a bit of "blackout cake" or peanut-butter pie. The food is still home-cooking good, especially the seafood—and the blackout cake has lost none of its appeal. Though the lines grow ever longer, nothing much has changed at this beloved spot. Eggs Galveston for breakfast is still one of the ultimate Vineyard experiences—come early, when it first opens, and sit on the porch, where the views are perfect.

Beach St. Ext. (on the harbor). ℂ **508/693-9223**. Reservations not accepted. Main courses $14–$27. AE, MC, V. June to early Sept Mon–Sat 7–11am, 11:30am–2:30pm, and 5–10pm; Sun 7am–1pm and 5–10pm; call for off-season hours. Closed Dec–Feb.

Zephrus at the Tisbury Inn ✶✶ INTERNATIONAL   This chic, high-energy restaurant seats guests outside on Main Street or inside by the hearth. Entree winners include pan-roasted pork tenderloin, served with sweet 'tater tots, and shrimp and farfalle pasta. Though the menu is in constant flux, there is always a good vegetarian choice, such as delicious risotto with truffle vinaigrette. Bring your favorite wine; the corkage fee is $5 per table.

Tisbury Inn, Main St. (in the center of Vineyard Haven). ℂ **508/693-3416**. Reservations recommended. Main courses $18–$35. AE, DC, DISC, MC, V. Daily 11:30–2:30pm and 5:30–10pm. Open year-round.

CHILMARK (INCLUDING MENEMSHA) & WEST TISBURY
Expensive

Ice House Restaurant ✶✶ NEW AMERICAN   This pricey up-island restaurant is earning raves for the high quality of its food and service. It's also a hip venue, attracting insiders who wouldn't be caught dead in the down-island towns. Chef/owner Keith Korn combines unusual ingredients with island produce, meats, and locally caught fish. His specialty appetizer is a golden fried tomato with a lobster salad and avocado. As a main course, look no further than the pan-roasted halibut with sweet corn and fava bean succotash.

688 State Rd., West Tisbury. ℂ **508/645-9239**. Main courses $25–$36. AE, MC, V. July–Aug Mon–Sat 6–10pm, Sun 11am–2pm and 6–10pm; call for off-season hours. Closed Jan–Mar.

Moderate

The Bite ✶✶ *Finds* SEAFOOD   It's usually places like this that we crave when we think of New England. This is your quintessential "chowdah" and clam shack, flanked by picnic tables and serving up superlative chowder, potato salad, fried fish, and so forth.

Basin Rd. (off North Rd., about a ¼ mile/0.4km northeast of the harbor), Menemsha. ℂ **508/645-9239**. Main courses $18–$30. No credit cards. July–Aug daily 11am–9pm; call for off-season hours. Closed late Sept to Apr.

MARTHA'S VINEYARD AFTER DARK

BARS & CLUBS   All towns except for Oak Bluffs and Edgartown are dry, and last call at bars and clubs is at midnight. Hit Oak Bluffs for the rowdiest bar scene and best nighttime street life. In Edgartown, you may have to hop around before you find the evening's most happening spot.

Disco lives! As do karaoke and comedy, on occasion, at **Atlantic Connection,** 124 Circuit Ave., Oak Bluffs (ℂ **508/693-7129**). There's entertainment nightly in season. Cover ranges from free to $12.

Young and loud are the watchwords at **The Lampost** and the **Rare Duck,** 111 Circuit Ave., Oak Bluffs (© **508/696-9352**), a pair of clubs in the center of town. The Lampost features live bands and a dance floor; the Rare Duck, acoustic acts. Entertainment includes such prospects as "'80s night" and "male hot-body contest." Cover is from $1 to $5.

The Vineyard's first and only brewpub, **Offshore Ale Company,** 30 Kennebec Ave., Oak Bluffs (© **508/693-2626**), is an attractively rustic place, with oak booths and peanut shells strewn on the floor. Local acoustic acts entertain 6 nights a week in season. The cover is $2.

The **Ritz Café,** 1 Circuit Ave., Oak Bluffs (© **508/693-9851**), is a down-and-dirty hole-in-the-wall that features live music nightly in season and on weekends year-round. The cover is $2 to $3.

THE PERFORMING ARTS The magnificent 1843 **Old Whaling Church,** 89 Main St., Edgartown (© **508/627-4442**), functions primarily as a performing-arts center offering films, plays, and concerts. Ticket prices vary; call for the schedule.

The **Vineyard Playhouse,** 24 Church St., Vineyard Haven (© **508/696-6300** or 508/693-6450; www.vineyardplayhouse.org), is an intimate black-box theater where Equity professionals put on a rich season of favorites and challenging new work, followed, on summer weekends, by musical or comedic cabaret in the gallery/lounge. Children's theater selections are performed on Saturdays at 10am. Townspeople often get involved in the outdoor Shakespeare production, a 3-week run starting in mid-July at the Tashmoo Overlook Amphitheatre about 1 mile (1.6km) west of town. The season runs from June to September; call for an off-season schedule.

2 Nantucket ★★★

Once the whaling capital of the world, this tiny island, 30 miles (48km) off the coast of Cape Cod, still counts its isolation as a defining characteristic. At only 3½ by 14 miles (6 by 23km) in size, Nantucket is smaller and more insular than Martha's Vineyard. But charm-wise, Nantucket stands alone, providing 21st-century amenities wrapped in an elegant 19th-century package.

Sophisticated Nantucket Town features bountiful stores, quaint inns, interesting historic sights, and pristine beaches. The rest of the island is mainly residential, but for a couple of notable villages. **Siasconset** ★★★ (nicknamed 'Sconset), on the east side of the island, is a tranquil community with picturesque cottages and a handful of businesses, including a pricey French restaurant. Sunset aficionados head to **Madaket** ★, on the west coast of the island, for the evening spectacular.

The lay of the land on Nantucket is rolling moors, cranberry bogs, and miles of exquisite public beaches. The vistas are honeymoon-romantic: an operating windmill, three lighthouses, and a skyline dotted with church steeples.

ESSENTIALS
GETTING THERE
BY FERRY From Hyannis Ferry service to Nantucket is fairly hassle-free, unless you're bringing a car in summer. But first-time visitors will find a car more of a nuisance than a convenience, unless they're staying outside of Nantucket Town.

From Hyannis (South St. Dock), the **Steamship Authority** (© **508/477-8600,** or 508/228-3274 from Nantucket; www.islandferry.com) operates

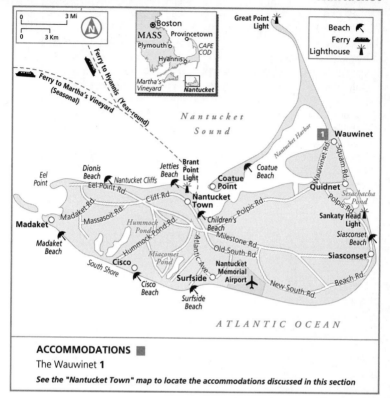

ACCOMMODATIONS ◼

The Wauwinet **1**

See the "Nantucket Town" map to locate the accommodations discussed in this section

year-round regular ferry service (for cars, passengers, and bicycles) to Steamship Wharf in Nantucket. Trip time is 2 hours and 15 minutes. A round-trip fare for a car costs $320 from mid-May to mid-October, $200 the rest of the year. Car rates do not include drivers or passengers. Passenger tickets are $13 one-way ($26 round-trip) for adults, $6.50 one-way ($13 round-trip) for children 5 to 12; bikes cost $10 round-trip. Parking costs $8 to $10 per day; you do not need to make parking reservations.

No advance reservations are needed for passengers on the regular ferry. But if you bring your car in summer, you must reserve *months in advance*—only six boats make the trip daily, and they fill up fast. Arrive at least 1 hour before departure to avoid having your space given away. There is a $10 fee for canceling a reservation.

The Steamship Authority's fast ferry, the *Flying Cloud* (© **508/495-3278**), is for passengers only; reservations are highly recommended. It takes 1 hour and runs five to six times a day in season. It is cheaper than the Hy-Line ferry (see below), at $24 one-way ($48 round-trip) for adults, $18 one-way ($36 round-trip) for children 5 to 12. AAA members get a $4 discount. Parking costs $8 to $10. Watch for the ferry parking signs on Route 6; if lots next to the dock are full, you'll need to take Exit 6 for a satellite lot, instead of Exit 7 for the main lot.

Tips Ferry Parking

Because you won't need a car on Nantucket, consider parking your car in Hyannis before boarding the ferry to the island. For all **Hy-Line** ferry service, Ocean Street Dock (© **888/778-1132** or 508/778-2602), in July and August, it's a good idea not only to reserve tickets in advance, but also to reserve a parking spot ahead of time. The all-day parking fee is $10 in season. Travelers on **Steamship Authority** (© **508/477-8600**) vessels do not need a parking reservation, but when the lots near the ferry terminal are full, satellite lots are used and passengers must take shuttle buses to the terminal. Be sure to arrive at least 1 hour before sailing time to allow for parking.

Hy-Line Cruises, Ocean Street Dock (© **888/778-1132** or 508/778-2600; for high-speed ferry reservations, call © **800/492-8082** or 508/778-0404; www.hy-linecruises.com), offers two types of passenger-only ferries from the Ocean Street Dock in Hyannis to Nantucket's Straight Wharf.

The *Grey Lady II,* a year-round high-speed passenger, makes the trip in 1 hour. The cost is $33 one-way ($58 round-trip) for adults, $25 one-way ($41 round-trip) for children 1 to 12, and $5 extra for bicycles. The boat seats 70 and makes five to six round-trips daily in season; reserve in advance.

From early May to October, Hy-Line runs its standard 1-hour-and-50-minute ferry service. Round-trip tickets are $27 for adults, $13.50 for children 4 to 12, and $10 extra for bikes. On busy holiday weekends, the slow ferry fills up, too, so order tickets in advance. Buy or pick up your tickets at least half an hour before sailing time.

Hy-line also runs slow crossings on the **MV *Great Point,*** which has a first-class section with a private lounge, restrooms, bar, and snack bar. The fare is $22 one-way ($44 round-trip) for adults and children. The comfortable seats on the *Great Point* are a far cry from the unforgiving benches on the regular slow ferry. No pets are allowed on the *Great Point.*

Hy-Line's "Around the Sound" cruise is a 1-day round-trip excursion from Hyannis with stops on Nantucket and Martha's Vineyard. It runs from early June to late September. The price is $36 for adults, $18 for children 4 to 12, and $15 extra for bikes.

From Martha's Vineyard   From Oak Bluffs (on Martha's Vineyard), Hy-Line runs three passenger-only ferries to Nantucket from early June to mid-September (there is no car-ferry service between the islands). Trip time is 2 hours and 15 minutes. The one-way fare is $13.50 for adults, $6.75 for children 5 to 12, and $5 extra for bikes.

From Harwich Port   You can avoid the summer crowds in Hyannis by boarding a passenger-only ferry with **Freedom Cruise Line,** 702 Rte. 28, across from Brax Landing, Harwich Port (© **508/432-8999;** www.nantucketislandferry. com). From mid-May to mid-October, boats leave from Saquatucket Harbor in Harwich Port; the trip takes 1½ hours. Round-trip tickets are $43 for adults, $36 for children 2 to 11, $6 for children under 2, and $10 extra for bikes. Parking is free for the first 24 hours, $12 per night thereafter. Reservations are highly recommended.

BY PLANE You can fly into **Nantucket Memorial Airport** (℡ 508/325-5300), about 3 miles (5km) south of Nantucket Road on Old South Road. The flight to Nantucket takes 30 to 40 minutes from Boston, 15 minutes from Hyannis, and a little over an hour from New York City airports.

Airlines providing service to Nantucket include: **Business Express/Delta Connection** (℡ 800/221-1212), year-round from Boston and seasonally from New York; **Cape Air/Nantucket Air** (℡ 800/352-0714), year-round from Hyannis ($74 round-trip), Boston (about $220 round-trip), Martha's Vineyard ($76 round-trip), and New Bedford ($71 round-trip); **Continental Express** (℡ 800/525-0280), seasonally from Newark (about $325 round-trip); **Island Airlines** (℡ 508/228-7575), year-round from Hyannis ($74 round-trip); and **US Airways Express** (℡ 800/428-4322), year-round from Boston ($210–$235 round-trip). Island Airlines and Nantucket Air both offer year-round charter service to the island.

GETTING AROUND

Nantucket is easily navigated by bike, moped, or on foot, and also by shuttle bus or taxi. The chamber of commerce strongly suggests that visitors leave their cars behind in order to minimize congestion and environmental impact. If you're staying outside of Nantucket Town, however, or if you plan to explore the outer reaches of the island, you might want to bring your own car or rent one here. Keep in mind, in-town traffic can reach gridlock in peak season, and parking can be a nightmare.

BY BICYCLE & MOPED Biking is a great way to get around Nantucket. The island is relatively flat, and paved bike paths abound—they'll get you from Nantucket Town to Siasconset, Surfside, and Madaket. There are also many unpaved back roads to explore, which make mountain bikes a wise choice. Mopeds are also available, but be aware that local rules and regulations are strictly enforced. Mopeds are not allowed on sidewalks or bike paths. You'll need a driver's license to rent a moped, and state law requires that you wear a helmet.

You can bring your own bike over on the ferries for a small additional charge. Otherwise, shops that rent bikes and mopeds (all within walking distance of the ferries) include **Cook's Cycle Shop, Inc.,** 6 S. Beach St. (℡ 508/228-0800); **Holiday Cycle,** 4 Chester St. (℡ 508/228-3644), which rents just bikes; **Nantucket Bike Shops,** at Steamboat Wharf and Straight Wharf (℡ 508/228-1999); and **Young's Bicycle Shop,** at Steamboat Wharf (℡ 508/228-1151), which also does repairs.

BY SHUTTLE BUS From June to September, inexpensive shuttle buses, with bike racks and wheelchair lifts, make a loop through Nantucket Town and to a few outlying spots; for routes, contact the **Nantucket Regional Transit Authority** (℡ 508/228-7025; www.nantucket.net/trans/nrta) or pick up a schedule at the visitor center on Federal Street or the Chamber Office on Main Street. The cost is 50¢ to $1, exact change required. A 3-day pass can be purchased at the visitor center for $10. Dogs are allowed on the bus as long as they are relatively clean and dry.

BY CAR & JEEP We recommend a car if you'll be here for more than a week or if you're staying outside Nantucket Town. Remember, though, there are no in-town parking lots; parking, although free, is limited.

Rental agencies on the island include **Affordable Rentals of Nantucket,** 6 S. Beach Rd. (℡ 508/228-3501); **Budget,** at the airport (℡ 800/527-0700 or

508/228-5666); **Hertz,** at the airport (© **800/654-3131** or 508/228-9421); **Nantucket Windmill Auto Rental,** at the airport (© **800/228-1227** or 508/228-1227); **Thrifty Car Rental,** at the airport (© **508/325-4616**); and **Young's 4 × 4 & Car Rental,** Steamboat Wharf (© **508/228-1151**). A four-wheel-drive rental costs about $180 per day (including an over-sand permit).

BY TAXI   You'll find taxis (many are vans that can accommodate groups or those traveling with bikes) waiting at the airport and at all ferry ports. During the busy summer months, we recommend reserving a taxi in advance to avoid a long wait upon arrival. Rates are flat fees, based on one person riding before 1am, with surcharges for additional passengers, bikes, and dogs. A taxi from the airport to Nantucket Town hotels will cost about $10. Reliable cab companies include **A-1 Taxi** (© **508/228-3330**), **Aardvark Cab** (© **508/728-9999**), **All Point Taxi** (© **508/228-5779**), and **Lisa's Taxi** (© **508/228-5779**).

VISITOR INFORMATION

Contact the **Nantucket Island Chamber of Commerce,** 48 Main St. (© **508/228-1700;** www.nantucketchamber.org). When you arrive, stop by the **Nantucket Visitors Service and Information Bureau,** 25 Federal St. (© **508/228-0925**). It's open daily from June to September, and Monday through Saturday from October to May. There are also information booths at Steamboat Wharf and Straight Wharf. Check the island's newspaper, the *Inquirer & Mirror* (known locally as "The Inky"), for information on events and activities around town.

   Nantucket Accommodations (© **508/228-9559;** fax 508/325-7009; www.nantucketaccommodation.com), a 30-year-old private service, arranges reservations for inns, cottages, guesthouses, B&Bs, and hotels; it has access to 95% of the island's lodgings, in addition to houses and cottages available by the night or week (as opposed to most realtors, who will only handle rentals for 2 weeks or more). The charge for the service is $15, assessed only when a reservation is made. Last-minute travelers should keep in mind that **Nantucket Visitors Service and Information Bureau** (© **508/228-0925**) operates a daily referral service for available rooms. It's not a booking service, but it always has the most updated list of lodging availability and cancellations.

   ATMs can be difficult to locate on Nantucket. **Nantucket Bank** (© **508/228-0580**) has three locations: 2 Orange St., 104 Pleasant St., and the airport lobby, all open 24 hours. **Pacific National Bank** has four locations: the A&P supermarket (next to the wharves), the Stop & Shop (open 24 hours seasonally), the Steamship Wharf Terminal, and Pacific National Bank lobby (open during bank hours only).

   In case of a medical emergency, the **Nantucket Cottage Hospital,** 57 Prospect St. (© **508/228-1200**), is open 24 hours.

BEACHES & OUTDOOR PURSUITS

BEACHES   In distinct contrast to Martha's Vineyard, virtually all of Nantucket's 110-mile (177km) coastline is open to the public.

- **Children's Beach:** This small beach is a protected cove just west of busy Steamship Wharf. Appealing to families, it has a park, playground, restrooms, lifeguards, snack bar, and even a bandstand for free weekend concerts.
- **Cisco Beach** 🌟🌟: About 4 miles (6km) from town, in the southwestern quadrant of the island (from Main St., turn onto Milk St., which becomes Hummock Pond Rd.), Cisco enjoys vigorous waves—great for the surfers who flock here. Restrooms and lifeguards are available.

- **Coatue Beach** 🏖: This fishhook-shaped barrier beach, on the northeastern side of the island at Wauwinet, is Nantucket's outback, accessible only by four-wheel-drive vehicles, watercraft, or the very strong legged. Swimming is strongly discouraged because of fierce tides.
- **Dionis Beach** 🏖🏖🏖: About 3 miles (5km) out of town (take the Madaket bike path to Eel Point Rd.) is Dionis, which enjoys the gentle sound surf and steep, picturesque bluffs. It's a great spot for swimming, picnicking, and shelling, and you'll find fewer children than at Jetties or Children's beaches. Stick to the established paths to prevent further erosion. Lifeguards patrol here, and restrooms are available.
- **Jetties Beach** 🏖🏖🏖: Located about a ½ mile (0.8km) west of Children's Beach on North Beach Street, Jetties is about a 20-minute walk, or a short bike ride, shuttle ride, or drive, from town (there's a large parking lot, but it fills up early on summer weekends). It's another family favorite for its mild waves, lifeguards, bathhouse, restrooms, and relatively affordable restaurant, the Jetties Cafe & Grille (© **508/325-6347**). Facilities include the town tennis courts, volleyball nets, a skate park, and a playground; watersports equipment and chairs are available to rent. In August, Jetties hosts an intense sand-castle competition, and the Fourth of July fireworks are held here.
- **Madaket Beach** 🏖🏖🏖: Accessible by Madaket Road, the 6-mile (10km) bike path that runs parallel to it, and by shuttle bus, this westerly beach is narrow and subject to pounding surf and sometimes serious crosscurrents. Unless it's a fairly tame day, you might content yourself with wading. It's the best spot on the island for admiring the sunset. Facilities include restrooms, lifeguards, and mobile food service.
- **Siasconset ('Sconset) Beach** 🏖🏖: The easterly coast of 'Sconset is as pretty as the town itself and rarely, if ever, crowded, perhaps because of the water's strong sideways tow. You can reach it by car, by shuttle bus, or via the Polpis or Milestone bike paths, about an 8-mile (13km) trip. There are usually lifeguards on duty, but the closest facilities (restrooms, grocery store, and cafe) are back in the center of the village.
- **Surfside Beach** 🏖🏖🏖: Three miles (5km) south of town via a popular bike/skate path, broad Surfside—equipped with lifeguards, restrooms, and a surprisingly accomplished little snack bar—is appropriately named and very popular. It draws thousands of visitors a day in high season, from college students to families, but the free parking lot can fit only about 60 cars—you do the math, or better yet, ride your bike or take the shuttle bus.

BICYCLING 🚴🚴🚴 Several paved bike paths radiate out from the center of town to outlying beaches. The main paths run about 6 miles (10km) west to Madaket, 3½ miles (6km) south to Surfside, and 8 miles (13km) east to Siasconset. To avoid backtracking from Siasconset, continue north through the charming village, and return on the **Polpis Road bike path** 🚴🚴. Strong riders could do a whole circuit of the island in a day, but most will be content to combine a single route with a few hours at a beach.

For a free map of the island's bike paths, stop by **Young's Bicycle Shop,** at Steamboat Wharf (© **508/228-1151**). It's definitely the best place for bike rentals. See "Getting Around," above, for other rental options.

FISHING For shellfishing, you'll need a permit from the **harbormaster's office,** 34 Washington St. (© **508/228-7261**). You'll see surf casters all over the island (no permit is required); for a guided trip, try Mike Monte of **Surf & Fly**

Fishing Trips (© **508/228-0529**). Deep-sea charters heading out of Straight Wharf include Captain Bob DeCosta's *Albacore* (© **508/228-5074**) and Captain David Martin's *Flicka* (© **508/325-4000**).

NATURE TRAILS   Through preservationist foresight, about a third of Nantucket is protected from development. Contact the **Nantucket Conservation Foundation,** 118 Cliff Rd. (© **508/228-2884**), for a map of its holdings ($4), which include the 205-acre (83-hectare) **Windswept Cranberry Bog,** off Polpis Road, and a portion of the 1,100-acre (446-hectare) **Coskata-Coatue Wildlife Refuge** ★★, comprising the barrier beaches beyond Wauwinet (see "Organized Tours," below). The **Maria Mitchell Association** (see "Museums & Historic Landmarks," below) also sponsors guided birding and wildflower walks in season.

WATERSPORTS   Nantucket Community Sailing manages the concession at Jetties Beach (© **508/228-5358**), which offers lessons and rents out kayaks, sailboards, sailboats, and more. **Sea Nantucket,** on tiny Francis Street Beach off Washington Street (© **508/228-7499**), also rents kayaks; it's a quick sprint across the harbor to beautiful Coatue.

MUSEUMS & HISTORIC LANDMARKS

Hadwen House ★★   During Nantucket's most prosperous years, whaling merchant Joseph Starbuck built the "Three Bricks" (nos. 93, 95, and 97 Main St.) for his three sons. His daughter married businessman William Hadwen, owner of the candle factory that is now the Whaling Museum, and Hadwen built this grand Greek Revival home across the street from his brothers-in-law in 1845. Although locals (mostly Quakers) were scandalized by the opulence, the local outrage spurred Hadwen on, and he decided to make the home even grander than he had originally intended. It soon became a showplace for entertaining the Hadwens' many wealthy friends. The home has been furnished with period pieces, while the gardens have been maintained in period style.

96 Main St. (at Pleasant St., a few blocks southwest of the town center). © **508/228-1894.** Admission included in Nantucket Historical Association pass ($12 adults, $8 children; $35 per family). June–Sept daily 10am–5pm; call for off-season hours. Closed mid-Oct to late May.

Jethro Coffin House ★   This 1696 saltbox is the oldest building left on the island. A National Historical Landmark, the brick design on its central chimney has earned it the nickname "The Horseshoe House." It was struck by lightning and severely damaged (in fact, nearly cut in two) in 1987, prompting a long-overdue restoration. It's filled with period furniture such as a trundle bed on wooden wheels.

Sunset Hill Rd., off W. Chester Rd., about a ½ mile (0.8km) northwest of the town center. © **508/228-1894.** Admission included in Nantucket Historical Association pass ($12 adults, $8 children; $35 per family). Mid-June to early Sept daily 10am–5pm; call for off-season hours. Closed mid-Oct to late May.

The Maria Mitchell Association ★★ *Kids*   This is a group of six buildings organized and maintained in honor of distinguished astronomer and Nantucket native Maria Mitchell (1818–89). The science center consists of astronomical observatories, with a lecture series, children's seminars, and stellar observation opportunities (when the sky is clear) from the **Loines Observatory,** 59 Milk St. (© **508/228-8690**), and the **Vestal Street Observatory,** 3 Vestal St. (© **508/228-9273**).

The **Hinchman House Natural Science Museum,** 7 Milk St. (© **508/228-0898**), houses a visitor center and offers lectures, bird-watching, wildflower

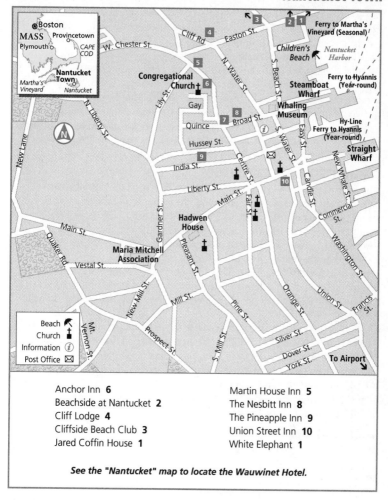

Anchor Inn **6**
Beachside at Nantucket **2**
Cliff Lodge **4**
Cliffside Beach Club **3**
Jared Coffin House **1**

Martin House Inn **5**
The Nesbitt Inn **8**
The Pineapple Inn **9**
Union Street Inn **10**
White Elephant **1**

See the "Nantucket" map to locate the Wauwinet Hotel.

and nature walks, and discovery classes for children and adults. The **Mitchell House,** 1 Vestal St. (© **508/228-2896**), the astronomer's birthplace, features a children's history series and adult-artisan seminars. The **Science Library** is at 2 Vestal St. (© **508/228-9219**), and the tiny, child-oriented **aquarium** is at 28 Washington St. (© **508/228-5387**).

4 Vestal St., at Milk St., about a ½ mile (0.8km) southwest of the town center. © 508/228-9198. www.mmo.org. Museum pass (for birthplace, aquarium, science museum, and Vestal Street Observatory) $7 adults, $5 seniors and children 6–14. Early June to late Aug Tues–Sat 10am–4pm; call for off-season hours.

Nantucket Life-Saving Museum ⚐ *Finds* Housed in a replica of the Nantucket Life-Saving Station, the museum has loads of interesting exhibits, including historic photos and newspaper clippings, as well as one of the last remaining Massachusetts Humane Society surf boats and its horse-drawn carriage.

158 Polpis Rd. © 508/228-1885. Admission $5 adults, $2 children. Mid-June to mid-Oct daily 9:30am–4pm.

Whaling Museum ★★★ (*Kids*) Housed in a former spermaceti (a waxy fluid extracted from sperm whales) candle factory, this museum is a must-visit, if not for the awe-inspiring skeleton of a 43-foot (13m) finback whale, then for the exceptional collections of scrimshaw and nautical art. Check out the action painting *Ship Spermo of Nantucket in a Heavy Thunder-Squall on the Coast of California 1876,* executed by a captain who survived the storm. The price of admission includes daily lectures on the brief and colorful history of the industry, like the beachside "whalebecue" feasts that natives and settlers once enjoyed.

13 Broad St. (in the center of town). ① 508/228-1894. www.nha.org. Admission included in Nantucket Historical Association pass ($12 adults, $8 children; $35 per family). Late May to mid-Oct daily 10am–5pm; call for off-season hours. Closed early Dec to mid-Apr.

ORGANIZED TOURS & CRUISES

The 1926 *Christina* ★★, at Slip 1019, Straight Wharf (① 508/325-4000), is a classic mahogany cat boat. A sail around the harbor is probably the best entertainment bargain on Nantucket ($25 for a 1½-hour trip). The sunset trips ($35) tend to sell out a day or two in advance. No sailings November through April.

Endeavor Sailing Excursions ★★, at Slip 15, Straight Wharf (① 508/228-5585), offers jaunts across the harbor on the *Endeavor,* a 31-foot (9m) replica of an historic Friendship sloop. Skipper James Genthner will gladly drop you off for a bit of sunbathing or beachcombing. Rates are $22.50 to $35 for a 1½-hour sail; reservations are recommended. No sailings November through April.

The Trustees of Reservations, a statewide conservation organization, runs the 3-hour **Coskata–Coatue Wildlife Refuge Natural History Tour** ★★★ (① 508/228-6799). The trip, via Ford Expedition, takes you over sand dunes and through rare habitat out to the Great Point Lighthouse, a replica of the 1818 original. On the way, you might spot snowy egrets, ospreys, and terns. Tours are offered from mid-May to mid-October, daily at 9:30am and 1:30pm. The cost is $30 for adults, $15 for children 15 and under; call to reserve.

SHOPPING ★★★

All of the shops listed below are located right in the center of Nantucket Town.

ANTIQUES & COLLECTIBLES Tonkin of Nantucket ★, 33 Main St. (① 508/228-9697), specializes in English and French antiques. Its offerings include silver, china, ship models, and Majolica.

ART & CRAFTS Exquisite art glass, as well as ceramics, jewelry, and basketry, can be found at **Dane Gallery** ★, 28 Centre St. (① 508/228-7779). The **Artists' Association of Nantucket** ★ has the widest selection of work by locals, and the gallery at 19 Washington St. (① 508/228-0294) is impressive. Open April through January, and by appointment only February and March.

Sailor's Valentine ★, in the Macy Warehouse on lower Main Street (① 508/228-2011), houses a collection of contemporary fine art, folk art, and "outsider art." There are also new versions of the namesake craft, a boxed design of colorful shells, which 19th-century sailors used to bring back from the Caribbean for their sweethearts at home.

FASHION Martha's Vineyard may have spawned "Black Dog" fever, but this island boasts the inimitable "Nantucket reds"—cotton clothing that starts out tomato-red and washes out to salmon-pink. The fashion originated at **Murray's Toggery Shop** ★, 62 Main St. (① 800/368-2134 or 508/228-0437).

WHERE TO STAY

As with Martha's Vineyard, we've given only summer rates here, because Nantucket is so seasonal. However, if you do visit in the off-season, you can find substantial discounts at any of the places that remain open. Note, though, that lodging rates on Nantucket are at high-season levels during the popular Christmas Stroll in December and Daffodil Festival in April.

VERY EXPENSIVE

Cliffside Beach Club ★★★ *(Finds)*   Right on the beach and within walking distance of town, this is surely the premier lodging on the island. It may not be as fancy as some, but there's a sublime beachy-ness to the whole setup, from the simply decorated rooms and the cheerful, youthful staff to the colorful umbrellas lined up on the beach. All bedrooms have such luxuries as French milled soaps, thick towels, and exceptional linens. Lucky guests on the Fourth of July get front-row seats for the fireworks staged at nearby Jetties Beach.

46 Jefferson Ave. (about 1 mile/1.6km from town center), Nantucket, MA 02554. ✆ **800/932-9645** or 508/228-0618. Fax 508/325-4735. www.cliffsidebeach.com. 26 units. Summer $355–$565 double; $695–$1,385 suite; $705 apartment; $895 cottage. Rates include continental breakfast. AE. Closed mid-Oct to late May. **Amenities:** Restaurant (elegant French bistro); exercise facility (Cybex equipment and a trainer); hydrotherapy spa; sauna; concierge; massage room; babysitting. *In room:* A/C, TV/VCR, fridge, coffeemaker, hair dryer.

The Wauwinet ★★★   This ultra-deluxe beachfront retreat is Nantucket's only Relais & Châteaux property. The inn is next to a wildlife sanctuary and is nestled between the Atlantic Ocean and Nantucket Bay. Each lovely room has a unique decor, with pine armoires, plenty of wicker, exquisite Audubon prints, and handsome fabrics. Extras include robes, bottled water, and a personalized set of engraved note cards. If you order up a video from the extensive library, it is delivered on a tray with complimentary popcorn. The staff goes to great lengths to please, ferrying you into town, for instance, in a 1946 "Woody," or dispatching you on a 21-foot (6m) launch across the bay to your own private strip of beach.

120 Wauwinet Rd. (about 8 miles/13km east of Nantucket center), Nantucket, MA 02554. ✆ **800/426-8718** or 508/228-0145. Fax 508/325-0657. www.wauwinet.com. 30 units. Summer $400–$890 double; $750–$1,500 cottage. Rates include full breakfast and afternoon wine and cheese. AE, DC, MC, V. Closed Nov to mid-May. **Amenities:** Restaurant (fine dining); tennis courts with pro shop; boats and bikes for guests' use; concierge; croquet lawn. *In room:* A/C, TV/VCR, CD player, hair dryer, iron.

White Elephant ★★★   This luxury property, right on the harbor, is the ultimate in-town lodging and has been newly renovated by the owners of the Wauwinet (see above). Guest rooms, distributed among one main building and 12 cottages, are large and airy (the most spacious rooms on Nantucket), with country-chic decor. About half have fireplaces, and most have harbor views. The same company owns Breakers, a 25-unit hotel next door that offers a less bustling atmosphere.

50 Easton St. (P.O. Box 1139), Nantucket, MA 02554. ✆ **800/475-2673** or 508/228-2500. Fax 508/638-2327. www.whiteelephanthotel.com. 66 units. Summer $400–$750 double; $350–$1,160 cottage. Rates include full breakfast. AE, DC, DISC, MC, V. Closed Jan–Mar. **Amenities:** Restaurant (lobster/steakhouse); outdoor heated pool; fitness center; concierge; business lounge; room service; laundry and dry-cleaning service; extensive video library. *In room:* A/C, TV, VCR or DVD player, stereo, dataport, hair dryer, safe.

EXPENSIVE

Beachside at Nantucket ★   No ordinary motel, the Beachside has been lavished with Provençal prints and handsome rattan and wicker furniture; the patios and decks overlooking the courtyard have been prettified with French doors and latticework. If you prefer the laissez-faire lifestyle of a motel to the sometimes constricting rituals of a B&B, you might find this the ideal base.

30 N. Beach St. (about ¾ of a mile/1.2km west of the town center), Nantucket, MA 02554. © **800/322-4433** or 508/228-2241. Fax 508/228-8901. www.thebeachside.com. 90 units. Summer $240–$285 double. Rates include continental breakfast. AE, DC, DISC, MC, V. Closed early Dec to late Apr. **Amenities:** Heated outdoor pool. *In room:* A/C, TV, fridge, hair dryer.

Jared Coffin House ⭐⭐ *(Kids* This grand brick manse built in 1845 is the social center of town. Accommodations range from well-priced singles (rare in these parts) to spacious doubles. The central location does have drawbacks: Front rooms can be quite noisy, and 20-minute waits for breakfast are not unusual because locals come here, too. It's the best breakfast in town, though not included in the rates; we suggest calling ahead to get your name put on the list.

29 Broad St. (at Centre St.), Nantucket, MA 02554. © **800/248-2405** or 508/228-2400. Fax 508/228-8549. www.jaredcoffinhouse.com. 60 units. Summer $175–$375 double. AE, DC, DISC, MC, V. Open year-round. **Amenities:** 2 restaurants; concierge. *In room:* TV, dataport, coffeemaker, hair dryer, iron.

The Pineapple Inn ⭐⭐ This beautifully renovated inn has quickly become one of the premier places to stay on the island. The graceful Quaker entrance of the 1838 home leads to spacious bedrooms decorated with fine reproductions and antiques, Oriental rugs, marble bathrooms, and many four-poster canopy beds. Breakfast features baked goods, cappuccino, and freshly squeezed orange juice. The garden patio with climbing roses is a fine place to enjoy an afternoon cocktail and contemplate dinner plans.

10 Hussey St. (in the center of town), Nantucket, MA 02554. © **508/228-9992.** Fax 508/325-6051. www.pineappleinn.com. 12 units. Summer $175–$325 double. Rates include continental breakfast. AE, MC, V. Closed early Dec to mid-Apr. Children 8 and over welcome. *In room:* A/C, TV, dataport, hair dryer, iron.

Union Street Inn ⭐⭐ *(Finds* Innkeepers Deborah and Ken Withrow have a terrific location for their 1770s property, just steps from Main Street yet in a quiet, residential section. Ken's experience in big hotels shows in the full concierge service offered here. Many guest rooms have canopied or four-poster beds; half have fireplaces. All are outfitted with antique furniture and fixtures. Unlike many Nantucket inns whose zoning laws forbid them to serve a full breakfast, this inn's location allows a superb complete breakfast on the garden patio. In the afternoon, there are usually home-baked goodies to sample as well.

7 Union St. (in the center of town), Nantucket, MA 02554. © **800/225-5116** or 508/228-9222. Fax 508/325-0848. www.unioninn.com. 12 units. Summer $160–$295 double; $395 suite. Rates include full breakfast. AE, MC, V. Closed Jan–Mar. **Amenities:** Concierge. *In room:* A/C, TV, hair dryer.

MODERATE

Anchor Inn ⭐ *(Value* This historic gem, an 1806 captain's home, is located next to the Old North Church. Authentic details can be found throughout the house, in the antique hardware and paneling, wide-board floors, and period furnishings. In the morning, guests enjoy home-baked muffins at individual tables on the enclosed porch.

66 Centre St./P.O. Box 387 (in the center of town), Nantucket, MA 02554. © **508/228-0072.** www. anchor-inn.net. 11 units. Summer $165–$215. Rates include continental breakfast. AE, MC, V. Closed Jan–Feb. *In room:* A/C (in season), TV, hair dryer.

Cliff Lodge ⭐⭐ *(Finds* Debby and John Bennett have freshened up this charming 1771 captain's house with their own countrified style. The cheerful interiors feature colorful quilts and splatter-painted floors. Rooms range from a first-floor beauty with king-size bed, paneled walls, and fireplace to the tiny third-floor rooms tucked under the eaves. The spacious apartment in the rear of the house is a sunny delight. The continental breakfast, of home-baked breads and muffins on the garden patio, is congenial. Chat with Debby for a wealth of island info, and then climb up to the roof walk for a bird's-eye view of the town and harbor.

9 Cliff Rd. (a few blocks from the center of town), Nantucket, MA 02554. ✆ **508/228-9480.** Fax 508/228-6308. www.nantucket.net/lodging/clifflodge. 12 units. Summer $115 single; $165–$225 double; $425 apartment. Rates include continental breakfast. MC, V. Open year-round. Children 12 and over welcome. *In room:* A/C, TV.

Martin House Inn ★★ *Value*   This is one of the lower-priced B&Bs in town, but also one of the most stylish, with a formal parlor and spacious side porch, complete with hammock. Charming innkeeper Debbie Wasil, who also owns the nearby Centerboard B&B, keeps this 1803 mariner's home in shipshape condition. The garret single rooms with shared bathroom are a bargain. Higher-priced rooms have four-posters and working fireplaces. Breakfasts include Martin's famous granola, as well as home-baked breads, muffins, and fresh fruits.

61 Centre St. (between Broad and Chester sts., a couple blocks from town center), Nantucket, MA 02554. ✆ **508/228-0678.** Fax 508/325-4798. www.nantucket.net/lodging/martinn. 13 units, 4 with shared bathroom. Summer $75–$85 single; $125–$295 double. Rates include continental breakfast. MC, V. Open year-round. *In room:* No phone.

INEXPENSIVE

The Nesbitt Inn *Value*   This Victorian-style inn has been run by the same family for 95 years. It's quite old-fashioned, and a bargain for Nantucket. All rooms have sinks and share bathrooms. There's a friendly atmosphere to the place, and beloved innkeepers Dolly and Nobby Noblit are salt-of-the-earth Nantucketers who will cheerfully fill you in on island lore.

21 Broad St. (in the center of town), P.O. Box 1019, Nantucket, MA 02554. ✆ **508/228-0156** or 508/228-2446. 13 units (all with shared bathroom), 2 apartments. Summer $75 single; $85–$125 double; $1,200 per week for apartment. Rates include continental breakfast. MC, V. Closed mid-Dec to Mar. *In room:* No phone.

WHERE TO DINE
VERY EXPENSIVE

Chanticleer Inn ★★ FRENCH   A contender for the priciest restaurant on the Cape and Islands, this rose-covered cottage-turned-auberge has fans who insist they'd have to cross an ocean to savor the likes of this classic French cuisine. A few glamorous options on the fixed-price menu include a frogs' legs "cake" in a potato crust, a gingered monkfish scaloppini with a lemon-rum sauce and sweet garlic fritters, and a very classy bread pudding with white-chocolate ice cream and apricot sauce. The stellar wine cellar is stocked with 38,000 bottles. Unfortunately, this kind of luxury comes with beaucoup d'attitude, so whether you're royalty or hoi polloi, prepare to be snubbed.

9 New St., Siasconset. ✆ **508/257-6231** or 508/257-9756. Reservations recommended. Jackets required for men. Main courses $42–$45; fixed-price dinner $70. AE, DC, MC, V. Mid-May to mid-Oct Wed–Sun noon–2:30pm and 6:30–9:30pm. Closed mid-Oct to mid-May.

Club Car ★★★ CONTINENTAL   For decades one of the top restaurants on Nantucket, this posh venue is popular with locals. Executive chef Michael Shannon is chummy with Julia Child, and the menu has classic French influences. Interesting offerings include roast rack of lamb Club Car, with fresh herbs, honey-mustard glaze, and minted Madeira sauce. Some nights, seven-course tasting menus are available for $65. The lounge area is within an antique car from the old Nantucket railroad; you'll want to have a pre- or post-dinner drink while cuddled in the red-leather banquettes. Lunch at the Club Car is a great deal for those on a budget.

1 Main St. ℭ **508/228-1101.** Reservations recommended. Main courses $32–$38. MC, V. July–Aug daily 11am–3pm and 6–10pm; call for off-season hours. Closed Jan–Apr.

The Pearl 🐾🐾 NEW AMERICAN   It's Miami Beach on Nantucket at this swank establishment with numerous stylish touches: appetizers and desserts served in martini glasses; a contemporary look with bluish lighting and large fish tanks; and an extensive champagne list. Skip the *grande deluxe plateau de mer;* it's not a lot of shellfish for a lot of money. But do choose the wild mushroom galette with white truffle cream. As a main course, look no further than the pan-roasted striped bass with citrus tomato infusion.

12 Federal St. ℭ **508/228-9701.** Reservations recommended. Main courses $34–$40. AE, MC, V. Late June to early Sept daily 6:30–9:30pm; call for off-season hours. Closed Jan–Mar.

Straight Wharf 🐾🐾 NEW AMERICAN   Straight Wharf, on the waterfront in the center of town, has long been known for its creative cuisine. Choices may include fancy appetizers like seared beef carpaccio with white truffle oil, or main courses such as native lobster "a la nage," which is prepared with a champagne sauce. Devoted regulars, of whom there are many, swear by the smoked bluefish paté served with herb focaccia. A more affordable "summer grill" menu, served in the bar area, features simpler fare. Make your reservation for 8pm on the deck so you can watch the sun set over the harbor.

Straight Wharf. ℭ **508/228-4499.** Reservations recommended. Main courses $31–$38; "summer grill" menu $16–$22. AE, MC, V. July–Aug Tues–Sun 6–10pm; call for off-season hours. Closed late Sept to May.

The Summer House 🐾🐾 *Finds* NEW AMERICAN   The classic 'Sconset-style atmosphere distinguishes this fine-dining experience from others on the island: wicker and wrought iron, roses and honeysuckle. A pianist plays nightly—often Gershwin standards—and the pounding Atlantic is just over the bluff. Distinctive main courses include unusual lobster cutlets with coconut-jasmine risotto timbale and mint-tomato relish. If it's in season, end your meal with the blueberry pie.

17 Ocean Ave., Siasconset. ℭ **508/257-9976.** Reservations recommended. Main courses $30–$42. AE, MC, V. July–Aug daily 6–10pm; mid-May to June and Sept to mid-Oct Wed–Sun 6–10pm. Closed mid-Oct to Apr.

EXPENSIVE

American Seasons 🐾🐾 REGIONAL AMERICAN   This romantic little restaurant has a great theme: Choose your region (New England, Pacific Coast, Wild West, or Down South) and select creative offerings. Start, for instance, with Louisiana crawfish risotto with fire-roasted onion and fried parsnips in a sweet-corn purée; then move on to the Pacific Coast's aged beef sirloin with caramelized shallot and Yukon potato hash.

80 Centre St. (2 blocks from the center of town). ℭ **508/228-7111.** Reservations recommended. Main courses $23–$28. AE, MC, V. Apr–Nov daily 6–9pm. Closed early Dec to mid-Apr.

Boarding House 🐾🐾 NEW AMERICAN   This centrally located fine-dining restaurant doubles as one of the most popular bars in town. You can head for the romantic dining room or the hopping upstairs bar, but on clear summer nights, you'll want to try for a table out on the patio. The menu has definite Asian and Mediterranean influences in choices like seared yellowfin tuna with sesame sushi rice cake and wasabi aioli. The award-winning wine list has a range of prices.

12 Federal St. © **508/228-9622**. Reservations recommended. Main courses $26–$36. AE, MC, V. July–Aug daily 6–10pm; call for off-season hours. Open year-round.

Company of the Cauldron ★★★ CONTINENTAL This intimate,
candlelit dining room features a classical harpist several nights a week in season. There is one distinct fixed-price meal each night, so check the menu out front or call ahead to see which night to go. Dietary preferences can be accommodated with advance notice. Don't miss the soft-shell crab appetizer, offered in season. The main course could be seafood, such as a special swordfish preparation, or a meat dish, like rack of lamb or beef Wellington.

5 India St. (between Federal and Centre sts.). © **508/228-4016**. Reservations required. Fixed-price $48–$50. MC, V. Early July to early Sept Tues–Sun seatings at 6:45 and 8:45pm; call for off-season hours. Closed late Oct to mid-May, except Thanksgiving weekend and the 1st 2 weeks of Dec.

DeMarco ★★ NORTHERN ITALIAN Come to this frame house, carved
into a cafe/bar and loft, for the best Italian food on the island. A forward-thinking menu and attentive service ensure a superior meal, which might include *antipasto di salmone* (house-smoked salmon rollantini, lemon-herb cream cheese, cucumber-and-endive salad with chive vinaigrette) and delicate capellini with rock shrimp, tomato, olives, capers, and hot pepper.

9 India St. (between Federal and Centre sts.). © **508/228-1836**. Reservations recommended. Main courses $18–$32. AE, MC, V. Mid-June to Sept daily 6–10pm; call for off-season hours. Closed mid-Oct to mid-May.

Òran Mór ★★★ *Finds* INTERNATIONAL Chef Peter Wallace runs this
second-floor waterfront venue, which has quickly become the premier restaurant on the island. The unusual name is Gaelic and means "great song"; it's the name of Wallace's favorite single-malt Scotch. Menu standouts are the lobster risotto appetizer and the grilled buffalo tenderloin entree. There are always local seafood specials. Some say the grilled breast of duck with savory tapioca and local nectar jus is the best duck dish on the island. Sundays off-season feature a scrumptious brunch.

2 S. Beach St. (in the center of town). © **508/228-8655**. Reservations recommended. Main courses $22–$34. AE, MC, V. July–Aug Thurs–Tues 6–10pm; Sept–June Thurs–Sat and Mon–Tues 6–9pm, Sun noon–9pm. Open year-round.

Ropewalk ★ SEAFOOD This open-air restaurant on the harbor is Nan-
tucket's only outdoor raw bar, and it's where the yachting crowd hangs out after a day on the boat. While the food is a bit overpriced, the location is prime. This is a good place to enjoy a light meal or appetizers, such as fried calamari, crab cakes, or fried oysters. The dinner menu includes grilled swordfish with rata-touille and grilled breast of chicken with roasted garlic and rosemary jus.

1 Straight Wharf. © **508/228-8886**. Reservations not accepted. Main courses $23–$33. MC, V. Apr to mid-Dec daily 11:30am–10pm (raw bar daily 3–10pm). Closed mid-Oct to Apr.

21 Federal ★★★ NEW AMERICAN Agreeable host Chick Walsh has
created an institution popular with locals, particularly for the happening bar scene. With many *Wine Spectator* awards to its credit, 21 Federal features about 11 wines available by the glass each night. Meanwhile, chef Russell Jaehnig seems to get better and more refined every year. For melt-in-your-mouth pleasure, start with the tuna tartare with wasabi crackers and cilantro aioli. The fish entrees are most popular here, although you might opt for the fine breast of duck accompanied by pecan wild rice and shiitake mushrooms. We love the pan-crisped salmon with champagne cabbage and beet-butter sauce, which has been a staple on the menu for years.

21 Federal St. (in the center of town). © **508/228-2121.** Reservations recommended. Main courses $27–$37. AE, MC, V. Apr to mid-Dec daily 6–10pm. Closed mid-Dec to Mar.

MODERATE

Black Eyed Susan's ★★ ETHNIC/ECLECTIC   This is supremely exciting food in a funky bistro atmosphere. Reservations are accepted for the 6pm seating only, and these go fast. Others must line up outside—the line starts forming around 5:30pm. The menu is in constant flux, as the chef's mood and influences change every 3 weeks. We always enjoy the spicy Thai fish cake and the tandoori chicken with green mango chutney. There's usually a Southwestern touch like the Dos Equis beer-battered catfish quesadilla with mango slaw and jalapeños; mop up the sauce with the delectable organic sourdough bread. There's no liquor license, but you can BYOB.

10 India St. (in the center of town). © **508/325-0308.** Reservations accepted for 6pm seating only. Main courses $15–$25. No credit cards. Apr–Oct daily 7am–1pm, Mon–Sat 6–10pm; call for off-season hours. Closed Nov–Mar.

Bluefin ★★ *(finds)* ASIAN/INTERNATIONAL   This new restaurant, an intimate spot a short walk from the center of town, offers great prices and tasty food, including sushi and tapas. The crispy crab rangoons come with the perfect hot-and-sour sauce. Lobster ravioli served with sweet basil crème is the ultimate in wretched excess. Keep in mind the bar scene here, too—if you're sitting near the bar area, it can get loud.

15 S. Beach St. © **508/228-2033.** Reservations recommended. Main courses $9–$16. AE, MC, V. June–Aug daily 5:30–10pm; call for off-season hours. Open year-round.

Le Languedoc Cafe ★★ FRENCH/NEW AMERICAN   Nantucket's most authentic French cafe offers a cozy atmosphere and reasonable prices. An expensive dining room is upstairs, but locals prefer the casual bistro downstairs and out on the terrace. There's a clubby feel here as diners come and go, greeting each other and enjoying themselves. Soups are superb, as are the Angus-steak burgers. More elaborate dishes include roasted tenderloin of pork stuffed with figs and pancetta and lobster with polenta (outrageous!).

24 Broad St. © **508/228-2552.** Reservations not accepted for cafe; reservations recommended for main dining room. Main courses $9–$19. AE, MC, V. June–Sept Tues–Sun noon–2pm, daily 6–10pm; call for off-season hours. Closed mid-Dec to Apr.

MODERATE

The Brotherhood of Thieves ★ PUB   This classic whaling bar housed in the basement of an early-19th-century brick building is a Nantucket institution. The specialty drink list is longer than the food menu and includes such playful concoctions as the "Dirty Girl Scout." In July and August, tourists line up to chow on burgers and hand-cut curly fries. Come fall and winter, locals enjoy the decently priced dinner offerings (chicken teriyaki, fried Cajun shrimp) while sitting beside the cozy hearth.

23 Broad St. (in the center of town). No phone. Main courses $9–$18. No credit cards. Mid-May to mid-Oct Sun–Thurs 11:30am–midnight, Fri–Sat 11:30am–12:30am; mid-Oct to mid-May Sun–Thurs 11:30am–10:30pm, Fri–Sat 11:30am–11:30pm. Closed Feb.

Fog Island Cafe ★★ NEW AMERICAN   You'll be wowed by the creative breakfasts and lunches at this sassy cafe. Homemade soups and salads are healthy and yummy. The dinner menu, served late June through August only, features fresh seafood, pastas, and a vegetarian alternative.

7 S. Water St. ☏ **508/228-1818.** Reservations recommended for dinner. Dinner main courses $10–$20. MC, V. Late June–Aug Mon–Sat 7am–2pm and 5–10pm, Sun 7am–1pm and 5–10pm; call for off-season hours. Open year-round.

TAKEOUT & PICNIC FARE

A terrific value on pricey Nantucket, **Something Natural,** 50 Cliff Rd. (☏ **508/ 228-0504**), turns out gigantic sandwiches. Save room for the addictive chocolate chip cookies. Stock up for a day at the beach, or eat your lunch right at the picnic tables on the grounds.

You can get fresh-picked produce right in town from **Bartlett's Ocean View Farm** ⚓, 33 Bartlett Farm Rd. (☏ **508/228-9403**). The truck is parked on Main Street in season.

Juice Guys, 4 Easy St. (☏ **508/228-4464**), is the spot to get your Nantucket Nectars fix. High-tech blenders mix potent combinations of fresh juice with vitamins, sorbet, yogurt, and holistic enhancers. Closed from late December to April.

The **Juice Bar** ⚓⚓, 12 Broad St. (☏ **508/228-5799**), is a humble hole-in-the-wall that scoops up some of the best homemade ice cream and frozen yogurt around, complemented by superb homemade hot fudge. Closed from mid-October to mid-April.

NANTUCKET AFTER DARK

Acoustic performers from all over the country hold forth in the **Brotherhood of Thieves,** 23 Broad St., in the center of Nantucket Town (no phone), an atmospheric pub where you'll find live folk music just about every night in season; no cover. Closed in February. The **Chicken Box,** 12 Dave St. (☏ **508/228-9717**), is the rocking spot for the 20-something crowd. It sometimes seems like the entire population of the island is shoving their way in here. Jimmy Buffett shows up late at night about once a summer, unannounced, and jams with the band. The cover varies. The **Rose and Crown,** 23 S. Water St. (☏ **508/228-2595**), draws all ages with its live, loud music for dancing. Closed January through March. The **Hearth Pub and Patio,** at the Harbor House, 23 S. Water St. (☏ **508/228-1500**), is a handsome venue with elegant appointments. There's live music most nights in season from 5pm to midnight; no cover.

The **Nantucket Arts Alliance** (☏ **800/228-8118** or 508/228-8118) operates Box Office Nantucket, offering tickets for all sorts of cultural events around town. It operates out of the Macy Warehouse on Straight Wharf, in season daily from 10am to 4pm.

Theater buffs will want to spend an evening at the **Actors' Theatre of Nantucket,** Methodist Church, 2 Centre St. (☏ **508/228-6325**). This shoe-box theater assays thought-provoking plays as readily as summery farces. The season runs from mid-May to mid-September. Tickets are $15. You can catch the children's productions ($10) from mid-July to mid-August.

8

Central & Western Massachusetts

by Herbert Bailey Livesey

While Boston and its maritime appendages of Cape Ann and Cape Cod face the sea and embrace it, inland Massachusetts turns in upon itself. Countless ponds and lakes shimmer in its folds and hollows, often hidden by deep forests and granite outcroppings. Farming and industry grew along the north-south valleys of the Connecticut and Housatonic rivers.

The heartland Pioneer Valley, bordering the Connecticut River, earned its name in the early 18th century, when European trappers and farmers first began to push west from the colonies clinging to the edges of Massachusetts Bay. They were followed by ambitious capitalists who erected red-brick mills along the river for the manufacture of textiles and paper. Most of those enterprises failed or faded in the post–World War II movement to the milder climate and cheaper labor of the South, leaving a miasma of economic hardship that has yet to be remedied. But those industrialists also helped fund several distinguished colleges for which the valley is now known; their educated populations provide much energy and a rich cultural life.

Roughly the same pattern applied in the Berkshires, the twin ranges of rumpled hills that define the western band of the state. There is only one college of note here, however, and the development of this region in the 19th century was prompted mainly by the construction of the railroad from New York and Boston. Artistic and literary folk made a favored summer retreat of it, followed by wealthy urbanites attracted by the region's reputation for creativity and Bohemianism. Many of their extravagant mansions, dubbed "Berkshire Cottages," still survive, and to this day the region attracts the town-and-country crowd, who support a vibrant summer schedule of the arts, then steal away as the crimson leaves fall and the Berkshires grow quiet beneath six months of snow.

1 Sturbridge & Old Sturbridge Village

18 miles (29km) SW of Worcester; 32 miles (52km) E of Springfield

First things first: Sturbridge and Old Sturbridge Village aren't a single entity. The former is an organic community, populated by working people with real lives. But why are there so many motels and restaurants in a town of fewer than 8,000 residents? That's because of the latter, a fabricated early-19th-century village comprised of authentic buildings moved here from other locations and peopled by docents pretending to follow the pursuits of 170 years past. It is deservedly popular, one of the two most prominent tourist destinations in central Massachusetts.

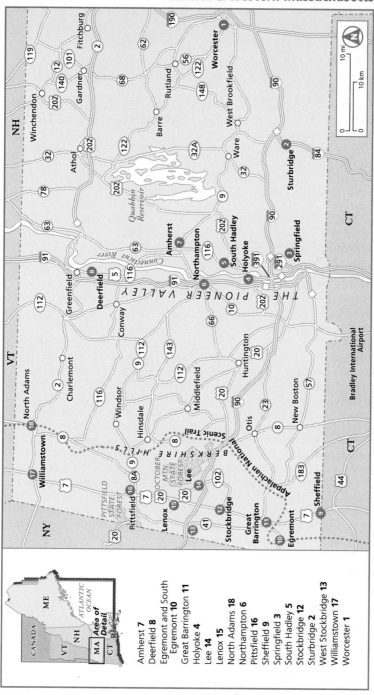

Amherst 7
Deerfield 8
Egremont and South
  Egremont 10
Great Barrington 11
Holyoke 4
Lee 14
Lenox 15
North Adams 18
Northampton 6
Pittsfield 16
Sheffield 9
Springfield 3
South Hadley 5
Stockbridge 12
Sturbridge 2
West Stockbridge 13
Williamstown 17
Worcester 1

ESSENTIALS

GETTING THERE   Take the east-west Massachusetts Turnpike (I-90) to Exit 9, or take I-84 to Exit 3B.

VISITOR INFORMATION   The **Sturbridge Area Visitors Center,** 380 Main St. (✆ **508/347-2761**), is open Monday through Friday during regular business hours.

SPECIAL EVENTS   Highly popular annual occasions are the **Brimfield Antique and Collectible Shows** ✪ (✆ **800/628-8379** or 508/347-2761; www.brimfieldshow.com), when over 6,000 dealers gather along a mile-long strip for up to 6 days (Tues–Sun) in mid-May, mid-July, and early September. Brimfield is an otherwise sleepy village adjoining Sturbridge on the west. Because it has few hotels, most of the dealers and seekers stay in Sturbridge, so you'll need to reserve your room at least 6 months in advance during show periods.

Thanksgiving and Christmas weeks at Old Sturbridge Village bring traditional New England dinners, concerts, and candlelit nights. Call ✆ **800/ 733-1830** or 508/347-3362 for details.

EXPLORING A 19TH-CENTURY VILLAGE

There is only one sight of significance in this otherwise pleasantly unremarkable town. Expect crowds on holiday weekends in summer and during the October foliage season.

Old Sturbridge Village ✪✪✪ *(Kids*   Only one of the more than 40 restored structures in the complex stands on its original site—the Oliver Wight House, now part of the Old Sturbridge Village Lodges (see below). The rest were transported here from as far away as Maine. All are authentic buildings, not re-creations, and they represent the living quarters and places of trade and commerce of a rural settlement of the 1830s. Among these are a Quaker meeting-house, sawmill, bank, country store, blacksmith shop, school, cooperage, and printing office. At the edges of the village are a working farm and herb garden.

Costumed docents demonstrate hearth cooking, sheep shearing, heirloom gardening, maple sugaring, musketry, carpentry, and more. "Residents" include children who roll hoops and play games true to the period. At the children's museum, kids 3 to 7 can dress up in costumes and use their imaginations in a pretend farm kitchen and one-room school. Special events mark such dates as the Fourth of July, Thanksgiving, and the Christmas season. Weddings, militia drills, and a harvest fair are staged. The 20-minute boat ride on the adjacent Quinebaug River is popular with younger visitors.

1 Old Sturbridge Rd. ✆ **800/733-1830** or 508/347-3362. Fax 508/347-0375. www.osv.org. Admission (2-day pass) $20 adults, $18 seniors, $10 children 6–15. Summer daily 10am–6pm; somewhat shorter hours the rest of the year, but schedule varies, so call ahead. Closed Dec 25. Take Exit 3B off I-84 or Exit 9 off I-90, drive west on Rte. 20, and bear right into the turnaround just before the entrance to the village.

WHERE TO STAY

If the choices below are full, try the **EconoLodge,** 262 Main St. (✆ **508/347-2324**), the **Colonial Quality Inn,** on Route 20 (✆ **508/347-3306**), or the **Sturbridge Coach Motor Lodge,** 408 Main St. (✆ **508/347-7327**). The first two are located near Exit 9 off I-84, the third near the entrance to Old Sturbridge Village.

Old Sturbridge Village Lodges   Apart from the centerpiece Oliver Wight House, which is more than 200 years old, these six barnlike structures arranged around a common green and pool are of post–World War II origin. Rooms are fresh, spacious, and straightforward, outfitted with colonial reproductions.

Rte. 20 E., Sturbridge, MA 01566. ℂ **508/347-3327**. Fax 508/347-3018. www.osv.org. 59 units. May–Oct $85–$130 double; Nov–Apr $80–$95 double. Extra person $5. AE, DISC, MC, V. **Amenities:** Heated outdoor pool; access to nearby health club. *In room:* A/C, TV, coffeemaker.

Publick House ☆ This complex is the high-profile lodging in the Sturbridge area. The main structure is a tavern built in 1771. Rooms are rustic, some with canopy beds, rag rugs, and colonial reproductions. A 1786 Federal-style farmhouse called the Colonel Ebenezer Crafts Inn, a mile (1.6km) from the hotel, has its own pool.

Rte. 131 (P.O. Box 187), Sturbridge, MA 01566. ℂ **800/782-5425** or 508/347-3313. Fax 508/347-5073. www.publickhouse.com. 126 units. $75–$160 double. AE, DC, DISC, MC, V. From Exit 3B off I-84, drive 1½ miles (2.4km) south of Rte. 20 on Rte. 131. Pets accepted in some rooms of Country Motor Lodge ($5 per night). **Amenities:** 2 restaurants (American), bar; 2 heated outdoor pools; tennis courts; access to nearby health club; dry cleaning. *In room:* A/C, TV, hair dryer.

WHERE TO DINE

In addition to the establishments listed below, you might sample either of the two restaurants associated with the **Publick House** (see above).

Rom's ☆ ITALIAN/AMERICAN This was once a hot dog and fried-clam roadside stand that has grown over nearly 50 years like a multigenerational New England farmhouse. Today, it seats 750 diners and remains a near-ideal family restaurant, with something to please everyone, from homemade pastas and pizzas to full seafood dinners. The lobster roll is twice the size but about the same price as those offered on the coast. Buffets at Wednesday dinner and Thursday lunch are crowd pleasers. A takeout window ladles "buckets of rigatoni" and fish-and-chips.

Rte. 131, 2 miles (3.2km) south of Rte. 20. ℂ **800/ROM-1952** or 508/347-3349. Main courses $8.95–$16.95. AE, DISC, DC, MC, V. Daily 11:30am–9pm.

The Whistling Swan ☆ CONTINENTAL/AMERICAN This 1855 Greek Revival mansion houses two restaurants that share a kitchen. On the main floor is the Cygnet Room, with wall sconces, Sheraton-style chairs, and dishes such as escargot and clams fra diavolo. The execution is safe and careful, and the service efficient if sometimes unsophisticated. Upstairs, the Ugly Duckling Loft packs tables together under the rough-cut board roof. Patrons strive to be heard over the live piano—it's loud, even boisterous. The food is simple and hearty, from fish-and-chips to meatloaf. Which venue to choose? We'd mount the stairs, in a New York minute.

502 Main St. (Rte. 20). ℂ **508/347-2321**. Reservations suggested on weekends. Main courses $16.95–$28.95 Cygnet Room; $6.95–$26.95 Ugly Duckling. AE, DC, MC, V. Cygnet Room Mon–Fri 11:30am–2:30pm and 5:30–9:30pm; Sat 11:30am–2:30pm and 5:30–10pm; Sun noon–8pm. Ugly Duckling Tues–Thurs 11:30am–11pm; Fri–Sat 11:30am–11:30pm.

2 Springfield

89 miles (143km) W of Boston; 32 miles (52km) N of Hartford

Times have been tough in this once-prosperous manufacturing city on the east bank of the Connecticut River. But its loyal citizens haven't given in to the consequences of job flight and high unemployment, and there is evidence of redevelopment throughout downtown, with recycled loft and factory buildings standing beside modern glass towers. Springfield remains the most important city in western Massachusetts and has enjoyed some success in attracting new enterprises. Vacationers can pass a few hours here, but Springfield is primarily a stop on the way north or south.

ESSENTIALS

GETTING THERE Springfield is located near the juncture of the east-west Massachusetts Turnpike (I-90) and north-south I-91.

Bradley International (© **203/627-3000**), in Windsor Locks, Conn., is the nearest major airport, about 20 miles (32km) to the south. Rent a car here from any of the major companies or catch a bus, cab, or limo into Springfield. Major airlines serving Bradley include **American** (© **800/433-7300**), **Continental** (© **800/525-0280**), **Delta** (© **800/221-1212**), **Northwest** (© **800/225-2525**), **United** (© **800/241-6522**), and **US Airways** (© **800/247-8786**).

Amtrak (© **800/USA-RAIL;** www.northeast.amtrak.com) trains stop daily both ways in Springfield on routes between Boston and Chicago; Boston and Washington, D.C.; and New York and St. Albans, Vt. (where there are connecting buses from Montréal), with intermediate stops in Philadelphia, New York, and Hartford, among others.

VISITOR INFORMATION The new **Riverfront Visitor Information Center** of the Greater Springfield Convention and Visitors Bureau (© **413/787-1548;** www.valleyvisitor.com) is at 1200 West Columbus Ave., next to the Basketball Hall of Fame.

SPECIAL EVENTS The mid-September **Eastern States Exposition** (© **413/737-2443**) is a huge old-fashioned agricultural fair with games, rides, a midway, and entertainment. It's held on a fairground on the opposite side of the Connecticut River in West Springfield. Also on the grounds is the **Old Storrowtown Village,** a collection of restored colonial buildings, accessible by guided tour Monday through Saturday from June to Labor Day, and by appointment the rest of the year.

MUSEUMS & HISTORIC SITES

Basketball Hall of Fame ★★ Dr. James Naismith invented basketball in Springfield in 1891, providing the logic for this center. A must for fans, it is painless even for those who regard the game as a blur of 7-foot armpits. Take the elevator to the third floor and work your way down. Up here are the displays recalling the history of the game—remember the Waterloo Hawks? On the ground floor are a shooting court and virtual-reality display, in which visitors can insert themselves on a large screen and play against the pros. A new facility (on the other side of the parking lot) may be open by the time you get here.

1150 W. Columbus Ave. (at Union St.). © 413/781-6500. Fax 413/781-1939. www.hoophall.com. Admission $10 adults, $6 seniors and children 7–15. Daily 10am–5pm. Closed Thanksgiving, Dec 25, New Year's Day.

Springfield Museums at the Quadrangle ★ *Kids* Four museums and a library surrounding a quadrangle constitute this worthwhile resource. Enter the library from State Street and walk through to the back. On the right is the first museum; the others around the quad make a counterclockwise circuit. Before setting out, note the somewhat limited hours below.

The **George Walter Vincent Smith Art Museum** is housed in an 1896 Italian Renaissance–style mansion. Upstairs are largely sentimental pastoral scenes, with a few small landscapes by George Inness, Thomas Cole, and Albert Bierstadt. On the main floor are cases of Japanese samurai weaponry surrounding a carved 1805 Shinto shrine.

⌐Fun Fact *And to Think That I Saw It on Mulberry Street*

Interest in the man who called himself Dr. Seuss spiked with the recent opening of a new Broadway show, *Seussical,* and the hit movie *The Grinch.* The grandparents of Theodor Seuss Geisel lived on Springfield's Mulberry Street, and in 1937, the writer and illustrator named the first of his dozens of children's books for the neighborhood. He followed up with such classics as *The Cat in the Hat* and *How the Grinch Stole Christmas.* Over 100 million copies of his books have been sold, and every title is still in print.

Geisel spent most of his adult life in California, the result of a nearly 2-decade career in documentary films, during which he won two Academy Awards. But much of his inspiration for the children's books to which he returned can be traced to Springfield. His drawing of Bartholomew Cubbins's castle bears a strong resemblance to the Howard Street Armory, now a community center, and certain of his landscapes look as if they were recalled from his playtimes in Forest Park, near his boyhood home at 74 Fairfield St.

Alas, Mulberry Street is no longer the august avenue it once must have been, its Victorian manses now crowded by undistinguished apartment blocks and commercial strips—and the former Central High School from which Geisel graduated is now a condominium.

Kids will enjoy the **Science Museum,** which contains a planetarium (showtime at 2:45pm), dioramas of African animals, and the Monsanto Eco-Center.

Enter the **Connecticut Valley Historical Museum** through a gateway that is a representation of the headgear worn by Dr. Seuss's famous Cat in the Hat. (The children's author grew up in Springfield.) There are examples of weapons made by the city's firearms manufacturers, including a blunderbuss and an unusual 1838 rifle with a revolving cartridge chamber.

The strongest of the lot is the **Museum of Fine Arts** 🖈, with examples of colonial paintings through Gilbert Stuart and John Copley to early-20th-century realists George Bellows and Reginald Marsh, culminating with magic realists and Abstract Expressionists—Frank Stella, Helen Frankenthaler, Don Eddy, and George Sugarman. Make a particular effort to view the remarkable serigraph of lower Manhattan by Richard Estes.

220 State St. (at Chestnut St.). ℂ **413/263-6800.** www.quadrangle.org. Combined admission for all 4 museums $6 adults, $3 seniors and college students, $2 children 6–18; $1 extra for the planetarium. Wed–Fri noon–5pm (also Tues in July–Aug).

WHERE TO STAY

Sheraton Springfield 🖈🖈   Just off the Springfield Center exit of I-91, this can be a treat after a few nights in idiosyncratic New England B&Bs. Predictable, yes, but curl up in a room with all these conveniences, and lack of charm can suddenly seem unimportant—especially when it's combined with room service and a capable restaurant. Executive-level rooms are sometimes cheaper than standard units, so be sure to inquire.

1 Monarch Place, Springfield, MA 01114. ℂ **800/426-9004** or 413/781-1010. Fax 413/734-3249. info@sheratonspringfield.com. 310 units. $101–$189 double. AE, DC, DISC, MC, V. **Amenities:** Restaurant (Continental), bar; heated indoor pool; health club; Jacuzzi; sauna; business center; shopping arcade; limited room service; same-day dry cleaning. *In room:* A/C, TV w/ pay movies, dataport, coffeemaker, hair dryer, iron.

Springfield Marriott ★★   Directly across the street from the Sheraton (see above), this representative of the widespread chain shares, even duplicates, most of its rival's attributes. One of its perks is poolside food service.

1500 Main St., Springfield, MA 01105. ℂ 800/228-9290 or 413/781-7111. Fax 413/731-8932. www. marriotthotels.com. 264 units. $160–$190 double. AE, DC, DISC, MC, V. **Amenities:** Restaurant (Continental), 2 bars; heated indoor pool; health club; Jacuzzi; sauna; business center; limited room service; same-day dry cleaning. *In room:* A/C, TV w/ pay movies, dataport, coffeemaker, hair dryer, iron.

WHERE TO DINE

Pioneer Valley Brew Pub ECLECTIC AMERICAN   This "Deco diner" is a welcome exception to the largely forlorn dining scene. The ales and lagers on tap will wash down such tasty dishes as grilled pork loin with apple-raisin chutney. Subtlety isn't a strong suit, not with flavors and portions this big.

5159 Taylor St. (near Dwight St.). ℂ 413/732-2739. Main courses $11.95–$17.95. AE, DISC, MC, V. Tues–Fri 11:30am–9pm; Sat 5–10pm.

Student Prince and the Fort GERMAN/AMERICAN   In 1935, German immigrants opened the Student Prince and began serving schnitzels and sauerbraten. That might not have seemed the precise historical moment to ensure the success of such an enterprise, but it thrived. In 1946, the Fort dining room was added next door. The result is the most popular place in town. Monster portions are the rule, with veal shanks as thick as a linebacker's forearm.

8 Fort St. (west of Main St.). ℂ 413/734-7475. Main courses $9.75–$23.75. AE, DC, DISC, MC, V. Daily noon–10pm.

SPRINGFIELD AFTER DARK

Symphony Hall, at Court Street and East Columbus Avenue (ℂ **413/ 788-7033;** tickets@citystage.symphonyhall.com), is the venue for concerts by the Springfield Symphony Orchestra, touring performers and musicals, and productions meant for children.

A strip of beer-and-pool joints, music bars, and hip eateries has developed along downtown Worthington Street. Check out the food and weekend live jazz at **Caffeine's Downtown,** 260 Worthington St. (ℂ **413/788-6646**), or puff an hour away in its adjacent cigar lounge, **Nicotine's** (ℂ **413/781-0386**).

3 The Pioneer Valley

Low hills and quilted fields channel the Connecticut River as it runs south toward Long Island Sound, forming the Pioneer Valley. The earliest European settlers came here for what proved to be uncommonly fertile soil and were followed in the 19th century by men who harnessed the power of the river and became wealthy textile and paper manufacturers.

These industrialists took the lead in funding the institutions of higher learning that are now the pride of the region. Prestigious Smith, Mount Holyoke, and Amherst are here, as are innovative Hampshire College and the sprawling main campus of the University of Massachusetts, with its enrollment of more than 25,000 students. All five contribute mightily to the cultural life of the valley, and the towns of **Northampton, Amherst,** and **South Hadley** are invigorated by the vitality of thousands of college-age young people.

In the north, near Vermont, the living village of **Deerfield** preserves the architecture and atmosphere of colonial New England, but without the whiff of sterility that often afflicts artificial gatherings of old buildings with costumed docents.

Interstate 91 and Route 5 both traverse the valley from south to north. The trip from edge to edge on the interstate takes less than an hour, while Route 5 tenders more of the flavor of pastoral vistas and colorful mill towns.

There are plenty of motels along the way, but if you're looking for lodgings more representative of the character of the region, contact the **Folkstone Bed & Breakfast Reservation Service** (© **800/762-2751** or 508/480-0380).

ESSENTIALS

GETTING THERE   From Boston and upstate New York, take the Massachusetts Turnpike (I-90) to Springfield, then follow I-91 or Route 5 north. While there are local buses, you'll want a car.

The nearest major airport is **Bradley International** (© **203/627-3000**), just south of Springfield, in Windsor Locks, Conn. (See "Springfield," earlier in this chapter, for a list of airlines that serve Bradley.) **Valley Transporter** (© **800/ 872-8752** or 413/549-1350) offers van shuttles between the airport and Amherst, Northampton, Hadley, Holyoke, and Deerfield.

Amtrak (© **800/USA-RAIL;** www.northeast.amtrak.com) *Vermonter* trains stop in Amherst and Northampton on the route between St. Albans, Vt., and Washington, D.C.

VISITOR INFORMATION   The **Pioneer Valley Tourist Information Center** (© **413/665-7333**) is at the intersection of Routes 5 and 10 in South Deerfield, at Exit 24 off I-91.

HOLYOKE

Once an important paper-manufacturing center, Holyoke (8 miles/13km north of Springfield, 88 miles/142km west of Boston) has suffered a long economic slide since World War II. Abandoned factories and the dissolute air of the commercial center don't bolster first impressions. Still, there are a couple of modestly worthwhile sights.

Canals dug during the city's heyday still cut through downtown. (They were intended to allow access to the mills.) Running beside one of the canals is long and narrow **Heritage State Park,** with its entrance at 221 Appleton St. (© **413/534-1723**). Its interpretive center offers walking tours and exhibits; a restored antique merry-go-round and the Volleyball Hall of Fame are also in the park. On most Sundays from mid-June to late August, the ancient locomotive of the **Heritage Park Railroad** pulls train buffs on a 2-hour trip downriver to Holyoke Mall at Ingleside. Call Heritage State Park (see above) for more information.

WHERE TO STAY & DINE

Yankee Pedlar Inn ⊕   If you're looking for a sedate, tranquil country inn, this isn't it. Business is thriving, and the place bustles with weddings, tour groups, and corporate get-togethers. The dining room is highly popular with locals as well as travelers. Of the five buildings in the largely Victorian complex, the 1850 House has the most modern rooms, while the Carriage House has the least expensive. Live music is presented on weekends.

1866 Northampton St. (Rte. 5), Holyoke, MA 01040. © **413/532-9494.** Fax 413/536-8877. www. yankeepedlar.com. 28 units. $79–$109 double; $115–$139 suite. Rates include breakfast. AE, DC, MC, V. Take Exit 16 off I-91 and head east 5 blocks. **Amenities:** Restaurant (American), bar; access to nearby health club; video rentals. *In room:* TV/VCR.

SOUTH HADLEY

Pioneer educator Mary Lyon founded Mount Holyoke Female Seminary, one of the Seven Sisters group, here in 1836. Strung along the eastern side of Route 116 (College St.), the college is the essential reason for the existence of this small town (pop. 13,600). It lies 15 miles (24km) north of Springfield and 7 miles (11km) south of Amherst.

On the campus is a worthy **Art Museum** ✿ (© **413/538-2245**), which focuses on art of the Orient, Egypt, and the Mediterranean. Hours are Tuesday through Friday from 11am to 5pm, Saturday and Sunday from 1 to 5pm. Admission is free. To find it, take Park Street from the east side of the Y intersection in the center of town and follow the signs. It's been closed for renovation and expansion, so call ahead before making a special trip.

Joseph Skinner State Park (© **413/586-0350**) straddles the border between South Hadley and Hadley. On its 390 acres (158 hectares) are miles of trails, picnic grounds, and the historic Summit House (open Sat and Sun May–Oct), with panoramic views of the valley.

NORTHAMPTON ✿✿

Smith College, with its campus sprawling along Main Street slightly west of the commercial center, is Northampton's dominating physical and spiritual presence. One of the original Seven Sisters, Smith is the largest female liberal-arts college in the United States.

Northampton was long the home of Calvin Coolidge, who pursued his law practice here before and after his occupancy of the Oval Office. A room maintained by the **Forbes Library,** 20 West St. (© **413/584-6037**), contains many of his papers. Coolidge lived in houses at 21 Massasoit St. and on Hampton Terrace, but the homes are not open to the public.

Much else is open to visitors, however, and Northampton supplies many of the diversions of a thriving college town. Cultural events range from chamber music to art exhibitions, the number and diversity of restaurants and bars are far greater than most cities its size can flaunt, and its many stores are as kicky as any devout shopper might ask. Try to allow at least a long day and overnight in the area.

Just so you know, some folks like to call the town "NoHo." A well-received book by Tracy Kidder, *Home Town* (Random House; 1999), profiles Northampton and a number of its people.

SEEING THE SIGHTS

Note: The **Smith College Museum of Art,** with a permanent collection of paintings by Degas, Monet, Seurat, Picasso, and Winslow Homer, closed in 2000 for major renovations and isn't expected to reopen before the fall of 2002. Call © **413/585-2760** for updates.

Historic Northampton ✿   Among Northampton's most popular attractions are the Museum Houses—three historic homes still standing on their original sites. They are the 1730 Parsons House, the 1796 Shepherd House, and the 1812 Isaac Damon House, which contains a furnished parlor true to 1820.

46 Bridge St. (east of the railroad bridge). © 413/584-6011. www.historic-northampton.org. Tours $3 adults, $2 seniors and students, $1 children 12 and under. Museum Tues–Fri 10am–4pm, Sat–Sun noon–4pm; house tours given Sat–Sun noon–4pm only.

Smith College ✿   To a considerable extent, the campus buildings that line Elm Street are a testament to the excesses of late-19th-century architecture.

Their often egregious admixtures of Gothic, Greco-Roman, Renaissance, and medieval esthetic notions lend a Teutonic sobriety to the west end of town. On the other hand, Frederick Law Olmsted, famed for his design of New York's Central Park, laid out much of the original landscaping, and the campus contains many wooded walks and gardens.

Elm St. ℂ 413/584-2700. www.smith.edu.

OUTDOOR PURSUITS

Three miles (5km) southwest of town on Route 10 is **Arcadia Nature Center and Wildlife Sanctuary,** 127 Combs Rd., Easthampton (ℂ 413/584-3009), a 700-acre (284-hectare) preserve operated by the Massachusetts Audubon Society. It contains marshes and woods bordering the Connecticut River, with 5 miles (8km) of trails. The sanctuary is open Tuesday through Sunday from dawn to dusk, trails from 9am to 3pm. Admission is $3 for adults, $2 for seniors and children 3 to 15.

The 8½-mile (14km) **Norwottuck Rail Trail Bike Path** follows a former railroad bed running between Northampton and Amherst. Access is via Damon Road and at Mount Farms Mall. Bicyclists, skaters, and cross-country skiers are all welcome. Bikes can be rented at **Valley Bicycles,** 319 Main St. (ℂ 413/256-0880), across the river in Amherst.

Look Memorial Park, 300 N. Main St. (ℂ 413/584-5457), is northwest of town off Route 9, with 157 acres (64 hectares) of woods, a lake (with boats for rent), miniature golf, tennis, picnic grounds, and a small zoo. Musical and theatrical events, including puppet shows, are held in summer.

SHOPPING

In a town with a bookstore at every other corner, **Raven Used Books,** 4 Old South St., down the hill from Main Street (ℂ 413/584-9868), shines. Along with the usual categories, it has shelves devoted to shamanism, prophecy, and erotica.

In addition to an abundance of bookstores, Northampton enjoys the most diverse shopping in the valley. The **Antiques Center of Northampton,** 9½ Market St. (ℂ 413/584-3600), contains the stalls of more than 60 dealers; closed Wednesdays. **Ten Thousand Villages,** 82 Main St. (ℂ 413/582-9338), is part of a nonprofit Mennonite program selling handicrafts from more than 30 Third World countries.

A former department store has been reconfigured into **Thorne's Marketplace,** 150 Main St. (ℂ 413/584-5582), now containing more than 30 boutiques and a box office for theatrical and musical events. Next to the side entrance of the marketplace is **Herrell's,** 7 Old South St. (ℂ 413/586-9700), home base of a mini-chain of New England ice-cream emporia.

Northampton has a reputation as a small town with an unusually vigorous arts community. Burnishing that image is the prestigious **R. Michelson Gallery,** 132 Main St. (ℂ 413/586-3964), which occupies a grand former bank.

WHERE TO STAY

Anticipate higher rates and limited vacancies during graduation and homecoming, in addition to the usual holiday weekends.

Autumn Inn A genteel motel with a vaguely Georgian style, the Autumn is conveniently situated opposite the quieter northern end of the Smith campus. The breakfast room has a huge wood-burning fireplace.

259 Elm St., Northampton, MA 01060. ☎ **413/584-7660.** Fax 413/586-4808. www.hampshire hospitality.com. 30 units. Apr–Nov $88–$112 double, $150 suite; Dec–Mar $78–$88 double, $120 suite. AE, DC, MC, V. **Amenities:** Unheated outdoor pool (summer only). *In room:* A/C, TV, dataport, coffeemaker, hair dryer, iron.

Hotel Northampton ✰ Built in 1927, this brick building at the center of town looks older. Rooms of varying sizes contain wicker and colonial reprodu tions, feather duvets, and assorted Victoriana. Many front rooms have balconies overlooking King Street, some have fridges, and a few have Jacuzzis. Downstairs, Wiggins Tavern is a colonial watering hole with dark beams and three stone fireplaces.

36 King St., Northampton, MA 01060. ☎ **800/547-3529** or 413/584-3100. Fax 413/584-9455. www.hotel northampton.com. 99 units. $105–$235 double. Rates include continental breakfast. AE, DISC, MC, V. Free parking. **Amenities:** 2 restaurants (American), 2 bars; exercise room; business center; limited room service; same-day dry cleaning/laundry. *In room:* A/C, TV, dataport, hair dryer, iron.

Inn at Northampton ✰ There's a new sign out by the road, making it easier to find this inn, which is hidden behind a Mobil gas station. Renovations have elevated it from a standard motel to something closer to a modest resort and conference center.

Rte. 5 and I-91 (just west of Exit 18), Northampton, MA 01060. ☎ **800/582-2929** or 413/586-1211. Fax 413/586-0630. www.hampshirehospitality.com. 122 units. $109–$139 double; $149 suite. Rates include continental breakfast Mon–Fri. AE, DC, DISC, MC, V. **Amenities:** Restaurant (steakhouse); bar; heated indoor pool; outdoor pool; lighted tennis court; Jacuzzi; business center; limited room service. *In room:* A/C, TV, dataport, coffeemaker, hair dryer, iron.

WHERE TO DINE

Eastside Grill ✰✰ REGIONAL AMERICAN The consensus choice for tops in town, this white-clapboard building with a nautical look is a retreat for the 40-plus set from the prevailing collegiate tone of Northampton. The far-reaching menu has bayou riffs, such as duck étouffée and shrimp and andouille jambalaya. But while the Cajun/Creole dishes absorb much of the kitchen's attention, there are ample alternatives. Seafood is impressive, especially the curried fried oysters and macadamia-crusted halibut.

19 Strong Ave. (1 block south of Main St.). ☎ **413/586-3347.** Reservations recommended. Main courses $9.95–$15.95. AE, DC, DISC, MC, V. Mon–Thurs 5–10pm; Fri 5–10:30pm; Sat 4–10:30pm; Sun 4–9pm.

Fitzwilly's ✰ AMERICAN Occupying an 1898 building, this ingratiating pub makes the most of its stamped-tin ceilings and ample space. Copper brewing kettles signal an intriguing selection of beers. Beyond the two bars are curtained booths where patrons dive into pizzas, ribs, pastas, and such pub faves as blooming onion and fried calamari. Appetizers are half price during the 4-to-7pm happy hour. Everything is available for takeout.

23 Main St. (near Pleasant St.). ☎ **413/584-8666.** Reservations not accepted. Main courses $9.25–$14.50. AE, DC, DISC, MC, V. Daily 11:30am–1am.

Green Street Café ✰✰ NEW AMERICAN Julia Child dined here, and the chef is a graduate of the French Culinary Institute. That accounts for the Gallic tilt of the menu and the excellent baguettes, baked right here, served with both butter and tapenade. Don't overdose on the bread, though, for there are any number of delectables emerging from the kitchen—salmon in parchment and chicken in sauternes with spätzle, for two. The restaurant grows its own vegetables in season, and the emphasis throughout the year is on fresh ingredients. All that, and a fireplace, too. *Note:* An odd state blue law restricts its sale of wine and beer to the months of April through January.

64 Green St. *(℃)* **413/586-5650.** Reservations recommended. Main courses $16–$26. MC, V. Mon–Fri noon–2pm and 5:30–10pm; Sat 5:30–10pm; Sun 10:30am–2:30pm and 5:30–10pm. Follow Main St. toward the Smith campus, straight into West St., turning right on Green St.

La Cazuela ✿✿ SOUTHWESTERN/MEXICAN   Although La Cazuela has moved up the hill to this more accessible address, opposite the Academy of Music, its menu continues to mix recipes of the American Southwest with those of Mexico—and while the kitchen takes its job seriously, strict authenticity isn't the point. In addition to the predictable enchiladas and chimichangas, dinner specials explore regional cuisines with such dishes as *pollo en adobo* (chicken marinated in a chili and garlic paste, charbroiled with peppers and onions). The bar features tequila drinks.

271 Main St. *(℃)* **413/586-0400.** Reservations recommended. Main courses $9.25–$15.95. AE, DISC, MC, V. Sun–Thurs 5–9pm; Fri–Sat 5–11pm.

Vermont Country Deli & Cafe ✿ ECLECTIC   Tantalizing options include sesame chicken, pesto tortellini, and maple-barbecued pork ribs. Nearly 20 imaginative sandwiches, including three of the strictly vegetarian persuasion, are made to order. Also on offer are plump sticky buns and sourdough baguettes.

48 Main St. (near Pleasant St.). *(℃)* **413/586-7114.** Main courses $5.50–$8.95. MC, V. Mon–Sat 7am–7pm; Sun 8am–6pm.

NORTHAMPTON AFTER DARK

The presence of Smith and four other area colleges only partially accounts for the large number of bars and clubs in town, making Northampton the nightlife magnet of the valley. In April, the **Loud Music Festival** rattles walls with more than 250 alternative rock bands from around the country. For a rundown of what's happening, pick up a copy of the *Valley Advocate.*

Still thriving after 100-plus years, the **Academy of Music,** 74 Main St. (*(℃)* **413/584-8435**), shows arthouse and foreign films, and provides a venue for opera, ballet, and pop performers on tour.

Another old favorite, the **Iron Horse Music Hall,** 20 Center St. (*(℃)* **413/586-8686**), has played host to a variety of artists, from Bonnie Raitt to Dave Brubeck to grunge rockers. Cover is typically between $8 and $18.

Live bluegrass, jam rock, and soul-funk alternate with DJs at the **Pearl Street Nightclub,** 10 Pearl St. (*(℃)* **413/584-0610**). There are often dance nights targeted at teenagers, as well as gay nights. Nearby is the funky bar of the **Bay State Hotel,** 41 Strong Ave. (*(℃)* **413/584-8513**). It's a refuge for smokers, with live rock Thursday through Saturday.

The **Calvin Theatre and Performing Arts Center,** 19 King St. (*(℃)* **401/586-0851**), offers touring performers as diverse as the Pat Metheny Group, flamenco troupes, and children's theater.

AMHERST

Yet another Pioneer Valley town defined by its educational institutions, this one has an even larger student population than most, with distinguished Amherst College occupying much of its center, the large University of Massachusetts campus to its immediate northwest, and Hampshire College off South Pleasant Street. All three—and Smith College and Mount Holyoke, on the other side of the Connecticut River—combine to provide a full September-to-June slate of artistic and musical events.

On the edge of the town green is a seasonal **information booth.** Its hours vary, but if it's closed, visitors can call the **Chamber of Commerce (℗ 413/253-0700)** for information.

HISTORIC HOMES & COLLEGES

Most of the historic homes are within a few blocks of the Amity/Main/Pleasant street crossing. Amherst College lies mostly along the east side of the town green. At the northeast corner is the **Town Hall,** another fortress-like Romanesque Revival creation of Boston's H. H. Richardson.

Amherst College   Named for Baron Jefferey Amherst, a British general during the last of the French and Indian Wars, the illustrious liberal-arts college was founded in 1821, with Noah Webster on its first board of trustees. Robert Frost was a member of the faculty for more than a decade.

Amherst's campus cuts through the heart of the town and contains two museums open to the public. The **Pratt Museum** 𝕽, at the southeast corner of the main quad (℗ **413/542-2165**), contains dinosaur tracks collected from sedimentary rocks of the valley, as well as fossils and a mastodon skeleton. The **Mead Art Museum** 𝕽, Routes 116 and 9 (℗ **413/542-2335**), displays sculptures, paintings, photographs, and antiquities. Its strengths lie in the works of 19th- and 20th-century American artists and French Impressionists. Admission to both museums is free.

S. Pleasant and College sts. ℗ 413/542-2000. www.amherst.edu.

Dickinson Homestead 𝕽   Designated a National Historic Monument, this is the house where Emily Dickinson was born in 1830 and where she lived until her family moved in 1840. They returned in 1855, and the famous poet stayed here until her death 31 years later. The "Belle of Amherst" was the granddaughter and daughter of local movers and shakers, the source of her support while she produced the poetry that was to be increasingly celebrated even as she withdrew into near-total seclusion.

280 Main St. (2 blocks east of the Town Hall). ℗ 413/542-8161. www.dickinsonhomestead.org. Admission $5 adults, $4 seniors and students, $3 children 6–18, free for children under 6 and students from the 5 area colleges. Guided tours only, Mar to mid-Dec Wed and Sat 1–4pm on the hour; Apr–May and Sept–Oct Wed–Sat 1–4pm on the hour; June–Aug Wed–Sun 1–4pm on the half hour, Sat 10:30 and 11:30am. Reservations recommended.

University of Massachusetts   Though the university was founded in 1863, this sprawling 1,200-acre (486-hectare) campus north of the town center dates mainly from the 1960s. Several of its buildings top out at over 20 stories. Its 25,000 students study for degrees in 90 academic fields. Six art galleries are scattered around the campus; foremost among these is the University Gallery in the **Fine Arts Center** 𝕽, beside the pond in the quad. It focuses on 20th-century artists. The center also mounts productions in dance, music, and theater. Call the box office (℗ **413/545-2511**) for information on upcoming performances.

Rte. 116. ℗ 413/545-4237 for tour information. Campus tours available daily at 11am and 1:15pm, except Sat–Sun in June–July, Mar break, and most holidays.

OUTDOOR PURSUITS

An 8½-mile (14km) bicycle trail follows an old rail bed from Warren Wright Road in Belchertown, passing through Amherst, and on to Elder Island in the Connecticut River adjacent to Northampton. Bikes can be rented at **Valley Bicycles,** 319 Main St., Amherst (℗ **800/831-5437** or 413/256-0880).

It operates a seasonal shop, **Valley Bicycles Trailside,** 8 Railroad St. (©584-4466), directly on the trail.

SHOPPING

Atticus/Albion Bookstore, 8 Main St. (© 413/256-1547), has a rumpled aspect that is catnip for readers who like to take a seat on the window sofa to skim their finds. The nearby **Jefferey Amherst Bookshop,** 55 S. Pleasant St. (© 413/253-3381), is tidier, specializing in Emily Dickinson and academic texts.

WHERE TO STAY

Allen House Victorian Inn ⚘ The colorful exterior makes this Queen Anne–style Victorian, built in 1886, easy to spot. The interior is fitted out in the manner of the Aesthetic artistic movement, which lasted barely 10 years. In any event, the parlor and bedrooms are lovingly decorated, embellished with tracery and curlicues that are somehow Arabic in feel. The carriage house in back serves as bicycle storage for guests who want to take advantage of the nearby Norwottuck Trail.

599 Main St. (5 blocks east of the Town Hall), Amherst, MA 01002. © 413/253-5000. www.allenhouse.com. 7 units. $75–$175 double. Rates include breakfast. AE, DISC, MC, V. No children under 10. *In room:* A/C, TV, dataport, hair dryer.

Lord Jeffery Inn ⚘⚘ It's a running battle to keep the principal lodging in a college town from looking a little battered. At the moment, the Lord Jeff is winning, thanks to almost constant renovation and redecorating. So despite the wear and tear of more than 75 years of graduations and homecomings, the inn offers an environment that is as warm as its several fireplaces. The Sorbonne-trained chef has turned the Windowed Hearth into Amherst's event restaurant, open for dinner and Sunday brunch.

30 Boltwood Ave. (next to the Town Hall), Amherst, MA 01002. © 800/742-0358 or 413/253-2576. Fax 413/256-6152. www.pinnacle-inns.com/lordjefferyinn. 48 units. $89–$128 double; $219 suite. AE, MC, V. Pets accepted ($15). **Amenities:** 2 restaurants (creative regional), bar; access to nearby health club; limited room service. *In room:* A/C, TV, dataport.

WHERE TO DINE

Another option is the **Windowed Hearth,** at the Lord Jeffery Inn, above.

Judie's ⚘⚘ ECLECTIC AMERICAN Don't leave Amherst without eating at Judie's. The vivacious owner does her best to suit every taste. Just to keep things ticking, for example, there's a "Munchie Madness" period from 3 to 6pm, with a half-price snacks menu. Throughout the day, folks drop by for a cup of seafood bisque and one of the trademark popovers. A typical dinner entree is seafood gumbo with shrimp, sausage, scallops, salmon, and lobster. This being a college town, portions run from really big to immense, the better to assuage raging young metabolisms.

51 N. Pleasant St. (north of Amity and Main sts.). © 413/253-3491. Main courses $9–$16.50. AE, DISC, MC, V. Sun, Tue–Thurs 11:30am–10pm; Fri–Sat 11:30am–11pm.

AMHERST AFTER DARK

Students and other young adults tend to gravitate toward the livelier music scene in Northampton, but Amherst does offer some nighttime entertainment. Close at hand is the **Black Sheep Cafe,** 79 Main St. (© 413/253-3442), active with singers, readings, chamber music—a broad, unpredictable selection. The beer is good, the food indifferent, and the music varied at the **Amherst Brewing Company,** 24–36 N. Pleasant St. (© 413/253-4400).

Amherst College's **Buckley Recital Hall** (© **413/542-2195**) and the **Mullins Center** (© **413/733-2500**) at UMass mount a variety of performances that might include, for example, the Cincinnati Symphony, Mummenschantz, or Elton John.

DEERFIELD ★★★

Meadows cleared and plowed more than 330 years ago still surround this historic town between the Connecticut and Deerfield rivers. Every morning, tobacco and dairy farmers leave houses fronting the main street to work their land nearby. Students attend the distinguished prep school, Deerfield Academy, founded in 1797. Deerfield is an invaluable fragment of American history, and it isn't one of those New England village exhibits with costumed performers who go home to their condos at night.

A town still exists here, 16 miles (26km) north of Northampton and 16 miles (26km) northwest of Amherst, because the earliest English settlers were determined to thrive despite their status as a frontier pressure point in the wars that tormented colonial America. Massacres of Deerfield's settlers by the French and Indian enemies of the British nearly wiped out the town in 1675 and again in 1704. In the latter raid, 47 people were killed and another 112 were taken prisoner and marched to French Québec.

The main thoroughfare, simply called "The Street," is lined with more than 80 houses built in the 17th, 18th, and 19th centuries. Most are private, but 14 of them can be visited through tours conducted by Historic Deerfield, a local tourism organization (see below).

MUSEUMS & HISTORIC HOMES

"The Street" is a mile long, with most of the museum houses concentrated along the long block north of the central town common. There are two buildings operated by organizations other than Historic Deerfield. One is Memorial Hall Museum, east of the town common on Memorial Street, for which a separate admission is charged. (For the slightly larger fee of $12 adults, $5 children and students, tours of the 14 museum houses can be combined with a visit to Memorial Hall through Historic Deerfield.) The other is the Indian House Memorial, north of the Deerfield Inn, also maintained by a separate organization. Because it is only a 1929 reproduction of an earlier house, it is of less interest than the other structures.

Special celebrations in the town are held on Patriot's Day (the 3rd Mon in Apr), Washington's Birthday, Thanksgiving, and the Christmas holidays. Call the information center (© **413/774-5581;** see below) for details.

Historic Deerfield ★★★   Begin with a visit to the Hall Tavern, opposite the post office, where tickets are sold and brochures are available. A particularly useful booklet outlines a walking tour of 88 historic locations in the village. This is also the departure point for guided tours. While there are no charges for simply strolling the Street, the only way to get inside the museum houses is by tour.

The 14 houses on the tour were constructed between 1720 and 1850. They contain furnishings, textiles, ceramics, silver and pewter, and implements used from the early 17th century to 1900. Included are imports from China and Europe as well as items made in the Connecticut River Valley during its prominence as an industrial center.

The judicious selection at the **Museum Store,** between the post office and the Deerfield Inn (© **413/774-5581**), includes weather vanes, hand-dipped candles, and reproductions of light fixtures found in the village houses.

A stone building behind the Dwight House contains the **Flynt Center of Early American Life** ⭐, with galleries for changing exhibitions of paintings, textiles, and decorative arts relevant to the local history.

A free attraction is the **Channing Blake Meadow Walk.** Open from 8am to 6pm in good weather, the interpretive trail begins beside the Rev. John Farwell Moors House, a Historic Deerfield holding on the west side of the Street. It goes through a working farm, past the playing fields of Deerfield Academy, and through pastures beside the Deerfield River. Along the trail, sheep and cattle are seen up close; for that reason, dogs aren't allowed.

Information Center, Hall Tavern, The Street. (📞 413/774-5581. grace@historic-deerfield.com. Admission to all museum houses (good for 2 consecutive days) $12 adults, $6 children 6–17. Daily 9:30am–4:30pm.

Memorial Hall Museum ⭐ Deerfield Academy's original 1798 building was converted into this museum of village history in 1880. A popular, if suggestively grisly, exhibit is the door of a 1698 home that shows the gashes made by weapons of the French and Indian raiders in 1704. Should the point be too muted, a hatchet is also embedded in the door. Five period rooms are also on view. Special events—plays, crafts fairs, lectures, and even ice-cream socials—are held monthly.

8 Memorial St. (between the Street and Rtes. 5 and 10). (📞 413/774-3768, or 413/774-7476 off-season. Admission $6 adults, $3 children and students, free for children under 6. May–Oct daily 10am–4:30pm.

WHERE TO STAY & DINE

Deerfield Inn ⭐⭐ Built in 1884, this inn is located in the middle of the Street and is one of the stellar stopping places in the valley. The innkeepers restlessly scour the establishment, over the last few years replacing all the bathroom fixtures, refinishing the older furniture, and installing new carpeting. Antiques and reproductions are judiciously mixed throughout.

81 Old Main St., Deerfield, MA 01342. (📞 800/926-3865 or 413/774-5587. Fax 413/775-7221. www.deerfieldinn.com. 23 units. May–Oct $235–$255 double; Nov–Apr $188–$235 double. Rates include breakfast and afternoon tea. Midweek discounts available. AE, DC, MC, V. **Amenities:** Restaurant (American), cafeteria, bar. In room: A/C, TV, dataport, coffeemaker, hair dryer, iron..

4 The Berkshires

More than hills but less than mountains, the Taconic and Hoosac ranges that define this region at the western end of the state go by the collective name "The Berkshires." The hamlets, villages, and two small cities that have long drawn sustenance from the region's kindly Housatonic River and its tranquil tributaries are as New England as New England can be.

Mohawks and Mohegans lived and hunted here, and while white missionaries established settlements at Stockbridge and elsewhere in an attempt to Christianize the native tribes, the Indians eventually moved on west. Farmers, drawn to the narrow but fertile floodplains of the Housatonic, were supplanted in the 19th century by manufacturers, who erected the brick mills that drew their power from the river.

At the same time, artists and writers were drawn by the mild summers and seclusion that these hills and lakes offered. Nathaniel Hawthorne, Herman Melville, and Edith Wharton were among those who put down temporary roots. By the late 19th century and the arrival of the railroad, wealthy New Yorkers and Bostonians had discovered the region and begun to erect extravagant summer "cottages." With their support, culture and the performing arts found a hospitable reception. By the 1930s, theater, dance, and music performances had established themselves as regular summer fixtures. Tanglewood, Jacob's Pillow, and the Berkshire and Williamstown Theatre festivals draw tens of thousands of visitors every summer.

Note that many inns routinely stipulate minimum 2- or 3-night stays in summer and over holiday weekends and often require advance deposits.

ESSENTIALS

GETTING THERE   The Massachusetts Turnpike (I-90) runs east-west from Boston to the Berkshires, with an exit near Lee and Stockbridge. From New York City, the scenic Taconic State Parkway connects with I-90 not far from Pittsfield.

Amtrak (© **800/USA-RAIL;** www.northeast.amtrak.com) operates several trains daily between Boston and Chicago, stopping in Pittsfield each way.

VISITOR INFORMATION   The **Berkshire Visitors Bureau,** Berkshire Common (off South St., near the entrance to the Hilton), Pittsfield (© **800/ 237-5747** or 413/443-9186), can assist with questions and lodging reservations. Local chambers of commerce maintain information booths at central locations in Great Barrington, Lee, Lenox, Pittsfield, Stockbridge, and Williamstown (see the sections that follow). Also check out **www.berkshires.com** and **www.western massvisit.net.**

SHEFFIELD ☙

The first settlement of any size encountered when approaching from Connecticut on Route 7 is Sheffield, known as the "Antiques Capital of the Berkshires." It occupies a floodplain beside the Housatonic River, 11 miles (18km) south of Great Barrington, with the Berkshires rising to the west.

Agriculture has long been the principal occupation of its residents, and still is, to a degree. Everyone else sells antiques, or so it might seem driving along Route 7 (also known as Main St. or Sheffield Plain). The meticulously maintained houses cultivate an impression of prosperous tranquility.

May through October, stop by the **Colonel Ashley House,** Cooper Hill Road, in Ashley Falls (© **413/229-8600**). Built by the colonel himself in 1735, this modified saltbox is believed to be the oldest house in Berkshire County. Ashley was a person of considerable repute in colonial western Massachusetts, a pioneer settler, an officer in one of the French and Indian Wars, and later a lawyer and a judge. The house is open from 1 to 5pm on Saturday, Sunday, and holiday Mondays in June, September, and October; Wednesday through Sunday from July to Labor Day. To find it, drive south from Sheffield on Route 7, then veer onto Route 7A toward Ashley Falls. Bear right on Rannapo Road. At the Y intersection, turn right on Cooper Hill Road.

OUTDOOR PURSUITS

The 278-acre (113-hectare) nature reservation called **Bartholomew's Cobble** ☙, on Route 7A (© **413/229-8600**), lies beside an oxbow bend in the Housatonic. Its 6 miles (10km) of trails cross pastures, penetrate forests, and provide vistas of the river valley from the area's high point, Hurlburt's Hill. Picnicking is permitted. Birders should take binoculars. Trails are open from sunrise to sunset, and the small natural-history museum is open daily from 8:30am to 4:30pm. Requested donations are $3 for adults and $1 for children 6 to 12. To get here, follow the directions for the Colonel Ashley House (see above), except at the end of Rannapo Road, bear left on Weatogue Road.

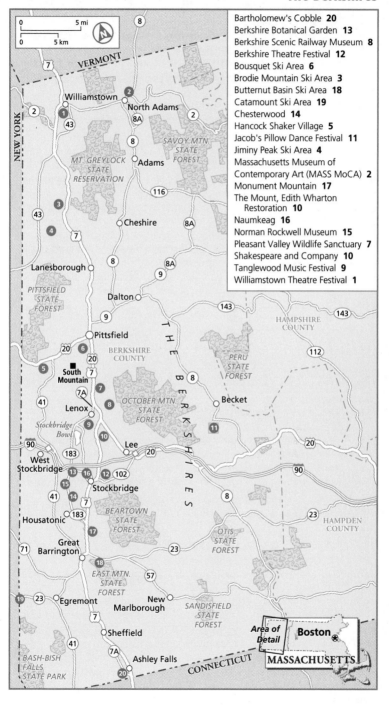

The Berkshires

Bartholomew's Cobble **20**
Berkshire Botanical Garden **13**
Berkshire Scenic Railway Museum **8**
Berkshire Theatre Festival **12**
Bousquet Ski Area **6**
Brodie Mountain Ski Area **3**
Butternut Basin Ski Area **18**
Catamount Ski Area **19**
Chesterwood **14**
Hancock Shaker Village **5**
Jacob's Pillow Dance Festival **11**
Jiminy Peak Ski Area **4**
Massachusetts Museum of
Contemporary Art (MASS MoCA) **2**
Monument Mountain **17**
The Mount, Edith Wharton
Restoration **10**
Naumkeag **16**
Norman Rockwell Museum **15**
Pleasant Valley Wildlife Sanctuary **7**
Shakespeare and Company **10**
Tanglewood Music Festival **9**
Williamstown Theatre Festival **1**

Sheffield on Stage

From late June to late August, the **Barrington Stage Company** (℃ **413/ 528-8888;** www.barringtonstageco.org) mounts musicals, comedies, and dramas at the **Consolati Performing Arts Center,** on Berkshire School Road. On five Saturday evenings in July and August, the **Berkshire Choral Festival,** 245 N. Undermountain Rd. (℃ **413/229-3522;** www.chorus.org), performs classical works at the Berkshire School in Sheffield.

ANTIQUING

Sheffield lays justifiable claim to the title of "Antiques Capital of the Berk-shires"—no small feat, given what seems to be an effort by half the population of the Berkshires to sell collectibles, oddities, and true antiques to the other half. These are canny, knowledgeable dealers who know exactly what they have, so expect high quality and few bargains.

Darr Antiques and Interiors, 34 S. Main St. (℃ **413/229-7773**), specializes in 18th- and 19th-century English and American furniture. Farther north along Route 7, **Dovetail Antiques,** 440 Sheffield Plain (℃ **413/229-2628**), features American clocks. Continuing along Route 7, on the left at the edge of town, is **Susan Silver** (℃ **413/229-8169**), with meticulously restored 18th- and 19th-century English library furniture (desks, reading stands) and French accessories.

There are at least two dozen other dealers along this route. Most of them stock the **free directory** of the Berkshire County Antiques Dealers Association, which lists member dealers from Sheffield to Cheshire and across the border in Connecticut and New York. Look, too, for the pamphlet called *The Antique Hunter's Guide to Route 7.*

SOUTH EGREMONT

If you're coming to the Berkshires from the Taconic Parkway in New York, you can't help but drive through the town of Egremont. Its larger, busier half is South Egremont, once a stop on the stagecoach route between Hartford and Albany. It retains many structures from that era, including mills that utilized the stream that still rushes by. Those circumstances make it a magnet for antiques dealers and restaurateurs. In the former category, seek out **The Splendid Peas-ant,** on Route 23 (℃ **413/528-5755**), which specializes in folk art.

OUTDOOR PURSUITS

HIKING   Scenic **Bash-Bish Falls State Park** 🕊🕊, on Route 23 (℃ **413/ 528-0330**), makes a rewarding day outing for hiking, birding, and fishing (no picnicking, though). To get here, drive west on Route 23 from town, turning south on Route 41, and immediately right on Mount Washington Road. Watch for signs directing the way to Mount Washington State Forest and Bash-Bish Falls. After 8 miles (13km), a sign indicates a right turn toward the falls; look for it opposite a church with an unusual steeple. The road begins to follow the course of a mountain stream, going downhill. In about 3 miles (5km) is a large parking place next to a craggy promontory.

The sign also points off to a trail down to the falls, which should be negoti-ated only by reasonably fit adults. First, mount the promontory for a splendid view across the plains of the Hudson Valley to the pale-blue ridgeline of the Catskill Mountains. The falls can be heard, but not yet seen, down to the left. If this trail seems too steep, continue driving down the road to another parking area, on the left. From here, a gentler trail a little over a mile (1.6km) long leads to the falls. The falls themselves are quite impressive, crashing down from more than 80 feet (24m). The park is open from dawn to dusk. It has 15 campsites.

SKIING   At the western edge of the township, touching the New York border, is the **Catamount Ski Area,** on Route 23 (© **413/528-1262;** www. catamountski.com). About 2 hours from Manhattan, it is understandably popular with New Yorkers. It has 28 trails, including the daunting Catapult (the steepest run in the Berkshires) and four double chairlifts. Night skiing and rentals are available.

WHERE TO STAY

Egremont Inn 🐾   Slip into this friendly former stagecoach stop as easily as into a favorite old flannel robe. The Egremont has been a tavern and inn since 1780. That longevity shows, in tilting floors and a grand brick fireplace. Dinner is served Wednesday through Sunday year-round. A singer-guitarist performs Thursday nights, a jazz ensemble Saturday evenings. Kids are welcome.

Old Sheffield Rd. (1 block off Rte. 23), South Egremont, MA 01258. © 413/528-2111. Fax 413/528-3284. www.egremontinn.com. 19 units. Weekdays $90–$145 double; weekends $105–$170 double. Rates include breakfast. Weekend packages available. AE, DISC, MC, V. **Amenities:** Restaurant (American), tavern; outdoor pool; golf course nearby; 2 tennis courts; bike rental. *In room:* A/C.

Weathervane Inn   An affectionate cat welcomes new arrivals to a building that began as a 1735 farmhouse, but was renovated in Greek Revival style in 1835. Many guest rooms have four-poster beds with quilts; fireplaces have been added to two units.

Rte. 23, South Egremont, MA 01258. © 800/528-9580 or 413/528-9580. Fax 413/528-1713. www. weathervaneinn.com. 10 units. $125–$165 double; $225–$245 suite. Rates include breakfast and afternoon tea. AE, DC, MC, V. **Amenities:** Unheated outdoor pool; public golf course next door. *In room:* A/C, dataport.

GREAT BARRINGTON

Even with a population well under 8,000, this pleasant retail center, 7 miles (11km) south of Stockbridge, is the largest town in the southernmost part of the county. Rapids in the Housatonic provided power for a number of mills in centuries past, most of which are now gone, and in 1886 this was one of the first communities in the world to have electricity on its streets and in its homes.

Great Barrington has no sights of particular significance, leaving time to browse its many antiques galleries and specialty shops. Convenient as a home base for excursions to such nearby attractions as Monument Mountain, Bash-Bish Falls, Butternut Basin, Tanglewood concerts, and the historic houses of Stockbridge, it has a number of unremarkable but entirely adequate motels north of the center along or near Route 7 that tend to fill up more slowly on weekends than the better-known inns in the area. It is something of a dining destination, too, compared with other Berkshire towns—it has *four* sushi bars!

The **Southern Berkshire Chamber of Commerce** maintains an information booth at 362 Main St. (© **413/528-1510;** www.greatbarrington.org), near the town hall. It's open Tuesday through Saturday from 9am to 5pm. *Note:* The local Board of Health has banned smoking in *any* public space in town.

OUTDOOR PURSUITS

The **Egremont Country Club,** on Route 23 (© **413/528-4222**), is open to the public. Its facilities include an 18-hole golf course, tennis courts, and an Olympic-size pool.

Butternut Basin, on Route 23, 2 miles (3km) east of town (© **413/ 528-2000,** or 800/438-7669 for snow conditions; www.skibutternut.com), is known for its strong family ski programs. There's day care for kids 2½ to 6 from December 23 until the end of the season, and the SKIwee program for children 4 to 12 offers packages that include lunch, instruction, and lift tickets. Six double and quad chairlifts provide access to 22 trails. There are also 5 miles (8km) of cross-country trails. On weekends, lift tickets cost $41 for adults, $30 for seniors and children 7 to 14, and $10 for children 6 and under. A 2-day jazz festival is presented in late August.

A little over 4 miles (6km) north of town, west of Route 7, is **Monument Mountain,** with two trails to the summit. The easier route is the Indian Monument Trail, about an hour's hike to the top; the more difficult one, the Hickey Trail, isn't much longer but takes the steep way up. The summit, called Squaw Peak, offers splendid views.

SHOPPING

Head straight for Railroad Street, the town's best shopping strip. Start on the corner with Main Street, at **T. P. Saddle Blanket & Trading Co.** (© **413/ 528-6500**). An unlikely emporium that looks as if it had been lifted whole from the Rockies, it's packed with boots, hats, Indian jewelry, blankets, and jars of salsa.

Mistral's, 6 Railroad St. (© **413/528-1618**), stocks Gallic tableware, linens, fancy foods, and furniture. Nearby, **Nahuál,** 9 Railroad St. (© **413/528-2423**), offers folk arts and handicrafts, primarily from Africa and Latin America. **Church Street Trading Company,** 4 Railroad St. (© **413/528-6120**), defies easy categorization, with walking sticks, dog collars, and candles all on display. The primary wares are sturdily stylish North Country sweaters, shirts, and pants.

Around the corner, **The Chef's Shop,** 290 Main St. (© **413/528-0135**), features a bounty of gadgets and cookbooks. Walking in the other direction, crossing Railroad Street, you'll encounter **Sappa,** 306 Main St. (© **413/528-6098**), presenting luxury bath products, vases, and flax-filled eye pillows. Across the street, **La Pace,** 313 Main St. (©**413/528-1888**), is an upmarket bed, bath, and beyond with an Italian tilt.

In the north end of town, just before Route 7 turns right across a short bridge, Route 41 goes straight, toward the village of Housatonic. In about 4 miles (6km) you'll see a shed that houses the kiln of **Great Barrington Pottery** (© **413/274-6259**). Owner Richard Bennett has been throwing pots according to ancient Japanese techniques for more than 30 years.

Stay on Route 7, going north, and you'll pass a large mall with an anchoring Kmart. In that unlikely location is one of the best (and few) bookstores in the Berkshires, **The Bookloft,** Barrington Plaza (© **413/528-1521**).

WHERE TO STAY

North of town on Route 7 is **Monument Mountain Motel,** 249 Stockbridge Rd. (© **413/528-3272;** fax 413/528-3132), which has a pool, tennis courts, and a riverside location. The **Chamber of Commerce** operates a lodging hot line at © **800/269-4825** or 413/528-4006.

The Old Inn on the Green & Gedney Farm ★★ This growing establishment comprises a former 1760 tavern/general store and the 18th-century Thayer House, both on the village green; a pair of converted dairy barns; and the latest addition, 1906 Gedney Manor, with a spa and fitness center now under construction. Among the most desirable units are those in Thayer House, some with fireplaces and all with air-conditioning, and in the barn, where contemporary furnishings are combined with Oriental rugs. All five intimate dining rooms have fireplaces; reservations are advised.

Rte. 57, New Marlborough, MA 01230. ✆ **800/286-3139** or 413/229-3131. Fax 413/229-8236. www.oldinn.com. 26 units. $175–$290 double; $245–$285 suite; $325–$365 Thayer House unit. Rates include breakfast. Mon–Wed 25% discount. AE, MC, V. Take Rte. 23 east from Great Barrington, picking up Rte. 57 after 3.4 miles (5.5km). After 5.7 miles (9km), the Old Inn is on the left. Continue to the barns on the left; registration is on the ground floor of the gray barn. **Amenities:** Restaurant (creative American); courtyard pool at Thayer House. *In room:* Hair dryer.

Windflower Inn　A roadside lodging built in the middle of the last century in Federal style, the Windflower commands a large plot of land opposite the Egremont Country Club, on Route 23 between Great Barrington and South Egremont. Six rooms have fireplaces; four have canopy beds.

684 S. Egremont Rd. (P.O. Box 25), Great Barrington, MA 01230. ✆ **800/992-1993** or 413/528-2720. Fax 413/528-5147. www.windflowerinn.com. 13 units. $100–$200 double. Rates include breakfast and afternoon tea. Children stay in parents' room for $25. AE. **Amenities:** Unheated outdoor pool. *In room:* A/C, TV, dataport.

WHERE TO DINE

In addition to the places listed below, you might check out the restaurant at the **Old Inn on the Green & Gedney Farm** (see above).

Barrington Brewery ⚸ ECLECTIC AMERICAN　Nothing detracts from the primary function of this brewery in a converted barn. All of its beers and ales are made upstairs and funneled directly to the taps in the tavern. Grub, of the burger and pizza variety, is secondary but tasty enough.

Rte. 7 (in the Jennifer House complex, north of town). ✆ **413/528-8282.** Main courses $7.95–$15.95. AE, DISC, MC, V. Daily 11:30am–10pm (bar open later, depending on business).

Castle Street Cafe ⚸⚸ NEW AMERICAN　This storefront bistro has ruled the Great Barrington roost for some time now, and has expanded into the next building, installing what it calls a "Celestial Bar," with live jazz piano 6 nights a week in summer and on weekends the rest of the year. While a Francophilic inclination is apparent in the main room, what with duck breast with potato galette and steak au poivre, it isn't overpowering. Have a drink at the bar in the new room while you're checking out the night's menu, or stay there for such casual eats as burritos, burgers, and pizzas. An award-winning wine list is another reason to stop in.

10 Castle St. (near the Town Hall). ✆ **413/528-5244.** Main courses $18–$24. AE, DISC, MC, V. Daily 5–10pm (until 10:30pm Fri–Sat).

Hudson's AMERICAN BISTRO　At the corner where Route 7 turns north from Great Barrington toward Stockbridge, this fetching wayside stop is run by two dedicated chef/owners who play with curries and pastas and Cajun seasonings. Both are graduates of the Culinary Institute of America; that campus is on the banks of the Hudson River, thus this restaurant's name. The dining room is spare, with bare wood floors, bentwood chairs, and framed food posters. Keep it in mind for a quality lunch of gumbo or jambalaya, not easy to find in these parts.

50 Stockbridge Rd. (Rte 7). ✆ **413/528-2002.** Main courses $14–$23.50. AE, DC, MC, V. Summer Tues–Sun noon–2:30pm and 5–9:30pm; winter Wed–Sat noon–2:30pm and 5–10pm.

Union Bar & Grill ⚸ NEW AMERICAN　One might associate the industrial-chic interior, with exposed ceiling ducts and brushed-metal trim, with New York's TriBeCa. The menu might have been transplanted, too, given, for one example, the grilled swordfish with black beans, bok choy, and green mango and cashew salad. At lunch, even the ordinarily prosaic sandwich list turns up a duck confit number, with caramelized onions on sourdough bread. The young and hip mingle easily with seniors and families, accompanied by live jazz at Saturday lunch and Sunday brunch.

293 Main St. © 413/528-6228. Main courses $17–$26. MC, V. Summer Thurs–Tues 11:30am–11pm (bar until 1am); winter daily 5–11pm.

GREAT BARRINGTON AFTER DARK

The **Aston Magna Festival** features classical music performed on period instruments. Concerts are held on five Sundays in July and August at St. James Church, Main Street and Taconic Avenue (© **800/875-7156** or 413/528-3595).

The **Triplex Cinema,** 70 Railroad St. (© **413/528-8886**), shows a mixed bag of independent and foreign flicks as well as major studio releases.

STOCKBRIDGE 🕸🕸

Stockbridge's ready accessibility to Boston and New York (about 2½ hours from each and reachable by rail since the mid–19th century) transformed the original frontier settlement into a Gilded Age summer retreat for the rich. The town has long been popular with artists and writers as well. Illustrator Norman Rockwell, who lived here for 25 years, rendered the Main Street of his adopted town in a famous painting. Along and near Main Street are a number of historic homes and other attractions, enough to fill up a long weekend, even without the Tanglewood concert season in nearby Lenox. One of the Berkshires' hottest destinations, Stockbridge is inevitably jammed on warm weekends and during foliage season.

Stockbridge lies 7 miles (11km) north of Great Barrington and 6 miles (10km) south of Lenox. The **Stockbridge Chamber of Commerce (© 413/298-5200;** www.stockbridgechamber.org) maintains an information booth opposite the row of stores depicted by Rockwell. It's open May through October.

SEEING THE SIGHTS

Berkshire Botanical Garden These 15 acres (6 hectares) of flower beds, ponds, and herb gardens are an inviting destination for strollers and picnickers. The first weekend in October features a harvest festival.

Rtes. 102 and 183. © 413/298-3926. www.berkshirebotanical.org. Admission $5 adults, $4 seniors, $3 students, free for children under 12. May–Oct daily 10am–5pm. Tours offered Sat–Sun June–Aug. Drive west from downtown Stockbridge on Main St., picking up Church St. (Rte. 102) northwest for about 2 miles (3.2km).

The Berkshire Theatre Festival 🕸🕸 From June to August, and occasionally at other times during the year, the Berkshire Theatre Festival holds its season of classic and new plays, often with marquee names starring or directing. Dianne Wiest and Joanne Woodward have been participants. Its venue is a "casino" built in 1887 to plans by architect Stanford White. A second venue, the Unicorn Theatre, opened in 1996.

P.O. Box 797, Main St. © 413/298-5576. www.berkshiretheatre.org. Tickets $36–$52 Main Stage, $15 Unicorn Theatre.

Chesterwood 🕸 Sculptor Daniel Chester French, best known for the Lincoln Memorial in Washington, D.C., used this estate as his summer home for more than 30 years. His *Minute Man* statue at the Old North Bridge in Concord, completed in 1875 at the age of 25, launched his highly successful career. The

122-acre (49-hectare) grounds are used for an annual show of contemporary sculpture.

4 Williamsville Rd. ℂ **413/298-3579**. www.chesterwood.org. Admission $8.50 adults ($6.50 for grounds only), $5 children 13–18, $3 children 6–12. May–Oct daily 10am–5pm. Drive west on Main St., south on Rte. 183 about 1 mile (1.6km) to the Chesterwood sign.

Mission House ⍟   The Rev. John Sergeant had the most benevolent, if paternalistic, of intentions: He sought to build a house among the members of the Housatonic tribe, hoping to convert them to civilized (i.e., English) ways through proximity to his godly self and his small band of settlers. The weathered Mission House, built in 1739, was the site of this Christianizing process.

Main and Sergeant sts. (Rte. 102). ℂ **413/298-3239**. www.thetrustees.org. Admission $5 adults, $3 children. Memorial Day to Columbus Day daily 10am–5pm. Visits are by guided tour only.

Naumkeag   In 1886, Stanford White designed this 26-room house for Joseph Hodge Choate, who served as U.S. ambassador to the Court of St. James. The client dubbed it "Naumkeag," a Native American name for Salem, Mass., his childhood home. His house of many gables and chimneys is largely of the New England shingle style, surrounded by impressive gardens. Admission is by guided tour only, worth it for the glimpses of the rich interior.

Prospect Hill. ℂ **413/298-3239**. www.thetrustees.org. Admission $9 adults, $3 children. Memorial Day to Columbus Day daily 10am–5pm. From the Cat & Dog Fountain in the intersection next to the Red Lion Inn, drive north on Pine St. to Prospect Hill Rd. about ½ a mile (0.8km).

Norman Rockwell Museum ⍟⍟   This striking building opened in 1993, at a cost of $4.4 million, to house the works of Stockbridge's favorite son. The illustrator used both his neighbors and the town where he lived to tell stories about an America now rapidly fading from memory. Most of Rockwell's paintings adorned covers of the *Saturday Evening Post:* warm and often humorous depictions of homecomings, first proms, and visits to the doctor. He addressed serious concerns, too, notably with his poignant portrait of a little African-American girl being escorted by U.S. marshals into a previously segregated school. Critics long derided his paintings as saccharine and sentimental, but today a revision of sorts has led to widespread appreciation for his deft brushwork. The lovely 36-acre (15-hectare) grounds also contain Rockwell's last studio (closed Nov–Apr).

Rte. 183. ℂ **413/298-4100**. www.nrm.org. Admission $9 adults, $2 children 6–18; $20 per family. May–Oct daily 10am–5pm; Nov–Apr Mon–Fri 10am–4pm, Sat–Sun 10am–5pm. Take Main St. (Rte. 102) west to the junction with Rte. 183, then turn left (south) at the traffic signal. In about ½ a mile (0.8km), you'll see the entrance to the museum on the left.

WHERE TO STAY

Inn at Stockbridge ⍟   A mile (1.6km) north of Stockbridge center, this 1906 building with a grandly columned porch is set well back from the road on 12 acres (5 hectares). The innkeepers are eager to please, serving full breakfasts by candlelight and afternoon spreads of wine and cheese. Four new bedrooms have fireplaces and whirlpools.

30 East St. (Rte. 7), Stockbridge, MA 01262. ℂ **888/466-7865** or 413/298-3337. Fax 413/298-3406. www.stockbridgeinn.com. 12 units. June–Oct $130–$310 double; Nov–May $125–$250 double. Rates include full breakfast and afternoon refreshments. AE, DISC, MC, V. No children under 12. **Amenities:** Outdoor pool. *In room:* A/C, TV, hair dryer, iron.

The Red Lion Inn ⍟⍟   So well known that it serves as a symbol of the Berkshires, this busy inn had its origins as a stagecoach tavern in 1773. The rocking chairs on the porch are the perfect place to while away an hour reading or people-watching. Six satellite buildings have gradually been added, all within 3 miles (5km) of the inn. Jackets are required for men in the pricey main dining room, but not in the casual Widow Bingham Tavern nor, in good weather, in the courtyard out back. The wine cellar has been recognized with important awards. The Lion's Den has nightly live entertainment, usually of the folk-rock variety. Book your room reservations far in advance.

Main St., Stockbridge, MA 01262. (C) 413/298-5545. Fax 413/298-5130. www.redlioninn.com. 110 units (16 with shared bathrooms). Mid-Apr to late May $125–$190 double, $195–$295 suite; June–late Oct $175–$215 double, $260–$345 suite; late Oct to mid-Apr $110–$179 double, $179–$335 suite. Packages available. AE, DC, DISC, MC, V. **Amenities:** 3 restaurants (eclectic/American), 2 bars; outdoor pool; golf and tennis privileges nearby; exercise room; limited room service; massage; babysitting; laundry; dry cleaning. *In room:* A/C, TV/VCR, dataport, hair dryer.

Taggart House 🏵🏵   Ordinarily, an inn with only four guest rooms wouldn't merit space here. But what rooms! The decor of this outwardly sedate 1850 Victorian/colonial mansion provides guests with a breathtaking immersion in the Gilded Age. Start with the theatrical main floor—the inlaid mahogany dining table was once a centerpiece in an Argentine palace. There's a paneled library, a ballroom, a harpsichord, and nine beguiling fireplaces. And upstairs, beds are decorated with fur throws, East Indian silk coverlets, and velvet canopies.

Main St. (1 block west of the Red Lion), Stockbridge, MA 01262. (C) and fax **413/298-4303.** www.taggart house.com. 4 units. Weekdays $235–$355 double; weekends $265–$355. Rates include breakfast. Packages available. 2- to 3-night minimum stay on summer and fall weekends. MC, V. Young children not accepted. *In room:* A/C, dataport.

WHERE TO DINE

See also the dining options at the **Red Lion Inn,** reviewed above.

Michael's 🏵 ELECTIC AMERICAN   This tavern with a pronounced sports tilt is one of the few nearby alternatives to the Red Lion Inn. Bar snacks served around two big-screen TVs are of the chili and nachos variety, while entrees in the dining room run to steaks, chicken Dijon, and scallops marinara. The food is pretty good, the greeting friendly, and the place stays open throughout the day.

9 Elm St. (off Main St.). (C) 413/298-3530. Main courses $12.95–$22.95. AE, DC, MC, V. Mon–Sat 11:30am–9pm (bar until 1am); Sun noon–1am.

WEST STOCKBRIDGE

The hills around this Stockbridge satellite (just 5 miles/8km northwest) are alive with creativity. Potters, painters, writers, sculptors, weavers, and glass blowers pursue their compulsions, selling the results from their studios and several galleries. A pamphlet called *The Art of West Stockbridge,* available in display racks throughout the area, describes the work of some of the more important artisans and where it can be found.

One of the most ambitious enterprises is the **Berkshire Center for Contemporary Glass** 🏵, 6 Harris St. ((C) **413/232-4666**), in the heart of the village. Kids find the process fascinating and are even allowed to participate. The center is open daily, from 10am to 10pm May through October, from 10am to 6pm November through April.

WHERE TO STAY

The Inn at Richmond 🏵   This used to be a horse farm, and animals are still boarded in the barns at the back of the 27-acre (11-hectare) property. The library is irresistible, with its fireplace, piano, video library, and waiting bottles of port and sherry. Six guest rooms have sofa beds, five have fireplaces, and two have Jacuzzis. Three cottages feature full kitchens. The inn is about 5 miles (8km) north of West Stockbridge, and Tanglewood and Hancock Shaker Village are only 20 minutes away.

802 State Rd. (Rte. 41), Richmond, MA 01254. © **888/968-4748** or 413/698-2566. Fax 413/698-2100. www.innatrichmond.com. 10 units. Memorial Day to Oct $135–$195 double, $185–$275 suite; Nov–May $125–$145 double, $155–$175 suite. Cottage $850–$1,000 per week in winter; $1,300–$1,500 per week in summer and fall. Room rates include full breakfast. AE, MC, V. Children 8 and over welcome. *In room:* A/C, TV, dataport, hair dryer, iron.

WHERE TO DINE
La Bruschetta ★★ NEW ITALIAN   The chef/owners grew weary of gearing up for the frantic summer business, then downstaffing and cutting back during the slow winter—so they now operate a fine food and wine store, providing quality takeout stews, rotisserie chicken, osso buco, and the best (and only) pizzas in West Stockbridge.

1 Harris St. © **413/232-7141**. Pizzas and main courses $8.99–$11.99. AE, MC, V. Tues–Sun 11am–9pm.

Truc Orient Express ★★ VIETNAMESE   The menu is full of revelatory taste sensations. *Mai tuyet nhi* is a soup adrift with snow mushrooms and lobster meat, a suitable lead-in to the extravaganza called *lauthap cam-chap pin loo*, a hot pot crowded with meatballs, shrimp, squid, scallops, and assorted veggies ladled over rice noodles. Tables are set up on the deck in summer, and takeout is available.

2 Harris St. © **413/232-4204**. Main courses $7.50–$18. AE, DISC, MC, V. Summer daily 11am–3pm and 5–10pm; winter Wed–Mon 5–9:30pm.

LEE
While Stockbridge and Lenox were developing into luxurious recreational centers for the upper crust of Boston and New York, Lee was a thriving papermill town. That meant that it was shunned by the wealthy summer people and thus remained essentially a town of workers and merchants. It has a somewhat raffish though not unappealing aspect, its center bunched with shops and offices and few of the stately homes that characterize neighboring communities.

The town's contribution to the Berkshire cultural calendar is the Jacob's Pillow Dance Festival, which first thrived as "Denishawn," a fabled alliance between founders Ruth St. Denis and Ted Shawn.

Lee is located 5 miles (8km) southeast of Lenox. In summer and early fall, the **Lee Chamber of Commerce** (© **413/243-0852;** www.leechamber.org) operates an **information center** on the town common, Route 20 (© **413/243-4929**). It can help you find lodging, often in guesthouses and B&Bs—rarely as grand as those in neighboring Lenox, but nearly always cheaper. That's something to remember when every other place near Tanglewood is either booked or quoting prices of $200 a night.

SEEING THE SIGHTS
The Jacob's Pillow Dance Festival ★★★   In 1933, Ted Shawn decided to put on a show in the barn, and so was born Jacob's Pillow. After decades of advance and retreat and evolution, Jacob's Pillow is now to dance what Tanglewood is to classical music. Once a regular summer venue for Shawn and famed dancer and choreographer Martha Graham, one of his early disciples, the theater has long welcomed troupes of international reputation, including the Mark Morris Dance Group, Twyla Tharp, and the Paul Taylor Dance Company. The season runs from mid-June to late August, and tickets go on sale April 1.

The more prominent companies are seen in the main Ted Shawn Theatre, while other troupes are assigned to the Doris Duke Studio Theatre. Admission is free to the Inside/Out, an outdoor stage. The growing campus includes a store, pub, dining room, tent restaurant, and exhibition space. Picnic lunches can be pre-ordered 24 hours in advance.

P.O. Box 287, George Carter Rd., Becket. © 413/243-0745. www.jacobspillow.org. Tickets $20–$50. From Lee, take Rte. 20 east about 9 miles (14km), then turn north on Rte. 8 toward Becket.

Santarella 🏵 With no obligatory historic homes or museums to see in Lee, visitors often make the short excursion to a curious fairy-tale structure called Santarella, but known by most as the "Gingerbread House." Conical turrets top towers, while the shingled roof rolls like waves on the ocean. It served as a studio for sculptor Henry Hudson Kitson from 1930 to 1947, and now houses galleries showcasing the works of Berkshire artists.

Tyringham Rd. © 413/243-3260. www.santarella.org. May–Oct daily 10am–5pm. Admission $4 adults, free for children under 6. Take Rte. 20 south from Lee to Rte. 102, near the no. 2 interchange of the Massachusetts Tpk. Following the signs through the complicated intersection, pick up Tyringham Rd. on the other side and drive south about 4 miles (6km).

OUTDOOR PURSUITS
October Mountain State Forest offers 50 campsites (with showers) and more than 16,000 acres (6,480 hectares) for hiking, canoeing, cross-country skiing, and snowmobiling. To get here, drive northwest on Route 20 into town, turn right on Center Street, and follow the signs.

WHERE TO STAY
On the road to Lenox, the lakeside **Best Western Black Swan,** 435 Laurel St./Rte. 20 (© **413/243-2700;** www.travelweb.com), has a pool and restaurant; some rooms have fireplaces.

Applegate 🏵 This B&B utilizes a gracious 1920s Georgian colonial manse to full advantage. The top unit has a canopy bed, Queen Anne reproductions, sunlight filtering through gauzy curtains, a steam shower, and a fireplace (with real wood). Two new suites have been completed and two more are planned; all will have TVs, Jacuzzis, and gas fireplaces. Most rooms have phones with dataports. Breakfast is by candlelight, and the innkeepers set out wine and cheese in the afternoon.

279 W. Park St., Lee, MA 01238. © **800/691-9012** or 413/243-4451. www.applegateinn.com. 8 units. June–Oct $125–$295 double; Nov–May $95–$245 double. MC, V. From Stockbridge, drive north on Rte. 7 about ½ a mile (0.8km); take a right on Lee Rd. The inn is 2¼ miles (3.6km) ahead. No children under 12. **Amenities:** Heated outdoor pool; 9-hole golf course across the street; tennis court; access to nearby health club; bikes. *In room:* A/C.

Chambéry Inn 🏵 This was the Berkshires' first parochial school (1885), named for the French hometown of the nuns who ran it. That accounts for the extra-large bedrooms, which were formerly classrooms. Six of them, with 13-foot (4m) ceilings and the original woodwork and blackboards, are equipped with whirlpool tubs and gas fireplaces. Some rooms have TV/VCRs, CD players, and fridges. A breakfast basket is delivered to your door each morning.

199 Main St., Lee, MA 01238. © **413/243-2221.** Fax 413/243-0039. www.berkshireinns.com. 9 units. July–Aug and Oct $99–$160 double, $135–$259 suite; Sept and last 2 weeks in June $85–$220 double, $129–$195 suite; Nov to mid-June $85–$220 double, $119–$179 suite. Rates include breakfast. AE, DISC, MC, V. No children under 18. **Amenities:** Limited room service from the neighboring restaurant. *In room:* A/C, TV, coffeemaker, hair dryer, iron.

Federal House ⭐ Built in 1824 in the Federal style, including a portico with fluted columns, this distinguished inn still sports antiques belonging to the original family in its bedrooms, which are perfectly nice if pricey. Four units have TVs. Breakfast is served by candlelight, the new owners have upgraded bedding and window treatments, and gas fireplaces are being installed in three rooms.

Main St. (Rte. 102), South Lee, MA 01260. ② 800/243-1824 or 413/243-1824. www.berkshireweb.com. 10 units. July–Aug and Oct $145–$245 double; Sept and Nov–May $100–$175 double. Rates include breakfast. AE, DISC, MC, V. Children over 12 welcome. **Amenities:** Restaurant (contemporary French). *In room:* A/C.

LENOX ⭐⭐ & TANGLEWOOD

Stately homes and fabulous mansions mushroomed in this former agricultural settlement from the 1890s until 1913, when the 16th Amendment, authorizing income taxes, put a severe crimp in that impulse. But Lenox remains a repository of extravagant domestic architecture surpassed only in such fabled resorts of the wealthy as Newport and Palm Beach. And because many of the cottages have been converted into inns and hotels, it is possible to get inside some of these beautiful buildings, if only for a cocktail or a meal.

The reason for so many lodgings in a town with a population of barely 5,000 is Tanglewood, a nearby estate where a series of concerts by the Boston Symphony Orchestra are held every summer.

Lenox lies 7 miles (11km) south of Pittsfield. The **Lenox Chamber of Commerce** (② **413/637-3646;** www.lenox.org) provides visitor information and lodging referrals.

SEEING THE SIGHTS

Frelinghuysen Morris House & Studio ⭐ Built on 46 acres (19 hectares) next to the Tanglewood property in the early 1940s, this Bauhaus-influenced house was the home of abstract artists Suzy Frelinghuysen and George L. K. Morris. Their chosen style was Cubism, which they pursued long after it had been abandoned by better-known practitioners. Works by some of those artists—Braque, Léger, Gris, and Picasso—can be viewed alongside the canvases of the owners. Visits are by tour only.

92 Hawthorne St. ② 413/637-0166. www.frelinghuysen.org. Admission $8 adults, $3 children 5–16. July 4th to Labor Day Thurs–Sun 10am–4pm; Sept–Columbus Day Thurs–Sat 10am–4pm. Drive south from Tanglewood on Rte. 183, turn left on Hawthorne Rd., then left again on Hawthorne St. (note 2 different streets).

The Mount, Edith Wharton Restoration ⭐ Wharton, who won a Pulitzer for her novel *The Age of Innocence,* was singularly equipped to write that deftly detailed examination of the upper classes of the Gilded Age and the first decades of the 20th century. She was born into that stratum of society in 1862 and traveled in the circles that made the Berkshires a regular stop on their restless movements between New York, Florida, Newport, and the Continent. Wharton had her villa built on this 130-acre (53-hectare) lakeside property in 1902 and lived here 10 years before leaving for France, never to return. She took an active hand in the creation of the Mount, which makes the mansion a notable rarity—one of the few designated National Historic Landmarks designed by a woman. Wharton was, after all, the author of an upscale 1897 how-to guide called *The Decoration of Houses.* A $15-million restoration campaign is under way, with work so far completed on the terrace and greenhouse and continuing on the interior and gardens.

2 Plunkett St. (at the intersection of Rtes. 7 and 7A). ② 413/637-1899. www.edithwharton.org. Admission $7.50 adults, $7 seniors, $5 students and children 13–18, $3 children 6–12. Guided tours given Memorial Day–Oct 31 daily 9am–5pm.

Shakespeare & Company ✸ The repertory company has long used buildings and amphitheaters on the grounds of the Mount (see above) to stage its May-to-October season of plays by the Bard, works by Edith Wharton and George Bernard Shaw, and efforts by new American playwrights. After increasingly bitter conflict with the custodians of the Wharton property, officials of the company have offered to purchase the National Music Foundation on Kemble Street. This is expected to take place in a series of staggered moves up until 2003, when the lease at the Mount expires. In the meantime, performances take place Tuesday through Sunday (weekends only after Labor Day). Lunch and dinner picnic baskets can be purchased on site.

70 Kemble St. ⓒ 413/637-1199. www.shakespeare.org. Tickets $14.50–$33.50.

Tanglewood Music Festival ✸✸✸ Lenox is filled with music every summer, and the undisputed headliner is the Boston Symphony Orchestra (BSO). Concerts are given at the famous Tanglewood estate, usually beginning in July and ending the weekend before Labor Day. The estate is on West Street (actually in Stockbridge township, although it's always associated with Lenox). From Lenox, take Route 183 1½ miles (2.4km) southwest of town.

While the BSO is Tanglewood's 800-pound cultural gorilla, the program features a menagerie of other performers and musical idioms. These run the gamut from popular artists (like James Taylor and Bonnie Raitt) and jazz musicians (including Dave Brubeck and Wynton Marsalis) to such guest soloists as Itzhak Perlman and Yo-Yo Ma.

The Koussevitzky Music Shed is an open auditorium that seats 5,000, surrounded by a lawn where an outdoor audience lounges on folding chairs and blankets. Chamber groups and soloists appear in the smaller Ozawa Hall. Major performances are on Friday and Saturday nights and Sunday afternoon.

Tentative programs are available after January 1; the schedule is usually locked in by March. Tickets can sell out quickly, so get yours as far in advance as possible. If you decide to go at the last minute, take a blanket or lawn chair and get tickets for lawn seating, which is almost always available. You can also attend open rehearsals during the week, as well as the rehearsal for the Sunday concert on Saturday morning.

The estate itself (ⓒ **413/637-5165** June–Aug), with more than 500 acres (203 hectares) of lawns and gardens, much of it overlooking the lake called Stockbridge Bowl, was put together starting in 1849 by William Aspinwall Tappan. Admission to the grounds is free when concerts aren't scheduled.

In 1851, a structure on the property called the Little Red Shanty was rented to Nathaniel Hawthorne, who stayed here long enough to write a children's book, *Tanglewood Tales,* and meet Herman Melville, who lived in nearby Dalton. The existing Hawthorne Cottage is a replica (and isn't open to the public). On the grounds is the original Tappan mansion, with fine views.

West St., Stockbridge. For recorded information, call ⓒ **617/266-1492** from Sept–June 10 (note that information on upcoming Tanglewood concerts is not available until the program is announced in Mar or Apr). www.bso.org (tentative program info available after Jan 1). Tickets $14–$85 Shed and Ozawa Hall, $13–$16 lawn. Lawn tickets for children under 12 are free; children under 5 not allowed in the Shed or Ozawa Hall. Higher prices apply for some special appearances. To order tickets by mail before June, write the Tanglewood Ticket Office at Symphony Hall, 301 Massachusetts Ave., Boston, MA 02115. After June 1, write the Tanglewood Ticket Office, 297 West St., Lenox, MA 01240. Tickets can be charged to a credit card through **Symphony Charge** (ⓒ **888/266-1200** outside Boston, or 617/266-1200) or at www.bso.org.

OUTDOOR PURSUITS

Pleasant Valley Wildlife Sanctuary, 472 West Mountain Rd. (© **413/637-0320**), has a small museum and 7 miles (11km) of hiking and snowshoeing trails crossing its 1,500 acres (608 hectares). Beaver lodges and dams can be glimpsed from a distance, and waterfowl and other birds are found in abundance—bring binoculars. Hours are Tuesday through Saturday from dawn to sunset; admission is $3 for adults and $2 for children 3 to 15. To get here, drive north 6.6 miles (11km) on Routes 7 and 20 and turn left on West Dugway Road.

In town, **Main Street Sports & Leisure,** 48 Main St. (© **413/637-4407**), rents bikes, canoes, skates, snowshoes, cross-country skis, and tennis rackets. The staff can recommend routes and trails, give you preprinted driving directions to area state parks and forests, and arrange guided trips. **Kennedy Park,** right down the street from the store, is a favorite spot for cross-country skiing in winter, or for a ramble in any season. Dogs are allowed off-leash throughout the 12 miles (19km) of trails.

More extensive trails can be found at **October Mountain State Forest** (see "Outdoor Pursuits" under the section on Lee, above) or at **Beartown State Forest,** 69 Blue Hill Rd., in nearby Monterey. The Appalachian Trail, which runs from Maine to Georgia, connects with a loop trail around a small pond with a nice swimming area. To get here, take Route 7 south for 3½ miles (5.6km), then turn left onto West Road. After 2½ miles (4km), turn left at the T intersection onto Route 102 east. Turn right over the bridge onto Meadow Street, then turn right onto Pine Street and follow the signs.

SHOPPING

The Bookstore, 9 Housatonic St. (© **413/637-3390**), helps fill a yawning need in the Berkshires, which are curiously lacking in comprehensive bookstores. Those in pursuit of art and antiques, on the other hand, cannot easily exhaust the possibilities. Among them: **La Vie en Rose,** 67 Church St. (© **413/637-3663**), known for hand-painted furniture and vintage jewelry; the **Ella Lerner Gallery,** 17 Franklin St. (© **413/637-3315**), specializing in European and American painters of the 19th and 20th centuries; and the **Hoadley Gallery,** 21 Church St. (© **413/637-2814**), which shows American crafts and ceramics. For fashion-forward clothing for men and women, much of it Italian-made, check in at **Casablanca,** 21 Housatonic St. (© **413/637-2680**). L.L.Bean, it isn't. Out on Route 7, heading toward Pittsfield, serious cooks should watch for **The Cook's Resource,** 374 Pittsfield Rd. (© **413/637-0606**).

WHERE TO STAY

The list of lodgings below is only partial, and most can accommodate only small numbers of guests. The Tanglewood concert season is a powerful draw, so prices are highest in summer as well as the brief foliage season. Rates are of Byzantine complexity, set according to wildly varying combinations of seasons and days of the week as well as facilities offered. Minimum 2- or 3-night stays are usually required during the Tanglewood weeks, foliage, weekends, and holidays. *Note:* For visits during the Tanglewood season, reserve far in advance—February isn't too soon.

Given the substantial number of lodgings and limited space to describe them, admittedly arbitrary judgments have been made to winnow the list. Some inns, for example, are so rule-ridden and facility-free that they come off as crabby—no kids, no pets, no phones, no credit cards, no breakfast before 9am, shared bathrooms—and they cost twice as much as nearby motels that have all those conveniences. Let them seek clients elsewhere.

Others are open only 6 or 7 months a year and charge the world for a bed or a meal. In this latter category, though, one place demands at least a mention: **Blantyre,** 16 Blantyre Rd. (🕐 **413/637-3556** in summer, 413/298-3806 in winter), in its 1902 Tudor-Norman mansion, cossets its guests with a soak in undeniable luxury, both in dining room and bedchamber. Rates are $330 to $395 double, up to $1,100 for the top suite.

If all the area's inns are booked or if you want to be assured the full quota of 21st-century conveniences, Routes 7 and 20 north and south of town harbor a number of motels, including the **Mayflower Motor Inn** (🕐 **413/443-4468**), the **Susse Chalet** (🕐 **413/637-3560**), the **Lenox Motel** (🕐 **413/499-0324**), and the **Comfort Inn** (🕐 **413/443-4714**).

Very Expensive

Canyon Ranch in the Berkshires ★★★ Resorts successfully melding turn-of-the-last-century opulence and contemporary impulses for fitness and healthy living are rare, so for those with the discretionary income or others who'd like to splurge just once, this is the place. A guard turns away the unconfirmed at the gate, so there's no popping in for a look around. The core facility is the 1897 mansion modeled after Le Petit Trianon at Versailles. A fire in 1949 left only the magnificent library untouched, but that loss has been offset by major renovations. Sweat away the pounds in the huge spa complex, with 40 exercise classes a day, weights, an indoor track, racquetball, squash, and all the equipment you might want. Canoeing and hiking are added possibilities. Guest rooms are in contemporary New England style, with every hotel convenience except tempting minibars. After being steamed, exhausted, pummeled, and showered, the real events of each day are mealtimes: "nutritionally balanced gourmet," naturally.

P.O. Box 2170, 165 Kemble St., Lenox, MA 01240. 🕐 **800/726-9900** or 413/637-4100. Fax 413/637-0057. www.canyonranch.com. 126 units. All-inclusive 3- to 7-night packages from $1,080–$4,540 double. Rates include meals and allowances for health, beauty, and fitness services. Taxes and 18% service charge extra. AE, DC, DISC, MC, V. **Amenities:** Restaurant (spa cuisine); heated indoor and outdoor pools; outdoor and indoor tennis courts; extensive health club and spa; bikes; business center; salon; limited room service; in-room massage; same-day dry cleaning/laundry. *In room:* A/C, TV/VCR, dataport, hair dryer, iron, safe.

Cranwell Resort & Golf Club ★★★ The main building of this all-season resort looks like a castle in the Scottish Highlands, but no 17th-century laird lived this well. It stands at the center of a 380-acre (154-hectare) property, ringed by views of the surrounding hills. That's where the most expensive rooms are; the rest are in four smaller outlying buildings. Accommodations are outfitted with less concern for adherence to a particular style than for surrounding guests in immediate comfort. In addition to the lovely grounds (which serve as cross-country ski trails in winter), there is a 60-acre (24-hectare) golf school. Three dining rooms range from formal to pubby, and live jazz is featured Friday and Saturday nights. Construction of an enormous spa with pool should be complete by the time of your visit.

55 Lee Rd. (Rte. 183), Lenox, MA 01240. 🕐 **800/272-6935** or 413/637-1364. Fax 413/637-4364. www. cranwell.com. 107 units. July–Oct $209–$459 double; Nov–Apr $99–$239 double. Golf and ski packages available. AE, DC, DISC, MC, V. From Lenox Center, go north to Rte. 20 E. The resort is on the left. **Amenities:** 3 restaurants (eclectic); bar; heated outdoor and indoor pools; 18-hole golf course; 4 tennis courts; extensive new health club; bike rental; salon; limited room service; in-room massage; babysitting; same-day dry cleaning. *In room:* A/C, TV/VCR, fax, dataport, fridge, coffeemaker, hair dryer, iron, safe.

Wheatleigh ✿✿   Glamorous young New Yorkers and Europeans drape themselves in Gatsbyesque poses around the lavishly appointed great hall. Much of the time, they look elaborately bored, no easy feat in this persuasive 1893 replica of a 16th-century Tuscan palazzo, which aspires to the highest standards of the moneyed Berkshires. Happily, the interior decor is muted, not florid, utilizing neutral colors and restrained shapes. Wheatleigh has always been very expensive, even though the cheapest rooms average only 11 by 13 feet (3.3 × 4m). But other places are catching up, and the manager is striving to give requisite value. The dining room rounds out the experience, with painstakingly conceived food in superb presentation.

Hawthorne Rd., Lenox, MA 01240. ✆ **413/637-0610.** Fax 413/637-4507. www.wheatleigh.com. 19 units. $215–$725 double. AE, DC, MC, V. **Amenities:** 2 restaurants (eclectic), lounge; heated outdoor pool; tennis court; exercise room; bike rental; concierge; in-room massage; babysitting; laundry service; dry cleaning. *In room:* A/C, TV/VCR, fax, hair dryer.

Expensive

Cliffwood Inn ✿   One of the relatively compact manses of the Vanderbilt era, this inn has a long veranda in back overlooking the pool. Antiques and reproductions of many styles and periods fill the common and private spaces. Six guest rooms have working fireplaces (including one in a bathroom!). Three units have TVs.

25 Cliffwood St., Lenox, MA 01240. ✆ **800/789-3331** or 413/637-3330. Fax 413/637-0221. www.cliffwood.com. 7 units. July–Labor Day and foliage season $159–$254 double; May 15–June 30 and Sept after Labor Day $136–$200; Nov–May 14 $118–$173. Rates include breakfast daily in high season, Sat–Sun only in shoulder season, Sun and holiday weekends only in low season. No credit cards. Children over 10 welcome. **Amenities:** Outdoor pool and indoor counter-current workout pool; Jacuzzi. *In room:* A/C.

Gateways Inn ✿✿   Harley Procter, who hitched up with a man called Gamble and made a bundle, had this house built in 1912. Its most impressive feature is the staircase that winds down into the lobby. Designed by McKim, Mead & White, it's a stunner, just the thing for a grand entrance. Equally impressive is the suite named for conductor Arthur Fiedler, with not one but two fireplaces, a big four-poster on the sun porch, and a Jacuzzi. Eight rooms have working fireplaces. Dining here is one of Lenox's greater pleasures. The tiny bar is being expanded and a terrace has been added for after-concert light meals and desserts. Lunch is offered on summer weekends.

51 Walker St., Lenox, MA 01240. ✆ **800/492-9466** or 413/637-2532. Fax 413/637-1432. www.gatewaysinn.com. 12 units. June–Oct $120–$260 double, $275–$400 suite; Nov–May $90–$180 double, $230–$320 suite. Rates include breakfast. AE, DC, DISC, MC, V. No children under 12. **Amenities:** Restaurant (eclectic), bar. *In room:* A/C, TV.

Whistler's Inn   Both innkeepers are compulsive travelers who bring things back from every trip, filling the rooms of their 1820 Tudor mansion with cut glass, painted screens, grandfather clocks, Persian rugs, and shelf after shelf of books. The result: rooms that are not so much decorated as gathered, without a single boring corner. Most units have TVs and air-conditioning; some have fireplaces as well. The carriage house has one room decked out in African style, the other suggesting Santa Fe. A bottle of sherry or port is kept in the library for guests to enjoy along with tea and cookies. Facilities for children are limited.

5 Greenwood St., Lenox, MA 01240. ✆ **413/637-0975.** Fax 413/637-2190. www.whistlersinnlenox.com. 11 units. June 16–Oct $130–$275 double; Nov–June 15 $100–$210 double. Rates include breakfast. AE, DISC, MC, V.

Moderate

Brook Farm Inn "There is poetry here," insist the owners of this picture-pretty 1870 farmhouse, and an afternoon idle in the hammock overlooking the pool or a curled-up read by the fireplace will have you agreeing. Six rooms have wood-burning fireplaces. Breakfast is an ample buffet.

15 Hawthorne St., Lenox, MA 01240. © 800/285-7638 or 413/637-3013. Fax 413/637-4751. www.brookfarm.com. 12 units. Mid-June to Labor Day $140–$230 double; Labor Day–Nov and Memorial Day to early June $105–$180; Nov–June $105–$165. Rates include breakfast and afternoon tea. AE, DISC, MC, V. From the town center, go south 1 block on Old Stockbridge Rd.; turn right. No children under 15. **Amenities:** Heated outdoor pool; access to nearby health club. *In room:* A/C.

Candlelight Inn A folksy gathering place for locals as well as guests, the bar in this 1885 Victorian enjoys a convivial nightly trade, and the dining rooms are often full. In winter, sit beside a crackling fire; in summer, lunch out in the courtyard. On summer weekends, the basement pub is open for after-concert drinks and snacks. While the Candlelight does most of its business on the restaurant side, the upstairs bedrooms are homey and unpretentious.

35 Walker St., Lenox, MA 01240. © 800/428-0580 or 413/637-1555. www.candlelightinn-lenox.com. 8 units. $75–$195 double. Rates include breakfast. AE, DISC, MC, V. Often closed for a week or so in Jan. Accommodations unsuitable for children under 10. **Amenities:** Restaurant (eclectic), bar. *In room:* A/C, no phone.

Gables Inn ★★ Edith Wharton, who spent more than 2 decades in Lenox, made this Queen Anne mansion her home for 2 years while her house, the Mount, was being built. That may be enough to interest fans of the novelist, but there's much more to appeal to potential guests, including the canopied four-poster in Edith's bedroom. Meticulously maintained Victoriana and antiques are found in every corner. Many rooms have fireplaces, and suites have VCRs and fridges.

81 Walker St., Lenox, MA 01240. © 800/382-9401 or 413/637-3416. Fax 413/637-3416. www.gables lenox.com. 19 units. $90–$200 double; $160–$250 suite. Rates include breakfast. DISC, MC, V. No children under 12. **Amenities:** Heated outdoor and indoor pools; tennis court. *In room:* A/C, TV.

Village Inn An inn off and on since 1775, this place hasn't a whiff of pretense. Its rooms come in considerable variety and are categorized as Deluxe, Superior, Standard, or Economy. That means four-posters in the high-end rooms, some of which have fireplaces and/or Jacuzzis, and constricted quarters with double beds at the lower prices. Claw-foot tubs are common in all categories. Ask about rooms on the renovated third floor. Afternoon tea and dinner are served in the restaurant, light meals in the tavern.

16 Church St., Lenox, MA 01240. © 800/253-0917 or 413/637-0020. Fax 413/637-9756. www.villageinn-lenox.com. 32 units. Summer–fall $135–$255 double, $480–$530 suite; winter–spring $65–$185 double, $350–$390 suite. Discount of 30% during midweek in winter/spring. AE, DC, DISC, MC, V. No children under 6. **Amenities:** Restaurant, bar; free video library. *In room:* A/C, TV/VCR.

WHERE TO DINE

See also "Where to Stay," above, as many inns have dining rooms. In particular, **Blantyre** (© 413/637-3556) is worth a splurge. In high season, **Spigalina,** 80 Main St. (© 413/637-4455), serves imaginative Mediterranean cooking. Note that three of the restaurants listed below serve lunch, in a region where most restaurants don't open until evening.

Café Lucia ★★ REGIONAL ITALIAN Here on Lenox's Restaurant Row, the post-preppie crowd of regulars and weekend refugees from the city is attired in country-casual cashmere and tweed, a taste no doubt honed at campuses of the Ivy League and Seven Sisters. The waitresses display a professionalism rarely experienced in these hills, bringing satisfying starters—carpaccio, bruschetta, and the like—followed by superior renditions of *saltimbocca alla Romana* and eight pastas. Dine out on the broad deck in warmer months.

80 Church St. (C) 413/637-2640. Reservations recommended. Main courses $17–$32. AE, DC, DISC, MC, V. Tues–Sun 5:30–10pm. Closed 3 weeks Mar or Apr. Winter hours fluctuate, especially around holiday weekends; call ahead.

Church Street Cafe ⭐⭐ ECLECTIC AMERICAN   The most popular place in town delivers fanciful combinations that please the eye and pique the taste buds. Creative appearances on past menus have included seared salmon on a crisp noodle cake and a pizza topped with lobster and mascarpone drizzled with white truffle oil. Lunch is a busy time here, with crab-cake sandwiches among the favorites. The decor is rudimentary, the service friendly but rushed. A large deck fills up whenever the weather allows.

65 Church St. (C) 413/637-2745. Reservations recommended on weekends. Main courses $17.50–$28.50. MC, V. May–Oct daily 11:30am–2pm and 5:30–9pm; Nov–Apr Tues–Sat 11:30am–2pm and 5:30–9pm.

Roseborough Grill AMERICAN/GLOBAL   Inside the rambling old farmhouse are plain wooden tables unadorned at lunch but dressed with linen and candles at night. Serious jazz drifts out of the stereo, and often-surprising food issues from the kitchen. Past dishes have included pan-seared Chilean sea bass escabeche, lobster linguine, and shrimp and white bean stew, all of which demonstrate that the chefs gambol in many scented fields, usually emerging with dignity intact.

71 Church St. (C) 413/637-2700. Main courses $17–$27. AE, DC, DISC, MC, V. Thurs–Mon 11:30am–3pm and 5–9pm (until 10pm Fri–Sat). Call ahead in winter. Closed Feb–Mar.

Zinc ⭐⭐ CONTEMPORARY BISTRO   With its eponymous zinc bar, butcher paper over white tablecloths, tile floor, and waitresses in ankle-length aprons, this recent entry has leapt in a single bound to the upper echelon of Berkshires dining. That is, if you admire not only the setting but also a cuisine and wine list that adhere with some rigor to the French-bistro canon. Menus have listed such appetizers as boneless quail stuffed with polenta, continuing with steak frites, sautéed skate wing, and lobster bouillabaise. A remarkable 24 wines are available by the glass.

56 Church St. (C) 413/637-8800. Reservations suggested. Main courses $18–$27. AE, MC, V. Wed–Mon 11:30am–3pm and 5:30–10pm (bar until 12:30am).

PITTSFIELD

Berkshire County's largest city (pop. 48,000) gets little attention in most tourist literature, and for good reason. A commercial and industrial center, it presents little of the charm that marks such popular destinations as Stockbridge and Lenox. Still, it is a convenient base for day excursions to attractions elsewhere in the region. In summer, the Pittsfield Mets play minor-league baseball at Wahconah Park, a 1919 stadium with real wooden box seats.

Pittsfield lies 137 miles (221km) west of Boston, 7 miles (11km) north of Lenox. The **Berkshire Visitors Bureau** ((C) **800/237-5747** or 413/443-9186; www.berkshires.org) is located in the same block of buildings as the Crowne Plaza Hotel, on Berkshire Common.

Movers & Shakers

Mother Ann arrived in 1774 with eight disciples just as the disgruntled American colonies were about to burst into open rebellion. The former Ann Lee, once imprisoned in England for her excess of religious zeal, had anointed herself leader of the United Society of Believers in Christ's Second Coming. The austere Protestant sect was dedicated to simplicity, equality, and celibacy. They were popularly known as "the Shakers" for their spastic movements when in the throes of religious ecstasy. By the time of her death in 1784, Mother Lee had made many converts, who then fanned out across the country to form communal settlements from Maine to Indiana. One of the most important Shaker communities, Hancock, edged the Massachusetts–New York border, near Pittsfield.

Shaker society produced dedicated, highly disciplined farmers and craftspeople whose products were much in demand in the outside world. They sold seeds, invented early agricultural machinery and hand tools, and erected large buildings of several stories and exquisite simplicity. Their spare, clean-lined furniture and accessories anticipated the so-called Danish Modern style by a century and in recent years have drawn astonishingly high prices at auction.

All of these accomplishments required a verve owed at least in part to sublimation of sexual energy, for a fundamental Shaker tenet was total celibacy for its adherents. They kept going with converts and adoption of orphans (who were free to leave, if they wished). But by the 1970s, the inevitable result of this policy left the movement with a bare handful of believers. The string of Shaker settlements and museums that remain is testament to their dictum, "Hands to work, hearts to God."

SEEING THE SIGHTS

Arrowhead   Herman Melville bought this 18th-century house in 1850 and lived here until 1863. It was during this time that he wrote *Moby Dick*. A nature trail and shop are on site. In truth, however, the house is of limited interest to visitors other than literature students and avid readers.

780 Holmes Rd. (©) 413/442-1793. www.mobydick.org. Admission $6 adults, $2 seniors and children. From Fri before Memorial Day to Oct 31 daily 9:30am–5pm; rest of year by appointment only. Visits are by guided tour only, given on the hour. Drive east from Park Sq. on East St., turn right on Elm St., and turn right on Holmes Rd.

Berkshire Museum ⭐   It began in 1903 as the "Museum of Natural History and Art," words chiseled in stone above the entrance. The holdings bounce from Babylonian cuneiform tablets to tanks of live fish to archaeological artifacts like a delicate necklace from Thebes dating to at least 1500 B.C. An auditorium seating 300 serves as the "Little Cinema," which shows art and foreign films during the warmer months.

39 South St. (Rte. 7, 1 block south of Park Sq.). (©) 413/443-7171. www.berkshiremuseum.org. Admission $7 adults; $5 seniors, students, and Mon matinee; $4 children 3–18. Mon–Sat 10am–5pm; Sun noon–5pm.

Hancock Shaker Village ★★★   Of the 20 restored buildings that make up the village, its signature structure is easily the 1826 round stone barn. The Shaker preoccupation with functionalism joined with purity of line and respect for materials has never been clearer than it is in the design of this building—its round shape expedited the chores of feeding and milking livestock by arranging cows in a circle, and the precise joinery of the roof beams and support pillars is a joy to observe.

The second must-see is the brick dwelling that contained the communal dining room, kitchens, and sleeping quarters. Sexes were separated at meals, work, and religious services, and such features as the opposing staircases leading to male and female "retiring rooms" served equality.

While artisans and docents demonstrate Shaker crafts and techniques, they are not in costume, nor do they pretend to be Shaker inhabitants. They are knowledgeable about their subject, though, and dispense such nuggets as explanations of the Shaker discipline that required members to dress the right side first, to button from right to left, and to step with the right foot first.

The museum shop is excellent, and a cafe serves lunches in summer and fall, with some dishes based on Shaker recipes. On Saturday nights from July to October, the village presents tours and Shaker four-course dinners at a cost of about $40. Reservations for these are essential.

Rtes. 20 and 41, Pittsfield. ℂ **800/817-1137** or 413/443-0188. www.hancockshakervillage.org. Admission Memorial Day to late Oct $13.50 adults, $5.50 children 6–17, $33 per family; rest of year (by guided tour only) $10 adults, $5 children 6–17, $25 per family. Memorial Day to late Oct daily 9:30am–5pm; rest of year daily 10am–3pm (tours on the hour). Call ahead in winter for hours and events.

OUTDOOR PURSUITS

Plaine's Bike, Ski, & Snowboard, 55 W. Housatonic St., at Center Street (ℂ **413/499-0294**), rents bikes and carries equipment for all the sports its name suggests. It's on Route 20, west of downtown.

Pittsfield State Forest, entered on Cascade Street (ℂ **413/442-8992**), is a little over 3 miles (5km) west of the center of town. Its 10,000 acres (4,050 hectares) have 31 campsites, boat ramps, streams for canoeing and fishing, and trails for hiking, biking, riding, and cross-country skiing. It's open daily from 8am to 8pm. Admission is $2 per car.

BOATING **Onota Boat Livery,** 463 Pecks Rd. (ℂ **413/442-1724**), rents canoes and motorboats for use on Onota Lake, conveniently located at the western edge of the city.

SKIING South of the city center, off Route 7 near the Pittsfield city limits, is the **Bousquet Ski Area,** Dan Fox Drive (ℂ **413/442-8316** business office, 413/442-2436 snow phone; www.bousquets.com). Bousquet (pronounced "Bos-kay") has 21 trails, with a vertical drop of 750 feet (225m), two double lifts, and two rope tows. Night skiing is available Monday through Saturday. Rentals and lessons are offered. Lift tickets cost $25.

About 10 miles (16km) north of Pittsfield on Route 7, in New Ashford, is **Brodie Mountain Ski Area** (ℂ **413/443-4752;** www.skibrodie.com), with a vertical drop of 1,250 feet (375m). Night skiing is available, and in summer the ski area offers racquetball, tennis, 150 campsites, and a heated pool. Lift tickets are $29 for adults, $19 for seniors and children.

Alternatively, turn west a mile (1.6km) short of Brodie Mountain on Brodie Mountain Road and continue 2 miles (3km) to **Jiminy Peak** ★, Hancock (ℂ **413/738-5500,** or 413/738-7325 for ski reports; www.jiminypeak.com).

This expanding resort aspires to four-season activity, so skiing on 28 trails (18 open at night) with seven lifts is supplemented the rest of the year by horseback riding, trapshooting, fishing in a stocked pond, a rock-climbing wall, six tennis courts, mountain biking, pools, and golf at the nearby Waubeeka Springs course.

WHERE TO STAY

The Country Inn at Jiminy Peak *(Kids)* This is one of the better lodging deals in the Berkshires, if your idea of luxury is space. All units are one-bedroom suites with full kitchens and sofa beds. Recent renovations have enhanced the resort's reputation as a family destination, with its on-site downhill skiing and abundant recreational facilities (see "Outdoor Pursuits," above).

Brodie Mountain Rd. (near Rte. 43), Hancock, MA 01237. © 800/882-8859 or 413/738-5500. Fax 413/738-5513. www.jiminypeak.com. 105 units. $150–$330 suite. Winter rates include lift tickets. AE, DC, DISC, MC, V. **Amenities:** 2 restaurants (eclectic); 2 bars; heated outdoor and indoor pools; 6 tennis courts; exercise room; Jacuzzi; sauna; children's programs; game room; babysitting; coin-op washers and dryers. *In room:* A/C, TV/VCR, kitchenette, coffeemaker, hair dryer, iron.

WILLIAMSTOWN 🎭🎭

This community and its prestigious liberal-arts college were both named for Col. Ephraim Williams, who was killed in 1755 in one of the French and Indian Wars. He bequeathed the land for creation of a school and a town. His college grew, spreading east from the central common along both sides of Main Street (Rte. 2). Over the town's long history, buildings have been erected in several styles of the times. That makes Main Street a virtual museum of institutional architecture, with representatives of the Georgian, Federal, Gothic Revival, Romanesque, and Victorian modes, as well as a few that are yet to be labeled. They stand at dignified distances from one another, so what might have been a tumultuous visual hodgepodge is a stately lesson in historical design. The impressive Clark Art Institute is the best reason to make a special trip, perhaps in conjunction with a performance at the increasingly ambitious Williamstown Theatre Festival.

A free weekly newspaper, the *Advocate* (© **413/664-7900**), produces useful guides to both the northern and southern Berkshires. For a copy, write to the *Advocate,* 87 Marshall St., North Adams, MA 01267. An unattended **information booth,** at North Street (Rte. 7) and Main Street (Rte. 2), has an abundance of pamphlets and brochures free for the taking.

SEEING THE SIGHTS

Sterling and Francine Clark Art Institute 🎭🎭🎭 Within these walls are canvases by Renoir (34 of them), Degas, Gauguin, Toulouse-Lautrec, Pissarro, and their predecessor, Corot. Also on display is the famed Degas sculpture *Little Dancer,* believed to be his only three-dimensional piece and a signature work of the Institute. While they are the stars, there are also works by 15th- and 16th-century Dutch portraitists, European genre and landscape painters, and Americans Sargent and Homer, as well as fine porcelain, silver, and antiques. This qualifies as one of the great cultural resources of the Berkshires and of the state.

Apart from the collection itself, the Clarks' farsighted endowment funded the modern wing added to the original neoclassical building and has covered all acquisitions, upkeep, and renovations. His stipulation that there be no admission fee was finally breached, but the charge applies only to adults, 4 months a year. A substantial bookstore in the lobby has been joined by a snack counter and an attractive cafe. An additional wing is being contemplated.

Pittsfield on Stage

The **Berkshire Opera Company,** 297 North St. (℗ **413/443-7400**), stages its July and August productions of both established and new operas at the Koussevitzky Arts Center of Berkshire Community College in Pittsfield. That venue is also employed by the **Albany Berkshire Ballet,** 51 North St. (℗ **413/445-5382**), with up to 14 performances of two ballets from early July to mid-August.

Special exhibitions scheduled for 2003 include *Renoir and Algeria* and *Turner: The Late Seascapes.*

225 South St., Williamstown. ℗ **413/458-2303**. www.clarkart.edu. Admission mid-June–Oct $5 adults, free for students and children; free to all Tues and Nov–June. Sept–June Tues–Sun 10am–5pm; July–Aug daily 10am–5pm.

Williams College Museum of Art ✪ The second leg of Williamstown's two prominent art repositories exists in large part thanks to the college's collection of almost 400 paintings by the American modernists Maurice and Charles Prendergast. The museum also has works by Gris, Léger, Whistler, Picasso, Warhol, and Hopper.

15 Lawrence Hall Dr., Williamstown. ℗ **413/597-2429**. www.williams.edu/WCMA. Free admission. Tues–Sat (and some Mon holidays) 10am–5pm; Sun 1–5pm.

OUTDOOR PURSUITS

Waubeeka Golf Links, Routes 7 and 43, South Williamstown (℗ **413/ 458-5869**), is open to the public, with weekend greens fees of $35.

Mount Greylock State Reservation ✪ contains the highest peak (3,487 ft./ 1,046m) in Massachusetts as well as a section of the Appalachian Trail. A road allows cars almost to the summit, where War Memorial Tower affords vistas of the Taconic and Hoosac ranges, far into Vermont and New York. Trails radiate from the parking lot near **Bascom Lodge,** North Main Street off Route 7 in Lanesboro (℗ **413/743-1591** or 413/443-0011), a grandly rustic creation of the Civilian Conservation Corps in the New Deal 1930s. Simple dormitory beds and four private rooms are available for rent from mid-May to late October. Dinners are available by reservation.

SHOPPING

In the small downtown shopping district, **Library Antiques,** 70 Spring St. (℗ **413/458-3436**), is filled with a wealth of English chess sets, African carvings, Peruvian alpaca sweaters, and antique American fishing lures and creels. South of the town center on Route 7, **Saddleback Antiques,** 1395 Cold Spring Rd. (℗ **413/458-5852**), features country, wicker, and Victorian furniture. Slightly north of town on Route 7, **Collectors Warehouse,** 105 North St. (℗ **413/458-9686**), has a little bit of everything—jewelry, books, dolls, furniture, and glassware.

WHERE TO STAY

This is a college town, so in addition to the usual Berkshires peak periods of July, August, and the October foliage season, accommodations fill up during graduation and on football weekends. The largest lodging in town is the 100-unit **Williams Inn,** 1090 Main St. (℗ **800/828-0133** or 413/458-9371). Despite the name, it is a standard motel, with a dining room, tavern, and indoor pool. **The Orchards,** 222 Adams Rd. (© **800/225-1517** or 413/458-9611), a more sedate choice, has a competent restaurant, a pool, and an exercise room. Three miles (5km) south of town at Routes 2 and 7 is the brookside **Berkshire Hills Motel** (© **413/458-3950**), with a heated pool. See also the section on North Adams, below.

Field Farm Guesthouse ⋆   After an extended vacation of B&B-hopping, there may come a time when one more tilted floor or wobbly Windsor chair will send even a devout inn lover over the edge. Here's an antidote. This pristine example of postwar modern architecture rose in 1948 on a spectacular 296-acre (120-hectare) estate with 4 miles (6km) of trails. The living room is equipped with a telescope to view the beavers and waterfowl on the lake. Most guest rooms look over meadows to Mount Greylock, most of the Scandinavian Modern furniture was made to order for the house, and three units have decks while two have fireplaces. Breakfasts are hearty meals of waffles and five-cheese omelets utilizing fruits, herbs, and vegetables grown on the property. Well-behaved children are welcome.

554 Sloan Rd., Williamstown, MA 01262. © and fax **413/458-3135**. www.thetrustees.org. 5 units. $125–$165 double. Rates include breakfast. DISC, MC, V. Follow Rte. 7 to Rte. 43 and turn west, then make an immediate right on Sloan Rd. Continue 1 mile (1.6km) to the Field Farm entrance, on the right. **Amenities:** Heated outdoor pool; tennis court. *In room:* Hair dryer.

WHERE TO DINE
Fire destroyed **Mezze,** previously recommended here, but the owners have opened **Eleven,** described in the section on North Adams, below.

Main Street Café ⋆ CREATIVE ITALIAN   Dominating the otherwise woe-begone local dining scene is this transplant from Vermont, which brought along its name from Bennington. The bar, more often used for eating than extended drinking, has a tasty menu of snacks. There are imaginative pizzas from the brick oven, plus daily special risottos and raviolis. Ten wines are available by the glass. In good weather, meals are served on the deck. Jazz combos play on Friday nights.

16 Water St. © **413/458-3210**. Main courses $16.95–$24.95. AE, DC, MC, V. Daily noon–midnight. Shorter hours may apply in winter; call ahead.

WILLIAMSTOWN AFTER DARK
The Williams College Department of Music sponsors diverse concerts and recitals. Call its **Concertline** (© **413/597-3146**) to learn of upcoming events. In addition, the Clark Art Institute (see above) hosts frequent classical-music events.

The Williamstown Theatre Festival ⋆⋆   Williamstown's premier attraction each summer, the festival performs in the Adams Memorial Theatre. Staging classic and new plays during its season from late June to August, the festival attracts many top actors and directors, among them Gwyneth Paltrow, Frank Langella, Ethan Hawke, and Bebe Neuwirth. The Main Stage presents works by major playwrights, while the Nikos Stage often features more experimental productions. The schedule is usually announced by April. It's not too difficult to get tickets, but if a particular performance is said to be sold out, there are often cancellations in the 30 minutes before curtain.

Main St. (P.O. Box 517). © **413/597-3400** for box office, 413/597-3399 for recorded information. www.wtfestival.org. Tickets $3–$50.

NORTH ADAMS
Barely 5 years ago, there was not a wisp of hope that this comatose mill town could be pulled back from the brink of near-death. Its unemployment rate was

the highest in the state, and over two-thirds of its storefronts were empty. A land developer once even suggested that the town be flooded to create lakefront property.

In no time at all, North Adams has experienced a whiplash rebirth, its storefronts filling up with restaurants and galleries and high-tech start-ups. The thoroughly unlikely reason, to almost everyone's agreement, is an art museum. An abandoned industrial complex has been converted, despite hoots of derision, into a center for the visual and performing arts. It is called the Massachusetts Museum of Contemporary Art, and it has strikingly altered the socio-economic dynamic of North Adams.

Massachusetts Museum of Contemporary Art ⚘ A lot of excitement and anticipation surrounded this ambitious project, the conversion of an empty 27-building textile factory into a center for the arts. Even before its official opening, it had a nickname—MASS MoCA—and hosted performances by David Byrne, Patti Smith, and the Merce Cunningham Dance Company. Works on display are often outsized, crossing traditional esthetic boundaries to marry elements of both performing and visual arts.

Its chief virtue—from the standpoint of those contemporary artists who choose to work on a grand scale—is the vastness of the spaces available. But additionally, the museum has hosted a variety of musical events, experimental films, even dance parties, and is attracting small tenant companies working the vineyards of technology, including software, video, and e-commerce. MASS MoCA has attracted hundreds of thousands of visitors and is certainly worth the short detour east from neighboring Williamstown.

87 Marshall St., North Adams. ✆ 413/662-2111. www.massmoca.org. Admission June–Oct $8 adults, $3 children 6–16; Nov–May $7 adults, $5 seniors and students, $2 children 6–16. June–Oct daily 10am–6pm; Nov–May Wed–Mon 11am–5pm.

WHERE TO STAY

Blackinton Manor ⚘ Music informs this 1849 Greek Revival house, hardly surprising since one of the owners is a classical pianist and his wife an opera singer and invested cantor. They hold a number of chamber concerts throughout the year, many of them to benefit favorite causes. But they don't neglect their hospitality functions for a minute, be assured—this is one of the most gracious inn experiences in the northern Berkshires. You'll know after passing an evening before the fire with a glass of sherry. All of the bedrooms are grandly furnished, but try for the lavishly appointed Music Room, spacious enough to contain its own piano. A typical breakfast consists of fresh fruit, an herbed omelet, and freshly baked pastries.

1391 Massachusetts Ave., North Adams, MA 01247. ✆ 800/795-8613 or 413/663-5795. www.blackinton-manor.com. 5 units. $110–$250 double. Rates include breakfast. MC, V. Children over 7 welcome. Follow Rte. 2 east from Williamstown into North Adams, turn left on Ashton, and turn right after railroad bridge. **Amenities:** Unheated outdoor pool. *In room:* A/C, TV.

The Porches ⚘⚘ In this entertaining melding of vintage and contemporary, a row of five detached 19th-century workingmen's houses has been stitched together by an uninterrupted streetside veranda, the spaces in between roofed over and fitted with indoor catwalks and patios. Rooms are witty tributes to the past, with kitschy lamps and paint-by-numbers pictures on the walls, but are also equipped with DVD players and high-speed DSL Internet access. Down duvets, bathrobes, and cushy sofas add to guests' comfort. Ask for one of the second-floor king rooms with balcony.

231 River St., North Adams, MA 01247. © **413/664-0400.** Fax 413/664-0401. www.porches.com. 50 units. June to mid-Nov $150–$260 double, $225–$430 suite; mid-Nov to late May $125–$209 double, $175–$329 suite. Rates include breakfast. Packages available. AE, DC, MC, V. Find it behind the MASS MoCA complex, half a block west of Marshall St. **Amenities:** Heated outdoor pool; Jacuzzi; sauna; computer for guests' use (laptop rentals also available); in-room massage; laundry service (Mon–Fri); free DVD library. *In room:* A/C, TV/DVD, dataport, minibar, hair dryer, iron.

WHERE TO DINE

Eleven FRENCH BISTRO   After fire razed their popular restaurant, Mezze, in Williamstown, the owners plunged back into the fray with this enterprise, located just before the entrance to MASS MoCA. Its industrial spareness suggests the cafeteria of a struggling dot-com, but the background of beige, white, and gray is meant eventually to backdrop contemporary artworks. Patrons are a mix of artistic folks and office workers at lunch, couples and gangs of friends at night. The menu adheres to the contemporary bistro model of steak frites, pan-seared cod with white beans, and yellowfin tuna with wasabi and celery purée. Skip the uninspired appetizer plate of New England cheeses; the fried ricotta ravioli with wild mushrooms is more interesting.

1111 MASS MoCA Way. © **413/622-2004.** Main courses $13–$18. AE, MC, V. Mon–Sat 11:30am–4pm and 5–10pm (daily Memorial Day to Columbus Day).

Il Tesoro ITALIAN   Opened in 2001, this airy corner space in a restored downtown building features a floor painted in patterns meant to evoke a Venetian palazzo. Expect the likes of veal piccata and clams in white wine, preceded by good bread that arrives warm from the oven with a roasted eggplant spread. Veal is a specialty, but seafood is worth a look, notably the *frutta di mare*—shrimp, clams, mussels, and calamari sautéed in white wine and garlic.

34 Holden St. © **413/664-6400.** Main courses $17.95–$27.95. AE, DC, MC, V. Mon–Thurs 5–10pm; Fri–Sat 5–11pm.

9

Connecticut

by Herbert Bailey Livesey

Connecticut resists generalization and confounds spinners of superlatives. It doesn't rank at the top or bottom of any important chart of virtues or liabilities, which makes it impossible to stuff into pigeonholes. The nation's second-smallest state is certainly compact—only 90 miles (145km) wide and 55 miles (89km) top to bottom—but it is still three times the size of the most diminutive of all, which happens to lie right next door. While parts of it are clogged with humanity, some corners are as empty and undeveloped as inland Maine.

By many measures, Connecticut's citizens are as wealthy as any in the country, but dozens of its towns are only shells of their prosperous 19th-century selves, beset by poverty as intractable as it gets. It can boast no dramatic geographical feature, and its highest elevation is only 2,380 feet (714m). Established in 1635 by disgruntled English settlers who didn't like the way things were going at Plymouth Colony, it has long seemed spiritually divorced from the rest of New England—an appendage of New York, or a place to be traversed on the way from there to Boston.

All this might appear to constitute an identity crisis and hardly makes Connecticut seem an appealing vacation destination. But a closer look reveals an abundance of reasons to slow down and linger.

To a great extent, the state owes its existence to the presence of water. In addition to having Long Island Sound along its entire southern coast, several significant rivers and their tributaries slice through the hills and coastal plain—the Housatonic, Naugatuck, Quinnipiac, Connecticut, and Thames. They provided power for the mills along their courses and the towns and cities that grew around them. Industry still drives most of the economy, despite the bucolic image that mention of the state often conjures, and the pollution that industry has caused in the rivers and the sound is being scoured away.

Development, too, appears to have slowed, helping to preserve for a little longer Connecticut's scores of classic colonial villages, from the Litchfield Hills in the northwest to the Mystic coast in the opposite corner. They are as placid and timeless as they have been for more than 3 centuries, or as polished and sophisticated as transplanted urbanites can make them. And the state's salty maritime heritage is palpable in the old boat-building and fishing villages at the mouths of its rivers, especially those east of New Haven.

Connecticut is New England's front porch. Pull up a chair and stay awhile.

1 Fairfield County

Mansions, marinas, and luxury apartment blocks elbow for space right up to the deeply indented Long Island Sound shoreline in the southwestern corner of the state. This is one of the most heavily developed stretches of the coast, and, in terms of family income, one of the wealthiest. As the land rises slowly inland from the water's edge, woods thicken, roads narrow, and pockets of New England unfold. Yacht country becomes horse country.

The first suburbs began to form in the middle of the last century, when train rails started radiating north and east from New York's Grand Central Terminal into the countryside. This part of the state was made accessible for summertime refugees from the big city, and eventually weekend houses became permanent dwellings. Corporate executives liked the life of the gentry, so after World War II, they started moving their companies closer to their new homes. Stamford became a city; Greenwich, New Canaan, Darien, and Westport were the bedrooms of choice—pricey, haughty, redolent of the good life. (Of course, Fairfield County also contains Bridgeport, a depressed city that once considered filing for bankruptcy.)

But for visitors, the fashionable exurbs and their beaches, restaurants, and upscale shops are the draw, along with the villages farther north, especially Ridgefield, that hint of Vermont, all within 1½ hours of Times Square.

ESSENTIALS

GETTING THERE   From New York and points south, take I-95 or, preferably, the Hutchinson and Merritt parkways. From eastern Massachusetts and northern Connecticut, take I-84 south to Danbury, then Route 7 south into Fairfield County.

The **Metro North** (© **800/METRO-INFO** or 212/532-4900; www.mta.nyc.ny.us/mnr) commuter line has many trains daily from New York's Grand Central Terminal, with stops at Greenwich, Stamford, Darien, Norwalk, Westport, and additional stations all the way to New Haven. Express trains make the trip in 45 to 65 minutes.

VISITOR INFORMATION   Information on the northern part of the county is available from the **Housatonic Valley Tourism District** (© **800/841-4488;** www.housatonic.org), while the **Coastal Fairfield County Convention and Visitor Bureau** (© **800/473-4868;** www.visitfairfieldco.org) can provide materials about the coastal towns.

STAMFORD

A trickle of corporations started moving their headquarters from New York 38 miles (61km) northeast to Stamford in the 1960s. That flow became a steady stream by the 1980s, and more than a dozen Fortune 500 companies continue to direct their operations from here. They have erected shiny mid-rise towers that give the city of 108,000 residents an appearance more like the new urban centers of the Sun Belt than those of the Snow Belt.

One result is a lively downtown that other, less prosperous Connecticut cities surely envy. Roughly contained by Greylock Place, Tresser Boulevard, and Atlantic and Main streets, it has two theaters, tree-lined streets with many shops and a large mall, pocket parks and plazas, and a number of stylish restaurants, sidewalk cafes, and nightclubs.

For further information, contact the **Greater Stamford Convention & Visitors Bureau,** 1 Landmark Sq. (© **203/359-4761**).

Stamford Museum & Nature Center ⭐ *Kids*   About 5 miles (8km) north of the city center is this fine family-oriented resource. The center has a large lake, an open pen with a pair of river otters, and a real working farm with goats, sheep, cattle, and peacocks. May and June mark the arrival of newborn chicks,

Connecticut

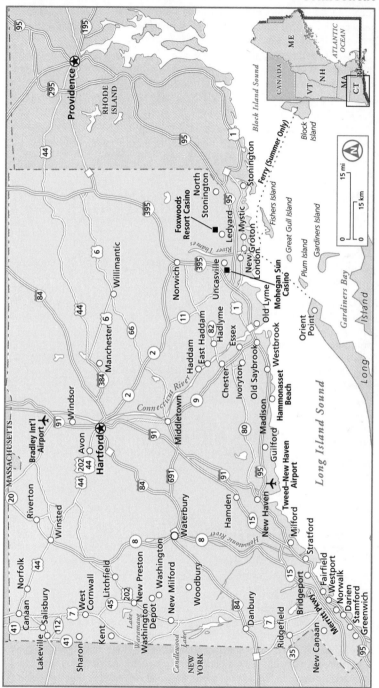

kids, calves, and lambs. On the grounds are a country store, nature trails, a small planetarium, and an oddball Tudor-Gothic house with galleries of art, natural history, and Indian lore.

39 Scofieldtown Rd. ⦿ 203/322-1646. Admission $6 adults, $4 seniors and children 4–13. Mon–Sat and holidays 9am–5pm; Sun 1–5pm. Feeding time is 9am. The center is 1 mile (1.6km) north of Exit 35 off the Merritt Pkwy. (Rte. 15).

Whitney Museum of American Art, Fairfield County   This outpost of the parent institution in New York is housed on the ground floor of one of Stamford's office towers. It displays the kind of cutting-edge art that routinely infuriates and amuses critics and art lovers at the mother museum. There is no permanent collection, just traveling exhibitions.

400 Atlantic St. (at Tresser Blvd.). ⦿ 203/358-7630 or 203/358-7652. Free admission. Tues–Sat 11am–5pm.

OUTDOOR PURSUITS

Recreational sailors might want to consider the bare-boat charters at **Brewer Yacht Haven,** Washington Boulevard (⦿ **203/359-4500**), while less experienced folk may prefer joining the crew of the *Sound Waters* (⦿ **203/ 323-1978**), an 80-foot (24m) three-masted schooner. The 3-hour sailing trips are intended as educational sojourns on the ecology of the sound. There are also a handful of sunset dinner cruises and singles sails. Fees are $10 to $25.

SHOPPING

United House Wrecking *(Finds)*   Dedicated antiques hounds will want to make time for this sprawling emporium of oddments. The name may not sound promising, but the company got its start selling architectural remnants salvaged from demolitions. For years, it featured such items as 1930s gas pumps, stone pigs, and pagodas. Now it showcases far less bizarre imported antiques and reproductions. Open Monday through Saturday from 9:30am to 5:30pm, Sunday from noon to 5pm. (It's tough to find. From Exit 9 of I-95, pick up Rte. 1, then Rte. 106 north; make a left on Glenbrook Rd., which becomes Church St., and turn right on Hope St. Be sure you have a map or detailed directions.) 535 Hope St. ⦿ 203/348-5371.

WHERE TO STAY

Westin Stamford ⟨★★⟩   This outpost of the always reliable international chain does nothing to diminish the expectations of business travelers. Everything is in place, from the executive floors with club lounge to the airport shuttle van. The more expensive rooms have high-speed Internet connections.

1 Stamford Place (Exit 7, I-95), Stamford, CT 06902. ⦿ 800/937-8461 or 203/967-2222. Fax 203/351-1910. www.westin.com. 481 units. $114–$289 double. AE, DC, DISC, MC, V. **Amenities:** Restaurant (international); heated indoor pool; tennis court; health club; concierge; business center; 24-hr. room service; same-day dry cleaning/laundry. *In room:* A/C, TV, dataport, minibar, coffeemaker, hair dryer, iron, safe.

WHERE TO DINE

Beacon ⟨★⟩ AMERICAN   Chef Waldy Malouf gathered acclaim at three New York restaurants for championing the use of regional ingredients and uncomplicated cooking methods. His exurban outpost was receiving hosannas from reviewers within days of its initial shakedown period. What you get here is a multi-tiered space with outdoor decks directly over the water, accompanied by substantial platters of fish, fowl, and beef subjected to "open-fire cooking"—that is, grilled, smoked, and/or wood-roasted. Upstairs is a bar where snacks are available. Tasty, the food certainly is, and simple. Think of this not for romantic interludes but rather for groups who don't want to be distracted by inventive formulations meant to push the gastronomic envelope.

183 Harbor Dr. ✆ **203/327-4600.** Reservations strongly advised. Main courses $18–$29. AE, DC, MC, V. Mon–Sat noon–2:30pm and 5:30–10pm (Fri–Sat until 11pm); Sun noon–2:30pm and 5–9pm. Take Exit 8 from I-95 north, merging with State St. Turn right on Elm St., right again on Jefferson St., left on Magee Ave., and right on Harbor Dr.

Oceans 211 ✹✹ NEW AMERICAN/SEAFOOD   First, know that the hands-on owner put in his apprenticeship at the venerable Oyster Bar in New York's Grand Central Terminal. It shows: The ground-floor bar has a Manhattan sheen, with a curving black marble bar and a long display case of featured wines (mostly from California). The menu is deceptively plain, the entrees listed only by their central ingredients—halibut, mahimahi, shrimp. The delights come with what shows up on the plate. Tilapia, for example, arrives with an olive-and-fig vinaigrette, sweet sausage, orzo, and oyster mushrooms. You might have trouble getting past the delectable appetizers—the curried shrimp quesadilla with annato cream, for one. Upstairs is a less cozy dining room that seats up to 70.

211 Summer St. ✆ **203/973-0494.** Reservations suggested on weekends. Main courses $20–$26. AE, DC, MC, V. Mon–Fri noon–2:30pm and 5:30–9:30pm; Sat 5:30–10:30pm.

Smokey Joe's BARBECUE   This used to be called Buster's, but apart from a paint job and a new sign, nothing much has changed. Smack on the Stamford–Darien line, it wouldn't pass an Amarillo authenticity test, but it's close enough. Upstairs is a down-and-dirty bar with pool table; downstairs is a classic barbecue joint. Stand in the cafeteria line and select from confusing lists of ribs, brisket, pulled pork, sausage, and birds; then retire to the oilclothed picnic tables to gorge.

1308 E. Main St. (Rte. 1). ✆ **203/406-0605.** Main courses $9.95–$24.50. Mon–Thurs 11:30am–9:30pm; Fri–Sat 11:30am–10:30pm; Sun 11:30am–9pm (bar daily until 1:30am).

STAMFORD AFTER DARK

The **Rich Forum/Stamford Center for the Arts,** Atlantic Street and Tresser Boulevard (✆ **203/325-4466;** www.onlyatsca.com), presents professional productions, with name actors, of successful Broadway and off-Broadway plays as well as new ones, while the **Palace Theatre,** 61 Atlantic St. (✆ **203/325-4466;** www.onlyatsca.com), offers musicals; rotating appearances by the Stamford Symphony Orchestra, the Connecticut Grand Opera and Orchestra, and the Connecticut Ballet; and one-night stands by solo acts and traveling troupes like Willie Nelson and the Alvin Ailey Dance Theater.

Among the handful of downtown clubs is the long-standing **Art Bar,** 84 W. Park Place (✆ **203/973-0300**), which features a subterranean maze of lounge rooms, a bar, and a DJ. Open Thursday through Sunday nights; a dress code is enforced. The **Terrace Club,** 1938 W. Main St. (✆ **203/961-9770**), features live acts and DJ nights—country, Latin, and ballroom dancing all get their turn. The aptly named **Next Door Cafe,** 1990 W. Main St. (✆ **203/961-9770**), has DJs most nights. In summer, there's live Latin music on the patio.

NORWALK

Given the despair that grips many New England cities, the continuing betterment of this city's once notorious South Norwalk neighborhood gladdens the heart. The rehabilitation of several blocks of 19th-century row houses is transforming the waterfront into a trendy precinct that has come to be called, inevitably, "SoNo." The Norwalk Seaport Oyster Festival, held in early September, attracts over 90,000 visitors to its tall ships and oyster boats, crafts show, and food court. The district, bounded roughly by Washington, Water, and North and South Main streets, is readily accessible from the South Norwalk railroad station.

Lockwood-Mathews Mansion Museum Erected in 1864, this granite mansion in the Second Empire style is covered with peaked and mansard slate roofs and has 62 rooms arranged around a stunning skylit octagonal rotunda. Marble, gilt, marquetry, and frescoes were commissioned and incorporated with abandon. It has been designated a National Historic Landmark.

295 West Ave. ✆ **203/838-1434**. Admission $8 adults, $5 seniors, free for children under 12. Visits are by 1-hour guided tour only. Mid-Mar to New Year's Day Wed–Sun noon–5pm. From I-95 southbound, take Exit 15; from I-95 northbound, take Exit 14.

The Maritime Aquarium at Norwalk ★★ This facility remains the centerpiece of revitalized SoNo. The present name isn't inclusive, as part of the complex includes a section of boat-builders at work as well as exhibits of model ships and full-size vessels, including the *Tango,* which was *pedaled* across the Atlantic. The main attractions, though, are the marine creatures and mammals on view. Five harbor seals are fed at 11:45am, 1:45pm, and 3:45pm, when they wriggle up on the rocks and all but rest their heads in their handler's lap. Additional exhibits include a pair of river otters, an open pool of cow-nosed rays, and tanks alive with creatures found in sound waters. A new sea-turtle exhibit opened in 2001. Finally, a giant IMAX screen shows nature films that aren't necessarily confined to the seven seas.

10 N. Water St. ✆ **203/852-0700**. www.maritimeaquarium.org. Admission $8.75 adults, $8 seniors, $7.25 children 2–12; IMAX $6.75 adults, $5.75 seniors, $5 children; combination packages (aquarium plus IMAX movie) $13.25 adults, $11.50 seniors, $10 children. July–Aug daily 10am–6pm; Sept–June daily 10am–5pm.

CRUISES

Excursions to **Sheffield Island** and its historic lighthouse are offered by the *Seaport Islander* (✆ **888/547-6863** or 203/854-4656), a 60-passenger vessel that departs from Hope Dock, near the Maritime Aquarium. Weather permitting, the boat sets out two to four times daily, on Saturdays and Sundays from Memorial Day weekend to late September and Monday through Friday from late June to Labor Day. The round-trip takes about 2½ hours, with a 15-minute layover on the island. Fares are $15 for adults, $7 for children 3 to 12, and $5 for children under 3. Special outings include sunset cruises and occasional Sunday picnics. Call ahead.

Similarly, the oyster sloop *Hope* has "creature cruises" in winter to spot seals and bird life, as well as marine study cruises at other times, a service of the Maritime Aquarium. Fares are $15 per person. Reserve ahead by calling ✆ **203/852-0700,** ext. 206.

SHOPPING

Serious shoppers have several choices, primarily among the boutiques and galleries along Washington and Main streets. One shop that may produce a bargain or at least a surprise is **Saga,** 119 Washington St. (✆ **203/855-1900**). It specializes in folk arts and crafts as well as jewelry and furnishings from the southwestern United States, Mexico, and points south.

WHERE TO DINE

Amberjacks Coastal Grill ✿ CONTEMPORARY AMERICAN   The chef/ owner used to run a restaurant in Key West, and this room looks as if he trucked it up intact from Duval Street. The bar is shaped like the prow of a boat, while maritime paintings adorn the walls. The food is boldly flavored, with frequent use of Asian spices and Creole staples. Examples are the Thai tuna steak with wasabi mashed potatoes at dinner and the po' boy sandwich at lunch. Jazz, blues, and local bands appear Thursdays, Fridays, and some Saturdays. The lively Friday happy hour draws 30-ish singles who move out onto the deck in summer.

99 Washington St. (between Broad and Main sts.). © 203/853-4332. Reservations suggested on weekends. Main courses $10.95–$25. AE, DC, MC, V. Mon–Sat noon–3pm and 5:30–10pm (Fri–Sat until 11pm); Sun noon–10pm.

Barcelona ✿✿ MEDITERRANEAN   Tapas are the featured attraction here, but the kitchen isn't doctrinaire about recipes, which range all over the Mediterranean and even down to South America for inspiration. The day's delectables might include mussels al Diabla, chorizo with sweet and sour figs, or triangular piquillo peppers stuffed with potato-cod brandade. Other options include paella, steaks, and roast monkfish. Tapas cost 25% less before 6:30pm. The patio is open year-round.

63–65 N. Main St. (north of Washington St.). © 203/899-0088. Reservations suggested on weekends. Tapas $3.50–$7.50. Main courses $16–$24. AE, DC DISC, MC, V. Daily 5pm–1am.

WESTPORT

After World War II, the housing crunch had young couples scouring the metropolitan area for affordable housing lying along the three main routes of what is now known as the Metro North transit system. Some of them wound up in this pretty village beside the Saugatuck River, several miles inland from Long Island Sound (47 miles/76km northeast of New York City, 29 miles/47km southwest of New Haven). Most of the new commuter class found Westport to be too far away from Manhattan (1–1½ hours each way on the train), and it was deemed the archetype of the far-out bedroom communities that were dubbed the "exurbs"—beyond suburban.

Notable for its large contingent of people in the creative crafts, primarily commercial artists, advertising copywriters, art directors, and their fellows, the town was also appealing to CEOs and higher-level executives, many of whom solved their commuting problem by moving their offices to nearby Stamford. The result is a bustling community with surviving elements of its rural New England past wrapped in a sheen of Big Apple panache.

For further information, contact the **Westport Chamber of Commerce,** 180 Post Rd. E. (© **203/227-9234**).

OUTDOOR PURSUITS

Sherwood Island State Park, Green Farms (© **203/566-2305**), has two long swimming beaches separated by a grove of trees sheltering dozens of picnic tables with grills. Surf fishing is a possibility from designated areas, and the park has concession stands, restrooms, and an amateurish "nature center." The park is open from Memorial Day to Labor Day, daily from 8am to sunset. Pets are not allowed. By car, take Exit 18 off I-95 or U.S. 1, following the road called the Sherwood Island Connector. Admission for out-of-state cars is $8 Monday through Friday, $12 Saturday and Sunday.

You can get to Sherwood Island by taking a train to Westport and a taxi from the station to the park. If you don't have a car, you might prefer to use that method to get to **Compo Beach,** the long municipal strand not far from downtown.

West of the town center is the **Nature Center for Environmental Activities,** 10 Woodside Lane (© **203/227-7253**). Its 62 acres (25 hectares) offer several trails, a wildlife rehab center, and a building with live animals and an aquarium. Open Monday through Saturday from 9am to 5pm, Sunday from 1 to 4pm. Admission is $1 for adults, 50¢ for children 3 to 14; donations are welcome.

The Nature Conservancy oversees **Devil's Den Preserve,** Old Route 7 (© **203/226-4991**), in Weston, north of Westport (take Route 7 to Old Route 7). An undeveloped tract of more than 1,500 acres (608 hectares) in the heart of densely populated Fairfield County, this is a refuge of rare value. It has 15 miles (24km) of trails beside ponds and waterways rich with birds and other wildlife. Cross-country skiing is permitted, but there are no picnic or toilet facilities. Open daily from sunrise to sunset. Admission is free, but donations are welcome.

Rent a sailboat or arrange a lesson at the **Longshore Sailing School,** Longshore Club Park, 260 S. Compo Rd. (© **203/226-4646**), about 2 miles (3km) south of the Boston Post Road (U.S. 1).

SHOPPING

Circa Antiques   Here is as eclectic a selection as two owners from Ontario and west Texas might contrive. They unload containers from France every 3 months or so, most of it furniture from the 19th and early 20th centuries. Biedermeier pieces are increasingly evident. 11 Riverside Ave. © **203/222-8642.**

Lillian August   Less conventional than other Westport stores, Lillian August displays a large collection of paintings, rugs, overstuffed chairs, and related accessories. Owing allegiance to no specific style, it looks as if it were conceived by Laura Ashley on speed. 17 Main St. © **203/629-1539.**

The Stuart Collection   On the west end of the bridge over the Saugatuck is a row of fetching shops. This one trumpets its taste for dazzlingly colorful ceramics and blown glassware, most of it Italian, such as the ornate Venetian chandeliers. 11 Winter St. © **203/221-7102.**

WHERE TO STAY

Inn at National Hall ★★★   A playful elegance is on display throughout this riverside hotel, starting as soon as you enter the elevator, which turns out to be a *trompe l'oeil* representation of an estate library. The 1873 brick building has finally realized its destiny as an exquisitely decorated hotel. Voluptuous furnishings, antiques, and canopied beds fill the public rooms and duplex suites—it's improbable that you've seen anything like this elsewhere. But those prices!

2 Post Rd. (at west end of Saugatuck Bridge), Westport, CT 06880. © **800/628-4255** or 203/221-1351. Fax 203/221-0276. www.innatnationalhall.com. 16 units. $275–$485 double; $465–$850 suite. Rates include breakfast. AE, DC, MC, V. Valet parking $20. **Amenities:** Restaurant (Mediterranean), lounge; access to nearby health club; spa; concierge; limited room service; in-room massage; babysitting; same-day dry cleaning/laundry. *In room:* A/C, TV w/ pay movies, dataport, hair dryer, safe.

WHERE TO DINE

In addition to the following choices, consider the restaurant at the **Inn at National Hall** (see above).

Acqua ★ MEDITERRANEAN/SEAFOOD   A light touch does wonders with such immaculately fresh ingredients as striped bass, halibut, crab, skate, and clams. Presentations are marvelously inviting, yet without the appearance of excessive pushing and prodding in the kitchen. The decor consists of murals depicting cherubim, aged-looking tiles, and a bar arching around the wood-burning oven, used for pizzas and the customer favorite, roasted chicken.

43 Main St. (near east end of Saugatuck Bridge). ✆ 203/222-8899. Reservations recommended on weekends. Main courses $16–$28. AE, DC, MC, V. Mon–Thurs noon–2:30pm and 5:30–10pm; Fri–Sat noon–2:30pm and 5:30–10:30pm; Sun noon–3pm and 5:30–9:30pm.

Tavern on Main ✍ AMERICAN BISTRO   Westporters don't come in too many different ages, sizes, or colors, but most of them mount the Tavern's front steps with regularity. Local merchants, widows who lunch, executives, and young moms crowd into the clubby bar to wait for a table. The main room has fragments of the building's earliest years—hand-hewn beams and a brick fireplace. Menu items suffer from neither gushing elaboration nor daring. But the kitchen toys with convention, as with the trademark lobster roll: The center of a seeded roll is scooped out, the cavity filled with warm (not cool) buttery chunks and shreds of the crustacean. Similar turns are taken with coconut shrimp, five-vegetable couscous, and potato-wrapped sea bass.

146 Main St. ✆ 203/221-7222. Reservations recommended. Main courses $6–$20 lunch; $15–$25 dinner. AE, DC, MC, V. Daily 11:30am–10pm (Fri–Sat until 11pm).

WESTPORT AFTER DARK

One of the oldest theaters on the straw-hat circuit, the **Westport Country Playhouse,** 25 Powers Ct. (✆ **203/227-4177**), has passed its 70th year. Revitalized under the leadership of Joanne Woodward and other new administrators, the theater produces comedies, dramas, and musicals from June to mid-September. Famous or at least vaguely familiar actors appear in almost every production. A Sunday music series brings in such diverse acts as Arlo Guthrie, the Preservation Hall Jazz Band, and doo-wop groups. Single tickets go on sale May 29, priced from $17 to $48.

The **White Barn Theatre,** Newtown Avenue (✆ **203/227-3768**), is a respected venue with a slightly shorter summer season than the Playhouse. From late June to August, outdoor musical performances are given at **Levitt Pavilion,** off Jesup Green near the center of town (✆ **203/226-7600**).

RIDGEFIELD

No town in Connecticut has a more imposing main street. Ridgefield's is almost 100 feet (30m) wide, lined with ancient elms, maples, and oaks, and bordered by massive 19th-century houses. Impressive at any time of the year, it is in its glory during the brief blaze of the October foliage season. Only a little over an hour from New York City (58 miles/93km northeast), the town is nonetheless a true evocation of the New England character.

Aldrich Museum of Contemporary Art ★★   This superb collection of paintings and sculptures from the second half of the 20th century was begun decades ago by Larry Aldrich, a fashion designer who died in 2001. The original 18th-century clapboard structure has more than doubled in size with a harmonious addition. Three major exhibitions are held a year, as well as concerts, films, and lectures. The outdoor sculptures can be viewed even when the museum itself is closed.

258 Main St. (near the intersection of Rtes. 35 and 33 at the south end of Main St.). ✆ 203/438-4519. www.aldrichart.org. Admission $5 adults, $2 seniors and students, free for children under 12; free to all Tues. Tues–Sun noon–5pm (but hours fluctuate with the season and current exhibitions; call ahead). Free guided tours Sun 2pm.

Keeler Tavern   This 1713 stagecoach inn was providing sustenance to travelers between Boston and New York long before the Revolutionary War, but that conflict provided it with its object of greatest note. A British cannonball is imbedded in one of its walls, presumably fired during the Battle of Ridgefield in 1777. It's now a museum of colonial life, with period furnishings and costumed guides. And the tavern has another claim to fame: It was long the summer home of architect Cass Gilbert (1849–1934), who designed the Supreme Court Building in Washington, D.C., and who was a key figure in the construction of the George Washington Bridge in New York.

132 Main St. ✆ **203/438-5485.** Admission $4 adults, $2 seniors, $1 children. Wed and Sat–Sun 1–4pm.

SHOPPING

Hay Day Market   Apart from the usual antiques shops and the strip malls north of town on Route 35, this is a most interesting stop for devoted food lovers. Hidden in a shopping center behind Main Street, it is about as fancy a food market as exists outside of Manhattan. Sections are devoted to produce, prepared foods, baked goods, charcuterie, cheeses, and fresh flowers. 21 Governor St. ✆ **203/431-4400.**

WHERE TO STAY & DINE

Bernard's ✵   New proprietors have breathed life into the tired old Inn at Ridgefield. The piano still stands in the main dining parlor, and it's played Friday and Saturday nights and for the festive Sunday brunch, but the primary interests of the owners clearly lie in the kitchen. Imagine fricassee of snails with wild mushrooms, asparagus, and fava beans in a potato basket with red currant tomatoes! Given an occasional tendency to overcook the fish, the main courses of veal, lamb, or game are often better choices. Several dinner choices appear as half-priced versions at lunch, but the romance of music and flickering lights is in the evenings.

20 West Lane (near the junction with Rte. 7). ✆ **203/438-8282.** Reservations recommended on weekends. Main courses $23.50–$31.50. AE, DC, MC, V. Tues–Sun noon–2:30pm and 6:30–9pm.

The Elms ✵   Ridgefield's oldest (1799) operating inn has the ambience of a small contemporary hotel with the conveniences most travelers desire, as well as newly decorated guest rooms with canopied beds. The **dining room and tavern** ✵✵ (✆ **203/438-9206**) are now in the hands of Manhattan chef Brendan Walsh, whose ministrations have freshened the award-winning restaurant and lower-priced tavern without masking their origins. His food utilizes regional ingredients, as in the Connecticut seafood stew. Mixed grill of lamb, venison, and sausage is a Sunday dinner fixture. Reservations are essential on weekends.

500 Main St. (Rte. 35, at the north end of town), Ridgefield, CT 06877. ✆ and fax **203/438-2541.** www.elmsinn.com. 20 units. $150–$210 double. Rates include breakfast. AE, DC, MC, V. **Amenities:** Restaurant (creative American), tavern. *In room:* A/C, TV.

West Lane Inn ✵✵   An inn to fit most images of a romantic country getaway, this also works for businesspeople, as it offers modem jacks, voice mail, and express checkout. Some rooms have fireplaces, and all have four-poster beds. The 1849 house stands on a property blessed with giant shade trees. You can take breakfast on the terrace in good weather. Bernard's (see above), just across the driveway, serves lunch and dinner.

22 West Lane (off Rte. 35), Ridgefield, CT 06877. ✆ **203/438-7323.** Fax 203/438-7325. www.west laneinn.com. 18 units. $110–$225 double. Rates include breakfast. AE, DC, DISC, MC, V. Driving north from

Wilton on Rte. 33, turn west on Rte. 35 at the edge of town. **Amenities:** Concierge; limited room service; laundry service; dry cleaning. *In room:* A/C, TV/VCR, dataport, kitchenette, fridge, coffeemaker, hair dryer.

2 The Litchfield Hills ✦✦

When the Hamptons got too pricey, too visible, and too chichi back in the 1980s, a lot of stockbrokers, CEOs, and celebs started discovering the Litchfield Hills, arguably the most fetchingly rustic yet sophisticated part of Connecticut.

The topography and, to an extent, the microculture of the region are defined by the river that runs through it, the Housatonic. Broad but not deep enough for vessels larger than canoes, it waters farms and villages and forests along its course, provides opportunities for recreational angling and float trips, and, over the millennia, has helped to shape these foothills, which merge with the Massachusetts Berkshires.

Men in overalls and CAT caps still stand on the porches of general stores, their breath steaming in the bracing autumn air. Churches hold pancake-breakfast fundraisers; neighbors squabble about development. That's one side of these bucolic hills, less than 2 hours from Times Square.

Increasingly, the other side is fashioned by refugees from New York. These chic seekers of tranquility and real estate fled to pre-Revolutionary saltboxes and Georgian colonials on Litchfield's warren of back roads and brought Manhattan-bred expectations with them. Boutiques fragrant with designer coffees and cachets opened in spaces once occupied by luncheonettes and feed stores. Restaurants discovered sushi and sun-dried tomatoes and just how much money they could get away with charging the newcomers.

Compromises and city-country conflicts aside, the Litchfield Hills remain a satisfying all-season destination for day trips and overnights from metropolitan New York and Connecticut.

ESSENTIALS

GETTING THERE   From New York City, take the Hutchinson River Parkway to I-684 north to I-84 east, taking Exit 7 onto Route 7 north. Continue on Route 7 for New Milford, Kent, West Cornwall, and Canaan. For Washington Depot, New Preston, and Litchfield, branch off onto Route 202 at New Milford. An especially attractive entrance into the region is Route 44 from the Taconic Parkway, through Millerton and into Lakeville and Salisbury.

From Boston, take the Massachusetts Turnpike west to the Lee exit, picking up Route 7 south from nearby Stockbridge.

VISITOR INFORMATION   The useful 40-page *Unwind* brochure is produced by the **Litchfield Hills Visitors Bureau** (© **860/567-4506;** fax 860/567-5214; www.litchfieldhills.com). Also see **www.housatonic.org** and **www.litchfieldcty.com**.

NEW MILFORD

A gateway to the Litchfield Hills, this town was founded in 1703 and functions as a commercial center for the smaller villages that surround it—Roxbury, Bridgewater, Washington, and Brookfield. It is also at the high end of a long stretch of overdeveloped Route 7, which is clogged with strip malls.

New Milford is a welcome stop on the drive north, if only for lunch and a short stroll. Turn right on Route 202 where it splits from Route 7 and crosses the Housatonic River and a railroad track. Up on the left is one end of the long town green. A 1902 fire destroyed many of the buildings around the green, so this isn't one of those picture-book New England settings. Rather, it is a mix of late Victoriana, early Greek Revival, and Eisenhower-era architecture, not to ignore the requisite Congregational church.

Otherwise, there are no obligatory sights, so a walk down Bank Street, west of the green and along Railroad Street, with its crafts shops, a bookstore, and an Art Moderne movie house, won't take long.

OUTDOOR PURSUITS

Candlewood Lake (© 860/354-6928) is the third-largest man-made lake in the eastern United States. It has a finger that pokes into New Milford, but the area with the most recreational facilities is a few miles to the west. From New Milford, drive north on Route 7 about 2½ miles (4km), turn west on Route 37 toward and through Sherman, then south on Route 39 to **Squantz Pond State Park** (© 860/424-3200). With over 170 acres (69 hectares) along the lakeshore, it offers swimming, ice-skating, fishing, hiking and cycling trails, picnic grounds, rental canoes, and a boat launch.

WHERE TO STAY

There are good reasons for families to consider making New Milford their base for exploring the Litchfield Hills. Inns in the towns farther north typically exclude smokers, pets, and children, and their rates fluctuate wildly according to day and season. The following establishment is more tolerant and relatively inexpensive.

Heritage Inn *(Kids)*   This building started life as a tobacco warehouse in 1870, but looks more like a railroad hotel in the Old West, with its high ceilings and long central hall. The old beams were left exposed, a nice touch, for the decor is otherwise uninspired, though perfectly comfortable. The upstairs rooms pull together better visually. Breakfast goes well beyond the usual, with French toast and made-to-order omelets. While the inn stands next to the railroad tracks, only an occasional freight train rumbles past, since commuter service was ended years ago.

34 Bridge St. (opposite Railroad Station), New Milford, CT 06776. © 800/311-6294 or 860/354-8883. Fax 860/350-5543. www.bedandbreakfast.com. 20 units. $110–$125 double. Rates include breakfast. Children under 5 stay free in parents' room; older kids sharing parents' room pay $15. AE, DC, DISC, MC, V. **Amenities:** Coin-op washers and dryers; dry cleaning. *In room:* A/C, TV, dataport, hair dryer, iron.

WHERE TO DINE

There are many dining choices along Bank and Railroad streets and out on nearby Route 7.

The Cookhouse *(Kids)*   SOUTHERN/BARBECUE   Inexplicably, Connecticut has been home to some thumpingly good barbecue joints. This is the current champ. It's set, appropriately enough, in a converted barn on often tacky Route 7. Ribs, chicken, pulled pork, and beef brisket are slow-smoked for 10 hours or more. Heaping portions come with sides such as baked beans, collard greens, and mashed potatoes. There's also sweet potato pie, Louisiana meat pie, and the catfish po' boy.

31 Danbury Rd. (Rte. 7). © 860/355-4111. Main courses $12.95–$19.95. AE, DC, MC, V. Sun–Thurs 11:30am–10pm; Fri–Sat 11:30am–11pm.

WOODBURY *(Kids)*

The chief distinction of this attractive town strung along Route 6, west of Waterbury, is its number of high-end antiques stores. On weekends in good weather, the main road is clogged with cars trolling for treasures, and progress can be slow.

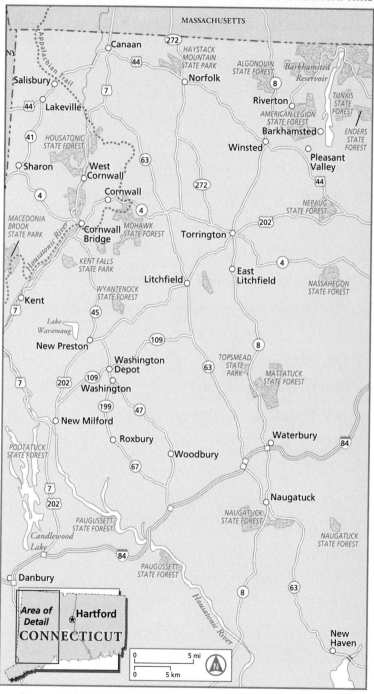

ANTIQUING

Shoppers are drawn here for antiques and collectibles of every sort, from funky to obscure to elegant. To winnow down the list, pick up the directory produced by the **Woodbury Antiques Dealers Association** 🏵🏵 (www.antiqueswood bury.com) at one of the member stores.

Start off in the building at 289 Main St., at the intersection of Routes 6 and 317, which contains **Jennings & Rohn Antiques** (© **203/263-3775**). European paintings and furnishings from the 16th century to 1960 are on view, as well as lighting fixtures and some Art Deco. At **Martell & Suffin Antiques** (© **203/263-1913**), the owners favor 18th- and early-19th-century European furniture as well as Asian works of art.

Drive south on Main Street (Rte. 6) to the notable **Wayne Pratt Antiques,** 346 Main St. (© **203/263-5676**), which specializes in 18th-century American furniture, much of it museum-level Chippendale and Queen Anne pieces. Some items are within reach for the rest of us, like the keepsake Chinese porcelain boxes for $12.

Of similar high order are the offerings at **Country Loft Antiques,** 557 Main St. (© **203/266-4500**), largely 19th-century French furnishings and *objets* displayed in a fine old barn. Wares run from biscuit tins to carved armoires, bolts of fabric to 18th-century dining tables. Be sure to look into the basement, outfitted as a wine cellar.

On most Saturdays in decent weather, the **Woodbury Antiques & Flea Market** (© **203/263-2841**) sets up in a parking lot at the south end of town.

SEEING THE SIGHTS

Flanders Nature Center   North of Woodbury on Route 6, watch for Flanders Road forking to the left. Three miles (5km) along, on the right, is the office building for this nature center. Yearly events include maple syrup and wreath making, along with a fall festival. Maps of hiking trails are available.

Church Hill and Flanders Rd. © **203/263-3711**. Free admission. Office Mon–Fri 9am–5pm; trails daily dawn to dusk.

Glebe House   About the only scrap of surviving history worth mentioning is this 1750 house of an Episcopal bishop, west of Route 6 on a street of fine 18th-century houses. A *glebe* was a property given to a preacher as partial compensation for his services. Inside are furnishings true to the period; outside is the Gertrude Jekyll Garden.

Hollow Rd. © **203/263-2855**. Admission $4 adults, $1 children under 12. Apr–Oct Wed–Sun 1–5pm; Nov Sat–Sun 1–4pm.

WHERE TO STAY

Longwood Country Inn 🏵   South of the town center, this 2-century-old house has been a B&B since 1951, until recently known as Merryvale. One of the current owners is an architect and the other worked in fashion, accounting for the spare good taste evident throughout. The considerably upgraded accommodations include room 3, with a four-poster bed and a fireplace, and the smaller but country-elegant room 2. In addition, the owners have pushed out the walls for a new 48-seat restaurant. Meals are contemporary in execution, but with "historic colonial inspiration."

1204 Main St. (Rte. 6), Woodbury, CT 06798. © **203/266-0800**. Fax 203/263-4479. www.longwood countryinn.com. 5 units. $115–$250 double. Rates include breakfast. AE, DC, MC, V. **Amenities:** Restaurant (regional American). *In room:* A/C, TV.

WHERE TO DINE

Another option is the **Longwood Country Inn,** described above.

Good News Café ★★ NEW AMERICAN   This is a fun spot, with a cheery staff and rooms doused in blazing primary colors. The food? Make it Europe meets Asia, touching down in various parts of the Americas along the way. The results are spirited, but never bizarre. Examples: spiced venison chop with celery root purée and grilled swordfish with tomato herb bread pudding and wilted broccoli rabe. Most of the entrees qualify as heart-healthy, and ingredients, whenever possible, are purchased from local farmers. Desserts, however, tend to be rich, gooey, and caloric. Saturday nights feature live jazz, and there's outdoor dining in summer.

694 Main St. (Rte. 6). ℂ 203/266-4663. Reservations recommended on weekends. Main courses $15–$29. AE, DC, MC, V. Wed–Mon 11:30am–10pm.

WASHINGTON ★★ & WASHINGTON DEPOT

Settled in 1734, its name changed in 1779 to honor the first American president, Washington occupies the crown of a hill beside Route 47. Its village green, with the impressive 1802 Congregational Meeting House surrounded by white buildings and sheltered by shade trees, is an example of a municipal arrangement found all over New England—but rarely to such near-perfection. The traveling series of musical events known as the **Armstrong Chamber Concerts** (ℂ **860/868-0522**) usually alights in Washington on four Sunday afternoons in spring and fall (other appearances are in Greenwich, Conn., and Lenox, Mass.). Performances are in the Congregational church.

Adjacent Washington Depot, down the hill beside the Shepaug River, serves as the commercial center, with a bank and a small cluster of shops. Stop in at the beguiling **Hickory Stick Bookshop,** 2 Greenhill Rd. (ℂ **860/868-0525**).

Nearby **Steep Rock Reservation** (ℂ **860/868-9131**) is a lovely spot for hiking, fly-fishing, or cross-country skiing. (Unfortunately for pet owners, dogs must now be leashed.)

Institute for American Indian Studies   A worthwhile detour takes drivers down Curtis Road to this small repository of Native American crafts and artifacts. They are presented with sensitivity and, for the most part, without polemics. Down a nearby path is a re-creation of an Algonquian village. There's a picnic area on the grounds.

Rte. 199. ℂ 860/868-0518. Admission $4 adults, $2 children 6–16. Mon–Sat 10am–5pm; Sun noon–5pm (closed Mon–Tues Jan–Mar).

WHERE TO STAY

Mayflower Inn ★★   Galaxies of stars have already been scattered in abundance over this, one of the state's courtliest manor inns. While the main building is almost entirely new, some elements survive from the original 1894 structure, the most delightful of which is the richly paneled library. Porches look out across manicured lawns to deep woods. Most bedrooms have fireplaces, the bathrooms are done with tapestry rugs and mahogany wainscoting—all is as close to perfection as such an enterprise is likely to be, *almost* justifying the breathtaking prices. The clientele can't be described as youthful.

The accomplished restaurant features top-drawer ingredients drawn from New England producers and Atlantic fisheries. Perhaps needless to say, the cellar is extensive, meticulously chosen, and pricey.

118 Woodbury Rd. (Rte. 47), Washington, CT 06793. ℂ 860/868-9466. Fax 860/868-1497. inn@mayflower inn.com. 25 units. $400–$600 double; $650–$1,300 suite. AE, MC, V. Take Rte. 202 north 2 miles (3km) past

New Preston, turn south on Rte. 47 through Washington Depot and up the hill past Washington Common. The entrance is on the left. Children over 12 welcome. **Amenities:** Restaurant (eclectic); pub; heated outdoor pool; nearby golf course; tennis court; extensive health club; sauna; bike rental; massage; same-day dry cleaning/laundry. *In room:* A/C, TV w/ pay movies, fax, dataport, minibar, hair dryer.

WHERE TO DINE

One dining option is the restaurant at the **Mayflower Inn** (described above). For a more casual meal, put together a picnic from the delectable array of quiches, pizzas, and salads at **The Pantry,** 5 Titus Rd., Washington Depot (© **860/868-0258**).

G. W. Tavern 🐾 ECLECTIC AMERICAN   The atmospheric bar has booths and a fireplace, while the simulated attached barn is airier, with a deck that looks down on the Shepaug River. The kitchen is dedicated to interpretations of such robust Americana as Cobb salad, prime beef, and fish-and-chips. There are spins on convention, though, exemplified by the fried-oyster tomato-basil soup and the Bass ale used in the batter for the onion rings. Weekend brunches are popular with stylish locals.

Rte. 47 (north of Washington Depot shopping center). © **860/868-6633.** Main courses $9–$28. AE, MC, V. Daily 11:30am–2:30pm and 5:30–10pm (Fri–Sat until 11pm).

NEW PRESTON & LAKE WARAMAUG 🐾🐾

Never more than a few houses and retailers at the junction of two country roads, the hamlet of New Preston long served primarily as a supplier for locals and, starting in the mid–19th century, the families who summered on nearby Lake Waramaug. More recently, New Preston's small grocery and hardware stores have been converted to antiques emporia of high order, and they find themselves surrounded on weekends by BMWs and Volvos.

EXPLORING THE LAKE WARAMAUG AREA

At the northwest tip of the L-shaped lake, 95-acre (38-hectare) **Lake Waramaug State Park,** Lake Waramaug Road (© **860/868-0220**), gives the public access to a beautiful body of water that is otherwise monopolized by the private homes and inns that border it. Canoes and paddleboats are for rent, and there's a swimming beach as well as picnic tables, food concessions, and a total of almost 80 camping and RV sites.

Hopkins Vineyard   A former dairy farm on a promontory above Lake Waramaug was converted in 1979 into a vineyard and winery. Headquartered in a 19th-century barn across the street from the Hopkins Inn (see "Where to Stay & Dine," below), it produces 11 bottlings. It won't make anyone forget the Napa Valley, but prices are fair. A wine bar overlooks the lake.

25 Hopkins Rd. © **860/868-7954.** www.hopkinsvineyard.com. Jan–Feb Fri–Sat 10am–5pm, Sun 11am–5pm; Mar–Apr Wed–Sat 10am–5pm, Sun 11am–5pm; May–Dec Mon–Sat 10am–5pm, Sun 11am–5pm.

SHOPPING

In no time, the intersecting streets that form the center of the village have gone from sleepy to spiffy. Notable among the shops is **J. Seitz & Co.,** Main Street/East Shore Road (© **860/868-0119**), featuring Indian blankets and clothing. Next door is **Del Mediterraneo,** selling pottery and home furnishings.

WHERE TO STAY & DINE

The Birches Inn 🐾   Enthusiastic reviews were lavished upon the latest refiguring of the in-house restaurant before the paint was dry. Less remarked upon were the restored bedrooms, five of them in the main house, up a slope from the road, and another three in the lakeside cottage. Comfort prevails over quaintness, and the results are superior to those found in most nearby lodgings. Take in the vista from the **dining room** ✿✿ or deck, almost a match for the satisfying food. The French-born chef/owner emphasizes grills, but marries often-disparate ingredients with panache.

233 West Shore Rd., New Preston, CT 06777. ✆ **888/590-7945** or 860/868-1735. Fax 860/868-1815. www.thebirchesinn.com. 8 units. May–Oct $125–$300 double; Nov–Apr $95–$225 double. Rates include breakfast. AE, MC, V. Drive to the left of the town beach on West Shore Rd. about a mile (1.6km). *In room:* A/C, TV.

The Boulders ✿✿ This once rustic lakeside inn, with a private swimming beach, has scrambled steadily upward in both price and quality. The outlying "guesthouses"—four buildings with two spacious units each plus a new carriage house—enjoy private decks, fireplaces, Jacuzzis, and refrigerators. These have contemporary furnishings, while the tone of the bedrooms in the 1895 main house is set by antiques and reproductions of country styles. Five rooms have TVs. A serious wine cellar complements the acclaimed cuisine.

E. Shore Rd. (Rte. 45), New Preston, CT 06777. ✆ **800/552-6853** or 860/868-0541. Fax 860/868-1925. www.bouldersinn.com. 17 units. $260–$320 double. Rates include breakfast. Rates are $50 lower midweek Nov–Apr, $60 higher Fri–Sat Memorial Day–Oct. AE, DISC, MC, V. Drive north from New Preston about 2 miles (3km) on Rte. 45. **Amenities:** Restaurant (regional American); golf course nearby; tennis court; access to nearby health club, on-site Jacuzzi, free canoes and rowboats; game room; limited room service; in-room massage. *In room:* A/C, hair dryer.

Hopkins Inn A family named Hopkins started farming this land in 1787, and its descendants turned the farm into a vineyard and winery in 1979. The farmhouse sits atop a hill with the best views of Lake Waramaug. Food is the main event, since most of the guest rooms are on the spartan side, with phones and TV only in the two-bedroom suite in the annex. Dishes from the Swiss and Austrian Alps are served in hefty portions.

22 Hopkins Rd., New Preston, CT 06777. ✆ **860/868-7295**. Fax 860/868-7464. www.thehopkinsinn.com. 13 units (11 with private bathroom). $77–$180 double. AE, DISC, MC, V. From New Preston, take Rte. 45 north about 2½ miles (4km) and look for the sign on the left. **Amenities:** Restaurant (closed Jan–late Mar). *In room:* A/C.

LITCHFIELD ✿✿

Possessed of a long common with stately trees reconfigured around the turn of the 20th century by the Frederick Law Olmsted landscaping firm (designers of New York's Central Park), Litchfield is testimony to the taste and affluence of the Yankee entrepreneurs who built it up in the late 18th and early 19th centuries from a colonial farm community to an industrial center. The factories and mills were dismantled toward the end of the 19th century, and the men who built them settled back to enjoy their riches in their uncommonly large homes.

In recent decades, the town has been discovered by fashionable New Yorkers, who find it less frenetic than the Hamptons. Their influence is seen both in the quality of store merchandise and restaurant fare, as well as in the lofty prices houses command.

Note: The best lodging in the area, the Tollgate Hill Inn, has closed and is currently up for sale.

A WALK THROUGH HISTORY

Litchfield's houses and tree-lined streets reward leisurely strollers. From the stores and restaurants along West Street, walk east (to the right when facing the common), and then turn right on South Street. On the opposite corner is the

Litchfield History Museum, at South and East streets (© **860/567-4501**), containing an eclectic array of local historical artifacts, including the world's largest collection of works by the 18th-century portraitist Ralph Earl. It's open from mid-April to November, Tuesday through Saturday from 11am to 5pm and Sunday from 1 to 5pm. Admission is $5 for adults, $3 for seniors, and free for children under 14.

Walking down South Street, on the right, are the **Tapping Reeve House and Law School** (© **860/567-4501**). One of the few historic houses regularly open to the public, the Reeve house was built in 1773, while the adjacent 1784 building was the earliest American law school, established before independence. It counted among its students Aaron Burr and Noah Webster. Hours are the same as those of the Litchfield History Museum, which maintains it; one ticket buys admission to both museums.

When the street starts to peter out into more modern houses, walk back toward the common and cross over to the north side. Over here on the right is the magisterial **First Congregational Church,** built in 1828. Turn left, then right on North Street, where the domestic architecture matches the quiet splendor of South Street.

NEARBY ATTRACTIONS

Haight Vineyard   Chardonnays and merlots don't spring to mind as likely Connecticut products, but this establishment, established in 1978, has grown and prospered, presently offering 11 drinkable bottlings. The tasting room is open year-round. There's a second winery in Mystic.

29 Chestnut Hill Rd. © **860/567-4045.** Mon–Sat 10:30am–5pm; Sun noon–5pm.

OUTDOOR PURSUITS

The **White Memorial Foundation,** Route 202 (© **860/567-0857**), is a 4,000-acre (1,620-hectare) wildlife sanctuary and nature conservancy about 3 miles (5km) southwest of Litchfield. It has campsites and 35 miles (56km) of trails for hiking, cross-country skiing, and horseback riding. On the grounds is a small museum of natural history. The Holbrook Bird Observatory looks out on a landscape specially planted to attract birds. The museum is open year-round, Monday through Saturday from 9am to 5pm and Sunday from noon to 4pm; free admission.

This is horse country, so consider a canter across the meadows and along the wooded trails of **Topsmead State Park,** Buell Road (© **860/567-5694**). The park has a wildlife preserve and a Tudor-style mansion that can be toured the second and fourth weekends of each month from June to October. To get here, follow Route 118 for a mile (1.6km) east of town. The grounds are open from 8am to sunset. Horses can be hired nearby at **Lee's Riding Stables,** 57 East Litchfield Rd., off Route 118 (© **860/567-0785**).

SHOPPING

Most of the interesting shops are in the row of late-19th-century brick buildings on the south side of the town green. In front of **Barnidge & McEnroe,** 7 West St. (© **860/567-4670**), is a coffee bar for muffins and lattes, which will keep you going as you browse through three entertaining floors of books, gifts, and ceramics.

WHERE TO DINE

West Street Grill NEW AMERICAN   When this contemporary bistro opened over a decade ago, it was dusted with stars by local and big-city reviewers. That was then. Known as an incubator for some of Connecticut's best chefs, several of whom went off to open their own places, it no longer merits raves. Entrees tend toward fusion renditions of meats, fowl, and fish, little of which knocks your socks off. Portions are substantial, though, and it remains the trendiest spot for miles.

43 West St. (on the green). ℂ **860/567-3885.** Reservations recommended for dinner, essential on weekends. Main courses $17–$27. AE, MC, V. Mon–Thurs 11:30am–3pm and 5:30–9pm; Fri–Sat 11:30am–4pm and 5:30–10:30pm.

KENT

A prominent prep school of the same name, a history as an iron-smelting center, and a continuing reputation as a gathering place of artists and writers define this town of fewer than 2,000. Noted 19th-century landscape painter George Inness helped establish that assessment, and several galleries represent the works of his creative descendants. They are joined by a multiplicity of antiques shops and bookstores, most of them strung along Route 7. South of town on the same road is the hamlet of Bull's Bridge, named for one of the two remaining covered bridges in the state that can be crossed by cars.

Four miles (6km) northeast of Kent is **Kent Falls State Park,** on Route 7 (ℂ **860/927-3849**). Its centerpiece, a 250-foot (75m) cascade, is clearly visible from the road, and picnic tables are set about the grounds. A path mounts the hill beside the falls. Restrooms are available. A parking fee of $8 per out-of-state car ($5 per Connecticut car) is charged on weekends and holidays between June and October.

WHERE TO STAY & DINE

Fife 'n Drum ECLECTIC   Reminiscent of the roadhouses depicted in Hollywood noir, this place is all dark wood and brick. There are two dining rooms (each with its own grand piano) with a big battered bar in between. Apart from daily specials and an appetizer list that bounces all over the place, from sushi to escargots, the set menu could date from the 1940s, too. Settle in for no-surprises herb-crusted pork loin, baked fish, or filet mignon au poivre.

A separate building contains eight guest rooms, which adhere to a colonial theme but offer TVs, air-conditioning, and private bathrooms.

53 N. Main St. (Rte. 7). ℂ **860/927-3509.** Main courses $14–$28. AE, DC, MC, V. Mon and Wed–Sat 11:30am–3pm and 5:30–10pm (Sat until 10:30pm); Sun 11:30am–9pm.

WEST CORNWALL

Not to be confused with Cornwall, 4 miles (6km) to the southeast, nor Cornwall Bridge, 7 miles (11km) to the south, this tiny village is best known for its picturesque covered bridge, one of only two in the state that still permit the passage of cars. The bridge connects Routes 7 and 128, crossing the Housatonic. With a state forest to the north and a state park to its immediate south, West Cornwall enjoys a piney seclusion that remains welcoming to passersby.

Housatonic Meadows State Park, on Route 7 (ℂ **860/672-6772** in summer, or 860/927-3238 the rest of the year), is comprised of 452 acres (183 hectares) bordering both sides of the Housatonic River immediately south of West Cornwall. With 95 campsites, it offers access to fishing, canoeing, and picnicking.

Housatonic Anglers, Route 7 (ℂ **860/672-4457;** www.housatonicanglers. com), offers float trips, fly-fishing schools, and guided fishing trips. **Clarke Outdoors,** 163 Rte. 7, Cornwall (ℂ **860/672-6365;** www.adventuresports. com), offers rentals of kayaks and rafts, as well as instruction and guided trips. Whitewater rafting in the Class IV-V section of the Housatonic costs $85.

Just outside Cornwall proper, off Route 4, is **Mohawk Mountain Ski Area,** 46 Great Hollow Rd. (ⓒ **800/895-5222** or 860/672-6100; www.mohawkmtn. com). "Mountain" is an overstatement, but this is the state's oldest ski resort, with five lifts, 23 trails, snowmakers, and night skiing. All-day lift tickets are $35 for adults.

SHARON

This hamlet near the New York border is primarily residential, a picturesque village with many houses made of brick or fieldstone in a region where wood-frame houses prevail.

Sharon Audubon Center   The 890-acre (360-hectare) nature preserve has gardens, a shop and interpretive center, and 11 miles (18km) of trails. Injured birds are brought to the center for rehabilitation, and there are usually several raptors recuperating in house.

Rte. 4. ⓒ **860/364-0520.** Trails $3 adults, $1.50 seniors and children. Main building Mon–Sat 9am–5pm, Sun 1–5pm; grounds dawn to dusk.

LAKEVILLE & SALISBURY

These two attractive villages share a main street lined with 19th-century houses stretching along Route 44. The "lake" in question is Wononscopomuc, slightly south of the town center.

The discovery in the area of a particularly pure iron ore led to the development of mines and forges as early as the mid-1700s. One of the ironworkers was the eccentric Ethan Allen, later to become the leader of the Green Mountain Boys and a hero for his capture of Fort Ticonderoga from the British in 1775.

Holley-Williams House   One wealthy forge owner, John Milton Holley, bought a 1768 mansion and doubled its size in 1808. The result is a Federal and Greek Revival mix. It contains furnishings assembled by Holley and his descendants over the 173 years the family lived there. There were a lot of them—the outhouse has seven holes.

15 Millerton Rd., Rte. 44. ⓒ **860/435-2878.** Free admission; guided tours $3 adults, $2 seniors and students, free for children under 5. Late June to Labor Day Sat–Sun and holidays noon–5pm.

WHERE TO STAY

Interlaken Inn ⓡ   Guest rooms here are divided among five different buildings—like Sunnyside, with its period furniture and B&B feel; the Main Building, with its standard but pleasant double rooms; and the Townhouse Suites, fully equipped with washer/dryers, fireplaces, and kitchens. Room sizes and styles can really vary—talk to the reservations staff about your needs before booking. If you're in the mood to splurge, try the Woodside building's Executive Suite, complete with two TV/VCRs, a granite bathroom with an oversized shower and dual showerheads, and French doors leading out to a private patio with hot tub. The restaurant, Morgan's, offers some of the best food in the area.

74 Interlaken Rd., Lakeville, CT 06039. ⓒ **800/222-2909** or 860/435-9878. Fax 860/435-2980. www. interlakeninn.com. 82 units. $149–$319 weekends; $129–$239 weekdays. AE, MC, V. Pets allowed in some units ($10). **Amenities:** Restaurant (New American), bar; outdoor pool; nearby golf course; 2 tennis courts; health club; 2 saunas; canoes, paddleboats, kayaks, and rowboats; game room; business center; limited room service; massage and facials by reservation; babysitting. *In room:* A/C, TV/VCR, dataport, coffeemaker, hair dryer, iron.

White Hart ⓡ   This inn's fortunes have fluctuated in its 180-plus years, but the white-clapboard lodging at the end of Salisbury's main street is continuing its recent rise without a bump. The front porch is a prime summertime perch.

Apart from the three suites and the large Ford Room, most of the guest rooms are on the small side. Both dining room and wine cellar have received excellent notices.

Village Green (P.O. Box 545), Salisbury, CT 06068. ℰ **800/832-0041** or 860/435-0030. Fax 860/435-0040. www.whitehartinn.com. 26 units. Apr–Nov $119–$249 double; Dec–Mar $109–$229 double. AE, DC, DISC, MC, V. Pets allowed ($10). **Amenities:** Restaurant (New American), cafe, bar. *In room:* A/C, TV, hair dryer.

WHERE TO DINE

You may also want to consider a meal at the **White Hart,** reviewed above.

West Main at Pocketknife Square ✮ FUSION   The team that started out together in a more modest setting in Sharon picked up and moved here a few years ago. This is a far more attractive venue, with the big beams and old stones of a former barn fitted out with a striking fireplace and what they claim is the longest bar in the state. Such items as summer rolls with sesame-chili-mustard sauce, sensational frites with aioli, and spicy Shandong noodles have caused a lot of oohing and cross-table sampling. Live jazz is featured Thursday through Saturday nights.

8 Holley Place, Lakeville ℰ **860/435-1450.** Main courses $18–$21. AE, MC, V. Wed–Mon 5:30–9pm (Fri–Sat until 10pm). Closed 2 weeks in Mar and 2 weeks in Nov.

NORFOLK

Founded in 1758, Norfolk was long popular as a vacation destination for industrialists who owned mills and factories along Connecticut's rivers. At the least, drive into the center for a look at the village green. It is highlighted by a monument that involved the participation of two of the late 19th century's most celebrated creative people—sculptor Augustus Saint-Gaudens and architect Stanford White.

At the opposite corner is the 90-year-old "Music Shed," the venue for an eagerly awaited series of summer events, the **Norfolk Chamber Music Festival** ✮ (ℰ **860/542-3000;** www.yale.edu/norfolk). Held from July to August, it hosts performances by such luminaries as the Tokyo String Quartet and the Vermeer Quartet.

Two prime recreational areas are near each other on Route 272, north of town. A mile (1.6km) from the village green is **Haystack Mountain State Park,** Route 272 (ℰ **860/482-1817**). Its chief feature is a short trail leading to a stone tower at the 1,715-foot (515m) crest. On clear days, the views from the top take in a panorama stretching from the Catskill Mountains to Long Island Sound.

Another 5 miles (8km) farther north, on the Massachusetts border, enjoy this abundance of streams, rapids, and cascades at **Campbell Falls,** Route 272 (ℰ **860/482-1817**). Fishing is a possibility, as are hiking and picnicking.

WHERE TO STAY

Manor House ✮   This gabled 1898 manse doesn't fit into a stylistic cubbyhole; just call it "Late Victorian Bavarian Tudor." Inside, it manages to be both stately and homey, with authentic Tiffany windows and fireplaces in the main salon, dining room, and four bedrooms. The most desirable rooms are on the second floor, notably the English Room, with a king-size bed, and the Lincoln Room, with a half-canopied antique queen bed. The least expensive room is on the third floor, tucked under the eaves—when the owner tells you it's very small, believe her.

69 Maple Ave., Norfolk, CT 06058. ℰ **860/542-5690.** Fax 860/542-5690. www.manorhouse-norfolk.com. 9 units. $100–$250 double. Rates include breakfast. AE, DISC, MC, V. *In room:* No phone.

3 New Haven

Much of what is worthwhile about New Haven can be credited to the presence of one of the world's most prestigious universities. Yale both enriches its community and exacerbates the usual town-gown conflicts—a paradox with which the institution and civic authorities have struggled since the colonial period.

The approach to New Haven via Interstate 95 isn't a paean to positive urban planning. At the waterfront are acres of railroad switchyards, storage tanks, and warehouses. Inland are a few half-hearted mid-rise office buildings reached by streets that radiate a sense of hope unfulfilled. It is easy to decide to drive on by.

That would be shortchanging both the city and yourself. For while New Haven suffers the afflictions of many of Connecticut's cities—nearly a quarter of its citizens live at or below the poverty line—it also has a great deal to offer the leisure traveler: performing-arts centers and theaters, outstanding museums, autumn renewals of college football rivalries that date back over 120 years, and a variety of ethnic restaurants.

Relatively little serious history has happened here, but there are a number of amusing "firsts" that boosters love to trumpet. The first hamburger was allegedly made and sold here, as was—even less certainly—the first pizza.

ESSENTIALS

GETTING THERE   Interstate 95 between New York and Providence skirts the shoreline of New Haven; I-91 from Springfield, Mass., and Hartford ends here. Connections can also be made from the south along the Merritt and Wilbur Cross parkways. Downtown traffic isn't too congested, except at the usual rush hours, and there are ample parking lots and garages near the green and Yale University, where most visitors spend their time.

Tweed–New Haven Airport receives feeder flights connecting with several major airlines, including **Continental** (© **800/525-0280**), **United** (© **800/241-6522**), and **US Airways** (© **800/428-4322**). It's located southeast of the city, near Exits 50 and 51 off I-95.

Amtrak (© **800/USA-RAIL;** www.amtrak.com) has several trains daily that run between Boston and New York and stop in New Haven. To or from New York takes 1½ hours; to or from Boston, about 3 hours. **Metro North** (© **800/METRO-INFO** or 212/532-4900; www.mta.nyc.ny.us/mnr) commuter trains make many daily trips between New Haven and New York. Metro North tickets are much cheaper than Amtrak's, but its trains take longer.

VISITOR INFORMATION   The **Greater New Haven Convention & Visitors Bureau** maintains an office at 1 Long Wharf Dr. (© **203/777-8550**), easily reached from Exit 46 off I-95. It's open from Memorial Day to Labor Day. An especially useful map is *Professor Pathfinder's Yale University & New Haven,* available at bookstores.

SPECIAL EVENTS   Important events are the new **International Festival of Arts & Ideas** (www.artidea.org), held at many sites around the city in late June, and a free **jazz festival** on the green from late July to early August. Call the visitor center for details.

EXPLORING YALE & NEW HAVEN

The major attractions are all associated with Yale University, and, except for the Peabody Museum, are within walking distance of one another near the **New Haven Green,** which is bounded by Elm, Church, Chapel, and College streets.

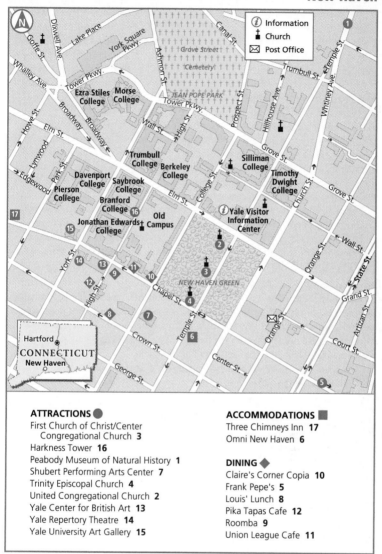

ATTRACTIONS ●

First Church of Christ/Center Congregational Church **3**
Harkness Tower **16**
Peabody Museum of Natural History **1**
Shubert Performing Arts Center **7**
Trinity Episcopal Church **4**
United Congregational Church **2**
Yale Center for British Art **13**
Yale Repertory Theatre **14**
Yale University Art Gallery **15**

ACCOMMODATIONS ■

Three Chimneys Inn **17**
Omni New Haven **6**

DINING ◆

Claire's Corner Copia **10**
Frank Pepe's **5**
Louis' Lunch **8**
Pika Tapas Cafe **12**
Roomba **9**
Union League Cafe **11**

The green, about a third the size of Boston Common, is divided into two unequal parts by north-south Temple Street. Government and bank buildings, including the Gothic Revival City Hall, border it on the east, a retail district on the south, and some older sections of the vast Yale campus to the north and west.

Facing Temple Street are three historic churches, all dating from the early 19th century. Next to Chapel Street is **Trinity Episcopal Church,** a brownstone Gothic Revival structure; the Georgian **First Church of Christ/Center Congregational Church;** and the essentially Federal-style **United Congregational.** The First Church of Christ is of greatest interest, built atop a crypt with tombstones inscribed as early as 1687. Tours are conducted Tuesday through Friday between 10:30am and 2:30pm.

The oldest house in New Haven is now the **Yale University Visitor Information Center,** a colonial facing the north side of the green at 149 Elm St., near College Street (© **203/432-2300**). While its primary mission is to familiarize prospective students and their parents with Yale on a 1-hour **guided walking tour,** the center also has an introductory video and maps for self-guided tours. It's open Monday through Friday from 9am to 4:45pm, Saturday and Sunday from 10am to 4pm. Guided tours are available Monday through Friday at 10:30am and 2pm, Saturday and Sunday at 1:30pm.

It is impossible to imagine New Haven without Yale, so pervasive is its physical and cultural presence. After all, it helped educate our last three presidents, as well as Gerald Ford, William Howard Taft, Noah Webster, Nathan Hale, and Eli Whitney. Established in 1702 in the shoreline town now known as Clinton, the young college was eventually moved here in 1718 and named for Elihu Yale, who made a major financial contribution.

The most evocative quadrangle of the sprawling institution is the **Old Campus,** which can be entered from College, High, or Chapel streets. Inside, the mottled green is enclosed by Federal and Victorian Gothic buildings and dominated by **Harkness Tower,** a 1920 Gothic Revival campanile that looks much older.

Peabody Museum of Natural History 🍷

Head to the third floor and work your way down, especially if a school group has just entered. Up at the top are dioramas with stuffed animals in various environments: bighorn sheep, Alaskan brown bears, bison, and musk oxen. On the same floor is a small but illuminating collection of ancient Egyptian artifacts. The second floor doesn't hold much of general interest, but down on the first is a "bestiary" of large stuffed animals, which leads logically into the Great Hall of Dinosaurs.

170 Whitney Ave. (at Sachem St.). © **203/432-5050**. Admission $5 adults, $3 seniors and children 3–15. Mon–Sat 10am–5pm; Sun noon–5pm.

Yale Center for British Art 🍷🍷

What looks like a parking garage from outside is a great deal more impressive inside. The museum, designed by Louis I. Kahn, claims to be the most important repository of British art outside the United Kingdom, with holdings of more than 1,400 paintings and sculptures. Most of the paintings in the permanent collection are from the 16th through the early 19th century. It's a dazzling array, with canvases by such luminaries as Hogarth, Gainsborough, Joshua Reynolds, and the glorious Turner.

1080 Chapel St. (at High St.). © **203/432-2800**. www.yale.edu/ycba. Free admission. Tues–Sat 10am–5pm; Sun noon–5pm.

Yale University Art Gallery 🍷🍷

The artworks of many epochs and regions are on display, but the museum is most noted for its collections of French Impressionists and American realists of the late 19th and early 20th centuries. It's a satisfying collection for connoisseurs, and won't test the patience of reluctant museumgoers. Architect Louis I. Kahn, responsible for the nearby Center for British Art, also designed the larger of these two buildings. Take the elevator to the fourth floor and work your way down. Asian arts and crafts command the top floor. The tiny Netsuke ivories at the center bear close examination. On the third floor are 14th- to 18th-century Gothic ecclesiastical panels and 16th-century Italian and Dutch portraits, among them paintings by Rubens and Frans Hals. In sharp contrast are adjoining galleries of 20th-century works—Rothko and Rauschenberg as well as Braque, Picasso, and Mondrian.

1111 Chapel St. (at York St.). © **203/432-0600**. www.yale.edu/artgallery. Free admission ($5 suggested donation). Tues–Sat 10am–5pm; Sun 1–6pm.

SHOPPING

Atticus Bookstore & Cafe It might as easily be listed under "Where to Dine," for half of this store consists of a lunch counter and takeout section, famous for its scones. The rest of the space is devoted to what many call the best bookstore in town. Open daily from 8am to midnight. 1082 Chapel St. ℭ **203/776-4040.**

WHERE TO STAY

New Haven lodgings are both limited and, with one notable exception, devoid of either charm or distinctiveness. Still, its motels and hotels fill up far in advance for football weekends, alumni reunions, and graduation.

Among the chains in town are the **Holiday Inn,** 30 Whalley Rd. (ℭ **203/777-6221**); **Grand Chalet Inn & Suites,** 400 Sargent Dr. (ℭ **203/562-1111**); and **Residence Inn,** 3 Long Wharf Dr. (ℭ **203/777-5337**). The visitor center has a **hotel reservations service** (ℭ **800/332-7829**).

Omni New Haven ✿✿ This is a conventional member of the reliable Omni chain. Its location couldn't be improved, next to the green and within walking distance of the theaters, much of the campus, and two of the Yale museums. Galileo's, the 19th-floor restaurant, offers fine views of the green and surrounding cityscape.

155 Temple St. (south of Chapel St.), New Haven, CT 06510. ℭ **800/THE-OMNI** or 203/772-6664. Fax 203/974-6780. www.omnihotels.com. 305 units. $119–$169 double. AE, DC, DISC, MC, V. **Amenities:** Restaurant, bar; exercise room; concierge; business center; limited room service; same-day dry cleaning/laundry. *In room:* A/C, TV, dataport, minibar, coffeemaker, hair dryer.

Three Chimneys Inn ✿✿ Once known as the Inn at Chapel West, this 1870 mansion is a favorite of Yalies and their parents. All rooms are outfitted with mahogany four-poster beds. On chilly days, gas fires burn in the dining room and parlor, where a tray of cordials is set out. Businesspeople are more in evidence than is usual at inns, many of them here to interview Yale students for jobs.

1201 Chapel St. (between Park and Howe sts.), New Haven, CT 06511. ℭ **800/443-1554** out of state, or 203/789-1201. Fax 203/776-7363. www.threechimneysinn.com. 11 units. $185–$200 double. Rates include full breakfast and afternoon tea. AE, DISC, MC, V. Children over 6 welcome. **Amenities:** Exercise room; access to nearby health club; same-day dry cleaning. *In room:* A/C, TV, dataport, hair dryer.

WHERE TO DINE

Claire's Corner Copia VEGETARIAN Few college towns are without at least one low-cost vegetarian restaurant. This one has ruled in New Haven since 1975. Options include curried couscous, eggplant rollatini, and a number of Mexican entrees, but the stars might well be the award-winning quiches. The operator stops short of vegan purity, with tuna salad and albacore melt sandwiches on the card. Breakfast brings a bounty of plump scones and massive muffins.

1000 Chapel St. (at College St.). ℭ **203/562-3888.** Main courses $5.25–$9.50. No credit cards. Sun–Thurs 8am–9pm; Fri–Sat 8am–10pm.

Frank Pepe's ✿ PIZZA On the scene for most of the last century, Pepe's has long claimed the local pizza crown while fighting off perpetual challenges. In exchange for super, almost unimaginably thin-crusted pies, pilgrims put up with long lines, a nothing decor, and a sullen staff.

If the wait looks to be especially long, you can do about as well at **Sally's** ✿, 237 Wooster St. (ℭ 203/624-5271), just down the street.

157 Wooster St. (between Olive and Brown sts.). ℭ **203/865-5762**. Pizzas $4.95–$12. No credit cards. Mon and Wed–Thurs 4–10pm; Fri–Sat 11:30am–11pm; Sun 2:30–10:30pm.

Louis' Lunch ☆ SANDWICHES The claim, unprovable but gaining strength as the decades roll on, is that America's very first hamburger sandwich was sold in 1900 at this little luncheonette. It moved from its original location to escape demolition, but not much else has changed. The wooden counter and tables are carved with the initials of a century of patrons. The beef is freshly ground each day, thrust into gas-fired ovens, and then served (medium rare, usually) on two slices of white toast. The only allowable garnishes are slices of tomato, onion, or cheese. There's no mustard and no ketchup, so don't even ask. And no fries, either, just potato chips.

261–263 Crown St. (between High and College sts.). ℭ **203/562-5507**. Burgers $3–$4.50. No credit cards. Tues–Wed 11am–4pm; Thurs–Sat noon–2am. Closed Aug.

Pika Tapas Cafe ☆ SPANISH Among the most common tapas are the *tortilla,* a firm potato-and-onion omelet; *pan Catalan,* thick slices of bread rubbed with tomato pulp and draped with Serrano ham and Manchego cheese; and *gambas al ajillo,* shrimp sautéed with garlic. These and another dozen or so are set out on the big semicircular bar at this sprightly enterprise. Keep it in mind for light meals before or after curtain at the nearby theaters.

39 High St. (south of Chapel St.). ℭ **203/865-1933**. Main courses $13.75–$19, tapas $2.25–$7.50. AE, DC, MC, V. Wed–Sat 11:30am–2:30pm and 5–10pm (Fri–Sat until 11pm); Sun–Tues 5–9pm.

Roomba ☆☆ NUEVO LATINO What you'll find here, thanks to the highly creative mind of the chef/owner, is the fusion of techniques and ingredients of at least half a dozen Latin American countries. Much of it you will never have seen before, but none of it requires courage to eat. Waiters in guayaberas are happy to explain the menu. They bring plates of marvelously fanciful construction, often utilizing fried strips of plantains and paper umbrellas. There's patio seating in summer.

1044 Chapel St. (south of Chapel St.). ℭ **203/562-7666**. Main courses $19–$24. AE, MC, V. Tues–Sat noon–2:30pm and 5:30–9:30pm (Fri–Sat until 10:30pm); Sun 5:30–8:30pm.

Union League Café ☆☆ CREATIVE FRENCH These grand salons retain an air of their aristocratic origins, which date back to 1854. Even the name fairly shrieks of its former status as a bastion of WASP privilege, the Union League Club. It has loosened up considerably, and denim-clad Yalies, their doting parents, philosophizing profs, and deal-making execs are all equally comfortable here. With waiters in aprons and tables covered with butcher paper, the atmosphere is now closer to an updated brasserie than to that of a gentlemen's sanctuary. The chef routinely tinkers with Gallic culinary tradition. Entrees on the order of duck breast with potato and white truffle gnocchi and Grenache sauce seem both familiar and fresh.

1032 Chapel St. (between High and College sts.). ℭ **203/562-4299**. Main courses $16.50–$23.75. AE, DC, MC, V. Mon–Fri 11:30am–2:30pm; Mon–Sat 5:30–9:30pm.

NEW HAVEN AFTER DARK

The presence of Yale and a highly educated faction of the general population ensures a cultural life equal to that of many larger cities. A reliable source of information on cultural events and nightlife is the free weekly newspaper, the *New Haven Advocate* (www.newhavenadvocate.com).

THE PERFORMING ARTS Within a couple of blocks of the green, the **Shubert Performing Arts Center,** 247 College St. (ℭ **800/228-6622** or

203/562-5666; www.shubert.com), presents musicals, opera, cabaret, concerts, and such touring troupes as the Alvin Ailey Dance Theater. A deconsecrated church west of the green is the home of the well-regarded **Yale Repertory Theatre,** 222 York St., at Chapel (✆ **203/432-1234;** www.yalerep.org), which mounts an October-to-May season of modern productions as well as classics by Shakespeare, George Bernard Shaw, and Tennessee Williams.

Away from downtown, but worth the cab fare, is the prestigious **Long Wharf Theatre,** 222 Sargent Dr. (✆ **203/787-4282**), known for its success in producing new plays that often make the jump to off-Broadway and even Broadway itself. The season runs from October to June. The Long Wharf spawned the smaller **Stage II.**

Several venues on the Yale campus, including **Sprague Memorial Hall,** 470 College St., and **Woolsey Hall,** College and Grove streets, host the performances of many resident organizations, including the New Haven Symphony Orchestra, New Haven Civic Orchestra, Yale Concert Band, Yale Glee Club, Yale Philharmonia, and Yale Symphony Orchestra. For upcoming events, call the **Yale Concert Information Line** (✆ **203/432-4157**).

THE CLUB & MUSIC SCENE   A newish venue for blues, jazz, and Latin soul, **The Blues,** 71 Whitney Ave. (✆ **203/498-2583**), keeps the scheduling and inducements fresh. There are jam sessions, salsa classes, and a generous—and free!—happy-hour buffet.

The biggest and best venue for live rock and pop is **Toad's Place,** 300 York St. (✆ **203/621-TOAD**), which has welcomed the likes of the Rolling Stones, U2, and Bob Dylan.

For something less frenetic, the popular **BAR,** 254 Crown St. (✆ **203/ 495-1111**), has a lounge in front—open to the street on warm nights—and a pool table, terrace, and dance floor in back. On Sundays, listen to live jazz or blues. **The Brü Rm,** a brewpub tacked onto the slightly older nightclub, produces rich beers and poses a naked challenge in the eternal New Haven pizza wars. Its thinnest-crust pies are leading contenders for the crown long held by Frank Pepe's.

4 Hartford

115 miles (185km) NE of New York; 103 miles (166km) SW of Boston

Dissidents, fleeing the rigid religious dictates of the Massachusetts Bay Colony, founded Hartford in 1636. Three years later, they drafted what were called the "Fundamental Orders," the basis of a subsequent claim that Connecticut was the first political entity on earth to have a written constitution, hence the nickname "Constitution State."

Unfortunately, Connecticut's capital and second-largest city endures a drooping uneasiness it hasn't been able to shake. There was hope for revival a few years ago when it appeared that the governor had persuaded the New England Patriots to move to downtown Hartford. A new stadium was to have been the centerpiece of a $1-billion, 35-acre (14-hectare) riverfront development. At the last contractual minute, the Patriots exercised an escape clause, choosing to remain in the Boston area. While it is possible that parts of the plan will yet be realized, there was a great whoosh of despair when the balloon burst.

It was uncertain that even the ambitious original scheme would have reversed decades of decline. Hartford continues to point gamely to its grand edifices—

the divinely overwrought gold-domed capitol, the High Victorian Mark Twain House, and the august Wadsworth Atheneum. Worthwhile as these sites certainly are, they don't prevent visitors from noticing the miles of distressed housing, weed-strewn lots, and hollow-eyed office structures that radiate out from the center.

It isn't as if efforts haven't been made to heal the wounds. A civic center was completed in 1975 in an attempt to attract business downtown, and a flyway connects it with the newer 39-story CityPlace. Both venues offer concerts and art exhibits, and the 489-seat Hartford Stage Company has a 10-month theatrical season in its own 1977 building cater-corner from the center. A block away, the gracious Old State House enjoyed a 4-year renovation. Across Main Street, a shed has been provided for a daily farmers' market; a local paper sponsors noontime rock concerts in summer. All these efforts have encouraged the establishment of a few cosmopolitan restaurants and a couple of good hotels, so most of a day trip or overnight visit can be contained within only a few square blocks.

ESSENTIALS

GETTING THERE Interstates 84 and 91 intersect in central Hartford, halfway between New York and Boston. Downtown Hartford has plenty of convenient parking, including the garage of the Civic Center.

Bradley International Airport, in Windsor Locks, about 12 miles (19km) north of the city, is served by several major airlines, including **American** (✆ 800/433-7300), **Continental** (✆ 800/525-0280), **Delta** (✆ 800/221-1212), **Northwest** (✆ 800/225-2525), **Southwest** (✆ 800/435-9792), **United** (✆ 800/241-6522), and **US Airways** (✆ 800/247-8786). Buses, cabs, and limousines shuttle passengers into the city and to other points in the state.

Amtrak (✆ 800/USA-RAIL; www.amtrak.com) has several trains daily following the inland route between New York City and Boston, stopping at Hartford and Windsor Locks. The trip to either New York or Boston takes about 2½ hours.

VISITOR INFORMATION An information counter on the main floor of the Civic Center, at Trumbull, Asylum, and Church streets, is staffed by members of the **Hartford Guides** (✆ 860/293-8105). Highly knowledgeable about their city, they not only provide information on sightseeing, shopping, restaurants, and hotels, but also conduct walking tours and can provide escort service for women and seniors from lodgings or restaurants to their cars or buses.

SPECIAL EVENTS Hartford makes the most of its association with one of America's most beloved authors, Mark Twain. His image is seen everywhere, and the city puts on **Mark Twain Days** in mid-August, with such events as frog jumping, riverboat rides, and performances of plays based on Twain's life or works. In late July, there's a **Festival of Jazz** with free performances at the pavilion in Bushnell Park.

SEEING THE SIGHTS

The Old State House After a 4-year, $12-million restoration, the 1796 State House opened in time to celebrate its bicentennial. Costumed interpreters stand ready to answer questions. Upstairs on the right is the Senate chamber, with a full-length painting of the first president by the indefatigable Washington portraitist Gilbert Stuart. These days, the building is used for temporary art exhibitions, changed two or three times yearly.

800 Main St. (at Asylum Ave.). ✆ 860/522-6766. Free admission. Mon–Fri 10am–4pm; Sat 11am–4pm.

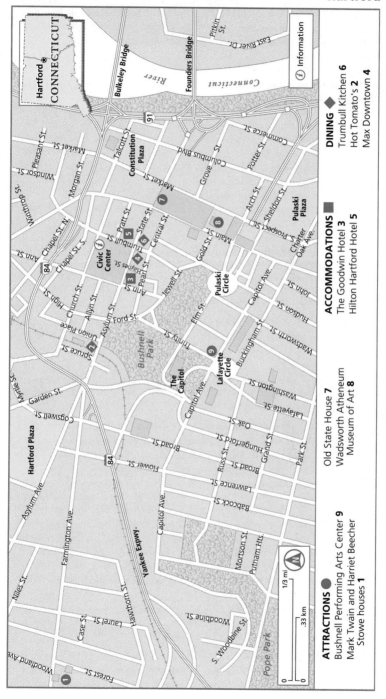

ATTRACTIONS ●
Bushnell Performing Arts Center **9**
Mark Twain and Harriet Beecher
Stowe houses **1**

Old State House **7**
Wadsworth Atheneum
Museum of Art **8**

ACCOMMODATIONS ■
The Goodwin Hotel **3**
Hilton Hartford Hotel **5**

DINING ◆
Trumbull Kitchen **6**
Hot Tomato's **2**
Max Downtown **4**

Mark Twain House ✪✪   This 19-room house is a fascinating example of the late-19th-century style sometimes known as "Picturesque Gothic," with several steeply peaked gables and brick walls whose varying patterns are highlighted by black or orange paint.

Samuel Clemens, whose pseudonym was a term used by Mississippi River pilots to indicate a water depth of 2 fathoms, lived here from 1874 to 1891. The High Victorian interior was the work of distinguished designers of the time, including Louis Comfort Tiffany, who provided both advice and stained glass. Twain's enthusiasm for newfangled gadgets—*Life On The Mississippi* is said to be the first novel written on a typewriter—led to the installation of a primitive telephone in the entrance hall. A guided tour takes about an hour and eventually leads to the top floor and the writer's main workroom, a large space that also has a pool table. Twain would often walk across the hall in the middle of the night and wake up his butler to play a few games.

A new education and visitor center is set to open in late 2003; it will house galleries, a small cinema, a cafe, and a shop. No doubt ticket prices will be raised at that time.

351 Farmington Ave. ✆ **860/247-0998.** www.marktwainhouse.org. Admission $9 adults, $8 seniors, $7 children 13–18, $5 children 6–12. May–Oct and Dec Mon–Sat 9:30am–4pm; Sun noon–4pm. Rest of the year, closed Tues. Visits by guided tour only; last tour begins at 4pm. Take Exit 46 off I-84, turn right onto Sisson Ave., then right onto Farmington Ave. The house is on the right. From downtown, drive west on Asylum St., bearing left on Farmington Ave. The house is on the left.

Harriet Beecher Stowe House   On the adjacent property, across the lawn from the Twain residence, this is a smaller version of its neighbor, built in 1871. Stowe, the author of *Uncle Tom's Cabin*, lived here for most of the time Twain resided in his house.

77 Forest St. ✆ **860/522-9258.** Admission $9.50 adults, $6 seniors, $2.75 children 6–16. Memorial Day to Columbus Day and Dec Mon–Sat 9:30am–4:30pm; Sun 11am–4:30pm. Rest of the year Sun noon–5pm; closed Tues. Visits by guided tour only; last tour begins at 4pm.

Wadsworth Atheneum Museum of Art ✪✪✪   Opened in 1842, this was the first public art museum in the United States and remains a repository with few equals in New England. The strength of the collection lies primarily in its American paintings, spanning the period from landscape artists of the 19th century through luminaries of the New York School of the mid–20th century. On the top floor are works by Thomas Cole, of the Hudson River School, and his contemporaries Frederick Church and Albert Bierstadt. On the balcony are more Americans—Frederic Remington, Andrew Wyeth, Milton Avery, Norman Rockwell. Watch for the shadow box by Joseph Cornell. The first floor contains rule-bending multimedia works, as well as canvases by Abstract Expressionists and pop and op artists of the 1950s and 1960s like de Kooning and Rauschenberg. The **Museum Cafe** has surprisingly good light items and tables out on the terrace in fair weather.

600 Main St. (1 block west of the Old State House). ✆ **860/278-2670.** www.wadsworthatheneum. org Admission $7 adults, $5 seniors and students, $3 children 6–17 (free all day Thurs and 11am–noon on Sat); surcharges for some special exhibitions. Tues–Sun 11am–5pm (until 8pm 1st Thurs of month).

WHERE TO STAY

The Goodwin Hotel ✪   This quiet hostelry opposite the Civic Center is housed in a Queen Anne–style Victorian built in 1881 as a residence for J. P. Morgan. Its understated public areas are attractive, while its cautiously decorated bedrooms are fully equipped. Valet parking is often slow, but still a blessing along this crowded block. The in-house restaurant has an erratic reputation, but some of the city's best dining options are short walks away.

1 Haynes St. (at Asylum St.), Hartford, CT 06103. © **800/922-5006** or 860/246-7500. Fax 860/244-2669. www.goodwinhotel.com. 124 units. $99–$247 double; $250–$750 suite. Weekend packages available. AE, DC, DISC, MC, V. Valet parking $15. **Amenities:** Restaurant (American), lounge; modest health club; concierge; limited room service; same-day dry cleaning. *In room:* A/C, TV w/ pay movies, VCR on request, dataport, hair dryer, iron.

Hilton Hartford Hotel ✦✦   This 22-story slab used to be a Sheraton. Guests will enjoy the results of the $4 million expended on largely cosmetic renovations. The hotel connects with the Civic Center and is readily visible to drivers entering the city from I-84.

315 Trumbull St., Hartford, CT 06103. © **800/445-8667.** Fax 860/240-7246. www.hartford.hilton.com. 390 units. $155–$189 double. AE, DC, DISC, MC, V. **Amenities:** Restaurant (international); sports bar; indoor pool; fully equipped health club; Jacuzzi; sauna; limited room service; same-day dry cleaning/laundry. *In room:* A/C, TV, dataport, coffeemaker, hair dryer, iron.

WHERE TO DINE

Hot Tomato's ✦ ITALIAN   The renovation of Union Station spawned this popular trattoria in one wing. Dine in the glass-sided dining room or on the terrace. A casually dressed crowd tucks into big bowls of garlicky pasta. Especially spicy dishes are marked with a star; two such are shrimp fra diavolo and ziti tossed with grilled chicken strips and bitter broccoli rabe.

1 Union Place (corner of Asylum St.). © **860/249-5100.** Reservations advised for patio and on weekends. Main courses $13–$24.95. AE, DISC, DC, MC, V. Mon–Fri 11:30am–11pm; Sat–Sun 4pm–midnight.

Max Downtown ✦✦ CONTEMPORARY AMERICAN   Hartford's primetime power epicenter has a crowd that looks essentially interchangeable with the one that frequents the Trumbull Kitchen (see below), albeit with a few more suits at midday and a lot of air-kissing at night. Too bad patrons don't pay much attention to the bar menu, for its treats are along the lines of mulligatawny and mahimahi with mango-papaya sauce. The main room has banquettes arrayed behind expanses of glass, with a flashy mural on the back wall. Diners are indulged with hefty chophouse favorites—thick veal chops and strip steaks—and flightier efforts, such as ahi tuna with spring roll, peppered pineapple, and kimchi.

185 Asylum St. (opposite City Center). © **860/522-2530.** Reservations advised on weekends. Main courses $16.95–$29.95. AE, DC, MC, V. Mon–Fri 11:30am–2:30pm and 5–10:30pm (Fri until 11:30pm); Sat 5–11:30pm; Sun 4:30–10pm.

Trumbull Kitchen ✦ ECLECTIC   Formerly the Civic Cafe, this latest addition to the highly successful Max chain (see Max Downtown, above) retains its popularity, and appears to be building upon it. Still looking like it belongs in a hipper city, young execs and lawyers continue to frequent it, observing or partaking in the ritual collisions of egos. The menu is sprinkled with such global grazing categories as fondues and tapas, noshes and dim sum. This is fun, diverting food—tasty enough without distracting from the primary mingling.

150 Trumbull St. (near Asylum St.). © **860/493-7412.** Main courses $16.95–$23.95. AE, DC, DISC, MC, V. Mon–Fri 11–1am; Sat 5pm–2am.

HARTFORD AFTER DARK

The free weekly *Hartford Advocate* (www.hartfordadvocate.com) provides useful information on cultural, sports, and musical events.

The **Bushnell Performing Arts Center,** 166 Capitol Ave. (© **860/987-5900;** www.bushnell.org), is in the midst of a $45-million expansion, including a new 918-seat theater added to the 2,800-seat main stage. They serve as venues for the Hartford Symphony, Connecticut Opera, Hartford Pops, and smaller traveling groups, when not hosting visiting symphony orchestras or road companies of Broadway plays such as *Ragtime* and *Kiss Me, Kate*. The **Hartford Stage,** 50 Church St. (©**860/527-5151,** www.hartfordstage.org), mounts a variety of mainstream plays.

Several downtown clubs host live bands, usually Thursday through Saturday. At the **Arch Street Tavern,** 85 Arch St. (© **860/246-7610**), nationally known bands of the second magnitude appear from time to time. The **Brickyard Cafe,** 113 Allyn St. (© **860/249-2112**), contains a bar, dance floor, and sports bar with pool tables. **Black-Eyed Sally's,** 350 Asylum St. (© **860/278-7427**), known for its ribs and other Southern-style gustatorial treats, presents live blues bands.

The lamented Hartford Brewery, the city's first brewery, has closed. A fresh alternative is the **City Steam Brewery,** 942 Main St. (© **860/525-1600**), serving food that goes well with the home brews. On the premises are pool tables, frequent live music, and the Brew HA HA Comedy Club (on weekends). For beer by the pitcher along with Monday Night Football or the Final Four, where better than **Coach's,** 187 Allyn St. (© **860/522-6224**), a place founded by the UConn basketball coach himself. It has 35 TVs, bar snacks, video games, and live music Thursday through Saturday.

5 From Guilford to Old Saybrook

Usually ignored by vacationers anxious to get on to Mystic and Essex and the casinos, the stretch of coast between New Haven and the Connecticut River, known simply as the Shoreline, has its gentle pleasures, enough to justify a short detour for lunch, a walk on a beach, a spell of shopping, or even a proper British high tea (in Madison). When lodgings are difficult to find at the better-known destinations, the Shoreline's inns and resorts are logical alternatives within easy driving distance.

ESSENTIALS

GETTING THERE   The Shoreline can be reached from Exit 57 off I-95. Pick up Route 1 (a.k.a. the Boston Post Rd.), which serves as the main street of several Shoreline towns.

Several daily **Amtrak** (© **800/USA-RAIL;** www.amtrak.com) trains stop at Old Saybrook. The **Shoreline East** (© **800/255-7433**) commuter line uses the same tracks to service towns between here and New Haven, but only Monday through Friday.

VISITOR INFORMATION   Contact the **Connecticut River Valley and Shoreline Visitors Council,** 393 Main St., Middletown (© **800/486-3346** or 860/347-0028; www.cttourism.org).

GUILFORD

One of the state's oldest colonial settlements (1639), this village, 13 miles (21km) east of New Haven, is embraced by the West and East rivers and has an uncommonly large public green. There are dozens of historic houses to see in town, most of them privately owned and a few others open to the public on a limited basis, typically from Memorial Day to Labor Day. **Hyland House,** 84 Boston St. (© **203/453-9477**), built around 1660, and the **Thomas Griswold House,** 171 Boston St. (© **203/453-3176**), from 1774, are two of these.

Henry Whitfield State Museum   The Whitfield Museum bills itself as the oldest house in Connecticut and the oldest stone house in New England. Most of what you see now, including the leaded windows, dates from a 1930s reconstruction and not from the mid-1600s. It is presented as a museum, not a historic home. The furnishings are authentic to the period.

248 Old Whitfield St. ℂ 203/453-2457. Admission $3.50 adults, $2.50 seniors, $2 children 6–17. Feb 1– Dec 14 Wed–Sun 10am–4:30pm; Dec 15–Jan 30 by appointment only.

MADISON

Madison, 19 miles (31km) east of New Haven, is home to a historic architectural district that stretches west of the business district along the Boston Post Road, from the main green to the town line, and contains many examples of 18th- and 19th-century domestic styles.

The well-to-do town has completed the transition from colony to seaside resort to year-round community, a process begun when the first house was built in 1651. Today, there are two dwellings from the early years that can be visited on limited summer schedules. **Deacon John Grave House,** 581 Boston Post Rd. (ℂ **203/245-4798**), dates from 1685, and the **Allis-Bushnell House,** 853 Boston Post Rd. (ℂ **203/245-4567**), from 1785.

Off the Boston Post Road east of the town center, also reached from Exit 62 off I-95, is **Hammonasset Beach State Park** (ℂ **203/245-1817**), a 900-plusacre (365-plus-hectare) peninsula jutting into Long Island Sound that has the only public swimming beach in the area, plus a nature center, picnic areas, campgrounds, and boating. Cars with Connecticut license plates get in for $5 Monday through Thursday and $7 Saturday and Sunday; out-of-state plates pay $8 and $12, respectively.

SHOPPING

Madison's commercial district may look ordinary at first glance, but several shops along Boston Post Road and intersecting Wall Street provide entertaining browsing. **R. J. Julia Booksellers,** 768 Boston Post Rd. (ℂ **203/245-3959**), holds frequent author readings and poetry slams.

The British Shoppe, 45 Wall St. (ℂ **203/245-4521**), stocks such favorites as kippers, pork pies, and sublime cheeses. Classic ploughman's lunches recall those in English pubs. (Tough licensing requirements don't allow for pints of English beer, but you can bring your own.)

Exit 63 off 1-95 west leads directly to **Clinton Crossing,** 20-A Killingsworth Tpk. (ℂ **860/664-0700**), a "premium" outlet mall with more than 80 shops. Clothing by such designers as Calvin Klein, Donna Karan, and Ralph Lauren are augmented by Coach leather goods and Le Creuset cookware.

WHERE TO STAY

All rooms in the nine-unit **Tidewater Inn,** 949 Boston Post Rd. (ℂ **203/245-8457;** fax 203/318-0265), have air-conditioning, TVs, and phones.

The Inn at Lafayette ⨳/Cafe Allegre ⨳⨳   The stately Greek Revival portico in the middle of the business district promises a touch of elegance, and the interior delivers. Since 1998, the ground floor has housed Cafe Allegre, a soothing setting for northern Italian food of considerable accomplishment. The bar is a low-key gathering place, popular for lunch, with a piano player on Thursday and Friday nights. The new owners haven't done much with the guest rooms upstairs, but they were already comfortable enough, with marble baths and king- or queen-size beds.

725 Boston Post Rd., Madison, CT 06443. ℂ **866/623-7498** or 203/245-7773. Fax 203/245-6256. www. allegrecafe.com. 5 units. Late May to mid-Oct $125–$175 double; mid-Oct to mid-May $95–$150 double. AE, DC, MC, V. Children over 12 welcome. **Amenities:** Restaurant (Italian), bar. *In room:* A/C, TV, dataport, hair dryer.

WHERE TO DINE

See above for a review of **Cafe Allegre.**

Lenny & Joe's Fish Tale ⍟ SEAFOOD   At this rough-and-ready fish shack, fish rules, most of it fried. And while it is sure to elevate triglyceride counts, the nutty coating on super-fresh clams, oysters, shrimp, and calamari is hard to resist. There's another branch at 1301 Boston Post Rd. (ℂ 860/245-7289).

86 Boston Post Rd., Westbrook ℂ **860/669-0767.** Main courses $11.95–$15.95. Daily 11am–10pm (Sun until 9pm).

OLD SAYBROOK

Its location at the mouth of the Connecticut River (35 miles/56km east of New Haven, 26 miles/42km west of Mystic) is this otherwise nondescript town's principal lure. Get off Route 1 to see it at its best. Pick up Route 153 south at the western edge, following the nearly circular route as it touches the shore and passes through the hamlets of Knollwood and Fenwick and across the causeway to Saybrook Point before ending up back in the main business district.

WHERE TO DINE

Cuckoo's Nest ⍟ MEXICAN/CAJUN/CREOLE   Sticklers for gastronomic verisimilitude can look elsewhere. The rest of us can have a good time at this raffish roadhouse, which comes with beat-up wooden chairs and tables that have been on site since 1976. A jazz duo performs Thursday nights, a pianist on Sundays. As for the food, pasta jambalaya with shrimp, chicken, and sausage is hardly Creole, nor is the chicken and rice with jalapeños precisely Mexican, but they taste mighty good. The Sunday brunch is only $10.95. Start off with a mango margarita out on the terrace.

1712 Boston Post Rd. (Rte. 1). ℂ **860/399-9060.** Main courses $13.95–$16.95. AE, DC, DISC, MC, V. Mon–Thurs 11:30am–10pm; Fri–Sat 11:30am–11pm; Sun 11am–10pm.

6 The Connecticut River Valley

New England's longest river originates in the far north near the Canadian border, 407 miles (655km) from Long Island Sound. It separates Vermont from New Hampshire, splits Massachusetts in half, then takes a 45-degree turn at Middletown, south of Hartford, to make its final run to the sea.

Native Americans of the region called the river *Quinnetukut,* which, to the tin ears of the English settlers, sounded like "Connecticut." The colonists encroached upon Indian territory as far north as present-day Windsor, which ignited a brief war with the Pequot, who occupied the land.

Because the river was navigable by relatively large ships as far as Hartford, the sheltered lower Connecticut became important for boat-building and industries associated with the international clipper trade. The Connecticut River retains that nautical flavor, and the valley has miraculously avoided the industrialization, development, and decay that afflict most of the state's other rivers.

Cruising, boating, and kayaking are obvious attractions, supplemented by rides on a steam-powered train, a selection of worthy B&Bs, antiques shops, a venerable musical theater, even a bizarre castle on a hilltop.

ESSENTIALS

GETTING THERE Limited-access state highway 9 runs parallel to the river, along the west side of the valley, connecting I-91 south of Hartford with I-95 near Old Saybrook. The lower valley is therefore readily accessible from all points in New England and from the New York metropolitan area and points south.

Amtrak (© 800/USA-RAIL; www.amtrak.com) trains stop at Old Saybrook, at the mouth of the river, several times daily on runs between New York and Boston. In addition, **Shoreline East** (© 800/255-7433) commuter trains operate Monday through Friday between New Haven and Old Saybrook.

VISITOR INFORMATION The **Connecticut River Valley and Shoreline Visitors Council,** 393 Main St., Middletown (© 800/486-3346 or 860/347-0028; www.cttourism.org), is a source of pamphlets, maps, and related materials.

OLD LYME

As quiet a town as the coast can claim, Old Lyme (40 miles/64km east of New Haven, 21 miles/34km west of Mystic) was the favored residence of generations of seafarers and ship captains. Many of their 18th- and 19th-century homes have survived, some as inns and museums. With its many tree-lined streets largely free of traffic, stressless biking is an attractive option here.

Florence Griswold Museum Once the shipbuilding and merchant trade had all but flickered out at the end of the 19th century, artists who came to be known as the "American Impressionists" took a fancy to this area. They received encouragement, patronage, and even food and shelter from Ms. Griswold, the wealthy daughter of a sea captain. Her 1817 mansion was the temporary home for a number of painters, many of whom left samples of their work in gratitude, sometimes painting directly on the walls of the dining room. Rotating exhibits are held; the studio of William Chadwick is also on view. Visitors can walk across the mansion's 6 acres (2.4 hectares) to the Lieutenant River.

96 Lyme St. (Rte. 1). © 860/434-5542. www.flogris.org. Admission $7 adults, $6 seniors and students, $4 children 6–12. Apr–Dec Tues–Sat 10am–5pm, Sun 1–5pm; Jan–Mar Wed–Sun 1–5pm.

OUTDOOR PURSUITS

One of several state parks located at the edge of Long Island Sound, **Rocky Neck State Park,** Route 156 (© 860/739-5471), east of Old Lyme, has a crescent-shaped beach and over 560 acres (227 hectares) for camping, picnicking, fishing, and hiking. Take I-95 to Exit 72 and follow Route 156 south. Open daily from 8am to sunset.

Although headquartered in New York's Hudson Valley, **Atlantic Kayak Tours,** 320 W. Saugerties Rd., Saugerties (© 914/246-2187), conducts many

---

(*Tips* **A Note on Accommodations**

There aren't a great many motels between Haddam and Old Lyme (the southernmost segment of the valley that is of greatest interest to visitors), but there are several excellent full-service inns and many small B&Bs—some of which can be found only through referral agencies. Two such companies are **Bed & Breakfast, Ltd.** (© 203/469-3260) and **Nutmeg Bed & Breakfast Agency** (© 800/727-7592 or 860/236-6698).

tours along Connecticut's rivers and shoreline, as well as crossings to Long Island. Most tours are $80.

WHERE TO STAY & DINE

Bee and Thistle Inn 🐝 Situated on more than 5 acres (2 hectares) beside the Lieutenant River, the Bee and Thistle has a core structure that dates from 1756, with the usual later wings and additions. Every corner of the place is an enjoyable jumble of antiques and collectibles. A detached cottage is the best lodging, with the only in-room TV. It has a fireplace, as does one room in the main house. Year after year, the inn's **dining room** 🐝🐝 is voted "best overall" and "most romantic" in the state by reader polls. Musicians are on hand weekend evenings; appropriate attire is requested.

100 Lyme St. (Rte. 1), Old Lyme, CT 06371. ✆ **800/622-4946** or 860/434-1667. Fax 860/434-3402. www.beeandthistleinn.com. 12 units. $79–$189 double; $210 cottage. AE, DC, DISC, MC, V. From the south, take Exit 70 off I-95; turn left, then right on Rte. 1 (Halls Rd.) north. Children over 12 welcome. **Amenities:** Restaurant (creative American). *In room:* A/C.

Old Lyme Inn 🐝🐝 This expansive 1850s farmhouse is more a small hotel than a conventional inn. Most of the spacious bedrooms are furnished in part with attractive Victorian pieces, including four-poster beds. The dining rooms are even more impressive, especially the Grill, which features an antique Victorian bar and marble-mantled fireplace as well as live music on weekends. Admirers of venerable taverns might not want to leave. Pets are accepted, a rare policy among New England inns.

85 Lyme St. (Rte. 1), Old Lyme, CT 06371. ✆ **800/434-5352** or 860/434-2600. Fax 860/434-5352. www.oldlymeinn.com. 13 units. $135–$185 double. Rates include breakfast. AE, DC, DISC, MC, V. To get here, follow directions for the Bee and Thistle, above. **Amenities:** 2 restaurants (creative American), bar. *In room:* A/C, TV, hair dryer.

ESSEX 🐝🐝

It is difficult to imagine what improvements might be made to bring this dream of a New England town any closer to perfection. In fact, a published survey, *The 100 Best Small Towns in America,* ranks the waterside village number one. Among the criteria were low crime rates, per-capita income, proportion of college-educated residents, and numbers of physicians.

Tree-bordered streets are lined with shops and homes that retain an early-18th-century flavor without the unreal frozen-in-amber quality that often afflicts other towns as postcard-pretty as this. People live and work and play here, and bustle busily along a Main Street that runs down to Steamboat Dock and its flotilla of working vessels and pleasure craft.

Clustered along the harbor end of Main Street are three historic houses that are open to the public on limited seasonal schedules. No. 40 is the **Richard Hayden House,** an 1814 brick Federal. Next door, at no. 42, is the **Noah Tooker House,** an 18th-century center-hall colonial. And at no. 51 is the **Robert Lay House,** completed around 1730 and thought to be the oldest original structure in town.

Connecticut River Museum 🐝 Anglers cast lines from the dock while gulls and ducks hang around hoping for a discarded tidbit. Steamboat service was fully operational here from 1823, and the existing dock dates from 1879. Designated a National Historic Site, the museum proper features model ships, marine paintings, and artifacts that relate the story of shipbuilding in the valley, which began in 1733 and helped make this a center of world trade far into the

19th century. The museum usually has walking-tour maps ($1) of Essex, making this a good first stop on your visit.

Steamboat Dock (at foot of Main St.). ℂ 860/767-8269. www.ctrivermuseum.org. Admission $4 adults, $3 seniors, $2 children 6–12. Tues–Sun 10am–5pm.

Essex Steam Train   Steam locomotives from the 1920s chug along to a boat landing in the hamlet of Deep River, a mildly engrossing excursion of about an hour. It can be combined with an optional cruise on the river.

1 Railroad Ave. (Rte. 154). ℂ 860/767-0103. www.essexsteamtrain.com. Train and boat $18.50 adults, $9.50 children 3–11; train only $10.50 adults, $5.50 children 3–11. Daily trips mid-June to Labor Day, less frequently Sept–May.

WHERE TO STAY & DINE

Griswold Inn ★★   Gloss over the assertion that "the Griz" is the oldest inn in America (there are other claimants). What's more important is that local people have rescued the inn from outside buyers. That's a relief, for it is difficult to imagine this corner of New England without the Griz. Rumpled, cluttered, folksy, and forever besieged by drop-in yachtspeople, anglers, locals, and tourists, the main building dates to 1776. The atmospheric taproom started life as a schoolhouse and was moved here in 1800. There's live entertainment every night, be it a Dixieland band or just a man with a banjo. The colorful dining rooms are named for their displays of books, antique weapons, or marine paintings. The food is hearty, no-foolin' victuals—turkey with stuffing, roast loin of pork. The often plain and unadorned bedrooms scattered throughout six buildings are slowly being upgraded; some have fireplaces. Viva Griz!

36 Main St. (center of town), Essex, CT 06426. ℂ 860/767-1776. Fax 860/767-0481. www.originalinns.com. 30 units. $95–$200 double. Rates include breakfast. AE, MC, V. **Amenities:** Restaurant (American), bar. *In room:* A/C.

IVORYTON

Once a center for the ivory trade, where factories fabricated piano keys and hair combs, Ivoryton has since subsided into a residential quietude. A virtual suburb of the only slightly larger Essex, a few miles east, the town perks up a bit in summer, when the **Ivoryton Playhouse,** 103 Main St. (ℂ 860/767-3075; www.riverrep.com) conducts its theatrical season. The repertoire runs to revivals of Broadway comedies and mysteries.

WHERE TO STAY & DINE

Copper Beech Inn ★★   Despite comparisons with the Griswold Inn in nearby Essex, these are two very different animals. Where the Griz is decidedly populist and perennially busy, the stately Copper Beech has much less traffic, without a single figurative hair out of place. The rooms in the converted barn have ample elbowroom, TVs, Jacuzzis, and decks. The rooms in the 19th-century main building have most of the character, with original bathroom fixtures and plenty of antiques. These have phones but no TVs, and staying here can be as nostalgic as a visit to Aunt Edna's. The Copper Beech is also home to one of the most honored restaurants in the region, where French techniques are applied to high-quality seasonal ingredients. Service is seamless, the wine list impressive.

46 Main St., Ivoryton, CT 06442. ℂ 888/809-2056 or 860/767-0330. www.copperbeechinn.com. 13 units. $120–$190 double. Rates include breakfast. AE, DC, MC, V. Closed 1st week in Jan. Take Exit 3 from Rte. 9 and head west on Main St. Children over 10 welcome. **Amenities:** Restaurant (country French), bar. *In room:* A/C.

CHESTER

Hardly more than a 3-block business center, Chester can be dismissed easily enough. But pause a moment, for this riverside hamlet deserves savoring. Along Main Street are antiques shops, galleries, and several eateries. **Naturally, Books and Coffee,** 16 Main St. (© **860/526-3212**), offers a small selection of books, an espresso bar, and live acoustic performers on weekends. **Ceramica,** 36–38 Main St. (© **860/526-9978**), an outlet of a small chain, carries a line of uniformly gorgeous hand-painted bowls, pitchers, vases, and teapots.

WHERE TO DINE

The Wheatmarket (© **860/526-9347**), next door to Fiddlers (see below), will make up picnic baskets, or you can put together your own from the appetizing array of breads, cheeses, soups, salads, and sandwiches.

Fiddlers 🏕 SEAFOOD Have your fish any way you want—poached, sautéed, broiled, baked, or grilled over mesquite—or leave it up to the skillful kitchen staff, for they can come up with some eye-openers. If "lobster au pêché" (fat chunks of lobster meat married to peach nubbins, shallots, mushrooms, cream, and peach brandy) is still on the menu, go for it. Not for lobster purists, certainly, but a revelatory example of what an imaginative chef can do. The dining rooms are cheerfully unremarkable.

4 Water St. (behind Main St.). © 860/526-3210. Main courses $13.95–$21.95. DC, MC, V. Tues–Thurs 11:30am–2pm and 5:30–9pm; Fri 11:30am–2pm and 5:30–9:30pm; Sat 5:30–10pm; Sun 4–9pm.

EAST HADDAM

Hadlyme (a jurisdiction of the town of East Haddam), hardly more than a wide spot in a country road, wouldn't have attracted much attention at all if a wealthy thespian hadn't decided to build his hilltop redoubt here.

To get here, take the **Chester-Hadlyme Ferry,** at the end of Route 148, slightly less than 2 miles (3km) from Chester. A ferry has operated here since 1769, and the current version takes both cars and pedestrians ($2.25 for vehicles plus $1.50 for trailers, 75¢ for walk-on passengers). It operates (when it feels like it) from 7am to 6:45pm in the warmer months. If it's closed, there will be a sign posted at the intersection of Routes 148 and 154, in which case you'll have to drive north on Route 154 to Haddam and take the bridge.

Gillette Castle State Park 🏕 William Gillette was a successful actor and playwright known primarily for his portrayals of Sherlock Holmes. He took the money and ran to this hill rearing above the Connecticut River, where he had his castle built. It's difficult to believe that he really thought the result resembled the Norman fortresses that allegedly were his inspiration. Rock gardens by roadside eccentrics in South Dakota or Death Valley are closer relations. Gillette felt it necessary, for one example, to design a dining-room table that slid into the wall, an inexplicable space-saving effort by a bachelor rattling around in 24 oddly shaped rooms.

But whatever Gillette's deficiencies as an architect and designer, no one can argue with his choice of location. The castle sits atop a hill above the east bank, with superlative vistas upriver and down. Nowhere else is the blessed underdevelopment of the estuary more apparent.

The 184-acre (75-hectare) grounds have picnic areas, nature trails, and fishing sites. Because the terrace of the "castle" can be entered for free, many visitors come just to take in those **views** 🏕🏕. *Note:* The castle itself has been closed the last 2 years for renovations. It's scheduled to reopen in 2002, but inquire locally to be sure. The grounds have remained open to visitors.

67 River Rd. ℂ **860/526-2336.** www.cttourism.org. Admission $4 adults, $2 children 6–11. Grounds daily 8am–sunset; castle Memorial Day to Labor Day Fri–Sun 10am–5pm.

RIVER CRUISES

A voyage on the river is an irresistible outing. Cruises of a variety of lengths, times, and themes are offered by **Camelot Cruises,** 1 Marine Park (ℂ **860/345-8591;** www.camelotcruises.com). The pride of its fleet is the MV *Camelot,* a 160-foot (48m) vessel carrying as many as 500 passengers. In addition to dinner and mystery cruises, there are summer and fall excursions to Sag Harbor, Long Island.

A competing company, **Mark Twain Cruises,** River Street, Deep River (ℂ **877/658-9246;** www.deeprivernavigation.com), uses six boats for winter eagle-spotting, fall foliage, fireworks, birding, meal, and jazz cruises. Embarkations are from State Street and Charter Oak Landings in Hartford as well as from Saybrook Point and other ports along the river.

EAST HADDAM AFTER DARK

From Gillette Castle State Park, turn north on Route 82 and make the short drive to East Haddam proper. The dominant building is a restored 1877 Victorian of splendid proportions that is now the **Goodspeed Opera House** ★★, Goodspeed Landing (ℂ **860/873-8668;** www.goodspeed.org). It mostly stages revivals of Broadway musicals on the order of *Man of La Mancha,* but always makes room for more experimental or original shows that have often made it all the way to the Big Apple. The season is usually April through October. Tours are given June through October, Monday from 1 to 3pm and Saturday from 11am to 1:30pm; these cost $2 for adults and $1 for children.

7 Mystic & the Southeastern Coast

Mystic: 55 miles (89km) E of New Haven

This section of the shoreline is studded with towns that still bear the stamp of their maritime pasts, a string of fishing ports and inlets that segues into the mainland beach resorts of Rhode Island. Inland are a number of still semirural villages, but their futures are unpredictable due to the presence of two enormously successful and steadily expanding Indian casino complexes, Foxwoods and Mohegan Sun. They produce gushers of money that are altering forever the character of this region.

The town of Mystic and its twin attractions, Mystic Aquarium and the living museum that is Mystic Seaport, are the prime reasons for a stay—the Seaport alone can easily occupy most of a day, and the two-part town itself sustains a nautical air, with fun shops and restaurants to suit most tastes.

But that's not a complete list of the region's charms. The tranquil neighboring village of Stonington is home to a small but active commercial fishing fleet, the last in the state; there are several enchanting inns in the area; and many companies offer their vessels for whale-watching, dinner cruises, and deep-sea fishing excursions. And yes, for those with a taste for the adrenaline rush of a winning streak, there are those casinos.

If at all possible, avoid July, August, and weekends from May to Columbus Day, when the crowds are oppressive, restaurants are packed, and rooms are booked months in advance at very high rates.

ESSENTIALS

GETTING THERE   From New York City, take I-95 to Exit 84 (New London), Exit 86 (Groton), Exit 90 (Mystic), or Exit 91 (Stonington). Or, to avoid the heavy truck and commercial traffic of the western segment of I-95, use the Hutchinson River Parkway, which becomes the Merritt Parkway (Rte. 15) and merges with the Wilbur Cross Parkway. Continue to Exit 54, connecting with I-95 for the rest of the trip. From Boston, take the Massachusetts Turnpike to I-395 south to Exit 75, then south on Route 32 to New London and I-95.

Amtrak (© 800/USA-RAIL; www.amtrak.com) runs several trains daily on its Northeast Direct route between New York, Providence, and Boston, with intermediate stops at New Haven, Old Saybrook, New London, and Mystic.

SEAT (© 860/886-2631), the regional bus company, connects the more important towns and villages of the district, except for North Stonington.

A new way to get from the metropolitan New York region to New London, and from there to the Foxwoods casino complex, is via the super-fast tri-catamaran ferries operated by **Fox Navigation** (© 888/724-5369; www.fox navigation.com). Embarkation is at Glen Cove, on the north shore of Long Island, and the trip takes about 2 hours 15 minutes. Pass the time on reclining airline-type seats with on-board movies and food service. Passengers debark at the State Pier in New London and are transported from there to Foxwoods. There are four round-trips, 4 days per week.

VISITOR INFORMATION **Mystic Coast & Country** (© 800/692-6278; www.mycoast.com) can provide vacation planning kits. If the many motels off I-95 aren't for you, ask for the folder describing the loosely affiliated **Bed & Breakfasts of Mystic Coast,** which lists 23 establishments in the area, including four just across the Rhode Island state line.

NEW LONDON

New London's protected deep-draft harbor at the mouth of the Thames River was responsible for its long and influential history as a whaling port. That heritage lingers, although its years of great prosperity seem to be behind it. That may change, for the opening of a global headquarters of the Pfizer corporation in 2001 has provoked hopes for a rosier economic future.

Possessed of an architecturally interesting but largely somnolent downtown district, New London, which lies 46 miles (74km) east of New Haven and 45 miles (72km) southeast of Hartford, is of note to travelers primarily because it's a transit point for three ferry lines connecting Block Island, R.I., and Long Island, N.Y., with the mainland, as well as the new high-speed ferries connecting with Martha's Vineyard and Glen Cove, Long Island. **Connecticut College** has a large campus at the northern edge of the city, along Route 32 and Williams Street.

An **information booth** is located downtown at the corner of Eugene O'Neill Drive and Golden Street (© 860/444-7264). It's open June through August, daily from 10am to 4pm; May, September, and October, Friday through Sunday from 10am to 4pm.

Coast Guard Academy Visitors are directed to a pavilion overlooking the Thames. It doesn't offer much except views of the river and shores. A full-rigged sailing vessel, the *Eagle,* is the academy's principal attraction, with boarding allowed usually only in April and May. It was built as a training ship for German Naval cadets in 1936 and taken as a war prize after World War II.

15 Mohegan Ave. (off Williams St., north of Exit 84 off I-95). © 860/444-8611. Free admission. Grounds daily 9am–5pm; Visitors Pavilion May–Oct daily 10am–5pm, Apr Sat–Sun 10am–5pm. Pavilion closed Nov–Mar.

Lyman Allyn Museum of Art   This neoclassical granite pile stands on a hill looking across Route 32 toward the Coast Guard Academy. Its holdings are the result of the enthusiasms of private collectors and therefore stick to no specific curatorial vision. The basement contains detailed room settings of Victorian dollhouse furniture, right down to tiny ladles on the kitchen counter. On the main floor are colonial American paintings, including landscapes by Frederic Edwin Church and Albert Bierstadt. Upstairs are exhibits as diverse as Asian temple castings and Japanese lacquerware.

625 Williams St. ☏ **860/443-2545**. Admission $4 adults, $3 seniors and students, free for children under 6. Tues–Sat 10am–5pm; Sun 1–5pm. From Exit 83 off I-95, follow brown signs to museum.

OUTDOOR PURSUITS

Not far from downtown is **Ocean Beach Park,** at the south end of Ocean Avenue (☏ **800/510-7263** or 860/447-3031), a 40-acre (16-hectare) recreational facility with a broad sand beach, boardwalk, 50-meter saltwater pool, miniature golf, water slide, bathhouse with lockers and showers, concession stands, and lounge. Open Memorial Day weekend through Labor Day, daily from 9am to 10pm.

June through September, excursions run by **Thames River Cruises** (☏ **860/444-7827**) carry passengers up past the *Nautilus* submarine base (see section on Groton, below). The Thames can't be compared to the Rhine or even the lower Connecticut River for scenic diversion, but it's a pleasant enough outing. (The submarine base can also be reached by car.) Daily departures are made hourly from 9am to 5pm; home dock is the City Pier at the foot of State Street, behind the railroad station. The fare is $10 for adults, $6 for children 6 to 13.

The ferries that ply the Long Island Sound from New London have a recreational aspect, as well as simply serving as transport between Block Island and Long Island. **Cross Sound Ferry** (☏ **631/323-2525** for reservations, 860/443-5281 for information; www.longislandferry.com) provides year-round service to Orient Point on Long Island. Departures are every hour or two during the day, and the one-way voyage takes about an hour and 20 minutes. Call ahead to make reservations, especially when taking a car. The **Fishers Island Ferry** (☏ **860/443-6851**) also has daily departures for Long Island. From mid-June to early September, **Nelseco Navigation Co.** (☏ **860/442-7891** or 860/442-9553) operates its ferry once a day (with an extra trip Fri evenings) between New London and the Old Harbor on Block Island. The one-way trip takes about 2 hours. Call ahead to determine fares and sailing times; advance reservations for cars are essential.

WHERE TO DINE

Timothy's ☆☆ NEW AMERICAN   Although you are invited to dip your bread in olive oil, and three or four perky pastas are listed on the menu, this isn't an overtly Italian restaurant. Think of it as a contemporary bistro. The lobster and crabmeat bisque with a splash of sherry is a signature dish, and items like the sautéed flounder coated in crushed pecans and the semi-boneless duckling are regulars. All of it is brightly seasoned, with daring combinations of fresh herbs. New London needs more operations like this.

181 Bank St. ☏ **860/437-0526**. Reservations recommended for dinner. Main courses $14.95–$25.95. Tues–Fri 11:30am–2:30pm and 5:30–9:30pm (Fri until 10pm); Sat 5:30–10pm.

GROTON

The future is uncertain for this naval-industrial town on the opposite side of the Thames from New London. It has long been dependent on the presence of the

Electric Boat division of General Dynamics and the Navy's submarine base, and cutbacks in military budgets have adversely affected both. Whatever happens, the principal tourist attraction remains the USS *Nautilus,* the world's first nuclear-powered vessel.

After a visit to the submarine museum, history buffs may wish to stroll around **Fort Griswold Battlefield State Park,** Monument Street and Park Avenue (© **860/445-1729** or 860/449-6877). It was here, in 1781, that the traitor Benedict Arnold led a British force against American defenders, ruthlessly ordering the massacre of his 88 prisoners after they had surrendered. The free museum is open from Memorial Day to Labor Day, daily from 10am to 5pm; and from Labor Day to Columbus Day, Saturday and Sunday from 10am to 5pm.

Submarine Force Museum   The entry hall and adjoining galleries display models of submarines, torpedoes, missiles, deck guns, periscopes, and a full-scale cross-section of Bushnell's *Turtle,* the "first submersible ever used in a military conflict," in 1776. Out back, the USS *Nautilus* itself stands at its mooring, ready for inspection. The somewhat claustrophobic walk through the control rooms, attack center, galley, and sleeping quarters is aided by listening devices handed out to each visitor.

Naval Submarine Base, 1 Crystal Lake Rd. © **800/343-0079** or 860/694-3174. www.submarinemuseum. Free admission. May 15–Oct 31 Wed–Mon 9am–5pm, Tues 1–5pm; Nov 1–May 14 Wed–Mon 9am–4pm. Take Exit 86 from I-95, drive north on Rte. 12, and follow signs to the USS *Nautilus.*

FISHING TRIPS

A number of companies offer full- and half-day fishing trips. Typical of the party boats is the 114-foot (34m) *Hel-Cat II,* 181 Thames St. (© **860/535-2066** or 860/535-3200), operating from its own pier about 2 miles (3km) south of Exit 85 north or Exit 86 south off I-95. Trips are from 6 to 8½ hours at fares of $30 to $48.

Both charter and party boats are available from the **Sunbeam Fleet,** based at **Captain John's Sport Fishing Center,** 15 First St., Waterford (© **860/443-7259;** wwwsunbeamfleet.com). Fishing party boats sail twice daily Friday through Sunday in June, Thursday through Tuesday from July to Labor Day. The same firm has whale-watching voyages three times a week in July and August. Nature cruises go eagle-watching in February and March, and search for harbor seals March through May. Adult fares are $30 to $40. Waterford is the town immediately south of New London; the dock is next to the Niantic River Bridge.

WHERE TO STAY

Clarion Inn *Kids*   A solid possibility for families planning to spend a few days in the region, 34 of these units have minimally equipped kitchens, and most are suites that sleep up to four people.

156 Kings Hwy., Groton, CT 06340. © **800/252-7466** or 860/446-0660. Fax 860/445-4082. 69 units. $78–$189 double. Lower rates Nov–May. AE, DC, DISC, MC, V. **Amenities:** Restaurant, bar; heated indoor pool; exercise room; sauna. *In room:* A/C, TV.

Mystic Marriott Hotel & Spa 🕸🕸   Filling a perceived gap in area lodgings, Marriott brings a measure of big-town pizzazz to an otherwise colorless intersection in a triangle occupied at the other corners by the casinos and Mystic. Rooms adhere to corporate cookie-cutter standards, but are no less comfortable for that. The big deal is the Elizabeth Arden spa, which shares facilities with the excellent fitness center. In addition to the nail, skincare, and hair salons are two hydrotubs, supplemented by seaweed wraps, herbal mud masks, and stone therapy. Food and service in the Octagon dining room are less impressive than the surroundings.

625 North Rd. (Rte. 117), Groton, CT 06340. ℂ **860/446-2600.** Fax 860/446-2696. www.marriott hotels.com. 285 units. Memorial Day to Columbus Day $169–$239 double; rest of year $149–$189 double. Packages available. AE, DC DISC, MC, V. **Amenities:** Restaurant (steakhouse), bar; heated indoor 50m pool; exhaustively equipped health club and spa; business center; 24-hr. room service; same-day dry cleaning/ laundry. *In room:* A/C, TV w/ pay movies, Sony PlayStation, dataport, coffeemaker, hair dryer, iron, safe.

MYSTIC ★★★

The spirit and texture of the maritime life and history of New England are captured in many ports along its indented coast, but nowhere more cogently than beside the Mystic River estuary and its harbor. This was a dynamic whaling and shipbuilding center during the colonial period and into the last century, but the discontinuation of the first industry and the decline of the second haven't adversely affected the community. No derelict barges or rotting piers degrade the views and waterways (or at least not many).

Mystic and West Mystic are stitched together by a drawbridge, the raising of which, mostly for sailboats, causes traffic stoppages at a quarter past every hour but rarely shortens tempers, except for visitors who don't leave their urban impatience behind. There are complaints by some that the two-part town has been commercialized, but the incidence of T-shirt shops and related tackiness is limited, and the more garish motels and attractions have been restricted to the periphery, especially up near Exit 90 off I-95.

The town is home to one of New England's most singular attractions, the Mystic Seaport museum village. Far more than the single building the name might suggest, it is a re-created seaport of the mid-1800s, with dozens of buildings and watercraft of that romantic era of clipper ships and the China trade.

A **visitor center** is located in Building 1D of the Olde Mistick Village shopping center, at Route 27 and Coogan Boulevard, near the Interstate (ℂ **860/536-1641**).

SEEING THE SIGHTS

Mystic Seaport ★★★   Few visitors fail to be enthralled by this evocative museum village. It encompasses an entire waterfront settlement, more than 60 buildings on and near a 17-acre (7-hectare) peninsula poking into the Mystic River. Plan to set aside at least 2 or 3 hours—if not an entire day—for a visit. A useful map guide is available at the ticket counter in the **visitor center** in the building opposite the museum stores (which stay open later than the village most of the year, so make them your last stop).

Exit the visitor center and bear right along the path leading between the Galley Restaurant and the village green. It bends to the left, intersecting with a street of shops, public buildings, and houses. At that corner is an 1870s hardware and dry-goods store.

Turning right here, you'll pass a schoolhouse, a chapel, and an 1830s home. Stop at the **children's museum,** which invites youngsters to play games characteristic of the seafaring era. It faces a small square that is the starting point for **horse-drawn wagon tours.**

From here, the three-masted barque *Charles W. Morgan,* one of the proudest possessions of the Seaport fleet of over 400 craft, is only a few steps away. It was built in 1841.

If you're a fan of scrimshaw and ship models, continue along the waterfront to the right until you reach the **Stillman Building,** which contains fascinating exhibits of both. Otherwise, head left toward the lighthouse. Along the way, you'll encounter a tavern, an 1833 bank, a cooperage, and other shops and services that did business with the whalers and clipper ships that put in at ports such as this.

The friendly docents in the village are highly competent at the crafts they demonstrate and are always ready to impart as much information as visitors care to absorb. The fact that they aren't dressed in period costumes paradoxically enhances the village's feeling of authenticity by avoiding the contrived air of many such enterprises.

The next vessel encountered is the iron-hulled square-rigger *Joseph Conrad,* which dates from 1881. Up ahead is a small **lighthouse,** which looks out across the water toward the large riverside houses that line the opposite shore. Round the horn, go past the boat sheds, the fishing shacks, and the ketches and sloops that are moored along here in season until you come to the dock for the perky 1908 **SS Sabino.** This working ship gives half-hour river rides from mid-May to early October, daily from 11am to 4pm, and 1½-hour evening excursions Monday through Thursday leaving at 5pm, Friday and Saturday at 7pm. A few steps away is the 1921 fishing schooner *L. A. Dunton.*

And still the village isn't exhausted. A few steps south is the **Henry B. Du Pont Preservation Shipyard,** where the boats are painstakingly restored. One recent project was the re-creation of the schooner *Amistad,* which inspired an exhibit exploring the historical incident.

Also on the grounds are the **Galley Restaurant,** which serves pretty good fish-and-chips, fried clam strips, and lobster rolls; and **Sprouter's Tavern,** which offers snacks and sandwiches.

When you exit for the day, ask the gatekeeper to validate your ticket so you can come back the next day for free.

Across the brick courtyard with the giant anchor is a building containing several **museum stores** as well as an art gallery. These superior shops stock books, kitchenware, fresh-baked goods, nautical prints and paintings, and ship models.

75 Greenmanville Ave. (Rte. 27). ☎ **888/9-SEAPORT** or 860/572-5315. www.mysticseaport.org. Admission $17 adults, $9 children 6–12 (2nd day included with validation). AE, MC, V. Ships and exhibits Apr–Oct daily 9am–5pm, Nov–Mar daily 10am–4pm; grounds 9am–5pm. Closed Dec 25. Take Exit 90 off I-95, going about 1 mile (1.6km) south on Rte. 27 toward Mystic. Parking lots are on the left, the entrance on the right.

Mystic Aquarium ★★ *Kids*   If you've never seen a dolphin or orca show, this is the place. Less gimmicky than similar commercial enterprises in Florida and California, the show illuminates as it entertains, and at 15 minutes in length, doesn't test the attention spans of the very young. The adorable mammals squawk, click, roll up onto the apron of their pool, tail walk, and joyously splash the nearer rows of spectators.

While the rest of the exhibits necessarily fall in the shadow of the stars, they are enough to occupy at least another hour. Near the entrance is a tank of fur seals, and out back are sea lions and African black-footed penguins. A $52-million expansion was completed in 1999 under the direction of the legendary undersea explorer Robert Ballard, who discovered the sunken *Titanic.* It includes a 1-acre (0.4-hectare) outdoor habitat called the Alaskan Coast, which contains a pool for resident white beluga whales and harbor seals. Visitors are practically eye to eye with such creatures as sea horses, jellyfish, and the pugnacious yellow-head jaw fish, which spends its hours digging fortifications in the sand.

55 Coogan Blvd. (at Exit 90 off I-95). (C) **860/572-5955**. www.mysticaquarium.org. Admission $16 adults, $15 seniors, $11 children 3–12. July–Labor Day daily 9am–6pm; after Labor Day–Nov and mid-Mar to June daily 9am–5pm; Dec–late Mar Mon–Fri 10am–4pm, Sat–Sun 9am–5pm.

OUTDOOR PURSUITS

For a change from salt air and ship riggings, drive inland to the **Denison Pequotsepos Nature Center,** 109 Pequotsepos Rd. ((C) **860/536-1216**), a 125-acre (51-hectare) property with more than 7 miles (11km) of trails. The center building has a thrown-together quality, with dog-eared books beside the live boa constrictor and worm farm. Younger children are nonetheless fascinated. Outside are picnic tables and flight cages of rehabilitating raptors. There are five nature trails, none of which merit special effort—but they can serve as gentle diversion for a half hour or so. Admission is $6 for adults, $4 for seniors and children 12 and under. Open Monday through Saturday from 9am to 5pm, Sunday from 10 to 4pm (closed Sun Jan–Apr, Mon Sept–Apr). To get here, take Route 27 north from Mystic, make a right on Mistuxet Avenue, and turn left on Pequotsepos Road.

Several operators offer **sailing and fishing cruises.** One of the most convenient is the *Argia* ((C) **860/536-0416**), a replica of a 19th-century schooner that docks 100 feet (30m) south of the drawbridge in Mystic. Fares are $32 to $34 for adults, $22 to $24 for children. For longer trips, outings on the *Mystic Whaler* ((C) **800/697-8420;** fax 860/536-4219; www.mysticwhaler.com) include dinner sails, day trips, and extended cruises that can last 2, 3, or 5 days. Corresponding rates go from $65 up to $735. Voyages set out from a pier at 7 Holmes St., off Route 27, 1 mile (1.6km) south of Mystic Seaport.

SHOPPING

Downtown Mystic has limited shopping, a situation made worse by a fire in 2000 that destroyed a 19th-century building with eight storefronts next to the famous drawbridge. Of the survivors, an engaging choice is **Bank Square Books,** 53 W. Main St. ((C) **860/536-3795**).

WHERE TO STAY

There are plenty of ho-hum but adequate area motels that can soak up the traffic at all but peak periods, meaning weekends from late spring to early fall plus weekdays in July and August, when it is necessary to have reservations. Pick of the litter may be the **Best Western Sovereign,** north of Exit 90 ((C) **800/528-1234**), with a pool and restaurant. Nearby competitors are the **Comfort Inn** ((C) **800/228-5150** or 860/572-8531), **Days Inn** ((C) **800/325-2525** or 860/572-0574), and **Residence Inn** ((C) **800/331-3131** or 860/536-5150).

Hilton Mystic (★)   Unlike the motels clustered around the I-95 interchange, this is a full-service hotel, providing the amenities expected of its big-city cousins, though without much personality. The front desk is often willing to negotiate prices. A pianist entertains many evenings in the lounge. The hotel is owned by the Pequot tribe, so it's no surprise that there are posters announcing coming attractions at Foxwoods Casino and a shuttle van to take you there.

20 Coogan Blvd., Mystic, CT 06355. (C) **800/445-8667** or 860/572-0731. Fax 860/572-0328. www.hilton.com. 183 units. $95–$250 double. AE, DC, DISC, MC, V. Free valet parking. Take Exit 90 off I-95 and drive south, following signs to the Mystic Aquarium; the hotel is opposite. **Amenities:** Restaurant (Continental), lounge; heated indoor pool; fitness room; bike rental; children's programs; video arcade; limited room service; same-day dry cleaning/laundry. *In room:* A/C, TV w/ pay movies, dataport, coffeemaker, hair dryer, iron.

The Inn at Mystic 🐾🐾 A variety of lodgings are on offer at this property occupying 13 acres (5 hectares) overlooking Long Island Sound. The complex also incorporates one of the area's best restaurants, Flood Tide (see "Where to Dine," below). At the crest of the hill is the impressive inn, a 1904 Classical Revival mansion with rooms as grand as the exterior, enhanced by Jacuzzis, fireplaces, and canopied beds. Down the hill is the intimate Gatehouse, similarly accoutered with a scattering of antiques. Some of the units in the new motel sections are equally well appointed, including a few with balconies; others are modest and conventional. Don't miss the bounteous breakfasts.

Rtes. 1 and 27, Mystic, CT 06355. ℂ 800/237-2415 or 860/536-9604. www.innatmystic.com. 67 units. $75–$175 motel double; $140–$295 mansion or gatehouse double. Rates include afternoon tea. Packages available. AE, DC, DISC, MC, V. Pets accepted in 6 units ($10). **Amenities:** Restaurant (Continental), bar; outdoor pool; 2 putting greens; tennis court; access to nearby health club; free kayaks and boats; limited room service; same-day dry cleaning/laundry. *In room:* A/C, TV, dataport, fridge, coffeemaker, hair dryer.

Steamboat Inn 🐾🐾 Mystic's most appealing lodging is easily overlooked from land, but readily apparent from the river. Perched on the riverbank, the yellow-clapboard structure has apartment-size downstairs bedrooms, with Jacuzzis and wet bars, while the upstairs units have wood-burning fireplaces. Every room is decorated uniquely—Laura Ashley must have been a muse—and all but one have water views. They are, it must be said, starting to look just a bit tired. The inn commissioned the 97-foot (29m) luxury yacht, *Valiant*, that is moored at its dock. The staterooms can be rented when the yacht isn't chartered.

73 Steamboat Wharf, Mystic, CT 06355. ℂ 860/536-8300. Fax 860/536-9528. www.visitmystic.com/steamboat. 10 units. Late May–Nov $200–$285 double; Dec–late May $125–$245 double. Rates include breakfast. AE, DISC, MC, V. Validated parking available in a gated lot. Look for the sign pointing down an alley on the west bank of the Mystic River, just before the drawbridge. Children over 9 welcome. *In room:* A/C, TV, dataport, fridge, coffeemaker, hair dryer, iron.

Taber Inne 🐾 Not quite an inn but more than a motel, this place has something to suit most tastes and budgets, with seven immaculate buildings containing both simple units and hedonistic suites with fireplaces and decks. A new cottage with a cathedral ceiling has two bedrooms, a sitting room, and a kitchen.

66 Williams Ave. (Rte. 1; 2 blocks east of the intersection with Rte. 27), Mystic, CT 06355. ℂ 860/536-4904. Fax 860/572-9140. www.taberinne.com. 25 units. Mid-Apr to Nov $125–$155 double; $225–$365 suite; Nov to mid-Apr $95–$139 double, $225–$340 suite. AE, MC, V. **Amenities:** Heated indoor pool; access to nearby health club with tennis court; exercise room. *In room:* A/C, TV, dataport, coffeemaker, hair dryer.

WHERE TO DINE

Abbott's Lobster in the Rough SEAFOOD It's as if a wedge of the Maine coast has been punched into the Connecticut shore. This nitty-gritty lobster shack has plenty of picnic tables and not a frill to be found. While there are many options, including hot dogs and chicken, the classic shore dinner rules. That means clam chowder, boiled shrimp, steamed mussels, and a tasty lobster, with coleslaw, chips, and drawn butter thrown in. Bring your own beer.

117 Pearl St., Noank. ℂ 860/536-7719. Reservations not accepted. Main courses $15–$23 (lobster dinners $18–$30). AE, MC, V. First Fri in May to Memorial Day Fri–Sun noon–7pm; Memorial Day to Labor Day weekend daily noon–9pm; after Labor Day weekend to Columbus Day weekend Fri–Sun noon–7pm. From downtown Mystic, go south on Rte. 215 and cross a railroad bridge. At Main St. in Noank, turn left, and take an immediate right on Pearl St. Be prepared to ask for directions anyway.

Flood Tide 🐾🐾 CONTINENTAL Peel back about 3 decades: They still do tableside preparations here, like Caesar salad, beef Wellington with foie gras, and rack of lamb, carved showily before your eyes. The retro performance reminds us why we used to relish this celebratory stuff in the days before Nouvelle-Pan-Asian-Fusion food was invented. The new chef is expected to perk things up, though. Lunch is less fussy, and breakfast is a particular treat, with such offerings as eggs Benedict with lobster. A pianist plinks at the baby grand nightly and at Sunday brunch. The dining rooms look out over the sound, so ask for a table by the window.

The Inn at Mystic, Rtes. 1 and 27. ℂ **860/536-8140.** Reservations recommended. Main courses $22–$36. AE, DC, DISC, MC, V. Daily 7pm–midnight.

Go Fish ⟨⟩ SEAFOOD   Brash and boisterous, Go Fish is dominated by a sprawling granite bar. To one side are the young smokers; on the other, older folks and families. Ask for fish cooked just about any way possible—baked, roasted, grilled, deep-fried, or pan-blackened. Entrees are abundant, so you might want to skip appetizers, enticing though they are (the creamy bisque, for one). Wines are served by the glass, in sizes "full," "half," or "taste."

Olde Mistick Village, at Exit 90 off I-95. ℂ **860/536-2662.** Reservations not accepted. Main courses $14.95–$24.95. AE, DC, DISC, MC, V. Sun–Thurs 11:30am–9:30pm; Fri–Sat 11:30am–10:30pm.

Kitchen Little ⟨⟩ AMERICAN   Not much more than a shack by the water, this is the sort of place dismissed and passed every day by hundreds of tourists hurrying on to the Seaport. They're missing not only 45 distinct breakfast choices but also some of the coast's tastiest clam and scallop dishes. At lunch, you must have the definitive clear broth clam chowder, maybe the whole belly clam rolls, and absolutely the fried scallop sandwich. Expect a wait in summer and tight quarters inside. Try to snare a table out back, in view of the tall ships.

Rte. 27, 1 mile (1.6km) south of I-95. ℂ **860/536-2122.** Reservations not accepted. Main dishes $3.45–$13.95. MC, V. Daily 6:30am–2pm.

STONINGTON & NORTH STONINGTON

Not much seems to happen in these slumbering villages, only lightly brushed by the 21st century despite all the thrashing about in heavily touristed Mystic. That suits the residents just fine, explaining why most of them are not thrilled by the continual rumors of projected expansions of the nearby Foxwoods complex, not to mention a third tribe now seeking federal recognition.

It is difficult to imagine what the flexing of that gambling empire will do eventually to inland North Stonington, as peaceful a New England retreat as can be found, with hardly any commercialization beyond a couple of inns. Soundside Stonington has a pronounced maritime flavor, sustained by the presence of the state's only remaining (albeit dwindling) fishing fleet. Its two lengthwise streets are lined with well-preserved Federal-style and Greek Revival homes.

EXPLORING THE AREA

For an introduction, drive south to **Cannon Square** along Stonington's **Water Street.** Standing in the grassy main square are two cannons that were used to fight off an attack by British warships during the War of 1812. Opposite is a lovely old granite house and, on the corner, a neoclassical bank.

Continue south to the end of Water Street, where there's a small **town beach** (admission $2–$3, or $5–$6 per family). The misty blue headland directly south across the sound is Montauk Point, the eastern extremity of New York's Long Island. Return along Main Street, which is almost exclusively residential except for a few government buildings.

You might check out the **Old Lighthouse Museum,** 7 Water St. (ℂ **860/535-1440**). Built of stone in 1823, it was moved here from 100 yards (91m) away and deactivated. Most of its exhibits relate to the maritime past of the area, with scrimshaw tusks and the export porcelain that constituted much of the 19th-century China trade. Most interesting is the carved ivory pagoda. Admission is $4 for adults, $2 for children 6 to 12. Open May through October, Tuesday through Sunday from 11am to 4pm.

One of the Nutmeg State's handful of earnest wineries, **Stonington Vineyards,** 523 Taugwonk Rd., Stonington (© **860/535-1222**), has a tasting room in a barn beside its vineyard. There are usually six or seven pressings to be sampled, with a chardonnay leading the pack. Open daily from 11am to 5pm, with a cellar tour at 2pm. To get here, take Exit 91 off I-95 and drive north 2½ miles (4km).

WHERE TO STAY

Antiques & Accommodations 🌟   Gardens, porches, and patios invite lounging at these three 19th-century houses. Rooms and suites vary substantially: The bridal suite has a canopied bed, five rooms have fireplaces, and three have phones with dataports, so make your needs known at the outset. An adjacent 1840 farmhouse has two more rooms, each with fireplace and Jacuzzi. The four-course breakfast brings such surprises as cantaloupe soup, turkey hash, and walnut-and-banana waffles. Guests who take a liking to any of the antique pieces will be pleased to know that just about everything is for sale.

32 Main St., North Stonington, CT 06359. © 800/554-7829 or 860/535-1736. Fax 860/535-2613. www.visitmystic.com/antiques. 10 units. May–Dec $129–$229 double, $199–$249 suite; Jan–Apr $99–$199 double, $187–$229 suite. Rates include breakfast. MC, V. Sometimes closed Jan. Take Exit 92 off I-95, drive west on Rte. 2 for 2½ miles (4km), and turn right onto Main St. at the sign. **Amenities:** Access to nearby health club. *In room:* A/C, TV, hair dryer.

The Inn at Stonington 🌟🌟   Newly built on the site of a restaurant leveled by fire, this inn harmonizes nicely with its neighbors on the town's main street. Combining the intimacy of a small inn with the comforts of a luxury hotel, it abounds in felicitous flourishes that exceed the expected. Every unit has a gas fireplace, six have balconies, and 10 have Jacuzzis. While rooms reflect a single design sensibility, with tailored contemporary interpretations of country decor, no two are alike.

60 Water St., Stonington, CT 06378. © 860/535-2000. Fax 860/535-8193. www.innatstonington.com. 12 units. Spring/summer $149–$295 double; fall/winter $135–$295 double. Rates include breakfast and evening wine and cheese. AE, DC, MC, V. Take Exit 91 off I-95; follow signs into Stonington village. **Amenities:** Small, well-equipped exercise room; bikes and kayaks available; computer for guests' use. *In room:* A/C, TV, dataport, hair dryer.

Randall's Ordinary 🌟   The oldest structure on this 27-acre (11-hectare) estate dates from 1685. The three bedrooms upstairs have fireplaces and four-poster or canopied beds, though no TVs or phones. Those conveniences are provided in the rooms in the nearby 1819 barn. All meals are cooked at an open hearth and served by a staff in period costumes. Considering the primitive circumstances under which the food is prepared, it is always hearty, if simple. Go for the romantic setting, not gastronomy.

Rte. 2, North Stonington, CT 06359. © 877/599-4540. Fax 860/599-3308. www.randallsordinary.com. 18 units. $140–$250 double. AE, MC, V. Take Exit 92 off I-95 and head north on Rte. 2. *In room:* A/C.

WHERE TO DINE

Boom 🌟 NEW AMERICAN   With a spate of area closings in recent years, it's a challenge picking new restaurants that have the necessaries to survive. This one, though, looks likely to have a respectable life span ahead. It's a companionable, underdecorated little room looking out over a marina. There are irresistible fried oysters among the appetizers, and entrees of scallops and shrimp in tomato-vodka sauce over penne; salmon with artichoke hearts, Kalamata olives, and capers in lemon beurre blanc; and tangy bouillabaise. In good weather, tables are set up outside with a raw bar. Local purveyors are employed for seafood, and the restaurant moves a lot of lobster in summer. Help keep it around awhile.

Dodson Boatyard, 194 Water St. ℂ 860/535-2588. Reservations recommended on weekends. Main courses $14.50–$23.50. AE, MC, V. Tues–Sat 11:30am–3pm; Sun 10am–3pm; Tues–Sun 5:30–9:30pm. Closed Mar.

Stonecroft ✦✦ ECLECTIC   This 1807 inn is home to Drew Egy, a gifted chef who works wonders with dishes that have become familiar in the past 2 decades of America's food revolution. His realm is a converted barn, with linen-dressed tables and a fireplace. Warm focaccia with caramelized onion butter is a nice elevation over the usual rolls. Wine is generously poured in anticipation of such starters as Camembert baked in pastry with rum pecan pears. A favorite entree is black cherry–ancho braised venison osso buco. Other dishes come in a remarkable variety of colors, textures, and ingredients—a touch too many, in some cases—but you'll likely be delighted with most choices.

There are also 10 rooms at the inn, four in the 1807 Georgian main house and six in the converted barn. Many have fireplaces; rates are $140 to $250.

515 Pumpkin Hill Rd., Ledyard. ℂ 860/572-0771. www.stonecroft.com. Reservations recommended on weekends. Main courses $19–$28. AE, DC, MC, V. Wed–Sun 6–10pm. Take Exit 89 north from I-95, onto Cow Hill Rd., which shortly becomes Pumpkin Hill Rd.

FOXWOODS RESORT CASINO

This casino-hotel complex (ℂ 800/752-9244 or 860/885-3000; www.foxwoods. com) is forever changing, adding, renovating, and expanding. There are six cavernous gambling rooms, one of the most popular being the hall containing 4,500 slot machines (out of a total of 6,400). The 3,200-seat Bingo Hall is huge, and the high-tech horse parlor is a dazzler. All the usual methods of depleting wallets are at hand—blackjack, bingo, keno, craps, baccarat, roulette, money wheels, and several variations of poker.

SEEING THE SIGHTS

Mashantucket Pequot Museum and Research Center ✦✦   A $139-million trickle of the floods of cash washing over southeastern Connecticut and its resurgent Indian Nation has been diverted to create this museum. Opened in 1998 to substantial fanfare, it has justified the hoopla with a carefully conceived mix of film, murals, models, dioramas, and re-creations of scenes of Native American life. The Pequot Village exhibit is complete with wigwams and life-size figures shown fishing, hunting, cooking, butchering game, and making baskets and ceramics. An observation tower supplies views of the reservation. Lunch and snacks are served in the restaurant, and there's a shop with books, jewelry, and crafts.

110 Pequot Trail. ℂ 800/411-9671. www.mashantucket.com. Admission $12 adults, $10 seniors, $8 children 6–15. Memorial Day to Labor Day daily 10am–7pm; rest of year Wed–Mon 10am–6pm.

WHERE TO STAY

The resort has three hotels, the newest and most luxurious of which became operational in 1998, more than doubling Foxwoods' housing capacity. Unlike Las Vegas and other gambling centers, rates aren't kept artificially low as an inducement to gamblers, although that policy may change depending upon competitive pressures from the rival Mohegan Sun Resort.

To get to the resort from Boston, take I-95 south to Exit 92 onto Route 2 west. From New Haven and New York, take I-95 to I-395 north to Exit 79A

A Casino in the Woods

What has been wrought in the woodlands north of the Mystic coast in the last decade is nothing less than astonishing. There was little but trees here when the Mashantucket Pequot tribe received clearance to open a gambling casino on their ancestral lands in rural Ledyard. Virtually overnight, the tribal bingo parlor was expanded into a full-fledged casino, and a hotel was built.

That was in 1992. Within 3 years, it had become the single most profitable gambling operation in the world, with a reported 40,000 visitors a day. Money cascaded over the Pequot (pronounced *Pee*-kwat) in a seemingly endless torrent. Expansion was immediate—another hotel, then a third, more casinos, golf courses, and the $139-million **Mashantucket Pequot Museum and Research Center,** devoted to Native American arts and culture. The tribe bought up adjacent lands and at least four nearby inns and hotels, and then opened a shipworks to build high-speed ferries. All that hasn't sopped up the floods of profit, and the tribe has made major contributions to the Mystic Aquarium and Smithsonian Museum of the American Indian.

All this prosperity came to a tribe of fewer than 520 acknowledged members, nearly all of them of mixed ethnicity. Residents of surrounding communities were ambivalent, to put the best face on it. When it was learned that one of the tribe's corporate entities was to be called Two Trees Limited Partnership, a predictable query was, "Is that all you're going to leave us? Two trees?"

But while there is a continuing danger of damage to the fragile character of this authentically picturesque corner of Connecticut, it is also a fact that because of the recent development, thousands of non-Pequots have found employment in their various enterprises.

The complex is reached through forested countryside of quiet hamlets that give little hint of the behemoth rising above the trees in Ledyard township. There are no signs screaming FOXWOODS. Instead, watch for

onto Route 2A east, picking up Route 2 east. Don't bother trying to park your car in the huge garage. It takes forever, and the valet parking at the front door is swift and free.

Grand Pequot Tower ★★   The Grand Pequot Tower handily takes its place among New England's elite resort hotels. The newest of Foxwoods' hotels (so far) is the grandest in space and concept, yet it is also the most tasteful of the three. Polished granite and imported woods and marbles feature extensively in the handsome lobby. The tower's main restaurants, Fox Harbour and Al Dente, surpass all the resort competition. In back is a 50,000-square-foot casino, containing a plush Club Newport International open only to big-money players.

Rte. 2, Mashantucket, CT 06339. © **800/369-9663** or 860/885-3000. Fax 860/312-7474. www.foxwoods. com. 824 units. July–Labor Day $220–$295 double, from $400 suite; Sept–June $195–$270 double, from $400 suite. AE, DC, DISC, MC, V. Free valet parking. **Amenities:** 2 restaurants (seafood, Italian), bars; indoor pool; golf course on property; health club and spa; video arcade; shopping arcade; concierge; 24-hr. room service; babysitting; same-day dry cleaning/laundry. *In room:* A/C, TV, dataport, hair dryer.

plaques with the symbols of tree, wolf, and fire above the word RESERVATION. As you enter the property, platoons of attendants point the way to parking and hotels. Ongoing construction surrounds the glassy, turquoise-and-violet towers of the hotels and casino. Though bustling, it doesn't look like Vegas from the outside—happily, there are no sphinxes, no fake volcanoes, and no neon palm trees.

Inside, the glitz gap narrows, but it is still relatively restrained as such temples to chance go. The gambling rooms have windows, for example, even though the prevailing wisdom among casino designers is that they should not give customers any idea of what time of day or night it is.

And no one is allowed to forget that this whole eye-popping affair is owned and operated by Native Americans. Prominently placed around the main buildings are larger-than-life sculptures by artists of Chiricahua and Chippewa descent, depicting Amerindians in a variety of poses and artistic styles. One other Indian-oriented display is *The Rainmaker,* a glass statue of an archer shooting an arrow into the air. Every hour on the hour, he is the focus of artificial thunder, wind-whipped rain, and lasers pretending to be lightning bolts, the action described in murky prose by a booming voice-of-Manitou narrator. That's as close as the chest thumping gets to going over the top, although some visitors might reflect upon the political correctness of the non-Indian cocktail waitresses outfitted in skimpy Pocahontas minidresses with feathers in their hair.

The pace of all this is slowing somewhat, at least temporarily. The Pequots are watching closely as the new Mohegan Sun Resort, barely 6 miles (10km) away as the crow flies, continues to crowd in on their territory.

Two dozen bus companies provide daily service to Foxwoods from Boston, Hartford, Providence, New York, Philadelphia, and Albany, among many other cities—too many to list here. For information on transit from particular destinations, call ⓒ **860/885-3000.**

Great Cedar Hotel ⭐ Well maintained despite the heavy foot traffic, this hotel has eight floors adjoining the casinos. Guest rooms are colorful, but not too gaudy (except for the suites for high rollers on the top floor).

Rte. 2, Mashantucket, CT 06339. ⓒ **800/369-9663** or 860/885-3000. Fax 860/885-4040. www.foxwoods. com. 312 units. July–Labor Day $170–$22 double, $500 suite; Sept–June $195–$265 double, $500 suite. AE, DC, DISC, MC, V. Free valet parking. **Amenities:** Restaurant, bars; indoor pool; golf course on the property; health club and spa; video arcade; shopping arcade; limited room service; babysitting; same-day dry cleaning/laundry. *In room:* A/C, TV, dataport.

Two Trees Inn This was the first Foxwoods lodging, built in less than 3 months, now a short shuttle-bus ride or 10-minute walk from the casino complex. A conventional motor hotel, it attracts large numbers of bus tours.

240 Lantern Hill Rd. (off Rte. 2), Mashantucket, CT 06339. ⓒ **800/369-9663** or 860/312-3000. Fax 860/885-4050. www.foxwoods.com. 280 units. July–Nov $160–$195 double, $185–$220 suite; Sept–June $135–$160 double, $160–$185 suite. AE, DC, DISC, MC, V. **Amenities:** Restaurant, bar; heated indoor pool; fitness room; sauna; same-day dry cleaning/laundry. *In room:* A/C, TV.

WHERE TO DINE

Twenty-four restaurants and fast-food operations situated throughout the hotel-casino complex cover the most popular options. Only a couple aspire to even moderately serious culinary achievement, and there are no bargains as found in Atlantic City or Vegas. Expect to pay at least $50 for dinner for two, not including drinks, taxes, or tip.

Cedars Steak House (✆ 860/885-3000, ext. 4252) grills beef and seafood; **Al Dente** (ext. 4090) does designer pizzas and pastas; and **Fox Harbour** (ext. 2445) specializes in seafood. All three expect guests to be dressed at least a notch better than tank tops and jeans. They are the only ones that accept reservations.

The most popular dining room is the **Festival Buffet** (ext. 3172), which charges $10 for an all-you-can-eat spread. Other self-explanatory possibilities are **Han Garden** (ext. 4093), **Pequot Grill** (ext. 2690), and **The Deli** (ext. 5481).

FOXWOODS AFTER DARK

Just as in Vegas and Atlantic City, big showbiz names are whisked onto the premises, usually on weekends. Even Wayne Newton makes the scene, as do the likes of Regis Philbin, Tony Bennett, Reba McEntire, the Dixie Chicks, and Jay Leno. For information, call ✆ 800/200-2882.

UNCASVILLE & THE MOHEGAN SUN CASINO

About halfway between New London and Norwich, this blue-collar town once hardly provided sufficient reason even to downshift your car. That's changed, for good.

In 1996, the barely extant Mohegan tribe opened its gambling casino, **Mohegan Sun,** Mohegan Sun Boulevard (✆ 888/226-7711; www.mohegan sun.com). Sitting in the middle of a potential $1-billion annual market, it was drawing 20,000 gamblers a day away from Foxwoods within a few weeks of opening. Obviously, the initial outlay of over $300 million for land and construction paid off handsomely, for the tribe announced soon after its inauguration that it was committing another $400 million for a new 1,200-room hotel, a marina, and nongambling entertainment facilities. The projected expenditure was soon more than doubled, and now includes a completed 10,000-seat sports arena, a planetarium, and a second "Casino of the Sky."

The original casino building bulges with eager gamblers. It is circular, with four entrances named for the seasons. The core of 150,000 square feet is devoted to the games, everything from blackjack to craps, supplemented by 3,000 slot machines. In the center is a nightclub, the Wolf Den, featuring weekend headliners on the order of Seal and Crystal Gayle. Overhead are simulated log constructions meant to suggest ancient lodge houses. It's an aesthetically

---

Kids A Break from Gambling

If you want to temporarily escape the whirring of slots, or simply need to occupy underage kids, check out **Cinetropolis,** an entertainment center that looks like a cleaned-up futuristic Gotham. **Turbo Ride** lets you pretend you're experiencing the rumbling takeoffs and powerful G-forces of jets taking off. **Fox Giant Screen Theatre** is an IMAX-like production that features front-row rock concerts and exploding volcanoes, and **Virtual Adventures** lets you take control of an undersea vessel.

Tips   Which Casino?

When Mohegan Sun first opened, it seemed unlikely to mount a serious challenge to Foxwoods. It was, after all, only a single building, with no big-name entertainment, hotel, or facilities to occupy children. But it was easier to reach, just off I-395, a major highway between Boston and New York, and the essentially childless environment no doubt made it appealing to resolute gamblers. Now a hotel, marina, sports arena, and planetarium are completed or underway, and the headliners in the showroom are of Vegas stature.

Mohegan Sun has a less frantic environment than Foxwoods, comparatively speaking, but it is smaller, with fewer choices in games and restaurants, and until current construction is completed, it has no significant nongambling attraction, while Foxwoods has its heralded museum of Pequot life.

pleasing space, as casinos go, although few of the avid players seem to notice. They can even park their kids in the child-care center.

Of the score of dining options in the two casinos, the relatively ambitious **Longhouse** proffers mostly prime beef and seafood, while other eateries feature Asian, barbecue, Italian, steaks, and just-about-everything-else chow. With an outpost of **Michael Jordan's Steakhouse** now open and celebrity chefs Jasper White and Todd English adding their efforts with their new restaurants, **Summer Shack** and **Tuscany,** respectively, the quality of the food is unexpectedly good.

The casino is right off I-395, Exit 79A, which makes for easy on/off access for gamblers who don't want to deal with that onerous 20-minute drive to Foxwoods before emptying their bank accounts.

NORWICH

There is tourist potential here, where the Yantic and Shetucket rivers converge to form the Thames. Blocks of Broadway and Union Street are lined with substantial mansions from the city's golden era. There is no pretending, however, that this old mill town isn't in the doldrums, and so far, the presence of the nearby Mohegan Sun casino hasn't had much spillover effect. Until efforts to reverse that decline take hold, the principal reason for a visit is the fine lodging described below.

WHERE TO STAY & DINE

The Spa at Norwich Inn ★★★   Reopened after extensive renovations, this is now an even more desirable property. The complex is set on 40 acres (16 hectares), the main building augmented by outlying "villas" with 160 condo units. A typical suite has a kitchen, a sitting area with fireplace, a separate bedroom, and a deck overlooking the woods and a pond. Inn rooms aren't as large and don't have fireplaces, but they are hardly spartan. Kensington's, the dining room, enjoys a versatile kitchen staff capable of producing meals either conventional or fitness-minded. The property is owned by the Pequot tribal organization, and its Foxwoods Casino is about 15 minutes away, making this inn a soothing and convenient respite from the glitz.

607 W. Thames St. (Rte. 32), Norwich, CT 06360. © **800/267-4772** or 860/886-2401. Fax 860/886-9483. www.thespaatnorwichinn.com. 103 units. May–Oct $175–$375 double; Nov–Apr $125–$325 double. AE, DC, MC, V. From New Haven, take Exit 76 off I-95 onto I-395 north, Exit 79A onto Rte. 2A east, then exit onto Rte.

32 north and drive 1½ miles (2.4km) to the inn. **Amenities:** Restaurant, bar; indoor and outdoor pools; golf course on property; fully equipped health club and spa (with exercise classes, steam rooms, sauna, and massage); concierge; limited room service; babysitting; same-day dry cleaning/laundry. *In room:* A/C, TV, dataport, fridge, coffeemaker, hair dryer, iron.

10

Rhode Island

by Herbert Bailey Livesey

Water defines "Little Rhody" as much as mountain peaks characterize Colorado. The Atlantic thrusts all the way to the Massachusetts border, cleaving the state into unequal halves and filling the geological basin that is Narragansett Bay. That leaves 400 miles of coastline and several large islands.

A string of coastal towns runs in a northeasterly arc from the Connecticut border up to Providence, the capital, which lies at the point of the bay, 30 miles (48km) from the open ocean. It was here that Roger Williams, banned from the Massachusetts Bay Colony in 1635 for his outspoken views on religious freedom, established his colony. Little survives from that first century, but a large section of the city's East Side is composed almost entirely of 18th- and 19th-century buildings.

Another group of Puritan exiles established their settlement a couple of years after Providence, on an island known to the Narragansett tribe as "Aquidneck." Settlers thought their new home resembled the Isle of Rhodes in the Aegean, so the official name became "Rhode Island and Providence Plantations," a moniker that was subsequently applied to the entire state and remains the official name.

The most important town on Aquidneck is Newport, and it's the best reason for an extended visit to the state. Its first era of prosperity was during the colonial period, when its ships not only plied the new mercantile routes to China but also engaged in the reprehensible "Triangular Trade" of West Indies molasses for New England rum for African slaves. Their additional skill at smuggling and evading taxes brought them into conflict with their British rulers, whose occupying army all but destroyed Newport during the Revolution.

After the Civil War, the town began its transformation from commercial outpost to resort, with the arrival of the millionaires whose lives spawned what Mark Twain sneeringly described as the "Gilded Age." They built astonishingly extravagant mansions, their contribution to Newport's bountiful architectural heritage. Winning the America's Cup and subsequent defenses of yachting's most famous trophy made the town into a recreational sailing center with a packed summer cultural calendar. As a result, travelers who want nothing more than a deep tan by Monday can coexist with history buffs and music lovers, who come to attend concerts held against a seductive backdrop of waves hissing across packed sand.

Finally, there is Block Island, which is a 1-hour ferry ride from Point Judith. A classic summer resort, it has avoided the imposition of Martha's Vineyard chic and Provincetown clutter. It has also sidestepped history (even though it was first settled in 1661), so there are few mandatory sights. That leaves visitors free simply to explore its lighthouses, hike its cliffside trails, and hit the beach.

1 Providence ★ ★

45 miles (72km) S of Boston; 55 miles (89km) NE of New London

Providence delights in its new sobriquet, "Renaissance City," and is beside itself over the success of the TV series named for it. No question, this city is moving on up, counter to the trend of so many small and mid-sized New England cities. *Money* magazine even declared it the "Best Place to Live in the East." Revival is in the air and prosperity is returning, especially evident in the resurgent "downcity" business district. Rivers have been uncovered to form canals and waterside walkways; gondolas glide beneath graceful bridges; distressed buildings of the last century have been reclaimed; and continued construction includes a new hotel behind Union Station as well as Providence Place, a monster mall that brings national department stores to town for the first time. Advance buzz on the new Heritage Harbor Museum, Rhode Island's first state history museum, is tremendous. This affiliate of the venerable Smithsonian Institution, being developed on the sprawling site of a former power plant, is scheduled to open in 2002.

Much of the credit for Providence's boom, grudging or exuberant, goes to the ebullient six-term mayor, Vincent A. "Buddy" Cianci, Jr. Despite the airing of some incriminating taped phone conversations, Cianci has to date escaped the net cast by an FBI probe into the bribery of local officials. Called Operation Plunder Dome, the investigation has revived Providence's reputation for tolerance of corruption at high levels. A regular guest on the *Imus in the Morning* radio and cable TV show, Cianci recently laughed off a 97-page federal indictment charging him and others with racketeering, extortion, witness tampering, and mail fraud.

Still, local pride in the city's revitalization is palpable. A burgeoning dining scene includes ambitious new restaurants that are nearly always less expensive than their counterparts in Boston and New York. College Hill is one of only 26 National Historic Districts, the calendar is full of special events, and the presence of the young people attending the city's 12 colleges and universities guarantees a lively nightlife.

Roger Williams knew what he was doing. Admired for his fervent advocacy of religious and political freedom in the early colonial period, he obviously had good instincts for town building as well. He planted the seeds of his settlement on a steep rise overlooking a swift-flowing river at the point where it widened into a large protected harbor. That part of the city, called the East Side and dominated by the ridge now known as College Hill, remains the most attractive district of a New England city second only to Boston in the breadth of its cultural life and rich architectural heritage.

College Hill is so named because it is the site of Rhode Island College, which started life in 1764 and was later renamed Brown University. The Hill is further enhanced by the presence of the highly regarded Rhode Island School of Design, whose buildings are wrapped around the perimeter of the Brown campus. In and around these institutions are several square miles of 18th- and 19th-century houses, colonial to Victorian, lining often gaslit streets. At the back of the Brown campus is the funky shopping district along Thayer Street, while at the foot of the Hill is the largely commercial Main Street.

While most points of interest are found on the East Side, the far larger collection of neighborhoods west of the river has its own attractions. The level downtown area is the center for business, government, and entertainment, with

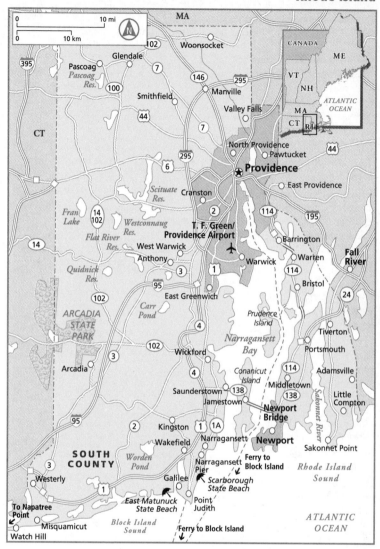

City Hall, a new convention center, the two best large hotels, some small parks and historic buildings, and several venues for music, dance, and theatrical productions. To its north, across the Woonasquatucket River, is the imposing State House and the Amtrak station. And to its west, on the other side of Interstate 95, is Federal Hill, a residential area bearing a strong ethnic identity, primarily Italian, but increasingly leavened by numbers of more recent immigrant groups.

ESSENTIALS

GETTING THERE I-95, which connects Boston and New York, runs right through the city. From Cape Cod, pick up I-195 west.

T. F. Green/Providence Airport (© **888/268-7222** or 401/737-8222; www.pvdairport.com) in Warwick, south of Providence (Exit 13, I-95), is served by major airlines such as **American** (℃ **800/433-7300**), **Continental** (℃ **800/ 525-0280**), **Delta** (℃ **800/221-1212**), **Northwest** (℃ **800/225-2525**), **Southwest** (℃ **800/435-9792**), **United** (℃ **800/241-6522**), and **US Airways** (℃ **800/428-4322**). The Rhode Island Public Transit Authority (RIPTA) provides transportation between the airport and the city center. Taxis are also available, costing about $20 for the 20-minute trip.

Amtrak (℃ **800/USA-RAIL;** www.amtrak.com) runs several trains daily between Boston and New York, stopping at the attractive new station at 100 Gaspee St., near the State House.

GETTING AROUND   Traffic on local streets isn't bad, even at rush hour. Taxis are not easy to come by, with few to be found outside even the largest hotels. They can take 15 minutes or more when called from restaurants.

VISITOR INFORMATION   For advance information, contact the **Providence Warwick Convention & Visitors Bureau,** 1 West Exchange St. (℃ **800/233-1636** or 401/274-1636; www.providencecvb.com). In town, consult the new visitor center in the Rhode Island Convention Center, 1 Sabin St. (℃ **800/233-1636** or 401/751-1177), or check with the helpful park rangers at the visitor center of the Roger Williams National Park, at the corner of Smith and North Main streets, open daily from 9am to 4:30pm.

EXPLORING PROVIDENCE
STROLLING THE HISTORIC NEIGHBORHOODS
This is a city of manageable size—the population is about 170,000—that can easily occupy 2 or 3 days of a Rhode Island vacation. Two leisurely walks, one short, another longer, pass most of the prominent attractions and offer up a sense of the city's evolution from a colony of dissidents to a contemporary center of commerce and government.

Downtown, chart a route from the 1878 City Hall on Kennedy Plaza along Dorrance Street 1 block to Westminster. Turn left, then right in 1 block, past the Arcade (see "Quick Bites," later in this section), then left on Weybosset.

To extend this into a longer walk, follow Weybosset until it joins Westminster and continue across the Providence River. Turn right on the other side, walking along South Water Street as far as James Street, just before the I-195 overpass. Turn left, cross South Main, and then turn left on Benefit Street. This is the start of the so-called **Mile of History** ⚬⚬. Lined with 18th- and 19th-century houses, it is enhanced by gas streetlamps and sections of brick herringbone sidewalks. Along the way are opportunities to visit, in sequence, the 1786 **John Brown House,** the **First Unitarian Church** (1816), the **Providence Athenaeum,** and the **Museum of Art, Rhode Island School of Design.**

SEEING THE SIGHTS
Boosters are understandably proud of their new **Waterplace Park & Riverwalk** ⚬⚬, which encircles a tidal basin and borders the Woonasquatucket River down past where it joins the Moshassuck to become the Providence River. It incorporates an amphitheater, boat landings, landscaped walkways, and vaguely Venetian bridges that cross to the East Side. Summer concerts and other events are held here, among them the enormously popular **WaterFires** ⚬⚬ (℃ **401/ 272-3111**), when 97 bonfires are set ablaze in the basin of Waterplace Park and along the river on New Year's Eve and on more than 20 other dates July through October, their roar accentuated by amplified music.

Providence

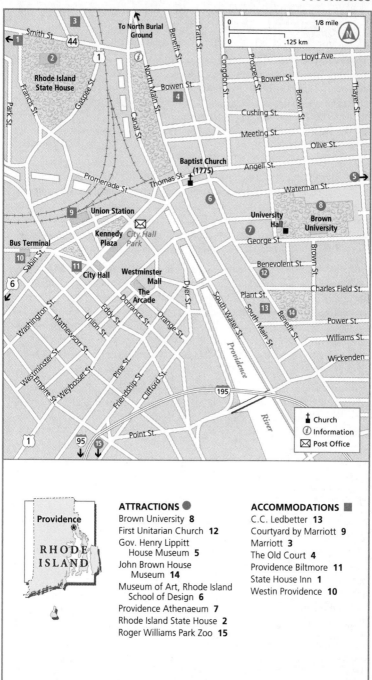

ATTRACTIONS ●
Brown University **8**
First Unitarian Church **12**
Gov. Henry Lippitt
  House Museum **5**
John Brown House
  Museum **14**
Museum of Art, Rhode Island
  School of Design **6**
Providence Athenaeum **7**
Rhode Island State House **2**
Roger Williams Park Zoo **15**

ACCOMMODATIONS ■
C.C. Ledbetter **13**
Courtyard by Marriott **9**
Marriott **3**
The Old Court **4**
Providence Biltmore **11**
State House Inn **1**
Westin Providence **10**

Nearby, in Kennedy Plaza, the new **Fleet Skating Center** has an ice rink twice the size of the one in New York's Rockefeller Center, fully utilized almost every winter evening. Skate rentals, lockers, and a snack bar are available.

Brown University   The nation's seventh-oldest college was founded in 1764 and has a reputation as the most experimental institution among its Ivy League brethren. The evidence of its pre-Revolutionary origins is seen in **University Hall,** built in 1771. Tours of the campus are intended primarily for prospective students, but anyone can join (call ahead).

Office of Admissions, 45 Prospect St. (corner of Angell St.). ✆ **401/863-1000.** Free admission. Tours, late Nov to early Sept Mon–Fri at 10am, 11am, 1pm, 3pm, and 4pm (11am and 3pm only during Christmas and spring vacations); mid-Sept to mid-Nov, Sat 10am, 11am, and noon.

Gov. Henry Lippitt House Museum ⭐   This house is as magnificently true to its grandiose Victorian era as any residence on the Continent. Meticulously detailed stenciling, expanses of stained glass, and inlaid floors make this mansion one of the treasures of College Hill. Visits are by guided tour only.

199 Hope St. (at Angell St.). ✆ **401/453-0688.** Admission $4 adults, $2 seniors and students. Tours Apr–Dec Tues–Fri 11am–3pm on the hour; Sat–Sun and Jan–Mar by appointment only.

John Brown House Museum   Quite unlike the fiery 19th-century abolitionist of the same name, *this* John Brown was an 18th-century slave trader who amassed a fortune in the China trade. He contributed much of that fortune to the university that bears the family name. The style of his 1786 mansion is Georgian, although after the Revolution, Brown no doubt preferred to think of it as Federal. Visits are by guided tour only.

52 Power St. (at Benefit St.). ✆ **401/331-8575.** Admission $6 adults, $4.50 seniors and students, $3 children 7–17. Tues–Sat 10am–5pm; Sun noon–4pm.

Museum of Art, Rhode Island School of Design ⭐⭐   Prestigious RISD (pronounced *Riz*-dee) supports this ingratiating center of fine and decorative arts. The holdings include Chinese terra cotta, Greek statuary, and French Impressionist paintings. Probably of greatest interest are the works by such masters as Monet, Cézanne, Rodin, Picasso, and Matisse. But allow time for the American wing, which contains paintings by Gilbert Stuart, John Singleton Copley, and John Singer Sargent.

224 Benefit St. (between Waterman and College sts.). ✆ **401/454-6500.** Admission $5 adults, $4 seniors, $2 ages 5–18, $1 children 5–18. Tues–Sun 10am–5pm (Thurs until 9pm).

Providence Athenaeum   The Providence Athenaeum commissioned this 1838 Greek Revival building to house its lending library, the fourth oldest in the United States and an innovative concept at the time. Edgar Allan Poe courted Sarah Whitman, his "Annabel Lee," between these shelves. Glances through the old card catalog reveal handwritten cards dating well back into the 1800s. Bibliophiles will lose themselves in this marvelous place. Rotating exhibits of rare books and works by local artists are additional attractions.

251 Benefit St. (at College St.). ✆ **401/421-6970.** Free admission. Mon–Thurs 9am–7pm; Fri–Sat 9am–5pm; Sun 1–5pm. Closed first 2 weeks in Aug.

Rhode Island State House   Constructed of Georgian marble that blazes in the sun, the 1900 capitol dominates the city center. This near-flawless example of neoclassical governmental architecture (by McKim, Mead & White, 1891–92) boasts one of the largest self-supported domes in the world. The gilded figure on top represents "Independent Man," the state symbol. Inside, a portrait of George Washington is given pride of place, one of many depictions painted by Gilbert Stuart, a Rhode Island native son.

82 Smith St. (between Francis and Hayes sts.). © **401/277-2357**. Free admission. Guided tours by appointment Mon–Fri 8:30am–noon.

Roger Williams Park Zoo ⭐⭐ *Kids*   Situated in a 430-acre (174-hectare) park that also contains a museum of natural history and a planetarium, the zoo is divided into three principal habitats: Tropical America, the Farmyard, and the Plains of Africa. A newer exhibit is devoted to Australia, with the zoo's first salt-water aquarium. A walk-through aviary and underwater viewing areas with polar bears, sea lions, and harbor seals are additional attractions.

1000 Elmwood Ave. (at Exit 17 off I-95). © **401/785-3510**. www.rogerwilliamsparkzoo.org. Admission $7 adults, $4.50 seniors and children 3–12. Mid-May to mid-Oct Mon–Fri 9am–5pm, Sat–Sun 9am–6pm; late Oct to early May daily 9am–4pm. Driving south on I-95, take Exit 17; driving north, take Exit 16.

SHOPPING

Thayer Street, the main commercial district for the university, is home to the official **Brown Bookstore,** at no. 244 (at the corner of Olive St.), and the **College Hill Bookstore,** at no. 252, funkier and wider-ranging in its selections. Also in the vicinity are **Silverberry's,** at no. 220, with dressy and casual clothes for college-age women, and **Hillhouse,** no. 135, long in the business of providing male Brownies with Ivy dress-up clothes for interview weeks and parents' days.

WHERE TO STAY

The clusters of motels around most of the exits from I-95 and I-195 offer decent value. Among these possibilities are the **Days Hotel,** 220 India St. (© **401/ 272-5577**), and the **Ramada Inn,** 940 Fall River Ave., Seekonk, Mass. (© **508/ 336-7300**).

Alternatives are provided by B&B referral agencies such as **Bed & Breakfast of Rhode Island** (© **800/828-0000** or 401/849-1298). These are rooms in private homes, so sometimes quirky rules apply. Lodgings in the historic districts are required to provide off-street parking, and it's free at the three East Side inns (C. C. Ledbetter, the Old Court, and the State House Inn) recommended below. There's a charge for parking at the big downtown hotels. Rates at most area inns and motels go up on alumni and parents' weekends and during graduation weeks.

C. C. Ledbetter   There's no sign out front, as Ms. Ledbetter doesn't want to bother her neighbors. Look for the 1780 clapboard building with the olive-green exterior. Things are more colorful inside, with lots of books and contemporary artwork. One bedroom might be the only one in the state to contain a rowing machine. A hearty continental breakfast is served around a common table downstairs, where the two resident dogs usually linger. It's only a couple of blocks from Brown and RISD, so graduation weekends are already booked deep into this new century.

326 Benefit St. (between Charlesfield and Power), Providence, RI 02903. © and fax **401/351-4699**. 5 units (2 with private bathroom). $85–$130 double. Rates include breakfast. MC, V. *In room:* A/C, TV, hair dryer, no phone.

Courtyard by Marriott ⭐   This new addition to the downcity lodging scene is welcome both for its lower rates and for the extra rooms provided in a city still short on accommodations. As a mid-priced entry designed primarily for businesspeople, its rooms are equipped with two-line phones, high-speed Internet access, and well-lit desks. It is just as comfortable for leisure travelers, with several of our recommended restaurants, the new Providence Place mall, and WaterFires only minutes away.

32 Exchange Terrace, Providence, RI 02903. ℂ **800/321-2211** or 401/272-1191. Fax 401/272-1416. www.courtyard.com. 216 units. $129–$199 double. AE, DC, DISC, MC, V. **Amenities:** Cafe/bar (breakfast and cocktails); indoor pool with Jacuzzi; exercise room; business center; coin-op laundry; same-day dry cleaning. *In room:* A/C, TV w/ pay movies, dataport, coffeemaker, hair dryer, iron.

Marriott   This busy motor hotel is popular with both business and leisure travelers. It's north of downtown, but within a 10-minute drive of most of the city's attractions. Shuttle service to and from the airport and the bus and train stations can be arranged when booking.

1 Orms St., Providence, RI 02904. ℂ **800/937-7768** or 401/272-2400. Fax 401/273-2686. www.marriott hotels.com/pvdri. 68 units. $179–$276 double. AE, DC, DISC, MC, V. Free parking. **Amenities:** 2 restaurants, bar; indoor/outdoor pool; modest exercise room with Jacuzzi and sauna; concierge; business center; limited room service; dry cleaning. *In room:* A/C, TV w/ pay movies, dataport, coffeemaker, hair dryer, iron.

The Old Court   This was once a rectory, built in 1863, and the furnishings reflect that use and period. There are secretaries embellished with marquetry, Oriental rugs, and more familiar Victoriana. Most traces of its tenure as a boardinghouse for students have been expunged. Families or longer-term visitors may be interested in the apartment across the street.

144 Benefit St., Providence, RI 02903. ℂ **401/751-2002.** Fax 401/272-4830. www.oldcourt.com. 10 units. $115–$155 double. Rates include breakfast. AE, DISC, MC, V. No children under 12. *In room:* A/C, TV.

Providence Biltmore ★★   A grand staircase beneath the stunning Deco bronze ceiling dates the centrally located building to the 1920s, and a plaque in the lobby shows the nearly 7-foot-high (2m) water level of the villainous 1938 hurricane. From the lobby, the dramatic glass elevator literally shoots skyward, exiting outdoors to scoot up the side of the building. Most guest rooms are large, half of them with more than 600 square feet of floor space; some of the 23 suites have kitchenettes. The entire property has received more than $10 million of overdue attention over the last 3 years, and another 50 rooms have been added.

11 Dorrance St., Providence, RI 02903. ℂ **800/294-7709** or 401/421-0700. Fax 401/455-3127. www. providencebiltmore.com. 289 units. $165–$225 double; $275 suite. AE, DC, MC, V. Valet parking $15. **Amenities:** Restaurant, bar; fitness center; concierge; business center; limited room service; babysitting; laundry; dry cleaning. *In room:* A/C, TV, VCR available, dataport, coffeemaker, hair dryer.

State House Inn   The neighborhood isn't the best, but it isn't scary, either, and downtown restaurants are only minutes away. In compensation, the owners lay out lower rates and hotel conveniences. Some rooms in the 1889 house have canopy beds or fireplaces, and new and antique furnishings have been added in the last couple years. Children are welcome.

43 Jewett St., Providence, RI 02908. ℂ **401/351-6111.** Fax 401/351-4261. www.providence-inn.com. 10 units. May–Oct $129–$159 double; Nov–Apr $139–$189 double. Ask about lower weekday corporate rates. Rates include full breakfast. AE, DISC, MC, V. From the State House, drive west on Smith St., over I-95, then left on Holden and right on Jewett. *In room:* A/C, TV, VCR available, dataport, hair dryer, iron.

Westin Providence ★★★   The city's best hotel by far, this property does nothing to diminish the solid reputation of the Westin chain, and even with a luxurious interior and downtown location, the rates are lower than those of its siblings in Boston and New York. Skyways connect the hotel with the new Providence Place mall and the convention center. The architectural grandeur of the lobby rotunda and other public spaces doesn't seem to dampen the sunny dispositions of the staff. Off the lobby is a lounge with the buffed glow of an exclusive men's club.

1 West Exchange St., Providence, RI 02903. ✆ **800/937-8461** or 401/598-8000. Fax 401/598-8200. www.westin.com. 364 units. $209–$284 double. Valet parking $15. AE, DC, MC, V. **Amenities:** 2 restaurants, 2 bars; indoor pool; fully equipped health club with Jacuzzi and sauna; concierge; business center; limited room service; babysitting; same-day dry cleaning/laundry. In room: A/C, TV w/ pay movies, VCR available, Sony PlayStation, dataport, minibar, coffeemaker, hair dryer, iron.

WHERE TO DINE

Providence has a sturdy Italian heritage, resulting in a profusion of tomato-sauce and pizza joints, especially on Federal Hill, the district west of downtown and I-95. Because they are so obvious, the suggestions below focus on restaurants that break away from the red-gravy imperative.

One fruitful strip to explore for dining options is that part of **Thayer Street** that borders the Brown University campus. It counts Thai, Tex-Mex, barbecue, Indian, and even Egyptian restaurants among its possibilities.

Cafe Nuovo ★★★ MEDITERRANEAN FUSION   This spacious room of glass, marble, and burnished wood occupies part of the ground floor of a downtown office tower that overlooks the confluence of the Moshassuck and Woonasquatucket rivers. Unlike its local competitor, Al Forno, which gets the greater share of largely undeserved ink, Cafe Nuovo takes reservations, is open for lunch *and* dinner, and impresses with every course, from dazzling appetizers to stunning pastries. The fare is grounded in the Italian repertoire, but skips lightly among other inspirations, too—Thai, Greek, and Portuguese among them. That culinary restlessness leads to dishes like duck with cranberry chutney and persimmon pudding, or ginger-crusted salmon with Key lime beurre blanc and jasmine rice. Afterward, consider the remarkable crème brûlée, gussied up with gold leaf and tiered with spun sugar. There's music on weekends and outdoor dining in warm weather. This is the hottest observation point for the nearly two dozen WaterFires events.

1 Citizens Plaza (access is from the Steeple St. bridge). ✆ **401/421-2525.** Reservations advised. Main courses $17.50–$29.95. AE, DC, DISC, MC, V. Mon–Fri 11:30am–4pm; Mon–Thurs 5–10:30pm; Fri–Sat 5–11pm. Closed first week in Jan.

Cafe Paragon ★ ECLECTIC AMERICAN   Located in the heart of the shopping and eating street edging the Brown campus, this spot is understandably popular with faculty, students, and neighbors. In deference to a core clientele with neither fat salaries nor expense accounts, management has kept prices within reason, yet still manages to serve food that equals that found in many downtown emporia. There are burgers and pastas, of course, but also full menus of some imagination, from soups and bruschettas to such specials as roast mahimahi with a tomato-caper-onion salsa. Portions are ample—the individual pizzas fill 12-inch plates, and the exceptional salads are meal-sized. In the warmer months, there's sidewalk seating.

234 Thayer St. (at Angell St.). ✆ **401/421-2525.** Main courses $9–$18. AE, DISC, MC, V. Daily 11am–1am (Fri–Sat until 2am).

CAV ★★ ECLECTIC   No corporate design drudge had a hand in *this* warehouse interior, another Jewelry District pioneer. CAV is an acronym for "Coffee/Antiques/Victuals," and patrons are surrounded by tribal rugs, primitive carvings, and assorted antiques (most for sale). Your server is likely to be a hunk taking a break from auditions. He'll bring dishes prepared by folks more accomplished at their craft than he, selected from such strenuous menu swings as Peking dumplings to the overkill seafood risotto packed with shrimp, scallops, salmon, tuna, haddock, mussels, and sausage. The small stage has an open mike on Mondays and live jazz or blues on Fridays and Saturdays. On those nights, there's a $5 cover.

14 Imperial Place (near Basset St.). ⓒ **401/751-9164**. Reservations recommended. Main courses $13–$24. DISC, MC, V. Mon–Thurs 11:30am–10pm; Fri–Sat 11:30am–1am; Sun 10:30am–10pm.

The Gatehouse ★★ NEW AMERICAN   Step into a refined taproom with a green marble bar on the left, a fireplace and elegantly set tables over to the right. Downstairs is a candlelit lounge and a deck perched above the Seekonk River. Jazz musicians perform down here Wednesday through Saturday, and a pub menu offers burgers and pastas. Service and cuisine are more polished on the main floor. Imagine just this one signature appetizer: duck confit wrapped in prosciutto topped with foie gras combined with the tastes of tangerine honey, blackberry, and caramelized chardonnay sauce. Unlikely as it may sound, it's a perfect marriage of flavors. Many of the entrees are grilled, such as the pecan-smoked pork loin rubbed with maple and tarragon. There are daily pasta and fish specials. Presentation is careful but not fussy. On summer Fridays, the party moves to an outdoor patio for live music and free bar snacks.

4 Richmond Sq. (east end of Pitman St.). ⓒ **401/521-9229**. Reservations recommended on weekends. Main courses $18.95–$32.95. AE, DC, DISC, MC, V. Mon–Sat 5:30–10pm (bar until 1am); Sun noon–3pm and 5–10pm.

Pot au Feu ★ TRADITIONAL FRENCH   If English weren't being spoken all around, you'd think this restaurant was on a village square in Provence. Dishes like *escargot a la Bourguignonne* are exactly as they should be, reminders of what made Gallic cooking memorable long before the excesses of the food revolution set in. Unless you simply must have a tablecloth, there's no reason not to head straight downstairs, especially at dinner, when the price gap widens between the fancier salon and the basement bistro.

44 Custom House St. (off Weybosset St.). ⓒ **401/273-8953**. Reservations recommended. Main courses $22–$29 salon, $14–$22 bistro. AE, DC, MC, V. Salon Tues–Fri noon–1:30pm and 6–9pm; Sat 6–9:30pm. Bistro Mon–Fri 11:30am–2pm; Mon–Thurs 5:30–9pm; Fri–Sat 5:30–10pm; Sun 4–9pm. Closed Sun in July–Aug and last week in July.

Prov ★ ECLECTIC   This is one of a number of enterprises helping to transform the distressed Jewelry District into Providence's SoHo. In this case, the Atomic Grill has been re-tooled into a more upscale version of its former self. The environment has been slicked down and made less frantic—the better to attract a slightly older professional group rather than the slacker set that once dominated. Nothing that arrives at the table looks or tastes exactly as it does anywhere else, which isn't to say that it all works. Misses are almost as frequent as hits; fish and shellfish seem safest. Live entertainment is provided several nights a week.

99 Chestnut St. (at Clifford St.). ⓒ **401/621-8888**. Main courses $13–$26. AE, MC, V. Dining room Tues 5–10pm; Wed–Thurs and Sat 5–10:30pm; Fri 11:30am–3pm and 5–10:30pm; Sun bar only 8pm–1am.

QUICK BITES

Providence claims the invention of the diner, starting with a horse-drawn wagon transporting food down Westminster Street in 1872. The tradition is carried forward by the likes of the **Seaplane Diner,** 307 Allens Ave. (ⓒ **401/941-9547**), a silver-sided classic with tableside jukeboxes, and **Richard's Diner,** 377 Richmond St. (ⓒ **401/331-8541**), so small you can walk across it in six strides.

A bona fide National Historic Landmark is an unlikely venue for snarfing up cookies, souvlaki, and egg rolls. But **The Arcade,** 65 Weybosset St. (ⓒ **401/598-1199**), is a 19th-century progenitor of 20th-century shopping malls, an

1828 Greek Revival structure that runs between Weybosset and Westminster streets. Its main floor is given over largely to fast-food stands and snack counters of the usual kinds—yes, the Golden Arches, too—while the upper floor is primarily boutiques and souvenir shops.

Another local culinary institution arrives in Kennedy Plaza on wheels every afternoon around 4:30pm. The grungy aluminum-sided **Haven Bros.** (© 401/861-7777) is a food tractor-trailer with a counter and six stools inside and good deals on decent burgers and even better fries sold from its parking space next to City Hall. No new frontiers here, except that it hangs around until way past midnight to dampen the hunger pangs of clubgoers, lawyers, night people, and workaholic pols. (The mayor is a regular.)

PROVIDENCE AFTER DARK

This being a college town, there is no end of music bars, small concert halls, and pool pubs. A good source of information is the free weekly *Providence Phoenix* (www.providencephoenix.com).

THE PERFORMING ARTS The **Ocean State Lyric Opera** (© 401/331-6060) stages three or four productions a season at various locations, including the Veterans Memorial Auditorium. The **Rhode Island Philharmonic** (© 401/831-3123) usually appears at the Providence Performing Arts Center or the Veterans Memorial Auditorium. Big-ticket touring musicals on the order of *Cabaret*, as well as traveling dance companies and other attractions, are showcased at the **Providence Performing Arts Center,** 220 Weybosset St. (© 401/421-ARTS), while new plays share space with Ibsen and Shakespeare at the **Trinity Repertory Company,** 201 Washington St. (© 401/521-1100).

THE CLUB & MUSIC SCENE The southern end of Water and Main streets, known as India Point, has several bar/restaurants functioning essentially as nightspots. **The Hot Club,** 575 S. Water St. (© 401/861-9007), sits out over the water, with two bars and two terraces. It's open from noon until well past midnight. **Fish Company,** 515 S. Water St. (© 401/769-2220), is popular primarily with 20-somethings.

South of downtown, in the Jewelry District, **The Complex** ☆, 180 Pine St. (© 401/751-4263), offers four distinctive dance clubs for only one cover: techno at Liquid Assets, disco at Polly Esta's, Top 40 at Algiers, and dance rock at Club Uranus. It's open Wednesday through Saturday. Not far away, sharing a building with Prov (p. 384), is **Snooker's,** 99 Chestnut St. (© 401/351-7665), a pool hall with live music Friday and Saturday nights. in its **Green Room.** Behind the restaurant is the **Reactor Room,** where a DJ pushes a Latin beat, geared to a somewhat older crowd.

Lupo's Heartbreak Hotel, 239 Westminster St. (© 401/272-5876), hosts a variety of live concerts. Tickets are sold around the corner at the **Met Café,** 130 Union St. (© 401/828-4889), which has its own stage and frequent performances by local bands.

The Call, 15 Elbow St. (© 401/751-2255), showcases mostly regional bands, supplemented by acts in the attached **Century Lounge,** 150 Chestnut St. (same phone). Jazz and indie rock are often staged at **AS220,** 115 Empire St. (© 401/831-9327).

Gay clubs on the scene include **Gerardo's,** 1 Franklin Sq. (© 401/274-5560), with dancing Thursday through Sunday, and **MiraBar,** 35 Richmond St. (© 401/331-6761).

Many restaurants in the city engage musical groups two or more nights a week. These include the Gatehouse, CAV, and the Viva! annex to Cafe Paragon, all described under "Where to Dine," above. At the **Trinity Brewhouse,** 186 Fountain St. (© **401/453-2337**), live jazz and blues share attention with boutique beers, a pool table, and a deck.

MOVIES   For art-house films and midnight cult movies, there is the **Avon Repertory Cinema,** 260 Thayer St., near Meeting Street (© **401/421-3315**).

2 A Bucolic Detour to Sakonnet Point

As a break from the urbanity of Providence or the concentration of sights and activities that is Newport, a side trip down the length of the oddly isolated southeastern corner of the state is a soothing excursion.

No one has thought to throw a bridge or run a ferry across the water between Newport and Sakonnet Point, prospects the reclusive residents would no doubt resist to the last lawsuit. They have been known to steal away with road signs to discourage summer visitors, and there are almost no enterprises specifically geared to attract tourists. Things are quiet in these parts, and they intend to keep it that way.

To get here from Providence or Boston, pick up I-195 east, then Route 24 south, toward Newport. Take Exit 4 for Route 77 south, just before the Sakonnet River Bridge. From Newport, take Route 138 toward Fall River, and exit on Route 77 south immediately after crossing the bridge.

After a welter of small businesses, most of them involved in some way with the ocean, Route 77 smoothes out into a pastoral Brigadoon, not quite rural, but more rustic than suburban. Colonial farmhouses, real or replicated, bear sidings of weathered shakes the color of wood smoke. They are centered in tidy lawns, bordered by miles of low stone walls. No plastic deer, no tomato plants in front yards—it's as if a requirement of residence were attendance at a school of good taste.

There are a few antiques shops and roadside farm stands along the way, and a cluster of stores at the enclave of Tiverton Four Corners, about halfway down the point, but none are commercially intrusive enough to sour the pastoral serenity.

One of the rare good reasons to pull off the road is **Sakonnet Vineyards** ⊕, 162 W. Main Rd. (© **401/635-8486;** www.sakonnetwine.com), with an entrance road on the left, about 3 miles (5km) south of Tiverton Four Corners. In operation for more than 20 years, it is one of New England's oldest wineries, and produces 50,000 cases of creditable wines annually. Types range from a popular pinot noir to an honored vidal blanc. Bring along a picnic lunch, then buy a bottle and retire to one of the tables beside the pond. The hospitality center is open daily from 10am to 6pm in summer, 11am to 5pm in winter, with tours on the hour.

Continuing south on Route 77, the road skirts Little Compton and heads on to **Sakonnet Point,** where the inland terrain gives way to stony beaches and coastal marshes. There's a wetlands wildlife refuge, a small harbor with working boats, and not much else.

Now head back north on Route 77, watching for the sign pointing toward Adamsville. Take the right turn at the triangular traffic island just beyond, onto a road that seems to have neither name nor number. Shortly, it arrives at a T intersection surrounded by a church, some shops, and the **Common's** restaurant (see below). This is downtown **Little Compton** ⊕. Turn left (north) and you're back in the country. In about 4 miles (6km), the road ends at Peckham Road. Turn right, in the faith that you are heading toward **Adamsville;** you'll arrive in about 8 miles (13km). It's here that you'll come across **Abraham Manchester's** (see below).

From Adamsville, return to Route 77 via Route 179 to Tiverton Four Corners to get back to Newport, or take Route 81 to Route 24 if returning to Providence or Boston.

WHERE TO STAY ALONG THE WAY

Stone House Club   From the last stop in Sakonnet Point, return along Route 77, and you'll shortly note the entrance to this restaurant/tavern/inn. It's open to the public, but it must observe the wink-wink subterfuge of proclaiming itself a private club because it serves spirits and there's a church next door. That means a $25 membership fee for individuals and $40 for couples, in addition to room rates. Furnishings are worn and unstylish, but look oddly right for their location. Two private beaches are available to guests. The cellar Tap Room and the more formal restaurant upstairs traipse all over the gastronomic map, with an emphasis on seafood. They are open Tuesday through Sunday in summer, Friday through Sunday from October to December and March to April.

122 Sakonnet Point Rd., Little Compton, RI 02837. ℂ **401/635-2222.** Fax 401/635-2822. www.stone houseclub.com. 14 units (4 with shared bathroom). Summer and holidays $58–$125 double, $125–$200 suite; Nov–Apr $48–$80 double, $90–$150 suite. Rates include breakfast. *Note:* Additional membership fee as noted above. MC, V. Closed Sept–Oct. **Amenities:** Restaurant, bar. *In room:* No phone.

WHERE TO DINE ALONG THE WAY

Another dining option is the **Stone House Club,** described above.

Abraham Manchester's ECLECTIC   Adamsville is a less pristine hamlet than Little Compton, with a disheveled aspect and more pickup trucks than SUVs. At its heart is Abraham Manchester's, which serves as the town's social center. The building is a former general store, but not much attention is paid the niceties of historic preservation. A mounted stag head and wagon wheel are typical of the decor. The menu is unexpectedly imaginative, with, for example, a production called the "Manchester Medley Platter," a jumble of shrimp marinated in red wine, blackened swordfish, barbecued chicken, and a slab of tenderloin.

The owner's daughter runs **Breakfast in the Barn (ℂ 401/635-2985)** on the other side of the parking lot, offering fresh breads and pastries with her elaborate breakfasts. It's open Monday through Friday from 6 to 11:30am, Saturday and Sunday from 7am to 12:30pm.

Main Rd. ℂ **401/635-2700.** Main courses $6.85–$21.95. MC, V. Daily 11:30am–9pm (Sat–Sun until 10pm)

Common's REGIONAL AMERICAN   This is the place to sample a few Rhode Island specialties: johnnycakes (lacy pancakes of stoneground cornmeal as thin as playing cards) and stuffies (chopped Quahog [*KWAH*-og or *KOE*-hog] clams mixed with minced bell peppers and bread crumbs, and packed into both halves of the shell for baking). A satisfying lunch is the chock-full lobster roll, which comes with fries for $10.95; add Quahog chowder and fritters for another $4.95. Everyone here knows everyone else, filling the place with joshing and laughter.

On the Little Compton Commons. ℂ **401/635-4388.** Main courses $5.95–$13.95. No credit cards. Daily 5am–6pm (Fri–Sat until 7pm).

3 Newport ✶✶✶

75 miles (121km) S of Boston; 115 miles (185km) NE of New Haven

"City by the Sea" is the singularly unimaginative nickname an early resident unloaded on Newport. At least it was accurate, because for a time during the colonial period it rivaled Boston and even New York as a center of New World trade and prosperity. Newport occupies the southern tip of Aquidneck Island in Narragansett Bay, and is connected to the mainland by three bridges and a ferry.

Wealthy industrialists, railroad tycoons, coal magnates, financiers, and robber barons were drawn to the area in the 19th century, especially between the Civil War and World War I. They bought up property at the ocean's rim to build what they called summer "cottages"—which were in fact mansions of immoderate design and proportions patterned after European palaces.

The principal toys of the Newport elite were equally extravagant yachts meant for pleasure, not commerce, and competition among them established Newport's reputation as a sailing center. In 1851, the schooner *America* defeated a British boat in a race around the Isle of Wight. The prize trophy became known as the America's Cup, which remained in the possession of the New York Yacht Club (with an outpost in Newport) until 1983. In that shocking summer, *Australia II* snatched the Cup away from *Liberty* in the last race of a four-out-of-seven series. An American team regained the cup in 1987, but in 1995 a New Zealand crew won it back. The strong U.S. yachting tradition has endured despite the loss of the Cup, and Newport continues as a bastion of world sailing and a destination for long-distance races.

The perimeter of the city resembles a heeled boot, its toe pointing west, not unlike Italy. About where the laces of the boot would be is the downtown business and residential district. Several wharves push into the bay, providing support and mooring for flotillas of pleasure craft. Much of the strolling, shopping, eating, quaffing, and gawking is done along this waterfront and its parallel streets: America's Cup Avenue and Thames Street. (The latter used to be pronounced "Tems," in the British manner, but was Americanized to "Thaymz" after the Revolution.)

The navy pulled out its battleships, causing a decline in the local economy, but it hasn't proven to be the disaster predicted by some, and Newport has been spared the coarser intrusions that afflict so many coastal resorts. Monster RVs rarely add to the heavy traffic of July and August, and T-shirt emporia have kept within reasonable limits—a remarkable feat, considering that Newport has nearly 4 million visitors a year.

Immediately east and north of the business district are blocks of colonial, Federal, and Victorian houses of the 18th and 19th centuries, many of them designated National Historic Sites. Happily, they are not frozen in amber but are very much in use as residences, restaurants, offices, and shops. Taken together, they are as visually appealing in their own way as the 40-room cottages of the super-rich.

So, despite Newport's prevailing image as a collection of stupefyingly ornate mansions and regattas of sailing ships inaccessible to all but the rich and famous, the city is, for the most part, middle class and moderately priced. Scores of inns and B&Bs assure lodging even during festival weeks, at rates and fixtures from budget to luxury level. In almost every respect, this is the "First Resort" of the New England coast.

ESSENTIALS

GETTING THERE   From New York City, take I-95 to the third Newport exit, picking up Route 138 east (which joins briefly with Route 4) and crossing the Newport toll bridge slightly north of the downtown district. From Boston, take Route 24 through Fall River, picking up Route 114 into town.

Newport

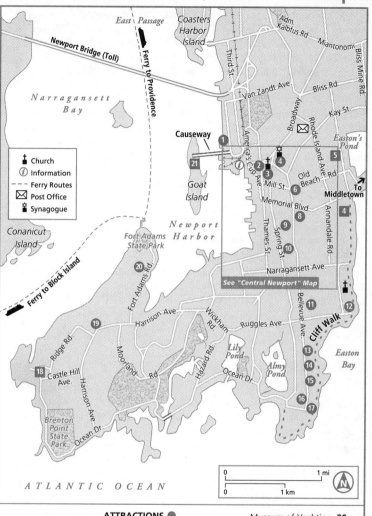

East Passage

Coasters Harbor Island

Newport Bridge (Toll)

Ferry to Providence

Narragansett Bay

Causeway

Goat Island

Newport Harbor

Fort Adams State Park

Ferry to Block Island

Conanicut Island

Adm. Kalbfus Rd.
Miantonomi
Third St.
Van Zandt Ave.
Bliss Rd.
Bliss Mine Rd.
Broadway
Kay St.
Rhode Island Ave.
Easton's Pond
America's Cup Ave.
Mill St.
Old Beach Rd.
To Middletown
Memorial Blvd.
Thames St.
Spring St.
Annandale Rd.
Narragansett Ave.
See "Central Newport" Map

- ✝ Church
- ⓘ Information
- - - Ferry Routes
- ✉ Post Office
- ✡ Synagogue

Fort Adams Rd.
Harrison Ave.
Wickham Rd.
Ruggles Ave.
Lily Pond
Hazard Rd.
Ocean Dr.
Almy Pond
Bellevue Ave.
Cliff Walk
Ridge Rd.
Moorland Rd.
Easton Bay
Castle Hill Ave.
Harrison Ave.
Ocean Dr.
Brenton Point State Park

ATLANTIC OCEAN

| 0 | | 1 mi |
| 0 | | 1 km |

N

Providence
⊛
RHODE ISLAND
Newport

ATTRACTIONS ●

The Astors' Beechwood **14**
Belcourt Castle **16**
The Breakers **12**
Chateau-sur-Mer **11**
The Elms **10**
Hammersmith Farm **19**
Hunter House **1**
International Tennis Hall of Fame **8**
Kingscote **9**
Marble House **15**
Museum of Newport History **2**

Museum of Yachting **20**
Newport Art Museum **6**
Rosecliff **13**
Rough Point **17**
Touro Park **5**
Touro Synagogue **4**
Trinity Church **3**

ACCOMMODATIONS ■

Castle Hill **18**
Cliffside Inn **7**
Elm Tree Cottage **5**
Hyatt Regency Newport **21**

See "Central Newport" map for additional accommodations.

T. F. Green/Providence Airport (© 401/737-8222) in Warwick, south of Providence (Exit 13, I-95), handles national flights into the state. Major airlines serving this airport include **American** (© 800/433-7300), **Continental** (© 800/525-0280), **Delta** (© 800/221-1212), **Northwest** (© 800/225-2525), **United** (© 800/241-6522), and **US Airways** (© 800/428-4322). A few of the larger Newport hotels provide shuttle service, as does **Cozy Cab** (© 401/846-2500).

The **Rhode Island Public Transit Authority,** or **RIPTA** (© 800/244-0444 or 401/781-9400; www.ripta.com), runs up to 28 buses a day on the 70-minute ride between Providence's Kennedy Plaza and the Newport Gateway Visitor Center. One-way fare is $1.25.

RIPTA has inaugurated **ferry service** between Point Street Landing in Providence and Perrotti Park. From mid-April to early October, there are five departures daily; the rest of the year, three departures Monday through Friday only. One-way fare is $4. The operator is Boston Harbor Cruises; call © **617/227-4321** for information.

The **Interstate Navigation Company** (© 401/783-4613) provides ferry service between Providence, Block Island, and Newport's Fort Adams.

VISITOR INFORMATION For advance information available 24 hours, call **visitor information** (© 800/976-5122 outside R.I., 800/556-2484 in R.I.). In town, stop by the excellent **Newport Gateway Visitor Center,** 23 America's Cup Ave. (© 800/326-6030 or 401/849-8048; www.gonewport.com). Open daily from 9am to 5pm (until 6pm Fri–Sat), it has attendants on duty, brochures, a lodging-availability service, a cafe, a souvenir stand, restrooms, and panoramic photos showing the locations of mansions, parks, and other landmarks. The building is shared with the bus station.

PARKING & GETTING AROUND Most of Newport's attractions, except for the mansions, can be reached on foot, so leaving your car at your hotel or inn is wise. Parking lots aren't cheap, especially at the waterfront, and many streets are narrow. The metered parking along Thames Street is closely monitored by police, and fines are steep (although in the off-season, the meters are hooded and parking is free for up to 3 hr.). Renting or bringing a bicycle is an attractive option.

The **Rhode Island Public Transit Authority,** or **RIPTA** (© 401/781-9400), has a free shuttle bus that follows a roughly circular route through town, making stops at major sights.

SPECIAL EVENTS Arrive any day in summer and expect to find at least a half dozen festivals, competitions, or other events in progress. Following is only a partial list. (Call ahead to confirm dates: © **800/263-4636** outside R.I., or 401/848-2000 in R.I.).

While there are a few substantive events in the off-season, notably **Christmas in Newport** (© 401/849-6454; www.christmasinnewport.org) and the **February Winter Festival** (© 888/976-5122; www.newportevents.com), which focuses on food and winter sports, the pace ratchets up in June, starting with the **Great Chowder Cook-Off** (© 401/846-1600; www.newportfestivals.com). In the third week of June, the gardens of the Point section of town are open to visitors during the **Secret Garden Tour** (© 401/847-0514; www.secretgardentour.com).

During 2 weeks in July, the **Newport Music Festival** (© 401/846-1133; www.newportmusic.org), offers classical concerts daily at various venues. In the

ACCOMMODATIONS ■
Turner Inn **8**
Admiral Fitzroy Inn **17**
Francis Malbone House **16**
Jailhouse Inn **3**
La Farge Perry House **1**
Mill Street Inn **7**
Pilgrim House **5**
Vanderbilt Hall **6**
The Victorian Ladies **14**

*See the "Newport" map for
additional accommodations.*

DINING ◆
Asterix & Obelix **20**
Black Pearl **12**
Bouchard **19**
Brick Alley Pub **4**
Cheeky Monkey **13**
Clarke Cooke House **11**
Le Bistro **10**
Rhode Island Quahog Company **9**
Salas **15**
Scales & Shells **18**
White Horse Tavern **2**

third week is the **Black Ships Festival** (© 401/846-5600; www.newportevents. com), a celebration of all aspects of Japanese culture.

August brings the **Ben & Jerry's Folk Festival** (www.newportfolk.com) and the **JVC Jazz Festival** (© 401/847-3700 for both), both held at Fort Adams State Park. Things wind down after Labor Day, though there's still the **Waterfront Irish Festival** (© 401/846-1600; www.newportfestivals.com) in early September and the **Bowen's Wharf Seafood Festival** (© 401/849-2120) in the third week of October.

THE COTTAGES

That's what wealthy summer people called the almost unimaginably sumptuous mansions they built in Newport in the last decades before the 16th Amendment to the Constitution permitted an income tax.

Say this for the wealthy of the Gilded Age, many of whom obtained their fortunes by less than honorable means: They knew a good place to put down roots when they saw it. These are the same ones, after all, who developed Palm Beach in winter, the Hudson Valley in spring, the Berkshires in autumn, and Newport in summer, sweeping from house to luxurious house with the insouciance of a bejeweled matron dragging her sable down a grand staircase.

When driving or biking through the cottage district (walking its length is impractical for most people), consider the fact that most of these astonishing residences are still privately owned. That's almost as remarkable as the grounds and interiors of the nine that are open to the public.

Also, resolve to visit only one or two estates per day: The sheer opulence of the mansions can soon become numbing. Each residence requires 45 minutes to an hour for its guided tour. If at all possible, go during the week to avoid crowds and traffic.

Six of the mansions are maintained by the **Preservation Society of Newport County,** 424 Bellevue Ave. (© 401/847-1000; www.newportmansions.org), which also operates the 1748 Hunter House, the 1860 Italianate Chepstow villa, the 1883 Isaac Bell House, and the Green Animals Topiary Gardens in Portsmouth. The Society sells a **combination ticket,** good for a year, to five of its properties; the cost is $29 for adults, $10 for children 6 to 17. Individual tickets for the Breakers are $15 for adults, $4 for children, while individual tickets for Kingscote, the Elms, Chateau-sur-mer, Marble House, Hunter House, and Rosecliff are $10 for adults, $4 for children. They can be purchased at any of the properties. Credit cards are accepted at most, but not all, of the cottages. Special events, such as the festive Thanksgiving and Christmas celebrations, cost extra. Parking is free at all the Society properties.

The mansions that aren't operated by the Preservation Society but are open to the public are Belcourt Castle, Beechwood, and Rough Point.

Following are descriptions of the cottages in the order in which they're encountered when driving south from Memorial Boulevard along Bellevue Avenue, then west on Ocean Drive.

Kingscote ✪ This mansion (on the right side of the avenue) is a reminder that well-to-do Southern families often had second homes north of the Mason-Dixon line to avoid the sultry summers of the Deep South. Kingscote was built in 1839, nearly 40 years before the Gilded Age (usually regarded as the era between the end of the Civil War and the beginning of World War I). But it is considered one of the Newport Cottages because it was acquired in 1864 by the sea merchant William Henry King, who furnished it with porcelains and textiles accumulated in the China trade. Architect Richard Upjohn designed the mansion in the same Gothic Revival style he used for Trinity Church in New York. The firm of McKim, Mead & White was commissioned to design the 1881 dining room, notable for its Tiffany glass panels. As you drive down Bellevue, the Isaac Bell House is between Kingscote and the Elms.

Bowery St. (west of Bellevue Ave.). Late Mar–Apr Sat–Sun 10am–5pm; May–Columbus Day daily 10am–5pm. See above for admission details.

The Elms ★★   Architect Horace Trumbauer is said to have been inspired by the Château d'Asnieres outside Paris, and a first look at the ornate dining room of the Elms, suitable for at least a marquis, buttresses that claim. So, too, do the sunken gardens, laid out and maintained in the formal French manner. The owner was a first-generation millionaire, a coal tycoon named Edward J. Berwind. His cottage was completed in 1901, and he filled it with genuine Louis XIV and XV furniture as well as paintings and accessories true to the late 18th century. It was one of the first fully electrified mansions in Newport.

Bellevue Ave. Daily 10am–5pm. Closed Thanksgiving, Dec24–25. See above for admission details.

Chateau-sur-mer ★   William S. Wetmore was yet another merchant who made his fortune in the China trade. The entrance to this "Castle by the Sea" is on the left side of Bellevue, driving south. High Victorian in style, which means it drew from many inspirations (including Italian Renaissance and French Second Empire), the Chateau features a central atrium with a skylight and balconies at every level. A park designed in a style true to the period of the cottage has copper beech and weeping willow trees standing around its garden pavilion.

Bellevue Ave. Jan to mid-Apr Sat–Sun and holidays 10am–4pm; late Apr–Oct daily 10am–5pm. See above for admission details.

The Breakers ★★★   After Chateau-sur-mer, turn left on Ruggles Avenue, then left again on Ochre Point Avenue. The Breakers is on the right; a parking lot is on the left.

If you have time to see only one of the cottages, make it this one. Architect Richard Morris Hunt was commissioned to create this replica of a generic Florentine Renaissance palazzo, replacing a wood structure that burned down in 1892. He was unrestrained by cost considerations. The high iron entrance gates alone weigh over 7 tons. The 50-by-50-foot (15m-by-15m) great hall has 50-foot-high (15m) ceilings, forming a giant cube, and is sheathed in marble. Such mind-numbing extravagance shouldn't really be surprising—Hunt's patron was, after all, Cornelius Vanderbilt II, grandson of railroad tycoon Commodore Vanderbilt.

Had Vanderbilt been European royalty, the Breakers would have provided motive for a peasant revolt. Vanderbilt's small family and their staff of 40 servants had 70 rooms in which to roam. The mansion's foundation is approximately the size of a football field, and the Breakers took nearly 3 years to build (1892–95). Platoons of artisans were imported from Europe to apply gold leaf, carve wood and marble, and provide mural-sized baroque paintings. The furnishings on view are original. The bathrooms, far from common at the time, were provided with both fresh and salt running water, hot and cold.

Ochre Point Ave. (east of Bellevue Ave.). ✆ **401/847-1000.** Mid-Apr to Jan 1 daily 10am–5pm (until 6pm Fri–Sat in July–Aug); Nov 24 and Dec 1, 8, 15 and 29 also 6–8pm. See above for admission details.

Rosecliff ★   From the Breakers, return to Bellevue Avenue and turn left (south); Rosecliff is on the left. Stanford White thought the Grand Trianon of

Louis XVI at Versailles a suitable model for this 1902 commission for the flamboyant heiress Tessie Fair Oelrichs. With a middling 40 rooms, it doesn't overwhelm, at least not on the scale of the Breakers. But it has the largest ballroom of all the cottages, not to mention a storied heart-shaped grand staircase. All this was made possible by one James Fair, an immigrant who made his fortune after he unearthed the thickest gold and silver vein of Nevada's Comstock Lode and bought this property for his daughters.

In 1941, the mansion and its contents were sold for $21,000. It was used as a setting for some scenes in the Robert Redford movie of Fitzgerald's *The Great Gatsby* (1974) and for a ballroom scene in Arnold Schwarzenegger's *True Lies* (1994).

Bellevue Ave. Mid-Apr to late Oct daily 10am–5pm. See above for admission details.

The Astors' Beechwood ★★ Mrs. William Backhouse Astor—*the* Mrs. Astor, as every brochure and guide feels compelled to observe—was, during her active life, the arbiter of exactly who constituted New York and Newport society. "The 400" list of socially acceptable folk was influenced or perhaps even drawn up by her, and that roster bore meaning, in some quarters, well into the second half of the 20th century. Being invited to Beechwood was absolutely critical to a social pretender's sense of self-worth, and elaborate machinations were set in motion to achieve that goal.

Rebuilt in 1857 after a fire destroyed the original version, the mansion isn't as large or impressive as some of its neighbors. But unlike those managed by the Preservation Society, it provides a little theatrical pizzazz with a corps of actors who pretend to be friends, children, and servants of Mrs. Astor. In set pieces, they share details about life in the late Victorian era. Frequent special events are held, often replicating those that took place when she held court, including costume balls and specially decorated banquets with Victorian music and dancing.

580 Bellevue Ave. ✆ 401/846-3772. www.astors-beechwood.com. Admission $10 adults, $8.50 seniors and children 6–12; $30 per family. Mid-May to early Nov daily 10am–5pm (tours every 20 min.); Christmas events Nov–Dec Wed–Sun; Feb to mid-May Fri–Sun 10am–4pm (tours every 30 min.).

Marble House ★★★ Architect Richard Morris Hunt outdid himself for his clients William and Alva Vanderbilt. Several types of marble were used both outside and in, with a lavish hand that rivals the palaces of the Sun King, especially Le Petit Trianon at Versailles. It reaches its apogee in the ballroom, which is encrusted with three kinds of gold. It cost William $11 million to build and decorate Marble House, but Alva divorced him 4 years after the project was finished. She got the house, which she soon closed after marrying William's friend and neighbor. When her second husband died, Alva discovered the cause of female suffrage, and reopened Marble House in 1913 to hold a benefit for the campaign for women's right to vote. (Dishes in the scullery bear the legend "Votes for Women.")

Bellevue Ave. Mid-Apr to Jan 1 daily 10am–5pm (Fri–Sat until 6pm); Nov Sat–Sun 10am–4pm; Jan–Mar Sat–Sun and holidays 10am–4pm. See above for admission details.

Belcourt Castle ★★ This was the only slightly less grand mansion down the road from Marble House to which Alva Vanderbilt repaired after her second marriage. While the Vanderbilts were avid yachtsmen, her new husband, Oliver Hazard Perry Belmont, was a fanatical horseman. His 60-room house contained extensive stables on the ground floor where his beloved steeds slept under monogrammed blankets (the Belmonts were instrumental in building New York's famed Belmont Racetrack).

The castle, intended to resemble a European hunting lodge, has a ponderously masculine character, understandable in that it was designed for the bachelor Belmont before he won over vivacious Alva. It contains artifacts from the medieval era through the 19th century, including stained glass, Japanese and Chinese cabinetry, a full-size replica of a gaudy Portuguese coronation carriage, and French Renaissance furniture. Thomas Edison designed the lighting. There are 14 secret doors and a tunnel to the kitchens, which were located 2 blocks away for fear of fire.

The castle sold for a mere $25,000 in the early 1940s to the family of Harold B. Tinney, members of which still live here.

657 Bellevue Ave. (at Lakeview Ave.). ⓒ 401/846-0669. Admission $10 adults, $8 seniors and college students, $7 children 13–18, $3.50 children 6–12. Feb–May Sat–Sun and holidays 10am–3pm; Memorial Day to mid-Oct daily 9:30am–4:30pm; mid-Oct to Nov daily 10am–4pm; Dec (special tours) 10am–3pm. Closed Jan.

Rough Point ⍟⍟   The fabled 1887 Gothic-Tudor home of the late tobacco heiress Doris Duke made its long-awaited opening in 2000. Of its 105 rooms, only 11 are currently open for viewing, and by only 96 visitors per day. They are likely to be greeted by Chairman Mao, the last of Duke's many pets. The heiress's collections include a wealth of Ming-dynasty vases, Flemish and French tapestries, and paintings by Van Dyck and Gainsborough. Watch for the ivory inset side tables bearing the marks of Catherine the Great in what is called the Yellow Room.

While those who knew her reject suggestions that Duke was reclusive or troubled, hers was, at the least, an often darkly eventful life. It was here at Rough Point in 1967 that the story of the tobacco heiress and her interior decorator/companion unfolded. Eduardo Tirella was killed after being crushed against the iron entrance gates by Duke's station wagon. Duke later claimed that Tirella had gotten out of the car to open the gates when she accidentally hit the accelerator. The police chief declared it "an unfortunate accident," but local tongues wagged.

Duke died in 1993, bequeathing Rough Point to the Newport Restoration Foundation, along with all clothing, jewelry, and furniture in the house. To get here from Belcourt Castle, continue south on Bellevue. Rough Point is on the left, just before a sharp turn west along what becomes Ocean Drive. Individual visits aren't allowed. The only source for tickets is the Newport Gateway Visitor Center, where parking is also available. Minibuses shuttle visitors to Rough Point; tours take about 70 minutes.

Bellevue Ave. ⓒ 401/849-7300. www.newportrestoration.org. Admission $25. Visits by guided tour only; mid-Apr to early Nov daily at 9:45am, 11:30am, 1:30pm, and 3:30pm.

ADDITIONAL ATTRACTIONS

Historic Hill is the large district of colonial Newport that rises from America's Cup Avenue, along the waterfront, to Bellevue Avenue, the beginning of Victorian Newport. **Spring Street** ⍟ serves as the Hill's main drag, and it's a treasure trove of colonial, Georgian, and Federal structures. Chief among its visual delights is the 1725 **Trinity Church** ⍟, at the corner of Church Street. Said to have been influenced by the work of the legendary British architect Christopher Wren, it certainly reflects that inspiration in its belfry and distinctive spire, seen from all over downtown Newport and dominating Queen Anne Square, a greensward that runs down to the waterfront.

Hammersmith Farm   Built for John W. Auchincloss in 1887, this shingled Victorian mansion was used for the wedding reception of Jacqueline Bouvier (whose mother was married to an Auchincloss), in 1953. It subsequently became the unofficial summer White House of the short Kennedy presidency. Hammersmith was sold in 1997 for over $6.6 million to a Chicago businessman who sold it again 2 years later, and it is no longer open to the public. The house can still be seen from the road, however.

Ocean Dr. (past Castle Hill Ave.).

Hunter House ⭐ Another property of the Preservation Society, this 1754 Georgian colonial is one of the most impressive dwellings in the neighborhood known as the Point, north of downtown. Above the doorway is a carved wooden pineapple. This symbol of welcome derived from the practice of placing a real pineapple at the door to announce that the sea-captain owner had returned from his long voyage and was ready to receive guests. The interior displays furniture crafted by Newport's famed 18th-century cabinetmakers, Townsend and Goddard.

54 Washington St. (at Elm St.). ☎ 401/847-1000. See "The Cottages," above, for admission details. Late May to early Oct daily 10am–5pm.

International Tennis Hall of Fame On Bellevue Avenue, there was (and is) an exclusive men's club called the Newport Reading Room. One member was James Gordon Bennett, Jr., the wealthy publisher of the *New York Herald*. He persuaded a friend to ride a horse into the club. The outraged members reprimanded Bennett, who had an instant snit that they hadn't enjoyed his little jest. He went right out and bought a property on the other side of Memorial Boulevard, and ordered a structure built for his own social and sports club.

McKim, Mead & White produced a shingle-style edifice of lavish proportions, with turrets and verandas and an interior piazza for lawn games, equestrian shows, and a new game called tennis. It is now given to a permanent grass court. As Bennett hoped, his Newport Casino swiftly became the premier gathering place of his privileged compatriots.

Now the pavilion hosts professional tournaments, and its courts are open to the public for play (call ahead to make reservations between May–Oct). The building itself houses the Hall of Fame, of interest primarily to fans of the game. A restaurant (☎ 401/847-0418) serves lunch, sunset dinners, and weekend brunch.

194 Bellevue Ave. (at Memorial Blvd.). ☎ 401/849-3990. www.tennisfame.org. Admission $8 adults, $6 seniors and students, $4 children 16 and under; $20 per family. Daily 9:30am–5pm (except during tournaments).

Museum of Newport History Maintained by the Newport Historical Society, this museum is in the refurbished 1772 Brick Market (not to be confused with the nearby shopping mall Brick Marketplace). The architect was Peter Harrison, also responsible for the Touro Synagogue (see below). The museum houses boat models, marine charts, antique silverware, and a ship figurehead, and also features videos on Newport history.

127 Thames St. (at Touro St.). ☎ 401/841-8770. www.newporthistorical.org. Admission $5 adults, $4 seniors, $3 children 6–18. Apr–Oct Mon and Wed–Sat 10am–5pm, Sun 1–5pm; Nov–Mar Fri–Sat 10am–4pm, Sun 1–4pm.

Newport Art Museum Across the avenue from Touro Park, this was the first Newport commission of Richard Morris Hunt, who went on to design many of the cottages along Bellevue Avenue. Unlike most of his later Newport houses, the 1862 main structure is in the Victorian stick style, a wood construction that had origins in earlier Carpenter Gothic. It now mounts art exhibitions and serves as a venue for concerts.

76 Bellevue Ave. (at Old Beach Rd.). ℂ **401/848-8200.** Admission $4 adults, $3 seniors, $2 students, free for children under 5. Only a voluntary donation charged for entrance Sat 10am–noon. Memorial Day to Columbus Day Mon–Sat 10am–5pm, Sun noon–5pm; Columbus Day to Memorial Day Mon–Tues and Thurs–Sat 10am–4pm, Sun noon–4pm.

Touro Park   Opposite the Newport Art Museum, this small park provides a shaded respite. Its center is the Old Stone Mill. Dreamers like to believe that its eight columns were erected by Vikings. Realists say it was built by Benedict Arnold, a governor of the colony long before his great-great-grandson committed his infamous act of treason during the War of American Independence.

Bellevue Ave. (between Pelham and Mill sts.).

Touro Synagogue   This is the oldest existing synagogue in the United States, dating from 1763. A Sephardic Jewish community, largely refugees from Portugal, lived in Newport from the mid–17th century, over 100 years before this building was erected. It was designed by Peter Harrison, who was also responsible for the Brick Market (see Museum of Newport History, above). The synagogue was designated a National Historic Site in 1946.

Next door is the **Newport Historical Society,** 82 Touro St. (ℂ **401/846-0813**), which features displays of colonial furnishings and sponsors walking tours (see "Organized Tours & Cruises," below).

85 Touro St. (Spring St.). ℂ **401/847-4794.** Free admission. July 1–Sept 7 Sun–Fri 10am–5pm; Sept 8–June 30 Sun 11am–3pm, Mon–Fri 1–3pm; Nov 1–Apr 30 Sun 11am–3pm, Mon–Fri at 1pm (groups of 10 or more by appointment only). Guided tours only, beginning every half hour.

OUTDOOR PURSUITS: THE BEACH & BEYOND

Fort Adams State Park, Harrison Avenue (ℂ **401/847-2400**), is on the thumb of land that partially encloses Newport Harbor. It can be seen from the downtown docks and reached by driving or biking south on Thames Street and west on Wellington Avenue (a section of Ocean Dr., which becomes Harrison Ave.). The sprawling 1820s fort for which the park is named is under restoration, but can be viewed up close from outside; inquire about tours. Boating, ocean swimming, fishing, and sailing are all possible in the park's 105 acres (43 hectares). Open from Memorial Day to Labor Day; admission is $4 per car ($2 for Rhode Islanders and seniors). Tours are conducted from the visitor center in summer, daily from 10am to 4pm. Also on the grounds is the **Museum of Yachting** (ℂ **401/847-1018**), housed in a stone barracks from the early 19th century. Open from mid-May to October daily from 10am to 5pm, by appointment the rest of the year. Admission is $4 for adults, $3 for seniors and children under 12.

Farther along Ocean Drive, past Hammersmith Farm, is **Brenton Point State Park** 👯, a scenic preserve that borders the Atlantic, with nothing to impede the waves rolling in and collapsing on the rock-strewn beach. Scuba divers are often seen surfacing offshore, anglers enjoy casting from the long breakwater, and on a windy day the sky is dotted with colorful kites.

There are other beaches more appropriate for swimming. The longest and most popular is **Easton's Beach** 👯, which lies along Route 138A, the extension of Memorial Boulevard, east of town. There are plenty of facilities, including a bathhouse, eating places, picnic areas, lifeguards, a carousel, and the **Newport Aquarium** (ℂ **401/849-8430**).

On Ocean Drive, less than 2 miles (3km) from the south end of Bellevue Avenue, is **Gooseberry Beach** 👯, which is privately owned but open to the public. Parking costs $8 Monday through Friday, $12 Saturday and Sunday.

Cliff Walk 🎯🎯 skirts the edge of the southern section of town where most of the cottages were built, and provides better views of many of them than can be seen from the street. Traversing its length, high above the crashing surf, is more than a stroll but less than an arduous hike. For the full 3½-mile (5.6km) length, start at the access point near the intersection of Memorial Boulevard and Eustis Avenue. For a shorter walk, start at the Forty Steps, at the end of Narragansett Avenue, off Bellevue. Leave the walk at Ledge Road and return via Bellevue Avenue. Figure 2 to 3 hours for the round-trip, and be warned that there are some mildly rugged sections to negotiate, no facilities, and no phones. The walk is open from 9am to 9pm.

A new enterprise, the outdoor **Born Family Skating Center,** is set up at the Newport Yachting Center, on America's Cup Avenue (© **401/846-1600**). An oval rink about 40 yards (36m) long, it's open from late October into March, depending upon weather. Skate rentals are available.

Biking is one of the best ways to get around town, especially out to the mansions and along **Ocean Drive** 🎯🎯. Among several rental shops are **Firehouse Bicycle,** 25 Mill St. (© **401/847-5700**); **Ten Speed Spokes,** 18 Elm St. (© **401/847-5609**); and **Fun Rentals,** 1 Commercial Wharf (© **401/846-3474**). The last firm also rents mopeds.

Adventure Sports Rentals, at the Inn on Long Wharf, 142 Long Wharf (© **401/849-4820**), rents not only bikes and mopeds, but also outboard boats, kayaks, and sailboats; parasailing outings can be arranged.

Guided fly-fishing trips and fly-casting instruction are offered by the **Saltwater Edge,** 561 Lower Thames St. (© **401/842-0062;** www.saltwateredge.com). Anglers are taken out on half- and full-day quests for yellowfin tuna, bluefish, striped bass, and white marlin.

ORGANIZED TOURS & CRUISES

Several organizations conduct tours of the mansions and the downtown historic district. Between May 15 and October 15, the **Newport Historical Society,** 82 Touro St. (© **401/846-0813**), offers two itineraries. Tours of Historic Hill leave on Thursday and Friday at 10am and tours of the Point on Saturday at 10am; each takes about 1½ hours. Tours of Cliff Walk leave on Saturday at 10am and take about 2 hours. Tickets cost $7 and can be purchased at the Society or at the Gateway Visitor Center (see "Visitor Information," earlier in this section).

Newport on Foot (© **401/846-5391**) leaves the Gateway Visitor Center twice daily on 90-minute tours. Call for details and times. Tickets are $7 per person, free for children under 12.

If your car has a cassette deck or you have a portable player, **CCInc Auto Tape Tours** produces a 90-minute recorded tour of the mansions, with an intelligent narration backed by music and sound effects. The tapes are available at the Museum Store in the Gateway Visitor Center for $12.95 each or directly from the company (© **201/236-1666**).

Viking Tours, based at the Gateway Visitor Center, 23 America's Cup Ave. (© **401/847-6921**), has narrated bus tours of the mansions and harbor cruises on the excursion boat *Viking Queen.* Bus tours—daily in summer, Saturdays from November to March—are 1½ to 4 hours and cost $18 to $38 for adults, $10 to $17 for children 5 to 11. Boat tours, from late May to early October, are 1 hour in length and cost $10 for adults, $8 for seniors, and $5 for kids.

Classic Cruises of Newport 🎯, Bannister's Wharf, schedules narrated cruises on its 72-foot (22m) schooner *Madeleine* (© **401/847-0298**) and its classic powerboat *RumRunner II* (© **401/847-0299**). They're offered daily in summer, Saturdays and Sundays in spring and fall.

The *Spirit of Newport* ✪, 2 Bowen's Wharf (© **401/849-3575**), offers 1½-hour cruises of the bay and harbor. Another possibility is the *Adirondack* ✪, a 78-foot (23m) schooner that makes 2-hour cruises from the Newport Yachting Center (© **401/846-3018**). Its ticket booth is on America's Cup Avenue at Commercial Wharf; reservations must be made in advance.

The **Old Colony & Newport Railway,** 19 America's Cup Ave. (© **401/624-6951;** www.ocnrr.com), features 80-minute round-trip excursions in vintage trains along the edge of the bay. Fares are $6 for adults, $5 for seniors, and $3.50 for children under 14.

SHOPPING

At the heart of the downtown waterfront, **Bannister's Wharf, Bowen's Wharf,** and **Brick Marketplace** have about 60 stores among them, few of them especially compelling.

More interesting, if only for their quirky individuality, are the shops along **Lower Thames Street.** For example, **J. T.'s Ship Chandlery** (no. 364) outfits recreational sailors with sea chests, ship lanterns, and foul-weather gear. **Aardvark Antiques** (no. 475) specializes in salvaged architectural components. Books, nautical charts, and sailing videos are offered at **Armchair Sailor** (no. 543); for vintage clothing, visit **Cabbage Rose** (no. 493).

Spring Street is noted for its antiques shops and purveyors of crafts, jewelry, and folk art. One of these is **MacDowell Pottery** (no. 140), a studio selling ceramics and gifts by Rhode Island artisans; the nearby **J. H. Breakell & Co.** (no. 132) is a good source for handcrafted jewelry. Antique boat models are displayed along with marine paintings and navigational instruments at **North Star Gallery** (no. 105). **The Drawing Room/The Zsolnay Store** (nos. 152–154) stocks estate furnishings and specializes in Hungarian Zsolnay ceramics. Folk art and furniture are the primary goods at **Liberty Tree** (no. 104).

Spring intersects with **Franklin Street,** which harbors even more antiques shops in its short length. **Newport China Trade Co.** (no. 8) deals in export porcelain and objects associated with 19th-century China. Take a fat wallet to the **John Gidley House** (no. 22) for European antiques of high order. **Patina** (no. 26) is another dealer in Americana and folk art.

WHERE TO STAY

The **Gateway Visitor Center** (© **800/976-5122** or 401/849-8040; www.gone wport.com) lists vacancies in motels, hotels, and inns. Most can be called from free direct-line phones located nearby. Less impulsive travelers should reserve in advance, especially on weekends (2 months ahead for weekends from Memorial Day to Labor Day).

Newport Reservations (© **800/842-0102** or 401/842-0102) is a free service representing a number of hotels, motels, inns, and B&Bs. **Anna's Victorian Connection** (© **401/849-2489**) is similar, but charges a fee and doesn't represent hotels or motels. **Bed & Breakfast Newport, Ltd.** (© **800/800-8765** or 401/846-5408) claims to offer 350 choices of accommodation.

Many of the better motels are located in Middletown, about 2 miles (3km) north of downtown Newport. Possibilities include the **Courtyard by Marriott,** 9 Commerce Dr. (© **401/849-8000**); **Newport Ramada Inn,** 936 W. Main Rd. (© **401/846-7600**); **Newport Gateway Hotel,** 31 W. Main Rd.

(© 401/847-2735); and **Howard Johnson,** 351 W. Main Rd. (© **401/849-2000**). Newport itself has a **Marriott,** 25 America's Cup Ave. (© **401/849-1000**).

The rates given below generally have very wide ranges depending upon seasonal demand, so a $200 room on weekends in July might be half that in spring. The summer season is usually defined as Memorial Day to Columbus Day, with lower prices in effect the rest of the year.

VERY EXPENSIVE

Castle Hill 🏰🏰 The setting—40 oceanfront acres (16 hectares) on a near-island—is the overwhelming attraction of this venerable resort. But now that sorely needed renovations of the 1874 Victorian mansion and its outbuildings are finished, even a visit in foul weather is a treat. The best values are the Harbor Houses, which have been gutted and overhauled, with new furniture, Jacuzzis, and porches overlooking the bay. The handsome taproom offers a riveting view (shared by the dining room, deck, and many of the bedrooms) of sailing ships on Narragansett Bay. Breakfast buffets are expansive. A herd of young drinkers crowds the immense lawn for live jazz on summer Sundays.

590 Ocean Dr., Newport, RI 02840. © **888/466-1355** or 401/849-3800. Fax 401/849-3838. www.castle hillinn.com. 27 units. Summer $225–$395 double; $350–$495 suite; fall–spring $145–$285 double, $225–375 suite. Rates include breakfast. AE, DISC, MC, V. Open weekends only Nov–Apr. Closed Jan. Children under 12 not accepted in main house. **Amenities:** Restaurant (regional), bar; laundry; dry cleaning. *In room:* A/C, TV, hair dryer.

Cliffside Inn 🏰🏰🏰 Assuming that money is no object, this tops the list of places to stay in Newport. All units now have at least one working fireplace. A new suite in the Seaview Cottage has a bathroom that has to be seen: The tub features both standard and hand-held showerheads, eight spray nozzles, and a built-in TV and CD player! Antiques are generously deployed, including Eastlake and Tiffany originals and Victorian fancies that include (in room 11) an amusing "bird cage" shower from 1890. A favorite unit is the Garden Suite, a duplex with private garden and big double bathroom with radiant heat beneath the Peruvian tile floors. Coffee, juice, and the newspaper of your choice are delivered to your room even before the full breakfast.

2 Seaview Ave. (near Cliff Ave.), Newport, RI 02840. © **800/845-1811** or 401/847-1811. Fax 401/848-5850. www.cliffsideinn.com. 16 units. $235–$375 double; $325–$545 suite. Rates include breakfast. AE, DISC, MC, V. No children under 13. **Amenities:** Limited room service; laundry; same-day dry cleaning. *In room:* A/C, TV/VCR, dataport, hair dryer, iron.

Francis Malbone House 🏰🏰 A few years ago, nine modern rooms were added in a wing attached to the original 1760 colonial house. They are very nice, with king-size beds and excellent reproductions of period furniture. Four of them share two sunken gardens, and three have Jacuzzi tubs built for two. But given a choice, take a room in the old section, where antiques outnumber repros, Oriental rugs adorn buffed wide-board floors, and silks and linens are deployed unsparingly. All but two units enjoy gas fireplaces. The most interesting parts of the waterfront are right outside the door.

392 Thames St. (east of Memorial Blvd.), Newport, RI 02840. © **800/846-0392** or 401/846-0392. Fax 401/848-5956. www.malbone.com. 20 units. Apr–Oct $215–$425 double; Nov–Mar $155–$245 double. Mid-week discounts available. Rates include breakfast and afternoon tea. AE, MC, V. No children under 12. *In room:* A/C, TV/VCR, CD player, dataport, hair dryer, iron.

Hyatt Regency Newport 🏰 More than 25 years old, the Hyatt is notable for its complete roster of hotel services, its location on an island at the northern end of Newport Harbor, and its full-service spa. You might expect such a place to be impersonal, but the staff endeavors to be pleasant. There are delightful views of the harbor and town from the restaurant and most of the guest rooms.

1 Goat Island, Newport, RI 02840. © 800/233-1234 or 401/851-1234. Fax 401/846-7210. www.hyatt.com. 264 units. Summer $290–$365 double; winter $99–$225 double. AE, DC, DISC, MC, V. Valet parking $9. **Amenities:** 2 restaurants (American, regional), bar; indoor freshwater and outdoor saltwater pools; 2 tennis courts; well-equipped health club and spa; concierge; airport courtesy van; business center; limited room service; massage; babysitting; laundry; dry cleaning. *In room:* A/C, TV, dataport, coffeemaker, hair dryer.

La Farge Perry House ★★ The first thing you're likely to notice upon entering this 1852 Federal-style home is the pristine standard of housekeeping, and immediately after, the muted elegance of the superb furnishings. Crystal chandeliers, plush fabrics, and nautical artifacts fill both public and private rooms. That isn't to imply early-19th-century austerity: Unlike many of Newport's lesser B&Bs, no sacrifices in new-millennium conveniences are made. All units are suites with poster or sleigh beds; two have double Jacuzzis and one has a fireplace. Breakfasts are memorable.

24 Kay St. (at Bull St.), Newport, RI 02840. © 877/736-1100 or 401/847-2223. www.lafargeperry.com. 5 units. May–Oct $300–$350 suite; Nov–Apr $225–$300 suite. Rates include full breakfast. Midweek discounts available. AE, MC, V. No children under 12. *In room:* A/C, TV/VCR, dataport, fridge, hair dryer.

Vanderbilt Hall ★★ After its $11-million renovation, this 1908 Georgian Revival manse gives no hint of its origins as a YMCA. Built with a donation by Alfred Vanderbilt, it would now suit its benefactor as one of his own residences. Public rooms contain antiques and paintings. Bedrooms have armoires, fabrics with period patterns, and, in the older wing, 18-foot (5m) ceilings. Rosenthal crystal and Wedgwood china set the tone in the acclaimed Alva Restaurant. The less formal Orangery, in a glass conservatory and an adjoining terrace, features three daily meals and afternoon tea. You'll be reminded to watch the sunset from the rooftop deck. An 18% service charge is added to your room bill, so you needn't tip any of the staff.

41 Mary St. (west of Bellevue), Newport, RI 02840. © 401/846-6200. Fax 401/846-0701. www.vanderbilt hall.com. 50 units. Summer $195–$565 double, $445–$795 suite; fall–spring $155–$445 double, $335–$645 suite; winter $95–$365 double, $295–$495 suite. Rates include afternoon tea. Midweek discounts available. AE, DISC, DC, MC, V. No children under 12. **Amenities:** 2 restaurants, bar; indoor pool; small fitness room with Jacuzzi and sauna; billiards room. *In room:* A/C, TV, dataport, hair dryer.

EXPENSIVE

Adele Turner Inn ★★ The 1855 Admiral Benbow was recently transformed into a sister property of the estimable Cliffside Inn (see above). That meant that surroundings and services took an instant upward turn. While it is unlikely that the Adele Turner will ever match its sibling virtue for virtue—its rooms are smaller, for one thing—it comes close enough to merit this high recommendation. And in one area, it is preferable: Once you are here, most of the downtown attractions are within walking distance. Old fireplaces have been restored and new ones installed. Some of the units have hot tubs. Full breakfasts and afternoon teas are nothing less than sumptuous.

93 Pelham St., Newport, RI 02840. © 800/845-1811 or 401/857-1811. Fax 401/848-5850. www.adele turnerinn.com. 13 units. $135–$355 double. Extra person $50. AE, DC, MC, V. **Amenities:** Concierge; limited room service; same-day dry cleaning/laundry; free video library. *In room:* A/C, TV/VCR, hair dryer.

Admiral Fitzroy Inn ★ The Admiral Fitzroy attracts Europeans and Australians drawn to the international yachting events and festivals held here. Despite the current name, the antique barometers, and the ship model at the reception desk, this used to be a nunnery—but that doesn't mean spartan gloom. Many rooms have "peek" harbor views, but you'll get a better look from the roof deck. In addition to the breakfast buffet, the kitchen serves a choice of hot dishes. The staff is unfailingly pleasant. Children are accepted here, so lots of families make this home base.

398 Thames St. (south of Memorial Blvd.), Newport, RI 02840. ✆ **866/848-8780** or 401/848-8000. Fax 401/848-8006. www.admiralfitzroy.com. 17 units. May–Oct $110–$225 double; Nov–Apr $85–$165 double. Rates include breakfast. AE, DISC, MC, V. *In room:* A/C, TV, fridge, coffeemaker, hair dryer.

Elm Tree Cottage 🏵   Only a couple of blocks from the beach and the Cliff Walk, this flamboyant Victorian manse is routinely ranked among Newport's most-loved inns. Many of the furnishings are French, with Louis XV as a central inspiration. All but one of the bedrooms have fireplaces. The Library room on the ground floor, with its horsey tackroom tone, is in manly counterpoint to the flounces and curlicues of the other units.

336 Gibbs Ave., Newport, RI 02840. ✆ **888/356-8733** or 401/849-1610. Fax 401/849-2084. www.elmtreebnb.com. 6 units. Spring–summer $225–$295 double, $450 suite; fall–winter $165–$195 double, $325 suite. Rates include breakfast. AE, MC, V. No children under 14. *In room:* A/C, TV, no phone.

The Victorian Ladies   The owners of these four small buildings have chosen a version of Victorian decor in keeping with the age of the main house, but updated to suit contemporary tastes. Every room is different, but most have queen beds, often four-posters. Six units have phones. Pocket gardens and patios are an added welcome for chats and idles. Newport's main shopping district is nearby.

63 Memorial Blvd. (east of Bellevue Ave.), Newport, RI 02840. ✆ **401/849-9960.** Fax 401/849-9960. www.victorianladies.com. 11 units. $125–$225 double. Rates include full breakfast. MC, V. Closed Jan. Children over 10 welcome. *In room:* A/C, TV.

MODERATE

Mill Street Inn 🏵   Something different from most Newport inns, this 19th-century sawmill was scooped out and rebuilt from the walls in. Apart from exposed expanses of brick and an occasional wood beam, all of it is new. An all-suite facility, even the smallest unit has a queen-size bed and a sofa bed. The duplexes have private balconies, but everyone can use the rooftop decks, where breakfast is served on warm days.

75 Mill St. (2 blocks east of Thames), Newport, RI 02840. ✆ **800/392-1316** or 401/849-9500. Fax 401/848-5131. www.millstreetinn.com. 23 units. June–Sept $125–$345 suite; Oct–May $65–$245 suite. Rates include breakfast and afternoon tea. Children under 16 stay free in parents' room. Packages available. AE, DC, MC, V. Free adjacent parking. **Amenities:** Access to nearby health club; dry cleaning. *In room:* A/C, TV w/ pay movies, dataport, minibar, hair dryer, safe.

INEXPENSIVE

Jailhouse Inn   They claim that this was once a colonial jail, although it doesn't look as if it's that old or served that purpose. In any case, the management has toned down the incarceration theme. What remains, including the caged reception desk, isn't as cute as someone thinks, but there are compensations—the prices, primarily.

13 Marlborough St. (east of Thames St., on same block as White Horse Tavern), Newport, RI 02840. ✆ **800/427-9444** or 401/847-4638. Fax 401/849-0605. www.historicinnsofnewport.com. 22 units. Summer $85–$250 double; winter $79–$115 double. Rates include breakfast and afternoon tea. AE, DC, DISC, MC, V. **Amenities:** Access to nearby health club; bike rental; business center; dry cleaning. *In room:* A/C, TV, dataport, fridge.

Pilgrim House   This narrow, four-story, elevatorless mid-Victorian has a rooftop deck with unobstructed harbor views—its top selling point. On good days, you can have your continental breakfast out here. The common room has a fireplace, a TV, and a VCR.

123 Spring St. (between Mary and Church sts.), Newport, RI 02840. 🕐 **800/525-8373** or 401/846-0040. Fax 401/848-0357. www.pilgrimhouseinn.com. 11 units. Summer $90–$220 double; winter $65–$135 double. Rates include breakfast. MC, V. No children under 12. *In room:* A/C, no phone.

WHERE TO DINE

There are far too many restaurants in Newport to give full treatment even to only the best among them. Equal in many ways to those recommended below are **Canfield House,** 5 Memorial Blvd. (🕐 **401/847-0416**); **Yesterday's & the Place,** 28 Washington Sq. (🕐 **401/847-0116**); and **The West Deck,** 1 Waites Wharf (🕐 **401/847-3610**).

Winter hours and days of operations vary considerably. Call ahead to avoid disappointment.

EXPENSIVE

Asterix & Obelix ★★ CONTEMPORARY FRENCH   Named for the famous French cartoon characters for no obvious reason, this cheerful place does render classic Gallic bistro dishes. Come and remember how delectable a near-perfect roast herbed chicken or sole meunière can be. To add a note of Lyonnaise authenticity, bluepoints, Wellfleets, and littlenecks are opened to order as starters. Daily specials are considerably more venturesome, such as the swordfish steak encrusted with Kalamata olives in cabernet sauce. A short bar menu lists sandwiches, pizzas, and pastas. What was once a car-repair shop has been given great splashes of color, with an open kitchen in back. Sunday dinners are served to live jazz from 7pm. Breads are provided by the chef/owner's **Boulangerie Obelix,** 382 Spring St. (🕐 401/846-3377).

599 Lower Thames St. 🕐 **401/841-8833.** Reservations recommended on summer weekends. Main courses $18–$28. MC, V. Daily 5–10pm (Sat–Sun until 11pm).

Black Pearl ★ SEAFOOD/AMERICAN   This long building near the end of the wharf has two sections. The Tavern contains an atmospheric bar and a room with marine charts on the walls. The pricier Commodore's Room is more formal, with linens and candles. In either setting, most of the preparations of fish, duck, and beef are familiar but of good quality, with an occasional lurch in exotic directions, such as the ostrich in red-wine sauce. In the more popular Tavern, don't miss the definitive Newport chowder, followed by a Pearlburger or one of the other overstuffed sandwiches. In summer, the menu is similar at the patio and open-air bar out on the wharf.

30 Bannister's Wharf. 🕐 **401/846-5264.** Reservations and jackets for men required for dinner in Commodore's Room. Main courses $13.75–$21.50 in Tavern, $17.50–$30 in Commodore's Room. AE, MC, V. Tavern daily 11:30am–1am; Commodore daily 11:30am–3pm and 6–10pm. Closed Jan and first 2 weeks in Feb.

Bouchard ★★ CREATIVE FRENCH   Settle in for the evening on comfortable Empire chairs, while an efficient waiter takes your coat and your cocktail order. It's a polished performance, under the alert eye of the hostess, wife of the chef, and what issues from the kitchen validates that promise. Presentations are thoughtfully conceived, attractive without voguish excesses. Here come duck breasts redolent with a peppery currant sauce or red snapper in parchment with a delicate Asian sweet-and-sour sauce. You are asked when you place your order if you'll be having the Grand Marnier soufflé. If you do, you won't regret it. This is dining in a grand tradition.

505 Lower Thames St. © **401/846-0123.** Reservations recommended in high season. Main courses $23.50–$28. AE, DISC, MC, V. Wed–Mon 6–9pm (Sat–Sun until 10pm). Closed 1st 2 weeks in Jan.

Cheeky Monkey ⭐⭐ ECLECTIC The canny owners of the Gatehouse in Providence brought a star chef on board to open this enterprise in 1997. His successor, Jeff Cruff, is no slouch, either. His takes on the menu stalwarts are explosions of flavor—witness the paella with lobster, mussels, scallops, and chorizo. The decor is frisky: Water glasses bear female nudes in relief, and there are leopard-print dadoes and paintings of anthropomorphic simians bearing resemblances to George Burns and Diana Vreeland. Recent additions include a new bistro with lighter fare and alfresco dining.

14 Perry Mill Wharf. © **401/845-9494.** Reservations recommended in high season. Main courses $22–$28. AE, DC, MC, V. June–Sept Wed–Sun noon–2:30pm; May–Oct daily 5:30–10pm (Fri–Sat until 11pm); Nov–May Tues–Sat 5:30–10pm.

Clarke Cooke House ⭐⭐⭐ ECLECTIC For many, this is the quintessential Newport restaurant. The picturesque 19th-century structure was moved to the wharf from America's Cup Avenue in the 1970s. Most of its several levels are open to the air in summer and glassed-in in winter. Several bars lubricate conversation. Up on the formal third floor, the staff sautés your lobster out of the shell while you put away such appetizers as stuffed zucchini blossoms, perhaps moving on to a four-spice duck leg confit with an apple-rhubarb compote. If that seems too rich, spare the walk upstairs and stop in at the Grille, which wraps around a fireplace and center bar. Opt, if possible, for the braised lamb shank with black trumpet mushrooms and squash risotto. The main floor, called the Candy Store, serves snacks, sandwiches, and drinks, and below that is the Boom Boom Room, with dancing to Top-40 tunes from 9pm to whenever.

Bannister's Wharf. © **401/849-2900.** Reservations recommended on summer weekends. Main courses $13–$23 in Candy Store and Grille, $22–$30 in the Porch. AE, DC, DISC, MC, V. Candy Store and Grille, summer daily 11:30am–10:30pm, winter Fri–Sun 11:30am–10:30pm; dining rooms, summer daily 6–10pm, winter Wed–Sun 6–10pm.

Le Bistro ⭐ FRENCH This capable kitchen assembles lightened versions of French country standards. Nibble at crusty bread while checking out the congenial, privileged lot that frequents the place. Rolexes peek out from the cuffs of Ralph Lauren sweatshirts, and it isn't difficult to imagine that all have 50-footers moored in the harbor. Eventually come the excellent bouillabaisse, the scallops paella, the rack of lamb garnished with grilled eggplant and marinated portobello mushrooms. The third-floor cafe serves lighter fare. Lunch is a treat—check out the "Montagnard" sandwich with prosciutto, blue cheese, and sautéed pears on toasted rye.

41 Bowen's Wharf (near America's Cup Ave.). © **401/849-7778.** Reservations recommended on summer weekends. Main courses $18.95–$29. AE, DC, DISC, MC, V. Daily 11:30am–11pm.

White Horse Tavern ⭐ NEW AMERICAN Still going strong after almost 330 years, the White Horse makes a credible claim to be the oldest operating tavern in America. On the ground floor are a bar and two dining rooms, with a big fireplace once used for cooking. Given the setting, the kitchen could have chosen to coast on New England boiled dinners and Indian pudding. But the food is quite good, from the daily lunch specials to the spice-rubbed venison with pears poached with rosemary. About a third of the dishes involve seafood. Prices are significantly lower on the Tavern menu, available from 5pm Sunday through Thursday.

25 Marlborough St. (at Farewell). © **401/849-3600**. Reservations recommended, essential for dinner. Jackets required for men at dinner. Lunch specials $12–$18; sandwiches $9; dinner main courses $23–$35. AE, DC, DISC, MC, V. Sun 11am–2pm; Wed–Mon noon–3pm; daily 6–9:30pm.

MODERATE

Brick Alley Pub ✿ ECLECTIC   Just so you know what you're getting into, the cab of a Chevy pickup truck is next to the soup-and-salad bar. It's loud and good-natured, Newport's favorite hangout. Families, tourists, working stiffs, and yachtsmen squeeze through the doors into the thronged dining rooms, the bar, and the terrace. The voluminous menu is pub grub squared: stuffed clams, Cajun catfish, nachos, burgers, pizzas, and "triple-hot buffalo shrimp pasta."

140 Thames St. © **401/849-6334**. Reservations recommended for dinner. Main courses $5.95–$24.95. AE, DISC, MC, V. Mon–Fri 11:30am–11pm; Sat–Sun 11am–midnight.

Rhode Island Quahog Company ✿ SEAFOOD   This casual temple to the treasured regional clam (pronounced *KOE*-hog) replaced a somnolent Tex-Mex cantina. It retained the terrace and the sturdy bar; otherwise, brace for prodigious platters of seafood, not fajitas. The $17.95 price may sound steep for a simple plate of fried clams, slaw, and fries, but it will serve two, and the extra-fresh clams still taste of the sea. Other must-haves are the chowder and the fisherman's stew. Filling the chairs Sunday through Thursday are special $9.95 dinners, while Thursday, Friday, and Saturday nights (in summer) bring live combos playing blues, jazz, or folk-rock.

250 Thames St. © **401/848-2330**. Reservations recommended on weekends. Main courses $9.95–$24.95. AE, DC, DISC, MC, V. Mon–Thurs noon–3pm and 5:30–10pm; Fri–Sat noon–3pm and 5:30–1am; Sun 11am–9pm.

Scales & Shells ✿✿ SEAFOOD   That graceless name reflects the uncompromising character of this clangorous fish house. Diners who insist on a modicum of elegance should head for the upstairs room, called Upscales. Myriad fish and shellfish, listed on the blackboard, are offered in guileless preparations that allow the natural flavors to prevail. Substantial portions, too: The "large" appetizer of fried calamari is enough for four. Swordfish grilled over hardwood and topped with roasted sweet peppers is typical. Expect no meat or fowl, but there are some vegetarian pastas.

527 Lower Thames St. © **401/846-3474** for main floor, 401/847-2000 for Upscales. Reservations recommended May–Sept. Main courses downstairs $12.25–$20.25, Upscales $16.25–$26.95. No credit cards. Sun–Thurs 5–10pm; Fri–Sat 5–11pm; Sun 4–10pm (slightly shorter hours in winter). Closed Mon Jan–May and from last week in Dec to first 2 weeks in Jan.

INEXPENSIVE

Flo's Clam Shack SEAFOOD   Located just past Easton's Beach over the Newport/Middletown line, this old-timer is more than a lopsided strandside shanty—but not *much* more. Step up to the order window, choose from the handwritten menu, and receive a stone with a number painted on it. What you'll get, if you're wise, are clams, on a plate or on a roll. Cooked swiftly to order, they're as tender as any to which you might have set your teeth. This is the place, also, to sample "chowda" and that Rhode Island specialty, stuffies. Upstairs are a raw bar and deck even more happily ramshackle than below. All entrees are reduced to $9.95 on Sundays, which also feature live music from 2 to 6pm.

4 Wave Ave. © **401/847-8141**. Main courses $9.95–$14.95. No credit cards. Apr to mid-May Thurs–Sun 11am–9pm; late May–Aug daily 11am–10pm; Sept–Jan 1 Thurs–Sun 11am–9pm. Closed Jan–Feb.

Salas ITALIAN *Value* A pure bargain dining establishment, not a wisp of pretense touches this family restaurant. Get this: A standard special gives a choice of lasagna, eggplant or chicken parmigiana, linguine with clams, or mussels marinara, with salad, for $13.95—*for two*. And while none of this will set a gourmet's pulse racing, neither is it the expected runny sauce on flaccid pasta too often encountered. In one choice, eight brightly sauced fresh littlenecks (not canned or chopped) nestle atop a twirled nest of al dente pasta. You'll be hard-pressed to finish it all.

Thames St. © 401/846-8772. Main courses $8.95–$15.95. AE, DC, DISC, MC, V. Daily 5–10pm.

NEWPORT AFTER DARK

The most likely places to spend an evening lie along **Thames Street.** One of the most obvious possibilities, **The Red Parrot,** 348 Thames St., near Memorial Boulevard (© **401/847-3140**), has the look of an Irish saloon and features jazz combos Thursday through Sunday. **One Pelham East** ⊛, at Thames and Pelham streets (© **401/847-9460**), has a cafe, a small dance floor, a pool table, and another bar upstairs, with mostly college-age patrons attending to rockers on the stage at front. **Park Place Tavern,** at Thames and Church streets (© **401/847-1767**), makes room for jazz duos Thursday through Sunday.

A full schedule of live music is on the plate at the **Newport Blues Café** ⊛, 286 Thames St., at Green Street (© **401/841-5510**), plus a Sunday gospel brunch. With its fireplace, dark wood, and massive steel back door that used to guard the safe of this former bank, the cafe has a lot more class than most of the town's bars. Meals are available nightly in summer, Thursday through Sunday nights off-season. It might close for 2 or 3 months in winter.

The Garden, 206 Thames St. (© **401/849-9300**), has pool, foosball, and live rock 3 to 4 nights a week. Folk and rock duos play at **Sully's Pub,** 108 Williams St. (© **401/849-4747**), for under-35 singles more interested in each other than in the music. The pool table stays busy. Upstairs is **Señor Frog's,** with a DJ who spins indie rock 6 nights a week.

Several restaurants occasionally offer music, as with the three-piece combo at Asterix & Obelix, disco at the Clarke Cooke House's Boom Boom Room, and jazz, folk, and rock at the Rhode Island Quahog Company (see "Where to Dine," above, for all three).

4 South County: From Wickford to Watch Hill

Narragansett: 32 miles (52km) SW of Providence; 14 miles (23km) W of Newport

Travelers rushing along the Boston–New York corridor inevitably choose I-95 to get from Providence to the Connecticut border. They either do not have the time for a detour or don't know that the nearby shore has some of the best beaches and most congenial fishing and resort villages of New England. This is called South County, a designation that has no official status, but refers to the coast that is the southerly edge of Bristol County. Bypassed by the inland I-95, it has escaped much of the commercial development that besets many parts of the New England coast.

Rhode Islanders certainly know about the beguilements of South County, though, so try to avoid weekends in July and August, when the crush of day-trippers can turn these two-lane roads into parking lots.

Definitions are fuzzy, but for our purposes, South County runs from Wickford, near Providence, to Westerly, nudging Connecticut. See the map on p. 377 to locate towns discussed in this section.

ESSENTIALS

GETTING THERE   To get to South County from Providence or Boston, take I-95 south, leaving it at Exit 9 to pick up Route 4, also a limited-access highway. In about 7 miles (11km), exit onto Route 102 east, and you'll soon arrive in Wickford. From Newport, cross the Newport and Jamestown bridges on Route 138 to Route 1A north, and follow it to Wickford. Narragansett, at the center of South County's beach country, is 32 miles (52km) southwest of Providence and 14 miles (23km) west of Newport.

VISITOR INFORMATION   The attendants at the **tourist information office** (© **401/783-7121**), in the landmark Towers on Route 1A in Narragansett, can help visitors find lodging. Contact the **South County Tourism Council,** 4808 Tower Hill Rd., Wakefield (© **800/548-4662** or 401/789-4422; www.south countyri.com), to request the useful brochure *South County Style.*

WICKFORD

Apart from those crowded summer weekends, a day or two in South County is as laid-back as an outing can be. There is nothing that can be regarded as a must-see sight, hardly any museums to speak of, and only a couple of historic houses to divert from serious cafe-sitting, sunbathing, and shopping—and these are the chief pursuits in Wickford, a tidy village that crowds the cusp of a compact harbor.

Sailors and fishermen, artists and craftspeople are among the residents, all of them evident within a block on either side of the **Brown Street** bridge that crosses the narrow neck of the waterway connecting Academy Cove with the harbor. Most of the shopping of interest clusters here, slipping over to adjoining **Main Street.**

One place that catches the eye is **Nautical Impressions,** 16 W. Main St. (© **401/294-7779**), a second-floor shop that features sextants, ships' bells, banded chests, and model yachts. On the ground floor, at the same street address, is **Seaport Tavern** (© **401/294-5771**). Its deck is just the spot for a snack, a light meal, or a glass of iced tea.

Proceed south on Route 1A, known through here as Boston Neck Road. About a mile (1.6km) south of Hamilton, watch for the side street on the right marked for the **Gilbert Stuart Birthplace,** 815 Gilbert Stuart Rd. (© **401/ 294-3001**). This may be the one historic homestead in South County that is worth a detour, and not because the painter famous for his portraits of George Washington was born here. Rather, it's the setting and the two preserved build-ings that reward a visit. First is a weathered gristmill dating from the late 1600s; second, the Stuart birthplace, built over his father's snuff mill. Admission is $3 for adults, $1 for children 6 to 12; visits are by guided tour only between April and October, Thursday through Monday from 11am to 4pm.

Still on Route 1A, on the right, south of Saunderstown, is the **Casey Farm** (© **401/295-1030**). The working 300-acre (122-hectare) farmstead is a hand-some 18th-century complex of barns and houses. Free-range chickens hop along the carefully laid stone walls that section the fields. Visits are by guided tour. The farm is open from June 1 to October 15, Tuesday, Thursday, and Saturday from 1 to 5pm. Admission is $3 for adults, $1.50 for children 6 to 12.

NARRAGANSETT & THE BEACHES ⊛⊛

Continuing south on 1A from the Casey Farm, the pace quickens, at least from late spring to foliage season. After crossing the Narrow River Inlet, the road bends around toward **Narragansett Pier.** Along here and several miles on south to Port Judith and Jerusalem are some of the most desirable beaches in

New England, with swaths of fine sand, relatively clean waters, and summer water temperatures that average about 70°F (21°C).

After a few blocks, Route 1A makes a sharp right turn (west), but stick to the shore, proceeding south on Ocean Road. Straight ahead is the **Towers,** a massive stone structure that spans the road between cylindrical towers with conical roofs. It is all that remains of the Gilded Age Narragansett Casino, designed by McKim, Mead & White, but lost in a 1900 fire. In the seaward tower is the Narragansett **tourist information office** (see "Essentials," above).

WHERE TO STAY

Stone Lea   Situated near the crest of a cliff that falls into the ocean, this renovated 1884 McKim, Mead & White commission is an antiques-filled delight to wander through, if a bit formal in tone. The terrace is a special treat at sunset. Some bedrooms have TVs. Breakfasts are substantial.

40 Newton Ave., Narragansett, RI 02882. ✆ 401/783-9546. 6 units. $150–$225 double. Rates include breakfast. MC, V. Open weekends only Apr–May and Oct–Nov; closed Dec–Mar. *In room:* No phone.

Village Inn ✪   There are several inns and hotels in the vicinity, many of them looking out over the water across wide lawns. This is one of the largest and most obvious, a couple of blocks from the Towers. Despite the humble name, it is large and almost new, part of a complex that incorporates a cinema, a gas station, and a dozen shops. It has an oceanview deck, ready access to the beach, and modest resort facilities.

1 Beach St., Narragansett, RI 02882. ✆ 800/843-7437 or 401/783-6767. Fax 401/782-2220. 61 units. Nov–Mar $70–$90; Apr to mid-May $85–$120; late May to late June and early Sept to late Oct $110–$145; late June to Labor Day $145–$220. Packages available. Closed Nov–Apr. **Amenities:** Restaurant (Spanish/Continental), bar; heated indoor pool with Jacuzzi. *In room:* A/C, TV, fridge, coffeemaker, hair dryer, iron, microwave.

WHERE TO DINE

Coast Guard House ✪ SEAFOOD/AMERICAN   Adjacent to the Towers is this 1888 former Coast Guard headquarters, now a well-regarded restaurant that enjoys unobstructed views of the beach and breakers crashing a few feet below its windows. Despite the venue, the menu features as many meat dishes as seafood, but all are executed with a measure of sophistication. Sample the Rhode Island clam chowder, prepared with broth. There's another bar on the deck upstairs.

40 Ocean Rd. ✆ 401/789-0700. Main courses $13–$22. AE, DC, DISC, MC, V. Mon–Thurs 11:30am–3pm and 5–9pm; Fri–Sat 11:30am–3pm and 5–11pm; Sun 10am–2pm and 4–10pm. Closed Jan.

Spain ✪✪ SPANISH   South of Scarborough Beach, this restaurant is deservedly the most popular on this stretch of shore. Partly it's the congenial staff, partly the terraces overlooking the sea. But the greater share of credit goes to the stellar interpretations of the Spanish tapas tradition and such favorites as *paella Valenciana*. Authenticity doesn't head the list of the kitchen's concerns: The irresistible fried calamari are tossed with very un-Spanish hot peppers. Do sample the *espinacas a la Catalana*—spinach sautéed with garlic, raisins, and pine nuts. The nightly land rush suggests that an early arrival is wise.

1144 Ocean Rd. ✆ 401/783-9770. Reservations accepted only for parties of 6 or more. Main courses $13.95–$18.95. AE, DISC, DC, MC, V. Tues–Sat 4–10pm (bar until midnight); Sun 1–9pm.

FROM NARRAGANSETT TO POINT JUDITH

Follow scenic Ocean Road south from the Towers, soon arriving at **Scarborough State Beach** ✪✪. Noticeably well kept, with a row of pavilions for picnicking and changing, it has ample parking and surroundings unsullied by brash commercial enterprises. The beach is largely hard-packed sand. While it has a mild surf that makes it good for families with young children, sections of it are often also jammed with teenagers and college-age folks.

Continuing on Ocean Road to the end, you'll reach the **Point Judith Lighthouse,** 1460 Ocean Rd. (© **401/789-0444**). Built in 1816, the brick beacon is a photo op that can be approached but not entered.

GALILEE

Backtrack along Ocean Road, turning left on Route 108, then left again on Sand Hill Cove Road, past the dock of the only year-round ferries to Block Island, and into the Port of Galilee. At the end, past a cluster of restaurants beside the channel connecting Point Judith Pond with the ocean, is the **Salty Brine State Beach.** Though small, it is protected by a breakwater and is a good choice for families with younger children. On the opposite side of the channel is popular **East Matunuck State Beach,** where waves break upon the sand at an angle, producing enough action to permit decent surfing on some summer days.

To get a better sense of the area from the water, consider the 1¾-hour tour on the *Southland* (© **401/783-2954;** www.southlandcruises.com), which departs from State Pier in Galilee. Cruises are on Saturday and Sunday only from Memorial Day to mid-June and after Labor Day until mid-October; there are daily departures from late June to Labor Day. Prices are $10 to $14 for adults, $6 to $8 for children 4 to 12.

Numerous **party and charter boats** leave for fishing expeditions from Point Judith. Another possible excursion is a **whale-watching cruise** with the **Frances Fleet,** 2 State St., Point Judith (© **800/662-2824** or 401/783-4988; www.francesfleet.com). Cruises are made from July to Labor Day, Monday through Saturday from 1 to about 6pm. It isn't cheap, at $32 for adults and $20 for children under 12, but the sight of a monster humpback leaping from the water is unforgettable.

WHERE TO DINE

George's of Galilee SEAFOOD/AMERICAN   The impulse to drive as far as you can without winding up in the drink may account for the popularity of George's, in business for over 50 years. It can't be the food, which is ordinary. Anyway, the decks serve as a good vantage point to watch the boat traffic in the channel. As for food, give the fried smelts, stuffies, fish-and-chips, and clam and cod cakes a thought, perhaps carrying them over to the picnic tables by the beach.

250 Sand Hill Cove Rd. © 401/783-2306. Main courses $8.95–$29.95 (market prices for lobster). AE, DISC, MC, V. May–Oct daily noon–10pm; Nov–Apr Thurs–Sun noon–2:30pm and 6–9:30pm.

WATCH HILL ☞

Although much of Westerly township remains peacefully semirural, it contains more than a dozen villages, notably the peninsular resort of Watch Hill, and several contiguous public beaches on slender barrier islands enclosing large saltwater ponds.

A beautiful land's-end village that achieved its resort status during the post–Civil War period, Watch Hill has retained it ever since. It helped that it is the closest of South County's beach towns to New York. Many grand summer mansions and Queen Anne gingerbread houses remain from that time. The north side of the point occupied by the village is the harbor, packed with pleasure boats. Stretching from the eastern edge of Westerly township to the southwesternmost tip of the state at Watch Hill are **Dunes Park Beach** and **Atlantic Beach,** followed by **Misquamicut State Beach**, a gathering place for large numbers of adolescents, and **Napatree Point Barrier Beach**, a wildlife preserve notable for its white crescent beach. While you can enter the Napatree preserve for free, there are no facilities, a reason for its generally sparser crowds. All the beaches are noted for their fine-grained sand and swimming in gentle surf with slow drop-offs.

South of town on Watch Hill Road is the picturesque 1856 **Watch Hill Lighthouse,** open from 1 to 3pm Tuesday and Thursday. Back in town at the small **Watch Hill Beach,** younger kids get a kick out of the nearby **Flying Horse Carousel,** which dates to 1867. Only kids are allowed to ride; tickets are 50¢. The carousel is open daily from mid-June to early September. Parents will have to settle for the more than 50 boutiques that fill the commercial blocks.

To get to Watch Hill from Providence and points north, take Exit 1 off I-95, south on Route 3, which passes through Westerly and continues to Watch Hill. From Connecticut, take Exit 92 from I-95, going south briefly on Route 2, picking up Route 78 (the Westerly Bypass) down along Airport Road into Watch Hill. Free parking is extremely limited, so if you arrive after 8am, expect to pay up to $15 in the commercial lot behind the main street.

Amtrak trains from Boston and New York stop in Westerly several times daily. There is a pull-over **information office** on I-95 near the Connecticut border, and a **Chamber of Commerce** office at 74 Post Rd. in Westerly (© **800/ 732-7636**).

WHERE TO STAY

Pleasant View Inn Two miles (3km) east of Watch Hill, this is a small resort with a private strand that adjoins 4 miles (6km) of Misquamicut Beach. The front desk can arrange guaranteed tee times at a nearby course. Five categories of rooms are assigned, most of the better ones facing the ocean, with balconies; some have fridges and microwaves.

65 Atlantic Inn, Westerly, RI 02891. © 800/782-3224 or 401/348-8200. www.pvinn.com. 112 units. May–June and Sept–Oct $75–$150; July–Aug $140–$240. Closed Nov–Apr. Packages available. AE, MC, V. **Amenities:** 2 restaurants (American), bar; heated outdoor pool and Jacuzzi; fitness room with Jacuzzi and sauna; game room. *In room:* A/C, TV.

Shelter Harbor Inn If it's time to stop for the night, for dinner, or for a spectacular Sunday brunch (reservations essential), watch for the entrance to this venerable inn off U.S. 1, about 6 miles (10km) east of Westerly. Parts of the main building date to 1810, and a genteel tone prevails. Several bedrooms have fireplaces, decks, or both. A shuttle takes guests to the private beach a mile (1.6km) away. A creative restaurant and honored wine cellar round out the picture, sullied only by uneven service. The inn is more permissive than most: Children are welcome and smoking is allowed.

10 Wagner Rd., Westerly, RI 02891. © 800/468-8883 or 401/322-8883. Fax 401/322-7907. www.shelter harborinn@earthlink.net. 24 units. May–Oct $126–$176 double; Nov–Apr $88–$146 double. Rates include breakfast. AE, DC, DISC, MC, V. **Amenities:** Restaurant (New American); rooftop Jacuzzi. *In room:* A/C, TV.

The Villa A Dutch colonial manor with many Italianate overlays on Route 1A outside of town, the Villa is most often recommended for its extensive gardens and warm hospitality. All units are suites—three have Jacuzzi tubs built for two, and a couple have fireplaces. The breakfasts are continental during the week, but enhanced with hot dishes on weekends.

190 Shore Rd., Westerly, RI 02891. ✆ **800/722-9240** or 401/596-1054. Fax 401/596-6268. www.the villaatwesterly.com. 6 units. Memorial Day to Columbus Day $150–$255 double; Columbus Day to Memorial Day $95–$195 double. Rates include breakfast. Packages available. AE, DISC, MC, V. **Amenities:** Outdoor pool with Jacuzzi. *In room:* A/C, TV, fridge, coffeemaker, hair dryer.

Watch Hill Inn   Savor sunsets from the veranda of this century-old clapboard lodge. Bedrooms are mostly of good size, with nothing special by way of decor, apart from the four-posters and occasional antiques. There's access to a beach. Meals are largely in the seafood-and-pasta tradition, but with superb views.

38 Bay St., Watch Hill, RI 02891. ✆ **800/356-9314** or 401/348-6300. Fax 401/348-6301. www.watch hillinn.com. 16 units. Mid-June to early Sept $175–$250 double; Sept–early June $100–$175 double. Rates include breakfast. Packages available. MC, V. **Amenities:** Restaurant. *In room:* A/C, TV, dataport.

WHERE TO DINE

Additional dining options include the restaurants at the **Pleasant View Inn, Shelter Harbor Inn,** and **Watch Hill Inn** (see above).

Olympia Tea Room ⭐ NEW AMERICAN   The genteel tone of Watch Hill is undergirded by the Olympia, long a favorite meet-and-eat retreat. This version of an even older restaurant opened in 1939, and long retained its soda fountains and wooden booths. The fountain is now a full bar, but the kitchen continues to crank out pretty imaginative food. If available, jump for the appetizer of plump, lightly fried oysters on wilted spinach and corn salsa. The stuffies and lobster rolls are as good as you're likely to enjoy in coastal New England.

74 Bay St. ✆ **401/348-8211.** Reservations not accepted. Main courses $12–$28. AE, MC, V. June–Columbus Day daily 11am–10pm; mid-Oct to Nov and Apr–May Fri–Sun 11am–9pm. (Hours may vary; call ahead.) Closed Dec–Easter.

5 Block Island ⭐⭐

Viewed from above or on a map, Block Island looks like a pork chop with a big bite taken out of the middle. Only 7 miles (11km) long and 3 miles (5km) wide, it is edged with long stretches of beach lifting at points into dramatic bluffs. The interior is dimpled with undulating hills, only rarely reaching above 150 feet (45m) in elevation. Its hollows and clefts cradle over 300 sweet-water ponds, some no larger than a backyard swimming pool. That "bite" out of the western edge of the "chop" is **Great Salt Pond,** which almost succeeds in cutting the island in two, but, as it is, serves as a fine protected harbor for fleets of pleasure boats.

The only significant concentration of houses, businesses, hotels, and people is at **Old Harbor,** on the lower eastern shore, where the ferries from the mainland arrive and most of the remaining commercial fishing boats moor.

Named for Adrian Block, a Dutch explorer who briefly stepped ashore in 1641, the island's earliest European settlement was in 1661, and it has since attracted the kinds of people who nurture fierce convictions of independence, fueled in part by the streaks of paranoia that lead them to live on a speck of land with no physical connection to the mainland. In the past, that has meant farmers, pirates, fishermen, smugglers, scavengers, and entrepreneurs, all of them willing to deal with the realities of isolation, lonely winters, and occasional killer hurricanes. Today, there are about 875 permanent residents of similar pluck and enterprise who tough it out 9 months a year waiting for the sun to stay awhile.

The challenges of island living aren't readily apparent to the tens of thousands of visitors who arrive every summer. They aren't likely to worry that the water supply is fragile or that generator-provided electricity is hugely expensive.

Vacationers are wont to describe this as paradise—and they are correct, at least if sun and sea and zephyrs are paramount considerations. Those elements transformed the island from an offshore afterthought into an accessible summer retreat for the urban middle class after the Civil War, in America's first taste of mass tourism.

Unlike other such regions throughout the country that have lost their sprawling Victorian hotels to fire or demolition, Block Island has preserved many of its buildings from that time. They crowd around Old Harbor, providing most of the lodging base. Smaller inns and B&Bs add more tourist rooms, most in converted houses built at the same time as the great hotels. There are only a few establishments that even resemble motels, and building stock is marked, with few exceptions, by tasteful Yankee understatement. Despite the ominous presence of a few houses that resemble those plunked down in potato fields in ultra-chic precincts of New York's Long Island, development so far remains under control, and there are no franchised eateries or shops of any kind—not the place to have a Big Mac attack.

Away from the sand and surf, it is an island of peaceful pleasures and gentle observations. Police officers wear Bermuda shorts and ride bikes. Children tend lemonade stands in front of picket fences and low hedges. Clumps of hydrangeas tangle with beach roses and honeysuckle, hiding the foundations of saltboxes and Victorian farmhouses with shingles scoured gray by sea winds. There are no squirrels, chipmunks, possums, or raccoons on the Block, but the island is in the middle of a prominent flyway for migratory birds, and egrets, ducks, goldfinch, and kingfisher are seen in abundance. Deer were introduced about 30 years ago, to the islanders' current regret, bringing Lyme disease and an enthusiasm for turning flower beds into salad bars.

ESSENTIALS

GETTING THERE The **Nelseco & Interstate Navigation Company,** New London, Conn. (© **401/783-4613;** www.blockislandferry.com), provides most of the surface service, including passenger-only ferries on daily triangular routes between Providence, Newport, and Block Island from late June to early September. Bicycles may be taken on board for a small fee. While reservations aren't required for passengers, get to the dock early, as the boats tend to fill up quickly.

Getting a car to Block Island is something of a hassle and considerably more expensive—at press time, $52.60 per vehicle round-trip in addition to fares of $16.80 per adult and $9.20 for each child under 12, or a total of $104.60 for a family of four. It can be assumed that these fares will continue to increase from year to year. Car ferries depart from the Port of Galilee at Point Judith, R.I. Apart from blacked-out days from Christmas to New Year's, there are daily departures year-round, as few as one or two a day in winter to as many as nine a day from early June to late August. Sailing time is about an hour. Drivers, be prepared: You are expected to *back* your car into the close quarters of the ferry's main deck.

The same company provides service from New London, Conn., daily from early June to Labor Day at 9am (extra trips at 7:15pm on Fri), with a return at 4:30pm. Sailing time is a little over 2 hours; round-trip passenger fare is $19.

Given the cost of taking a car, consider parking in one of the nearby long-term lots at Point Judith or New London. Block Island is small, rental bicycles and mopeds are readily available, there are cabs for longer distances, and most hotels and inns are within a few blocks of the docks. There are even car rental

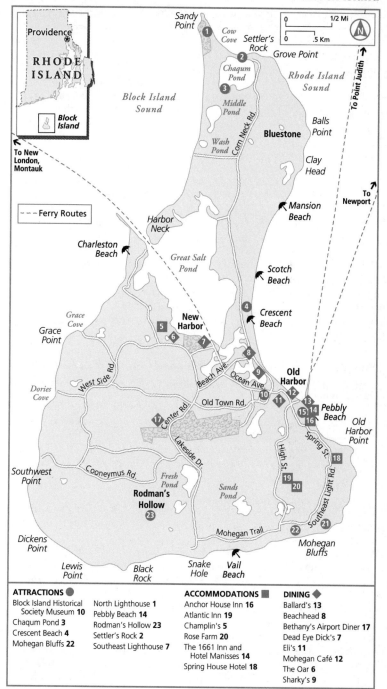

Block Island

Sandy Point ①
Cow Cove
Settler's Rock ②
Grove Point
Chaqum Pond ③
Middle Pond
Rhode Island Sound
Balls Point
Wash Pond
Block Island Sound
Bluestone
Clay Head
Corn Neck Rd.
Mansion Beach
Harbor Neck
Charleston Beach
Great Salt Pond
Scotch Beach
Crescent Beach ④
Grace Cove
New Harbor ⑤ ⑥ ⑦
Grace Point
⑧
West Side Rd.
Dories Cove
⑨
Old Harbor
Beach Ave.
Ocean Ave.
⑩ ⑪ ⑫
Old Town Rd.
⑬
⑮ ⑭
Pebbly Beach
⑰
Center Rd.
⑯
Old Harbor Point
Southwest Point
Cooneymus Rd.
Lakeside Dr.
Fresh Pond
Spring St.
⑱
High St.
Sands Pond
⑲ ⑳
Rodman's Hollow
㉓
Dickens Point
㉒
Southeast Light Rd.
㉑
Mohegan Trail
Mohegan Bluffs
Lewis Point
Black Rock
Snake Hole
Vail Beach

To Point Judith
To Newport
To New London, Montauk

- - - Ferry Routes

Providence ⊛
RHODE ISLAND
Block Island

0   1/2 Mi
0   .5 Km

ATTRACTIONS ●
Block Island Historical Society Museum **10**
Chaqum Pond **3**
Crescent Beach **4**
Mohegan Bluffs **22**
North Lighthouse **1**
Pebbly Beach **14**
Rodman's Hollow **23**
Settler's Rock **2**
Southeast Lighthouse **7**

ACCOMMODATIONS ■
Anchor House Inn **16**
Atlantic Inn **19**
Champlin's **5**
Rose Farm **20**
The 1661 Inn and Hotel Manisses **14**
Spring House Hotel **18**

DINING ◆
Ballard's **13**
Beachhead **8**
Bethany's Airport Diner **17**
Dead Eye Dick's **7**
Eli's **11**
Mohegan Café **12**
The Oar **6**
Sharky's **9**

agencies on the island. If you intend to take a car anyway, understand that it's important to make ferry reservations well in advance—2 months isn't too early for weekend departures.

High-speed, passenger-only ferry service from Point Judith was inaugurated in 2001 by **Island Hi-Speed Ferry** (© 877/733-9425; www.islandhighspeed ferry.com). The boat is equipped with airline-style seating and a cash bar; it makes the trip in 30 minutes, putting in at Payne's Dock in New Harbor. Service is available from June 1 to September 3, with five to six departures each day (the schedule may be expanded if the venture proves successful). Round-trip fares are $26 for adults and $12 for children 4 to 12; reservations are recommended.

Finally, service is also provided between Block Island and Montauk, at the eastern end of New York's Long Island, by **Viking Star,** Montauk, N.Y. (© 516/668-5700). From late May to mid-October, there are daily departures at 9am, returning from Block Island at 4:30pm. Despite what the company might say, the trip usually takes over 2 hours, landing at Champlin's Marina in New Harbor. Only passengers and bicycles can be accommodated; parking is available in Montauk. Reservations aren't required, but arrive early to make sure you get onboard. Round-trip fare is $35.

Westerly State Airport, near the Connecticut border, is the base for over a dozen regular flights to and from Block Island by **New England Airlines** (© 800/243-2460, 401/596-2460 in Westerly, or 401/466-5881 on Block Island; www.block-island.com/nea). Flights depart hourly, taking 12 to 15 minutes; the round-trip fare is $69. Make advance reservations and allow for the possibility that not-infrequent coastal fogs or high winds will delay or cancel flights.

VISITOR INFORMATION   The **Block Island Chamber of Commerce** has a year-round information office at the ferry landing at Old Harbor (© 800/383-BIRI or 401/466-2474; www.blockislandchamber.com). Its knowledgeable attendants can answer questions and help visitors find lodging. In the same building are lockers and one of the island's few ATMs. A new building at Corn Neck Road and Ocean Avenue contains the only bank, which also has an ATM.

Most streets on Block Island have no house numbers, and some roads have no names. Leave your dog at home: Hotels, inns, and B&Bs won't accept them, they are banned from the beaches, and they are supposed to be leashed at all times.

GETTING AROUND   Cars are allowed on the island, but roads are narrow, winding, and without shoulders, and drivers must contend with runners and flocks of bicycles and mopeds. Unless your party includes people with mobility problems or small children, we recommend leaving your car on the mainland and joining the two-wheelers. If you'd like to rent a car after you arrive by boat or plane, **Block Island Bike & Car Rental,** on Ocean Avenue (© 401/466-2297), has offices near Payne's Dock and at the airport; reserve ahead. If you decide to bring your car to the island, top off the gas tank before rolling onto the ferry. There is only one rudimentary gas station—no signs, nameless pumps—behind Sharkey's restaurant.

Rental bikes and mopeds are available at several shops and stands. Convenient sources near Old Harbor include **The Moped Man,** Water Street (© 401/466-5444), on the main business street, renting bikes as well as mopeds; **Old Harbor Bike Shop,** at the ferry dock (© 401/466-2029); and **Island Bike & Moped,** Chapel Street, behind the Harborside Inn (© 401/466-2700). Rates for bikes are typically $28 to $30 a day, less with widely available discount coupons.

Tips **A Note on Accommodations**

If you arrive on Block Island without reservations, one approach to getting a bed for the night is to show up at an inn an hour or so after the last ferry has departed, when management will often lower quoted rates if rooms are still available.

Moped rates vary, but are usually from $30 to $60 for half to full days. Bargaining often brings prices down, especially early in the week after the weekenders have left, or for 3 or more days. Keep in mind that mopeds aren't allowed on dirt roads, which provide access to many beaches.

Some inns also rent bicycles, so a possible plan is to take a taxi from the ferry or airport to your inn, drop off luggage, and get around by bike after that. Two such inns are the **Seacrest,** 207 High St. (© **401/466-2882**), and **Rose Farm,** on Roslyn Road (© **401/466-2034**), but inquire about rentals when making room reservations at other places as well.

EXPLORING THE ISLAND

Little on the island distracts from the central missions of sunning, cycling, hiking, lolling, and ingesting copious quantities of lobster, clams, chowder, and alcohol. There is no golf course, and the lone museum takes only about 20 minutes to cover. Add a couple of lighthouses, a wildlife refuge, and three topographical features of note, and that's about it, enough to provide destinations for a few leisurely bike trips. A driving tour of every site on that list takes no more than 2 hours.

A couple of miles (3km) south of Old Harbor on what starts out as Spring Street is the **Southeast Lighthouse.** A tablet by the road claims that in 1590, the Manisseans, the Indians of Block Island, drove a war-party of 40 Mohegans over the bluffs. An undeniably appealing Victorian structure, built in 1874, the lighthouse's claim for attention lies primarily in the fact that it had to be moved 245 feet (74m) back from the eroding precipice a few years ago to save it. That was expensive, and now another $1 million is desperately needed for renovation. That the building was designated a National Historic Landmark in 1997 might help in fundraising. There's a free small exhibit on the ground floor, but the admission fee to the top is $5.

Continuing along the same road, which goes through other names and soon makes a sharp right turn inland, watch for the left turn onto West Side Road. In a few hundred yards, pull over near the sign for **Rodman's Hollow,** a geological dent dug by a passing glacier. It's deeper than it looks, the bottom a few feet below sea level and laced with walking trails beneath a thick mantle of low trees. Much of what you see here is designated forever wild, for the Nature Conservancy has purchased about a third of the island's surface to protect it from development. A map of the 12-mile (19km) trail network can be purchased for $1.50 at the Chamber of Commerce building at the ferry landing.

From Old Harbor, proceed north on Corn Neck Road, skirting Crescent Beach, on the right. The paved road eventually ends at **Settler's Rock** ★★★, with a plaque naming the English pioneers who landed here in 1661. This is one of the loveliest spots on the island, with mirrored **Chaqum Pond** (suitable for swimming) behind the Rock and a scimitar beach curving out to **North Lighthouse,** erected in 1867. In between is a **national wildlife refuge** that is of particular interest to birders. The lighthouse, best reached by foot along the rocky beach, is now an interpretive center of local ecology and history, open from late June to Labor Day daily from 10am to 5pm.

Back in Old Harbor, the **Block Island Historical Society Museum,** Old Town Road and Ocean Avenue (© **401/466-2481**), was an 1871 inn that now contains a miscellany of photos, ship models, and tools. Upstairs is a room set up to reflect the Victorian period.

There are beaches on Block Island to suit every taste. Immediately south of the Old Harbor, past the breakwater, is the northern end of **Pebbly Beach,** a section informally known as **Ballard's Beach** for the popular restaurant located there (see "Where To Dine," below). Crowded with sunbathers and swimmers, it is one of only two on the island with lifeguards. The surf is often rough. Drinks are served at your towel. North of Old Harbor, beyond the Surf Hotel, starts the 3-mile-long (5km) **Crescent Beach** (a.k.a. Frederick J. Benson Town Beach or simply Town Beach). The southern section, with a sandy bottom that stays shallow well out into the gentle surf, is known as **Kid Beach** because of its relative safety for children. Farther along is the main part, a broad strand served by a pavilion with a snack bar, bathrooms, and showers ($1). Chairs, umbrellas, and boogie boards can be rented. The surf is higher along here and rolls straight in; lifeguards are on duty. Continuing north, and with a small parking lot reached by a dirt road off Corn Neck Road, is **Scotch Beach.** Consider this grown-up and R-rated, dominated by young summer workers and residents. Still further north is **Mansion Beach,** with a dirt road of the same name leading in from Corn Neck Road. Somewhat more secluded, it is usually less crowded than the others. On the west side of the island, running south from the jetty that marks the entrance to New Harbor, is **Charlestown Beach.** Uncrowded and relatively tranquil during the day, it draws anglers from dusk and into the night surfcasting for striped bass.

Apart from sunbathing, the island's most popular pursuit is **bicycling.** The ferries allow visitors to bring their own bikes (for a small fee), but several local agencies rent bikes as well (see "Getting Around," above).

Parasailing has become popular here, and chutes can be seen lifting riders up to heights of 1,200 feet (360m) above the ocean. Call **Block Island Parasail** (© **401/864-2474**) with questions, but you must make reservations in person at the office near the Old Harbor ferry landing.

A more old-fashioned form of transportation is provided by **Rustic Rides Farm,** on West Side Road (© **401/466-5060**). A walking attendant handles the reins and protects the littlest ones on the trail.

Fishing, kayaking, and canoeing are hugely popular, and the name to know is **Oceans & Ponds,** at Ocean and Connecticut avenues (© **401/466-5131**). The owners possess encyclopedic knowledge of the island; their quality stock features Orvis clothing and fishing gear. Rental kayaks and canoes put in at the head of the gentle inland ponds off the Great Salt Pond (New Harbor). Charters can be arranged on three sportfishing boats. Another source of boat rentals is **Champlin's Resort,** on Great Salt Pond (© **401/466-5811**), which has bumper boats and Zodiacs as well as kayaks.

WHERE TO STAY

Anchor House Inn 🖈   A huge anchor out front marks this former eyesore. The recently added units don't have as many steep stairs to negotiate. Room decor is spare and restful, avoiding froufrou. Breakfasts are of the hearty continental variety; take your coffee out to one of the rocking chairs on the porch.

253 Spring St., Block Island, RI 02807. © **800/730-0181** or 401/466-5021. Fax 401/466-8887. www. blockisland.com/anchorhouseinn. 6 units. Mar–Nov $110–$200 double. Rates include breakfast. AE, MC, V. Parking is limited. Closed Dec–Feb. No children under 12. *In room:* TV.

Atlantic Inn ★★

Perched upon 6 rolling acres (2 hectares) south of downtown, this 1879 Victorian hotel beguiles with its long veranda and broad views. Bedrooms are furnished mostly with antiques. Drawn by the promise of spectacular sunsets and the restaurant's changing menu of tapas joined with the most diverse beer and wine selection on the island, people start assembling on the veranda and lawn at 4pm each summer day. President Clinton stopped by for dinner a few years ago, drawn by the reputation of the kitchen, one of the two most accomplished on Block Island. He had no trouble getting a table, it can be assumed, but the rest of us need reservations from June to September. Fish, fowl, and vegetables are smoked on the premises, and the chef comes up with such attractions as grilled striped bass with orzo salad.

High St., Box 188, Block Island, RI 02807. © **800/224-7422** or 401/466-5883. Fax 401/466-5678. www.atlanticinn.com. 21 units. Mid-June to Labor Day and weekends Sept–Nov $150–$245 double; late Apr to mid-June and Labor Day to Oct $130–$175. Rates include breakfast. Children under 12 stay free in parents' room. DISC, MC, V. Closed Nov–Apr. **Amenities:** Restaurant (eclectic), bar; 2 tennis courts; bike rental. *In room:* Dataport.

Champlin's ★★ *Kids*

Families are welcome at this all-inclusive resort, with 225 slips in the marina for visiting yachtspeople (call © **800/762-4541** for information). Those who are put off by the idiosyncratic adornments of Victorian inns will be pleased by the clean lines and muted fabrics of the bedrooms here. There's live music in the bars on weekends, picnic grounds with grills, a pizza bar and ice-cream parlor, even a theater showing first-run movies. Once you've unpacked, there isn't much to compel you to leave, but a shuttle van is provided for trips to other parts of the island. With all that in its favor, the people in the chaotic reception area are annoyingly distracted and offhanded.

Great Salt Pond, P.O. Box J, Block Island, RI 02807. © **800/762-4541** or 401/466-7777. Fax 401/466-2638. www.champlinsresort.com. 30 units. Summer $150–$325 double; spring and fall $85–$200 double. AE, MC, V. Closed mid-Oct to early May. From Old Harbor, drive west on Ocean Ave. and turn left on West Side Rd. The entrance road to Champlin's is on the right. The ferry from Long Island docks here. **Amenities:** Restaurant, 2 bars; large outdoor pool; 2 tennis courts; kayak, bumper boat, and paddleboat rentals; moped and bike rentals; game room; car rental; coin-op washers and dryers. *In room:* A/C, TV, fridge.

Rose Farm ★

The 1897 farmhouse that was the original inn is complemented by an additional house across the driveway. Four of the rooms in the new building feature Jacuzzis and decks. Some have canopied beds, most have ocean views, and their furnishings are often antique. Afternoon refreshments, usually iced tea and pastries, are served.

Roslyn Rd., Box E, Block Island, RI 02807. © **401/466-2034.** Fax 401/466-2053. www.blockisland.com/ rosefarm. 19 units (2 with shared bathroom). $99–$250 double. Rates include breakfast. AE, DISC, MC, V. Closed Nov–Mar. From Old Harbor, drive west on High St. and turn left on paved driveway past the Atlantic Inn. Children over 12 welcome. **Amenities:** Bike rental; coin-op washers and dryers.

The 1661 Inn & Hotel Manisses ★★★

Emus, llamas, black swans, and a Scottish Highland ox graze in the meadow behind the Victorian Hotel Manisses, only the most visible part of a small hospitality empire. Other properties include the 1661 Inn & Guest House, up the hill, and the Dodge, Dewey, and Nicholas Ball cottages. (Children are welcome in five of the six buildings; smoking is allowed in one.) Guest rooms in the hotel utilize oak antiques and lots of wicker; some units have TVs and/or fireplaces. The median age in the hotel is noticeably

> ## Tips DIY Shore Dinners
>
> Should you have housekeeping facilities in your lodging, you might wish to put together a New England shore dinner. Lobster is the central component, of course, and you can buy yours straight off the fishing boats. Each afternoon from about 4 to 5:30pm, boats put in at both Old Harbor and the Great Salt Pond. Depending upon their catches of the day, they charge from $6 to $8 per pound. A more reliable source is **Finn's Fish Market,** at the Old Harbor ferry landing (© **401/466-2102**). Its lobster prices are similar, and it also carries oysters, clams, shrimp, and fish.
>
> For the other fixings—corn, tomatoes, bread, sausage, chicken—stop at either the **Block Island Grocery** (known as the B.I.G.) near Ocean Avenue and Corn Neck Road (©**401/466-2949**), a conventional supermarket; or **Block Island Depot,** Ocean Avenue (© **401/466-2403**), which carries a line of cheeses and organic foods. The best-stocked wine and liquor store is the **Red Bird Package Store,** on Dodge Street (© **401/466-2441**), around the corner from the north end of Water Street. **Seaside Market,** toward the other end of Water Street (© **401/466-5876**), has a good wine selection and some grocery products.

grayer than in the other buildings, where families tend to gather. Common rooms in the 1661 Inn host an afternoon "wine and nibble" hour, while the Manisses parlor serves desserts and flaming coffees in the evening. Stylish dining is featured in the main dining room, with comparable fare in the more casual Gatsby Room. Picnic lunches are also prepared for guests. The inn is now open year-round, although the restaurants are closed in winter.

1 Spring St., P.O. Box 1, Block Island, RI 02807. © **800/626-4773** or 401/466-2421/2063. Fax 401/466-3162. www.blockislandresorts.com. 17 units in hotel, plus 43 units (some with shared bathroom) in satellite buildings. $60–$370 double. Rates include breakfast. MC, V. **Amenities:** 2 restaurants, bar; concierge; babysitting. *In room:* Minibar, hair dryer, no phone.

Spring House Hotel ⚝   Marked by its mansard roof and wraparound porch, the island's oldest hotel (1852) has hosted the Kennedy clan, Ulysses S. Grant . . . and Billy Joel. The young staff is congenial, if occasionally a bit scattered. There are three styles of bedrooms, most of good size, with queen-size beds and pullout sofas. A considerable attraction is the all-you-can-eat barbecue lunch on the veranda. Swimming is allowed in the freshwater pond on the property. The hotel sponsors concerts of classical and pop music on its grounds in July and August.

902 Spring St., P.O. Box 902, Block Island, RI 02807. © **800/234-9263** or 401/466-5844. springhouse@ids.net. 63 units. Summer $175–$375 double; spring and fall $75–$285. Rates include breakfast. AE, MC, V. Closed mid-Oct to Mar. **Amenities:** Restaurant, bar.

WHERE TO DINE

Expect mostly lobsters, fried and grilled fish and chicken, and routine burgers and beef cuts. Chowders are usually surefire, especially the creamy New England version. Clam cakes appear less frequently on menus than before, but are still a staple. Actually deep-fried fritters containing more dough than clams, they are still fun eating, especially when dipped in tartar sauce.

Several inns and hotels have dining rooms worth noting (see "Where to Stay," above, for reviews of the **Atlantic Inn,** the **1661 Inn & Hotel Manisses,** and **Spring House Hotel**), but even there, neither jackets nor ties are required. Due to the seasonal nature of the resort island, its restaurants can change policies, menus, and, most important, chefs in a twinkling. Keep that in mind if any of the observations below prove to undervalue or overstate a restaurant's virtues.

You can get takeout or eat in at the **Black Rock Café,** in the Figurehead Building at the south end of Water Street (© **401/466-8500**). It has a coffee bar along with an appetizing menu of cheeses, salads, entrees, and fresh baked goods.

Ballard's ⭐ *Kids* AMERICAN/SEAFOOD   Sooner rather than later, everyone winds up at Ballard's. Behind the long front porch is a warehouse-like hall where a monster whale skeleton hangs, and beyond that a terrace beside a crowded beach. Several bars and frequent live bands fuel drinkers and diners from lunch until midnight. The menu is all over the map, with something for everyone. Complementing the lobster rolls and fish-and-chips are yellowfin tuna *au poivre* and roasted monkfish medallions with shrimp and sweet pepper dressed in a tarragon hollandaise. Kids have their own menu, and they can make as much noise and mess as they want.

Old Harbor. © **401/466-2231.** Main courses $7.25–$18.95. AE, MC, V. Daily 11:30am–11pm. Closed Oct to mid-May.

Beachhead ⭐ *Kids* ECLECTIC   After changes in management, the menu has been expanded from the former tavern limitations to one of the more ambitious slates on the island. The casual atmosphere remains, making this another likely destination for families in afternoon and early evening (dinner prices are steep, though). In peak season, at least, the noise level is high enough to mask childish squeals. There's plenty of seating inside and on the porch. Seafood and meats are prepared in more imaginative ways than before, and the selection of beers and wines is attractive.

Corn Neck Rd. © **401/466-2249.** Main courses $9.95–$26.95. MC, V. Daily 11:30am–9pm (later in summer).

Bethany's Airport Diner *Kids* AMERICAN   "Ramshackle" is too grand a word for this relic of the 1940s. That's good, if your party includes little ones, for even the most destructive 2-year-old can't do much damage, especially out at the tables beside the runway. Decent chili and chowder come in Styrofoam cups, preceding tuna melts and quesadillas. Such specials as the Monte Cristo—a toasted ham and cheese sandwich—are about as fancy as it gets. Apart from the stools at the counter and the wooden benches around the few tables, decor is confined to the model airplanes hanging from the ceiling, several of them fashioned from beer cans.

Center Rd. (at the airport). © **401/466-3100.** All items under $10. Daily 5:30am–5pm (shorter hr. in off-season).

Dead Eye Dick's ⭐ SEAFOOD/AMERICAN   Despite the name and the logo of a shark with an eyepatch, which might suggest beer blasts and wet T-shirt contests, this is a PG-rated restaurant with good eats and a welcome for all ages. Swordfish is high on the honors list, often grilled with a tomato-ginger relish. A twist on the Rhode Island stuffie is the minced Quahog crammed back into its shell with andouille sausage and sweet pepper. Lunch is mostly tasty wraps and meat salads. The kids' menu suggests pasta with butter or chicken tenders. Arrive early for a table on the deck.

Water St. (near Payne's Dock). © **401/466-2473.** Main courses $15.95–$19.95. AE, MC, V. Memorial Day to Labor Day daily 5–10pm (Sun until 9pm); July–Aug also open noon–3pm. Closed rest of the year.

Eli's ITALIAN/AMERICAN   This place used to be just a spaghetti-and-grinders drop-in, but it's evolved into one of the island's most popular eateries. Problem is, it can serve only 50 voracious diners at a time, and the no-reservations policy means waits of up to 2 hours. But it can be worth it. Choices like "Hunter's Dastardly Duck" bring a half of that bird together with apples, pheasant sausage, brandy, and demi-glace. Such combinations are undeniably full-flavored, although the diverse ingredients are often mashed together as if in a thick stew, losing some of their individuality. Huge portions defy anyone to finish.

456 Chapel St. ✆ 401/466-5230. Main courses $14–$29. AE, MC, V. May–Oct daily 5:30–10pm (Sat–Sun until 11pm); Nov–Dec Sat–Sun 5:30–10pm. Closed Jan–Apr.

Mohegan Café & Brewery ECLECTIC   Walk straight across from the Old Harbor ferry landing to this agreeable tavern—most people do. Featured microbrews are listed on the blackboard. Most of the daytime menu is standard pub fare, with chowder, burgers, and fried clams featured. That's the time to go, for the kitchen has a sure hand with its luncheon familiars, but looks too far afield for dinner ideas (Korean bulgogi, pad Thai, and red curried chicken). This is one of the few public places with air-conditioning, something to remember on a muggy July day.

Water St. ✆ 401/466-5911. Main courses $16.95–$21.95. AE, DISC, MC, V. Summer Sun–Thurs 11:30am–9pm, Fri–Sat 11am–10pm; shorter hours during spring and fall shoulder seasons.

The Oar ✯ AMERICAN   This good-time bar is now open for breakfast and lunch, and the menu has been plumped up with a few more dinner dishes. Grilled swordfish and sirloin flesh out the old roster of nachos, lobster rolls, and calamari. There's a deck and a bar with a picture window to take in dramatic views of storms over the mainland and of the fleet of pleasure boats in the Great Salt Pond. The ceiling and walls are hung with scores of oars—all of them painted with cartoons, graffiti, and assorted messages of obscure or ribald intent.

West Side Rd. (Block Island Marina). ✆ 401/466-8820. Main courses $7.50–$15. AE, MC, V. Daily 8am–midnight (bar until 1am). Closed late Oct–May.

Sharkey's AMERICAN   With its kicked-back atmosphere and pub-style menu, this entry opposite Crescent Beach has a clear kinship with at least a dozen casual eateries on the island. Expect the usual burgers and cheesesteak pretenders, but know that the people handling the fried-fish dishes have a superbly light hand—go for the definitive fish-and-chips. Daily specials lean to the likes of blackened this or that—mako shark, for one—while dinner entrees run to fettuccine and prime rib. Children are welcome.

Corn Neck Rd. ✆ 401/466-9900. Main courses $8.95–$21.95. MC, V. Summer daily 11:30am–10pm; hours vary substantially spring and fall. Closed late Oct to mid-May.

BLOCK ISLAND AFTER DARK

Nightlife isn't of the raunchy, rollicking, south Florida variety, but the bars don't close at sunset, either. Among the prime candidates for a potential rockin' good time is **Captain Nick's,** on Ocean Avenue (✆ 401/466-5670), opposite the Block Island Grocery. It has pool tables inside, plus live music most nights in season out on the terrace. A block away, **Yellow Kittens,** on Corn Neck Road (✆ 401/466-5855), also presents live bands in summer, inside or out on the deck. Darts, pool tables, foosball, and video games help fill the winter nights. Pub food, pool tables, video games, and foosball are also attractions at **Club Soda,** on Connecticut Avenue (✆ 401/466-5397), supplemented by live music once or twice a week.

Ballard's (see "Where to Dine," above) has live rock or pop most afternoons out on the terrace and nightly inside. An occasional live-music venue is the lounge of the **National Hotel,** on Water Street (© **401/466-2901**). Yachtsmen and other sailors docked or moored at Champlin's Marina settle in on the end of the main dock at **Trader Vic's,** at New Harbor (© **401/466-2641**). The bar is downstairs, with a DJ or band out on the deck most afternoons. In addition to the sunset drinks and tapas on the front lawn of the **Atlantic Inn** (see "Where to Stay," earlier in this chapter), many visitors settle in on the porch of the equally well-situated (and less expensive) **Narragansett Inn,** on Water Street (© **401/466-2626**).

Island residents try to keep **Mahagony Shoals,** on Payne's Dock at the end of Water Street (© **401/466-5572**), to themselves. What they come for is the barbed humor of Wally McDonough. He sings Irish folk ballads and banters with the audience, invariably giving better than he gets. Wally occupies his corner Wednesday, Thursday, Saturday, and Sunday nights, as well as Fridays, when he feels like it. Get there around 10pm.

11

Vermont

by Wayne Curtis

Vermont is the Green Mountain State, and the rolling hills, shaggy peaks, and towns clustered along river valleys give the state its distinct sense of place. Still a predominantly rural state, Vermont is filled with dairy farms, dirt roads, and small-scale enterprises. The towns and hills are home to an intriguing mix of old-time Vermonters and back-to-the-landers who showed up in VW microbuses in the 1960s and stayed.

Without feeling in the least like a theme park, Vermont captures a sense of America as it once was. Vermonters still share a strong sense of community, and they still respect the ideals of thrift and parsimony. They prize their small villages and towns, and they understand what makes them special. Five-term governor Howard Dean once said that one of Vermont's special traits was in knowing "where our towns begin and end." It seems a simple notion, but that speaks volumes when one considers the erosion of identity that has afflicted many small towns swallowed up by one creeping megalopolis after another.

For travelers, Vermont is a great destination for long drives, mountain rambles, and overnights at country inns. It's not hard to get a taste of Vermont's way of life: You'll find it in almost all of the small towns and villages. And they are small—let the numbers tell the story: Burlington, Vermont's largest city, has just 39,127 residents; Montpelier, the state capital, 8,247; Brattleboro, 8,612; Bennington, 9,532; Woodstock, 1,037; and Newfane, 164. The state's entire population is just 608,000—making it one of a handful of states with more senators than representatives in Congress.

Of course, numbers don't tell the whole story. You have to let the people do that. One of Vermont's better-known former residents, Nobel Prize–winning author Sinclair Lewis, wrote more than 70 years ago: "I like Vermont because it is quiet, because you have a population that is solid and not driven mad by the American mania—that mania which considers a town of 4,000 twice as good as a town of 2,000. Following that reasoning, one would get the charming paradox that Chicago would be 10 times better than the entire state of Vermont, but I have been in Chicago and not found it so."

With all respect to readers from Chicago, that still holds true today.

1 Bennington, Manchester & Southwestern Vermont

Southwestern Vermont is the turf of Ethan Allen, Robert Frost, Grandma Moses, and Norman Rockwell. As such, it may seem familiar even if you've never been here before. Over the decades, it has subtly managed to work itself into America's cultural consciousness.

The region is sandwiched between the Green Mountains to the east and the rolling hills along the Vermont–New York border to the west. If you're coming

Vermont

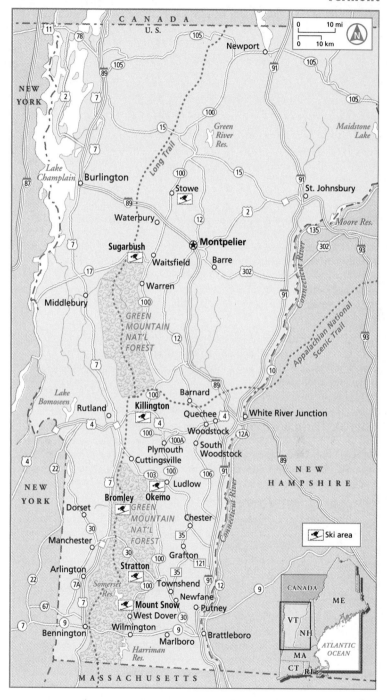

from Albany or the southwest, the first town you're likely to hit is Bennington—a commercial center that offers up low-key diversions for residents and tourists alike. Northward toward Rutland, the terrain is more intimate than intimidating, with towns clustered in broad and gentle valleys along rivers and streams. Former 19th-century summer colonies and erstwhile lumber and marble towns exist side by side, offering pleasant accommodations, delightful food, and—in the case of Manchester Center—world-class shopping.

BENNINGTON

Bennington owes its fame (such as it is) to a handful of eponymous moments, places, and things: like the Battle of Bennington, fought in 1777 during the American War of Independence; Bennington College, a small but prestigious liberal-arts school; and Bennington pottery, which traces its ancestry back to the first factory here in 1793, and remains prized by collectors for its superb quality.

Today, visitors will find two Benningtons. Historic Bennington with its regal homes sits atop a hill just west of town off Route 9. (Look for the mini–Washington Monument.) Modern downtown Bennington is a pleasant, no-frills commercial center with restaurants and stores that still sell things people actually need. It's not so much a tourist destination as a handy supply depot. (It's actually Vermont's third-largest city.) The downtown is compact, low, and handsome, and boasts a fair number of architecturally striking structures, including the stern marble Federal building at 118 South St., with its six fluted columns.

ESSENTIALS

GETTING THERE   Bennington is located at the intersection of Routes 9 and 7. If you're coming from the south, the nearest interstate access is via the New York Thruway at Albany, N.Y., about 35 miles (56km) away. From the east, I-91 is about 40 miles (64km) away at Brattleboro. **Vermont Transit (© 800/451-3292** or 802/442-4808) offers bus service to Bennington from Albany, Burlington, and other points. Buses arrive and depart from 126 Washington St.

VISITOR INFORMATION   The **Bennington Area Chamber of Commerce,** 100 Veterans Memorial Dr. (© **802/447-3311;** www.bennington.com), maintains an information office on Route 7 North near the veterans complex. It's open Monday through Friday from 8:30am to 4:30pm year-round; in summer and fall, also on Saturday and Sunday from 9am to 4pm.

EXPLORING THE TOWN

One of Bennington's claims to history is the fabled Battle of Bennington, which took place on August 16, 1777. This relatively minor skirmish would have major implications for the outcome of the American Revolution. British general John Burgoyne was ordered to attack the settlement of Bennington, where he came upon colonial forces led by Gen. John Stark. After a couple of days playing cat and mouse, Stark ordered the attack on August 16. The battle was over in under 2 hours—the British and their Hessian mercenaries were defeated, with more than 200 troops killed; the colonials lost but 30 men. This cleared the way for another vital colonial victory at the Battle of Saratoga.

You can't miss the **Bennington Battle Monument** ✦ if you're passing through the surrounding countryside. This 306-foot (92m) obelisk of blue limestone atop a low rise was dedicated in 1891. It resembles a shorter, paunchier Washington Monument. Note that it's actually about 6 miles (10km) from the site of the actual battle; the monument marks the spot where the munitions were

---

(Moments "I Had a Lover's Quarrel with the World."

That's the epitaph on the tombstone of Robert Frost, who's buried with his family in the cemetery behind the impressive 1806 First Congregational Church. (It's where Rte. 9 makes two quick bends just west of downtown, and down the hill from the Bennington Monument.) Travelers often stop here to pay their respects to the man considered by many to be the voice of New England. Signs point to the Frost family grave. Closer to the church itself, look for the wondrously carved early tombstones (some with urns and skulls) of the voiceless and forgotten.

---

stored. The monument's viewing platform, which is reached by elevator, is open April through October, daily from 9am to 5pm. A fee of $1 is charged.

Bennington Museum 🐾🐾   This eclectic and intriguing collection traces its roots back to 1875, although the museum has occupied the current stone-and-column building overlooking the valley only since 1928. The galleries feature a wide range of exhibits on local arts and industry, including early Vermont furniture, glass, paintings, and Bennington pottery. Of special interest are the colorful primitive landscapes by Grandma Moses (1860–1961), who lived much of her life nearby. (The museum has the largest collection of Moses paintings in the world.) Look also for the glorious 1925 luxury car called the Wasp, 16 of which were handcrafted in Bennington between 1920 and 1925. A $2-million renovation in 1999 added new galleries and an expanded gift shop.

W. Main St. (Rte. 9 between Old Bennington and the current town center). ✆ 802/447-1571. www. benningtonmuseum.com. Admission $6 adults, $5 students and seniors, free for children under 12; $13 per family. Daily 9am–6pm (until 5pm Nov 1–May 31).

WHERE TO STAY

Four Chimneys 🐾   This striking Colonial Revival building will be among the first to catch your eye as you arrive in Bennington from the west. Set off from Route 7 on a nicely landscaped, 11-acre (4-hectare) lot, it's an imposing white structure with—no surprise—four prominent chimneys. The inn, built in 1912, is at the edge of Historic Bennington; the towering Bennington Monument looms over the backyard. Guest rooms are inviting and homey, but the overall sensibility can be mildly offputting, as if you were visiting somebody else's relatives.

21 West Rd., Bennington, VT 05201. ✆ 802/447-3500. Fax 802/447-3692. www.fourchimneys.com. 11 units. Weekends, holidays, and summer midweek $125–$205 double; winter midweek $100–$180 double. Rates include breakfast. 2-night minimum stay foliage and holiday weekends. AE, DISC, MC, V. Children 12 and over accepted. **Amenities:** Restaurant (Continental). *In room:* A/C, TV, dataport, hair dryer, iron.

Paradise Motor Inn 🐾 *(Value)*   This is Bennington's best motel, with tidy and generously sized accommodations. We'd opt for the North Building, despite its dated 1980s styling—each room here has a terrace or balcony. The more up-to-date Office Building has a richer Colonial Revival style. It's across from the Hemming's gas station, and within walking distance of town.

141 West Main St., Bennington, VT 05201. ✆ 802/442-8351. Fax 802/447-3889. www.bennington.com/ paradise. 76 units. Summer and winter $57–$100 double (discounts in off-season). DISC, MC, V. **Amenities:** Outdoor heated pool; tennis courts. *In room:* A/C, TV.

South Shire Inn 🐾🐾   Architect William Bull designed this impressive Victorian home in 1880. The spacious downstairs features leaded glass on the bookshelves

Southern Vermont

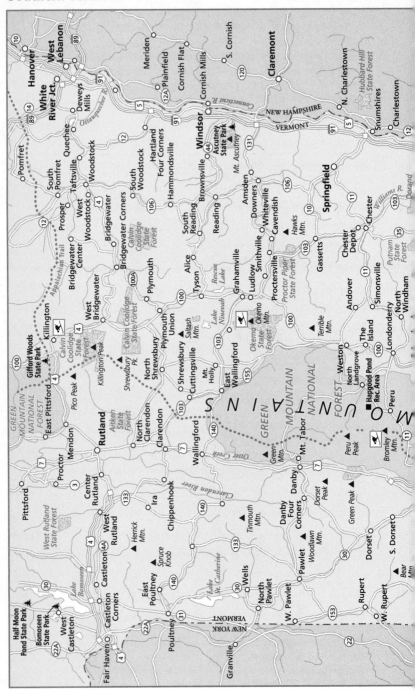

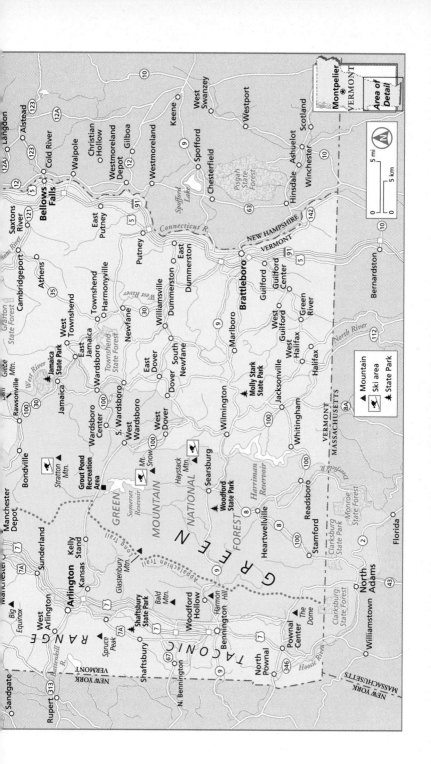

and intricate plasterwork in the dining room. The guest rooms are richly hued, and most have canopy beds and fireplaces (Duraflame-type logs only). The best of the bunch is the old master bedroom, which has a king-size canopy bed, a tile-hearth fireplace, and a beautiful bathroom with hand-painted tile. Four more modern rooms are in the carriage house. The carriage house's downstairs units are slightly more formal; the upstairs rooms are more intimate, with low eaves and skylights over the tubs.

124 Elm St., Bennington, VT 05201. © 802/447-3839. Fax 802/442-3547. www.southshire.com. 9 units. $110–$165 double; foliage season $130–$185 double. Rates include breakfast. AE, MC, V. Children over 12 welcome. *In room:* A/C, hair dryer.

WHERE TO DINE

Alldays & Onions ECLECTIC   This casual spot was named after an early-20th-century British automobile manufacturer. Locals flock here to enjoy the wholesome sandwiches, filling salads, and tasty soups. The more ambitious dinner entrees include Southwest cowboy steak with skillet corn sauce and soba with stir-fried vegetables. The atmosphere is that of a small-town restaurant gussied up for a big night out.

519 Main St. © 802/447-0043. Reservations accepted for dinner, but not often needed. Breakfast $2–$8; sandwiches $2.50–$7.25; dinner $10.95–$19.95. AE, DISC, MC, V. Mon–Sat 7:30am–4pm; Fri–Sat 5:30–8:30pm.

Blue Benn Diner ★ *Value* DINER   Diner aficionados make pilgrimages to enjoy the ambience of this 1945 Silk City classic. Blue-plate dinner specials include vegetables, rice, soup or salad, rolls, and rice pudding for dessert. A bit incongruously, fancier and vegetarian fare is also available; especially good is the grilled portobello on sourdough. There's also a great selection of pies, such as blackberry, pumpkin, and chocolate cream.

North St. (Rte. 7). © 802/442-5140. Breakfast $1.50–$5.95; sandwiches and entrees $1.95–$5.75; dinner specials $7.95–$8.95. No credit cards. Mon–Tues 6am–5pm; Wed–Fri 6am–8pm; Sat 6am–4pm; Sun 7am–4pm.

ARLINGTON ★, MANCHESTER ★★ & DORSET ★★

The rolling Green Mountains are rarely out of view from this cluster of hamlets. And in midsummer, the lush green hereabouts gives Ireland a good run for its money—verdant hues are found in the forests blanketing the hills, the valley meadows, and the mosses along the tumbling streams, making it obvious how these mountains earned their name.

This trio of quintessential Vermont villages makes an ideal destination for romantic getaways, aggressive antiquing, and serious outlet shopping. Each of the towns is worth visiting, and each has its own unique charm.

Arlington has a town center that borders on microscopic; with its auto-body shops and redemption center (remnants of a time when the main highway artery passed through town), it gleams a bit less than its sibling towns to the north.

To the north, **Manchester** and **Manchester Center** share a blurred town line, but maintain distinct characters. The more southerly Manchester has an old-world, old-money elegance with a campus-like town centered around the resplendently columned Equinox Hotel. Just to the north, Manchester Center is a major mercantile center with dozens of national outlets offering discounts on brand-name clothing, accessories, and housewares.

A worthy detour off the beaten track is **Dorset,** an exquisitely preserved town of white-clapboard architecture and marble sidewalks.

One caveat: With its proximity to the New York Thruway just 40 miles (64km) east at Albany, the area attracts a disproportionate number of affluent weekenders from New York City—thus the prices for inns and restaurants tend to be higher throughout this region.

ESSENTIALS

GETTING THERE Arlington, Manchester, and Manchester Center are located north of Bennington on Historic Route 7A, which runs parallel to and west of the more modern, less scenic Route 7. Dorset is north of Manchester Center on Route 30, which departs from Route 7A in Manchester Center. **Vermont Transit** (© **800/451-3292** or 802-362-1226) offers bus service to Manchester.

VISITOR INFORMATION The **Manchester and the Mountains Chamber of Commerce,** 5046 Main St., Suite 1, Manchester Center (© **802/362-2100;** www.manchestervermont.net), maintains an information center in Manchester Center. Hours are Monday through Saturday from 9:30am to 5pm. From Memorial Day weekend to October, it's also open Sunday from 9:30am to 5pm.

For information on outdoor recreation, the **Green Mountain National Forest** maintains a district ranger office (© **802/362-2307**) in Manchester on Routes 11 and 30 east of Route 7. It's open Monday through Friday from 8am to 4:30pm.

EXPLORING THE AREA

Arlington has long been associated with painter and illustrator Norman Rockwell, who lived here from 1939 to 1953. Arlington residents were regularly featured in Rockwell covers for the *Saturday Evening Post.* "Moving to Arlington had given my work a terrific boost. I'd met one or two hundred people I wanted to paint . . . the sincere, honest, homespun types that I love to paint," Rockwell wrote in his autobiography.

Visitors can catch a glimpse of this long relationship in a 19th-century Carpenter Gothic–style church in the middle of town, called the **Norman Rockwell Exhibition** ✦ (© **802/375-6423**). This small museum features a variety of displays, including many of those famous covers, along with photographs of the original models. You'll sometimes find the models working as volunteers. Reproductions are available at the gift shop. It's open daily, in summer from 9am to 5pm and in the off-season from 10am to 4pm (closed Jan). Admission is $2 for adults and free for children under 12.

Manchester has long been one of Vermont's moneyed resorts, attracting prominent summer residents like Mary Todd Lincoln and Julia Boggs Dent, the wife of Ulysses S. Grant. This town is worth visiting just to wander its quiet streets, bordered by distinguished homes dating from the early Federal period. It feels a bit like a time warp here, and the cars driving past the green seem strangely out of place. Be sure to note the sidewalks made of irregular marble slabs. The town is said to have 17 miles (27km) of such sidewalks, composed of the castoffs from Vermont's marble quarries.

On Route 30, 7 miles (11km) north of Manchester, is the village of **Dorset.** Fans of American architecture owe themselves a visit. While not as grand as Manchester, this quiet town of white clapboard and black and green shutters has a quiet and appealing grace. The elliptical green is fronted by early homes that are modest by Manchester standards, but nonetheless imbued with a subtle elegance. In the right light, Dorset feels more like a Norman Rockwell painting than many Norman Rockwell paintings.

MUSEUMS & HISTORIC HOMES

American Museum of Fly Fishing ✦   This is the place for serious anglers. The museum includes exhibits on the evolution of the fly-fishing reel, paintings and sculptures of fish and anglers, and dioramas depicting fishing at its best. You can see the tackle of some of the nation's more notable anglers, including Herbert Hoover, Andrew Carnegie, and Ernest Hemingway. And, naturally, there are extensive exhibits of beautifully tied flies.

Rte. 7A (1 block north of the Equinox Hotel), Manchester. 📞 **802/362-3300.** Admission $3 adults, free for students and children under 12. Jan–Apr Mon–Fri 10am–4pm; May–Dec daily 10am–4pm (sometimes closed weekends in summer; call first).

Hildene ✦✦   Robert Todd Lincoln was the only son of Abraham and Mary Todd Lincoln to survive to maturity. But he's also noted for his own achievements: He earned millions as a prominent corporate attorney, and he served as secretary of war and ambassador to Britain under three presidents. He was president of the Pullman Company (makers of deluxe train cars) from 1897 to 1911, stepping in after the death of company founder George Pullman.

What did one do with millions of dollars in an era when a million bucks was more than chump change? Build lavish summer homes, for the most part. And Lincoln, the son of a man who grew up in famously modest circumstances, was no exception. He summered in this stately, 24-room Georgian Revival mansion between 1905 and 1926 and delighted in showing off its remarkable features, including a sweeping staircase and a 1908 Aeolian organ with 1,000 pipes (you'll hear it played on the tour). Still, it's more regal than ostentatious, and made with an eye to quality. Lincoln had formal gardens designed after the patterns in a stained-glass window and planted on a gentle promontory with outstanding views of the flanking mountains. The home is viewed on group tours that start at an informative visitor center; allow time following the tour to explore the grounds.

Rte. 7A, Manchester. 📞 **802/362-1788.** www.hildene.org. Admission $8 adults, $4 children 6–14. Tours given mid-May through Oct daily 9:30am–4pm; grounds close at 5:30pm. Special holiday tours Dec 27–29.

Southern Vermont Art Center ✦✦   This fine art center is well worth the short detour from town. Located partly in a striking Georgian Revival home surrounded by 400 pastoral hillside acres (162 hectares)—and overlooking land that once belonged to Charles Orvis of fly-fishing fame—the galleries display works from the center's well-regarded collection, as well as changing exhibits of contemporary Vermont artists. An inventive modern building across the drive, designed to display more of the 800-piece permanent collection, opened in 2000. (It was designed by noted contemporary architect Hugh Newell Jacobsen.) Leave time to enjoy a light lunch at the Garden Cafe and to wander the grounds, exploring both the sculpture garden and the woods beyond.

West Rd. (P.O. Box 617), Manchester. 📞 **802/362-1405.** www.svac.org. Summer admission $6 adults, $3 students, free for children under 13; winter admission (one building open) $3 adults, free for students and children. Mid-May to Oct Tues–Sat 10am–5pm, Sun noon–5pm; Nov to mid-May Mon–Sat 10am–5pm.

ALPINE SKIING

Bromley Mountain Ski Resort ✦   Bromley is a great place to learn to ski. Gentle and forgiving, the mountain also features long, looping intermediate runs that are tremendously popular with families. The slopes are mostly south-facing, which means they receive the warmth of the sun and some protection from the harshest winter winds. (It also means the snow may melt quicker than at other ski resorts.) The base lodge scene is more mellow than at many resorts, and your experience is almost guaranteed to be relaxing.

P.O. Box 1130, Manchester Center, VT 05255. 📞 **800/865-4786** for lodging, or 802/824-5522. www.
bromley.com. Vertical drop: 1,334 ft. (400m). Lifts: 6 chairlifts (including 1 high-speed detachable quad), 3
surface lifts. Skiable acreage: 175. Lift tickets: $51 Sat–Sun, $46 Mon–Fri.

Stratton 🎿🎿 Founded in the 1960s, Stratton labored in its early days under
the belief that Vermont ski areas had to be Tyrolean to be successful—hence
Swiss chalet architecture, and the overall feel of being Vail's younger, less
affluent sibling. In recent years, Stratton has worked to leave the image of Alpine
quaintness behind in a bid to attract a younger, edgier set. New owners added
$25 million in improvements, mostly in snowmaking, with coverage now up
over 80%. The slopes are especially popular for snowboarding, a sport that was
invented here when bartender Jake Burton slapped a big plank on his feet and
aimed down the mountain. Expert skiers should seek out Upper Middlebrook,
a fine, twisting run off the summit.

Stratton Mountain, VT 05155. 📞 **800/843-6867** for lodging, or 802/297-2200. www.stratton.com. Vertical
drop: 2,003 ft. (601m). Lifts: 1 tram, 9 chairlifts (including 2 6-person high-speed), 2 surface lifts. Skiable
acreage: 583. Lift tickets: $64 holidays, $63 Sat–Sun, $57 Mon–Fri.

OTHER OUTDOOR PURSUITS

CANOEING **Battenkill Canoe Ltd.,** in Arlington (📞 **800/421-5268** or
802/362-2800; www.battenkill.com), offers canoe rentals for exploring the
scenic Battenkill and surrounding areas. Trips range from 2 hours to a full day
($45 per canoe including shuttle), but the firm specializes in 5-day inn-to-inn
canoe packages. It's open daily from 9am to 5:30pm May through October, with
limited hours the rest of the year.

FLY-FISHING Aspiring anglers can sign up for fly-fishing classes taught by
instructors affiliated with **Orvis** (📞 **800/548-9548**). The 2½-day classes
include instruction in knot tying and casting; students practice catch-and-release
fishing on the company pond and the Battenkill River. Classes are held from
mid-April to Labor Day.

HIKING & BIKING Scenic hiking trails ranging from challenging to relaxing
can be found in the hills a short drive from town. At the Green Mountain
district ranger station (see "Visitor Information," above), ask for the brochure
Day Hikes on the Manchester Ranger District.

A scenic drive northwest of Manchester Center will take you to the **Delaware
and Hudson Rail-Trail,** approximately 20 miles (32km) of which have been
built in two sections in Vermont. The southern section of the trail runs about
10 miles (16km) from West Pawlet to the state line at West Rupert, over trestles
and past vestiges of former industry, such as the old Vermont Milk and Cream
Co. Like most rail-trails, this is perfect for exploring by mountain bike. To reach
the trailhead, drive north on Route 30 from Manchester Center to Route 315,
then continue north on Route 153. In West Pawlet, park across from Duchie's
General Store (a good place for refreshments), then set off on the trail southward
from the old D&H freight depot across the street.

SHOPPING

Manchester Center has the best concentration of high-end outlets in New England. Among the noted retailers with a presence here are Baccarat, Armani,
Coach, Cole-Haan, Brooks Brothers, Timberland, Tommy Hilfiger, J. Crew, and
Circa 50 (modernist furnishings). The shops are located in tasteful minimall
clusters in and around a T intersection in the heart of Manchester Center.

One hometown favorite is worth seeking out if your interests include fishing or outdoorsy fashion. Orvis has crafted a worldwide reputation for manufacturing top-flight fly-fishing equipment, and happens to be based in Manchester. The **Orvis Catalog Store** (© 802/362-3750) is located between Manchester and Manchester Center and offers housewares, sturdy clothing, and—of course—fly-fishing equipment. Two small ponds allow prospective customers to try the gear before buying.

Near the middle of Manchester Center, at the intersection of Route 7A and Route 30, is the **Northshire Bookstore** (© 802/362-2200; www.northshire. com), one of the best bookshops in New England. Call or check the website for upcoming readings.

WHERE TO STAY

Arlington Inn 🌟🌟   This stout, columned 1848 Greek Revival would be perfectly at home in the Virginia countryside. But it anchors this village well, set back from Historic Route 7A on a lawn bordered with sturdy maples. Inside, the inn boasts a similarly courtly feel, with unique wooden ceilings adorning the first-floor rooms and a tavern that borrows its atmosphere from an English hunt club. If you prefer modern comforts, ask for a room in the 1830 parsonage next door, where you'll find phones and TVs. The quietest units are in the detached carriage house, which is most removed from the sound of Route 7A.

Rte. 7A (P.O. Box 369), Arlington, VT 05250. © **800/443-9442** or 802/375-6532. Fax 802/375-6534. www.arlingtoninn.com. 17 units. $115–$265 double. Rates include breakfast. 2-night minimum stay most weekends. AE, DISC, MC, V. **Amenities:** Restaurant (regional); tennis court; babysitting. *In room:* A/C.

Barnstead Inn 🌟   If you're looking for a bit of history with your lodging but are shell-shocked by area room rates, consider this congenial place within walking distance of Manchester. All but two of the guest rooms are located in an 1830s hay barn; many are decorated in a rustic country style, some with exposed beams. Expect vinyl bathroom floors, industrial carpeting, and a mix of motel-modern and antique furniture. Among the more desirable units are room B, which is the largest, and the two rooms (12 and 13) above the office, each with original round beams.

Rte. 30 (P.O. Box 988), Manchester Center, VT 05255. © **800/331-1619** or 802/362-1619. www.barnstead inn.com. 15 units. Summer and fall $89–$150 double, $150–$200 suite; off-season from $80. AE, MC, V. Children over 12 welcome. **Amenities:** Heated pool (summer only). *In room:* A/C, TV, dataport, coffeemaker.

Barrows House 🌟🌟   Within strolling distance of the village of Dorset stands this compound of eight buildings set on 12 acres (5 hectares) studded with birches, firs, and maples. The main house was built in 1784, and it's been an inn since 1900. The primary distinctions of Barrows House are its historic lineage and the convenience to Dorset; the rooms are more comfortable than elegant, though some have fireplaces. A few units have phones. This place will please history buffs; those looking for more pampering may prefer the Equinox or the Inn at Ormsby Hill (see reviews for both, below).

Rte. 30, Dorset, VT 05251. © **800/639-1620** or 802/867-4455. Fax 802/867-0132. www.barrowshouse.com. 28 units. $185–$255 double. Rates include breakfast and dinner. B&B rates also available. Midweek and off-season discounts available. 2-night minimum stay on weekends and some holidays. AE, DISC, MC, V. Pets allowed in 2 cottages. **Amenities:** Restaurant (contemporary New England); outdoor heated pool; tennis courts; sauna; bike rental; game room. *In room:* A/C, no phone (except for in a few units).

1811 House 🌟🌟🌟   This is one of our favorite inns in New England, and is certain to appeal to anyone drawn to early regional history. The historic home was built in the mid-1770s, and began taking in guests in 1811 (hence the name). And it seems that not much has changed in the intervening centuries. The cozy, warren-like common rooms are steeped in the past—the pine floors are uneven, the doors are out of true, and everything is painted in earthy, colonial tones. The antique furniture re-creates the feel of the house during the Federal period, and a delightful pub lies off the entryway, complete with tankards hanging from the beams. Among our favorite units is the Robinson Room, with a private deck and great view. The chocolate-chip cookies set out each afternoon are memorable.

Rte. 7A, Manchester Village, VT 05254. ✆ **800/432-1811** or 802/362-1811. Fax 802/362-2443. www.1811house.com. 14 units. $200–$260 double. Rates include breakfast. AE, DISC, MC, V. *In room:* A/C.

The Equinox ✿✿✿   Since 2000, the Equinox has been owned and managed by the upscale Rockresorts, which manages a respected international group of resorts. It remains a blue-blood favorite, with acres of white clapboard behind a long row of stately columns that define lovely Manchester Village. Its roots extend back to 1769, but don't be misled by its lineage: The Equinox is a full-blown modern resort. You'll find extensive sports facilities scattered about its 2,300 acres (932 hectares), four dining rooms, scheduled events (such as guided hikes up Mount Equinox), and a sense of settled graciousness. The rooms are tastefully appointed, although not terribly large. Alas, the restaurants don't quite live up to the near-perfection of the inn, so leave nights open to sample other area establishments.

Rte. 7A (P.O. Box 46), Manchester Village, VT 05245. ✆ **800/362-4747** or 802/362-4700. Fax 802/362-1595. www.equinoxresort.com. 183 units. $189–$339 double; $499–$599 suite. Ask about packages. AE, DISC, MC, V. **Amenities:** 4 restaurants (contemporary/regional, pub fare); indoor and outdoor pools; 18-hole golf course; tennis courts; health club; sauna; concierge; shopping arcade; salon; limited room service; babysitting; laundry service; dry cleaning; croquet; falconry school. *In room:* A/C, TV, dataport, hair dryer, iron.

Inn at Ormsby Hill ✿✿   The oldest part of the striking Inn at Ormsby Hill dates to 1764. (The revolutionary Ethan Allen was rumored to have hidden out here.) Today, it's a harmonious medley of eras and styles, with inspiring views of the Green Mountains. Guests enjoy those views along with gourmet breakfasts in the dining room, which was built by prominent 19th-century attorney Edward Isham to resemble the interior of a steamship. Among the best units are the Taft Room, with its vaulted wood ceiling, and the Library, with many of Isham's books still lining the shelves. Nine rooms feature two-person Jacuzzis and fireplaces.

Rte. 7A (near Hildene, south of Manchester Village), Manchester Center, VT 05255. ✆ **800/670-2841** or 802/362-1163. Fax 802/362-5176. www.ormsbyhill.com. 10 units. Weekends $215–$310 double; weekdays $170–$245 double; foliage and holidays $315–$370 double. Rates include breakfast. 2-night minimum stay on weekends. DISC, MC, V. Closed briefly in Apr. Children 14 and over welcome. *In room:* A/C, hair dryer.

Palmer House Resort ✿   This is actually a motel, but several notches above the run-of-the-mill. It's been owned and operated by the same family for nearly 50 years, and the rooms are furnished with antiques and other niceties you might not expect. Ask for one of the somewhat larger rooms in the newer rear building. Added in 2000 were eight spacious suites, each with gas fireplace, wet bar, and private deck overlooking a trout-stocked pond and the mountains beyond. The buildings are set on 22 nicely tended acres (9 hectares), and the motel even has its own small golf course. Rooms tend to book up early in the season, so call ahead to avoid disappointment.

Rte. 7A, Manchester Center, VT 05255. ✆ **800/917-6245** or 802/362-3600. www.palmerhouse.com. 58 units. Summer $150–$175 double, $220–$230 suite; off-season from $85 double, from $180 suite. 2-night minimum stay some weekends. **Amenities:** Pool; 9-hole golf course; tennis courts; Jacuzzi, sauna; fishing pond and free fishing rods. *In room:* A/C, TV, fridge, coffeemaker, hair dryer.

West Mountain Inn ☆   Sitting atop a grassy bluff at the end of a dirt road a ½ mile (0.8km) from Arlington center, the West Mountain Inn's rambling, white-clapboard building dates back a century and a half. It's a perfect place for travelers striving to get away from the irksome hum of modern life. Guest rooms are nicely furnished with country antiques and Victorian reproductions. The rooms vary widely in size and shape, but even the smallest has plenty of charm and character.

River Rd., Arlington, VT 05250. ✆ **802/375-6516.** Fax 802/375-6553. www.westmountaininn.com. 18 units. Spring/winter weekends and summer, $198–$280 double; winter midweek $169–$189 double; foliage season $223–$300 double. Rates include breakfast and dinner. 2-night minimum stay on weekends. AE, DISC, MC, V. **Amenities:** Restaurant (contemporary New England); nearby health club; in-room massage (by prior arrangement); babysitting. *In room:* A/C, no phone.

Wilburton Inn ☆☆   This impressive 1902 Tudor estate is sumptuously appointed, the common spaces filled with European antiques, Persian carpets, and even a baby grand. Throughout the brick manor house you'll find works from the modern-art collection amassed by the inn's owners. The guest rooms are divided amongst the main house and several outbuildings of various vintages. In the outbuildings, our favorite unit is spacious room 24, with a private deck with views of Mount Equinox and quirky outdoor sculptures. Three rooms have fireplaces; the units in the mansion lack TVs. One note: The inn hosts weddings virtually every weekend in summer, so travelers looking for quiet are best off booking midweek.

River Rd., Manchester Village, VT 05254. ✆ **800/648-4944** or 802/362-2500. www.wilburton.com. 35 units (1 with private hall bathroom). Weekends $150–$250 double; midweek $125–$205 double; holidays and foliage $180–$315 double. Rates include breakfast. 2- to 3-night minimum stay on weekends and holidays. AE, MC, V. **Amenities:** Restaurant (regional contemporary); pool; tennis courts. *In room:* A/C, TV, hair dryer, iron.

WHERE TO DINE

Chantecleer ☆☆☆   CONTINENTAL   If you like superbly prepared Continental fare but are put off by the stuffiness of highbrow Euro-wannabe restaurants, this is the place for you. Rustic elegance is the best description for this century-old dairy barn. The oddly tidy exterior, which looks as if it could house a chain restaurant, doesn't offer a clue to just how pleasantly romantic the interior is. Chef Michel Baumann specializes in game and might feature veal with a roasted garlic, sage, and balsamic demi-glace. Especially good is the whole Dover sole, which is filleted tableside.

Rte. 7A, 3½ miles (5.6km) north of Manchester Center. ✆ **802/362-1616.** Reservations recommended. Main courses $26–$35. AE, MC, V. Wed–Mon 6–9:30pm. Also closed Mon in winter and for 2–3 weeks in both Nov and Apr.

Little Rooster Cafe ☆   CONTEMPORARY/REGIONAL   This appealing spot near the outlets is the best choice in town for breakfast or lunch. Start the day with flapjacks, a Cajun omelet, or a luscious corned-beef hash (go ahead— your doctor won't know). Lunches feature a creative sandwich selection, such as a commendable roast beef with pickled red cabbage and a horseradish dill sauce.

Rte. 7A South, Manchester Center. ✆ **802/362-3496.** Breakfast items $4.50–$6.75; lunch $6.50–$8.25. No credit cards. Daily 7am–2:30pm (closed Wed in off-season).

Mistral's at Toll Gate ☆☆   FRENCH   The best tables at Mistral's are along the windows, which overlook a lovely creek that's spotlit at night. Located in a

---

⌐*Tips* Looking for More Information?

The single best source of information on the region is the **state visitor center** (☏ **802/254-4593**) right off I-91 in Guilford, just south of Brattleboro. The beautiful new building, inspired by Vermont's barns, is filled with maps, brochures, and videos on activities in the region.

---

tollhouse of a long-since-bypassed byway, the restaurant is a romantic mix of modern and old. The menu changes seasonally, with dishes like salmon cannelloni stuffed with lobster. The kitchen is run with great aplomb by chef/owner Dana Markey. The restaurant has been recognized with the *Wine Spectator* award of excellence since 1994.

Toll Gate Rd. (east of Manchester off Rte. 11/30). ☏ **802/362-1779.** Reservations recommended. Main courses $22–$32. AE, MC, V. July–Oct Thurs–Tues 6–9pm; Nov–June Thurs–Mon 6–9pm.

2 Brattleboro & the Southern Green Mountains

The southern Green Mountains are New England writ large. If you've developed a notion in your head of what New England looks like but haven't ever been here, this may be the place you've envisioned. You half expect to walk into an inn and bump into Bob Newhart, the mild-mannered innkeeper.

The hills and valleys around the bustling town of Brattleboro in Vermont's southeast corner contain some of the state's best-hidden treasures. Driving along the main valley floors—on roads along the West or Connecticut rivers, or on Route 100—tends to be fast and only moderately interesting. To really soak up the region's flavor, turn off the main roads and wander up and over rolling ridges and into the narrow folds in the mountains that hide peaceful villages. If it seems to you that the landscape hasn't changed all that much in the past 2 centuries, well, you're right. It hasn't.

This region is well known for its pristine and historic villages. You can't help but stumble across them as you explore. A good strategy is to stop for a spell in Brattleboro to stock up on supplies or sample some local food or music. Then head for the southern Green Mountains, settle in at a remote inn, and continue your explorations on foot or by bike. In winter, you can plumb the snowy white hills by cross-country ski or snowshoe.

THE WILMINGTON/MOUNT SNOW REGION

Set high in the hills on the winding mountain highway midway between Bennington and Brattleboro, Wilmington has managed to retain its charm as an attractive village despite its location on two busy roads. It's definitely a town for tourists—if you want to get a light bulb or haircut, you're better off in Bennington or Brattleboro. What Wilmington does have is a nice selection of antiques shops, boutiques, and pizza joints. Except on busy holiday weekends, Wilmington still manages to feel like a gracious mountain village untroubled by the times.

From Wilmington, the ski resort of Mount Snow/Haystack is easily accessible to the north via Route 100, which is brisk, busy, and close to impassable on sunny weekends in early October. Heading north, you'll first pass through West Dover, a classically New England town with a prominent steeple and acres of white clapboard.

ESSENTIALS

GETTING THERE Wilmington is located at the junction of Route 9 and Route 100. Route 9 offers the most direct access. The Mount Snow area is north of Wilmington on Route 100.

VISITOR INFORMATION The **Mount Snow/Haystack Region Chamber of Commerce** (© **877/887-6884** or 802/464-8092; www.visitvermont.com) maintains a visitor center at 21 West Main St., Wilmington; open daily from 10am to 5pm. Its room booking service is especially helpful for smaller inns and B&Bs; call © **877/887-6884.** For on-mountain accommodations, check with **Mount Snow Lodging Bureau and Vacation Service** (© **800/245-7669**).

THE MARLBORO MUSIC FESTIVAL 𐂷𐂷𐂷

The renowned Marlboro Music Festival offers classical concerts performed by accomplished masters as well as highly talented younger musicians on weekends from mid-July to mid-August in the agreeable town of Marlboro, east of Wilmington on Route 9. The retreat was founded in 1951 and has hosted countless noted musicians, including Pablo Casals, who participated between 1960 and 1973. Concerts take place in the 700-seat auditorium at Marlboro College, and advance ticket purchases are strongly recommended. Prices range from $5 to $25. Between September and June, contact the festival's winter office at Marlboro Music, 135 S. 18th St., Philadelphia, PA 19103 (© **215/569-4690**). In summer, write Marlboro Music, Marlboro, VT 05344, or call the box office (© **802/254-2394**). The website is www.marlboromusic.org.

MOUNTAIN BIKING

Mount Snow was among the first resorts to foresee the widespread appeal of mountain biking, and the region remains one of the leading destinations for those whose vehicle of choice has knobby tires. The first mountain-bike school in the country was established here in 1988, and still offers a roster of classes that are especially helpful to novices. Clinics and guided tours are also available.

The **Mountain Bike Center** 𐂷 (call Crisports at © **802/464-4040**), open from late May to mid-October at the base of the mountain, offers rentals, maps, and advice. The resort itself has some 45 miles (72km) of trails; bikers can also explore an additional 140 miles (225km) of trails and abandoned roads that lace the region. For a fee, you can take your bike to the mountaintop by gondola and coast your way down along marked trails, or earn the ride by pumping out the vertical rise to the top. Fanning out from the mountain are numerous abandoned town roads that make for less challenging but no less pleasant excursions.

ALPINE SKIING

Mount Snow 𐂷 Mount Snow is noted for its widely cut runs on the front face (disparaged by some as "vertical golf courses"), yet remains an excellent destination for intermediates and advanced intermediates. More advanced skiers migrate to the North Face, which is its own little world of bumps and glades. Because it's the closest Vermont ski area to Boston and New York (it's a 4-hr. drive from Manhattan), the mountain can be especially crowded on weekends.

Mount Snow's village is attractively arrayed along the base of the mountain. The most imposing structure is the balconied hotel overlooking a small pond, but the overall character is shaped more by the unobtrusive smaller lodges and homes. Once famed for its groovy singles scene, Mount Snow's post-skiing activities have mellowed somewhat and embraced the family market, although 20-somethings will still find a good selection of après-ski diversions.

Tips **Open Slopes**

Haystack Mountain, which is owned by Mount Snow and located about 10 miles (16km) away up a quiet valley, offers less crowded, old-fashioned skiing at its best. Not only will you avoid the thickest of crowds on weekends, but you'll also save some money: Lift tickets are $38 here throughout the week, compared to $56 on weekends and holidays at Mount Snow.

Mount Snow, VT 05356. ℂ **800/245-7669** for lodging, or 802/464-3333. www.mountsnow.com. Vertical drop: 1,700 ft. (510m). Lifts: 18 chairlifts (3 high-speed), 5 surface lifts. Skiable acreage: 749. Lift tickets: $56 weekends and holidays, $49 midweek.

CROSS-COUNTRY SKIING

The Mount Snow area offers excellent cross-country ski centers. The 9 miles (14km) of groomed trail at **Timber Creek Cross-Country Touring Center** (ℂ **802/464-0999**), in West Dover near the Mount Snow access road, are popular with beginners and hold snow nicely thanks to the high elevation. Tickets are $15. The **Hermitage Ski Touring Center** (ℂ **802/464-3511**) attracts more advanced skiers to its varied terrain and 30 miles (48km) of trails. A pass here costs $14. The **White House Ski Touring Center,** at the inn by the same name on Route 100 (ℂ **800/541-2135** or 802/464-2135), has easy access to the Vermont woods, a good range of terrain, and 25 miles (40km) of trails. A pass costs $12. The center also maintains snowshoe trails and offers rentals.

WHERE TO STAY

The Mount Snow area has a surfeit of lodging options, ranging from basic motels to luxury inns to slopeside condos. In winter, the high prices reflect relatively easy access for skiers from New York and Boston. Rates drop quite a bit in summer, when the region slips into a pleasant lethargy. Call Mount Snow's lodging line (ℂ **800/245-7669**) to ask about packages and condo accommodations.

The Hermitage 🌟🌟 We love this place not so much for its unpretentious sense of style—the 19th century as interpreted by the 1940s—but for the way it combines the stately with the quirky. The inn is located on 25 acres (10 hectares) of meadow and woodland, and feels a bit like one of those British summer estates that P. G. Wodehouse wrote about. Out back are cages filled with game birds, some quite exotic, that are raised for eating, hunting, and show. The guest rooms are designed to satisfy basic comfort more than a thirst for elegance, and some are a bit past their prime. But they're still far from shabby—and the faded charm is part of the inn's appeal. The dining room is best known for its selection of wines, but the Continental cuisine holds its own quite nicely.

Coldbrook Rd. (P.O. Box 457), Wilmington, VT 05363. ℂ 802/464-3511. Fax 802/464-2688. www.hermitageinn.com. 15 units. $225–$250 double. Rates include breakfast and dinner. 2- or 3-night minimum stay on weekends and holidays in winter. AE, MC, V. **Amenities:** Restaurant (Continental); access to outdoor pool and tennis court (1 mile/1.6km away); cross-country ski center; sporting clays; stocked trout pond; private hunting preserve. *In room:* TV.

Inn at Quail Run 🌟 Quail Run is a hybrid of the sort New England could use more of: an intimate B&B that welcomes families (and even pets). Set on 13 acres (5 hectares) in the hills east of Route 100, the converted ski lodge was renovated in 1997, with guest rooms done up in a contemporary country style.

Family accommodations include king and bunk beds; four rooms have gas fire-places.

106 Smith Rd., Wilmington, VT 05363. ✆ **800/343-7227** or 802/464-3362. 13 units. Summer $120–$160 double; foliage $165–$200 double; ski season $135–$180 double. Rates include full breakfast. 3-night minimum stay on holiday weekends; 2-night minimum stay in foliage season. AE, DISC, MC, V. Pets allowed in some rooms ($15 per night). **Amenities:** Heated outdoor pool; Jacuzzi; sauna; game room. *In room:* TV.

Inn at Sawmill Farm ★★

The Inn at Sawmill Farm is a Relais & Chateaux property spread over 28 acres (11 hectares), and one of the first inns in New England to cater to affluent travelers. Guest rooms in this old farmhouse, parts of which date back to 1797, are each different, but all share similar contemporary country styling and colonial reproduction furniture. Among the best are Cider House No. 2, with its rustic beams and canopy bed, and the Woodshed, a quiet cottage with a beautiful brick fireplace and cozy loft. Some guests report that in recent years the inn has lost a bit of its burnish, and especially given the high room rates, service is no longer as crisp as it once was.

Crosstown Rd. and Rte. 100 (P.O. Box 367), West Dover, VT 05356. ✆ **800/493-1133** or 802/464-8131. Fax 802/464-1130. www.vermontdirect.com/sawmill. 21 units. Weekends $362–$850 double; weekdays $360–$750 double. Rates include breakfast and dinner. AE, DC, MC, V. Closed Apr–May. **Amenities:** Restaurant (see review below); outdoor pool; tennis court. *In room:* A/C, hair dryer, iron.

Trail's End ★

Trail's End, a short drive off Route 100 on 10 nicely tended acres (4 hectares), is located in an updated 1960s ski lodge. Guest rooms are spotlessly clean, styled in a modern country fashion. Six feature fireplaces, two have Jacuzzis, and the suites are perfect for midwinter cocooning, with microwaves, fridges, and VCRs. Our favorite? Room 6, with a lovely fireplace and nice oak accents. Other good places to linger include the main common room with 22-foot (6.5m) stone fireplace, the stone-floored library and game room, and the informal second-floor loft.

5 Trail's End Lane (look for turn between Haystack and Mount Snow), Wilmington, VT 05363. ✆ **800/ 859-2585** or 802/464-2727. Fax 802/464-5532. www.trailsendvt.com. 15 units. Winter $130–$190 double; fall $120–$180 double; summer $110–$160 double. Rates include breakfast. 2- to 3-night minimum stay on weekends and holidays. AE, DISC, MC, V. Children over 7 welcome. **Amenities:** Heated outdoor pool (summer only); tennis court; Jacuzzi; game room. *In room:* TV, no phone.

Vintage Motel *Value*

This is a good budget choice for those planning to spend little time in their rooms. It has basic, motel-size units with industrial carpeting, durable furniture, and a few nice touches like quilts on the beds. There's a family room with microwave and VCR. Bathrooms have curious square tubs (with showers), which are weird and appealing at the same time. The place is popular with both snowmobilers and skiers.

195 Rte. 9, Wilmington, VT 05363. ✆ **800/899-9660** or 802/464-8824. www.vintagemotel.com. 18 units. Winter $65–$95 double; summer $60[nd[$75 double. 2-night minimum stay some weekends; 3-night minimum stay on holidays. AE, DISC, MC, V. Pets accepted in 4 rooms. **Amenities:** Outdoor pool. *In room:* TV.

White House of Wilmington ★

This grand Colonial Revival mansion sits atop the crest of an open hill just east of Wilmington. Built in 1915, the interior features hardwood floors, arched doorways, and nice detailing throughout. It's often a lively place, especially in winter, with cross-country skiers, snowshoers, and snow tubers (there's a great hill out front) all milling about. Guest rooms are simply furnished in Colonial Revival style; nine have fireplaces and four feature Jacuzzis. We love room 1, a corner unit with fireplace and vintage white-tile bathroom, and room 3, which has its own balcony and sitting room with fireplace. The dining room, which serves Continental fare, is one of the region's more popular fine-dining restaurants. The inn is often booked for weekend weddings in summer.

178 Rte. 9, East Wilmington, VT 05363. ✆ **800/541-2135** or 802/464-2135. Fax 802/464-5222. www. whitehouseinn.com. 25 units. Weekends $162–$262 double; weekdays $148–$240 double. Rates include breakfast. 2-night minimum stay on weekends. AE, MC, V. Children 8 and over welcome in main inn; all ages welcome in guesthouse. **Amenities:** Restaurant (Continental); indoor and outdoor heated pools; tennis courts; sauna; steam room; snowshoe rental; 25 miles (40km) of groomed cross-country ski trails. *In room:* No phone.

WHERE TO DINE

Dot's ✿ *Value* DINER   Wilmington is justly proud of Dot's, an institution that has stubbornly remained loyal to its longtime clientele, offering good, cheap food in the face of creeping boutique-ification elsewhere in town. (There's a second, more modern Dot's in Dover.) Located right in the village, Dot's is a classic, with pine paneling, swivel counter stools, and checkerboard linoleum tile. It's famous for its chili and pancakes, but don't overlook the Cajun skillet—a medley of sausage, peppers, onions, and home fries sautéed and served with eggs and melted Jack cheese.

West Main St., Wilmington. ✆ **802/464-7284.** Breakfast $2.95–$7.25; lunch $2.75–$7.50; dinner $2.75–$12.95. DISC, MC, V. Daily 5:30am–8pm (Fri–Sat until 9pm).

Inn at Sawmill Farm ✿✿ CONTINENTAL   More than 32,000 bottles of wine lurk in the custom-made wine cellar of this inn, which earned a coveted "Grand Award" from *Wine Spectator* magazine. The wine is only one of the reasons the inn consistently attracts well-heeled diners. The food is deftly prepared, with entrees ranging from pheasant breast and roasted salmon to potato-crusted sea bass with wild mushrooms. The converted barn-and-farmhouse atmosphere is romantic and the service superb, although the formality of the servers puts some relaxed folks on edge.

Crosstown Rd. and Rte. 100, West Dover. ✆ **802/464-8131.** www.vermontdirect.com/sawmill. Reservations recommended. Main courses $28–$39. AE, DC, MC, V. Daily 6–9:30pm. Closed mid-Apr to Memorial Day weekend.

Le Petit Chef ✿✿ FRENCH   Situated in an antique Cape Cod–style farmhouse, Le Petit Chef has attracted legions of satisfied customers who flock here to sample Betty Hillman's creative fare. The interior has been modernized at the expense of some historic character, but the quality of the food usually makes diners overlook the made-for-ski-crowds ambience. By all means, start with the signature "Bird's Nest," an innovative mélange of shiitake mushrooms and onions cooked in a cream sauce and served in a deep-fried-potato basket. Main courses include salmon with a citrus glaze, loin of venison with fruit chutney, and beef with merlot sauce and wild mushrooms.

Rte. 100, Wilmington. ✆ **802/464-8437.** Reservations recommended. Main courses $18–$32. AE, MC, V. Wed–Thurs and Sun–Mon 6–9pm; Fri–Sat 6–10pm. Closed late fall and early spring.

Maple Leaf Malt & Brewing Co. PUB FARE   This is the place for those nights you don't feel like anything fancy, but Dot's seems a bit too, well, authentic for your mood. This neighborly bar, just around the corner from Dot's, features sandwiches, burgers, wraps, and the occasional pasta special. It's all perfectly fine, if unexciting, and the food makes a nice accompaniment to the brews crafted on the far side of the glass walls in the dining room. Expect it to be clamorous on winter weekends.

3 North Main St., Wilmington. ✆ **802/464-9900.** Main courses $6.95–$15.95. AE, DISC, MC, V. Daily 11:30am–10pm (sometimes later).

Piero's Trattoria ✦ PASTA/ITALIAN   This appealingly informal spot is located at the Orchard Inn. The oddly styleless dining room is small and dim, with just seven tables located off the lobby of the upstairs B&B. Not a promising appearance, but both chefs come from central Italy, the pastas are homemade, and other entrees might include veal stuffed with prosciutto and mozzarella served over polenta with a Sambuca sage sauce.

53 North Main St. (Rte. 100), Wilmington. ✆ 802/464-7147. www.theorchardinn.com. Reservations recommended. Main courses $14.95–$17.95. AE, MC, V. Summer Tues–Sat 5:30–9:30pm; winter Thurs–Sat 5:30–9:30pm. Call ahead to check for possible openings other nights.

BRATTLEBORO

Deeply set in a scenic river valley, the commercial town of Brattleboro not only is a good spot for provisioning, but also has a funky, slightly dated charm that's part 19th century, part 1960s. The rough brick texture of this compact, hilly city has aged nicely, its flavor only enhanced since it was adopted by "feral hippies" (as a friend calls them), who live in and around town and operate many of the best local enterprises.

While Brattleboro is very much part of the 20th century, its heritage runs much deeper. In fact, Brattleboro was Vermont's first permanent settlement. (The first actual settlement, which was short-lived, was at Isle La Motte on Lake Champlain in 1666.) Soldiers protecting the Massachusetts town of Northfield built an outpost here in 1724 at Fort Dummer, about 1½ miles (2.4km) south of the current downtown. The site of the fort is now a small state park with a campground. In later years, Brattleboro became a center of trade and manufacturing, and was the home of the Estey Organ Co., which once supplied countless home organs carved in ornate Victorian style to families across the nation.

Brattleboro is the commercial hub of southeastern Vermont, located at the junction of I-89, Routes 5 and 9, and the Connecticut River. It's also the most convenient jumping-off point for those arriving from the south via the interstate. If you're looking for supplies, a strip-mall area with grocery and department stores is just north of town along Route 5. For more interesting shopping, take the time to explore downtown.

Brattleboro has long seemed immune from the vexations of modern life, but one modern inconvenience has made a belated appearance: traffic jams. Lower Main Street (near the bridge from New Hampshire) can back up heading into town, leading to honking horns and frustration. It's the source of considerable local grousing.

ESSENTIALS

GETTING THERE   From the north or south, Brattleboro is easily accessible by car via Exits 1 and 2 on I-91. From the east or west, Brattleboro is best reached via Route 9. Brattleboro is also a stop on the **Amtrak** (✆ **800/872-7245;** www.amtrak.com) line from Boston to northern Vermont.

VISITOR INFORMATION   The **Brattleboro Chamber of Commerce,** 180 Main St. (✆ **802/254-4565;** www. brattleboro.com), dispenses information Monday through Friday between 8:30am and 5pm.

EXPLORING THE TOWN

Here's a simple, straightforward strategy for exploring Brattleboro: Park. Walk.

The vibrant downtown is blessedly compact, and strolling around is the best way to appreciate its human scale and handsome commercial architecture. It's a town of cafes, bookstores, antiques dealers, and outdoor-recreation shops, and it invites browsing. One stop of note is **Sam's Outdoor Outfitters,** 74 Main St. (© **802/254-2933**), which is filled to the eaves with camping and fishing gear.

Enjoyable for kids and curious adults is the **Brattleboro Museum & Art Center,** Union Railroad Station, near the bridge to New Hampshire (© **802/257-0124;** www.brattleboromuseum.org). Wonderful exhibits highlight the history of the town and the Connecticut River Valley. It's open from mid-May to October, Tuesday through Sunday from noon to 6pm. Admission is $3 for adults, $2 for seniors and students, and free for children under 18.

About 1½ miles (2.4km) outside of town on Route 30 is **Tom and Sally's Handmade Chocolates,** 485 West River Rd. (© **802/254-4200**), a boutique chocolate shop with delicious handmade confections. Of note is the chocolate body-paint kit, which comes complete with two brushes.

OUTDOOR PURSUITS

A soaring aerial view of Brattleboro can be found atop **Wantastiquet Mountain,** which is just across the Connecticut River in New Hampshire (figure on a round-trip of about 3 hr.). To reach the base of the "mountain" (a term that's just slightly grandiose), cross the river on the two green steel bridges, then turn left on the first dirt road; go 0.2 miles (0.3km) to a parking area on your right. The trail begins here via a carriage road (stick to the main trail and avoid the side trails) that winds about 2 miles (3km) through forest and past open ledges to the summit, which is marked by a monument dating from 1908. From here, you'll be rewarded with sweeping views of the river, the town, and the landscape beyond.

Vermont Canoe Touring Center, at the intersection of Route 5 and the West River north of town (© **802/257-5008**), is a fine spot to rent a canoe or kayak for a couple of hours ($10 for two people). Explore locally, or arrange for a shuttle upriver or down. Among the best spots, especially for birders, are the marshy areas along the lower West River and a detour off the Connecticut River locally called "the Everglades." Get a lunch to go at the Brattleboro Food Co-op (see "Where to Dine," below) and make a day of it.

Bike rentals and advice are available at the **Brattleboro Bicycle Shop,** 165 Main St. (© **800/272-8245** or 802/254-8644; www.bratbike.com). Hybrid bikes ideal for exploring area back roads can be rented by the day ($20) or week ($100).

WHERE TO STAY

Several chain motels flank Route 5 north of Brattleboro. The top choice is **Quality Inn & Suites,** 1380 Putney Rd. (© **800/228-5151** or 802/254-8701; www.qualityinnbrattleboro.com), with a restaurant and indoor/outdoor pools.

Chesterfield Inn ⋆⋆ Located a 10-minute drive east of Brattleboro in New Hampshire, this attractive inn sits in a field just off a busy state highway, but inside it's more quiet and refined than you'd imagine. The original farmhouse dates back to the 1780s, but has been expanded and modernized and today has a casual contemporary sensibility with antique accents. Nine guest rooms are located in the main inn, with an additional six in cottages nearby. All are spacious and comfortably appointed. Eight have wood-burning fireplaces, while two have gas fireplaces. The priciest units feature fireplaces, double Jacuzzis, and private decks.

Rte. 9, Chesterfield, NH 03443. © **800/365-5515** or 603/256-3211. Fax 603/256-6131. www.chesterfield inn.com. 15 units. $110–$275 double. 2-night minimum stay foliage and holidays. AE, DC, DISC, MC, V. Pets allowed with advance permission. **Amenities:** Restaurant (New American); babysitting. *In room:* A/C, TV, dataport, minibar, coffeemaker, hair dryer, iron.

Colonial Motel & Spa *Value* Operated by the same family since 1975, this sprawling compound is well maintained and offers the town's best value. Opt for the back building's slightly larger and quieter rooms. The motel's best feature is the 75-foot (23m) indoor lap pool in the freestanding spa building.

Putney Rd., Brattleboro, VT 05301. ℂ **800/239-0032** or 802/257-7733. www.colonialmotelspa.com. 73 units. $65–$85 double; $120 suite. Rates include continental breakfast Mon–Fri. AE, DISC, MC, V. Take Exit 3 off I-91; turn right and proceed half a mile (0.8km). **Amenities:** Restaurant (Italian); indoor lap pool; limited fitness equipment; Jacuzzi; sauna. *In room:* A/C, TV.

40 Putney Road *★★* Built in the early 1930s, this compact French château–style home features guest rooms that are attractively appointed with a mix of modern country furnishings and reproductions. Two units have gas fireplaces. The cottage suite, with a sofa bed in the living room, is popular with families and pairs of couples traveling together. You can stroll to town within a few minutes, but the inn is situated along a busy road, diminishing the pastoral qualities somewhat.

40 Putney Rd., Brattleboro, VT 05301. ℂ **800/941-2413** or 802/254-6268. Fax 802/258-2673. www. putney.net/40putneyrd. 5 units. High season $125–$230 double; off-season $100–$175 double. Rates include breakfast. AE, DISC, MC, V. Pets allowed with advance permission. **Amenities:** Pub. *In room:* A/C, TV/VCR, dataport, fridge, hair dryer, iron.

Latchis Hotel *★* This downtown hotel fairly leaps out in Victorian-brick Brattleboro. Built in 1938 in an understated Art Deco style, the Latchis was once the cornerstone for a small chain of hotels and theaters. It no longer has its own orchestra or commanding dining room (although the theater remains), but it still has an authentic if funky and somewhat outdated flair. For the most part, the guest rooms are compact and comfortable, but not luxurious. Most of the rooms have limited views of the river, but those come with the sounds of cars on Main Street. If you want quiet, sacrifice the view and ask for a room in back. From the hotel, it's easy to explore town on foot, or you can wander the first-floor hallways to take in a first-run movie at the historic Latchis Theatre or quaff a fresh pint at the Windham Brewery.

50 Main St., Brattleboro, VT 05301. ℂ **802/254-6300.** Fax 802/254-6304. www.brattleboro.com/latchis. 30 units. $75–$155 double. AE, MC, V. **Amenities:** Restaurant (eclectic/brewpub); movie theater. *In room:* A/C, TV, fridge, coffeemaker.

WHERE TO DINE

Brattleboro Food Co-op DELI The Co-op has been selling wholesome foods since 1975, and its location, downtown near the New Hampshire bridge (with plenty of parking) features a deli counter and seating area. The emphasis is on natural foods, although it's not all tofu and sprouts—you can get a smoked turkey and Swiss cheese sandwich, or opt for a crispy salad. Check out the eclectic wine selection and the award-winning Vermont Shepherd cheeses, made nearby in Putney.

Brookside Plaza, 2 Main St. ℂ **802/257-0236.** Sandwiches $3.50–$6; prepared foods around $4–$5 per pound. Mon–Sat 9am–9pm; Sun 9am–8pm.

The Common Ground VEGETARIAN The Common Ground opened 2 years after the Woodstock music festival, which establishes it both chronologically and spiritually. This culinary landmark occupies a funky, sometimes chaotic space on the second floor of a downtown building. A meal might include grilled tofu with tahini, brown rice with tamari ginger sauce, or a marinated sea-vegetable salad. The Common Ground has long been a worker-owned cooperative and has been suffering some upheaval and wrenching shifts in management, but as press time it looked as if it had turned the corner and might finally get its act together. Still, call ahead to make sure it's open, or arrive with a backup plan.

25 Elliot St., #2 ✆ **802/257-0855.** Reservations not accepted. Lunch $3–$7.50; dinner $3.50–$8. No credit cards. Summer Mon–Thurs 11:30am–8pm, Fri–Sat 11:30am–9pm, Sun 11am–2pm and 5–9pm; rest of year Thurs–Sat 5–9pm, Sun 11am–2pm and 5–9pm, Mon 11am–9pm.

Lucca Bistro & Brasserie ⭐ BISTRO   The Lucca Bistro, beneath the Latchis Theatre and Latchis Hotel, is a comfortable, urbane space featuring informal French and Italian cuisine. Sample the excellent ales, stouts, and lagers made on site by the Windham Brewery, or go a bit more cosmopolitan with the oyster and martini bar near the entrance. The menu includes country French dishes like a rustic paté, onion soup au gratin, and escargot. There's also a meaty "bistro burger" for those disinclined to travel abroad.

6 Flat St. ✆ **802/254-4747.** Reservations suggested. Pastas $5–$8.95; bistro menu $9–$26. AE, DISC, MC, V. Wed–Mon 5:30–10pm; Sat–Sun 11:30am–3:30pm.

Peter Havens Restaurant ⭐⭐ REGIONAL/AMERICAN   Chef-owned Peter Havens has been serving up consistently reliable fare since it opened in 1989. Situated downtown in a pleasantly contemporary building, Peter Havens may not bowl you over with its menu, but you will be impressed by what you're served. You're likely to feel instantly at home in this friendly spot, which has just 10 tables. Meals are prepared with choice ingredients and are served with panache. Seafood is the specialty, with such offerings as salmon with a chipotle pepper rémoulade.

32 Elliot St. ✆ **802/257-3333.** Reservations strongly recommended. Main courses $19–$24. MC, V. Tues–Sat 6–9pm.

T. J. Buckley's ⭐⭐⭐ NEW AMERICAN   This is Brattleboro's best restaurant, and one of the better choices in all of Vermont. The lilliputian T. J. Buckley's is housed in a classic old diner on a dim side street. Renovations like slate floors and golden lighting have created an intimate spot that seats about 20. The menu is limited, with just four entrees each night—beef, poultry, shellfish, and fish—but the food has absolutely nothing in common with simple diner fare. The ingredients are fresh and select, the preparation more concerned with melding flavors than dazzling with architectural flourishes. If you want to sample chef Michael Fuller's inventiveness, we'd recommend the fish or shellfish. Vegetarians can request a veggie platter.

132 Elliot St. ✆ **802/257-4922.** Reservations usually essential. Main courses $25–$32. No credit cards. Winter Thurs–Sun 6–9pm; rest of year Wed–Sun 6–9pm (sometimes later on busy nights).

NEWFANE ⭐⭐⭐ & TOWNSHEND

These two villages, about 5 miles (8km) apart on Route 30, are the picture-perfect epitome of Vermont. Both are set deeply within the serpentine West River Valley, and both are built around open town greens. Both towns consist of impressive white-clapboard houses and public buildings that share the grace and scale of the surrounding homes. Both boast striking examples of Early American architecture, notably Greek Revival.

Don't bother looking for strip malls, McDonald's, or garish video outlets hereabouts. Newfane and Townshend feel as if they've been idling on a sidetrack for decades while the rest of American society steamed blithely ahead. But these villages certainly don't have the somber feel of a mausoleum. On one visit during a breezy autumn afternoon, a swarm of teenagers skateboarded off the steps of the courthouse in Newfane, and a lively basketball game was underway at the edge of the green in Townshend. There's life here.

(Fun Fact **Recent History**

That handsome gazebo on the village green in Townshend? It looks like it's been here forever, but it actually dates back only to 1988, when the Chevy Chase movie *Funny Farm* was filmed here. A production crew built it for the movie, but the townspeople liked it well enough to keep it.

For visitors, inactivity is often the activity of choice. Guests find an inn or lodge that suits their temperament, then spend the days strolling the towns, driving the back roads, soaking in a mountain stream, hunting for antiques, or striking off on foot for one of the rounded, wooded peaks that overlook villages and valleys.

ESSENTIALS
GETTING THERE Newfane and Townshend are located on Route 30 northwest of Brattleboro. The nearest interstate access is off Exit 3 from I-91.

VISITOR INFORMATION There's no formal information center serving these towns. Brochures are available at the **state visitor center** (© **802/254-4593**) on I-91 in Guilford, south of Brattleboro.

EXPLORING THE AREA
Newfane was originally founded on a hill a few miles from the current village in 1774; in 1825, it was moved to its present location on a valley floor. Some of the original buildings were dismantled and rebuilt, but most date from the early to mid–19th century. The **National Historic District** ★★ comprises some 60 buildings around the green and on nearby side streets. You'll find styles ranging from Federal to Colonial Revival, although Greek Revival appears to carry the day. A strikingly handsome courthouse—where cases are still heard, as they have been for nearly 2 centuries—dominates the shady green. This structure was originally built in 1825. For more information on area buildings, get a copy of the free walking-tour brochure at the Moore Free Library on West Street or at the Historical Society, below.

Newfane's history is explored at the engaging **Historical Society of Windham County** ★, on Route 30 across from the village common, in a handsome 1930s Colonial Revival brick building. There's an eclectic assemblage of local artifacts (dolls, melodeons, rail ephemera), along with changing exhibits that feature intriguing snippets of local history. It's open from late May to mid-October, Wednesday through Sunday from noon to 5pm; admission is by donation.

More than two dozen **antiques shops** are located on or near Route 30 in the West River Valley. They provide good grazing on lazy afternoons, and are a fine resource for serious collectors. At any of the shops, look for the brochure *Antiquing in the West River Valley*, which provides a good overview. Among the options: the **Riverdale Antiques Center** ★ (© **802/365-4616**), with about 65 dealers selling some country furniture but mostly smaller collectibles, and **Schommer Antiques** ★★, on Route 30 in Newfane Village (© **802/365-7777**), which carries a good selection of 19th-century furniture and accessories in a shop that's listed on the National Register of Historic Places.

Treasure hunters should time their visit to hit the **Newfane Flea Market** ★ (© **802/365-4000**), which features 100-plus tables of assorted stuff, including much of the 12-tube-socks-for-8-bucks variety. The flea market is held on Sundays from May to October on Route 30 just north of Newfane Village.

On Route 30 between Townshend and Jamaica, you'll pass the **Scott Covered Bridge** below the Townshend Dam (closed to car traffic). It dates from 1870, and is an example of a Towne lattice-style bridge, with an added arch. At 166 feet (50m) long, it has the distinction of being the longest single-span bridge in the state.

WHERE TO STAY & DINE

Four Columns Inn   You can't help but notice the Four Columns Inn in Newfane: It's the regal white-clapboard building with four Ionic columns just off the green. This perfect village setting hides an appealing inn within. Rooms in the Main House and Garden Wing are larger (and more expensive) than those above the restaurant. Four units have been made over as luxury suites. The best choice in the house is room 12, with a Jacuzzi, skylight, gas fireplace, and private deck with a view of a small pond. Low beams and white damask table-cloths characterize the inn's well-regarded dining room, which features creative New American cooking.

West St. (P.O. Box 278), Newfane, VT 05345. ℂ **800/787-6633** or 802/365-7713. Fax 802/365-0022. www.fourcolumnsinn.com. 15 units. Weekends $135–$290; weekdays $115–$230. Rates include continental breakfast. AE, DISC, MC, V. Pets accepted with prior permission ($10 per night). **Amenities:** Restaurant (New American); outdoor pool; babysitting; hiking trails on 150 acres (61 hectares). *In room:* A/C, hair dryer.

Three Mountain Inn   The lovely Three Mountain Inn is located in the middle of the appealing village of Jamaica, housed in a historic white-clapboard home. It's benefited from a major upgrading under ambitious innkeepers, who are refurbishing the rooms one by one in a restrained country style. Accommodations range from the cozy and basic to the outright sumptuous, with Jacuzzis, gas fireplaces, and TV/VCRs. The inn is well located as a base for exploring southern Vermont; in winter, skiing at Stratton is a short drive away. Guests can walk from the inn to Jamaica State Park, where there's an easy hike along the river on an old rail bed.

Rte. 30 (P.O. Box 180), Jamaica, VT 05343. ℂ **800/532-9399** or 802/874-4140. Fax 802/874-4745. www.threemountaininn.com. 15 units. $125–$235 double, $275 cottage; foliage and holidays $145–$255 double, $295 cottage. Rates include breakfast. AE, MC, V. Children over 12 welcome. Pets allowed with restrictions (call first). **Amenities:** Restaurant (New American). *In room:* A/C, dataport, hair dryer.

Windham Hill Inn   The Windham Hill Inn is about as good as it gets, especially if you're in search of a romantic getaway. Situated on 160 acres (65 hectares) at the end of a dirt road in a high upland valley, the inn was originally built in 1823 as a farmhouse and remained in the same family until the 1950s, when it was converted to an inn. The Windham Hill today melds the best of the old and the new. The guest rooms are wonderfully appointed in an elegant country style; six have Jacuzzis or soaking tubs, nine have balconies or decks, 13 have gas fireplaces, and all have views. Especially nice are the Jesse Lawrence Room, with a soaking tub and gas woodstove, and Forget-Me-Not, with a soaking tub and four-poster bed. The excellent dining room features creative cooking with a strong emphasis on local ingredients.

Windham Hill Rd., West Townshend, VT 05359. ℂ **800/944-4080** or 802/874-4080. Fax 802/874-4702. www.windhamhill.com. 21 units. $185–$355 double; foliage season $250–$375 double. Rates include breakfast. 2- to 3-night minimum stay on weekends and some holidays. AE, DISC, MC, V. Closed the week prior to Dec 27. Children over 12 welcome. Turn uphill across from the country store in West Townshend and climb 1¼ (2km) miles to a marked dirt road; turn right and continue to end. **Amenities:** Restaurant (New American); heated pool; tennis court; game alcove; 6 miles (10km) of groomed cross-country ski trails. *In room:* A/C, hair dryer, iron.

GRAFTON ✦✦✦ & CHESTER ✦

One of Vermont's most scenic villages, Grafton was founded in 1763 and soon grew into a thriving settlement. By 1850, the town was home to some 10,000 sheep, and boasted a handsome hotel that provided shelter for guests on the stage between Boston and Montréal. A cheese cooperative was organized in 1890, and the soapstone industry flourished. But as agriculture and commerce shifted west and to the cities, Grafton became a mere shadow of a town—by the Depression, many of the buildings were derelict; for 3 decades afterwards, much of the town could be purchased for a song.

In 1963, Hall and Dean Mathey of New Jersey created the Windham Foundation. A wealthy relative who had recently died entrusted these two brothers to come up with a worthy cause for her fortune. It took a few years, but they eventually hit on Grafton, where their family had summered, and began purchasing and restoring the dilapidated center of town, including the old hotel. The foundation eventually came to own some 55 buildings and 2,000 acres (810 hectares) around the town—even the cheese cooperative was revived. Within time the village again came to life, although it's now teeming with history buffs and tourists rather than farmers and merchants.

To the north, more commercial Chester is less pristine and more lived in. The downtown area has a pleasant neighborly feel; there's also a handful of boutiques and shops along the main road. Chester is a great destination for antiquing, with several good dealers in the area. When heading north of town on Route 103, be sure to slow through the Stone Village, a neighborhood of austere stone homes. Many of these are rumored to have been stopping points on the Underground Railroad.

ESSENTIALS

GETTING THERE   Take I-91 to Bellows Falls (Exit 5 or 6), and follow signs to town via Route 5. From here, take Route 121 west for 12 miles (19km) to Grafton. For a more scenic route, take Route 35 north from Townshend.

VISITOR INFORMATION   The **Grafton Information Center** (© 802/843-2255) is located in the Daniels House on Townshend Road, behind the Grafton Inn. For information on Chester, call the **Chester Area Chamber of Commerce** (© 802/875-2939).

EXPLORING GRAFTON

Grafton is best seen at a languorous pace, on foot, when the weather is welcoming. A picnic is a good idea, especially if it involves the excellent local cheddar. There are no imposing historic homes open for tours; it's more a village to be enjoyed with aimless walks outdoors. Don't expect to be overwhelmed by grandeur. Instead, keep a keen eye out for telling historical details.

Start at the **Grafton Village Cheese Co.** (© 800/472-3866), where you can buy a snack of award-winning cheese and peer through plate-glass windows to observe the cheese-making process. It's open Monday through Friday from 8am to 4pm, Saturday and Sunday from 10am to 4pm.

From here, follow the trail over the nearby covered bridge, and then bear right on the footpath along the cow pasture to the **Kidder Covered Bridge.** Head into town via Water Street, continuing on to Main Street. Toward the village center, white-clapboard homes and shade trees abound. This is about as New England as New England gets.

On Main Street, stop by the **Grafton Historical Society Museum** (© 802/ 843-2584; open weekends only) to peruse photographs, artifacts, and memorabilia of Grafton. Afterwards, take a look at the **Old Tavern at Grafton,** the impressive building that anchors the town and has served as a social center since 1801, and partake of a beverage at its rustic lounge (see "Where to Stay & Dine," below). From here, you can make your way back to the cheese company by wandering on pleasant side streets. To see Grafton from a different perspective, inquire at the inn about horse-and-buggy rides.

More active travelers should head for the **Grafton Ponds Nordic Ski and Mountain Bike Center** (© 802/843-2400), just south of the cheese factory on Route 35. Managed by the Old Tavern, Grafton Ponds offers bike rentals and access to a hillside trails system summer and fall. Come winter, it grooms 18 miles (29km) of trails and maintains a warming hut near the ponds, where you can sit by a woodstove and enjoy a steaming bowl of soup. The Big Bear loop runs high up the flanks of a hill and is especially appealing; travel counterclockwise so that you can walk up the steep hill and enjoy the rolling descent. Ski and snowshoe rentals are available; a trail pass costs $15 for adults, $10 for seniors and students, and $5 for children 7 to 12.

WHERE TO STAY & DINE

Fullerton Inn ⭐   The Fullerton Inn is more of a hotel than a country inn, located in a tall building (well, relatively speaking) smack in the middle of Chester's one-street downtown. The lobby has the feel of an informal old roadhouse, but with its polished maple floors, handsome fieldstone fireplace, and piano, it's a welcoming spot. The eclectically furnished guest rooms vary in size and decor, although most have small bathrooms. There's little soundproofing, so noises from neighbors can carry. Room 17 is quiet and faces the rear of the property. For the more socially inclined, rooms 8 and 10 have doors onto a balcony that overlooks the street.

40 Common (P.O. Box 589), Chester, VT 05143. © 802/875-2444. Fax 802/875-6414. www.fullertoninn. com. 21 units. $99–$149 double. Rates include continental breakfast. 2-night minimum stay foliage and holiday weekends. AE, DISC, MC, V. Children over 12 welcome. **Amenities:** Restaurant (traditional New England). *In room:* No phone.

Hugging Bear Inn ⭐ *Kids*   Young kids love this place. It's a turreted, Queen Anne–style home on Chester's Main Street that's filled with teddy bears: There's a 5-foot (1.5m) teddy in the living room and some 250 of them scattered about the inn. And in the attached barn are another *10,000* bears for sale at the Hugging Bear Shoppe, which attracts serious collectors from around the world. The guest rooms are themed around—no surprise—teddy bears. Expect bear sheets, bear shower curtains, and more. Pandamonium has a panda theme, while the Winnie the Pooh Room is all Pooh, all the time.

244 Main St., Chester, VT 05143. © 800/325-0519 or 802/875-2412. Fax 802/875-3823. www.hugging bear.com. 6 units. $90–$135 double. Rates include breakfast. AE, DISC, MC, V. *In room:* A/C, no phone.

Old Tavern at Grafton ⭐⭐   This beautiful historic inn seems much more intimate than its 63 guest rooms would suggest, because the rooms are spread throughout the town. Fourteen rooms are in the handsome colonnaded main inn, which dates from 1801, while another 22 are across the street in the Homestead Cottage. The remaining units are scattered among seven historic guesthouses in and around the village. All are decorated with antiques and an upscale-country sensibility; the rooms in the Homestead Cottage (which is actually two historic homes joined together) have a more modern, hotel-like character (if you want more history, ask for the main inn).

Rtes. 35 and 121, Grafton, VT 05146. ℭ **800/843-1801** or 802/843-2231. Fax 802/843-2245. www.old-tavern.com. 63 units. Weekends $185–$270 double; weekdays $135–$195 double; suites to $390. Rates include breakfast. 2- to 3-night minimum stay on winter weekends, on some holidays, and in foliage season. MC, V. Closed Apr. **Amenities:** Restaurant (contemporary New England), pub; sand-bottomed swimming pond; tennis court; platform tennis; Jacuzzi; bike rental; game room; coin-op washers and dryers; cross-country skiing. *In room:* No phone.

LUDLOW ⚸ & OKEMO

Centered around a former mill that produced fabrics and, later, aircraft parts, Ludlow has an unpretentious made-in-mill-town-Vermont character that seems quite distant from the prim grace of white-clapboard Grafton. Low-key and unassuming, it draws skiers by the busload to Okemo Mountain, a once-sleepy ski resort that's come to life in recent years. Ludlow is also notable as one of the few ski towns in New England that didn't go through an unfortunate Tyrolean identity crisis. It lacks splashy nightlife and fancy restaurants, and longtime visitors like it that way.

ESSENTIALS

GETTING THERE Ludlow is situated at the intersection of Routes 193 and 100. The most direct route from an interstate is Exit 6 off I-91; follow Route 103 west to Ludlow. **Vermont Transit** (ℭ **800/451-3292**) offers bus service to Ludlow.

VISITOR INFORMATION The **Ludlow Area Chamber of Commerce** (ℭ **802/228-5830;** www.vacationinvermont.com) staffs an information booth at the Okemo Marketplace, at the foot of Mountain Road. It's usually open Tuesday through Sunday from 10am to 4pm, with some seasonal variation.

ALPINE SKIING

Okemo ⚸⚸ Okemo fans like to point out a couple of things. First, this is one of the few family-owned mountains remaining in Vermont. Second, it features more varied and challenging terrain, yet doesn't attract as many yahoos as does Killington to the north. As such, it's first and foremost a mountain for families, who like the welcoming slopes and the friendly, unintimidating base area. Well-maintained half-pipes with music are popular with younger snowboarders. Okemo has plans to expand its slopes to adjacent Jackson Gore Peak, a move that will also include new base development. Families should note that the mountain offers three levels of ticket prices, with discounts for young adults and juniors.

Ludlow, VT 05149. ℭ **800/786-5366** for lodging or 802/228-4041. www.okemo.com. Vertical drop: 2,150 ft. (645m). Lifts: 10 chairlifts (3 high-speed), 4 surface lifts. Skiable acreage: 520. Lift tickets: $59 Sat–Sun, $54 Mon–Fri.

WHERE TO STAY

During ski season, contact the **Okemo Mountain Lodging Service** (ℭ **800/786-5366** or 802/228-5571) for reservations in slopeside condos. More information is available at www.okemo.com.

The Governor's Inn ⚸ This regal village home was built in 1890 by Vermont governor William W. Stickney and is the picture of Victorian elegance. The lobby and common room are richly hued with time-worn hardwood. Guest rooms vary in size (some are quite small), but all are comfortably appointed with antiques; three have gas fireplaces. Dinner in the cozy dining rooms is served weekends only by reservation (dates may expand beyond weekends; call first). The fixed-price meal is $45 for inn guests.

86 Main St., Ludlow, VT 05149. 📞 800/468-3766 or 802/228-8830. Fax 802/228-2961. www.the governorsinn.com. 9 units. $105–$225 double; $230–$315 suite. Rates include breakfast. AE, DISC, MC, V. Children over 12 welcome. *In room:* Hair dryer, no phone (except in suite).

The Inn at Water's Edge ⍟ Located a 10-minute drive north of Okemo Mountain, this 150-year-old house on the banks of the Black River, just off Route 100, has been thoroughly updated in a florid Victorian style. The innkeepers have focused on making this a destination for romantic getaways. The attached barn features a lounge and bar perfect for relaxing, with an oak pool table, a chess set, leather couches, a TV, and a mahogany bar imported from England. The guest rooms in the barn over the bar tend toward the cozy and dark. Room 11, upstairs in the main house, would be our choice—it's bright and appealingly furnished, with corner windows and wood floors. The dining room serves four-course meals nightly.

45 Kingdom Rd., Ludlow, VT 05149. 📞 888/706/9736 or 802/228-8143. Fax 802/228-8443. www.innat watersedge.com. 11 units. $200–$275 double. Rates include breakfast and dinner. AE, MC, V. Children over 12 welcome. **Amenities:** Canoes; free bikes. *In room:* A/C, no phone.

WHERE TO DINE

See also the **Governor's Inn,** described above.

Harry's Cafe ⍟ ECLECTIC Along a dark stretch of road north of Ludlow, you'll pass a brightly lit roadside cafe with a red neon "Harry's" over the door. It may look like a hamburger joint, but it's not. Rather, it's an appealing family restaurant with a menu that spans the globe. Entrees are a veritable culinary United Nations, with New York sirloin, jerk pork, spicy Thai curry, and fish-and-chips. Your best bet is the Thai fare, the house specialty. On the downside, the restaurant's interior is more blandly efficient than cozy, and service can bog down on busy nights.

Rte. 103 (5 miles/8km north of Ludlow), Mount Holly. 📞 802/259-2996. Reservations recommended in winter. Main courses $10.95–$16.95. AE, MC, V. Daily 5–10pm.

Nikki's ⍟ NEW ENGLAND Nikki's is the best choice in town for a pleasant if not overly creative dinner. It's a friendly local spot that's been serving up tasty meals since 1976, and is divided between an older section with a crackling fireplace and a new addition that's bright and modern. Think of the fare as updated comfort food, with familiar favorites like grilled swordfish and Black Angus steak. The wine selection is several notches above the usual ski-resort fare; the restaurant has won an award of excellence from *Wine Spectator* magazine.

Rte. 103, Ludlow. 📞 802/228-7797. www.nikkisrestaurant.com. Reservations not accepted. Main courses $12.95–$28.95 (most under $20). AE, DC, MC, V. Spring and summer daily 5:30–9:30pm; fall and winter daily 5–9pm (Fri–Sat until 10pm). Closed mid-Apr to late June and early Nov.

3 Woodstock ⍟⍟⍟

For more than a century, the resort community of Woodstock has been considered one of New England's most exquisite villages. Even the surrounding countryside is by and large unsullied—you simply can't drive to Woodstock on a route that *isn't* pastoral and scenic. The downtown is compact and neat, populated largely by galleries and boutiques. The village green is surrounded by handsome homes, creating what amounts to a comprehensive review of architectural styles of the 19th and early 20th centuries.

Woodstock, which sits on the banks of the gentle Ottaquechee River, was first settled in 1765, rose to some prominence as a publishing center in the mid–19th century (no fewer than five newspapers were published here in 1830), and began to attract wealthy families who summered here in the late 19th century. To this day, Woodstock feels as if it should have a prestigious prep school just off the green, and it comes as some surprise that it doesn't. A Vermont senator in the late 19th century noted that "the good people of Woodstock have less incentive than others to yearn for heaven," and that still applies today.

Much of the town is on the National Register of Historic Places, and the Rockefeller family has deeded 500 acres (203 hectares) surrounding Mount Tom to the National Park Service. In fact, locals sometimes joke that downtown Woodstock itself could be renamed Rockefeller National Park, given the attention and cash the Rockefeller family have lavished on the town in the interest of preservation.

Other wealthy summer rusticators were also instrumental in preserving the character of the village, and today the very wealthy have turned their attention to the handsome farms outside town. Few of these former dairy farms still produce milk; barns that haven't been converted into architectural showcase homes more than likely house valuable collections of cars or antiques.

Woodstock is also notable as a historic center of winter recreation. The nation's first ski tow (a rope tow powered by an old Buick motor) was built in 1933 at the Woodstock Ski Hill near today's Suicide Six ski area. While no longer the skiing center of Vermont, Woodstock remains a worthy destination for skating, cross-country skiing, and snowshoeing.

One caveat: Woodstock's excellent state of preservation hasn't gone unnoticed, and it draws hordes of travelers. During foliage season, the town green is perpetually obscured by tour buses slowly circling around it.

ESSENTIALS

GETTING THERE   Woodstock is 13 miles (21km) west of White River Junction on Route 4 (take Exit 1 off I-89). From the west, Woodstock is 20 miles (32km) east of Killington on Route 4. **Vermont Transit** (© **800/451-3292**) offers bus service from Boston and Burlington.

VISITOR INFORMATION   The **Woodstock Area Chamber of Commerce,** 18 Central St. (© **888/496-6378** or 802/457-3555; www.woodstockvt.com), staffs an information booth on the green, open June through October daily from 9:30am to 5:30pm.

EXPLORING THE AREA

The heart of the town is the shady, elliptical green. The famous Admiral George Dewey spent his later years in Woodstock, and local folks may explain very convincingly that the green was laid out in the shape of Dewey's flagship. This is such a fine and believable explanation for the odd, cigar-shaped green that it causes us no small amount of distress to note that the green was in place by 1830, or 7 years before Dewey was born.

To put local history in perspective, stop by the **Woodstock Historical Society** 😿, 26 Elm St. (© **802/457-1822**). Housed in the beautiful 1807 Charles Dana House, it has rooms furnished in Federal, Empire, and Victorian styles. It's open late May through October, plus weekends in December. Hours are Monday through Saturday from 10am to 5pm and Sunday from noon to 4pm. Admission is $2.

Billings Farm and Museum ★★★   This remarkable working farm offers a glimpse of a grander era, as well as an introduction to the oddly interesting history of scientific farming. This extraordinary spot was the creation of Frederick Billings, who is credited with completing the Northern Pacific Railroad. (Billings, Montana, is named after him.) The 19th-century dairy farm was once renowned for its scientific breeding of Jersey cows and its fine architecture, especially the gabled 1890 Victorian farmhouse. A tour includes hands-on demonstrations of farm activities, exhibits of farm life, a look at an heirloom kitchen garden, and a visit to active milking barns.

Elm St., about ½ a mile (0.8km) north of town on Rte. 12. © 802/457-2355. www.billingsfarm.org. Admission $8 adults, $7 seniors, $6 children 13–17, $4 children 5–12, $1 children 3–4. May–Oct daily 10am–5pm.

Marsh-Billings-Rockefeller National Historic Park ★★   The Billings Farm and the National Park Service have teamed up to manage the new Marsh-Billings-Rockefeller National Historic Park, the first and only national park focusing on the history of conservation. You'll learn about the life of George Perkins Marsh, the author of *Man and Nature* (1864), which is considered one of the first and most influential books in the history of the environmental movement. You'll also learn how Woodstock native and rail tycoon Frederick Billings, who read *Man and Nature,* eventually returned and purchased Marsh's boyhood farm, putting into practice many of the principles of good stewardship that Marsh espoused. The property was subsequently purchased by Mary and Laurance Rockefeller, who in 1982 established the nonprofit farm; a decade later they donated more than 500 acres (203 hectares) of forest land and their mansion, filled with exceptional 19th-century landscape art, to the National Park Service. Visitors can tour the elaborate Victorian mansion, walk the carriage roads surrounding Mount Tom, and view one of the oldest professionally managed woodlands in the nation.

P.O. Box 178, Woodstock. © 802/457-3368. www.nps.gov/mabi. Free admission to grounds; mansion tours $6 adults, $3 children 16 and under. Advance reservations recommended for mansion tours. Late May–Oct daily 10am–5pm.

NEARBY SIGHTS

Birders will enjoy a trip to the **Vermont Raptor Center** ★ (© 802/457-2779), home to 25 species of birds of prey that have been injured and can no longer survive in the wild. The winged residents typically include bald eagles, great horned owls, peregrine falcons, and an array of hawks. The birds are located outside in spacious cages along a horseshoe-shaped walkway set on a hillside. (*Tip:* Start at the top and work down.) Other attractions include an herbarium and trails in the Bragdon Nature Preserve. The institute is located 1½ miles (2.4km) southwest of the village on Church Hill Road. (Look for the turn at the west end of the green.) May through October, it's open Monday through Saturday from 9am to 5pm; November through April, Monday through Saturday from 10am to 4pm. Admission is $7 for adults, $4 for youths 12 to 18, and $3 for children 5 to 11.

About 5 miles (8km) east of Woodstock is the riverside village **Quechee** ★★. This picturesque town still revolves spiritually and economically around the restored brick mill building along the falls. **Simon Pearce Glass** ★★ (© 802/295-2711) makes exceptionally fine glassware and pottery from the former Downer's Mill, a historic structure that now houses a glassmaking operation, store, and well-regarded restaurant (p. 455). Visitors can watch glass blowing on weekdays and summer weekends. Hours are daily from 9am to 9pm.

⌒Overrated Quechee Gorge

Five miles (8km) east of town, Route 4 crosses Quechee Gorge, a venerable if somewhat disappointing tourist attraction. The sheer power of the glacial runoff that carved the gorge some 13,000 years ago must have been dramatic, but the 165-foot (50m) gorge isn't all that impressive today. More impressive is its engineering history: The chasm was first spanned in 1875 by a wooden rail trestle. The current steel bridge was constructed in 1911 for the railroad, but the tracks were torn up in 1933 and replaced by Route 4.

The best view of the bridge is from the bottom of the gorge, which is accessible by a well-graded gravel path that descends south from the parking area on the gorge's east rim. The round-trip requires no more than half an hour. If the day is warm enough, you might also follow the path northward, then descend to the river to splash around in the rocky swimming hole near the spillway.

OUTDOOR PURSUITS

Outdoor activities in the Woodstock area aren't as rugged as those you'll find in the Green Mountains to the west, but they'll easily occupy travelers for an afternoon or two.

BIKING The hilly terrain around Woodstock is ideal for exploring by road bike for those in reasonably good shape. Few roads don't lead to great rides; just grab a map and go. Mountain bikes are available for rent ($20 per day) at **Woodstock Sports,** 30 Central St. (© 802/457-1568).

HIKING **Mount Tom** is the prominent hill overlooking Woodstock, and its low summit has great views over the village and to the Green Mountains to the west. (It's part of the Marsh-Billings-Rockefeller National Historic Park, described above.) You can ascend the mountain right from the village: Start at Faulkner Park. To reach the trailhead from the green, cross Middle Covered Bridge and continue straight on Mountain Avenue. The road bends left and soon arrives at the grassy park at the base of Mount Tom.

The trail winds up the hill, employing one of the most lugubrious sets of switchbacks you're ever likely to experience. Designed after the once-popular "cardiac walks" in Europe, the trail makes hikers feel they are walking miles only to gain a few feet in elevation. But persevere. This gentle trail eventually arrives at a clearing overlooking the town. A steeper, rockier, and more demanding trail continues 100 yards (91m) or so to the summit. From the top, you can follow the carriage path down to Billings Farm or retrace your steps back to the park and village.

HORSEBACK RIDING Equestrians head to the **Kedron Valley Stables** ⋒ (© 802/457-1480; www.kedron.com), about 4½ miles (7km) south of Woodstock on Route 106. A full menu of options is available, ranging from a 1-hour beginner ride ($35) to a 5-night inn-to-inn excursion ($1,475 per person including all meals and lodging, double occupancy). The stables rent horses to experienced riders for local trail rides, offer sleigh and carriage rides, and have an indoor riding ring for inclement weather. Credit cards are not accepted.

SKIING The area's best cross-country skiing is at the **Woodstock Ski Touring Center** ⋒⋒ (© 800/448-7900 or 802/457-6674), at the Woodstock Country

Club, just south of town on Route 106. The center maintains 36 miles (58km) of trails, including 12 miles (19km) of trails groomed for skate-skiing. And it's not all flat; the high and low points along the trail system vary by 750 feet (225m) in elevation. There's a lounge and restaurant at the ski center and a large fitness center accessible via ski trail. Lessons and picnic tours are available. The trail fee is $12.50 for adults and $8.25 for children under 14.

The ski area **Suicide Six** 🎿, 2 miles (3km) north of Woodstock on Pomfret Road (✆ **802/457-6661**), has an intimidating name, but at just 650 vertical feet (195m) it doesn't pose much of a threat to either life or limb. Owned and operated by the Woodstock Inn, this family-oriented ski resort (it first opened in 1934) has two double chairs, a complimentary J-bar for beginners, and a base lodge. Beginners, intermediates, and families with young children will be content here. Lift tickets are $44 for adults, $28 for seniors and children under 14. (Inn guests ski free midweek.)

WHERE TO STAY

Jackson House Inn 🎿🎿🎿   This is a truly comfortable choice, located a 5-minute drive west of the village center. The home was built in 1890 by a lumber baron who hoarded the best wood for himself; the cherry and maple floors are so beautiful you'll feel guilty for not taking off your shoes. The guest rooms are well appointed with antiques, although some of the older rooms are rather small. A well-executed addition (1997) created four suites with fireplaces and Jacuzzis. The inn welcomes guests with a series of pleasant surprises, including complimentary evening hors d'oeuvres and champagne and a 3-acre (1-hectare) backyard with formal English gardens. This inn deserves three stars for its elegance and attentive service; only its location, a stone's throw off a busy stretch of Route 4, detracts from the graceful tranquility.

114–3 Senior Lane, Woodstock, VT 05091. ✆ **800/448-1890** or 802/457-2065. Fax 802/457-9290. www.jacksonhouse.com. 15 units. $195–$260 double; $290–$380 suite. Higher rates in foliage season. Rates include breakfast. 2-night minimum stay most weekends. AE, MC, V. Children 14 and over welcome. **Amenities:** Restaurant (see "Where to Dine," below); small fitness room; steam room. *In room:* A/C, hair dryer, no phone (except in suites).

Shire Motel 🎿   The convenient Shire Motel is within walking distance of the green and the rest of the village, and with its attractive colonial decor is better appointed than your average motel. The rooms are bright and have more windows than you might expect, with most facing the river that runs behind the property. (The downside: thin sheets and some scuffed walls.) At the end of the second-floor porch is an outdoor kitchen where you can sit on rockers overlooking the river and enjoy a cup of coffee. The yellow-clapboard house next door has three modern suites, all with gas fireplaces and Jacuzzis.

46 Pleasant St., Woodstock, VT 05091. ✆ **802/457-2211**. www.shiremotel.com. 36 units. Summer $78–$145 double; holidays and foliage $125–$175 double; off-season $58–$95 double; suite $150–$250. AE, MC, V. *In room:* A/C, TV, dataport, fridge.

Three Church St. *(Value*   This sturdy brick Greek Revival B&B with a white-clapboard ell is located just off the west end of the Woodstock green, and is well situated for launching an exploration of the village. It offers excellent value, especially if you don't mind sharing a bathroom and can overlook small imperfections like the occasional water stain on the ceiling. In the back is a lovely porch overlooking the inn's 3 acres (1 hectare). Guest rooms are furnished comfortably and eclectically with country antiques. A night here feels more like staying with a relative than at a fancy inn.

3 Church St., Woodstock VT 05091. © **802/457-1925.** Fax 802/457-9181. 11 units (5 share 2 bathrooms). $85–$115 double. Higher rates during foliage season and Christmas week. Rates include breakfast. MC, V. Closed Apr. Pets allowed ($5 per night). **Amenities:** Pool; tennis court. *In room:* No phone.

Twin Farms 🌸🌸🌸 Twin Farms offers uncommon luxury at an uncommon price. Housed on a 300-acre (122-hectare) farm that was once home to Nobel Prize–winning novelist Sinclair Lewis and his journalist wife, Dorothy Thompson, Twin Farms is a very private, exceptionally tasteful small resort. The compound consists of the main inn, with four guest rooms, and 10 outlying cottages, each with fireplace. The owners are noted art collectors, and some of the work on display includes originals by David Hockney, Roy Lichtenstein, Milton Avery, and William Wegman. Rates include everything, from gourmet meals and open bar to use of all recreational equipment.

> *Tips* **Breadworks**
>
> Right in the village center is **Pane Salute**, 61 Central St. (© **802/457-4882**), a bakery that specializes in delectable Italian breads.

Barnard, VT 05031. © **800/894-6327** or 802/234-9999. Fax 802/234-9990. www.twinfarms.com. 14 units. $900–$1,050 inn room double; $1,350–$2,400 cottage. Rates include all meals and liquor. AE, MC, V. Closed Apr. No children under 18. **Amenities:** Restaurant (New American); lake swimming; tennis courts; fitness center; Jacuzzi; canoes; bike rental; game room; concierge; car rental; free shuttle to rail or plane; limited room service; in-room massage. *In room:* A/C, TV/VCR, minibar, coffeemaker, hair dryer, iron.

Woodstock Inn & Resort 🌸🌸🌸 The Woodstock Inn is central Vermont's best full-scale resort. Located in an imposing brick structure set off the town green, the inn appears to be a venerable and long-established institution at first glance. But it's not—it wasn't built until 1969. The inn adopted a dignified Colonial Revival look well suited for Woodstock. Guest rooms are tastefully decorated in either country pine or a Shaker-inspired style. The best units, in the wing built in 1991, feature plush carpeting, fridges, and fireplaces.

14 The Green, Woodstock, VT 05091. © **800/448-7900** or 802/457-1100. Fax 802/457-6699. www.woodstockinn.com. 141 units, 3 town houses. $179–$339 double; $454–$559 suite. Ask about packages and off-season rates. 2-night minimum stay on weekends. AE, MC, V. **Amenities:** 2 restaurants (traditional/regional, cafe); indoor and outdoor pools; Robert Trent Jones–designed golf course (at inn-owned Woodstock Country Club); tennis courts; free shuttle to fitness center (squash, racquetball, steam rooms); bike rental; concierge; limited room service; babysitting; laundry service; dry cleaning; cross-country ski trails. *In room:* A/C, TV w/ pay movies, dataport, hair dryer, iron, safe.

WHERE TO DINE

Jackson House Inn 🌸🌸🌸 CONTINENTAL The Jackson House dining room is a modern addition to the original country inn (see above). Its centerpiece is a 16-foot (4.75m) stone fireplace, and it boasts soaring windows offering garden views. Men might feel most comfortable in a sports coat, although a jacket is not required. Once settled, you'll sample some of the most exquisite dishes in New England, deftly prepared and artfully arranged. The three-course meals begin with offerings like Maine crabmeat and field greens with shaved fennel. Main courses do an equally good job combining the earthy with the celestial. Expect dishes like crispy-skin salmon with a shiitake compote, or Angus filet with creamy white-corn polenta and a three-onion marmalade. For dessert, the banana-walnut soufflé is surprisingly delicate. This is a meal that will linger in your memory.

114–3 Senior Lane. © **800/448-1890** or 802/457-2065. Reservations highly recommended. 3-course prix-fixe dinner $55 (chef's tasting menu $65). AE, MC, V. Wed–Sun 6–9pm.

The Prince and the Pauper 🏃🏃 NEW AMERICAN   It takes a bit of sleuthing to find the Prince and the Pauper, located down Dana Alley (next to the Woodstock Historical Society's Dana House)—but it's worth the effort. This is one of Woodstock's more inviting restaurants, with an intimate but informal setting. (It's quite a bit more casual than the Jackson House.) Ease into the evening with a libation in the taproom, then move over to the rustic-but-elegant dining room. The menu changes daily, but you might start with a Cuban black-bean soup, then move on to baked swordfish with a roasted pepper aioli, or perhaps boneless rack of lamb baked in puff pastry with spinach and mushroom duxelles. The fixed-price dinner menu offers good value; those on a tighter budget should linger in the lounge and order from the bistro menu, with selections like crab cakes, meatloaf, and tasty wood-fired pizzas.

24 Elm St. ℂ **802/457-1818.** www.princeandpauper.com. Reservations recommended. 3-course dinners $38. AE, DISC, MC, V. Sun–Thurs 6–9pm; Fri–Sat 6–9:30pm. Lounge opens at 5pm.

Simon Pearce Restaurant 🏃🏃 NEW AMERICAN   The setting can't be beat. Housed in a restored 19th-century woolen mill with wonderful views of a waterfall (spotlit at night), Simon Pearce is a collage of exposed brick, pine floorboards, and handsome wooden tables and chairs. Meals are served on Simon Pearce pottery and glassware—if you like your place setting, you can buy it afterward at the sprawling retail shop in the mill. The atmosphere is a wonderful concoction of formal and informal, ensuring that everybody feels comfortable whether in white shirt and tie or (neatly laundered) jeans. Lunch features dishes like crispy calamari with field greens. At dinner, look for entrees such as crispy roast duck with shiitake ginger sauce, or barbecued salmon with roasted corn salad.

The Mill, Quechee. ℂ **802/295-1470.** www.simonpearce.com. Reservations recommended for dinner. Lunch items $8.75–$14.50; dinner main courses $18–$34.50. AE, DC, DISC, MC, V. Daily 11:30am–2:45pm and 6–9pm.

Wild Grass 🏃 ECLECTIC   Wild Grass is located in a small business complex that lacks the quaintness of much of the rest of Woodstock—yet the menu rises above the prosaic surroundings, offering creative fare and good value for this often overpriced town. Especially appealing are the unique crispy sage leaves with tangy dipping sauces. Fish is grilled to perfection, and sauces are pleasantly zesty. Other entrees include roast duckling with a shallot port sauce, Caribbean pork with a black-bean corn salsa, and, for vegetarians, marinated tempeh served with a spicy peanut sauce.

Rte. 4 (east of the village). ℂ **802/457-1917.** Reservations recommended during peak season. Main courses $14.25–$19.25. DISC, MC, V. Tues–Sat 6–9pm (also open Sun in summer).

4 Killington 🏃

In 1937, a travel writer described the town near Killington Peak as "a small village of a church and a few undistinguished houses built on a highway three corners." The area was rugged and remote, isolated from the commercial center of Rutland to the west by imposing mountains and accessible only through daunting Sherburne Pass.

That was before Vermont's second-highest mountain was developed as the Northeast's largest ski area. And before a 5-mile (8km) access road was slashed through the forest to the mountain's base. And before Route 4 was widened and improved, improving access to Rutland. In fact, that early travel writer would be hard-pressed to recognize the region today.

Killington is plainly not the Vermont pictured on calendars and placemats. But the region around the mountain boasts Vermont's most active winter scene, with loads of distractions both on and off the mountain. The area has a frenetic, where-it's-happening feel in winter. (That's not the case in summer, when empty parking lots can trigger mild melancholia.) Those most content here are skiers who like their skiing BIG, singles in search of aggressive mingling, and travelers who want a wide selection of amenities and are willing to sacrifice the quintessential New England charm in exchange for a broader choice of diversions.

ESSENTIALS

GETTING THERE   Killington Road extends southward from Routes 4 and 100 (marked on some maps as Sherburne). It's about 12 miles (19km) east of Rutland on Route 4. Many inns offer shuttles to the Rutland airport. **Amtrak** (© 800/USA-RAIL; www.amtrak.com) offers service from New York to Rutland, with connecting shuttles to the mountain and various resorts. The **Marble Valley Regional Transit District** (© 802/773-3244) operates the **Skibus,** offering service between Rutland and Killington ($1).

VISITOR INFORMATION   The **Killington & Pico Areas Association** (© 802/773-4181) supplies information on lodging and packages. It also staffs an information booth on Route 4 at the base of the access road; open Monday through Friday from 9am to 5pm, Saturday and Sunday from 10am to 2pm. For information on accommodations and travel to Killington, contact the **Killington Lodging and Travel Service** (© 800/621-6867).

ALPINE SKIING

Killington ★★   Killington is a love-it or hate-it kind of place. It's New England's largest and most bustling ski area, offering greater vertical drop than any other New England mountain. You'll find the broadest selection of slopes, with trails ranging from long, narrow, old-fashioned runs to killer bumps high on its flanks. Thanks to this diversity, it has long been the destination of choice for serious skiers.

That said, it's also the skier's equivalent of the Mall of America: a huge operation run with bland efficiency and not much of a personal touch. It's not a particularly friendly place. It's easy to get lost and separated from your friends and family, and it seems to attract boisterous groups of young adults. To avoid getting lost, ask about the free tours of the mountain, led by the ski ambassadors based at Snowshed. If you're looking for the big mountain experience, with lots of evening activities and plenty of challenging terrain, it's a good choice. If you're looking for a less overwhelming experience and a more local sense of place, more intimate resorts like Sugarbush, Stowe, and Suicide Six are better options.

Killington, VT 05751. © 800/621-6867 for lodging, or 802/422-3261. www.killington.com. Vertical drop: 3,050 ft. (915m). Lifts: 2 gondolas, 30 chairlifts (6 high-speed), 2 surface lifts. Skiable acreage: 1,182. Lift tickets: $62.

CROSS-COUNTRY SKIING

Nearest to the ski area (just east of the Killington Rd. on Rte. 100/Rte. 4) is **Mountain Meadows Cross Country Ski Resort** ★ (© 800/221-0598 or 802/775-7077), with 34 miles (55km) of trails groomed for both skating and classic skiing. The trails are largely divided into three pods, with beginner trails closest to the lodge, an intermediate area a bit further along, and an advanced 6-mile (10km) loop farthest away. Rentals and lessons are available. A 1-day pass is $14, a half-day pass (after 1pm) $11.

Tips **A Classic Compromise**

If you're in search of classic New England, consider staying in quaint Woodstock (see "Woodstock," earlier in this chapter) and commuting the 20 miles (32km) to the slopes at Killington.

The intricate network of trails at the **Mountain Top Inn** ✦✦ (© **802/483-6089**) activity center has a loyal local following. The 66-mile (106km) network runs through mixed terrain with pastoral views and is groomed for both traditional and skate-skiing. The area is often deep with snow owing to its high ridge-top location in the hills east of Rutland, and snowmaking along key portions of the trail ensure that you won't have to walk across bare spots during snow droughts. The resort maintains three warming huts along the way, and lessons and rentals are available. The trails have a combined elevation gain of 670 feet (201m). Adults pay $14 for 1-day passes, $11 for half-day passes (after 1pm). With more challenging and picturesque terrain, Mountain Top offers the better value of the two options.

OTHER OUTDOOR PURSUITS

MOUNTAIN BIKING   Biking comes in two forms at Killington—organized on the mountain, or on-your-own on the back roads. On Killington's mountain, around 45 miles (72km) of trails are open for biking, and one eight-passenger gondola is equipped to haul bikes and riders to the summit, delivering great views. A trail pass is $8; a trail pass with a two-time gondola ride is $20; unlimited gondola rides are $30 per day.

The **Mountain Bike Shop,** at the Killington Base Lodge (© **802/422-6232**), is open from June to mid-October. Bike rentals start at $30 for 2 hours, up to $45 for a full day. Rentals and trail advice are also available from **True Wheels Bike Shop,** in the Basin Ski Shop near the top of the Killington access road (© **802/422-3234**). Rates range from $25 to $60 a day. Bikes are available from April to mid-October; reservations are helpful during busy times.

HIKING   Hikers often set their sights on **Deer Leap Mountain** ✦✦ and its popular 3-hour loop to the summit and back. The trail departs from the Inn at Long Trail off Route 4 at Sherburne Pass. Leave your car across from the inn, then head north through the inn's parking lot onto the Long Trail/Appalachian Trail and into the forest. Follow the white blazes. (You'll return on the blue-blazed trail you'll see entering on the left.) In ½ a mile (0.8km), you'll arrive at a crossroads. The Appalachian Trail veers right to New Hampshire's White Mountains and Mount Katahdin in Maine; Vermont's Long Trail runs to the left. Follow the Long Trail; after a ½ mile (0.8km) or so, turn left at the signs for Deer Leap Height. Great views of Pico and the Killington area await you in ⅔ of a mile (0.6km). After a snack break here, continue down the blue-blazed descent back to Route 4 and your car. The entire loop is about 2½ miles (4km).

A HISTORIC SITE

President Calvin Coolidge State Historic Site ✦✦   When told that Calvin Coolidge had died, literary wit Dorothy Parker is said to have responded, "How can they tell?" Even in his death, the nation's most taciturn president had to fight for respect. A trip to the Plymouth Notch Historic District should at least raise Silent Cal's reputation among visitors, who'll get a strong sense of the president reared in this mountain village, a man shaped by harsh weather, unrelieved isolation, and a strong sense of community and family.

Situated in a high upland valley, the historic district consists of a group of about a dozen buildings open to the public and a number of private residences. It was at the Coolidge Homestead (open for tours) that in August 1923 Vice President Coolidge, on a vacation from Washington, was awakened in the middle of the night and informed that President Warren Harding had died. His own father, a notary public, administered the presidential oath of office.

Coolidge is buried in the cemetery across the road. He remains the only president to have been born on Independence Day, and every July 4th a wreath is laid at his simple grave in a quiet ceremony.

Be sure to stop by the **Plymouth Cheese Factory** (© **802/672-3650**), just uphill from the Coolidge Homestead. Founded in the late 1800s by President Coolidge's father, the business was owned by the president's son until the late 1990s. Excellent cheeses here include a spicy pepper cheddar. Hours are daily from 9:30am to 5pm; in winter, it's best to call ahead.

Rte. 100A, Plymouth. © 802/672-3773. Admission $6.50 adults, free for children under 15. Daily 9:30am–5pm. Closed mid-Oct to late May.

WHERE TO STAY

Skiers headed to Killington for a week or so should consider the condo option. A number of condo developments spill down the hillside and along the low ridges flanking the access road. These vary in elegance, convenience, and size. **Highridge** features units with saunas and Jacuzzis, along with access to a compact health club. **Sunrise Village** has a more remote setting, along with a health club and easy access to the Bear Mountain lifts. **The Woods at Killington** is farthest from the slopes (free shuttle) but offers access to the finest health club and the road's best restaurant. Rates fluctuate widely, depending on time of year, number of bedrooms, and length of stay. But figure on prices ranging from around $100 to $130 and up per person per day, which includes lift tickets. You can line up a vacation by contacting the **Killington Lodging and Travel Bureau** (© **800/621-6867;** www.killington.com), which also arranges stays at area inns and motels.

Blueberry Hill Inn ✦✦✦   The wonderfully homey Blueberry Hill Inn lies in the heart of the Moosalamoo recreation area, on 180 acres (73 hectares) along

---

(**Tips** **Budget Choices**

Budget travelers who don't mind a commute to the slopes (you can take the $1 bus) should look into staying in Rutland, a commercial city about 11 miles (18km) west of the access road. Here you'll find a cluster of basic motels and chain hotels, mostly on or along Route 7 south of town. Rates at the **Comfort Inn at Trolley Square**, 19 Allen St. (© **800/228-5150** or 802/775-2200), include continental breakfast. The **Holiday Inn,** 476 U.S. Rte. 7 South (© **800/462-4810** or 802/775-1911), has an indoor pool, Jacuzzi, and sauna. Likewise, the **Howard Johnson Rutland,** 401 U.S. Rte. 7 South (© **802/775-4303**), features an indoor pool and sauna, with the familiar orange-roofed restaurant next door. The **Best Western Hogge Penny Inn,** on Route 4 East (© **800/828-3334** or 802/773-3200), has a pool and tennis court.

a quiet road about 45 minutes northwest of Killington (about midway to Middlebury). With superb hiking, biking, canoeing, swimming, and cross-country skiing, it's an extraordinary destination for those inclined toward spending time outdoors. The inn dates to 1813; one graceful addition is the greenhouse walkway, which leads to the cozy guest rooms. Family-style meals are served in a rustic dining room, with a great stone fireplace and homegrown herbs drying from the wooden beams.

Goshen–Ripton Rd., Goshen, VT 05733. ✆ **800/448-0707** or 802/247-6735. Fax 802/247-3983. www. blueberryhillinn.com. 12 units. $230–$300 double. Rates include breakfast and dinner. MC, V. **Amenities:** Lake swimming nearby; sauna; bike rental; babysitting; cross-country ski trails. *In room:* No phone.

Butternut on the Mountain Motor Inn
Butternut is a short remove from the access road, just enough to lend a little quiet, although winter guests tend to make up for that with a dose of boisterousness. It's more a recommended budget choice than an especially noteworthy spot. The rooms are motel-size with motel decor, but the inn's unexpected facilities make it a good option. Eleven rooms have air-conditioning.

Killington Rd., Killington, VT 05751. ✆ **800/524-7654** or 802/422-2000. Fax 802/422-3937. www.butternut lodge.com. 18 units. Winter $70–$160 double. Lower off-season rates. AE, DISC, MC, V. **Amenities:** Restaurant (pub fare), lounge; tiny indoor pool; Jacuzzi; game room; coin-op laundry. *In room:* TV.

Killington Grand ★★
This is a good (though pricey) choice for travelers seeking contemporary accommodations right on the mountain. More than half of the units have kitchen facilities, and most are quite spacious though decorated in a generic country-condo style. The resort has placed an emphasis on catering to families. You pay a premium for convenience compared with other spots near the mountain, but that convenience is hard to top during ski season. The helpful service is a notch above that typically experienced at large ski hotels.

228 East Mountain Rd. (near Snowshed base area), Killington, VT 05751. ✆ **802/422-5001.** Fax 802/422-6881. www.killington.com. 200 units. Ski season $250 midweek, $300 weekend, $350 holiday; rest of year $175–$195 double. Ask about packages. 5-night minimum stay during Christmas and school holidays; 2-night minimum stay on weekends. AE, DISC, MC, V. **Amenities:** 2 restaurants (upscale American, cafe); heated outdoor pool; tennis courts; fitness center; Jacuzzi; sauna; children's programs; concierge; limited room service; massage; coin-op laundry; dry cleaning. *In-room:* A/C, TV, coffeemaker, hair dryer, iron.

Mountain Top Inn ★★
The Mountain Top Inn was carved out of a former turnip farm in the 1940s but has left its root-vegetable heritage long behind. Situated on 1,300 ridgetop acres (527 hectares) with expansive views of the rolling countryside, it's a modern inn with country charm, and has the feel of a classic, small Poconos resort hotel, where the hosts make sure you've got something to do every waking minute. Guest rooms are unremarkable but comfortable, with understated accents like quilts and pine furnishings. Deluxe rooms have views of the lake. Overall, the Mountain Top doesn't offer much value to travelers simply looking for room and board, but those who like to keep active outdoors and who prefer to stay in one place during their vacation can keep busy for their money. Killington's slopes are about a 25-minute drive away. The dining room, with heavy beams and rustic chairs, features regional American cuisine with a Continental twist.

195 Mountain Top Rd., Chittenden, VT 05737. ✆ **800/445-2100** or 802/483-2311. Fax 802/483-6373. www.mountaintopinn.com. 55 units. Summer and fall $176–$268 double; winter $176–$268 midweek, $196–$268 weekends and holidays; off-season $168–$268. AE, MC, V. **Amenities:** Restaurant (contemporary American); outdoor pool; beach swimming; 5-hole golf course; driving range; horseback riding; shooting clays; 66 miles (106km) of cross-country skiing trails. *In room:* A/C, dataport.

The Summit Lodge ⚜ Think plaid carpeting and Saint Bernards. Those two motifs seem to set the tone at this inviting spot on a knoll just off the access road. Although built only in the 1960s, the inn has a more historic character, with much of the common space constructed of salvaged barn timbers. The guest rooms are less distinguished, with clunky pine furniture and little ambience, although all have balconies or terraces. The Summit has more character than most self-styled resorts along the access road, and offers decent value.

Killington Rd. (P.O. Box 119), Killington, VT 05751. ℂ **800/635-6343** or 802/422-3535. Fax 802/422-3536. www.summitlodgevermont.com. 45 units. Summer $95 double; winter $116–$198 double. Winter rates include breakfast. Minimum-stay policy on holidays. AE, DC, MC, V. **Amenities:** Restaurant (American); 2 pools (small outdoor heated pool in winter, larger pool in summer); tennis courts; indoor Jacuzzi; game room; limited room service; massage; coin-op laundry. *In room:* TV.

WHERE TO DINE

The mere mention of the restaurants along Killington's access road no doubt provokes a deep horror at poultry farms across the nation. It's our impression that *every* Killington restaurant serves up chicken wings, and plenty of them. If you love wings, especially free wings, you'll be in heaven. Alas, if you're looking for something more adventurous, the access road is home to an astonishing level of culinary mediocrity—bland pasta, soggy nachos—capped off with indifferent, harried service. Most restaurants are okay spots to carbo-load for a day on the slopes, and if you're with a group of friends, you may not mind the middling quality—but for the most part, don't expect much of a dining adventure.

Charity's PUB FARE   Rustic and boisterous, Charity's is the place if you like your food big and your company young. The barn-like restaurant is adorned with stained-glass lamps, Victorian prints, and a handsome old bar. The menu offers a good selection of burgers, plus vegetarian entrees such as red pepper ravioli.

Killington Rd. ℂ **802/422-3800.** Reservations not accepted. Lunch items $5.95–$8.95; dinner main courses $12.95–$18.95. AE, MC, V. Daily 11:30am–10pm.

Choices Restaurant and Rotisserie ⚜ BISTRO   One of the locally favored spots for unpretentious fare is Choices, located on the access road across from the Outback. Full dinners come complete with salad or soup and bread and will amply restore calories lost on the slopes or the trail. Fresh pastas are a specialty; other inviting entrees include meats from the rotisserie. The atmosphere is nothing to write home about and the prices are higher than at nearby burger joints, but the high quality of the food makes up for that.

Killington Rd. (at Glazebook Center). ℂ **802/422-4030.** Reservations not accepted. Main courses $12.50–$21.95. AE, MC, V. Sun–Thurs 5–10pm; Fri–Sat 5–11pm; Sun 11am–2:30pm.

Hemingway's ⚜⚜⚜ NEW AMERICAN   Hemingway's is an uncommonly elegant spot—and one that ranks among the very best restaurants in New England. Located in the 1860 Asa Briggs House, a former stagecoach stop, guests are seated in one of three formal areas. The two upstairs rooms are appointed with damask linen, crystal goblets, and fresh flowers. Diners tend to dress casually but neatly (no shorts or T-shirts). The three- or four-course dinners are priced rather reasonably given the quality of the kitchen and the unassailable service. A typical meal might start with cured salmon on a crispy potato waffle; then it's on to the splendid main course, perhaps red snapper with grilled shrimp and a risotto of bacon and chanterelles.

Rte. 4 (between Rte. 100 N. and Rte. 100 S.). ℂ **802/422-3886.** www.hemingwaysrestaurant.com. Reservations strongly recommended. Fixed-price menu $48–$60; vegetarian menu $45[nd$50; wine-tasting menu $75–$80. AE, MC, V. Wed–Thurs and Sun 6–9pm; Fri–Sat 6–10pm. (Also open selected Mon–Tues during ski and foliage seasons; call first.) Closed mid-Apr to mid-May and early Nov.

Mother Shapiro's *(Kids* PUB FARE   Mother's is a great place for breakfast or brunch. You'll find omelets, lox, corned-beef hash, and pancakes. At Sunday brunch during peak season, there's a unique Bloody Mary bar—you get a glass with vodka and formulate your own spicy concoction from a lineup of ingredients. It's a fun place that kids adore, done up in a comic-book Victorian vaudeville/brothel look. Dinners, by comparison, tend to be so-so, and service more harried.

Killington Rd. ℂ 802/422-9933. www.mothershapiros.com. Reservations not accepted. Breakfast $4.59–$8.99; sandwiches $5.99–$7.99; dinner entrees $6.99–$17.99. AE, DISC, MC, V. Daily breakfast 7–11am; lunch and munchies 11am–3pm; dinner 4:30–10pm.

KILLINGTON AFTER DARK

Mother Shapiro's   This popular restaurant often features live blues later in the evening. It's also a good choice for late-night snacking. Killington Rd. ℂ 802/422-9933.

Outback/Nightspot   The music tends to be mellower here than at the other hot spots in town, with acoustic musicians often heading the lineup. It's the place to go if you want to chat with friends while enjoying music and wood-fired pizza. Killington Rd. ℂ 802/422-9885.

Pickle Barrel   The Pickle Barrel is Killington's largest and loudest club, and lures in B-list national acts like Eddie Money, Little Feat, and the Mighty Mighty Bosstones. Killington Rd. ℂ 802/422-3035. www.picklebarrelnightclub.com.

Wobbly Barn   The Wobbly is best known for its happy hour, but it also packs in the crowds for dancing. Expect bands that play good, hard-driving rock. The American Skiing Company (owners of the mountain) own this pioneer establishment, located in an old barn. Killington Rd. ℂ 802/42-3392. www.wobblybarn.com.

5 Middlebury *(★(★*

Middlebury is a gracious college town set amid rolling hills and pastoral countryside. The town center is idyllic in a New-England-as-envisioned-by-Hollywood sort of way. All that's lacking is Jimmy Stewart wandering about, muttering confusedly to himself.

The town centers on an irregular sloping green. Above the green is the commanding Middlebury Inn; shops line the downhill slopes. In the midst of the green is a handsome chapel, and the whole scene is lorded over by a white-steepled Congregational church, built between 1806 and 1809. Otter Creek tumbles dramatically through the middle of town and is flanked by a historic district that feature vestiges of former industry. In fact, Middlebury has 300 buildings listed on the National Register of Historic Places. About the only disruption to the historical perfection is the growl of trucks downshifting as they drive along the main routes through town.

Middlebury College, which is within walking distance at the edge of downtown, doesn't so much dominate the village as coexist nicely alongside it. The college has a sterling reputation for its liberal-arts education, but may be best known for its intensive summer language programs. Don't be surprised if you hear folks gabbing uncertainly in exotic tongues while walking through town in summer. Students commit to total immersion, taking the "Language Pledge," which prohibits the use of English while they're enrolled in the program.

ESSENTIALS

GETTING THERE   Middlebury is located on Route 7 about midway between Rutland and Burlington. **Vermont Transit** (© **800/451-3292** or 802/388-4373) offers bus service to town.

VISITOR INFORMATION   The **Addison County Chamber of Commerce,** 2 Court St. (© **800/733-8376** or 802/388-7951; www.midvermont. com), is located in a historic white building just off the green, facing the Middlebury Inn. Assistance is available Monday through Friday during business hours, and often on weekends from early June to mid-October as well.

EXPLORING THE TOWN

The best place to begin a tour of Middlebury is the Addison County Chamber of Commerce (see above), where you can request the self-guided walking-tour brochure.

The **Vermont Folklife Center** ☆, 3 Court St. (© **802/388-4964;** www. vermontfolklifecenter.org), is located in the 1823 Masonic Hall, a short walk from the Middlebury Inn. You'll see changing displays of various folk arts from Vermont and beyond. The gift shop has intriguing items, such as heritage foods and traditional crafts. Hours are 11am to 4pm Tuesday through Saturday in summer, Thursday through Saturday in spring, late fall, and winter. Admission is by donation.

The historic **Otter Creek** ☆☆ district, set along a steep hillside by the rocky creek, is well worth exploring. While here, you can peruse top-flight crafts at the **Vermont State Crafts Center at Frog Hollow** ☆☆, 1 Mill St. (© **802/388-3177;** www.froghollow.org). The center, picturesquely situated overlooking the tumbling stream, is open daily (closed Sun in winter) and features the work of some 300 craftspeople, ranging from extraordinary carved wood desks to metal-work to glass and pottery. The Crafts Center also maintains shops in Manchester Village and at the Church Street Marketplace in Burlington. Visit its website for a listing of exhibits.

Located atop a low ridge with beautiful views of both the Green Mountains to the east and farmlands rolling toward Lake Champlain to the west, prestigious **Middlebury College** ☆☆ has a handsome campus of gray-limestone and white-marble buildings that's best explored on foot. The architecture of the college, founded in 1800, is primarily Colonial Revival, which lends it a rather stern Calvinist demeanor. Especially appealing is the prospect from the marble Mead Memorial Chapel, built in 1917 and overlooking the campus green.

At the edge of campus is the **Middlebury College Center for the Arts,** which opened in 1992. This architecturally engaging center houses the small **Middlebury College Museum of Art** ☆ (© **802/443-5007**), with a selective sampling of European and American art, both ancient and new. Classicists will savor the displays of Greek urns and vases; modern-art aficionados can check out the museum's permanent and changing exhibits. The museum is located on Route 30 (South Main St.) and is open Tuesday through Friday from 10am to 5pm, Saturday and Sunday from noon to 5pm. Admission is free.

Two miles (3.2km) outside of Middlebury is the **Morgan Horse Farm** ☆☆ (© **802/388-2011**), which dates back to the late 1800s and is now owned and administered by the University of Vermont. Col. Joseph Battell, owner of the farm from the 1870s to 1906, is credited with preserving the Morgan breed, a horse of considerable beauty and stamina that has served admirably in war and exploration. The farm is open for guided tours May through October, daily from 9am to 4pm. There's also a picnic area and gift shop. At press time, admission is $4 for adults, $3 for teens, and $1 for children 5 to 12. Take Route 125 to Weybridge Street (Rte. 23 North), head north for ¾ mile (1.2km), and turn right at the sign for the farm.

Brewhounds should schedule a stop at the **Otter Creek Brewing Co.** ✿, 793 Exchange St. (© **800/473-0727;** www.ottercreekbrewing.com), for a tour and free samples of the well-regarded beverages, including the flagship Copper Ale. The visitor center is open Monday through Saturday from 10am to 6pm. Tours are given at 1, 3, and 5pm.

OUTDOOR PURSUITS

HIKING   The Green Mountains roll down to Middlebury's eastern edge, making for easy access to the mountains. Stop by the **U.S. Forest Service's Middlebury Ranger District office,** south of town on Route 7 (© **802/388-4362**), for information on area trails.

One recommended walk for people of all abilities—and especially those of poetic sensibilities—is the **Robert Frost Interpretive Trail,** dedicated to the memory of New England's poet laureate. Frost lived in a cabin on a farm across the road for 23 summers. (The cabin is now a National Historic Landmark.) Located on Route 125 approximately 6 miles (10km) east of Middlebury, this relaxing loop is just a mile (1.6km) long, and excerpts of Frost's poems are placed on signs along the trail.

SKIING   Downhill skiers looking for a low-key mountain invariably head to **Middlebury College Snow Bowl** (© **802/388-4356**), near Middlebury Gap on Route 125 east of town. This historic ski area, founded in 1939, has a vertical drop of just over 1,000 feet (300m) served by three lifts. The college ski team uses the ski area for practice, but it's also open to the public at rates of about half what you'd pay at Killington. Adult tickets are $32 on weekends, $26 midweek.

There's cross-country skiing nearby at the **Rikert Ski Touring Center** (© **802/388-2759**), at Middlebury's Bread Loaf Campus on Route 125. The center offers 24 miles (39km) of machine-groomed trails through a lovely winter landscape. Adult ski passes are $10, while students and children pay $5. Half-day passes are also available ($6 and $3, respectively).

WHERE TO STAY

The outskirts of Middlebury are home to a handful of motels. The **Blue Spruce Motel,** 2428 Rte. 7 South (© **800/640-7671** or 802/388-4091), has 22 basic units; families may like room 122, a suite with kitchen, sleeping loft, and carport. Rates start at $75 ($125 for the suite). The **Greystone Motel,** 1395 Rte. 7 South (© **802/388-4935**), has 10 rooms going for $75 to $95 in summer, $55 to $75 in winter.

Inn on the Green ✿✿✿   This is one of our favorites in Vermont. The handsome inn, occupying a house that dates to 1803, is both historic and comfortable, and our recommendation for those wishing to be in downtown Middlebury. The rooms are furnished with a mix of antiques and reproductions; lustrous wood floors and boldly colored walls of harvest yellow, peach, and burgundy lighten the architectural heaviness of the house. Units in the front of the house are flooded with afternoon light.

71 South Pleasant St., Middlebury, VT 05753. © **888/244-7512** or 802/388-7512. Fax 802/388-4075. www.innonthegreen.com. 11 units. $125–$225 weekends and summer; $175–$240 foliage season; $98

winter midweek. Rates include continental breakfast. 2-night minimum stay on weekends. AE, DC, DISC, MC, V. *In room:* A/C, TV, dataport, hair dryer, iron.

The Middlebury Inn ⭐

The historic Middlebury Inn traces its roots back to 1827, when Nathan Wood built a brick public house he called the Vermont Hotel. The modern guest rooms are on the large side, and most are outfitted with a sofa or upholstered chairs, reproduction furniture, and some vintage bathroom fixtures. Rooms 116 and 246 are spacious corner units entered via a dark foyer/sitting room. Room 129, while smaller, has a four-poster bed, a view of the green, and a Jacuzzi. The 10 guest rooms in the Porterhouse Mansion next door also have a pleasant, historic feel. An adjacent motel with 20 units is decorated in an Early American motif, but it feels like veneer—underneath it's just a standard-issue motel. Stick with the main inn if you're seeking a taste of history.

14 Courthouse Sq., Middlebury, VT 05753. ☎ **800/842-4666** or 802/388-4961. www.middleburyinn.com. 75 units. Weekends $98–$220 double; midweek $88–$200 double; $156–$375 suite. Rates include continental breakfast. AE, DC, MC, V. Pets accepted in some rooms. **Amenities:** Restaurant (traditional New England), tavern (pub fare); laundry service. *In room:* A/C, TV, dataport, hair dryer, iron.

Swift House Inn ⭐⭐

The Swift House Inn is a compound of three historic buildings set in a residential area just a few minutes' walk from the town green. The main Federal-style inn dates back to 1814; inside, it's decorated in a simple, historical style that still has a modern crispness. Guest rooms are appointed with antique and reproduction furnishings. Especially appealing is the Swift Room, with its oversize bathroom, Jacuzzi, and terrace. About half of the rooms have fireplaces or Jacuzzis or both; all but two have TVs. Light sleepers may prefer the main inn or the Carriage House rather than the Gate House down the hill; the latter is on Route 7, and the truck noise can be a minor irritant at night.

25 Stewart Lane, Middlebury, VT 05753. ☎ **802/388-9925.** Fax 802/388-9927. www.swifthouseinn.com. 21 units (1 with detached bathroom). Weekends $100–$235 double; midweek $90–$225 double. Rates include continental breakfast. 2-night minimum stay some weekends. AE, DISC, MC, V. **Amenities:** Restaurant (eclectic). *In room:* A/C, TV, dataport, hair dryer, iron.

WHERE TO DINE

Storm Cafe ⭐ NEW AMERICAN

This tiny spot tucked on the ground floor of a stone mill in Frog Hollow is popular with locals and travelers alike. The menu is beguilingly simple, but tremendous care has been taken in the selection of ingredients and the preparation of the dishes; the salads are especially good. Lunches include smoked salmon and jerk chicken; dinner is takeout only, and you need to arrive early for the delicious pasta, fish, or chicken dishes.

3 Mill St. ☎ **802/388-1063.** Reservations recommended, especially on weekends. Main courses $7–$12.95. MC, V. Tues–Sat 11am–3:30pm and 4–6pm.

Tully and Marie's ⭐ NEW AMERICAN/GLOBAL

Tully and Marie's is not Ye Olde New Englande. It's a bright and colorful Art Deco–inspired restaurant overlooking the creek, made all the more appealing by its surprising location down a small, dark alley. It's the kind of fun, low-key place destined to put you in a good mood. The menu shows clear influences from Asia and Mexico. At lunch, expect pad Thai, vegetable linguine, and a variety of hearty meals. At dinner, there's chicken saltimboca, bourbon shrimp, and grilled strip steak with carmelized shallots and leeks.

7 Bakery Lane (on Otter Creek just upstream from the bridge in the middle of town). ☎ **802/388-4182.** www.tullyandmaries.com. Reservations recommended on weekends and during college events. Lunch items $6.25–$9.50; dinner main courses $13–$20. AE, MC, V. Summer daily 11:30am–3pm and 5–10pm. Winter daily 11:30am–3pm; Sun–Mon and Thurs 5–9pm; Fri–Sat 5–10pm.

6 Mad River Valley ★★

The Mad River Valley is one of Vermont's better kept secrets. This scenic valley surrounding the towns of Warren and Waitsfield has something of a Shangri-La quality to it. In places, it has changed little since first settled in 1789 by Gen. Benjamin Wait and a handful of Revolutionary War veterans, including half a dozen said to have served as Minutemen at the battles of Concord Bridge and Lexington.

Since 1948, ski-related development has competed with the early farms that were the backbone of the region for 2 centuries, but the newcomers haven't been too pushy or overly obnoxious, at least so far. Save for a couple of telltale signs, you could drive Route 100 past the sleepy villages of Warren and Waitsfield and not realize that you've passed close to some of the choicest skiing in the state. The region hasn't fallen prey to unbridled condo or strip-mall developers, and the valley seems to have learned the lessons of haphazard development that afflicted Mount Snow and Killington to the south. Other towns could still learn a lot from Waitsfield: Note the Mad River Green, a tidy strip mall disguised as an old barn on Route 100 just north of Route 17. It's scarcely noticeable from the main road. Longtime Vermont skiers say the valley today is like Stowe used to be 25 years ago.

ESSENTIALS

GETTING THERE Warren and Waitsfield are on Route 100 between Killington and Waterbury. The nearest interstate access is from Exit 10 (Waterbury) on I-89; drive south on Route 100 for 14 miles (23km) to Waitsfield.

VISITOR INFORMATION The **Sugarbush Chamber of Commerce** (✆ **800/828-4748** or 802/469-3409; www.madrivervalley.com) is at 4601 Main St. (Route 100) in the General Wait House, next to the school. It's open daily from 9am to 5pm; during slow times, expect limited hours and days.

ALPINE SKIING

Sugarbush ★★ Sugarbush is a fine intermediate-to-advanced resort, comprised of two ski mountains linked by a 2-mile (3km), 10-minute high-speed chairlift that crosses three ridges. (A shuttle bus offers a warmer way to connect one ski mountain to the other.) The large number of high-speed lifts and excellent snowmaking make this a desirable destination for serious skiers. While the improved Sugarbush has generated some buzz since large-scale improvements began in the mid-1990s, it remains a pleasantly low-key area with great intermediate cruising runs on the north slopes and some challenging, old-fashioned expert slopes on Castlerock. Sugarbush is a good choice if you find the sprawl of Killington overwhelming, but don't want to sacrifice great skiing in the search for a quieter and more intimate resort area.

Warren, VT 05674. ℂ 800/537-8427 for lodging, or 802/583-6100. www.sugarbush.com. Vertical drop: 2,650 ft. (795m). Lifts: 14 chairlifts (4 high-speed), 4 surface lifts. Skiable acreage: 432. Lift tickets: $57.

Mad River Glen ✿✿✿   Mad River Glen is the curmudgeon of the Vermont ski world—just what you'd expect from a place whose motto is "Ski it if you can." High-speed detachable quads? Forget it. The main lift is a 1948 *single-chair* lift that creaks its way 1 mile (1.6km) to the summit. Snowmaking? Don't count on it. Only 15% of the terrain benefits from the fake stuff; the rest is dependent on Mother Nature. Snowboarding? Nope, it's forbidden here. Mad River's slopes are twisting and narrow and hide some of the steepest drops you'll find in New England (nearly half of the slopes are classified as expert). Mad River Glen long ago attained the status of a cult mountain among serious skiers, and its fans seem bound and determined to keep it that way. The ski area is today owned and operated by a cooperative of Mad River skiers (and has been since 1995), making it the only cooperative-owned ski area in the country. The owners are proud of the mountain's funky traditions (how *about* that single chair?) and say they're determined to maintain that spirit.

Waitsfield, VT 05763. ℂ 802/496-3551. www.madriverglen.com. Vertical drop: 2,000 ft. (600m). Lifts: 4 chairlifts. Skiable acreage: 115. Lift tickets: $32 midweek, $40 weekends, $42 holidays.

EXPLORING THE VALLEY

An unique way to see the region is atop an Icelandic pony. The **Vermont Icelandic Horse Farm** ✿ (ℂ 802/496-7141; www.icelandichorses.com) specializes in tours on these small, sturdy horses. Full- and half-day rides are available daily, but to really appreciate both the countryside and the horses, sign up for one of the multi-day treks, which range from 1 to 5 nights and include lodging at area inns, all meals, and a guide. In winter, there's also **skijoring,** which can best be described as sort of like water-skiing behind a horse. Call for prices and reservations.

BIKING   A rewarding 14-mile (23km) **bike trip** ✿✿ along paved roads begins at the village of Waitsfield. Park your car near the covered bridge, then follow East Warren Road past the Inn at Round Barn Farm and up into the farm-filled countryside. (Don't be discouraged by the unrelenting hill at the outset.) Near Warren, turn right at Brook Road to connect back to Route 100. Return north on bustling but generally safe and often scenic Route 100 to Waitsfield.

   Clearwater Sports, Route 100, north of the covered bridge, Waitsfield (ℂ 802/496-2708; www.clearwatersports.com), offers mountain-bike rentals from a blue-and-white Victorian-era house. The staff is helpful with suggestions for other routes and tours.

HIKING   Hikers in search of a spectacular view should strike out for **Mount Abraham** ✿✿, west of Warren. Drive west up Lincoln Gap Road (it leaves Rte. 100 just south of Warren Village) and continue until the crest, where you'll cross the intersection with the Long Trail. Park here and head north on the trail; about 2 miles (3km) along you'll hit the Battell Shelter. Push on another ⅘ of a mile (1.3km) up a steep ascent to reach the panoramic views atop 4,006-foot (1,202m) Mount Abraham. Enjoy. Retrace your steps back to your car. Allow 4 to 5 hours for the round-trip.

   For a less demanding adventure, head *south* from Lincoln Gap Road on the Long Trail. In about ⅗ of a mile (1km), look for a short spur trail to **Sunset Rock** ✿, with sweeping westward vistas of the farms of the Champlain Valley, along with Lake Champlain and the knobby Adirondacks beyond. The round-trip requires a little more than an hour.

WINTER SPORTS   Clearwater Sports, Route 100, Waitsfield (© 802/496-2708; www.clearwatersports.com), offers telemark ski rentals and advice in winter, and also leads guided snowshoe hikes into the backcountry. Ask about the Mad River Rocket Sled trips, which involves snowshoeing up and sledding back down a nearby hill.

WHERE TO STAY

While Sugarbush isn't overrun with condos and lodges, it has its share. Some 200 of the condos nearest the mountain are managed by the **Sugarbush Resort** (© **800/537-8427** or 802/583-3333; www.sugarbush.com). Guests have access to a slew of amenities, including a health club and five pools. The resort also manages the attractive 46-unit Sugarbush Inn, right on the access road. Shuttle buses deliver guests to and from the mountain and other facilities. During major winter holidays, there's a minimum stay of 5 days. Rates vary widely, and most rooms are sold as packages that include lift tickets in winter.

Inn at the Mad River Barn ★ *Value*   This classic 1960s-style ski lodge attracts a clientele that's nearly fanatical in its devotion to the place. It's best not to come here expecting anything fancy—carpets and furniture both tend toward the threadbare. Do come expecting to have some fun once you're settled in. It's all knotty pine, with spartan guest rooms and rustic common areas where visitors feel at home putting their feet up. Accommodations are in the barn behind the white-clapboard main house and in an annex up the lawn, which is a bit fancier but has less character. Most rooms have TVs; plans for 2002 include the installation of air-conditioning in about half of the units. In winter, boisterous family-style dinners are offered ($15). In summer, the mood is slightly more sedate, but enhanced by a beautiful pool a short walk away in a grove of birches.

2849 Millbrook Rd., Rte. 17, Waitsfield, VT 05673. © **800/631-0466** or 802/496-3310. Fax 802/496-6696. www.madriverbarn.com. 15 units. Winter $110 double; summer $74–$95 double. Midweek discounts available. Rates include breakfast. 2-night minimum stay holiday and winter weekends. AE, DISC, MC, V. **Amenities:** Restaurant (winter only), lounge; outdoor pool; fitness room; sauna; game room. *In room:* No phone.

Inn at Round Barn Farm ★★   This ranks among our favorite romantic B&Bs in northern New England. You arrive after passing through a covered bridge just off Route 100; 2 miles (3.2km) later you come upon a regal barn and farmhouse, set on 235 sloping acres (95 hectares). The centerpiece of the inn is the Round Barn, a striking 1910 structure that's used for weddings, art exhibits, and church services. Guest rooms are furnished with an understated country elegance. The less expensive rooms are in the older part of the house and are comfortable, if small; the larger luxury units in the attached barn feature soaring ceilings, steam showers, gas fireplaces, and phones. These are worth a splurge.

1661 E. Warren Rd., Waitsfield, VT 05673. © **802/496-2276.** Fax 802/496-8832. www.innattheround barn.com. 11 units. $130–$265 double. Rates include breakfast. 3-night minimum stay and $20 surcharge during holidays and foliage season. AE, DISC, MC, V. Closed Apr 15–30. No children under 15. **Amenities:** 60-foot (18m) indoor lap pool; game room; 18-mile (29km) cross-country ski center. *In room:* Hair dryer, no phone (except in luxury rooms).

The Pitcher Inn ★★★   This Relais & Châteaux property is one of Vermont's finest. Set in the timeless village of Warren, the inn was newly built in the 1990s from the ground up following a fire that leveled a previous home; only the barn is original. But architect David Sellars has created an inn that seamlessly blends modern conveniences, whimsy, and classic New England styling. The common areas fuse several styles: a little Colonial Revival, a little Mission, and a little Adirondack sporting camp to top it off. There's not a bad room in the house, and all are designed with such wit that they're like elegant puzzles. (Our favorite feature: The carved goose in flight on the ceiling of the Mallard Room is attached to a weather vane on the roof, and it rotates to indicate wind direction.) Nine units have fireplaces, while five have steam showers.

275 Main St., Warren, VT 05674. © **888/867-8424** or 802/496-6350. Fax 802/496-6354. www.pitcherinn. com. 11 units. $300–$550 double; $600 suite. Rates include breakfast. Minimum stay applies on weekends (2 nights), holidays (3 nights), and Dec 25 (5 nights). AE, MC, V. Children under 16 accepted in suites only. **Amenities:** Restaurant (New American/regional); Jacuzzi; game room; limited room service; in-room massage; babysitting. *In room:* A/C, TV/VCR, dataport, hair dryer.

West Hill House ★   This is among the more casual inns in the valley, in part because of its quiet hillside location, and in part because of the easy camaraderie among guests. Set on a lightly traveled country road, the 1850s farmhouse offers the quintessential New England experience within a few minutes' commute of the slopes at Sugarbush. Guest rooms are decorated in an updated country style, all with gas fireplaces or gas woodstoves; three have air-conditioning. The more modern units include steam showers and Jacuzzis.

1496 West Hill Rd., Warren, VT 05674. © **800/898-1427** or 802/496-7162. Fax 802/496-6443. www. westhillhouse.com. 7 units. $125–$190 double. Rates include full breakfast. Check website for specials. 3-night minimum stay foliage and holiday weekends; 2-night minimum stay on other weekends. AE, DISC MC, V. Children 12 and over welcome. **Amenities:** Honor bar; in-room massage; snowshoes. *In room:* TV/VCR, hair dryer, iron.

WHERE TO DINE

Bass Restaurant ★★ *Value* NEW AMERICAN   The Bass Restaurant is a quiet and romantic spot that offers excellent value. It's located in a former dinner theater with a circular stone fireplace and a handsome blond-wood bar. Light jazz plays in the background, and modern sculpture enlivens the space. Main courses range from oven-roasted duck with black currant and orange jus to macadamia-crusted tuna on coconut rice.

527 Sugarbush Access Rd., Warren. © **802/583-3100.** www.bassrestaurant.com. Main courses $12.50–$21.50 (most under $16). AE, MC, V. Sun–Thurs 5–10pm; Fri–Sat 5–11pm.

The Den ★ AMERICAN   Good food, decent service, no frills: That's the Den in a nutshell. A local favorite since 1970 for its well-worn, neighborly feel, it's the kind of spot where you can plop yourself down in a pine booth, help your-self to the salad bar while awaiting your main course, then cheer on the Red Sox on the tube over the bar. The menu offers the usual pub fare, including burgers, Reubens, and pork chops with applesauce and fries.

Junction of Rtes. 100 and 17, Waitsfield. © **802/496-8880.** Lunch items $4.95–$6.95; dinner main courses $8.95–$13.95. AE, MC, V. Daily 11:30am–11pm.

The Spotted Cow ★★ FRENCH-INSPIRED NEW AMERICAN   Set in a small, rustic retail complex in Waitsfield, the Spotted Cow is a low-ceilinged, modern, natural-wood spot with cherry banquettes. The place has the cozy feel of a bistro only locals know about, with a more cultivated than funky air. The inventive lunch menu features brie sandwiches, shiitake soup, and vegetarian paté. At dinner, the kitchen shines with creative approaches to old favorites. Venison is always on the menu, as is fresh fish. The duck and lamb cassoulet is a good choice, as is the Bermuda fish chowder, made with a splash of black rum. A vegetarian special is always available.

Bridgestreet Marketplace (at corner of Rte. 100 and East Warren Rd.), Waitsfield. ℂ 802/496-5151. Reservations recommended. Main courses $8.95–$10.95 lunch, $17.95–$23.95 dinner. MC, V. Tues–Sat 11:30am–3pm and 5:30–9pm; Sun 10:30am–3pm and 5:30–9pm.

7 Montpelier ★★ & Barre

Montpelier may very well be the most down-home, low-key state capital in the United States. There's a hint of that in every photo of the glistening gold dome of the capitol. Rising up behind it isn't a bank of mirror-sided skyscrapers, but a thickly forested hill. Montpelier, it turns out, isn't a self-important center of politics, but a small town that happens to be home to state government.

The state capitol is worth a stop, as is the local historical society. But more than that, Montpelier is worth visiting if only to experience a small, clean New England town that's more than a little friendly. Montpelier centers on two main boulevards: State Street, which is lined with state government buildings, and Main Street, where many of the town's shops are located. It's all very compact, manageable, and cordial.

The downtown has a pair of hardware stores next door to each other, well-stocked bookstores, and the **Savoy,** 26 Main St. (ℂ 802/229-0509), one of the best art movie houses in northern New England. At the Savoy, a large cup of cider and popcorn slathered with real, unclarified butter cost less than a small popcorn with nastily flavored oil at a mall cinema.

Nearby Barre (pronounced "Barry") is more commercial and less charming, but shares an equally vibrant past. Barre has more of a blue-collar demeanor than Montpelier. The historic connection to the thriving granite industry is glimpsed occasionally, from the granite curbstones lining the long Main Street to the signs for commercial establishments carved out of locally hewn rock. Barre attracted talented stone workers from Scotland and Italy (there's even a statue of Robert Burns), who helped give the turn-of-the-20th-century town a lively, cosmopolitan flavor.

ESSENTIALS

GETTING THERE   Montpelier is accessible via Exit 7 off I-89. For Barre, take Exit 8. Waterbury is located at Exit 10 off I-89. For bus service to Montpelier or Waterbury, contact **Vermont Transit** (ℂ 800/451-3292 or 802/223-7112). For train service to Waterbury, contact **Amtrak** (ℂ 800/872-7245; www.amtrak.com), whose *Vermonter* makes daily departures from New York.

VISITOR INFORMATION   The **Central Vermont Chamber of Commerce** (ℂ 802/229-5711; www.central-vt.com) is located on Stewart Road off Exit 7 of I-89. Turn left at the first light; it's a ½ mile (0.8km) on the left. The chamber is open Monday through Friday from 9am to 5pm.

EXPLORING THE AREA

Start your exploration of Montpelier with a visit to the gold-domed **State House** ★ (ℂ 802/828-2228), guarded out front by the statue of Ethan Allen. Three capitol buildings have risen on this site since 1809; the present building retained the impressive portico designed during the height of Greek Revival style in 1836. It was modeled after the temple of Theseus in Athens, and is made of Vermont granite. Self-guided tours are offered when the building is open, Monday through Friday from 7:45am to 4:15pm; in summer, it's also open Saturday from 11am to 3pm. Guided tours are run between late June and late October,

Central Vermont & the Champlain Valley

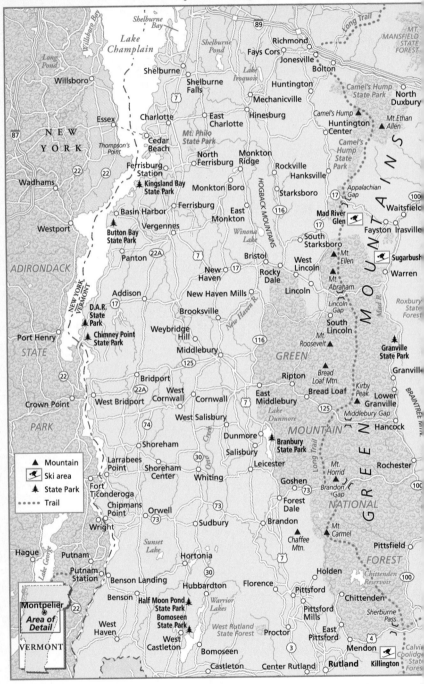

Lake Champlain
Shelburne Bay
Shelburne Pond
Long Trail
MT. MANSFIELD STATE FOREST
Long Pond
Willsboro
Shelburne
Shelburne Falls
Fays Cors
Richmond
89
Jonesville
Bolton
Huntington
Mechanicville
Hinesburg
Camel's Hump State Park
North Duxbury
Lake Iroquois
Essex
Charlotte
East Charlotte
Camel's Hump
Mt. Ethan Allen
Huntington Center
Mt Philo State Park
7
Cedar Beach
Thompson's Point
North Ferrisburg
Monkton Ridge
Rockville
Hanksville
Camel's Hump State Park
Appalachian Gap
NEW YORK
87
Ferrisburg Station
Monkton Boro
Starksboro
17
100
Waitsfield
Kingsland Bay State Park
Ferrisburg
East Monkton
116
Mad River Glen
Fayston Irasville
Wadhams
22
22
Basin Harbor
Vergennes
Winona Lake
South Starksboro
17
Sugarbush
Westport
Button Bay State Park
Panton
22A
7
Bristol
West Lincoln
Mt. Ellen
Warren
ADIRONDACK
New Haven
17
Rocky Dale
Mt. Abraham
Roxbury State Forest
Addison
17
New Haven Mills
Lincoln
Lincoln Gap
Port Henry
NEW YORK VERMONT
D.A.R. State Park
Brooksville
New Haven R.
South Lincoln
STATE
Chimney Point State Park
Weybridge Hill
116
Mt. Roosevelt
Granville State Park
22
Middlebury
125
GREEN
Granville
Crown Point
Bridport
22A
West Cornwall
Cornwall
7
Ripton
Bread Loaf Mtn.
Bread Loaf
Kirby Peak
Lower Granville
BRAINTREE Mtn.
PARK
West Bridport
74
West Salisbury
East Middlebury
Lake Dunmore
125
Middlebury Gap
Hancock
Shoreham
Dunmore
Branbury State Park
MOUNTAIN
Mt. Horrid
Rochester
Larrabees Point
30
Salisbury
Leicester
Long Trail
100
Fort Ticonderoga
Shoreham Center
Whiting
Goshen
73
Brandon Gap
Mt. Carmel
NATIONAL
Chipmans Point
Orwell
73
Forest Dale
Brandon
Wright
Sudbury
7
Chaffee Mtn.
Pittsfield
100
Hague
Putnam
Sunset Lake
Hortonia
Holden
Chittenden Reservoir
Putnam Station
Benson Landing
30
Florence
Pittsford
Chittenden
FOREST
Lake George
Benson
Hubbardton
Warrior Lakes
Pittsford Mills
Sherburne Pass
Montpelier
Area of Detail
22
Half Moon Pond State Park
Bomoseen State Park
West Rutland State Forest
Proctor
East Pittsford
4
Calvin Coolidge State Forest
VERMONT
West Haven
West Castleton
Bomoseen
3
Mendon
Killington
Castleton
Center Rutland
Rutland

Mountain ▲
Ski area ⛷
State Park ♠
Trail ·····

470

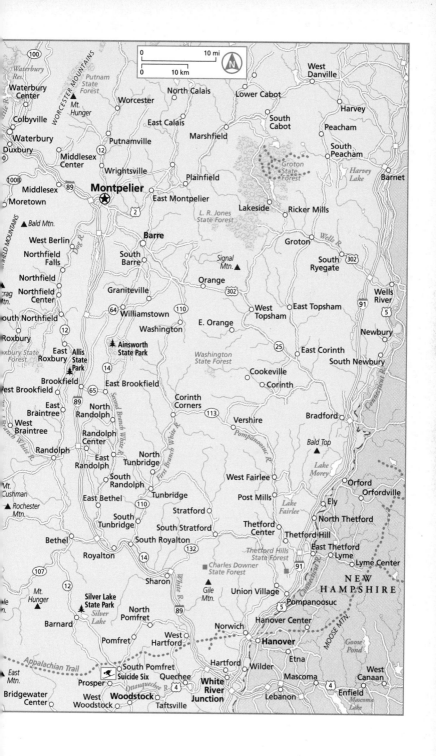

Monday through Friday from 10am to 3:30pm and Saturday from 11am to 2:30pm, every half hour. The tour is informative and fun; it's worth your while if you're in the area, but probably not worth a major detour.

A short stroll from the State House is the **Vermont Historical Society** ⊛, 109 State St. (✆ **802/828-2291**). The museum is housed in a replica of the elegant old Pavilion Building, a prominent Victorian hotel, and contains a number of artifacts, including a gun once owned by Ethan Allen. It's open Tuesday through Friday from 9am to 4:30pm, Saturday from 9am to 4pm, and Sunday from noon to 4pm. Admission is $3 for adults, $2 for students and seniors. *Note:* The museum will be closed until late 2002 and possibly beyond for extensive renovations; call first to make sure it has reopened.

Rock of Ages Quarry ⊛⊛   When in or around Barre, listen for the deep, throaty hum of industry. That's the Rock of Ages Quarry, set on a hillside high above town near the aptly named hamlet of Graniteville. A free visitor center presents informative exhibits, a video about quarrying, and a glimpse of an old granite quarry (no longer active). Self-guided tours of the old quarry are free. For a look at the active quarry (the world's largest), sign up for a guided half-hour tour. An old bus groans up to a platform high above the 500-foot (150m) canyon, where workers cleave huge slabs of granite and hoist them out using 150-foot (45m) derricks anchored with a spider's web of 15 miles (24km) of steel cable. It's an operation to behold.

773 Graniteville Rd., Graniteville. ✆ **802/476-3119.** www.rockofages.com. Guided tours $4 adults, $3.50 seniors, $1.50 children 6–12. Visitor center (free) May–Oct Mon–Sat 8:30am–5pm, Sun noon–5pm (in foliage season, Sun 8:30am–5:30pm); guided tours offered June to mid-Oct Mon–Fri 9:15am–3pm. Closed July 4. From Barre, drive south on Rte. 14; turn left at lights by McDonald's; watch for signs.

WHERE TO STAY

Capitol Plaza Hotel ⊛   This is the favored hotel of visitors on business with the state government, but is also well located (across from the capitol) to serve folks exploring the town. The guest rooms adopt a light, faux-colonial tone, with more amenities than one might expect. It's nothing fancy, but is clean, comfortable, and convenient.

100 State St., Montpelier, VT 05602. ✆ **800/274-5252** or 802/223-5252. Fax 802/229-5427. www.capitolplaza.com. 58 units. $98 double; foliage season from $119 double; $118–$168 suite. AE, DISC, MC, V. **Amenities:** Restaurant (steakhouse). *In room:* A/C, TV, dataport, hair dryer, iron.

Inn at Montpelier ⊛   Two in-town homes constitute the Inn at Montpelier, and both offer welcoming accommodations and an appeal for those who enjoy historic architecture. The main Federal-style inn, built in 1827, features a mix of historical and up-to-date furnishings, along with a sunny sitting room and deck. (Room 27 is especially pleasant and features a private deck.) The property is somewhat more sparely furnished than other historic inns in the area (head to Waitsfield or Warren if you're in search of the quintessential Vermont inn), but it offers comfortable lodging an easy stroll from downtown.

147 Main St., Montpelier, VT 05602. ✆ **802/223-2727.** Fax 802/223-0722. www.innatmontpelier.com. 19 units. $94–$177 double (higher during foliage season). Rates include continental breakfast. AE, DC, DISC, MC, V. **Amenities:** Bike rental; in-room massage; dry cleaning. *In room:* A/C, TV, dataport.

WHERE TO DINE

A creation of the New England Culinary Institute, **La Brioche Bakery & Cafe,** at State and Main streets (✆ **802/229-0443**), is a little bit of Europe in one of New England's more Continental cities. Get a croissant or baguette to go, or settle into an outdoor table in the afternoon sun.

Main Street Grill & Bar ★★ AMERICAN/ECLECTIC   This comfortable, modern restaurant serves as classroom and ongoing exam for students of the New England Culinary Institute, located just down the block. It's not unusual to see knots of students, toques at a rakish angle, walking between the restaurant and class. You can eat in the first-level dining room, watching street life through the broad windows, or burrow in the homey bar downstairs. Dishes change every 3 months, but might include roasted rabbit paella, pan-seared rainbow trout, or leg of venison with celery root and parsnips. One or two vegetarian dishes are always on the menu.

Also of note is the second-floor **Chef's Table,** which is owned by the culinary institute but operates on a different schedule. (It's open Mon through Fri for lunch and dinner, and Sat for dinner only.) This intimate dining room offers more refined fare, such as a smoked pork chop with apple-fennel salad and grilled yellowfin tuna with an olive-caper sauce.

118 Main St. ✆ 802/223-3188. Limited reservations accepted. Lunch items $6.50–$8.95; dinner entrees $11.75–$16.75. AE, DISC, MC, V. Mon–Sat 11:30am–2pm and 5:30–9pm; Sun 10am–2pm and 5:30–9pm.

8 Stowe

Stowe is a wonderful destination, summer, fall, and winter. It was one of Vermont's first winter destination areas, but it has managed the decades-long juggernaut of growth with patience and aplomb. There are condo developments andstrip mall–style restaurants, to be sure. Yet the village has managed to preserve its essential character nicely, including trademark views of the surrounding mountains and vistas across the fertile farmlands of the valley floor. Thanks to its history and charm, Stowe tends to attract a more affluent clientele than, say, Killington or Okemo.

Stowe is quaint, compact, and home to what may be Vermont's most gracefully tapered church spire, located atop the Stowe Community Church. Because the mountain is a few miles from the village, the town doesn't suffer that woebegone emptiness that many ski villages do come summer. You can actually park your car and explore on foot or by bike, which isn't the case at ski resorts that have developed around large parking lots and condo clusters.

This small town of just 3,400 has more depth and breadth of accommodations and restaurants than do comparably sized ski towns—some 62 lodging establishments and more than 50 eateries. Most of the growth in recent decades has taken place along Mountain Road (Rte. 108), which runs northwest of the village to the base of Mount Mansfield and the Stowe ski area. Here you'll find an array of motels, restaurants, shops, bars, and even a three-screen cinema, with many establishments nicely designed or at least tastefully tucked out of view. The road has all the convenience of a strip-mall area, but with little of the aesthetic blight.

The chief complaint about Mountain Road: traffic. It invariably backs up at the end of the ski day in winter and on foliage weekends, and can make a trip into the village an interesting experiment in blood-pressure management. Fortunately, a free trolley bus connects the village with the mountain during ski season, so you can let your car get snowed in and prevent outbreaks of village traffic from getting under your skin.

ESSENTIALS

GETTING THERE   Stowe is located on Route 100 north of Waterbury and south of Morrisville. In summer, Stowe may also be reached via Smugglers

The Saga of Ben & Jerry

The doleful cows standing amid a bright green meadow on pints of Ben & Jerry's ice cream have become almost a symbol for Vermont, but Ben & Jerry's cows—actually, they're Vermont artist Woody Jackson's cows—have also become a symbol for friendly capitalism ("hippie capitalism," as some prefer).

The founding of the company has become a legend in business circles. Two friends from Long Island, New York, Ben Cohen and Jerry Greenfield, started up their company in Burlington in 1978 with $12,000 and a few mail-order lessons in ice-cream making. The pair experimented with the flavor samples they obtained free from salesmen and sold their products out of an old downtown gas station. Embracing the outlook that work should be fun, they gave away free ice cream at community events, staged free outdoor films in summer, and plowed profits back into the community. Their free-spirited approach, along with the exceptional quality of their product, built a successful corporation with sales rising to the hundreds of millions of dollars.

While competition from other gourmet ice-cream makers and a widespread consumer desire to cut back fat consumption have made it tougher to have fun and turn a profit at the same time, Ben and Jerry are still at it, expanding their manufacturing plants outside New England and concocting new products. Even though Ben & Jerry sold their interest to outside buyers recently, the company's heart and soul remains in Vermont.

The main factory in Waterbury, about 10 miles (16km) south of Stowe, is among the most popular tourist attractions in Vermont. The plant is located about a mile (1.6km) north of I-89 on Route 100, and the grounds have a festival marketplace feel to them, despite the fact that there's no festival and no marketplace. During peak summer season, crowds mill about waiting for the 30-minute factory tours. These are first-come, first-served, and run daily from 9am to 8pm in July and August (with somewhat more limited hours in the off-season); afternoon tours fill up quickly, so get here early if you want to avoid a long wait. Tours are $2 for adults, $1.75 for seniors, and free for children under 12.

Once you've got your ticket, browse the small ice cream museum (learn the long, strange history of Cherry Garcia), buy a cone of your favorite flavor at the scoop shop, or lounge along the promenade, which is scattered with Adirondack chairs and picnic tables. For kids, there's the "Stairway to Heaven," which leads to a playground, and a "Cow-Viewing Area," which is pretty much self-explanatory. The tours are informative and fun, and conclude with a sample of the day's featured product. For more information, call ℂ **802/244-8687.**

Notch on Route 108. This pass, which squeezes narrowly between rocks and is not recommended for RVs or trailers, is closed in winter.

There is no direct train or bus service to Stowe. Travel to Waterbury, 10 miles (16km) south of Stowe, via **Vermont Transit** (ℂ **800/451-3292** or

802/244-6943) or **Amtrak** (© **800/872-7245;** www.amtrak.com), then con-
nect to Stowe via a rental car from **Thrifty** (© **802/244-8800**), **Richard's
Limousine Service** (© **800/698-3176** or 802/253-5600), or a taxi from **Peg's
Pick Up** (© **800/370-9490** or 802/253-9490).

VISITOR INFORMATION   The **Stowe Area Association** (© **877/467-8693**
or 802/253-7321; www.stoweinfo.com) maintains an office on Main Street in
the village center, open Monday through Friday from 9am to 8pm, Saturday and
Sunday from 10am to 5pm (limited hours during slower seasons).

The **Green Mountain Club** (© **802/244-7037**), a venerable statewide association devoted to building and maintaining backcountry trails, has a visitor center
on Route 100 between Waterbury and Stowe. It's open Monday through Friday.

SPECIAL EVENTS   The **Stowe Winter Carnival** (© **802/253-7321**) takes
place at the end of January, as it has since 1921. The fest features a number of
wacky events involving skis, snowshoes, and skates, as well as nighttime entertainment in area venues. Don't miss the snow sculpture contest or "turkey bowling," which involves sliding frozen birds across the ice.

ALPINE SKIING

Stowe Mountain Resort ✦✦✦   Stowe was one of the first, one of the
classiest, and one of the most noted ski resorts in the world when it opened in
the 1930s. Its regional dominance has eroded somewhat in the intervening
decades—Killington, Sunday River, and Sugarloaf, among others, have all
captured large shares of the New England market. But this historic resort still
has loads of charm and plenty of excellent runs. It's one of the best places for the
full New England ski experience, it's one of the most beautiful ski mountains,
and it offers tremendous challenges to advanced skiers with winding, old-style
trails. Especially notable are its legendary "Front Four" trails (National, Starr,
Lift Line, and Goat) that have humbled more than a handful of skiers attempting to grope their way from advanced intermediate to expert. The mountain has
four good, long lifts that go from bottom to top—not the usual patchwork of
shorter lifts you find at other ski areas. Beginners can start out across the road at
Spruce Peak, which features gentle, wide trails.

Stowe, VT 05672. © **800/253-4754** for lodging, or 802/253-3000. www.stowe.com. Vertical drop: 2,360 ft.
(708m). Lifts: 1 gondola, 8 chairlifts (1 high-speed), 2 surface lifts. Skiable acreage: 480. Lift tickets: $60
holidays, $58 nonholidays.

CROSS-COUNTRY SKIING

Stowe is an outstanding destination for cross-country skiers, with three groomed
ski areas featuring a combined total of more than 100 miles (161km) of trails
traversing everything from gentle valley floors to challenging mountain peaks.

The **Trapp Family Lodge Cross-Country Ski Center,** on Luce Hill Road, 2
miles (3.2km) from Mountain Road (© **800/826-7000** or 802/253-8511;
www.trappfamily.com), was the nation's first cross-country ski center. It remains
one of the most gloriously situated in the Northeast, set atop a ridge with views
across the broad valley and into the folds of the mountains flanking Mount
Mansfield. The center features 27 miles (43km) of groomed trails, plus 60 miles
(97km) of backcountry trails, on its 2,700 acres (1,094 hectares) of rolling
forestland. Rates are $16 for a trail pass, $18 for equipment rental.

The **Edson Hill Manor Ski Touring Center** (© **800/621-0284** or
802/253-8954) has 33 miles (53km) of wooded trails just off Mountain Road
($10 for a day pass). Also offering appealing ski touring is the **Stowe Mountain**

Resort Cross-Country Touring Center (© **800/253-4754** or 802/253-7311), with 48 miles (77km) at the base of Mount Mansfield ($12).

SUMMER OUTDOOR PURSUITS

Stowe's history is linked to winter recreation, but it's also an outstanding fair-weather destination, surrounded by lush, rolling green hills and open farmlands and towered over by craggy **Mount Mansfield,** at 4,393 feet (1,318m) Vermont's highest peak.

Deciding how to get atop Mount Mansfield is half the challenge. The **toll road** ⚓ (© **802/253-7311**) traces its lineage back to the 19th century, when it served horse-drawn vehicles bringing passengers to the old hotel sited near the mountain's crown. (The hotel was demolished in the 1960s.) Drivers now twist their way up this road and park below the summit of Mansfield; a 2-hour hike along well-marked trails will bring you to the top for unforgettable views. The toll road is open from late May to mid-October. The fare is $14 per car with up to six passengers, $2 per additional person. Ascending on foot or by bicycle is free.

Another option is the Stowe **gondola** ⚓ (© **802/253-7311**), which whisks visitors to within 1½ miles (2.4km) of the summit at the Cliff House Restaurant. Hikers can explore the rugged, open ridgeline, and then descend before twilight. The gondola runs from mid-June to mid-October and costs $11 round-trip for adults, $7 for children 6 to 12.

The budget route up Mount Mansfield (and in our mind the most rewarding) is on foot, and you have at least nine choices for an ascent. The easiest but least pleasing route is up the toll road. Other options require local guidance and a good map. Ask for information from knowledgeable locals (your inn might be of help), or stop by the Green Mountain Club headquarters, on Route 100 about 4 miles (6km) south of Stowe; open Monday through Friday. GMC can also assist with advice on other area trails.

One of the most understated local attractions is the **Stowe Recreation Path** ⚓⚓, which winds approximately 5 miles (8km) from behind the Stowe Community Church up the valley toward the mountain, ending behind the Topnotch Tennis Center. This exceptionally appealing pathway, completed in 1989, is heavily used by locals for transportation and exercise in summer; in winter, it serves as a cross-country ski trail. Connect to the pathway at either end or at points where it crosses side roads that lead to Mountain Road. No motorized vehicles or skateboards are allowed.

All manner of recreational paraphernalia is available for rent at the **Mountain Sports & Bike Shop** (© **802/253-7919**), which is right on the Rec Path. This includes full-suspension demo bikes, baby joggers, and bike trailers. Basic bike rentals are $16 for 4 hours, which is plenty long enough to explore the path. The shop is on Mountain Road (across from the Golden Eagle Resort) and is open daily from 9am to 6pm in summer. (This is also a good spot for cross-country ski and snowshoe rentals in winter.)

Fans of paddle sports should seek out **Umiak Outdoor Outfitters,** 849 South Main St., in Stowe (© **802/253-2317**). The folks here offer guided river trips (flatwater or light rapids) and instruction, ranging from 1 hour ($20) to 3 days ($225). Also available are canoe, kayak, and raft rentals ($25 to $35 per day).

WHERE TO STAY

The **Sun and Ski Motor Inn,** 1613 Mountain Rd. (© **800/448-5223** or 802/253-7159), has 26 units (all with air-conditioning, phones, TVs, and fridges) and a heated pool. Rates are $69 to $142.

Edson Hill Manor ★★ The Edson Hill Manor sits atop a long, quiet drive 2 miles (3km) from Mountain Road and features an ineffably quirky charm. The main lodge dates to the 1940s; the four carriage houses just up the hill are of newer vintage. The whole compound is set amid a rolling landscape of lawns, hemlocks, and maples. The comfortable common room in the main house is like a movie set for a country retreat—tapestries, pastels, and oils adorn the walls. Most of the nine guest rooms in the main lodge have pine floors, wood-burning fireplaces, colonial maple furnishings, wingback chairs, and four-poster beds. The carriage-house rooms are somewhat larger, but lack the cozy charm of the main inn and feel more like motel units (note that we mean *really* nice motel units). Some units have TVs; manor rooms are air-conditioned.

1500 Edson Hill Rd., Stowe, VT 05672. ✆ **800/621-0284** or 802/253-7371. www.stowevt.com. 25 units. High season $209–$269 double (including breakfast and dinner); regular season $139–$199 double (including breakfast); off-season (Apr–May and Nov) $80–$95 double. AE, DISC, MC, V. Pets and young children welcome in carriage house units only. **Amenities:** Restaurant (New American); pool nearby; riding stables (private lessons available).

Green Mountain Inn ★★★ This handsome structure sits right in the village, and it's the best choice for those seeking a sense of New England history along with a bit of pampering. The sprawling hostelry has 100 guest rooms spread among several buildings, but it feels far more intimate, with accommodations tastefully decorated in an early-19th-century motif. More than a dozen units feature Jacuzzis and/or gas fireplaces, and the Mill House has rooms with CD players, sofas, and Jacuzzis that open into the bedroom from behind folding wooden doors. The luxe Mansfield House features double Jacuzzis, marble bathrooms, and 36-inch TVs with DVD players. The most expensive rooms are uniformly superb; some of the lower-priced rooms in the main inn feature minor irritants, like balky radiators or views of noisy kitchen ventilators.

Main St. (P.O. Box 60), Stowe, VT 05672. ✆ **800/253-7302** or 802/253-7301. Fax 802/253-5096. www.greenmountaininn.com. 100 units. $99–$299 double; $299–$399 suite. Premium charged during foliage season and Christmas week. 2-night minimum stay summer/winter weekends and in foliage season. AE, DISC, MC, V. Dogs under 50 lbs. allowed in some rooms ($20 per night). **Amenities:** Restaurant (creative pub fare); heated outdoor pool; well-equipped fitness room; Jacuzzi; sauna; steam room; game room; limited room service, in-room massage; laundry service. *In room:* A/C, TV w/ pay movies, hair dryer.

Stowehof ★ Stowehof is situated high on a hillside and feels far removed from the hubbub of the valley floor. The exterior is an example of that aggressive neo-Tirolean ski-chalet styling, but inside, the place comes close to magical—it's pleasantly rustic, with heavy beams and pine floors, ticking clocks, and massive tree trunks carved into architectural elements. Guests may feel a bit like characters in *The Hobbit*. The rooms are furnished without a lot of fanfare: Some are bold and festive, others subdued and quiet. Four have wood-burning fireplaces, 24 have air-conditioning, and all have views. Among the best are rooms 43 and 44, both with high ceilings and balconies. The lodge is next to Wiessner Woods, with 80 acres (32 hectares) laced with hiking and cross-country ski trails.

434 Edson Hill Rd. (P.O. Box 1139), Stowe, VT 05672. ✆ **800/932-7136** or 802/253-9722. Fax 802/253-7513. www.stowehofinn.com. 46 units. Ski season $138–$250 double; summer $69–$125 double; off-season $35–$70 double. Rates include full breakfast. Higher rates during holidays. 4-night minimum stay during holidays; 2-night minimum stay on some weekends. AE, DC, MC, V. **Amenities:** Restaurant (New American); outdoor heated pool; tennis courts; nearby health club; Jacuzzi; sauna; game room; business center; in-room massage; laundry service; dry cleaning; horseback riding (extra fee). *In room:* TV.

Stowe Motel This is one of Stowe's best choices for those traveling on a budget. The motel has 60 units spread among three buildings; rooms are basic but slightly larger than average, with some comfortable touches like couches and coffee tables.

2043 Mountain Rd., Stowe, VT 05672. ℂ **800/829-7629** or 802/253-7629. Fax 802/253-9971. www. stowemotel.com. 60 units. Standard room $79–$89 double (winter holidays from $122, foliage from $94); efficiency unit $89–$126. Ask about ski packages. Pets accepted in some rooms ($10). **Amenities:** Heated pool (summer only); Jacuzzi; game room; free snowshoes. *In room:* A/C, TV, dataport, fridge.

Topnotch ★★★ A boxy, uninteresting exterior hides a creatively designed interior at this upscale resort and spa. The lobby is ski-lodge modern, with lots of stone and wood and a huge moose head hanging on the wall. Guest rooms are attractively appointed, most in country pine. Ten units have wood-burning fireplaces; 18 have Jacuzzis; and third-floor rooms have cathedral ceilings. The main attractions here are the resort's spa and activities, which range from horseback riding in summer to cross-country skiing and indoor tennis in winter. There are nice touches throughout, like fireplaces in the spa's locker rooms.

4000 Mountain Rd., Stowe, VT 05672. ℂ **800/451-8686** or 802/253-8585. Fax 802/253-9263. www. topnotch-resort.com. 92 units. Ski season and midsummer $220–$310 double, $355–$710 suite; off-season $160–$230 double, $280–$550 suite. Higher rates and 6-night minimum stay Christmas week. Town-home accommodations $185–$715 depending on season and size. AE, DC, DISC, MC, V. Pets allowed. **Amenities:** 2 restaurants (Continental, family fare); indoor and outdoor pools; indoor and outdoor tennis courts; fitness room; full spa; Jacuzzi; sauna; concierge; limited room service; horseback riding. *In room:* A/C, TV/VCR w/ pay movies, dataport, fridge, coffeemaker, hair dryer, iron, safe.

Trapp Family Lodge The Trapp family of *Sound of Music* fame bought this sprawling farm in 1942, just 4 years after fleeing the Nazi takeover of Austria. The Tyrolean-flavored lodge, on 2,700 mountainside acres (1,094 hectares), is a comfortable resort hotel, though designed more for efficiency than elegance. The guest rooms are a shade better than run-of-the-mill hotel rooms, and most come complete with fine views and balconies. Room prices are high here; they offer access to nice facilities, but little else. Better value can be found elsewhere in the valley. The restaurant offers well-prepared Continental fare; Sunday concerts are held in the meadow in summer.

700 Trapp Hill Rd., Stowe, VT 05672. ℂ **800/826-7000** or 802/253-8511. Fax 802/253-5740. www. trappfamily.com. 116 units. Winter and summer $245–$275 double, $320–$615 suite; off-season from $180 double. Higher rates during holidays and foliage season (includes meals). 5-night minimum stay Christmas week; 3-night minimum stay Presidents' week and foliage season. AE, DC, MC, V. Depart Stowe westward on Rte. 108; in 2 miles (3.2km) bear left at fork near white church; continue up hill following signs for lodge. **Amenities:** 2 restaurants (Continental, informal Austrian); heated indoor pool; 2 outdoor pools (one for adults only); tennis courts; fitness center; sauna; children's programs; game room; limited room service; in-room massage; babysitting; coin-op laundry; dry cleaning. *In room:* TV.

WHERE TO DINE

Blue Moon Cafe ★★★ NEW AMERICAN The delectable bread on the table, Frank Sinatra crooning in the background, and vibrant local art on the walls offer clues that this isn't your typical ski-area pub-fare restaurant. Located a short stroll off Stowe's main street in a contemporary setting in an older home, the Blue Moon serves up the village's finest dining. The menu changes weekly, but count on lamb, beef, and veggie options, plus a couple of seafood offerings. The kitchen staff creates inventive dishes like sirloin strip steak with caramelized onions and blue cheese. Desserts are simple yet pure delights: profiteroles with espresso ice cream, Belgian chocolate pot, three sorbets with cookies.

35 School St. ℂ 802/253-7006. Reservations recommended. Main courses $16–$26. AE, DISC, MC, V. Daily 6–9:30pm. Usually open weekends only in shoulder seasons; call first.

Miguel's Stowe-Away ☆ MEXICAN/SOUTHWESTERN   Located in an old farmhouse midway between the village and the mountain, Miguel's packs in folks looking for the tangiest Mexican and Tex-Mex food in the valley. Start off with a margarita or Vermont beer, then order up appetizers like crab cakes with chipotle aioli. Follow up with sizzling fajitas or one of the filling combo plates. Desserts range from the complicated (apple-mango compote with cinnamon tortilla and ice cream) to the simple (chocolate-chip cookies). Miguel's has grown popular enough to offer its own brand of chips, salsa, and other products, which turn up in specialty shops and grocery stores throughout the Northeast. Expect a loud and boisterous atmosphere on busy nights.

Mountain Rd. ✆ 800/254-1240 or 802/253-7574. www.miguels.com. Reservations recommended on weekends and in ski season. Main courses $8.95–$17.95 (most under $14). AE, DISC, MC, V. Daily 5–10pm (from 5:30pm in summer).

Mr. Pickwick's ☆ BRITISH PUB FARE   Mr. Pickwick's is a pub and restaurant that's part of Ye Old English Inne. It could justly be accused of being a theme-park restaurant, with the theme being, well, ye olde Englande. But it's been run since 1983 with such creative gusto by British expats Chris and Lyn Francis that it's hard not to enjoy yourself. Start by admiring the Anglo gewgaws while relaxing at handsome wood booths. Sample from the 150 beers before ordering house specialties like bangers and mash, fish-and-chips, and beef Wellington. A new deck offers great expanded seating.

433 Mountain Rd. ✆ 802/253-7558. www.mrpickwicks.com. Main courses $6.95–$12.95 lunch, $13.95–$23.95 dinner. AE, DC, MC, V. Daily 11am–1am.

The Shed ☆ PUB FARE   Stowe has plenty of options for pub fare, but the Shed is the most reliable. Since it first opened more than 3 decades ago, this friendly place has won fans by the sleighload with its filling fare and feisty camaraderie. Meals are pub-fare eclectic: nachos (a little soggy), burgers (including a veggie option), grilled tuna, prime rib, and stir-fry noodles.

1859 Mountain Rd. ✆ 802/253-4364. Reservations recommended on weekends and holidays. Lunch items $5–$9.95; dinner main courses $10.95–$18.95. AE, DC, DISC, MC, V. Daily 11:30am–midnight (light fare only 10pm–midnight); Sun brunch 10am–2pm.

9 Burlington

Burlington is a vibrant college town—home to the University of Vermont, known as UVM—that's continually, valiantly resisting the onset of middle age. It's the birthplace of hippies-turned-corporation Ben & Jerry's. (Look for the sidewalk plaque at the corner of St. Paul and College streets commemorating the first store, which opened in 1978.) It elected a socialist mayor in 1981, Bernie Sanders, who's now Vermont's lone representative to Congress. Burlington was also the birthplace of the eclectic rock band Phish, which for a time was heir to the Grateful Dead hippie-rock tradition.

It's no wonder that Burlington has become a magnet for those seeking alternatives to big-city life with its big-city problems. Burlington has a superb location overlooking Lake Champlain and the Adirondacks of northern New York. To the east, visible on your way out of town, the Green Mountains rise dramatically, with two of the highest points (Mount Mansfield and Camel's Hump) stretching above the undulating ridge.

In the mid–20th century, Burlington turned its back for a time on its spectacular waterfront. Urban redevelopment focused on parking garages and a few high-rises; the waterfront lay fallow, and was developed for light industry. In recent years, the city has sought to regain a toehold along the lake, acquiring and redeveloping parts for commercial and recreational use. It's been successful in some sections (especially the bike path, discussed below), less so in others.

In contrast, the downtown section is thriving. The pedestrian mall (Church St.), a creation that has failed in so many other towns, works here. New construction has brought large-scale department stores (Filene's, for one) right smack downtown, reversing the flight to the mall that has plagued so many other small cities. The city's scale is pleasantly skewed toward pedestrians—it's best to park your car and walk as soon as you can.

ESSENTIALS

GETTING THERE   Burlington is at the junction of I-89, Route 7, and Route 2. **Burlington International Airport,** about 3 miles (5km) east of downtown, is served by **Continental Express** (© **800/732-6887**), **Delta** (© **800/221-1212**), **Jet Blue** (© **800/538-2583**), **United** (© **800/241-6522**), and **US Airways** (© **800/428-4322**).

The **Amtrak** (© **800/872-7245;** www.amtrak.com) *Vermonter* offers daily departures for Burlington from Washington, Baltimore, Philadelphia, New York, New Haven, and Springfield, Mass.

Vermont Transit (© **800/451-3292** or 802/864-6811), with a depot at 345 Pine St., offers bus connections from Albany, Boston, Hartford, New York's JFK Airport, and other points in Vermont, Massachusetts, and New Hampshire.

VISITOR INFORMATION   The **Lake Champlain Regional Chamber of Commerce,** 60 Main St. (© **802/863-3489;** www.vermont.org), maintains an information center in a stout 1929 brick building just up from the waterfront and a short walk from Church Street Market. Hours are Monday through Friday from 8:30am to 5pm. On weekends, maps and brochures are left in the entryway for visitors. A summer-only information booth is also staffed on the Church Street Marketplace at the corner of Church and Bank streets (no phone).

The free weekly *Seven Days* (www.sevendaysvt.com) carries topical and lifestyle articles, along with a very good list of events.

SPECIAL EVENTS   The **Vermont Mozart Festival** (© **800/639-9097** or 802/862-7352; www.vtmozart.com) takes place in and around Burlington from mid-July to August. (Three's also a winter series.) Tickets range from $19 to $32. Call or check the website for upcoming concerts.

EXPLORING THE REGION

Ethan Allen Homestead 🦌   A quiet retreat on one of the most idyllic stretches of the Winooski River, the Ethan Allen Homestead is a shrine to Vermont's favorite son. While Allen wasn't born in Burlington, he settled here later in life on property confiscated from a British sympathizer during the Revolution. The reconstructed farmhouse is an enduring tribute to this Vermont hero; an orientation center offers an intriguing multimedia accounting of Allen's life. The house is open for tours from mid-October to mid-May by appointment only. (A day's notice is required.) The grounds are open year-round daily from dawn to dusk. Admission to the park is free.

Rte. 127. © 802/865-4556. Admission $5 adults, $4 seniors, $2.50 children 5–17; $14 per family. Mid-May to mid-June daily 1–5pm; mid-June to mid-Oct Mon–Sat 10am–5pm, Sun 1–5pm. Take Rte. 127 northward from downtown; look for signs.

Burlington

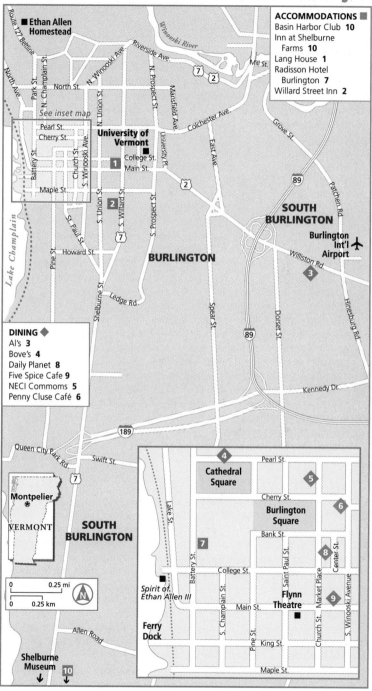

Ethan Allen: Patriot & Libertine

In 1749, the governor of New Hampshire began giving away land to settlers willing to brave the howling wilderness of what is now Vermont. Two decades later, the New York State courts decreed those grants void, which opened the door for New York speculators to flood into the region vowing to push the original settlers out of the valleys and up into the Green Mountains.

Not surprisingly, this didn't sit well with those already there. They established a network of military units called the Green Mountain Boys, who promised to drive out the New Yorkers. A hale fellow named Ethan Allen headed up new militia, which launched a series of effective harrying raids against the impudent New Yorkers. Green Mountain Boys destroyed their homes, drove away their livestock, and chased the New York sheriffs back across the border.

The American Revolution soon intervened, and Ethan Allen and the Green Mountain Boys took up the revolutionary cause with vigor. They helped sack Fort Ticonderoga in New York in 1775, rallied to the cause at the famed Battle of Bennington, and continued to make splendid nuisances of themselves to the British effort throughout the war.

Allen's fame grew as word spread about him and his Green Mountain Boys. A hard-drinking, fierce-fighting, large-living sort of guy, Allen became a legend in his own time. He could bite the head off a nail, one story claimed; another said that he was once bit by a rattlesnake, which promptly belched and died.

While Allen's apocryphal exploits lived on following his death in 1789, he also left a more significant legacy. Vermont's statehood in 1791 was due in large part to the independence and patriotism the region showed under Allen. And today you can't drive very far in Vermont without a reminder of Allen's historic presence—parks are named after him, inns boast that he once slept there, and you'll still hear the occasional story about his bawdy doings.

Lake Champlain Ferries *Car* ferries chug across the waters of Lake Champlain from Burlington to New York State between late spring and foliage season. It's a good way to cut out miles of driving if you're heading west toward the Adirondacks. It's also a great way to see the lake and mountains on a pleasant, inexpensive cruise. Between June and mid-October, a 90-minute narrated lake cruise is also offered; the cost is $7.75 for adults and $3.75 for children. No reservations are accepted; travelers are advised to arrive 20 to 30 minutes in advance of departure.

Ferries also cross Lake Champlain between Grande Isle, Vt., and Plattsburgh, N.Y. (year-round), and Charlotte, Vt., and Essex, N.Y. (Apr–early Jan). Call the following number for more information.

King St. Dock. ☎ **802/864-9804.** www.ferries.com. Fares $13.25 one-way for car and driver from Burlington to Port Kent; $6.50 round-trip for adult passengers; $3 for children 6–12. Burlington ferry operates mid-May to mid-Oct. Frequent departures in summer between 7:30am and 7:30pm. Schedule varies in spring, fall, and foliage season; call or check the website for departure times.

Finds **Garage Sale**

One of our favorite spots is the **Architectural Salvage Warehouse,** 53 Main St. (© **802/658-5011**). Anyone who owns an old home will enjoy browsing this store, located at the corner of Maple and Battery streets southwest of the Church Street Marketplace. You'll see claw-foot tubs, plenty of old doors, and mantels, but also souvenirs for those who'd rather travel light: crystal doorknobs, brass hardware, and other portable items you can toss in the trunk.

Shelburne Museum 🟊🟊🟊   Established in 1947, the Shelburne contains one of the nation's most singular collections of American decorative, folk, and fine art, occupying some 37 buildings spread over 45 rolling acres (18 hectares) 7 miles (11km) south of Burlington. The more mundane exhibits include quilts, early tools, and weather vanes. But the museum also collects and displays *whole* buildings from around New England and New York. These include an 1890 railroad station, a lighthouse, an Adirondack lodge, and a round barn. There's even an eerily landlocked 220-foot (66m) steamship. Additions in the past several years include a wonderful 1950s ranch house furnished in period style, as well as an architecturally engaging "Collector's House" (new in 2001), made creatively of prefab metal structures and other materials.

Rte. 7 (P.O. Box 10), Shelburne. © **802/985-3346.** www.shelburnemuseum.org. Summer admission $17.50 adults, $8.75 students and children 6–14; spring and late fall admission (only selected buildings open) $10 adults, $5 children. Late May to mid-Oct daily 10am–5pm. Only selected buildings open Apr–late May and mid-Oct to Dec; call for information.

The Spirit of Ethan Allen 🟊   Accommodating 500 passengers on three decks, the new *Ethan Allen III* (brought to Lake Champlain in summer 2002 and 40 percent larger than its predecessor) offers a more genteel touring alternative to the ferry. The vistas of Lake Champlain and the Adirondacks haven't changed much since Samuel de Champlain, who first reached here in 1609, explored the area. The enclosed decks are air-conditioned, and food is available on all cruises, including nightly dinners and a Sunday brunch. The scenic cruise departs daily every other hour beginning at 10am until 4pm. Parking is available at additional cost.

Burlington Boathouse. © **802/862-8300.** www.soea.com. Narrated cruises (1½ hours) $9.95 adults, $3.95 children 3–11. Sunset cruises (2½ hours) $11.95 adults, $4.95 children. Specialty cruises (dinner, brunch, mystery theater) priced higher; call for details. Late May to mid-Oct daily.

SHOPPING

The **Church Street Marketplace** is one of the more notable success stories of downtown development. Situated along 4 blocks that extend southward from the austerely elegant 1816 Congregational church, the marketplace buzzes with the sort of downtown energy that makes urban planners everywhere envious. While the marketplace has been discovered by the national chains (Banana Republic, Borders, Urban Outfitters), it still makes room for used bookstores and homegrown shops. In summer, leave time to be entertained by buskers, sidewalk vendors, and knots of young folks just hanging out.

OUTDOOR PURSUITS

Burlington is blessed with numerous attractive city parks. Most popular is **Leddy Park** 🟊🟊, on North Avenue (© **802/864-0123**), with an 1,800-foot

(540m) beach, tennis courts, ball fields, walking trails, and an indoor skating rink. **North Beach** ⚓ (© 802/862-0942) also features a long sandy beach, plus a campground for tents and RVs.

On the downtown waterfront, look for the **Burlington Community Boathouse** ⚓ ((© 802/865-3377). A lot of summer action takes place at this city-owned structure and along the boardwalk. You can rent a sailboat or rowboat, sign up for kayaking lessons, or just enjoy the sunset.

One of Burlington's hidden but beguiling attractions is the **Burlington Bike Path** ⚓⚓⚓, which runs 9 miles (14km) on an old rail bed along the picturesque shores of Lake Champlain to the mouth of the Winooski River. It's an easy and quiet trip, passing through parks, past backyards, and along sandy beaches. You can pick it up near the Community Boathouse and head north toward the Winooski River. It's worth packing a picnic lunch and exploring for a few hours on a sunny afternoon.

This is just one segment of an ambitious project to create a 350-mile (564km) bikeway around Lake Champlain. Several key links were recently made in the Burlington area, first in fall 2000 when an experimental bike ferry was established across the Winooski River.

From the north shore of the Winooski, you can peddle northward, picking up the Causeway Park trail, which is (no surprise) a causeway that lets you seemingly skim across the lake's surface by bike. A ferry was also recently established across the Colchester Cut, a boater's break in the causeway that prevented bikers from making through-trips. (*Note*: Burlington Bikeways, a local nonprofit, has been working to find funding to keep both ferries operating during bike season, and biking advocates hope that both will soon be permanent features. Ask at the Burlington visitor center for the current ferry status, or contact **Burlington Parks and Recreation** at © 802/864-0123.)

Bike rentals are available downtown at the **Skirack,** 85 Main St. (© 802/658-3313; www.skirack.com). Rates are $14 to $16 for 4 hours (enough time to do the whole trail). Skirack also rents in-line skates ($10 for 4 hours). **North Star Cyclery,** 100 Main St. (© 802/863-3832), rents bicycles at comparable rates. When at the bike shops or the visitor center, ask for the free map *Cycling the City,* which will help you plot a course around town.

WHERE TO STAY

A number of chain motels are located along Route 7 (Shelburne Rd.) in South Burlington, a 5- to 10-minute drive from downtown. While they lack any trace of New England charm, they're modern, clean, and reliable.

Among the better choices are these three, which are clustered together: **Holiday Inn Express,** 1712 Shelburne Rd. (© 800/874-1554 or 802/860-1112); **Smart Suites,** 1700 Shelburne Rd. (© 877/862-6800); and **Howard Johnson,** 1720 Shelburne Rd. (© 800/874-1554 or 802/860-6000).

On and around Route 2 near I-89 (west of downtown, near the airport) are several other chains, including the **Holiday Inn,** 1068 Williston Rd. (© 802/863-6363), and **Best Western Windjammer Inn,** 1076 Williston Rd. (© 800/371-1125 or 802/863-1125). Our choice for a low-end overnight is the **Swiss Host Motel and Village,** 1272 Williston Rd. (© 802/862-5734), which has the excellent good fortune of being across from Al's French Frys.

Basin Harbor Club ⚓⚓⚓ Situated on 700 rolling lakeside acres (284 hectares) 30 miles (48km) south of Burlington, the Basin Harbor Club offers a detour into a slower-paced era. Established in 1887, this is the kind of resort where you can spend a week and not get bored—at least if you're a self-starter and don't need a perky recreational director to plan your day. The property also features historic gardens, including the largest collection of annuals in Vermont. Best of all are the trademark Adirondack chairs, which are scattered all over the property and invite the most exquisite indolence (bring books!). Thirty-eight rooms are located in the main lodge, but we prefer the rustic cottages, which are tucked along the shore and in shady groves of trees. Nothing's too fancy, yet nothing's too shabby; it's all comfortable in a New England old-money kind of way. (The occasional battered Venetian blind seem to add to the charm.)

Basin Harbor Rd., Vergennes, VT 05491. ℂ **800/622-4000** or 802/475-2311. Fax 802/475-6545. www.basin harbor.com. 105 units. Summer $270–$345 double, to $425 suite (including breakfast, lunch, and dinner); early summer and fall $185–$285 double, to $315 suite (including breakfast and dinner). Closed mid-Oct to mid-May. 2-night minimum stay on weekends. MC, V. Pets allowed in cottages with additional charge. **Amenities:** 2 restaurants (traditional American, pub fare); heated outdoor pool; 18-hole golf course; tennis courts; fitness room; aerobics classes; marina with boat rentals (windsurfers, kayaks, canoes, day sailors, outboards); lake cruises; bike rental; children's programs (summer); concierge; limited room service; babysitting; laundry service; dry cleaning; art workshops; lecture series; airfield. *In room:* A/C, dataport, hair dryer, iron.

The Inn at Shelburne Farms ⭐⭐
The numbers behind this elaborate mansion on the shores of Lake Champlain tell the story: 60 rooms, 10 chimneys, 1,400 acres (567 hectares). Built in 1899, this sprawling Edwardian "farmhouse" is the place to fantasize about the lifestyles of the *truly* rich and famous. From the first glimpse of the mansion as you come up the winding drive, you'll know you've left the grim world behind. That's by design—noted landscape architect Frederick Law Olmsted had a hand in shaping the grounds. Guest rooms vary in terms of decor and upkeep; some are overdue for a makeover. If you're feeling flush, ask for Overlook, with great views of the grounds. Among the budget units, we like Oak Room with its lake view.

Harbor Rd., Shelburne, VT 05482. ℂ **802/985-8498.** www.shelburnefarms.org. 24 units (7 units share 4 bathrooms). Fall $105–$365 double; spring and summer $95–$315 double. 2-night minimum stay on weekends. Closed mid-Oct to mid-May. AE, DC, DISC, MC, V. **Amenities:** Restaurant (New England regional); lake swimming; tennis court; children's farmyard; babysitting; farm tours. *In room:* No phone.

Lang House ⭐
This stately Queen Anne mansion (1881) sits on the hillside between downtown and the University of Vermont. It's not as extravagant as the Willard Street Inn (the owners there are co-owners here), but it's comfortably appointed and lavish with rich cherry and maple woodwork. Guest rooms vary, but most have small bathrooms and small TVs. Room 101 has a wonderfully old-fashioned bathroom with wainscoting, while room 202 has a cozy sitting area tucked in the turret, which gets lots of afternoon light.

360 Main St., Burlington, VT 05401. ℂ **877/919-9799** or 802/652-2500. Fax 802/651-8717. www.langhouse. com. 9 units. $125–$185 double. Rates include breakfast. AE, DISC, MC, V. *In room:* A/C, TV.

Radisson Hotel Burlington ⭐⭐
The nine-story Radisson offers the best views (if you spend the extra $20 on a lakeside room) as well as the best downtown location. The sleek glass box was built in 1976, but renovations have kept the weariness at bay. The hotel is located between the waterfront and Church Street Marketplace, both a 5-minute walk away. Five cabana rooms, which open up to the pool area, are ideal for families.

60 Battery St., Burlington, VT 05401. ℂ **802/658-6500.** Fax 802/658-4659. www.radisson.com/burlingtonvt. 256 units. Summer $159–$269 double; winter $139–$179 double. Ask about packages. AE, DISC, MC, V. Parking in attached garage $5 per day. **Amenities:** 2 restaurants (family, New American); indoor pool; small fitness room; Jacuzzi; concierge; free airport shuttle; limited room service; babysitting; laundry service; dry cleaning. *In room:* A/C, TV w/ pay movies, dataport, coffeemaker, hair dryer, iron, safe.

Willard Street Inn ★★ This impressive choice is located in a splendid 1881 Queen Anne–style brick mansion a few minutes' walk from the university. The historic inn has soaring first-floor ceilings, cherry woodwork, and a beautiful window-lined breakfast room. Among the best units are room 12, which boasts a small sitting area and views of the lake, and the spacious room 4, which has a sizable bathroom and lake views.

349 S. Willard St. (2 blocks south of Main St.), Burlington, VT 05401. ✆ 800/577-8712 or 802/651-8710. Fax 802/651-8714. www.willardstreetinn.com. 14 units (1 with private hall bathroom). $125–$225 double. Rates include breakfast. 2-night minimum stay on weekends. AE, DC, DISC, MC, V. *In room:* A/C, TV, dataport.

WHERE TO DINE

Al's ★ BURGERS & FRIES Al's is where Ben and Jerry (*the* Ben and Jerry) go when they need to sate their cravings for french fries. This classic roadside joint is both fun and efficient. The vats of fries draw people back time and again; the other offerings (hamburgers, hot dogs, and sloppy-joe-like barbecue on a bun) are okay, but nothing special.

1251 Williston Rd. (Rte. 2, just east of I-89), South Burlington. ✆ 802/862-9203. Sandwiches $1–$3.95. No credit cards. Mon–Wed 10:30am–11pm; Thurs–Sat 10:30am–midnight; Sun 11am–10pm.

Bove's ★ *Value* ITALIAN A Burlington landmark since 1941, Bove's is a classic red-sauce joint just a couple of blocks from the Church Street Marketplace. The facade is stark black and white, its octagonal windows closed to prying eyes by Venetian blinds. Step through the doors and into a lost era; grab a seat at one of the vinyl booths and browse the menu, which offers spaghetti with meat sauce, spaghetti with meatballs, spaghetti with sausage, and . . . well, you get the idea. The red sauce is rich and tangy, while the garlic sauce will knock you clear out of your booth. Cocktails include old chestnuts like stingers, pink ladies, and sloe gin fizzes.

68 Pearl St. ✆ 802/864-6651. www.boves.com. Sandwiches $1.40–$4.15; dinner items $4.45–$7.70. No credit cards. Tues–Sat 10am–8:45pm.

Daily Planet ★ ECLECTIC This popular spot is often brimming with students and downtown workers on evenings and weekends. The mild mayhem adds to the charm. The meals are better prepared than one might expect from a place that takes its cues from a pub. A bar menu features fajitas, grilled eggplant sandwiches, and chicken wings. In the dining room, look for lunch dishes like lamb stew and creative salads; at dinner, there's strip steak with a Gorgonzola–green peppercorn sauce or rainbow trout with peach–red onion relish.

15 Center St. ✆ 802/862-9647. Reservations recommended for parties of 5 or more. Lunch items $5.75–$7.95; dinner main courses $11.25–$19.95. AE, DISC, MC, V. Mon–Fri 11:30am–3pm; Sun–Thurs 5–9:30pm; Fri–Sat 5–10pm. Sept–May also Sat–Sun brunch 11am–3pm.

Five Spice Cafe ★★ PAN-ASIAN Located upstairs and down in an intimate setting with rough wood floors and aquamarine wainscoting, Five Spice is a popular spot among students and professors. But customers are drawn here for the exquisite food, not for the scene. The cuisine draws on the best of Thailand, Vietnam, China, and beyond. Try the superb hot-and-sour soup, then gear up for Thai red snapper. The dish with the best name on the menu—Evil Jungle Prince with Chicken—is also one of our favorites, made with a light sauce of coconut milk, chilies, and lime leaves.

175 Church St. ✆ 802/864-4045. Reservations recommended on weekends and in summer. Lunch items $4.50–$9.95; dinner main courses $11.95–$17.95. AE, DISC, MC, V. Mon–Fri 11:30am–3pm and 5–9pm (Fri until 10pm); Sat 11am–10pm; Sun 11am–9:30pm.

NECI Commons ★★ (Value) BISTRO NECI Commons is a popular stop for foodies sniffing out new trends and for those who like good value. Yet another in the New England Culinary Institute empire (the Inn at Essex and Montpelier's Main Street Grill & Bar are others), this lively spot is a training ground for aspiring chefs and restaurateurs. You can eat upstairs in the main dining room, which has windows overlooking the Church Street Marketplace, or downstairs, where you can watch the chef-trainees prepare meals in the open kitchen. Sunday brunch features a wood-fired breakfast pizza, with eggs, bacon, tomato, and cheddar. Lunchtime brings delectable sandwiches (crab cake with chipotle sauce on a toasted roll), crispy calamari salad, and chicken satay. At dinner, look for blackened sea bass with wilted spinach or sirloin served with the restaurant's famous Vermont cheddar potatoes. The prices are reasonable, the service excellent.

25 Church St. ℭ **802/862-6324.** Call before arrival for priority seating. Brunch $5.95–$7.95; lunch $6.95–$8.95; bistro $6.50–$8.95; dinner $8.50–$18.95. AE, DC, DISC, MC, V. Daily 11:30am–4pm (bistro menu 2–4pm only) and 5:30–9pm; Sun brunch 11am–3pm.

Penny Cluse Cafe ★★ CAFE/LATINO This bright, casual spot gets our vote as the city's best choice for lunch or breakfast. We like the Zydeco breakfast with eggs, black beans, andouille sausage, and corn muffins. Lunch ranges from salads to sandwiches (the veggie Reuben with mushrooms, spinach, and red onions is excellent) to more elaborate fare like adobo pork chops with a plantain cake. Equally well-prepared dinners are served Tuesday through Friday nights.

169 Cherry St. (a block off the Church Street Marketplace). ℭ **802/651-8834.** Reservations recommended for dinner. Breakfast dishes $3.50–$6.50; sandwiches and lunch dishes $6.25–$8. MC, V. Mon–Fri 6:45am–3pm; Sat–Sun 8am–3pm; Tues–Fri 6–10pm.

BURLINGTON AFTER DARK

THE PERFORMING ARTS The nonprofit **Flynn Theatre for the Performing Arts,** 153 Main St. (ℭ **802/652-4500;** www.flynntheatre.org), is the anchor for the downtown fine-arts scene. Housed in a wonderful Art Deco theater (1930), the Flynn stages events ranging from touring productions of Broadway shows (Penn and Teller) to concerts (Diana Krall) and dance performances (Paul Taylor).

Plays are performed by the University of Vermont theater department and local theater groups at the handsome **Royall Tyler Theatre,** on campus (ℭ **802/ 656-2094**). Shows ranging from Shakespeare to student-directed one-act plays are staged throughout the year.

THE CLUB & MUSIC SCENE Burlington has a thriving local music scene. Check the weeklies for information on festivals and concerts during your visit, as well as to find out who's playing at the clubs.

Nectar's, 188 Main St. (ℭ **802/658-4771**), is an odd amalgam—part funky cafeteria-style restaurant, part no-frills lounge. No wonder this is the place Phish got its start. Live bands play nightly, and there's never a cover. Look for the revolving neon sign (the last of its kind in Vermont). Upstairs is **Club Metronome,** 188 Main St. (ℭ **802/865-4563**), a loud and loose nightspot that showcases a wide array of local talent, some of which is actually pretty impressive (although Saturday nights often feature recorded music). Cover is $3 to $15.

For gay nightlife, head to **135 Pearl** (ℭ **802/863-2343**), located naturally enough at 135 Pearl St. Open Monday through Thursday from 7:30pm to 1am, Friday and Saturday from 5pm to 1am.

10 The Northeast Kingdom

Vermont's Northeast Kingdom has a more wild and remote character than much of the rest of the state. Consisting of Orleans, Essex, and Caledonia counties, the region was given its memorable nickname in 1949 by Sen. George Aiken, who understood the area's allure at a time when few others paid it much heed. What gives this region its character is its stubborn, old-fashioned insularity.

In contrast to the dusky narrow valleys of southern Vermont, the Kingdom's landscape is open and spacious, with rolling meadows ending abruptly at the hard edge of dense boreal forests. The leafy woodlands of the south give way to spiky forests of spruce and fir. Accommodations and services for visitors aren't as plentiful or easy to find here as in the southern reaches of the state, but a handful of inns are tucked among the hills and in the forests.

This section includes a loose, somewhat convoluted driving tour of the Northeast Kingdom, along with suggestions for outdoor recreation. If your time is limited, make sure you at least stop in St. Johnsbury, which has two of our favorite Vermont attractions—the Fairbanks Museum and St. Johnsbury Athenaeum. The total tour, from Hardwick to St. Johnsbury by way of Newport, Derby Line, and Lake Willoughby, is approximately 90 miles (145km). Allow a full day, or more if you plan to take advantage of hiking and biking in the region.

Visitor information is available from the **Northeast Kingdom Chamber of Commerce,** 357 Western Ave., Suite 2, St. Johnsbury (© **800/639-6379** or 802/748-3678; www.nekchamber.com).

| DRIVING TOUR | **TOURING THE NORTHEAST KINGDOM** |

Begin at:

① Hardwick

This is a small town with rough edges set along the Lamoille River. It has a compact commercial main street, some quirky shops, and a couple of casual, family-style restaurants.

From here, head north on Route 14 a little over 7 miles (11km) to the turnoff toward Craftsbury and

② Craftsbury Common

This uncommonly graceful village is home to a small academy and many historic buildings spread along a sizable green and a broad main street. The town occupies a wide upland ridge and offers sweeping views to the east and west. Be sure to stop by the old cemetery on the south end of town, where you can wander among the historic tombstones of pioneers, dating back to the 1700s. Craftsbury is an excellent destination for mountain biking and cross-country skiing and is

home to the region's finest inn (see below).

From Craftsbury, continue north to reconnect to Route 14. You'll wind through the towns of Albany and Irasburg as you head north. At the village of Coventry, veer north on Route 5 to the lakeside town of

③ Newport

This commercial outpost (pop. 4,400) is set on the southern shores of Lake Memphremagog, a stunning 27-mile-long (43km) lake that's just 2 miles (3km) wide at its broadest point and the bulk of which lies across the border in Canada. From Newport, continue north on Route 5, crossing under I-91, for about 7 miles (11km) to the border town of Derby Line (pop. 2,000), with a handful of restaurants and antiques shops. You can park and walk across the bridge to poke around the Canadian town of Rock Island with just some simple ID like a driver's license. (That's for U.S.

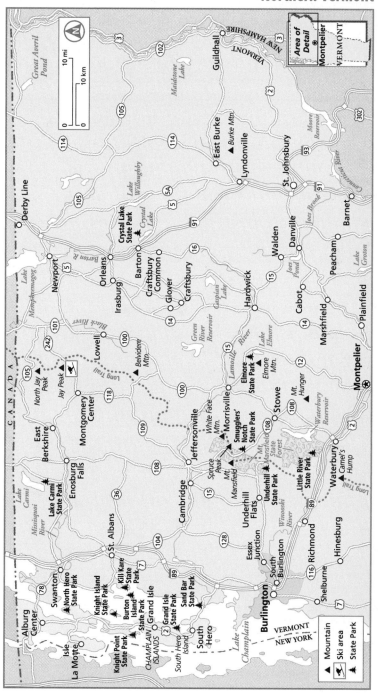

Tips **Recommended Reading**

Howard Frank Mosher's magical 1994 novel *Northern Borders* is ostensibly about a young boy living with his taciturn grandparents in northern Vermont, but the book's central character is really Vermont's Northeast Kingdom.

---

residents; foreign travelers might ask at the U.S. Customs booth about returning before crossing the line.)

Back in Derby Line, look for the

4 Haskell Free Library and Opera House

Sitting at the corner of Caswell Avenue and Church Street (© **802/ 873-3022**), this handsome neoclassical building contains a public library and an elegant opera house modeled after the old Boston Opera House. This much-adorned theater opened in 1904 with advertisements promoting a minstrel show featuring "new songs, new jokes, and beautiful electric effects."

What's most curious about the structure, however, is that it's one of few buildings that lie half in Canada and half in the United States. (The Haskell family donated the building jointly to the towns of Derby Line and Rock Island.) A thick black line runs beneath the seats of the opera house, indicating who's in the United States and who's in Canada. Because the stage is set entirely in Canada, apocryphal stories abound of frustrated U.S. officers watching fugitives perform on stage. More recently, the theater has been used for the occasional extradition hearing.

From Derby Line, retrace your path south on Route 5 to Derby Center and the juncture of Route 5A. Continue south on Route 5A to the town of Westmore on the shores of

5 Lake Willoughby

This glacier-carved lake is best viewed from the north, with the shimmering sheet of water pinching between the base of two low mountains at the

southern end. There's a distinctive Alpine feel to the whole scene, and this underappreciated lake is certainly one of the most beautiful in the Northeast. Route 5A along the eastern shore is lightly traveled and well suited to biking or walking.

Head southwest on Route 16, which departs from Route 5A just north of the lake. Follow Route 16 through the peaceful villages of Barton and Glover. From Glover, continue south through serene farmlands to Lyndonville, where you pick up Route 5 south to

6 St. Johnsbury

This town of 7,600 inhabitants is the largest in the Northeast Kingdom and the region's center of commerce. First settled in 1786, the town enjoyed a buoyant prosperity in the 19th century, largely stemming from the success of platform scales, invented here in 1830 by Thaddeus Fairbanks and still manufactured here today. Luckily, the town has not suffered from the depredations of tourist boutiques and brewpubs, and retains an abundance of fine commercial architecture in two distinct areas, which are joined by steep Eastern Avenue. The north end of Main Street is also notable for its grand residential architecture.

At the corner of Main and Prospect streets in St. Johnsbury, look for

7 The Fairbanks Museum

In 1889, this imposing Romanesque, red-sandstone structure was built at 1302 Main St. (© **802/748-2372;** www.fairbanksmuseum.com) to hold the accumulations of obsessive amateur collector Franklin Fairbanks, the grandson of the inventor of the platform scale. Fairbanks was once described as "the kind of little boy who came home with his pockets full of worms." In adulthood, his propensity to collect continued unabated. His artifacts include four stuffed bears, a huge moose, art from Asia, and 4,500 stuffed birds. And that's just the tip of the iceberg.

The soaring, barrel-vaulted main hall embodies Victorian grandeur. Among the assorted clutter, look for the unique mosaics by John Hampson, who crafted scenes of American history—such as Washington bidding his troops farewell—entirely of *mounted insects*. In the Washington scene, for instance, iridescent green beetles form the epaulets, while the regal great coat is comprised of hundreds of purple moth wings. Words fail us here; you must see these works, which alone are worth the price of admission.

Hours are Monday through Saturday from 9am to 5pm, Sunday from 1 to 5pm. Admission is $5 for adults, $4 for seniors, $3 for children 5 to 17, and $12 per family.

Also in town, just south of the museum on Main Street, is the

❽ St. Johnsbury Athenaeum

The Athenaeum is in an Edward Hopper–esque brick building with a truncated mansard tower and prominent keystones over the windows. This is the town's public library, but it also houses an extraordinary gallery dating to 1873. It claims to be the oldest unadulterated art gallery in the nation, and we see no reason to question that claim.

Your first view of the gallery is spectacular: After winding through the cozy library with its ticking regulator clock, you round a corner and find yourself gazing across Yosemite National Park. Noted Hudson River School painter Albert Bierstadt created this luminous 10-by-15-foot (3m-by-4.5m) oil, and the gallery was built specifically to accommodate this work. (Local lore says the small balcony in the gallery was built for Bierstadt to better view his work on subsequent visits.) In 1999, the gallery received the donation of another Bierstadt painting, *The Cove.*

Some 100 other works fill the walls. Most are copies of other paintings (a common teaching tool in the 19th century), but look for originals by other Hudson River School painters, including Asher B. Durand, Thomas Moran, and Jasper Cropsey.

The Athenaeum (✆ **802/748-8291**) is open Monday and Wednesday from 10am to 8pm; Tuesday, Thursday, and Friday from 10am to 5:30pm; and Saturday from 9:30am to 4pm. Admission is free, but donations are encouraged.

ALPINE SKIING

Jay Peak ✸✸ Located just south of the Canadian border, Jay is Vermont's best choice for those who prefer to avoid the glitz and clutter that seem to plague ski resorts elsewhere. While some new condo development has been taking place at the base of the mountain, Jay still has the feel of a remote destination, accessible by a winding road through unbroken woodlands. Thanks to its staggering snowfall (an average of 340 in./864cm, more than any other New England ski area), Jay has developed extensive glade skiing; the ski school also specializes in running the glades, making it a fitting place for advanced intermediates to learn how to navigate these exciting, challenging trails.

Rte. 242, Jay, VT 05859. ✆ **800/451-4449** for lodging, or 802/988-2611. www.jaypeakresort.com. Vertical drop: 2,153 ft. (646m). Lifts: 1 60-person tram, 4 chairlifts, 2 surface lifts. Skiable acreage: 385 acres. Lift tickets: $52.

OTHER OUTDOOR PURSUITS

CROSS-COUNTRY SKIING   The same folks who offer mountain biking at the Craftsbury Outdoor Center (see below) also maintain 61 miles (98km) of groomed cross-country trails through the gentle hills surrounding Craftsbury. The forgiving, old-fashioned trails, maintained by **Craftsbury Nordic Center** 👥👥 (© **800/729-7751** or 802/586-7767), emphasize pleasing landscapes rather than fast action. Trail passes are $14 for adults, $9 for seniors, and $7 for children 6 to 12. Another option is **Highland Lodge** 👥, on Caspian Lake (© **802/533-2647**), which offers 36 miles (58km) of trails (about 10 miles/16km groomed) through rolling woodlands and fields.

HIKING   At the southern tip of Lake Willoughby, two rounded peaks rise above the lake's waters. These are the biblically named Mount Hor and Mount Pisgah, both of which lie within Willoughby State Forest. Both summits are accessible via footpaths that are somewhat strenuous but yield excellent views.

For **Mount Pisgah** (elevation 2,751 ft./825m), look for parking on the west side of Route 5A about 5.7 miles (9.2km) south of the junction with Route 16. The trail departs from across the road and runs 1.7 miles (2.7km) to the summit. To hike **Mount Hor** (elevation 2,648 ft./794m), drive 1.8 miles (3km) down the gravel road on the right side of the aforementioned parking lot, veering right at the fork. Park at the small lot and continue on foot past the parking lot a short distance until you spot the start of the trail. Follow the trail signs to the summit, a round-trip of about 3½ miles (5.6km).

MOUNTAIN BIKING   The Craftsbury ridge features several excellent variations for bikers in search of easy terrain. Most of the biking is on hard-packed dirt roads through sparsely populated countryside. The views are sensational, and the sense of being well out in the country very strong. The **Craftsbury Outdoor Center at Craftsbury Common** (© **800/729-7751** or 802/586-7767; www.craftsbury.com) rents bikes and is an excellent source for information on area roads. Rentals are $25 to $35 per day. A small fee is charged for using bikes on the cross-country ski trail network.

WHERE TO STAY

Comfort Suites 👥   Built in 2000, this property has a number of nice touches, like granite vanity counters and high-backed desk chairs. The rooms are pleasantly appointed (more like an inn than a motel), and in the basement are an appealing if small swimming pool and fitness room, along with a game room outfitted with air hockey and a pool table.

703 Rte. 5 South (off Exit 20 of I-91), St. Johnsbury, VT 05819. © **800/228-5150** or 802/748-1500. Fax 802/748-1243. 107 units. Summer $109–$169 double; foliage season from $139 double; off-season from $79 double. Rates include continental breakfast. AE, DISC, MC, V. **Amenities:** Indoor pool; fitness room; game room; coin-op laundry. *In room:* A/C, TV, dataport, coffeemaker, hair dryer, iron.

Inn on the Common 👥👥👥   This exceedingly handsome complex of three Federal-era buildings anchors the charming ridgetop village of Craftsbury Common, one of the most quintessential of New England villages. The inn offers just the right measures of both history and pampering. It tends to be a rather social place, attracting both families and couples seeking a romantic getaway. Dinner starts with cocktails at 6pm, with guests seated family-style amid elegant surroundings at 7:30pm. The menu changes nightly, but includes well-prepared contemporary American fare. Some deluxe guest rooms contain fireplaces.

Craftsbury Common, VT 05827. © **800/521-2233** or 802/586-9619. Fax 802/586-2249. www.innonthe common.com. 16 units. $250–$270 double; foliage season $280–$300 double. Rates include breakfast and dinner. 2-night minimum stay during foliage and Christmas week. AE, MC, V. Pets accepted by prior arrangement ($15). **Amenities:** Outdoor heated pool (summer only); tennis court; bike rental nearby; in-room massage; babysitting (by advance arrangement); croquet. *In room:* Hair dryer, no phone.

Willoughvale Inn ★★   This is the sister property of the well-managed Green Mountain Inn in Stowe (p. 477), and a similar attention to detail prevails. The elegant inn, set on a low rise at the north end of Lake Willoughby, has stunning views across the water to the twin mountains at the south end of the lake. The 11 rooms in the lodge are tastefully appointed, with much of the furniture crafted in Vermont. Willoughvale is an ideal location for a quiet retreat, especially if you reserve one of the four rustic cottages right on the water. What we like most about this place is that it lacks ostentation, but pays close attention to clean design and small touches of elegance. It's hard to imagine a better place to spend a few days with books and a bicycle. The restaurant is likewise unpretentious, serving well-prepared meals along with a superb view of the lake.

793 Rte. 5A, Orleans, VT 05860. © **800/594-9102** or 802/525-4123. Fax 802/525-4514. www.willough vale.com. 15 units. Winter $109–$179 double; summer $149–$249 double. Rates include continental breakfast. 2-night minimum stay July, Aug, and foliage weekends. Cottages available by the week only in July–Aug. AE, MC, V. One pet (under 50 lbs.) permitted per room or cottage ($20 per night). **Amenities:** Restaurant (American); watersports equipment (canoes, kayaks); bike rental. *In room:* A/C, TV.

12

New Hampshire

by Wayne Curtis

New Hampshire's state symbol is the Old Man of the Mountains, an icon you'll see just about everywhere you look—on state highway signs, on brochures, on state police cars. And it's an apt symbol for a state that relishes its cranky-old-man demeanor. New Hampshire has long been a magnet for folks who speak of government—especially "big government"—in tones normally reserved for bowel ailments. That "Live Free or Die" license plate? It's for real. New Hampshire stands behind its words. This is a state that still regards zoning as a nefarious conspiracy to undermine property rights. Note that New Hampshire does not have a bottle-deposit law, nor a law banning billboards. (Heathen Vermont has both, as does its other godless neighbor, Maine.)

New Hampshire savors its reputation as an embattled outpost of plucky and heroic independents fighting the good fight against intrusive laws and irksome bureaucrats. Without a state sales tax or state income tax, it's had to be creative in financing its limited government. Many government services are funded through the "tourist tax" (an 8% levy on meals and rooms at restaurants and hotels) along with a hefty local property tax. In fact, candidates for virtually every office must take "The Pledge," which means they'll vow to fight any effort to impose sales or income tax. To shirk The Pledge is tantamount to political suicide.

Get beyond New Hampshire's affable crankiness, though, and you'll find pure New England. Indeed, New Hampshire may represent the New England ethic distilled to its essence. At its core is a mistrust of outsiders, a premium placed on independence, a belief that government should be frugal above all else, and a laconic acceptance that, no matter what, you just can't change the weather. Travelers exploring the state with open eyes will find these attitudes in spades.

Visitors will also find wonderfully diverse terrain—from ocean beaches to broad lakes to the region's impressive mountains. Without ever leaving the state's borders, you can toss a Frisbee on a sandy beach, ride bikes along quiet country lanes dotted with covered bridges, hike rugged granite hills blasted by some of the most severe weather in the world, and canoe on a placid lake in the company of moose and loons. You'll also experience good food and country inns you won't ever want to leave. But most of all, you'll find vestiges of that feisty independence that has defined New England since the first settlers ran up their flag 3½ centuries ago.

1 Portsmouth ✦✦✦

Portsmouth is a civilized seaside city of bridges, brick, and seagulls. Filled with elegant architecture that's more intimate than intimidating, this bonsai-size city projects a strong and proud sense of its heritage without being overly precious about it.

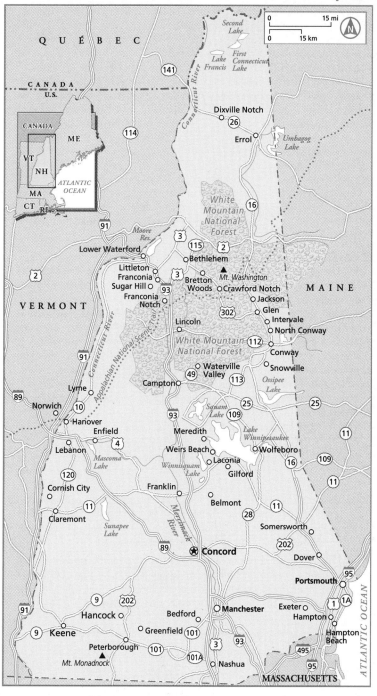

Part of the city's appeal is its variety. Upscale coffee shops and fancy art galleries exist alongside old-fashioned barber shops and tattoo parlors. A steady gentrification in recent years has brought with it some twee shops and businesses, but the town still has a fundamental earthiness. Portsmouth's humble waterfront must actually be sought out, and when found it's rather understated.

Portsmouth's history runs deep, a fact that is instantly evident on a walk through town. For the past 3 centuries, the city has served as a hub for the region's maritime trade. In the 1600s, Strawbery Banke (it wasn't renamed Portsmouth until 1653) was a center for the export of wood and dried fish to Europe. In the 19th century, it prospered as a center of regional trade. Across the river in Maine, the Portsmouth Naval Shipyard was founded in 1800, and evolved into a prominent base for the building and repair of U.S. Navy submarines. Today, Portsmouth's maritime tradition continues with a lively trade in bulk goods. (Look for scrap metal and minerals stockpiled along the shores of the Piscataqua River on Market Street.) The city's de facto symbol is the tugboat, one or two of which are almost always tied up near the waterfront's picturesque "tugboat alley."

ESSENTIALS

GETTING THERE   Portsmouth is served by Exits 3 through 7 on I-95. The most direct access to downtown is via Market Street (Exit 7), which is the last New Hampshire exit before crossing the river to Maine.

In 2000, discount airline **Pan Am** (© **800/359-7262;** www.flypanam.com) launched operations out of a former military base on Portsmouth's outskirts. The only airline that serves Portsmouth (don't expect onward connections), it has flights to a limited but growing roster of second-tier airports, including Gary, Ind.; Sanford, Fla.; and Baltimore, Md. Call or check the carrier's website for an updated list of airports currently served.

By bus, Portsmouth is served by **Concord Trailways** (© **800/639-3317**) and **Vermont Transit** (© **800/451-3292**).

VISITOR INFORMATION   The **Greater Portsmouth Chamber of Commerce,** 500 Market St. (© **603/436-1118;** www.portcity.org), operates an information center between Exit 7 and downtown. From Memorial Day to Columbus Day, it's open Monday through Wednesday from 8:30am to 5pm, Thursday and Friday from 8:30am to 7pm, and Saturday and Sunday from 10am to 5pm. The rest of the year, hours are Monday through Friday from 8:30am to 5pm. In summer, the chamber staffs a second information booth at Market Square in the middle of the historic district. Online, you can find extensive information on the region at **www.seacoastnh.com**.

PARKING   Most of Portsmouth can be easily reconnoitered on foot, so you need park only once. Parking can be tight in and around the historic district in summer. The municipal garage, on Hanover Street between Market and Fleet streets, costs 50¢ per hour. Strawbery Banke Museum (see below) also offers limited parking for visitors.

A MAGICAL HISTORY TOUR

Portsmouth's 18th-century prosperity is evident in the regal Georgian-style homes that dot the city. Strawbery Banke occupies the core of the historic area, and is well worth visiting. If you don't have the budget, time, or inclination to spend half a day at Strawbery Banke, a walking tour will bring you past many other significant homes, some of which are open to the public. A helpful

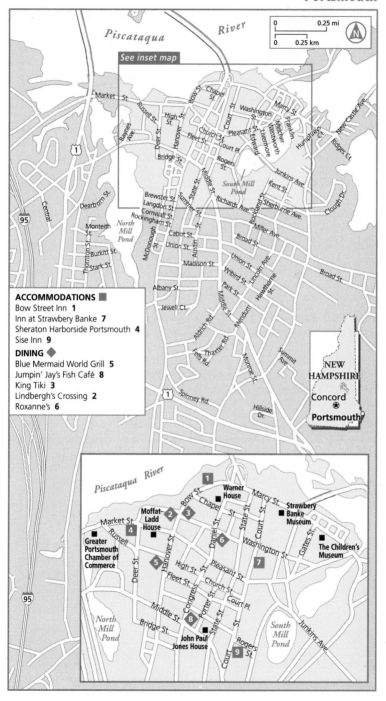

ACCOMMODATIONS ■
Bow Street Inn **1**
Inn at Strawbery Banke **7**
Sheraton Harborside Portsmouth **4**
Sise Inn **9**

DINING ◆
Blue Mermaid World Grill **5**
Jumpin' Jay's Fish Café **8**
King Tiki **3**
Lindbergh's Crossing **2**
Roxanne's **6**

brochure, *The Portsmouth Trail: An Historic Walking Tour,* is available at visitor centers.

Strawbery Banke Museum ✿✿✿   In 1958, the city planned to raze this venerable neighborhood, first settled in 1653, to make way for urban renewal. A group of local citizens resisted and won, establishing an outdoor history museum that's grown to become one of the largest in New England. Today it consists of 10 downtown acres (4 hectares) and 46 historic buildings. Ten of these have been restored with period furnishings; eight others feature exhibits. (The remainder may be seen from the exterior only.) While Strawbery Banke employs staffers to assume the character of historic residents, the emphasis is more on the buildings, architecture, and historic accoutrement, and less on living history as practiced at Sturbridge Village or Plimoth Plantation in Massachusetts.

The neighborhood surrounds an open lawn and has a settled, picturesque quality to it. At three crafts shops on the grounds, you can watch coopers, boat builders, and potters at work. The most intriguing home is the split-personality Drisco House, half of which depicts life in the 1790s, and half of which shows life in the 1950s, nicely demonstrating how houses grow and adapt to each era.

Hancock St. ✆ 603/433-1106. www.strawberybanke.org. Admission $12 adults, $11 seniors, $8 children 7–17; $28 per family. May 1–Oct 29 daily 10am–5pm. Special events held first 2 weekends of Dec; otherwise closed Nov–Apr. Look for directional signs posted around town.

John Paul Jones House ✿✿   Revolutionary War hero John Paul ("I have not yet begun to fight") Jones lived in this handsome 1758 home during the Revolutionary War. He was here to oversee the construction of his sloop, *Ranger,* believed to be the first ship to sail under the United States flag. (There's a model of it on display.) Costumed guides offer tours of 45 minutes to an hour.

43 Middle St. ✆ 603/436-8420. Admission $4 adults, $2 children 6–14. Mon–Sat 10am–4pm; Sun noon–4pm. Closed late Oct–May.

Moffatt-Ladd House ✿✿   The Moffatt-Ladd House, built for a family of prosperous merchants and traders, is as notable for its elegant garden as for its 1763 home, with its great hall and elaborate carvings throughout. The house belonged to one family between 1763 and 1913, when it became a museum, and many of the furnishings have never left the premises. It will especially appeal to aficionados of Early American furniture and painting.

154 Market St. ✆ 603/436-8221. Admission $5 adults, $2.50 children under 12. June 15–Oct 15 Mon–Sat 11am–5pm; Sun 1–5pm. Closed mid-Oct to mid-June.

Warner House ✿   The Warner House, built in 1716, was the governor's mansion in the mid–18th century when Portsmouth served as state capital. This stately brick structure with graceful Georgian elements is a favorite among architectural historians for its wall murals from around 1716 (said to be the oldest murals still in place in the U.S.), the early wall marbleizing, and the original white pine paneling.

150 Daniel St. ✆ 603/436-5909. www.warnerhouse.org. Admission $5 adults, $2.50 children 7–12. Tues–Sat 10am–4pm; Sun 1–4pm. Closed Nov–May.

Wentworth-Gardner House ✿✿✿   The Wentworth-Gardner is arguably the most handsome mansion in the entire Seacoast region, and is widely considered to be one of the best examples of Georgian architecture in the nation. Built in 1760, the home features many of the classic period elements, including very pronounced quoins (the blocks on the building's corners), pedimented window caps, plank sheathing (meant to make the home appear as if made of masonry), and an elaborate doorway featuring Corinthian pilasters, a broken scroll, and a paneled door topped with a pineapple, the symbol of hospitality. The inside is no less impressive, with hand-painted Chinese wallpaper and a vast fireplace in the kitchen. Perhaps most memorable is its human scale—although this was one of the grandest homes of the colonial era, it's very modest in scope, and in some circles today might not be considered much more than a pool house.

50 Mechanic St. ℂ **603/436-4406.** Admission $4 adults, $2 children 6–14. Tues–Sun 1–4pm. Closed mid-Oct to mid-June. From rose gardens on Marcy St. across from Strawbery Banke, walk south 1 block, turn left toward bridge, make right before crossing bridge; house is down the block on your right.

BOAT TOURS

Portsmouth is especially attractive seen from the water. A small fleet of tour boats ties up at Portsmouth, offering scenic tours of the Piscataqua River and the historic Isle of Shoals throughout the summer and fall.

The **Isle of Shoals Steamship Co.** ★★ (ℂ **800/441-4620** or 603/431-5500) sails from Barker Wharf on Market Street and is the most established of the tour companies. It offers a variety of tours on the 90-foot (27m) *Thomas Laighton* (a modern replica of a late-19th-century steamship) and the 70-foot (21m) *Oceanic.* A popular excursion to the Isle of Shoals allows passengers to disembark and wander about the dramatic, rocky Star Island, far out in the off-shore swells. Reservations are encouraged. Other options include 6-hour whale-watching voyages and a sunset lighthouse cruise. Fares range from $10 to $25 for adults, $6 to $16 for children. Parking is an additional $3.

Portsmouth Harbor Cruises ★ (ℂ **800/776-0915** or 603/436-8084) specializes in tours of the historic Piscataqua River aboard the *Heritage,* a 49-passenger ship. Cruise by five old forts, or enjoy the tidal estuary of inland Great Bay, a scenic trip upriver from Portsmouth. Reservations are suggested. Fares are $8.50 to $16 for adults, $6 to $9 for children.

ESPECIALLY FOR KIDS

The Children's Museum of Portsmouth ★★ *Kids*   This bright, lively museum offers a morning's worth of hands-on exhibits of interest to younger artisans and scientists. (It's designed to appeal to children between 1 and 11.) Among the more popular displays are exhibits on earthquakes, dinosaur digs, and lobstering, along with the miniature yellow submarine and space shuttle cockpit, both of which invite clambering.

280 Marcy St., 2 blocks south of Strawbery Banke. ℂ **603/436-3853.** www.childrens-museum.org. Admission $5 adults and children, $4 seniors, free for children under 2. Tues–Sat 10am–5pm; Sun 1–5pm. Also open Mon during summer and school vacations.

SHOPPING

Portsmouth's compact historic district is home to dozens of unique boutiques. The **N. W. Barrett Gallery,** 53 Market St. (ℂ **603/431-4262**), offers a classy selection of ceramics, glass, lustrous woodworking, and handmade jewelry by area craftspeople. The **Robert Lincoln Levy Gallery,** operated by the New Hampshire Art Association, 136 State St. (ℂ **603/431-4230**), has frequently changing shows of fine art produced by New Hampshire artists.

Chaise Lounge, 104 Congress St. (ℂ **603/430-7872**), offers an eclectic range of home furnishings—sort of Empire meets modern—while **Nahcotta,** 110 Congress St. (ℂ **603/433-1705**), sells quietly edgy and entertaining paintings and sculptures.

Bibliophiles and collectors of cartography should plan a detour to the **Portsmouth Bookshop,** 1–7 Islington St. (© **603/433-4406**), which specializes in old and rare books and maps.

Bailey Works, 146 Congress St. (© **603/430-9577**), makes its own rugged, waterproof bike messenger bags in several styles and colors. The attention to detail is superb.

Paradiza, 63 Penhallow St. (© **603/431-0180**), has an array of very clever greeting cards, along with exotica like soaps and bath products from Israel and Africa. **Macro Polo,** 89 Market St. (© **603/436-8338**), specializes in retro-chic gifts, toys, magnets, and gadgets.

WHERE TO STAY

Downtown accommodations are preferred, because everything is within walking distance. For those on a budget, less-stylish chain hotels are located at the edge of town along I-95. Among them are the **Anchorage Inn,** 417 Woodbury Ave. (© **800/370-8111** or 603/431-8111); **Fairfield Inn,** 650 Borthwick Ave. (© **603/436-6363**); and **Holiday Inn of Portsmouth,** 300 Woodbury Ave. (© **603/431-8000**).

In addition to the options listed below, see the **Inn at Portsmouth Harbor** (p. 544).

Inn at Strawbery Banke 🦋 This historic inn, in a home built around 1814, is ideally located for exploring Portsmouth. Strawbery Banke is but a block away, and Market Square is just 2 blocks away. The innkeepers have done a nice job taking a cozy antique home and making it comfortable for guests. Rooms are tiny but bright and feature stenciling, wooden shutters, and beautiful pine floors. Common areas include two sitting rooms with TVs.

314 Court St., Portsmouth, NH 03801. © **800/428-3933** or 603/436-7242. www.innatstrawberybanke.com. 7 units (1 with bathroom down the hall). Summer and early fall $145–$150 double; off-season $100–$115 double. Rates include full breakfast. 2-night minimum stay Aug and Oct weekends. AE, DISC, MC, V. Children 10 and over welcome. *In room:* A/C, no phone.

Sheraton Harborside Portsmouth 🦋🦋 This is a well-maintained, well-managed property popular with business travelers, as well as leisure travelers looking for the amenities of a larger hotel. The modern five-story brick building is nicely located—the attractions of downtown Portsmouth are virtually at your doorstep (Strawbery Banke is a 10-min. walk)—and with parking underground and across the street, a stay here can make for a relatively stress-free visit. Some guest rooms have views of the harbor.

250 Market St., Portsmouth, NH 03801. © **603/431-2300.** Fax 603/431-7805. 200 units. Summer $149–$205 double; ask about discounts in off-season. AE, DISC, MC, V. **Amenities:** Restaurant (American); fitness room; business center; limited room service. *In room:* A/C, TV w/ pay movies, dataport, minibar, coffeemaker, hair dryer, iron.

Sise Inn 🦋🦋 The Sise Inn is an elegant hotel in the guise of a country inn. This solid Queen Anne–style home was built in 1881; the hotel addition was constructed in the 1980s. The effect is happily harmonious, with antique stained glass and copious oak trim meshing well with the more contemporary elements. An elevator serves the three floors, and there's modern carpeting throughout, but many of the rooms feature antique armoires and an updated Victorian styling. We like room 406, a suite with a soaking tub and sitting room, and room 216, with its own sauna and lovely natural light. An elaborate continental breakfast is served in the huge old kitchen and adjoining sunroom. This is a popular hotel for business travelers, but if you're on holiday you won't feel out of place.

40 Court St. (at Middle St.), Portsmouth, NH 03801. ℂ 877/747-3466 or 603/433-1200. Fax 603/433-1200. 34 units. June–Oct $145–$225 double; Nov–May $110–$175 double. Rates include continental breakfast. AE, DISC, MC, V. **Amenities:** Access to health club (within walking distance); laundry. *In room:* A/C, TV, iron.

WHERE TO DINE

The funky **Ceres Bakery,** 51 Penhallow St. (ℂ **603/436-6518**), on a quiet side street, has just a handful of tables, so you might be better off getting a cookie to go and then walking to the waterfront rose gardens. **Cafe Brioche,** 14 Market Sq. (ℂ **603/430-9225**), is often crowded with folks attracted by not only the central location but also the delectable baked goods.

Blue Mermaid World Grill ★★ GLOBAL/ECLECTIC   The Blue Mermaid ranks among our favorites in Portsmouth for its good food, good value, and refusal to take itself too seriously. It's a short stroll from Market Square, in a historic area called the Hill. It's not a pretentious place—locals congregate here, Tom Waits drones on in the background, and the service is casual but professional. The menu is adventurous in a low-key global kind of way: Try lobster and shrimp pad Thai or halibut with a wasabi cream sauce. There's also burgers, pasta, and pizza from the wood grill, along with a fun cocktail menu (mojitos, margaritas) and homemade fire-roasted salsa.

The Hill (at Hanover and High sts. facing the municipal parking garage). ℂ 603/427-2583. www.blue mermaid.com. Reservations recommended for parties of six or more. Lunch items $5.95–$13.95; dinner main courses $12.95–$21.95 (most around $15–$17). AE, DISC, MC, V. Sun–Thurs 11:30am–9pm; Fri–Sat 11:30am–10pm.

Jumpin' Jay's Fish Café ★★ SEAFOOD   One of Portsmouth's more urbane eateries, Jay's is a welcome destination for those who like their seafood more sophisticated than simply deep-fried. A sleek and spare spot, it has an open kitchen and a handsome polished-steel bar. The day's fresh catch is posted on blackboards; you pick the fish and pair it with sauces like salsa verde, ginger-orange, or roasted red pepper. Pasta dishes are an option—add scallops, mussels, chicken as you like. The food's great, and the attention to detail admirable.

150 Congress St. ℂ 603/766-3474. Reservations recommended (call by Wed for weekends). Main courses $13.95–$24.95. AE, DISC, MC, V. Mon–Thurs 5:30–9:30pm (closes at 9pm in winter); Fri–Sat 5–10pm; Sun 5–9pm.

King Tiki POLYNESIAN   Fun and aggressively retro, King Tiki throws together kitschy velvet paintings, rattan furniture, loud music, and a good lineup of finger foods (expect faux exotica like Hawaiian tempura). Come to get drinks, soak up the atmosphere, and gawk at people inside and out. If you don't set your expectations for the food too high, you won't be disappointed.

2 Bow St. ℂ 603/430-5228. Main courses $8–$12. MC, V. Mon 6pm–1am; Tues–Thurs 5pm–1am; Fri–Sun 3pm–1am.

Lindbergh's Crossing ★ BISTRO   Located in an old waterfront warehouse, this intimate restaurant has a bistro menu that's subtly creative without calling too much attention to itself. The almond-crusted halibut is served over salad Niçoise; another popular dish is the seafood (shrimp, mussels, scallops, and whitefish) served in a saffron shrimp broth over couscous. If you don't have reservations, ask about seating in the bar.

29 Ceres St. ℂ 603/431-0887. Reservations recommended. Main courses $14–$24. AE, DC, MC, V. Sun–Thurs 5:30–9:30pm; Fri–Sat 5:30–10pm. Bar opens at 4pm daily; light menu available.

Roxanne's ★★ ECLECTIC   Roxanne's is easily overlooked, but worth seeking out. You'll find fresh ingredients creatively prepared. For breakfast, indulge in homemade corned-beef hash with poached eggs. At lunch, expect offerings like a tangy smoked-seafood chowder. Dinners include fresh ravioli that changes with the seasons, along with hearty meals like pork tenderloin with red cabbage, turnip, sweet potato, and caramelized pineapple. Roxanne's is the best bet for a visiting vegetarian, offering several dishes nightly for the non-carnivore.

105 Daniel St. © **603/431-1948.** Reservations strongly recommended for dinner. Main courses $4.95–$7.50 breakfast; $5.95–$7.95 lunch; $14.95–$19.95 dinner. MC, V. Mon–Fri 7:30am–2:30pm; Wed–Fri 5:30–9:30pm; Sat 8am–2pm and 5:30–9:30pm; Sun 8am–2pm and 4–8pm.

2 Hanover & Environs ★★★

If your idea of New England involves a sweeping green edged with stately brick buildings, be sure to visit Hanover, a thriving university town agreeably situated in the Connecticut River Valley. First settled in 1765, the town was home to early pioneers who were granted a charter by King George III to establish a college. It was named after the second Earl of Dartmouth, the school's first trustee. Since its founding, Dartmouth College has had a large hand in shaping the community.

This Ivy League school has produced more than its share of celebrated alumni, including poet Robert Frost, Vice President Nelson Rockefeller, former surgeon general C. Everett Koop, and children's-book author Dr. Seuss.

Today, a handsome village green marks the permeable border between college and town. In summer, the green is an ideal destination for strolling and lounging. The best way to explore Hanover is on foot, so your first endeavor is to park your car, which can be trying during peak seasons. Try the municipal lots west of Main Street.

ESSENTIALS

GETTING THERE   Hanover is north of Lebanon, N.H., and I-89 via Route 10 or Route 120. Amtrak serves White River Junction, Vt., across the river.

VISITOR INFORMATION   Dartmouth College alumni and chamber volunteers maintain a seasonal **information center** (© **603/643-3512**) on the green. It's open daily, from 10am to 5pm in June and September, and from 9:30am to 5pm in July and August. Off-season, head to the **Hanover Chamber of Commerce,** on Main Street across from the post office (© **603/643-3115**); open Monday through Friday from 9am to 4:30pm.

SPECIAL EVENTS   In mid-February, look for the fantastical ice sculptures of the **Dartmouth Winter Carnival;** call Dartmouth College (© **603/646-1110**) for more information on this traditionally beer-soaked event.

EXPLORING HANOVER

Hanover is a superb town to explore on foot, by bike, and even by canoe. Start by picking up a map of the campus, available at the information center on the green or at the Hanover Inn. (Free guided tours are also offered in summer.) The expansive, leafy campus is a delight to walk through.

Dartmouth's **Baker Memorial Library** harbors a wonderful treasure: a set of murals by Latin American artist José Orozco, who painted *The Epic of American Civilization* while teaching here between 1932 and 1934. The huge paintings wrap around a basement study room, and are as colorful as they are densely metaphorical. Ask for the printed interpretation at the front desk.

South of the green next to the Hanover Inn is the modern **Hopkins Center for the Arts** ✹ (✆ **603/646-2422**; www.dartmouth.edu/~hop). The center attracts national acts to its 900-seat concert hall and stages top-notch performances at the Moore Theater. The building was designed by Wallace Harrison, who later went on to fame for his Lincoln Center in New York.

Enfield Shaker Museum ✹✹   This cluster of historic buildings on peaceful Lake Mascoma is about a 20-minute drive southeast of Hanover. "The Chosen Vale," as its first inhabitants called it, was founded in 1793; by the mid-1800s it had 350 members and 3,000 acres (1,215 hectares). From that peak, the community dwindled, and by 1927 the Shakers abandoned the Chosen Vale and sold the village lock, stock, and barrel. Today, much of the property is owned by either the state of New Hampshire or the museum.

Dominating the village is the imposing Great Stone Dwelling, an austere but gracious granite structure erected between 1837 and 1841. When constructed, it was the tallest building north of Boston, and it remains the largest dwelling house in any of the Shaker communes. The Enfield Shakers lived and dined here, with as many as 150 Shakers at a time eating at long trestle tables. In 1997, the museum acquired the stone building, and in 1998 a new restaurant and inn opened to the public (see Shaker Inn at the Great Stone Dwelling, p. 504). The self-guided walking tour of the village is free with admission. The overall historic feel is compromised by a recent condominium development along the lakeshores, although the scale and design of these structures are sympathetic to the original village.

Rte. 4A, Enfield. ✆ **603/632-4346.** www.shakermuseum.org. Admission $7 adults, $6 seniors, $5 students, $3 children 10–18. Memorial Day–Halloween Mon–Sat 10am–5pm, Sun noon–5pm; winter and spring Sat 10am–4pm, Sun noon–4pm.

Hood Museum of Art ✹   This modern, open building next to the Hopkins Center houses one of the oldest college museums in the nation. Its current incarnation—an austere three-story structure—was built in 1986 and features special exhibits as well as examples from the permanent collection, which includes superb 19th-century American landscapes.

Wheelock St. ✆ **603/646-2808.** www.dartmouth.edu/~hood. Free admission. Tues, Thurs, and Fri–Sat 10am–5pm; Wed 10am–9pm; Sun noon–5pm.

Ledyard Canoe Club ✹✹   An idyllic way to spend a lazy afternoon is to drift along the Connecticut River in a canoe. Dartmouth's historic boating club is located just down the hill from the campus. While much of the club's focus is on competitive racing, it's a good place for visitors to rent a boat for a few hours and explore the tree-lined river. Instruction is available.

Off West Wheelock St. (turn upstream at the bottom of the hill west of the bridge; follow signs to the club-house). ✆ **603/643-6709.** www.dartmouth.edu/~lcc. Canoe and kayak rentals $5 per hour, $15 per day ($25 on weekends). Summer Mon–Fri 10am–8pm, Sat–Sun 9am–8pm; spring and fall Mon–Fri noon–6pm, Sat–Sun 10am–6pm. Open when river temperature is higher than 50°F (10°C).

Montshire Museum of Science ✹✹ *Kids*   This is not your average New England science museum of dusty stuffed animals in a creaky building. Located on the border between New Hampshire and Vermont (hence the name), the Montshire is a modern, architecturally engaging, hands-on museum that draws kids back time and again. It's set on a beautiful 100-acre (41-hectare) property sandwiched between I-91 and the Connecticut River. Exhibits are housed in an open, soaring structure inspired by the region's barns. The museum contains some live animals (don't miss the leaf-cutter ant exhibit on the second floor), but it's the fun, interactive exhibits that involve kids deeply, teaching them the principles of math and science on the sly. Even preschoolers are entertained here at "Andy's Place," a play area with aquariums, bubble-making exhibits, and other magical things. Outside, there's a new science park masquerading as a playground, plus four nature trails that wend through the riverside property of tall trees and chirpy birds.

Montshire Rd., Norwich. ℂ **802/649-2200.** www.montshire.org. Admission $6.50 adults, $5.50 children 3–17. MC, V. Daily 10am–5pm. Take Exit 13 off I-91 and head east; look for museum signs almost immediately.

WHERE TO STAY

Several lodgings are located off the interstate in Lebanon and West Lebanon, about 5 miles (8km) south of Hanover. Try the **Airport Economy Inn,** 45 Airport Rd. (Exit 20 off I-89; ℂ **800/433-3466** or 603/298-8888); **Days Inn,** 135 Rte. 120 (Exit 18 off I-89; ℂ **603/448-5070**); **Fireside Inn and Suites,** 25 Airport Rd. (Exit 20 off I-89; ℂ **603/298-5906**); or **Sunset Motor Inn,** 305 N. Main St. (Rte. 10, 4 miles/6km off Exit 19 off I-89; ℂ **603/298-8721**).

The Hanover Inn ★★★ The Upper Connecticut River Valley's most up-to-date hotel is perfectly situated for exploring campus and town. Established in 1780, most of the current inn was added at later dates—1924, 1939, or 1968—and this large, modern hotel now features professional service, attractive rooms, excellent dining, and subterranean walkways to the art museum and performing-arts theater. Yet the inn somehow manages to maintain an appealing old-world graciousness, informed by that mildly starchy neo-Georgian demeanor trendy in the 1940s. Most rooms have canopy or four-poster beds and down comforters; some overlook the green.

Wheelock St. (P.O. Box 151), Hanover, NH 03755. ℂ **800/443-7024** or 603/643-4300. Fax 603/643-4433. www.hanoverinn.com. 92 units. $257–$297 double. AE, DISC, MC, V. Valet parking $12 per day. Pets accepted ($15 per night). **Amenities:** 2 dining rooms (see review of the Daniel Webster Room, below); limited room service; massage; babysitting; dry cleaning. *In room:* A/C, TV, dataport, coffeemaker, hair dryer, iron.

Home Hill Inn ★★ The Home Hill Inn offers French flair in a gracious 1811 Federal-style house set on 25 acres (10 hectares) near the Connecticut River. Since 1996, its owners have made the property into one of the region's most inviting retreats. The rooms are elegantly appointed in a style that's not too delicate, not too rustic. The main house has five guest rooms; six more are in the carriage house, with another (seasonal) in the pool house. Most units have fireplaces. Co-owner and executive chef Victoria du Roure serves fare mostly from the south of France.

River Rd. (15 miles/24km south of Hanover), Plainfield, NH 03781. ℂ **603/675-6165.** Fax. 603/675-5220. www.homehillinn.com. 12 units. $150–$325 double. Rates include continental breakfast. AE, DISC, MC, V. **Amenities:** Restaurant (French); pool; putting green; clay tennis court; bikes. *In room:* A/C.

Shaker Inn at the Great Stone Dwelling ★★ Part of the Enfield Shaker Museum, the Shaker Inn opened in 1998 and offers a unique destination for those curious about the Shakers and American history. The rooms are spread among the upper floors of the massive stone dwelling house built by the Enfield Shaker community in the 1830s. All units are furnished with simple and attractive Shaker reproductions. Some rooms have original built-in Shaker cabinets (you can stow your socks in something that would bring 5 figures at a New York auction house). Room 1, the most expensive, boasts the most original detail. The restaurant features upscale regional fare that draws on Shaker traditions.

Rte. 4, Enfield, NH 03748. ✆ **888/707-4257** or 603/632-7810. Fax 603/632-7922. www.theshakerinn.com. 24 units. $105–$155 double. Rates include breakfast. AE, DC, DISC, MC, V. **Amenities:** Restaurant (Shaker-inspired cuisine); lake swimming. *In room:* Dataport.

WHERE TO DINE

Daniel Webster Room ✿✿ CONTEMPORARY AMERICAN   The Daniel Webster Room of the Hanover Inn will appeal to those looking for fine dining in a formal New England atmosphere. The inn's Colonial Revival dining room is reminiscent of a 19th-century resort hotel, with fluted columns and regal upholstered chairs. Produce from the college's organic farm is used seasonally. The eclectic changing entrees might include braised rabbit leg with truffled pappardelle. Off the inn's lobby is the more informal Zins, a wine bistro that serves 30 wines by the glass.

Hanover Inn, Wheelock St. ✆ **603/643-4300.** Reservations recommended. Breakfast items $3.95–$10.95; lunch items $4.50–$14.50; dinner main courses $19–$28. AE, DISC, MC, V. Restaurant Mon 7–10:30am and 11:30am–1:30pm; Tues–Fri 7–10:30am, 11:30am–1:30pm, and 6–9pm; Sat 7–10:30am and 6–9pm; Sun 8–10am and 11am–1:30pm. Bistro daily 11:30am–10pm.

La Poule à Dents ✿✿ FRENCH   In the sleepy town of Norwich just across the river from Hanover, this fine restaurant wakes up guests with the valley's most exquisite dining. The 1820 home with a canopied terrace has the feel of an intimate French auberge, the perfect spot for a romantic evening. The sumptuous meals begin with an inviting array of appetizers, such as a meaty charcuterie of three homemade sausages served with fig bread. Entrees might include seared sea scallops on barley risotto with ginger and miso.

Carpenter St. (off Main St. across from the Citgo station), Norwich, Vt. ✆ **802/649-2922.** www.lapoule.com. Reservations recommended. Main courses $18–$27. AE, DISC, MC, V. Daily 6–8:30pm.

Lou's ✿ *Value* BAKERY/COMFORT FOOD   Lou's has been a Hanover institution since 1947, attracting crowds for breakfast on weekends and a steady local clientele for lunch throughout the week. The mood is no-frills, with a linoleum floor, maple-and-vinyl booths, and a harried but efficient crew of waiters. Breakfast is served all day, and the sandwiches, made with fresh-baked bread, are huge and delicious.

30 S. Main St. ✆ **603/643-3321.** Breakfast items $3–$7; lunch items $5–$8. AE, MC, V. Mon–Fri 6am–3pm; Sat 7am–3pm; Sun 7am–3pm (opens 8am Sun in winter). Bakery open for snacks until 5pm.

3 The Lake Winnipesaukee Region

Lake Winnipesaukee is the state's largest lake, convoluted with coves and dotted with islands. Yet when you're out on the water, it rarely seems all that huge. That's because the 180-mile (290km) shoreline is edged with dozens of inlets, coves, and bays, and further fragmented by 274 islands. As a result, intermittent lake views from the shore give the illusion you're viewing a chain of smaller lakes and ponds rather than one massive body of water that measures 12 by 20 miles (19km by 32km) at its broadest points.

How to best enjoy the lake? If you're traveling with kids, Weirs Beach is a fun base. If you're looking for isolation, consider renting a cabin on the eastern shore for a week or so, track down a canoe or sailboat, then explore much the same way travelers did a century ago. If your time is limited, a driving tour around the lake with a few well-chosen stops will give you a nice taste of the region's woodsy flavor.

The White Mountains & Lake Winnipesaukee

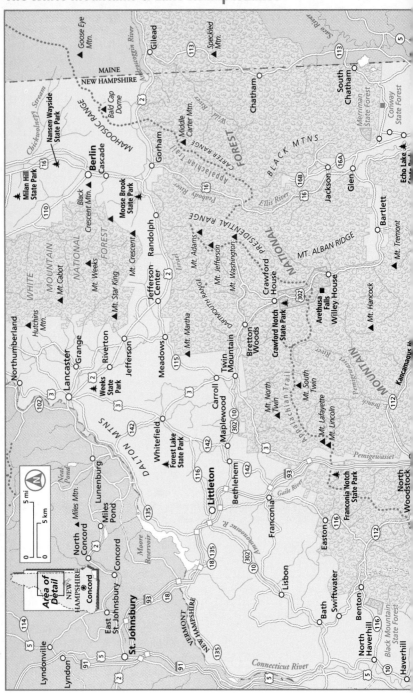

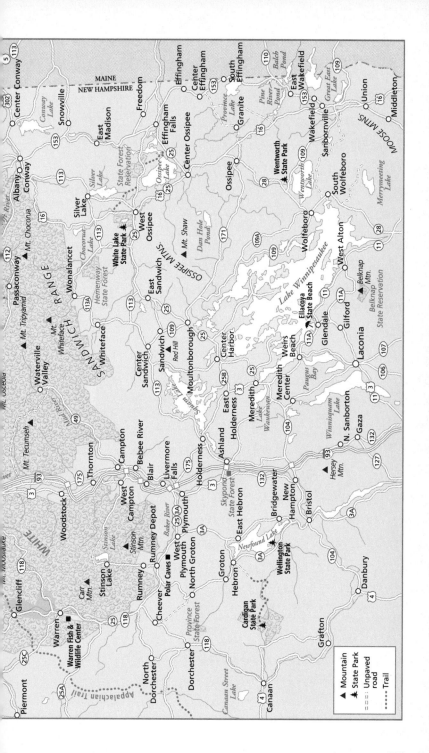

Lake Winnipesaukee's western shore has a more frenetic, working-class atmosphere than its refined sibling shore across the lake. That's partly for historic reasons—the main stage and rail routes passed along the western shore—and partly for modern reasons: I-93 runs west of the lake, serving as a sluice for harried visitors streaming in from Boston to the south.

WEIRS BEACH ⊛

Weirs Beach is a compact, blue-collar resort town that still shows its Victorian heritage. Unlike beach towns that sprawl for miles, Weirs Beach clusters in that classic pre-automobile fashion, spread along a boardwalk near a sandy beach. At the heart of the town is a working railroad that still connects to the steamship line—a nice throwback to an era when summer vacationers used mass transportation. The town attracts a mix of visitors, from history and transportation buffs to beach nuts.

But most of all, it attracts families. Lots of families, many of whom start the morning at sunny Endicott Beach, at the south edge of town, swimming in the clear waters of Winnipesaukee, then taking a train or boat excursion before switching over to afternoon video games at nearby arcades. Weirs Beach hasn't been gentrified—it has a historic authenticity that some find charming, and others find a bit too down-at-the-heels for their tastes.

ESSENTIALS

GETTING THERE   Interstate access to Weirs Beach is from I-93 at Exit 20 or Exit 23. From Exit 20, follow Route 3 north through Laconia to Weirs Beach. From the north, take Exit 23 and drive 9 miles (14km) east on Route 104 to Meredith, then head south on Route 3.

VISITOR INFORMATION   The **Greater Laconia/Weirs Beach Chamber of Commerce,** 11 Veterans Sq., Laconia (© 603/524-5531; www.laconia-weirs. org), maintains a seasonal information booth on Business Route 3 about halfway between Laconia and Weirs Beach. It's open daily in summer from 10am to 6pm. The **Lakes Region Association** (© 800/605-2537; www.lakesregion.org) has offices at Exit 23 off I-93 and is also happy to send out a vacation kit with maps and information.

SIGHTSEEING BY LAND & BY LAKE

Train rides leave from town on the **Winnipesaukee Scenic Railroad** ⊛ (© 603/279-5253 or 603/745-2135; www.hoborr.com), which offers 1- and 2-hour excursions in summer. It's a pleasing way to enjoy great views of lake and forest; kids are provided a hobo lunch packed in a bundle on a stick ($6.95). The 2-hour ride is $8.50 for adults and $6.50 for children 4 to 11.

The **MV** *Mount Washington* ⊛⊛ (© 603/366-2628; www.cruisenh.com) is an exceptionally handsome 230-foot (69m) vessel with three decks and a capacity of 1,250 passengers. This ship, by far the largest of the lake tour boats, offers excellent views of the shoreline and the knobby peaks of the White Mountains rising over the lake's northern end. Departing daily from Weirs Beach are a 2-hour tour ($16 for adults, $8 for children 4–12) and a 2½-hour excursion ($19 for adults, $9 for children). Occasional dinner cruises offer different themes—most feature classic rock, oldies nights, and country-and-western. The ship also runs tours from other ports around the lake, including Wolfeboro, Alton Bay, Center Harbor, and Meredith (call for details). The season runs from the end of May to mid-October.

EXPLORING WEIRS BEACH

In addition to the beach, the arcades, and the boat and train rides, Weirs Beach is home to a number of activities that delight young kids. The **Surfcoaster USA,** on Route 11B just outside Weirs Beach (© **603/366-4991;** www.surfcoaster usa.com), has a huge assortment of wave pools, water slides, and other wet diversions. Day passes cost $25 for adults, $18 for kids under 4 feet (1.2m) tall. Afternoon passes ($17 and $13, respectively) go on sale at 2pm.

The **Funspot** (© **603/366-4377**) will keep kids occupied with 500-odd games, including video games, candlepin bowling, bingo, and a driving range. There's no charge to enter. Games are priced individually (e.g., bowling is $2.75 per game per person). Also in town on Route 11B is **Daytona Fun Park** (© **603/366-5461**), which has go-carts, miniature golf, and batting cages.

Kellerhaus ☆ (© **603/366-4466**), located in a storybook-like stone-and-half-timber structure on Route 3, just north of Endicott Beach, features an ice-cream buffet where fanatics can select from a battery of toppings. Open in peak season from 8am to 11pm daily; call for off-season hours.

Come evening, complete the trip back in time with a movie at the wonderfully old-fashioned **Weirs Drive-In Theater,** on Route 3 (© **603/366-4723**).

WHERE TO STAY

Naswa Resort *Kids*   This old-fashioned (ca. 1936) lakefront resort features motel units, suites, and brightly colored, knotty-pine cabins. Most of the activity revolves around the sandy 1,000-foot (300m) beach, which fronts Winnipesaukee and teems with kids. Buildings are crowded in along the beach, and no one would confuse this with a romantic getaway. But it's a good destination for families, with easy access to boating and the activities of nearby Weirs Beach. Guest rooms are furnished comfortably but without much style.

1086 Weirs Blvd., Laconia, NH 03246. © **603/366-4341.** Fax 603/366-5731. www.naswaresort.com. 84 units. $149–$189 weekend double; $79–$149 midweek double. Discounts available in spring and fall. 2-night minimum stay on weekends. AE, DISC, MC, V. Closed mid-Oct to May. **Amenities:** Restaurant (beach bar/grill); watersports equipment rental (canoes, powerboats, jet skis). *In room:* A/C, TV.

MEREDITH ☆

The pleasant village of Meredith sits at the northwest corner of Winnipesaukee, with views across Meredith Bay from throughout the town. It lacks both the quaintness and the selection of activities that many travelers seek—a busy road cuts off the tidy downtown from the lakeshore, and small strip malls have intruded—but has good services and is home to several desirable inns. Foremost among its appeal is its superb location. We'd choose Meredith as a home base if we were looking to explore the lakes area and the White Mountains in just 2 or 3 days, because both are within striking distance for day trips. (Franconia Notch is about 50 miles/81km north.)

ESSENTIALS

GETTING THERE   Interstate access to Meredith is via Exit 23 off I-93. Drive 9 miles (14km) east on Route 104 to Route 3, then turn left down the hill into town.

VISITOR INFORMATION   The **Meredith Area Chamber of Commerce** (© **603/279-6121**) maintains an office in the white house on Route 3 (on the left when driving down the hill from Rte. 104). It's open daily from 9am to 5pm (closed weekends in winter).

EXPLORING THE AREA

Meredith's attractive though now largely bypassed Main Street ascends a hill from Route 3 at an elbow in the middle of town. A handful of galleries and boutiques offers low-key browsing. The creative re-adaptation of an early mill at the **Mill Falls Marketplace** ⚘ (✆ **800/622-6455**) features 18 shops, including a well-stocked bookstore. It's connected to the Inns at Mill Falls, at the intersection of Routes 3 and 25.

An excellent fair-weather trip is an excursion to 112-acre (45-hectare) **Stonedam Island** ⚘⚘, one of the largest protected islands in the lake. The island, owned by the Lakes Region Conservation Trust (✆ **603/279-3246**), has a trail that winds through wetlands and forest. Located approximately 2½ miles (4km) southeast of downtown Meredith, it's an ideal destination for a picnic, although it takes some doing to get here. Rent a canoe or kayak at **Sports & Marine Parafunalia,** Route 25, Meredith Shopping Center (✆ **603/279-8077**), and make a day of it.

Note also that the **MV *Mount Washington*** (see "Sightseeing by Land & by Lake," above) makes a stop once weekly in Meredith.

WHERE TO STAY

The Inns at Mill Falls ⚘⚘   This ever-expanding complex is gradually dominating downtown Meredith, but has managed its growth with considerable flair. The accommodations are spread among three uncommonly well-tended buildings (with a fourth slated to open in 2004). The main inn is located in a former mill complex (a small, tasteful shopping mall is adjacent), and features attractive but less elaborate rooms. All rooms in the more upscale Chase House have gas fireplaces; most also have balconies and porch rockers with views of the lake across Route 3. The Inn at Bay Point is located smack on 2,000 feet (600m) of lakefront, and most of its rooms feature balconies with sensational views. Ten units have Jacuzzis. The property is not especially well suited for kids.

Rte. 3, Meredith, NH 03253. ✆ **800/622-6455** or 603/279-7006. www.millfalls.com. 101 units. Summer $149–$279 double; winter $99–$269 double. AE, DC, DISC, MC, V. Minimum stay required some weekends. **Amenities:** 5 restaurants (casual dining); small indoor pool; fitness room; shopping arcade; limited room service; massage; babysitting; laundry service; dry cleaning. *In room:* A/C, TV, dataport, hair dryer, iron.

Manor on Golden Pond ⚘⚘⚘   This regal stucco-and-shingle mansion, 9 miles (14km) north of Meredith in Holderness, was built between 1903 and 1907 and sits on a low hill overlooking Squam Lake. It's wonderfully situated on 14 landscaped acres (6 hectares) studded with white pines. Inside, it has the feel of an English manor house, with rich oak paneling and leaded windows. The larger, more expensive guest rooms are creatively furnished and far more inviting than the motel-sized units along the first-floor wing. Most units have wood-burning fireplaces. Among our favorite rooms: Savoy Court, Buckingham, and Stratford, all lavishly appointed. Four recently constructed annex suites have French doors that open onto views of the lake. The top-notch dining room is "dressy casual" (no shorts or jeans).

Rte. 3, Holderness, NH 03245. ✆ **800/545-2141** or 603/968-3348. Fax 603/968-2116. www.manoron goldenpond.com. 27 units. Summer $210–$375 double; winter $150–$375 double. Rates include breakfast. 2-night minimum stay weekends and foliage season. AE, DISC, MC, V. No children under 14. **Amenities:** Restaurant (New American); outdoor pool; lake swimming; clay tennis court; free canoes and paddleboat; limited room service; massage; croquet; horseshoes; shuffleboard. *In room:* A/C, TV, dataport, hair dryer, iron (plus fridge and coffeemaker in annex rooms).

WHERE TO DINE

Abondante ☆ ITALIAN/DELI   This storefront market and deli has a delightful atmosphere—copper-topped tables, herbs drying from the joists overhead, and classical music. Both table service and to-go orders are available, with an inviting selection of fresh pastas (the lobster ravioli is popular) and rustic breads. This is a good spot for a casual dinner or a takeout picnic lunch.

30 Main St. ✆ **603/279-7177**. Main courses $4.95–$8.95 lunch, $7.95–$18.95 dinner. AE, DISC, MC, V. Summer daily 11am–2pm and 5–9pm (Fri–Sat until 10pm); off-season Wed–Sun 11am–2pm and 4–8pm (Fri–Sat 5–9pm).

Hart's Turkey Farm Restaurant TURKEY/AMERICAN   Hart's is bad news if you're a turkey. On a typical day, this place dishes up more than a ton of America's favorite bird. Judging by name alone, Hart's Farm sounds more rural than it is. In fact, it's in a nondescript building on busy Route 3. Inside, it's comfortable in a faux–Olde New Englande sort of way—a classic family restaurant (founded 1954) that borders on kitsch, but with turkey too good to write off as merely a retro experience. The service is afflicted with that sort of rushed efficiency found in places that attract bus tours. But diners don't return time and again to Hart's for the charm—they come for the turkey.

Junction of Rtes. 3 and 104. ✆ **603/279-6212**. www.hartsturkeyfarm.com. Main courses $9.50–$21.95 (most under $15). AE, DISC, MC, V. Daily 11:15am–8pm (until 9pm in summer).

WOLFEBORO ☆☆

The lovely town of Wolfeboro on Lake Winnipesaukee's eastern shore claims to be the first summer resort in the United States, and the documentation makes a pretty good case for it. In 1763, John Wentworth, the nephew of a former governor, built a summer estate on what's now called Lake Wentworth (just east of Winnipesaukee). The house burned in 1820, and the site now largely attracts archaeologists.

Where western Winnipesaukee tends to be more raucous with the populist attractions of Weirs Beach, Wolfeboro has more of a blue-blood sensibility. You'll find impeccably maintained 19th-century architecture, attractive shops, and a more refined sense of place.

ESSENTIALS

GETTING THERE   Lake Winnipesaukee's east shore is best explored on Route 28 (from Alton Bay to Wolfeboro) and Route 109 (from Wolfeboro to Moultonborough).

VISITOR INFORMATION   The **Wolfeboro Chamber of Commerce** (✆ **800/516-5324** or 603/569-2200; www.wolfeboroonline.com) offers information from its offices in a converted railroad station at 32 Central Ave., a block off Main Street. It's open in summer daily from 10am to 5pm, off-season Monday through Friday from 10am to 3pm.

EXPLORING THE AREA

Wolfeboro (pop. 2,800) has a vibrant, homey downtown that's easily explored on foot. Park near Depot Square and the Victorian train station, then stock up on brochures and maps at the Chamber of Commerce office inside. Behind the train station, running along the former tracks of the rail line, is the **Russell C. Chase Bridge-Falls Path** ☆, a rail-trail that runs along Back Bay to a set of small cascades.

Several boat tours depart from docks behind the shops of Main Street. Our favorite option: a wind-in-the-face, half-hour tour on the *Millie B.* ☆☆

Tips **Worthwhile Views**

For a sweeping view of Winnipesaukee's eastern shore, drive 7 miles (11km) north of Wolfeboro on Route 109 to the **Abenaki Tower**. (Look for a parking lot and wooden sign on the right side of the road at the crest of a hill.) From the lot, it's an easy 5-minute hike to the sturdy log tower, which rises about 80 feet (24m) high and is ascended by a steep staircase (not a good destination for acrophobes). Those who soldier on to the top are rewarded with excellent views of nearby coves, inlets, and the Belknap Mountains southwest of the lake.

((C) **603/569-1080**), a rare 28-foot (8.4m) mahogany speedboat constructed by Hacker-Craft ($10 for adults, $5 for children under 5). Also available are 1½-hour excursions on the ***Winnipesaukee Belle*** (C) **603/569-3796**), a 65-foot (20m) faux steamship with a canopied upper deck, owned and operated by the Wolfeboro Inn. And the impressive **MV *Mount Washington*** (see "Sightseeing by Land & by Lake," above) sails out of Wolfeboro four times weekly in summer.

For a self-propelled afternoon, kayak rentals and guided tours are available from **Winnipesaukee Kayak** , 17 Bay St., at Back Bay Marina ((C) **603/569-9926**). On a relatively windless day, little beats exploring by paddle from Wolfeboro Bay to the cluster of islands just to the south.

Quieter lake swimming is available at **Wentworth State Beach** , 5 miles (8km) east of Wolfeboro on Route 109 ((C) **603/569-3699**), which also features a shady picnic area.

Castle in the Clouds About 15 miles (24km) north of Wolfeboro is a rather unusual sight. In 1913, cranky millionaire Thomas Gustav Plant built an eccentric stone edifice high atop a mountain overlooking Lake Winnipesaukee, at a cost of $7 million. The home is a sort of rustic, smaller San Simeon East, with cliff-hugging rooms, stained-glass windows, and unrivaled views of the surrounding hills and lakes. Visitors drive to the carriage house, where they park and are taken in groups through the house by knowledgeable guides. Even if the castle holds no interest, the 5,200-acre (2,106-hectare) grounds are worth the admission. The long access road is harrowingly narrow and winding, with wonderful vistas and turnouts for stopping along the way. Take your time to explore on the way up; the separate exit road is fast, straight, and uninteresting.

Rte. 171 (4 miles/6km south of Rte. 25), Moultonborough. (C) **800/729-2468** or 603/476-2352. www.castle springs.com. Admission $12 adults, $10 seniors, $8 students, free for children under 6. Grounds only $6 adults, free for children. Mid-May to mid-June Sat–Sun 9am–5pm; mid-June to Labor Day daily 9am–5pm; Labor Day to 3rd week of Oct daily 9am–4pm. Closed Nov–Apr.

New Hampshire Antique and Classic Boat Museum Winnipesaukee is synonymous with classic wooden powerboats—sleek Chris-Crafts and other icons of a more genteel era. This museum is located in a barn about 2 miles (3.2km) from downtown. Check the website for upcoming events: The summer regattas bring boat restorers and aficionados out of the woodwork to show off their obsessions.

397 Center St., Wolfeboro. (C) **603/569-4554**. www.nhacbm.org. Admission $5 adults, $4 seniors, $3 students, free for children under 12. Summer Mon–Sat 10am–4pm, Sun noon–4pm; call for off-season hours. Drive north on Rte. 109/28 from downtown.

WHERE TO STAY & DINE

Wolfeboro Inn ★★ This small, elegant resort hotel strives to mix modern and traditional, and succeeds quite admirably. Located an easy stroll from downtown, the inn dates back to 1812 but was extensively expanded in the 1980s. The modern lobby features a small atrium with wood beams, a slate floor, and a brick fireplace, but retains an old-world elegance. Most of the comfortable guest rooms are furnished with reproductions and quilts. Deluxe units have better views, and a dozen have balconies as well. Rooms 200 and 300 are especially nice, with sofas, fridges, and two balconies. The downside: For an inn of this price and quality, it has only a disappointing sliver of lakeshore and just a tiny beach.

90 N. Main St., Wolfeboro, NH 03894. ℂ **800/451-2389** or 603/569-3016. Fax 603/569-5375. www.wolfeboroinn.com. 44 units. Mid-May to Oct $159–$299 double; Nov to mid-May $89–$279 double. Rates include continental breakfast. 2-night minimum stay in peak season. AE, MC, V. **Amenities:** 2 restaurants (steakhouse; pub fare); lake swimming; rowboat; boat tours; concierge; limited room service; babysitting; laundry service; dry cleaning. *In room:* A/C, TV, coffeemaker, hair dryer, iron.

4 The White Mountains

The White Mountains are northern New England's outdoor-recreation capital. This cluster of ancient mountains is a sprawling, rugged playground that attracts kayakers, mountaineers, rock climbers, skiers, mountain bikers, bird-watchers, and, especially, hikers.

The **White Mountain National Forest** encompasses some 773,000 acres (313,065 hectares) of rocky, forested terrain, more than 100 waterfalls, dozens of remote backcountry lakes, and miles of clear brooks and cascading streams. An elaborate network of 1,200 miles (1,932km) of hiking trails dates back to the 19th century, when the urban gentry took to the mountains in droves to build character, build trails, and experience nature's sublimity. Trails ranging from easy to demanding lace the hillside forests, run along remote valley rivers, and traverse barren, windswept ridgelines where the weather can change dramatically in less time than it takes to eat your lunch.

The center of the White Mountains—in spirit if not in geography—is its highest point: 6,288-foot (1,886m) **Mount Washington,** an ominous, brooding peak that's often cloud-capped and mantled with snow both early and late in the season. This blustery peak is accessible by cog railroad, car, and foot, making it one of the more popular destinations in the region. You won't find utter wilderness here, but you will find abundant natural drama.

Flanking this colossal peak is the brawny **Presidential Range** of the White Mountains, a series of wind-blasted granite peaks named after U.S. presidents and offering spectacular views. Surrounding these are numerous other rocky ridges that lure hikers looking for challenges and a place to experience nature at its most elemental.

Travelers whose idea of fun doesn't involve steep cliffs or icy dips in mountain streams can enjoy the mountain scenery via spectacular drives. North of North Conway, Route 302 carries travelers through Crawford Notch to the pleasant towns of Bethlehem and Littleton. Route 16 travels from southern New Hampshire through congested North Conway before twisting up dramatic Pinkham Notch at the base of Mount Washington. Wide and fast, Route 2 skirts the northern edge of the mountains, offering wonderful views en route to the town of Jefferson. I-93 may be the most scenic interstate in northern New England, passing through spectacular Franconia Notch as it narrows to a two-lane road in deference to its natural surroundings (and local political will). The most scenic

Guides to Exploring the White Mountains

For serious exploration of the White Mountains, you'll need supplemental guides and maps to keep you on track. Here's a short list of recommended guides, most of which are available at area bookstores:

- *AMC White Mountain Guide* (Appalachian Mountain Club, 1998, $21.95). This comprehensive 576-page book is chock-full of detailed information on all the hiking trails in the White Mountains. It's the definitive hiker's bible for the region.
- *White Mountains Map Book* (Map Adventures, 2000, $16.95). This colorful, sharply printed map features 386 hiking trails, distances, and a GPS grid. The text offers an overview of what you'll find on 76 day hikes, along with information on camping. It's a good choice for those planning 2 or 3 days of hiking.
- *50 Hikes in the White Mountains* (Backcountry Publications, 1997, $14.95). The fifth edition of this popular guide, written by Daniel Doan and Ruth Doan MacDougall, offers a good selection of mountain rambles in the high peaks region around Mount Washington. You'll find everything from easy strolls to overnight backpack trips.
- *Waterfalls of the White Mountains* (Backcountry Publications, 1999, $18). Waterfall lovers will get their money's worth from Bruce and Doreen Bolnick's guide to 100 mountain waterfalls, including roadside cascades and backcountry cataracts.

drive in the Whites, though, is the **Kancamagus Highway,** which links Conway with Lincoln and provides frequent roadside pull-offs for casual explorers to admire cascades, picnic along rivers, and enjoy sweeping mountain views.

Where to base yourself? North Conway is the motel capital of the region, with hundreds of rooms—many quite charmless, but usually available at reasonable rates. The Loon Mountain and Waterville Valley areas have a sort of planned condo-village graciousness that delights some travelers and gives others the creeps. Jackson, Franconia Notch, Crawford Notch, and the Bethlehem-Littleton area are the best destinations for old-fashioned hotels and inns.

BACKCOUNTRY FEES The White Mountain National Forest requires anyone using the backcountry—whether for hiking, biking, skiing, or picnicking—to pay a recreation fee. Anyone parking at a trailhead must display a backcountry permit on the dashboard of his car. Permits are available at ranger stations and many stores in the region. An annual permit costs $20, while a 7-day pass is $5. (You can also buy a day pass for $3, but it covers only one site. If you drive somewhere else later in the afternoon and park, you'll have to pay $3 again.) For information, contact the Forest Service's White Mountains office at © **603/ 528-8721.**

RANGER STATIONS & INFORMATION The Forest Service's **central White Mountains office** is at 719 Main St. in Laconia (© **603/528-8721**), which is near Lake Winnipesaukee. Your best general source of information is the **Saco Ranger Station,** 33 Kancamagus Hwy., 100 yards (91m) west of Route 16, Conway (© **603/447-5448**). Other district offices are **Androscoggin Ranger Station,** 300 Glen Rd., Gorham (© **603/466-2713**); **Ammonoosuc**

Ranger Station, 660 Trudeau Rd., Bethlehem (℃ **603/466-2713**); and **Pemigewasset Ranger Station,** Route 175, Holderness, near the Plymouth town line (℃ **603/536-1315**). The **Evans Notch Ranger Station** (℃ **207/ 824-2134**), which covers the Maine portion of the White Mountains (about 50,000 acres/20,250 hectares), is in Bethel at 18 Mayville Rd., off Route 2 just north of town.

Additional information and advice on recreation are available at the **Appalachian Mountain Club's Pinkham Notch Camp** (℃ **603/466-2727**), on Route 16 between Jackson and Gorham. The center is open daily from 6am to 10pm.

CAMPING The White Mountain National Forest maintains 19 drive-in campgrounds scattered throughout the region, with the number of sites at each ranging from 7 to 176. Campsites are $12 to $16 per night, plus an additional fee if you reserve in advance. Reservations are accepted at about half of these through National Recreation Reservation Service (℃ **877/444-6777; www.reserveamerica.com**). Most sites are very basic (some with pit toilets only), but all are well maintained.

Dolly Copp Campground (℃ **603/466-2713**), near the base of Mount Washington, is the largest and least personal of the campgrounds, but has a superior location and great views from the open sites. Along the Kancamagus Highway, we're partial to the **Covered Bridge Campground** (℃ **603/ 447-5448**), which is adjacent to an 1858 covered bridge and a short drive to delightful river swimming at the Rocky Gorge Scenic Area.

Backcountry tent camping is free throughout the White Mountains, and no permit is needed. (You will need to purchase a parking permit to leave your car at the trailhead; see above.) Check with one of the ranger stations for current restrictions. Log lean-tos are also scattered throughout the backcountry, providing overnight shelter for campers. Shelters are sometimes free, or sometimes a backcountry manager will collect a small fee. Ask at any ranger station for details and locations.

NORTH CONWAY & ENVIRONS

North Conway is the commercial heart of the White Mountains. Shoppers are drawn by the outlets along Routes 302 and 16. (The highways overlap through town.) Outdoor purists abhor it, considering it a garish interloper to be avoided at all costs, except when seeking pizza and beer.

North Conway itself won't strike anyone as nature's wonderland. The shopping strip south of the village is basically one long turn lane flanked by outlet malls, motels, and chain restaurants. On rainy weekends and during the foliage season, the road can resemble a linear parking lot.

Sprawl notwithstanding, North Conway is beautifully situated along the eastern edge of the broad and fertile Saco River Valley (also called the Mount Washington Valley). Gentle, forest-covered mountains, some with sheer cliffs that suggest the distant, stunted cousins of Yosemite's rocky faces, border the bottomlands. Northward up the valley, the hills rise in a triumphant crescendo to the blustery heights of Mount Washington.

The village is trim and attractive (if often congested), with an open green, some colorful shops, Victorian frontier-town commercial architecture, and a distinctive train station. It's a good place to park, stretch your legs, and find a cup of coffee or a snack. (There's a Ben & Jerry's ice-cream shop off the green near the train station.)

ESSENTIALS

GETTING THERE   North Conway and the Mount Washington Valley are on Route 16 and Route 302. Route 16 connects to the Spaulding Turnpike, which intersects with I-95 outside of Portsmouth, N.H. Route 302 begins in Portland, Maine. **Concord Trailways** (© **800/639-3317**) provides service from points south, including Boston.

Traffic can be vexing in the Mount Washington Valley on holiday weekends in summer and foliage weekends in fall, when backups of several miles aren't uncommon. Try valiantly to plan around these busy times in order to preserve your own sanity.

VISITOR INFORMATION   The **Mount Washington Valley Chamber of Commerce** (© **800/367-3364** or 603/356-3171; www.4seasonresort.com) operates a seasonal information booth opposite the village green. The staff can help arrange accommodations. It's open in summer, daily from 9am to 6pm; in winter, on Saturday and Sunday only. The chamber's main office is at 2617 Main St.

The state of New Hampshire also operates an **information booth** with restrooms and phones at a vista with fine views of Mount Washington, on Routes 16 and 302 north of North Conway.

RIDING THE RAILS

The **Conway Scenic Railroad** ★★ (© **800/232-5251** or 603/356-5251; www.conwayscenic.com) offers mountain excursions in comfortable rail cars (including a dome car) pulled by either steam or early diesel engines. Trips depart from a distinctive 1874 train station just off the village green. The 1-hour excursion heads south to Conway; you're better off signing up for the more picturesque 1¾-hour trip northward to the village of Bartlett. For the best show, select the 5½-hour excursion through dramatic Crawford Notch, with stupendous views of the mountains from high along this beautiful glacial valley. Ask also about the railway's dining excursions.

The train runs from mid-April to mid-December, with more frequent trips scheduled daily in midsummer. Coach and first-class fares are available; first-class passengers sit in "Gertrude Emma," an 1898 parlor car with wicker and rattan chairs, mahogany woodwork, and an observation platform. Tickets are $9.50 to $19 for adults ($33–$45 for the Crawford Notch trip), $7 to $14 for children 4 to 12 ($18–$30 for Crawford Notch). Kids under 4 ride free on the two shorter trips. Reservations are accepted for the dining car and the Crawford Notch train.

SHOPPING

North Conway was one of northern New England's first major outlet centers. As many as 200 shops are located along the strip, which extends about 3 miles (5km) northward from the junction of Routes 302 and 16 in Conway into the village of North Conway itself.

That said, it should be noted that the outlet scene has lagged somewhat in recent years—the selection is not as upscale as in Freeport or Kittery, Maine, or in Manchester, Vt. The strip is starting to be plagued by empty storefronts, largely because of the success of one rapidly expanding outlet center, which has absorbed much of the surrounding business into a village-like minimall.

That place is **Settler's Green Outlet Village Plus** (© **603/356-7031**; www.settlersgreen.com), and shoppers should start here. The center features more than 50 shops, including J. Crew, Nike, Levi's, and Orvis.

Just north of Settler's Green is the popular **L.L.Bean** (📞 **603/356-2100**) at the Tanger Outlet Center. Next to L.L.Bean is **Chuck Roast** (📞 **800/533-1654**), a notable local manufacturer of fleecewear that's worth a browse.

Also of note is **Yield House** (📞 **800/659-2211**), the nationally known manufacturer of colonial reproduction furniture. It's located on Route 3 at the south end of the strip, where it merges with Route 302. Some excellent discounts may be found in the warehouse next to the main showroom.

Three good outdoor-equipment suppliers are located in and around North Conway. **International Mountain Equipment** (📞 **603/356-7013**) and **Eastern Mountain Sports** (📞 **603/356-5433**) are both on Main Street, just north of the green. Our favorite for its good selection and friendly staff is **Ragged Mountain Equipment** (📞 **603/356-3042**), 3 miles (5km) north of town in Intervale on Routes 16 and 302.

ALPINE SKIING

Cranmore Mountain Resort ⭐ *Value* Mount Cranmore is the oldest operating ski area in New England. The slopes are unrepentantly old-fashioned, but the mountain has restyled itself as a snow-sports mecca—look for extensive snow tubing, snow-scooters, and ski-bikes. The slopes aren't likely to challenge advanced skiers, but the resort will delight beginners and intermediates, as well as those who like a little diversion from the skiing with the ski toys. It's highly recommended for families, thanks to the relaxed attitude, range of activities, and budget ticket prices (kids 6–12 pay $15).

North Conway Village, NH 03860. 📞 **603/356-5544**. www.cranmore.com. Vertical drop: 1,200 ft. (360m). Lifts: 7 chairlifts (1 high-speed quad), 2 surface lifts. Skiable acreage: 192. Lift tickets: $32.

WHERE TO STAY

Briarcliff Motel Among North Conway's dozens of roadside motels, the Briarcliff is one of the better choices. It's a basic motel with standard-size units, but all have been redecorated in rich colors, more like B&B rooms. There's a $10 premium for a room with a "porch," but these are a little peculiar—the porches are really part of a long enclosed sitting area with each unit separated from its neighbor by cubicle-height partitions. (Save your money.) Get over the traffic noise, and the Briarcliff offers decent value.

Rte. 16 (P.O. Box 504), ½ a mile (0.8km) south of village center, North Conway, NH 03860. 📞 **800/338-4291** or 603/356-5584. www.briarcliffmotel.com. 30 units. Summer $59–$125 double; off-season $49–$79 double. 2-night minimum stay holidays and foliage season. AE, DISC, MC, V. **Amenities:** Small pool. *In room:* A/C, TV, fridge.

The Buttonwood Inn ⭐⭐ Located just a couple minutes' drive from the outlets and restaurants, the Buttonwood has more of a classic country-inn feel than any other North Conway inn. It's set on 17 quiet acres (7 hectares) on the side of Mount Surprise in an 1820s-era home, and has a tastefully appointed interior inspired by Shaker style. Most bedrooms tend toward the small and cozy, but two common areas allow guests plenty of space to unwind. Two units have gas fireplaces, and one of these has a Jacuzzi as well. Hosts Claudia and Peter Needham are uncommonly helpful with the planning of day trips. Peter prepares breakfasts that tend toward the country-elegant (think cornmeal waffles with strawberry-rhubarb sauce).

Mt. Surprise Rd., North Conway, NH 03860. 📞 **800/258-2625** or 603/356-2625. Fax 603/356-3140. www.buttonwoodinn.com. 10 units (2 with private hall bathroom). $95–$250 double; from $130 foliage season; from $85 off-season. Rates include breakfast. 2- to 3-night minimum stay on weekends and holidays. AE, DISC, MC, V. Closed Apr. Children over 6 welcome. **Amenities:** Pool; cross-country ski trails. *In room:* A/C, dataport.

Comfort Inn & Suites ✿ *Kids* This tidy all-suite (mostly large single rooms, actually) chain hotel opened in 2000, giving travelers a bit more elbowroom than at most area motels. It's a good choice for families: It's close to the outlet shopping and has its own elaborate pirate-themed miniature golf course on the property. Two rooms have gas fireplaces.

2001 White Mountain Hwy. (Rte. 16), North Conway, NH 03860. © **800/228-5150** or 603/356-8811. Fax 603/356-7770. 58 units. $99–$199 double; to $249 executive suite. Rates include continental breakfast. AE, DISC, MC, V. **Amenities:** Small indoor pool; limited fitness room; game room; coin-op laundry. *In room:* A/C, TV, dataport, fridge, coffeemaker, hair dryer, iron.

Cranmore Inn ✿ The Cranmore Inn has the feel of a 19th-century board-inghouse—which is appropriate, because that's what it is. Open since 1863, this Victorian home is a short walk from North Conway's center. Its heritage adds charm and quirkiness, but comes with drawbacks, like sometimes-uneven water pressure in the showers. That said, it offers good value thanks to its handy location and the hospitality of the innkeepers.

80 Kearsarge St., North Conway, NH 03860. © **800/526-5502** or 603/356-5502. www.cranmoreinn.com. 18 units (3 with private hall bathroom). Summer $68–$88 double; foliage season and ski weekends $86–$128 double; off-season $59–$88 double. Rates include breakfast. Kitchen units $99–$159, not including breakfast. 2-night minimum stay weekends, holidays, and foliage season. AE, DISC, MC, V. **Amenities:** Heated outdoor pool (summer only). *In room:* No phone.

The Forest Country Inn ✿ Just 10 minutes north of North Conway is a spur road that leads through the village of Intervale, which has several lodges and a feeling removed from the clutter of the outlet shops. The Forest Country Inn was built in 1850, with a mansard-roofed third floor added in 1890. Typical for the era, the rooms are more cozy than spacious, and today are decorated mostly with reproductions and some antiques. The best units are the two in the nearby stone cottage; ask for the Cottle Room, with its wood-burning fireplace, wing chairs, and small porch.

Rte. 16A (P.O. Box 37), Intervale, NH 03845. © **877/854-6535** or 603/356-9772. Fax 603/356-5652. www.forest-inn.com. 11 units. July–Oct and mid-Dec to Mar $95–$140 double ($20 surcharge in foliage season); off-season $70–$100 double. Rates include breakfast. 2-night minimum stay most weekends and holidays. AE, DISC, MC, V. Children 6 and over welcome. Closed Apr. **Amenities:** Small pool. *In room:* A/C.

Stonehurst Manor ✿ This imposing, architecturally eclectic Victorian stone-and-shingle mansion, originally built for the family that owned Bigelow carpet, is set amid white pines on a rocky knoll above Route 16, north of North Conway. It wouldn't seem at all out of place in either the south of France or the moors of Scotland. One's immediate assumption is that it caters to the stuffy and affluent—but the main focus here is on outdoor adventure, and it attracts a youngish crowd. Request one of the 14 rooms in the regal 1876 mansion (another 10 are in a comfortable but less elegant wing built in 1952).

Rte. 16, 1.2 miles (2km) north of North Conway Village (P.O. Box 1937), North Conway, NH 03860. © **800/525-9100.** Fax 603/356-3217. www.stonehurstmanor.com. 24 units (2 with shared bathroom). $80–$140 double; $106–$166 double with breakfast and dinner included. (7% fuel and energy surcharge in winter; $10 surcharge weekends; $20–$30 surcharge foliage season.) 2-night minimum stay on weekends. MC, V. Pets accepted in limited rooms ($25 per night). **Amenities:** Restaurant (wood-fired pizza/eclectic); outdoor pool; tennis court; Jacuzzi. *In room:* A/C, TV, no phone.

White Mountain Hotel and Resort 🐾🐾 This resort has the best location of any hotel in the North Conway area. Sited at the base of dramatic White Horse Ledge near Echo Lake State Park amid a contemporary golf-course community, the White Mountain Hotel was built in 1990, but its style borrows from classic area resorts. Its designers have managed to take some of the more successful elements of a friendly country inn—a nice deck with a view, a clubby tavern area—and incorporate them into a thoroughly modern resort. The bedroom appointments are a solid notch or two above standard hotel furnishings.

West Side Rd. (5.4 miles/8.7km west of North Conway), P.O. Box 1828, North Conway, NH 03860. ℂ 800/533-6301 or 603/356-7100. Fax 603/356-7100. www.whitemountainhotel.com. 80 units. Summer $139–$199 double; foliage $169–$199 double; winter $79–$129 double; other times $59–$99 double. 2-night minimum stay on weekends. AE, DISC, MC, V. **Amenities:** Dining room (Continental/regional); tavern; outdoor heated pool; 9-hole golf course; tennis courts; fitness center; Jacuzzi; sauna; game room; limited room service; babysitting; coin-op washers and dryers; laundry service; dry cleaning. *In room:* A/C, TV, data-port, coffeemaker, hair dryer, iron.

WHERE TO DINE

North Conway is the turf of family-style restaurants, fast-food chains, and bars that happen to serve food. If you're looking for more refined dining, head for the Inn at Thorn Hill in Jackson, about 10 minutes north (p. 523).

Bellini's 🐾 SOUTHERN ITALIAN Bellini's has a fun, quirky interior that's more informal than its Victorian exterior might suggest. It's run by the third generation of the Marcello family, who opened their first place in Rhode Island in 1927. The food runs the gamut from fettuccine chicken pesto to *braciola,* and most everything is homemade—soups, breads, pastas, and desserts. Particularly good: the toasted ravioli appetizer.

33 Seavey St., North Conway. ℂ 603/356-7000. www.bellinis.com. Reservations not accepted. Main courses $12–$22. AE, DISC, MC, V. Sun, Wed, and Thurs 5–10pm; Fri–Sat 5–11pm.

Chinook Cafe 🐾 ECLECTIC The Chinook Cafe opened in 1998 in Conway (a 10-min. drive south of North Conway) as a small, mostly takeout place, but its popularity forced it to move down the street and expand. You'll find healthy fare for breakfast and lunch, with a good selection of vegetarian items. The chicken wraps are delicious (try Thai style with peanut sauce), the smoothies nicely sippable while driving, and the homemade baked goods a fitting conclusion to a hike. The more upscale dinners include maple-smoked duck breast or seared sea scallops with braised leeks and toasted pecans.

80 Main St. (across from the fire station), Conway. ℂ 603/447-6300. Main courses $1.75–$3.75 breakfast, $4.25–$5.75 lunch, $14–$19 dinner. MC, V. Mon–Tues 8am–4pm; Wed–Sat 8am–9:30pm.

Moat Mountain Smoke House and Brewing Co. 🐾 BARBECUE/PUB FARE Moat Mountain is the place for fresh beer, smoked meat, and wood-fired pizza. It has a more intriguing variety of eats than other North Conway beer joints. Options include barbecued meats, burgers, quesadillas, wraps, and several dishes that feature smoked trout and salmon. A dozen beers are on tap. There's also a children's menu.

3378 White Mountain Hwy. (Rte. 16), about 1 mile (1.6km) north of North Conway. ℂ 603/356-6381. Reservations not accepted. Main courses $5.75–$18.95. AE, MC, V. Daily 11:30am–9pm (Fri–Sat until 10pm).

JACKSON & ENVIRONS 🐾🐾

Jackson is a quiet village situated in a picturesque valley just off Route 16, about 15 minutes north of North Conway. The village center, approached on a single-lane covered bridge, is tiny, but touches of old-world elegance remain—vestiges of a time when Jackson was a favored destination for the East Coast upper middle class, who fled the summer heat in the cities to relax at rambling wooden hotels or shingled country homes.

With the Depression and the rise of the motel trade in the '40s and '50s, Jackson and its old-fashioned hostelries slipped into a lasting slumber. Then along came the 1980s, which brought condo projects sprouting in fields where cows once roamed, vacation homes flanking the hills, and the resuscitation of the two vintage wooden hotels that didn't burn or collapse during the dark ages.

Thanks to a revamped golf course and one of the most elaborate and well-maintained cross-country ski networks in the country, Jackson is again a thriving year-round resort. While no longer undiscovered, it still feels a shade out of the mainstream and is a peaceful spot, especially when compared to commercial North Conway.

ESSENTIALS

GETTING THERE   Jackson is just off Route 16 about 11 miles (18km) north of North Conway. Look for the covered bridge on the right when heading north.

VISITOR INFORMATION   The **Jackson Chamber of Commerce (© 800/ 866-3334** or 603/383-9356; www.jacksonnh.com) can provide information and make lodging reservations.

ASCENDING MOUNT WASHINGTON

Mount Washington, located just north of Jackson amid the national forest, is home to numerous superlatives. At 6,288 feet (1,886m), it's the highest mountain in the Northeast. It's said to have the worst weather in the world outside of the polar regions. It holds the world's record for the highest surface wind speed ever recorded—231 miles (372km) per hour, in 1934. Winds over 150 miles (242km) per hour are routinely recorded every month except June, July, and August, in part the result of the mountain's location at the confluence of three major storm tracks.

Mount Washington may also be the mountain with the most options for getting to the summit. Visitors can ascend by cog railroad (see "Crawford Notch," later in this chapter), by car, by guide-driven van, or on foot.

Despite the raw power of the weather, the summit of Mount Washington is not the best destination for those seeking wilderness wild and untamed. The summit is home to a train platform, a parking lot, a snack bar, a gift shop, a museum, and a handful of outbuildings, some of which house the weather observatory. And there are the crowds, which can be thick on a clear day. Then again, on a clear day the views can't be beat, with vistas extending into four states and to the Atlantic Ocean.

The best place to learn about Mount Washington and its approaches is the rustic **Pinkham Notch Camp** (© **603/466-2721**), operated by the Appalachian Mountain Club. Located at the crest of Route 16 between Jackson and Gorham, Pinkham Notch offers overnight accommodations and meals (see "Joe Dodge Lodge at Pinkham Notch," below), maps, and plenty of advice from the helpful staff. A number of hiking trails depart from Pinkham Notch, allowing for several loops and side trips.

About a dozen trails lead to the mountain's summit, ranging in length from 3.8 to 15 miles (6km–24km). (Detailed trail information is available at Pinkham Notch Camp.) The most direct and dramatic is the **Tuckerman Ravine Trail** ★★★, which departs from Pinkham Notch. Healthy hikers should allow 4 to 5 hours for the ascent, an hour or two less for the return trip. Be sure to allow enough time to enjoy the dramatic glacial cirque of Tuckerman Ravine, which attracts extreme skiers to its snowy chutes and sheer drops as late as June.

The **Mount Washington Auto Road** ★★ (© **603/466-3988;** www. mt-washington.com) opened in 1861 as a carriage road, and has since remained one of the most popular White Mountain attractions. The steep, winding 8-mile (13km) road (with an average grade of 12%) is partially paved and incredibly dramatic; your breath will be taken away at one curve after another. The ascent will test your iron will; the descent will test your car's brakes. The trip's not worth doing if the summit is in the clouds; wait for a clear day.

If you'd prefer to leave the driving to someone else, van tours ascend throughout the day, allowing you to relax, enjoy the views, and learn about the mountain from informed guides. The cost is $22 for adults and $10 for children 5 to 12, including a half-hour stay on the summit.

The Auto Road, which is on Route 16 north of Pinkham Notch, is open from mid-May to late October from 7:30am to 6pm (limited hours early and late in the season). The cost is $16 for car and driver, $6 for each additional adult ($4 for children). The fee includes audiocassette narration pointing out sights along the way. Management has imposed some curious restrictions on cars; for instance, Acuras and Jaguars with automatic transmissions must show a "1" on the shifter to be allowed on the road, and no Lincoln Continentals from before 1969 are permitted.

One additional note: The average temperature atop the mountain is 30°F (−1°C). (The warmest temperature ever recorded atop the mountain, in August, was 72°F, or 22°C.) Even in summer, visitors should come prepared for blustery conditions.

EXPLORING PINKHAM NOTCH

Pinkham Notch Camp is at the height of land on Route 16. Just south, look for signs for **Glen Ellis Falls** ★★, a worthwhile 10- to 15-minute stop. From the parking area, you'll pass through a pedestrian tunnel and walk along the Glen Ellis River for a few minutes until it seemingly falls off the face of the earth. The stream plummets 64 feet (19m) down a sheer cliff; observation platforms are located at the top and near the bottom of the falls. The whole trip from parking lot to base of the falls is less than a ½ mile (0.8km). After a torrential rain, this is one of the region's most impressive falls.

From Pinkham Notch Camp, it's about 2.4 miles (3.9km) up to **Hermit Lake and Tuckerman Ravine** ★★★ via the Tuckerman Ravine Trail (see above). Even if you're not planning to continue on to the summit, the ravine with its sheer sides and lacey cataracts may be the most dramatic destination in the White Mountains. It's well worth the 2-hour ascent in all but the most miserable weather. The trail is only moderately demanding. Bring a picnic and lunch on the massive boulders that litter the ravine's floor.

In summer, an enclosed **gondola** ★ at Wildcat ski area (see below) hauls passengers up the mountain for a view of Tuckerman Ravine and Mount Washington's summit. The lift operates Saturday and Sunday from Memorial Day to mid-June, then daily through October. The base lodge is just north of Pinkham Notch on Route 16.

ALPINE SKIING

Black Mountain ★ Dating back to the 1930s, Black Mountain is one of the White Mountains' pioneer ski areas. It remains the quintessential family mountain—modest in size, thoroughly nonthreatening, ideal for beginners—although there's also glade skiing for more advanced skiers. A day here feels a bit as though you're trespassing onto a farmer's unused hayfield, which adds to the charm. The ski area also offers two compact terrain parks for snowboarders, as well as lessons, rentals, a nursery, and a base lodge with cafeteria and pub.

Jackson, NH 03846. ✆ **800/698-4490** or 603/383-4490. www.blackmt.com. Vertical drop: 1,100 ft. (330m). Lifts: 2 chairlifts, 2 surface lifts. Skiable acreage: 143. Lift tickets: $32 Sat–Sun, $20 Mon–Fri.

Wildcat ★★   Set high within Pinkham Notch, Wildcat has a rich heritage as a venerable New England ski mountain with the best views of any ski area in the Whites. Visitors will discover a bountiful supply of pleasing intermediate trails, as well as some challenging expert terrain. This is skiing as it used to be everywhere—there's no base area clutter, just a simple lodge. While that also means there's no on-slope accommodations, there's an abundance of choices within a 15-minute drive. Skiers can save a few dollars by purchasing advance lift tickets online through the mountain's website.

Rte. 16, Pinkham Notch, NH 03846. ✆ **800/255-6439** or 603/466-3326. www.skiwildcat.com. Vertical drop: 2,100 ft. (630m). Lifts: 4 chairlifts (1 high-speed). Skiable acreage: 225. Lift tickets: $52 Sat–Sun and holidays, $42 Mon–Fri.

CROSS-COUNTRY SKIING

Jackson regularly ranks among the top five cross-country ski resorts in the nation. The reason for that: the nonprofit **Jackson Ski Touring Foundation** ★★★ (✆ **603/383-9355;** www.jacksonxc.com), which created and now maintains the trail network of 93 miles (150km), 56 miles (90km) of which are regularly groomed. The terrain is wonderfully varied; many of the trails are rated "most difficult," which will keep advanced skiers from getting bored. Novice and intermediate skiers have good options spread out along the valley floor.

Start at the base lodge near the Wentworth Resort in the center of Jackson. There's parking, and you can ski through the village and into the hills. Gentle trails traverse the valley floor, with more advanced trails winding up the flanking mountains. If you're interested, ask about one-way ski trips with shuttles back to Jackson. Given how extensive the trails are, passes are a good value at $14 on Saturdays and holidays, $12 all other days. Rentals are available in the ski center ($16 per day). Snowshoe rentals and trails specifically for snowshoers are available.

ESPECIALLY FOR KIDS

Parents with children 10 and under can buy peace of mind at **StoryLand** ★★, at the northern junction of Routes 16 and 302 (✆ **603/383-4293**). This old-fashioned (ca. 1954) fantasy village is filled with 30 acres (12 hectares) of improbably leaning buildings, magical rides, and fairy-tale creatures. A "sprayground" features a 40-foot (12m) water-spurting octopus—if they're so inclined, kids can get a good summer soaking. StoryLand is open from Memorial Day to mid-June, Saturday and Sunday only from 10am to 5pm; mid-June to Labor Day, daily from 9am to 6pm; and Labor Day to Columbus Day, Saturday and Sunday only from 10am to 5pm. Admission is $19 for all visitors 4 and older.

WHERE TO STAY

Covered Bridge Motor Lodge ★ *Value*   This pleasant, family-run motel is situated on 5 acres (2 hectares) between Route 16 and the burbling river, right next to Jackson's famous covered bridge. Rooms are priced well for this area. The best units have balconies that overlook the river; the noisier rooms facing the

Moments   Jackson Falls

A warm weekday afternoon, a fat book, and Jackson Falls equals a truly memorable combination. This wonderful cascade tumbles down out of Carter Notch just above the village of Jackson (head up Carter Notch Rd. in front of the Wentworth resort). Park along the road, and then find a sunny patch of ledge near the water, with views out to the valley. A few natural pools offer great splashing around. Two caveats: It can be buggy early in the summer, and it can be crowded on weekends all summer long.

road are a bit cheaper. Ask about the two-bedroom apartments with kitchen and fireplace. While pretty basic, the lodge features lovely gardens and other appealing touches that make it a good value.

Rte. 16, Jackson, NH 03846. ✆ **800/634-2911** or 602/383-9151. www.jacksoncoveredbridge.com. 33 units. Summer $79–$98 double; from $59 off-season. Rates include continental breakfast. AE, DISC, MC, V. **Amenities:** Outdoor pool; tennis court; Jacuzzi. In room: A/C, TV.

Eagle Mountain House ★★   The Eagle Mountain House is a handsome relic that happily survived the ravages of time, fire, and the capricious tastes of tourists. Built in 1916, this gleaming white wooden classic is set in an idyllic valley above Jackson. Guest rooms are furnished in a country pine look with stenciled blanket chests, armoires, and feather comforters. There's a premium for rooms with mountain views, but it's not really worth the extra cash. Just plan to spend your free time lounging on the wide porch with its views across the golf course toward the mountains beyond.

Carter Notch Rd., Jackson, NH 03846. ✆ **800/966-5779** or 603/383-9111. Fax 603/383-0854. www.eaglemt.com. 93 units. Summer $109–$149 double, $139–$179 suite; winter $79–$129 double, $109–$159 suite. Ask about packages. AE, DISC, MC, V. **Amenities:** Dining room (New England), tavern; outdoor pool (summer only); 9-hole golf course; tennis courts; small health club; Jacuzzi; sauna; game room; massage; dry cleaning. In room: TV.

Inn at Thorn Hill ★★★   This truly elegant inn is a great choice for a romantic getaway. The classic shingle-style home (now swathed in yellow siding) was designed by famed architect Stanford White in 1895, and sits just outside the village center surrounded by wooded hills. Inside, there's a comfortable Victorian feel and luxuriously appointed guest rooms. Our favorites include Catherine's Suite, with a fireplace and two-person Jacuzzi, and Notch View Cottage, with a screened porch and a Jacuzzi with a view of the forest. The hospitality is warm and top-notch, and the meals are among the best in the valley.

Thorn Hill Rd. (P.O. Box A), Jackson, NH 03846. ✆ **603/383-4242.** www.innatthornhill.com. 19 units. $190–$300 double; foliage and Christmas $225–$345 double; $275–$300 cottage. Rates include breakfast and dinner. 2- to 3-night minimum stay on weekends and some holidays. AE, DISC, MC, V. Children 8 and over welcome. **Amenities:** Restaurant (see below); outdoor pool; Jacuzzi; limited room service; babysitting; laundry service. In room: A/C, TV.

Joe Dodge Lodge at Pinkham Notch   Guests come to Pinkham Notch Camp more for the camaraderie than the accommodations. Situated spectacularly at the base of Mount Washington, far from commercial clutter and with easy access to numerous hiking and skiing trails, the lodge is operated by the Appalachian Mountain Club like a tightly run youth hostel, with guests sharing spartan bunk rooms, dorm-style bathrooms, and boisterous meals at family-style tables in the main lodge. (Some private rooms offer double beds or family accommodations.) The pluses: a festive atmosphere and a can't-be-beat location for outdoor forays.

Rte. 16, Pinkham Notch, NH. (Mailing address: AMC, P.O. Box 298, Gorham, NH 03581.) ℂ 603/466-2727. www.outdoors.org. 108 beds in bunk rooms of 2, 3, and 4 beds; all with shared bathroom. Peak season $49 per adult, $33 per child (discount for AMC members); off-season $46 per adult, $30 per child. Rates include breakfast and dinner. MC, V. Children 3 and over welcome. **Amenities:** Cafeteria/dining room; weekend activities; outdoor store. *In room:* No phone.

WHERE TO DINE

Inn at Thorn Hill ✦✦✦ NEW AMERICAN The romantic Inn at Thorn Hill is a great spot for a memorable meal. The candlelit dining room faces the forested hill behind the inn. Start with a glass of fine wine (the restaurant has won the *Wine Spectator* award of excellence), and then browse the menu, which changes weekly. Appetizers might include a roulade of duck breast with basil and ginger. Entrees feature choices such as toasted cashew and coconut salmon, or perhaps pecan-crusted lamb loin with an apple rum demi-glace. If quail's on the menu, it's a great choice.

Thorn Hill Rd., Jackson. ℂ 603/383-4242. www.innatthornhill.com. Reservations recommended. Main courses $22.95–$27.95. AE, DISC, MC, V. Daily 6–9pm.

Thompson House Eatery ✦✦ ECLECTIC This friendly, old-fashioned spot in a 19th-century farmhouse at the edge of Jackson's golf course attracts crowds not only for its well-prepared fare, but also for the reasonable prices. There's dining indoor and out, with lunches including six different salads (the

---

⟨Value Gorham: Budget Beds, Low-Cost Lunches

White Mountain travelers on a lean budget would do well to look at **Gorham** as a base for mountain explorations. This tidy commercial town 10 minutes north of Pinkham Notch lacks charm, but has a great selection of clean mom-and-pop motels and family-style restaurants that won't break the bank. After all, if you're planning to spend your days hiking or canoeing, where you rest your head at night won't much matter.

The top motel choice is the **Royalty Inn,** 130 Main St. (ℂ 800/437-3529 or 603/466-3312; www.royaltyinn.com), which has a restaurant, larger-than-average if plain rooms, two pools, and a fitness club; summer rates are $75 to $90. **Top Notch Motor Inn,** 265 Main St. (ℂ 800/228-5496 or 603/466-5496), has an outdoor pool, Jacuzzi, and in-room fridges. Rates start at $69; small pets are accepted.

For basic family dining, there's **Wilfred's,** 117 Main St. (ℂ 603/466-3315), serving steaks, chops, and a variety of seafood. For healthier fare, try the **Loaf Around Bakery,** 19 Exchange St. (ℂ 603/466-2706), which is open for breakfast and lunch (a visit to the antique bathroom is mandatory). **Libby's Bistro,** 111 Main St. (ℂ 603/466-5330), is located in a handsomely renovated bank building and serves dinners better than anything you'll turn up in North Conway.

Moriah Sports, 101 Main St. (ℂ 603/466-5050), sells a wide range of sporting equipment (bikes, cross-country skis, and raingear) and is a good stop for suggestions on area activities.

Tips **Take a Dip**

During the lazy days of summer, the **Saco River**—which runs through the valley—offers several good swimming holes just off the highway. They're unmarked, but watch for local cars parked off the side of the road for no apparent reason, and you should be able to find your way to a good spot for soaking and splashing.

---

curried chicken and toasted almonds is great), knockwurst, frittatas, and basic sandwiches (tuna, grilled cheese). Come dinnertime, there's fresh fish, steak, and several vegetarian entrees. The adjacent ice-cream parlor is worth a stop.

Rte. 16A (near north intersection with Rte. 16), Jackson. *C* 603/383-9341. Reservations recommended for dinner. Main courses $4.95–$7.95 lunch, $6.95–$18.95 dinner. AE, DISC, MC, V. Summer daily 11:30am–3:30pm and 5:30–9pm (Fri–Sat until 10pm); winter Fri–Sun 11:30am–3:30pm, Wed–Mon 5:30pm–9pm. Call for open days/hours in shoulder seasons.

CRAWFORD NOTCH

Crawford Notch is a wild, rugged mountain valley that angles through the heart of the White Mountains. Within the notch itself is a surplus of legend and history. For years after its discovery by European settlers in 1771, it was an impenetrable wilderness, creating a barrier to commerce by blocking trade between the prosperous Upper Connecticut River Valley and commercial harbors in Portland and Portsmouth. This was eventually surmounted by a plucky crew who hauled the first freight through.

Nathaniel Hawthorne immortalized the notch with a short story about a real-life tragedy that struck in 1826. One dark and stormy night (naturally), the Willey family fled its home when they feared an avalanche would roar toward the valley floor. As fate would have it, the avalanche divided above their home and spared the structure; the seven who fled were killed in tumbling debris. You can still visit the site today; watch for signs when driving through the notch.

The notch is accessible via Route 302 (which is wide and speedy on the lower sections), becoming steeper as it approaches the narrow defile of the notch itself. Modern engineering has taken most of the kinks out of the road, so you need to remind yourself to stop from time to time to enjoy the panoramas. The views up the cliffs from the road can be spectacular on a clear day; on an overcast or drizzly day, the effect is nicely foreboding.

ESSENTIALS

GETTING THERE   Route 302 runs through Crawford Notch for approximately 25 miles (40km) between the towns of Bartlett and Twin Mountain.

VISITOR INFORMATION   The **Twin Mountain Chamber of Commerce** (*C* **800/245-8946** or 603/846-5407; www.twinmountain.org) offers information and lodging referrals at its booth near the intersection of Routes 302 and 3. Open year-round; hours vary.

WATERFALLS & SWIMMING HOLES

Much of the mountainous land flanking Route 302 falls under the jurisdiction of **Crawford Notch State Park**, which was established in 1911 to preserve land that elsewhere had been decimated by overly aggressive logging. The headwaters of the Saco River form in the notch, and what's generally regarded as the first permanent trail up Mount Washington also departs from here. Several turnouts and trailheads invite a more leisurely exploration of the area. The trail network on both sides of Crawford Notch is extensive; consult the *AMC White Mountain Guide* or *White Mountains Map Book* for detailed information.

Up the mountain slopes that form the valley, hikers will spot a number of lovely waterfalls, some more easily accessible than others. Two to start with:

Arethusa Falls ★★ has the highest single drop of any waterfall in the state, and the trail to the falls passes several attractive smaller cascades. These are especially beautiful in the spring or after a heavy rain. The trip can be done as a 2⅔-mile (4.3km) round-trip to the falls and back on Arethusa Falls Trail, or as a 4½-mile (7.2km) loop that includes views from Frankenstein Cliffs. (These are named not after the creator of the monster, but after a noted landscape painter.)

If you're arriving from the south, look for signs to the trail parking area shortly after passing the Crawford Notch State Park entrance sign. From the north, the trailhead is a ½ mile (0.8km) south of the Dry River Campground. At the parking lot, look for the sign and map to get your bearings, and then cross the railroad tracks to start up the falls trail.

Continue northward on Route 302 to the trailhead for tumultuous **Ripley Falls** ★. This easy hike is a little more than 1 mile (1.6km) round-trip. Look for the sign to the falls on Route 302 just north of the trailhead for Webster Cliff Trail. (If you pass the Willey House site, you've gone too far.) Park at the site of the Willey Station. Follow signs for the Ripley Falls Trail, and allow about a half hour to reach the cascades. The most appealing swimming holes are at the top of the falls.

A HISTORIC RAILWAY

Mount Washington Cog Railway ★★ *(Kids)* The cog railway was a marvel of engineering when it opened in 1869, and it remains so today. Part moving museum, part slow-motion roller-coaster ride, the cog railway steams to the summit with a determined "I think I can" pace of about 4 miles (6km) per hour. But there's still a frisson of excitement on the way up and back, especially when the train crosses Jacob's Ladder, a rickety-seeming trestle 25 feet (7.5m) high that angles upward at a grade of more than 37%. Passengers enjoy the expanding view on this 3-hour round-trip. (There are stops to add water to the steam engine, to check the track switches, and to allow other trains to ascend or descend.) There's also a 20-minute stop at the summit to browse around. Be aware that the ride is noisy and sulfurous, and you should dress warmly and expecting to acquire a patina of cinder and soot.

Rte. 302, Bretton Woods. © **800/922-8825** or 603/846-5404. www.thecog.com. Fare $49 adults, $35 children 6–12. MC, V. Memorial Day to late Oct daily, plus Sat–Sun in May. Frequent departures; call for schedule. Reservations recommended.

ALPINE SKIING

Attitash Bear Peak ★★ This is a good mountain for families and skiers who are at the intermediate-edging-to-advanced level; look for great cruising runs and a handful of more challenging drops. Attitash Bear Peak includes two peaks, 1,750-foot (525m) Attitash and the adjacent 1,450-foot (435m) Bear Peak, and is among New England's most scenic ski areas—it's dotted with rugged rock outcroppings, and you'll get sweeping views of Mount Washington and the Presidentials. (There's an observation tower on the main summit.) The base area tends to be sleepy in the evenings, but those looking for nightlife can head 15 minutes away to North Conway.

Rte. 302, Bartlett, NH 03812. (℃) **800/223-7669** or 603/374-2368. www.attitash.com. Vertical drop: 1,750 ft. (525m). Lifts: 12 chairlifts (including 2 high-speed quads), 3 surface lifts. Skiable acreage: 280. Lift tickets: $49 Sat–Sun, $53 holidays, $42 Mon–Fri.

Bretton Woods ⚞ Bretton Woods continues its aggressive expansion, most recently in 2000 with the addition of another high-speed quad and 30 acres (12 hectares) of expert glade skiing. The new trails and lifts bring a welcome vitality to the mountain, which has long been popular with beginners and families. (Note that the challenge level here still doesn't rival the more demanding slopes of Vermont or Maine.) The resort does a fine job with kids and offers a pleasantly low-key attitude that families adore. Accommodations are available on the mountain and nearby, notably at the Mount Washington Hotel, but evening entertainment tends to revolve around Jacuzzis, TVs, and going to bed early. There's an excellent cross-country ski center nearby.

Rte. 302, Bretton Woods, NH 03575. (℃) **800/232-2972** or 603/278-3307. www.brettonwoods.com. Vertical drop: 1,500 ft. (450m). Lifts: 8 chairlifts (including 2 high-speed quads), 2 surface lifts. Skiable acreage: 375. Lift tickets: $53 Sat–Sun and holidays, $44 Mon–Fri.

WHERE TO STAY & DINE

Mount Washington Hotel ⚞⚞ This resort, with its gleaming white clapboards and cherry-red roof, was built in 1902. In its heyday, it attracted luminaries like Babe Ruth, Thomas Edison, and Woodrow Wilson. Guest rooms vary in size and decor; many have grand views of the surrounding mountains and countryside. A 900-foot (270m) veranda makes for relaxing afternoons. Meals are enjoyed in an impressive octagonal dining room. (Men should wear jackets at dinner.) A house orchestra provides entertainment, and guests often dance between courses. The decor isn't lavish, and while the innkeepers are making overdue improvements, the hotel can feel a bit unfinished in parts. That said, this remains one of our favorite spots in the mountains, partly for the sheer improbability of it all, and partly for its direct link to a lost era.

Rte. 302, Bretton Woods, NH 03575. (℃) **800/258-0330** or 603/278-1000. www.mtwashington.com. 200 units. Weekends and holidays $259–$529 double. Midweek $219–$469 double; suites to $1,299. Rates include breakfast and dinner. Minimum stay during holidays. AE, DISC, MC, V. **Amenities:** 2 restaurants (Continental, pub fare); indoor and outdoor pools; two PGA golf courses (27 holes); 12 clay tennis courts; shuttle to nearby health club; Jacuzzi; sauna; bike rental; summer children's programs; game room; concierge; shopping arcade; room service; babysitting; coin-op laundry. *In room:* TV.

Notchland Inn ⚞⚞ Located off Route 302 in a wild section of Crawford Notch, this inn looks every bit like a redoubt in a Sir Walter Scott novel. Built of hand-cut granite between 1840 and 1862, Notchland is classy yet informal, perfectly situated for exploring the wilds of the White Mountains. Guest rooms are outfitted with antiques, wood-burning fireplaces, high ceilings, and individual thermostats; three suites have Jacuzzis. Two units are located in the adjacent schoolhouse, where the upstairs room has a wonderful soaking tub. All but three rooms have air-conditioning. The inn is also home to affable Bernese mountain dogs and llamas. Guests are recommended to add the five-course dinner to their plan ($30 per person). It's a good value—and the next nearest restaurant is a long, dark drive away.

Rte. 302, Hart's Location, NH 03812. (℃) **800/866-6131** or 603/374-6131. Fax 603/374-6168. www.notchland.com. 13 units. $180–$240 double; foliage and holidays $230–$290 double. Rates include breakfast. 2- to 3-night minimum stay on weekends, foliage, and some holidays. AE, DISC, MC, V. Children over 12 welcome. **Amenities:** Restaurant (global); river swimming (across road); Jacuzzi; babysitting. *In room:* Hair dryer, iron, no phone.

WATERVILLE VALLEY

In the southwestern corner of the White Mountains is the town of Waterville Valley, which occupies a lovely, remote valley at the head of a 12-mile (19km) dead-end road. Incorporated as a town in 1829, Waterville Valley became a popular destination for summer visitors in the late 19th century. Skiers first started descending the slopes in the 1930s, when the Civilian Conservation Corps and local ski clubs carved a few trails out of the forest. But it wasn't until 1965, when a skier named Tom Corcoran bought 425 acres (172 hectares) in the valley, that Waterville began to assume its current air.

Few traces of that history remain, and Waterville Valley today has a modern, manufactured character. The "village" is reasonably compact (although you need to drive or take a shuttle to the ski slopes). Modern lodges, condos, and a handful of restaurants are located within a loop road. In the center is the "Town Square," a sort of minor mall complex with a restaurant and a few shops.

Our chief complaint is that Waterville Valley has the unnatural, somewhat antiseptic quality of planned communities everywhere. You don't feel like you're in New England in the least, but rather a sort of 1970s time warp. This is a reasonable choice for a weeklong family vacation—the resort is practiced at planning activities for kids—but those in search of classic New England won't miss anything by not venturing here.

ESSENTIALS

GETTING THERE   Waterville Valley is located 12 miles (19km) northwest of Exit 28 or Exit 29 off I-93 via Route 49.

VISITOR INFORMATION   The **Waterville Valley Chamber of Commerce** (© **800/237-2307** or 603/726-3804; www.watervillevalleyregion.com) staffs a year-round information booth on Route 49 in Campton, just off Exit 28 of I-93.

ALPINE SKIING

Waterville Valley ⭐   Waterville Valley is a classic intermediate skier's mountain. The trails are uniformly wide and well groomed, and the ski area is compact enough that no one will get confused and end up staring down a double-diamond trail. Improvements in recent years have made it a fine place to learn to ski or brush up on your skills. Advanced skiers have some black-diamond trails, but the selection and steepness don't rival that of the larger ski mountains to the north. A new terrain park served by a Poma lift above the base lodge is popular with boarders. In 2001, Waterville Valley bucked the trend and lowered regular ticket prices by $10; whether this welcome change sticks beyond one season remains to be seen.

Waterville Valley, NH 03215. © 800/468-2553 or 603/236-8311. www.waterville.com. Vertical drop: 2,020 ft. (606m). Lifts: 8 chairlifts (2 high-speed), 4 surface lifts. Skiable acreage: 255. Lift tickets: $39 nonholidays (including most weekends), $47 holidays.

WHERE TO STAY

Guests at hotels in Waterville Valley pay a mandatory 15% resort tax (13% in winter), which gains them access to the Valley Athletic Club. If you don't plan to use the complex, think about staying in Lincoln or North Woodstock instead.

Snowy Owl Inn ⭐   The Snowy Owl will appeal to those who like the amiable character of a country inn but prefer modern conveniences. A four-story resort project near Town Square, the inn offers a number of nice touches like a towering fieldstone fireplace in the lobby, a handsome octagonal indoor pool, and a rooftop observatory reached via spiral staircase. The rooms are a notch above basic motel-style units; five have kitchens.

Village Rd., Waterville Valley, NH 03215. ⓒ 800/766-9969 or 603/236-8383. Fax 603/236-4890. www.snowyowlinn.com. 80 units. Winter $109–$249 double (school holidays from $199); summer $99–$219 double. Rates include continental breakfast. AE, DISC, MC, V. **Amenities:** Indoor and outdoor pools; access to Valley Athletic Club; Jacuzzi; sauna; game room. *In room:* TV, dataport, hair dryer.

The Valley Inn   The Valley Inn is one of the smaller complexes in the valley, and thus somewhat more intimate than its neighbors. Most rooms feature a sitting area and tiny dining table in a bay window as well as a wet bar; suites have kitchenettes. The inn is conveniently located near the village center and within walking distance of the Athletic Club and Town Square. There's a shuttle to the slopes in winter.

Tecumseh Rd. (P.O. Box 1), Waterville Valley, NH 03215. ⓒ 800/343-0969 or 603/236-8336. Fax 603/236-4294. www.valleyinn.com. 52 units. Winter weekends $94–$217 double, $263 suite; winter midweek $83–$193 double, $263 suite (premium charged during winter holidays); discounts in summer and off-season. Minimum stay during certain holidays. AE, DISC, MC, V. **Amenities:** 2 restaurants (American, pub fare); indoor/outdoor heated pool; tennis courts; access to Valley Athletic Club; Jacuzzi; sauna; game room; limited room service; coin-op laundry. *In room:* A/C, TV.

WHERE TO DINE

The good news is that Waterville Valley's accommodations often include kitchens, so you can prepare your own meals. The bad news? There's a limited selection of restaurants, and no place is outstanding. The Athletic Club has its own restaurant on the second floor, **Wild Coyote Grill** (ⓒ 603/236-4919), which offers regional favorites like potato-crusted salmon and grilled sirloin with mashed potatoes. Basic pub fare can be enjoyed in the **Red Fox Tavern,** in the basement of the Valley Inn (ⓒ 603/236-8336).

LINCOLN, NORTH WOODSTOCK ⚶ & LOON MOUNTAIN

Some 25 miles (40km) north of Waterville Valley are the towns of Lincoln and North Woodstock, as well as the Loon Mountain ski resort (located just east of Lincoln). These towns are also the start (or end) of the Kancamagus Highway, a 35-mile (56km) route that's one of the White Mountains' most scenic drives.

At the former mill town of Lincoln and the adjacent village of North Woodstock, you'll find mundane stores, fast-food chains, and no-frills motels. Lincoln has embraced strip-mall development; North Woodstock has retained some of its native charm in a vestigial village center. Neither will win any awards for quaintness. Loon Mountain opened in 1966 and was criticized early on for its mediocre skiing, though some upgrading since then has brought the mountain greater respect.

Clusters of condos now blanket the lower hillsides of this narrow valley. The Loon Mountain base village is usually lively with skiers in winter, but in summer has a post-nuclear-fallout feel to it, with few people in evidence. The ambience is also compromised by that peculiar style of resort architecture that's simultaneously aggressive and bland.

As with Waterville Valley, we think there are other areas of the White Mountains that are more distinctly New England. You're better off pressing on.

ESSENTIALS

GETTING THERE   Lincoln is accessible off I-93 from Exits 32 and 33.

VISITOR INFORMATION   The **Lincoln-Woodstock Chamber of Commerce** (ⓒ **800/227-4191** or 603/745-6621; www.linwoodcc.org) has an information office open daily at Depot Plaza on Route 112 in Lincoln. More comprehensive is the **White Mountains Visitor Center** (© **800/346-3687** or 603/745-8720), located just east of Exit 32 off I-93; open daily from 9am to 5pm.

THE KANCAMAGUS HIGHWAY ★★★

The Kancamagus Highway—locally called "the Kanc"—is among the White Mountains' most spectacular drives. Officially designated a national scenic byway by the U.S. Forest Service, the 35-mile (56km) roadway joins Lincoln and Conway through 2,860-foot (858m) Kancamagus Pass.

The route begins and ends along wide, tumbling rivers on relatively flat plateaus. The two-lane road rises steadily to the pass. Several rest areas allow visitors to pause and enjoy the mountain views. The highway also makes a good destination for hikers; any number of day and overnight trips may be launched from the roadside. One simple, short hike along a gravel pathway (it's less than ⅓ mile, or 0.5km, each way) leads to **Sabbaday Falls** ★★, a cascade that's especially impressive after a downpour. Six national forest campgrounds are also located along the highway.

To get the most out of the road, take your time and make frequent stops. Think of it as a scavenger hunt as you look for a covered bridge, cascades with good swimming holes, a historic home with a quirky story behind it, and spectacular mountain panoramas.

ALPINE SKIING

Loon Mountain ★ Located on U.S. Forest Service land, Loon had long been stymied in expansion efforts by environmental concerns regarding land use and water withdrawals from the river. The ski mountain has been slowly reshaped, adding uphill capacity, 15 acres (6 hectares) of glade skiing (in 2000), and improved snowmaking. The expansion has reduced some of the congestion of this popular area, but it's still very crowded on weekends. Most of the trails cluster toward the bottom, and most are solid intermediate runs. Experts head to the north peak, which has a challenging selection of advanced trails served by a triple chairlift. For kids, there's a new snow-tubing park off the Little Sister lift.

Rt. 112, Lincoln, NH 03251. © **800/227-4191** for lodging, or 603/745-8111. www.loonmtn.com. Vertical drop: 2,100 ft. (630m). Lifts: 6 chairlifts, 1 high-speed gondola, 2 surface lifts. Skiable acreage: 250. Lift tickets: $51 Sat–Sun, $43 Mon–Fri.

WHERE TO STAY

Mountain Club at Loon ★★ Set at the foot of Loon Mountain's slopes, the Mountain Club is a contemporary resort of prominent gables and glass built during the real-estate boom of the 1980s. It was managed for several years as a Marriott, and the inoffensive but unexciting decor tends to reflect its chain-hotel heritage. Guest rooms are designed to be rented either individually or as two-room suites. The high rates reflect the proximity to the slopes and the excellent health club facilities connected to the hotel via covered walkway.

Rte. 112 (R.R. #1; Box 40), Lincoln, NH 03251. © **800/229-7829** or 603/745-2244. Fax 603/745-2317. www.mtnclubonloon.com. 234 units. Winter weekend $209–$429 double; midweek $169–$399 double; summer and off-season $114–$259 double. AE, DISC, MC, V. **Amenities:** 2 restaurants (New England, pub fare); indoor and outdoor pools; tennis courts; fitness center (with basketball court and aerobics); Jacuzzi; sauna; concierge; limited room service; coin-op laundry. *In room:* A/C, TV, coffeemaker, hair dryer.

Wilderness Inn ★ The Wilderness Inn is located at the southern edge of North Woodstock village—not quite the wilderness that the name suggests. It's a friendly, handsome bungalow-style home that dates to 1912, and the interior features heavy timbers in classic Craftsman style, a spare mix of antiques and reproductions, and games to occupy an evening. Five bedrooms have TVs; the second-floor units are air-conditioned. The nearby cottage is a fine spot to relax, with a gas fireplace and Jacuzzi. If you're arriving by bus in Lincoln, the innkeepers will pick you up at no charge.

Rte. 3 (just south of Rte. 112), North Woodstock, NH 03262. ✆ **800/200-9453** or 603/745-3890. www.thewildernessinn.com. 8 units. Winter $80–$150 double; off-season $60–$90 double. Rates include breakfast. AE, MC, V. *In room:* TV, no phone.

Woodstock Inn   The Woodstock Inn has a Jekyll-and-Hyde thing going on. In the front, it's a white Victorian set in Woodstock's commercial downtown—one of the few older inns in the land of condos and resorts. In the back, it's a modern, boisterous brewpub that serves up hearty fare. The inn's guest rooms are spread among three houses. If you're on a tight budget, go for the shared-bathroom units in the main house and the nearby Deachman house; the slightly less personable Riverside building offers rooms with private bathrooms. Accommodations are individually decorated in a country Victorian style. Three units have Jacuzzis.

Main St. (P.O. Box 118), North Woodstock, NH 03262. ✆ **800/321-3985** or 603/745-3951. Fax 603/745-3701. www.woodstockinnnh.com. 24 units (2 with shared bathroom). $68–$150 double (shared bathroom from $59); foliage $97–$180 double; off-season $59–$165 double. Rates include breakfast. AE, DISC, MC, V. **Amenities:** 2 restaurants (see below); coin-op laundry. *In room:* A/C, TV, dataport.

WHERE TO DINE

Clement Room Grille/Woodstock Station AMERICAN/PUB FARE Dine in the casually upscale Clement Room on the enclosed porch of the Woodstock Inn, or head to the brewpub out back, housed in an old train station. In the Clement Room, there's an open grill and fare that aspires toward some originality (ostrich quesadilla, venison with wild mushrooms). The pub has high ceilings, knotty pine, and a decor that draws on vintage winter recreational gear. The pub menu rounds up the usual suspects, like nachos, chicken wings, burgers, and pasta, none of which is prepared with much creative flair. Better are the porters, stouts, and ales brewed on the premises.

Main St. ✆ **603/745-3951**. Reservations accepted for Clement Room only. Breakfast items $3.95–$9.50; lunch and dinner items $5.49–$22.95. AE, DISC, MC, V. Clement Room daily 7–11:30am and 5:30–9:30pm; Woodstock Station daily 11:30am–10pm.

FRANCONIA NOTCH ★★★

Franconia Notch is rugged New Hampshire writ large. As travelers head north on I-93, the Kinsman Range to the west and the Franconia Range to the east begin to converge, and the road swells upward. Soon, the flanking mountain ranges press in on either side, forming dramatic Franconia Notch, which offers little in the way of civilization and services but a whole lot in the way of natural drama. Most of the notch is included in a well-managed state park that to most travelers will be indistinguishable from the national forest. Those seeking the sublime should plan on a leisurely trip through the notch, allowing enough time to get out of the car and explore forests and craggy peaks. Franconia Notch is more developed for recreation (and thus more crowded with day-trippers) than equally rugged Crawford Notch to the northeast (see "Crawford Notch," earlier in this chapter).

ESSENTIALS

GETTING THERE   I-93 runs through Franconia Notch, gearing down from four lanes to two (where it becomes the Franconia Notch Parkway) in the most scenic and sensitive areas of the park. Several roadside turnoffs dot the route.

VISITOR INFORMATION   Information on the park and surrounding area is available at the **Flume Information Center** (© 603/745-8391), at Exit 1 off the parkway. It's open in summer daily from 9am to 4:30pm. North of the notch, head to the **Franconia Notch Chamber of Commerce,** on Main Street next to the town hall (© 800/237-9007 or 603/823-5661; www.franconian otch.org). It's open spring through fall, Tuesday through Sunday from 10am to 5pm (days and hours often vary).

EXPLORING FRANCONIA NOTCH STATE PARK

Franconia Notch State Park's 8,000 acres (3,240 hectares), nestled within the surrounding White Mountain National Forest, hosts an array of scenic attractions easily accessible from I-93 and the Franconia Notch Parkway. At the Flume Information Center (see above), there's a free 15-minute video that summarizes the park's attractions. For information on any of the following, contact the park offices (© 603/823-8800).

The most famous park landmark is the **Old Man of the Mountains** ★★, located near Cannon Mountain. From the right spot on the valley floor, this 48-foot (14m) rock formation bears an uncanny resemblance to the profile of a craggy old man—early settlers said it was Thomas Jefferson. If it looks vaguely familiar, it's because this is the logo you see on all the New Hampshire state highway signs. The profile, which often surprises visitors by just how tiny it is when viewed from far below (bring binoculars), is best seen from the well-marked roadside viewing area at Profile Lake.

The Flume ★★ is a rugged gorge through which the Flume Brook tumbles. The gorge, a massively popular attraction in the mid–19th century, is 800 feet (240m) long, 90 feet (27m) deep, and as narrow as 20 feet (6m) at the bottom; visitors explore by means of a network of boardwalks and bridges on a 2-mile (3.2km) walk. Early photos of the chasm show a boulder wedged in overhead; this was swept away in an 1883 avalanche. If you're looking for easy, quick access to natural grandeur, it's worth the money. Otherwise, set off into the mountains and seek your own drama with fewer crowds and less expense. Admission is $8 for adults, $5 for children 6 to 12.

Echo Lake ★ is a picturesquely situated recreation area, with a 28-acre (11-hectare) lake, a handsome swimming beach, and picnic tables scattered about all within view of Cannon Mountain on one side and Mount Lafayette on the other. A bike path runs alongside the lake and meanders up and down the notch for a total of 8 miles (13km). Mountain bikes, canoes, and paddleboats can be rented for $10 per hour. Admission to the park is $3 for all visitors over 12.

For a high-altitude view of the region, set off for the alpine ridges on the **Cannon Mountain Tramway** ✿✿. The old-fashioned cable car serves skiers in winter; in summer, it whisks up to 80 travelers at a time to the summit of the 4,180-foot (1,254m) mountain. Once at the top, you can strike out on foot along the Rim Trail for superb views. Be prepared for cool, gusty winds. The tramway costs $10 round-trip for adults, $6 for children 6 to 12. It's located at Exit 2 off the parkway.

HIKING

The Franconia Notch region is one of the most varied and more challenging destinations for White Mountain hikers. It's easy to plan hikes ranging from gentle valley walks to arduous ascents of blustery granite peaks. Consult the *AMC White Mountain Guide* for a comprehensive directory of area trails, or ask for suggestions at the information center.

Among our recommendations: A pleasant woodland detour of 2 hours or so can be found at the **Basin-Cascades Trail** ✿✿ (look for well-marked signs off I-93 about 1½ miles/2.4km north of the Flume). A popular roadside waterfall and natural pothole, the Basin attracts crowds who come to see pillows of granite scoured smooth by glaciers and water. Relatively few visitors continue to the series of cascades beyond. Look for signs for the trail, and then head off into the woods. After about a ½ mile (0.8km) of easy hiking, you'll reach **Kinsman Falls,** a beautiful 20-foot (6m) cascade. Continue another ½ mile (0.8km) beyond that to **Rocky Glen,** where the stream plummets through a craggy gorge.

For a more demanding hike, set off for rugged **Mount Lafayette,** with its spectacular views of the western White Mountains. Hikers should be experienced, well-equipped, and in good physical condition. Allow 6 to 7 hours to complete the hike. A popular and fairly straightforward ascent begins up the **Old Bridle Trail,** which departs from the Lafayette Place parking area off the parkway. This trail climbs steadily to the AMC's **Greenleaf Hut** (2.9 miles/4.7km) with expanding views along the way. From here, continue to the summit of Lafayette on the **Greenleaf Trail.** It's only 1.1 miles (1.8km) further, but it covers rocky terrain and can be demanding and difficult, especially if the weather turns on you. If in doubt about conditions, ask advice of other hikers or the AMC staff at Greenleaf Hut.

ALPINE SKIING

Cannon Mountain ✿   One of New England's first ski mountains, Cannon remains famed for its challenging runs and exposed faces, and the mountain still attracts skiers serious about getting down the hill in style. (During skiing's formative years, this state-run ski area was *the* place to ski in the East.) Many of the old-fashioned New England–style trails are narrow and fun (if often icy, scoured by the notch's winds), and the enclosed tramway is an elegant way to get to the summit. There's no base scene to speak of; skiers retire to inns around Franconia or retreat southward to the condo villages of Lincoln.

Franconia Notch Pkwy., Franconia. ✆ **603/823-8800.** Vertical drop: 2,146 ft. (644m). Lifts: 70-person tram, 5 chairlifts, 1 surface lift. Skiable acreage: about 175. Lift tickets: $44 Sat–Sun, $32 Mon–Fri.

A HISTORIC HOME

The Frost Place ✦   Robert Frost lived in New Hampshire from the time he was 10 until he was 45. This humble farmhouse is where Frost lived with his family. Wandering the grounds, it's not hard to see how his granite-edged poetry evolved at the fringes of the White Mountains. First editions of Frost's works are on display; a nature trail in the woods nearby is posted with excerpts from his poems.

Ridge Rd., Franconia. ✆ **603/823-5510.** Admission $3 adults, $1.50 children 6–15. Late May–June Sat–Sun 1–5pm; July to mid-Oct Wed–Mon 1–5pm. Head south on Rte. 116 from Franconia 1 mile (1.6km) to Ridge Rd. (gravel); follow signs a short way to the house; park in lot below the house.

WHERE TO STAY & DINE

Franconia Inn ✦   This pleasant, welcoming inn is set in a bucolic valley 2 miles (3.2km) from the village of Franconia. Built in 1934 after a fire destroyed the original 1886 structure, the inn has an informal feel, with wingback chairs around the fireplace and jigsaw puzzles half completed in the paneled library. Guest rooms are appointed in a relaxed country fashion; three feature gas fireplaces, while four have Jacuzzis. The inn is a haven for cross-country skiers—38 miles (61km) of groomed trails start right outside the front door.

1300 Easton Rd., Franconia, NH 03580. ✆ **800/473-5299** or 603/823-5542. Fax 603/823-8078. www. franconiainn.com. 32 units. Weekends $126–$186 double; midweek $116–$176 double. Rates include breakfast. MAP rates available. 3-night minimum stay on holiday weekends. AE, MC, V. Closed Apr to mid-May. **Amenities:** Restaurant (traditional/New American); heated outdoor pool; tennis courts; Jacuzzi; sauna; free mountain bikes; game room; bridle trails and horse rentals; cross-country ski trails. *In room:* No phone.

Sugar Hill Inn ✦✦   This classic inn with wraparound porch and sweeping mountain panoramas occupies 16 acres (6 hectares) on lovely Sugar Hill. It makes a great base for exploring the western White Mountains. Guest rooms are graciously appointed in an antique country style, some influenced by a Shaker sensibility. Most have gas Vermont Castings stoves for heat and atmosphere. The restaurant, featuring upscale regional fare, is one of the area's best.

Rte. 117, Franconia, NH 03580. ✆ **800/548-4748** or 603/823-5621. Fax 603/823-5639. www.sugar hillinn.com. 18 units. $130–$225 double; $175–$265 suite; $135–$195 cottage. Rates include breakfast. AE, MC, V. Closed Apr. Children over 12 welcome. **Amenities:** Restaurant (New England). *In room:* No phone.

BETHLEHEM ✦ & LITTLETON ✦

More than a century ago, Bethlehem was as populous as North Conway to the south, and home to numerous sprawling resort hotels, summer retreats, and even its own semiprofessional baseball team. Bethlehem subsequently lost the race for the riches (or won, depending on your view of outlet shopping), and today is again a sleepy town high on a hillside.

Once famed for its lack of ragweed and pollen, Bethlehem teemed with vacationers seeking respite from the ravages of hay fever in the late 19th and early 20th centuries. When antihistamines and air-conditioning appeared on the scene, the sufferers stayed home. Empty resorts burned down one by one until the 1920s, when Hasidim from New York City discovered Bethlehem. They soon arrived in number to spend summers in the remaining boardinghouses. Indeed, that tradition has endured, and it's not uncommon today to see resplendently bearded men in black walking the village streets or rocking on the porches of Victorian-era homes.

Nearby Littleton, set in a broad valley along the Ammonoosuc River, is the area's commercial hub, but it still has plenty of small-town charm. The long main street has an eclectic selection of shops—you can buy a wrench, a foreign magazine, locally brewed beer, whole foods, or camping supplies.

Neither town offers much in the way of must-see attractions, but both have good lodging, decent restaurants, and pleasing environs. Either town makes a more economical alternative for travelers seeking to avoid the commercial tourist bustle to the south. *Note:* Some visitors find Bethlehem melancholy and full of unpolished charm; others find it a bit eerie and prefer to push on.

ESSENTIALS

GETTING THERE   Littleton is best reached via I-93; get off at Exit 41 or 42. Bethlehem is about 3 miles (5km) east of Littleton on Route 302. Get off I-93 at Exit 40 and head east. From the east, follow Route 302 past Twin Mountain to Bethlehem.

VISITOR INFORMATION   The **Bethlehem Chamber of Commerce** (© **603/869-3409**) maintains a summer information booth on Main Street across from town hall. The **Littleton Area Chamber of Commerce** (© **603/ 444-6561;** www.littletonareachamber.com) offers information from its office at 120 Main St.

EXPLORING BETHLEHEM

Bethlehem consists of Main Street and a handful of side streets. Several antiques stores clustered in what passes for downtown are worth browsing. Bethlehem was once home to 38 resort hotels; little evidence of them remains today. For a better understanding of the town's rich history, pick up a copy of *An Illustrated Tour of Bethlehem, Past and Present,* available at many shops around town. This informative guide brings to life many of the graceful old homes and buildings of the past.

Just west of Bethlehem on Route 302 is **The Rocks** ★★ (© **603/444-6228;** www.therocks.org), a classic Victorian gentleman's farm that today is the head-quarters for the Society for the Protection of New Hampshire Forests. Set on 1,200 acres (486 hectares), this 1883 estate contains a well-preserved shingled house, an uncommonly handsome barn, and trails that meander through mead-ows and woodlands. It's a peaceful spot, perfect for a picnic. The society also oper-ates a Christmas-tree farm here. Admission is free; open daily from dawn to dusk.

WHERE TO STAY

Worth noting is a major new restoration of a grand old North Country classic, slated to open in summer 2002. The **Mountain View Grand** (© **603/837-2100;** www.mountainviewgrand.com) in Whitefield, north of Bethlehem, was a popular destination in the late 19th century, and gradually grew into a sprawl-ing resort with golf course and tremendous mountain views. After years of aban-donment and likely demolition, the hotel was rescued in 1998, and over the past few years has benefited from a $20-million overhaul, including the replacement of 38 miles (61km) of plumbing and the peeling away of seven layers of wall-paper in guest rooms. The newly refurbished hotel has 146 units, indoor and outdoor pools, a fitness center, and spa treatments. Rates are $149 to $359 in summer, $79 to $179 in winter.

Adair ★★★   Adair opened a decade ago, yet remains one of New England's better-kept secrets. The peaceful Georgian Revival home dates from 1927 and is set on 200 acres (81 hectares). Its memorable Granite Tap Room is a huge, won-derfully informal, granite-block-lined rumpus room with a VCR, antique pool table, and fireplace. The guest rooms are impeccably well furnished with a mix of antiques and reproductions; six have fireplaces. The best of the lot is the Kinsman suite, with a Jacuzzi the size of a small swimming pool, a gas woodstove, and a petite balcony looking out toward the Dalton Range. The service is top-rate. Cocktail lovers should bring their own liquor; set-ups and mixers are free.

80 Guider Lane (off Exit 40 on Rte. 93), Bethlehem, NH 03574. © **888/444-2600** or 603/444-2600. Fax 603/444-4823. www.adairinn.com. 10 units. $175–$295 double; cottage $355. Rates include breakfast, tax, and gratuity. 2-night minimum stay weekends and foliage season. AE, DISC, MC, V. Children 12 and over welcome. **Amenities:** Restaurant (see review of Tim-Bir Alley, below); tennis court; game room. *In room:* A/C, hair dryer, no phone.

Hearthside Village Cottage Motel 🐾 🅺ids

A little weird and a little charming, Hearthside claims to be the first motor court built in New Hampshire. A colony of steeply gabled miniature homes, the village was constructed by a father and son in the 1930s and late 1940s. The six 1940s-era cottages are of somewhat better quality, with warm knotty-pine interiors. Many of the cottages have fireplaces (Duraflame-style logs only), some have kitchenettes, and several are suitable for families. There's an indoor playroom filled with toys for tots, and another rec room with video games and Ping-Pong.

Rte. 302 (midway between Bethlehem Village and I-93), Bethlehem, NH 03574. © **603/444-1000**. www.hearthsidevillage.com. 16 cottages. $59.95–$69.95 ($10 less in off-season). 2- to 3-night minimum stay in foliage season. MC, V. Closed mid-Oct to mid-May. **Amenities:** Small pool; game rooms. *In room:* TV, fridge, coffeemaker (on request), no phone.

Rabbit Hill Inn 🐾🐾

A short hop across the Connecticut River from Littleton is the lost-in-time Vermont village of Lower Waterford, with its perfect 1859 church and tiny library. Amid this cluster of buildings is the stately Rabbit Hill Inn, constructed in 1795. With its prominent gabled roof and imposing columns, this romantic retreat easily ranks among the most refined structures in the Connecticut River Valley. More than half of the rooms have gas fireplaces, and several feature Jacuzzis. Rates include breakfast and dinner in the creative dining room, where proper attire is expected (jacket and tie are "appropriate," but not required). The inn is halfway between Littleton, N.H., and St. Johnsbury, Vt., allowing guests to easily explore both states.

Rte. 18, Lower Waterford, VT 05848. © **800/762-8669** or 802/748-5168. Fax 802/748-8342. www.rabbit hillinn.com. 19 units. $260–$410 double. Rates include breakfast, dinner, afternoon tea, and gratuities. 2-night minimum stay on weekends. AE, MC, V. Closed early Apr and early Nov. From I-93, take Rte. 18 northwest from Exit 44 for approximately 2 miles (3.2km). Children over 12 welcome. **Amenities:** Swimming pond; golf club membership nearby; in-room massage. *In room:* A/C, coffeemaker, hair dryer, iron.

Thayers Inn 🐾 🆅alue

Thayers may offer the best value of any White Mountains inn. It's a clean, well-run hostelry in an impressive Greek Revival downtown building that dates to 1850. You'll find a mix of rooms furnished comfortably if eclectically with high-quality flea-market furniture. The $60 rooms aren't especially spacious, but are perfectly adequate and comfortable. The top floor is a bit of a hike—but room 47 ($40) is a true bargain for those on a budget, with air-conditioning, in-room sink, and shared bathroom. The cupola is worth a visit for the panoramic view of the town.

Main St., Littleton, NH 03561. © **800/634-8179** or 603/444-6469. www.thayersinn.com. 48 units (3 with shared bathroom). $40 double with shared bathroom; $60–$120 double with private bathroom. Rates include continental breakfast. AE, DISC, MC, V. Pets accepted if not left alone in room. **Amenities:** Restaurant (casual dining); free video library. *In room:* A/C, TV, no phone.

WHERE TO DINE

Tim-Bir Alley 🐾🐾 REGIONAL/CONTEMPORARY

The White Mountains' best dining is at Tim-Bir Alley, housed in the area's most gracious country inn.

In this romantic setting, owners Tim and Biruta Carr prepare meals from wholesome, basic ingredients. You might start with pork and pecan dumplings with an apple-hoisin sauce. Afterwards, tuck into a main course of lamb chops with a wild mushroom and merlot sauce, or sea bass served with a smoked Mediterranean relish. Save room for the superb desserts, which might include a peach-blueberry tart. Attentive service isn't a strong suit here, so expect to enjoy a leisurely meal.

Adair Country Inn, 80 Guider Lane, Bethlehem. ✆ **603/444-6142.** Reservations required. Main courses $15.95–$23.95. No credit cards. Summer Wed–Sun 5:30–9pm; winter Wed–Sat 5:30–9pm. Closed Apr and Nov.

5 The North Country

New Hampshire's North Country is an ideal destination for those who find the White Mountains too commercialized. The tiny communities of the region—like Errol, at a crossroads of two routes to nowhere—regard change with high suspicion, something that held true even during the go-go times of the 1980s. The land surrounding the town remains an outpost of rugged, raw grandeur that has been little compromised.

Of course, the problem with these lost-in-time areas is the nothing-to-see-nothing-to-do syndrome, one that especially seems to afflict families with young children. You can drive for miles and not see much other than spruce and pine, an infrequent bog, a glimpse of a shimmering lake, and—if you're lucky—a roadside moose chomping on sedges.

But there *is* plenty to do if you're self-motivated and oriented toward the outdoors. There's white-water kayaking on the Androscoggin River, canoeing on Lake Umbagog, and bicycling along the wide valley floors. You can also visit one of the Northeast's grandest, most improbable historic resorts, which continues to thrive against considerable odds. Some recent advances are encouraging for those who'd like to see the area remain unchanged. The piney shoreline around spectacular Lake Umbagog was protected as a National Wildlife Refuge in the 1990s. The upshot? Umbagog should remain in its more-or-less pristine state for all time.

ESSENTIALS

GETTING THERE   Errol is at the junction of Route 26 (accessible from Bethel, Maine) and Route 16 (accessible from Gorham, N.H.). **Concord Trailways** (✆ **800/639-3317**) provides service to Berlin from points south, including Boston.

VISITOR INFORMATION   The **Northern White Mountains Chamber of Commerce,** 164 Main St., Berlin (✆ **800/992-7480** or 603/752-6060; www.northernwhitemountains.com), offers information Monday through Friday between 8:30am and 4:30pm.

OUTDOOR PURSUITS

Dixville Notch State Park ✿ (✆ **603/788-2155**) has several hiking trails, including a delightful 2-mile (3.2km) round-trip to Table Rock. Look for the small parking area just east of the Balsams Resort on the edge of Lake Gloriette. The loop hike (it connects with a ½-mile/0.8km return along Rte. 26) ascends a scraggy trail to an open rock with fine views of the resort and the flanking wild hills.

A great place to learn the fundamentals of white water is at **Saco Bound's Northern Waters** ✿✿ (✆ **603/447-2177;** www.sacobound.com) white-water school, located where the Errol Bridge crosses the Androscoggin River. The school offers 2- to 5-day workshops in the art of getting downstream safely. Classes involve videos, dry-land training, and frequent forays onto the river—both at the Class I to III rapids at the bridge and the more forgiving rips downstream. Two-day classes are $180, including equipment and a riverside campsite.

Excellent lake canoeing may be found at Lake Umbagog, which sits between Maine and New Hampshire. The lake, which is home to the **Lake Umbagog Wildlife Refuge** 🏕🏕 (© 603/482-3415), has some 40 miles (64km) of shoreline, most of which is wild and remote. You'll need a boat of some sort to properly see the lake. Canoes and flatwater kayaks are available for rent at Saco Bound's Errol outpost for $27 per day (see above). Saco Bound also offers pontoon boat tours to get a glimpse of the complex river system that feeds both into and out of the lake.

The area around Errol offers excellent roads for **bicycling**—virtually all routes out of town make for good exploring (although it's mighty hilly heading east). An especially nice trip is south on Route 16 from Errol. The occasional logging truck can be unnerving, but mostly it's an easy and peaceful riverside trip. Consider pedaling as far as what's locally called the Brown Co. Bridge—a simple wooden logging road bridge that crosses the Androscoggin River. It's a good spot to leap in the water and float through a series of gentle rips before swimming to shore. Some small ledges on the far side of the bridge provide a good location for sunning and relaxing. Biking information and rentals ($18 per day) are available in Gorham at **Moriah Sports,** 101 Main St. (© 603/466-5050).

WHERE TO STAY & DINE

Balsams Grand Resort Hotel 🏕🏕🏕 The Balsams is a grand gem hidden deep in the northern forest. Located on 15,000 acres (6,075 hectares) in a valley surrounded by 800-foot (240m) cliffs, it's one of a handful of the great 19th-century New England resorts still in operation, and its survival is all the more extraordinary given its stunningly remote location. What makes this Victorian grande dame even more exceptional is its refusal to compromise or bend to the trend of the moment. Bathing suits and jeans are prohibited in the public areas, you'll be ejected from the tennis courts or golf course if you're not neatly attired, and men are *required* (not requested) to wear jackets at dinner. The resort has also maintained strict adherence to the spirit of the "American plan"—everything but booze is included in the room rates, from greens fees to boats on Lake Gloriette to evening entertainment in the lounges. (In winter, even ski tickets at the inn's own downhill area are included.) Meals are an event—especially the summer luncheon buffet. (When did you last gorge on chocolate éclairs?)

Dixville Notch, NH 03576. © 800/255-0600, 800/255-0800 in N.H., or 603/255-3400. Fax 603/255-4221. www.thebalsams.com. 204 units. Summer $420–$500 double (including all meals, entertainment, greens fees, etc.); winter $350–$390 double (including breakfast, dinner, and lift tickets). 4-night minimum stay on weekends July–Aug. AE, DISC, MC, V. Closed early Apr to late May and mid-Oct to mid-Dec. **Amenities:** Restaurant; 3 lounges; heated outdoor pool; 18-hole and 9-hole golf courses; tennis courts; health club; Jacuzzi; sauna; free watersports equipment; bike rental; summer children's programs; game room; concierge; shopping arcade; salon; limited room service; massage; babysitting; laundry service; dry cleaning; 45 miles (72km) of groomed cross-country ski trails; downhill ski area. *In room:* Dataport, iron (TVs in suites).

Philbrook Farm Inn 🏕🏕 *Finds* Philbrook Farm is a wonderful retreat, well out of the tourist mainstream, and worthy of protection as a local cultural landmark. It's a classic New England period piece that traces its lineage to the 19th century, when farmers opened their doors to summer travelers to earn some extra cash. Set on 1,000 acres (405 hectares) between the Mahoosuc Range and the Androscoggin River, this country inn has been owned and operated by the Philbrook family since 1853. It has expanded haphazardly, with additions in 1861, 1904, and 1934. As a result, the cozy rooms are eclectic—some have a country farmhouse feel, others a more Victorian flavor. Guests spend their days swimming, playing croquet, exploring trails in the nearby hills, or just reading on the porch.

881 North Rd. (off Rte. 2 between Gorham, N.H., and Bethel, Maine), Shelburne, NH 03581. © **603/466-3831.** www.nettx.com/philbrook. 24 units (6 with shared bathroom). $115–$150 double, including breakfast and dinner; cottage (no meals) $750 per week. No credit cards. Closed Apr and Nov–Dec 25. Pets allowed in cottages. **Amenities:** Restaurant (traditional New England); pool; game room; badminton; shuffleboard. *In room:* No phone.

13

Maine

by Wayne Curtis

Professional funny guy Dave Barry once suggested that Maine's state motto should be "Cold, but damp."

Cute, but true. There's spring, which tends to last a few blustery, rain-soaked days. There's November, during which Arctic winds alternate with gray sheets of rain. And then winter brings a character-building mix of blizzards and ice storms to the fabled coast and rolling mountains.

Then there's summer. Summer in Maine brings osprey diving for fish off wooded points, cumulus clouds building over the rounded peaks of the western mountains, and the haunting whoop of loons echoing off the dense forest walls bordering the lakes. It brings languorous days when the sun rises well before most visitors, and by 8am it seems like noontime. Maine summers bring a measure of gracious tranquility, and a placid stay in the right spot can rejuvenate even the most jangled nerves.

The trick comes in finding that right spot. Those who arrive without a clear plan may find themselves ruing their decision. Maine's Route 1 along the coast has its moments, but for the most part it's rather charmless—an amalgam of convenience stores, tourist boutiques, and restaurants catering to bus tours. Acadia National Park can be congested, Mount Katahdin's summit overcrowded, and some of the more popular lakes have become de facto racetracks for jet skis.

But Maine's size works to the traveler's advantage. Maine is roughly as large as the other five New England states combined. It has 3,500 miles (5,635km) of coastline, some 3,000 coastal islands, and millions of acres of undeveloped woodland. With all this space and a little planning, you'll be able to find your piece of Maine.

1 The South Coast

Maine's southern coast runs from the state line at Kittery to about Portland. Thanks to quirks of geography, nearly all of Maine's sandy beaches are located in this 60-mile (97km) stretch of coastline. This is the place to head for a relaxing sandy spot amid the lulling sound of the surf. It's not wilderness here—most beaches have beach towns nearby, and these range from classic 19th-century villages to more honky-tonkish resorts. One thing all the beaches share in common: They're washed by the frigid waters of the Gulf of Maine. Swimming sessions tend to be brief and accompanied by shrieks, whoops, and agitated hand-waving. These beaches are more suited for early-morning walks than for swimming.

The beach season itself is also brief and intense, running from the Fourth of July to Labor Day. At an increasing number of beach towns, the season is stretching into fall (Columbus Day is generally when the remaining businesses

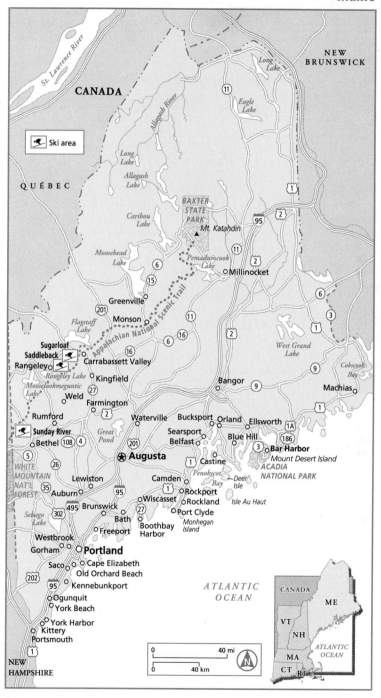

shutter up), and the post–Labor Day pace at these shorefront communities is slower and less frenetic—for some, the perfect atmosphere for a laid-back beach-side respite.

KITTERY & THE YORKS

Kittery ✦ is the first town you'll come to if you're driving to Maine from the south. Kittery was once famous for its naval yard (it's still operating), but regionally it's now better known for its dozens of factory outlets. Maine has the second-highest number of outlet malls in the nation (second only to California), and Kittery is home to a good many of them.

"The Yorks," just to the north, are comprised of three towns that share a name but little else. In fact, it's rare to find three such well-defined and diverse New England archetypes in such a compact area. **York Village** is redolent with early American history and architecture. **York Harbor** ✦✦ reached its zenith during America's late Victorian era, when wealthy urbanites constructed rambling cottages at the ocean's edge. **York Beach** ✦ has an early-20th-century beach-town feel, with loud amusements, taffy shops, and small gabled summer homes set in crowded enclaves near the beach.

ESSENTIALS

GETTING THERE   Kittery is accessible from well-marked exits off I-95 or Route 1. The Yorks are reached most easily from Exit 1 off the Maine Turnpike; look for Route 1A just south of the turnpike exit. This route connects all three York towns. Contact **Amtrak** (*©* **800/872-7245;** www.amtrak.com) for information on train service from Boston to southern Maine.

VISITOR INFORMATION   The **Kittery Information Center** (*©* **207/439-1319**) is located at a well-marked rest area on I-95. It's open daily from 8am to 6pm in summer, from 9am to 5:30pm the rest of the year. The **York Chamber of Commerce** (*©* **207/363-4422**) operates an information center at 571 Rte. 1, a short distance from the turnpike exit. It's open in summer daily from 9am to 5pm (until 6pm Fri); limited hours the rest of the year.

SHOPPING

Kittery's consumer mecca is 4 miles (6km) south of York on Route 1. Some 120 factory outlets flank the highway, including Calvin Klein, Coach, Crate & Barrel, Le Creuset, DKNY, Polo/Ralph Lauren, and Tommy Hilfiger.

In summer, navigating the area can be frustrating owing to the four lanes of heavy traffic and capricious restrictions on turns. (A free shuttle bus links the

---

⟨Finds The Wiggly Bridge

Just west of Route 103 outside of York Harbor, you'll see a tiny bridge at the edge of a marsh. (It's said, not implausibly, to be the smallest suspension bridge in the world.) That's the **Wiggly Bridge,** and it's part of Fisherman's Walk, a lovely footpath that connects York Village and York Harbor. The trail begins near the Stage Neck Inn and tracks upriver past lobster shacks and along lawns leading up to grand shingled homes. Across Wiggly Bridge, it passes into the woods and connects with a dirt lane, which emerges at Lindsay Road near Hancock Wharf. The entire walk is about 1 mile (1.6km).

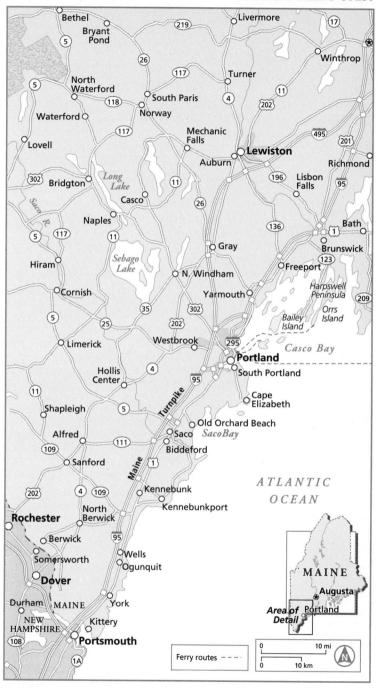

Bethel
Bryant
Pond
5
Livermore
17
Winthrop
26
219
117
North
Waterford
5
118
Turner
4
11
202
South Paris
Norway
117
Mechanic
Falls
495
201
Waterford
Lovell
302
Bridgton
Long
Lake
Auburn
Lewiston
Richmond
196
Lisbon
Falls
95
Saco R.
Casco
11
136
Bath
5
117
Naples
11
Gray
Brunswick
1
Sebago
Lake
26
Freeport
123
Hiram
N. Windham
Harpswell
Peninsula
209
Cornish
Yarmouth
Orrs
Island
35
302
Bailey
Island
Casco Bay
25
202
Limerick
Westbrook
295
11
Hollis
Center
4
Portland
South Portland
Shapleigh
5
95
Cape
Elizabeth
Alfred
111
Old Orchard Beach
Saco
Saco Bay
109
Sanford
Biddeford
202
4
109
North
Berwick
Kennebunk
Kennebunkport
ATLANTIC
OCEAN
Rochester
Berwick
95
Somersworth
Wells
Ogunquit
Dover
Durham
MAINE
York
NEW
HAMPSHIRE
Kittery
108
Portsmouth
1A

MAINE

Augusta
Portland

*Area of
Detail*

Ferry routes ─ ─ ─

0   10 mi
0   10 km

N

outlets and lessens some of the frustration.) The selection of outlets is slightly more diverse than in Freeport, a little more than an hour north, which is more clothing oriented. But Freeport's quaint village setting is far more appealing than the congested sprawl zone of Kittery. Information on current outlets is available from the **Kittery Outlet Association** (© **888/548-8379;** www.thekittery outlets.com).

DISCOVERING LOCAL HISTORY

Old York Historical Society 🚗🚗 John Hancock is famous for his oversized signature on the Declaration of Independence and the insurance company named after him. What's not so well known is his checkered past as a businessman. Hancock was the proprietor of Hancock Wharf, a failed enterprise that's but one of the intriguing historic sites in York Village.

First settled in 1624, York Village has several early buildings open to the public. A good place to start is **Jefferds Tavern,** across from the handsome old burying ground. Changing exhibits here document various facets of early life. Next door is the **School House,** furnished as it might have been in the last century. A 10-minute walk along Lindsay Road will bring you to **Hancock Wharf,** which is next door to the **George Marshall Store.** Also nearby is the **Elizabeth Perkins House,** with its well-preserved Colonial Revival interiors. The one don't-miss structure is the intriguing **Old Gaol,** built in 1719 with musty dungeons for criminals. (The jail is the oldest surviving public building in the U.S.) Just down the knoll is the **Emerson-Wilcox House,** built in the mid-1700s. Added to periodically over the years, it's a virtual catalog of architectural styles and early decorative arts.

5 Lindsay Rd., York. © 207/363-4974. Admission $7 adults, $3 children 6–16. Tues–Sat 10am–5pm; Sun 1–5pm (last tour at 4pm). Closed mid-Oct to mid-June.

BEACHES

York Beach consists of two beaches—**Long Sands Beach** 🚗 and **Short Sands Beach**—separated by a rocky headland and a small island capped by scenic **Nubble Light** 🚗🚗. Both offer plenty of room for sunning and throwing Frisbees when the tide is out. When the tide is in, they're both cramped. Short Sands fronts the town of York Beach, with its candlepin bowling and video arcades. It's the better bet for families with kids. Long Sands runs along Route 1A, across from a profusion of motels and convenience stores. Changing rooms, restrooms, and parking (50¢ per hr.) are available at both beaches; other services, including snacks, are provided by local restaurants and vendors.

WHERE TO STAY

York Beach has a proliferation of motels facing Long Sands Beach. Reserve ahead during prime season. Simple options on or near the beach include the **Anchorage Motor Inn** (© 207/363-5112), the **Long Beach Motor Inn** (© 207/363-5481), and the wonderfullly vintage but somewhat threadbare **Nevada Motel** (© 207/363-4504), which is still run by the same man who built it in 1953.

In Kittery

Inn at Portsmouth Harbor 🚗🚗 This 1899 home is just across the river from Portsmouth, N.H., a pleasant ½-mile (0.8km) walk away. Guests here get a taste of small-town life, yet still have access to the restaurants and shopping of Portsmouth. Rooms are tastefully furnished with eclectic antiques, though most are on the small side. Valdra has ruby-red walls and a bathroom with historic

---

Finds **Sayward-Wheeler House**

For those who'd like a taste of local history but lack the stamina for the full-court Old York visit, consider a stop by the Sayward-Wheeler House in York Harbor, owned by the Society for the Preservation of New England Antiquities (SPNEA). It's a well-preserved merchant's home dating to 1760. Inside, you'll see china captured as booty during the 1745 Seige of Louisbourg, which routed the French out of Nova Scotia. Open weekends only from June to mid-October, with tours hourly from 11am to 4pm. Admission is $5 for adults, $4 for seniors, and $2.50 for children. For information, call the SPNEA's office in New Hampshire at *C* **603/436-3205.**

---

accents; Royal Gorge has limited skylight views of the harbor and a cast-iron tub. Breakfasts are flat-out great: fresh-squeezed juice and selections like corn pancakes with smoked salmon.

6 Water St., Kittery, ME 03904. *C* 207/439-4040. Fax 207/438-9286. www.innatportsmouth.com. 5 units. Apr–Oct $135–$175 double; Nov–Mar $85–$155 double. Rates include breakfast. 2-night minimum stay summer and holidays. MC, V. Children over 12 welcome. *In room:* A/C, TV, dataport, hair dryer, iron.

In the Yorks

Dockside Guest Quarters *R*   David and Harriet Lusty established this quiet retreat in 1954, and recent additions haven't changed the friendly maritime flavor of the place. Situated on a 7-acre (3-hectare) peninsula, the inn occupies grounds shaded with maples and white pines. Five rooms are in the main house (1885), but most of the accommodations are in small, modern town house–style cottages. These are bright and airy, and all have private decks that overlook the entrance to York Harbor.

Harris Island (P.O. Box 205), York, ME 03909. *C* 207/363-2868. Fax 207/363-1977. www.docksidegq.com. 25 units. Feb–Apr $95–$120 double; May–Oct $100–$230; Nov–Dec $95–$120. Continental breakfast $4. 2-night minimum stay July–Sept. DISC, MC, V. Drive south on Rte. 103 from Rte. 1A in York Harbor; after bridge over York River, turn left and follow signs. **Amenities:** Restaurant (traditional New England/seafood); ocean swimming; rowboats; bike rental; laundry service; badminton; croquet. *In room:* TV, dataport, iron.

Stage Neck Inn *RR*   A hotel in one form or another has been housing guests on this windswept bluff, located between the harbor and the open ocean, since about 1870. The most recent incarnation was constructed in 1972 and furnished with an understated elegance. Rooms were renovated in 2000. The hotel is modern yet offers an old-fashioned sense of intimacy lacking in other contemporary resorts. Almost every unit has a view of the water. York Harbor Beach is but a few steps away.

Stage Neck (P.O. Box 70), York Harbor, ME 03911. *C* 800/222-3238 or 207/363-3850. www.stageneck.com. 60 units. May–Labor Day $205–$335 double; early fall $165–$245; winter $135–$180; spring $155–$195. Ask about off-season packages. AE, DC, DISC, MC, V. Head north on Rte. 1A from Rte. 1; make second right after York Harbor post office. **Amenities:** 2 dining rooms (fine dining, pub fare); indoor and outdoor pools; ocean swimming; tennis courts; fitness room; Jacuzzi; sauna; game room, limited room service; in-room massage; coin-op laundry; dry cleaning. *In room:* A/C, TV/VCR, CD player, dataport, fridge, coffeemaker, hair dryer.

WHERE TO DINE
In Kittery

Chauncey Creek Lobster Pier *RR* LOBSTER POUND   It's not on the wild open ocean, but Chauncey's is one of the best lobster pounds in the state, not least because the Spinney family, which has been selling lobsters here since

---

Tips **Trolley Ho**

From mid-May to Columbus Day, a number of trackless "trolleys" run all day between Perkins Cove and the Wells town line to the north, with detours to the sea down Beach and Ocean streets. The cost is $1 per adult, 50¢ per child. It's well worth the small expense to avoid the hassles of driving and parking.

---

the 1950s, takes such pride in the place. You reach the pound by walking down a wooden ramp to a broad deck on a tidal inlet, where some 42 festively painted picnic tables await. Lobster is the specialty, of course, but steamed mussels (in wine and garlic) and clams are also available. It's BYOB.

Chauncey Creek Rd. (between Kittery Point and York off Rte. 103; watch for signs), Kittery Point. ℂ 207/ 439-1030. Reservations not accepted. Lobsters priced to market; other items $1.50–$12.95. MC, V. Daily 11am–8pm (until 7pm during shoulder seasons); closed Mon after Labor Day. Closed Columbus Day to Mother's Day. Limited parking.

In the Yorks

Cape Neddick Inn Restaurant 𝕽𝕽 COUNTRY GOURMET   This elegant inn, located on a fairly quiet stretch of Route 1, is the best choice for a memorably exquisite meal south of Ogunquit. The inn was purchased in 2001 by Johnathan Pratt, who has worked at such noted establishments as Restaurant Daniel and Jean George in New York City. His French-inspired American fare features dishes such as poached lobster in vermouth cream or venison stew in a red-currant sauce. The wine list has about 125 selections, many of which offer good value.

1233 Rte. 1, Cape Neddick. ℂ 207/363-2899. Reservations recommended. Main courses $18–$28. DISC, MC, V. Tues–Sun 5:30–10pm. Closed Mar.

Goldenrod Restaurant 𝕽 FAMILY STYLE   This beach-town classic is the place for local color—it's been a summer institution in York Beach since 1896. It's easy to find: Look for visitors gawking through plate-glass windows at the ancient taffy machines hypnotically churning out taffy in volumes, enough (9 million candies a year) to make busloads of dentists wealthy. Behind the taffy and fudge operation is the restaurant, short on gourmet fare but long on atmosphere. Diners sit around a stone fireplace or at the antique soda fountain. The meals are basic and filling; expect waffles, griddle cakes, club sandwiches, and deviled egg and bacon sandwiches.

Railroad Rd. and Ocean Ave., York Beach. ℂ 207/363-2621. www.thegoldenrod.com. Breakfast $2.75–$5.50; lunch and dinner entrees $2.95–$8. MC, V. Memorial Day to Labor Day daily 8am–10pm (until 9pm in June); Labor Day to Columbus Day Wed–Sun 8am–3pm. Closed Columbus Day to Memorial Day.

OGUNQUIT

Ogunquit is a bustling beachside town that's attracted vacationers and artists for more than a century. While notable for its elegant summer-resort architecture, Ogunquit is most famous for its 3½-mile (5.6km) white-sand beach, backed by grassy dunes. The beach serves as the town's front porch, and most everyone drifts over here at least once a day when the sun is shining.

Ogunquit's fame as an art colony dates to around 1890, when Charles H. Woodbury arrived and declared the place an "artist's paradise." He was followed by artists Walt Kuhn, Elihu Vedder, Yasuo Kuniyoshi, and Rudolph Dirks, the last of whom was best known for creating the "Katzenjammer Kids" comic strip.

In the latter decades of the 19th century, the town found quiet fame as a destination for gay travelers. Ogunquit has retained its appeal for gays through the years, and many local enterprises are run by gay entrepreneurs. The scene is very low-key compared to Provincetown, Mass. It's more like an understated family resort, where a good many family members happen to be gay.

Despite the architectural gentility and the overall civility of the place, the town can feel overrun with tourists during summer, especially on weekends. The teeming crowds are part of the allure for some Ogunquit regulars. If you're not a crowd person, you would probably do well to visit here in the off-season.

ESSENTIALS

GETTING THERE   Ogunquit is located on Route 1 between York and Wells. It's accessible from either Exit 1 or Exit 2 off the Maine Turnpike.

VISITOR INFORMATION   The **Ogunquit Welcome Center** (© 207/646-5533 or 207/646-2939; www.ogunquit.org) is on Route 1 south of the village center. It's open from April to Columbus Day, daily from 9am to 5pm (until 8pm in peak season), and the rest of the year, daily from 10am to 2pm.

GETTING AROUND   The village is centered around an intersection that seems fiendishly designed to cause massive traffic foul-ups in summer. Parking is tight and relatively expensive for small-town Maine ($6 per day or more). As a result, Ogunquit is best navigated on foot or by bike.

EXPLORING OGUNQUIT

The village center is good for an hour or two of browsing among the boutiques, or sipping a cappuccino at one of the several coffee emporia.

From the village, you can walk to scenic Perkins Cove along **Marginal Way,** a mile-long (1.6km) oceanside pathway once used for herding cattle to pasture. The pathway departs across from the Seacastles Resort on Shore Road. It passes tide pools, pocket beaches, and rocky bluffs, all of which are worth exploring. The seascape can be spectacular (especially after a storm), but Marginal Way can also be spectacularly crowded on fair-weather weekends. To elude the crowds, head out in the very early morning.

Perkins Cove ⟡, accessible either from Marginal Way or by driving south on Shore Road and veering left at the Y intersection, is a small, well-protected harbor that seems custom-designed for a photo opportunity. As such, it attracts visitors by the busload and boatload, and is often heavily congested. A handful of touristy galleries, restaurants, and T-shirt shops occupy a cluster of quaint buildings between the harbor and the sea. An intriguing pedestrian drawbridge is operated by whoever happens to be handy, allowing sailboats to come and go.

Excursions Coastal Maine Outfitting Co. ⟡, Route 1, Cape Neddick (© 207/363-0181; www.excursionsinmaine.com), runs sea-kayaking tours on rivers and out along the coast daily in summer. Ask about sunrise, sunset, and full-moon trips. Perkins Cove is also home to a handful of deep-sea fishing and tour-boat operators. Try the *Deborah Ann* (© 207/-361-9501) for whale-watching or the *Ugly Anne* (© 207/646-7202) for deep-sea fishing.

Not far from the cove is the **Ogunquit Museum of American Art** ⟡⟡, 183 Shore Rd. (© **207/646-4909**), one of the best small art museums in the nation. The engaging modern building is set in a glen overlooking the shore. The curators have a track record for staging superb shows and attracting national attention. Open July through September, Monday through Saturday from 10:30am to 5pm and Sunday from 2 to 5pm. Admission is $4 for adults, $3 for seniors and students, and free for children under 12.

For evening entertainment, head to the **Ogunquit Playhouse,** Route 1 (© **207/646-5511;** www.ogunquitplayhouse.org), a 750-seat summer-stock theater that has garnered a solid reputation for its serious attention to stagecraft. The theater has entertained Ogunquit since 1933, attracting noted actors such as Bette Davis and Tallulah Bankhead. Tickets are $28.

BEACHES

Ogunquit's **main beach** ⭐⭐ is 3½ miles (5.6km) long, and three parking lots ($2 per hr.) are located along its length. The beach appeals to everyone—there's a more lively scene at the south end near the town itself, and it's more unpopulated as you head north, where it's backed with dunes and, beyond them, clusters of summer homes. The most popular access point is at the foot of Beach Street, which runs into Ogunquit Village. The beach ends at a sandy spit, where the Ogunquit River flows into the sea; here you'll find a handful of informal restaurants. It's also the most crowded part of the beach. Less congested options are at **Footbridge Beach** (turn on Ocean Ave. off Rte. 1 north of the village center) and **Moody Beach** (turn on Eldridge Ave. in Wells). Restrooms and changing rooms are maintained at all access points.

WHERE TO STAY

Just a few steps from Ogunquit's main downtown intersection is the meticulously maintained **Studio East Motel,** 267 Main St. (© **207/646-7297**). It's open from April to mid-November, with rates running from $99 to $119 in high season.

Beachmere Inn ⭐ The Beachmere Inn sprawls across a grassy 4-acre (1.6-hectare) hillside, and nearly every room has a view northward up Ogunquit's famous beach, which is a 10-minute walk via footpath. The Beachmere Victorian dates to the 1890s and is all turrets and porches; next door is the mid-century-modern Beachmere South, a motel-like structure whose spacious rooms have balconies or patios. When the main buildings are full, guests are offered one of five rooms in the Bullfrog Cottage, a short drive away. These units are less impressive, but are spacious and appropriate for families.

62 Beachmere Place, Ogunquit, ME 03907. © 800/336-3983 or 207/646-2021. Fax 207/646-2231. www.beachmereinn.com. 53 units. Peak season $90–$230; mid-season $70–$175; off-season $60–$125. Rates include continental breakfast. 3-night minimum stay in summer. AE, DC, DISC, MC, V. Closed mid-Dec to Apr 1. *In room:* A/C, TV, dataport, coffeemaker.

The Dunes ⭐⭐ This classic motor court (ca. 1936) has made the transition to the modern age more gracefully than any other vintage motel we've seen. There's one motel-like building, but most of the rooms are found in gabled cottages, all white clapboard and green shutters. The kitchens and bathrooms have been updated in the past 10 years, but there's still plenty of old-fashioned charm in the vintage furnishings, braided rugs, fireplaces, and knotty-pine paneling. The Dunes is set on 12 peaceful acres (5 hectares) away from Route 1, with Adirondack chairs overlooking a lagoon; at high tide, guests can borrow a rowboat to get across to the beach.

518 U.S. Rte. 1, Ogunquit, ME 03907. © 207/646-2612. www.dunesmotel.com. 36 units. Peak season $85–$175; off-season $68–$125. MC, V. July–Aug 1-week minimum stay in cottages, 3-night minimum stay in motel. Closed late Oct to late Apr. **Amenities:** Pool; rowboats. *In room:* A/C, TV, dataport, fridge, coffeemaker.

Nellie Littlefield House ⭐ The prime location and the handsome Queen Anne architecture are the main draws at this 1889 home near the village center.

All rooms feature a mix of modern and antique reproduction furnishings. Four units have private decks, but views are limited (mostly of the unlovely motel next door). Most spacious is the J. H. Littlefield suite, with two TVs and a Jacuzzi. The most unique? The circular Grace Littlefield room, located in the upper turret.

9 Shore Rd., Ogunquit, ME 03907. © **207/646-1692.** Fax 207/361-1206. 8 units. Peak season $155–$210; mid-season $95–$160; off-season $80–$125. Rates include breakfast. 2- or 3-night minimum stay weekends and holidays. DISC, MC, V. Closed late Oct—Apr. Children over 12 welcome. **Amenities:** Small fitness room. *In room:* A/C, TV, fridge.

WHERE TO DINE

For breakfast (served daily until 1pm), it's hard to beat **Amore,** 178 Shore Rd. (© **207/646-6661**). This isn't the place for dainty pickers and waist-watchers, but hey . . . you're on vacation.

Arrows ★★★ NEW AMERICAN This restaurant put Ogunquit on the national culinary map by serving up some of the most innovative cooking in New England. The emphasis is on local products—often very local, including many ingredients from the organic gardens. The menu depends on what's in season or available from the fishing boats, but tends to be informed by an Asian way of thinking, sometimes overtly, sometimes not. Recent entrees have included duck confit with caramelized ginger and lemon-grass sauce. Arrive a half hour or so before your reservation to stroll the gardens with a glass of wine.

Berwick Rd. © **207/361-1100.** www.arrowsrestaurant.com. Reservations recommended. Main courses $39–$42. MC, V. Mid-Apr to Memorial Day weekend Fri–Sun 6–9:30pm; June–Columbus Day Tues–Sun 6–9:30pm; Columbus Day to mid-Dec Fri–Sun 6–9:30pm. Closed mid-Dec to mid-Apr. Turn uphill at the Key Bank in the village; the restaurant is 1.9 miles (3km) on your right.

Hurricane ★★ NEW AMERICAN Tucked away in Perkins Cove is one of southern Maine's more enjoyable dining experiences. The plain-shingled exterior of the building, set along a curving, narrow lane, doesn't hint at what you'll find inside. Owner Brooks MacDonald is known for his consistently creative concoctions, like the pizza appetizer of grilled boar sausage topped with fresh tomato and provolone. For dinner, there's delectable lobster cioppino, an Asian-style yellowfin tuna, and fire-roasted red snapper on mint couscous.

Reservations are sometimes hard to come by in this small restaurant; if so, there's a newly opened branch on Dock Square in downtown Kennebunkport (© 207/967-9111) that has more seating (with a view of a tidal creek).

Oarweed Rd., Perkins Cove. © **800/649-6348** in Maine and N.H., or 207/646-6348. www.perkinscove.com. Reservations recommended. Lunch items $7–$15; dinner main courses $15–$35; lobster dishes priced daily (to $39). AE, DC, DISC, MC, V. Daily 11:30am–3:30pm and 5:30–9:30pm (until 10:30pm May–Oct). Closed briefly in Jan (call ahead).

THE KENNEBUNKS

"The Kennebunks" consist of the side-by-side villages of **Kennebunk** and **Kennebunkport,** both situated along the shores of small rivers, and both claiming a portion of rocky coast. The region was first settled in the mid-1600s and flourished after the American Revolution, when ship captains, boatbuilders, and merchants constructed imposing, solid homes. The Kennebunks are famed for their striking architecture and expansive beaches.

ESSENTIALS

GETTING THERE Kennebunk is located off Exit 3 of the Maine Turnpike. Kennebunkport is 3½ miles (5.6km) southeast of Kennebunk on Port Road (Rte. 35).

VISITOR INFORMATION The **Kennebunk-Kennebunkport Chamber of Commerce** (© 800/982-4421 or 207/967-0857; www.kkcc.maine.org) can answer questions year-round by phone or at its office on Route 9 next to Meserve's Market. The **Kennebunkport Information Center** (© 207/967-8600), operated by an association of local businesses, is off Dock Square (next to Ben & Jerry's) and is open daily in summer and fall.

GETTING AROUND The local trolley (© 207/967-3686; www.intown trolley.com)—a bus, really—makes stops in and around Kennebunkport and also serves the beaches. The fare is $8 per day for unlimited trips.

EXPLORING KENNEBUNKPORT ★★

Kennebunkport is the summer home of President George Bush the Elder, whose family has summered here for decades. As such, it's possessed of the tweedy, upper-crust feel that one might expect. The tiny downtown, whose streets were laid out during days of travel by boat and horse, is subject to monumental traffic jams. If the municipal lot off the square is full, head north on North Street a few minutes to the free long-term lot and catch the trolley back into town. Or go about on foot—it's a pleasant walk of about 10 to 15 minutes from the satellite lot to Dock Square.

Dock Square ★ has an architecturally eclectic wharf-like feel to it, with low buildings of mixed vintages and styles, but the flavor is mostly clapboard and shingles. Today it's *haute tourist,* with boutiques featuring some creative arts and crafts and a lot of trinkets. Kennebunkport's deeper appeal is found in the surrounding blocks, where the side streets are lined with Federal-style homes; many have been converted to B&Bs (see "Where to Stay," below).

The **Richard A. Nott House** ★, 8 Maine St., at the head of Spring Street (© 207/967-2751), is an imposing Greek Revival structure built in 1853. It was donated to the local historical society with the stipulation that it remain forever unchanged. It still has the original wallpaper, carpeting, and furnishings. Open from mid-June to mid-October on Tuesday and Friday from 1 to 4pm, Saturday from 10am to 1pm. Admission is $5 for adults, $2 for children under 18.

To get a clear view of the coast, sign up for a 2-hour sail aboard the **Schooner Eleanor** ★★, at the Arundel Wharf Restaurant (© 207/967-8809). If the weather's willing, you'll have a perfect view of the Bush compound and Cape Porpoise. The fare is $38 per person.

A bit further afield, in the affluent neighborhood around the Colony Hotel (about 1 mile/1.6km east of Dock Square on Ocean Ave.), is a fine collection of homes of the uniquely American shingle style. It's worth a detour on foot or by bike to ogle these icons of the 19th- and early-20th-century leisure class.

Ocean Drive from Dock Square to **Walkers Point** ★ and beyond is lined with opulent summer homes overlooking surf and rocky shore. You'll likely recognize the former president's home at Walkers Point when you arrive (look for the shingle-style Secret Service booth at the head of a drive). There's nothing to do here but park for a minute, take a picture of the house, then push on.

The Seashore Trolley Museum ★★★ A short drive north of Kennebunkport is a local marvel: a scrapyard-masquerading-as-a-museum. This quirky museum was founded in 1939 to preserve a disappearing way of life, and today contains one of the largest collections in the world—more than 200 trolleys, including specimens from Glasgow, Moscow, San Francisco, and Rome. (Naturally, there's a streetcar named "Desire" from New Orleans.) About 40 cars still operate, and admission includes rides on a 2-mile (3.2km) track. This is an uncommonly intriguing spot, and at times feels like a scrapyard that's come to life.

195 Log Cabin Rd., Kennebunkport. 🕐 **207/967-2800.** www.trolleymuseum.org. Admission $7.25 adults, $5.25 seniors, $4.75 children 6–16; $24 per family. May 29–Oct 21 daily 10am–5pm; May 6–27 and Oct 21–Nov 5 Sat–Sun 10am–5pm. Closed early Nov to early May. Drive north from Kennebunkport on North St. for 1.7 miles (2.7km); look for signs.

BEACHES

The coastal area around Kennebunkport is home to several of the state's best beaches. Southward across the river (technically this is Kennebunk, although it's much closer to Kennebunkport) are **Gooch's Beach** ⨀⨀ and **Kennebunk Beach** ⨀⨀. Head eastward on Beach Street (from the intersection of Rtes. 9 and 35) and you'll soon wind into a handsome colony of shingled summer homes. The narrow road twists past sandy beaches and rocky headlands. It's congested in summer; avoid gridlock by exploring on foot or by bike.

 Goose Rocks Beach ⨀⨀⨀ is north of Kennebunkport off Route 9 (watch for signs), and is a good destination for those who like their crowds light. You'll find an enclave of summer homes set amid rustling oaks just off a fine-sand beach. Offshore is a narrow barrier reef that has historically attracted flocks of geese. *Note:* No restrooms are available here.

WHERE TO STAY

Captain Jefferds Inn ⨀⨀   Fine antiques abound throughout this 1804 Federal home, and guests will need some persuading to come out of their wonderful rooms once they've settled in. Among the best are Manhattan, with a four-poster bed, fireplace, and beautiful afternoon light; and Assisi, with a restful indoor fountain and rock garden (weird, but it works). Winterthur is the only unit with a TV, though there's also one in the common room. An elaborate breakfast is served before the fire on cool days, and on the terrace when weather permits.

5 Pearl St. (P.O. Box 691), Kennebunkport, ME 04046. 🕐 **800/839-6844** or 207/967-2311. Fax 207/967-0721. www.captainjefferdsinn.com. 15 units. $145–$295 double. Rates include breakfast. 2-night minimum stay on weekends. AE, MC, V. Pets allowed by advance reservation ($20). *In room:* A/C, hair dryer, no phone.

Captain Lord ⨀⨀⨀   Housed in a Federal-style home that peers down a shady lawn toward the river, this is one of the most architecturally distinguished inns in New England. You'll know immediately that this is the genuine article once you spot the grandfather clocks and Chippendale highboys in the front hall. Guest rooms are furnished with splendid antiques; all feature gas fireplaces. There's not a single unappealing room (although the Union is a little dark). Among our favorites: Excelsior, a corner unit with a massive four-poster and a

---

🄵 *Tips* Beach Parking

Finding a spot is often difficult, and all beaches require a parking permit, which may be obtained at the town offices or from your hotel. You can avoid parking hassles by renting a bike and leaving your car at your lodging. **Cape Able Bike Shop** (🕐 **800/220-0907** or 207/967-4382) offers three-speeds for $10 a day or $40 per week. The shop is on North Street north of Kennbunkport at Arundel Road. The trolley also offers beach access (see "Getting Around," above); the fare is $8 per day for unlimited trips.

two-person Jacuzzi; Hesper, the best of the lower-priced rooms; and Merchant, a spacious suite with a large Jacuzzi.

Pleasant and Green sts. (P.O. Box 800), Kennebunkport, ME 04046. © **207/967-3141.** Fax 207/967-3172. www.captainlord.com. 16 units. Summer and fall $199–$399 double; winter and spring from $99 midweek, from $175 weekends. Rates include breakfast. 2- or 3-night minimum stay weekends and holidays. DISC, MC, V. Children 12 and over welcome. *In room:* A/C, dataport, minibar, hair dryer, iron.

The Colony Hotel 🎔🎔
The Colony is one of the handful of oceanside resorts that have preserved intact the classic New England vacation experience. This mammoth white Georgian Revival (1914) lords over the ocean and the mouth of the Kennebunk River. All rooms in the main inn have been renovated over the last 3 years (but still no air-conditioning or TVs in most). They're bright and cheery, simply furnished with cottage antiques. Rooms in two of the three outbuildings carry over the rustic elegance of the main hotel; the exception is the East House, a 1950s-era hotel at the edge of the property with 20 uninteresting motel-style rooms (with TVs). A staff naturalist leads coastal ecology tours on Saturdays in July and August; on Fridays, there's a lobster buffet dinner.

140 Ocean Ave. (P.O. Box 511), Kennebunkport, ME 04046. © **800/552-2363** or 207/967-3331. Fax 207/967-8738. www.thecolonyhotel.com/maine. 123 units. $180–$430 double July–Aug; off-season rates available. Rates include breakfast. 3-night minimum stay summer weekends and holidays in main hotel. AE, MC, V. Closed mid-Oct to mid-May. Pets allowed ($25 per night). **Amenities:** Restaurant (traditional resort fare), lounge; heated saltwater pool; putting green; tennis courts; bike rental; limited room service; shuffleboard court; social director. *In room:* Dataport, hair dryer, iron.

Franciscan Guest House *Value*
This former dormitory on the grounds of St. Anthony's Monastery is a unique budget choice. Rooms are all rather institutional, with industrial carpeting and inexpensive paneling. On the other hand, all have private (if small) bathrooms, and guests can stroll the lovely riverside grounds or walk over to Dock Square, about 10 minutes away. A Lithuanian breakfast (cheese, oatmeal, salami, fruit, juice, and homemade bread) is served downstairs. Although this is one of the most spartan lodgings we've seen, the fact that reservations are often needed a year in advance tells the story.

Beach St. (P.O. Box 980), Kennebunk, ME 04046. © **207/967-2011.** 60 units. $65–$88 double. Breakfasts available; payment by donation. No credit cards. Closed mid-Sept to mid-June. *In room:* A/C, TV.

The Lodge at Turbat's Creek 🎔
The Lodge at Turbat's Creek is a classy, clean motel in a quiet residential neighborhood at the north end of Ocean Drive, about 5 minutes by car from Dock Square. The leafy grounds are scattered with Adirondack chairs. The standard motel-size rooms are decorated with pine furniture and painted a cheerful yellow.

Turbat's Creek Rd., Kennebunkport, ME 04046. © **207/967-8700.** 26 units. June–Aug $99–$169 double; off-season $79–$169 double. Rates include continental breakfast. AE, MC, V. Closed late-Oct to Apr (open 2 weeks in Dec). Limited pets allowed; ask when booking. From Dock Sq., take Rte. 9 north; turn right on Maine St., left at first fork, right at second. **Amenities:** Heated pool; free bikes. *In room:* A/C, TV, dataport.

The Tides Inn 🎔
This is the best bet in the region for a quiet getaway. Located across the street from Goose Rocks Beach, the Tides Inn is an 1899 yellow-clapboard and shingle affair that retains a seaside boardinghouse feel while providing up-to-date comfort. The rooms tend toward the small side but are nonetheless comfortable, and you can hear the lapping of the surf from all of them. Among the most popular are rooms 11, 15, 24, and 29, some of which have bay windows. The cozy pub features a woodstove and dartboard, while the parlor has old wicker, a TV, and chess for those rainy days. The Belvidere Room

offers upscale dining in a Victorian setting, with options such as scallops with ginger chive polenta.

Goose Rocks Beach, Kennebunkport, ME 04046. © 207/967-3757. www.tidesinnbythesea.com. 22 units (4 share 2 bathrooms). Peak season $155 double with shared bathroom, $195–$295 double with private bathroom; off-season from $135 double. 3-night minimum stay July–Aug. AE, MC, V. Closed mid-Oct to mid-May. **Amenities:** Restaurant (New American). *In room:* No phone.

White Barn Inn ★★★ Part of the exclusive Relais & Châteaux group, the White Barn Inn pampers its guests like no other in Maine. Upon checking in, guests are shown to one of the parlors and offered port or brandy while valets gather luggage and park cars. The atmosphere is distinctly European, with an emphasis on service. Rooms are decorated in an upscale country style; nearly half have wood-burning fireplaces. We're not aware of any other inn of this size that offers as many unexpected niceties, like robes, fresh flowers, and turn-down service at night. Guests can avail themselves of the inn's free bikes (including a small fleet of tandems) to head to the beach, or stroll across the street to explore the grounds of St. Anthony's Franciscan Monastery.

Beach Ave., ¼ mile (0.4km) east of junction of Rtes. 9 and 35 (P.O. Box 560-C), Kennebunkport, ME 04046. © 207/967-2321. Fax 207/967-1100. www.whitebarninn.com. 25 units. $230–$250 double; $365–$550 suite. Rates include continental breakfast and afternoon tea. 2- or 3-night minimum stay weekends and holidays. AE, MC, V. **Amenities:** Restaurant (see below); heated pool; free canoes; free bikes; concierge; limited room service; massage. *In room:* A/C, TV/VCR (on request).

The Yachtsman Lodge & Marina ★★ The White Barn Inn took over this motel in 1997 and made it a remarkably appealing base for exploring the southern Maine coast. It's within walking distance of Dock Square, and nice touches abound, like down comforters, high ceilings, and French doors that open onto patios just above the river. All rooms are of standard motel size, but are a far cry from anything you'd find in a chain.

Ocean Ave. (P.O. Box 2609), Kennebunkport, ME 04046. © 207/967-2511. Fax 207/967-5056. www.yachts manlodge.com. 30 units. Peak season $195–$255 double; off-season $129–$253 double. Rates include continental breakfast. 2-night minimum stay weekends and holidays. AE, MC, V. *In room:* A/C, TV/VCR, CD player, dataport, fridge, coffeemaker, hair dryer, iron.

WHERE TO DINE

Prices for lobster in the rough tend to be a bit more expensive around Kennebunkport than at other casual lobster joints further up the coast. But if you can't wait, **Nunan's Lobster Hut,** on Route 9 north of Kennebunkport at Cape Porpoise (© **207/967-4362**), is a good choice. It's often crowded with diners and full of atmosphere, which helps make up for sometimes lackluster food and disappointments like potato chips (rather than a baked potato) served with the lobster dinner. Open daily for dinner, starting at 5pm in summer.

Grissini ★★ TUSCAN Run by the folks of the White Barn Inn (see review above), Grissini is a handsome trattoria that offers good value. The mood is elegant but rustic Italian writ large: Oversized Italian advertising posters line the walls of the soaring, barn-like space, while the handsome stone fireplace takes the chill off a cool evening. The menu includes a wide range of pastas and pizza, served with considerable flair. More far-ranging entrees include osso buco, served over garlic mashed potatoes, and fried calamari served with a spicy tomato sauce. Expect an exceedingly pleasant experience.

27 Western Ave., Kennebunkport. © 207/967-2211. www.restaurantgrissini.com. Reservations recommended. Main courses $11.95–$22.95. AE, MC, V. Sun–Fri 5:30–9:30pm; Sat 5–9pm (closed Wed Jan–Mar).

Seascapes ✿✿ CONTEMPORARY NEW ENGLAND   A tony restaurant with a wonderful ocean view, Seascapes is decorated in what might be termed traditional country-club bamboo. It's fancy but not fussy, with food several notches above the tried and true. The fish is fresh, and the breads and desserts are made on the premises. The menu offers traditional favorites along with more adventurous dishes like cashew-crusted Chilean sea bass served with a citrus-tamari sauce. The restaurant has garnered *Wine Spectator*'s award of excellence annually since 1993.

77 Pier Rd., Cape Porpoise, Kennebunkport. ✆ 207/967-8500. www.seascapesrestaurant.com. Reservations recommended. Main courses $19–$28. Daily 12:30–2:30pm and 5–9pm (until 10pm Fri–Sat in peak season). Closed late Oct–Apr.

White Barn Inn ✿✿✿ REGIONAL/NEW AMERICAN   The White Barn Inn regularly attracts gourmands from New York and Boston. It's pricey, but worth it. The restaurant (attached to an inn; see "Where to Stay," above) is housed in a rustic barn with a soaring interior and an eclectic collection of country antiques displayed in a hayloft. The setting is magical, the service is astonishingly attentive, and the kitchen rarely produces a flawed dish. You might start with a lobster spring roll, then graduate to roasted pheasant breast with butternut squash, or perhaps rack of lamb on creamed Swiss chard with a red onion marmalade. Anticipate a meal to remember.

Beach Ave., Kennebunkport. ✆ **207/967-2321.** Reservations recommended. Fixed-price dinner $77. AE, MC, V. Daily 6–9pm. Closed 2 weeks in Jan.

2 Portland ✶✶

106 miles N of Boston

Portland, Maine's largest city, is located on a peninsula extending into scenic Casco Bay. It's easy to speed right past on I-295, admire the skyline, and be on your way to the villages and headlands further up the coast. After all, urban life isn't what one usually thinks of when one thinks of Maine.

But Portland is well worth an afternoon's detour or an overnight. This historic city has plenty of charm—especially the renovated Old Port section with its brick sidewalks and cobblestone streets—but there are also ferries to islands, boutique shops, historic homes, and graceful neighborhoods. And there's the food: Portland is blessed with an uncommonly high number of excellent restaurants for a city its size (just 65,000, or roughly half that of Peoria, Ill.), making it a culinary mecca of Maine.

ESSENTIALS

GETTING THERE   Portland is off the Maine Turnpike (I-95). From the south, downtown is most easily reached by taking Exit 6A off the turnpike, then following I-295. Exit at Franklin Street and follow this eastward until you arrive at the waterfront at the Casco Bay Lines terminal. Turn right on Commercial Street and you'll be at the lower edge of the Old Port. Continue several blocks to the visitor center (see below).

In December 2001, **Amtrak** (✆ **800/872-7245;** www.amtrak.com) launched its long-delayed *Downeaster* service from Boston's North Station to Portland. The train makes four round-trips daily.

Concord Trailways (✆ **800/639-3317** or 207/828-1151) and **Vermont Transit** (✆ **800/537-3330** or 207/772-6587) offer bus service from Boston and Bangor. The Vermont Transit terminal (next to the Amtrak terminal) is at 950 Congress St. Concord Trailways, which is slightly more expensive, offers movies

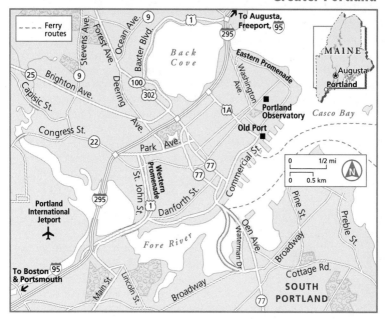

and headsets on its trips; its terminal is on Sewall Street (a 35-min. walk from downtown).

The **Portland International Jetport,** across the Fore River from downtown (© **207/772-0690;** www.portlandjetport.org), is served by scheduled flights on **Air Nova** (© **902/873-5000;** www.airnova.ca), **American Airlines** (© **800/ 433-7300;** www.aa.com), **Continental** (© **800/525-0280;** www.continental. com), **Delta/Business Express** (© **800/638-7333;** www.delta.com), **North-west** (© **800/225-2525;** www.nwa.com), **US Airways** (© **800/428-4322;** www.usairways.com), and **United** (© **800/241-6522;** www.ual.com). Buses ($1) connect the airport to downtown; cab fare runs about $15.

VISITOR INFORMATION The **Convention and Visitor's Bureau of Greater Portland,** 305 Commercial St. (© **207/772-5800** or 207/772-4994; www.visitportland.com), is open in summer Monday through Friday from 8am to 6pm, Saturday and Sunday from 10am to 5pm; shorter hours in the off-season. Portland has two free weekly alternative newspapers—*Casco Bay Weekly* and the *Portland Phoenix*—both of which offer listings of local events, nightclub performances, and the like.

EXPLORING THE CITY

Any visit to Portland should start with a stroll around the historic **Old Port.** Bounded by Commercial, Congress, Union, and Pearl streets, this area near the waterfront contains the city's best commercial architecture, a plethora of fine restaurants, a mess of boutiques, and one of the thickest concentrations of bars on the Eastern Seaboard. The narrow streets and intricate brick facades reflect the mid-Victorian era; most of the area was rebuilt following a devastating fire in 1866. Leafy, quaint Exchange Street is the heart of the Old Port, with other attractive streets running off and around it.

The city's finest harborside stroll is along the **Eastern Prom Pathway** 🏵🏵, which wraps for about a mile (1.6km) along the waterfront beginning at the Casco Bay Lines ferry terminal (at Commercial and Franklin sts). The paved pathway is suitable for walking or biking, and offers expansive views out toward the islands. The pathway skirts the lower edge of the **Eastern Promenade** 🏵, a 68-acre (28-hectare) hillside park with broad, grassy slopes extending down to the water. Tiny East End Beach is located here, but the water is often unhealthy for swimming (look for signs). The pathway continues on to Back Cove Pathway, a 3½-mile (5.6km) loop around tidal Back Cove.

Atop Munjoy Hill (above the Eastern Promenade) is the distinctive **Portland Observatory** 🏵, 138 Congress St. (© **207/774-5561**), a quirky shingled tower dating from 1807 and used to signal the arrival of ships into port. Exhibits provide a quick glimpse of Portland past, but the real draw is the view of city and harbor from the top. From Memorial Day to Columbus Day, it's open daily from 10am to 5pm; admission is $3 for adults, $2 for children.

On the other end of the Portland peninsula is the **Western Promenade** 🏵🏵. (From the Old Port, follow Spring Street westward to Vaughan; turn right and then take the first left on Bowdoin Street.) A narrow strip of lawn atop a forested bluff is the actual promenade; it has views across the Fore River, which is lined with less-than-scenic light industry and commercial buildings, with the White Mountains in the distance. The neighborhood around is also called the "Western Prom," and a walk through here reveals the grandest houses in the city, in a wide array of architectural styles from Italianate to shingle to stick.

Children's Museum of Maine 🏵🏵 *Kids* The centerpiece exhibit is the camera obscura, a room-size "camera" located on the top floor of this stout, columned downtown building next to the art museum. Children gather around a white table in a dark room, where they see magically projected images that include cars driving on city streets, boats plying the harbor, and seagulls flapping by. Other attractions range from running a supermarket checkout counter to sliding down the firehouse pole.

142 Free St. (next to the Portland Museum of Art). © 207/828-1234. www.kitetails.com. Admission $5 adults and children, free for children under 1. Mon–Sat 10am–5pm; Sun noon–5pm. Closed Mon fall–spring. Discounted parking at Spring St. Parking Garage.

Maine Narrow Gauge Railroad Co. & Museum 🏵 *Kids* In the late 19th century, Maine was home to several narrow-gauge railways, which operated on rails 2 feet (0.6m) apart. Most of these versatile trains have disappeared, and this nonprofit organization is dedicated to preserving the examples that remain. The museum itself is free; there's a charge for a short ride on the trains, which chug on a rail line along Casco Bay at the foot of the Eastern Prom. The views of the islands are outstanding; the ride itself is slow-paced and somewhat yawn-inducing unless you're very young.

58 Fore St. © 207/828-0814. Free museum admission; train fare $5 adults, $4 seniors, $3 children. Daily 10am–4pm; trains run on the hour from 11am. Closed Jan to mid-Feb. From I-295, take Franklin St. exit and follow to Fore St.; turn left and continue to museum, on right.

Portland Head Light & Museum 🏵🏵🏵 Just a 10-minute drive from downtown is this 1794 lighthouse, easily one of the most picturesque in the nation. The light marks the entrance to Portland Harbor, and was occupied continuously from its construction until 1989, when it was automated and the graceful keeper's house (1891) was converted to a small museum. Still active, the lighthouse is closed to the public, but visitors can stop by the museum, wander the

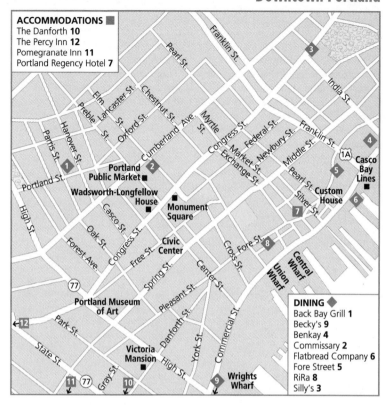

ACCOMMODATIONS ■
The Danforth **10**
The Percy Inn **12**
Pomegranate Inn **11**
Portland Regency Hotel **7**

DINING ◆
Back Bay Grill **1**
Becky's **9**
Benkay **4**
Commissary **2**
Flatbread Company **6**
Fore Street **5**
RiRa **8**
Silly's **3**

grounds, and watch the boats come and go. The park has a pebble beach, grassy lawns, and picnic areas for informal barbecues.

Fort Williams Park, 1000 Shore Rd., Cape Elizabeth. ℂ 207/799-2661. www.portlandheadlight.com. Free entrance to park grounds; museum admission $2 adults, $1 children 6–18. Park grounds open year-round, daily from sunrise–sunset (until 8:30pm in summer); museum open June–Oct daily 10am–4pm, spring and late fall Sat–Sun 10am–4pm. From Portland, follow State St. across the Fore River; continue straight on Broadway. At third light, turn right on Cottage Rd., which becomes Shore Rd.; follow until you arrive at the park, on your left.

Portland Museum of Art ⊛⊛   This bold, modern museum was designed by I. M. Pei & Partners in 1983, and features selections from its own fine collections along with touring exhibits. The museum is particularly strong in American artists with Maine connections, including Winslow Homer, Andrew Wyeth, and Edward Hopper. Colby College and the museum share the Joan Whitney Payson Collection, which includes works by Renoir, Degas, and Picasso. In October 2002, the museum will reopen the McLellan-Sweat House, a stunning 1801 Federal-style building attached to the modern wing.

7 Congress Sq. (corner of Congress and High sts.). ℂ 207/775-6148. Fax 207/773-7324. www.portland museum.org. Admission $8 adults, $6 students and seniors, $2 children 6–12. Tues–Wed and Sat–Sun 10am–5pm, Thurs–Fri 10am–9pm; June to mid-Oct also open Mon 10am–5pm. Guided tours daily at 2pm.

Portland Public Market ⊛⊛   The Portland Public Market, which opened in 1998, features more than two dozen vendors selling fresh foods and flowers.

Finds **Play Ball!**

The **Portland Sea Dogs,** an AA team affiliated with the Florida Marlins, plays throughout the summer at Hadlock Field, a compact stadium near downtown that retains an old-time feel despite aluminum benches and other updates. Activities are geared towards families, with lots of entertainment between innings. Tickets are priced at $5 to $7 for adults, $3 to $6 for seniors and children under 16. The season runs from April to Labor Day. For information, call © **800/936-3647** or 207/879-9500, or check www.portlandseadogs.com.

The distinctive building is at once classic and modern, and houses fishmongers, butchers, a seafood cafe, a wine shop, and an upscale restaurant called Commissary (p. 561). The market is a much-recommended spot to lay in supplies for a picnic.

25 Preble St. (half a block west of Monument Sq.). © 207/228-2000. www.portlandmarket.com. Mon–Sat 9am–7pm; Sun 10am–5pm. Free parking (with validated ticket) at connected garage on the west side of Cumberland Ave.

Victoria Mansion ★★   Widely regarded as one of the most elaborate brownstones ever built in the United States, this mansion (also known as the Morse-Libby House) is a remarkable display of High Victorian style. Built between 1858 and 1863, it's a prime example of the opulent Italianate style. Inside, it appears that not a square inch of wall space was left untouched by craftsmen or artisans (11 painters were hired to create the murals). The decor is ponderous and somber, but it offers an engaging look at a bygone era.

109 Danforth St. (at Park St.). © 207/772-4841. www.victoriamansion.org. Admission $7.50 adults, $3 children 6–17. May–Oct Tues–Sat 10am–4pm, Sun 1–5pm; tours offered at quarter past and quarter of each hour. Closed Nov–Apr, except for holiday tours from late Nov to mid-Dec. From the Old Port, head west on Fore St., veer right on Danforth St. at light near Stonecoast Brewing; go 3 blocks to the mansion.

Wadsworth-Longfellow House & Center for Maine History ★   Maine Historical Society's "history campus" on busy Congress Street includes the austere brick Wadsworth-Longfellow House (1785), built by Gen. Peleg Wadsworth, father of poet Henry Wadsworth Longfellow. It's furnished in an early-19th-century style. Adjacent is the Maine History Gallery, located in a garish postmodern building.

489 Congress St. © 207/879-0427. www.mainehistory.com. Gallery and Longfellow house tour $6 adults, $2 children 6–18. Gallery only $4 adults, $2 children. June–Oct gallery daily 10am–5:30pm, Longfellow House daily 10am–4pm; Nov–May gallery only Wed–Sat noon–4pm.

BOAT TOURS

Casco Bay Lines ★   Six Casco Bay islands have year-round populations and are served by scheduled ferries from downtown Portland. Except for Long Island, the islands are part of the city of Portland. The ferries offer a reasonably priced way to view the bustling harbor and get a taste of island life. Trips range from a 20-minute (one-way) excursion to Peaks Island (the closest thing to an island suburb with 1,200 year-round residents) to a 5½-hour round-trip cruise to Bailey Island (connected by bridge to the mainland south of Brunswick). All of the islands are well-suited for walking; Peaks Island has a rocky back shore that's easily accessible via the island's paved perimeter road. (Bring a picnic lunch.) Cliff Island is the most remote of the bunch.

Commercial and Franklin sts. (C) **207/774-7871.** www.cascobaylines.com. Fares vary depending on the run and season, but summer rates typically $5.25–$13.75 round-trip. Frequent departures 6am–10pm.

Eagle Island Tours 🎯🎯 Eagle Island was the summer home of Arctic explorer and Portland native Robert E. Peary, who claimed in 1909 to be the first person to reach the North Pole. (His accomplishments have been the subject of exhaustive debate among Arctic scholars.) In 1904, Peary built a simple home on a remote 17-acre (7-hectare) island at the edge of Casco Bay. After his death in 1920, his family kept up the home before eventually donating it to the state. It's now open to the public, maintained much the way it was when Peary lived here. Eagle Tours offers one trip daily from Portland. The 4-hour excursion includes a 1½-hour stopover on the island.

Long Wharf (Commercial St.). (C) **207/774-6498.** Tour $18 adults, $14 seniors, $10.50 children under 12 (includes state park fee of $1.50 adults, 50¢ children). Departures daily at 10am.

Old Port Mariner Fleet 🎯 The *Indian II* offers deep-sea fishing trips far beyond Portland Harbor, while the *Odyssey* is a cruise boat that offers whale-watching as well as evening music parties, including a 2-hour "floating Irish pub" on Saturday and Sunday evenings.

Commercial St. (Long Wharf and Custom House Wharf). (C) **207/775-0727.** www.marinerfleet.com. Excursions $10–$75. Several departures daily.

WHERE TO STAY

The **Holiday Inn by the Bay** 🎯, 88 Spring St. ((C) **207/775-2311**), offers great views of the harbor from half of the rooms. Doubles are about $150 in high season. Budget travelers seeking chain hotels can head toward the area around the Maine Mall in South Portland, about a 10-minute drive from downtown. Try **Days Inn** ((C) **207/772-3450**) or **Coastline Inn** ((C) **207/772-3838**).

The new **Extended Stay America,** 2 Ashley Dr., Scarborough ((C) **207/883-0554;** www.exstay.com), is a few minutes' drive south of the Maine Mall and 6 miles (10km) from downtown. We're partial to this fast-growing chain for its well-maintained rooms, usually available at a reasonable price. Doubles here start at about $50.

Black Point Inn 🎯🎯🎯 Located a 15-minute drive from downtown Portland, the Black Point is a Maine classic. Situated on 9 acres (4 hectares) on a point with views along the coast both north and south, the inn was built in 1873 in an area enshrined in some of the work of Winslow Homer. Sixty rooms are located in the main shingled lodge; the others are spread among four tidy cottages. The cottage units have more of a rustic feel; our pick would be the Sprague Cottage, with its flagstone floors in the common area and five rooms with private balconies. Note that the inn is popular for weddings on summer weekends.

510 Black Point Rd., Prouts Neck, ME 04074. (C) **800/258-0003** or 207/883-2500. Fax 207/883-9976. www.blackpointinn.com. 80 units. July–Labor Day $390–$560 double, $440–$600 cottage double; spring and fall from $290; winter from $250. Rates include breakfast and dinner. AE, DC, DISC, MC, V. **Amenities:** Restaurant (New England); outdoor pool; small indoor pool; ocean swimming at 2 adjacent beaches; shuttle to 5 area golf courses; fitness room; Jacuzzi; sauna; summer children's programs; limited room service (delivery charge); massage; babysitting; laundry service; dry cleaning; social director. *In room:* A/C, TV, VCR (on request), dataport, fridge (on request), hair dryer, iron.

The Danforth 🎯🎯 Located in an unusually handsome brick home constructed in 1821, this is one of Portland's more desirable small inns. The extra touches are welcome throughout, from the working fireplaces (in all guest rooms but one) to the richly paneled billiards room. Especially appealing is room 1, with a sitting area and private deck, and room 2, with high ceilings and abundant morning light. The inn is at the edge of the Spring Street Historic District, a 10-minute walk from downtown. It's popular for weddings, so if you're in search of a quiet weekend retreat, ask if anything is planned.

163 Danforth St., Portland, ME 04102. ℭ **800/991-6557** or 207/879-8755. Fax 207/879-8754. www. danforthmaine.com. 9 units. Summer $135–$285 double; off-season $119–$229 double. Rates include continental breakfast. AE, MC, V. Pets sometimes allowed ($10). **Amenities:** Passes to in-town health club; bike rental; billiards room; in-room massage. *In room:* A/C, TV, dataport, hair dryer, iron.

The Percy Inn 𝖗𝖗 The Percy Inn, at the edge of Portland's West End, is housed in a pair of handsome early-19th-century brick town houses in an up-and-coming but not-quite-there-yet area. It's close to good restaurants and is about a 15-minute walk to the Old Port. Guest rooms in the main building are reached via a narrow and twisting staircase. The Henry W. Longfellow Room has wonderful random-width floorboards, a small snack room with fridge, and a sitting area with a marble cafe table. Pine Suite 1 is the largest of the lot. For families, there's another two-bedroom suite in the carriage house. Nice touches abound: All rooms have weather radios, complimentary soft drinks, and coolers with beach blankets for day trips.

15 Pine St., Portland ME 04104. ℭ **207/871-7638.** Fax 207/775-2599. www.percyinn.com. 8 units. June–Oct $129–$275 double; Nov–May $89–$250 double. Higher rates during foliage season and special events. Rates include continental breakfast. MC, V. Limited lot parking plus street parking. *In room:* A/C, TV/VCR, CD player.

Pomegranate Inn 𝖗𝖗𝖗 This imposing 1884 Italianate home in the architecturally distinctive Western Prom neighborhood surprises guests with interiors that are both whimsical and elegant—a fatally cloying combination when attempted by anyone without impeccably good taste. Expect bold artwork and eclectic antiques. Most units have gas fireplaces; the best of the lot is the carriage house, with its own terrace and fireplace. Tea and wine are served upon arrival, and breakfasts are tasty. Downtown is a 20-minute walk away.

49 Neal St., Portland, ME 04102. ℭ **800/356-0408** or 207/772-1006. Fax 207/773-4426. www.pomegranate inn.com. 8 units. Summer and fall $135–$225 double; winter and spring $95–$165 double. Rates include breakfast. 2-night minimum stay summer weekends; 4-night minimum stay Christmas and Thanksgiving. AE, DISC, MC, V. On-street parking. Children 16 and over welcome. From the Old Port, take Middle St. (which turns into Spring St.) to Neal St. in the West End (about 1 mile/1.6km); turn right. On-street parking. *In room:* A/C, TV, dataport, hair dryer.

Portland Regency Hotel 𝖗𝖗 Centrally located on a cobblestone courtyard in the trendy Old Port, the Regency boasts the city's premier hotel location. The architects have had to work within the quirky layout of the 1895 brick armory building; as a result, top-floor rooms lack windows but have skylights, and windows are at knee-height in some other units. For a splurge, ask for room 332 or 336, both corner units with handsome (nonworking) fireplaces. The interior walls can be thin; on weekends, the Old Port revelry sometimes penetrates even the dense brick outer walls.

20 Milk St., Portland, ME 04101. ℭ **800/727-3436** or 207/774-4200. Fax 207/775-2150. www.theregency.com. 95 units. Summer $209–$309 double; off-season $159–$249 double. AE, DC, DISC, MC, V. Valet parking $8 per day. **Amenities:** Restaurant (contemporary American); extensive health club; Jacuzzi; sauna; courtesy car to airport; limited room service; massage; babysitting; dry cleaning. *In room:* A/C, TV, dataport, minibar, hair dryer, iron.

WHERE TO DINE
EXPENSIVE
Back Bay Grill 𝖗𝖗 NEW AMERICAN Back Bay Grill has long been one of Portland's best regarded restaurants, offering an upscale, contemporary

ambience in a somewhat downscale neighborhood. Diners might start off with the popular terrine of house-cured gravlax and smoked salmon with marinated red onions. Among main courses, look for heavenly dishes like rack of lamb with porcini-infused potato gratin and lavender demi-glace, or halibut with a chorizo-saffron sauce.

65 Portland St. ℂ 207/772-8833. www.backbaygrill.com. Reservations recommended. Main courses $18–$33. AE, DC, DISC, MC, V. Mon–Thurs 5–9pm; Fri–Sat 5–9:30pm.

Commissary ★★ NEW AMERICAN Commissary brought an unaccustomed gloss to the Portland restaurant scene when it opened in 2000. It's the handiwork of Maine native Matthew Kenney, a chef/entrepreneur noted in foodie circles for his several Manhattan restaurants. The soaring space is urbane (if noisy), and the menu employs fresh fare from the public market and beyond. Among the typical offerings: wood-roasted char, chicken stuffed with foie gras and pears, and risotto of wild mushrooms.

25 Preble St. (in Portland Public Market). ℂ 207/228-2057. Reservations recommended. Main courses $18–$25. AE, DC, DISC, MC, V. Tues–Sat 5–10pm; Sun–Mon 5–9pm.

Fore Street ★★★ CONTEMPORARY/GRILL Fore Street has lately emerged from the shadows to take its place as one of New England's most celebrated restaurants—in 2001, chef Sam Hayward was profiled in *Saveur* and *House Beautiful*, and was also listed on *Gourmet*'s list of the 100 best restaurants. His secret is simplicity—local ingredients are used whenever possible, and the kitchen shuns fussy presentations. The space is equally honest: Light floods in through huge windows in this loft-like space, and the open kitchen is filled with a team of chefs stoking the wood-fired oven and grilling fish and meats. Some of the most memorable dishes are prepared over an applewood grill, like Maine pheasant or two-texture duckling with grilled pears.

288 Fore St. ℂ 207/775-2717. Reservations recommended. Main courses $14.95–$25.95. AE, MC, V. Mon–Thurs 5:30–10pm; Fri–Sat 5:30–10:30pm; Sun 5:30–9:30pm. Parking in lot off Commercial St.

MODERATE

Benkay ★ *Value* JAPANESE/SUSHI Of Portland's handful of sushi restaurants, Benkay is the hippest. It's usually teeming with a lively crowd lured by good value. Ask about $1 sushi nights (usually weeknights). The regular sushi platter delivers a lot for the money, although nothing very exotic. Expect harried service on busy nights.

2 India St. (at Commercial). ℂ 207/773-5555. Reservations not accepted. Main courses $7.95–$16.95. Mon–Fri 11:30am–2pm; Mon–Sat 5–10pm; Sun noon–9pm.

Flatbread Company ★ PIZZA This upscale, hippie-chic pizzeria—an off-shoot of the original Flatbread Company in Waitsfield, Vt.—may have the best waterfront location in town. It sits on a slip overlooking the Casco Bay Lines terminal, so you can watch fishermen at work while you eat. (There are picnic tables on the deck.) The inside brings to mind a Phish concert, with Tibetan prayer flags and long-haired staffers stoking wood-fired ovens and slicing nitrate-free pepperoni and organic vegetables.

72 Commercial St. ℂ 207/772-8777. Reservations accepted for parties of 10 or more. Pizzas $12–$15. AE, MC, V. Mon–Tues 5–9pm; Wed–Sun 11:30am–9pm.

RiRa ★ IRISH PUB This fun spot is styled after an Irish pub, and the owners have gone to great lengths to achieve that effect. The doors were imported from Kilkenny, and the bar from County Louth. The old and new blend seamlessly, and the place sometimes seems more Irish than the real thing—save for the lack of smoke and the TV blaring sports that aren't soccer. The upstairs dining room has a great view of the ferry slip; look for basic pub fare like smoked turkey wrap and cheeseburgers, along with specialties like shepherd's pie and Guinness bread pudding. This is part of a small chain, with other RiRas in North Carolina, Rhode Island, and Vermont.

72 Commercial St. (next to the Flatbread Company). © 207/761-4446. www.rira.com. Pub fare $6–$10; dinner main courses $11–$20. AE, MC, V. Daily 11:30am–10pm.

INEXPENSIVE

Becky's ★★ Value DINER   Becky's got a glowing write-up in *Gourmet* magazine in 1999, but it obviously hasn't gone to the proprietor's head. This local institution is in a squat concrete building on the non-quaint end of the waterfront, and has drop ceilings, fluorescent lights, and scruffy booths. It's populated very early by fishermen grabbing a plate o' eggs before setting out; later in the day it attracts students and businessmen. The menu offers about what you'd expect, like inexpensive sandwiches (fried haddock and cheese, corn dogs, or tuna melt). It's most noted for breakfast, which includes 13 different omelets. Where else can you find five different types of home fries? Dinner brings favorites like lobster rolls and fried clams.

390 Commercial St. © 207/773-7070. www.beckysdiner.com. Breakfast items $2.25–$7.50; sandwiches $1.95–$4.95; dinners $2.25–$7.95. AE, DISC, MC, V. Sun–Mon 4am–3pm; Tues–Sat 4am–9pm.

Silly's ★★ ECLECTIC/TAKEOUT   Silly's is the favored cheap-eats joint among even jaded Portlanders. Situated on a ragged commercial street, the interior is bright and funky. The place is noted for its roll-ups, which consist of tasty fillings in fresh tortillas. Among our favorites: the shish kebab with feta, and the sloppy "Diesel," with pulled pork barbecue and coleslaw. The fries are hand cut, and the milkshakes huge. Homemade ice creams vary, but tend to be, um, unique, such as cinnamon basil or avocado and lime.

40 Washington Ave. © 207/772-0360. Lunch and dinner items $3.25–$7.50; pizzas $8.50–$10.95. MC, V. Mon–Sat 10am–10pm.

PORTLAND AFTER DARK

Portland is usually lively in the evenings, especially on summer weekends when the testosterone level in the Old Port seems to rocket into the stratosphere, with young folks prowling the dozens of bars and spilling out into the streets.

Among the Old Port bars favored by locals are **Three-Dollar Dewey's,** at Commercial and Union streets (try the great fries); **Gritty McDuff's Brew Pub,** on Fore Street near Exchange Street; and **Brian Ború,** on Center Street. All three are casual and pubby, with customers sharing long tables with new companions.

Beyond the active Old Port bar scene, a number of clubs offer a mix of live and recorded entertainment. These establishments come and go, sometimes quite rapidly. Check one of the free weekly newspapers, *Casco Bay Weekly* or the *Portland Phoenix,* for current venues, performers, and showtimes.

Among the more reliable spots for live music is **Stone Coast Brewing Co.,** 14 York St. (© 207/773-2337), a brewpub at the edge of the Old Port. Downstairs, there's a no-smoking bar and restaurant overlooking the brewery. Upstairs is "The Smoking Room," with pool tables, sales of hand-rolled cigars, and live music (local acts as well as touring bands). The cover ranges from $1 to $20, but is typically $3 to $5 for regional acts.

Portland still has downtown movie houses, allowing travelers in the mood for a flick to avoid the disheartening slog out to the boxy, could-be-anywhere mall octoplexes. **Nickelodeon Cinemas,** 1 Temple St. (© **207/772-9751**), has six screens and offers an eclectic mix of first- and second-run films. **The Movies,** 10 Exchange St. (© **207/772-9600**), is a compact art-film showcase in the heart of the Old Port.

3 The Mid Coast

Veteran Maine travelers contend this part of the coast is fast losing its native charm—it's too commercial, too developed, too much like the rest of the United States. The grousers do have a point, especially regarding Route 1's roadside, but get off the main roads and you'll catch glimpses of another Maine. Back-road travelers will stumble upon quiet inland villages, dramatic coastal scenery, and a rich sense of history, especially maritime history.

The best source of general information for the region is the **Maine State Information Center** (© **207/846-0833**), off Exit 17 of I-95 in Yarmouth. This state-run center is stocked with hundreds of brochures and staffed by a helpful crew that can provide information on the entire state (but is particularly well-informed about the mid-coast region).

Just across the road from the state information center is the **DeLorme Map Store** (© **888/227-1656**). Here you'll find a wide selection of maps, including the firm's trademark state atlases and a line of CD-ROM map products. The store is fun to browse even if you're not a map buff, but what makes the place worth a detour is Eartha, "the world's largest rotating and revolving globe." The 42-foot-diameter (13m) globe, which occupies the whole of the atrium lobby, is constructed on a scale of 1:1,000,000, and is the largest satellite image of the earth ever produced.

FREEPORT

If Freeport were a mall (and that's not a far-fetched analogy), L.L.Bean would be the anchor store. It's the business that launched Freeport, elevating its status from just another town off the interstate to one of the two outlet capitals of Maine (the other is Kittery). Freeport still has the form of a classic Maine village, but it's a village that's been largely taken over by the national fashion industry. Most of the old homes and stores have been converted to upscale shops. Banana Republic occupies an exceedingly handsome brick Federal-style home; even the McDonald's is in a tasteful Victorian farmhouse—you really have to look for the golden arches.

While a number of more modern structures have been built to accommodate the outlet boom, strict planning guidelines have managed to preserve much of the local charm, at least in the village section. Huge parking lots off Main Street are hidden from view, making this one of the more aesthetically pleasing places to shop; but even with these large lots, parking can be scarce during peak season, especially on rainy summer days when every cottage-bound tourist between York and Camden decides that a trip to Freeport is a winning idea. Bring a lot of patience, and expect crowds if you come at a busy time.

ESSENTIALS

GETTING THERE   Freeport is on Route 1 but is most commonly reached via I-95 from either Exit 19 or 20.

VISITOR INFORMATION   The **Freeport Merchants Association,** 23 Depot St. (© **800/865-1994** or 207/865-1212; www.freeportusa.com), publishes a free map and directory of businesses, restaurants, and accommodations; it's widely available around town.

SHOPPING

Freeport has more than 100 retail shops between Exit 19 off I-95 at the far lower end of Main Street and Mallett Road, which connects to Exit 20. Shops have recently begun to spread south of Exit 19 toward Yarmouth. Get off at Exit 17 and head north on Route 1 if you don't want to miss a single shop. Hours are typically daily from 9am to 9pm during the busy summer season.

Among national chains with a presence in Freeport are Levi's, Calvin Klein, Patagonia, North Face, Nike, J. Crew, Timberland, and many others.

L.L.Bean ★★★ Monster outdoor retailer L.L.Bean traces its roots to the day Leon Leonwood Bean decided that what the world really needed was a good weatherproof hunting shoe. He joined a watertight gum shoe with a laced leather upper. Hunters liked it. The store grew. An empire was born. Today, L.L.Bean sells millions of dollars worth of clothing and outdoor goods to customers nationwide through its catalogs. This modern store is the size of a regional mall, but tastefully done with its own indoor trout pond and lots of natural wood. It's open 365 days a year, 24 hours a day, and it's a popular spot even in the dead of night. Selections include Bean's own trademark clothing, home furnishings, books, shoes, and outdoor gear. A good place to start is the L.L.Bean factory store, which may have items you're looking for at discounted prices. It's located between Main and Depot streets—ask at the front desk of the main store for directions. Main and Bow sts. ℭ 800/341-4341. www.llbean.com.

WHERE TO STAY

Harraseeket Inn ★★ The Harraseeket deftly mixes traditional and modern in a personable property 2 blocks north of L.L.Bean. A late-19th-century home is the soul of the hotel, but most of the rooms are in modern additions. Guests can relax in the well-regarded dining room, enjoy afternoon tea in the common room, or sip a cocktail in the rustic Broad Arrow Tavern and order snacks from its wood-fired oven. Bedrooms are tastefully appointed with a mix of contemporary and antique furniture. About a quarter have fireplaces, and more than half feature single or double Jacuzzis.

162 Main St., Freeport, ME 04032. ℭ 800/342-6423 or 207/865-9377. www.harraseeketinn.com. 84 units. Summer and fall $195–$265 double; spring and early summer $140–$235; winter $110–$215. Rates include breakfast. AE, DC, DISC, MC, V. Take Exit 20 off I-95 to Main St. **Amenities:** 2 restaurants (New American, grill); indoor heated lap pool; concierge; limited room service; laundry service; dry cleaning. *In room:* A/C, TV, dataport, coffeemaker, hair dryer.

Kendall Tavern ★ This cheerful yellow farmhouse is out of the bustle of Freeport, but only a ½ mile (0.8km) from downtown shopping. Guest rooms are decorated in a bright and airy style with a mix of antique and new furniture. Rooms facing Route 1 are noisier than others, but the traffic isn't likely to be too disruptive. There's a piano in one of the two parlors, and a Jacuzzi in a spacious private room in the back.

213 Main St. (Rte. 1), Freeport, ME 04032. ℭ 800/341-9572 or 207/865-1338. 7 units. High season $100–$125 double; off-season $75–$95 double. Rates include breakfast. AE, DISC, MC, V. **Amenities:** Jacuzzi. *In room:* No phone.

Maine Idyll Motor Court ★ 𝒱𝑎𝑙𝑢𝑒 This 1932 motor court is a Maine classic—20 cottages scattered about a grove of beech and oak trees. Each has a tiny porch, modest kitchen facilities, and time-worn furniture. Fourteen have fireplaces, with birch logs provided more for atmosphere than warmth. The only interruption to an idyll here is the omnipresent sound of traffic: I-95 is just through the trees on one side, Route 1 on the other side.

1411 Rte. 1, Freeport, ME 04032. © 207/865-4201. www.freeportusa.com/maineidyll. 20 units. $49–$72 double; $70–$90 2- or 3-bedroom cottage. Rates include continental breakfast. No credit cards. Closed early Nov to mid-Apr. Pets allowed. Located 2½ miles (4km) north of L.L. Bean. *In room:* TV, kitchenette, no phone.

WHERE TO DINE

A short walk from L.L.Bean is **Chowder Express & Sandwich Shop,** 2 Mechanic St. (© **207/865-3404**), a hole-in-the-wall with counter seating. Fish, lobster, and clam chowder are served in paper bowls with plastic spoons. It's convenient for a quick bite between shops.

Harraseeket Lunch & Lobster ★★ LOBSTER POUND   Located at a boatyard on the Harraseeket River about a 10-minute drive from Freeport's main shopping district, this lobster pound is a popular destination on sunny days—although with its heated dining room, it's a worthy destination any time. Be prepared for big crowds; a good alternative is to come in late afternoon between the crushing lunch and dinner hordes.

Main St., South Freeport. © 207/865-4888. Reservations not accepted. Lobsters market price (typically $8–$12). No credit cards. Daily 11:30am–8:30pm. Closed mid-Oct to May 1. From I-95, take Exit 17 and head north on Rte. 1; turn right on S. Freeport Rd. at the large Indian statue; continue to stop sign in South Freeport; turn right to waterfront. From Freeport, take South St. (off Bow St.) to Main St. in South Freeport; turn left to water.

Jameson Tavern ★ REGIONAL   Located in a handsome farmhouse literally in the shadow of L.L.Bean, the Jameson Tavern touts itself as the birthplace of Maine. In 1820, the papers legally separating Maine from Massachusetts were signed here. Today, it's a two-part restaurant under single ownership. The Tap Room offers fare like crab-cake burgers and lobster croissants (sit out on the patio if the weather's good), while the Dining Room serves more sedate meals, with an emphasis on steaks and hearty fare.

115 Main St. (just north of L.L.Bean). © 207/865-4196. Reservations encouraged. Tap Room main courses $7.95–$17.95; Dining Room main courses $5.95–$11.95 lunch, $11.95–$22.95 dinner. AE, DC, DISC, MC, V. Tap Room daily 11am–11pm; Dining Room summer daily 11am–10pm, winter daily 11:30am–9pm.

BRUNSWICK ★ & BATH ★

Brunswick and Bath are two handsome, historic towns that share a strong commercial past. Brunswick was once home to several mills along the Androscoggin River; these have since been converted to offices and the like, but the town's broad Maine Street still bustles with activity. Brunswick is also home to Bowdoin College. The school was founded in 1794 and has since amassed an illustrious

---

Tips **Recommended Reading**

E. B. White was a sometime resident of a saltwater farm on the Maine coast and frequent contributor to the *New Yorker*. His essays in *One Man's Meat,* composed in the late 1930s and early 1940s, are only incidentally about Maine, but you get a superb sense of place by observing the shadows. For more specific information on the life of a lobsterman, look into James M. Acheson's exhaustively researched 1988 book *Lobster Gangs of Maine*. It will answer every question you have, and then some.

roster of prominent alumni, including Nathaniel Hawthorne, Henry Wadsworth Longfellow, President Franklin Pierce, and Arctic explorer Robert E. Peary.

Eight miles (13km) to the east, Bath is pleasantly situated on the Kennebec River, and is a noted center of shipbuilding. The first U.S.-built ship was constructed downstream at the Popham Bay colony in the early 17th century. Bath shipbuilding reached its heyday in the late 19th century, but the business of shipbuilding continues to this day. Bath Iron Works is one of the nation's preeminent boatyards, constructing and repairing ships for the Navy. The scaled-down military has left Bath shipbuilders in a somewhat tenuous state, but it's still common to see the steely gray ships in the dry dock. (The best view is from the bridge over the Kennebec.)

ESSENTIALS

GETTING THERE   Brunswick and Bath are both on Route 1. Brunswick is accessible via Exits 22 and 23 off I-95. If you're bypassing Brunswick and heading north up Route 1 to Bath or beyond, continue up I-95 and take the "coastal connector" exit in Topsham, which avoids some of the slower going through Brunswick. For bus service from Portland or Boston, contact **Vermont Transit** (© 800/451-3292) or **Concord Trailways** (© 800/639-3317).

VISITOR INFORMATION   The **Bath-Brunswick Region Chamber of Commerce,** 59 Pleasant St., near downtown Brunswick (© 207/725-8797 or 207/443-9751), offers information and lodging assistance Monday through Friday from 8:30am to 5pm. The chamber also staffs a summer-only information center on Route 1 between Brunswick and Bath; open daily from 10am to 7pm.

EXPLORING THE AREA

Collectors flock to **Cabot Mill Antiques,** 14 Maine St., in downtown Brunswick (© 207/725-2855; www.cabotiques.com), which features the stuff of 140 dealers.

Bowdoin Museum of Art 👣👣   This stern, neoclassical building on the Bowdoin campus was designed by McKim, Mead & White in 1894. While the collections are relatively small, they include a number of exceptional paintings from Europe and America. The artists include Andrew and N. C. Wyeth, Marsden Hartley, Winslow Homer, and John Singer Sargent.

Walker Art Building, Bowdoin College, Brunswick. © 207/725-3275. Free admission. Tues–Sat 10am–5pm; Sun 2–5pm.

Maine Maritime Museum & Shipyard 👣👣 *Kids*   This museum on the banks of the Kennebec River (just south of the very obvious Bath Iron Works shipyard) features a wide array of displays related to the boatbuilder's art. It's sited at the former shipyard of Percy and Small, which built some 42 schooners in the late 19th and early 20th centuries. The largest wooden ship ever built in America—the 329-foot (99m) *Wyoming*—was constructed on this lot in 1909. The Maritime History Building houses changing exhibits of maritime art and artifacts. The 10-acre (4-hectare) property contains a fleet of additional displays, including a complete boatbuilding shop where you can watch wooden boats take shape. Kids enjoy the play area, where they can search for pirates from the crow's nest of the play boat. Occasional river cruises ($30) are offered from the dock.

243 Washington St., Bath. © 207/443-1316. www.bathmaine.com. Admission $9 adults, $6 children 6–17; $27 per family. Daily 9:30am–5pm.

Peary-MacMillan Arctic Museum 👣   While Admiral Robert E. Peary (class of 1887) is well known for his accomplishments (he discovered the North Pole at age 53 in 1909), Donald MacMillan (class of 1898) also racked up an impressive string of achievements in Arctic research and exploration. You can learn about both men in this intriguing museum on the Bowdoin College campus. The front room features mounted Arctic animals; a second room outlines Peary's historic 1909 expedition, complete with excerpts from his journal. The last room includes varied displays of Inuit arts and crafts, some historic, some modern. This compact museum can be visited in about 20 minutes; the art museum (see above) is just next-door.

Hubbard Hall, Bowdoin College, Brunswick. © 207/725-3416. Free admission. Tues–Sat 10am–5pm; Sun 2–5pm.

BEACHES
This part of Maine is better known for rocky cliffs and lobster pots than swimming beaches, with two notable exceptions.

Popham Beach State Park (© 207/389-1335), at the tip of Route 209 (head south from Bath), has a long and sandy strand, plus great views of knobby offshore islands such as Seguin Island, capped with a lonesome lighthouse. Parking and changing rooms are available. Admission is $2 for adults, 50¢ for children 5 to 11.

At the tip of the next peninsula to the east is idyllic **Reid State Park** (© 207/371-2303). Arrive early enough and you can stake out a picnic table among the wind-blasted pines. The mile-long beach is great for strolling. Services include changing rooms and a small snack bar. Admission is $2.50 for adults, 50¢ for children 5 to 11. To get here, follow Route 127 south from Bath and Route 1.

WHERE TO STAY
In Bath
Moses Galen House ⭐   The 1874 Moses Galen House is an extravagant Italianate home done up in exuberant colors. The whole of the spacious first floor is open to guests and includes a TV room, lots of loudly ticking clocks, and an appropriately cluttered Victorian double parlor. Note the old friezes and stained glass original to the house. Guest rooms vary in size and decor, but all are welcoming. The Victorian Room occupies a corner and gets lots of afternoon light, although its bathroom is dark; the Suite is ideal for families, with two sleeping rooms and a small kitchen.

1009 Washington St., Bath, ME 04530. © 888/442-8771. www.galenmoses.com. 5 units. $119–$225 double. Rates include full breakfast. 2-night minimum stay on summer weekends. AE, DISC, MC, V. *In room:* A/C, hair dryer, iron.

On the Coast
Driftwood Inn & Cottages ⭐ *Value*   The Driftwood Inn dates back to 1910, and not a lot seems to have changed since then. A family-run retreat on 3 acres (1 hectare), the inn is a compound of four shingled buildings and a handful of cottages on a rocky, oceanside property. The spartan rooms have a simple turn-of-the-last-century flavor that hasn't been gentrified in the least. Most units share bathrooms, but some have sinks and toilets. Cottages are nothing fancy: Expect industrial carpeting, plastic shower stalls, and a few beds that could stand replacing. Bring plenty of books and board games.

Washington Ave., Bailey Island, ME 04003. © 207/833-5461, or 508/947-1066 off-season. 30 units (most share hall bathrooms). $70–$110 double; weekly $400 per person, including breakfast and dinner (July–Aug only); cottages $600–$635 per week. No credit cards. Closed mid-Oct to mid-May. **Amenities:** Dining room (New England; open late June to Labor Day); ancient saltwater pool. *In room:* No phone.

Grey Havens ✹✹ This is the inn first-time visitors to Maine fantasize about. Located on Georgetown Island off the beaten track southeast of Bath, this 1904 shingled home with prominent turrets sits on a rocky bluff overlooking the sea. Inside, it's all richly mellowed pine paneling. Guest rooms are simply but comfortably furnished. The oceanfront units command a premium, but are worth it. (Save a few dollars by requesting an oceanfront room with private bathroom across the hall.) One caveat: The inn has been only lightly modernized, which is generally good but means rather thin walls.

Seguinland Rd., Georgetown Island, ME 04548. ✆ **207/371-2616.** Fax 207/371-2274. www.greyhavens. com. 13 units (2 with private hall bathrooms). $130–$220 double. Rates include continental breakfast. MC, V. Closed Nov–May. No children under 12. From Rte. 1, head south on Rte. 127 and follow signs for Reid State Park; watch for inn on left. **Amenities:** Free canoes and bikes. In room: No phone.

WHERE TO DINE

Five Islands Lobster Co. ✹ LOBSTER POUND The drive alone makes this rustic lobster pound a worthy destination. It's about 12 miles (19km) south of Route 1 down winding Route 127, past bogs and spruce forests with glimpses of azure ocean inlets. (Head south from Woolwich, which is just across the bridge from Bath.) Drive until you pass a cluster of clapboard homes, and then keep going until you can't go any farther. This is a down-home affair, owned jointly by local lobstermen and the proprietors of the Grey Havens inn (see above). Wander next door to the Love Nest Snack Bar for extras like soda or (recommended) onion rings. Settle in at one of the picnic tables, or head over to a grassy spot at the edge of the dirt parking lot. Despite its edge-of-the-world feel, the lobster pound can be crowded on weekends.

Rte. 127, Georgetown. ✆ **207/371-2990.** Typically $8–$10 per lobster. MC, V. July–Aug daily 11am–8pm; shorter hours in off-season. Closed Columbus Day to Mother's Day.

Robinhood Free Meetinghouse ✹✹ NEW AMERICAN Chef Michael Gagne's menu features between 30 and 40 entrees, and they're wildly eclectic—from scallops Niçoise in puff pastry to Wiener schnitzel with lingonberries. Ordering from the menu is like playing stump the chef: Let's see you make *this!* And Gagne almost always hits his notes. He has attracted legions of local followers who appreciate the extraordinary attention paid to detail, like the foam baffles glued discreetly to the underside of the seats to dampen the echoes in the sparely decorated 1855 Greek Revival meetinghouse. Even the sorbet served between courses is homemade.

Robinhood Rd., Robinhood. ✆ **207/371-2188.** www.robinhood-meetinghouse.com. Reservations encouraged. Main courses $18–$25. AE, DISC, MC, V. May–Oct daily 5:30–9pm; rest of year, limited days (call first).

WISCASSET ✹ & THE BOOTHBAYS ✹

Wiscasset is a lovely riverside town on Route 1. Although the sluggish line of traffic snaking through diminishes the charm, it makes a good stop en route to coastal destinations further along.

The Boothbays, 11 miles (18km) south of Route 1 on Route 27, consist of several small and scenic villages—**East Boothbay, Boothbay Harbor,** and **Boothbay,** among them—which are closer than Wiscasset to the open ocean.

The former fishing port of Boothbay Harbor was discovered in the 19th century by wealthy rusticators who retreated here each summer. Having embraced the tourist dollar, the harborfront village never really looked back, and in more recent years it has emerged as one of the premier destinations of travelers in search of classic coastal Maine. This has had an obvious impact: The

Tips **Escaping the Crowds**

Boothbay Harbor is overrun with summer visitors, but at nearby **Ocean Point,** you can leave most of the crowds behind as you follow a picturesque lane that twists along the rocky shore and past a colony of vintage summer homes. Follow Route 96 southward east of Boothbay Harbor, and you'll pass through the sleepy village of East Boothbay before continuing on toward the point. The narrow road runs through piney forests before arriving at the rocky finger; it's one of a handful of Maine peninsulas with a road edging its perimeter, which allows for fine oceanviews. The colorful Victorian-era cottages bloom along the roadside like wildflowers. Ocean Point makes for a good **bike loop.** Mountain-bike rentals are available at Tidal Transit (see below).

village is a mandatory stop for bus tours, which have in turn attracted kitschy shops and a slew of mediocre restaurants serving baked stuffed haddock. If Boothbay Harbor is stuck in a time warp, it's Tourist Trap circa 1974—bland and boxy motels hem in the harbor, and shops hawk mass-market trinkets. However, if you avoid the touristy claptrap of the downtown harbor area itself, some of the outlying areas are strikingly beautiful.

ESSENTIALS

GETTING THERE   Wiscasset is on Route 1 midway between Bath and Damariscotta. Boothbay Harbor is south of Route 1 on Route 27. Coming from the west, look for signs shortly after crossing the Sheepscot River at Wiscasset.

VISITOR INFORMATION   Wiscasset lacks an information booth, but you can get questions answered by calling the **Wiscasset Regional Business Association** (© 207/882-9617). The Boothbay area has three visitor centers in and around town, reflecting the importance of tourist dollars to the region. At the intersection of Routes 1 and 27 is a center that's open May through October and is a good place to stock up on brochures. A mile (1.6km) before you reach the village is the seasonal **Boothbay Information Center** on your right, open June through October. The year-round **Boothbay Harbor Region Chamber of Commerce** (© 207/633-2353) is at the intersection of Routes 27 and 96.

EXPLORING WISCASSET

Aside from enjoying the town's handsome architecture and vaunted prettiness, you'll find a handful of worthwhile shops that range from spare art galleries to antiques stores cluttered with architectural salvage.

Castle Tucker ★   This fascinating mansion overlooking the river at the edge of town was built in 1807, then radically added to in a more ostentatious style in 1860. The home remains more or less in the same state it was when reconfigured by cotton trader Capt. Richard Tucker; his descendant Jane Tucker still lives on the top floor. Tours of the lower floor are offered by the Society of New England Antiquities. The highlight is the detailing; be sure to note the extraordinary elliptical staircase and the painted plaster trim (it's not oak).

Lee and High sts. © 207/882-7364. Admission $5 adults, $2.50 children. July–Aug Wed–Sun tours leave on the hour 11am–4pm. Closed Sept–June.

Musical Wonder House ⍟⍟   Danilo Konvalinka has been collecting music boxes both grand and tiny for decades, and nothing seems to delight him more than to show them off for visitors. The collection ranges from massive music boxes that sound as resonant as an orchestra (an 1870 Girard from Austria) to the tinnier sounds of the smaller contraptions. They're displayed in four rooms in a stately 1852 home. A full tour is pricey; if you're undecided, visit the gift shop and sample some of the coin-operated 19th-century music boxes. Intrigued? Sign up for the next tour.

18 High St. ℂ 207/882-7163. Tours $8 for half of downstairs, $15 for full downstairs, $30 for full house. Late May to mid-Oct daily 10am–5pm. Closed late Oct to late May.

EXPLORING THE BOOTHBAY REGION

Parking in Boothbay Harbor in midsummer will require either great persistence or the forking over of a few dollars. A popular local attraction is the long, narrow **footbridge** across the harbor, first built in 1901. It's more of a destination than a link—other than a couple unnotable restaurants and motels, there's not much on the other side. The winding streets that weave through the town are filled with shops that cater to tourists. Don't expect much merchandise beyond the usual trinkets and souvenirs.

If dense fog or rain socks in the harbor, bide your time at the vintage **Romar Bowling Lanes** ⍟ (ℂ 207/633-5721). This log-and-shingle building near the footbridge has a harbor view and has been distracting travelers with traditional New England candlepin bowling since 1946.

In good weather, stop by one of the Boothbay region information centers (see above) and request a free guide to the holdings of the **Boothbay Region Land Trust** ⍟⍟ (ℂ 207/633-4818). Eight pockets of publicly accessible lands dot the peninsula, and most feature quiet trails good for a stroll or a picnic. Among the best: the Linekin Preserve, a 95-acre (38-hectare) parcel en route to Ocean Point (drive south from Route 1 in Boothbay Harbor on Route 96 for 3.8 miles/6km; look for parking on the left) with 600 feet (180m) of riverfront. A hike around the loop trail (about 2.1 miles/3.4km) will occupy a pleasant hour.

Coastal Maine Botanical Garden   This 128-acre (52-hectare) waterside garden remains a work in progress, but makes for a peaceable oasis. It's not a fancy, formal garden, but rather a natural habitat that's being coaxed into a more mannered state. Several short trails lead through the mossy forest, good for half an hour's worth of exploring.

Barters Island Rd., Boothbay (near Hogdon Island). ℂ 207/633-4333. Free admission. Open daylight hours. From Rte. 27 in Boothbay Center, bear right at the monument at the stop sign, then make the first right on Barters Island Rd.; drive 1 mile (1.6km); look for the stone gate on your left.

Marine Resources Aquarium ⍟ (Kids)   This compact aquarium offers context for life in the sea around Boothbay and beyond. Kids will be enthralled by the rare albino and blue lobsters, and can get their hands wet in a 20-foot (6m) touch tank. Parking is tight at the aquarium, which is located on a point across the water from downtown Boothbay Harbor, so visitors are urged to use the free shuttle bus (look for the Rocktide trolley) that connects to downtown.

McKown Point Rd., West Boothbay Harbor. ℂ 207/633-9542. Admission $3 adults, $2.50 children 5–18. Daily 10am–5pm. Closed late Oct to Memorial Day weekend.

BOAT TOURS

The best way to see the Maine coast around Boothbay is on a boat tour. Nearly two dozen tour boats berth at the harbor or nearby, offering trips ranging from an hour's outing to a full-day excursion to Monhegan Island.

Balmy Day Cruises ✦ (**℘ 800/298-2284** or 207/633-2284) runs several trips from the harbor, including an excursion to Monhegan Island on the *Balmy Days II,* which allows passengers 4 hours to explore the island before returning (see "Monhegan Island," below). The cost is $30 for adults, $18 for children. If you'd rather be sailing, ask about the 90-minute cruises on the 15-passenger *Bay Lady* ($18). It's a good idea to make reservations.

A more intimate way to tour the harbor is via sea kayak. **Tidal Transit Kayak Co.** ✦ (**℘ 207/633-7140**) offers morning, afternoon, and sunset tours for $30 (sunset's the best bet). Kayaks may also be rented for $12 per hour or $50 per day. Tidal Transit is open daily in summer (except when it rains); it's located on the waterfront at 47 Townshend Ave. (walk down the alley).

WHERE TO STAY

Five Gables Inn ✦✦   This handsome inn sits proudly amid a small colony of summer homes on a quiet road above a peaceful cove. It's nicely isolated from the hubbub of Boothbay Harbor. Room 8 is a corner unit with brilliant morning light; most requested is room 14, with a fine view and a fireplace with marble mantle. (Note that some of the first-floor rooms open onto a common deck and lack privacy, and all but five rooms have showers only.) The breakfast buffet is sumptuous, with offerings like tomato-basil frittata and blueberry-stuffed French toast.

207 Murray Hill Rd. (P.O. Box 335), East Boothbay, ME 04544. ℘ **800/451-5048** or 207/633-4551. www.fivegablesinn.com. 16 units. $130–$195 double. Rates include breakfast. MC, V. Closed Nov to mid-May. Children 12 and over welcome. Drive through East Boothbay on Rte. 96; turn right after crest of hill on Murray Hill Rd. *In room:* Hair dryer.

The Inn at Lobsterman's Wharf ✦ *Value*   This is our budget pick for the Boothbay region. A clean, no-frills place adjacent to a working boatyard, this inn was originally a coal depot and later a boardinghouse. It still has some boardinghouse informality to it (although all rooms now have small bathrooms), but you get a lot for your money. Seven rooms face the water; Hodgon Suite is the largest, with a view of the boatyard.

Rte. 96, East Boothbay. ℘ **207/633-5481.** 9 units. $60–$90 double. Rates include continental breakfast. MC, V. Limited pets allowed. **Amenities:** Restaurant (see below). *In room:* TV, no phone.

Newagen Seaside Inn ✦   This small, 1940s-era resort has seen more glamorous days, but it's still a superb, low-key establishment. The white-shingled Colonial Revival–style inn is furnished simply in country pine. There's a classically austere dining room, narrow hallways with pine wainscoting, and a lobby with a fireplace. New innkeepers Corinne and Scott Larson have made some strides in updating the place, which has long been known (and even favored) for its plain and occasionally threadbare rooms. Guests return every year to the 85-acre (34-hectare) grounds filled with decks, gazebos, and walkways that border on the magical. It's hard to convey the magnificence of the ocean views, which may be the best of any inn in Maine.

Rte. 27 (P.O. Box 29), Cape Newagen, ME 04576. ℘ **800/654-5242** or 207/633-5242. Fax 207/633-5340. www.newagenseasideinn.com. 26 units. $140–$240 double. Rates include breakfast. Ask about off-season discounts. AE, MC, V. Closed mid-Oct to mid-May. Take Rte. 27 from Boothbay Harbor and continue south until the tip of Southport Island; look for sign. **Amenities:** Restaurant (traditional New England); freshwater and saltwater pools; tennis courts; Jacuzzi; rowboats; bike rental; game room (hand-set pin bowling, darts, Ping-Pong, pool); badminton; croquet; horseshoes. *In room:* TV/VCR on request.

Spruce Point Inn ★★ (Kids)   The Spruce Point Inn, originally built as a hunting and fishing lodge in the 1890s, turned into a summer resort in 1912. Those looking for historic authenticity may be disappointed. Those seeking modern facilities with some historic accents will be delighted. (Those who prefer their gentility a bit less glossy should consider the Newagen Seaside Inn, above.) The rooms in the main inn are basic and comfortable; the newer wings are somewhat more condo-like. This is a great choice for families, and offers plenty of activities to fill each day.

Atlantic Ave. (P.O. Box 237), Boothbay Harbor, ME 04538. ℂ 800/553-0289 or 207/633-4152. www.sprucepointinn.com. 93 units. Mid-July to Aug $165–$350 double; fall $140–$250; spring $125–$225; early summer $150–$265. 2- or 3-night minimum stay weekends and holidays. AE, DISC, MC, V. Closed mid-Oct to Memorial Day. Pets accepted ($50 deposit, $100 cleaning fee). Turn seaward on Union St. in Boothbay Harbor; go 2 miles (3.2km) to inn. **Amenities:** Restaurant (upscale New England); 2 outdoor pools (1 heated); tennis courts; small fitness center; Jacuzzi; game room; concierge; boat tours; free shuttle to downtown Boothbay Harbor; in-room massage; babysitting; self-service laundry; laundry service; dry cleaning; lawn games (shuffleboard, tetherball, croquet, and others). *In room:* TV, fridge, coffeemaker, iron.

WHERE TO DINE
In Wiscasset

Red's Eats ★ LOBSTER ROLLS/SANDWICHES   This roadside stand has received more than its share of media ink about its famous lobster rolls. (They often crop up in "Best of Maine" surveys.) And they *are* good, consisting of moist chunks of chilled lobster placed in a roll served with a little mayo on the side. Be aware that they're at the pricey end of the scale—you can find less expensive (although less meaty) versions elsewhere.

Water St. (Rte. 1 just before the bridge). ℂ 207/882-6128. Sandwiches $2.50–$5.75; lobster rolls typically around $11. No credit cards. Mon–Thurs 11am–11pm; Fri–Sat 11am–2am; Sun noon–6pm. Closed Oct–Apr.

Sarah's ★ SANDWICHES/TRADITIONAL   This hometown favorite overlooks the Sheepscot River and is usually crowded at lunch, with offerings like pita pockets, croissant sandwiches, wraps, and something called a whaleboat (like a calzone). The lobsters are fresh, hauled in daily by Sarah's brother and father. This is the best choice for an informal lunch break when motoring along Route 1.

Water St. and Rte. 1 (across from Red's). ℂ 207/882-7504. Sandwiches $4.45–$6.25; pizzas $4.95–16.95. AE, DISC, MC, V. Daily 11am–8pm (Fri–Sat until 9pm).

In the Boothbays

In Boothbay Harbor, look for **"King" Brud** and his famous hot-dog cart. Brud started selling hot dogs in 1943, and he's still at it. June through October, he's usually at McKown and Commercial streets from 10am to 4pm.

Boothbay Region Lobstermen's Co-op SEAFOOD   WE ARE NOT RESPONSIBLE IF THE SEAGULLS STEAL YOUR FOOD, reads the sign at the ordering window of this lobster joint. And that sets the casual tone pretty well. Situated across the harbor from downtown Boothbay, the co-op offers no-frills food served at picnic tables on a dock and inside a crude shelter. This is the best pick from among the cluster of lobster-in-the-rough places that line the waterfront. The salty atmosphere is the draw here; it's a fair-weather destination that should be avoided in rain or fog.

Atlantic Ave., Boothbay Harbor. ℂ 207/633-4900. Fried and grilled foods $2–$10.25; lobsters priced to market, typically $8–$12. DISC, MC, V. May to mid-Oct daily 11:30am–8:30pm. On foot, cross footbridge and turn right; follow road for ⅓ of a mile (0.5km).

Tips **Lobster Pricing**

Travelers sometimes get a rude surprise when they receive their bill for a meal at a casual wharfside lobster restaurant. Prices posted for lobsters are *per pound*, not per lobster. At times this can be inadvertently misleading, since there's often a range of prices listed—for example, $6.99 for 1¼ lobsters, $7.99 for 1½ lobsters, and so on. (This just reflects the fact that larger lobsters are harder to come by, and thus priced higher.) The prices are still per pound; you'll just need to do a little quick math to figure out the price of your lobster.

Christopher's Boathouse ★★ NEW AMERICAN/WOOD GRILL Christopher's is a happy exception to the generally unexciting fare found in town. Scenically located at the head of the harbor, the restaurant is bright and modern. (There's also deck dining.) The chef has a deft touch with spicy flavors, and nicely melds the expected with the unexpected (for instance, lobster and mango bisque with spicy lobster won tons). The meals from the grill are excellent, and include a venison flank with wild mushroom sauce. The restaurant is noted for its lobster succotash, which is better than it sounds.

25 Union St., Boothbay Harbor. © 207/633-6565. www.christophersboathouse.com. Reservations recommended in peak season. Main courses $5–$9 lunch, $18.50–$25 dinner. DISC, MC, V. June–Aug daily 11:30am–2pm; July–Sept daily 5:30–9pm; Oct–June Thurs–Sat 5:30–9pm.

Lobsterman's Wharf ★ SEAFOOD Located on the water in East Boothbay, the Lobsterman's Wharf has the comfortable feel of a neighborhood bar, complete with pool table. If the weather cooperates, sit at a picnic table on the dock and admire the views of a spruce-topped peninsula across the Damariscotta River. Entrees include a mixed-seafood grill and a barbecued shrimp-and-ribs platter.

Rte. 96, East Boothbay. © 207/633-3443. Reservations accepted for parties of 6 or more. Lunch from $4.50–$13.95; dinner $13.95–$22.95 (mostly $14–$16). AE, MC, V. Daily 11:30am–midnight. Closed mid-Oct to mid-May.

MONHEGAN ISLAND ★★★

Monhegan Island is Maine's premier island destination. Visited by Europeans as early as 1497, the wild, remote island was first settled by fishermen attracted to the sea's bounty in offshore waters. Starting in the 1870s, noted artists discovered the island and came to stay for a spell. The roster included Rockwell Kent, George Bellows, Edward Hopper, and Robert Henri. The artists gathered in the kitchen of the lighthouse to chat and drink coffee; it's said that the wife of the lighthouse keeper accumulated a tremendously valuable collection of paintings. Today, Jamie Wyeth, scion of the Wyeth clan, claims the island as his part-time home.

It's not hard to figure out why artists have been attracted to the place: There's a mystical quality to it, from the thin light to the startling contrasts of dark cliffs and foamy white surf. There's also a remarkable sense of tranquility here, which can only help focus one's inner vision. In addition, it's a superb destination for hikers, because most of the island is undeveloped and laced with trails.

Be aware that this is not Martha's Vineyard—no ATMs, few pay phones, even electricity is scarce. That's what repeat visitors like about it. An overnight at one of the hostelries is strongly recommended. Day trips are easily arranged, but the island's true character doesn't start to emerge until the last day boat sails away and the quiet, rustic appeal of the place percolates to the surface.

ESSENTIALS

GETTING THERE   Access to Monhegan Island is via boat from New Harbor, Boothbay Harbor, or Port Clyde. The picturesque trip from Port Clyde is the favored route among longtime visitors; the boat passes through a series of spruce-clad islands before setting out on the open sea.

Two boats make the run to Monhegan from Port Clyde. The *Laura B.,* which takes 70 minutes, is a doughty workboat (building supplies and boxes of food are loaded on first; passengers fill in the available niches on the deck and in the small cabin). The newer, faster (50 min.), passenger-oriented *Elizabeth Ann* offers a heated cabin and more seating. You'll need to leave your car behind, so pack lightly and wear sturdy shoes. The round-trip fare is $27 for adults, $14 for children 2 to 12, and $2 for pets. Reservations are advised; contact **Monhegan Boat Line** (© **207/372-8848;** www.monheganboat.com). Parking near the dock costs $4 per day.

VISITOR INFORMATION   Monhegan Island has no formal visitor center, but it's small and friendly enough that you can make inquiries of just about anyone you meet on the island paths. The clerks at the ferry dock in Port Clyde are also quite helpful. Be sure to pick up the inexpensive map of the island's hiking trails at the boat ticket office or at the various shops around the island.

Note: Because wildfire could destroy this breezy island in short order, smoking is prohibited outside the village.

EXPLORING MONHEGAN ISLAND

Walking is the chief activity on the island, and it's surprising how much distance you can cover on these 700 acres (284 hectares), about 1½ miles (2.4km) long and ½ mile (0.8km) wide. The village clusters tightly around the harbor; the rest of the island is mostly wildland, laced with **17 miles (27km) of trails** ★★★. Much of the island is ringed with high, open bluffs atop fissured cliffs. Pack a picnic and hike the perimeter trail, and plan to spend much of the day just sitting and reading. The inland trails are appealing in a far different way. Deep, dark **Cathedral Woods** ★★ is mossy and fragrant; sunlight only dimly filters through the evergreens to the forest floor.

Birding is a popular activity in the spring and fall. Monhegan Island is on the Atlantic flyway, and a wide variety of birds stop at the island along their migration routes.

The sole formal attraction on the island is the **Monhegan Museum** ★, located next to the 1824 lighthouse on a high point above the village. The museum, open July through September, has a quirky collection of historic artifacts and provides some context for this rugged island's history. Also near the lighthouse is a small and select art museum featuring the works of Rockwell Kent and other island artists.

The spectacular view from the grassy slope in front of the lighthouse is the real prize. The vista sweeps across a marsh, past one of the island's historic hotels, past melancholy Manana Island and across the sea beyond. Get here early if you want a good seat for the sunset.

Artists are still attracted here in great number, and in summer many open their **studios** to visitors during posted hours. Some of the artwork runs along the lines of predictable seascapes and sunsets, but much of it rises above the banal. Look for the bulletin board along the main pathway in the village for walking directions to the studios and a listing of the days and hours they're open.

Moments Quiet Time

Pack a picnic lunch and an engrossing book and plan to spend a lazy, sunny afternoon lounging on the cliffs that line Monhegan's eastern shore. You haven't experienced utter indolence until you've kicked back a few hours here, relaxing to the calls of seagulls and lulling surf crashing against the rocks. Type A personalities who find this lack of activity unnerving can profitably occupy themselves by scanning the waters for whales, which feed just offshore.

WHERE TO STAY & DINE

Monhegan House ⭐   The handsome Monhegan House has been accommodating guests since 1870, and it has the patina of a venerable lodging house. The rooms at this four-story walk-up are austere but comfortable; everyone shares clean, dormitory-style bathrooms. The lobby with fireplace is a welcome spot to sit and take the fog-induced chill out of your bones (even summers can be cool here), while the front deck is the place to lounge and keep an eye on the comings and goings of the village.

Monhegan Island, ME 04852. © 800/599-7983 or 207/594-7983. www.monheganhouse.com. Fax 207/596-6472. 33 units (all with shared bathrooms). $109–$119 double. Rates include breakfast. AE, DISC, MC, V. Closed Columbus Day to Memorial Day. **Amenities:** Restaurant (casual dining). *In room:* No phone.

Trailing Yew ⭐   This friendly, informal place, popular with hikers and birders, has been taking in guests since 1929. Guest rooms are simply furnished in a pleasantly dated summer-home style. Only one of the four buildings has electricity (most but not all bathrooms have electricity); those staying in rooms without power are provided a kerosene lamp (bring a small flashlight—just in case). Rooms are also unheated, so bring a sleeping bag if the weather's chilly. The Trailing Yew has more of an easygoing, youth-hostel camaraderie; if you're the private type, opt for the Monhegan House.

Monhegan Island, ME 04852. © 800/592-2520 or 207/596-0440. 37 units (all but 1 share bathrooms). $134 double. Rates include breakfast, dinner, taxes, and tips. No credit cards. Closed mid-Oct to mid-May. **Amenities:** Restaurant (New England/family style). *In room:* No phone.

4 Penobscot Bay

Traveling eastward along the Maine coast, those who pay attention to such things will notice they're suddenly heading almost due north around Rockland. The culprit behind this geographic quirk is Penobscot Bay, a sizeable bite out of the Maine coast that forces a lengthy northerly detour to cross the head of the bay where the Penobscot River flows in at Bucksport.

You'll find some of Maine's most distinctive coastal scenery in this region, which is dotted with broad offshore islands and high hills rising above the mainland shores. Although the mouth of Penobscot Bay is occupied by two large islands, its waters can still churn with vigor when the tides and winds conspire.

Penobscot Bay's western shore gets a heavy stream of tourist traffic, especially along Route 1 through the village of Camden. Nonetheless, this is a good destination to get a taste of the Maine coast. Services for travelers are abundant, although during peak season, a small miracle will be required to find a weekend guest room without a reservation.

Penobscot Bay

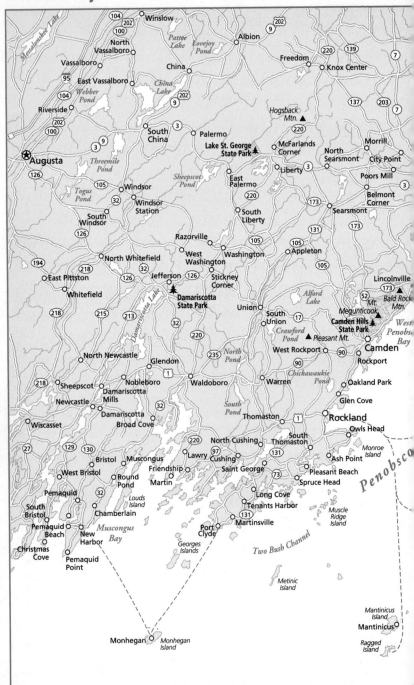

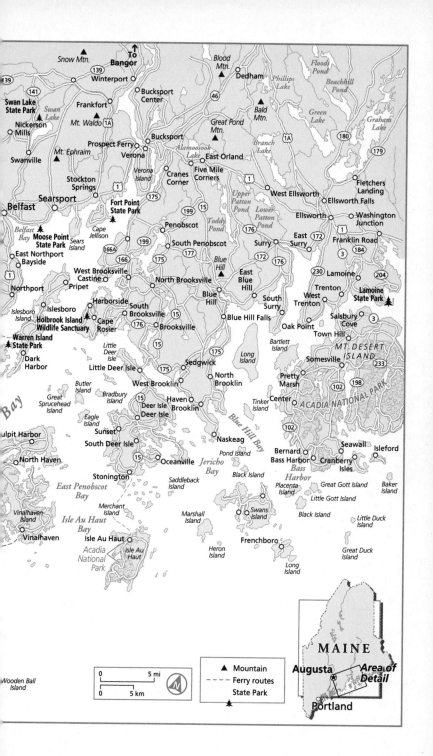

To Bangor

Snow Mtn.

Blood Mtn.

Dedham

Floods Pond

Beachhill Pond

Winterport

Phillips Lake

Bucksport Center

Green Lake

Graham Lake

Frankfort

Bald Mtn.

Swan Lake State Park

Swan Lake

Mt. Waldo

Great Pond Mtn.

180

179

Nickerson Mills

Prospect Ferry

Bucksport

Alamoosook Lake

East Orland

Branch Lake

Fletchers Landing

Swanville

Mt. Ephraim

Verona

Five Mile Corners

West Ellsworth

Ellsworth Falls

Washington Junction

Stockton Springs

Verona Island

Cranes Corner

Upper Patton Pond

Ellsworth

Searsport

Fort Point State Park

Lower Patton Pond

East Surry

172

Franklin Road

Belfast

199

Penobscot

Toddy Pond

Surry

184

Belfast Bay

Cape Jellison

South Penobscot

Blue Hill

East Blue Hill

172

230

Lamoine

204

Moose Point State Park

Sears Island

177

3

East Northport

Bayside

West Brooksville

North Brooksville

Blue Hill

South Surry

Oak Point

Trenton

West Trenton

Lamoine State Park

Northport

Castine

Pripet

Blue Hill Falls

Salsbury Cove

Town Hill

MT. DESERT ISLAND

Harborside

South Brooksville

Bartlett Island

Somesville

233

Islesboro Island

Holbrook Island Wildlife Sanctuary

Cape Rosier

Brooksville

Long Island

Pretty Marsh

102

198

Warren Island State Park

Dark Harbor

Little Deer Isle

Sedgwick

North Brooklin

Center

ACADIA NATIONAL PARK

Butler Island

West Brooklin

Tinker Island

102

Great Sprucehead Island

Bradbury Island

Haven Brooklin

Eagle Island

Deer Isle

Bernard

Bass Harbor

Seawall

Isleford

Pulpit Harbor

Sunset

South Deer Isle

Naskeag

Pond Island

Cranberry Isles

Bass Harbor

North Haven

Oceanville

Jericho Bay

Black Island

Placenta Island

Great Gott Island

Baker Island

Vinalhaven Island

Stonington

Saddleback Island

Little Gott Island

Black Island

Little Duck Island

East Penobscot Bay

Merchant Island

Marshall Island

Swans Island

Great Duck Island

Vinalhaven

Isle Au Haut Bay

Heron Island

Frenchboro

Little Duck Island

Bay

Acadia National Park

Isle Au Haut

Isle Au Haut

Long Island

Wooden Ball Island

MAINE

Augusta

Area of Detail

0   5 mi

0   5 km

▲ Mountain

--- Ferry routes

State Park

Portland

577

ROCKLAND 🖈

Located on the southwest edge of Penobscot Bay, Rockland has long been proud of its brick-and-blue-collar waterfront-town reputation. Built around the fishing industry, Rockland historically dabbled in tourism on the side, but with the decline of the fisheries and the rise of the tourist economy in Maine, the balance has shifted—in the last decade, Rockland has been colonized by creative restaurateurs, innkeepers, and other small-business folks who are painting it with an unaccustomed gloss.

There's a small park on the waterfront from which the fleet of windjammers comes and goes, but more appealing than Rockland's waterfront is its commercial downtown—basically one long street lined with historic brick architecture. If it's picturesque harbor towns you're seeking, head to Camden, Rockport, Port Clyde, or Stonington; but Rockland makes a great base for exploring this beautiful coastal region, especially if you like your towns a bit rough around the edges.

ESSENTIALS

GETTING THERE Route 1 passes directly through Rockland. Rockland's tiny airport is served by **Colgan Air** (📞 **800/272-5488** or 207/596-7604), with daily flights from Boston and Bar Harbor. **Concord Trailways** (📞 **800/639-3317**) offers bus service from Bangor and Portland.

VISITOR INFORMATION The **Rockland/Thomaston Area Chamber of Commerce** (📞 **800/562-2529** or 207/596-0376) staffs an information desk at Harbor Park. It's open from Memorial Day to Labor Day, daily from 9am to 5pm; the rest of the year, Monday through Friday from 9am to 5pm.

SPECIAL EVENTS The **Maine Lobster Festival** (📞 **800/562-2529** or 207/596-0376) takes place at Harbor Park the first weekend in August (plus the preceding Thurs and Fri). Entertainers and vendors of all sorts of Maine products fill the waterfront parking lot. The event includes the Maine Sea Goddess Coronation Pageant.

MUSEUMS

Farnsworth Museum 🖈🖈 Rockland, for all its rough edges, has long and historic ties to the arts. Noted sculptor Louise Nevelson grew up here, and in 1935 philanthropist Lucy Farnsworth bequeathed a fortune large enough to establish the Farnsworth Museum, which has since joined the ranks of the most respected art museums in New England. The Farnsworth has a superb collection of paintings and sculptures by renowned American artists with a connection to Maine. This includes not only Nevelson and three generations of Wyeths (N. C., Andrew, and Jamie), but also Rockwell Kent, Childe Hassam, and Maurice Prendergast. Just down the block in the former Pratt Memorial Methodist Church is the Farnsworth Center for the Wyeth Family, where you'll find Andrew and Betsy Wyeth's personal collection of Maine-related art.

The Farnsworth also owns two other buildings open to the public. The Farnsworth Homestead, behind the museum, offers a glimpse into the life of prosperous coastal Victorians. A 25-minute drive away in the village of Cushing is the Olson House, perhaps Maine's most famous home, which was immortalized in Andrew Wyeth's painting *Christina's World*. Ask at the museum for directions and information (closed in winter).

52 Main St., Rockland. 📞 207/596-6457. www.farnsworthmuseum.org. Admission $9 adults, $8 seniors, $5 students 18 and over, free for ages 17 and under (all prices discounted $1 in winter). Summer daily 9am–5pm; winter Tues–Sat 10am–5pm, Sun 1–5pm.

Windjammer Tours

During the long transition from sail to steam, captains of the fancy new steamships belittled the old-fashioned sailing ships as "windjammers." The term stuck, and through a curious metamorphosis, the name evolved into a term connoting adventure and romance.

Today, windjammer vacations combine adventure with limited creature comforts—sort of like lodging at a backcountry cabin on the water. Guests typically bunk in small two-person cabins, which usually offer cold running water and a porthole to let in fresh air, but not much else.

Maine is the capital of windjammer cruising in the United States, and the two most active Maine harbors are **Rockland** and **Camden** on Penobscot Bay. Cruises last from 3 days to 1 week, during which these handsome, creaky vessels poke around the tidal inlets and small coves that ring the beautiful bay. It's a superb way to see Maine's coast the way it's historically been explored—from the water, looking inland.

Cruises vary from ship to ship and from week to week, depending on the inclinations of the captain and the vagaries of the weather. The "standard" cruise often features a stop at one or more of the myriad spruce-studded Maine islands, hearty breakfasts, and a palpable sense of maritime history. A windjammer vacation demands you use all your senses, to smell the tang of the salt air, to hear the rhythmic creaking of the masts in the evening, and to feel the frigid ocean waters as you leap in for a bracing dip.

More than a dozen windjammers offer cruises in the Penobscot Bay region during the summer. Rates run between about $110 and $150 per person per day, with modest discounts early and late in the season. The ships vary widely in size and vintage; accommodations range from cramped and rustic to reasonably spacious and well-appointed. Ideally, you'll have a chance to look at a couple of ships to find one that suits you before signing up. If that's not practical, call ahead to the **Maine Windjammer Association** (© **800/807-9463;** www.sailmainecoast.com) and request a packet of brochures, which allows comparison shopping.

Owls Head Transportation Museum ⚐ You don't have to be a car buff or plane nut to enjoy this museum. It has an extraordinary collection of cars, motorcycles, bikes, and planes, displayed in a hangar-like building at the edge of the Knox County Airport. Look for the early Harley-Davidson and the sleek 1929 Rolls-Royce Phantom.

Rte. 73, 3 miles (5km) south of Rockland, Owls Head. © **207/594-4418.** www.ohtm.org. Admission $6 adults, $4 children 5–12; $16 per family. Apr–Oct daily 10am–5pm; Nov–Mar daily 10am–4pm.

WHERE TO STAY

Capt. Lindsey House Inn ⚐⚐ The brick Capt. Lindsey House (1835) is just a couple minutes' stroll from the Farnsworth Museum. Guests enter through a doorway a few steps off Main Street, and then pass into an opulent common area with a mix of antique and contemporary furniture. Bedrooms are decorated in a contemporary country style; bold colors meld with traditional design. Even the smaller units are comfortable; those on the third floor feature yellow pine floors and antique Oriental carpets. Note that rooms facing the street can be noisy.

5 Lindsey St., Rockland, ME 04841. © 800/523-2145 or 207/596-7950. Fax 207/596-2758. www.lindsey house.com. 9 units. Peak season $120–$175 double; Columbus Day to Memorial Day $65–$110 double. Rates include continental breakfast. AE, DISC, MC, V. **Amenities:** Restaurant (pub fare). *In room:* A/C, TV, dataport, hair dryer.

LimeRock Inn ★★   This beautiful 1890 Queen Anne–style inn is located on a quiet side street just 2 blocks from Main Street. The innkeepers have done a commendable job converting what could have been a gloomy manse into one of the region's better lodging choices. Attention has been paid to detail throughout, from the country Victorian furniture to the Egyptian-cotton linens. All units are welcoming, but among the best is the Island Cottage Room, an airy chamber converted from an old shed and featuring a private deck and Jacuzzi. If it's big elegance you're looking for, opt for the Grand Manan Room, which has a four-poster bed, fireplace, and double Jacuzzi.

96 Limerock St., Rockland, ME 04841. © 800/546-3762 or 207/594-2257. www.limerockinn.com. 8 units. $100–$195 double. Rates include breakfast. MC, V. *In room:* No phone.

Samoset Resort ★★   The Samoset is a something of a Maine coast rarity—a modern, self-contained resort that offers contemporary styling, ocean views, and lots of golf. Located on 230 acres (93 hectares) at the mouth of Rockland Harbor, the hotel and town houses are surrounded by the handsome 18-hole golf course. The lobby is constructed of massive timbers, and all guest rooms have balconies or terraces. Golfers love the place—it's been called Pebble Beach East—and families will find plenty of activities for the kids. The resort also has the best sunset stroll in the state—you can ramble across the golf course to a breakwater that leads out to a picturesque lighthouse. The one downside: For the high prices charged, the staff is less polished than you would expect.

Rockport, ME 04856. © 800/341-1650 or 207/594-2511. www.samoset.com. 250 units. Mid-July to August $269–$299 double, $349 suite; fall $189–$239 double, $289 suite; winter $119–$149 double, $199 suite; May to mid-June $159–$199 double, $249 suite; mid-June to early July $199–$239 double, $289 suite. AE, DISC, MC, V. Valet parking available. **Amenities:** 4 restaurants (3 casual/American, 1 Continental/fine dining); indoor and outdoor pools; golf course; tennis courts; health club; Jacuzzi; sauna; children's programs; concierge; courtesy car; business center; room service; massage; babysitting; laundry service; dry cleaning. *In room:* A/C, TV w/ pay movies, iron.

WHERE TO DINE

Cafe Miranda ★★ *(Value)* GLOBAL   Cafe Miranda provides the best value for the buck of any restaurant in Maine. Hidden away on a side street, this tiny restaurant draws liberally from cuisines from around the world, and given its wide-ranging culinary inclinations, it comes as something of a surprise just how well everything is prepared. The char-grilled pork and shrimp cakes with a ginger-lime-coconut sauce are superb, as are the barbecued pork ribs with a smoked jalapeño sauce.

15 Oak St. © 207/594-2034. www.cafemiranda.com. Reservations recommended. Main courses $10–$19.50. DISC, MC, V. Tues–Sat 5:30pm–9:30pm (until 8:30pm in winter).

Primo ★★★ MEDITERRANEAN/NEW AMERICAN   When Primo opened in 2000, it immediately attracted New York–size buzz, and with good reason. Executive chef Melissa Kelly graduated first in her class at the Culinary Institute of America, and won the 1999 James Beard Foundation award for "best chef in the Northeast." The restaurant occupies a century-old home a short drive south of downtown (no views to speak of). The menu draws from local products when available. You might choose from grilled duckling breast on a bed of mashed sweet potatoes with braised cabbage and a caramelized apple jus, or pepper-crusted venison with pecan wild rice.

2 South Main St. (Rte. 173). (© 207/596-0770. www.primorestaurant.com. Reservations recommended. Main courses $14–$28. AE, DISC, MC, V. Thurs–Mon 5:30–9:30pm; call for off-season days and hours.

CAMDEN ★★

Camden is a quintessential coastal Maine village. Set at the foot of the wooded Camden Hills on a picturesque harbor that no Hollywood movie set could improve, the affluent village has attracted the gentry of the Eastern Seaboard for more than a century. Elaborate mansions still dominate the shady side streets (many have been converted into bed-and-breakfasts), and Camden is possessed of a grace and sophistication that eludes many other coastal towns.

On the downside: All this attention and Camden's growing appeal to bus tours are having a deleterious impact. The merchandise at the shops seems to be trending downward in appeal to a lower common denominator, and the constant summer congestion distracts somewhat from the village's inherent charm. If you don't come expecting a pristine and undiscovered village, you're likely to enjoy the place all the more.

ESSENTIALS

GETTING THERE   Camden is on Route 1. Coming from the south, shave a few minutes off your trip by turning left onto Route 90, 6 miles (10km) past Waldoboro, bypassing Rockland. The most traffic-free route from southern Maine is to Augusta via the Maine Turnpike, then via Route 17 to Route 90 to Route 1. **Concord Trailways** (© **800/639-3317**) offers bus service from Bangor and Portland.

VISITOR INFORMATION   The **Rockport-Camden-Lincolnville Chamber of Commerce** (© **800/223-5459** or 207/236-4404) runs a visitor center at the Public Landing in Camden; open Monday through Friday from 9am to 5pm and Saturday from 10am to 5pm. In summer, it's also open Sunday from 10am to 4pm.

EXPLORING CAMDEN

Camden Hills State Park (© **207/236-3109**) is about 1 mile (1.6km) north of the village center on Route 1. This 6,500-acre (2,633-hectare) park features an oceanside picnic area, 112 campsites, a winding toll road up 800-foot (240m) Mount Battie with spectacular views from the summit, and well-marked hiking trails. The day-use fee is $2 for adults, 50¢ for children 5 to 11.

The 57-foot (17m) windjammer *Surprise* ★★ (© **207/236-4687**; www.camdenmainesailing.com), launched in 1918, departs on 2-hour cruises from the Camden Public Landing. Daily excursions ($28) are offered from June to October. Reservations are recommended; children must be 12 or older.

The *Schooner Lazy Jack* ★★ (© **207/230-0602**; www.schoonerlazyjack.com) has been plying the waters since 1947, and is modeled after the Gloucester fishing schooners of the late 19th century. There's a maximum of 13 passengers; children must be 10 or older. The 2-hour tours cost $25 per person.

Maine Sport Outfitters (© **800/722-0826** or 207/236-8797) offers **sea-kayaking tours** ★ of Camden's scenic harbor. The 2-hour beginners' excursion ($45) takes paddlers out to Curtis Island, an easy way to get a taste of the area's maritime culture. Longer trips and instruction are also available. Sign up for the

> ## ⌒Moments A Morning in the Park
>
> Camden Hills State Park attracts plenty of visitors, most of whom listlessly drive to the summit of Mount Battie, park for a few moments, then drive back down. Strive for more than that. The trail up the east side of **Mount Megunticook** is often magical early on a still summer morning—the low sun glints off the waters of Penobscot Bay, Camden Harbor looks like a perfect diorama, and the hollows of the hills behind you are muffled in low clouds. You're alone with the world.
>
> Here's how you do it: Get up early (*really* early—the summer sun doesn't dawdle in Maine). Park near the campground and follow the well-maintained trail to a set of open ledges, which requires only about 30 to 45 minutes' exertion to memorable views.

tours either at the store (on Rte. 1 in Rockport, a few minutes' drive south of Camden) or at the boathouse, located at the head of the harbor.

WHERE TO STAY

South of the village center are the **Cedar Crest Motel,** 115 Elm St. (© **800/ 422-4964** or 207/236-4839), a handsome compound with a shuttle-bus connection downtown ($109 to $132 in peak season); and longtime mainstay **Towne Motel,** 68 Elm St. (© **207/236-3377**), within walking distance of the village ($99–$115). Right in town, just across the footbridge, is the **Best Western Camden Riverhouse Hotel,** 11 Tannery Lane (© **800/755-7483** or 207/236-0500), with an indoor pool and fitness center ($159–$209).

Camden Harbour Inn   This 1871 inn sits in a quiet neighborhood with a great view of the harbor and mountains beyond. It's one of the few old-fashioned Victorian-era hotels in town that hasn't been extensively refurbished, and still retains something of a creaky holiday feel with its floral wallpaper, mix of simple antiques and ill-advised modern furnishings, and thin towels. Most rooms have views, eight have balconies or terraces, and six have fireplaces. The inn is within walking distance of downtown.

83 Bayview St., Camden, ME 04843. © 800/236-4266 or 207/236-4200. Fax 207/236-7063. www.camden harbourinn.com. 22 units. Peak season $195–$255 double (including full breakfast); off-season $135–$195 (including continental breakfast). 2-night minimum stay in peak season. AE, DISC, MC, V. Children 12 and over welcome. Pets accepted on ground floor. *In room:* TV.

Cedarholm Garden Bay 🏖🏖   Cedarholm began years ago with four simple cottages just north of Camden along Route 1. When Joyce and Barry Jobson took over in 1995, they built a road down to the 460 feet (138m) of dramatic cobblestone shoreline and constructed two modern, steeply gabled cedar cottages, each with two bedrooms. These are wonderful places, with great detailing like pocket doors, cobblestone fireplaces, and Jacuzzis. In 2001, they built two more cottages, called Osprey and Tern, which are smaller and have fewer amenities, but are no less dramatically sited. (Our two-star rating reflects the unique appeal of the shorefront cottages.) Guests staying up the hill in the smaller and older cottages can still wander down to the shore and lounge on the deck overlooking the bay. It's noisier up above, where it's closer to Route 1, and the rates reflect that.

Rte. 1, Lincolnville Beach, ME 04849. © 207/236-3886. 8 units. Oceanfront cottages $250–$295 double; oceanview cottages $85–$155 double. Rates include breakfast. 2-night minimum stay in some cottages. MC, V. *In room:* TV.

Inn at Sunrise Point ★★★   This peaceful sanctuary 4 miles (6km) north of Camden Harbor is a world apart from the bustling town. The service is helpful, and the setting can't be beat. Situated on the edge of Penobscot Bay, the inn consists of a cluster of contemporary yet classic shingled buildings. The predominant sounds here are of birds singing and waves lapping at the cobblestone shore. Bedrooms are full of amenities, including fireplaces and individual heat controls. The cottages are at the deluxe end of the scale, all with double Jacuzzis, fireplaces, fridges, and private decks.

Rte. 1 (P.O. Box 1344), Camden, ME 04843. ℂ 800/435-6278 or 207/236-7716. Fax 207/236-0820. www.sunrisepoint.com. 7 units. $175–$250 double room; $275–$395 cottage. Rates include breakfast. AE, MC, V. Closed Nov–late May. No children permitted. *In room:* TV/VCR, hair dryer.

Maine Stay ★★   The Maine Stay is known for its congenial hospitality. This classic slate-roofed New England home (dating back to 1802) is within walking distance of both downtown and Camden Hills State Park. All rooms have ceiling fans and antiques; four have TVs as well. The downstairs Carriage House Room is away from the buzz of traffic on Route 1 and boasts its own stone patio. Perhaps the most memorable part of a stay here is getting to know the three hosts—Peter Smith; his wife, Donny; and her twin sister, Diana Robson. They're genuinely interested in their guests' well-being, and will offer dozens of day-trip suggestions.

22 High St., Camden, ME 04843. ℂ 207/236-9636. www.mainestay.com. 8 units. $80–$165 double. Rates include breakfast. AE, MC, V. Children over 10 welcome. *In room:* Coffeemaker, hair dryer, no phone.

Norumbega ★★★   This Victorian-era stone castle is big enough to ensure privacy, but intimate enough to allow you to get to know the other guests— mingling often occurs in the afternoon, when the innkeepers put out fresh-baked cookies. Overlooking the bay, the Norumbega has remarkable architectural detailing—extravagant woodwork and a stunning oak-and-mahogany inlaid floor. Five guest rooms have fireplaces, most have TVs, and three "garden-level rooms" have private decks. Two rooms rank among the finest in New England—the Library Suite, with interior balcony, and the sprawling Penthouse, with its superlative views.

61 High St., Camden, ME 04843. ℂ 207/236-4646. Fax 207/236-0824. www.norumbegainn.com. 13 units. July to mid-Oct $160–$475 double; mid-May to June and late Oct $125–375; Nov to mid-May $99–$295. Rates include breakfast. 2-night minimum stay summer, weekends, and holidays. AE, DISC, MC, V. Children 7 and over welcome. *In room:* Dataport, hair dryer.

Whitehall Inn ★   The Whitehall is a distinguished and understated New England resort, listed on the National Register of Historic Places, where you half expect to find a young Cary Grant in a blue blazer tickling the ivories on the lobby's 1904 Steinway. Set at the edge of town in a structure that dates to 1834, the inn has a striking architectural integrity with its columns, gables, and long roofline. Accommodations are simple but appealing. (Ask for a room away from the Route 1 noise.) The Whitehall occupies a minor footnote in the annals of American literature—a young local poet recited her poems here for guests in 1912, stunning the audience with her eloquence. Her name? Edna St. Vincent Millay. The inn is quite popular with a more mature blue-blood clientele, many of whom have been coming every summer for generations.

52 High St., Camden, ME 04843. ℂ 800/789-6565 or 207/236-3391. Fax 207/236-4427. www.whitehall-inn.com. 50 units (8 units share 4 bathrooms). July to mid-Oct $135–$165 double with private bathroom, $105–$115 double with shared bathroom. Rates include breakfast. Discounts available in late May and June. AE, MC, V. Closed mid-Oct to late May. **Amenities:** Restaurant (traditional New England); tennis court; tour desk; babysitting. *In room:* No phone.

WHERE TO DINE

Atlantica ✦✦ CONTEMPORARY AMERICAN   Atlantica gets high marks for its innovative seafood menu and its consistently well-prepared fare. Located on the waterfront with a small indoor seating area and an equally small outdoor deck, Atlantica features creative dishes like pan-seared tuna, served with artichoke and smoked tomatoes, and scallops glazed with ginger and brown sugar. Start with a cup of the lobster-corn chowder.

1 Bayview Landing. ✆ 888/507-8514 or 207/236-6011. www.atlanticarestaurant.com. Reservations recommended. Main courses $8–$14 lunch, $18–$30 dinner. AE, MC, V. Summer Tues–Sun 10:30am–2pm and 5:30–9pm; off-season Thurs–Sat 10:30am–2pm, Tues–Sat 5:30–9pm.

Cappy's Chowder House SEAFOOD/AMERICAN   Cappy's is a local institution that's more memorable for its lively atmosphere than for its food. There's prime rib, a hearty seafood stew, and the famous chowder (which has gotten a nod from *Gourmet* magazine). "Old-time sodas" are a specialty.

1 Main St. ✆ 207/236-2254. Main courses $5.95–$14.95. MC, V. Daily 7:30am–midnight.

Peter Ott's ✦✦ AMERICAN   Peter Ott's opened in 1974 and has satisfied customers ever since with its no-nonsense fare. While it resembles a steakhouse with its wood tables and manly meat dishes (like char-broiled Black Angus), it's grown beyond that to satisfy more diverse tastes. In fact, it offers some of the better prepared seafood in town, including grilled salmon with a lemon caper sauce. Leave room for the lemon-almond crumb tart.

16 Bayview St. ✆ 207/236-4032. Main courses $13.95–$22.95. MC, V. Daily 5:30–9:30pm.

The Waterfront ✦ SEAFOOD   The Waterfront disproves the theory that "the better the view, the worse the food." Here you can watch yachts and windjammers come and go (angle for a seat on the deck), yet still be reasonably pleased with what you're served. Look for fried clams, crab cakes, and boiled lobster. On the more adventurous side, you'll find black sesame shrimp salad (served on noodles with a Thai vinaigrette) or seafood linguine with caramelized balsamic onions. A lighter pub menu is served between 2:30 and 5pm.

Bayview St. on Camden Harbor. ✆ 207/236-3747. Main courses $6.95–$13.95 lunch, $12.95–$22.95 dinner. AE, MC, V. Daily 11:30am–2:30pm and 5–10pm (closes earlier in off-season).

5 The Blue Hill Peninsula

The Blue Hill Peninsula is a back-roads paradise. If you're of a mind to get lost on country lanes that suddenly dead-end at the sea or inexplicably start to loop back on themselves, this is the place. In contrast to the western shores of Penobscot Bay, the Blue Hill Peninsula has more of a lost-in-time character. The roads are hilly, winding, and narrow, passing through leafy forests, along venerable saltwater farms, and touching on the edge of an azure inlet here or there.

CASTINE ✦✦

Castine gets our vote for the most gracious village in Maine. It's not so much the stunningly handsome mid-19th-century homes that fill the side streets, nor is it the location on a quiet peninsula, 16 miles (26km) south of RV-clotted Route 1.

No, what lends Castine its charm are the splendid, towering elm trees, which still overarch many of the village streets. Before Dutch elm disease ravaged the nation's tree-lined streets, much of the United States once looked like this, and it's easy to slip into a debilitating nostalgia for this most graceful tree, even if you're too young to remember America of the elms. Through perseverance and a measure of luck, Castine has managed to keep several hundred regal elms alive, and it's worth the detour for these alone.

For history buffs, Castine offers much more. This outpost served as a strategic town in various battles between British, Dutch, French, and feisty colonials in the centuries following its settlement in 1613. It was occupied by each of those groups at some point, and historical personages like Miles Standish and Paul Revere passed through during one epoch or another. The town has a dignified, aristocratic bearing, and it somehow seems appropriate that Tory-dominated Castine welcomed the British with open arms during the Revolution.

ESSENTIALS
GETTING THERE   Castine is 16 miles (26km) south of Route 1. Turn south on Route 175 in Orland (east of Bucksport) and follow this to Route 166, which winds its way to Castine. Route 166A offers an alternate route along Penobscot Bay.

VISITOR INFORMATION   Castine lacks a formal information center, but the clerk at the **Town Office** (✆ 207/326-4502) is often helpful with local questions.

EXPLORING CASTINE
The **Wilson Museum,** on Perkins Street (✆ 207/326-8753, or 207/326-8545 between 5 and 9pm), is an attractive and quirky anthropological museum constructed in 1921. It contains the collections of John Howard Wilson, an archaeologist and collector of prehistoric artifacts. His gleanings are neatly arranged in a staid, classical arrangement of the sort that proliferated in the late 19th and early 20th centuries. The museum is open from the end of May to the end of September, Tuesday through Sunday from 2 to 5pm; admission is free.

Next door is the **John Perkins House,** Castine's oldest home. It was occupied by the British during the Revolution and the War of 1812, and a tour features demonstrations of old-fashioned cooking techniques. It's open July and August on Wednesday and Sunday from 2 to 5pm. Admission is $2.

Castine is also home to the **Maine Maritime Academy** (✆ 207/326-8545), which trains sailors for the rigors of life at sea. The campus is on the western edge of the village, and the hulking gray S.S. *Maine* is often docked in Castine, almost overwhelming the village with its sheer size. Free half-hour tours of the ship are offered in summer (assuming the ship is in port) from 10am to noon and 1 to 4pm.

Castine sits on a lovely open harbor, with farmland and forest edging the watery expanse. **Castine Kayak Adventures** ☆ (© **207/326-9045;** www.castinekayak.com) offers 6-hour ($105) and 3-hour ($55) sea-kayak tours departing from Dennett's Wharf restaurant. Both trips are appropriate for those without experience. You'll often spot wildlife, including bald eagles, harbor seals, and ospreys.

WHERE TO STAY

Castine Harbor Lodge ☆ *Kids*   Housed in a grand 1893 mansion (the only inn on the water in Castine), this place is run with an informal good cheer that allows kids to feel at home amid the regal architecture. The parlor is dominated by a pool table, and there's Scrabble and Nintendo for the asking. The front porch, with views that extend across the bay to the Camden Hills, offers one of the best places in the state to unwind. The spacious guest rooms are eclectically appointed with antiques and modern furnishings. Families might consider the annex, where four rooms share two bathrooms. And if you're not traveling with a family? It's still a great spot if you prefer well-worn comfort to high-end elegance. Added in 2001 were a 250-foot (75m) dock and three guest moorings for those arriving by sea.

Perkins St. (P.O. Box 215), Castine, ME 04421. © 207/326-4335. www.castinemaine.com. 14 units (4 units in annex share 2 bathrooms). $85–$195 double. Rates include continental breakfast. DC, DISC, MC, V. Pets allowed ($10 per night). **Amenities:** Wine bar (pub fare). *In room:* No phone.

Castine Inn ☆   The Castine Inn is a Maine coast rarity—a hotel that was originally built (in 1898) as a hotel, not as a residence that was later converted. This handsome village inn, designed in an eclectic Georgian–Federal Revival style, has a fine front porch and attractive gardens. Inside, the lobby takes its cue from the 1940s, with wingback chairs and love seats. Guest rooms on the two upper floors (no elevator) are simply if unevenly furnished in a Colonial Revival style. Note that the innkeepers have revamped several units, adding luxe touches. These are markedly more inviting than the other rooms and are worth the extra splurge.

Main St. (P.O. Box 41), Castine, ME 04421. © 207/326-4365. Fax 207/326-4570. www.castineinn.com. 19 units. $90–$150 double; $215 suite. Rates include breakfast. 2-night minimum stay July–Aug. MC, V. Closed Nov–Apr. Children 8 and over welcome. **Amenities:** Restaurant (see below); sauna. *In room:* No phone.

Pentagöet Inn ☆☆   This quirky 1894 structure with its prominent turret is comfortable without being fussy, personal without being overly intimate. New owners took over in 2000 and gave it a touch of travel exotica, with decor that includes an intriguing photo of Gandhi that once hung in the Indian embassy in Zaire, as well as an oil painting of Lenin liberated from a flea market in Tajikistan. Guest rooms in the main house are furnished with a similarly eclectic eye and a splash of romance. Rooms in the adjacent Perkins Street building—a more austere Federal-era house—have also been done over; all have ceiling fans and a smattering of antiques.

Main St. (P.O. Box 4), Castine, ME 04421. © 800/845-1701 or 207/326-8616. Fax 207/326-9382. www. pentagoet.com. 16 units. $75–$150 double. Rates include breakfast. MC, V. Closed Nov–Apr. Pets accepted by reservation. Children 12 and older welcome. **Amenities:** Restaurant (regional/global). *In room:* No phone.

WHERE TO DINE

Castine Inn ☆☆ NEW AMERICAN   At this handsome hotel dining room, you'll find Castine's best fare and some of the better food in the state. Chef/owner Tom Gutow served stints at Bouley and Verbena in New York, and

isn't timid about experimenting with local meats and produce. E.
such as lobster with vanilla butter, mango mayonnaise, and tropical-fru.
One night each week, when the restaurant offers a buffet, you're better o.
heading to Dennett's Wharf.

Main St. ✆ 207/326-4365. Reservations recommended. Main courses $15–$26. MC, V. Daily 6–9pm. Closed mid-Dec to May.

Dennett's Wharf PUB FARE   Located in a soaring waterfront sail loft, Dennett's Wharf offers upscale bar food amid a lively setting leavened with a good selection of microbrews. If the weather's decent, there's outdoor dining with superb harbor views. Look for grilled sandwiches and salads at lunch; dinner brings lobster, stir-fry, and steak teriyaki.

Sea St. (next to the Town Dock). ✆ 207/326-9045. www.dennettswharf.com. Reservations recommended in summer and for parties of 6 or more. Main courses $5.50–$17.95 lunch, $8.95–$23.95 dinner. AE, DISC, MC, V. Daily 11am–midnight. Closed mid-Oct to Apr 30.

DEER ISLE

Deer Isle is well off the beaten path but worth the detour from Route 1 if your tastes run to pastoral countryside with a nautical edge. Winding roads cross through forest and farmland, and travelers are rewarded with sudden glimpses of the sun-dappled ocean and mint-green coves.

Deer Isle doesn't cater exclusively to tourists, as many coastal regions do. It's still occupied by fifth-generation fishermen, farmers, longtime rusticators, and artists who prize their seclusion. The village of **Deer Isle** has a handful of inns and galleries, but its primary focus is to serve locals and summer residents, not transients. The village of **Stonington,** on the southern tip, is a rough-hewn sea town. Despite serious incursions over the past 5 years by galleries and enterprises dependent on tourism, it remains dominated in spirit by fishermen and the occasional quarryworker.

ESSENTIALS

GETTING THERE   Deer Isle is accessible via several country roads from Route 1. Coming from the west, head south on Route 175 off Route 1 in Orland, then connect to Route 15 to Deer Isle. From the east, head south on Route 172 to Blue Hill, where you can pick up Route 15. Deer Isle is connected to the mainland via a high, narrow suspension bridge, built in 1938, which can be somewhat harrowing to cross in high winds.

VISITOR INFORMATION   The **Deer Isle–Stonington Chamber of Commerce** (✆ 207/348-6124) staffs a summer information booth just beyond the bridge on Little Deer Isle. It's open daily from 10am to 4pm, depending on volunteer availability.

EXPLORING DEER ISLE

Deer Isle, with its network of narrow roads to nowhere, is ideal for perfunctory rambling. It's a pleasure to explore by car and is also inviting to travel by bike, although hasty and careening fishermen in pickups can make this unnerving at times. Especially tranquil is the narrow road between Deer Isle and Sunshine to the east. Plan to stop and explore the rocky coves and inlets along the way. To get here, head toward Stonington on Route 15, and just south of the village of Deer Isle, turn east toward Stinson Neck and continue along this scenic byway for about 10 miles (16km).

Stonington, at the southern tip of Deer Isle, consists of one commercial street that wraps along the harbor's edge. While B&Bs and boutiques have made inroads here recently, it's still a mostly rough-and-tumble waterfront town. If you hear industrial sounds emanating from just offshore, that's probably the stone quarry on Crotch Island, which has been in operation for more than a century.

Haystack Mountain School of Crafts 🐦   The 40-acre (16-hectare) ocean-side campus of this respected summer crafts school, established in 1950, is visually stunning. Edward Larrabee Barnes, who set the buildings on a hillside overlooking the waters of Jericho Bay, designed it in the 1960s. Barnes managed to play up the views while respecting the delicate landscape by constructing a series of small structures on pilings that seem to float above the earth. The class-rooms and studios are linked by boardwalks, many of which are connected to a wide central staircase, ending at the "Flag Deck," a sort of open-air commons just above the shoreline. The buildings and classrooms are closed to the public, but summer visitors are welcome to walk to the Flag Deck and stroll the nature trail adjacent to the campus. The drive to the campus is outstanding.

Sunshine Rd. 🕐 207/348-2306. www.haystack-mtn.org. Donations appreciated. Summer daily 9am–5pm; tours Wed 1pm. Head south of the village of Deer Isle on Rte. 15; turn left on Greenlaw District Rd. and follow signs to school, approximately 7 miles (11km).

A DAY TRIP TO ISLE AU HAUT 🐦🐦🐦

Rocky and remote Isle au Haut offers one of the most unique hiking and camping experiences in northern New England. This 6 × 3-mile (10 × 5km) island, located 6 miles (10km) south of Stonington, was originally named Ille Haut—or High Island—in 1604 by French explorer Samuel de Champlain. The name and its pronunciation evolved—today, it's generally pronounced "aisle-a-ho"—but the island itself has remained steadfastly unchanged over the centuries.

About half of the island is owned by the National Park Service and main-tained as an outpost of Acadia National Park (see "Mount Desert Island & Acadia National Park," below). A mailboat makes a stop in the morning and late afternoon at Duck Harbor, allowing for a solid day of hiking. The National Park Service also maintains a cluster of five Adirondack-style lean-tos at Duck Harbor, available for camping. (Reservations are essential; write Acadia National Park, Bar Harbor, ME 04609, or call 🕐 **207/288-3338.**)

A network of hiking trails radiates out from Duck Harbor. Among the highlights: the trail up 543-foot (163m) **Duck Harbor Mountain** (the island's highest point) for exceptional views of the Camden Hills to the west and Mount Desert Island to the east. Also worth hiking are the **Cliff** or **Western Head trails,** which track along high bluffs and coastal outcroppings, periodically descending to cobblestone coves. A hand pump near Duck Harbor provides drinking water, but be sure to bring food.

The other half of the island is privately owned, some by fishermen who can trace their island ancestry back 3 centuries, and some by summer rusticators whose forebears discovered the bucolic splendor of Isle au Haut in the 1880s. The summer population of the island is about 300, with about 50 die-hards remaining year-round. The mailboat also stops at the small harborside village, which has a few old homes, a handsome church, and a tiny post office and store. Day-trippers would be better served ferrying straight to Duck Harbor.

Isle au Haut Boat Company (🕐 **207/367-6516;** www.isleauhaut.com) operates a ferry to the island; it leaves from the pier at the end of Sea Breeze Avenue in Stonington. From mid-June to mid-September, the *Miss Lizzie* departs for the village of Isle au Haut daily at 7am, 11:30am, and 4:30pm; the *Mink* departs for Duck Harbor daily at 10am and 4:30pm. (Limited trips to Isle au Haut are offered the rest of the year.) The round-trip fare to either destination is $30 for adults, $15 for children under 12. The crossing takes about 45 minutes to the village, 1 hour to Duck Harbor. Travelers should arrive at least half an hour before departure. Tickets may be purchased in advance through the company's website.

SEA KAYAKING

Old Quarry Ocean Adventures ★★ (© 207/367-8977; www.oldquarry.com), just outside the village of Stonington, offers guided kayak tours, as well as rentals to those with prior experience. Half-day tours cost $50 for a single kayak, $85 for a tandem. Overnight camping trips are also offered. Other services: parking and a launch site for those who've brought their own boats, sailboat tours and lessons, charter tours aboard a 38-foot (11m) lobster boat, shorefront camping, and a three-bedroom home available for rent by the week.

WHERE TO STAY

You'll find standard motel rooms at **Eggemoggin Landing,** on Route 15 (© **207/348-6115**), at a great location on the shores of Eggemoggin Reach at the south end of the bridge from the mainland to Little Deer Isle. Open May through October; rates are $69 to $80 in high season. Pets are allowed in spring and fall. Amenities include a restaurant, kayak and bike rentals, and sailboat cruises.

Goose Cove Lodge ★★ *Kids*   This rustic compound next to a nature preserve is a superb destination for families and lovers of the outdoors. Exploring the grounds offers an adventure every day. You can hike out at low tide to salty Barred Island, or mess around in boats in the cove. Twenty rooms offer fireplaces or Franklin stoves; two modern cottages sleep six and are available through the winter. Our favorites? Elm and Linnea, cozy cabins tucked away in the woods on a rise overlooking the beach. Meals are far above what you would expect to find at the end of a remote dirt road.

Goose Cove Rd. (P.O. Box 40), Sunset, ME 04683. © **207/348-2508.** Fax 207/348-2624. www.goosecove lodge.com. 23 units. Peak season $150–$320 double; off-season $124–$274 double. Rates include breakfast. Ask about off-season packages. 2-night minimum stay July–Aug (1-week minimum stay in cottages). MC, V. Closed mid-Oct to mid-May. **Amenities:** Restaurant (New American); free canoes, kayaks, and bikes. *In room:* No phone.

Inn on the Harbor ★   This quirky waterfront inn has the best location in town—perched over the harbor and right on the main street. This is an ideal spot for resting up before or after a kayak expedition, as well as a good base for a day trip out to Isle au Haut. Ten rooms overlook the harbor; all are nicely appointed with antiques and sisal carpets. Complimentary sherry and wine are served in the reception room or on the deck each afternoon. The inn operates a restaurant a short walk away called the **Cafe Atlantic** (© **207/367-6373**), which features seafood, pasta, and beef. Parking is on the street or at nearby lots and can be inconvenient during busy times.

Main St. (P.O. Box 69), Stonington, ME 04681. © **800/942-2420** or 207/367-2420. Fax 207/367-5165. www.innontheharbor.com. 13 units. $105–$135 double; from $80 off-season. Rates include continental breakfast. AE, DISC, MC, V. Children 12 and over welcome. **Amenities:** Espresso bar. *In room:* TV, dataport.

Oakland House Seaside Resort/Shore Oaks ★★   Located on the mainland just north of the bridge to Deer Isle, Oakland House is a classic resort that's been in the same family since the Revolution. The main draw is the cluster of 15 cottages, tucked along a ½ mile (0.8km) of shorefront with superlative views.

These are mostly set aside for 1-week stays (Sat–Sat). The cottages are of varying vintages, but most have fireplaces. For shorter visits, a grand 1907 shorefront home has been converted into a 10-room inn called Shore Oaks; innkeepers Jim and Sally Littlefield have made it over into an Arts and Crafts–inspired hostelry that's very comfortable. Boat charters and a lobster bake are options in summer.

435 Herrick Rd., Brooksville, ME 04617. (800/359-7352 or 207/359-8521. www.oaklandhouse.com. 25 units (3 inn rooms share 1 bathroom). Inn rooms $159–$295 double (including breakfast and dinner). Cottages $1,300–$2,300 double per week (including breakfast and dinner); off-season $500–$1,225 per week. 2-night minimum stay for inn on weekends. MC, V. Inn closed mid-Oct to early May; cottages closed Feb–Mar. No children accepted in inn. **Amenities:** Restaurant (American); lake and ocean swimming; watersports equipment (rowboats, canoes, kayaks); game room; business center; dock and moorings. *In room:* No phone.

WHERE TO DINE

For fine dining, **Goose Cove Lodge** (see above) serves meals to the public, reservations required.

Fisherman's Friend ☆ SEAFOOD   This is a boisterous place where you'll easily get your fill of local color. Simple tables fill a large room, while waitresses hustle to keep up with demand. The menu features basic home-cooked meals, with fresh fish prepared in a variety of styles. It's justly famous for its lobster stew. Desserts, including berry pies and shortcake, tend toward traditional New England. Bring your own wine or beer.

School St., Stonington. (207/367-2442. Reservations recommended in high season and on weekends. Sandwiches $2.50–$6.50; dinner main courses $6.95–$15.95. DISC, MC, V. July–Aug daily 11am–9pm; June and Sept–Oct daily 11am–8pm; Apr–May Tues–Sun 11am–8pm. Closed Nov–Mar. Located up the hill from the harbor past the Opera House.

BLUE HILL ☆

Blue Hill (pop. 1,900) is fairly easy to find—just look for gently domed Blue Hill Mountain, which lords over the northern end of Blue Hill Bay. Set between the mountain and the bay is the quiet and historic town of Blue Hill, which clusters along the bay shore and a burbling stream. There's never much going on in town, and that seems to be exactly what brings visitors back time and again—and may explain why two excellent independent bookstores are located here. It's a good destination for an escape and will especially appeal to those deft at crafting their own entertainment.

ESSENTIALS

GETTING THERE   Blue Hill is southeast of Ellsworth on Route 172. Coming from the west, take Route 15 south 5 miles (8km) east of Bucksport.

VISITOR INFORMATION   Blue Hill does not maintain a visitor center; for information, contact the **Blue Hill Peninsula Chamber of Commerce** ((207/374-3242; www.bluehillme.com).

EXPLORING BLUE HILL

From the open summit of **Blue Hill Mountain** ☆☆, you'll get superb views of the bay and the rocky balds on Mount Desert Island just across the way. To reach the trailhead from the village, drive north on Route 172, and then turn west (left) on Mountain Road at the Blue Hill Fairgrounds. Drive ⅘ of a mile (1.3km) and look for the marked trail. An ascent of the "mountain" (elevation 940 feet/282m) is about a mile (1.6km) and requires about 45 minutes. Bring a picnic and enjoy the vistas.

Blue Hill has attracted more than its fair share of artists—especially, it seems, potters. On Union Street, stop by **Rowantrees Pottery** ☆☆ ((207/374-5535), which has been a local institution for more than 50 years. The pottery here is richly hued, and the glazes are made from local resources. The family-run **Rackliffe Pottery** ⚡, on Ellsworth Road (📞 **207/374-2297**), uses native clay and lead-free glazes. The bowls and vases have a lustrous, silky feel. Visitors are welcome to watch the potters at work. Both shops are open year-round.

The intriguing **Parson Fisher House** ⚡ (📞 **207/374-2459**) was home to Blue Hill's first permanent minister, who settled here in 1796. He was a rustic Renaissance man: Educated at Harvard, Fisher delivered sermons in six different languages, and was also a gifted writer, painter, and inventor. On a tour of his home, which he built in 1814, you can see a clock with wooden works he made, as well as samples of the books he not only wrote but also published and bound himself. The house is located on Routes 176 and 15 a ½ mile (0.8km) west of the village. It's open from July to mid-September, Monday through Saturday from 2 to 5 pm. Admission is $5 for adults, free for children under 12.

The **Big Chicken Barn** ⚡ (📞 **207/667-7308**) is a sprawling antiques shop and bookstore with around 90,000 volumes, well organized by category. There's also a forest's worth of old magazines in plastic sleeves (great browsing on a rainy afternoon). The shop is on Route 1 between Ellsworth and Bucksport.

WHERE TO STAY

Blue Hill Farm Country Inn ⚡   Comfortably situated on 48 acres (19 hectares), this inn's strength is in its common areas. The first floor of a sprawling barn has been converted to a spacious living room for guests. In the adjoining farmhouse, you can curl up in the cozy common room, which is amply stocked with a good selection of books. In contrast, the guest rooms are rather small and lightly furnished. The more modern units, upstairs in the barn loft, are nicely decorated in a country farmhouse style, but these are a bit motel-like, with rooms set off a central hallway. The three older rooms in the farmhouse have more character, but share a single bathroom with a small tub and hand-held shower.

Rte. 15, 2 miles (3.2km) north of village (P.O. Box 437), Blue Hill, ME 04614. 📞 **207/374-5126.** www. bluehillfarminn.com 14 units (7 with shared bathroom). June–Oct $80–$95 double; off-season $70–$80 double (no shared bathroom in off-season). Rates include continental breakfast. AE, MC, V. *In room:* No phone.

Blue Hill Inn ⚡⚡   The handsome Blue Hill Inn has been hosting travelers with aplomb since 1840. Located on one of Blue Hill's main thoroughfares and within walking distance of village attractions, this Federal-style inn is colonial American throughout, with the authenticity enhanced by creaky floors and doorjambs slightly out of true. Guest rooms are furnished with antiques; four units have wood-burning fireplaces. A more contemporary luxury suite features cathedral ceilings, fireplace, and deck.

Union St. (P.O. Box 403), Blue Hill, ME 04614. 📞 **207/374-2844.** Fax 207/374-2829. www.bluehillinn.com. 12 units. $118–$185 double; $220–$255 suite. Rates include breakfast. 2-night minimum stay in summer. Ask about packages that include kayaking, hiking, or sailing. DISC, MC, V. Closed Dec to mid-May. Children 13 and over welcome. **Amenities:** Dining room (New American/organic). *In room:* No phone.

WHERE TO DINE

Jean-Paul's Bistro ⚡ UPSCALE SANDWICHES   You get a lot of atmosphere for a moderate price at Jean-Paul's, which serves only lunch and tea. This is an excellent choice on a sunny day; head for the tables on the stone terraces and lawn that overlook the bay. Lunches tend toward quiche, croissant sandwiches, and salads. (The walnut tarragon chicken salad is tasty.) The delicious desserts make liberal use of local blueberries.

Main St. (at the intersection of Rtes. 172 and 15). (℃) **207/374-5852.** Lunch $6.95–$9.95. MC, V. Daily 11am–5pm. Closed mid-Sept to June.

6 Mount Desert Island & Acadia National Park

Mount Desert Island is home to spectacular Acadia National Park, and for many visitors the two places are one and the same. Yet the park holdings are only part of the appeal of this immensely popular island, which is connected to the mainland via a short, two-lane causeway. Beyond the parklands are scenic harborside villages and remote backcountry roads, lovely B&Bs and fine restaurants, oversize 19th-century summer "cottages," and the historic tourist town of Bar Harbor.

Mount Desert (pronounced "de-*sert*") is divided into two lobes separated by Somes Sound, the only legitimate fjord in the continental U.S. (A fjord is a valley carved by a glacier that subsequently filled with rising ocean water.) Most of the parkland is on the east side, although large swaths of park exist on the west as well. The eastern side is more developed, with Bar Harbor the center of commerce and entertainment. The western side has a more quiet, settled air, and teems more with wildlife than tourists. The island isn't huge—it's only about 15 miles (24km) from the causeway to the southernmost tip at Bass Harbor Head—yet visitors can do a lot of adventuring in such a compact space. The best plan is to take it slowly, exploring whenever possible by foot, bicycle, canoe, or kayak.

ACADIA NATIONAL PARK

It's not hard to fathom why Acadia is one of the biggest draws in the U.S. national park system. The park's landscape offers a rich tapestry of rugged cliffs, restless ocean, and quiet woods. Acadia's terrain (like so much of the rest of northern New England) was carved by glaciers 18,000 years ago. A mile-high ice sheet shaped the land by scouring valleys into distinctive U shapes, rounding many of the once-jagged peaks, and depositing huge boulders around the landscape, including the famous 10-foot-high (3m) "Bubble Rock," which appears to be perched precariously on the side of South Bubble Mountain.

The park's more recent roots can be traced back to the 1840s, when noted Hudson River School painter Thomas Cole packed his sketchbooks and easels for a trip to this remote island, then home to a small number of fishermen and boat builders. His stunning renditions of the surging surf pounding against coastal granite were later displayed in New York and triggered an early tourism boom as urbanites flocked to the island to "rusticate." By 1872, national magazines were touting Eden (Bar Harbor's name until 1919) as a desirable summer resort. It attracted the attention of wealthy industrialists, and soon became summer home to Carnegies, Rockefellers, Astors, and Vanderbilts, who erected massive "cottages" with literally dozens of rooms.

By the early 1900s, the popularity and growing development of the island began to concern its most ardent supporters. Boston textile heir and conservationist George Dorr and Harvard president Charles Eliot, aided by the largesse of John D. Rockefeller, Jr., started acquiring large tracts for the public's enjoyment. These parcels were eventually donated to the government, and in 1919 the land was designated Lafayette National Park, the first national park east of the Mississippi. Renamed Acadia in 1929, the park has grown to encompass nearly half the island, with holdings scattered about piecemeal here and there.

Rockefeller purchased and donated about 11,000 acres (4,455 hectares)— about a third of the park. He was also responsible for one of the park's most

Mount Desert Island/Acadia National Park

extraordinary features. Around 1905, a dispute erupted over whether to allow noisy new motorcars onto the island. Resident islanders wanted these new conveniences to aid their mobility; John D. Rockefeller, Jr., whose fortune came from the oil industry (students of irony, take note), strenuously objected, preferring the tranquility of a car-free island. Rockefeller went down to defeat on this issue, and the island was opened to cars in 1913. In response, the multimillionaire set about building an elaborate 57-mile (92km) system of private carriage roads, featuring a dozen gracefully handcrafted stone bridges. These roads, open today to pedestrians, bicyclists, and equestrians, are concentrated most densely around Jordan Pond, but also wind through wooded valleys and ascend to some of the most scenic open peaks.

JUST THE FACTS

GETTING THERE Acadia National Park is reached from the town of Ellsworth via Route 3. *Tip:* If you're driving from southern Maine, avoid the coastal congestion along Route 1 by taking the Maine Turnpike to Bangor, picking up I-395 to Route 1A, then continuing south on Route 1A to Ellsworth. While this looks longer on the map, it's the quickest route in summer and you're not missing much scenery on "coastal" Route 1, which often isn't in sight of the ocean between late May and mid-September.

Daily flights from Boston to the airport in Trenton, just across the causeway from Mount Desert Island, are offered year-round by US Air affiliate **Colgan Air**

> ### Tips Provisions
>
> Before you set out to explore the park, pack a picnic lunch and keep it handy. Once you're in the park, there are few places (other than Jordan Pond House) to stop for lunch or snacks. Having drinks and a bite to eat at hand will allow you to avoid breaking up your day with backtracking into Bar Harbor or elsewhere to fend off starvation. The more food you bring with you, the more your options for the day will expand.

(☎ **800/523-3273** or 207/667-7171). In summer, **Concord Trailways** (☎ **888/741-8686** or 207/942-8686) offers van service between Bangor (including an airport stop), Ellsworth, and Bar Harbor; reservations are required.

GETTING AROUND A free islandwide **shuttle bus** service was inaugurated in 1999 as part of an effort to reduce the number of cars on the island's roads. The propane-powered buses, which are equipped with racks for bikes, serve seven routes that cover nearly the entire island, and will stop anywhere you request outside the village centers, including trailheads, ferries, small villages, and campgrounds. All routes begin or end at the village green in Bar Harbor, but you're encouraged to pick up the bus wherever you're staying, whether at motel or campground, to minimize the number of parked cars in town. Route 3 goes from Bar Harbor along much of the Park Loop Road, offering easy access to some of the park's best hiking trails. The buses operate from late June to early September.

GUIDED TOURS **Acadia National Park Tours** (☎ **207/288-3327**) offers 2½-hour park tours departing twice daily (10am and 2pm) from downtown Bar Harbor. The bus tour includes three stops (Sieur De Monts Springs, Thunder Hole, and Cadillac Mountain) and plenty of park trivia courtesy of the driver. This is an easy way for first-time visitors to get a quick introduction to the park before setting out on their own. Tickets are available at Testa's Restaurant, 53 Main St., in Bar Harbor, for $20 per adult, $7.50 per child under 14.

ENTRY POINTS & FEES A 1-week park pass, which includes unlimited trips on Park Loop Road, costs $10 per car; no additional charge per passenger. (No daily pass is available.) The main point of entry to Park Loop Road, the park's most scenic byway, is at the visitor center at **Hulls Cove** (see below). Mount Desert Island consists of an interwoven network of park and town roads, allowing visitors to enter the park at numerous points. A glance at a park map (available free at the visitor center) will make these access points self-evident. The entry fee is collected at a toll booth on Park Loop Road a ½ mile (0.8km) north of Sand Beach.

VISITOR CENTERS & INFORMATION Acadia staffs two visitor centers. The **Thompson Island Information Center,** on Route 3 (☎ **207/288-3411**), is the first you'll pass as you enter Mount Desert Island. The local chambers of commerce maintain this center; park personnel are usually on hand to answer inquiries. It's the best stop for general lodging and restaurant information. Open from mid-May to mid-October.

For more detailed information on park attractions, continue on Route 3 to the National Park Service's **Hulls Cove Visitor Center,** about 7½ miles (12km) beyond Thompson Island. This attractive stone-walled center includes park service displays, such as a large relief map of the island, natural-history exhibits, and a short film. You can request brochures on trails and carriage roads, or purchase postcards and guidebooks. The center is open mid-April through October. Plans were afoot as of 2002 to construct a new visitor center; park funding and other considerations make a timetable uncertain, but disruptions may be likely in the coming years.

AVOIDING THE CROWDS   Early fall is the best time to miss out on the mobs yet still enjoy the weather. If you do come midsummer, try to venture out in the early morning or early evening to see the most popular spots, like Thunder Hole or the summit of Cadillac Mountain. Setting off into the woods at every opportunity is also a good strategy. About four out of five visitors restrict their tours to the Park Loop Road and a handful of other major attractions, leaving the backcountry open for more adventurous spirits. The best guarantee of solitude is to head to the more remote outposts managed by Acadia, especially Isle au Haut and Schoodic Peninsula, located across the bay to the east. Ask for more information at the visitor centers.

DRIVING TOUR   **DRIVING THE PARK LOOP ROAD** ✦✦✦

The 20-mile (32km) Park Loop Road is to Acadia what Half Dome is to Yosemite—it's the park's premier attraction, and the magnet for the largest crowds. This remarkable roadway starts near the Hulls Cove Visitor Center and follows the high ridges above Bar Harbor before dropping down along the rocky coast. Here, the spires of spruce and fir cap dark granite, and the earthy tones contrast sharply with the frothy white surf and the steely blue sea. After following the picturesque coast and touching on several coves, the road loops back inland along Jordan Pond and Eagle Lake, with a detour to the summit of the island's highest peak.

Ideally, visitors will make two circuits on the Park Loop Road. The first is for the sheer exhilaration of it and to discern the lay of the land. On the second trip, plan to stop frequently and poke around on foot by setting off on trails or scrambling along the coastline. Scenic pull-outs are staggered at frequent intervals. The two-lane road is one-way along coastal sections; the right-hand lane is set aside for parking, so you can stop wherever you'd like to admire the vistas.

From about 10am to 4pm in July and August, anticipate large crowds along the Park Loop Road, at least on those days when the sun is shining. Parking lots may fill at some of the more popular destinations, including Sand Beach, Thunder Hole, and the Cadillac Mountain summit. Travel early or late in the day. Alternatively, make the best of wet days by donning rain gear and letting the weather work to your advantage. You'll discover that you have the place to yourself.

From the Hulls Cove Visitor Center, the Park Loop Road initially runs atop

1 Paradise Hill

The tour will start with sweeping views eastward over Frenchman Bay. You'll clearly see the town of Bar Harbor far below, and just beyond it the Porcupines, a cluster of islands that look like, well, porcupines.

Following the Park Loop Road clockwise, you'll dip into a wooded valley and soon come to

2 Sieur de Monts Spring

Here you'll find a rather uninteresting natural spring, unnaturally encased, along with a botanical garden with some 300 species showcased in 12 habitats. The original **Abbe Museum** (✆ **207/288-3519**) is here, featuring a small but select collection of Native American artifacts. Open daily from mid-May to mid-October; admission is $2 for adults, $1 for children. A larger branch of the museum opened in downtown Bar Harbor in 2001, with more exhaustive and better curated displays (see "Exploring Bar Harbor," later in this chapter).

The **Tarn** is the chief reason to stop here; a few hundred yards south of the springs via footpath, it's a slightly medieval-looking and forsaken pond sandwiched between steep hills. Departing from the south end of the Tarn is the fine **Dorr Mountain Ladder Trail** ★★ (see "Hiking," below).

Continue the clockwise trip on the Park Loop Road; views eastward over the bay soon resume, almost uninterruptedly.

③ The Precipice Trail

This is the park's most dramatic trail. It ascends sheer rock faces on the east side of Champlain Mountain. It's only about ⅘ of a mile (1.3km) to the summit, but it's rigorous, and involves scrambling up iron rungs and ladders in very exposed places. (Those with a fear of heights or under 5 feet/1.5m tall should avoid this trail.) Alas, the trail is often closed midsummer to protect nesting peregrine falcons. Rangers are often on hand in the trailhead parking lot to point out the birds and suggest alternatives.

Between the Precipice Trail and Sand Beach is a tollbooth, where visitors pay the park fee of $10 per car, good for 1 week.

Picturesquely set between the arms of a rocky cove is

④ Sand Beach

This is the only sand beach on the island. Swimming these cold waters (about 50°F, or 10°C) is best enjoyed on extremely hot days, or by those with a freakishly robust metabolism. When it's sunny out, the sandy strand is usually crowded at midday, often with picnickers and urban travelers.

Tip: The water at the far end of the beach—where a gentle stream enters the cove—is often a few degrees warmer than at the end closer to the access stairs.

Two worthwhile hikes depart from near the beach. The **Beehive Trail** ★★★ overlooks Sand Beach (see "Hiking," below); it starts from a trailhead across the loop road. From the east end of Sand Beach, look for the start of the **Great Head Trail** ★★, a loop of about 2 miles (3.2km) that follows on the bluff overlooking the beach, then circles back along the shimmering bay before cutting through the woods back to Sand Beach.

About a mile (1.6km) south of Sand Beach is

⑤ Thunder Hole

This is a shallow oceanside cavern into which the surf surges, compresses, and bursts out. (There's a walking trail along the road if you'd rather leave your car parked at the beach.) When the bay is as quiet as a millpond (and it often is during the lulling days of summer), it's a no-star drive-by. You're better off spending time elsewhere.

But on days when the seas are rough and large swells roll in off the Bay of Fundy, it's a must-see, three-star attraction; that's when you can feel the ocean's power and force resonating under your sternum. (*Tip:* The best viewing time is 3 hr. before high tide.)

Parents with overly inquisitive toddlers (or teenagers) needn't fear: Visitors walk down to the cusp of Thunder Hole on a path that's girded with stout steel railings; on the most turbulent days, rangers gate off parts of the walkway to keep visitors away from rogue waves.

Just before the road curves around Otter Point, you'll be driving atop

⑥ Otter Cliffs

This is a set of 100-foot-high (30m) precipices capped with dense spruce that plummet down into roiling seas.

Look for whales spouting in summer; in early fall, tens of thousands of eider ducks can sometimes be seen floating in flocks just offshore. A footpath follows the brink of the crags.

At Seal Harbor, the Park Loop Road veers north and inland back toward Bar Harbor. Along the route is

❼ Jordan Pond

Jordan Pond is a small but uncommonly beautiful body of water encased by gentle, forested hills. A 3-mile (5km) hiking loop follows the pond's shoreline (see "Hiking," below), and a network of splendid carriage roads converge at the pond. After a hike or mountain-bike excursion, spend some time at a table on the lawn of the **Jordan Pond House** restaurant (see "Where to Dine," below).

Shortly before the Park Loop Road ends, you'll pass the entrance to

❽ Cadillac Mountain

You can reach this mountain by car by ascending an early carriage road. Among the mountain's claims to fame: At 1,528 feet (458m), it's the highest peak on the Eastern Seaboard between Canada and Brazil. It's also the first place in the United States touched by the sun during much of the year. But because Cadillac Mountain is the only mountaintop in the park accessible by car, and because it's also the island's highest point, the parking lot at the summit can be jammed, and drivers testy. The views are undeniably great, but the shopping-mall-at-Christmas atmosphere puts a serious crimp in one's enjoyment of the place. Some of the lower peaks—like Acadia or Champlain mountains—offer equally excellent views and fewer crowds.

OUTDOOR PURSUITS

HIKING   Acadia National Park has 120 miles (193km) of hiking trails, plus 57 miles (92km) of carriage roads suitable for walking. The park is studded with low "mountains" (they'd be called hills elsewhere), and almost all have trails with superb views of the open ocean. Many pathways were crafted by experienced stonemasons and others with high aesthetic intent, and thus the routes aren't the most direct—but they're often the most scenic, taking advantage of fractures in the rocks, picturesque ledges, and sudden vistas.

The Hulls Cove Visitor Center offers a brief chart of area hikes; combined with the park map, this is all you'll need to explore the well-maintained, well-marked trails. It's not hard to cobble together loop hikes to make your trips more varied. Coordinate your hiking with the weather; if it's damp or foggy, you'll stay drier and warmer strolling the carriage roads. If it's clear and dry, head for the highest peaks with the best views.

Among our favorite hikes is the **Dorr Mountain Ladder Trail** ★★★, which departs from near the south end of the Tarn, a pond near Sieur de Monts Spring. (Park either at the spring or just off Rte. 3 south at the Tarn.) This trail begins with a series of massive stone steps that ascend along a vast slab of granite, and then passes through crevasses (not for the wide of girth) and up ladders affixed to the rock face. The views east and south are superb. The trip to the summit of Dorr Mountain is ⅗ of a mile (1km); although short, it's quite demanding. Allow about 1½ hours round-trip.

The **Beehive Trail** ★★★ departs from the Park Loop Road just across from Sand Beach. The trail begins with a fairly gentle climb of ⅓ of a mile (0.3km), then turns right and begins a demanding ascent up a series of vertiginous ledges, some of which are linked with iron ladders set in the rock. (The layers of ledges give the hill its beehive look—and its name, of course.) From the top (a ½ mile, or 0.8km, from the road), hikers get splendid views of Sand Beach and the ocean beyond. Those in dubious physical shape or fearful of heights should steer clear. Allow about 45 minutes for a round-trip hike.

The loop around **Jordan Pond** ⭐ is more like a long stroll. Depart from the Jordan Pond House. The east side of the pond features a level trail; the west side is edged by a carriage road. The total loop measures just over 3 miles (5km). At the north end of the pond are a pair of oddly symmetrical mounds called **The Bubbles.** Detours to atop these peaks add about 20 minutes each to the loop; look for signs for these spur pathways off the Jordan Pond Shore Trail. Finish up your hike with tea and popovers at the Jordan Pond House (see "Where to Dine," below).

On the island's west side, an ascent and descent of **Acadia Mountain** ⭐⭐ takes about 1½ hours, but hikers should allow plenty of time for enjoying the view of Somes Sound and the smaller islands off Mount Desert's southern shores. This 2½-mile (4km) loop begins off Route 102 at a trailhead 3 miles (5km) south of Somesville. Head eastward through rolling mixed forest, then begin an ascent over ledgy terrain. There are two peaks; the east peak has better views.

MOUNTAIN BIKING   The 57 miles (92km) of **carriage roads** ⭐⭐⭐ built by John D. Rockefeller, Jr., are among the park's most extraordinary hidden treasures. (See "Acadia National Park," earlier in this section, for a brief history.) These were maintained by Rockefeller until his death in 1960, after which they became shaggy and overgrown. A major restoration effort was launched in 1990, and the roads today are superbly restored and maintained. With their wide hard-packed surfaces, gentle grades, and extensive directional signs, they make for very smooth biking. Note that bikes are also allowed on the island's free shuttle buses (see "Getting Around," above).

A useful map of the carriage roads is available free at the visitor centers; more detailed guides may be purchased at area bookshops, but they aren't necessary. Where the carriage roads cross private land (generally between Seal Harbor and Northeast Harbor), they are closed to mountain bikes. Mountain bikes are also banned from hiking trails.

Two areas are especially well-suited for launching mountain-bike trips. Near **Jordan Pond,** a number of carriage roads converge, allowing for a series of loops; several famous stone bridges are in this area. Afterward, enjoy tea at the Jordan Pond House, a popular island destination for over a century (see "Where to Dine," below).

At the north end of **Eagle Lake,** there's parking just off Route 223. From here, carriage roads loop around Eagle Lake to the south, with gentle hills and fine views. To the north of this parking area is a wooded loop around Witch Hole Pond; one of the finest stone bridges is located over a small gorge just off the southeast corner of the loop.

To get a taste of mountain biking without having to load rented bikes onto your car, ask the clerk at any of the Bar Harbor bike-rental shops about the route to **Witch Hole Pond** via West Street. The route is very steep (don't get discouraged!), but relatively traffic-free and relaxing; take your time, and look forward to coasting back into town once you're done.

Mountain bikes may be rented along Cottage Street in Bar Harbor, with rates around $15 to $17 for a day. Ask about closing times, because you may be able to get in a couple extra hours of peddling with a later-closing shop. **Bar Harbor Bicycle Shop,** 141 Cottage St. (📞 **207/288-3886**), is the most convenient and friendliest; you might also try **Acadia Outfitters,** 106 Cottage St.

(© 207/288-8118), or **Acadia Bike & Coastal Kayak,** 48 Cottage St. (© 207/288-9605).

CANOEING 🛶   Mount Desert's several ponds offer scenic if limited canoeing, and most have public boat access. Canoe rentals are available at the north end of Long Pond (the largest pond on the island at 3 miles/5km long) in Somesville from **National Park Canoe Rentals** (© 207/244-5854). The cost is $22 for 4 hours. Much of the west shore and the southern tip lie within Acadia National Park. Jet skis are banned in the national park. Note that swimming is prohibited in those ponds that serve as public water reservoirs (which include Bubble, Jordan, Eagle, and the south end of Long Pond).

CARRIAGE RIDES 🐎🐎   Carriage rides are offered by **Wildwood Stables** (© 207/276-3622; www.acadia.net/wildwood), a park concessionaire located a ½ mile (0.8km) south of Jordan Pond House. The 1-hour trip departs three times daily and takes in sweeping oceanviews; it costs $13.50 for adults, $7 for children 6 to 12, and $4 for children 2 to 5. Longer tours are available, as is a special carriage designed to accommodate disabled passengers. Reservations are recommended.

ROCK CLIMBING   Rock climbing is allowed only at Otter Cliffs, home to spectacular oceanside rock faces that attract experienced climbers as much for the beauty as for the challenge. **Acadia Mountain Guides,** 198 Main St., at the corner of Mount Desert Street (© 207/288-8186; www.acadiamountainguides.com), offers climbing lessons and guide services, ranging from a half-day introduction to intensive multi-day workshops on self-rescue and instruction on how to lead climbs. It's open from mid-May to mid-October. (In winter, ice climbing is available by special arrangement.)

SEA KAYAKING 🛶🛶   Sea kayaking has boomed around Mount Desert Island over the past decade. Experienced kayakers arrive in droves with their own boats. Novices sign up for guided tours, which are offered by several outfitters. Many new paddlers have found their inaugural experiences gratifying; others have complained that the quantity of paddlers taken out on quick tours in peak season makes the experience a little too much like a cattle drive to truly enjoy.

A variety of options can be found on the island, ranging from a 2½-hour harbor tour to a 7-hour excursion. Details are available from the following outfitters: **Acadia Outfitters,** 106 Cottage St. (© 207/288-8118); **Coastal Kayaking Tours,** 48 Cottage St. (© 800/526-8615 or 207/288-9605); **Island Adventure Kayak Tours & Rentals,** 137 Cottage St. (© 207/288-3886); and **National Park Sea Kayak Tours,** 39 Cottage St. (© 800/347-0940 or 207/288-0342). Rates range from approximately $40 to $50 per person for a 2- to 3-hour harbor or sunset tour, up to $75 for a 1-day excursion.

Sea-kayak rentals are available from **Loon Bay Kayaks,** located in summer at Barcadia Campground, at the junction of Routes 3 and 102 (© 888/786-0676 or 207/288-0099), which will deliver a boat to you, and from **National Park Canoe Rental,** 1 West St., Bar Harbor (© 207/288-0007). Solo kayaks rent for $32 to $35 per day. With unpredictable weather and squirrelly tides, kayakers are advised to have some prior experience before attempting to set out on their own.

CAMPING

The national park itself offers no overnight accommodations other than two campgrounds. (See the "Bar Harbor" and "Elsewhere on the Island," later in this section, for inns, hotels, and motels.) Both campgrounds are extremely popular; in July and August, expect them to fill by early to mid-morning.

Blackwoods (© 207/288-3274), located on the island's eastern side, tends to fill first. It's got a better location—bikers and pedestrians are just off the Park Loop Road and the rocky shore via a short trail—and, more important, it's the only one of the two that accepts reservations (which are required from mid-May to mid-September). On the downside, the sites here are rather gloomy and dour, set in a dense forest of scrappy fir and spruce. No public showers are available, but an enterprising business just outside the campground entrance offers clean showers for a small fee. Blackwoods is open year-round; late fall through spring, sites are easy to come by. You can reserve up to 5 months in advance by calling © **800/365-2267.** (This is a national reservations service whose contract is reviewed from time to time by the park service; if it doesn't work, call the campground directly to ask for the current toll-free reservation number.) Reservations may also be made online, between 10am and 10pm only, at http://reservations.nps.gov. Fees are $18 per night.

First-come, first-served **Seawall** (© 207/244-3600) is on the quieter western half of the island, near the fishing village of Bass Harbor. This is a good base for road biking, and several short coastal hikes are within easy striking distance. Many of the tent sites are walk-ins, which require carrying gear a hundred yards (91m) or so. Drive-in RV sites are available, but none have hookups. The campground is open late May through September. In general, if you get here by 9 or 10am, you'll have little trouble securing a site, even in midsummer. (This is especially true if you're a tent camper.) No showers are on site, but they're available nearby. Fees are $12 to $18 per night.

Private campgrounds handle the overflow. The region south of Ellsworth has 14 private campgrounds; the **Thompson Island Information Center** (© 207/288-3411) posts up-to-the-minute information on vacancies. In our opinion, two private campgrounds stand above the rest: **Bar Harbor Campground,** Route 3, Salisbury Cove (© 207/288-5185), is on the main route between the causeway and Bar Harbor and doesn't accept reservations; it has 300 sites both wooded and open. At the head of Somes Sound is **Mount Desert Campground,** Route 198 (© 207/244-3710); it's especially good for tent campers, who should inquire about the walk-in sites at the water's edge.

WHERE TO DINE

Jordan Pond House ★★ AMERICAN   This is the only full-service restaurant within park boundaries, and it occupies a delightful location on a grassy lawn looking northward up Jordan Pond. Afternoon tea with popovers is a hallowed Jordan Pond House tradition. Ladies who lunch sit next to mountain bikers, and everyone feasts on huge, tasty popovers and strawberry jam served with a choice of teas or fresh lemonade. The lobster and crab rolls are abundant and filling; the lobster stew is expensive but very, very good. Dinners include classic resort fare like prime rib, steamed lobster, and baked scallops with a crumb topping.

Park Loop Rd. (near Seal Harbor), Acadia National Park. © 207/276-3316. Advance reservations not accepted; call before arriving to hold table. Lunch $6.50–$12.75; afternoon tea $6.25–$7.25; dinner main courses $13–$18. AE, DISC, MC, V. Mid-May to late Oct daily 11:30am–8pm (until 9pm July–Aug).

BAR HARBOR

Bar Harbor provides most meals and beds to travelers coming to the island, as it has since the grand resort era of the late 19th century. The region was discovered by wealthy rusticators; later, sprawling hotels and boardinghouses cluttered

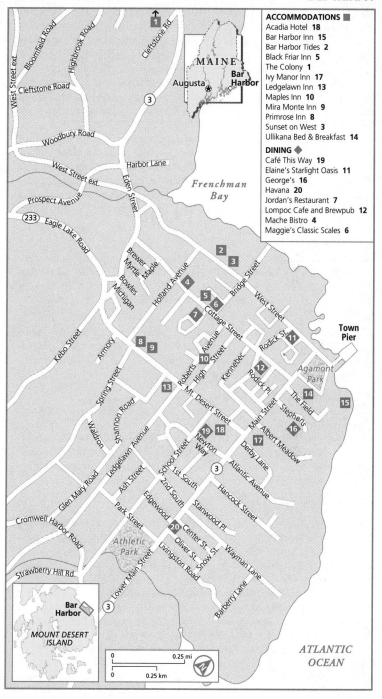

Bar Harbor

the shores and hillsides as the newly affluent middle class flocked here by steamboat and rail from Eastern Seaboard cities.

The tourist business continued to grow throughout the early 1900s, and then all but collapsed as the Depression and the growing popularity of car travel doomed the era of steamship travel and the extended vacation. Bar Harbor was dealt a further blow in 1947, when a fire leveled many opulent cottages and much of the rest of the town. In all, some 17,000 acres (6,885 hectares) of the island were burned, though downtown Bar Harbor and many in-town mansions along the oceanfront were spared.

After a period of quiet decay, Bar Harbor has been revived and rediscovered by both visitors and entrepreneurs. The less charitable regard Bar Harbor as just another tacky tourist mecca; crowds spill off the sidewalk and into the street in midsummer, and the traffic can be appalling. Yet Bar Harbor's history, distinguished architecture, and beautiful location along Frenchman Bay make it a desirable base for exploring the rest of the island, and it offers the most varied selection of lodging, meals, supplies, and services.

ESSENTIALS

GETTING THERE Bar Harbor is on Route 3 about 10 miles (16km) southeast of the causeway. **Concord Trailways** (© 800/639-3317) offers seasonal bus service from Boston and Portland. It also operates a seasonal van shuttle between Bar Harbor and Bangor International Airport; for details, call © **888/741-8686.**

VISITOR INFORMATION The **Bar Harbor Chamber of Commerce** (© **207/288-5103;** www.acadia.net/bhcc) stockpiles a huge arsenal of information on local attractions at its offices at 93 Cottage St. Call or e-mail in advance for a full guide to area lodgings and attractions.

EXPLORING BAR HARBOR

The best water views in town are from the foot of Main Street at grassy **Agamont Park,** which overlooks the town pier and Frenchman Bay. From here, set off past the Bar Harbor Inn on the **Shore Path** 👣👣, a winding trail that follows the shoreline for a ½ mile (0.8km) along a public right of way. The pathway passes in front of many elegant summer homes (some converted to inns), offering a superb vantage point to view the area's architecture.

From the path, you'll also have a fine view of **The Porcupines,** a cluster of spruce-studded offshore islands. This is a good spot to note the powerful force of glacial action. The south-moving glacier ground away at the islands, creating a gentle slope facing north. On the south shore, away from the glacial push (glaciers simply melted when they retreated north), is a more abrupt, clifflike shore. The resulting islands look like a small group of porcupines migrating southward—or so early visitors imagined.

In late 2001, the **Abbe Museum** 👣, 26 Mount Desert St. (© **207/288-3519;** www.abbemuseum.org), opened an extensive gallery that showcases a top-rate collection of Native American artifacts. (The original museum, next to Sieur de Monts Spring within the park itself, remains open and unchanged.) The new museum features an orientation center and a glass-walled lab where visitors can see archaeologists at work preserving recently recovered artifacts, along with changing exhibits and videos that focus largely on Maine and New England tribes. It's open in summer, daily from 10am to 5pm; late fall to Memorial Day, Thursday through Sunday from 10am to 5pm. Admission is $4.50.

Tips **Parking**

If parking spaces are scarce in downtown Bar Harbor, head to the end of Albert Meadow (a side street across from the village green). At the end of the road is a small waterfront park with free parking, great views of the bay, and foot access to Shore Path. It's not well marked or well publicized, so you can often find a place to park when much of the rest of town is filled up.

A short stroll around the corner from the new Abbe Museum is the **Bar Harbor Historical Society,** 33 Ledgelawn Ave. (© **207/288-0000** or 207/288-3807). Housed in this 1918 former convent are artifacts of life from the resort's glory days. Leave enough time to thumb through the scrapbooks about the devastating 1947 fire. The museum is open from mid-June to mid-October, Monday through Saturday from 1 to 4pm; admission is free.

One of downtown's quieter attractions is the 900-seat **Criterion Theater** ✪, on Cottage Street (© **207/288-3441;** www.criteriontheatre.com), built in 1932 in Art Deco style. In summer and fall, the theater shows first-run movies and hosts the occasional live concerts. The place is worth the price of admission for the fantastic if somewhat faded interiors. As was the case at most movie palaces in the past, it still costs extra to sit in the more exclusive loges upstairs, where you can now order from a light menu.

WHALE-WATCHING

Whales migrate to the cool waters offshore each summer to feast on the krill and plankton that well up toward the surface thanks to idiosyncratic ocean bottom topography, vigorous tides, and strong currents. Two outfitters offer tours aboard sleek catamarans. There's not much difference between the two boats (both have heated cabins and full galleys), so pick the one with the best schedule for you. Both will refund half the ticket price if no whales are spotted.

The *Friendship V* ✪ (© **800/942-5374** or 207/288-2386; www.whalesrus.com) operates from the municipal pier downtown. The 3-hour tour costs $39 per adult. (A puffin- and whale-watch tour is offered for $43.) **Acadian Whale Adventures,** 55 West St. (© **866/710-9800** or 207/288-9800; www.acadianwhaleadventures.com), offers catamaran tours that last between 3 and 3½ hours and cost $37. Free parking is available.

WHERE TO STAY

Bar Harbor is the bedroom community for Mount Desert Island, with hundreds of hotel, motel, and inn rooms. They're invariably filled in summer, when even the most basic of rooms can be expensive. It's essential to reserve as early as possible.

Expensive

Bar Harbor Inn ✪✪   This large, handsome complex is a combination of inn and motel, and has the best location of any lodging in Bar Harbor. Situated on shady waterfront grounds just off downtown Agamont Park and at the start of the Shore Path, it offers both convenience and charm. The rambling shingled inn dates back to the turn of the 19th century and has a settled, old-money feel. Guest rooms in the Oceanfront and Main Inn feature sweeping views of the bay, and many have private balconies; the less expensive Newport building lacks views but is comfortable and up-to-date.

Newport Dr. (P.O. Box 7), Bar Harbor, ME 04609. ℂ **800/248-3351** or 207/288-3351. www.barharborinn. com. 153 units. High season $175–$319 double; spring $75–$249; late fall $89–$225. Rates include continental breakfast. AE, DISC, MC, V. Closed Dec–late Mar. **Amenities:** 2 restaurants (formal dining room, outdoor grill); heated outdoor pool; fitness room; Jacuzzi; limited room service; babysitting; laundry service. *In room:* A/C, TV, coffeemaker, hair dryer.

Bar Harbor Tides ★★

The Bar Harbor Tides has just four guest rooms in a sprawling 1887 mansion. It's set at the head of a lush lawn that descends to the water's edge, all on 1½ in-town acres (0.6 hectares) in a neighborhood of imposing homes and within easy strolling distance of the village center. When you first enter, it feels as though you're visiting someone's great-aunt—someone's very rich great-aunt. But soon enough it starts to feels like home, as you unwind in the living room or, more likely, on the veranda, which has an outdoor fireplace. Plan to return here by sunset to wander down to the foot of the lawn and watch twilight settle in.

119 West St., Bar Harbor, ME 04609. ℂ **207/288-4968.** www.barharbortides.com. 4 units. $195–$375 double. Rates include full breakfast. AE, DISC, MC, V. Closed Nov to mid-June. *In room:* A/C, TV, dataport, hair dryer.

Sunset on West ★★★

This is exactly what a B&B should be, with gracious but unmeddlesome hosts, a splendid 1910 shingled cottage with views of the bay, a good downtown location, and lavish breakfasts. Everything comes together so expertly, you don't notice the lack of usual amenities, like TVs and phones. Common areas include a music room (with grand piano and fireplace) and a pantry with a guest fridge. Bedrooms feature the plushest towels we've come across, Hammacher Schlemmer robes, and down comforters. The Sunset Suite has a sitting room with a gas fireplace and a porch; Nocturne is a spacious suite perfect for those seeking a quiet getaway.

115 West St., Bar Harbor, ME 04609. ℂ **207/288-4242.** Fax 207/288-4545. www.sunsetonwest.com. 4 units. High season $175–$300 double; off-season $150–$230 double. Rates include full breakfast. MC, V. Closed Nov–Apr. Children 16 and over welcome. **Amenities:** Video library. *In room:* VCR, hair dryer, no phone.

Moderate

Black Friar Inn ★

This shingled structure with quirky pediments and an eccentric air offers good value for Bar Harbor. A former owner "collected" interiors and installed them throughout the house. Among them are a replica of the namesake Black Friar Pub in London, complete with elaborate carved-wood paneling (it serves as a common room); stamped tin walls in the breakfast room; and a doctor's office (now a guest room). Guest rooms, most of which are quite small, are furnished with a mix of antiques.

10 Summer St., Bar Harbor, ME 04609. ℂ **207/288-5091.** Fax 207/288-4197. www.blackfriar.com. 7 units (2 with private hall bathrooms). $95–$150 double. Rates include breakfast. DISC, MC, V. 2-night minimum stay mid-June to mid-Oct. Closed Dec–Apr. Children 12 and over welcome. *In room:* A/C, hair dryer, no phone.

Maples Inn ★★

This is a popular destination with outdoor enthusiasts. You'll often find guests swapping stories of the day's adventures on the front porch. The architecturally modest (by Bar Harbor standards) farmhouse-style inn is tucked away on a leafy side street, an easy walk from downtown. The innkeepers make guests feel comfortable, with board games and paperbacks scattered about. The bedrooms aren't huge, but you're not likely to feel cramped, either. The two-room White Birch has a fireplace and is the largest; White Oak has a private deck. Breakfasts are appropriately filling for a full day outdoors.

16 Roberts Ave., Bar Harbor, ME 04609. ✆ 207/288-3443. www.maplesinn.com. 6 units. Mid-June to mid-Oct $105–$160 double; off-season $65–$100 double. Rates include breakfast. DISC, MC, V. 2-night minimum stay mid-June to mid-Oct. No small children accepted. *In room:* A/C, no phone.

Ullikana Bed & Breakfast ⚴ This 1885 Tudor cottage is tucked on a side street near Agamont Park and the Bar Harbor Inn. The 10-bedroom "cottage" is solidly built, and the downstairs with its oak trim and wainscoting is dark in an English-gentleman's-club kind of way. Guest rooms are nicely decorated in a country Victorian mode, some with iron or brass beds. Audrey's Room has a pleasant, storybook feel to it, with pastel colors and a claw-foot tub. Summery room 6 has a deck with glimpses of the bay. Across the lane is the attractive Yellow House, which has six additional rooms simpler in style than those in the main cottage.

16 The Field, Bar Harbor, ME 04609. ✆ 207/288-9552. www.ullikana.com. 16 units (2 with detached bathroom). $155–$250 double. Rates include breakfast. MC, V. Closed mid-Oct to early May. Children 12 and over welcome. *In room:* No phone.

Inexpensive

Reputable motels in or near town that offer at least some rooms under $100 include the conveniently located **Villager Motel,** 207 Main St. (✆ **207/288-3211**); the in-town, pet-friendly **Rockhurst Motel,** 68 Mount Desert St. (✆ **207/288-3140**); and the smoke-free **Highbrook Motel,** 94 Eden St. (✆ **800/338-9688** or 207/288-3591). About 4 miles (6km) west of Bar Harbor on Route 3 is **Hanscom's Motel and Cottages** (✆ **207/288-3744;** www.hanscoms motel.com), an old-fashioned motor court with 12 well-maintained units (some two-bedroom).

The Colony ⚴ *⚴Value* This classic motor court consists of a handful of motel rooms and a battery of cottages arrayed around a long green. It will be most appreciated by those with a taste for the authentically retro; others might decide to look for something with updated amenities. The rooms are furnished in a simple '70s style that won't win any awards for decor, but all are comfortable; many have kitchenettes. It's just across Route 3 from a cobblestone beach, and a 10-minute drive from Bar Harbor.

Rte. 3, (P.O. Box 56) Hulls Cove, ME 04644. ✆ 800/524-1159 or 207/288-3383. www.acadia.net/thecolony. 55 units. $65–$105 double. AE, DC, DISC, MC, V. Closed mid-Oct to early June. *In room:* A/C, TV.

WHERE TO DINE

For a tasty ice-cream cone, head over to **Ben & Bill's Chocolate Emporium,** 66 Main St. (✆ **207/288-3281**). Visitors are often tempted to try the house novelty, lobster ice cream. Visitors often regret giving into that temptation.

Café This Way ⚴⚴ NEW AMERICAN Café This Way has the feel of a casually hip coffeehouse; bookshelves line one wall, and there's a small bar tucked in a nook. The breakfasts are excellent and mildly sinful, with offerings like eggs Benedict with spinach, artichoke, and tomato. The red-skinned potatoes are crispy and delicious; the robust coffee requires two creamers to lighten it. Dinners are equally appetizing, with tasty dishes like butternut-squash ravioli and filet mignon grilled with fresh basil.

14½ Mount Desert St. ✆ 207/288-4483. Reservations recommended for dinner. Main courses $3.25–$5.95 breakfast, $12–$19 dinner. MC, V. Mon–Sat 7–11am and 6–9pm; Sun 8am–1pm and 6–9pm. Closed Nov–Apr.

Elaine's Starlight Oasis ⚴ VEGETARIAN Bar Harbor's only fully vegetarian restaurant, Elaine's opened in 1998 and has been happily embraced by herbivorous visitors. Located near the waterfront in a cozy, contemporary space, the menu includes the house specialty of "beef" burgundy (made with seitan). Other offerings include mushroom lasagna, eggplant casserole, or tempeh Parmesan.

78 West St. ⓒ 207/288-3287. www.starlightoasis.com. Reservations not accepted. Main courses $6.95–$12.95. Wed–Mon 5–9:30pm (closes earlier in off-season). Closed Nov–May 1.

George's ★★★ CONTEMPORARY MEDITERRANEAN   For more than 2 decades, this has been a Bar Harbor classic, offering fine dining in elegant yet informal surroundings. George's captures the joyous feel of summer with four smallish dining rooms (with plenty of open windows) and a terrace. The service is upbeat, the meals wonderfully prepared. All entrees sell for one price, which includes salad, vegetable, and potato or rice. You won't go wrong with basic choices, but you're better off opting for more adventurous fare, like lobster strudel or mustard shrimp. The house specialty is lamb in its many incarnations, including chargrilled lamb tenderloin with a rosemary-infused three-bean ragout.

7 Stephens Lane. ⓒ 207/288-4505. www.georgesbarharbor.com. Reservations recommended. Entrees $25; appetizer, entree, and dessert $37–$40. AE, DC, DISC, MC, V. Daily 5:30–10pm; shorter hours after Labor Day. Closed Nov–early May.

Havana ★★★ LATINO/FUSION   Havana set a new creative standard for Bar Harbor when it opened in 1999. The spare but sparkling decor is as classy as you'll find in downtown Boston, and the menu could compete in any major urban area as well. Expect appetizers like crab and roasted corn cakes with a cilantro sour cream. Recent entrees included pork tenderloin with a chile and honey glaze, served with a chorizo and pepper hash, and adobo-marinated tuna with a pineapple coulis. We've yet to hear a report of anyone disappointed with a meal here.

318 Main St. ⓒ 207/288-2822. www.havanamaine.com. Reservations recommended. Main courses $16–$34. AE, DC, DISC, MC, V. Daily 5:30–10pm. Closed Mar; limited days and hours in off-season (call ahead).

Lompoc Cafe and Brewpub ☆ AMERICAN/ECLECTIC   The Lompoc Cafe has a neighborhood-bar feel to it, and it's little wonder that waiters and other workers from around Bar Harbor congregate here after hours. The adjacent microbrewery produces several unique beers, including the smooth Coal Porter. The menu has some pleasant surprises, like the Persian plate (hummus and grape leaves) and Szechuan eggplant wrap. Vegetarians will find a decent selection. Live music is offered some evenings, when there's a small cover.

36 Rodick St. ⓒ 207/288-9392. www.lompoc.com. Reservations not accepted. Sandwiches $5.25–$7.50; dinner main courses $9.95–$17.95. MC, V. May–Nov daily 11:30am–1am. Closed Dec–Apr.

ELSEWHERE ON THE ISLAND

There's plenty to explore outside of Acadia National Park and Bar Harbor. Quiet fishing villages, deep woodlands, and unexpected oceanviews are among the jewels that turn up when one peers beyond the usual places.

ESSENTIALS

GETTING AROUND   The eastern half of the island is best navigated on Route 3, which forms the better part of a loop from Bar Harbor through Seal Harbor and past Northeast Harbor before returning up the eastern shore of Somes Sound. Routes 102 and 102A provide access to the island's western half.

Pier, Beer & Lobster

The best lobster restaurants are those right on the water, where there's no pretension or frills. The ingredients for a proper feed at a local lobster pound are: a pot of boiling water, a tank of lobsters, some well-worn picnic tables, a good view, and a six-pack of Maine beer.

Beal's Lobster Pier, in Southwest Harbor (© **207/244-7178**), is one of the oldest pounds in the area. **Thurston's Lobster Pound,** in tiny Bernard, across the water from Bass Harbor (© **207/244-7600**), was atmospheric enough to be used as a backdrop for the 1999 Stephen King miniseries *Storm of the Century;* it's a fine place to linger toward dusk.

Abel's Lobster Pound, 5 miles (8km) north of Northeast Harbor on Route 198 (© **207/276-5827**), overlooks the deep-blue waters of Somes Sound; eat at a picnic table under the pines or indoors at the restaurant. At first glance it's quite a bit pricier than other lobster restaurants, but it doesn't charge for the extras like many other lobster joints—and some visitors claim that the lobsters here are more succulent.

See information on the free islandwide shuttle service under "Just the Facts," under "Acadia National Park," earlier in this chapter.

VISITOR INFORMATION   The best source of information on the island is the **Thompson Island Information Center** (© 207/288-3411), on Route 3 just south of the causeway connecting Mount Desert Island with the mainland. You can also contact the **Mount Desert Chamber of Commerce** (© **207/276-5040**).

EXPLORING THE REST OF THE ISLAND

On the tip of the eastern lobe of Mount Desert Island is the staid, prosperous community of **Northeast Harbor,** long one of the favored retreats among the Eastern Seaboard's upper crust. Those without personal invitations to come as house guests will need be satisfied with glimpses of the shingled palaces set in spruce forests and along the rocky shore; but the village itself is worth investigating. Situated on a narrow harbor, with the once-grand Asticou Inn at its head, Northeast Harbor is possessed of a refined sense of elegance that's best appreciated by finding a vantage point, then sitting and admiring.

One of the best, least-publicized places for enjoying views of the harbor is from the understatedly spectacular **Asticou Terraces** ✦ (© 207/276-5130). Finding the parking lot can be tricky: Head a ½ mile (0.6km) east on Route 3 from the junction with Route 198, and look for the small gravel lot on the water side of the road. Park here, cross the road on foot, and set off up a magnificent rock path that ascends the hillside with expanding views of the harbor and the town. This pathway, with its precise stonework and the occasional bench and gazebo, is one of the nation's hidden marvels of landscape architecture. Created by Boston landscape architect Joseph Curtis, the pathway seems to blend in almost preternaturally with its spruce-and-fir surroundings, as if it were created by an act of God rather than of man.

Continue on the trail at the top of the hillside and you'll soon arrive at Curtis's cabin (open to the public daily in summer), behind which lies the formal

Tips **A Scenic Drive**

Sargent Drive is the most scenic route out of Northeast Harbor. This one-way route runs through Acadia National Park lands along the shore of Somes Sound, affording some of the best views of this glacially carved inlet.

Thuya Gardens, which are as manicured as the terraces are natural. These wonderfully maintained gardens, designed by noted landscape architect Charles K. Savage, attract flower enthusiasts and local folks looking for a quiet place to rest. It's well worth the trip. A donation of $2 is requested of visitors to the garden; the terraces are free.

From the harbor, visitors can depart on a seaward trip to the remote **Cranberry Islands.** You have a couple of options: Either travel with a national park guide to Baker Island, the most distant of this small cluster of low islands, and explore the natural terrain; or, hop one of the ferries to either Great or Little Cranberry Island and explore on your own. On Little Cranberry, there's a small historical museum run by the National Park Service that's worth seeing. Both islands feature a sense of being well away from it all, but neither offers much in the way of shelter or tourist amenities, so travelers should head out prepared for the possibility of shifting weather.

WHERE TO STAY

The Claremont 🐦🐦   The Claremont offers nothing frilly or fancy—just simple, classic New England grace. Early prints of the 1884 building show an austere four-story wooden structure with a single gable overlooking Somes Sound from a grassy rise. And the place hasn't changed much since. It seems appropriate that the state's most combative croquet tournament takes place here in early August; all those folks in their whites are right at home. The common areas are appointed in a spare country style. There's a library with rockers, a fireplace, and jigsaw puzzles waiting to be assembled. Most guest rooms are bright and airy, furnished with antiques and some furniture that's simply old; bathrooms are modern. Guests opting for the full meal plan are given preference in reserving rooms overlooking the water; it's almost worth it, although dinners tend toward the lackluster.

P.O. Box 137, Southwest Harbor, ME 04679. 📞 **800/244-5036** or 207/244-5036. Fax 207/244/3512. www.theclaremonthotel.com. 42 units. July–Labor Day $159–$169 double including breakfast, $209–$229 double including breakfast and dinner; off-season $95–$135 double including breakfast, $145–$190 double including breakfast and dinner. Cottages $169–$230 June–Labor Day; $100–$155 off-season. 3-night minimum stay in cottages. No credit cards. Closed Nov to mid-May. **Amenities:** Clay tennis court; rowboats; free bikes; babysitting. *In room:* Hair dryer.

Inn at Southwest 🐦   This architecturally quirky inn is a mansard-roofed Victorian marvel at the leafy edge of the village. There's a decidedly late-19th-century air to this elegant home, but it's restrained on the frills. The hospitable guest rooms are named after Maine lighthouses and are outfitted with both contemporary and antique furniture. Among the most pleasant is Blue Hill Bay, with its large bathroom, sturdy oak bed, and glimpses of the scenic harbor.

371 Main St. (P.O. Box 593), Southwest Harbor, ME 04679. 📞 207/244-3835. www.innatsouthwest.com. 7 units. Summer and early fall $100–$160 double; off-season $70–$120. Rates include full breakfast. MC, V. Closed Nov–Apr.

Lindenwood Inn ★★   The Lindenwood is a refreshing change from the fusty, overly draperied inns often found along Maine's coast. Housed in a handsome 1902 Queen Anne–style home at the harbor's edge, the rooms are clean and uncluttered, the colors simple and bold. The adornments are few (those that do exist are mostly from the innkeeper's collection of African and Pacific art), but simple lines and bright natural light more than create a relaxing mood. Eight units have fireplaces; the spacious suite with its great harbor views is especially appealing. The boat dock is a pleasant stroll down the lawn.

118 Clark Point Rd. (P.O. Box 1328), Southwest Harbor, ME 04679. ✆ 207/244-5335. www.lindenwood. com. 15 units. June to mid-Oct $95–$245 double; mid-Oct to June $95–$275 double. Rates include breakfast. AE, MC, V. **Amenities:** Heated outdoor pool; Jacuzzi; boat dock. *In room:* TV.

WHERE TO DINE

For a quick bite or a picnic lunch, seek out the tiny **Docksider Restaurant,** 14 Sea St. (✆ **207/276-38965**), hidden a block off Northeast Harbor's compact downtown. The crab rolls and lobster rolls are outstanding.

The Burning Tree ★★ REGIONAL/ORGANIC   Located on busy Route 3 between Bar Harbor and Northeast Harbor, the Burning Tree is an easy restaurant to speed right by, but that would be a mistake. This low-key spot, with its bright, open, and sometimes noisy dining room, serves up the freshest food in the area. Much of the produce comes from its own gardens. Seafood is the specialty, and it's consistently prepared with imagination and skill. Typical entrees might include prosciutto-wrapped sea scallops or butternut-squash ravioli with rosemary cream.

Rte. 3, Otter Creek. ✆ 207/288-9331. Reservations recommended. Main courses $18–$23. Aug daily 5–9pm; mid-June to July and early fall Wed–Mon 5–9pm. Closed Columbus Day to mid-June.

Restaurant XYZ ★★ MEXICAN   Restaurant XYZ doesn't promise much at first: It's on the ground floor beneath a motel, and the interior is adorned with imports from Mexico that might best be described as "stuff." But the food! Drawing on the traditions of central Mexico and the Yucatan, the fare is spicy, earthy, and tangy. Expect a savory mole and a chipotle salsa that sings. Start with one of the standout margaritas and peruse the menu. Among the more inviting entrees are a pork loin baked in a sauce of ancho, guajillo, and chipotle chilies, and chilies stuffed with corn and cheese. Aficionados of authentic Mexican cooking will be delightfully surprised to find such intriguing dining deep behind the lines of boiled lobster and fried clams.

Shore Rd., Manset. ✆ 207/244-5221. Reservations recommended. Main courses $15–$16. MC, V. July–Aug daily 5:30–9pm; June and Sept–Oct Fri–Sat 5:30–9pm. Closed Columbus Day to Memorial Day.

7 The Western Lakes & Mountains

Maine's western mountains create a rugged, brawny region that stretches northeast from the White Mountains to the Carrabassett Valley. It isn't as commercialized as the Maine coast, and the villages aren't as quaint as you'll find in Vermont's Green Mountains—but visitors will find azure lakes, ragged forests of spruce and fir, and rolling hills and mountains that take on a distinct sapphire hue during the summer hiking season.

Cultural amenities are few here, but natural amenities are legion. Hikers have the famed Appalachian Trail, which crosses into Maine in the Mahoosuc Mountains (near where Rte. 26 enters into New Hampshire) and follows rivers and ridgelines northeast to Bigelow Mountain and beyond. Canoeists and anglers head to the noted Rangeley Lakes area, a chain of deepwater ponds and lakes that has attracted sportsmen for more than a century. And in winter, skiers can choose among several downhill ski areas, including the two largest in the state, Sunday River and Sugarloaf.

BETHEL 🎿🎿

Until relatively recently, Bethel was a sleepy resort town with one of those family-oriented ski areas that seemed destined for certain extinction. But then the sleepy Sunday River ski area was bought and dusted off by a brash young entrepreneur, who turned it into one of New England's most vibrant and challenging ski destinations.

With the rise of Sunday River, the white-clapboard town of Bethel (located about 7 miles/11km from the ski area) has been dragged into the modern era, although it hasn't (yet) taken on the artificial, packaged flavor of many other New England ski towns. The village (pop. 2,500) is still defined by the stoic buildings of the respected prep school Gould Academy, the broad village common, and the Bethel Inn, a sprawling, old-fashioned resort that's managed to stay ahead of the tide by adding condos, but without losing its pleasant, time-worn character.

ESSENTIALS

GETTING THERE   Bethel is located at the intersection of Routes 26 and 2. It's accessible from the Maine Turnpike by heading west on Route 26 from Exit 11. From New Hampshire, drive east on Route 2 from Gorham.

VISITOR INFORMATION   The **Bethel Area Chamber of Commerce,** 30 Cross St. (© **800/442-5826** for lodging reservations, or 207/824-2282; www.bethelmaine.com), has offices behind the Casablanca movie theater. It's open year-round, Monday through Friday from 8am to 8pm, Saturday from 10am to 6pm, and Sunday noon to 5pm.

Across Route 2 from the chamber, the **state tourism office,** 18 Mayville Rd. (© **207/824-4582**), has paired up with the White Mountain National Forest district office. You can stock up on brochures from across the state and get information on activities in the national forest. Open in peak season, daily from 8am to 6pm; off-season, Thursday through Tuesday from 8:30am to 5pm.

EXPLORING LOCAL HISTORY

Bethel's stately, historic homes ring the **Bethel Common,** a long greensward created in 1807 atop a low, gentle ridge. The town's **historic district** encompasses some 27 homes, which represent a wide range of architectural styles popular in the 19th century.

The **1813 Moses Mason House,** 14 Broad St., is now home of the collections and offices of the **Bethel Historical Society** (© **207/824-2908**). Mason was a doctor and a local civic leader, and was willing to try anything once, including building his Federal-style house on a stone foundation. His compatriots assured him that the house would topple over in a gale. It didn't, and all local houses were soon built on stone foundations. Mason also commissioned an itinerant painter—possibly the renowned landscape artist Rufus Porter—to paint his foyer and stairwell. The result is an engagingly primitive panorama of boats at anchor at a calm harbor flanked by a still forest of white pine. View this and numerous other artifacts of the early 19th century while exploring the home. It's open in July and August, Tuesday through Sunday from 1 to 4pm. Admission is $3 for adults and $1.50 for children.

ALPINE SKIING

Ski Mount Abram   Mount Abram is a welcoming and friendly intermediate mountain that's perfect for families still ascending skiing's learning curve. It has an informal atmosphere that sharply contrasts with bustling and impersonal Sunday River nearby. It's suffered from the usual financial ups and downs of small ski areas in recent years, but current owners seem to have put it on good course, adding a 500-foot (150m) snow tube park and capitalizing on its popularity among telemark skiers by offering telemark rentals and weekend lessons.

P.O. Box 240 Greenwood, ME 04255. ✆ 207/875-5002. www.skimtabram.com. Vertical drop: 1,030 ft. (309m). Lifts: 2 chairlifts, 3 T-bars. Skiable acreage: 135. Lift tickets (as of 2001): $35 Sat–Sun, $29 Mon–Fri.

Sunday River Ski Resort ★★★   Sunday River has grown at stunning speed in recent years, and in our opinion is the best ski mountain in New England for terrain and conditions. (The resort scene, however, sorely lags, and the staff can be brusque.) Unlike ski areas that have developed around a single tall peak, Sunday River expanded along an undulating ridge some 3 miles (5km) wide that encompasses seven peaks. Just traversing the resort, stitching runs together with chairlift rides, can take an hour or more. As a result, you'll rarely get bored making the same run time and again. The descents offer something for virtually everyone, from deviously steep bump runs to wide, wonderful intermediate trails. Sunday River is also blessed with plenty of water for snowmaking, and makes tons of the stuff using a proprietary snowmaking system. The superb skiing conditions are, alas, offset by an uninspiring base area. The lodges and condos (total capacity 6,000) tend toward the architecturally dull, and the less-than-delicate landscaping is of the sort created by bulldozers. Sunday River's trails are often crowded on weekends; weekdays you'll pretty much have the place to yourself.

P.O. Box 450, Bethel, ME 04217. ✆ 800/543-2754 for lodging, or 207/824-3000. www.sundayriver.com. Vertical drop: 2,340 ft. (702m). Lifts: 15 chairlifts (4 high-speed), 3 surface lifts. Skiable acreage: 654. Lift tickets: $52 Sat–Sun, $49 Mon–Fri.

OTHER OUTDOOR PURSUITS

Grafton Notch State Park ★★ straddles Route 26 as it angles northwest from Newry toward Errol, N.H. The dramatic 33-mile (53km) drive between the two towns is one of our favorites. You initially pass through farmland in a fertile river valley before ascending through bristly forest to a handsome glacial notch hemmed in by rough, gray cliffs on the towering hillsides above. Foreboding Old Speck Mountain towers to the south; views of Lake Umbagog open to the north as you continue into New Hampshire.

Public access to the park consists of a handful of roadside parking lots near scenic areas. The best of the bunch is **Screw Auger Falls,** where the Bear River drops through several small cascades before tumbling dramatically into a narrow, corkscrewing gorge. Picnic tables dot the forested banks upriver of the falls, and kids seem inexorably drawn to splash and swim in the smaller pools on warm days. Admission to the park is $1; look for self-pay stations at the parking lot.

HIKING   The **Appalachian Trail** ★★ crosses the Mahoosuc Mountains northwest of Bethel. Many of those who've hiked the entire 2,000-mile (3,220km) trail say this stretch is the most demanding on knees and psyches. The trail doesn't forgive; it generally foregoes switchbacks in favor of sheer ascents and descents. It's also hard to find water along the trail during dry weather. Still, it's worth the knee-pounding effort for the views and the unrivaled sense of remoteness.

One stretch crosses Old Speck Mountain, Maine's third-highest peak. Views from the summit are all but nonexistent since the old fire tower closed a while back, but an easy-to-moderate spur trail on the lower end of the trail ascends an 800-foot (240m) cliff called "The Eyebrow" and provides a good vantage point for Bear River Valley and the rugged terrain of Grafton Notch. Look for the well-signed parking lot where Route 26 intersects the trail in Grafton Notch State Park. Park your car, then head south on the A.T. toward Old Speck; in 0.1 mile (0.2km), you'll intersect the Eyebrow Trail, which you can follow to the overlook.

The Appalachian Mountain Club's *Maine Mountain Guide* is highly recommended for detailed information about other area hikes.

WHERE TO STAY

The Bethel Inn ⭐   The Bethel Inn is an old-fashioned resort set on 200 acres (81 hectares) in the village. It has a quiet, settled air, which is appropriate because it was built to house patients of Dr. John Gehring, who put Bethel on the map treating nervous disorders through a regimen of healthy country living. The quaint rooms aren't terribly spacious, but they are pleasingly furnished with country antiques. More luxurious are the 16 modern rooms added in the late 1990s. You give up some of the charm of the old inn, but gain elbowroom. The dining room remains the resort's Achilles' heel—the preparation and service often fail to live up to the promise of the surroundings.

On the Common, Bethel, ME 04217. ② 800/654-0125 or 207/824-2175. www.bethelinn.com. 62 units. Summer $198–$418 double; winter $158–$454 double. Rates include breakfast and dinner. 2-night minimum stay summer weekends and ski season; 3-night minimum stay during winter school vacations. Ski packages available. AE, DISC, MC, V. Pets accepted ($10 per night). **Amenities:** Dining room (Continental); outdoor heated pool; nearby lake swimming; 18-hole golf course; tennis courts; fitness center; Jacuzzi; sauna; canoes and kayaks; game room; babysitting; laundry service; cross-country skiing; shuttle to ski areas. *In room:* TV, hair dryer, iron.

Black Bear Bed & Breakfast ⭐   This 1830s farmhouse in a rural setting is a great choice for those seeking a casual spot to rest up between ski runs or hikes. Rooms are furnished in a simple country style with lots of light streaming through oversize windows. The upstairs great room looks out on the hills behind the inn; the downstairs common room is a good spot to chat with other guests. But the chief amenity is the location: It's on 8 acres (3 hectares) in a lovely dead-end valley. You can be on the slopes at Sunday River within 5 minutes, yet it feels like you're far off in the country by nightfall. In summer, guests splash around in the river or set off on mountain-biking and hiking rambles up the valley into the national forest.

Sunday River Rd. (P.O. Box 55), Bethel, ME 04217. ② 888/299-5487 or 207/824-0908. www.bbearbandb.com. 6 units. Winter $90–$105 double; summer $80–$90 double. Winter rates include breakfast. 2-night minimum stay on ski season weekends. AE, MC, V. Closed May. Pets allowed (ask first). **Amenities:** Heated pool (summer only); tennis court; Jacuzzi. *In room:* No phone.

The Victoria ⭐⭐   Built in 1895 and damaged by lightning some years back, the inn was restored in 1998 with antique lighting fixtures, period furniture, and the original oak doors. Guest rooms have a luxurious William Morris feel, with richly patterned wallpaper and handmade duvet covers. Room 1 is the master suite, with a turret window and a sizable bathroom; room 3 is the only unit with wood floors (the others are carpeted), but it has a tiny bathroom. Most intriguing are the four loft rooms in the carriage house, each with gas fireplace, Jacuzzi, and soaring ceilings.

32 Main St., Bethel, ME 04217. ② 888/774-1235 or 207/824-8060. www.thevictoria-inn.com. 15 units. High season, weekends, and holidays $99–$319 double; off-season $79–$189 double. Rates include breakfast and

(Finds Music in the Woods

Quisisana is not your average lakeside resort. Located on Kezar Lake in the village of Center Lovell (southwest of Bethel and north of Frye-berg Route 5), this spot features outstanding views to the White Mountains, but what makes a stay here really memorable is the music. It's everywhere. The 80-person staff consists of students recruited from conservatories from across the nation, and you're never far from waft-ing notes, whether it's someone practicing an aria in a rehearsal hall or a full-blown production number in a lakeside lodge. The guests (maximum of 150) usually stay for a week, and the musical menu changes day by day—Monday features musical theater, Tuesday piano recitals, Wednesday one-act operas, and so on. The recitals are per-formed by exuberant students who rarely slip up—an astonishing feat given that they practice in between sweeping, cooking, laundering, and the other mundane tasks of resort management.

The snug one-, two-, and three-bedrooms cabins are set among white pines along the lakeshore. They have the charm of an old sum-mer camp, but include amenities like private bathrooms (some shared bathrooms within family cabins) and comfortable furnishings. Days are spent canoeing, hiking, playing tennis, or simply sunning at the lake's edge. If it's rainy, the staff will often cobble together an extra recital to keep guests entertained. At dinnertime, creative, well-prepared entrees are served in a handsome dining hall in the main lodge.

During peak season, there's a 1-week minimum stay (Sat–Sat), with rates of $280 to $370 double per night, including all meals and enter-tainment. Credit cards aren't accepted, but personal checks are fine. For information, call © **207/925-3500** (or 914/833-0293 in winter) or go to www.quisisanaresort.com.

dinner. 2-night minimum stay weekends and holidays. Pets sometimes allowed ($30). AE, MC, V. **Amenities:** Restaurant (see below). *In room:* A/C, TV, hair dryer.

WHERE TO DINE
Great Grizzly/Matterhorn ⋆ STEAKHOUSE/PIZZA   These two restau-rants share a handsome timber-frame structure a couple of minutes from the ski area. It's casual and relaxed, with pinball, a pool table, and a handsome bar. You'll get two menus after you settle in: Great Grizzly offers mostly steaks, while Matterhorn specializes in very, very good wood-fired pizzas. The atmosphere is more relaxed and the food significantly better than at the Sunday River Brewing Company down the road.

Sunday River Rd. © **207/824-6271** or 207/824-6836. Pizzas from $7.95; other entrees $6.95–$16.95. MC, V. Daily pizza menu 3–10pm; steakhouse menu from 5–10pm. Open only during ski season.

The Victoria ⋆⋆ NEW AMERICAN   The dining room in Bethel's classiest inn happens to serve the town's best dinners. Guests choose from a menu that's simple but generally delivers on its high aspirations. Entrees include lobster ravi-oli and filet mignon served with a blueberry and port demi-glace. Desserts are a treat, both visually and to the tastebuds. This is Bethel's best pick for a romantic dinner out.

32 Main St. ☎ **888/774-1235** or 207/824-8060. www.thevictoria-inn.com. Reservations recommended on weekends. Main courses $9.95–$18.95. AE, MC, V. Wed–Mon 5:30–9pm.

RANGELEY LAKES ⭒⭒

Mounted moose heads on the walls, log cabins tucked into spruce forest, and cool August mornings that sometimes require not one sweater but two are the stuff of the Rangeley Lakes area. Although Rangeley Lake and its eponymous town are at the heart of the region, its borders extend much further, consisting of a series of lakes that feed into and flow out of the main lake.

The town of **Rangeley** (pop. 1,200) is the regional center for outdoor activities. It offers a handful of motels and restaurants, a bevy of fishing guides, a smattering of shops, and little else. Easy-to-see attractions in the Rangeley area are few, and most regular visitors and residents seem determined to keep it that way. The wise visitor rents a cabin or takes a room at a lodge, then explores the area with the slow pace that seems custom-made for the region. Rangeley is Maine's highest town at 1,546 feet (464m), and usually remains quite cool throughout the summer.

ESSENTIALS

GETTING THERE   Rangeley is 122 miles (196km) north of Portland, and 39 miles (63km) northwest of Farmington on Route 4. The most scenic approach is on Route 17 from Rumford.

VISITOR INFORMATION   The **Rangeley Lakes Region Chamber of Commerce** (☎ **800/685-2537** or 207/864-5364) maintains a year-round information booth in town at a small park near the lake. It's open Monday through Saturday from 9am to 5pm.

MUSEUMS & HISTORIC HOMES

Orgonon ⭒⭒⭒   Among the few notable historic sites in Maine relating to the 20th century is Orgonon, former home of the controversial Viennese psychiatrist Wilhelm Reich (1897–1957). An associate of Freud, Reich took his work a few steps further, building on the hypothesis that pent-up sexual energy resulted in numerous neuroses. Reich settled in Rangeley in 1942, where he developed the science of "orgonomy." According to Reich, living matter was animated by a sort of life force called "orgone," which floated freely in the atmosphere. To cure orgone imbalances, he invented orgone energy boxes, which were said to gather and concentrate ambient orgone. These boxes were just big enough to sit in. Reich was sentenced to federal prison for matters related to the interstate transport of his orgone boxes; he died in prison in 1957. While many dismissed Reich's theories as quackery, he still has dedicated adherents, including those who maintain the museum in his memory.

Orgonon, built in 1948 of native fieldstone, has a spectacular view of Dodge Pond and is designed in a distinctive mid-century-modern style, which stands apart from the local rustic-lodge motif. Visitors on the 1-hour guided tour can view the orgone boxes along with other intriguing inventions.

Dodge Pond Rd., 3½ miles (5.6km) west of Rangeley off Rte. 4. ☎ **207/864-3443.** Admission $4 adults, free for children under 12. July–Aug Tues–Sun 1–5pm; Sept Sun 1–5pm.

ALPINE SKIING

Saddleback Ski Area ⭒   With only two chairlifts, Saddleback qualifies as a small mountain, but it has an unexpectedly big-mountain feel. It offers a vertical drop of just 1,830 feet (549m), but what makes Saddleback so appealing is its rugged alpine setting (the Appalachian Trail runs across the high, mile-long ridge above the resort) and the old-fashioned cut of the trails. (The ski area was founded in 1960.) Saddleback offered glade skiing and narrow, winding trails well before the bigger ski areas sought to re-create these old-fashioned slopes. Condos and town houses offer limited on-mountain lodging; the ski mountain is about 7 miles (11km) from the village of Rangeley.

P.O. Box 490, Rangeley, ME 04970. ℂ 207/864-5671. www.saddlebackskiarea.com. Vertical drop: 1,830 ft. (549m). Lifts: 2 double chairlifts, 3 T-bars. Skiable acreage: 100. Lift tickets: $49 Sat–Sun, $38 Mon–Fri.

OTHER OUTDOOR PURSUITS

CANOEING The Rangeley Lakes region is a canoeist's paradise. Azure waters, dense forests, and handsome hills are all part of the allure. Rangeley Lake itself is populated along much of the lakeshore, but the cottages are well-spaced, and the lakeshore has a wild aspect to it. **Rangeley Lakes State Park** (ℂ 207/ 864-3858), on the south shore of the lake, has a cleared area for launching boats; a day-use fee is charged. You can also paddle right from downtown Rangeley, or use the public landing on the far northwest corner of the lake, at the intersection of Routes 16 and 4 near Oquossoc, which also offers easy canoe access to Cupsuptic and Mooselookmeguntic lakes from Haines Landing. For canoe rentals, try **Bald Mountain Camps,** in Oquossoc (ℂ 207/864-3671), or **Dockside Sports Center,** 90 Main St., in Rangeley (ℂ 207/864-2424).

In recent years, vast Mooselookmeguntic Lake suffered an unfortunate period of haphazard development on some of its southeastern coves, but much of the shore, especially along the west shore, is still remote and appealing. Note that capricious winds can come up suddenly, however, so be prepared and strive to stay close to shore. The **Stephen Phillips Wildlife Preserve** (ℂ 207/864-2003) on Mooselookmeguntic Lake rents canoes by the day and is one of the best jumping-off points to explore the wild lakes. A good day trip is out to the tip of Students Island, where there's an open field, spectacular views northwestward up the lake, and a great spot for a picnic.

HIKING The Appalachian Trail crosses Route 4 about 10 miles (16km) south of Rangeley. A strenuous but rewarding hike is along the trail northward to the summit of **Saddleback Mountain,** a 10-mile (16km) round-trip that ascends through thick forest and past remote ponds to open, arctic-like terrain with fine views of the surrounding mountains and lakes. Saddleback actually consists of two peaks over 4,000 feet (1,200m), hence the name. Be prepared for sudden shifts in weather, and for the high winds that often rake the open ridgeline.

An easier 1-mile (1.6km) hike may be found at **Bald Mountain** near the village of Oquossoc, on the northeast shore of Mooselookmeguntic Lake. Look for the trailhead 1 mile (1.6km) south of Haines Landing on Bald Mountain Road. The views have grown over in recent years, but you can still catch glimpses of the clear blue waters from above.

WHERE TO STAY & DINE

The Rangeley area has a scattering of B&Bs, but many visitors spend a week or more at a sporting camp or rented cottage. **Grant's Kennebago Camps** (ℂ 800/633-4815 or 207/864-3608) is 9 miles (14km) down a dusty logging road on Kennebago Lake—the biggest "fly-fishing only" lake east of the Mississippi. Rates are $150 per person, including all meals (with discounts for stays longer than 2 nights).

Rangeley Inn ⭐ The architecturally eclectic Rangeley Inn dominates Rangeley's miniature downtown. Parts of this hotel date back to 1877, but the main wing was built in 1907, with additions in the '20s and '40s. A motel annex is behind the inn on Haley Pond, but those looking for creaky floors and a richer sense of local heritage should request to stay in the main inn, where a handful of rooms come with claw-foot tubs. Some units in the motel have woodstoves, kitchenettes, and TVs. During the heavy tour season (especially fall), expect bus groups.

P.O. Box 160, Rangeley, ME 04970. ☎ **800/666-3687** or 207/864-3341. Fax 207/864-3634. www.rangeley inn.com. 50 units. $84–$120 double. 2-night minimum stay winter weekends. AE, DISC, MC, V. Pets allowed in 1 room ($8 per night). **Amenities:** 2 restaurants (traditional, pub fare). *In room:* No phone (in main inn).

Town & Lake Motel and Cottages   This old-fashioned compound offers a fine location right on the lake just outside Rangeley. Don't set your expectations too high for the motel rooms (ca. 1954)—they're worn but clean, and some beds are weary. Units with kitchens cost $10 extra. The cottages offer better value— all but one are right on the water, and these feature large windows with lake views, crate-style 1970s-era furnishings, porches, and kitchens.

112 Main St. (P.O. Box 47), Rangely, ME 04970. ☎ **207/864-3755.** 25 units. $85 double; $140–$160 cottage (sleeps up to 4). AE, DISC, MC, V. Pets allowed. **Amenities:** Lake swimming; free canoes; motorboat rental. *In room:* TV, coffeemaker.

CARRABASSETT VALLEY

The region in and around the Carrabassett Valley can be summed up in six words: big peaks, wild woods, deep lakes. The crowning jewel of the region is **Sugarloaf Mountain,** Maine's second-highest peak at 4,237 feet (1,271m). Distinct from nearby peaks because of its pyramidal shape, the mountain has been developed for top-notch skiing and offers the largest vertical drop in Maine, the best selection of winter activities, and a wide range of accommodations.

While Sugarloaf draws the lion's share of visitors, it's not the only game in town. Nearby **Kingfield** is an attractive, historic town with a venerable old hotel; it has more of the character of an Old West outpost than of classic New England. Other valley towns offering limited services for travelers include **Eustis, Stratton,** and **Carrabassett Valley.**

Outside the villages and ski resort, it's all rugged hills, tumbling streams, and spectacular natural surroundings. The muscular mountains of the **Bigelow Range** provide terrain for some of the state's best hiking, and Flagstaff Lake is the place for flatwater canoeing amid majestic surroundings.

ESSENTIALS

GETTING THERE   Kingfield and Sugarloaf are on Route 27. Skiers debate over the best route from the turnpike. Some exit at Auburn and take Route 4 north to Route 27; others exit in Augusta and take Route 27 straight through. It's a toss-up time-wise, but exiting at Augusta is marginally more scenic. **Maine Tour and Travel** (☎ **800/649-5071**) offers private shuttle service from state airports to the mountain.

VISITOR INFORMATION   For information on skiing or summer activities in the Sugarloaf area, contact the resort at ☎ **800/843-5623** or 207/237-2000. An information booth on Route 27 is staffed in summer and winter.

ALPINE SKIING

Sugarloaf/USA 🏂🏂🏂   Sugarloaf is Maine's big mountain, with the highest vertical drop in New England after Vermont's Killington. And thanks to quirks of geography, it actually feels bigger than it is. From the high, open snowfields or the upper advanced runs like Bubblecuffer or White Nitro, skiers develop vertigo looking down at the valley floor. Sugarloaf attracts plenty of experts to its hard-core runs, but it's also a fine intermediate mountain. This may be the friendliest resort in New England—the staff on the lifts, in the restaurants, and at the hotels all seem genuinely glad you're here. It's also a very welcoming family mountain, with lots of activities for kids. The main drawback? Wind. Sugarloaf seems to get buffeted regularly, with the higher lifts often closed because of gusting.

RR #1, Box 5000, Carrabassett Valley, ME 04947. © **800/843-5623** or 207/237-2000. www.sugarloaf.com. Vertical drop: 2,820 ft. (846m). Lifts: 13 chairlifts, including 2 high-speed quads; 1 surface lift. Skiable acreage: 1,410 (snowmaking on 475 acres). Lift tickets: $52.

CROSS-COUNTRY SKIING

The **Sugarloaf Outdoor Center** ★ (© **207/237-6830**) offers 63 miles (101km) of groomed trails that weave through the village at the base of the mountain and into the low hills and scrappy woodlands along the Carrabassett River. The trails are impeccably groomed for striding and skating, and wonderful views open here and there to Sugarloaf Mountain and the Bigelow Range. The base lodge is simple and attractive, all knotty pine with a cathedral ceiling, and features a cafeteria, towering stone fireplace, and well-equipped ski shop. Snowshoes are also available for rent. Trail fees are $16 for adults, $10 for seniors and children 12 and under. (Half-day tickets are also available.) The center is located on Route 27 about a mile (1.6km) south of the Sugarloaf access road. A shuttle bus serves the area in winter.

HIKING

The 12-mile (19km) Bigelow Range has some of the most dramatic high-ridge hiking in the state, a close second to Mount Katahdin. It consists of a handful of lofty peaks, with Avery Peak (the east peak) offering the best views. On exceptionally clear days, hikers can see Mount Washington to the southwest and Mount Katahdin to the northeast. This is terrain for experienced hikers, because it's not that hard to make a wrong turn and end up lost. Bring a compass or GPS.

A strenuous but rewarding hike for fit hikers is the 10.3-mile (17km) loop that begins at the **Fire Warden's Trail.** (The trailhead is at the washed-out bridge on Stratton Brook Pond Rd., a rugged dirt road that leaves eastward from Rte. 27 about 2.3 miles/3.7km north of the Sugarloaf access road.) Follow the Fire Warden's Trail up the steep ridge to the junction with the **Appalachian Trail (AT).** Head south on the AT, which tops the West Peak and South Horn, two open summits with stellar views. A ¼ mile (0.4km) past Horns Pond, turn south on **Horns Pond Trail** and descend back to the Fire Warden's Trail to return to your car. Allow about 8 hours for the loop; a topographical map and hiking guide are strongly recommended.

A less rigorous hike that still yields supremely rewarding views is to **Cranberry Peak,** the Bigelow peak furthest west. Plan on 4 to 5 hours to complete this hike along Bigelow Range Trail, which runs about 6½ miles (10km). The trailhead is just south of the town of Stratton (from the south, turn right ⅕ mile/03.km after crossing Stratton Brook, then drive on a dirt road a ½ mile/0.8km to a clearing). Follow the trail through woods and over a series of ledges to 3,213-foot (964m) Cranberry Peak. Retrace your steps to your car.

Detailed directions for these hikes and many others in the area can be found in the AMC's *Maine Mountain Guide.*

OTHER OUTDOOR PURSUITS

Sugarloaf's 18-hole **golf course** (© **207/237-2000**) is often ranked the number-one golf destination in the state by experienced golfers, who are lured here by the Robert Trent Jones, Jr., course design and dramatic mountain backdrop. Sugarloaf hosts a well-respected golf school in season.

Other outdoor activities are located in and around the **Sugarloaf Outdoor Center** (© 207/237-6830). Through the center, you can arrange for fly-fishing lessons, a mountain-bike excursion at the resort's mountain-bike park (rentals available), or hiking or white-water rafting in the surrounding mountains and valleys.

WHERE TO STAY

For convenience, nothing beats staying right on the mountain in winter. Many of the base-area condos are booked through the **Sugarloaf/USA Inn** (© 800/ 843-5623 or 207/237-2000). Sugarloaf also operates a lodging reservations service, booking guest rooms and private homes, mostly off mountain; call © 800/843-2732.

Grand Summit Hotel ⭐⭐ This is a great choice for skiers who want to be in the thick of it in winter, although it's pretty sleepy during the summer. Located next to the lifts in the heart of the Sugarloaf base area, this contemporary hotel offers three types of guest rooms. Standard rooms are tucked under sharply angled gables and are a bit dark; one-bedroom suites are divided between two floors, with an upstairs bedroom connected via a narrow spiral staircase. The superior rooms (best value) are brightest and most open. The odd-numbered rooms face the slopes, while even-numbered rooms face across the valley with views of distant hills. The ground floor features a lively pub; a free winter shuttle service connects to other restaurants around the resort.

Sugarloaf base area (RR 1, Box 2299), Carrabassett Valley, ME 04947. © 207/237-2222. Fax 207/237-2874. www.sugarloaf.com. 119 units. Peak ski season $145–$250 double, to $650 suite; off-season from $120. Minimum stay required some holiday weekends. AE, MC, V. **Amenities:** Restaurant (pub fare); 18-hole golf course; health club; Jacuzzi; sauna; nearby bike rental; babysitting. *In room:* A/C, TV, coffeemaker, hair dryer, iron.

The Herbert The Herbert has the feel of a classic North Woods hostelry—sort of Dodge City by way of Alaska. Built in downtown Kingfield in 1918, the hotel featured all of the finest accoutrements when it was constructed, including fumed oak paneling and incandescent lights in the lobby (look for the original brass fixtures), a classy dining room, and comfortable guest rooms. It's had ups and downs since then (with some downs more recently). Under new ownership since late 2001, the inn was in the process of getting a gradual makeover at press time. The Herbert is located about 15 miles (24km) from the slopes at Sugarloaf/ USA.

246 Main St. (P.O. Box 67), Kingfield, ME 04947. © 888/656-9922 or 207/265-2000. Fax 207/265-4594. www.herbertgrandhotel.com. 27 units. $95–$175 double. Rates include continental breakfast. AE, DISC, MC, V. **Amenities:** Restaurant (family style). *In room:* TV, no phone.

Three Stanley Avenue ⭐ *(Value* Three Stanley Avenue is the bed-and-breakfast annex to the well-known restaurant next door, One Stanley Avenue. Perched on a shady knoll in a quiet village setting just across the bridge from downtown Kingfield, this B&B has an old-fashioned Victorian boardinghouse feel to it. Guest rooms are comfortably if not luxuriously appointed.

3 Stanley Ave. (P.O. Box 169), Kingfield, ME 04947. © 207/265-5541. www.stanleyavenue.com. 6 units (3 units share 2 bathrooms). Dec–Mar $60–$65 double; Apr–Nov $55–$60 double. Rates include breakfast. 2-night minimum on winter weekends. DISC, MC, V. **Amenities:** Restaurant (New American). *In room:* No phone.

WHERE TO DINE

Hug's ⟨✿⟩ NORTHERN ITALIAN   This is a small place, set just off the high-way in a fairy-tale cottage, and the food is better than one would expect for a ski-area Italian restaurant. Dinner is preceded by a tasty basket of pesto bread, and entrees go beyond red sauce, offering a broad selection of pastas. (The wild-mushroom ravioli with walnut-pesto Alfredo is quite good.)

Rte. 27 (0.7 miles/1.1km south of the Sugarloaf access road), Carrabassett Valley. ⟨✆⟩ **207/237-2392.** Reservations recommended, especially on weekends. Main courses $9.95–$19.95. DISC, MC, V. Winter daily 5–10pm; summer and fall Wed–Sun 5–10pm. Closed May–late July and mid-Oct to early Dec.

8 Moosehead Lake Region ⟨★⟩⟨★⟩

Thirty-two miles (52km) long and 5 miles (8km) across at its widest point, Moosehead Lake is Maine's largest lake, and it's a great destination for hikers, boaters, and canoeists. The lake was historically the center of the region's logging activity; that history preserved the lake and kept it largely unspoiled by develop-ment. Timber companies still own much of the lakeside property (although the state has acquired a significant amount in the last few years), and the 350-mile (564km) shoreline is mostly unbroken second- or third-growth forest. The sec-ond-home building frenzy of the 1980s had an impact on the southern reaches of the lake, but the woody shoreline has absorbed most of the boom rather gracefully.

The first thing to know about the lake is that it's not meant to be seen by car. There are some great views from a handful of roads—especially from Route 6/15 as you near Rockwood, and from the high elevations on the way to Lily Bay—but for the most part the roads are a distance from the shores, and offer rather dull driving. To see the lake at its best, plan to get out on the water by steamship or canoe. If you prefer your sightseeing by car, you'll find more rewarding drives in the western Maine mountains or along the coast.

Greenville ⟨✿⟩ is the de facto capital of Moosehead Lake, scenically situated at the southern tip. Change is creeping into the North Woods—what was until recently a rugged outpost town is now orienting itself toward the tourist trade with boutiques and souvenir shops. Most shops now seem to stock a full line of T-shirts featuring moose. But the town's still a good place to base yourself for outdoor day excursions.

ESSENTIALS

GETTING THERE   Greenville is 158 miles (254km) from Portland. Take the turnpike to the Newport exit (Exit 39) and head north on Route 7/11 to Route 23 in Dexter, following that northward to Route 6/15 near Sangerville. Follow this to Greenville.

VISITOR INFORMATION   The **Moosehead Lake Chamber of Commerce** (⟨✆⟩ **207/695-2702;** www.mooseheadarea.com) maintains a helpful information center that's a recommended first stop. Not only will you find a good selection of the usual brochures, but the center also maintains files and shelves full of maps, trail information, wildlife guidebooks, and videos that visitors are free to use. From Memorial Day to mid-October, it's open Wednesday through Mon-day from 10am to 4pm; it's located on your right as you come into Greenville, next to the Indian Hill Trading Post.

EXPLORING THE MOOSEHEAD LAKE REGION

Northwood Outfitters, on Main Street in Greenville (⟨✆⟩ **207/695-3288;** www.maineoutfitter.com), is open daily and can help with planning a trip up the lake or into the woods, as well as load you up with enough equipment to stay out for weeks. It rents complete adventure equipment sets, which include canoe, paddles, life jacket, tent, sleeping bag, pad, camp stove, axe, cook kit, and more. The full kits start at $97 per person for 2 days, up to $272 per person for a week. Shuttle service and individual pieces of equipment are also available for rent, with canoes running $20 a day, mountain bikes from $20 to $30 a day.

One of our favorite hikes in the region is **Mount Kineo** ⟨⟨, marked by a massive, broad cliff that rises from the shores of Moosehead. This hike is accessible via water; near the town of Rockwood look for signs advertising shuttles across the lake to Kineo from the town landing. (Folks offering this service seem to change from year to year, so ask around; it usually costs about $5 round-trip.) Once on the other side, you can explore the grounds of the famed old Kineo Mountain House (alas, the grand, 500-room hotel was demolished in 1938), then cut across the golf course and follow the shoreline to the trail that leads to the 1,800-foot (540m) summit. The views from the cliffs are dazzling. Be sure to continue on the trail to the old fire tower, which you can ascend for a hawk's-eye view of the region.

MOOSE-WATCHING ⟨⟨

A number of outfitters offer to lead visitors along lakeshores and forest trails to view and photograph the wily moose, the region's most noted woodland resident. While you can see moose almost anywhere (keep a sharp eye out when driving!), a guided excursion will usually get you into some of the most beautiful spots in the region, hidden places you might not see otherwise. The moose-spotting batting average is quite high among all outfitters. Reservations are recommended, because guides often don't make plans to go out unless they have advance registrations. The folks at the visitor center can provide more information and help make arrangements.

Pontoon boats are perhaps the most comfortable vehicles in which to search for moose—it's like sitting in an outdoor living room that floats. **The Moose Cruise** ⟨, at the Birches Resort in Rockwood (© **207/534-7305**), offers three excursions daily, each lasting a bit over 2 hours.

Moose-watching excursions of 4 to 5 hours by canoe are offered by the **Maine Guide Fly Shop,** in Greenville (© **207/695-2266**), and **Ed Mathieu** ⟨ (© **207/876-4907**). Ed charges $110 per couple, which includes a trip to a pond via pick-up truck, plus lunch or snacks.

WHITE-WATER RAFTING ⟨⟨⟨

Big waves and boiling drops await rafters on the heart-thumping run through Kennebec Gorge at the headwaters of the **Kennebec River,** located southwest of Greenville. Dozens of rafters line up along the churning river below the dam, and then await the siren that signals the release. Your guide will signal you to hop in, and you're off, heading through huge, roiling waves and down precipitous drops with names like Whitewasher and Magic Falls. Most of the excitement is over in the first hour; after that, it's a lazy trip down the river, interrupted only by lunch and the occasional water fight with other rafts. Also nearby is the less thrilling but more technical Dead River, which offers about a half dozen release dates, mostly during early summer.

Commercial white-water outfitters offer trips in summer at a cost of about $85 to $115 per person (usually at the higher end on weekends). **Northern Outdoors** (© **800/765-7238;** www.northernoutdoors.com) is the oldest of the bunch, and offers rock-climbing, mountain-biking, and fishing expeditions as well, plus snowmobiling in winter. Other reputable companies include **Wilderness Expeditions** (© 800/825-9453), which is affiliated with the rustic Birches Resort, and the **New England Outdoor Center** (© 800/766-7238).

MOOSEHEAD BY STEAMSHIP ★★ & FLOATPLANE ★★

During the lake's golden days of tourism in the late 19th century, visitors could come by train from New York or Washington, then connect by steamship to the resorts and boardinghouses around the lake. A vestige of that era is found at the **Moosehead Marine Museum,** in Greenville (© 207/695-2716), where displays suggest the grandeur of life at Kineo Mountain House, a sprawling Victorian lake resort that once defined elegance. But the small museum's showpiece is the S.S. *Katahdin,* a 115-foot (35m) steamship that's been cruising Moosehead's waters since 1914. The two-deck ship (now run by diesel rather than steam) offers a variety of sightseeing tours, including a twice-a-week excursion up the lake to the site of the former Kineo Mountain House. Fares range from $20 to $26 for adults, $12 to $15 for children 6 and over.

Moosehead from the air is a memorable sight. Stop by **Folsom's Air Service** (© 207/695-2821), on the shores of the lake in Greenville, just north of the village center on Lily Bay Road. Folsom's has been serving the North Woods since 1946 and has a fleet of five floatplanes. A 15-minute tour of the southern reaches of the lake costs $20 per person; longer flights over the region run up to about $60 per person. A great adventure is the **canoe-and-fly package** ★★. For $100 per person, Folsom's will drop you and a canoe off at a remote river location; you then paddle to Lobster Lake, where you'll get picked up and returned to Greenville later that day.

WHERE TO STAY & DINE

Blair Hill Inn ★★★ This unexpectedly classy inn amid the wilds occupies an 1891 Queen Anne mansion with dazzling views of Moosehead Lake and the surrounding hills. It's been sparely decorated with a mix of rustic and classic appointments, like Oriental carpets and deer-antler lamps. The bright first-floor common rooms, the drop-dead-gorgeous porch, and the handsome guest rooms invite loafing. All units features robes, spring water, and locally made soaps. Room 1 is the best, featuring a panoramic sunset view and fireplace (Duraflame logs only). All guests can enjoy the outdoor Jacuzzi, Adirondack chairs on the lawn, and a small catch-and-release trout pond (ask about fly-fishing workshops).

Lily Bay Rd. (P.O. Box 1288), Greenville, ME 04441. © 207/695-0224. www.blairhill.com. 8 units. June–Oct $195–$395 double. Rates include breakfast. 2-night minimum stay on weekends. DISC, MC, V. Closed Nov and Apr. Children over 10 welcome. **Amenities:** Restaurant (fine dining); Jacuzzi. *In room:* Hair dryer, no phone.

Greenville Inn ★★ This 1895 Queen Anne lumber baron's home sits regally on a hilly side street above Greenville's commercial district. The interiors are sumptuous, with cherry and mahogany woodworking and a lovely stained-glass window over the stairwell. At the handsome small bar, you can order up a cocktail or Maine beer, then sit in front of the fire or retreat to the front porch to watch the evening sun slip over Squaw Mountain and the lake. Six modern cottages on the grounds have TVs and offer more privacy.

Norris St., Greenville, ME 04441. © 888/695-6000 or 207/695-2206. www.greenvilleinn.com. 12 units. Summer $135–$155 double, $165 cottage, $225 suite; off-season $125–$145 double, $155 cottage, $195 suite. Rates include continental breakfast. 2-night minimum stay on holiday weekends. DISC, MC, V. No children under 8. **Amenities:** Restaurant (Continental/regional). *In room:* No phone.

Little Lyford Pond Camps ⭐ This venerable backwoods logging camp is one of the more welcoming spots in the North Woods—at least for those looking to rough it a bit. Originally built to house loggers in the 1870s, each cabin contains a small woodstove, propane lantern, and cold running water, and has its own outhouse. At mealtimes, guests gather in the main lodge, which has books to browse and board games for evenings. During the day, activities aren't hard to find, from fishing for native brook trout (fly-fishing lessons available) and hiking with the lodge's llamas to canoeing at two nearby ponds or wandering on the Appalachian Trail to Gulf Hagas, a scenic gorge 2 miles (3.2km) away. In winter, the cross-country skiing on the lodging's private network is superb, and time spent in the sauna will make you forget the cold weather outside. Access is via rough logging road in summer (ski or snowmobile in winter), so factor in extra time in getting here.

P.O. Box 340, Greenville, ME 04441. ℂ 207/280-0016 (mobile phone). www.littlelyford.com. 8 units. $170 double. Rates include all meals. 2-night minimum stay on weekends and holidays. No credit cards. Pets allowed ($5 per day). **Amenities:** Sauna; free canoes. *In room:* No phone.

Appendix:
New England in Depth

by Wayne Curtis

Reduced to simplest terms, New England consists of two regions: Boston and Not-Boston.

Boston, of course, is in the same league as other major metropolitan areas, and boasts first-class hotels, restaurants, and historic and modern architecture. Of all U.S. cities, Boston has perhaps the richest history, ranging from the days of America's settlement in the 17th century through the War of Independence in 1776 and on into the nation's cultural renaissance in the mid- and late 19th century. The Boston area is also a national seat of education, with dozens of prestigious colleges and universities. The presence of so many august institutions lends the city a youthful air in contrast to its fusty heritage.

The extensive territory of Not-Boston arcs widely, from the Connecticut and Rhode Island shoreline through the rolling Berkshire Mountains of western Massachusetts on through the Green and White mountains and into the vast state of Maine. The Not-Boston region, while widely spread, traces it roots back to a Puritan ethic, and its longtime residents still tend to display shared traits and values, like a stubborn independence, a respect for thrift, and an almost genetic mistrust of outsiders.

New England's legendary aloofness is important to keep in mind when visiting the area, because getting to know the region requires equal amounts of patience and persistence. New England doesn't wear its attractions on its sleeve. It keeps its best destinations hidden in valleys and on the side streets of small villages. Your most memorable experience might come in cracking open a boiled lobster at a roadside lobster pound marked only with a scrawled paper sign, or exploring a cobblestone Boston alley that's not on the maps. There's no Disneyland or Space Needle or Grand Canyon here. New England is the sum of dozens of smaller attractions, and resists being defined by a few big ones.

Which isn't to say that New England lacks attractions. It has the mansions of Newport, the endless beaches of Cape Cod, the rolling Green Mountains of Vermont, the craggy White Mountains of New Hampshire, and magnificent Acadia National Park on the Maine coast. It has wonderful, lost-in-time towns like New Preston, Conn., and Woodstock, Vt. But attempting to explore New England as a "connect-the-dots" endeavor, linking the major sights with long drives, is a surefire recipe for disappointment. It's better to plan a slower itinerary that allows you to enjoy the desultory trips between destinations and explore the little villages and quiet byways.

Some writers maintain that New England's character is still informed by a grim Calvinist doctrine, which decrees nothing will change one's fate and that hard work is a moral virtue. The New Englander's dull acceptance that the Boston Red Sox will never be victorious is often trotted out as evidence of the region's enduring Calvinism, as is the inhabitants' perverse celebration of the often brutish climate.

But that's not to say travelers should expect rock-hard mattresses and nutritional but tasteless meals. On the contrary: Luxurious country inns and restaurants serving food rivaling what you'll find in Manhattan have become part of the landscape in the past 2 decades. Be sure to visit these places. But to get the most out of your trip, leave enough time to spend an afternoon rocking and reading on a broad inn porch, or to wander out of town on an abandoned county road with no particular destination in mind.

"There's nothing to do here," an inn manager in Vermont once explained to me. "Our product is indolence." That's an increasingly rare commodity these days. Take the time to savor it.

1 New England Today

It's a common question, so don't be embarrassed about asking it. You might be on Martha's Vineyard, or traveling through a pastoral Vermont valley, or exploring an island off the Maine coast. You'll see houses and people. And you'll wonder: "What do these people do to earn a living?"

As recently as a few decades ago, the answer was probably this: living off the land. They might have fished the seas, harvested timber, or managed a gravel pit. Of course, many still do operate such businesses, but this work is no longer the economic mainstay it once was. Today, scratch a rural New Englander and you're just as likely to find an editor for a magazine that's published in Boston or New York, a farmer who grows specialized produce for gourmet restaurants, or a banking consultant who handles business by fax and e-mail. And you'll find lots of folks dependent on tourism.

This change in the economy is but one of the tectonic shifts facing the region. The most visible and more wracking change involves development and growth. A region long familiar with economic poverty, the recent prosperity has threatened to bring to New England that curious sort of homogenization that has marked much of the nation. Instead of distinctive downtowns and courthouse squares, the landscape is starting to look a lot like suburbs everywhere—a pastiche of strip malls dotted with fast-food chains and big-box stores like Wal-Mart and Home Depot.

New England towns have long maintained their strong identities in the face of considerable pressure. The region has always taken a quiet pride in its low-key, practical approach to life. In smaller communities, town meetings are still the preferred form of government. Residents gather in a public space and vote on the important issues of the day, like funding for their schools, road improvements, and, at times, symbolic gestures, such as declaring their town a nuclear-free zone. "Use it up, wear it out, make do, or do without" is a well-worn phrase that aptly sums up the attitude of many in New England.

It's as yet unclear how town meetings and that sense of knowing where your town starts and the next one begins will survive the slow but inexorable encroachment of the Wal-Marts. Of course, suburban Connecticut communities in the orbit of New York City and Massachusetts towns just outside of Boston have long since capitulated to sprawl, as have pockets elsewhere in the region—including the areas near Hartford, Conn.; Portland, Maine; and Burlington, Vt.—where little regional identity can be discerned.

But the rest of New England is still figuring out how best to balance the principles of growth and conservation—how to allow the economy to edge into the modern age, without sacrificing those qualities that make New England such a distinctive place.

Development is a hot but not necessarily inflammatory issue—this isn't like the property rights movement in the West, where residents are manning the barricades and taking hostages for the cause. (At least not yet.) Few seem to think that development should be allowed at all costs. And few seem to think that the land should be preserved at all costs.

Pinching off all development means the offspring of longtime New England families will have no jobs, and New England will be fated to spend its days as a sort of quaint theme park. But if development continues unabated, many of the characteristics that make New England unique—and attract tourist dollars—will vanish. Will the Berkshires or the Maine coast be able to sustain their tourism industries if they're blanketed with strip malls and fast-food joints, making them look like every other place in the nation? Not likely. The question is how to respect the conservation ethic while leaving room for growth. And that question won't be resolved in the near future.

Except for a several-year slump in the early 1990s, New England has been enjoying an ongoing economic boom since the mid-1980s. Commentators point out that this change, while welcome after decades of slow growth, will bring new conflicts. The rise of the information culture will make it increasingly likely that those telecommuters and info-entrepreneurs will settle in remote and pristine villages, running their businesses via modem and satellite. How will these affluent migrants adapt to clear-cutting in the countryside or increasing numbers of tour buses cruising their village greens?

Change doesn't come rapidly to New England. But there's a lot to sort out, and friction will certainly build, one strip mall at a time.

2 History 101

Viewed from a distance, New England's history mirrors that of its namesake, England. The region rose from nowhere to gain tremendous historical prominence, captured a good deal of overseas trade, and became an industrial powerhouse and center for creative thought. And then the party ended relatively abruptly, as commerce and culture sought more fertile grounds to the west and south.

To this day, New England refuses to be divorced from its past. Walking through Boston, layers of history are evident at every turn, from the church steeples of colonial times (dwarfed by glass-sided skyscrapers) to verdant parklands that bespeak the refined sensibility of the late Victorian era.

History is even more inescapable in off-the-beaten-track New England. Travelers in Downeast Maine, northern New Hampshire, Connecticut's Litchfield Hills, the Berkshires of Massachusetts, and much of Vermont will find clues to what Henry Wadsworth Longfellow called "the irrevocable past" every way they turn,

Dateline

- **1000–15** Viking explorers land in Canada, and may or may not have sailed southward to New England. Evidence is spotty.
- **1497** John Cabot, seeking to establish trade for England, reaches the island of Newfoundland in Canada and sails south as far as Maine.
- **1602** Capt. Bartholomew Gosnold lands on the Massachusetts coast. Names Cape Cod, Martha's Vineyard, and other locations.
- **1604** French colonists settle on an island on the St. Croix River between present-day Maine and New Brunswick. They leave after a single miserable winter.
- **1614** Capt. John Smith maps the New England coast, names the Charles River after King Charles I of England, and calls the area a paradise.
- **1616** Smallpox kills large numbers of Indians between Maine and Rhode Island.
- **1620** The *Mayflower*, carrying some 100 colonists (including many Pilgrims, fleeing religious persecution in England), arrives at Cape Cod.

continues

from stone walls running through woods to spectacular Federal-style homes in the countryside.

Here's a brief overview of some historical episodes and trends that shaped New England:

INDIGENOUS CULTURE   Native Americans have inhabited New England since about 7000 B.C. While New York's Iroquois Indians had a presence in Vermont, New England was inhabited chiefly by Algonquins who lived a nomadic life. Connecticut was home to some 16 Algonquin tribes, who dubbed the region Quinnetukut.

After the arrival of the Europeans, French Catholic missionaries succeeded in converting many Native Americans, and most tribes sided with the French in the French and Indian Wars in the 18th century. Afterward, the Indians fared poorly at the hands of the British, and were quickly pushed to the margins. Today, they are found in greatest concentration at several reservations in Maine. The Pequots have established a thriving gaming industry in Connecticut. Other than that, the few clues left behind by Indian cultures have been more or less obliterated by later settlers.

THE COLONIES   In 1604, some 80 French colonists spent a winter on a small island on what today is the Maine–New Brunswick border. They did not care for the harsh weather of their new home and left in spring to resettle in present-day Nova Scotia. In 1607, 3 months after the celebrated Jamestown, Va. colony was founded, a group of 100 English settlers established a community at Popham Beach, Maine. The Maine winter demoralized these would-be colonists as well, and they returned to England the following year.

The colonization of the region began in earnest with the arrival of the Pilgrims at Plymouth Rock in 1620. The Pilgrims—a religious group that had split from the Church of England—established the first permanent

- **1630** Colonists led by John Winthrop establish the town of Boston, named after an English village.
- **1635–36** Roger Williams is exiled from Massachusetts for espousing liberal religious ideas; he founds the city of Providence, R.I.
- **1636** Harvard College is founded to educate young men for the ministry.
- **1638** America's first printing press is established in Cambridge.
- **1648** First labor unions are established by coopers and shoemakers in Boston.
- **1675–76** Native Americans attack colonists throughout New England in what is known as King Philip's war.
- **1692** The Salem witch trials take place. Twenty people (including 14 women) are executed before the hysteria subsides.
- **1704** America's first regularly published newspaper, the *Boston News Letter,* is founded.
- **1713** The first schooner, a distinctively American sailing ship, is designed and built in Gloucester, Mass.
- **1764** "Taxation without representation" is denounced in reaction to the Sugar Act.
- **1770** Five colonists are killed outside what is now the Old State House in an incident known as the Boston Massacre.
- **1773** British ships are raided by colonists poorly disguised as Indians during the Boston Tea Party. More than 300 chests of tea are dumped into the harbor from three British ships.
- **1775** On April 18, Paul Revere and William Dawes spread the word that the British are marching toward Lexington and Concord. The next day the "shot heard round the world" is fired. On June 17, the British win the Battle of Bunker Hill but suffer heavy casualties.
- **1783** Treaty of Paris is signed, formally concluding the American Revolution.
- **1788** Connecticut becomes the fifth, Massachusetts the sixth, and New Hampshire the ninth state to formally join the union.
- **1790** Rhode Island becomes the 13th state and the final colony to ratify the constitution.

colony, although it came at a hefty price: Half the group perished during the first winter. But the colony took root, and thrived over the years in part thanks to helpful Native Americans.

The success of the Pilgrims lured other settlers from England, who established a constellation of small towns outside of Boston that became the Massachusetts Bay Colony. Roger Williams was expelled from the colony for his religious beliefs; he founded the city of Providence, R.I. Other restless colonists expanded their horizons in search of lands for settlement. Throughout the 17th century, colonists from Massachusetts pushed northward into what is now New Hampshire and Maine, and southward into Connecticut. The first areas to be settled were lands near protected harbors along the coast and on navigable waterways.

The more remote settlements came under attack in the 17th and early 18th centuries in a series of raids by Indians against the British settlers—conducted both independently and in concert with the French. These proved temporary setbacks; colonization continued apace throughout New England into 18th century.

THE AMERICAN REVOLUTION
Starting around 1765, Great Britain launched a series of ham-handed economic policies to reign in the increasingly feisty colonies. These included a direct tax—the Stamp Act—to pay for a standing army. The crackdown provoked strong resistance. Under the banner of "No taxation without representation," disgruntled colonists engaged in a series of riots, resulting in the Boston Massacre of 1770, when five protesting colonists were fired upon and killed by British soldiers.

In 1773, the most infamous protest took place in Boston. The British had imposed the Tea Act (the right to collect duties on tea imports), which prompted a group of colonists dressed as Mohawk Indians to board three British ships and

- **1791** The short-lived Republic of Vermont (1777–91) ends and the state of Vermont joins the union.
- **1812** War of 1812 with England batters New England economy.
- **1814** The nation's first textile mill is built, in Waltham, Mass.
- **1820** Maine, formerly a district of Massachusetts, becomes a state.
- **1835** Samuel Colt of Connecticut develops the six-shooter pistol.
- **1861** Massachusetts Institute of Technology is founded.
- **1892** America's first gasoline-powered automobile is built in Chicopee, Mass.
- **1897** First Boston Marathon is run; Boston completes first American subway.
- **1903** The first World Series is played; Boston Red Sox win.
- **1918** The Red Sox celebrate another World Series victory. For the next 8 decades (and counting), they fail to repeat this feat.
- **1930** America's Cup sailing race is first held in Newport, R.I.
- **1930s** The Great Depression devastates New England's already reeling industrial base.
- **1938** A major hurricane sweeps into New England, killing hundreds and destroying countless buildings and trees.
- **1942** A fire at Boston's Cocoanut Grove nightclub kills 491 people.
- **1946** John F. Kennedy is elected to Congress to represent Boston's first congressional district.
- **1957** Boston Celtics win their first NBA championship, laying the groundwork for a reign that will eventually include 16 championships.
- **1963** New Hampshire becomes first state to establish a lottery to support education.
- **1966** Edward Brooke of Massachusetts becomes the first African American elected to the U.S. Senate since Reconstruction.
- **1972** Maine's Indians head to court, claiming the state illegally seized their land in violation of a 1790 act. They settle 8 years later for $81.5 million.

continues

dump 342 chests of tea into the harbor. This well-known incident was dubbed the Boston Tea Party.

Hostilities reached a peak in 1775, when the British sought to quell burgeoning unrest in Massachusetts. A contingent of British soldiers was sent to Lexington to seize military supplies and arrest two high-profile rebels—

- **1974** In Connecticut, Ella Grasso becomes the first elected woman governor.
- **1991** The Big Dig begins in Boston. Scheduled completion date: 2005.
- **2002** The New England Patriots win the Super Bowl, stunning New Englanders long accustomed to defeat.

John Hancock and Samuel Adams. The militia formed by the colonists exchanged gunfire with the British, thereby igniting the revolution ("the shot heard round the world").

Notable battles in New England included the Battle of Bunker Hill outside Boston, which the British won but at tremendous cost; and the Battle of Bennington in Vermont, in which the colonists prevailed. Hostilities formally ended in February 1783, and in September, Britain recognized the United States as a sovereign nation.

FARMING & TRADE As the new republic matured, economic growth in New England followed two tracks. Residents of inland communities survived by clearing the land for farming, and trading in furs. Vermont in particular has always been an agrarian state, and remains a prominent dairy producer to this day.

On the coast, boatyards sprang up from Connecticut to Maine, and ship captains made tidy fortunes trading lumber for sugar and rum in the Caribbean. Trade was dealt a severe blow following the Embargo Act of 1807, but commerce eventually recovered, and New England ships could be encountered everywhere around the globe.

The growth of the railroad in the mid–19th century was another boon. The train opened up much of the interior, and led to towns springing up overnight, such as White River Junction, Vt. The rail lines allowed local resources—such as the fine marbles and granites from Vermont—to be easily shipped to markets to the south.

INDUSTRY New England's industrial revolution found seed around the time of the embargo of 1807. Barred from importing English fabrics, Americans built their own textile mills. Other common household products were also manufactured domestically, especially shoes. Towns like Lowell, Mass.; Lewiston, Maine; and Manchester, N.H., became centers of textile and shoe production. In Connecticut, the manufacture of arms and clocks emerged as major industries. Today, industry no longer plays the prominent role it once did—manufacturing first moved to the South, then overseas.

TOURISM In the mid– and late 19th century, New Englanders discovered a new cash crop: the tourist. All along the Eastern Seaboard, it became fashionable for the gentry and eventually the working class to set out for excursions to the mountains and the shore. Regions such as the Berkshires, the White and Green mountains, and Block Island were lifted by the tide of summer visitors. The tourism wave crested in the 1890s in Newport, R.I., and Bar Harbor, Maine, both of which were flooded by the affluent. Several grand resort hotels from tourism's golden era still host summer travelers in the region.

ECONOMIC DOWNTURN While the railways allowed New England to thrive in the mid–19th century, the train played an equally central role in undermining its prosperity. The driving of the Golden Spike in 1869 in Utah, linking America's Atlantic and Pacific coasts by rail, was heard loud and clear in New England, and it had a discordant ring. Transcontinental rail meant farmers and manufacturers could ship goods from the fertile Great Plains and California to faraway markets, making it harder for New England's hardscrabble farmers to survive. Likewise, the coastal shipping trade was dealt a fatal blow by this new transportation network. And the tourists set their sights on the Rockies and other stirring sites in the West.

Beginning in the late 19th century, New England lapsed into an extended economic slumber. Families commonly walked away from their farmhouses (there was no market for resale) and set off for regions with more promising opportunities. The abandoned, decaying farmhouse became almost an icon for New England, and vast tracts of open farmland were reclaimed by forest. With the rise of the automobile, the grand resorts further succumbed, and many closed their doors as inexpensive motels siphoned off their business.

BOOM TIMES   In the last 2 decades of the 20th century, much of New England rode an unexpected wave of prosperity. A massive real-estate boom shook the region in the 1980s, driving land prices sky-high as prosperous buyers from New York and Boston acquired vacation homes or retired to the most alluring areas. In the 1990s, the rise of high-tech also sent ripples from Boston into the hinterlands. Tourism rebounded as harried urbanites of the Eastern Seaboard opted for shorter, more frequent vacations closer to home.

Travelers to the more remote regions will discover that many communities never benefited from the boom at all; they're still waiting to rebound from the economic malaise earlier in the century. Especially hard-hit have been places like northeastern Vermont and far Downeast Maine, where many residents still depend on local resources—timber, fisheries, and farmland—to eke out a living.

3 New England Style

You can often trace the evolution of a town by its architecture, as styles evolve from basic structures to elaborate Victorian mansions. The primer below should aid with basic identification.

- **Colonial** (1600–1700): The New England house of the 17th century was a simple, boxy affair, often covered in shingles or rough clapboards. Don't look for ornamentation; these homes were designed for basic shelter from the elements, and are often marked by prominent stone chimneys. You can see examples at Plimoth Plantation and in Salem, near Boston.
- **Georgian** (1700–1800): Ornamentation comes into play in the Georgian style, which draws heavily on classical symmetry. Georgian buildings were in vogue in England at the time, and were embraced by affluent colonists. Look for Palladian windows, formal pilasters, and elaborate projecting pediments. Deerfield (in the Pioneer Valley) is a good destination for seeing early Georgian homes; and Providence, R.I. and Portsmouth, N.H. have abundant examples of later Georgian styles.
- **Federal** (1780–1820): Federal homes (sometimes called Adams homes) may best represent the New England ideal. Spacious yet austere, they are often rectangular or square, with low-pitched roofs and little ornament on the front, although carved swags or other embellishments are frequently seen near the roofline. Look for fan windows and chimneys bracketing the building. Excellent Federal-style homes are found throughout the region in towns such as Kennebunkport, Maine.

A Literary Legacy

New Englanders have generated whole libraries, from the earliest days of hellfire-and-brimstone Puritan sermons to Stephen King's horror novels set in fictional Maine villages.

Among the more enduring writings from New England's earliest days are the poems of Massachusetts Bay Colony resident **Anne Bradstreet** (ca. 1612–1672) and the sermons and essays of **Increase Mather** (1639–1723) and his son, **Cotton Mather** (1663–1728).

After the American Revolution, Hartford dictionary writer **Noah Webster** (1758–1843) issued a call to American writers: "America must be as independent in literature as she is in politics, as famous for arts as for arms." He struck an early blow for pragmatism by taking the "u" out of British words like "labour" and "honour."

The tales of **Nathaniel Hawthorne** (1804–1864) captivated a public eager for a native literature. His most famous story, *The Scarlet Letter,* is a narrative about morality set in 17th-century Boston, but he wrote numerous other books that wrestled with themes of sin and guilt, often set in the emerging republic.

Henry Wadsworth Longfellow (1807–1882), the Portland poet who settled in Cambridge, caught the attention of the public with evocative narrative poems focusing on distinctly American subjects. His popular works included "The Courtship of Miles Standish," "Paul Revere's Ride," and "Hiawatha." Poetry in the mid-19th century was the equivalent of Hollywood movies today—Longfellow could be considered his generation's Steven Spielberg (apologies to literary scholars).

The zenith of New England literature occurred in the mid- and late 19th century with the Transcendentalist movement. These exalted writers and thinkers included **Ralph Waldo Emerson** (1803–1882), **Bronson Alcott** (1799–1888), and **Henry David Thoreau** (1817–1862). They fashioned a way of viewing nature and society that was uniquely American. They rejected the rigid doctrines of the Puritans, and found sustenance

- **Greek Revival** (1820–1860): The most easy-to-identify Greek Revival homes feature a bold projecting portico with massive columns, like a part of the Parthenon grafted onto an existing home. The less dramatic homes may simply be oriented such that the gable faces the street, accenting the triangular pediment. Greek Revival didn't catch on in New England quite the way it did in the South, but some fine examples exist, notably in Newfane, Vt.
- **Carpenter Gothic** and **Gothic Revival** (1840–1880): The second half of the 19th century brought a wave of Gothic Revival homes, which borrowed their aesthetic from the English country home. Aficionados of this style and its later progeny featuring gingerbread trim owe themselves a trip to Oak Bluffs at Martha's Vineyard, where cottages are festooned with scrollwork and exuberant architectural flourishes.
- **Victorian** (1860–1900): This is a catchall term for the jumble of mid- to late-19th-century styles that emphasized complexity and opulence. Perhaps the best-known Victorian style—almost a caricature—is the tall and narrow

in self-examination, the glories of nature, and a celebration of individualism. Perhaps the best known work to emerge from this period was Thoreau's *Walden.*

Among other regional writers who left a lasting mark on American literature was **Emily Dickinson** (1830–1886), a native of Amherst, Mass., whose precise and enigmatic poems placed her in the front rank of American poets. **James Russell Lowell** (1819–1891), of Cambridge, was an influential poet, critic, and editor. Later poets were imagist **Amy Lowell** (1874–1925), from Brookline, Mass., and **Edna St. Vincent Millay** (1892–1950), from Camden, Maine.

The bestselling *Uncle Tom's Cabin,* the book Abraham Lincoln half-jokingly accused of starting the Civil War, was written by **Harriet Beecher Stowe** (1811–1886) in Brunswick, Maine. She lived much of her life as a neighbor of **Mark Twain** (himself an adopted New Englander) in Hartford, Conn. Another bestseller was the children's book *Little Women,* written by **Louisa May Alcott** (1832–1888), whose father, Bronson, was part of the Transcendentalist movement.

New England's later role in the literary tradition may best be symbolized by the poet **Robert Frost** (1874–1963). Though born in California, he lived his life in Massachusetts, New Hampshire, and Vermont. In the New England landscape and community, he found a lasting grace and rich metaphors for life. (Among his most famous lines: "Two roads diverged in a wood, and I—I took the one less traveled by, / And that has made all the difference.")

New England continues to attract writers drawn to the noted educational institutions and the privacy of rural life. Prominent contemporary writers and poets who live in the region at least part of the year include **John Updike, Nicholson Baker, Christopher Buckley, P. J. O'Rourke, Bill Bryson, John Irving,** and **Donald Hall.** Maine is also the home of **Stephen King,** who is considered not so much a novelist as Maine's leading industry.

Addams-Family-style house, with mansard roof and prickly roof cresting. You'll find these scattered throughout the region.

The Victorian style also includes squarish **Italianate** homes with wide eaves and unusual flourishes, such as the Victoria Mansion in Portland, Maine.

Stretching the definition a bit, Victorian can also include the **Richardsonian Romanesque** style, which was popular for railroad stations and public buildings. The classic Richardsonian building, designed by H. H. Richardson himself in 1872, is Trinity Church, in Boston.

- **Shingle** (1880–1900): This uniquely New England style quickly became preferred for vacation homes on Cape Cod and the Maine coast. They're marked by a profusion of gables, roofs, and porches, and are typically covered with shingles from roofline to foundation.
- **Modern** (1900–present): Outside of Boston, New England has produced little in the way of notable modern architecture. In the 1930s, Boston became a center for the stark **International Style** with the appointment of Bauhaus

veteran Walter Gropius to the faculty at Harvard. Some intriguing experiments in this style are found on the MIT and Harvard campuses, including Gropius's Campus Center and Eero Saarinen's Kresge Auditorium.

4 A Taste of New England

All along the coast you'll be tempted by seafood in its various forms. You can get fried clams by the bucket at divey shacks along remote coves and busy highways. The more upscale restaurants offer fresh fish, grilled or gently sautéed.

Live lobster can be bought literally off the boat at lobster pounds, especially along the Maine coast. The setting is usually rustic—maybe a couple of picnic tables and a shed where huge vats of water are kept at a low boil.

Inland, take time to sample the local products. This includes delectable maple syrup, sold throughout the northern reaches. Check the label for Grade A syrup certification. Cheese is a Vermont specialty, especially cheddar. Look also for Vermont's famed apple cider, and Maine's wild blueberries.

In summer, small farmers across New England set up stands at the end of their driveways offering fresh produce straight from the garden. You can usually find berries, fruits, and sometimes home-baked breads. These stands are rarely tended; just leave your money in the coffee can.

Restaurateurs haven't overlooked New England's bounty. Many chefs serve up delicious meals consisting of local ingredients—some places even tend their own gardens. Some of the fine dishes we've enjoyed while researching this guide include curried pumpkin soup, venison medallions with shiitake mushrooms, and wild boar with juniper berries.

But you don't have to have a hefty budget to enjoy the local foods. A number of regional classics fall under the "road food" category. Here's an abbreviated field guide:

- **Beans:** Boston is forever linked with baked beans (hence the nickname "Beantown"), which are popular throughout the region. A Saturday-night supper traditionally consists of baked beans and brown bread.
- **Lobster rolls:** Lobster rolls consist of lobster meat plucked from the shell, mixed with just enough mayonnaise to hold it all together, then served on a hot-dog roll.
- **Moxie:** Early in this century, Moxie outsold Coca-Cola. Part of its allure was the fanciful story behind its 1885 creation: A traveler named Moxie was said to have observed South American Indians consuming the sap of a native plant, which gave them extraordinary strength. The drink was "re-created" by Maine native and Massachusetts resident Dr. Augustin Thompson. It's still popular in New England, although some folks liken the taste to a combination of medicine and topsoil.
- **Necco wafers:** Still made in Cambridge by the New England Confectionery Company, these powdery wafers haven't changed a bit since 1847. The candies are available widely throughout New England.

Finally, no survey of comestibles would be complete without mention of something to wash it all down: beer. New England has more microbreweries than any other region outside of the Pacific Northwest. Popular brewpubs that rank high on the list include the Great Providence Brewing Co., the Commonwealth Brewing Co. (Boston's first brewpub), the Portsmouth Brewery, Federal Jack's Brewpub (Kennebunkport), Vermont Pub & Brewery (Burlington), and the Windham Brewery at the Latchis Hotel (Brattleboro).

Index

Nature and wildlife areas (cont.)
   Great Meadows National Wildlife Refuge, 141
   Litchfield, 338
   Northampton, 289
   Parker River National Wildlife Refuge, 171
   Provincetown, 230
   Sandwich, 184
   Sheffield, 296
   Wellfleet, 224–225
   Yarmouth, 201–202
Nature Center for Environmental Activities, 328
Nature trails. See also Hiking; and specific trails
   Cape Cod National Seashore, 240
   Martha's Vineyard, 251, 253
   Nantucket, 270
   Provincetown, 230
Naumkeag, 303
Nauset Beach, 219–220
Nauset Light, 241
Nauset Light Beach, 239
Nauset Marsh Trail, 240
New Bedford, 170
   ferries to Martha's Vineyard, 245
New Bedford Whaling Museum, 170
New Bedford Whaling National Historical Park, 170
Newburyport, 169–171
New England Aquarium, 105, 110
New England Hiking Holidays, 46
New England Patriots, 117
New England Spring Flower Show, 28–29
Newes from America, 249
Newfane, 22, 443–445
Newfane Flea Market, 444
New Hampshire, 494–539
   visitor information, 24
   what's new in, 2–3
New Hampshire Antique and Classic Boat Museum, 512
New Haven, 2, 342–347
New Haven Green, 342–343
New London, 30, 360
New Milford, 331–332
Newport (RI), 2, 10–11, 21, 23, 387–406
   accommodations, 399–403
   beaches and outdoor activities, 397–398
   cottages, 392–395
   nightlife, 406
   organized tours and cruises, 398–399
   parking and getting around, 390
   restaurants, 403–406
   shopping, 399
   sights and attractions, 9, 392–397
   special events, 31, 32, 34, 390, 392
   traveling to, 388, 390
   visitor information, 390
Newport (VT), 488–490
Newport Aquarium, 397
Newport Art Museum, 396–397
Newport Folk Festival., 32
Newport Music Festival, 31, 390, 392
New Preston, 336–337
Newspapers and magazines, 53, 59
New Year's celebrations, 28
Nickerson State Park, 209, 210
Norfolk, 341
Norfolk Chamber Music Festival, 21, 341
Norman Rockwell Museum, 303
Norman's Woe, 157
North Adams, 2, 318–320
Northampton, 288–291
North Beach, 214
North Beach (Burlington), 484
North Bridge (Concord), 10
North Conway, 515–519
North Country, 537–539
Northeast Harbor, 607
Northeast Kingdom, 488–493
Northeast Kingdom Fall Foliage Festival, 33
Northfield, 31
North Lighthouse, 415
North Shore Arts Association, 161
North Trail (Brewster), 210
North Woods, 24
Norwalk, 325–327
Norwalk Oyster Festival, 32
Norwich, 373–374
Norwottuck Rail Trail Bike Path, 289

Nubble Light, 544
Nutcracker, The (Boston), 20

Oak Bluffs, 12–13
   accommodations, 258
   restaurants, 262
Oak Bluffs Town Beach, 251
Ocean Beach Park, 361
Ocean Point, 569
Ocean State Lyric Opera, 385
October Mountain State Forest, 306, 309
Ogunquit, 546–549
Ogunquit Museum of American Art, 547
Ogunquit Playhouse, 548
Okemo, 448–449
Old Bridle Trail, 533
Old Corner Bookstore Building, 106
Old Granary Burying Ground, 106
Old Harbor (Block Island), 411
Old Harbor Lifesaving Station, 240
"Old Ironsides" (Boston), 10
Old King's Highway (Route 6A), 21, 193
Old Lighthouse Museum, 367–368
Old Lyme, 355–356
Old Man of the Mountains, 532
Old Manse, 138
Old North Church, 107
Old Port (Portland), 555
Old Port Festival, 30
Old Revolutionary Monument, 133
Old Saybrook, 354
Old Sculpin Gallery, 248
Old Silver Beach, 188
Old South Meeting House, 106
Old Speck Mountain, 612
Old State House (Boston), 9, 106
Old State House (Hartford), 348
Old Storrowtown Village, 284
Old Sturbridge Village, 282
Old Tavern at Grafton, 447
Old Town (Marblehead), 144
Old Whaling Church, 248, 264

Wickedly honest guides for sophisticated travelers—and those who want to be.

HIT THE ROAD WITH
FROMMER'S DRIVING TOURS!

Frommer's
Portable Guides
Complete Guides for the Short-Term Traveler

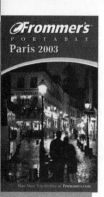

TRAVEL LIKE AN EXPERT WITH THE UNOFFICIAL GUIDES

For Travelers Who Want More Than the Official Line!

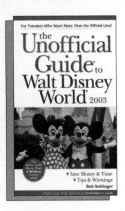

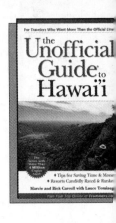

The Unofficial Guides®

Beyond Disney
Branson, Missouri
California with Kids
Chicago
Central Italy
Cruises
Disneyland®
Florida with Kids
Golf Vacations in the
  Eastern U.S.
The Great Smoky &
  Blue Ridge Region
Inside Disney
Hawaii
Las Vegas
London
Mid-Atlantic with Kids
Mini Las Vegas
Mini-Mickey
New England & New York
  with Kids
New Orleans
New York City

Paris
San Francisco
Skiing in the West
Southeast with Kids
Walt Disney World®
Walt Disney World®
  for Grown-Ups
Walt Disney World®
  with Kids
Washington, D.C.
World's Best Diving
  Vacations

Bed & Breakfasts and Country Inns in:
California
Great Lakes States
Mid-Atlantic
New England
Northwest
Rockies
Southeast
Southwest

The Best RV & Tent Campgrounds in:
California & the West
Florida & the
  Southeast
Great Lakes States
Mid-Atlantic States
Northeast
Northwest &
  Central Plains
Southwest & South
  Central Plains
U.S.A.

Available at bookstores everywhere.

FROMMER'S® COMPLETE TRAVEL GUIDES

Alaska
Alaska Cruises & Ports of Call
Amsterdam
Argentina & Chile
Arizona
Atlanta
Australia
Austria
Bahamas
Barcelona, Madrid & Seville
Beijing
Belgium, Holland & Luxembourg
Bermuda
Boston
Brazil
British Columbia & the Canadian Rockies
Budapest & the Best of Hungary
California
Canada
Cancún, Cozumel & the Yucatán
Cape Cod, Nantucket & Martha's Vineyard
Caribbean
Caribbean Cruises & Ports of Call
Caribbean Ports of Call
Carolinas & Georgia
Chicago
China
Colorado
Costa Rica
Denmark
Denver, Boulder & Colorado Springs
England
Europe
European Cruises & Ports of Call
Florida

France
Germany
Great Britain
Greece
Greek Islands
Hawaii
Hong Kong
Honolulu, Waikiki & Oahu
Ireland
Israel
Italy
Jamaica
Japan
Las Vegas
London
Los Angeles
Maryland & Delaware
Maui
Mexico
Montana & Wyoming
Montréal & Québec City
Munich & the Bavarian Alps
Nashville & Memphis
Nepal
New England
New Mexico
New Orleans
New York City
New Zealand
Northern Italy
Nova Scotia, New Brunswick & Prince Edward Island
Oregon
Paris
Philadelphia & the Amish Country
Portugal
Prague & the Best of the Czech Republic

Provence & the Riviera
Puerto Rico
Rome
San Antonio & Austin
San Diego
San Francisco
Santa Fe, Taos & Albuquerque
Scandinavia
Scotland
Seattle & Portland
Shanghai
Singapore & Malaysia
South Africa
South America
South Florida
South Pacific
Southeast Asia
Spain
Sweden
Switzerland
Texas
Thailand
Tokyo
Toronto
Tuscany & Umbria
USA
Utah
Vancouver & Victoria
Vermont, New Hampshire & Maine
Vienna & the Danube Valley
Virgin Islands
Virginia
Walt Disney World® & Orlando
Washington, D.C.
Washington State

FROMMER'S® DOLLAR-A-DAY GUIDES

Australia from $50 a Day
California from $70 a Day
Caribbean from $70 a Day
England from $75 a Day
Europe from $70 a Day

Florida from $70 a Day
Hawaii from $80 a Day
Ireland from $60 a Day
Italy from $70 a Day
London from $85 a Day

New York from $90 a Day
Paris from $80 a Day
San Francisco from $70 a Day
Washington, D.C. from $80 a Day

FROMMER'S® PORTABLE GUIDES

Acapulco, Ixtapa & Zihuatanejo
Amsterdam
Aruba
Australia's Great Barrier Reef
Bahamas
Berlin
Big Island of Hawaii
Boston
California Wine Country
Cancún
Charleston & Savannah
Chicago
Disneyland®
Dublin
Florence

Frankfurt
Hong Kong
Houston
Las Vegas
London
Los Angeles
Los Cabos & Baja
Maine Coast
Maui
Miami
New Orleans
New York City
Paris
Phoenix & Scottsdale

Portland
Puerto Rico
Puerto Vallarta, Manzanillo & Guadalajara
Rio de Janeiro
San Diego
San Francisco
Seattle
Sydney
Tampa & St. Petersburg
Vancouver
Venice
Virgin Islands
Washington, D.C.

FROMMER'S® NATIONAL PARK GUIDES

Banff & Jasper
Family Vacations in the National Parks
Grand Canyon

National Parks of the American West
Rocky Mountain

Yellowstone & Grand Teton
Yosemite & Sequoia/ Kings Canyon
Zion & Bryce Canyon

FROMMER'S® MEMORABLE WALKS

Chicago	New York	San Francisco
London	Paris	Washington, D.C.

FROMMER'S® GREAT OUTDOOR GUIDES

Arizona & New Mexico	Northern California	Vermont & New Hampshire
New England	Southern New England	

SUZY GERSHMAN'S BORN TO SHOP GUIDES

Born to Shop: France	Born to Shop: Italy	Born to Shop: New York
Born to Shop: Hong Kong, Shanghai & Beijing	Born to Shop: London	Born to Shop: Paris

FROMMER'S® IRREVERENT GUIDES

Amsterdam	Los Angeles	San Francisco
Boston	Manhattan	Seattle & Portland
Chicago	New Orleans	Vancouver
Las Vegas	Paris	Walt Disney World®
London	Rome	Washington, D.C.

FROMMER'S® BEST-LOVED DRIVING TOURS

Britain	Germany	Northern Italy
California	Ireland	Scotland
Florida	Italy	Spain
France	New England	Tuscany & Umbria

HANGING OUT™ GUIDES

Hanging Out in England	Hanging Out in France	Hanging Out in Italy
Hanging Out in Europe	Hanging Out in Ireland	Hanging Out in Spain

THE UNOFFICIAL GUIDES®

Bed & Breakfasts and Country Inns in:	Southwest & South Central Plains	Mid-Atlantic with Kids
California	U.S.A.	Mini Las Vegas
Great Lakes States	Beyond Disney	Mini-Mickey
Mid-Atlantic	Branson, Missouri	New England and New York with Kids
New England	California with Kids	New Orleans
Northwest	Chicago	New York City
Rockies	Cruises	Paris
Southeast	Disneyland®	San Francisco
Southwest	Florida with Kids	Skiing in the West
Best RV & Tent Campgrounds in:	Golf Vacations in the Eastern U.S.	Southeast with Kids
California & the West	Great Smoky & Blue Ridge Region	Walt Disney World®
Florida & the Southeast	Inside Disney	Walt Disney World® for Grown-ups
Great Lakes States	Hawaii	Walt Disney World® with Kids
Mid-Atlantic	Las Vegas	Washington, D.C.
Northeast	London	World's Best Diving Vacations
Northwest & Central Plains		

SPECIAL-INTEREST TITLES

Frommer's Adventure Guide to Australia & New Zealand
Frommer's Adventure Guide to Central America
Frommer's Adventure Guide to India & Pakistan
Frommer's Adventure Guide to South America
Frommer's Adventure Guide to Southeast Asia
Frommer's Adventure Guide to Southern Africa
Frommer's Britain's Best Bed & Breakfasts and Country Inns
Frommer's Caribbean Hideaways
Frommer's Exploring America by RV
Frommer's Fly Safe, Fly Smart
Frommer's France's Best Bed & Breakfasts and Country Inns
Frommer's Gay & Lesbian Europe

Frommer's Italy's Best Bed & Breakfasts and Country Inns
Frommer's New York City with Kids
Frommer's Ottawa with Kids
Frommer's Road Atlas Britain
Frommer's Road Atlas Europe
Frommer's Road Atlas France
Frommer's Toronto with Kids
Frommer's Vancouver with Kids
Frommer's Washington, D.C., with Kids
Israel Past & Present
The New York Times' Guide to Unforgettable Weekends
Places Rated Almanac
Retirement Places Rated

America Online Keyword: Travel
Booked seat 6A, open return.
Rented red 4-wheel drive.
Reserved cabin, no running water.
Discovered space.
th over 700 airlines, 50,000 hotels, 50 rental car companies and
00 cruise and vacation packages, you can create the perfect get-
ay for you. Choose the car, the room, even the ground you walk on.
Travelocity.com
A Sabre Company
Go Virtually Anywhere.
Travelocity,® Travelocity.com® and the Travelocity skyline logo are trademarks and/or servicemarks of Travelocity.com L.P.,

You Need
A Vacation.

700 Airlines, 50,00
Companies, And A Mill

Travelocity.com
A Sabre Company
Go Virtually Anywhere.